QUICKBOOKS® PRO 2006: A COMPLETE COURSE

Janet Horne, M.S.
Los Angeles Pierce College

PEARSON
Prentice Hall

UPPER SADDLE RIVER, NJ 07458

Cataloging data for this publication can be obtained from the Library of Congress.

AVP/Executive Editor: Wendy Craven
VP/Editorial Director: Jeff Shelstad
Product Development Manager: Pamela Hersperger
Project Manager: Kerri Tomasso
Media Product Development Manager: Nancy Welcher
AVP/Executive Marketing Manager: John Wannemacher
Associate Director, Production Editorial: Judy Leale
Senior Managing Editor, Production: Cynthia Regan
Production Editor: Denise Culhane
Permissions Coordinator: Charles Morris
Associate Director, Manufacturing: Vinnie Scelta
Manufacturing Buyer: Michelle Klein
Design/Composition Manager: Christy Mahon
Cover Design: Nancy Thompson
Cover Illustration/Photo: Photodisc
Printer/Binder: Bind-Rite

Pearson Education LTD.
Pearson Education Singapore, Pte. Ltd
Pearson Education, Canada, Ltd
Pearson Education–Japan
Pearson Education Australia PTY, Limited
Pearson Education North Asia Ltd
Pearson Educación de Mexico, S.A. de C.V.
Pearson Education Malaysia, Pte. Ltd.

PEARSON Prentice Hall

10 9 8 7 6 5 4 3
ISBN: 0-13-178982-1

To my husband and our sons
With thanks for their support, patience, and understanding

TABLE OF CONTENTS

Chapter 6—Payables and Purchases: Merchandising Business

PREFACE

QuickBooks® Pro 2006: A Complete Course is a comprehensive instructional learning resource. This text has been designed to respond to the growing trend toward adopting Windows applications and computerizing accounting systems. As a result of this trend, the text provides training using *Windows® XP* and the popular *QuickBooks® Pro 2006* accounting program. The text was written using Windows XP and QuickBooks® Pro 2006 but may be used with Windows 2000 and QuickBooks® Basic or Premier versions.

ORGANIZATIONAL FEATURES

QuickBooks® Pro 2006: A Complete Course is designed to present accounting concepts and their relationship to *QuickBooks® Pro 2006.* In addition to accounting concepts, students use a fictitious company and receive hands-on training in the use of *QuickBooks® Pro 2006* within each chapter. At the end of every chapter, the concepts and applications learned are reinforced by the completion of true/false, multiple-choice, fill-in, and essay questions plus an application problem using a different fictitious company. There are three practices sets in the text that utilize all the major concepts and transactions presented within an area of study. The third practice set is comprehensive and utilizes all the major concepts and transactions presented within the entire textbook.

The text introduces students to the computer, Windows, and QuickBooks accounting for a service business, a merchandising business, payroll, and company setup for QuickBooks. The appendices review Windows, disk duplication; back up files, and file restoration. QuickBooks Integration using Word and Excel; QuickBooks Features including QuickBooks Notes, Time Tracking, Job Costing, and Price Levels; and QuickBooks Online including online updates, Internet connection, payroll services, downloading a trial version of the software, online banking and payments, personalized web sites and domain names, credit check services, billing solutions, merchant services, online billing, online credit card billing, online backup services, and direct deposit.

DISTINGUISHING FEATURES

Throughout the text, emphasis has been placed on the use of QuickBooks' innovative approach to recording accounting transactions based on a business form rather than using the traditional journal format. This approach, however, has been correlated to traditional accounting through adjusting entries, end-of-period procedures, and use of the "behind the scenes" journal.

Unlike many other computerized accounting programs, QuickBooks is user-friendly when corrections and adjustments are required. The ease of corrections and the ramifications as a result of this ease are explored thoroughly.

Accounting concepts and the use of *QuickBooks® Pro 2006* are reinforced throughout the text with the use of graphics that show completed transactions, reports, and QuickBooks screens. The text helps students transition from textbook transaction analysis to "real-world" transaction analysis.

The text provides extensive assignment material in the form of tutorials; end-of-chapter questions (true/false, multiple-choice, fill-in, and essay); practice sets for a service business, a merchandising business, and a comprehensive practice set.

Students develop confidence in recording business transactions using an up-to-date commercial software program designed for small to mid-size businesses. With thorough exploration of the program in the text, students should be able to use *QuickBooks® Pro 2006* in a "real world situation" at the completion of the textbook training.

Students will explore and use many of the features of QuickBooks as it pertains to a service business and a merchandising business, including recording transactions ranging from simple to complex, preparing a multitude of reports, closing an accounting period, compiling charts and graphs, creating a company, and preparing the payroll. The transactions entered by students begin with simple entries and become more complex as they progress through the text. Students also learn ways in which QuickBooks can be customized to fit the needs of an individual company.

COURSES

QuickBooks® Pro 2006: A Complete Course is designed for a one-term course in microcomputer accounting. This text covers a service business, a merchandising business, a sole proprietorship, a partnership, payroll, and company setup to use QuickBooks. For a more basic text, ***QuickBooks® Pro 2006: Simplified*** may be used. It focuses on using QuickBooks Pro in a service/merchandising business and includes payroll, company creation, and a practice set. When using either text, students should be familiar with the accounting cycle and how it is related to a business. No prior knowledge of or experience with computers, Windows, or QuickBooks is required; however, an understanding of accounting is essential to successful completion of the coursework.

SUPPLEMENTS FOR THE INSTRUCTOR

*The **Instructor's Manual*** is a comprehensive printed answer key for all the exercises, the exams, and the practice sets. All computer assignments are printed in full and included for use in grading or as a student answer key. Please contact your Pearson Education Sales rep for a copy of this valuable resource. In addition to the printed Instructor's Manual, Prentice Hall maintains a web site where student and instructor materials may be downloaded for classroom use. **www.prenhall.com/compaccounting**.

- The instructor web site contains master data files for all the companies in the text
- Backup company files for each chapter that may be restored to a QuickBooks company file
- A sample syllabus/course outline
- Lectures for each chapter with a hands-on demonstration lecture
- Written exams for each area of study, a written final exam, and an exam for each practice set
- Suggestions for grading. Instructor materials include a lecture outline for each chapter
- Answers to the end-of-chapter questions
- Transmittal sheets that include the totals of reports and documents

- Excel files for all the reports prepared in the text.

SUPPLEMENTS FOR THE STUDENT

The data files for this text are available for download at www.prenhall.com/compaccounting.

ACKNOWLEDGMENTS

I wish to thank my colleagues for testing and reviewing the manuscript and my students for providing me with a special insight into problems encountered in training. Their comments and suggestions are greatly appreciated.

INTRODUCTION TO QUICKBOOKS® PRO 2006 AND COMPANY FILES

1

LEARNING OBJECTIVES

At the completion of this chapter, you will be able to:

1. Identify QuickBooks Pro desktop features, be familiar with the QuickBooks Centers, and understand the QuickBooks Home Page.
2. Recognize menu commands and use some keyboard shortcuts.
3. Recognize QuickBooks Pro forms and understand the use of lists and registers in QuickBooks Pro.
4. Access QuickBooks Pro reports and be familiar with QuickZoom.
5. Open and close QuickBooks Pro
6. Copy a company file and open a company
7. Add your name to a company name
8. Access QuickBooks Pro reports and be familiar with QuickZoom.
9. Prepare QuickBooks Pro graphs and use QuickReport within graphs.
10. Use QuickMath and the Windows Calculator.
11. Back up a company
12. Restore a company from a backup file
13. Close a company

MANUAL AND COMPUTERIZED ACCOUNTING

The work to be performed to keep the books for a business is the same whether you use a manual or a computerized accounting system. Transactions need to be analyzed, recorded in a journal, and posted to a ledger. Business documents such as invoices, checks, bank deposits, and credit/debit memos need to be prepared and distributed. Reports to management and owners for information and decision-making purposes need to be prepared. Records for one business period need to be closed before recording transactions for the next business period.

In a manual system, each transaction that is analyzed must be entered by hand into the appropriate journal (the book of original entry where all transactions are recorded) and posted to the appropriate ledger (the book of final entry that contains records for all the accounts used in the business). A separate business document such as an invoice or a check must be prepared and distributed. In order to prepare a report, the accountant/bookkeeper must go through the journal or ledger and look for the appropriate amounts to include in the report. Closing the books must be done item by item via closing entries, which are recorded in the journal and posted to the appropriate ledger accounts. After the closing entries are recorded, the ledger accounts must be ruled and balance sheet accounts must be reopened with Brought Forward Balances being entered. All of this is extremely time consuming.

When using a computerized system and a program such as QuickBooks, the transactions must still be analyzed and recorded. QuickBooks Pro operates from a business document point of view. As a transaction occurs, the necessary business document (an invoice or a check, for example) is prepared. Based on the information given on the business document, QuickBooks Pro records the necessary debits and credits behind the scenes in the Journal. If an error is made when entering a transaction, QuickBooks Pro allows the user to return to the business document and make the correction. QuickBooks Pro will automatically record the changes in the debits and credits in the Journal. If you want to see or make a correction using the actual debit/credit entries, QuickBooks Pro allows you to view the transaction register and make corrections directly in the register or use the traditional Journal. Reports and graphs are prepared by simply clicking “Report” on the menu bar.

VERSIONS OF QUICKBOOKS®

While this text focuses on training using QuickBooks® Pro 2006, it may also be used with the Premier version of the program. The Premier version offers some additional enhancements not available in the Pro version. The Premier version of the program is also available in industry specific versions; such as, Accountant, Contractor, Healthcare, Manufacturing and Wholesale, Nonprofit, Professional Services, and Retail. There is an Online Edition of QuickBooks that is available online for a monthly fee. However, the functions available are limited and many features of QuickBooks Pro cannot be utilized. In addition, there is also the Simple Start program, which is designed for first time QuickBooks users, and Enterprise Solutions, which is designed for larger businesses that want a great deal of customization.

For a comparison of features available among the different versions of the QuickBooks programs, access Intuit’s Web site at www.quickbooks.com.

BEGIN COMPUTER TRAINING

➤ When you see the arrow, it means you will be performing a computer task. Sometimes the computer task will have several steps. Continue until all steps listed are completed.

OPEN QUICKBOOKS® PRO

Once you are in Windows, opening QuickBooks Pro is as easy as point and click.

Open QuickBooks Pro

Click **Start**
Point to **All Programs**

Point to **QuickBooks Pro 2006** (or the program name given to you by your instructor)
On the drop-down list, click **QuickBooks Pro 2006**

HOW TO OPEN A COMPANY

To explore some of the features of QuickBooks Pro, you will work with a sample company that comes with the program. The company is Larry's Landscaping and is stored on the hard disk (C:) inside the computer.

Open a sample company

Click the **Open a sample file** button
Click **Sample service-based business**

When using the sample company for training, a warning screen will appear. This is to remind you NOT to enter the transactions for your business in the sample company.

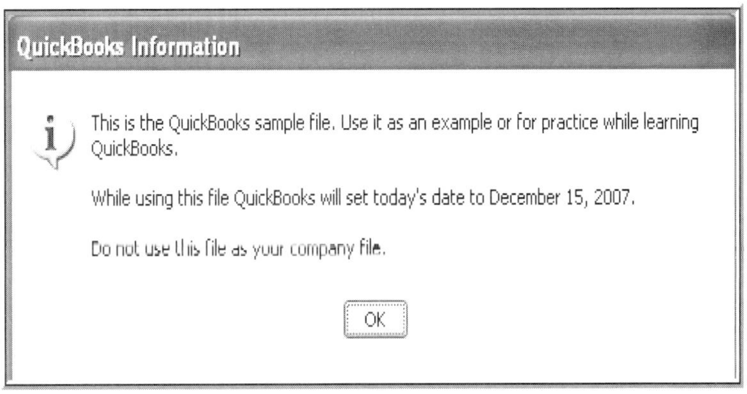

Click **OK** to accept the sample company data for use

When opening the sample company, you may get a screen for QuickBooks Learning Center. This allows you to obtain an overview of QuickBooks features and to work with tutorials regarding some of the basic areas of QuickBooks. If you do not want to see this screen every time you open QuickBooks, click the "Show this window at startup" box at the bottom of the Learning Center screen to remove the check mark. To continue, click the **Begin Using QuickBooks** button at the bottom of the Learning Center screen.

VERIFY AN OPEN COMPANY

It is important to make sure you have opened the data for the correct company. Always verify the company name in the title bar.

Verify an open company

Check the **title bar** at the top of the QuickBooks screen to make sure it includes the company name. The title bar should show:

QUICKBOOKS® PRO DESKTOP FEATURES

Once you have opened a company, and the title bar displays the **Company Name - QuickBooks Pro 2006**, you may give commands to QuickBooks by using the:

Menu bar. By pointing and clicking on a menu item or using the keyboard shortcut of Alt+ the underlined letter in the menu item you will give QuickBooks Pro the command to display the drop-down menu. For example, the File menu is used to open and close a company and may also be used to exit QuickBooks Pro.

QuickBooks Home. Below the Menu bar is a row of icons. The first icon says Home and is used to go to the Navigator screen

QuickBooks Command Centers. Next to Home is a list of Centers. Each center goes to a specific list within the program. For example, the Customer Center displays a list of customers and their current balances.

Icon bar. This optional bar contains small pictures that may be used to give commands by pointing to a picture and clicking the primary mouse button.

MENU COMMANDS

Menu commands can be the starting point for issuing commands in QuickBooks Pro. Many commands will be the same as the ones you can make using QuickBooks Home Page. Notice that available keyboard shortcuts are listed next to the menu item. Click outside the menu to close it

Access each of the menus by clicking or pointing to each menu item

File menu is used to access company files—new company, open company, close company, and switch from single to multi-user; create a portable company file; back up and restore company files; utilities, make accountant's copy of company files; printer setup and printing; send forms; shipping, and exit from the program.

Edit menu is used to make changes such as: Undo, Revert, Cut, Copy, Paste, Use Register, Use Calculator, Find, and Preferences.

View menu is used to select the use of an open window list, icon bar, and one or multiple windows.

Lists menu is used to show lists used by QuickBooks Pro. These lists include: Chart of Accounts (the General Ledger), Items, Fixed Asset Items, Price Level Items, Sales Tax Code List, Payroll Items, Class List, Workers Comp List, Other Names, Customer and Vendor Profiles, Templates, and Memorized Transactions.

Company menu is used to access the Home Page, change company information, set up users, change passwords, planning and budgeting, access the To Do list, access the Reminders screen, use the Alerts Manager, enter vehicle mileage, and access the Chart of Accounts. It is also used to make journal entries, and write letters with envelopes.

Customers menu is used to access the Customer Center, enter transactions and prepare business documents such as invoices, sales receipts, credit memos/refunds, statements and statement charges, finance charges, receive payments, and accept credit card payments. It is also used to access the Item List, and to change item prices.

Vendors menu is used to access the Vendor Center and the Item List. In addition, this menu is used to enter transactions for recording bills, paying bills, paying sales tax, creating purchase orders, receiving items, inventory activities, and printing 1099s/1096.

Employees menu is used to access the Employee Center and the Payroll Center, pay employees, edit/void paychecks, process payroll liabilities, perform payroll service activities, set up payroll services, get payroll updates, and access Workers Compensation to set up a Workers Comp List and create a Workers Comp Summary.

Banking menu is used to write checks, order checks and envelopes, use the check register, make deposits, transfer funds, enter credit card charges, use the loan manager, reconcile accounts, access online banking, and access the Other Names Lists.

Reports menu is used to access the Report Center and to prepare reports in the following categories: Company & Financial; Customers & Receivables; Sales; Jobs, Time & Mileage; Vendors & Payables; Purchases; Inventory; Employees & Payroll; Banking; Accountant & Taxes; Budgets; List; Custom Report Summary; Custom Transaction Detail Report; Transaction History; Transaction Journal; and Memorized Reports.

Window menu is used to switch between windows that have been opened and to arrange icons.

Help menu is used to access Help. The Help menu includes topics such as: QuickBooks Learning Center, Year-End Guide, Access Support Resources, Send Feedback Online, Internet Connection Setup, Add QuickBooks Services, Update QuickBooks, Manage My License, Buy QuickBooks Premier Edition, QuickBooks Privacy Statement, About Automatic Update, About QuickBooks Pro 2006.

QUICKBOOKS® PRO HOME PAGE

The QuickBooks Home Page allows you to give commands to QuickBooks Pro according to the type of transaction being entered. The Home Page tasks are organized into logical groups (Vendors, Customers, Employees, Company, and Banking).

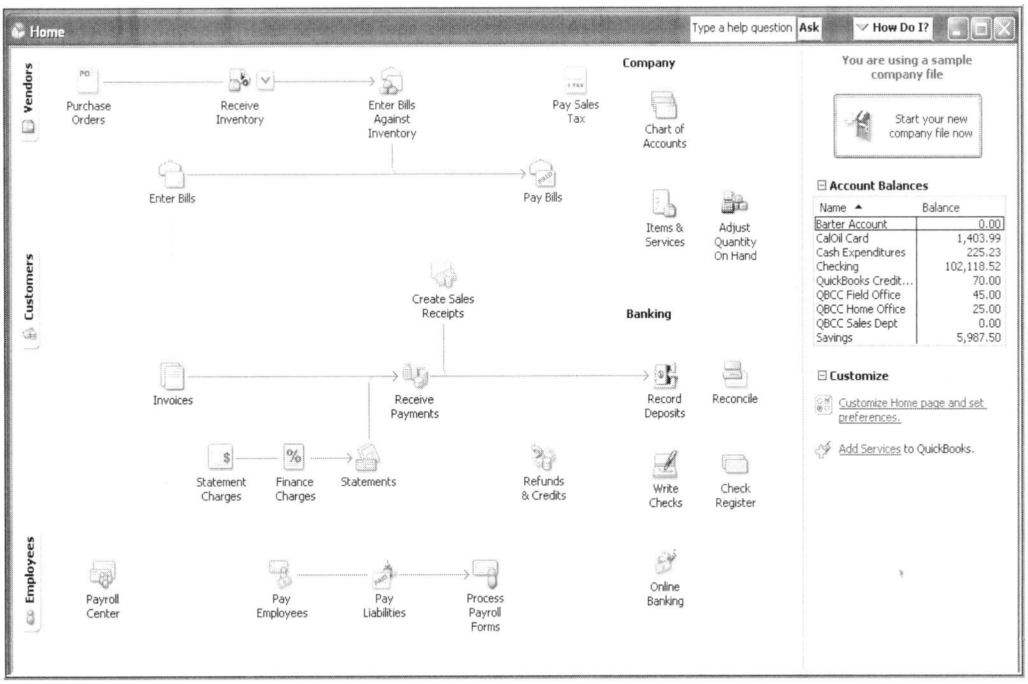

Each of the areas on the Home Page is used to enter different types of transactions. When appropriate, the Home Page shows a flow chart with icons indicating the major activities performed. The icons are arranged in the order in which transactions usually occur.

View each of the areas on the Home Page:

Company allows you to display information about your company. There are graphic icons used to display the Chart of Accounts, Items & Services, and to Adjust the Quantity on Hand.

Vendors allows you to enter your bills and to record the payment of bills. Companies with inventory can create purchase orders, record receipt of items, and pay sales tax.

Customers allows transactions associated with cash sales, credit sales, cash receipts, refunds and credits.

Employees allows paychecks to be created, payroll tax liabilities to be paid, and Forms 940, 941, and W2 to be printed.

Banking allows you to write checks, transfer money between accounts, use online banking, make bank deposits, reconcile the bank statement, and access the check register.

Customize allows you to customize your QuickBooks Preferences and to add services to QuickBooks.

QUICKBOOKS® PRO CENTERS

QuickBooks Pro 2006 has buttons that allow access to QuickBooks Centers. These are the Vendor, Customer, Employee, and Report centers. The centers focus on providing detailed information.

Vendor Center shows a list of vendors and the balances, vendor information and transactions for a selected vendor, a Vendors tab and a Transactions tab. The Vendors tab allows you to display information about the vendors and is the default tab. Clicking the Transactions tab displays transaction categories and allows you to get information about transaction groups. In addition, new vendors and transactions may be entered in the Vendor Center.

Customer Center shows a list of customers and the balances, customer information and transactions for a selected customer, a Customers tab and a Transactions tab. The Customers tab allows you to display information about the customers and is the default tab. Clicking the Transactions tab displays transaction categories and allows you to get information about transaction groups. In addition, new customers and transactions may be entered in the Customer Center.

Employee Center shows a list of employees, employee information and payroll transactions for a selected employee, an Employees tab, a Transactions tab, and a Payroll tab. The Employees tab allows you to display information about the individual employees. Clicking the Transactions tab displays transaction categories and allows you to get information about transaction groups. The Payroll tab provides information regarding payroll dates, payroll taxes, and payroll forms. In addition, new employees may be entered in the Employee Center.

Report Center accesses the Reports available in QuickBooks Pro and allows all of them to be prepared. These include specific reports, such as, Profit and Loss, Balance Sheet, Tax Reports, Transaction Detail Reports, Journal, General Ledger, Trial Balance, Income Tax Summary, Income Tax Detail, Journal, and an Audit Trail. There is also a variety of reports specific to payroll, customers, vendors, inventory, purchases, banking, and taxes.

Access each of the centers by clicking the appropriate Center icon beneath the menu bar
Close each Center before opening the next Center

KEYBOARD CONVENTIONS

When using Windows, there are some standard keyboard conventions for the use of certain keys. These keyboard conventions also apply to QuickBooks Pro and include the following.

Alt key is used to access the drop-down menus on the menu bar. Rather than click on a menu item, hold down the Alt key and type the underlined letter in the menu item name. Close the menu by simply pressing the Alt key. *Note*: Menu items do not have an underlined letter until you press the Alt key.

Tab key is used to move to the next field or, if a button is selected, to the next button.

Shift+Tab is used to move back to the previous field.

Esc key is used to cancel an active window without saving anything that has been entered. It is equivalent to clicking the Cancel button.

Practice using the keyboard conventions:

Access **Customer** menu: **Alt+U**
Access **Create Invoices**: type **I**
Press **Tab** key to move forward through the invoice
Press **Shift+Tab** to move back through the invoice
Press **Esc** to close the invoice

ICON BAR

Another way to give commands to QuickBooks Pro is to use the icon bar. If activated, the icon bar will be placed below the menu bar and next to the Centers bar. The icon bar has a list of buttons (icons) that may be clicked in order to access activities, lists, or reports. The icon bar may be turned on or off, it may be customized, and it may be moved beneath the Centers bar.

ON-SCREEN HELP

QuickBooks Pro has on-screen help, which is similar to having the QuickBooks Pro reference manual available on the computer screen. Help can give you assistance with a particular function you are performing. QuickBooks Pro Help also gives you information about the program using an on-screen index.

Help may be accessed to obtain information on a variety of topics, and it may be accessed in different ways:

To find out about the window in which you are working, press F1, type your question in the textbox for Ask a Help Question and click Ask, or click How Do I.

To learn about the new features available in QuickBooks Pro, click QuickBooks Help on the Help Menu, click Search tab, type "New Features" in the textbox, click Ask

To get additional information on how to use QuickBooks Pro or to enter a question and get immediate answers drawn from both the QuickBooks Help system and the technical support database, click the Help menu and click Access Support Resources.

To obtain information regarding specific items, access the Help Index by clicking QuickBooks Help on the Help menu and clicking the Index tab on the Help menu. QuickBooks Pro Help screen appears. There is a text box where you may type the first few letters of the name of the item with which you need help. As you key in the item name, QuickBooks Pro index displays items alphabetically. When the topic you need appears on the screen, double-click the topic to display it.

When the topic for Help has been located, information about the topic is provided in the Help window. If there is more information than can be shown on the screen, scroll bars will appear on the right side of the Help screen. A scroll bar is used to show or go through information. As you scroll through Help, information at the top of the Help screen disappears from view while new information appears at the bottom of the screen.

Sometimes words appear in blue and may be underlined in the QuickBooks Pro Help screen. Clicking on the blue word(s) will give you a pop-up definition of the word or display the corresponding icon. Clicking on blue underlined words will take you to other topics.

Often, the onscreen help provides links to an external Web site. To visit these links, you must have an Internet connection and be online. Links to sites outside the QuickBooks help are indicated with a lightning bolt symbol.

If you want to see a different topic, you may type in a different key word at the top of the screen. Index will give you the information on the new topic.

If you want to print a copy of the QuickBooks Pro Help screen, click the Printer icon at the top of the green title bar for the Help topic.

You may close a QuickBooks Pro Help screen by clicking the Close button (X) in the upper right corner of the screen.

PRACTICE USING HELP INDEX TO FIND KEYBOARD SHORTCUTS

Frequently, it is faster to use a keyboard shortcut to give QuickBooks Pro a command than it is to point and click the mouse through several layers of menus or icons. The list of common keyboard shortcuts may be obtained by using Help.

Use the Help Index

Click **Help** on the Menu bar
Click **QuickBooks Help**
Click the **Index** tab
Key in **k** in the textbox for "Type in keyword to find:"
keyboard shortcuts will be highlighted
Click the **Display** button
Click **General** in the listing displayed under keyboard shortcuts

- Notice the commands that may be given using the keyboard shortcuts

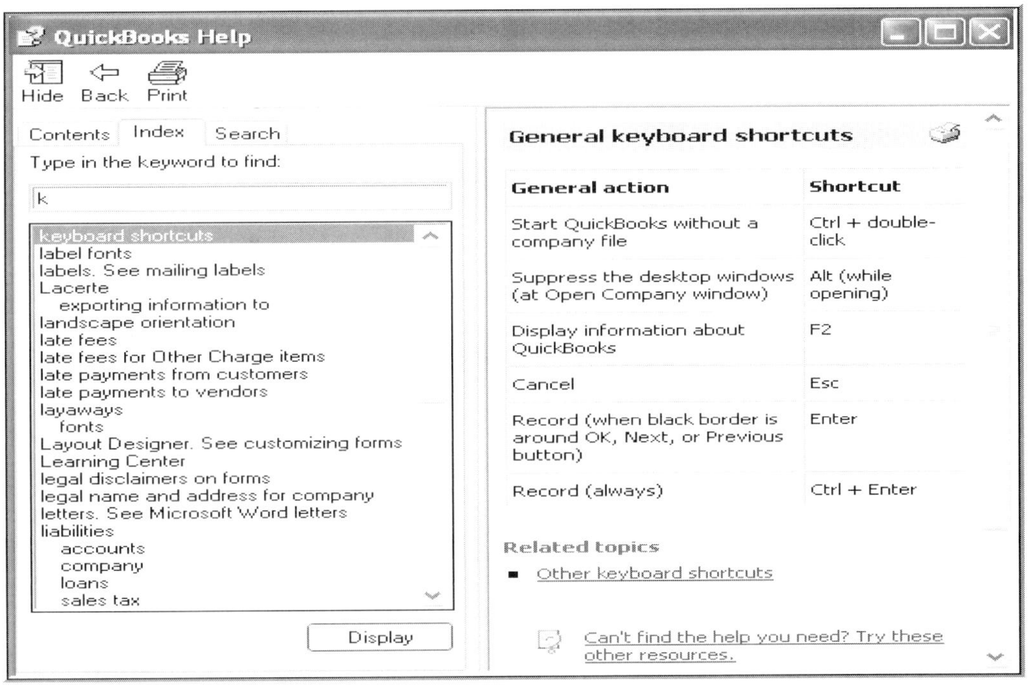

Click the **Close** button in the upper right corner of the Help screen

QUICKBOOKS® PRO FORMS

The premise of QuickBooks Pro is to allow you to focus on running the business, not deciding whether an account is debited or credited. Transactions are entered directly onto the business form that is prepared as a result of the transaction. Behind the scenes, QuickBooks Pro enters the debit and credit to the Journal and posts to the individual accounts.

QuickBooks Pro has several types of forms used to fill in your daily business transactions. They are divided into two categories: forms you want to send or give to people and forms you have received. Forms to send or give to people include invoices, sales receipts, credit memos, checks, deposit slips, and purchase orders. Forms you have received include payments from customers, bills, credits for a bill, and credit card charge receipts.

You may use the forms as they come with QuickBooks Pro, you may change or modify them, or you may create your own custom forms for use in the program.

➤ Examine the following invoice and note the terms, icons, and buttons listed as they apply to invoices. These terms will be used throughout the text when giving instructions for entries.

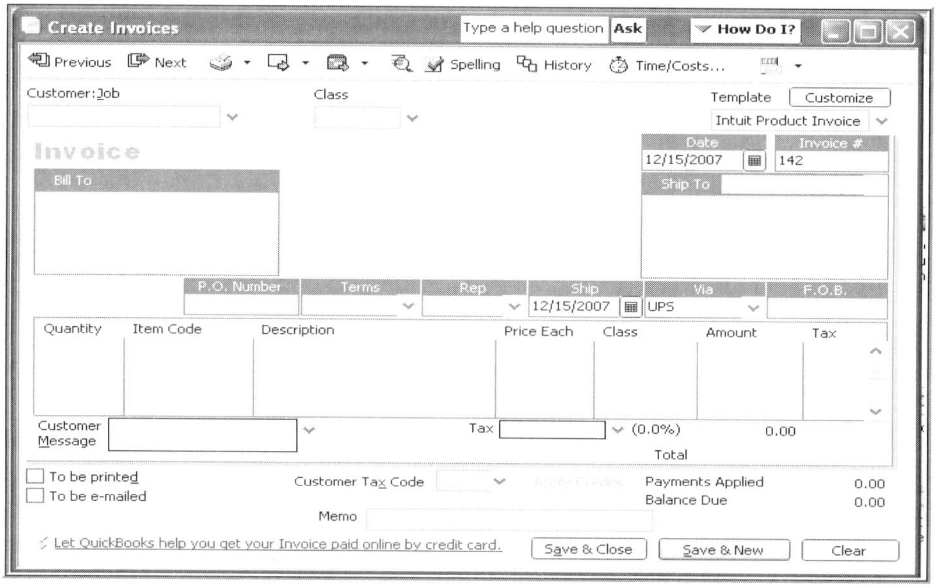

Field is an area on a form requiring information. Customer:Job is a field.

Text box is the area within a field where information may be typed or inserted. The area to be filled in to identify the Customer:Job is a text box.

Drop-down list arrow appears next to a field when there is a list of options available. On the invoice for Larry's Landscaping, clicking the drop-down list arrow for Customer:Job will display the names of all customers who have accounts with the company. Clicking a customer's name will insert the name into the text box for the field.

Title bar at the top of form indicates what you are completing. In this case, it says **Create Invoices**. The title bar also contains some buttons. They include:

Type a help question and an **Ask** button. To get assistance with a question, click in the Type a help question text box and type in your question; then, click the **Ask** button.
How Do I button that is clicked to obtain help.
Close button closes the current screen.

Toolbar at the top of the invoice has icons that are used to give commands to QuickBooks Pro or to get information regarding linked or related transactions.

Previous is clicked to go back to the previous invoice. This is used when you want to view, print, or correct the previous invoice. Each time the Previous icon is clicked, you go back one invoice. You may click the Previous icon until you go all the way back to invoices with opening balances.

Next is clicked to go to the next invoice after the one you entered. If the invoice on the screen has not been saved, this saves the invoice and goes to the next invoice. The next invoice may be one that has already been created and saved or it may be a blank invoice.

Print icon is used to print the invoice on paper, to view the invoice, to print a batch of invoices, to print postage, or to order business forms.

Send icon is used to fax or e-mail invoices.

Ship icon is used to ship merchandise.

Find is used to find invoices previously prepared.

Spelling is used to check the spelling in a business document.

History allows you to view information regarding any payments that have been made on the invoice.

Time/Costs opens the Choose Billable Time and Costs window where you can select which costs to include on the current invoice.

Letters icon is used to create letters for invoices.

Buttons on the bottom of the invoice are used to give commands to QuickBooks Pro.

Save & Close button is clicked when all information has been entered for the invoice and you are ready for QuickBooks Pro to save the invoice and exit the Create Invoices screen.

Save & New button is clicked when all information has been entered for the invoice and you are ready to complete a new invoice.

Clear button is clicked if you want to clear the information entered on the current invoice.

QUICKBOOKS® PRO LISTS

In order to expedite entering transactions, QuickBooks Pro uses lists as an integral part of the program. Customers, vendors, sales items, and accounts are organized as lists. In fact, the chart of accounts is considered to be a list in QuickBooks Pro. Frequently, information can be entered on a form by clicking on a list item.

Most lists have a maximum. However, it's unlikely that you'll run out of room on your lists. With so many entries available, there is room to add list items as you work. In fact, QuickBooks Pro allows items to be added to lists "on the fly." The vendors, customers, and employees lists are all provided in the related Centers. If you open the Customer Center, the Customer List will appear on the left side of the Center as follows:

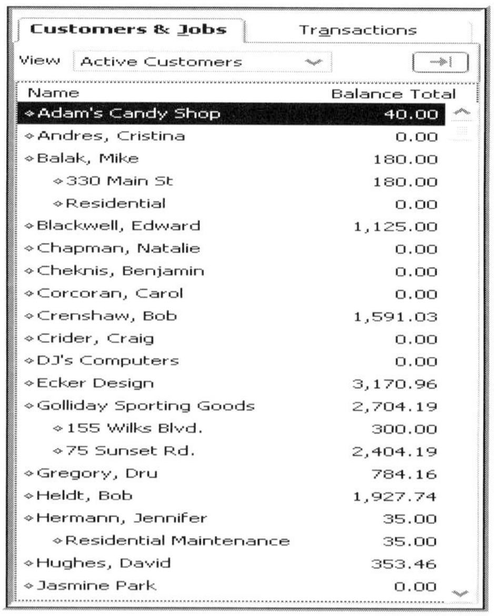

Use the **Lists** menu to examine several lists:

Click **Customer Center** to view the list of customers (in accounting concepts this is referred to as the Accounts Receivable Subsidiary Ledger), click the **Close** button to exit

Click the **Lists** menu, click **Chart of Accounts** to view the Chart of Accounts, click the **Close** button to exit

Click the **Vendor Center** to view the list of vendors(in accounting concepts this is referred to as the Accounts Payable Subsidiary Ledger), click the **Close** button to exit

QUICKBOOKS® PRO REGISTERS

QuickBooks Pro prepares a register for every balance sheet account. An account register contains records of all activity for the account. Registers provide an excellent means of looking at transactions within an account. For example, the Accounts Receivable register maintains a record of every invoice, credit memo, and payment that has been recorded for credit customers (in accounting concepts this is the Accounts Receivable account).

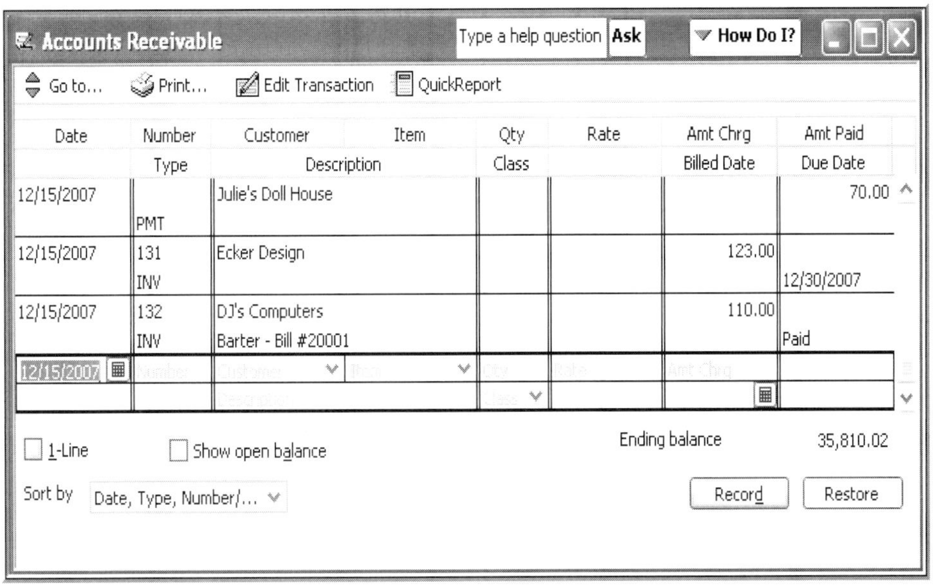

Examine the Accounts Receivable Register

Click **Chart of Accounts** in the Company section of the Home Page

Click **Accounts Receivable**

Click the **Activities** button at the bottom of the screen

Click **Use Register**

Scroll through the register

Look at the Number/Type column

Notice the types of transactions listed:

INV is for an invoice

PMT indicates a payment received from a customer
Click the **Close** button on the Register
Click the **Close** button on the Chart of Accounts List

QUICKBOOKS® PRO REPORTS

Reports are an integral part of a business. Reports enable owners and managers to determine how the business is doing and to make decisions affecting the future of the company. Reports can be prepared showing the profit and loss for the period, the status of the Balance Sheet (assets equal liabilities plus owner's equity), information regarding accounts receivable and accounts payable, and the amount of sales for each item. QuickBooks Pro has a wide range of reports and reporting options available. Reports may be customized to better reflect the information needs of a company. Reports may be generated in a variety of ways.

Reports menu includes a complete listing of the reports available in QuickBooks Pro and is used to prepare reports including: company and financial reports such as profit and loss (income statement), balance sheet; accounts receivable reports; sales reports; accounts payable reports; budget reports; transaction reports; transaction detail reports; payroll reports; list reports; custom reports; graphs showing graphical analysis of business operations; and several other classifications of reports.

Report Center includes a complete listing of the reports available in QuickBooks Pro.

Prepare reports from the Reports menu

Click **Reports** on the menu bar
Point to **Company & Financial**
Click **Profit & Loss Standard**
Scroll the Profit and Loss Statement for Larry's Landscaping
- Notice the Net Income for the period.

Click the **Close** button to exit the report

Prepare reports using the **Report Center**

Click **Report Center** button
Click **Company & Financial** in the list of reports on the left side of the navigator
Scroll through the list of reports available
Click **Balance Sheet Standard**
Scroll through the report
- Notice that assets equal liabilities plus equity.

Do not close the report

QUICKZOOM

QuickZoom allows you to view transactions that contribute to the data on reports or graphs.

Use QuickZoom

Scroll through the Balance Sheet on the screen until you see the fixed asset Truck Position the mouse pointer over the amount for **Total Truck**

- The mouse pointer turns into a magnifying glass with a Z.

Double-click the mouse to see the transaction detail for the Total Truck
Click the **Close** button to close the **Transactions by Account** report
Click the **Close** button to close the **Balance Sheet**
Do not close the Report Center

QUICKBOOKS® PRO GRAPHS

Using bar charts and pie charts, QuickBooks Pro gives you an instant visual analysis of different elements of your business. You may obtain information in a graphical form for Income & Expenses, Sales, Accounts Receivable, Accounts Payable, Net Worth, and Budget vs. Actual. For example, using the Report Center and Company & Financial as the type of report, clicking on Net Worth allows you to see an owner's net worth in relationship to assets and liabilities. This is displayed on a bar chart according to the month. To obtain information about liabilities for a given month, you may zoom in on the liabilities portion of the bar, double-click, and see the liabilities for the month displayed in a pie chart.

View a Graph

Report Center should be on the screen
Click **Company & Financial** as the **Type of Report**
Click **Net Worth Graph**

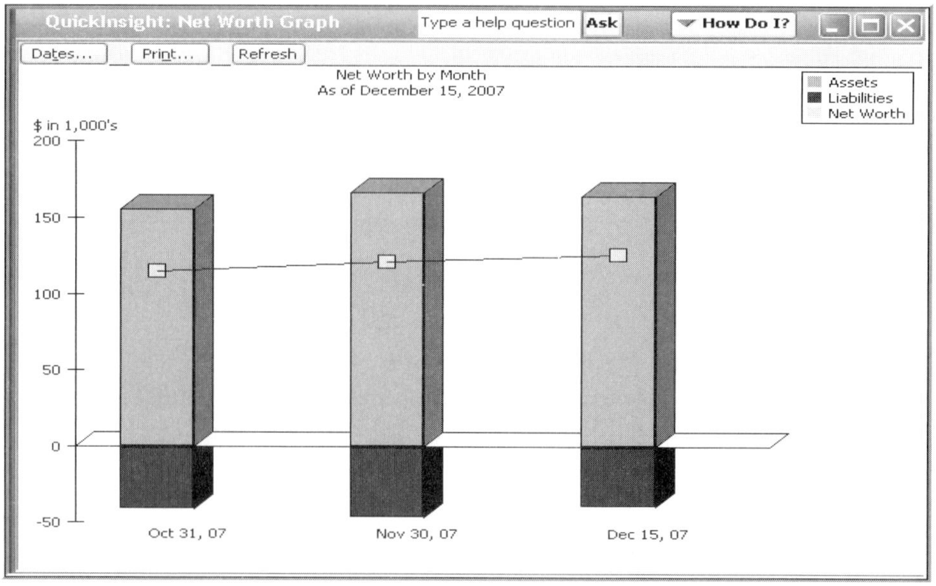

Zoom in on the Liabilities for October by pointing to the liabilities and double-clicking
View the pie chart for October's liabilities

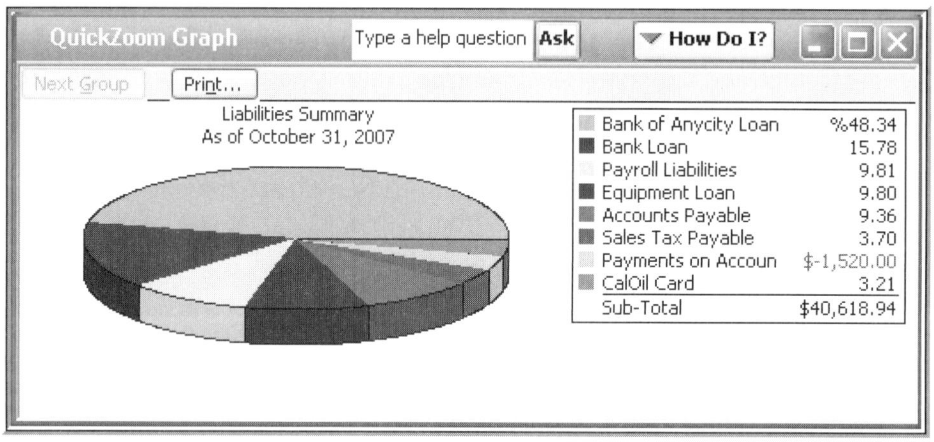

Click the **Close** button to close the pie chart
Zoom in on the Net Worth for December and double-click
View the pie chart for December's **Net Worth Summary**
Ctrl+F4 to close the pie chart
Click the **Close** button to close the **Net Worth** graph
Close **Report Center**

QUICKREPORT

QuickReports are reports that give you detailed information about items you are viewing. They look just like standard reports that you prepare but are considered "quick" because you don't have to go through the Reports menu to create them. For example, when you are viewing the Employee List, you can obtain information about an individual employee simply by clicking the employee's name in the list, clicking the Reports button, and selecting QuickReports from the menu.

View a QuickReport

Click **Lists** on the menu bar
Click **Chart of Accounts**
Click **Prepaid Insurance**
Click **Reports** button at the bottom of the Chart of Accounts List
Click **QuickReport: Prepaid Insurance**

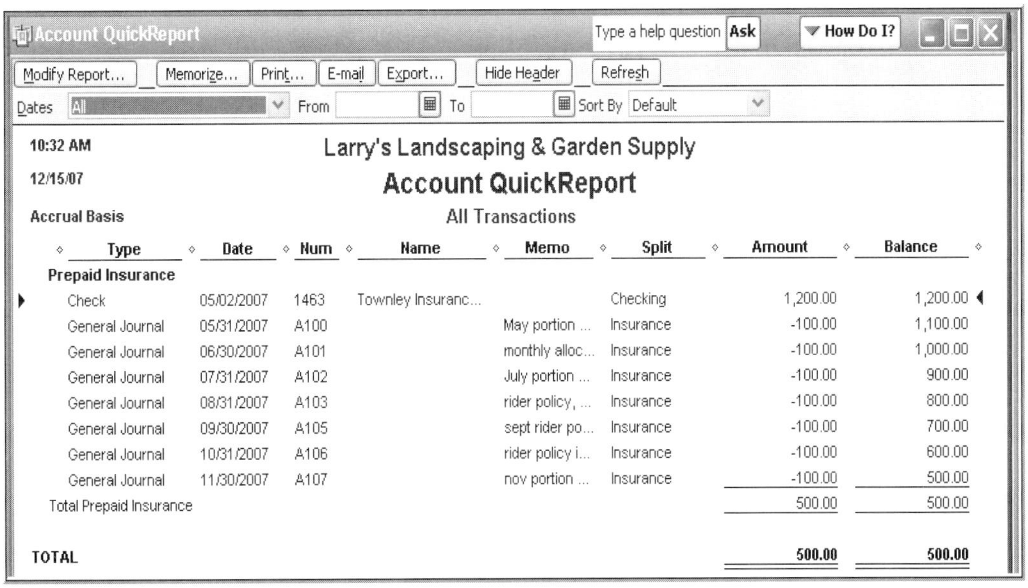

10:32 AM
12/15/07
Accrual Basis

Larry's Landscaping & Garden Supply
Account QuickReport
All Transactions

Type	Date	Num	Name	Memo	Split	Amount	Balance
Prepaid Insurance							
Check	05/02/2007	1463	Townley Insuranc...		Checking	1,200.00	1,200.00
General Journal	05/31/2007	A100		May portion ...	Insurance	-100.00	1,100.00
General Journal	06/30/2007	A101		monthly alloc...	Insurance	-100.00	1,000.00
General Journal	07/31/2007	A102		July portion ...	Insurance	-100.00	900.00
General Journal	08/31/2007	A103		rider policy, ...	Insurance	-100.00	800.00
General Journal	09/30/2007	A105		sept rider po...	Insurance	-100.00	700.00
General Journal	10/31/2007	A106		rider policy i...	Insurance	-100.00	600.00
General Journal	11/30/2007	A107		nov portion ...	Insurance	-100.00	500.00
Total Prepaid Insurance						500.00	500.00
TOTAL						**500.00**	**500.00**

Click **Close** to close the **QuickReport**
Click **Close** to close the **Chart of Accounts**

HOW TO USE QUICKMATH

QuickMath is available for use whenever you are in a field where a calculation is to be made. Frequently, QuickBooks Pro will make calculations for you automatically; however, there may be instances when you need to perform the calculation. For example, on an invoice, QuickBooks Pro will calculate an amount based on the quantity and the rate given for a sales item. If for some reason you do not have a rate for a sales item, you may use QuickMath to calculate the amount. To do this, you tab to the amount column, type an = or a number and the +. QuickBooks Pro will show a calculator tape on the screen. You may then add, subtract, multiply, or divide to obtain a total or a subtotal. Pressing the enter key inserts the amount into the column.

Use QuickMath

Click the **Invoices** icon on the Home Page
Click in the **Amount** column on the Invoice
Enter the numbers: **123+**
456+
789+

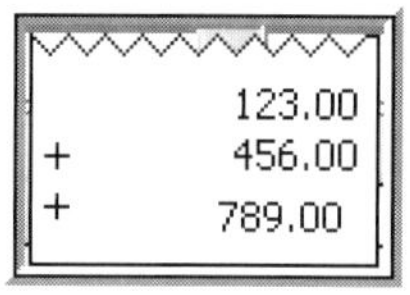

Press **Enter**
The total **1,368** is inserted into the Amount column
Click the **Clear** button to clear the Amount column
Click the **Close** button on the Invoice to close the invoice without saving

HOW TO USE WINDOWS® CALCULATOR

Windows includes accessory programs that may be used when working. One of these accessory programs is Calculator. Using this program gives you an on-screen calculator. To use the Calculator in Windows, click Start, point to Programs, point to Accessories, click Calculator. A calculator appears on your screen. The Windows calculator is also accessible through QuickBooks.

Access Windows Calculator through QuickBooks Pro

Click **Edit** on the menu bar
Click **Use Calculator**
Change from a standard calculator to a scientific calculator, click **View** menu, click **Scientific**

Change back to a standard calculator, click **View** menu, click **Standard**
Numbers may be entered by:
Clicking the number on the calculator
Keying the number using the numeric keypad
Typing the keyboard numbers
Enter the numbers: **123+**
456+
789+
The amount is added after each entry
After typing 789+, the answer 1368 appears automatically
Note: Using the Windows Calculator does not insert the amount into a QuickBooks form.
To clear the answer, click the **C** button on the calculator
Enter: **55*6**
Press **Enter** or click = to get the answer 330
Click **Control menu icon**, click **Close** to close the **Calculator**

HOW TO CLOSE A COMPANY

The sample company—Larry's Landscaping & Garden Supply—will appear as the open company whenever you open QuickBooks Pro. In order to discontinue the use of the sample company, you must close the company. In a classroom environment, you should always back up your work and close the company you are using at the end of a work session. If you use different computers when training, not closing a company at the end of each work session may cause your files to become corrupt, your disk to fail, or leave unwanted .qbi (QuickBooks In Use) files on your data disk.

Close a company

Click **File** menu, click **Close Company**
Close **QuickBooks**

DOWNLOAD COMPANY FILES

The company files for the text are available on the Prentice Hall web site www.prenhall.com/compaccounting.

Download company files

Open Internet Explorer
Enter the address www.prenhall.com/compaccounting on the URL
Click on the link for **QuickBooks**
Click on the link for **QuickBooks Pro 2006 Complete**

Click on the file name **qb06data**
Click **Save**
Insert your USB drive into your computer or ask you professor for specific directions to be used at your school
When the **Save As** screen appears, click the drop-down list arrow next to **Save In**
Click on the drive location for your USB drive

- In the example, my drive location is E:

Click **Save**
When the download is complete, click **Open**
Double-click the folder for **qb06data** to see the company files
Double-click the folder for **Computer** to see the company file
Continue with the next section

COPY A COMPANY FILE

A copy of the company files should be kept as a master. A master file is never used. It is set aside in case something happens to the file you are using to do your work. Work within the text will always be performed on a duplicate copy of the company data.

Make a duplicate of Computer

- Check with your instructor to make sure this is the procedure to be followed.

Click the **Folders** icon at the top of the screen

Scroll through the **All Folders** side on the left side of the Explorer screen
Point to the **Computer** company file
Hold down the right-mouse button and drag the file to **E:** (or the file location your instructor wants you to use)
Release the mouse button
Click **Copy Here**

- This will make a duplicate copy of the company file. This is the file you will use for training.

It is possible that the copy will be marked as "Read Only" and/or "Archive"
Once the file has been copied, right-click on the file
Click **Properties**
If there is a checkmark next to "Read Only" or "Archive" click the check box to remove the mark
The file is now ready for use.

YOUR NAME COMPUTER CONSULTANTS—COMPANY DESCRIPTION

In the text you will be recording transactions for a company that specializes in computer consulting. The company provides program installation, training, and technical support for today's business software as well as getting clients online and giving instruction in the use of the Internet. In addition, Your Name Computer Consulting will set up computer systems for customers and will install basic computer components, such as memory, modems, sound cards, disk drives, and CD and DVD drives.

This fictitious, small, sole proprietor company will be owned and run by you. You will be adding your name to the company name and equity accounts. This company will be used for training while completing Chapters 1 through 4.

OPEN A COMPANY—STUDENT'S NAME COMPUTER CONSULTANTS

Open a company

Open QuickBooks Pro as previously instructed
Click **Open an Existing Company** button at the bottom of the No Company Open screen
Click the drop-down list arrow for **Look in**
Click **Removable Disk (F:)** (or whatever drive your instructor wants you to use)
Locate **Computer** (under the **Look in** text box)

- Your company file may have an extension of **.qbw.** This is the file extension for your "QuickBooks Working" file. This is the company file that may be opened and used.

Double-click **Computer** to open, or click **Computer** and click **Open**

VERIFYING AN OPEN COMPANY

Verify the title bar heading:

Unless you tell QuickBooks Pro to create a new company, open a different company, or close the company, Student's Name Computer Consultants will appear as the open company whenever you open QuickBooks Pro. However, when you finish a work session, you should always close the company in order to avoid problems with the file in a future work session.

CLOSE THE QUICKBOOKS LEARNING CENTER

QuickBooks has an optional window that may be shown when a company is open. This is called the QuickBooks Learning Center. It contains information and short tutorials on how to use QuickBooks and lists new materials for the current version of the software. This may be shown whenever you open the company or you may select not to have it shown.

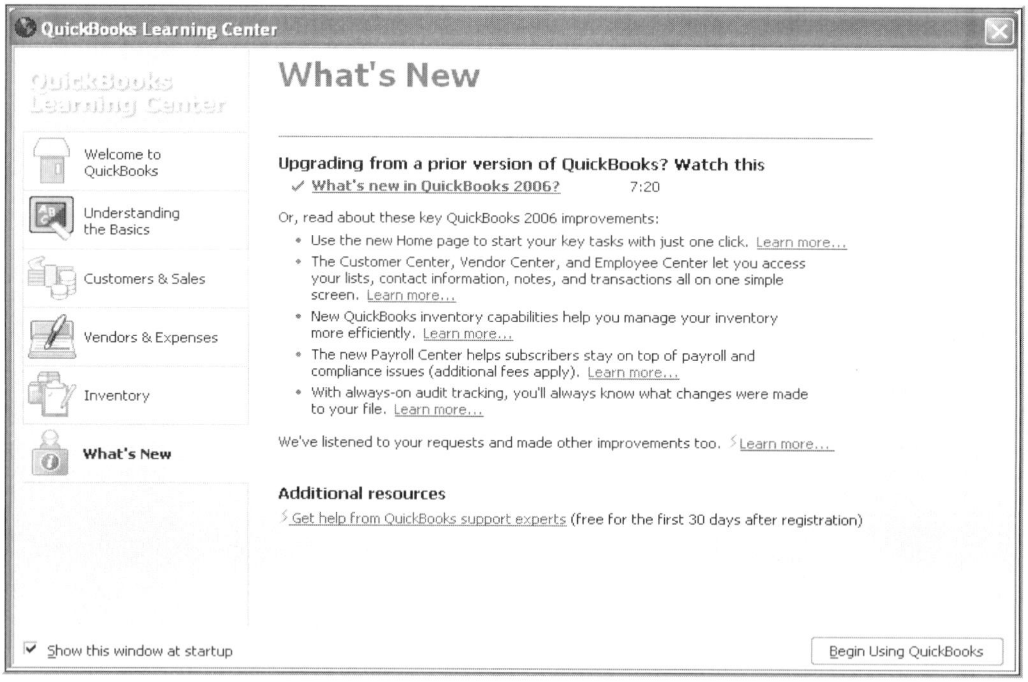

Turn off the QuickBooks Learning Center and begin using QuickBooks

Click the checkbox for **Show this window at startup** to remove the check
Click the **Begin Using QuickBooks** button

ADD YOUR NAME TO THE COMPANY NAME

Because each student in the course will be working for the same companies and printing the same documents, personalizing the company name to include your name will help identify many of the documents you print during your training.

Add your name to the company name

Click **Company** on the menu bar
Click **Company Information**
Click to the left of **Computer Consultants**
Replace the words **Student's Name** by holding down the left mouse button and dragging through the "Student's Name" to highlight
OR
Click in front of the S in Student's Name, press the **Delete** key to delete one letter at a time
Type your actual name, *not* the words *Your Name*. For example, Jeff Jones would type **Jeff Jones**
Repeat the steps to change the legal name to **Your Name Computer Consultants**
Click **OK**

- The title bar now shows **Your Name Computer Consultants**

HOW TO CREATE A QUICKBOOKS® PRO BACKUP FILE

As you work with a company and record transactions, it is important to back up your work. This allows you to keep the information for a particular period separate from current information. A backup also allows you to restore information in case your data disk becomes damaged. QuickBooks Pro has a feature to make a backup copy of your company file. A condensed file is created by QuickBooks. The file contains the essential transaction and account information. This file has a **.qbb** extension and is not usable unless it is restored to a company file that has a **.qbw** extension. This can be an existing company file or a company new file.

In this text, you will make a backup file at the end of each chapter. It will contain all the transactions entered up until the time you made the backup. At the end of each chapter, you will be instructed to make a backup file for the chapter. Future transactions will not be part of the backup file unless you make a new backup file. For example, Chapter 1 backup will not contain any transactions entered in Chapter 2. However, Chapter 2 backup will contain all the transactions for both Chapters 1 and 2. Chapter 3 backup will contain all the transactions for Chapters 1, 2, and 3, and so on.

Make a QuickBooks Pro backup of the company data for Your Name Computer Consultants.

Click **File** on the Menu Bar
Click **Back Up...**

- If you get a message for a Portable Company file, click the check box **Do not display this message in the future** to turn off the message, then click **OK**

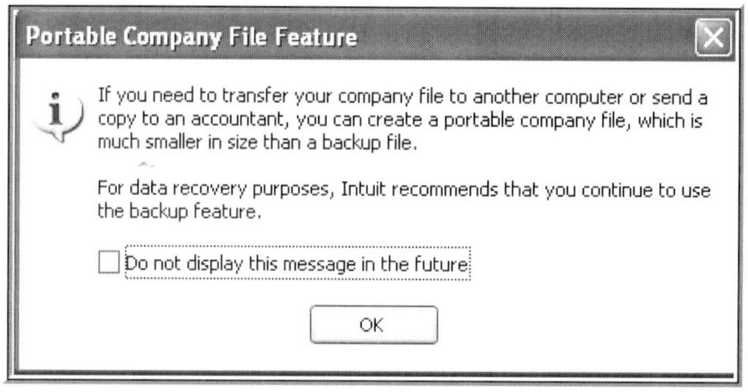

- QuickBooks Backup has two tabs: Back Up Company File and Schedule Backup.

The **Back Up Company File** tab should be active
Verify the Current Company information:
Filename is Computer.qbw
Location is F:\ or the location where your "working" file is stored
Backup Current Company should be to Disk
The circle in front of Disk should have a dot in it
Enter the filename **Computer Ch 1.qbb**
Location should be F:\ or the location where you want to store your backup file

- If it is not, click in the text box and enter the storage location

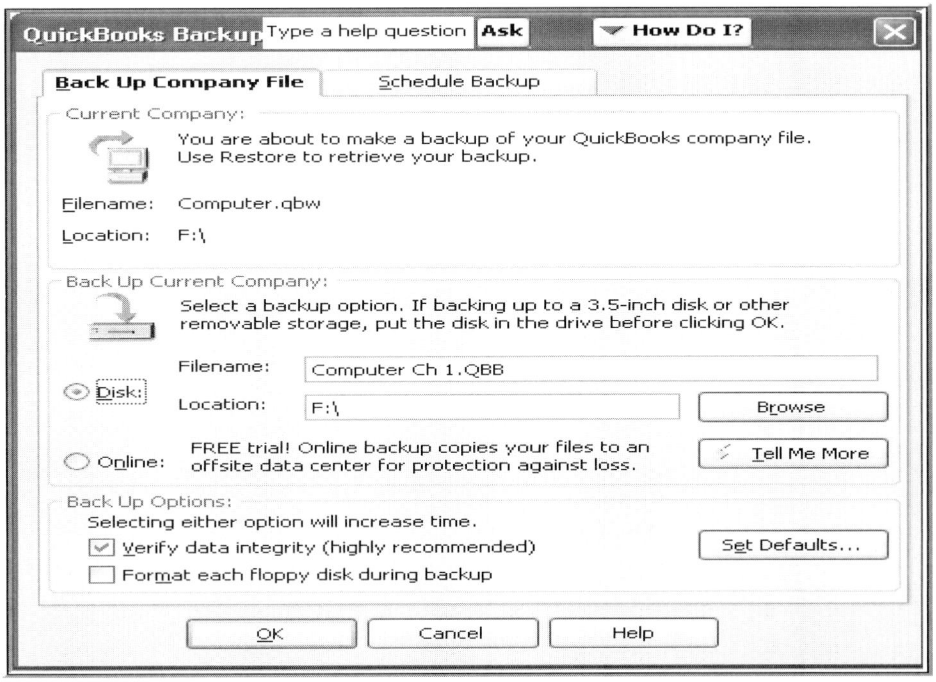

Click **OK**

- QuickBooks Pro will back up the information for Your Name Computer Consultants on the USB disk

Click the **OK** button in the dialog box stating that the backup was successful.

CHANGE THE NAME OF AN EXISTING ACCOUNT IN THE CHART OF ACCOUNTS

QuickBooks makes it easy to set up a company using the Easy Step Interview. You will create a company for use in Chapter 9 of the text. When creating a company using QuickBooks' Easy Step Interview, account names are assigned automatically. They might need to be changed to names more appropriate to the individual company.

Change account names

Access the **Chart of Accounts**:
Click **Lists** on the menu bar, click **Chart of Accounts**
Scroll through accounts until you see Student's Name Capital
Click **Student's Name Capital**
Click the **Account** button at the bottom of the Chart of Accounts
Click **Edit**
On the **Edit Account** screen, highlight **Student's Name**
Enter *your actual name*

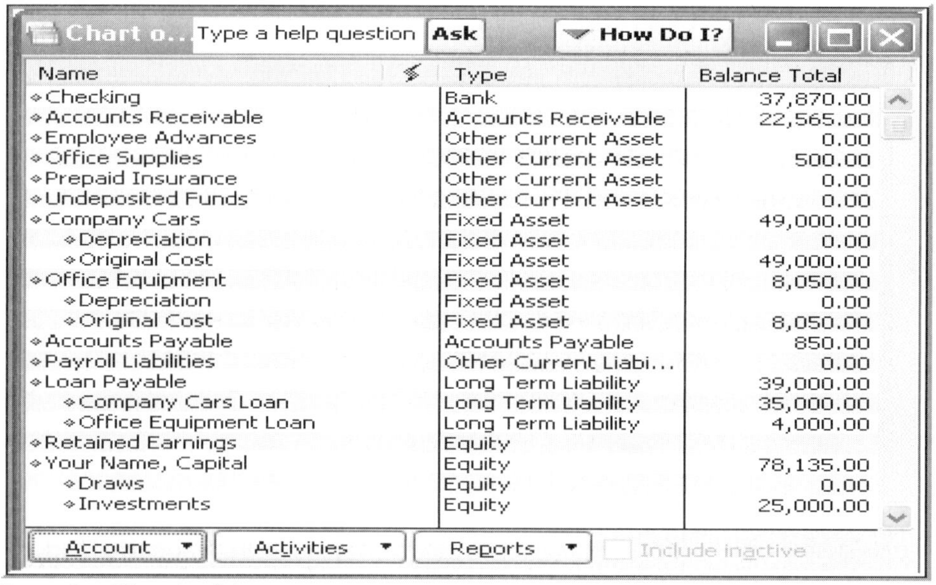

Name	Type	Balance Total
Checking	Bank	37,870.00
Accounts Receivable	Accounts Receivable	22,565.00
Employee Advances	Other Current Asset	0.00
Office Supplies	Other Current Asset	500.00
Prepaid Insurance	Other Current Asset	0.00
Undeposited Funds	Other Current Asset	0.00
Company Cars	Fixed Asset	49,000.00
Depreciation	Fixed Asset	0.00
Original Cost	Fixed Asset	49,000.00
Office Equipment	Fixed Asset	8,050.00
Depreciation	Fixed Asset	0.00
Original Cost	Fixed Asset	8,050.00
Accounts Payable	Accounts Payable	850.00
Payroll Liabilities	Other Current Liabi...	0.00
Loan Payable	Long Term Liability	39,000.00
Company Cars Loan	Long Term Liability	35,000.00
Office Equipment Loan	Long Term Liability	4,000.00
Retained Earnings	Equity	
Your Name, Capital	Equity	78,135.00
Draws	Equity	0.00
Investments	Equity	25,000.00

Close the **Chart of Accounts**

RESTORE A QUICKBOOKS® PRO BACKUP FILE

If you make an error in your training, you may find it beneficial to restore your .qbb backup file. The only way in which a .qbb backup file may be used is by restoring it to a .qbw company file. Using QuickBooks' Restore command on the File menu restores a backup file. A restored backup file replaces the current data in your company file with the data in the backup file so any transactions recorded after the backup was made will be erased.

Practice restoring a backup file after a change has been made in the company file

Click **File** on the menu bar
Click **Restore...**
Complete the **Get Company Backup From:** area of the screen
Insert **Computer Ch 1.qbb** for the Filename
Insert the Location as **F:** (or the location you are using for your files)
Complete the **Restore Company Backup To:** area of the screen
Insert **Computer.qbw** for the Filename
Insert the Location as **F:** (or the location you are using for your files)

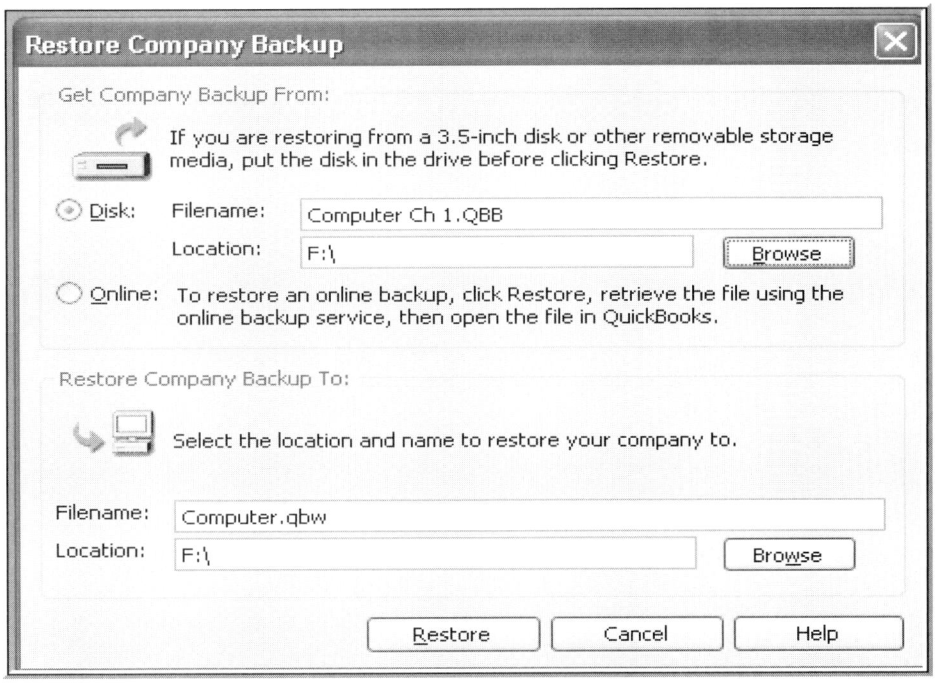

Click the **Restore** button

You will get a warning that you are choosing to overwrite an existing company file

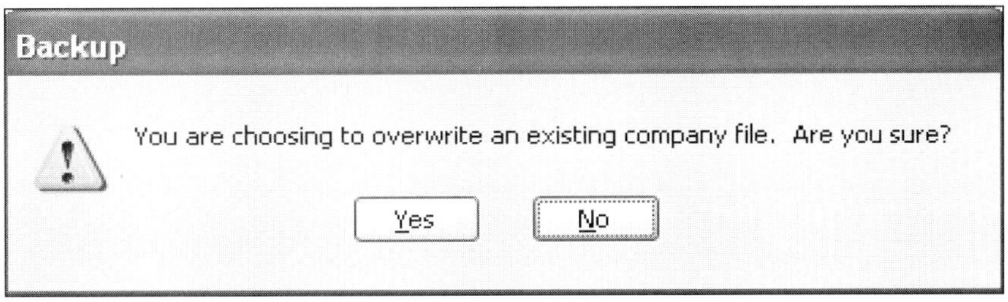

Click **Yes**

- You will get a screen telling you how much space you have available on the disk

Click **OK**

- You will get a **Delete Entire File** warning screen

Enter the word **Yes** and click **OK**

- When you restore a file to an existing company file, all the data contained in the company file will be replaced with the information in the backup file.

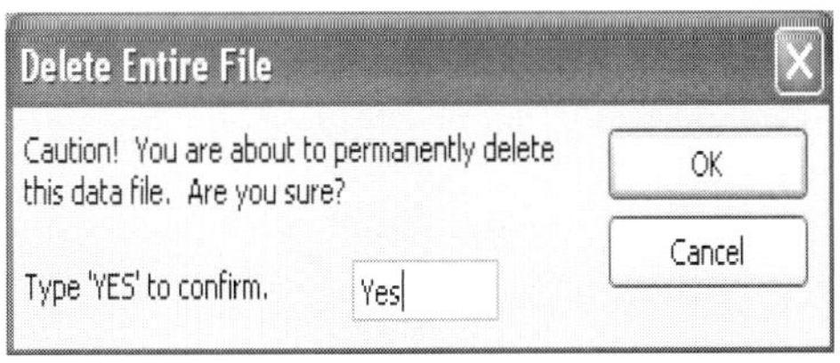

When the file has been restored, you will get the following

Press Enter or click **OK**
Open the **Chart of Accounts**
Verify that Student's Name Capital is the account name for the Owner's Capital account.

- Your Name Capital no longer shows because the company information was restored from the backup file made prior to changing the account name.

CREATE A DUPLICATE DISK

In addition to making a backup of the company file, you should always have a duplicate of the disk you use for your work. Refer to Appendix A: Introduction to Windows–Screens, Terminology, and Disk Duplication for instructions on how to use Windows Explorer to make a duplicate copy of your disk.

EXIT QUICKBOOKS® PRO AND REMOVE YOUR USB DRIVE

When you complete your work, you need to exit the QuickBooks Pro program. If you are saving work on a separate data disk or USB drive, you must not remove your disk until you exit the program. Following the appropriate steps to close and exit a program is extremely important. There are program and data files that must be closed in order to leave the program and company data so that they are ready to be used again. It is common for a beginning computer user to turn off the computer without exiting a program. This can cause corrupt program and data files and can make a disk or program unusable.

Close the company file for Your Name Computer Consultants, close QuickBooks, and stop the USB

Close the company file following the steps indicated earlier
Close QuickBooks by clicking the **Close** button in upper right corner of title bar
Click the icon for the USB drive in the lower right portion of the Taskbar

Click on the message 

When you get the message that it is safe to remove hardware, remove your USB

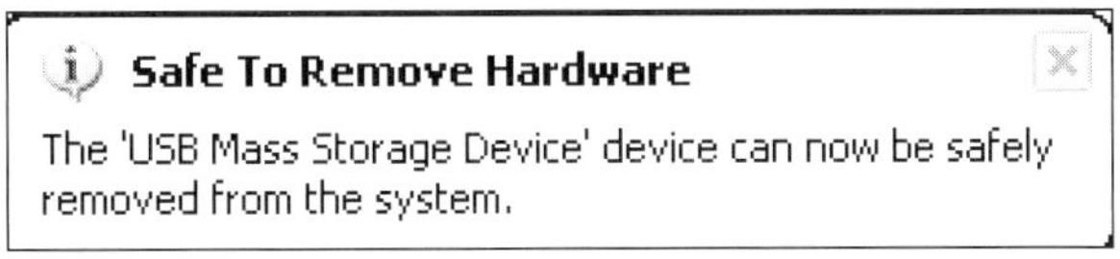

SUMMARY

Chapter 1 provides general information regarding QuickBooks Pro. In this chapter, various QuickBooks features were examined. A company file was opened, your name was added to the company name, an account name was changed. QuickBooks backup files were made and restored. Companies were closed, QuickBooks was closed, and USB drives were removed.

END-OF-CHAPTER QUESTIONS

TRUE/FALSE

ANSWER THE FOLLOWING QUESTIONS IN THE SPACE PROVIDED BEFORE THE QUESTION NUMBER.

_____ 1. There are various methods of giving QuickBooks Pro commands, including use of QuickBooks Home Page, icon bar, menu bar, and keyboard shortcuts.

_____ 2. A company file with a .qbw extension is used to record transactions.

_____ 3. Once an account has been used, the name cannot be changed.

_____ 4. If an error is made when entering a transaction, QuickBooks Pro will not allow the user to return to the business document and make the correction.

_____ 5. In a computerized accounting system, each transaction that is analyzed must be entered by hand into the appropriate journal and posted to the appropriate ledger.

_____ 6. QuickBooks Home Page appears beneath the title bar and has a list of drop-down menus.

_____ 7. If you use QuickBooks Pro to make a backup, you are actually having QuickBooks Pro create a condensed file that contains the essential transaction and account information.

_____ 8. The Alt key + a letter are used to access the drop-down menus on the menu bar.

_____ 9. When you end your work session, you must close your company, close QuickBooks, and remove your USB drive properly.

_____ 10. QuickBooks Learning Center must be shown whenever you open the company.

MULTIPLE CHOICE

WRITE THE LETTER OF THE CORRECT ANSWER IN THE SPACE PROVIDED BEFORE THE QUESTION NUMBER.

_____ 1. The extension for a company file that may be used is
   A. .qbi
   B. .qbb
   C. .qbw
   D. .qbc

_____ 2. A (n) ___ is considered to be a list in QuickBooks Pro.
   A. Invoice
   B. Chart of Accounts
   C. Company
   D. none of the above

_____ 3. QuickBooks Pro keyboard conventions ___.
   A. are keyboard command shortcuts
   B. use the mouse
   C. use certain keys in a manner consistent with Windows
   D. incorporate the use of QuickBooks Company Center

_____ 4. Buttons on the toolbar and on the bottom of an invoice are used to ___.
   A. give commands to QuickBooks Pro
   B. exit QuickBooks Pro
   C. prepare reports
   D. show graphs of invoices prepared

_____ 5. QuickMath displays ___.
   A. a calculator
   B. an adding machine tape
   C. a calculator with adding machine tape
   D. none of the above

_____ 6. QuickBooks Home Page ___.
   A. allows you to give commands to QuickBooks Pro according to the type of transaction being entered
   B. are icons shown in a row beneath the menu bar
   C. appears above the menu bar
   D. appears at the bottom of the screen

_____ 7. An icon is ___.
A. a document
B. a picture
C. a chart
D. a type of software

_____ 8. A way to find out the keyboard shortcuts for various commands is to look them up using the ___.
A. Internet
B. Help Index
C. File menu
D. Keyboard icon

_____ 9. A .qbb extension on a file name means that the file is ___.
A. open
B. the working file
C. a restored file
D. is a backup file

_____ 10. To verify the name of the open company, look at ___.
A. the icon bar
B. QuickBooks Home Page
C. the menu bar
D. the title bar

FILL-IN

IN THE SPACE PROVIDED, WRITE THE ANSWER THAT MOST APPROPRIATELY COMPLETES THE SENTENCE.

1. Whether you are using a manual or a computerized accounting system, transactions must still be __________ and __________.

2. The __________ menu is used to open and close a company and may also be used to exit QuickBooks Pro.

3. The name of the company file in use is displayed on the __________.

4. In QuickBooks you may change the company name by clicking Company Information on the __________ menu.

5. The __________ organizes tasks into logical groups (Vendors, Customers, Employees, Company, and Banking).

SHORT ESSAY

Describe the procedure of making a backup of a company file and explain its importance

____

____

____

END-OF-CHAPTER PROBLEM

At the end of each chapter, you will work with a different company and enter transactions that are similar to the ones you competed in the text. Follow the instructions given for transaction entry and printing. You may refer to the chapter for assistance.

YOUR NAME GARDEN & POOL MAINTENANCE

Your Name Garden & Pool Maintenance is owned and operated by you. Sally Jenkins and Ramon Garcia also work for the company. Sally manages the office and keeps the books for the business. Ramon provides lawn maintenance and supervises the lawn maintenance employees. You provide the pool maintenance. The company is located in Santa Barbara, California.

INSTRUCTIONS

- ► Download the company file for Your Name Garden & Pool Maintenance, **Garden.qbw**, as instructed in the chapter.
- ► Open the company.
- ► Click **Show this window at start up** to remove the check mark on the QuickBooks Learning Center, click **Begin Using QuickBooks**.
- ► Add your name to the company name. The company name will be **Your Name Garden & Pool Maintenance**. (Type your actual name, *not* the words *Your Name*. Do this whenever you are instructed to add *Your Name*.)
- ► Backup your file to **Garden Ch 1.qbb.** Mark the message for Portable Files so that it does not appear in the future.
- ► Change the name of Student's Name, Capital to **Your Name, Capital**
- ► Restore the Garden Ch 1.qbb backup file.

SALES AND RECEIVABLES: SERVICE BUSINESS

2

LEARNING OBJECTIVES

At the completion of this chapter, you will be able to:

1. Create invoices and record sales transactions on account.
2. Create sales receipts to record cash sales.
3. Edit, void, and delete invoices/sales receipts.
4. Create credit memos/refunds.
6. Add new customers and modify customer records.
7. Record cash receipts.
8. Enter partial cash payments.
9. Display and print invoices, sales receipts, and credit memos.
10. Display and print Quick Reports, Customer Balance Summary Reports, Customer Balance Detail Reports, and Transaction Reports by Customer.
11. Display and print Summary Sales by Item Reports and Itemized Sales by Item Reports.
12. Display and print Deposit Summary, Journal Reports, and Trial Balance.
13. Display Accounts Receivable Graphs and Sales Graphs.

ACCOUNTING FOR SALES AND RECEIVABLES

Rather than use a traditional Sales Journal to record transactions using debits and credits and special columns, QuickBooks Pro uses an invoice to record sales transactions for accounts receivable in the Accounts Receivable Register. Because cash sales do not involve accounts receivable, the transactions are recorded on a Sales Receipt. QuickBooks Pro puts the money received from a cash sale and from a customer's payment on account into the Undeposited Funds account. When a bank deposit is made the Undepositied Funds are placed in the Checking or Cash account. However, all transactions, regardless of the activity, are placed in the General Journal behind the scenes. A new customer can be added on the fly as transactions are entered. Unlike many computerized accounting programs, in QuickBooks Pro, error correction is easy. A sales form may be edited, voided, or deleted in the same window where it was created. Customer information may be changed by editing the Customer List. A multitude of reports are available when using QuickBooks Pro. Accounts receivable reports include Customer Balance Summary and Balance Detail reports. Sales reports provide information regarding the amount of sales by item. Transaction Reports by Customer are available as well as the traditional accounting reports such as Trial Balance, Profit and Loss, and Balance Sheet. QuickBooks Pro also has graphing capabilities so you can see and evaluate your accounts receivable and sales at the click of a button.

TRAINING TUTORIAL

The following tutorial is a step-by-step guide to recording sales (both cash and credit), customer payments, bank deposits, and other transactions for receivables for a fictitious company with fictitious employees. This company was used in Chapter 1 and is called Your Name Computer Consulting. In addition to recording transactions using QuickBooks Pro, we will prepare several reports and graphs for the company. The tutorial for Your Name Computer Consulting will continue in Chapters 3 and 4, where accounting for payables, bank reconciliations, financial statement preparation, and closing an accounting period will be completed.

TRAINING PROCEDURES

To maximize the training benefits, you should:

1. Read the entire chapter *before* beginning the tutorial within the chapter.
2. Answer the end-of-chapter questions.
3. Be aware that transactions to be entered are given within a **MEMO**.
4. Complete all the steps listed for the Your Name Computer Consulting tutorial in the chapter. (Indicated by:)
5. When you have completed a section, put a check mark next to the final step completed.
6. If you do not complete a section, put the date in the margin next to the last step completed. This will make it easier to know where to begin when training is resumed.
7. As you complete your work, proofread carefully and check for accuracy. Double-check amounts of money.
8. If you find an error while preparing a transaction, correct it. If you find the error after the Invoice, Sales Form, Credit Memo, or Customer:Job List is complete, follow the steps indicated in this chapter to correct, void, or delete transactions.
9. Print as directed within the chapter.
10. You may not finish the entire chapter in one computer session. Always use QuickBooks Pro to back up your work at the end of your work session as described in Chapter 1 and make a duplicate disk as described in Appendix A.
11. When you complete your computer session, always close your company. If you try to use a computer and a previous student did not close the company, QuickBooks Pro may freeze when you start to work. In addition, if you do not close the company as you leave, you may have problems with your company file, your disk may be damaged, and you may have unwanted .qbi (QuickBooks In Use) files that cause problems when using the company file.

COMPANY FILE

In Chapter 1, you began using the company. You changed the name from Student's Name Computer Consulting to Your Name Computer Consulting. A backup of the file was made. An account name was changed. The backup file was restored and you learned that the account name change had been replaced by the name in the backup file. During Chapters 2-4, you will continue to use the Computer.qbw file originally used in Chapter 1 to record transactions.

COMPANY PROFILE: YOUR NAME COMPUTER CONSULTING

As you learned in Chapter 1, Your Name Computer Consulting is a company specializing in computer consulting. The company provides program installation, training, and technical support for today's business software as well as getting clients online and giving instruction in the use of the Internet. In addition, Your Name Computer Consulting will set up computer systems for customers and will install basic computer components, such as memory, modems, sound cards, disk drives, and DVD and CD-ROM drives.

Your Name Computer Consulting is located in Southern California and is a sole proprietorship owned by you. You are involved in all aspects of the business and have the responsibility of obtaining clients. There are three employees: Justine Wong, who is responsible for software training; Silas Kaan, who handles hardware installation and technical support; and Consuelo Alcampo, whose duties include being office manager and bookkeeper and providing technical support.

Your Name Computer Consulting bills by the hour for training and hardware installation with a minimum charge of $95 for the first hour and $80 per hour thereafter. Clients with contracts for technical support are charged a monthly rate for service.

BEGIN TRAINING IN QUICKBOOKS® PRO

As you continue this chapter, you will be instructed to enter transactions for Your Name Computer Consulting. As you learned in Chapter 1, the first thing you must do in order to work is boot up or start your computer, open the program QuickBooks Pro, and open the company.

➤ Refer to Chapter 1 to Open QuickBooks Pro

OPEN A COMPANY—YOUR NAME COMPUTER CONSULTING

In Chapter 1, Your Name Computer Consulting was opened and a backup of the company file was made using QuickBooks Pro. Your Name Computer Consulting should have been closed in Chapter 1. To open the company for this work session you may click the Open an Existing Company button on the No Company Open screen or by clicking on File menu and Open Company. Verify this by checking the title bar.

Open **Your Name Computer Consulting**

Click **Open an Existing Company** button at the bottom of the No Company Open screen
OR
Click **File** on the Menu bar and click **Open Company**

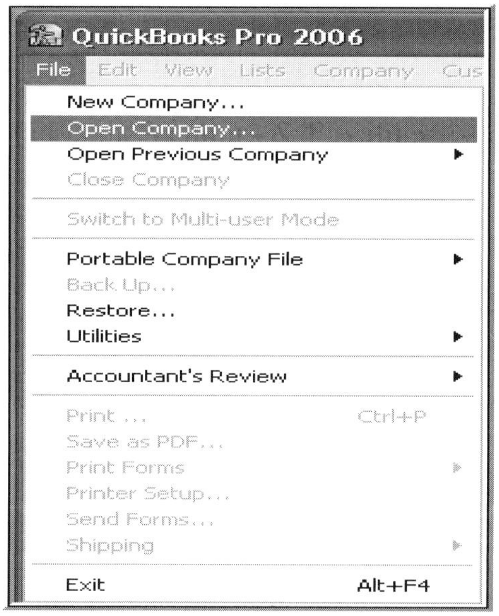

Click the drop-down list arrow for **Look in**
Click **Removable Disk (F:)** (or whatever drive your instructor wants you to use)
Locate **Computer** (under the **Look in** text box)

- Your company file may have an extension of **.qbw.** This is the file extension for your "QuickBooks Working" file. This is the company file that may be opened and used. As you learned in Chapter 1, you may not use a .qbb (backup) file for direct entry. A backup file must be restored to a .qbw (company) file.

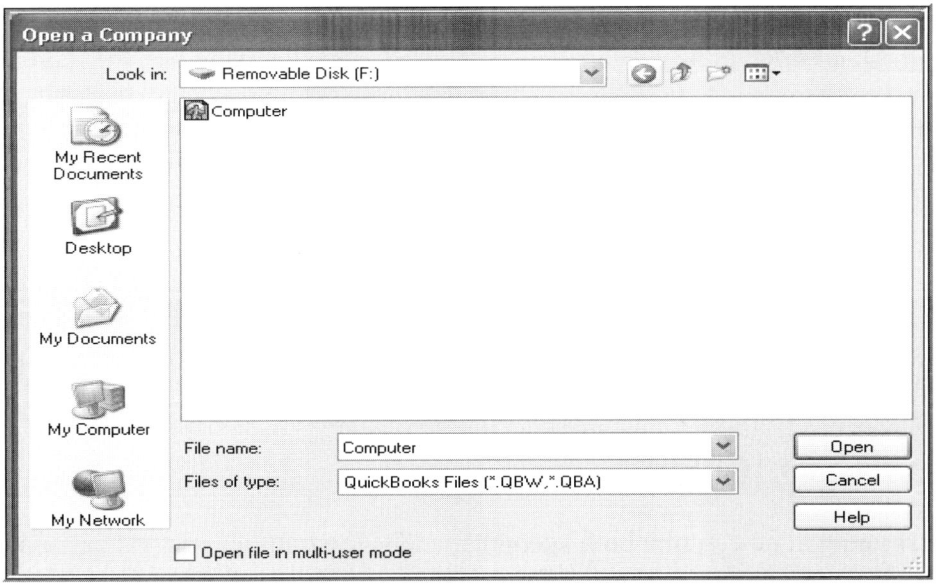

Double-click **Computer** to open, or click **Computer** and click **Open**

- Remember, this is the same file you used in Chapter 1.

VERIFYING AN OPEN COMPANY

Verify the title bar heading:

- The title bar should show **Your Name Computer Consulting** as the company name.
- *Note:* Unless you tell QuickBooks Pro to create a new company, open a different company, or close the company, Student's Name Computer Consultants will appear as the open company whenever you open QuickBooks Pro. However, when you finish a work session, you should always close the company in order to avoid problems with the file in a future work session.

QUICKBOOKS® HOME PAGE AND CENTERS

The QuickBooks Home Page allows you to give commands to QuickBooks Pro according to the type of transaction being entered. The Home Page tasks are organized into logical groups (Vendors, Customers, Employees, Company, and Banking). Each of the areas on the Home Page is used to enter different types of transactions. When appropriate, the Home Page shows a flow chart with icons indicating the major activities performed. The icons are arranged in the order in which transactions usually occur and are clicked to access screens to enter information or transactions in QuickBooks Pro. You may also choose to use the menu bar, the icon bar, or the keyboard to give commands to QuickBooks Pro. For more detailed information regarding the QuickBooks Home Page, refer to Chapter 1. Instructions in this text will be given primarily using the QuickBooks Home Page. However, the menu bar, the icon bar, and/or keyboard methods will be used as well.

At the top of the Home Page and below the menu bar, are a series of buttons that allow access to QuickBooks Centers. These are the Vendor, Customer, Employee, and Report centers. The centers focus on providing detailed information and accessing the lists associated with the center.

BEGINNING THE TUTORIAL

In this chapter you will be entering both accounts receivable transactions and cash sales transactions. Much of the organization of QuickBooks Pro is dependent on lists. The two primary types of lists you will use in the tutorial for receivables are a Customer:Job List and a Sales Item List.

The names, addresses, telephone numbers, credit terms, credit limits, and balances for all established credit customers are contained in the Customer:Job List. The Customer:Job List can also be referred to as the Accounts Receivable Ledger. QuickBooks Pro does not use this term; however, the Customer:Job List does function as the Accounts Receivable Ledger. A transaction entry for an individual customer is posted to the customer's account in the Customer:Job List just as it would be posted to the customer's individual account in an Accounts Receivable Ledger. The balance of the Customer:Job List will be equal to the balance of the Accounts

Receivable account in the Chart of Accounts, which is also the General Ledger. Invoices and accounts receivable transactions can also be related to specific jobs you are completing for customers. You will be using the following Customer:Job List for established credit customers.

Various types of income are considered to be sales. In Your Name Computer Consulting, there are several income accounts. In addition, there are categories within an income account. For example, Your Name Computer Consulting uses Training Income to represent revenues earned by providing on-site training. The sales items used for Training Income are Training 1 for the first or initial hour of on-site training and Training 2 for all additional hours of on-site training. As you look at the Item List, you will observe that the rates for the two items are different. Using lists for sales items allows for flexibility in billing and a more accurate representation of the way in which income is earned. The following Item List for the various types of sales will be used for the company.

Name	Description	Type	Account	Price
◊Tech Sup 1	5 Hours--Monthly Technical Support	Service	Income:Technical Suppo...	150.00
◊Tech Sup 2	10 Hours--Monthly Technical Support	Service	Income:Technical Suppo...	300.00
◊Tech Sup 3	15 Hours--Monthly Technical Support	Service	Income:Technical Suppo...	450.00
◊Training 1	Initial Hour of On-Site Training	Service	Income:Training Income	95.00
◊Training 2	Additional Hours of On-Site Training	Service	Income:Training Income	80.00

In the tutorial all transactions are listed on memos. The transaction date will be the same date as the memo date unless otherwise specified within the transaction. Always enter the date of the transaction as specified in the memo. By default, QuickBooks Pro automatically enters the current date or the last transaction date used. In many instances, this will not be the same date as the transaction in the text. Customer names, when necessary, will be given in the transaction. All terms for customers on account are Net 30 days unless specified otherwise. If a memo contains more than one transaction, there will be a horizontal line or a blank line separating the transactions.

MEMO

DATE: The transaction date is listed here

Transaction details are given in the body of the memo. Customer names, the type of transaction, amounts of money, and any other details needed are listed here.

Even when you are instructed how to enter a transaction step by step, you should always refer to the memo for transaction details. Once a specific type of transaction has been entered in a step-by-step manner, additional transactions will be made without having instructions provided. Of course, you may always refer to instructions given for previous transactions for ideas or for the steps used to enter those transactions. Again, always double-check the date and the year used for the transaction. QuickBooks automatically inserts the computer's current date, which will probably be quite different from the date in the text. Using an incorrect date will cause reports to have different totals and contain different transactions than those shown in the text.

ENTER SALE ON ACCOUNT

Because QuickBooks Pro operates on a business form premise, a sale on account is entered via an invoice. You prepare an invoice, and QuickBooks Pro records the transaction in the Journal and updates the customer's account automatically.

MEMO:
DATE: January 2, 2006

Bill the following: Invoice No. 1—Jose Mendoza has had several questions regarding his new computer system. He spoke with you about this and has signed up for 10 hours of technical support (Tech Sup 2) for January. Bill him for this and use Thank you for your business. as the message.

Record the sale on account shown in the invoice above. This invoice is used to bill a customer for a sale using one sales item:

Click the **Invoices** icon on the Home Page

- A blank invoice will show on the screen.

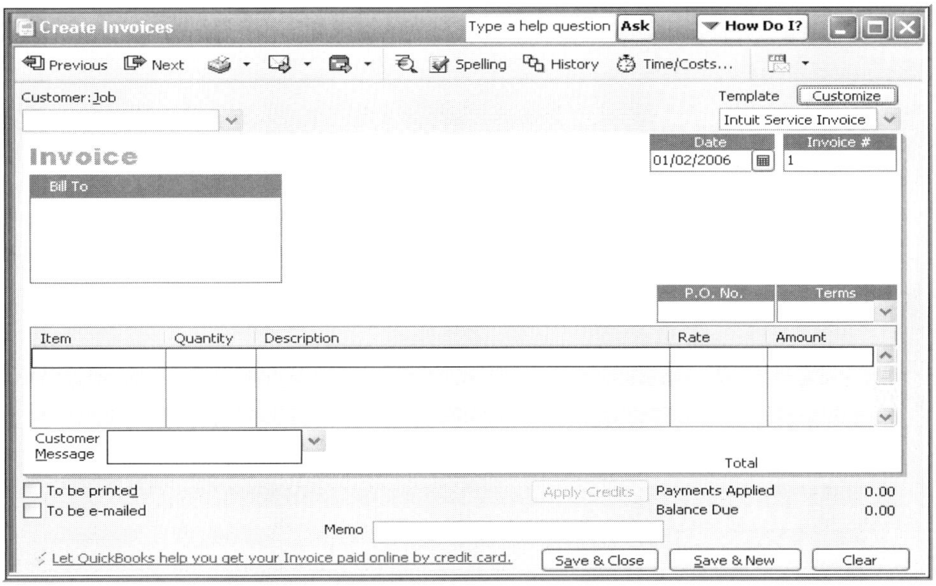

Click the drop-down list arrow next to **Customer:Job**

Click **Mendoza, Juan**

- His name is entered as Customer:Job, and Bill To information is completed automatically.

Tab two times to highlight **Intuit Service Invoice**

- Intuit Service Invoice should be displayed in the text box beneath Template. If it is not, click the drop-down list arrow next to the Customize button, click **Intuit Service Invoice**.

Tab to **Date**

- When you tab to the date, it will be highlighted. When you type in the new date, the highlighted date will be deleted.

Type **01/02/06** as the date

Invoice No. 1 should be showing in the **Invoice No.** box

- The Invoice No. should not have to be changed.

There is no PO No. to record

Terms should be indicated as **Net 30**

- If not, click the drop-down list arrow next to **Terms** and click **Net 30**.

Tab to or click the first line beneath **Item**

Click the drop-down list arrow next to **Item**

- Refer to the memo above and the Item List for appropriate billing information.

Click **Tech Sup 2** to bill for 10 hours of technical support

- Tech Sup 2 is entered as the Item.

Tab to or click **Qty**

Type **1**

- The quantity is one because you are billing for 1 unit of Tech Sup 2. As you can see on the Item List, Tech Sup 2 is for 10 hours of support. The total for the item and for the invoice is automatically calculated when you tab to the next item or click in a new invoice area. If you forget to tell QuickBooks Pro to use a quantity, it will automatically calculate the quantity as 1.

Click in the textbox for **Customer Message**
Click the drop-down list arrow next to **Customer Message**
Click **Thank you for your business.**

- Message is inserted in the Customer Message box.
- Look at the bottom portion of the Invoice. If there is a check mark in either the "To be printed" or To be e-mailed," boxes click to remove the check mark.

EDIT AND CORRECT ERRORS

If an error is discovered while entering invoice information, it may be corrected by positioning the cursor in the field containing the error. You may do this by clicking in the field containing the error, tabbing to move forward through each field, or pressing Shift+Tab to move back to the field containing the error. If the error is highlighted, type the correction. If the error is not highlighted, you can correct the error by pressing the backspace or the delete key as many times as necessary to remove the error, then typing the correction. (Alternate method: Point to the error, highlight by dragging the mouse through the error, then type the correction or press the Delete key to remove completely.)

➤ Practice editing and making corrections to Invoice No. 1

Click the drop-down list arrow next to **Customer:Job**
Click **Matthews, Timothy CPA**

- Name is changed in Customer:Job and Bill To information is also changed.

Click to the left of the first number in the **Date**—this is **0**
Hold down primary mouse button and drag through the date to highlight.
Type **10/24/06** as the date

- This removes the 01/02/2006 date originally entered.

Click to the right of the **1** in **Quantity**
Backspace and type a **2**
Press **Tab** to see how QuickBooks automatically calculates the new total
To eliminate the changes made to Invoice No. 1, click the drop-down list arrow next to **Customer:Job**
Click **Mendoza, Jose**
Click the cursor so it is in front of the **1** in the **Date**
Press the Delete key until the date is removed
Type **01/02/06**

Click to the right of the **2** in **Quantity**
Backspace and type a **1**
Press the **Tab** key

- This will cause QuickBooks Pro to calculate the amount and the total for the invoice and will move the cursor to the Description field.
- Invoice No. 1 has been returned to the correct customer, date, and quantity. Compare the information you entered with the information provided in the memo.

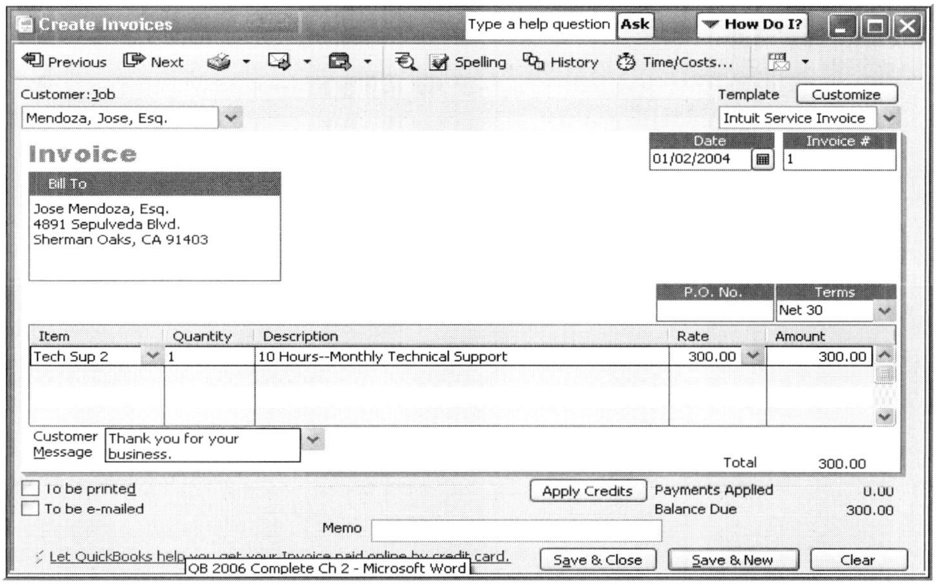

PRINT AN INVOICE

With Invoice No. 1 on the screen, print the invoice immediately after entering information

Click **Print** at the top of the **Create Invoices** screen

- If you click the drop-down list arrow for the Print button, you will get a list of printing options. Click the **Print** option.

Check the information on the **Print One Invoice Settings** tab:
Printer name (should identify the type of printer you are using):

- This may be different from the printer identified in this text.

Printer type: Page-oriented (Single sheets)
Print on: Blank paper

- The circle next to this should be filled. If it is not, click the circle to select.

Click the **Do not print lines around each field** check box to select.

- If there is a check in the box, lines will not print around each field.

- If a check is not in the box, lines will print around each field.

Number of copies should be 1

- If a number other than 1 shows:
  Click in the box
  Drag to highlight the number
  Type **1**

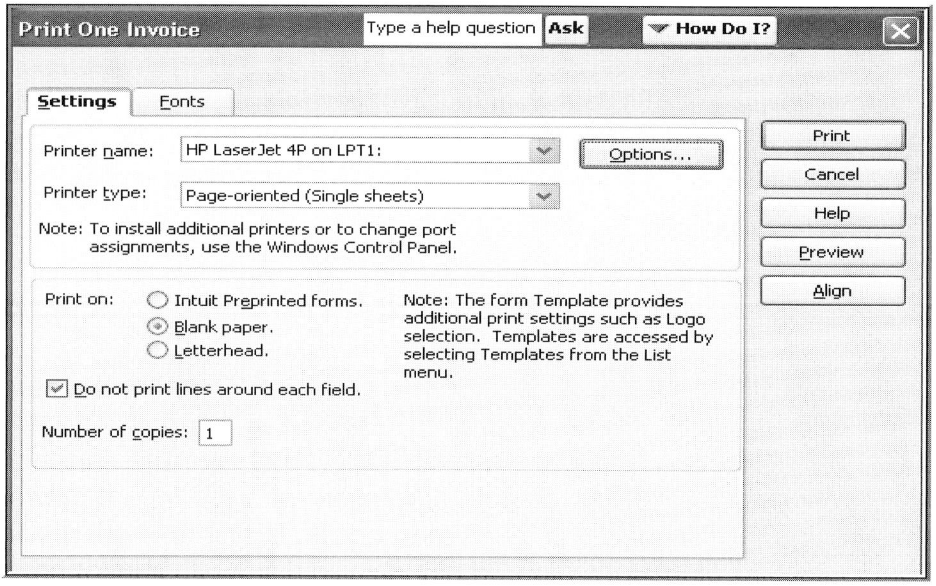

Click the **Print** button

- This initiates the printing of the invoice through QuickBooks Pro. However, because not all classroom configurations are the same, check with your instructor for specific printing instructions.
- If QuickBooks Pro prints your name on two lines, do not be concerned.

Click **Save & Close** button at the bottom of the **Create Invoices** screen to record and close the invoice

- If you did not remove the check from "To be e-mailed," you may get this message:

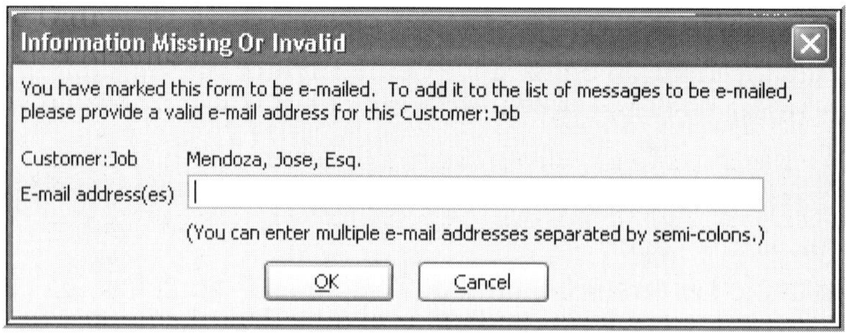

If you do, click **Cancel**

Click **To be e-mailed** on the Invoice to remove the check mark

ENTER TRANSACTIONS USING TWO SALES ITEMS

MEMO:
Date: January 3, 2006

Bill the following: Invoice No. 2—Timothy Matthews, CPA, spoke with you regarding the need for on-site training to help him get started using the Internet. Bill him for a 5-hour on-site training session with Justine Wong. Use Thank you for your business. as the message. (Remember to use Training 1 for the first hour of on-site training and Training 2 for all additional hours of training.)

Record a transaction on account for a sale involving two sales items

Click the **Invoices** icon on the QuickBooks Customers Navigator
Click the drop-down list arrow next to **Customer:Job**
Click **Matthews, Timothy, CPA**
- Name is entered as Customer:Job. Bill To information is completed automatically.

Tab to or click **Date**
Delete the current date
- Refer to instructions for Invoice No. 1 or to editing practice if necessary.

Type **01/03/06** as the date
Make sure that Invoice No. 2 is showing in the **Invoice No.** box
- The Invoice No. should not have to be changed.

There is no PO No. to record
Terms should be indicated as **Net 30**
Tab to or click the first line beneath **Item**
- Refer to Memo and Item List for appropriate billing information.
- *Note:* Services are recorded based on sales items and are not related to the employee who provides the service.

Click the drop-down list arrow next to **Item**
Click **Training 1**
- Training 1 is entered as the Item.

Tab to or click **Quantity**
Type **1**
- Amount will be calculated automatically and entered into the Amount Column when you go to the next line. Notice the amount is $95.00.

Tab to or click the second line for **Item**
Click the drop-down list arrow next to **Item**
Click **Training 2**
Tab to or click **Quantity**
Type **4**

- The total amount of training time is five hours. Because the first hour is billed as Training 1, the remaining four hours are billed as Training 2 hours. The total amount due for the Training 2 hours and the total for the invoice are automatically calculated when you go to the Customer Message box.

Click **Customer Message**
Click the drop-down list arrow next to **Customer Message**
Click **Thank you for your business.**

- Message is inserted in the Customer Message box.

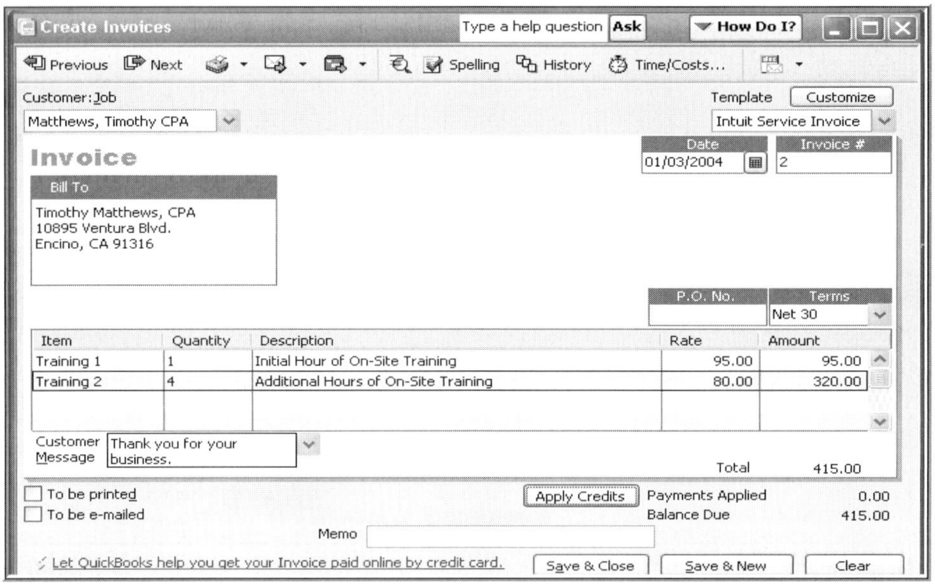

PRINT AN INVOICE

With Invoice No. 2 on the screen, print the invoice immediately after entering invoice information

Click **Print** button on the **Create Invoices** screen

- If you click the drop-down list arrow for the Print button, you will get a list of printing options. Click the **Print** option.

Check the information on the **Print One Invoice Settings** tab:

Printer name (should identify the type of printer you are using):
Printer type: Page-oriented (Single sheets)

Print on: Blank paper
Do not Print lines around each field check box should have a check mark
Click the **Print** button

After the invoice has printed, click the **Save & New** button at the bottom of the **Create Invoices** screen to record the Invoice 2 and go to a new invoice

PREPARE INVOICES WITHOUT STEP-BY-STEP INSTRUCTIONS

MEMO:
DATE: January 5, 2006

Bill the following: Invoice No. 3—Kala Jafrood needed to have telephone assistance to help her set up her Internet connection. Prepare an invoice as the bill for 10 hours of technical support for January. (Remember customers are listed by last name in the Customer List. Refer to Item List to select the correct Income account for billing.)

Invoice No. 4—Steele, Rhoades, Whitcomb, and Hinson have several new employees that need to be trained in the use of the office computer system. Bill them for 40 hours of on-site training from Justine Wong. (Your Name Computer Consulting does not record a transaction based on the employee who performs the service. It simply bills according to the service provided.)

Invoice No. 5—Grace, Anderson, and Binsley, CPA, need to learn the basic features of QuickBooks Pro, which is used by many of their customers. Bill them for 10 hours of on-site training and 15 hours of technical support for January so they may call and speak to Silas Kaan regarding additional questions. (Note: You will use three sales items in this transaction.)

Invoice No. 6—Yamashita, Bibey, and Iverson has a new assistant office manager. Your Name Computer Consulting Is providing 40 hours of on-site training for Beverly Wilson. To obtain additional assistance, the company has signed up for 5 hours technical support for January.

Enter the four transactions in the memo above. Refer to instructions given for the two previous transactions entered

- Remember, when billing for on-site training, the first hour is billed as Training 1, and the remaining hours are billed as Training 2.
- Always use the Item List to determine the appropriate sales items for billing.
- Use <u>Thank you for your business.</u> as the message for these invoices.
- If you make an error, correct it.
- Print each invoice immediately after you enter the information for it.

- To go from one invoice to the next, click the **Save & New** button.
- Click **Save & Close** after Invoice No. 6 has been entered and printed.

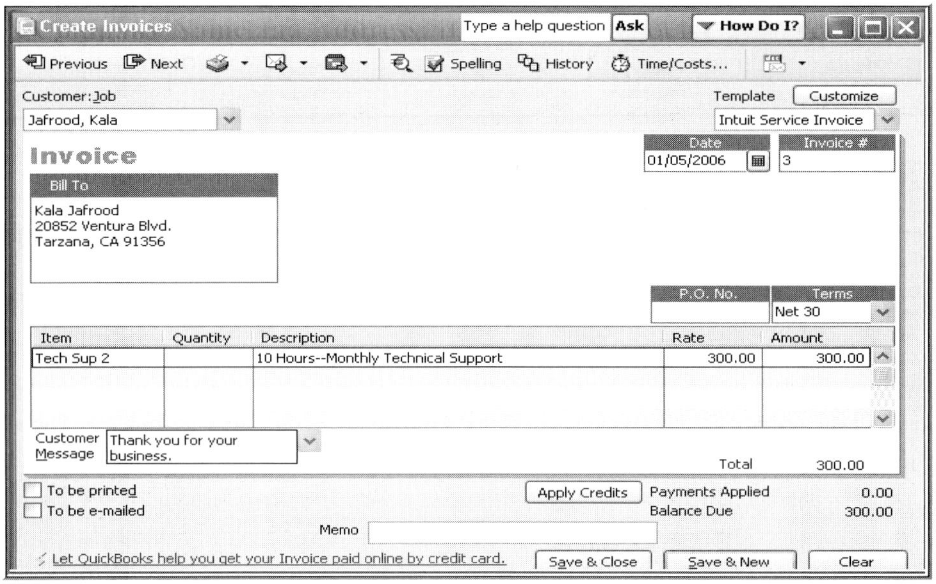

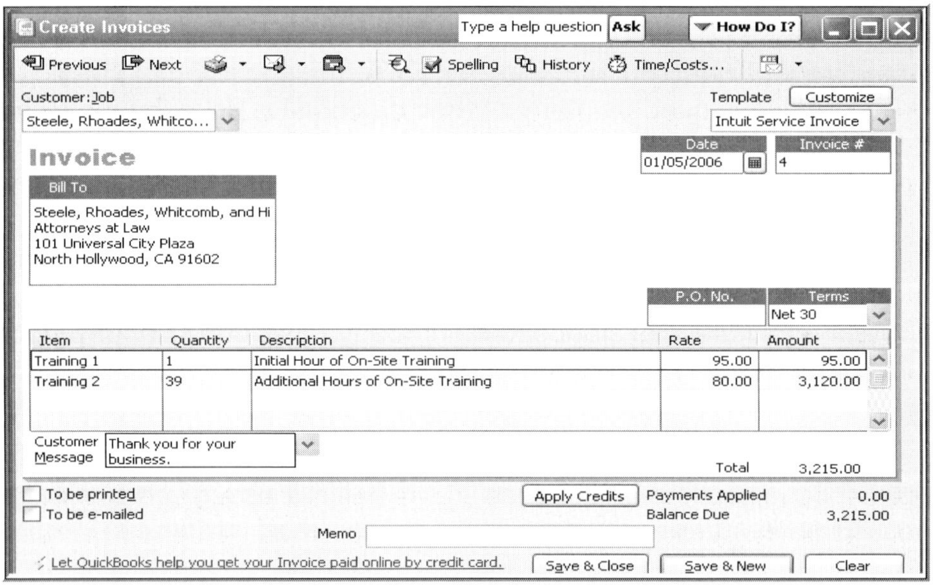

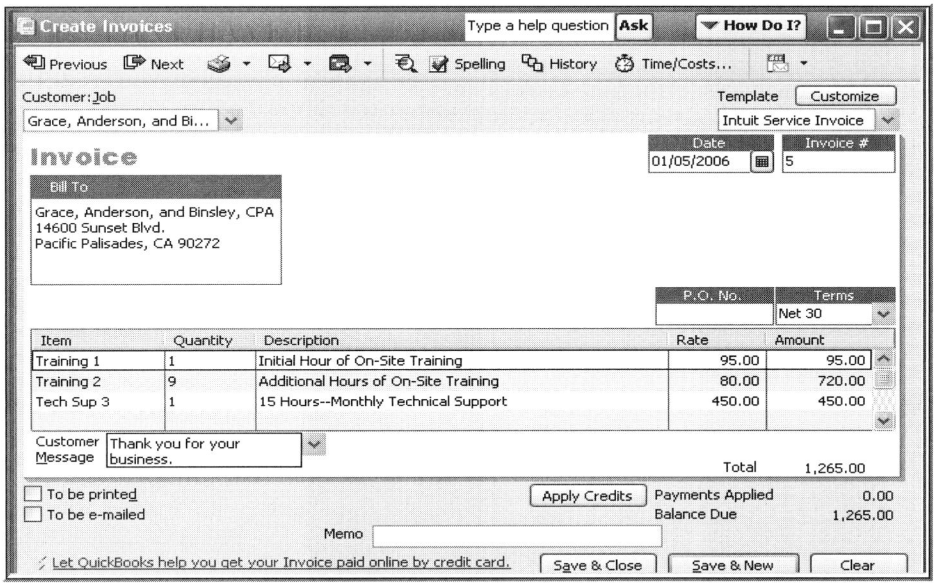

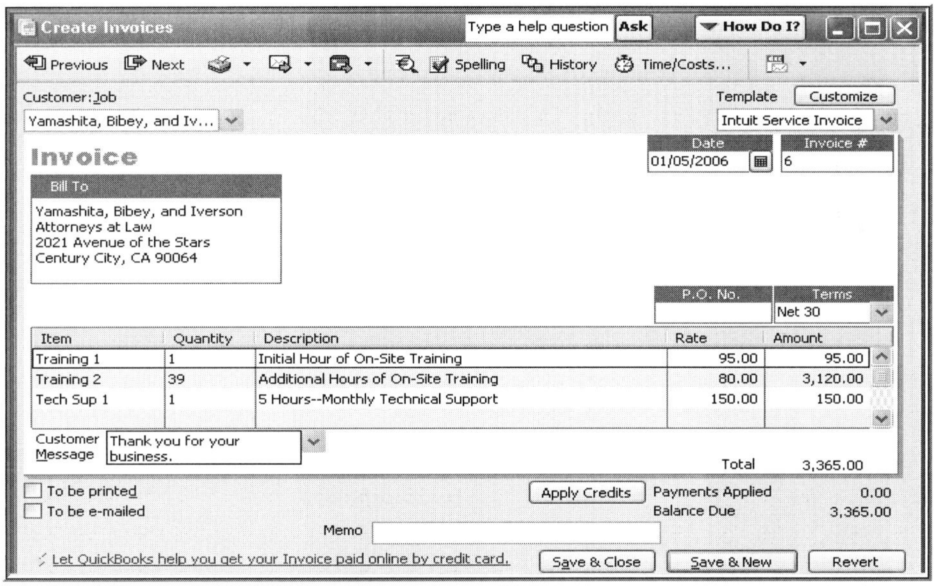

PRINT A/R REPORTS

QuickBooks Pro has several reports available for accounts receivable. One of the most useful is the Customer Balance Summary Report. It shows you the balances of all the customers on account.

Print the Customer Balance Summary Report

Click **Reports** on the menu bar
Point to **Customers & Receivables**
Click **Customer Balance Summary**

- The report should appear on the screen.
- The current date and time will appear on the report. Since the dates given in the text will not be the same date as the computer, it may be helpful to remove the date and time prepared from your report.

Remove the date prepared and the time prepared from the report:
Click **Modify Report**
Click the **Header/Footer** tab
Click the check box next to **Date Prepared** to deselect this option
Click the check box next to **Time Prepared** to deselect this option

- *Note:* Some reports will also have a Report Basis—Cash or Accrual. You may turn off the display of the report basis by clicking the check box for this option.

Click **OK** on the **Modify Report** screen
Change the Dates for the report:
Click in or tab to **From**
Enter **01/01/06**
Tab to **To**
Enter **01/05/06**
Press the Tab key

- After you enter the date, pressing the tab key will generate the report.
- This report lists the names of all customers with balances on account. The amount column shows the total balance for each customer. This includes opening balances as well as current invoices.

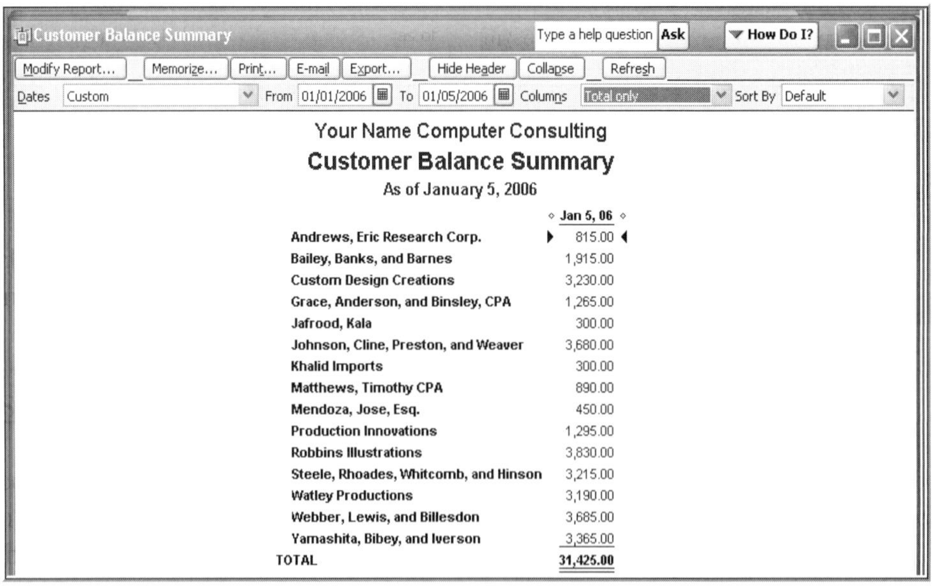

Your Name Computer Consulting
Customer Balance Summary
As of January 5, 2006

	Jan 5, 06
Andrews, Eric Research Corp.	815.00
Bailey, Banks, and Barnes	1,915.00
Custom Design Creations	3,230.00
Grace, Anderson, and Binsley, CPA	1,265.00
Jafrood, Kala	300.00
Johnson, Cline, Preston, and Weaver	3,680.00
Khalid Imports	300.00
Matthews, Timothy CPA	890.00
Mendoza, Jose, Esq.	450.00
Production Innovations	1,295.00
Robbins Illustrations	3,830.00
Steele, Rhoades, Whitcomb, and Hinson	3,215.00
Watley Productions	3,190.00
Webber, Lewis, and Billesdon	3,685.00
Yamashita, Bibey, and Iverson	3,365.00
TOTAL	31,425.00

Click the **Print** button at the top of the Customer Balance Summary Report
Complete the information on the **Print Reports Settings** tab:
Print To: The selected item should be **Printer**
Orientation: Should be Portrait. If it is not, click **Portrait** to select Portrait orientation for this report

- Portrait orientation prints in the traditional 8 ½- by 11-inch paper size.

Page Range: **All** should be selected; if it is not, click **All**
Page Breaks: Smart page breaks (widow/orphan control) should be selected
Number of copies should be **1**
If necessary, click on **Fit report to one page wide** to deselect this item

- When selected, the printer will print the report using a smaller font so it will be one page in width.

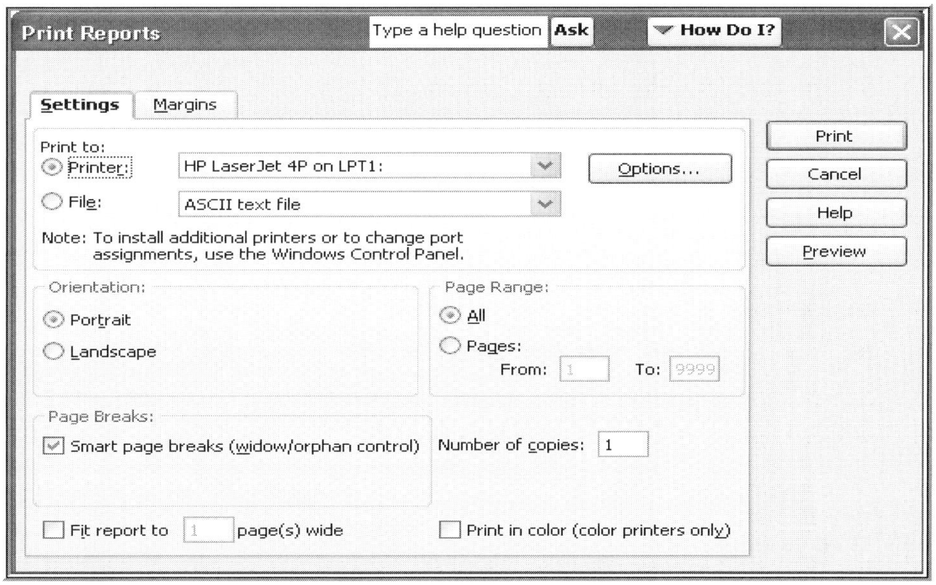

Click **Print** on the **Print Reports** screen
Do not close the **Customer Balance Summary Report**

USE THE QUICKZOOM FEATURE

You ask the office manager, Consuelo Alcampo, to obtain information regarding the balance of the Steele, Rhoades, Whitcomb, and Hinson account. To get detailed information regarding an individual customer's balance while in the Customer Balance Summary Report, use the Zoom feature. With the individual customer's information on the screen, you can print a report for that customer.

Use the QuickZoom

Point to the balance for **Steele, Rhoades, Whitcomb, and Hinson**

- Notice that the mouse pointer turns into a magnifying glass with a **Z** in it.

Click once to mark the balance **3,215.00**

- Notice the marks on either side of the amount.

Double-click to **Zoom** in to see the details

The report dates used should be from **01/01/06** to **01/05/06**

Remove the Date Prepared and Time Prepared from the header

- Follow the instructions previously listed for removing the current date from the header for the Customer Balance Summary Report.

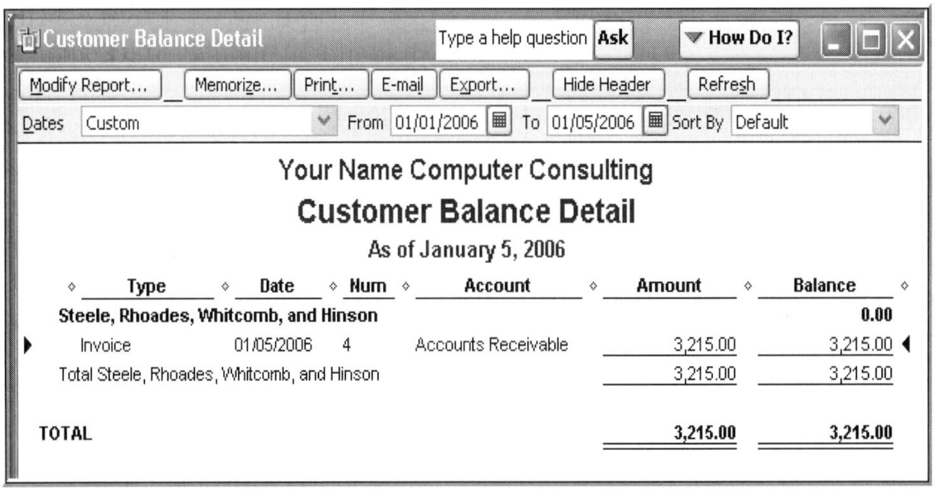

- Notice that Invoice No. 4 was recorded on 01/05/2006 for $3,215.
- To view Invoice No. 4, simply double-click on this transaction, and the invoice will be shown on the screen.

To exit Invoice No. 4 and return to the Customer Balance Detail Report, click the **Close** button on the title bar of the **Create Invoices** screen for Invoice No. 4.

Print the **Customer Balance Detail Report** for Steele, Rhoades, Whitcomb, and Hinson

- Follow the steps previously listed for printing the Customer Balance Summary Report.

Your Name Computer Consulting
Customer Balance Detail
As of January 5, 2006

Type	Date	Num	Account	Amount	Balance
Steele, Rhoades, Whitcomb, and Hinson					0.00
Invoice	1/5/2006	4	Accounts Receivable	3,215.00	3,215.00
Total Steele, Rhoades, Whitcomb, and Hinson				3,215.00	3,215.00
TOTAL				**3,215.00**	**3,215.00**

Click **Close** to close **Customer Balance Detail Report**

- If you get a screen for Memorize Report, always click **No**

Click **Close** to close **Customer Balance Summary Report**

CORRECT AN INVOICE AND PRINT THE CORRECTED FORM

Errors may be corrected very easily with QuickBooks Pro. Because an invoice is prepared for sales on account, corrections will be made directly on the invoice. We will access the invoice via the register for the Accounts Receivable account. The account register contains detailed information regarding each transaction made to the account. Therefore, anytime an invoice is recorded, it is posted to the Accounts Receivable register.

MEMO:
DATE: January 7, 2006

The actual amount of time spent for on-site training increased from 10 hours to 12 hours. Change Invoice No. 5 to Grace, Anderson, and Binsley, CPA, to correct the actual amount of training hours to show a total of 12 hours.

Correct an invoice using the Accounts Receivable Register

Correct the error described in the above memo and print a corrected invoice:
Click the **Chart of Accounts** icon in the Company sections of the Home Page
In the Chart of Accounts, click **Accounts Receivable**

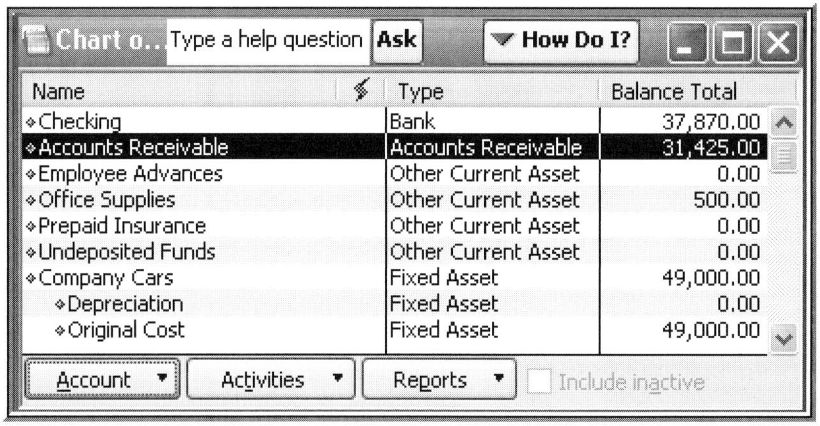

Click the **Activities** button
Click **Use Register**
OR
Double-click **Accounts Receivable** in the Chart of Accounts

- The Accounts Receivable Register appears on the screen with information regarding each transaction entered into the account.
- *Note:* This is the same as the Accounts Receivable General Ledger Account

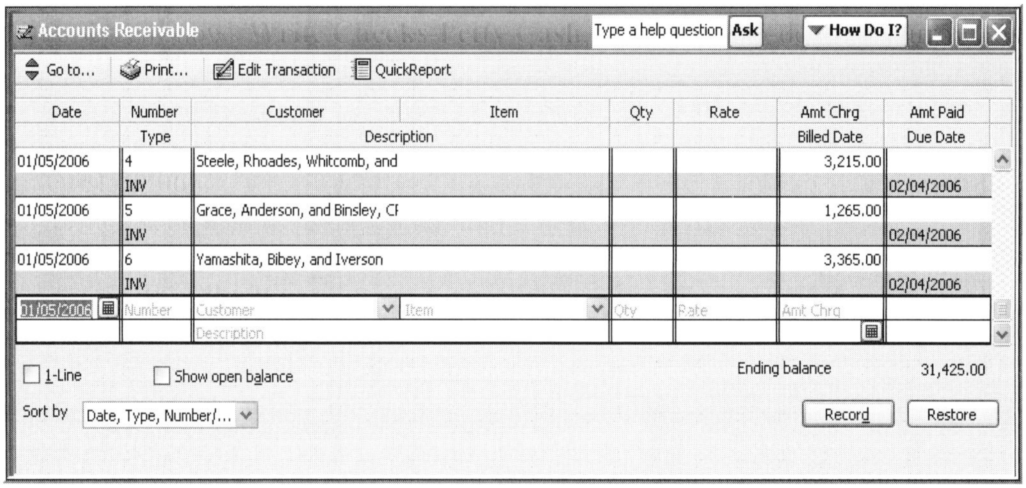

If necessary, scroll through the register until the transaction for **Invoice No. 5** is on the screen

- Look at the **Number/Type** column to identify the number of the invoice and the type of transaction.
- On the Number line you will see an invoice number or a check number.
- On the Type line, INV indicates a sale on account, and PMT indicates a payment received on account.

Click anywhere in the transaction for Invoice No. 5 to Grace, Anderson, and Binsley, CPA
Click **Edit Transaction** at the top of the register
- Invoice No. 5 appears on the screen.

Click the line in the **Quantity** field that corresponds to the **Training 2** hours
Change the quantity from 9 hours to 11 hours
Position cursor in front of the 9
Press **Delete**
Type **11**
Press **Tab** to generate a new total

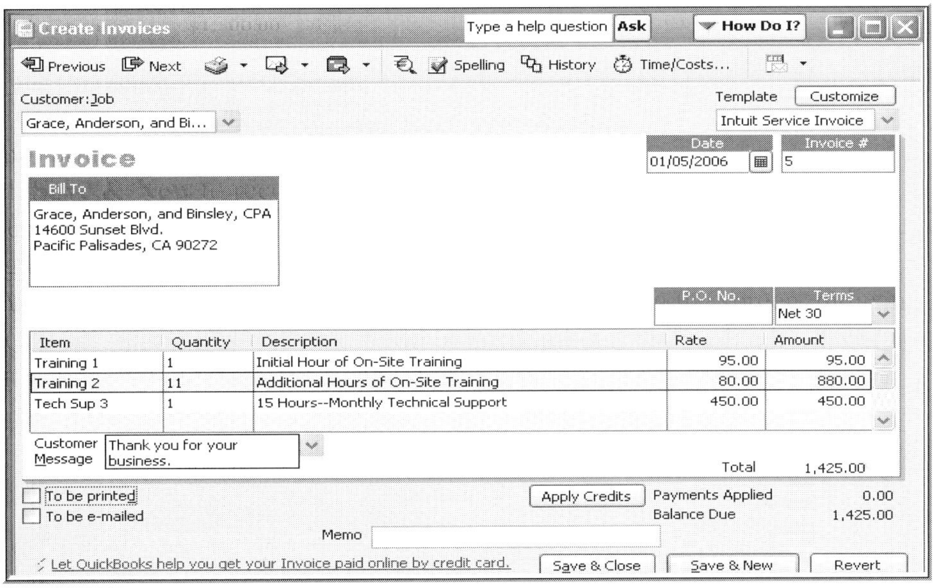

- Notice that the date remains 01/05/2006.

Click **Print** button on the **Create Invoices** screen to print a corrected invoice
Check the information on the **Print One Invoice Settings** tab
Click **Print**
Click **Save & Close** to record changes and close invoice
Click **Yes** on the Recording Transaction dialog box

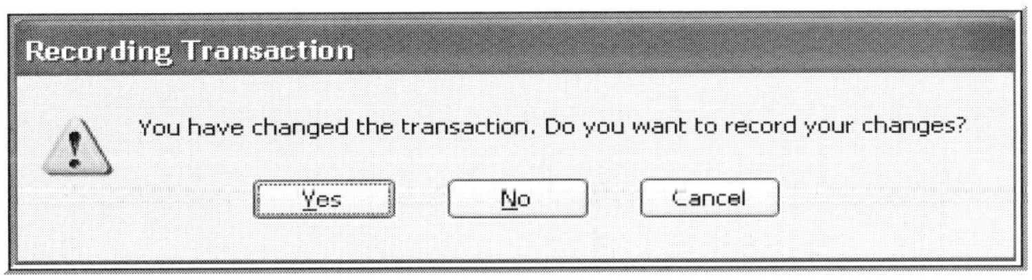

After closing the invoice, you return to the register.

VIEW A QUICKREPORT

After editing the invoice and returning to the register, you may get a detailed report regarding the customer's transactions by clicking the QuickReport button.

View a QuickReport for Grace, Anderson, and Binsley, CPA

Click the **QuickReport** button to view the **Grace, Anderson, and Binsley** account

Verify the balance of the account. It should be **$1,425.00**

- *Note:* You will get the date prepared, time prepared, and the report basis in the heading of your QuickReport.

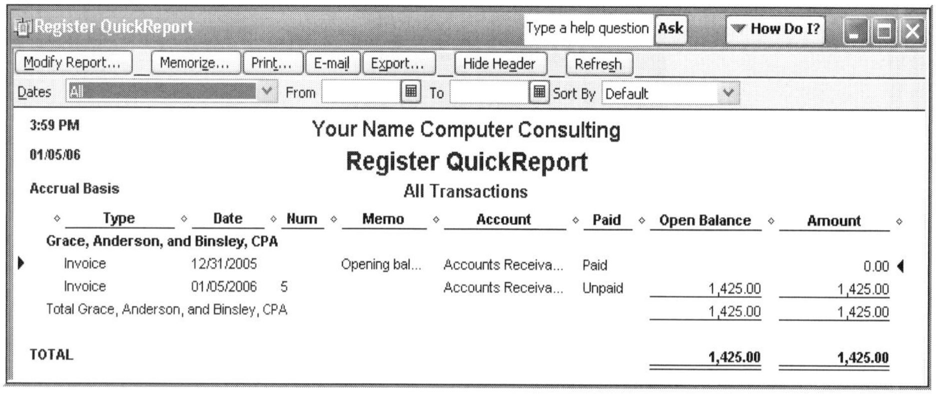

ANALYZE THE QUICKREPORT FOR GRACE, ANDERSON, AND BINSLEY

Analyze the QuickReport

Notice that the total of Invoice No. 5 is $1,425.00
Close the **QuickReport** without printing
Close the **Accounts Receivable Register**
Close the **Chart of Accounts**

VOID AND DELETE SALES FORMS

Deleting an invoice or sales receipt permanently removes it from QuickBooks Pro without leaving a trace. If you would like to correct your financial records for the invoice that you no longer want, it is more appropriate to void the invoice. When an invoice is voided, it remains in the QuickBooks Pro system with a zero balance.

VOID AN INVOICE

MEMO:
DATE: January 7, 2006

Kala Jafrood called to cancel the 10 hours of technical support for January. Because no support had been used, you decide to void Invoice 3.

Void the invoice above by going directly to the original invoice:

Use the keyboard shortcut **Ctrl+I** to open the Create Invoices screen
Click the **Previous** button until you get to **Invoice No. 3**
With Invoice No. 3 on the screen, click **Edit** on the menu bar
Click **Void Invoice**

- Notice that the amount and total for the invoice are no longer 300. They are both **0.00**. Find the Memo text box at the bottom of the screen and verify that the word VOID appears as the memo.

Click **Save & Close** on the **Create Invoices** screen
Click **Yes** on the Recording Transaction dialog box
Click the **Reports Center** button above the Home Page
Click **Customers & Receivables** as the Type of Report

- The report categories are displayed on the left side of the Report Center. To prepare a report, click the desired type of report, scroll through the list of reports, and click the desired report.

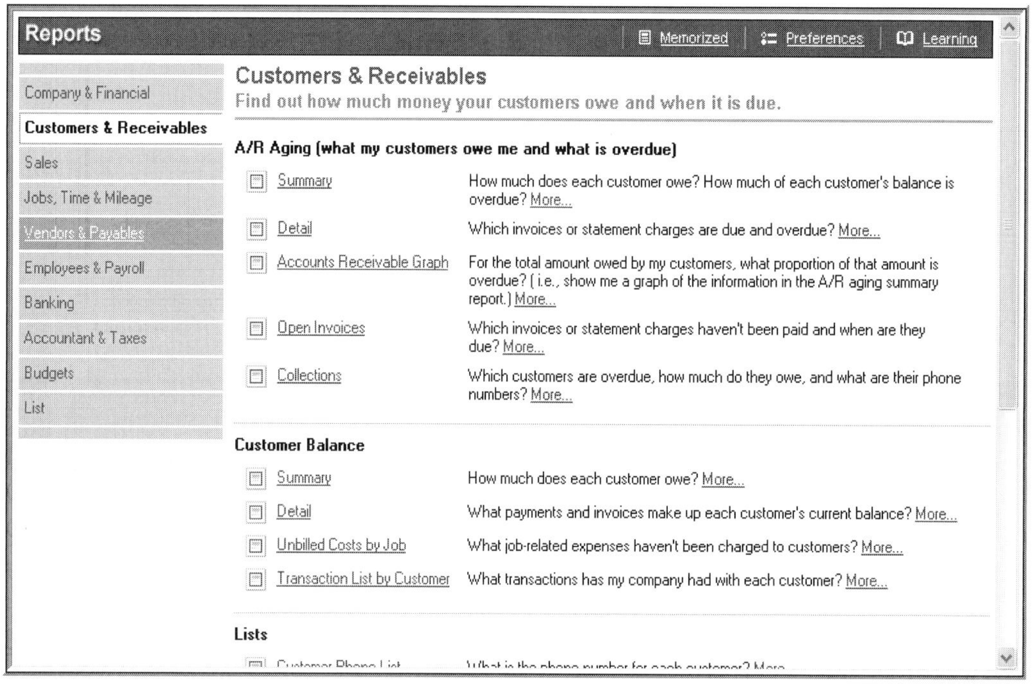

Click **Transaction List by Customer** in the Customer Balance section
Click in **From**
Enter **010106**
Tab to or click in **To**
Enter **010706**, press **Tab**
Remove the date prepared and the time prepared from the report heading:

Click **Modify Report**
Click **Header/Footer** tab
Click the check box next to **Date Prepared** and **Time Prepared** to deselect these options
Click **OK**

Your Name Computer Consulting
Transaction List by Customer
January 1 - 7, 2006

Type	Date	Num	Memo	Account	Clr	Split	Amount
Grace, Anderson, and Binsley, CPA							
Invoice	01/05/2006	5		Accounts Receivable		-SPLIT-	1,425.00
Jafrood, Kala							
Invoice	01/05/2006	3	VOID:	Accounts Receivable	✓	Technical Support Income	0.00
Matthews, Timothy CPA							
Invoice	01/03/2006	2		Accounts Receivable		-SPLIT-	415.00
Mendoza, Jose, Esq.							
Invoice	01/02/2006	1		Accounts Receivable		Technical Support Income	300.00
Steele, Rhoades, Whitcomb, and Hinson							
Invoice	01/05/2006	4		Accounts Receivable		-SPLIT-	3,215.00
Yamashita, Bibey, and Iverson							
Invoice	01/05/2006	6		Accounts Receivable		-SPLIT-	3,365.00

Print the **Transactions List by Customer Report** in Portrait orientation following printing instructions provided earlier in the chapter

- Do not use the option to fit the report to one-page wide. This report may print on two pages.
- This report gives the amount for each transaction with the customer.
- Notice that Invoice No. 3 is marked VOID in the Memo column and has a √ in the **Clr** column.
- The SPLIT column tells you which account was used to record the income. If the word **-SPLIT-** appears in the column, this means the transaction amount was split or divided among two or more accounts.

Close the **Transaction List by Customer Report**

- If you get a screen for Memorize Report, always click **No**

Close the **Report Center**

DELETE AN INVOICE AND USE FIND

When an invoice is deleted, it is permanently removed from QuickBooks. It will no longer be listed in any reports or shown as an invoice.

Find is useful when you have a large number of invoices and want to locate an invoice for a particular customer. Using Find will locate the invoice without requiring you to scroll through all the invoices for the company. For example, if customer Jimenez's transaction was on Invoice No. 3 and the invoice on the screen was Invoice No. 1,084, you would not have to scroll through 1,081 invoices because Find would locate Invoice No. 3 instantly. QuickBooks® Pro 2006 has two methods for finding transactions: simple find and advanced find.

Simple Find allows you to do a quick search using the most common transaction types. Transaction Types include Invoice, Sales Receipt, Credit Memo, Check, and others. The search results are displayed in the lower portion of the window. You can view an individual transaction by highlighting it and clicking Go To, or you can view a report by clicking Report.

Advanced Find is used to do a more detailed search for transactions than you can do using Simple Find. Advanced Find allows you to apply filters to your search criteria. When you apply a filter, you choose how you want QuickBooks to restrict the search results to certain customers, for example. QuickBooks then excludes from results any transactions that don't meet your criteria. You can apply filters either one at a time or in combination with each other. Each additional filter you apply further restricts the content of the search. The search results are displayed in the lower portion of the window. You can view an individual transaction by highlighting it and clicking Go To, or you can view a report by clicking Report.

MEMO:
DATE: January 7, 2006

Because of the upcoming tax season, Timothy Matthews has had to reschedule his 5-hour training session with Justine McBride three times. He finally decided to cancel the training session and reschedule it after April 15. Delete Invoice No. 2.

Delete Invoice 2 to Timothy Matthews, using Find to locate the invoice:

Use Simple Find by clicking **Edit** on the menu bar, clicking **Find** on the Edit menu and clicking the **Simple Find** tab

The Transaction Type should be **Invoice**.

- If it is not, click the drop-down list arrow for Transaction Type and click Invoice.

Click the drop-down list arrow for **Customer/Job:**

Click **Matthews, Timothy CPA**

- This allows QuickBooks Pro to find any invoices recorded for Timothy Matthews.

Click the **Find** button on the Find dialog box

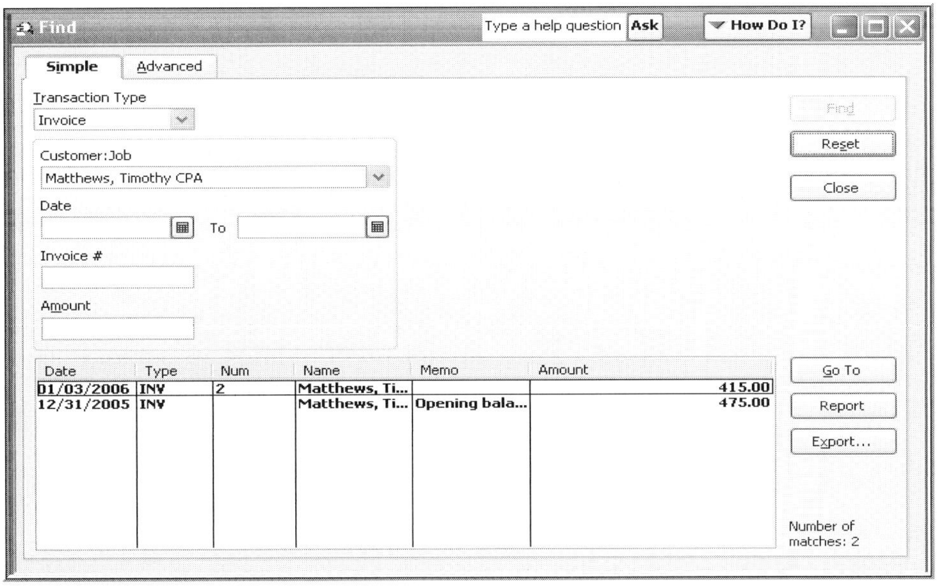

Click the line for **Invoice No. 2**

- Make sure you have selected Invoice No. 2 and not the invoice containing the opening balance.

Click **Go To**

- Invoice No. 2 appears on the screen.

With the invoice on the screen, click **Edit** on the menu bar

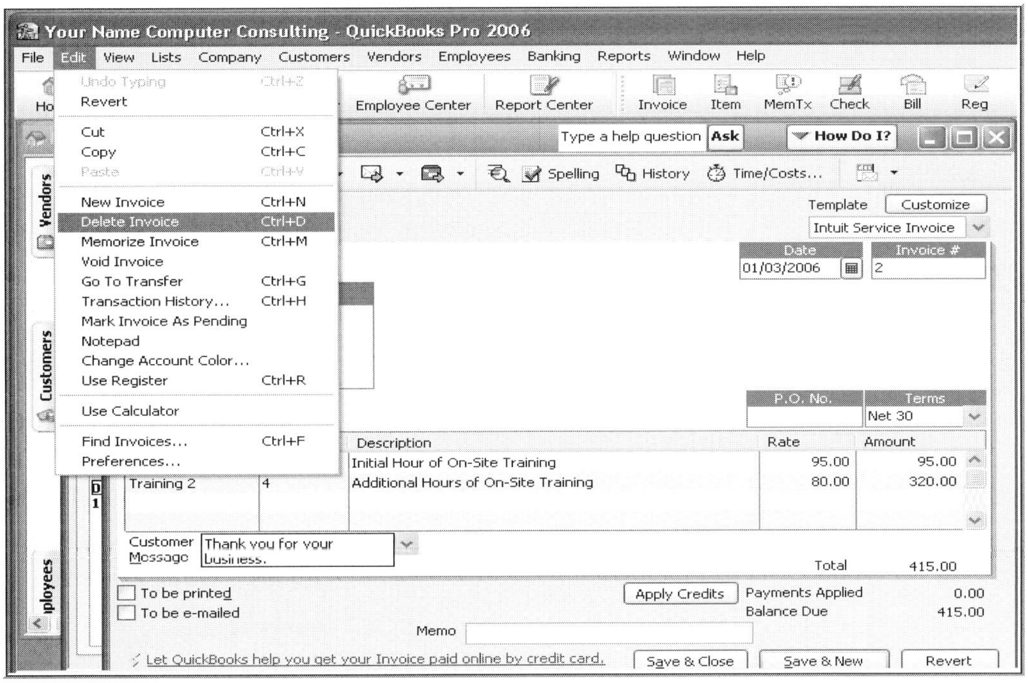

Click **Delete Invoice**
Click **OK** in the **Delete Transaction** dialog box

- Notice that the cursor is now positioned on Invoice No. 3 and that the voided invoice is marked Paid.

Click **Save & Close** button on the **Create Invoices** screen to close the invoice

- Notice that Invoice No. 2 no longer shows on Find.

Click **Close** button to close **Find**
Click **Reports** on the menu bar
Point to **Customers & Receivables**
Click **Customer Balance Detail**
Remove the **Date Prepared** and **Time Prepared** from the report header as previously instructed
Dates should be **All**
Print the report in Portrait orientation as previously instructed

Your Name Computer Consulting
Customer Balance Detail
All Transactions

Type	Date	Num	Account	Amount	Balance
Matthews, Timothy CPA					
Invoice	12/31/2005		Accounts Receivable	475.00	475.00
Total Matthews, Timothy CPA				475.00	475.00
Mendoza, Jose, Esq.					
Invoice	12/31/2005		Accounts Receivable	150.00	150.00
Invoice	01/02/2006	1	Accounts Receivable	300.00	450.00
Total Mendoza, Jose, Esq.				450.00	450.00
Production Innovations					
Invoice	12/31/2005		Accounts Receivable	1,295.00	1,295.00
Total Production Innovations				1,295.00	1,295.00
Robbins Illustrations					
Invoice	12/31/2005		Accounts Receivable	3,830.00	3,830.00
Total Robbins Illustrations				3,830.00	3,830.00

Partial Report

- Look at the account for Timothy Matthews. Notice that Invoice No. 2 does not show up in the account listing. When an invoice is deleted, there is no record of it anywhere in the report.
- Notice that the Customer Balance Detail Report does not include the information telling you which amounts are opening balances.
- The report does give information regarding the amount owed on each transaction plus the total amount owed by each customer.

Close the **Customer Balance Detail Report**

PREPARE A CREDIT MEMO

Credit memos are prepared to show a reduction to a transaction. If the invoice has already been sent to the customer, it is more appropriate and less confusing to make a change to a transaction by issuing a credit memo rather than void the invoice and issue a new one. A credit memo notifies a customer that a change has been made to a transaction.

MEMO:
DATE: January 8, 2006

Prepare the following: Credit Memo No. 7—Steele, Rhoades, Whitcomb, and Hinson did not need 5 hours of the training billed on Invoice No. 4. Issue a Credit Memo to reduce Training 2 by 5 hours.

Prepare a Credit Memo

Click the **Refunds and Credits** icon in the Customers area of the Home Page
Click the down arrow for the drop-down list box next to **Customer:Job**
Click **Steele, Rhoades, Whitcomb, and Hinson**
Tab twice to **Template** textbox

- It should say **Custom Credit Memo.**
- If not, click the drop-down list arrow and click **Custom Credit Memo**.

Tab to or click **Date**
Type in the date of the credit memo: **01/08/06**
The **Credit No.** field should show the number **7**

- Because credit memos are included in the numbering sequence for invoices, this number matches the number of the next blank invoice.

There is no PO No.

- Omit this field.

Tab to or click in **Item**
Click the drop-down list arrow in the Item column
Click **Training 2**
Tab to or click in **Quantity**
Type in **5**
Click the next blank line in the Description column
Type **Deduct 5 hours of additional training, which was not required. Reduce the amount due for Invoice #4.**

- This will print as a note or explanation to the customer.

Click the drop-down list arrow next to **Customer Message**
Click **It's been a pleasure working with you!**

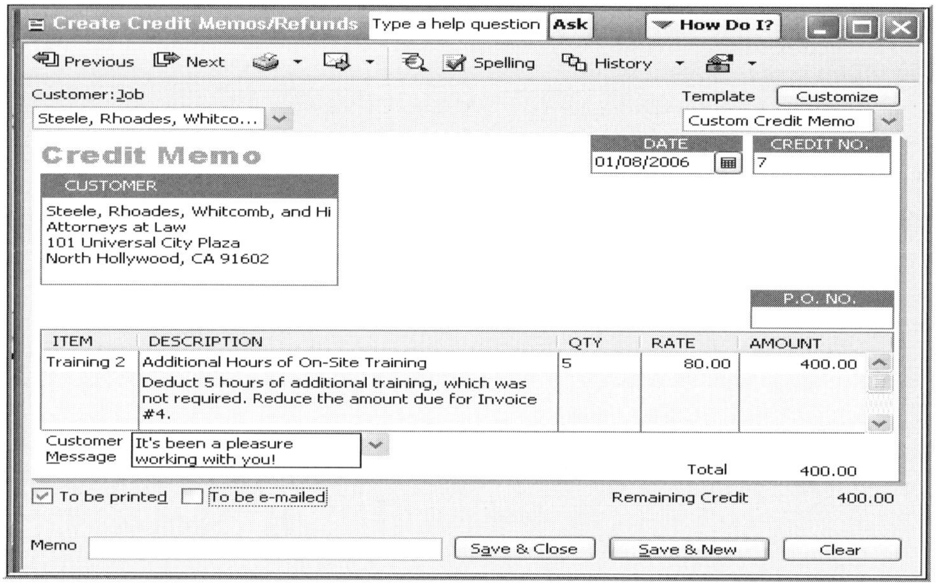

Click **Print** on **Create Credit Memos/Refunds**
Click **Print** on **Print One Credit Memo**
Click the **Save & Close** button
Click **Apply to an Invoice** on the Available Credit screen

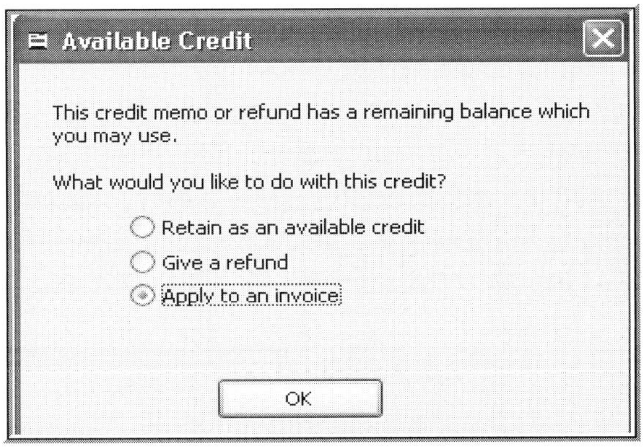

Click **OK**

- Make sure there is a check mark for Invoice 4.

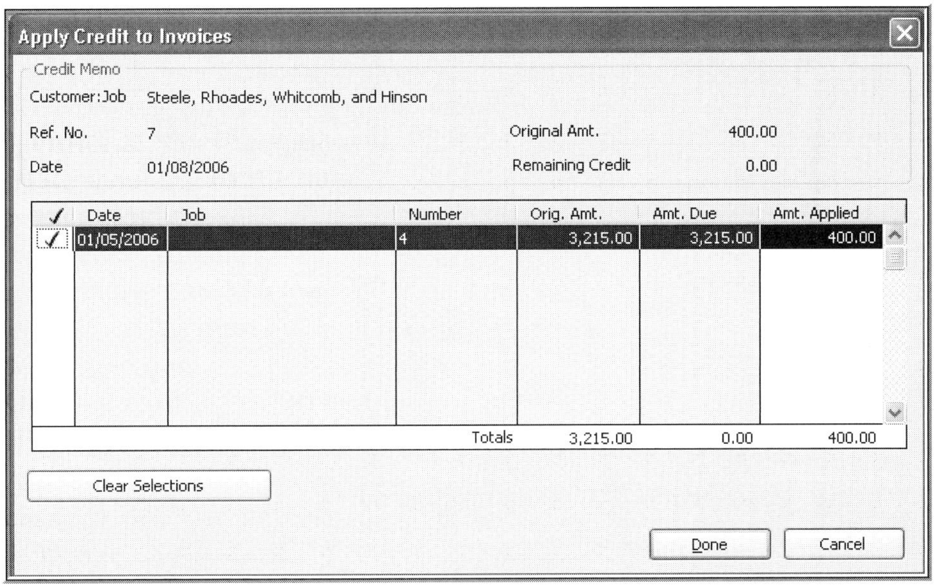

Click **Done**

VIEW CUSTOMER BALANCE DETAIL REPORT

Periodically viewing reports allows you to verify the changes that have occurred to accounts. The Customer Balance Detail report shows all the transactions for each *credit* customer. Cash customers must be viewed through sales reports.

View the Customer Balance Detail Report

Click the **Report Center** button
Click **Customers & Receivables** as the report type
Click **Customer Balance Detail** on the list of reports displayed
Scroll through the report

- Notice that the account for Steele, Rhoades, Whitcomb, and Hinson shows Credit Memo No. 7 for $400.00. The total amount owed was reduced by $400 and is $2,815.00.

Your Name Computer Consulting
Customer Balance Detail
All Transactions

Type	Date	Num	Account	Amount	Balance
Steele, Rhoades, Whitcomb, and Hinson					
Invoice	12/31/2005		Accounts Receivable	0.00	0.00
Invoice	01/05/2006	4	Accounts Receivable	3,215.00	3,215.00
Credit Memo	01/08/2006	7	Accounts Receivable	-400.00	2,815.00
Total Steele, Rhoades, Whitcomb, and Hinson				2,815.00	2,815.00
Watley Productions					
Invoice	12/31/2005		Accounts Receivable	3,190.00	3,190.00
Total Watley Productions				3,190.00	3,190.00
Webber, Lewis, and Billesdon					
Invoice	12/31/2005		Accounts Receivable	3,685.00	3,685.00
Total Webber, Lewis, and Billesdon				3,685.00	3,685.00
Yamashita, Bibey, and Iverson					
Invoice	12/31/2005		Accounts Receivable	0.00	0.00
Invoice	01/05/2006	6	Accounts Receivable	3,365.00	3,365.00
Total Yamashita, Bibey, and Iverson				3,365.00	3,365.00
TOTAL				**30,470.00**	**30,470.00**

Click **Close** to close the report without printing
Close the **Report Center**

ADD A NEW ACCOUNT TO THE CHART OF ACCOUNTS

Because account needs can change as a business is in operation, QuickBooks Pro allows you to make changes to the chart of accounts at any time. Some changes to the chart of accounts require additional changes to lists.

You have determined that Your Name Computer Consulting has received a lot of calls from customers for assistance with hardware installation. Even though Your Name Computer Consulting does not record revenue according to the employee performing the service, it does assign primary areas of responsibility to some of the personnel. Silas Kaan will be responsible for installing hardware for customers. As a result of this decision, you will be adding a third income account. This account will be used when revenue from hardware installation is earned. In addition to adding the account, you will also have to add two new sales items to the Item list.

MEMO:
DATE: January 8, 2006

Add a new account, Installation Income. It is a subaccount of Income.

Add a new income account for Hardware Installation

Click the **Chart of Accounts** icon in the Company section of the Home Page

- Remember that the Chart of Accounts is also the General Ledger.

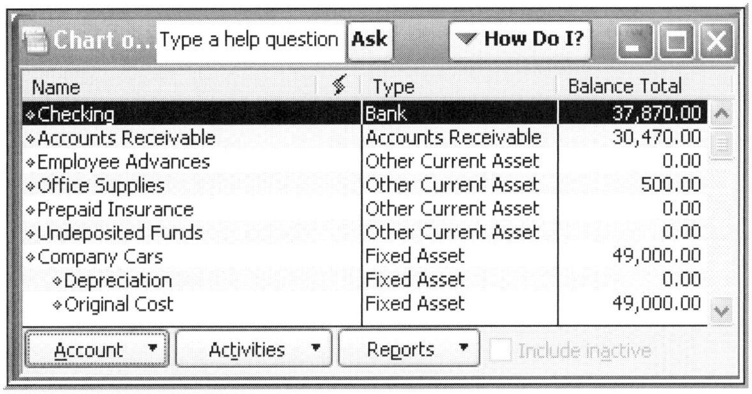

Click the **Account** button at the bottom of the Chart of Accounts screen

Click **New**
Click the drop-down list arrow next to **Type**

Click **Income**
Tab to or click in the text box for **Name**
Type **Installation Income**
Click the check box for **Subaccount of**
Click the drop-down list arrow for **Subaccount of**
Click **Income**
Tab to or click **Description**
Type **Hardware Installation Income**

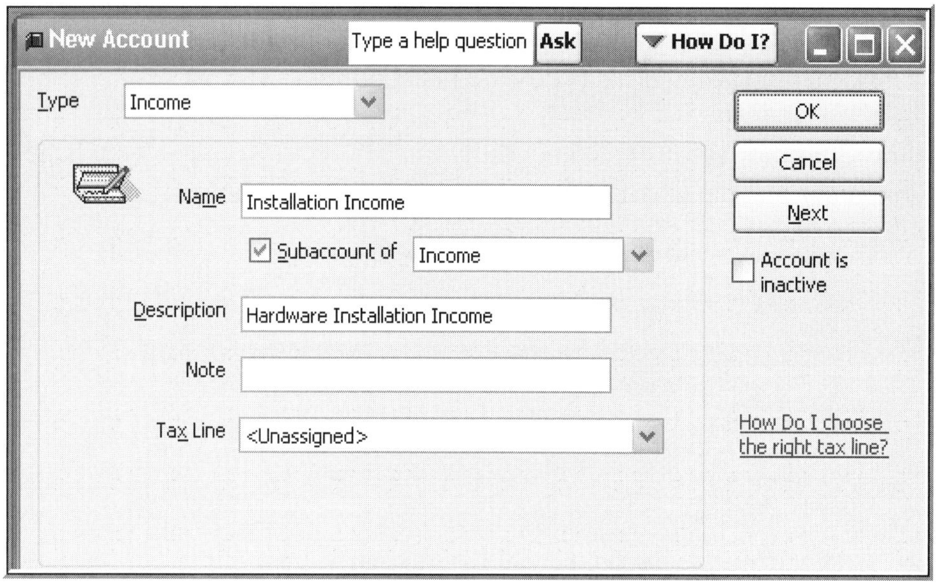

Click **OK** to record new account and close New Account screen
Scroll through the Chart of Accounts
Verify that Installation Income has been added under Income
Close **Chart of Accounts**

ADD NEW ITEMS TO THE ITEMS LIST

In order to accommodate the changing needs of a business, all QuickBooks Pro lists allow you to make changes at any time. The Item List stores information about the services Your Name Computer Consulting provides. In order to use the new Hardware Installation Income account, two new items need to be added to the Item List. When these items are used in a transaction, the amount of revenue earned on the transaction will be posted to the Installation Income account.

MEMO:
DATE: January 8, 2006

Add two Service items to the Item List—Name: Install 1, Description: Initial Hour of Hardware Installation, Rate: 95.00, Account: Installation Income; Name Install 2, Description: Additional Hours of Hardware Installation, Rate: 80.00, Account: Installation Income.

Add two new sales items

Click the **Items & Services** icon in the Company section of the Home Page
Click the **Item** button at the bottom of the **Item List** screen
Click **New**
Item Type is **Service**
Tab to or click **Item Name/Number**
Type **Install 1**
Tab to or click **Description**
Type **Initial Hour of Hardware Installation**
Tab to or click **Rate**
Type **95**
To indicate the general ledger account to be used to record the sale of this item, click the drop-down list arrow for **Account**
Click **Installation Income**

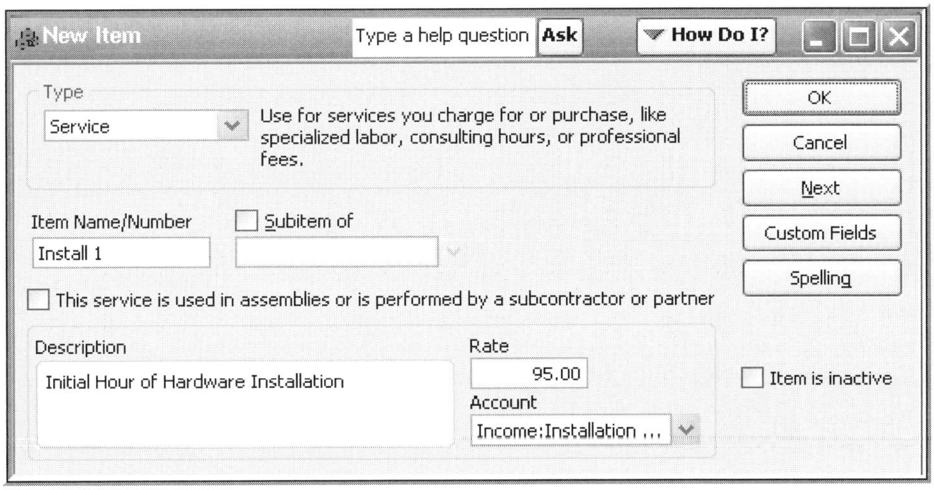

Click **Next** on the New Item dialog box
Repeat the steps above to add **Install 2**

The description is **Additional Hours of Hardware Installation**
The rate is **$80.00** per hour
When finished adding Install 2, click **OK** to add new items and to close **New Item** screen

- Whenever hardware installation is provided for customers, the first hour will be billed as Install 1, and additional hours will be billed as Install 2.

Verify the addition of Install 1 and Install 2 on the Item List

- If you find an error, click on the item with the error, click the **Item** button, click **Edit**, and make corrections as needed.

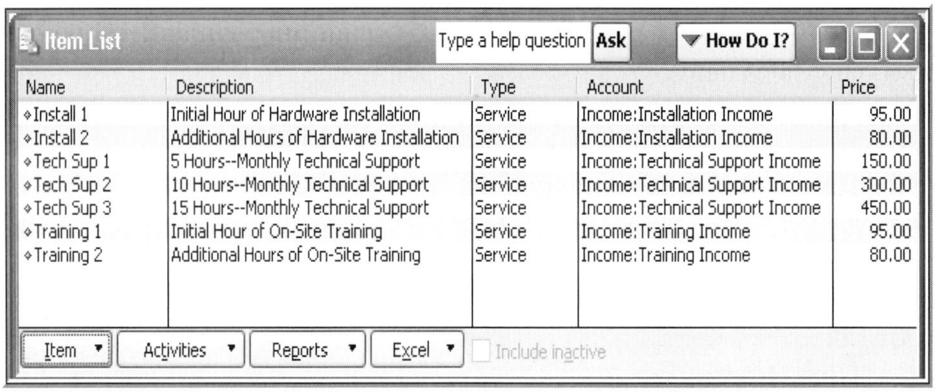

Name	Description	Type	Account	Price
◆Install 1	Initial Hour of Hardware Installation	Service	Income:Installation Income	95.00
◆Install 2	Additional Hours of Hardware Installation	Service	Income:Installation Income	80.00
◆Tech Sup 1	5 Hours--Monthly Technical Support	Service	Income:Technical Support Income	150.00
◆Tech Sup 2	10 Hours--Monthly Technical Support	Service	Income:Technical Support Income	300.00
◆Tech Sup 3	15 Hours--Monthly Technical Support	Service	Income:Technical Support Income	450.00
◆Training 1	Initial Hour of On-Site Training	Service	Income:Training Income	95.00
◆Training 2	Additional Hours of On-Site Training	Service	Income:Training Income	80.00

Close the **Item List**

ADD A NEW CUSTOMER

Because customers are the lifeblood of a business, QuickBooks Pro allows customers to be added "on the fly" as you create an invoice or a sales receipt. You may choose between Quick Add (used to add only a customer's name) and Set Up (used to add complete information for a customer).

> **MEMO:**
> **DATE:** January 8, 2006
>
> Prepare the following: Invoice No. 8—A new customer, Kendall Clark, has purchased several upgrade items for his personal computer but needed assistance with the installation. Silas Kaan spent two hours installing this hardware. Bill Mr. Clark for 2 hours of hardware installation. His address is: 20985 Ventura Blvd., Woodland Hills, CA 91371. His telephone number is: 818-555-2058. He does not have a fax. His credit limit is $1,000; and the terms are Net 30.

Add a new customer and record the above sale on account

Click the **Invoices** icon on the Home Page
In the Customer:Job dialog box, type **Clark, Kendall**
Press **Tab**

- You will see a message box for **Customer:Job Not Found** with buttons for three choices:
  Quick Add (used to add only a customer's name)
  Set Up (used to add complete information for a customer)
  Cancel (used to cancel the **Customer:Job Not Found** message box)

Click **Set Up**

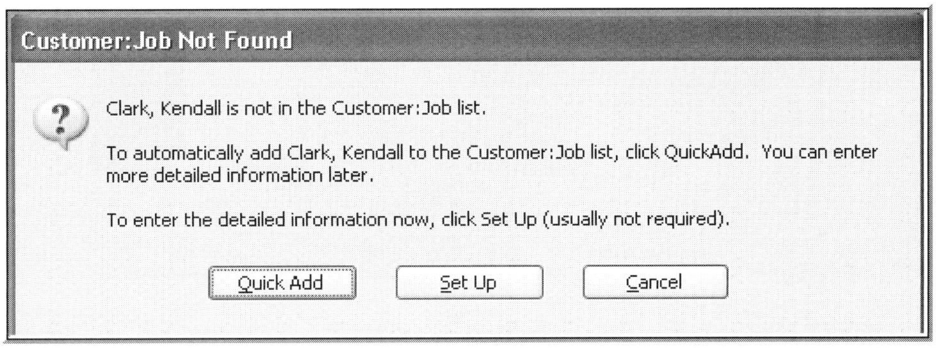

Complete the **New Customer** dialog box

- The name **Clark, Kendall** is displayed in the Customer Name field and as the first line of Bill To in the Address section on the Address Info tab.

There is no Opening Balance, so leave this field blank

- An opening balance may be given only when the customer's account is created. It is the amount the customer owes you at the time the account is created. It is not the amount of any transaction not yet recorded.

Complete the information for the **Address Info** tab
Tab to or click in First Name, type **Kendall**
Tab to or click in Last Name, type **Clark**
Tab to or click the first line for **Bill To**
If necessary, highlight **Clark, Kendall**
Type **Kendall Clark**

- Entering the customer name in this manner allows for the Customer:Job List to be organized according to the last name, yet the bill will be printed with the first name, then the last name.

Press **Enter** or click the second line of the billing address
Type the address **20985 Ventura Blvd.**
Press **Enter** or click the third line of the billing address
Type **Woodland Hills, CA 91371**

The Contact person is Kendall Clark
Tab to or click **Phone**
Type the phone number **818-555-2058**

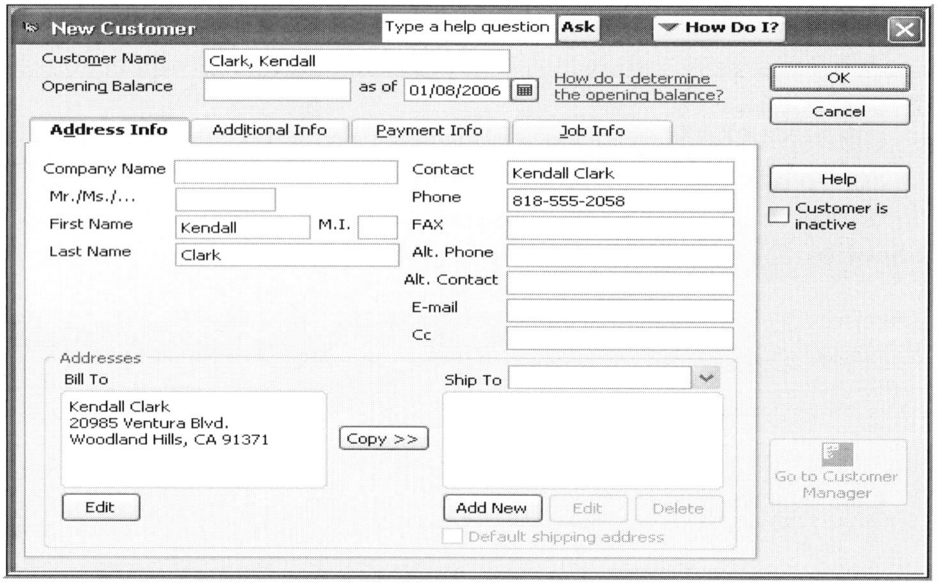

Click the **Additional Info** tab
Tab to or click **Terms**
Click the drop-down list arrow
Click **Net 30**

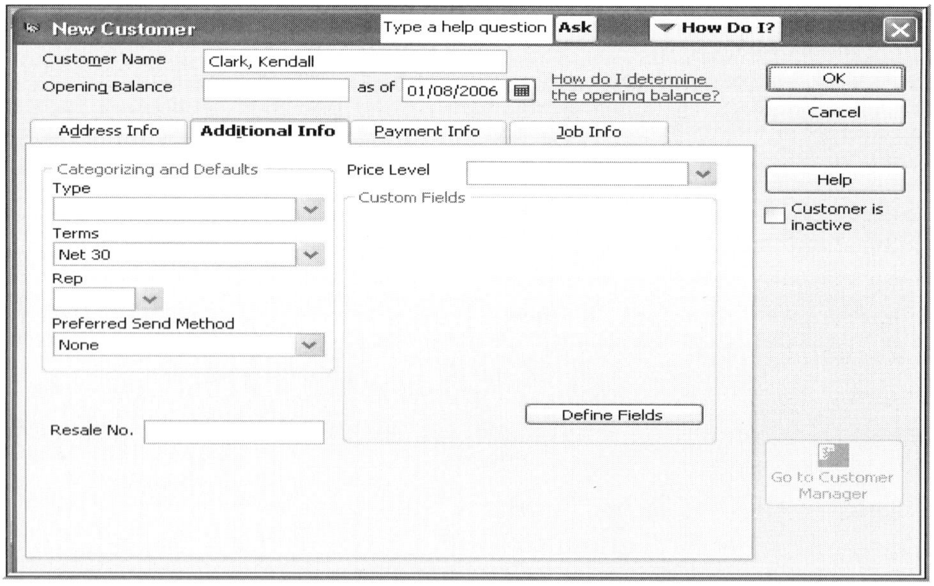

Click **Payment Info** tab
Tab to or click **Credit Limit**
Type the amount **1000**

- Do not use a dollar sign. QuickBooks Pro will insert the comma for you.

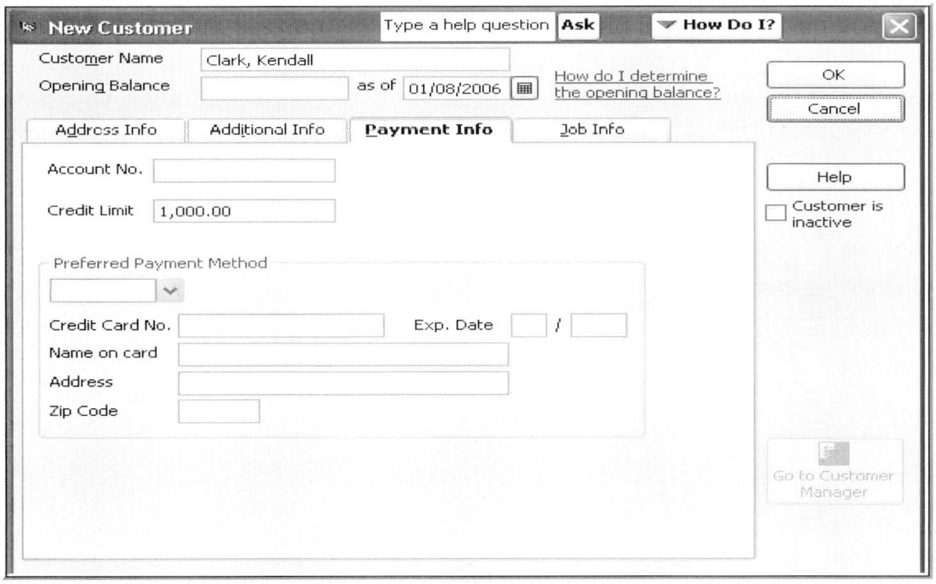

Click **OK** to return to the Invoice
Enter Invoice information as previously instructed
Date of the invoice is **01/08/06**
Invoice No. is **8**
The bill is for 2 hours of hardware installation

- Remember to bill for the initial or first hour, then bill the other hour separately.

The message is **Thank you for your business.**
The invoice total should be $175.00

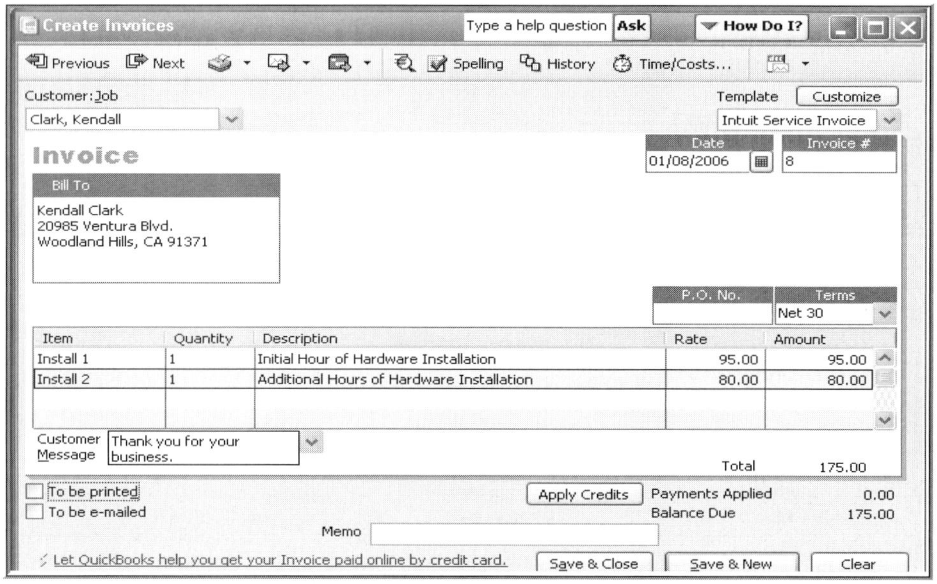

Print the invoice as previously instructed
Click **Save & Close** on the invoice to record and close the transaction

MODIFY CUSTOMER RECORDS

Occasionally, information regarding a customer will change. QuickBooks Pro allows you to modify customer accounts at any time by editing the Customer:Job List.

> **MEMO:**
> **DATE:** January 8, 2006
>
> Update the following account: Custom Design Creations has changed its fax number to 310-555-2109.

Edit the above account:

Access the Customer:Job List:

- There are several ways to access the Customer:Job List. Some are:
  Click the **Customer Center** icon.
  Use the keyboard shortcut: **Ctrl+J**
  Click the **Customer** icon left side of the Home Page

Click **Custom Design Creations** in the Customers & Job list in the Customer Center

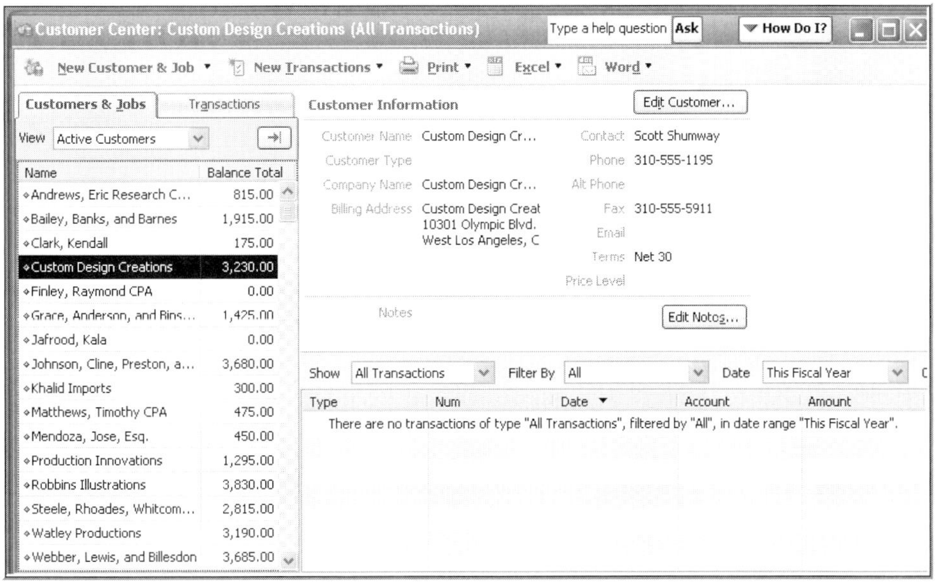

Edit the customer in one of three ways:

Click the **Edit Customer** button

Click **Custom Design Creations** on the **Customer:Job List**. Use the keyboard shortcut **Ctrl+E**.

Double-click **Custom Design Creations** on the **Customer:Job List**.

Change the fax number to 310-555-2109:

Click at the end of the fax number

Backspace to delete **5911**

Type **2109**

Click **OK**
Close the **Customer Center**

RECORD CASH SALES

Not all sales in a business are on account. In many instances, payment is made at the time the service is performed. This is entered as a cash sale. When entering a cash sale, you prepare a sales receipt rather than an invoice. QuickBooks Pro records the transaction in the Journal and places the amount of cash received in an account called Undeposited Funds. The funds received remain in Undeposited Funds until you record a deposit to your bank account.

MEMO:
DATE: January 10, 2006

Prepare the following to record cash sales: Sales Receipt No. 1—You provided 5 hours of on-site training to Raymond Finley, CPA, and received Ray's Check No. 3287 for the full amount due. Prepare Sales Receipt No. 1 for this transaction. Use It's been a pleasure working with you! as the message.

Record a Cash Sale

Click the **Create Sales Receipts** icon in the Customers section of the Home Page
Click **No** on the Merchant Account Service Message screen
Click the drop-down list arrow next to **Customer:Job**
Click **Finley, Raymond, CPA**
Tab to **Template**

- This should have **Custom Cash Sales** as the template. If not, click the drop-down list arrow and click **Custom Cash Sales**.

Tab to or click **Date**
Type **01/10/06**

- You may click on the calendar icon next to the date text box. Make sure the month is January and the year is 2006 then click 10

Sales No. should be **1**
Tab to or click **Check No.**
Type **3287**
Click the drop-down list arrow next to **Payment Method**
Click **Check**
Tab to or click the first line for **Item**

Click the drop-down list arrow next to **Item**
Click **Training 1**
Tab to or click **Qty**
Type **1**
Tab to or click the second line for **Item**
Click the drop-down list arrow next to **Item**
Click **Training 2**
Tab to or click **Qty**
Type **4**

- The amount and total are automatically calculated when you go to the Customer Message or tab past Qty.

Click **Customer Message**
Click the drop-down list arrow for **Customer Message**
Click **It's been a pleasure working with you!**

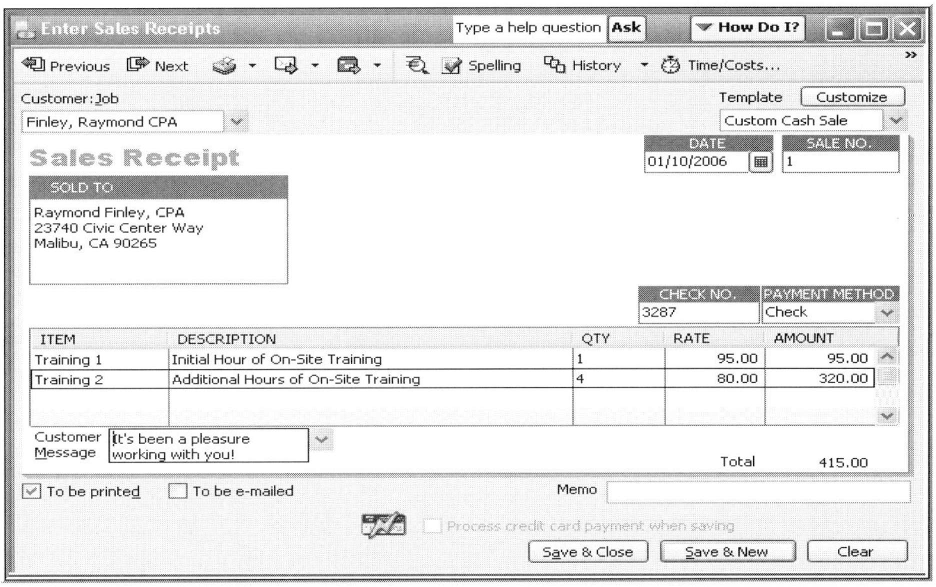

Do not close the Sales Receipt

PRINT SALES RECEIPT

Print the sales receipt

Click **Print** button on the top of the **Enter Sales Receipts** screen
Check the information on the **Print One Sales Receipt Settings** tab:
Printer name (should identify the type of printer you are using):
Printer type: Page-oriented (Single sheets)

Print on: Blank paper
Do not print lines around each field check box should be selected
Number of copies should be **1**
Click **Print**

- This initiates the printing of the sales receipt through QuickBooks Pro. However, since not all classroom configurations are the same, check with your instructor for specific printing instructions.

Once the Sales Receipt has been printed, click **Save & New** on the bottom of the **Enter Sales Receipts** screen

ENTER CASH SALES TRANSACTIONS WITHOUT STEP-BY-STEP INSTRUCTIONS

MEMO:
DATE: January 12, 2006

Sales Receipt No. 2—Raymond Finley needed additional on-site training to correct some error messages he received on his computer. You provided 1 hour of on-site training for Raymond Finley, CPA, and received Ray's Check No. 3306 for the full amount due. (Even though Mr. Finley has had on-site training previously, this is a new sales call and should have the first hour billed as Training 1.)

Sales Receipt No. 3—You provided 4 hours of on-site Internet training for Eric Andrews Research Corp. so the company could be online. Brian received Check No. 10358 for the full amount due.

Record the two transactions listed above

Use the procedures given when you entered Sales Receipt No. 1:

- Remember, the first hour for on-site training is billed as Training 1 and the remaining hours are billed as Training 2.
- Always use the Item List to determine the appropriate sales items for billing.
- Use Thank you for your business. as the message for these sales receipts.
- Print each sales receipt immediately after entering the information for it.
- If you make an error, correct it.
- To go from one sales receipt to the next, click the **Save & New** button on the bottom of the **Enter Sales Receipts** screen.
- Click **Save & Close** after you have entered and printed Sales Receipt No. 3.

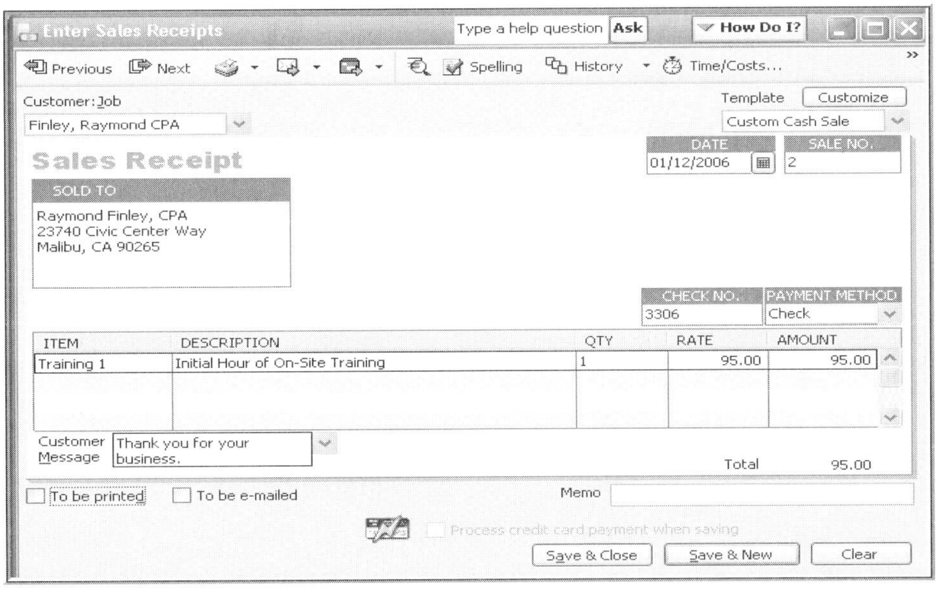

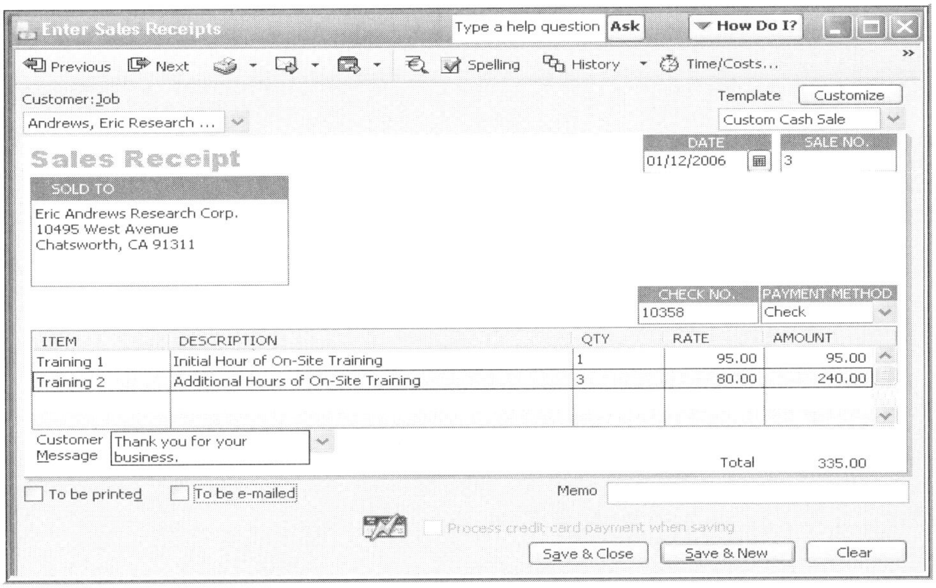

PRINT SALES BY CUSTOMER DETAIL REPORT

QuickBooks Pro has reports available that enable you to obtain sales information about sales items or customers. To get information about the total amount of sales to each customer during a specific period, print a Sales Report by Customer Detail. The total shown represents both cash and/or credit sales.

➤ Prepare and print a Sales by Customer Detail Report

Click **Reports** on the menu bar
Point to **Sales**
Click **Sales by Customer Detail**
To remove the **Date Prepared**, **Time Prepared**, and **Report Basis** from the report, click the **Modify Report** button and follow the instructions given previously for deselecting the date prepared, time prepared, and report basis
Change the dates to reflect the sales period from **01/01/06** to **01/14/06**
Tab to generate the report

- Notice that the report information includes the type of sales to each customer, the date of the sale, the sales item(s), the quantity for each item, the sales price, the amount, and the balance.
- The report does not include information regarding opening or previous balances due.
- The scope of this report is to focus on sales.

Your Name Computer Consulting
Sales by Customer Detail
January 1 - 14, 2006

Type	Date	Num	Memo	Name	Item	Qty	Sales Price	Amount	Balance
Andrews, Eric Research C...									
Sales Receipt	01/12/2006	3	Initial Hour of On-Sit...	Andrews, Eric Researc...	Training 1	1	95.00	95.00	95.00
Sales Receipt	01/12/2006	3	Additional Hours of ...	Andrews, Eric Researc...	Training 2	3	80.00	240.00	335.00
Total Andrews, Eric Research ...								335.00	335.00
Clark, Ke...									
Invoice	01/08/2006	8	Initial Hour of Hardw...	Clark, Kendall	Install 1	1	95.00	95.00	95.00
Invoice	01/08/2006	8	Additional Hours of ...	Clark, Kendall	Install 2	1	80.00	80.00	175.00
Total Clark, K...								175.00	175.00
Finley, Raymond...									
Sales Receipt	01/10/2006	1	Initial Hour of On-Sit...	Finley, Raymond CPA	Training 1	1	95.00	95.00	95.00
Sales Receipt	01/10/2006	1	Additional Hours of ...	Finley, Raymond CPA	Training 2	4	80.00	320.00	415.00
Sales Receipt	01/12/2006	2	Initial Hour of On-Sit...	Finley, Raymond CPA	Training 1	1	95.00	95.00	510.00
Total Finley, Raymond...								510.00	510.00

Click the **Print** button on the **Sales by Customer Detail** screen
On the **Print Report** screen, check the Settings tab to verify that **Print to**: Printer is selected and that the name of your printer is correct
Click **Landscape** to change the **Orientation** from Portrait

- Landscape changes the orientation of the paper so the report is printed 11-inches wide by 8½-inches long.

Verify that the **Range** is **All**
Make sure **Smart page breaks** have been selected
On the **Print Report** screen, click **Print**

- Do not select **Fit** report **to one page wide**. The printed report may require more than one page.

Close the **Sales by Customer Detail Report**

CORRECT A SALES RECEIPT AND PRINT THE CORRECTED FORM

QuickBooks Pro makes correcting errors user friendly. When an error is discovered in a transaction such as a cash sale, you can simply return to the form where the transaction was recorded and correct the error. Thus, to correct a sales receipt, you would open a Sales Receipt, click the Previous button until you found the appropriate sales receipt, and then correct the error. Because cash or checks received for cash sales are held in the Undeposited Funds account until the bank deposit is made, you can access the sales receipt through the Undeposited Funds account in the Chart of Accounts as well. Accessing the receipt in this manner allows you to see all the transactions entered in the account for Undeposited Funds.

When a correction for a sale is made, QuickBooks Pro not only changes the form, it also changes all journal and account entries for the transaction to reflect the correction. QuickBooks Pro then allows a corrected sales receipt to be printed.

MEMO:
DATE: January 14, 2006

After reviewing transaction information, you realize the date for the Sales Receipt No. 1 to Raymond Finley, CPA, was entered incorrectly. Change the date to 1/9/2006.

Correct the error indicated in the memo above and print a corrected sales receipt

Click the **Chart of Accounts** icon on the Home Page
Click **Undeposited Funds**

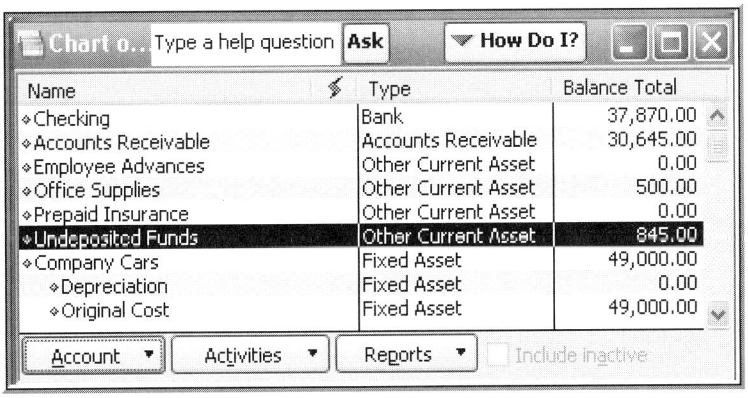

Click the **Activities** button
Click **Use Register**
- The register maintains a record of all the transactions recorded within the Undeposited Funds account.

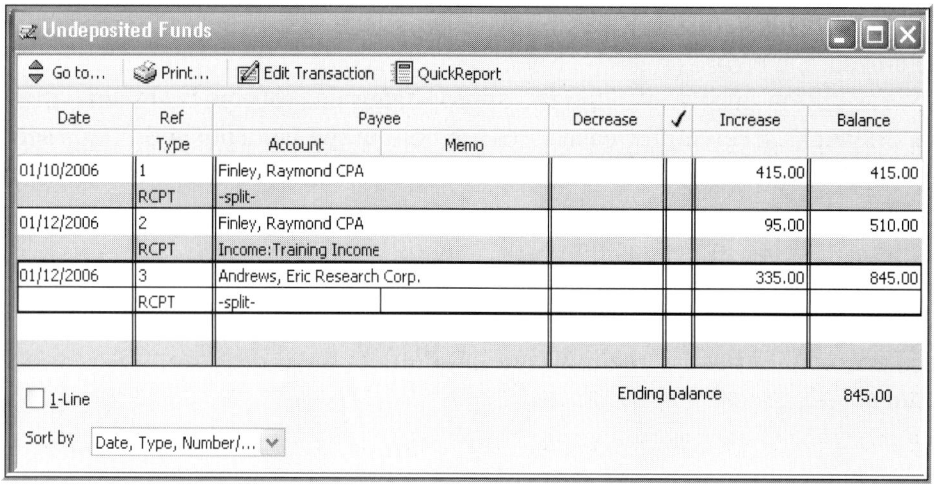

Click anywhere in the transaction for Sales Receipt No. 1 to Raymond Finley, CPA
- Look at the Ref/Type column to see the type of transaction.
- The number in the Ref line indicates the number of the sales receipt or the customer's check number.
- Type shows RCPT for a sales receipt.

Click the **Edit Transaction** button at the top of the register
- The sales receipt appears on the screen.

Tab to or click **Date** field
Change the Date to **01/09/06**
Tab to enter the date

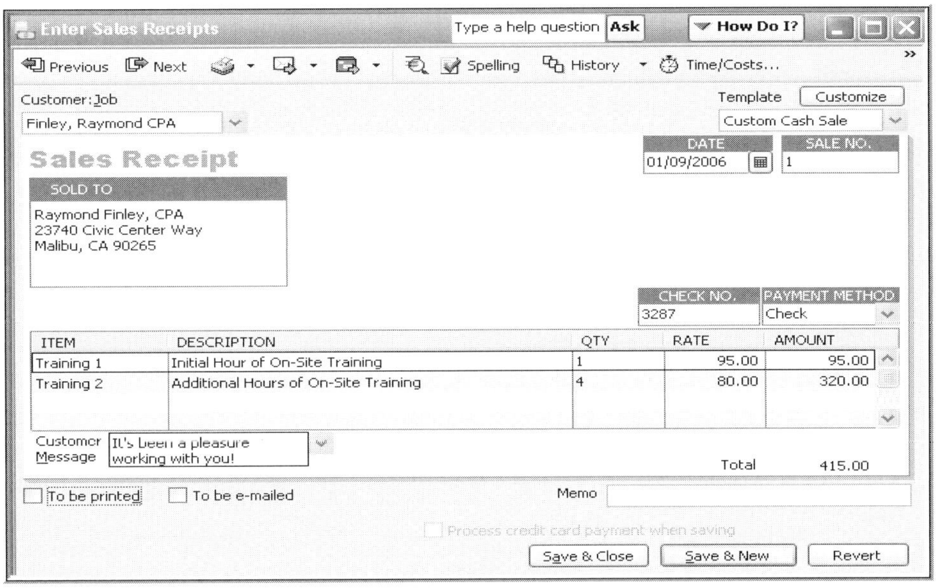

Print the Sales Receipt as previously instructed
Click **Save & Close**
Click **Yes** on the **Recording Transaction** dialog box
After closing the sales receipt, you are returned to the register for the Undeposited Funds account
Do not close the register

VIEW A QUICKREPORT

After editing the sales receipt and returning to the register, you may get a detailed report regarding the customer's transactions by clicking the QuickReport button.

Prepare a QuickReport for Raymond Finley

Click the **QuickReport** button to display the Register QuickReport for Raymond Finley, CPA

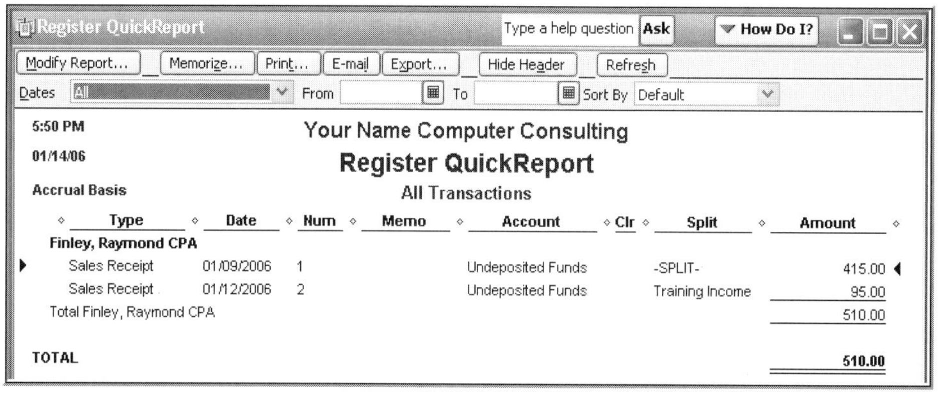

5:50 PM
01/14/06
Accrual Basis

Your Name Computer Consulting
Register QuickReport
All Transactions

Type	Date	Num	Memo	Account	Clr	Split	Amount
Finley, Raymond CPA							
Sales Receipt	01/09/2006	1		Undeposited Funds		-SPLIT-	415.00
Sales Receipt	01/12/2006	2		Undeposited Funds		Training Income	95.00
Total Finley, Raymond CPA							510.00
TOTAL							510.00

ANALYZE THE QUICKREPORT FOR RAYMOND FINLEY

Analyze the QuickReport

Notice that the date for Sales Receipt No. 1 has been changed to **01/09/2006**
- You may need to use the horizontal scroll bar to view all the columns in the report.

The account used is Undeposited Funds
The Split column contains the other accounts used in the transaction
- For Sales Receipt No. 2, the account used is **Training Income**.
- For Sales Receipt No. 1, you see the word **Split** rather than an account name.
- Split means that more than one sales item or account was used for this portion of the transaction.

View the sales items or accounts used for the Split by using QuickZoom to view the actual Sales Receipt
Use QuickZoom by double-clicking anywhere on the information for Sales Receipt No. 1
- The sales items used are Training 1 and Training 2.

Close the **Sales Receipt**
Close the **Register QuickReport** without printing
Close the **Register for Undeposited Funds**
Close the **Chart of Accounts**

ANALYZE SALES

To obtain information regarding the amount of sales by item, you can print or view sales reports. Sales reports provide information regarding cash and credit sales. When information regarding the sales according to the Sales Item is needed, a Sales by Item Summary Report is the appropriate report to print or view. This report enables you to see how much revenue is being generated by each sales item. This provides important information for decision making and managing the business. For example, if a sales item is not generating much income, it might be wise to discontinue that sales item.

Print a summarized list of sales by item

Click the **Report Center** icon
Click **Sales** as the type of report
Click **Summary** in the Sales by Item report list
The dates of the report are from **01/01/06** to **01/15/06**
Turn off the Date Prepared, Time Prepared, and Report Basis following instructions given previously
Tab to generate the report

Your Name Computer Consulting
Sales by Item Summary
January 1 - 15, 2006

	Jan 1 - 15, 06			
	Qty	Amount	% of Sales	Avg Price
Service				
Install 1	1	95.00	1.1%	95.00
Install 2	1	80.00	0.9%	80.00
Tech Sup 1	1	150.00	1.7%	150.00
Tech Sup 2	1	300.00	3.4%	300.00
Tech Sup 3	1	450.00	5%	450.00
Training 1	6	570.00	6.4%	95.00
Training 2	91	7,280.00	81.6%	80.00
Total Service		8,925.00	100.0%	
TOTAL		**8,925.00**	**100.0%**	

Click **Print**
The Orientation should be **Portrait**
Click **Print** on **Print Reports** dialog box
Close the report

View a sales report by item detail to obtain information regarding which transactions apply to each sales item

Click **Detail** on the Sales By Item report list
The dates of the report are from **01/01/06** to **01/15/06**
Turn off the Date Prepared, Time Prepared, and Report Basis following instructions given previously
Tab to generate the report
Scroll through the report to view the types of sales and the transactions that occurred within each category

- Notice how many transactions occurred in each sales item.

Your Name Computer Consulting
Sales by Item Detail
January 1 - 15, 2006

Type	Date	Num	Memo	Name	Qty	Sales Price	Amount	Balance
Service								
Install 1								
Invoice	01/08/2006	8	Initial Hour o...	Clark, Kendall	1	95.00	95.00	95.00
Total Install 1							95.00	95.00
Install 2								
Invoice	01/08/2006	8	Additional H...	Clark, Kendall	1	80.00	80.00	80.00
Total Install 2							80.00	80.00
Tech Sup 1								
Invoice	01/05/2006	6	5 Hours--Mo...	Yamashita, Bibey, and Iverson	1	150.00	150.00	150.00
Total Tech Sup 1							150.00	150.00
Tech Sup 2								
Invoice	01/02/2006	1	10 Hours--M...	Mendoza, Jose, Esq.	1	300.00	300.00	300.00
Invoice	01/05/2006	3	10 Hours--M...	Jafrood, Kala	0	300.00	0.00	300.00
Total Tech Sup 2							300.00	300.00

Close the report without printing
Close the **Report Center**

RECORD CUSTOMER PAYMENTS ON ACCOUNT

When customers make a full or partial payment of the amount they owe, QuickBooks Pro places the money received in an account called Undeposited Funds. The money stays in the account until a bank deposit is made. When you start to record a payment made by a customer, you see the customer's balance, any credits made to the account, and a complete list of outstanding invoices. QuickBooks Pro automatically applies the payment received to the oldest invoice.

MEMO:
DATE: January 15, 2006

Record the following cash receipt: Received Check No. 0684 for $815 from Eric Andrews Research Corp. as payment on account.

Record the receipt of a payment on account

Click the **Receive Payments** icon on the Customers section of the Home Page

- Notice the flow chart line from Invoices to Receive Payments. This icon is illustrated in this manner because recording a payment receipt is for a payment made on account. This is not a cash sale.

Click the drop-down list arrow for **Received From**
Click **Andrews, Eric Research Corp.**

- Notice that the current date or the last transaction date shows in the **Date** column and the total amount owed appears as the balance.
- Also note that previous cash sales to Eric Andrews Research Corp. are not listed. This is because a payment receipt is used only for payments on account.

Tab to or click **Amount**

- If you click, you will need to delete the 0.00. If you tab, it will be deleted when you type in the amount.

Enter **815**

- QuickBooks Pro will enter the **.00** when you tab to or click **Date**

Tab to or click **Date**

- If you click, you will need to delete the date. If you tab, the date will be deleted when you type 01/15/06.
- QuickBooks Pro automatically places a check in the check mark column for the oldest invoice and enters the payment amount is in the Payment column for the invoice being paid This means that the payment is applied to the oldest open invoice.

Type date **01/15/06**
Click the drop-down list arrow for **Pmt. Method**
Click **Check**
Tab to or click **Check No.**
Enter **0684**

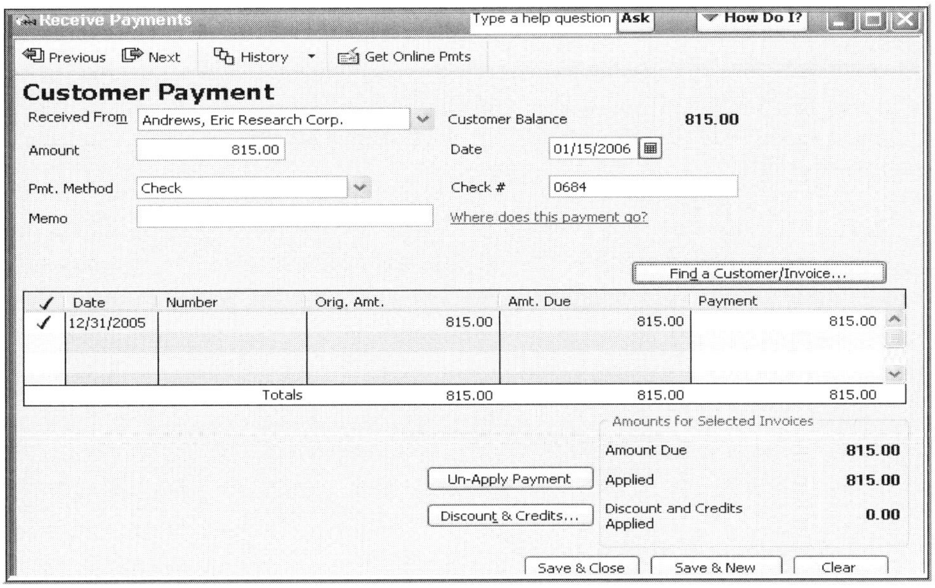

Click **Save & New**

RECORD ADDITIONAL PAYMENTS ON ACCOUNT WITHOUT STEP-BY-STEP INSTRUCTIONS

MEMO:
DATE: January 15, 2006

Received Check No. 1952 from Johnson, Cline, Preston, and Weaver for $3,680.
Received Check No. 8925 for $2,000 from Robbins Illustrations in partial payment of account. This receipt requires a Memo notation of Partial Payment. Make sure "Leave as an underpayment" is selected in the lower portion of the Customer Payment window.
Received Check No. 39251 from Timothy Matthews for $475.
Received Check No. 2051 for $2,190 from Watley Productions in partial payment of account. Record a Memo of Partial Payment for this receipt.
Received Check No. 5632 from Jose Mendoza for $150
Received Check No. 80195 from Webber, Lewis, and Billesdon for $3,685.

Enter the above payments on account; if necessary, refer to the previous steps listed

- Click **Save & New** to go from one Receive Payments Screen to the next
- Click the **Save & Close** button after all payments received have been recorded

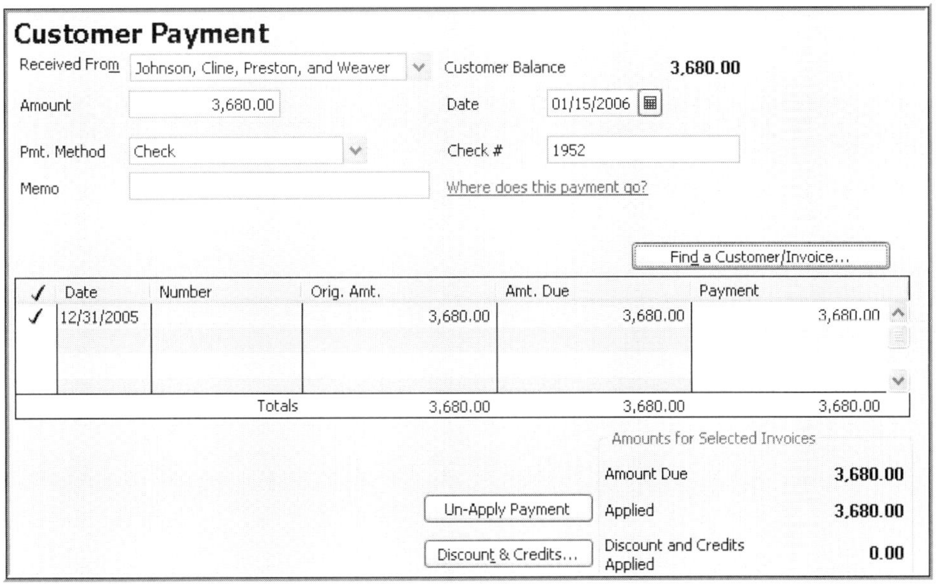
Customer Payment
Received From Johnson, Cline, Preston, and Weaver
Customer Balance 3,680.00
Amount 3,680.00
Date 01/15/2006
Pmt. Method Check
Check # 1952
Memo
Where does this payment go?
Find a Customer/Invoice...
✓ Date Number Orig. Amt. Amt. Due Payment
✓ 12/31/2005 3,680.00 3,680.00 3,680.00
Totals 3,680.00 3,680.00 3,680.00
Amounts for Selected Invoices
Amount Due 3,680.00
Un-Apply Payment
Applied 3,680.00
Discount & Credits...
Discount and Credits Applied 0.00

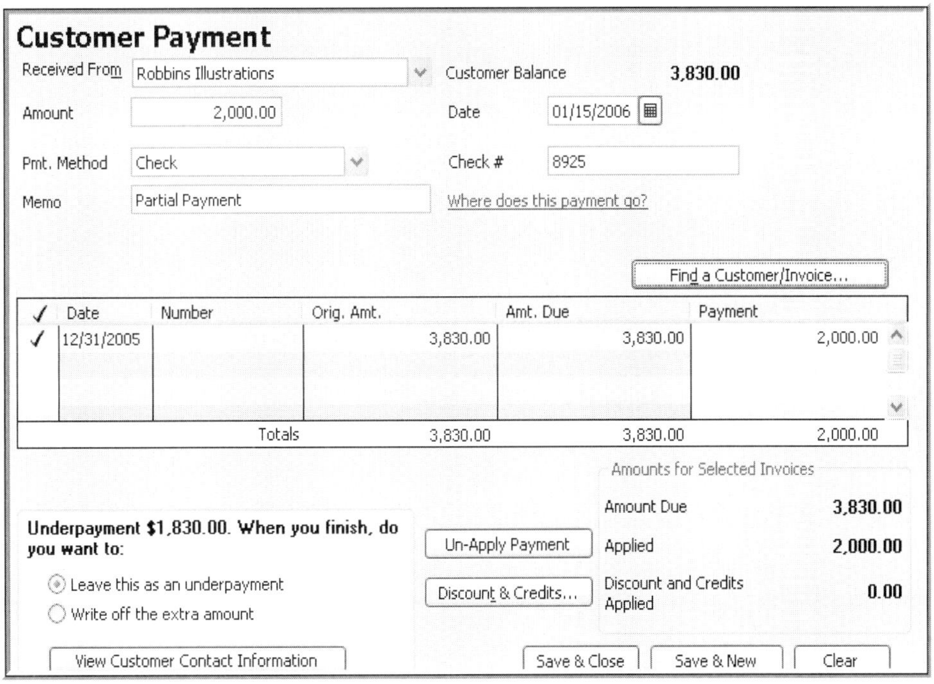
Customer Payment
Received From Robbins Illustrations
Customer Balance 3,830.00
Amount 2,000.00
Date 01/15/2006
Pmt. Method Check
Check # 8925
Memo Partial Payment
Where does this payment go?
Find a Customer/Invoice...
✓ Date Number Orig. Amt. Amt. Due Payment
✓ 12/31/2005 3,830.00 3,830.00 2,000.00
Totals 3,830.00 3,830.00 2,000.00
Amounts for Selected Invoices
Underpayment $1,830.00. When you finish, do you want to:
Leave this as an underpayment
Write off the extra amount
Amount Due 3,830.00
Un-Apply Payment
Applied 2,000.00
Discount & Credits...
Discount and Credits Applied 0.00
View Customer Contact Information
Save & Close
Save & New
Clear

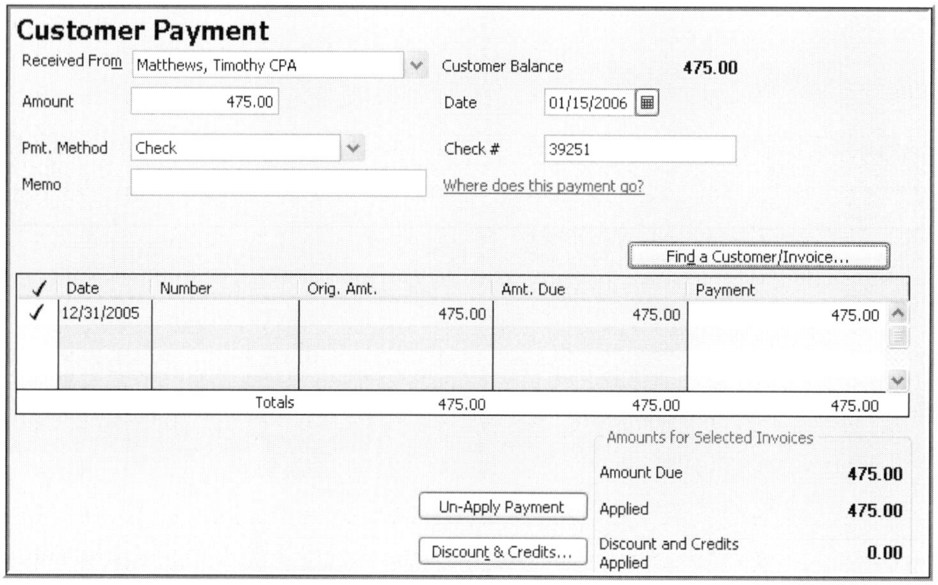

Customer Payment

Received From: Matthews, Timothy CPA | Customer Balance: **475.00**
Amount: 475.00 | Date: 01/15/2006
Pmt. Method: Check | Check #: 39251
Memo: | Where does this payment go?

Find a Customer/Invoice...

✓	Date	Number	Orig. Amt.	Amt. Due	Payment
✓	12/31/2005		475.00	475.00	475.00
		Totals	475.00	475.00	475.00

Amounts for Selected Invoices

Amount Due **475.00**
Un-Apply Payment | Applied **475.00**
Discount & Credits... | Discount and Credits Applied **0.00**

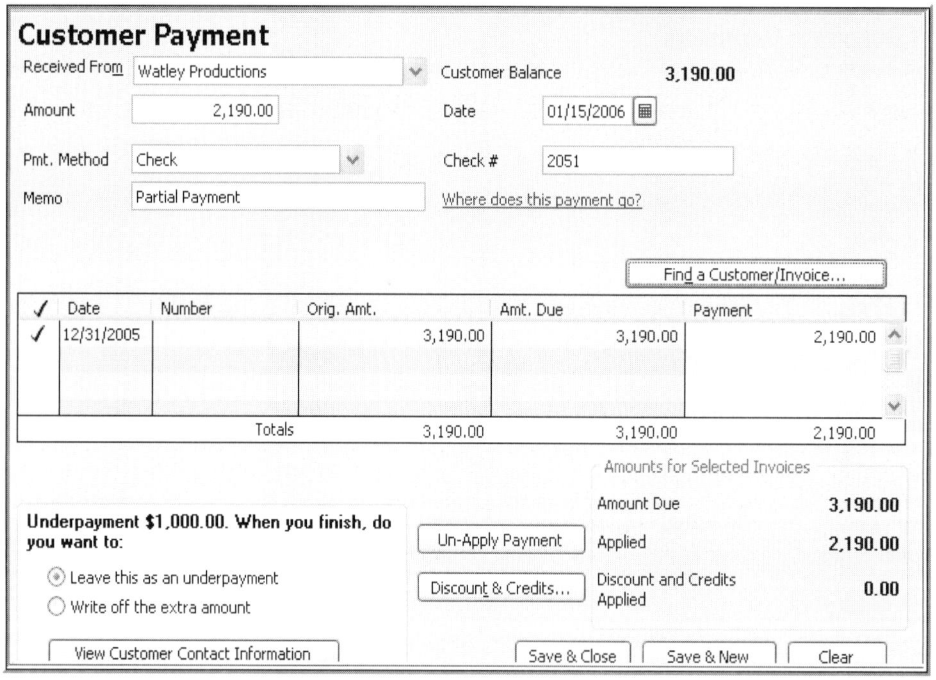

Customer Payment

Received From: Watley Productions | Customer Balance: **3,190.00**
Amount: 2,190.00 | Date: 01/15/2006
Pmt. Method: Check | Check #: 2051
Memo: Partial Payment | Where does this payment go?

Find a Customer/Invoice...

✓	Date	Number	Orig. Amt.	Amt. Due	Payment
✓	12/31/2005		3,190.00	3,190.00	2,190.00
		Totals	3,190.00	3,190.00	2,190.00

Amounts for Selected Invoices

Underpayment $1,000.00. When you finish, do you want to:

- Leave this as an underpayment
- Write off the extra amount

View Customer Contact Information

Amount Due **3,190.00**
Un-Apply Payment | Applied **2,190.00**
Discount & Credits... | Discount and Credits Applied **0.00**

Save & Close | Save & New | Clear

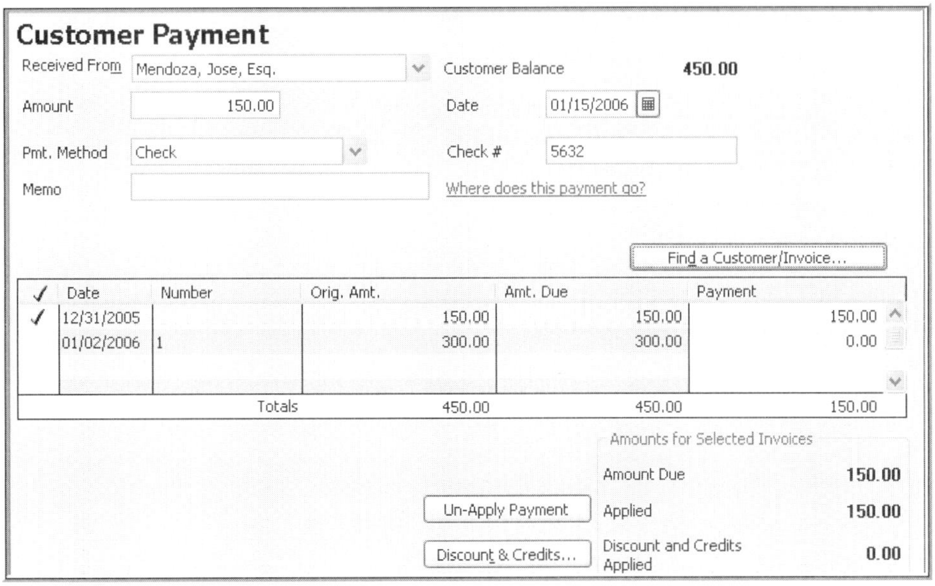

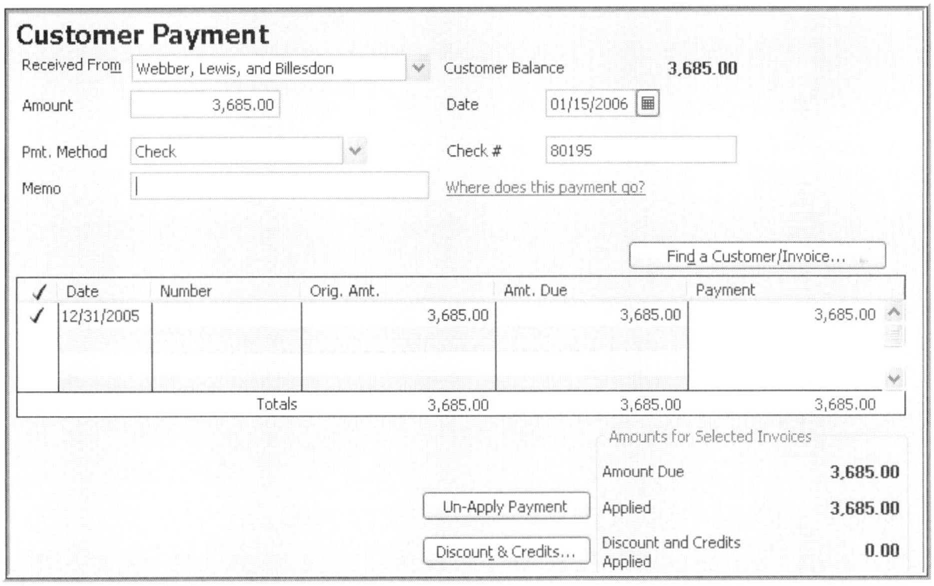

VIEW TRANSACTIONS BY CUSTOMER

In order to see the transactions for credit customers, you need to prepare a transaction report by customer. This report shows all sales, credits, and payments for each customer on account.

Prepare a Transaction List by Customer report

Click **Reports** on the menu bar

Point to **Customers & Receivables**
Click **Transaction List by Customer**

- Since you are only viewing the report, you do not need to remove the Date Prepared and the Time Prepared from the header

The dates are From **01/01/06** to **01/15/06**
Tab to generate the report
Scroll through the report

- Notice that information is shown for the invoices, cash sales, credit memo, and payments made on the accounts.
- Notice that the **Num** column shows the invoice numbers, sales receipt numbers, credit memo numbers, and check numbers.

10:18 AM
01/15/06

Your Name Computer Consulting
Transaction List by Customer
January 1 - 15, 2006

Type	Date	Num	Memo	Account	Clr	Split	Amount
Andrews, Eric Research Corp.							
Sales Receipt	01/12/2006	3		Undeposited Funds		-SPLIT-	335.00
Payment	01/15/2006	0684		Undeposited Funds		Accounts Receivable	815.00
Clark, Kendall							
Invoice	01/08/2006	8		Accounts Receivable		-SPLIT-	175.00
Finley, Raymond CPA							
Sales Receipt	01/09/2006	1		Undeposited Funds		-SPLIT-	415.00
Sales Receipt	01/12/2006	2		Undeposited Funds		Training Income	95.00
Grace, Anderson, and Binsley, CPA							
Invoice	01/05/2006	5		Accounts Receivable		-SPLIT-	1,425.00
Jafrood, Kala							
Invoice	01/05/2006	3	VOID:	Accounts Receivable	✓	Technical Support I...	0.00

Partial Report

Click the **Close** button to exit the report without printing

DEPOSIT CHECKS RECEIVED FOR CASH SALES AND PAYMENTS ON ACCOUNT

When you record cash sales and the receipt of payments on accounts, QuickBooks Pro places the money received in the Undeposited Funds account. Once the deposit is recorded, the funds are transferred from Undeposited Funds to the account selected when preparing the deposit.

MEMO:
DATE: January 15, 2006

Deposit all checks received for cash sales and payments on account.

Deposit checks received

Click the **Record Deposits** icon in the Banking section of the Home Page

- **Payments to Deposit** window shows all amounts received for cash sales and payments on account that have not been deposited in the bank.
- The column for **Type** contains RCPT, which means the amount is for a Sales Receipt (Cash Sale), and PMT, which means the amount received is for a payment on account.
- Notice that the √ column to the left of the Date column is empty.

Click the **Select All** button

- Notice the check marks in the √ column.

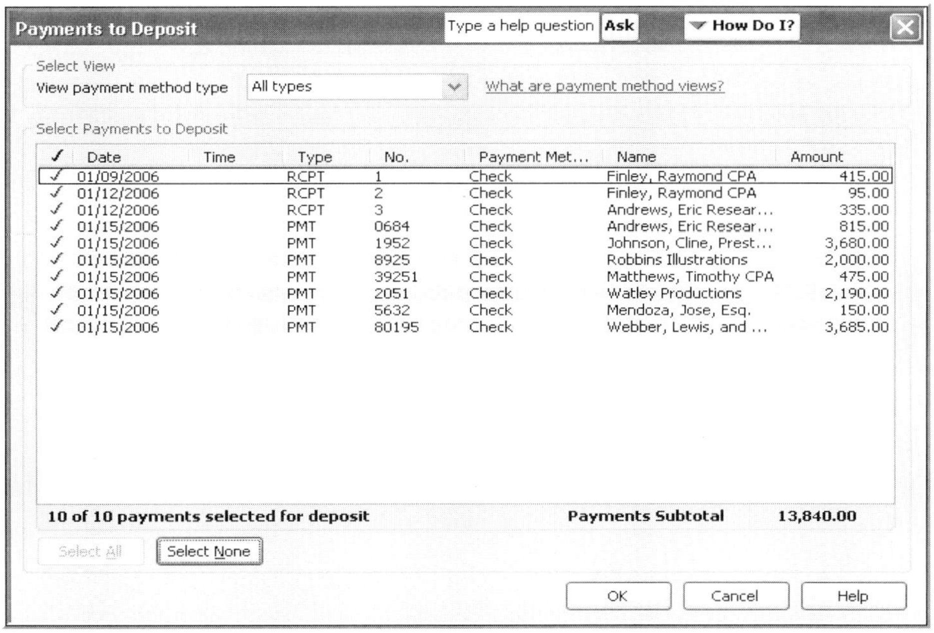
Payments to Deposit
Type a help question | Ask | How Do I?
Select View
View payment method type: All types — What are payment method views?
Select Payments to Deposit

✓	Date	Time	Type	No.	Payment Met...	Name	Amount
✓	01/09/2006		RCPT	1	Check	Finley, Raymond CPA	415.00
✓	01/12/2006		RCPT	2	Check	Finley, Raymond CPA	95.00
✓	01/12/2006		RCPT	3	Check	Andrews, Eric Resear...	335.00
✓	01/15/2006		PMT	0684	Check	Andrews, Eric Resear...	815.00
✓	01/15/2006		PMT	1952	Check	Johnson, Cline, Prest...	3,680.00
✓	01/15/2006		PMT	8925	Check	Robbins Illustrations	2,000.00
✓	01/15/2006		PMT	39251	Check	Matthews, Timothy CPA	475.00
✓	01/15/2006		PMT	2051	Check	Watley Productions	2,190.00
✓	01/15/2006		PMT	5632	Check	Mendoza, Jose, Esq.	150.00
✓	01/15/2006		PMT	80195	Check	Webber, Lewis, and ...	3,685.00

10 of 10 payments selected for deposit — Payments Subtotal 13,840.00
Select All | Select None
OK | Cancel | Help

Click **OK** to close **Payments to Deposit** screen and open **Make Deposits** screen

On the **Make Deposits** screen, **Deposit To** should be **Checking**

Date should be **01/15/2006**

- Tab to date and change if not correct.

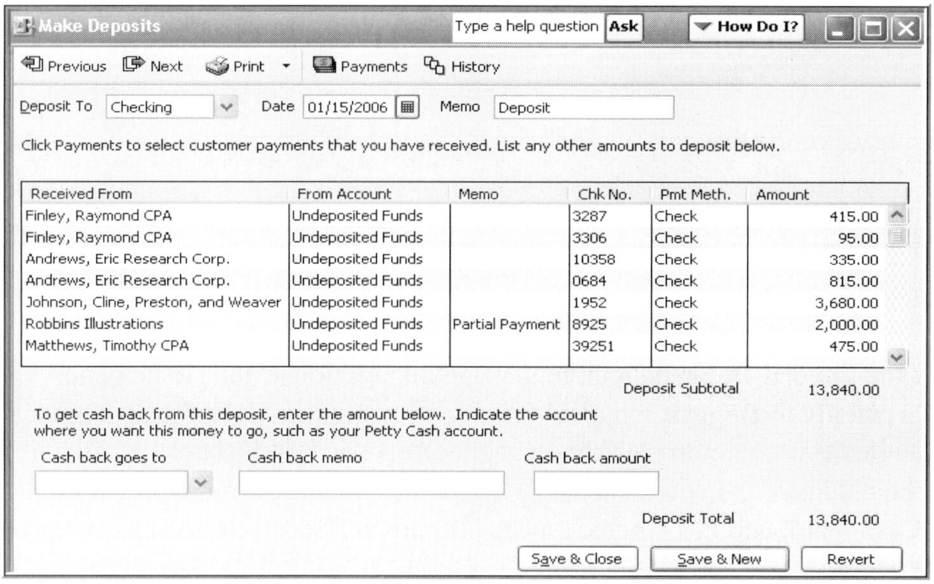

Click the **Print** button to print **Deposit Summary**
Select **Deposit summary only** on the **Print Deposit** dialog box, click **OK**

Check the **Settings** for **Print List**, click **Print**

- *Note:* QuickBooks Pro automatically prints the date that the Deposit Summary was printed on the report. It is the current date of your computer; and, therefore, it may not match the date shown in the answer key.

When printing is finished, click **Save & Close** on **Make Deposits** screen to record and close

PRINT JOURNAL

Even though QuickBooks Pro displays registers and reports in a manner that focuses on the transaction—for example, entering a sale on account via an invoice—it still keeps a General Journal. The Journal records each transaction and lists the accounts and the amounts for debit and credit entries. The Journal is very useful; especially, if you are trying to find errors. Always check the transaction dates, the account names, and the items listed in the Memo column. If a transaction does not appear in the Journal, it may be due to using an incorrect date. Remember, only the transactions entered within the report dates will be displayed.

Print the Journal

Open the **Report Center** as previously instructed
Click **Accountant & Taxes** as the Report type
Click **Journal**
The dates are from **01/01/06** to **01/15/06**
Modify the Report to change the **Header/Footer** so the **Date Prepared** and **Time Prepared** are not selected, click **OK**
Scroll through the report to view the transactions

- You may find that your Trans # is not the same as shown. QuickBooks automatically numbers all transactions recorded. If you have deleted and re-entered transactions more than directed in the text, you may have different transaction numbers. Do not be concerned with this.
- Also notice that not all names, memos, and accounts are displayed in full. You will learn how to change this later in training.

Click **Print**
On the Print Reports screen, the settings will be the same used previously except:
Click **Landscape** to select Landscape orientation
Click on **Fit report to one page wide** to select this item

- The printer will print the Journal using a smaller font so the report will fit across the 11-inch width.

Click Print

- The Journal will be several pages in length.

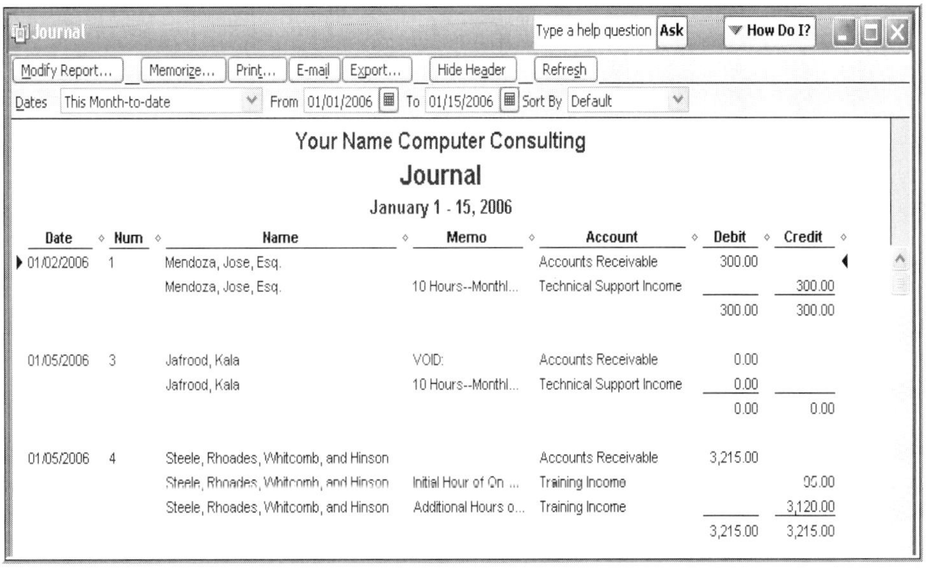

Close the report, do not close the Report Center

PRINT THE TRIAL BALANCE

When all sales transactions have been entered, it is important to print the Trial Balance and verify that the total debits equal the total credits.

Print the Trial Balance

Click **Trial Balance** on the Report Center list of Accountant & Taxes reports
Enter the dates from **010106** to **011506**
Click the **Modify Report** button and change **Header/Footer** so **Date Prepared**, **Time Prepared**, and **Report Basis** do not print
Print the report in **Portrait** orientation

- If necessary, click on **Fit report to one page wide** to deselect this item

Your Name Computer Consulting
Trial Balance
As of January 15, 2006

	Jan 15, 06	
	Debit	Credit
Checking	51,710.00	
Accounts Receivable	17,650.00	
Office Supplies	500.00	
Undeposited Funds	0.00	
Company Cars:Original Cost	49,000.00	
Office Equipment:Original Cost	8,050.00	
Accounts Payable		850.00
Loan Payable	0.00	
Loan Payable:Company Cars Loan		35,000.00
Loan Payable:Office Equipment Loan		4,000.00
Retained Earnings	0.00	
Student's Name, Capital		53,135.00
Student's Name, Capital:Investments		25,000.00
Income:Installation Income		175.00
Income:Technical Support Income		900.00
Income:Training Income		7,850.00
TOTAL	**126,910.00**	**126,910.00**

Close the report

GRAPHS IN QUICKBOOKS® PRO

Once transactions have been entered, transaction results can be visually represented in a graphic form. QuickBooks Pro illustrates Accounts Receivable by Aging Period as a bar chart, and it illustrates Accounts Receivable by Customer as a pie chart. For further details, double-click on an individual section of the pie chart or chart legend to create a bar chart analyzing an individual customer. QuickBooks Pro also prepares graphs based on sales and will show the results of sales by item and by customer.

PREPARE ACCOUNTS RECEIVABLE GRAPHS

Accounts Receivable graphs illustrate account information based on the age of the account and the percentage of accounts receivable owed by each customer.

Create graphs for accounts receivable:

Click **Customers & Receivables** in the Report Center list to select the type of report
Click **Accounts Receivable Graph** to select the report
Click **Dates** on the QuickInsight: Accounts Receivable Graph screen
On the **Change Graph Dates** change **Show Aging As of** to **01/15/06**
Click **OK**

- QuickBooks Pro generates a bar chart illustrating Accounts Receivable by Aging Period and a pie chart illustrating Accounts Receivable by Customer

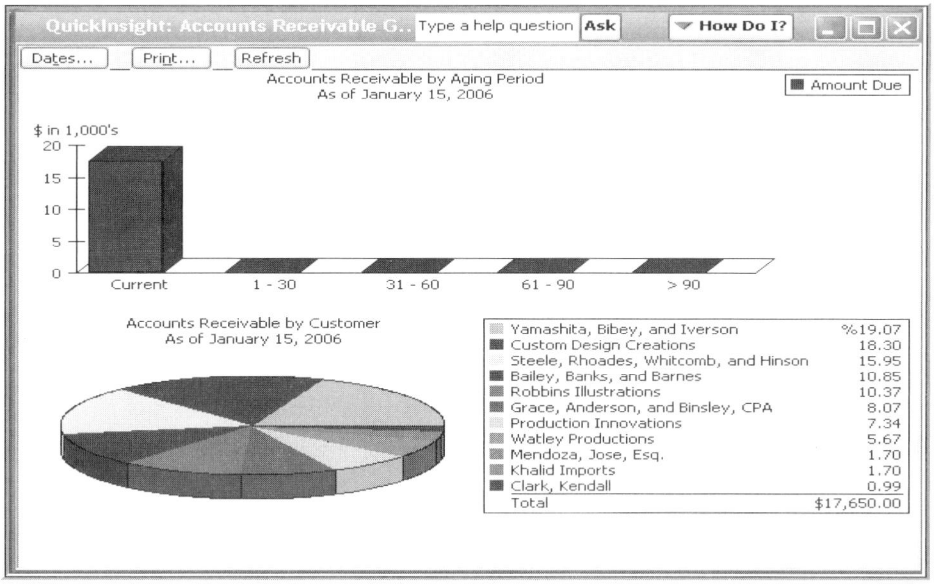

Printing is not required for this graph

- If you want a printed copy, click **Print** and print in Portrait mode

Click **Dates**
Enter **02/01/06** for the **Show Aging As of** date
Click **OK**

- Notice the difference in the aging of accounts.

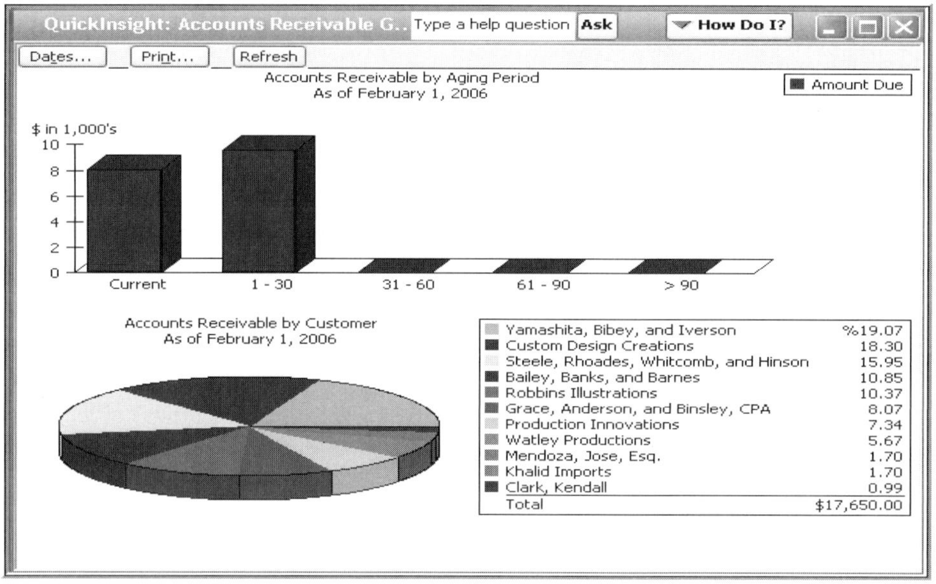

Click **Dates**
Enter **01/15/06**
Do not close the graph

USE QUICKZOOM FEATURE TO OBTAIN INDIVIDUAL CUSTOMER DETAILS

It is possible to get detailed information regarding the aging of transactions for an individual customer by using the QuickZoom feature of QuickBooks Pro.

Use QuickZoom to see information for Yamashita, Bibey, and Iverson

Double-click on the section of the pie chart for **Yamashita, Bibey, and Iverson**

- You get a bar chart aging the transactions of the customer.

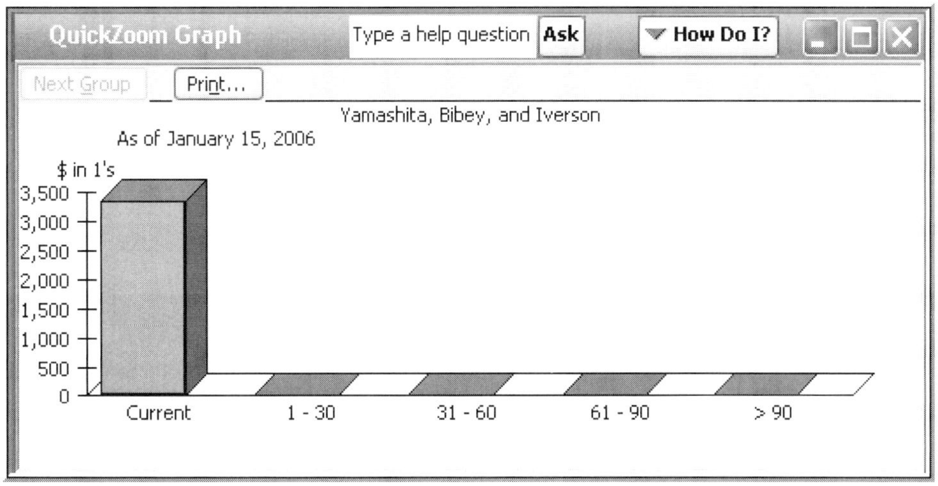

Printing is not required for this graph
Close the chart for Yamashita, Bibey, and Iverson and the Accounts Receivable graph

PREPARE SALES GRAPHS

Sales graphs illustrate the amount of cash and credit sales for a given period as well as the percentage of sales for each sales item.

Prepare a Sales Graph

Click **Sales** in the Report list
Click **Sales Graph**
Click the **Dates** button
Click in **From**
Enter **01/01/06**
Tab to **To**
Enter **01/15/06**
Click **OK**
The **By Item** button should be indented

- You will see a bar chart representing Sales by Month and a pie chart displaying a Sales Summary by item.
- If the **By Customer** button is indented, you will see the same bar chart but the pie chart will display a Sales Summary by customer.
- If the **By Rep** button is indented, you will see the same bar chart but the pie chart will display a Sales Summary by sales rep.

Printing is not required for this graph

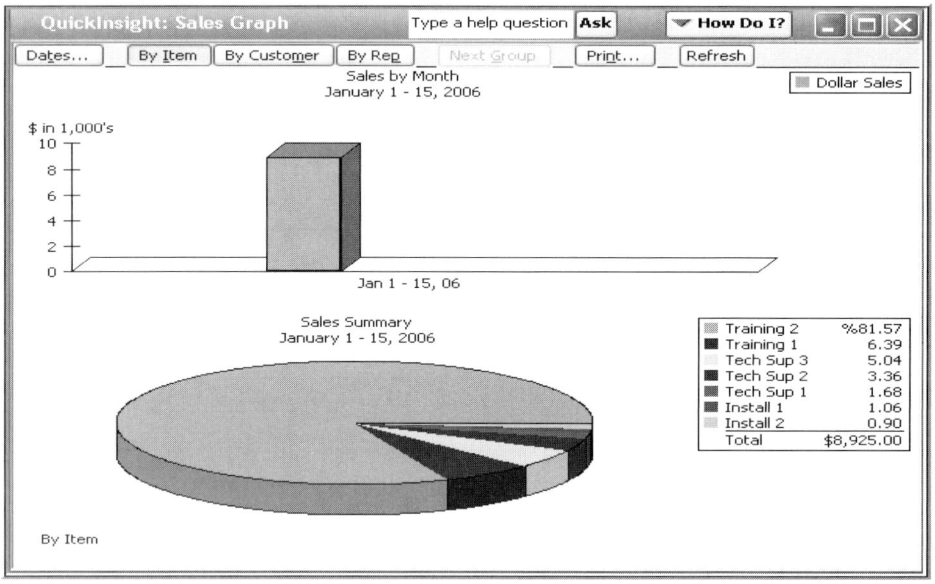

USE QUICKZOOM TO VIEW AN INDIVIDUAL ITEM

It is possible to use QuickZoom to view details regarding an individual item's sales by month.

Use QuickZoom to see information for Install 1

In the chart legend, double-click **Install 1**

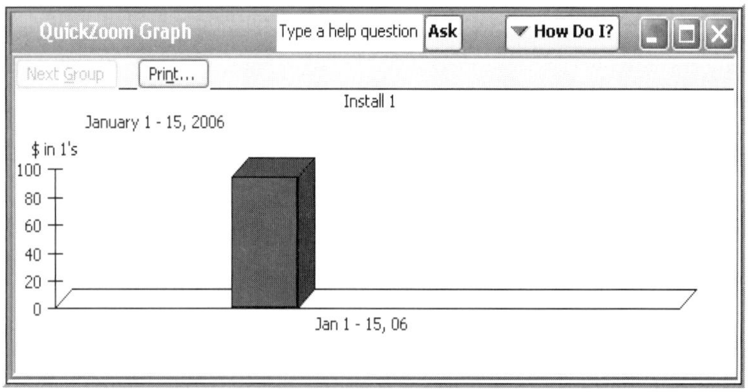

You will see the Sales by Month for Install 1
Do not print
Close Graphs

BACK UP AND CLOSE COMPANY

As you learned in Chapter 1, when you use QuickBooks Pro to make a back up file, the program creates a condensed file that contains all the data for the entries made up to the time of the backup file. This file has an extension **.qbb** and cannot be used to record transactions. When new transactions are recorded, a new backup file must be made. In training, it is wise to make a daily backup as well as an end-of-chapter backup. If errors are made in training, the appropriate backup file can be restored. For example, if you back up Chapter 2 and make errors in Chapter 3, the Chapter 2 backup may be restored to a company file with the extension **.qbw**. The data entered for Chapter 3 will be erased and only the data from Chapter 2 will appear.

A duplicate copy of the file may be made using Windows. Instructions for this procedure are given in Appendix A. You may hear the duplicate copy referred to as a backup file. This is different from the QuickBooks backup file.

➤ Back up the company

Follow the instructions provided in Chapter 1 to make your backup
The name of the backup file is **Computer Ch 2.qbb**

- Your Computer Ch 1.qbb file contains all of your work from Chapter 1
- Your Computer Ch 2.qbb file contains all your work from Chapters 1 and 2.
- The Computer Ch 2.qbb will not contain transactions from the work you do in Chapter 3.
- Keeping a separate backup file for each chapter is helpful for those times when you have made errors and cannot figure out how to correct them. Restoring your Chapter 2 back up file will restore your work from Chapters 1 and 2 and eliminate any work completed in Chapter 3. This will allow you to start over at the beginning of Chapter 3. If you do not have a back up file for Chapter 2, you would need to re-enter all the transactions for Chapter 2 before beginning Chapter 3.
- You may wish to make a daily back up file. If so, you should make a second backup to save your work each day. Use Computer.qbb as your daily backup file. This is helpful for those times when you have made errors and cannot figure out how to correct them but do not want to start over at the beginning of the chapter. Restoring your daily backup file will restore your work from the previous training session and eliminate the work completed in the current session.

EXIT QUICKBOOKS AND CLOSE THE COMPANY

After the backup file has been made, close the Company and QuickBooks

Follow the procedures given in Chapter 1 to close a company and to close QuickBooks

- Refer to Appendix A for the steps to follow to make a duplicate disk.

SUMMARY

In this chapter, cash and credit sales were prepared for Your Name Computer Consulting, a service business, using sales receipts and invoices. Credit memos were issued. Customer accounts were added and revised. Invoices and sales receipts were edited, deleted, and voided. Cash payments were received and bank deposits were made. All the transactions entered reinforced the QuickBooks Pro concept of using the business form to record transactions rather than enter information in journals. However, QuickBooks Pro does not disregard traditional accounting methods. Instead, it performs this function in the background. The Journal was accessed and changes to transactions were made via the Journal. The fact that the Customer:Job List functions as the Accounts Receivable Ledger and that the Chart of Accounts is the General Ledger in QuickBooks Pro was pointed out. The importance of reports for information and decision-making was illustrated. Exploration of the various sales and accounts receivable reports and graphs allowed information to be viewed from a sales standpoint and from an accounts receivable perspective. Sales reports emphasized both cash and credit sales according to the sales item generating the revenue. Accounts Receivable reports focused on amounts owed by credit customers. The traditional trial balance emphasizing the equality of debits and credits was prepared.

END-OF-CHAPTER QUESTIONS

TRUE/FALSE

ANSWER THE FOLLOWING QUESTIONS IN THE SPACE PROVIDED BEFORE THE QUESTION NUMBER.

_____ 1. A new customer can be added to a company's records on the fly.

_____ 2. In QuickBooks Pro, error correction for a sale on account can be accomplished by editing the invoice.

_____ 3. A Sales Item List stores information about products you purchase.

_____ 4. Once transactions have been entered, modifications to a customer's account may be made only at the end of the fiscal year.

_____ 5. In QuickBooks Pro all transactions must be entered with the traditional debit/credit method.

_____ 6. Checks received for cash sales are held in the Undeposited Funds account until the bank deposit is made.

_____ 7. When a correction for a transaction is made, QuickBooks Pro not only changes the form used to record the transaction, it also changes all journal and account entries for the transaction to reflect the correction.

_____ 8. QuickGraphs allow information to be viewed from both a sales standpoint and from an accounts receivable perspective.

_____ 9. QuickZoom allows you to print a report instantly.

_____ 10. A customer's payment on account is immediately recorded in the cash account.

MULTIPLE CHOICE

WRITE THE LETTER OF THE CORRECT ANSWER IN THE SPACE PROVIDED BEFORE THE QUESTION NUMBER.

_____ 1. To remove an invoice without a trace, it is ___.
A. voided
B. deleted
C. erased
D. reversed

_____ 2. To enter a cash sale, ___ is completed.
A. a debit
B. an invoice
C. a sales receipt
D. receive payments

_____ 3. Two primary types of lists used in this chapter are ___.
A. receivables and payables
B. invoices and checks
C. registers and navigator
D. customers and item

_____ 4. When you enter an invoice, an error may be corrected by ___.
A. backspacing or deleting
B. tabbing and typing
C. dragging and typing
D. all of the above

_____ 5. While in the Customer Balance Summary Report, it is possible to get an individual customer's information by using ___.
A. QuickReport
B. QuickZoom
C. QuickGraph
D. QuickSummary

_____ 6. Undeposited Funds represents ___.
A. cash or checks received from customers but not yet deposited in the bank
B. all cash sales
C. the balance of the accounts receivable account
D. none of the above

_____ 7. QuickBooks Pro uses graphs to illustrate information about ___.
A. the chart of accounts
B. sales
C. the cash account
D. supplies

_____ 8. Changes to the chart of accounts may be made ___.
A. at the beginning of a fiscal period
B. before the end of the fiscal year
C. at any time
D. once established, the chart of accounts may not be modified

_____ 9. To obtain information about sales by item, you can view ___.
A. the income statement
B. the trial balance
C. receivables reports
D. sales reports

_____10. When you add a customer using the Set Up method, you add ___.
A. complete information for a customer
B. only a customer's name
C. the customer's name, address, and telephone number
D. the customer's name and telephone number

FILL-IN

IN THE SPACE PROVIDED, WRITE THE ANSWER THAT MOST APPROPRIATELY COMPLETES THE SENTENCE.

1. The report used to view all the balances on account of each customer is the __________.

2. The form prepared to show a reduction to a sale on account is a(n) __________.

3. The report that proves that debits equal credits is the __________.

4. QuickBooks Pro shows icons on the __________ that may be clicked to open business documents used in recording transactions.

5. To verify the company being used in QuickBooks Pro, you check the __________.

SHORT ESSAY

Explain how the method used to enter an Accounts Receivable transaction in QuickBooks Pro is different from the method used to enter a transaction according to an accounting textbook.

____

____

____

____

____

NAME________________________

TRANSMITTAL

CHAPTER 2: YOUR NAME COMPUTER CONSULTING

Attach the following documents and reports:

Invoice No. 1: Jose Mendoza
Invoice No. 2: Timothy Matthews
Invoice No. 3: Kala Jafrood
Invoice No. 4: Steele, Rhoades, Whitcomb, and Hinson
Invoice No. 5: Grace, Anderson, and Binsley
Invoice No. 6: Yamashita, Bibey, and Iverson
Customer Balance Summary, January 5, 2006
Customer Balance Detail, Steele, Rhoades, Whitcomb, and Hinson
Invoice No. 5: Grace, Anderson, and Binsley
Transaction List by Customer, January 1-7, 2006
Customer Balance Detail Report
Credit Memo No. 7: Steele, Rhoades, Whitcomb, and Hinson
Invoice No. 8: Kendall Clark
Sales Receipt No. 1: Raymond Finley
Sales Receipt No. 2: Raymond Finley
Sales Receipt No. 3: Eric Andrews Research Corp.
Sales by Customer Detail Report, January 1-14, 2006
Sales Receipt No. 1 (corrected): Raymond Finley
Sales by Item Summary, January 1-15, 2006
Deposit Summary
Journal
Trial Balance, January 15, 2006

END-OF-CHAPTER PROBLEM

YOUR NAME GARDEN & POOL MAINTENANCE

Chapter 2 continues with the entry of both cash and credit sales, receipt of payment by credit customers, credit memos, and bank deposits. In addition, reports focusing on sales and accounts receivable are prepared.

INSTRUCTIONS

Use the company file **Garden.qbw** that you used for Chapter 1. The company name should be Your Name Garden & Pool Maintenance.

The invoices and sales receipts are numbered consecutively. Invoice No. 25 is the first invoice number used in this problem. Sales Receipt No. 15 is the first sales receipt number used in this problem. Each invoice recorded should contain a message. Choose the one that you feel is most appropriate for the transaction. Print each invoice and sales receipt as it is completed. Remember that payments received on account should be recorded as Receive Payments and not as a Sales Receipt.

When recording transactions, use the following Sales Item chart to determine the item(s) billed. If the transaction does not indicate the size of the pool or property, use the first category for the item; for example, LandCom 1 or LandRes 1 would be used for standard-size landscape service. Remember that PoolCom 1 and PoolRes 1 are services for spas—not pools. The appropriate billing for a standard-size pool would be PoolCom 2 or PoolRes 2.

When printing reports, always remove the Date Prepared, Time Prepared, and Report Basis from the Header/Footer.

YOUR NAME GARDEN & POOL MAINTENANCE
SALES ITEM LIST

ITEM	DESCRIPTION	AMOUNT
LandCom 1	Commercial Landscape Maintenance (Standard Size)	$150 mo.
LandCom 2	Commercial Landscape Maintenance (Medium)	250 mo.
LandCom 3	Commercial Landscape Maintenance (Large)	500 mo.
LandRes 1	Residential Landscape Maintenance (Standard Size)	$100 mo.
LandRes 2	Residential Landscape Maintenance (Medium)	200 mo.
LandRes 3	Residential Landscape Maintenance (Large)	350 mo.
PoolCom 1	Commercial Spa Service	$100 mo.
PoolCom 2	Commercial Pool Service (All pools unless specified as Large)	300 mo.
PoolCom 3	Commercial Pool Service (Large)	500 mo.
PoolRes 1	Residential Spa Service	$ 50 mo.
PoolRes 2	Residential Pool Service (All pools unless specified as Large)	100 mo.
PoolRes 3	Residential Pool Service (Large)	150 mo.
LandTrim	Trimming and Pruning	$75 hr.
LandPlant	Planting and Cultivating	50 hr.
LandWater	Sprinklers, Timers, etc.	75 hr.
LandGrow	Fertilize, Spray for Pests	75 hr.
PoolRepair	Mechanical Maintenance and Repairs	$75 hr.
PoolWash	Acid Wash, Condition	Price by the job
PoolStart	Startup for New Pools	500.00

RECORD TRANSACTIONS

January 1

- ▶ Billed Pacific View Motel for monthly landscape services and monthly pool maintenance services, Invoice No. 25. (Use LandCom 1 to record the monthly landscape service fee and PoolCom 2 to record the monthly pool service fee. The quantity for each item is 1.) Terms are Net 15.
- ▶ Billed Dr. Silverman for monthly landscape and pool services at his home. Both the pool and landscaping are standard size. The terms are Net 30.
- ▶ Billed Custom Creations for 2 hours shrub trimming. Terms are Net 30.
- ▶ Received Check No. 381 for $500 from Denise Ludlow for pool startup services at her home, Sales Receipt No. 15.
- ▶ Received Check No. 8642 from Kaan Padir for $150 as payment in full on his account.

January 15

- ▶ Billed a new customer: Matthew Ericsson (remember to enter the last name first for the customer name and change the billing name to first name first)—10824 Hope Ranch St., Santa Barbara, CA 93110, 805-555-9825, terms Net 30—for monthly service on his large pool and large residential landscape maintenance.
- ▶ Received Check No. 6758 from Pacific View Motel in full payment of Invoice No. 25.
- ▶ Received Check No. 987 from a new customer: Larry Bailey (a neighbor of Matthew Ericsson) for $75 for 1 hour of pool repairs. Even though this is a cash sale, do a complete customer setup: 10877 Hope Ranch St., Santa Barbara, CA 93110, 805-555-7175, fax 805-555-5717, E-mail lbailey@abc.com, terms Net 30.
- ▶ Billed Santa Barbara Bay Resorts for their large pool service and large landscaping maintenance. Also bill for 5 hours planting, 3 hours trimming, 2 hours spraying, and 3 hours pool repair services. Terms are Net 15.

January 30

- ▶ Received Check No. 1247 for $525 as payment in full from Custom Creations.
- ▶ Received Check No. 8865 from Sherri Somis for amount due.
- ▶ Billed Coast Resorts for large pool and large landscaping maintenance. Terms are Net 15.
- ▶ Billed Carillo Street Apartments for standard-size commercial pool service and standard-size commercial landscape maintenance. Terms are Net 30.
- ▶ Deposit all cash receipts. Print Deposit Summary.

PRINT REPORTS AND BACKUP

- ▶ Customer Balance Detail Report for all transactions. Portrait orientation.
- ▶ Sales by Item Summary Report for 1/1/2006 through 1/30/2006. Portrait orientation.
- ▶ Journal for 1/1/2006 through 1/30/2006. Print in Landscape orientation, fit to one page wide.
- ▶ Trial Balance for 1/1/2006 through 1/30/2006. Portrait orientation.
- ▶ Backup your work to **Garden Ch 2.qbb**

NAME ____________________

TRANSMITTAL

CHAPTER 2: YOUR NAME GARDEN & POOL MAINTENANCE

Attach the following documents and reports:

Invoice No. 25: Pacific View Motel
Invoice No. 26: Dr. Michael Silverman
Invoice No. 27: Custom Creations
Sales Receipt No. 15: Denise Ludlow
Invoice No. 28: Matthew Ericsson
Sales Receipt No. 16: Larry Bailey
Invoice No. 29: Santa Barbara Bay Resorts
Invoice No. 30: Coast Resorts
Invoice No. 31: Carillo Street Apartments
Deposit Summary
Customer Balance Detail
Sales by Item Summary
Journal
Trial Balance

3

PAYABLES AND PURCHASES: SERVICE BUSINESS

LEARNING OBJECTIVES

At the completion of this chapter you will be able to:

1. Understand the concepts for computerized accounting for payables.
2. Enter, edit, correct, delete, and pay bills.
3. Add new vendors and modify vendor records.
4. View Accounts Payable transaction history from the Enter Bills window.
5. View and/or print QuickReports for vendors, Accounts Payable Register, etc.
6. Use the QuickZoom feature.
7. Record and edit transactions in the Accounts Payable Register.
8. Enter vendor credits.
9. Print, edit, void, and delete checks.
10. Pay for expenses using petty cash.
11. Add new accounts.
12. Display and print the Accounts Payable Aging Summary Report, an Unpaid Bills Detail Report, a Vendor Balance Summary Report.
13. Display an Accounts Payable Graph by Aging Period.

ACCOUNTING FOR PAYABLES AND PURCHASES

In a service business, most of the accounting for purchases and payables is simply paying bills for expenses incurred in the operation of the business. Purchases are for things used in the operation of the business. Some transactions will be in the form of cash purchases, and others will be purchases on account. Bills can be paid when they are received or when they are due. Rather than use cumbersome journals, QuickBooks Pro continues to focus on recording transactions based on the business document; therefore, you use the Enter Bills and Pay Bills features of the program to record the receipt and payment of bills. QuickBooks Pro can remind you when payments are due and can calculate and apply discounts earned for paying bills early. Payments can be made by recording payments in the Pay Bills window or, if using the cash basis for accounting, by writing a check. A cash purchase can be recorded by writing a check or by using petty cash. Even though QuickBooks Pro focuses on recording transactions on the business forms used, all transactions are recorded behind the scenes in the General Journal. QuickBooks

Pro uses a Vendor List for all vendors with which the company has an account. QuickBooks Pro does not refer to the Vendor List as the Accounts Payable Ledger, yet that is exactly what it is. The total of the Vendor List/Accounts Payable Ledger will match the total of the Accounts Payable account in the Chart of Accounts/General Ledger. The Vendor List may be accessed through the Vendor Center.

As in Chapter 2, corrections can be made directly on the business form or within the Transaction Journal. New accounts and vendors may be added on the fly as transactions are entered. Reports illustrating vendor balances, unpaid bills, accounts payable aging, transaction history, and accounts payable registers may be viewed and printed. Graphs analyzing the amount of accounts payable by aging period provide a visual illustration of the accounts payable.

TRAINING TUTORIAL AND PROCEDURES

The following tutorial will once again work with Your Name Computer Consulting. As in Chapter 2, transactions will be recorded for this fictitious company. The tutorial for Your Name Computer Consulting will continue in Chapters 4, where accounting for bank reconciliations, financial statement preparation, and closing an accounting period will be completed. To maximize training benefits, you should follow the Training Procedures given in Chapter 2.

BEGINNING THE TUTORIAL

In this chapter, you will be entering bills incurred by the company in the operation of the business. You will also be recording the payment of bills, purchases using checks, and purchases/payments using petty cash.

The Vendor List keeps information regarding the vendors with whom you do business and is the Accounts Payable Ledger. Vendor information includes the vendor names, addresses, telephone numbers, payment terms, credit limits, and account numbers. You will be using the following list for vendors with which Your Name Computer Consulting has an account:

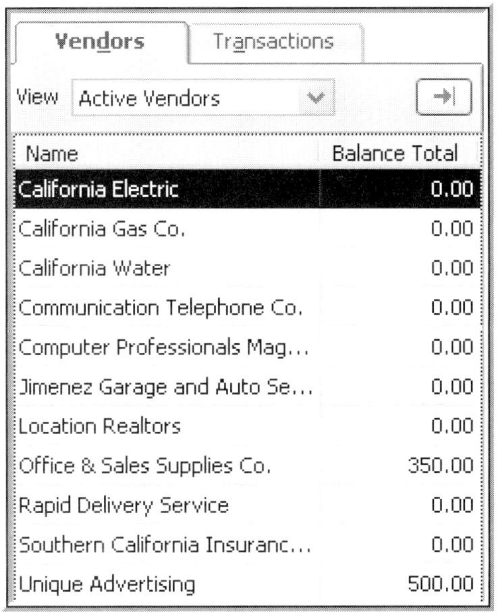

All transactions are listed on memos. The transaction date will be the same as the memo date unless specified otherwise within the transaction. Vendor names, when necessary, will be given in the transaction. Unless other terms are provided, the terms are Net 30. Once a specific type of transaction has been entered in a step-by-step manner, additional transactions of the same or a similar type will be made without having instructions provided. Of course, you may always refer to instructions given for previous transactions for ideas or for steps used to enter those transactions. To determine the account used in the transaction, refer to the Chart of Accounts. When you are entering account information on a bill, clicking on the drop-down list arrow will show a copy of the Chart of Accounts.

OPEN QUICKBOOKS® PRO AND YOUR NAME COMPUTER CONSULTING

➤ Open QuickBooks Pro as instructed in Chapters 1 and open Your Name Computer Consulting

ENTER A BILL

QuickBooks Pro provides accounts payable tracking. Entering bills as soon as they are received is an efficient way to record your liabilities. Once bills have been entered, QuickBooks Pro will be able to provide up-to-date cash flow reports, and will remind you when it is time to pay your bills. A bill is divided into two sections: a vendor-related section (the upper part of the bill that looks similar to a check and has a memo text box under it) and a detail section (the area that is divided into columns for Account, Amount, and Memo). The vendor-related section of the bill is where information for the actual bill is entered, including a memo with information about the transaction. The detail section is where the expense accounts, expense account amounts, and transaction explanations are indicated.

MEMO
DATE: January 16, 2006

Record the following bill: Unique Advertising prepared and placed advertisements in local business publications announcing our new hardware installation service. Received Unique's Invoice No. 9875 for $260 as a bill with terms of Net 30.

Record a bill

Click the **Enter Bills** icon in the Vendors section of the Home Page
Verify that Bill is marked at the top of the form and complete the Vendor-section of the bill:
Click the drop-down list arrow next to **Vendor**
Click **Unique Advertising**
- Name is entered as the vendor.

Tab to **Date**
- As with other business forms, when you tab to the date, it will be highlighted.
- When you type in the new date, the highlighted date will be deleted.

Type **01/16/06** as the date
Tab to **Ref. No.**
Type the vendor's invoice number: **9875**
Tab to **Amount Due**
Type **260**
- QuickBooks Pro will automatically insert the .00 after the amount.

Tab to **Terms**
Click the drop-down list arrow next to **Terms**
Click **Net 30**
- QuickBooks Pro automatically changes the Bill Due date to show 30 days from the transaction date.
- At this time nothing will be inserted as a memo in the text box between the vendor-related section of the bill and the detail section of the bill.

Complete the detail section of the bill using the **Expenses** tab
Tab to or click in the column for **Account**
Click the drop-down list arrow next to **Account**
Click **Advertising Expense**

- Based on the accrual method of accounting, Advertising Expense is selected as the account used in this transaction because this expense should be matched against the revenue of the period.

The **Amount** column already shows **260.00**—no entry required
Tab to or click the first line in the column for **Memo**
Enter the transaction explanation of **Ads for Hardware Installation Services**

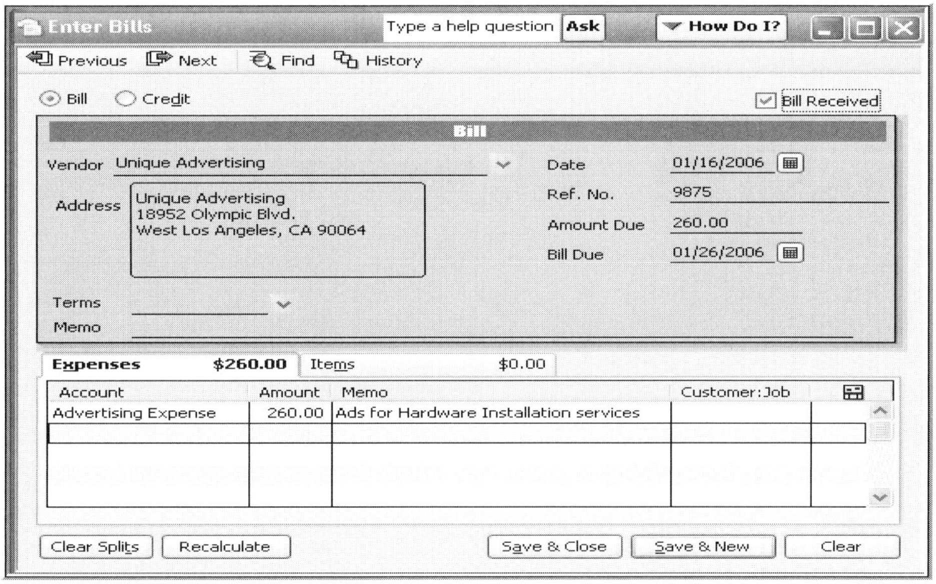

Do not click Save & Close

EDIT AND CORRECT ERRORS

If an error is discovered while you are entering information, it may be corrected by positioning the cursor in the field containing the error. You may do this by tabbing to move forward through each field or pressing Shift+Tab to move back to the field containing the error. If the error is highlighted, type the correction. If the error is not highlighted, you can correct the error by pressing the backspace or the delete key as many times as necessary to remove the error, then type the correction. (*Alternate method:* Point to the error, highlight it by dragging the mouse through the error, then type the correction.)

Practice editing and making corrections to the bill for Unique Advertising

Click the drop-down list arrow for **Vendor**
Click **Communication Telephone Co.**
Tab to **Date**
To increase the date by one day, press +

- You may press shift and the = key next to the backspace key, or you may press the + key on the numerical keypad.

Press + two more times

- The date should be **01/19/06**.

To decrease the date by one day, press -

- You may type a hyphen (-) next to the number **0**, or you may press the hyphen (-) key on the numerical keypad.

Press - two more times

- The date should be **01/16/06**.

Change the date by clicking on the calendar next to the date

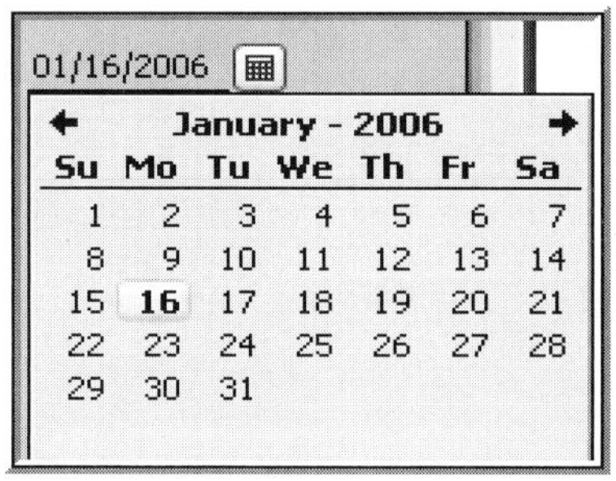

Click **19** on the calendar for January 2006
Click the calendar again
Click **16** to change the date back to 01/16/2006
To change the amount, click between the **2** and the **6** in **Amount Due**
Press the **Delete** key two times to delete the **60**
Key in **99** and press the **Tab** key

- The Amount Due should be **299.00**. The amount of 299.00 should also be shown in the Amount column in the detail section of the bill.

The transaction explanation was entered in the Memo column in the detail area of the bill and still shows the transaction explanation of "Ads for Hardware Installation Services."

- This memo prints on all reports that include the transaction.
- The same information should be in the Memo text box in the vendor-related area of the bill so it will appear as part of the transaction in the Accounts Payable account as well as all reports that include the transaction.

Copy **Ads for Hardware Installation Services** from the Memo column to the Memo text box:
Click to the left of the letter **A** in Ads
Highlight the memo text—**Ads for Hardware Installation Services**:
Hold down the primary mouse button
While holding down the primary mouse button, drag through the memo text **Ads for Hardware Installation Services**
Click **Edit** on the menu bar

Click **Copy**

- Notice that the keyboard shortcut **Ctrl+C** is listed. This shortcut could be used rather than using the Edit menu and Copy.
- This actually copies the text and places it in a temporary storage area of Windows called the Clipboard.

Click in the **Memo** text box beneath the **Terms**
Click **Edit** on the menu bar
Click **Paste**

- Notice the keyboard shortcut **Ctrl+V**.
- This inserts a copy of the material in the Windows Clipboard into the Memo text box—**Ads for Hardware Installation Services**
- This explanation will appear in the Memo area for the transaction in the Accounts Payable account as well as in any report that used the individual transaction information.

Click the drop-down list arrow for **Vendor**
Click **Unique Advertising**
Click to the right of the last **9** in **Amount Due**
Backspace two times to delete the **99**
Key in **60**

- The Amount **Due** should once again show **260.00**

Click the **Terms** drop-down list arrow
Click **Net 30**
Click **Save & Close** button to record the bill and return to the main screen
Click **No** on the **Name Information Changed** dialog box.

- The dialog box states: You have changed the Terms for Unique Advertising. Would you like to have this new information appear next time?

PREPARE A BILL USING MORE THAN ONE EXPENSE ACCOUNT

MEMO
DATE: January 18, 2006

On the recommendation of the office manager, Consuelo Alcampo, the company is trying out several different models of fax machines on a monthly basis. Received a bill from Office & Sales Supplies Co. for one month's rental of a fax machine, $25, and for fax supplies, which were consumed during January, $20, Invoice No. 1035A, Terms Net 10.

Record a bill using two expense accounts

Click the **Enter Bills** icon in the Vendors section of the Home Page and complete the vendor-related section of the bill
Click the drop-down list arrow next to **Vendor**
Click **Office & Sales Supplies Co.**
Tab to or click **Date**

- If you click in Date, you will have to delete the current date.

Enter **01/18/06**
Tab to or click **Ref. No.**
Key in the vendor's invoice number: **1035A**
Tab to or click **Amount Due**
Enter **45**
Tab to or click on the line for **Terms**
Type **Net 10** on the line for Terms, press the **Tab** key

- You will get a **Terms Not Found** message box.

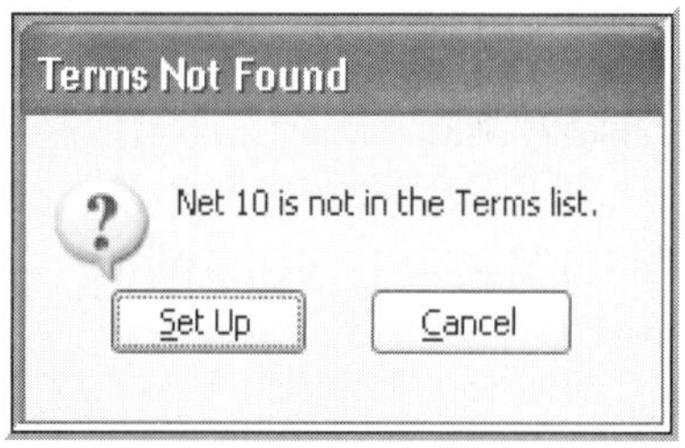

Click **Set Up**
Complete the information required in the **New Terms** dialog box:
Net 10 should appear as the Terms
Standard should be selected
Change the **Net due** from 0 to **10** days
Discount percentage should be **0**
Discount if paid within **0** days
Click **OK**

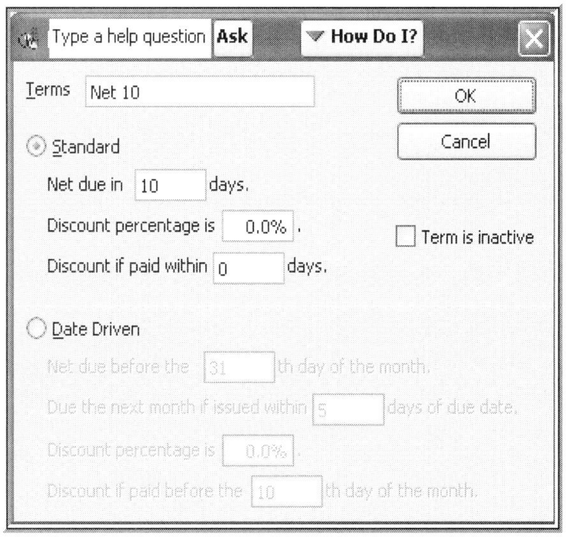

Tab to or click the **Memo** text box
Enter **Fax Rental and Fax Supplies for the Month** as the transaction description
To complete the **Detail Section** of the bill, tab to or click the first line for **Account**
Click the drop-down list arrow next to **Account**
Click **Equipment Rental**

- Because a portion of this transaction is for equipment that is being rented, Equipment Rental is the appropriate account to use.

Amount column shows **45.00**
Change this to reflect the actual amount of the Equipment Rental Expense
Tab to **Amount** to highlight
Type **25**
Tab to **Memo**
Enter **Fax Rental for the Month** as the transaction explanation
Tab to **Account**
Click the drop-down list arrow next to **Account**
Click **Office Supplies Expense**

- The transaction information indicates that the fax supplies will be used within the month of January. Using Office Supplies Expense account correctly charges the supplies expense against the period.
- If the transaction indicated that the fax supplies were purchased to have on hand, the appropriate account to use would be the asset Office Supplies.

The **Amount** column correctly shows **20.00** as the amount
Tab to or click **Memo**
Enter **Fax Supplies for the Month** as the transaction explanation

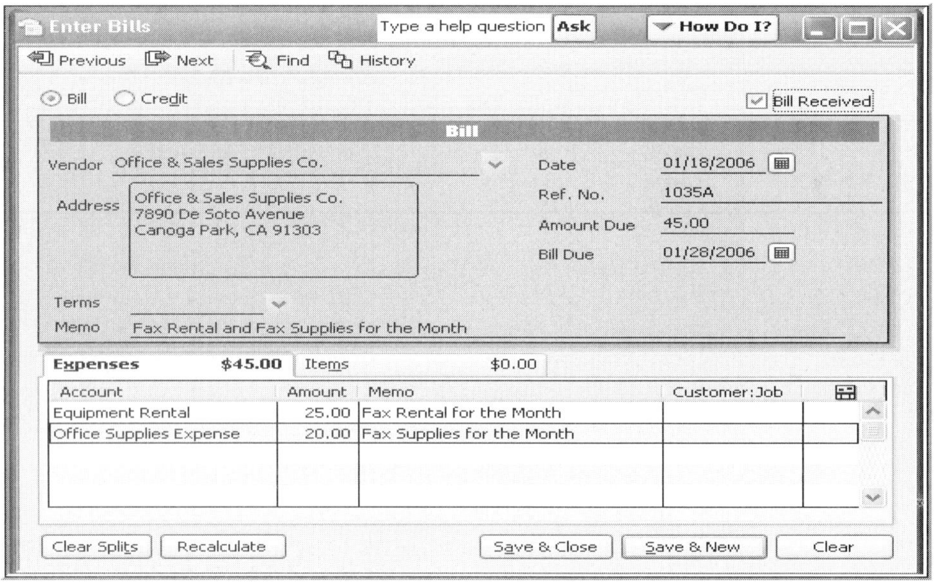

Click **Save & Close** to close the bill

- If you get a message regarding the change of Terms for Office & Sales Supplies Co., click **No**.

PRINT TRANSACTION BY VENDOR REPORT

To obtain information regarding individual transactions grouped by vendor, you prepare a transaction report by vendor. This allows you to view the vendors for which you have recorded transactions. The type of transaction is identified; for example, the word *Bill* appears when you have entered the transaction as a bill. The transaction date, any invoice numbers or memos entered when recording the transaction, the accounts used, and the transaction amount appear in the report.

Prepare a **Transaction by Vendor Report**

Click the **Report Center** icon
Click **Vendors & Payables**.to select the type of report
Click **Transaction List by Vendor**
Enter the Dates From **01/01/06** To **01/18/06**, press **Tab**
Once the report is displayed, click the **Modify Report** button
Click the **Header/Footer** tab
Click **Date Prepared** and **Time Prepared** to deselect these features
Click **OK**
Analyze the report:

- Look at each vendor account.

- Note the type of transaction, any invoice numbers, and memos.
- The **Account** column shows **Accounts Payable** as the account.
- As in any traditional accounting transaction recording a purchase on account, the Accounts Payable account is credited.
- The **Split** column shows the other accounts used in the transaction.
- If the word **-SPLIT-** appears in this column, it indicates that more than one account was used.
- The transaction for Office & Sales Supplies Co. has -SPLIT- in the Split Column. This is because the transaction used two accounts: Equipment Rental and Office Supplies Expense for the debit portion of the transaction.

Your Name Computer Consulting

Transaction List by Vendor

January 1 - 18, 2006

Type	Date	Num	Memo	Account	Clr	Split	Amount
Office & Sales Supplies Co.							
Bill	01/18/2006	1035A	Fax Rental and Fax Supplies for the Month	Accounts Payable		-SPLIT-	-45.00
Unique Advertising							
Bill	01/16/2006	9875	Ads for Hardware Installation	Accounts Payable		Advertising Expense	-260.00

Print the report in Landscape orientation as instructed in Chapter 2
Do not close the report

USE THE QUICKZOOM FEATURE

Consuelo Alcampo wants more detailed information regarding the accounts used in the Split column of the report. Specifically, she wants to know what accounts were used for the transaction of January 18, 2006 for Office & Sales Supplies Co. In order to see these account names, Consuelo will use the QuickZoom feature of QuickBooks Pro.

Use QuickZoom

Point to the word **-SPLIT-** in the Split column

- The mouse pointer turns into a magnifying glass with a **Z** in it.

Double-click to **Zoom** in to see the accounts used in the transaction

- This returns you to the *original bill* entered for Office & Sales Supplies Co. for the transaction of 01/18/2006.
- The accounts used are Equipment Rental Expense and Office Supplies Expense.

Click **Close** button to return to the Transaction by Vendor Report
Click **Close** button to close the report

- If you get a Memorize Report dialog box, click **No**

Close the Report Center

PREPARE BILLS WITHOUT STEP-BY-STEP INSTRUCTIONS

The accrual method of accounting matches the expenses of a period against the revenue of the period. Frequently, when in training, there may be difficulty in determining whether something is recorded as an expense or as a prepaid expense. When you pay something in advance, it is recorded as an increase (debit) to an asset rather than an increase (debit) to an expense. When you have an expense that is paid for in advance, such as insurance, it is called a prepaid expense. At the time the prepaid asset is used (such as one month's worth of insurance), an adjusting entry is made to account for the amount used during the period. Unless otherwise instructed, use the accrual basis of accounting when recording the following entries. (Notice the exception in the first transaction.)

MEMO **DATE:** January 19, 2006 Received a bill from Computer Professionals Magazine for a 6-month subscription for You, $74, Net 30 days, Invoice No. 1579-53. (Enter as an expense.)
Consuelo Alcampo received office supplies from Office & Sales Supplies Co., $450, terms Net 10 days, Invoice No. 8950S. These supplies will be used over a period of several months so enter as a prepaid expense. (Note: After you enter the vendor's name, the information from the previous bill appears on the screen. As you enter the transaction, simply delete any unnecessary information. This may be done by tabbing to the information and pressing the delete key until the information is deleted or by dragging through the information to highlight, then in either method entering the new information.)
While Justine Wong was on her way to a training session at Steele, Rhoades, Whitcomb, and Hinson, the company car broke down. It was towed to Jimenez Garage and Auto Services, where it was repaired. The total bill for the towing and repair is $575, Net 30 days, Invoice No. 630.
Received a bill from Southern California Insurance Company for the annual auto insurance premium, $2,850, terms Net 30, Invoice No. 3659 (Enter a memo for this bill.)

Enter the four transactions in the memo

- Refer to the instructions given for the two previous transactions entered.

- Remember, when recording bills, you will need to determine the accounts used in the transaction. To determine the appropriate accounts to use, refer to the Chart of Accounts/General Ledger as you record the above transactions.
- Enter information for Memos where an explanation is needed for clarification.
- To go from one bill to the next, click the **Save & New** button.
- After entering the fourth bill, click **Save & Close**

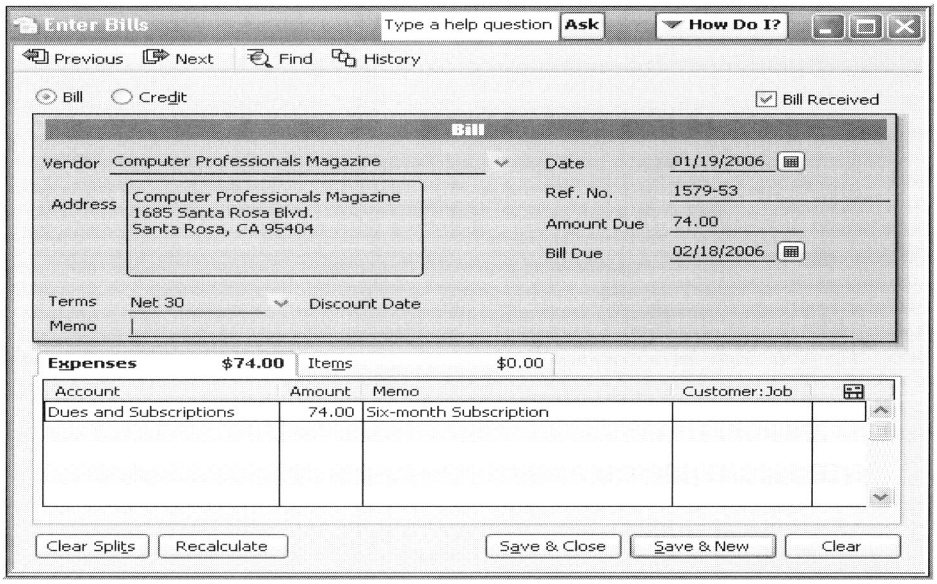

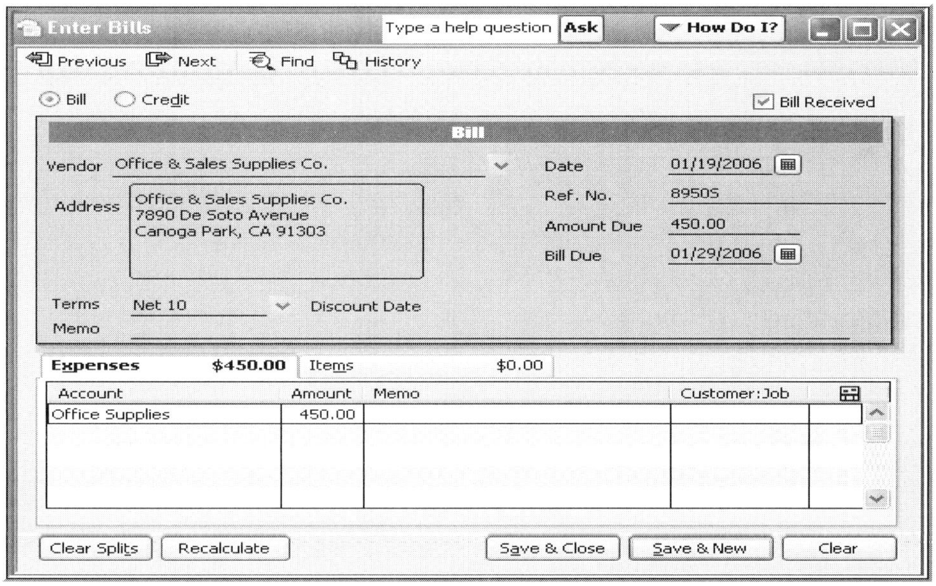

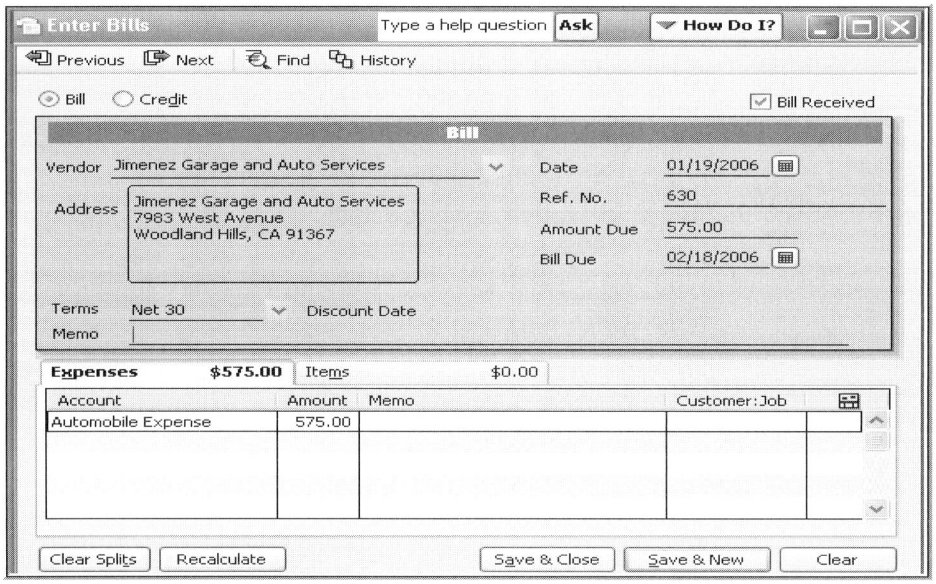

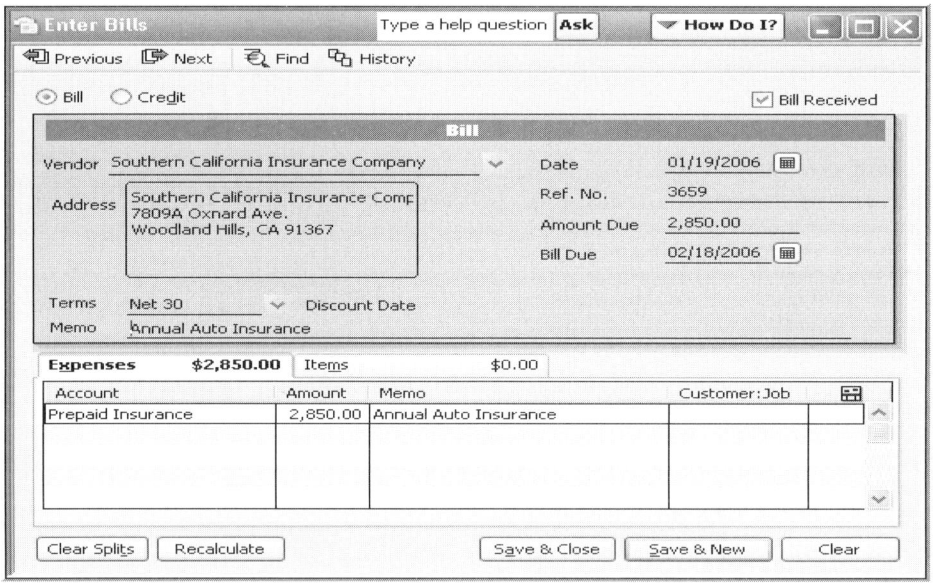

ENTER A BILL USING THE ACCOUNTS PAYABLE REGISTER

The Accounts Payable Register maintains a record of all the transactions recorded within the Accounts Payable account. Entering a bill directly into the Accounts Payable Register can be faster than filling out all of the information through Enter Bills.

MEMO

DATE: January 19, 2006

Rapid Delivery Service provides all of our delivery service for training manuals delivered to customers. Received monthly bill for January deliveries from Rapid Delivery Service, $175, terms Net 10, Invoice No. 88764.

Use the **Accounts Payable Register** to record the above transaction

Click the **Chart of Accounts** icon on the Home Page

OR

Use the keyboard shortcut **Ctrl+A**

Click **Accounts Payable**

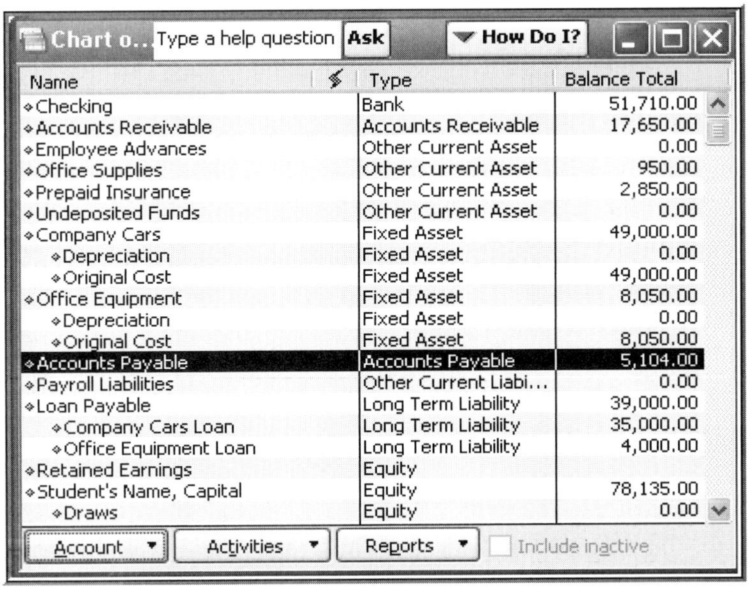

Click the **Activities** button at the bottom of the Chart of Accounts

Click **Use Register**

OR

Use the keyboard shortcut **Ctrl+R**

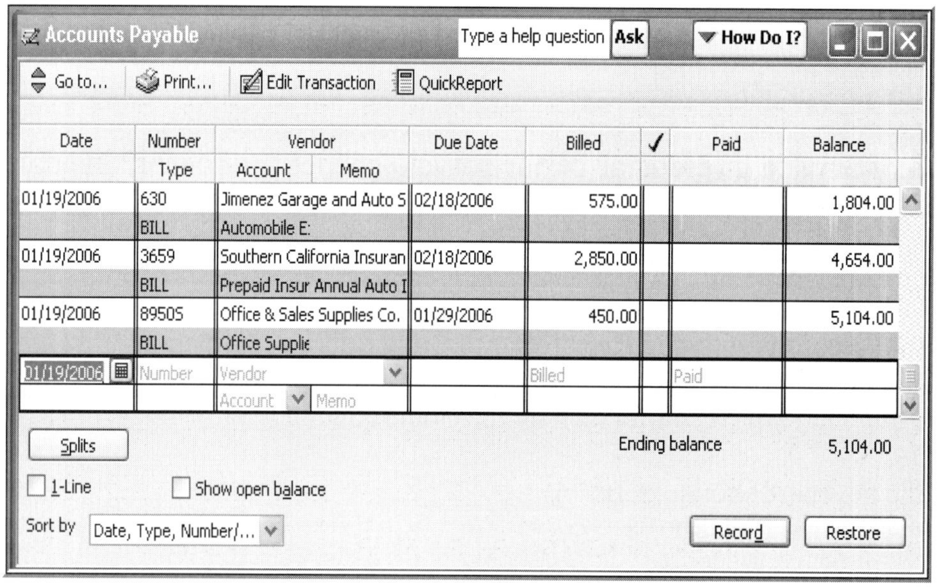

The date of **01/19/2006** is highlighted in the blank entry at the end of the Accounts Payable Register

- If it is not, click in the date column in the blank entry and key in **01/19/06** for the transaction date.

The word *Number* is in the next column

Tab to or click **Number**

- The word *Number* disappears.

Enter the Invoice Number **88764**

Tab to or click **Vendor**

Click the drop-down list arrow for **Vendor**

Click **Rapid Delivery Service**

Tab to or click **Due Date**

Verify the due date of **01/29/2006**

- If this is not the date showing, drag through the due date to highlight, then type **01/29/2006**.

Tab to or click **Billed**

Enter the amount **175**

Tab to or click **Account**

Click the drop-down list arrow for **Account**

Determine the appropriate account to use for the delivery expense

- If all of the accounts do not appear in the drop-down list, scroll through the accounts until you find the one appropriate for this entry.

Click **Postage and Delivery**

Tab to or click **Memo**

For the transaction memo, key **January Delivery Expense**

Click the **Record** button to record the transaction

01/19/2006	88764	Rapid Delivery Service	01/29/2006	175.00		5,279.00
	BILL	Postage and Delivery January Delivery Expense				

Do not close the register

EDIT A TRANSACTION IN THE ACCOUNTS PAYABLE REGISTER

Because QuickBooks Pro makes corrections extremely user friendly, a transaction can be edited or changed directly in the Accounts Payable Register as well as on the original bill. By eliminating the columns for Type and Memo, it is possible to change the register to show each transaction on one line. This can make the register easier to read.

MEMO
DATE: January 20, 2006

Upon examination of the invoices and the bills entered, Consuelo Alcampo discovers two errors: The actual amount of the invoice for Rapid Delivery Services was $195. The amount recorded was $175. The amount of the Invoice for *Computer Professionals Magazine* was $79, not $74. Change the transaction amounts for these transactions.

Correct the above transactions in the Accounts Payable Register

Click the check box for **1-line** to select
- Each Accounts Payable transaction will appear on one line.

Click the transaction for Rapid Delivery Service
Click between the **1** and **7** in the Amount column for the transaction
Press **Delete** to delete the 7
Type **9**
- The amount should be **195.00**.

Scroll through the register until the transaction for *Computer Professionals Magazine* is visible
Click the transaction for *Computer Professionals Magazine*
The **Recording Transaction** dialog box appears on the screen

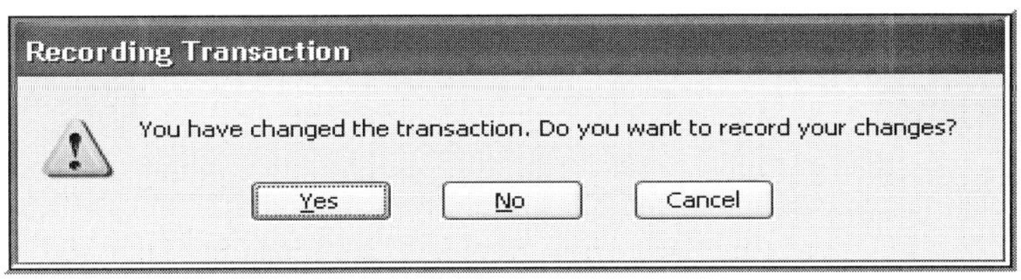

Click **Yes** to record the changes to the Rapid Delivery Service transaction

- The transaction for *Computer Professionals Magazine* will be the active transaction.

Click between the **4** and the **decimal point**
Press the **Backspace** key one time to delete the 4
Type **9**

- The amount for the transaction should be **79.00**.

Click the **Record** button at the bottom of the register to record the change in the transaction

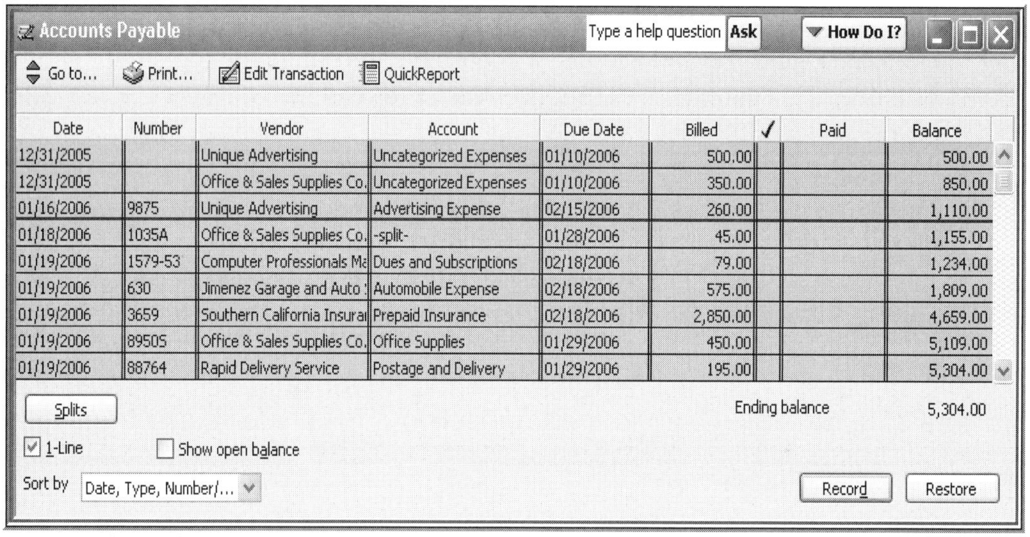

Date	Number	Vendor	Account	Due Date	Billed	✓	Paid	Balance
12/31/2005		Unique Advertising	Uncategorized Expenses	01/10/2006	500.00			500.00
12/31/2005		Office & Sales Supplies Co.	Uncategorized Expenses	01/10/2006	350.00			850.00
01/16/2006	9875	Unique Advertising	Advertising Expense	02/15/2006	260.00			1,110.00
01/18/2006	1035A	Office & Sales Supplies Co.	-split-	01/28/2006	45.00			1,155.00
01/19/2006	1579-53	Computer Professionals Ma	Dues and Subscriptions	02/18/2006	79.00			1,234.00
01/19/2006	630	Jimenez Garage and Auto	Automobile Expense	02/18/2006	575.00			1,809.00
01/19/2006	3659	Southern California Insura	Prepaid Insurance	02/18/2006	2,850.00			4,659.00
01/19/2006	89505	Office & Sales Supplies Co.	Office Supplies	01/29/2006	450.00			5,109.00
01/19/2006	88764	Rapid Delivery Service	Postage and Delivery	01/29/2006	195.00			5,304.00

Do not close the register

PREVIEW AND PRINT A QUICKREPORT FROM THE ACCOUNTS PAYABLE REGISTER

After editing a transaction, you may want to view information about a specific vendor. This can be done quickly and efficiently by clicking the vendor's name within a transaction and clicking the QuickReport button at the top of the Register.

MEMO
DATE: January 20, 2006

Several transactions have been entered for Office & Sales Supplies Co. You like to view transaction information for all vendors that have several transactions within a short period of time.

Prepare a QuickReport for Office & Sales Supplies Co.

Click any field in any transaction for Office & Sales Supplies Co.
Click the **QuickReport** button at the top of the Register

- The Register QuickReport for All Transactions for Office & Sales Supplies Co. appears on the screen.

Remove the **Date Prepared**, **Time Prepared**, and **Report Basis** as previously instructed
Click **Print**
Select Landscape orientation
Click **Preview** to view the report before printing

- The report appears on the screen as a full page.
- A full-page report on the screen usually cannot be read.

To read the text in the report, click the **Zoom In** button at the top of the screen
Use the scroll buttons and bars to view the report columns
Click **Zoom Out** to return to a full-page view of the report
When finished viewing the report, click **Close**

- You will return to the **Print Reports** screen.

If the report does not fit on one page, click **Fit report to one page wide** to select
Click **Print** button on the **Print Reports** screen

Your Name Computer Consulting
Register QuickReport
All Transactions

Type	Date	Num	Memo	Account	Paid	Open Balance	Amount
Office & Sales Supplies Co.							
Bill	12/31/2005		Opening balance	Accounts Payable	Unpaid	350.00	350.00
Bill	01/18/2006	1035A	Fax Rental and Fax Supplies for the Month	Accounts Payable	Unpaid	45.00	45.00
Bill	01/19/2006	8950S		Accounts Payable	Unpaid	450.00	450.00
Total Office & Sales Supplies Co.						845.00	845.00
TOTAL						**845.00**	**845.00**

Close the **Register QuickReport**, the **Accounts Payable Register**, and the **Chart of Accounts**

PREPARE UNPAID BILLS DETAIL REPORT

It is possible to get information regarding unpaid bills by simply preparing a report—no more digging through tickler files, recorded invoices, ledgers, or journals. QuickBooks Pro prepares an Unpaid Bills Report listing each unpaid bill grouped and subtotaled by vendor.

MEMO
DATE: January 25, 2006

Consuelo Alcampo prepares an Unpaid Bills Report for you each week. Even though Your Name Computer Consulting is a small business, you like to have a firm control over cash flow so you determine which bills will be paid during the week.

Prepare and print an Unpaid Bills Report

Click **Unpaid Bills Detail** in the **Vendors & Payables** list on the Report Menu
OR
Click the **Report Center** icon
The **Type of report** should be **Vendors & Payables**
In the list of reports, click **Unpaid Bills Detail**
Remove the Date Prepared and Time Prepared from the report header
Provide the report date by clicking in the text box for **Date**, dragging through the date to highlight, and typing **01/25/06**
Tab to generate the report

Your Name Computer Consulting
Unpaid Bills Detail
As of January 25, 2006

Type	Date	Num	Due Date	Aging	Open Balance
Computer Professionals Magazine					
Bill	01/19/2006	1579-53	02/18/2006		79.00
Total Computer Professionals Magazine					79.00
Jimenez Garage and Auto Services					
Bill	01/19/2006	630	02/18/2006		575.00
Total Jimenez Garage and Auto Services					575.00
Office & Sales Supplies Co.					
Bill	12/31/2005		01/10/2006	15	350.00
Bill	01/18/2006	1035A	01/28/2006		45.00
Bill	01/19/2006	8950S	01/29/2006		450.00
Total Office & Sales Supplies Co.					845.00
Rapid Delivery Service					
Bill	01/19/2006	88764	01/29/2006		195.00
Total Rapid Delivery Service					195.00

Partial Report

Print in Portrait orientation
Click **Close** to close the report
Click **No** if you get a Memorize Report dialog box
If necessary, click **Close** to close the **Report Center**

DELETE A BILL

QuickBooks Pro makes it possible to delete any bill that has been recorded. No adjusting entries are required in order to do this. Simply access the bill or the Accounts Payable Register and delete the bill.

> **MEMO**
> **DATE:** January 26, 2006
>
> After reviewing the Unpaid Bills Report, Consuelo realizes that the bill recorded for *Computer Professionals Magazine* should have been recorded for *Computer Technologies Magazine*.

Delete the bill recorded for *Computer Professionals Magazine*

Access the Chart of Accounts:
Click the **Chart of Accounts** icon on the Home Page
OR
Use the keyboard shortcut **Ctrl+A**
OR
Use the menu bar, click **List**, click **Chart of Accounts**
With the Chart of Accounts showing on the screen, click **Accounts Payable**
Open the Accounts Payable Register:
Use keyboard shortcut **Ctrl+R**
OR
Click **Activities Button**, click **Use Register**
Click on the bill for *Computer Professionals Magazine*
To delete the bill:
Click **Edit** on the menu bar, click **Delete Bill**

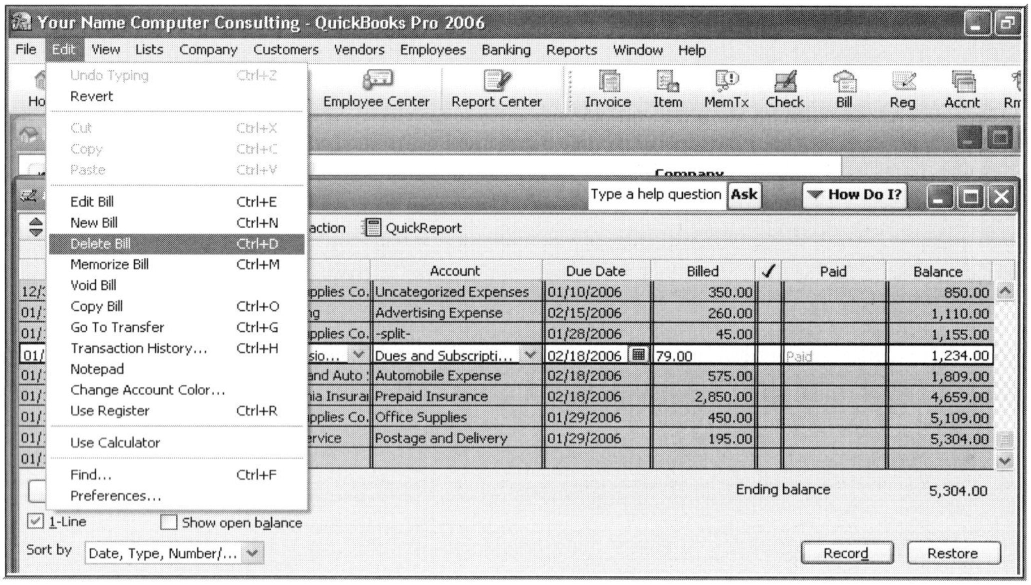

OR

Use the keyboard shortcut **Ctrl+D**

- The **Delete Transaction** dialog box appears on the screen.

Click **OK** to delete the bill

- Notice that the transaction no longer appears in the Accounts Payable Register.

Close the **Accounts Payable Register**

Close the **Chart of Accounts**

ADD A NEW VENDOR WHILE RECORDING A BILL

When entering bills, typing the first letter(s) of a vendor name enters the name on the Vendor line. If the vendor is not in the Vendor List, QuickBooks Pro allows you to add a new vendor on the fly while entering a bill. If you key in the vendor name, a QuickBooks Pro dialog box for Vendor Not Found appears with choices for a Quick Add—adding just the vendor name—or Set Up—adding the vendor name and all vendor account information. When the new vendor information is complete, QuickBooks Pro fills in the blanks on the bill for the vendor, and you finish entering the rest of the transaction.

MEMO
DATE: January 26, 2006

Record the bill for a 6-month subscription to *Computer Technologies Magazine*. The transaction date is 01/19/06, amount $79, Terms Net 30, Invoice No. 1579-53. This is recorded as an expense. The address and telephone for *Computer Technologies Magazine* is 12405 Menlo Park Drive, Menlo Park, CA 94025, 510-555-3829.

Record the above transaction

Access the **Enter Bills** screen

- Step-by-step instructions will be provided only for entering a new vendor.
- Refer to transactions previously recorded for all other steps used in entering a bill.
- When you key the first few letters of a vendor name, QuickBooks Pro will automatically enter a vendor name.

On the line for Vendor, type the **C** for *Computer Technologies Magazine*

- The vendor name **California Electric** appears on the vendor line and is highlighted.

Type **omp**

- The vendor name changes to **Computer Professionals Magazine**.

Finish typing **uter Technologies Magazine**

Press **Tab**

The **Vendor Not Found** dialog box appears on the screen with buttons for:

- **Quick Add**—adds only the name to the vendor list.
- **Set Up**—adds the name to the vendor list and allows all account information to be entered.
- **Cancel**—cancels the addition of a new vendor.

Click **Set Up**

- Computer Technologies Magazine is shown in the Vendor Name text box

If necessary, highlight the Vendor Name in the Vendor Name text box

Copy the name to the Company Name textbox by using the **Ctrl+C** keyboard shortcut for copy

Click in the Company Name textbox and use **Ctrl+V** to paste the name into the textbox

Tab to or click the first line for **Address**

- Computer Technologies Magazine appears as the first line of the address.

Position the cursor at the end of the name, press **Enter** or click the line beneath the company name (Do not tab)

Type the address listed in the transaction

Press **Enter** at the end of each line

When finished with the address, tab to or click **Phone**

Enter the telephone number

To enter the information for **Additional Info** tab, click **Additional Info** tab
Click drop-down list arrow next to **Terms**
Click **Net 30**

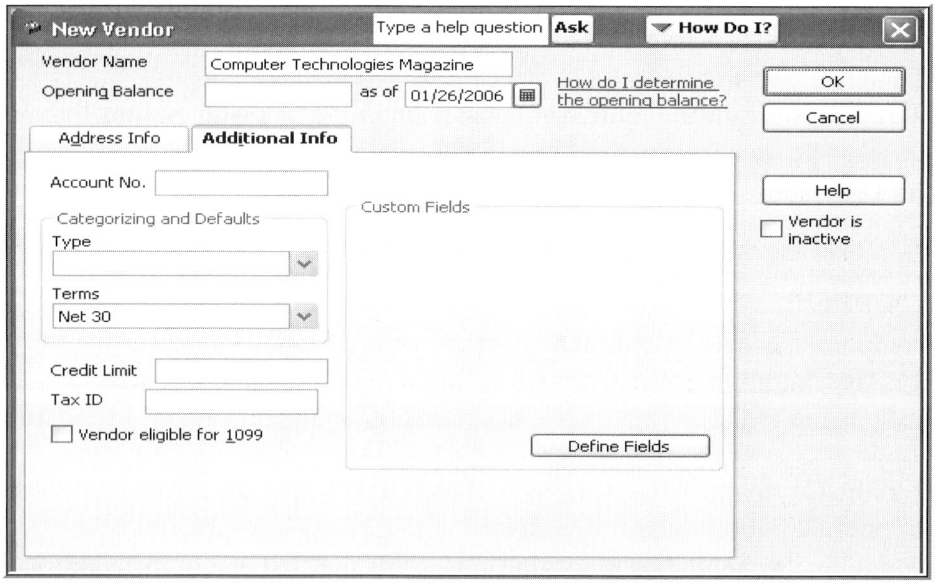

Click the **OK** button for **New Vendor** screen

- The information for Vendor, Terms, and the Dates is filled in on the Enter Bills screen.

If necessary, change the transaction date to **01/19/06**

Complete the bill using instructions previously provided for entering bills

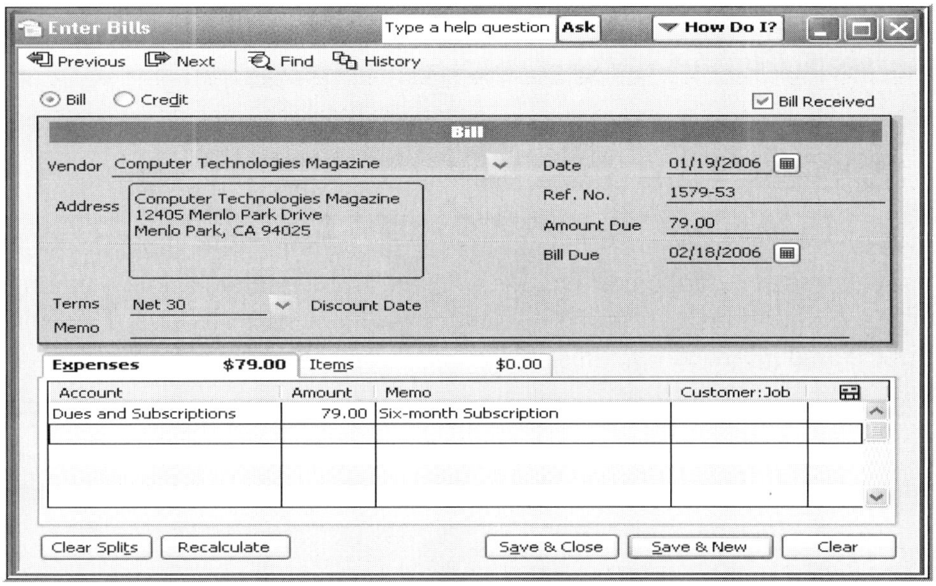

When finished, click **Save & Close** to close the bill and exit

MODIFY VENDOR RECORDS

Occasionally, information regarding a vendor will change. QuickBooks Pro allows vendor accounts to be modified at anytime by editing the Vendor List.

> **MEMO**
> **DATE:** January 26, 2006
>
> Because Linda Scott received a promotion, the contact person for Rapid Delivery Service has been changed to Brenda Hermosa.

Modify the vendor records for Rapid Delivery Service

Access the **Vendor List** by clicking the **Vendor Center** icon
Click **Rapid Delivery Service**
Click the **Edit Vendor** button
OR
Use the keyboard shortcut **Ctrl+E**

- The Edit Vendor screen appears.

Click the **Contact** text box

Drag through **Linda Scott** to highlight
Type **Brenda Hermosa**
Click **OK** to record the change
Click **Close** on **Vendor Center** to close

ENTER A CREDIT FROM A VENDOR

Credit memos are prepared to record a reduction to a transaction. With QuickBooks Pro, you use the Enter Bills window to record credit memos received from vendors acknowledging a return of or an allowance for a previously recorded bill and/or payment. The amount of a credit memo is deducted from the amount owed.

MEMO
DATE: January 26, 2006

Received Credit Memo No. 789 for $5 from Office & Sales Supplies Co. for a return of fax paper that was damaged.

Record the credit memo shown above

Access the **Enter Bills** window as previously instructed

On the **Enter Bills** screen, click **Credit** to select
- Notice that the word *Bill* changes to *Credit.*

Click the drop-down list arrow next to **Vendor**
Click **Office & Sales Supplies Co.**
Tab to or click the **Date**
Type **01/26/06**
Tab to or click **Ref. No.**
Type **789**
Tab to or click **Credit Amount**
Type **5**
Tab to or click in **Memo**
Enter **Returned Fax Paper**
Tab to or click the first line of **Account**
Click the drop-down list arrow
Because this was originally entered as an expense, click the account **Office Supplies Expense**
- The amount should show **5.00**; if not, enter **5**.
- The **Memo** column may be left blank.

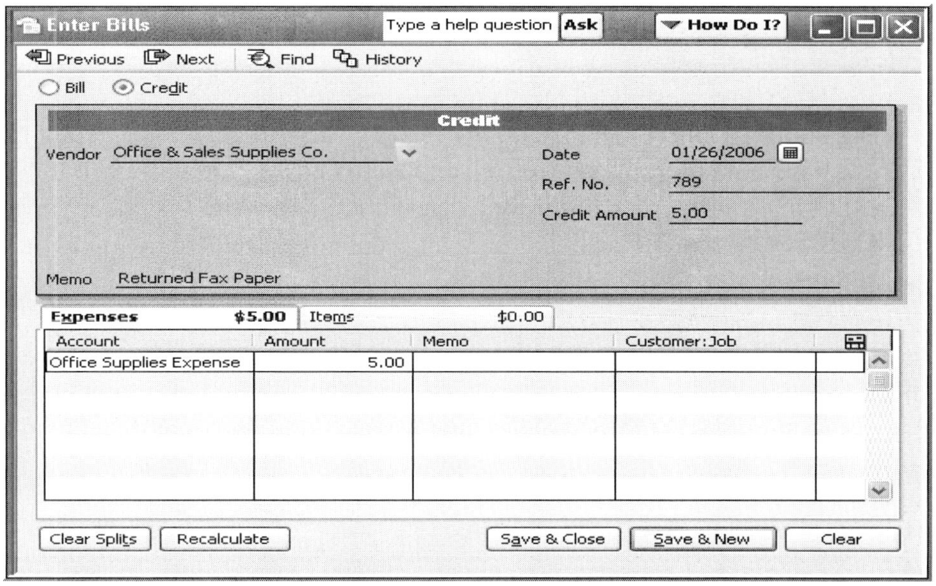

Click **Save & Close** to record the credit and exit **Enter Bills**

- QuickBooks Pro records the credit in the Accounts Payable account and shows the transaction type as BILLCRED in the Accounts Payable Register.

VIEW CREDIT IN ACCOUNTS PAYABLE REGISTER

When recording the credit in the last transaction, QuickBooks Pro listed the transaction type as BILLCRED in the Accounts Payable Register.

Verify the credit from Office & Sales Supplies Co.

Follow steps previously provided to access the Accounts Payable Register
If a check mark shows in the **1-Line** check box, remove it by clicking the check box

- This changes the display in the Accounts Payable Register from 1-Line to multiple lines.

Look at the **Number/Type** column and verify the type **BILLCRED**

01/26/2006	789	Office & Sales Supplies Co.					5.00	5,299.00
	BILLCRED	Office Supplies Expense Returned Fax Paper						

Close the **Accounts Payable Register**
Close the **Chart of Accounts**

PAYING BILLS

When using QuickBooks Pro, you should pay any bills entered through "Enter Bills" directly from the pay bills command and let QuickBooks Pro write your checks for you and mark the bills "Paid." If you have not entered a bill for an amount you owe, you will need to write the checks yourself. If you have recorded a bill for a transaction and write the check for payment yourself, the bill will not be marked as being paid and will continue to show up as an amount due.

Using the Pay Bills window enables you to determine which bills to pay, the method of payment—check or credit card—and the appropriate account. When determining which bills to pay, QuickBooks Pro allows you to display the bills by due date, discount date, vendor, or amount. All bills may be displayed, or only those bills that are due by a certain date may be displayed.

MEMO
DATE: January 26, 2006

Whenever possible, Consuelo pays the bills on a weekly basis. With the Pay Bills window showing the bills due for payment before 01/31/2006, Consuelo compares the bills shown with the Unpaid Bills Report previously prepared. The report has been marked by you to indicate which bills should be paid. Consuelo will select the bills for payment and record the bill payment for the week.

Pay the bills for the week

Click the **Pay Bills** icon in the Vendors section of the Home Page to access the **Pay Bills** window
Click **Show All Bills** to select
Sort Bills by **Due Date**
- If this is not showing, click the drop-down list arrow next to the **Sort Bills By** text box, click **Due Date**.

Scroll through the list of bills
Click the drop-down list arrow next to the **Sort Bills By** text box
Click **Vendor**
- This shows you how much you owe each vendor.

Again, click the drop-down list arrow next to the **Sort Bills** text box
Click **Amount Due**
- This shows you your bills from the highest amount owed to the lowest.

Click drop-down list arrow next to the **Sort Bills** text box, click **Due Date**
- The bills will be shown according to the date due.

Click **Show bills due on or before** to select this option
Click in the text box for the date
Drag through the date to highlight, enter **01/31/06** as the date
Scroll through the list of bills due
Select the bills to be paid

- The bills shown on the screen are an exact match to the bills you marked to be paid.

Click **Select All Bills**

- To pay some of the bills but not all of them, mark each bill to be paid by clicking on the individual bill or using the cursor keys to select a bill and pressing the space bar.

The **Select All Bills** button changes to **Clear Selections** so bills can be unmarked and the bills to be paid may be selected again
Apply the $5 credit for Office Supply Wholesale by clicking in the √ column for the $45 transaction for Office & Sales Supplies Co. with a due date of 01/28/2006

- This will deselect the bill

Click the √ column again to select the bill

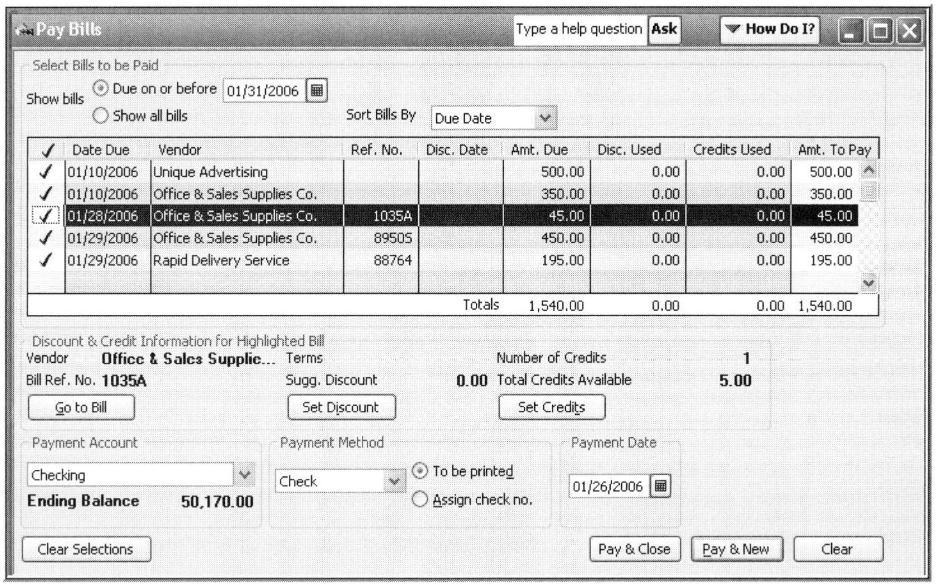

- Notice that the Set Credits button appears in bold and that a Total Credit of $5.00 is available.

Click the **Set Credits** button

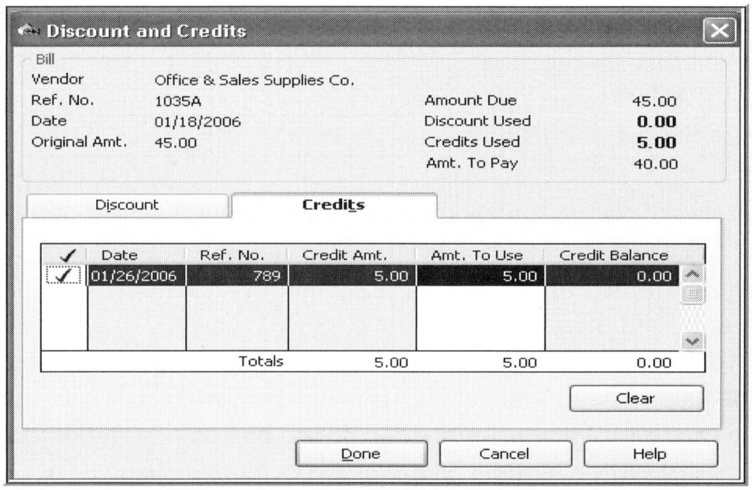

Click **Done** on the Discounts and Credits screen

- Notice that the Credits Used column for the transaction displays 5.00 and the Amt. To Pay for the bill is 40.00.

The **Payment Account** should be **Checking**

In the **Payment Method** section of the screen, make sure **Check** has been selected as the payment method

Make sure **To be printed** box has been selected

If it is not selected, click in the circle to select

Tab to or click **Payment Date**

Enter the Payment Date of **01/26/06**

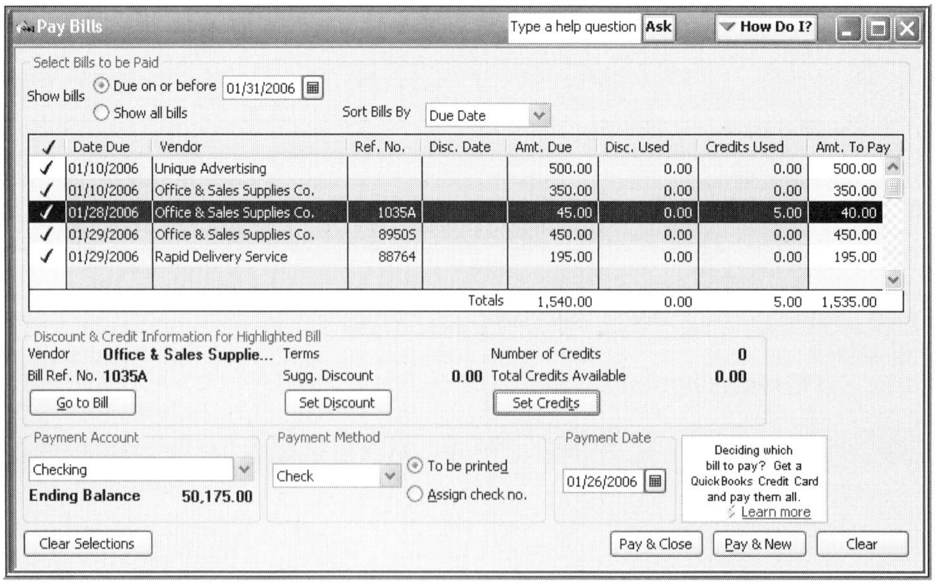

Click **Pay & Close** to record your payments and close the **Pay Bills** window

PRINTING CHECKS FOR BILLS

Once bills have been marked and recorded as paid, you may handwrite checks to vendors, or you may have QuickBooks Pro print the checks to vendors. If there is more than one amount due for a vendor, QuickBooks Pro totals the amounts due to the vendor and prints one check to the vendor.

Print the checks for the bills paid

Click the **File** menu
Point to **Print Forms**
Click **Checks**
Bank Account should be **Checking**

- If this is not showing, click the drop-down list arrow, click **Checking**.

The **First Check Number** should be **1**

- If not, delete the number showing, and key **1**.

In the √ column, the checks selected to be printed are marked with a check mark

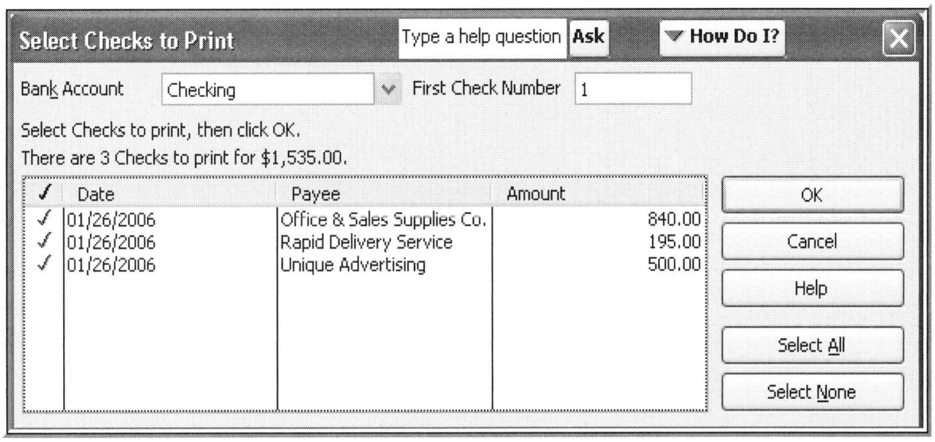

Click **OK** to print the checks

- The **Print Checks** screen appears.

Verify and if necessary change information on the **Settings** tab
Printer name: The name of your printer should show in the text box

- If the correct printer name is not showing, click the drop-down list arrow, click the correct printer name.

Printer type: Page-oriented (Single sheets) should be in the text box

- If this does not show or if you use Continuous (Perforated Edge) checks, click the drop-down list arrow, click the appropriate sheet style to select.

Check style: Three different types of check styles may be used: Standard, Voucher, or Wallet

If it is not in the check style text box, click **Standard Checks** to insert

Print Company Name and Address: If the box does not have a check mark, click to select

Use Logo should not be selected; if a check mark appears in the check box, click to deselect

Click **Print** to print the checks

- All three checks will print on one page.

Did check(s) print OK? dialog box appears

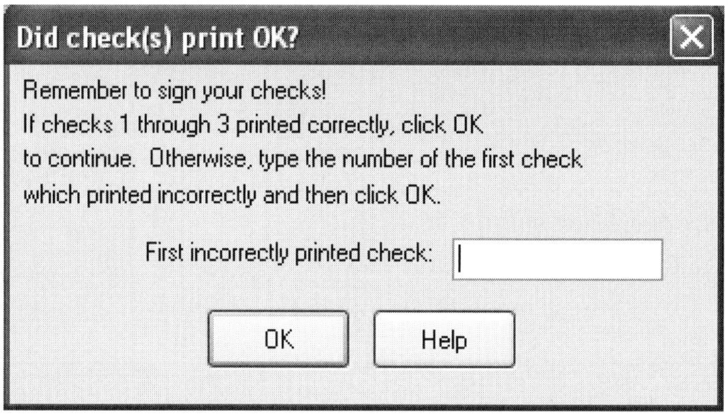

If checks **printed** correctly, click **OK**

- The checks have the address for Your Name Computer Consulting, the name and address of the company being paid, and the amount being paid.
- The actual checks will not have a check number printed because QuickBooks Pro is set up to work with preprinted check forms containing check numbers.
- In the memo section of the check, any memo entered on the bill shows.
- If there was no memo entered for the bill, the vendor account number appears as the memo.
- If you cannot get the checks to print on one page, it is perfectly acceptable to access the checks by clicking the **Write Checks** icon in the Banking section of the Home Page, and printing them one at a time. This method is also useful if you need to correct a check and reprint it.

If you get a message box regarding purchasing checks, click **No**

REVIEW BILLS THAT HAVE BEEN PAID

In order to avoid any confusion about payment of a bill, QuickBooks Pro marks the bill PAID. Scrolling through the recorded bills in the Enter Bills window, you will see the paid bills marked PAID.

Scroll the **Enter Bills** window to view PAID bills

Click **Enter Bills** on the Vendors Navigator
Click the **Previous** button to go back through all the bills recorded

- Notice that the bills paid for Office & Sales Supplies Co., Rapid Delivery Service, and Unique Advertising are marked **PAID**. The Credit from Office & Sales Supplies Co. remains unmarked even though it has been used.

Click the **Close** button

PETTY CASH

Frequently, a business will need to pay for small expenses with cash. These might include expenses such as postage, office supplies, and miscellaneous expenses. For example, rather than write a check for postage due of 75 cents, you would use money from petty cash. QuickBooks Pro allows you to establish and use a petty cash account to track these small expenditures. Normally, a Petty Cash Voucher is prepared; and, if available, the receipt for the transaction is stapled to it. It is important in a business to keep accurate records of the petty cash expenditures, and procedures for control of the Petty Cash fund need to be established to prohibit access to and unauthorized use of the cash. Periodically, the petty cash expenditures are recorded so that the records of the company accurately reflect all expenses incurred in the operation of the business.

ADD PETTY CASH ACCOUNT TO THE CHART OF ACCOUNTS

QuickBooks Pro allows accounts to be added to the Chart of Accounts list at any time. Petty Cash is identified as a "Bank" account type so it will be placed at the top of the Chart of Accounts along with other checking and savings accounts.

MEMO
DATE: January 26, 2006

Occasionally, there are small items that should be paid for using cash. Consuelo Alcampo needs to establish a petty cash account for $100

Add Petty Cash to the **Chart of Accounts**

Access **Chart of Accounts** as previously instructed
Click the **Account** button at the bottom of the Chart of Accounts, click **New**
Create a new account:
Type should be **Bank**

- If it is not, click the drop-down list arrow next to the text box for **Type**, then click **Bank**.

Enter **Petty Cash** in the **Name** text box
Leave the other items blank

- *Note:* The Opening Balance is used only when setting up QuickBooks Pro, not when adding an account. In this case, we will be transferring money from the checking account into the Petty Cash fund once the account has been created.
- Since there is no opening balance, the date of **01/26/06** does not have to be shown for the **as of** date.

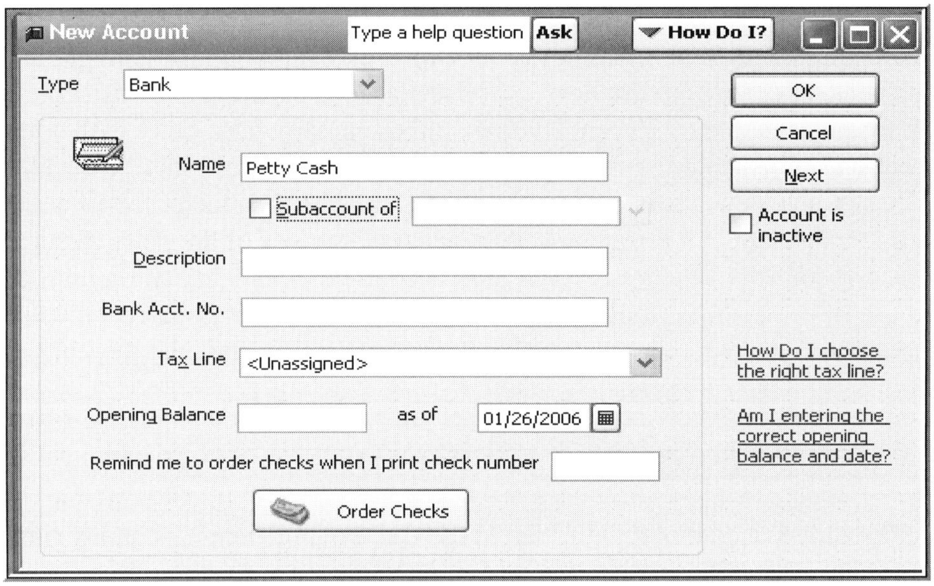

Click **OK** to record the new account
Do not close the **Chart of Accounts**

ESTABLISH PETTY CASH FUND

Once the account has been established, the petty cash fund must have money in order to pay for small expenses. A cash withdrawal from checking must be made or a check must be written and cashed to obtain petty cash funds. This may be recorded in the Checking Register.

Record the cash withdrawal of $100 from checking to establish petty cash:

To access the **Check Register**, click **Checking** account in the **Chart of Accounts**, click the **Activities** button, click **Use Register**

- The Check Register should be on the screen.
- If the cursor is not already in the Date column, click in the **Date** column for a new transaction at the end of the Check Register.
- The date should be highlighted; if it is not, drag through the date to highlight.

If the date is not 01/26/2006, enter **01/26/06**
Tab to or click **Number**
Enter **CASH**
Because this is a cash withdrawal, a Payee name will not be entered
Tab to or click **Payment**
Enter **100**
Tab to or click **Account**
Click the drop-down list arrow next to **Account**
Click **Petty Cash**

- The account shows Petty Cash and Type changed from CHK to TRANSFR.

Tab to or click **Memo**
Enter **Establish Petty Cash Fund**
Click **Record** button to record the withdrawal

01/26/2006	Cash		100.00			50,075.00
	TRANSFR	Petty Cash Establish Petty Cash Fund				

Close the **Checking Register**
Do not close the **Chart of Accounts**

RECORD PAYMENT OF AN EXPENSE USING PETTY CASH

As petty cash is used to pay for small expenses in the business, these payments must be recorded. QuickBooks Pro makes it a simple matter to record petty cash expenditures directly into the Petty Cash Register.

MEMO
DATE: January 30, 2006

Consuelo Alcampo needs to record the petty cash expenditures made during the week: postage due, 34 cents; purchased staples and paper clips, $3.57 (this is an expense); reimbursed Justine Wong for gasoline purchased for company car, $13.88.

In the Petty Cash account, record a compound entry for the above expenditures

Click **Petty Cash** on the **Chart of Accounts**
Use the keyboard shortcut **Ctrl+R** to access the **Register**:
Click in the **Date** column, highlight the date if necessary
Type **01/30/06**

- No entry is required for Number; QuickBooks Pro inserts **1** for the number.
- No entry is required for Payee.

Tab to or click **Payment**
Enter **17.79** (you must type the decimal point)
Tab to or click in **Account** text box
Click **Splits** at the bottom of the screen

- Splits is used because the total amount of the transaction will be split among three expense accounts.

In the **Account** column showing on the screen, click the drop-down list arrow
Scroll until you see **Postage and Delivery**
Click **Postage and Delivery**
Tab to **Amount** column

- Using the Tab key will highlight **17.79**.

Type **.34**

- Memo notations are not necessary because the transactions are self-explanatory.

Tab to or click the next blank line in **Account**
Repeat the steps listed above to record **3.57** for **Office Supplies Expense** and **13.88** for **Automobile Expense**

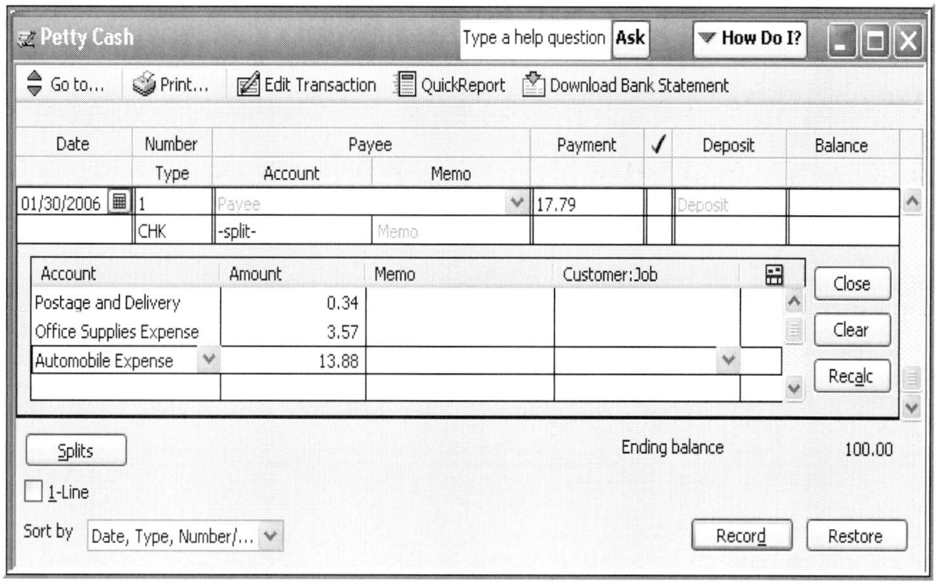

Click **Close** when all expenses have been recorded

Click **Record** to record the transaction

- Notice that the word "payee," the account name, and memo are removed from the transaction. The only item indicated is **-split-**.
- Verify the account Ending Balance of 82.21.

Close **Petty Cash** and the **Chart of Accounts**

PAY BILLS BY WRITING CHECKS

Although it is more efficient to record all bills in the Enter Bills window and pay all bills through the Pay Bills window, QuickBooks Pro also allows bills to be paid by writing a check. The check window is divided into two main areas: the check face and the detail area. The check face includes information such as the date of the check, the payee's name, the check amount, the payee's address, and a line for a memo—just like a paper check. The detail area is used to indicate transaction accounts and amounts.

MEMO
DATE: January 30, 2006

Since these items were not previously recorded as bills, write checks to pay the following:

Location Realtors—rent for the month, $1,500
Communication Telephone Co.—telephone bill for the month, $350
California Electric—electric bill for the month, $250
California Water—water bill for the month, $35
California Gas Co.—heating bill for the month, $175

Write checks to pay the bills listed above

Click the **Write Checks** icon in the Banking section of the Home Page
OR
Use the keyboard shortcut **Ctrl+W**
Verify the bank account used for the check
If the screen shows **Write Checks-Petty Cash**, click the drop-down list arrow for **Bank Account**, click **Checking**.

- If you get a message to set a default account, click **Ok**

Tab to or click **Date**
Enter **01/30/06**

- If the check has been written by hand, this will be left blank.

To complete the check face, click the drop-down list arrow next to **Pay to the Order of**
Click **Location Realtors**
Tab to or click **Amount**
Enter the amount of the rent
Tab to or click **Memo**
Enter **Monthly Rent**

- This memo prints on the check, not on reports. If you do not provide a memo on the check, QuickBooks will enter an account number or telephone number as the memo.

Click **To Be Printed** to indicate that the check needs to be printed

- When To Be Printed is selected, an icon for Order Checks appears on the check.

Use the **Expenses** tab to complete the detail area,
Tab to or click the first line of **Account**
Click the drop-down list arrow for **Account**
Click **Rent**

- The total amount of the check is shown in Amount column.

- If you want a transaction description to appear in reports, enter the description in the Memo column—no entry is required because these are standard transactions.

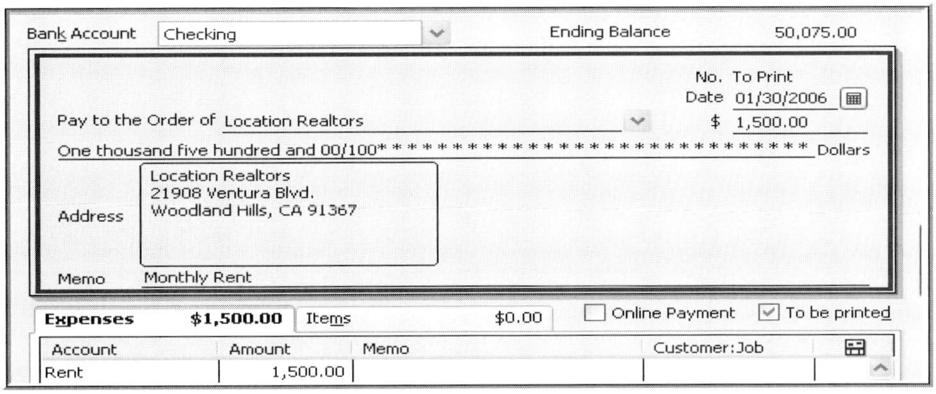

Do not print any of the checks being entered

Click **Save & New** to record the check and advance to the next check

Repeat the steps indicated above to record payment of the telephone, electric, water, and gas bills

- While entering the bills, you may see a dialog box on the screen, indicating that QuickBooks Pro allows you to do online banking. Online banking will not be used at this time. Click **OK** to close the dialog box.

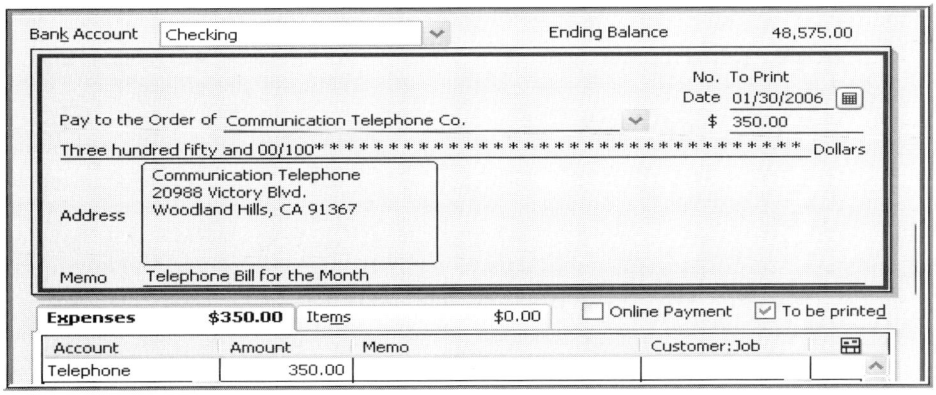

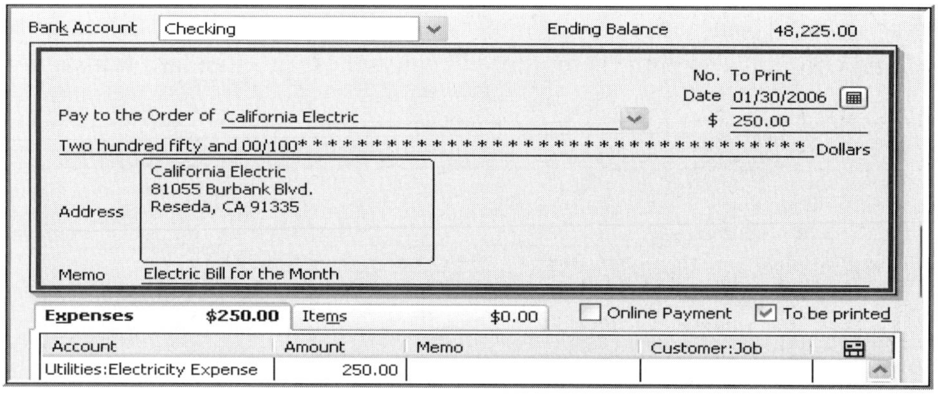

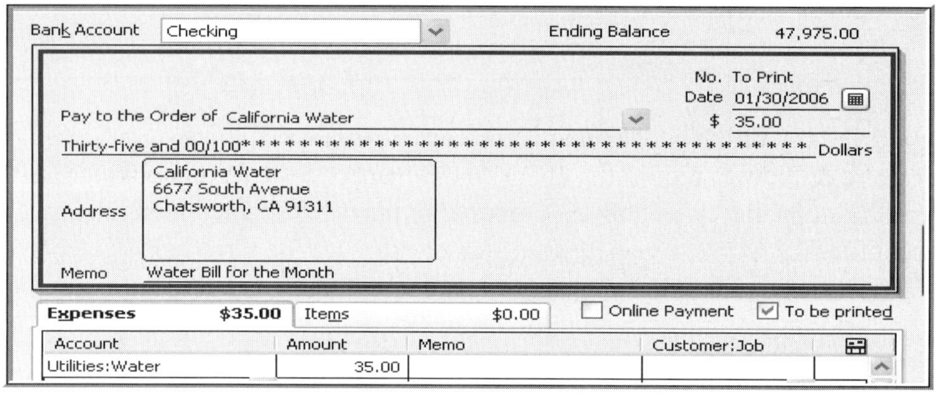

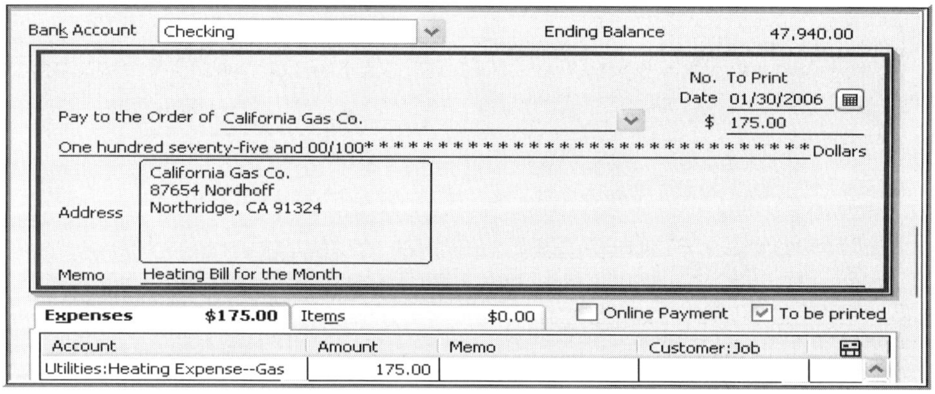

Duplicate Check

ENTER THE CHECK FOR THE ELECTRIC BILL A SECOND TIME

Click the drop-down list arrow and click **California Electric**

- The first payment entered for the payment of the bill for electricity appears on the screen.

Click **Save & Close** to record the second payment for the electric bill and exit the **Write Checks** window

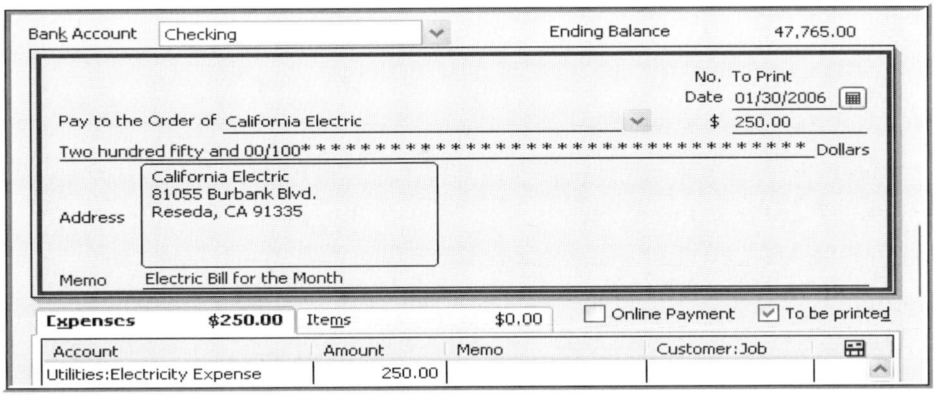

EDIT CHECKS

Mistakes can occur in business—even on a check. QuickBooks Pro allows for checks to be edited at anytime. You may use either the Check Register or the Write Checks window to edit checks.

MEMO
DATE: January 30, 2006

Once the check for the rent had been entered, Consuelo realized that it should have been for $1,600. Edit the check written to Location Realtors.

➤ Revise the check written to pay the rent

Open **Write Checks** as previously instructed
Click **Previous** until you reach the check for Location Realtors
Click between the **1** and the **5** in the **Amount** column
Press **Delete** to delete the **5**
Type **6**, press the **Tab** key

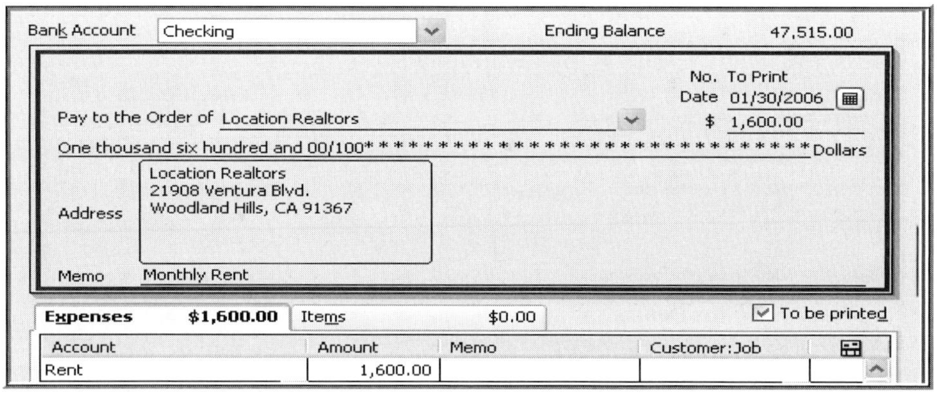

Do not print the check
Click **Save & Close**
Click **Yes** on the screen asking if you want to save the transaction that has been changed

VOID CHECKS

QuickBooks Pro allows checks to be voided. Rather than deleting the transaction, voiding a check changes the amount of the check to zero but keeps a record of the transaction.

> **MEMO**
> **DATE:** January 30, 2006
>
> The telephone bill should not have been paid until the first week of February. Void the check written for the telephone expense.

Use the steps given previously to access the Register for the **Checking** account

Void the check written for the telephone expense
Click anywhere in the check to Communication Telephone Co.
Click **Edit** on the menu bar at the top of the screen—not the Edit button
Click **Void Check**

- The amount of the check is now 0.00 and the memo shows VOID: Telephone Bill for the Month.

Click the **Record** button
Do not close the register for checking

DELETE CHECKS

Deleting a check completely removes it and any transaction information for the check from QuickBooks Pro. Make sure you definitely want to remove the check before deleting it. Once it is deleted, a check cannot be recovered. It is often preferable to void a check than to delete it because a voided check is maintained in the company records; whereas, no record is kept of a deleted check.

MEMO

DATE: January 30, 2006

In reviewing the register for the checking account, Consuelo Alcampo discovered that two checks were written to pay the electric bill. Delete the second check.

Delete the second entry for the electric bill

- Notice that there are two transactions showing for California Electric.

Click anywhere in the second entry to California Electric

Click **Edit** on the menu bar at the top of the screen, click **Delete Check**

OR

Use the keyboard shortcut **Ctrl+D**

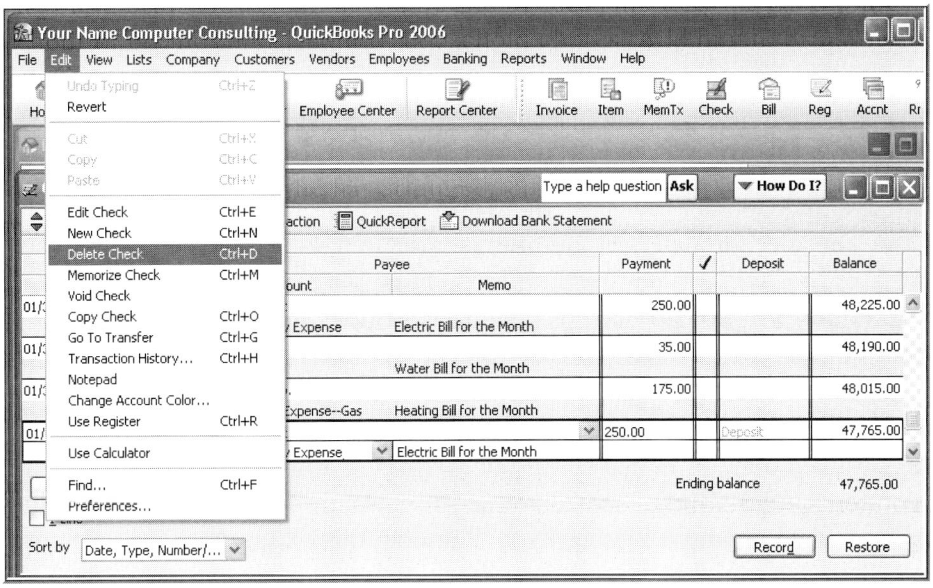

Click **OK** on the **Delete Transaction** dialog box

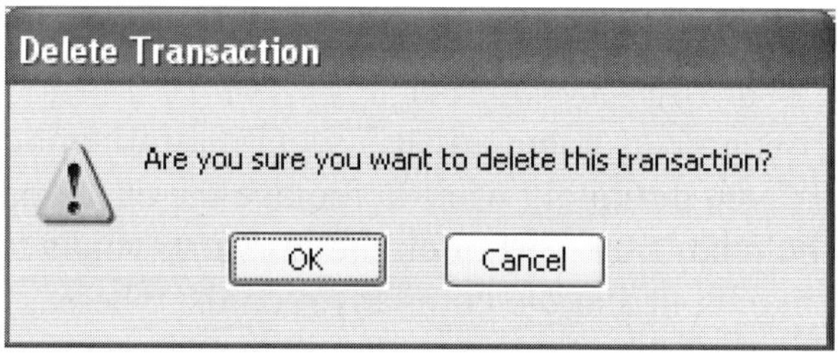

- After you have clicked the **OK** button, there is only one transaction in Checking for California Electric.

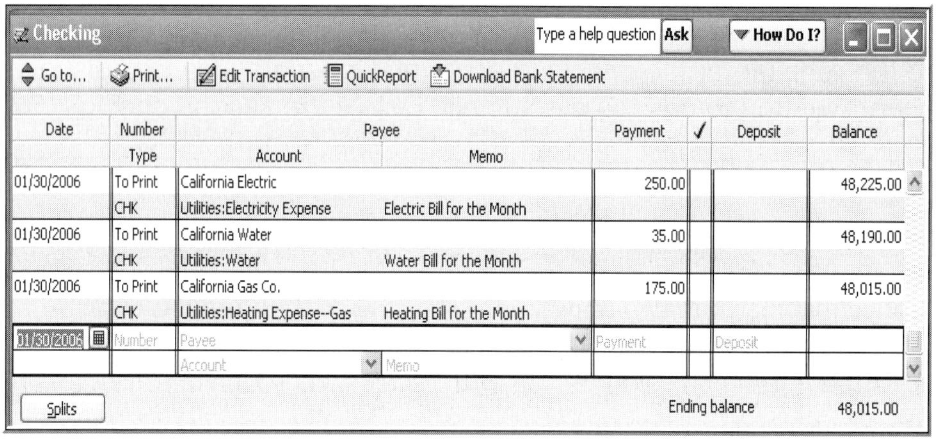

Close the **Checking Register** and the **Chart of Accounts**

PRINT CHECKS

Checks may be printed as they are entered, or they may be printed at a later time. When checks are to be printed, QuickBooks Pro inserts the words *To Print* rather than a check number in the Check Register. The appropriate check number is indicated during printing. Because QuickBooks Pro is so flexible, a company must institute a system for cash control. For example, if the check for rent of $1,500 had been printed, QuickBooks Pro would allow a second check for $1,600 to be printed. In order to avoid any impropriety, more than one person should be designated to review checks. As a matter of practice in a small business, the owner or a person other than the one writing checks should sign the checks. Pre-numbered checks should be used, and any checks printed but not mailed should be submitted along with those for signature. Lastly, QuickBooks optional audit trail feature detailing all transactions, including corrections, should be in use. This is turned on in the Preferences section on the Edit menu. The audit trail has not been turned on for use in training; however, it is strongly recommended that this feature be used in an actual business environment.

MEMO
DATE: January 30, 2006

Consuelo needs to print checks and obtain your signature so the checks can be mailed.

Print the checks for rent and utility bills paid by writing checks

Click the **File** menu, point to **Print Forms**, click **Checks**
Bank Account should be **Checking**
- If this is not showing, click the drop-down list arrow, click **Checking**

Because Check Nos. 1, 2, and 3 were printed previously, **4** should be the number in the **First Check Number** text box
- If not, delete the number showing, key **4**

In the √ column, the checks selected for printing are marked with a check mark
- If not, click the **Select All** button.

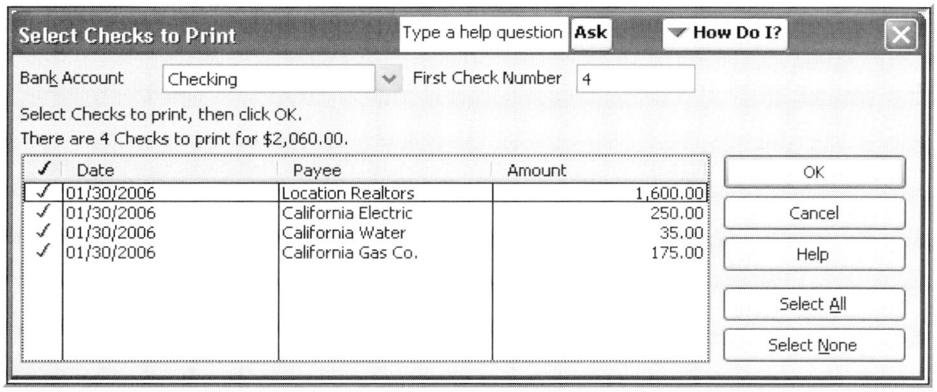

Click **OK** to print the checks
- The **Print Checks** screen appears.

Verify and if necessary change information on the **Settings** tab to use **Standard Checks** as previously shown in the chapter
Click **Print** to print the checks
Did check(s) print OK? dialog box appears
If the checks printed correctly, click **OK**
- The checks have the address for Your Name Computer Consulting, the name and address of the company being paid, and the amount being paid. There is no check number printed on the checks because QuickBooks Pro is set up to use pre-numbered checks.

- In the memo section of the check, any memo entered when preparing the check shows. If there was no memo entered for the bill, the vendor account number appears as the memo.
- If you run into difficulties or find you made an error and want to correct and/or print an individual check, you may do so by printing directly from the check.

PREPARE CHECK DETAIL REPORT

Once checks have been printed, it is important to review information about checks. The Check Detail Report provides detailed information regarding each check, including the checks for 0.00 amounts. Information indicates the type of transaction, the date, the check number, the payee, the account used, the original amount, and the paid amount of the check.

MEMO
DATE: January 30, 2006

Now that the checks have been printed, Consuelo prints a Check Detail Report. She will give this to You to examine when he signs the printed checks.

Print a Check Detail Report

Open the **Report Center**
The type of report should be **Banking**
Click **Check Detail** to select the report
Remove the **Date Prepared** and **Time Prepared** from the report header
The report is From **01/01/06** to **01/30/06**
Tab to **generate** report

- *Note:* You may find that the transaction for Petty Cash appears in a different order than the screen shot. The position of the transaction does not matter as long as the transaction is included in the report.

Print the report in **Landscape** Orientation

Your Name Computer Consulting
Check Detail
January 1 - 30, 2006

Type	Num	Date	Name	Item	Account	Paid Amount	Original Amount
Check		**01/30/2006**	**Communication Telephone...**		**Checking**		**0.00**
TOTAL						0.00	0.00
Bill Pmt -Check	**1**	**01/26/2006**	**Office & Sales Supplies Co.**		**Checking**		**-840.00**
Bill		12/31/2005			Uncategorized Expenses	-350.00	350.00
Bill	1035A	01/18/2006			Equipment Rental	-22.22	25.00
					Office Supplies Expense	-17.78	20.00
Bill	8950S	01/19/2006			Office Supplies	-450.00	450.00
TOTAL						-840.00	845.00
Check	**1**	**01/30/2006**			**Petty Cash**		**-17.79**

Partial Report

Click **Close** to close the report
Do not close the Report Center

VIEW MISSING CHECKS REPORT

A Missing Checks Report lists the checks written for a bank account in order by check number. If there are any gaps between numbers or duplicate check numbers, this information is provided. The report indicates the type of transaction, Check or Bill Payment-Check, check date, check number, payee name, account used for the check, the split or additional accounts used, and the amount of the check.

MEMO
DATE: January 30, 2006

To see a listing of all checks printed, view a Missing Checks Report for all dates.

View a Missing Checks Report

Click **Missing Checks** to select the report being prepared

- If **Checking** appears as the account on the **Missing Checks Report** dialog box, click **OK**.
- If it does not appear, click the drop-down list arrow, click **Checking**, click **OK**.

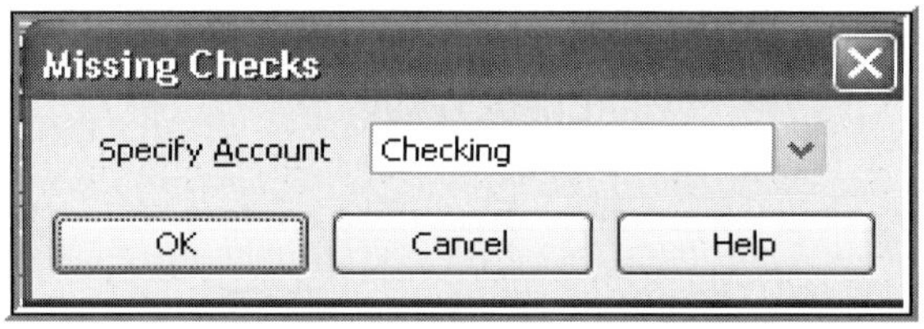

Examine the report:

Your Name Computer Consulting

Missing Checks

All Transactions

Type	Date	Num	Name	Memo	Account	Split	Amount
Bill Pmt -Check	01/26/2006	1	Office & Sales Supplies Co.	456-45623	Checking	Accounts Payable	-840.00
Bill Pmt -Check	01/26/2006	2	Rapid Delivery Service	January Delivery Expe...	Checking	Accounts Payable	-195.00
Bill Pmt -Check	01/26/2006	3	Unique Advertising	1-2567135-54	Checking	Accounts Payable	-500.00
Check	01/30/2006	4	Location Realtors	Monthly Rent	Checking	Rent	-1,600.00
Check	01/30/2006	5	California Electric	Electric Bill for the Month	Checking	Electricity Expense	-250.00
Check	01/30/2006	6	California Water	Water Bill for the Month	Checking	Water	-35.00
Check	01/30/2006	7	California Gas Co.	Heating Bill for the Month	Checking	Heating Expense--Gas	-175.00

- The **Account** in all cases is **Checking**.
- The **Split** column indicates which accounts in addition to checking have been used in the transaction.
- Look at the **Type** column.
- The checks written through Pay Bills indicate the transaction type as **Bill Pmt-Check**.
- The bills paid by actually writing the checks show **Check** as the transaction type.

Close the report without printing

Close the Report Center

PURCHASE AN ASSET WITH A COMPANY CHECK

Not all purchases will be transactions on account. If something is purchased and paid for with a check, a check is written and the purchase is recorded.

MEMO

DATE: January 30, 2006

Having tried out several fax machines from Office & Sales Supplies Co. on a rental basis, you decide to purchase a fax machine from them. Because the fax machine is on sale if it is purchased for cash, you decide to buy it by writing a company check for the asset for $486.

Record the check written for the purchase of a fax machine

Access **Write Checks - Checking** window as previously instructed

- You wrote the check by hand. It does not need printing.

Click the **To be printed** box to deselect.

- The **No.** shows as **1**.

Because Check Nos. 1 through 7 have been printed, enter **8** for the check number
Click the drop-down list arrow for **Pay to the Order of**
Click **Office & Sales Supplies Co.**
The **Date** should be **01/30/2006**
Enter **486** for the Amount
Tab to or click **Memo**
Enter **Purchase Fax Machine**
Tab to or click **Account** on the **Expenses** tab
Click the drop-down list arrow, scroll to the top of the **Chart of Accounts**, and click **Original Cost** under **Office Equipment**

- If you get a message to Track Fixed Assets, click **NO**
- **Amount** column shows the transaction total of **486.00**. This does not need to be changed.

Click **Memo**
Enter **Purchase Fax Machine**

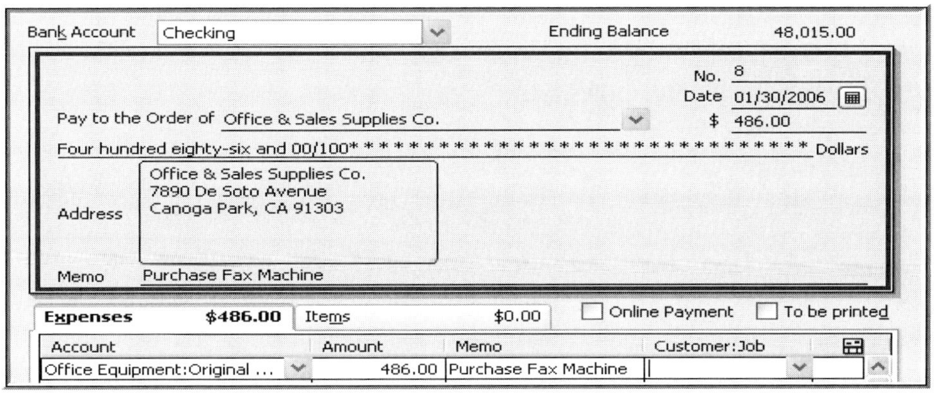

Click **Save & Close** to record the check and exit the **Write Checks - Checking** window without printing

CUSTOMIZE REPORT FORMAT

The report format used in one company may not be appropriate for all companies that use QuickBooks Pro. In order to allow program users the maximum flexibility, QuickBooks Pro makes it very easy to customize many of the user preferences of the program. For example, you may customize menus, reminder screens, and reports and graphs.

Customize the report preferences so the reports are automatically refreshed, and the date prepared, time prepared, and report basis do not print on reports

Click the **Edit** menu, click **Preferences**

Scroll through the items listed on the left side of the screen until you get to Reports and Graphs

Click the **Reports and Graphs** icon

Click **Refresh Automatically** on the **My Preferences** tab

- Whenever data is changed and a report appears on the screen, QuickBooks will automatically update the report to reflect the changes.

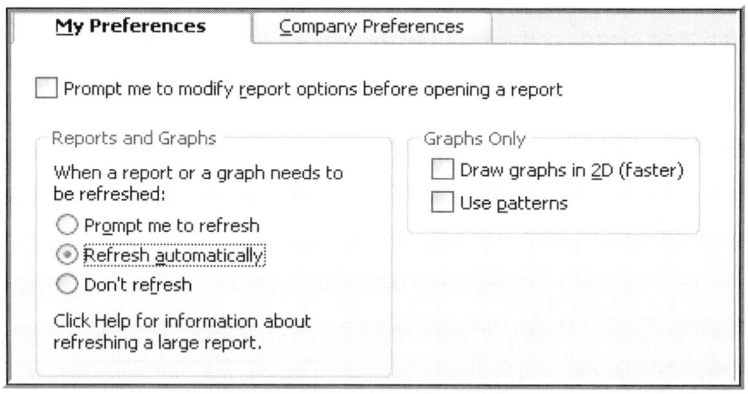

Click the **Company Preferences** tab

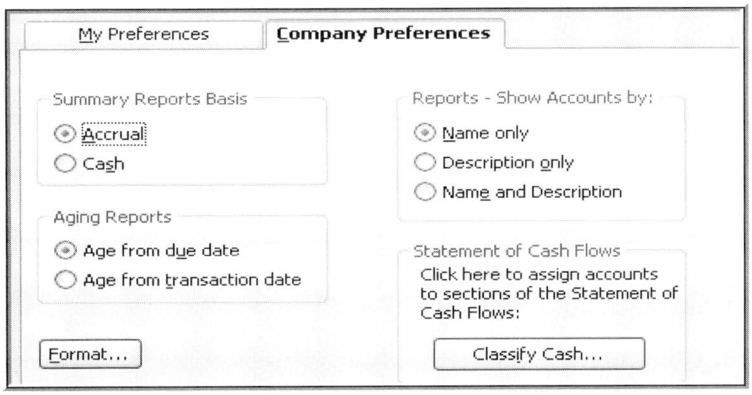

Click the **Format** button

- If necessary, click the **Header/Footer** tab

Click **Date Prepared**, **Time Prepared**, and **Report Basis** to deselect

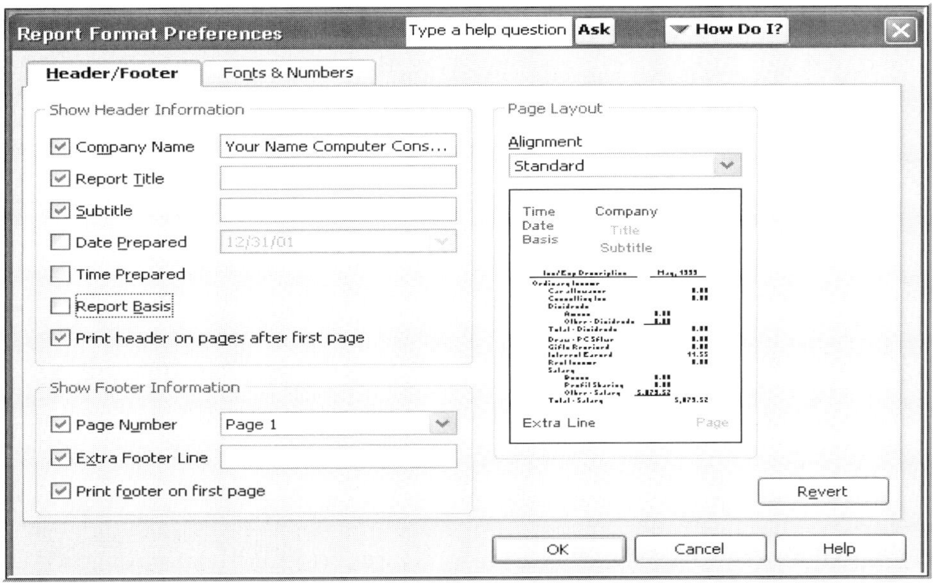

Click **OK** to save the change
Click **OK** to close **Preferences**

PRINT ACCOUNTS PAYABLE AGING SUMMARY

It is important in a business to maintain a good credit rating and to make sure that payments are made on time. In order to avoid overlooking a payment, the Accounts Payable Aging Summary lists the vendors to which the company owes money and shows how long the money has been owed.

MEMO
DATE: January 30, 2006

Prepare the Accounts Payable Aging Summary for Your Name Computer Consulting.

Prepare an **Accounts Payable Aging Summary**

Open the **Report Center** as previously instructed
Click **Vendors & Payables** to select the type of report, click **A/P Aging Summary**
- Notice that the date and time prepared do not appear as part of the heading information.

Tab to or click in the box for the **Date**
- If it is not highlighted, highlight the current date.

Enter **01/30/06**
- Tab through but leave Interval (days) as 30 and Through (days past due) as 90.
- The report will show the current bills as well as any past due bills.

Your Name Computer Consulting
A/P Aging Summary
As of January 30, 2006

	Current	1 - 30	31 - 60	61 - 90	> 90	TOTAL
Computer Technologies Magazine	79.00	0.00	0.00	0.00	0.00	79.00
Jimenez Garage and Auto Services	575.00	0.00	0.00	0.00	0.00	575.00
Southern California Insurance Company	2,850.00	0.00	0.00	0.00	0.00	2,850.00
Unique Advertising	260.00	0.00	0.00	0.00	0.00	260.00
TOTAL	3,764.00	0.00	0.00	0.00	0.00	3,764.00

Follow instructions provided earlier to print the report in Portrait orientation
Close the **A/P Aging Summary** screen
Do not close the Report Center

PRINT UNPAID BILLS DETAIL REPORT

Another important report is the Unpaid Bills Detail Report. Even though it was already printed once during the month, it is always a good idea to print the report at the end of the month.

MEMO
DATE: January 30, 2006

At the end of every month, Consuelo Alcampo prepares and prints an Unpaid Bills Detail Report for you.

Prepare and print the report

Follow instructions provided earlier in the chapter to prepare and print an **Unpaid Bills Detail Report** for **01/30/2006** in Portrait orientation

Your Name Computer Consulting
Unpaid Bills Detail
As of January 30, 2006

Type	Date	Num	Due Date	Aging	Open Balance
Computer Technologies Magazine					
Bill	01/19/2006	1579-53	02/18/2006		79.00
Total Computer Technologies Magazine					79.00
Jimenez Garage and Auto Services					
Bill	01/19/2006	630	02/18/2006		575.00
Total Jimenez Garage and Auto Services					575.00
Southern California Insurance Company					
Bill	01/19/2006	3659	02/18/2006		2,850.00
Total Southern California Insurance Company					2,850.00
Unique Advertising					
Bill	01/16/2006	9875	02/15/2006		260.00
Total Unique Advertising					260.00
TOTAL					**3,764.00**

Close the report
Do not close the Report Center

PRINT VENDOR BALANCE SUMMARY

There are two Vendor Balance Reports available in QuickBooks Pro. There is a Summary Report that shows unpaid balances for vendors and a Detail Report that lists each transaction for a vendor. In order to see how much is owed to each vendor, prepare a Vendor Balance Summary report.

MEMO
DATE: January 30, 2006

At the end of each month, Consuelo prepares and prints a Vendor Balance Summary Report to give to you.

Prepare and print a **Vendor Balance Summary Report**

Click **Vendor Balance Summary**

- The report should show only the totals owed to each vendor on January 30, 2006.
- If it does not, tab to or click **From**, enter **01/30/06**. Then tab to or click **To**, enter **01/30/06**.

Your Name Computer Consulting
Vendor Balance Summary
All Transactions

	Jan 30, 06
Computer Technologies Magazine	79.00
Jimenez Garage and Auto Services	575.00
Southern California Insurance Company	2,850.00
Unique Advertising	260.00
TOTAL	3,764.00

Follow steps listed previously to print the report in Portrait orientation
Close the report; do not close the **Report Center**

CREATE AN ACCOUNTS PAYABLE GRAPH BY AGING PERIOD

Graphs provide a visual representation of certain aspects of the business. It is sometimes easier to interpret data in a graphical format. For example, to determine if any payments are overdue for accounts payable accounts, use an Accounts Payable Graph to provide that information instantly on a bar chart. In addition, the Accounts Payable Graph feature of QuickBooks Pro also displays a pie chart showing what percentage of the total amount payable is owed to each vendor.

Prepare an Accounts Payable Graph

Click **Accounts Payable Graph** in the Vendors & Payables list of reports
Click the **Dates** button at the top of the report
Enter **01/30/06** for **Show Aging as of** in the **Change Graph Dates** text box

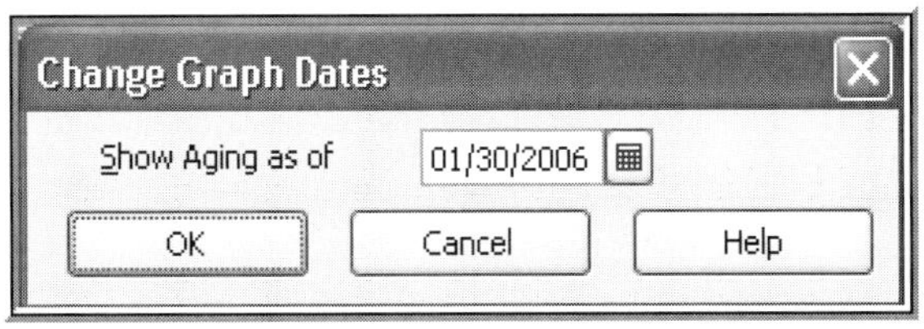

Click **OK**

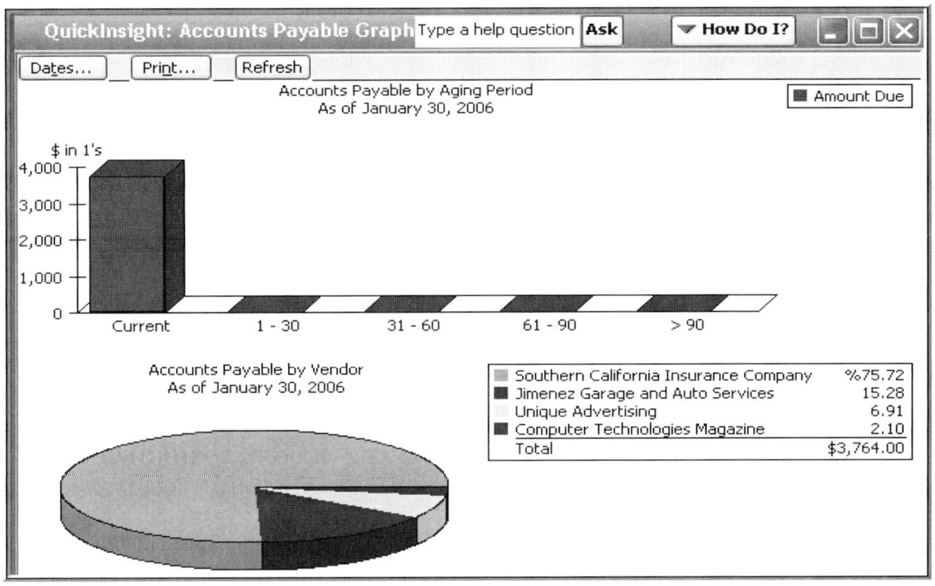

Click the **Dates** button again, enter **02/28/06** for the date
Click **OK**

- Notice that the bar moved from Current to 1-30. This means at the end of February the bills will be between 1 and 30 days overdue.

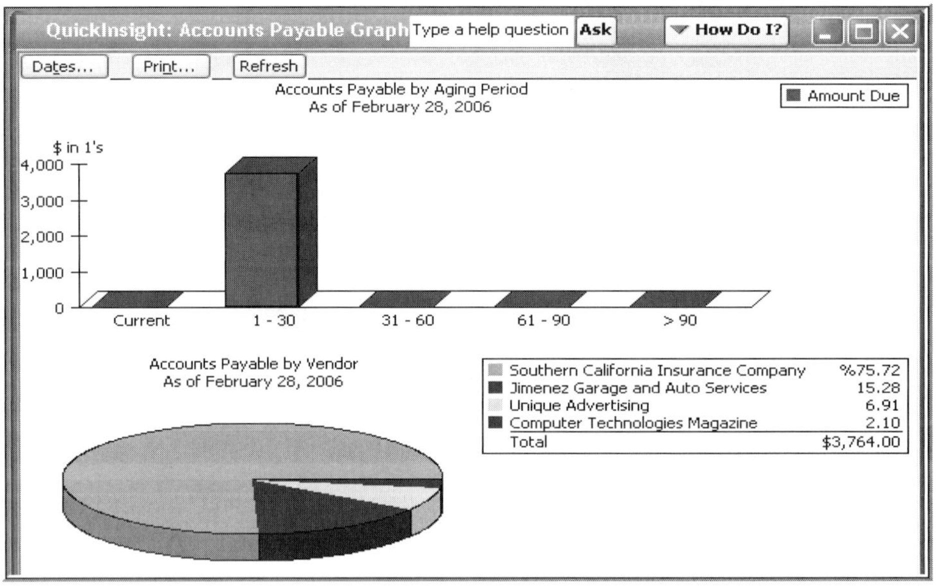

USE QUICKZOOM TO VIEW GRAPH DETAILS

To obtain detailed information from a graph, use the QuickZoom feature. For example, to see the overdue category of an individual account, double-click on a vendor in the pie chart, and this information will appear in a separate bar chart.

Use QuickZoom to see how many days overdue the Southern California Insurance Company's bill will be at the end of February

Point to the section of the pie chart for **Southern California Insurance Company**
Double-click

- The bar chart shows the bill will be in the 1-30 day category at the end of February.

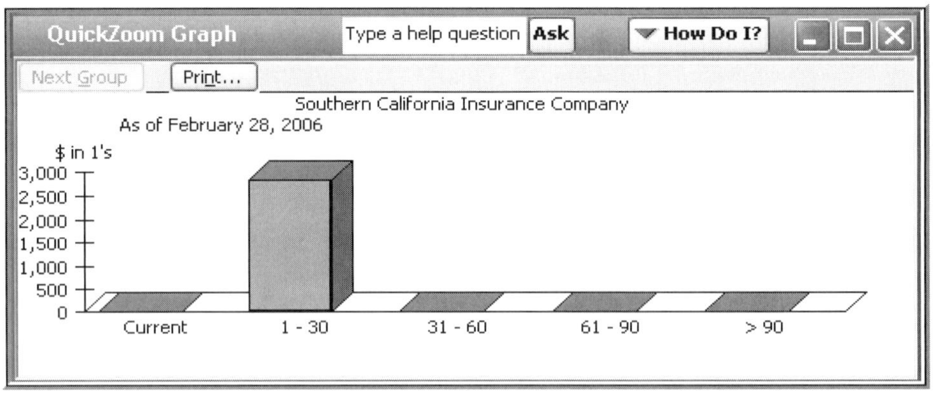

Close the QuickZoom Graph for Southern California Insurance Company

Close the **QuickInsight: Accounts Payable Graph**

BACK UP YOUR NAME COMPUTER CONSULTING DATA AND CLOSE COMPANY

Whenever an important work session is complete, you should always back up your data. If your data disk or company file is damaged or an error is discovered at a later time, the backup file (.qbb) may be restored to the same or a new company file and the information used for recording transactions. As in previous chapters, you should close the company at the end of each work session.

Follow the instructions given in Chapters 1 and 2 to back up data for Your Name Computer Consulting and to close the company and refer to Appendix A for instructions on making a duplicate disk

SUMMARY

In this chapter, bills were recorded and paid, checks were written, and reports were prepared. The petty cash fund was established and used for payments of small expense items. Checks were voided, deleted, and corrected. Accounts were added and modified. QuickReports were accessed in various ways, and QuickZoom was used to obtain transaction detail while in various reports. Reports were prepared for Missing Checks and Check Details. Unpaid Bills and Vendor Balance Summary Reports provided information regarding bills that had not been paid. The graphing feature of QuickBooks Pro allowed you to determine Accounts Payable by aging period and to see the percentage of Accounts Payable for each vendor.

END-OF-CHAPTER QUESTIONS

TRUE/FALSE

ANSWER THE FOLLOWING QUESTIONS IN THE SPACE PROVIDED BEFORE THE QUESTION NUMBER.

_____ 1. Credit Memos are prepared to record a reduction to a transaction.

_____ 2. When you use QuickBooks Pro, checks may not be written in a checkbook.

_____ 3. QuickZoom is a QuickBooks Pro feature that allows detailed information to be displayed.

_____ 4. A purchase can be recorded by writing a check or by using petty cash.

_____ 5. Once a report format has been customized as a QuickBooks Pro preference for a company, QuickBooks Pro will automatically use the customized format for the company.

_____ 6. In a service business, most of the accounting for purchases and payables is simply paying bills for expenses incurred in the operation of the business.

_____ 7. The accrual method of accounting matches the income of the period with the cash received for sales.

_____ 8. A Missing Check Report lists any duplicate check numbers or gaps between check numbers.

_____ 9. The Accounts Payable Register keeps track of all checks written in the business.

_____ 10. If a check has been edited, it cannot be printed.

MULTIPLE CHOICE

WRITE THE LETTER OF THE CORRECT ANSWER IN THE SPACE PROVIDED BEFORE THE QUESTION NUMBER.

_____ 1. When using QuickBooks Pro graphs, information regarding the percentage of accounts payable owed to each vendor is displayed as a ___.
A. pie chart
B. bar chart
C. line chart
D. both A and B

_____ 2. A check may be entered in ___.
A. the Write Checks window
B. the Check Register
C. both A and B
D. neither A nor B

_____ 3. When you enter a bill, typing the first letter(s) of a vendor's name on the Vendor line
A. enters the vendor's name on the line if the name is in the Vendor List
B. displays a list of vendor names
C. displays the Address Info tab for the vendor
D. indicates that you want to type the vendor name completely

_____ 4. To erase an incorrect amount in a bill, you may ___, then key the correction.
A. drag through the amount to highlight
B. position the cursor in front of the amount and press the delete key until the amount has been erased
C. position the cursor after the amount and press the backspace key until the amount has been erased
D. all of the above

_____ 5. When a document prints sideways, it is called __ orientation.
A. portrait
B. landscape
C. standard
D. horizontal

_____ 6. A correction to a bill that has been recorded can be made on the bill or ___.
A. not at all
B. on the Accounts Payable Graph
C. in the Accounts Payable Register
D. none of the above

_____ 7. When a bill is deleted, ___.

A. the amount is changed to 0.00
B. the word *deleted* appears as the Memo
C. it is removed without a trace
D. a bill cannot be deleted

_____ 8. To increase the date on a bill by one day, ___.

A. press the + key
B. press the - key
C. tab
D. press the # key

_____ 9. If a bill is recorded in the Enter Bills window, it is important to pay the bill by ___.

A. writing a check
B. using the Pay Bills window
C. using petty cash
D. allowing QuickBooks Pro to generate the check automatically five days before the due date

_____ 10. When entering several bills at once on the Enter Bills screen, it is most efficient to ___ to go to the next blank screen.

A. click Previous
B. click Save & New
C. click OK
D. click Preview

FILL-IN

IN THE SPACE PROVIDED, WRITE THE ANSWER THAT MOST APPROPRIATELY COMPLETES THE SENTENCE.

1. The ____________ section of a check is used to record the check date, payee, and amount for the actual check. The ____________ section of a check is used to record the accounts used for the bill, the amount for each account used, and transaction explanations.

2. An Accounts Payable Graph by Aging Period shows a ___________ chart detailing the amounts due by aging period and a ___________ chart showing the percentage of the total amount payable owed to each vendor.

3. Three different check styles may be used in QuickBooks Pro: ____________, __________, or ____________.

4. The keyboard shortcut to edit or modify a vendor's record is ____________.

5. Petty Cash is identified as a ____________ account type so it will be placed at the top of the Chart of Accounts along with checking and savings accounts.

SHORT ESSAY

When viewing a Transaction by Vendor Report that shows the entry of a bill for the purchase of office supplies and office equipment, you will see the term **-split-** displayed. Explain what the term **Split** means when used as a column heading and when used within the Split column for the bill indicated.

____

____

____

____

____

____

____

NAME____________________

TRANSMITTAL

CHAPTER 3: YOUR NAME COMPUTER CONSULTING

Attach the following documents and reports:

Transaction List by Vendor, January 1-18, 2006
Register QuickReport, Office & Sales Supplies Co.
Unpaid Bills Detail Report, January 25, 2006
Check No. 1: Office & Sales Supplies Co.
Check No. 2: Rapid Delivery Service
Check No. 3: Unique Advertising
Check No. 4: Location Realtors
Check No. 5: California Electric
Check No. 6: California Water
Check No. 7: California Gas Co.
Check Detail Report
A/P Aging Summary, Current and Total
Unpaid Bills Detail Report, January 30, 2006
Vendor Balance Summary

END-OF-CHAPTER PROBLEM

YOUR NAME GARDEN & POOL MAINTENANCE

Chapter 3 continues with the transactions for bills, bill payments, and purchases for Your Name Garden & Pool Maintenance. Cash control measures have been implemented. Sally prints the checks and any related reports; Ramon initials his approval of the checks; and you, the owner, sign the checks.

INSTRUCTIONS

Continue to use the company file that you used in Chapters 1 and 2 **Garden.qbw**. Record the bills, bill payments, and purchases as instructed within the chapter. Always read the transactions carefully and review the Chart of Accounts when selecting transaction accounts. Print reports and graphs as indicated. If a bill is recorded on the Enter Bills screen, it should be paid on the Pay Bills screen—not by writing the check yourself.

RECORD TRANSACTIONS

January 1—Use Enter Bills to record the following bills:

- ▶ Received a bill from Communications Services for cellular phone service, $485, Net 10, Invoice No. 1109, Memo: Cellular Telephone Services for January.
- ▶ Received a bill from the Office 'N Things for office supplies purchased to have on hand, $275, Net 30, Invoice No. 58-9826. (This is a prepaid expense so an asset account is used.) No memo is necessary.
- ▶ Received a bill from Grafton's Motors for truck service and repairs, $519, Net 10, Invoice No. 1-62, Memo: Truck Service and Repairs. (Use Automobile Expense as the account for this transaction. We will change the name to something more appropriate in Chapter 4.)
- ▶ Received a bill from Garden Street Gasoline for gasoline for the month, $375, Net 10, Invoice No. 853, Memo: Gasoline for Month.
- ▶ Received a bill from Ricardo's Cooler/Heating for a repair of the office air conditioner, $150, Net 30, Invoice No. 87626, Memo: Air Conditioner Repair. (The air conditioner is part of the building.)

January 15—Use Enter Bills to record the following bills:

- ▶ Add a new expense account: Disposal Expense, Description: County Dump Charges.
- ▶ Received a bill from Santa Barbara County Dump for disposing of lawn, tree, and shrub trimmings, $180, Net 30, Invoice No. 667, no memo necessary.
- ▶ Received a bill from California Water Co., $25, Net 10, Invoice No. 098-1, no memo.

- ► Change the QuickBooks Pro Company Preferences to customize the report format so that reports refresh automatically, and that the Date Prepared, the Time Prepared, and the Report Basis do not print as part of the header.
- ► Print an Unpaid Bills Detail Report for January 1-15 in Portrait orientation.
- ► Pay all bills *due on or before January 15*, print checks. (Use Pay Bills to pay bills that have been entered in the Enter Bills window.) Print the checks using standard style.
- ► Record the receipt of a bill from Quality Equipment Maintenance. Add this new vendor as you record the transaction. Additional information needed to do a complete Set Up is: 1234 State Street, Santa Barbara, CA 93110, 805-555-0770, Net 10. The bill was for the repair of the lawn mower, $75, Invoice No. 5-1256, no memo necessary.
- ► Change the telephone number for Santa Barbara County Dump. The new number is 805-555-3798.
- ► Prepare and print the Vendor Balance Detail Report for all transactions.

January 30—Enter the transactions:

- ► Received a $10 credit from Quality Equipment Maintenance. The repair of the lawn mower wasn't as extensive as originally estimated.
- ► Add Petty Cash to the Chart of Accounts.
- ► Use the Register for Checking to transfer $50 from Checking to Petty Cash, Memo: Establish Petty Cash Fund.
- ► Record the use of Petty Cash to pay for postage due 64 cents, and office supplies, $1.59 (this is a current expense). Memo notations are not necessary.
- ► Write Check No. 5 to Quality Equipment Maintenance to buy a lawn fertilizer spreader as a cash purchase of equipment, $349, Check Memo: Purchase of Lawn Fertilizer Spreader. Print the check. (If you get a dialog box indicating that you currently owe money to Quality Equipment Maintenance, click **OK** and continue writing the check.)
- ► Print an Unpaid Bills Detail Report for January 30.
- ► Pay all bills *due on or before January 30*; print the checks. (Note: There may be some bills that were due after January 15 but before January 30. Be sure to pay these bills now. If any vendor shows a credit and has a bill that is due, apply it to the bill prior to payment. You may need to click on each bill individually in order to determine whether or not there is a credit to be applied.) Print the checks using standard style.
- ► Prepare an Accounts Payable Graph as of 1/30/2006. Do not print.
- ► Prepare a QuickZoom Graph for Santa Barbara County Dump as of 1/30/2006. Do not print.
- ► Back up your data and close the company.

NAME____________________

TRANSMITTAL

CHAPTER 3: YOUR NAME GARDEN & POOL MAINTENANCE

Attach the following documents and reports:

Unpaid Bills Detail Report, January 15, 2006
Check No. 1: Communications Services
Check No. 2: Garden Street Gasoline
Check No. 3: Grafton's Motors
Check No. 4: Santa Barbara County Dump
Vendor Balance Detail
Check No. 5: Quality Equipment Maintenance
Unpaid Bills Detail Report, January 30, 2006
Check No. 6: California Water Co.
Check No. 7: Quality Equipment Maintenance

GENERAL ACCOUNTING AND END-OF-PERIOD PROCEDURES: SERVICE BUSINESS

4

LEARNING OBJECTIVES

At the completion of this chapter, you will be able to:

1. Complete the end-of-period procedures.
2. Change account names, delete accounts, and make accounts inactive.
3. View an account name change and its effect on subaccounts.
4. Record depreciation and enter the adjusting entries required for accrual-basis accounting.
5. Record owner's equity transactions for a sole proprietor including capital investment and owner withdrawals.
6. Reconcile the bank statement, record bank service charges, automatic payments, and mark cleared transactions.
7. Print Trial Balance, Profit and Loss Statement, and Balance Sheet.
8. Export a report to Microsoft® Excel
9. Perform end-of-period backup and close the end of a period.

GENERAL ACCOUNTING AND END-OF-PERIOD PROCEDURES

As previously stated, QuickBooks Pro operates from the standpoint of the business document rather than an accounting form, journal, or ledger. While QuickBooks Pro does incorporate all of these items into the program, in many instances they operate behind the scenes. QuickBooks Pro does not require special closing procedures at the end of a period. At the end of the fiscal year, QuickBooks Pro transfers the net income into the Retained Earnings account and allows you to protect the data for the year by assigning a closing date to the period. All of the transaction detail is maintained and viewable, but it will not be changed unless OK is clicked on a warning screen.

Even though a formal closing does not have to be performed within QuickBooks Pro, when you use accrual-basis accounting, several transactions must be recorded to reflect all expenses and income for the period. For example, bank statements must be reconciled and any charges or bank collections need to be recorded. During the business period, the CPA for the company will review things such as account names, adjusting entries, depreciation schedules, owner's equity adjustments, and so on. Sometimes the changes and adjustments will be made by the accountant on a separate disk called the Accountant's Copy of the business files. This disk is then merged with the company files that are used to record day-to-day business transactions, and all adjustments made by the CPA are added to the current company files. There are certain restrictions to the types of transactions that may be made on an Accountant's Copy of the business files.

Once necessary adjustments have been made, reports reflecting the end-of-period results of operations should be prepared. For archive purposes at the end of the fiscal year an additional backup disk is prepared and stored.

TRAINING TUTORIAL AND PROCEDURES

The following tutorial will once again work with Your Name Computer Consulting. As in Chapters 2 and 3, transactions will be recorded for this fictitious company. To maximize training benefits, you should follow the steps illustrated in Chapter 2.

OPEN QUICKBOOKS® PRO AND YOUR NAME COMPUTER CONSULTING

Open QuickBooks Pro

Open Your Name Computer Consulting

- This file should contain all the transactions that you recorded for Chapters 2 and 3.
- To close an open company and open your copy of the company, click **File**, click **Open Company**, click **Computer.qbw**, check to make sure you are using the correct storage location, click **Open**.

Check the title bar to verify that Your Name Computer Consulting is the open company

BEGINNING THE TUTORIAL

In this chapter, you will be recording end-of-period adjustments, reconciling bank statements, changing account names, and preparing traditional end-of-period reports. Because QuickBooks Pro does not perform a traditional "closing" of the books, you will learn how to assign a closing date and to protect transactions and data recorded during previous accounting periods.

As in the earlier chapters, all transactions are listed on memos. The transaction date will be the same as the memo date unless otherwise specified within the transaction. Once a specific type of transaction has been entered in a step-by-step manner, additional transactions of the same or a similar type will be made without instructions being provided. Of course, you may always refer to instructions given for previous transactions for ideas or for steps used to enter those transactions. To determine the account used in the transaction, refer to the Chart of Accounts, which is also the General Ledger.

CHANGE THE NAME OF EXISTING ACCOUNTS IN THE CHART OF ACCOUNTS

Even though transactions have been recorded during the month of January, QuickBooks Pro makes it a simple matter to change the name of an existing account. Once the name of an account has been changed, all transactions using the "old" name are updated and show the "new" account name.

> **MEMO**
> **DATE:** January 31, 2006
>
> Upon the recommendation from the company's CPA, you decided to change the names of several accounts: Student's Name, Capital to Your Name, Capital (Use your actual name); Company Cars to Business Vehicles; Company Cars Loan to Business Vehicles Loan; Automobile Expense to Business Vehicles Expense; Auto Insurance Expense to Business Vehicles Insurance; Office Equipment to Office furniture and Equipment; Office Equipment Loan to Office Furniture/Equipment Loan; Loan Interest to Interest on Loans

Change the account names

Access the **Chart of Accounts**:
Click **Lists**, click **Chart of Accounts** on the menu bar
OR
Click the **Chart of Accounts** icon on the Home page
OR
Use the keyboard shortcut Ctrl+A
OR
Click the **Acct** icon on the icon bar
Scroll through accounts until you see **Student's Name, Capital**, click the account
Click the **Account** button at the bottom of the Chart of Accounts, click **Edit**
OR
Use the keyboard shortcut **Ctrl+E**
On the **Edit Account** screen, highlight **Student's Name**
Enter the your name

- The balances of any subaccounts of Student's Name, Capital will be reflected in the account total on the Chart of Accounts and in reports.

Click **OK** to record the name change and to close the **Edit Account** screen

- Notice that the name of the account appears as Your Name, Capital in the Chart of Accounts and that the balance of $78,135.00 shows.

- The account name was changed in Chapter 1; however, the backup file was restored. This eliminated the account name change because the backup was made before changing the account name.

Follow the steps above to change the names of:

Company Cars to **Business Vehicles**
Company Cars Loan to **Business Vehicles Loan**
Automobile Expense to **Business Vehicles Expense**

- Delete the Description Automobile Expense.

Auto Insurance Expense to **Business Vehicles Insurance**
Office Equipment to **Office Furniture and Equipment**
Office Equipment Loan to **Office Furniture/Equipment Loan**

- Due to exceeding the allotted number of characters in an account name, the word "and" was omitted and the "/" was used.

Loan Interest to **Interest on Loans**

- Leave the description as Loan Interest Expense

Do not close the **Chart of Accounts**

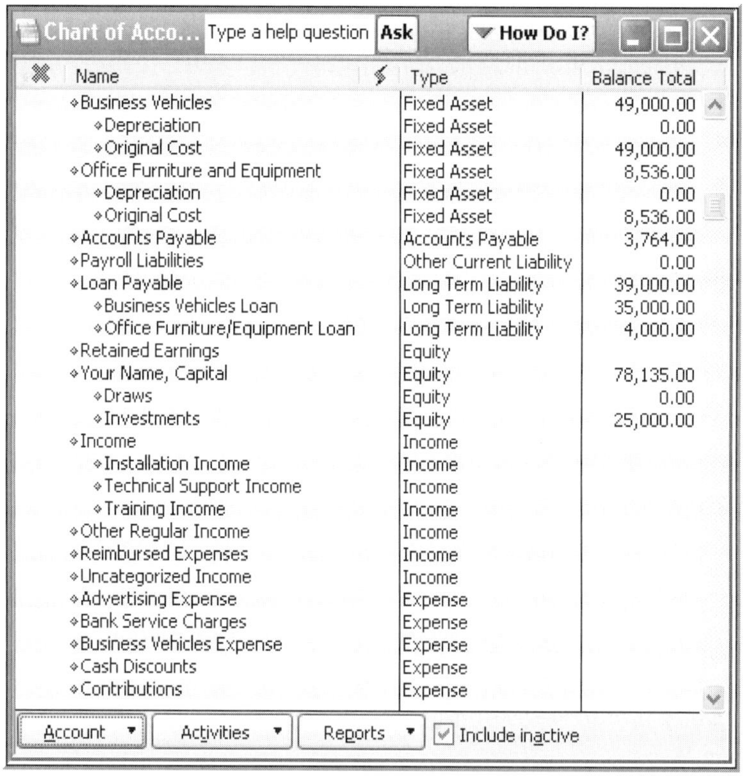

EFFECT OF AN ACCOUNT NAME CHANGE ON SUBACCOUNTS

Any account that uses Company Car as part of the account name needs to be changed. However, when the account name of Company Car was changed to Business Vehicles, the subaccounts of Company Car automatically became subaccounts of Business Vehicles.

Examine the Depreciation and Original Cost accounts for Business Vehicles

Click **Depreciation** under Business Vehicles
Use the keyboard shortcut **Ctrl+E**
The text box for **Subaccount of** shows as **Business Vehicles**

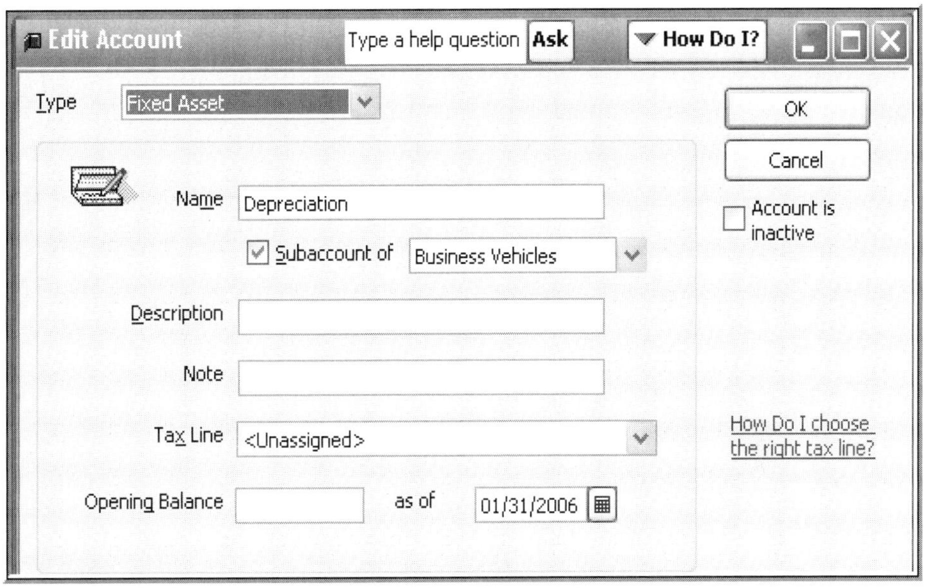

Click **Cancel**

- Repeat the above steps to examine the **Original Cost** account.
- Examine **Your Name, Capital** and **Office Furniture and Equipment** and their subaccounts.

Do not close the **Chart of Accounts**

MAKE AN ACCOUNT INACTIVE

If you are not using an account and do not have plans to use it in the near future, the account may be made inactive. The account remains available for use, yet it does not appear on your chart of accounts unless you check the Show All check box.

MEMO

DATE: January 31, 2006

At present, the company does not plan to purchase its own building. The accounts Interest Expense: Mortgage and Taxes: Property should be made inactive.

Make the accounts listed above inactive

Click **Mortgage** under Interest Expense
Click the **Account** button at the bottom of the **Chart of Accounts**
Click **Make Inactive**

- The account no longer appears in the Chart of Accounts.
- If you wish to view all accounts including the inactive ones, click the **Include Inactive** check box at the bottom of the **Chart of Accounts** and all accounts will be displayed.
- Notice the icon next to Mortgage. It marks the account as inactive.

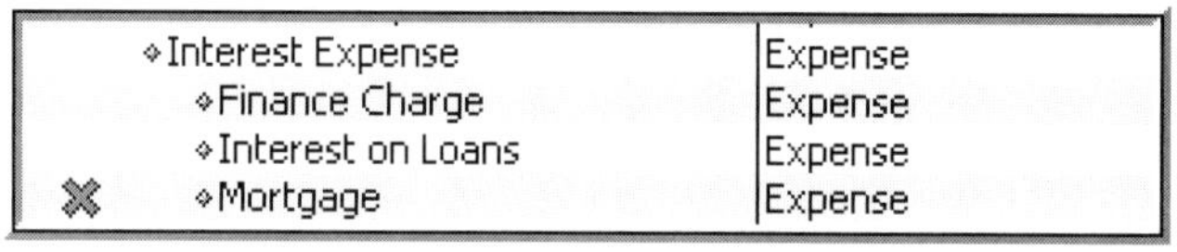

Repeat the above to make **Taxes: Property** inactive

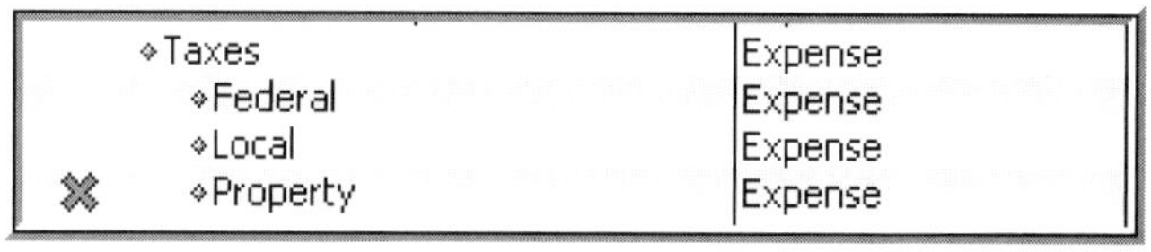

DELETE AN EXISTING ACCOUNT FROM THE CHART OF ACCOUNTS

If you do not want to make an account inactive because you have not used it and do not plan to use it at all, QuickBooks Pro allows the account to be deleted at anytime. However, as a safeguard, QuickBooks Pro prevents the deletion of an account once it has been used even if it simply contains an opening or an existing balance.

MEMO
DATE: January 31, 2006

In addition to previous changes to account names, you find that you do not use nor will use the expense account: Contributions. Delete this account from the Chart of Accounts. In addition, delete the Dues and Subscriptions account.

Delete the **Contributions** expense account

Scroll through accounts until you see Contributions, click **Contributions**
Click the **Account** button at the bottom of the Chart of Accounts, click **Delete**
OR
Use the keyboard shortcut **Ctrl+D**

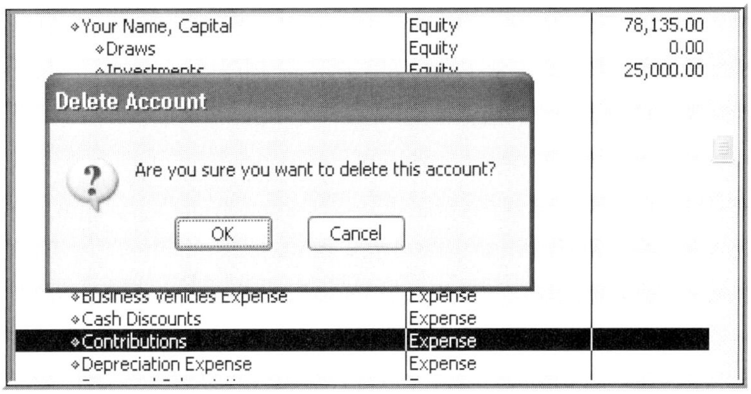

Click **OK** on the **Delete Account** dialog box

- The account has now been deleted.

Repeat the above steps for the deletion of **Dues and Subscriptions**

- As soon as you try to delete Dues and Subscriptions, a **QuickBooks Message** appears indicating that the account has a balance or is used in a transaction, an invoice item, or your payroll setup. QuickBooks offers a solution of making the account inactive.

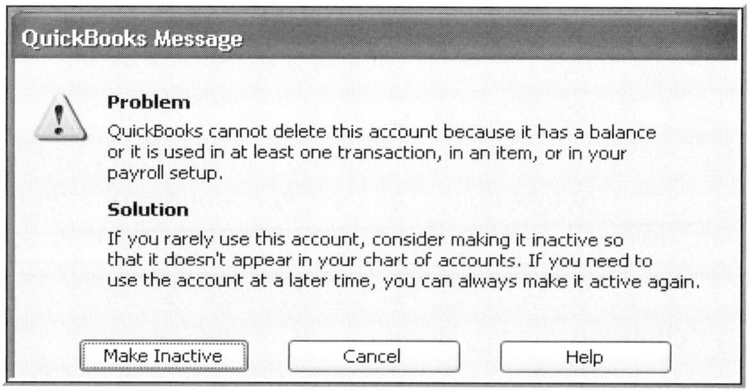

Click **Cancel**

- The account remains in the Chart of Accounts.

Close the **Chart of Accounts**

ADJUSTMENTS FOR ACCRUAL-BASIS ACCOUNTING

As previously stated, the accrual basis of accounting matches the income and the expenses of a period in order to arrive at an accurate figure for net income. Thus, the revenue is earned at the time the service is performed or the sale is made no matter when the actual cash is received. The cash basis of accounting records income or revenue at the time cash is received no matter when the sale was made or the service performed. The same holds true when a business buys things or pays bills. In accrual-basis accounting, the expense is recorded at the time the bill is received or the purchase is made regardless of the actual payment date. In cash-basis accounting, the expense is not recorded until it is paid.

There are several internal transactions that must be recorded when you are using the accrual basis of accounting. These entries are called adjusting entries. For example, equipment does wear out and will eventually need to be replaced. Rather than wait until replacement to record the use of the equipment, one makes an adjusting entry to allocate the use of equipment as an expense for a period. This is called depreciation. Certain items used in a business are paid for in advance. As these are used, they become expenses of the business. For example, insurance for the entire year would be used up month by month and should, therefore, be a monthly expense. Commonly, the insurance is billed and paid for the entire year. Until the insurance is used, it is an asset. Each month, the portion of the insurance used becomes an expense for the month.

ADJUSTING ENTRIES—PREPAID EXPENSES

During the operation of a business, companies purchase supplies to have on hand for use in the operation of the business. In accrual-basis accounting, unless the supplies are purchased for immediate use and will be used up within the month, the supplies are considered to be prepaid expenses (an asset because it is something the business owns) until they are used in the operation of the business. As the supplies are used, the amount used becomes an expense for the period. The same system applies to other things paid for in advance, such as insurance. At the end of the period, an adjusting entry must be made to allocate the amount of prepaid expenses (assets) used to expenses.

The transactions for these adjustments may be recorded in the register for the account by clicking on the prepaid expense (asset) in the Chart of Accounts, or they may be made in the General Journal.

MEMO
DATE: January 31, 2006

Consuelo, remember to record the monthly adjustment for Prepaid Insurance. The $2,850 is the amount we paid for the year. Also, we used $350 worth of supplies this month. Please adjust accordingly.

Record the adjusting entries for office supplies expense and business vehicle insurance expense in the General Journal.

Access the General Journal:
Click **Company** on the menu bar, click **Make General Journal Entries**
- If you get a screen regarding Assigning Numbers to Journal Entries, click **OK**

Record the adjusting entry for Prepaid Insurance
Enter **01/31/06** as the **Date**
- **Entry No.** is left blank unless you wish to record a specific number.
- Because all transactions entered for the month have been entered in the Journal as well as on an invoice or a bill, all transactions automatically have a Journal entry number.

Tab to or click the **Account** column
Click the drop-down list arrow for **Account**, click **Business Vehicles Insurance**
Tab to or click **Debit**
- The $2,850 given in the memo is the amount for the year; calculate the amount of the adjustment for the month by using QuickBooks QuickMath or the Calculator.

Use QuickBooks QuickMath
    Press the + key on the 10-key numerical keypad or at the top of the keyboard
    Enter **2850** by:
        Keying the numbers on the **10-key pad** (preferred)
        - Be sure Num Lock is on. There should be a light by Num Lock on/or above the 10-key pad. If not, press Num Lock to activate.
          OR

Using the mouse to click the numbers
OR
Typing the numbers at the top of the keyboard
Press / for division
Key **12**
Press **Enter** to close QuickMath and enter the amount in the Debit column
Or use the Calculator
Click **Edit** on the menu bar, click **Use Calculator**
Enter **2850**
Press / for division
Key **12**
Press = or **Enter**
Click the **Close** button to close the **Calculator**

- For additional calculator instructions refer to Chapter 1.

Enter the amount of the adjustment **237.5** in the **Debit** column

- Notice that the amount must be entered by you when using Calculator; QuickBooks Math automatically enters the amount.

Tab to or click the **Memo** column
Type **Adjusting Entry, Insurance**
Tab to or click **Account**
Click the drop-down list arrow for **Account**
Click the asset account **Prepaid Insurance**

- The amount for the Credit column should be entered automatically. However, there are several reasons why an amount may not appear in the Credit column; if 237.50 does not appear, type it in the Credit column.

Tab to or click the **Memo** column
Type **Adjusting Entry, Insurance**

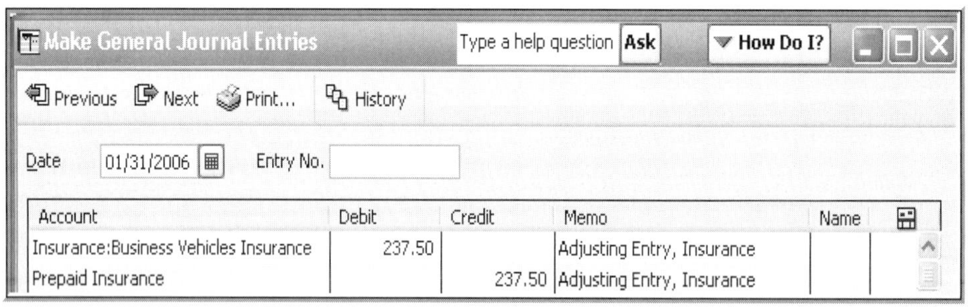

Click **Save & New** to record the adjustment and advance to the next **Make General Journal Entries** screen
Repeat the above procedures to record the adjustment for the office supplies used
Use the Memo **Supplies Used**

- The amount given in the memo is the actual amount of the supplies used in January.

- Remember, when supplies are purchased to have on hand, the original entry records an increase to the asset Office Supplies. Once the supplies are used, the adjustment correctly records the amount of supplies used as an expense.

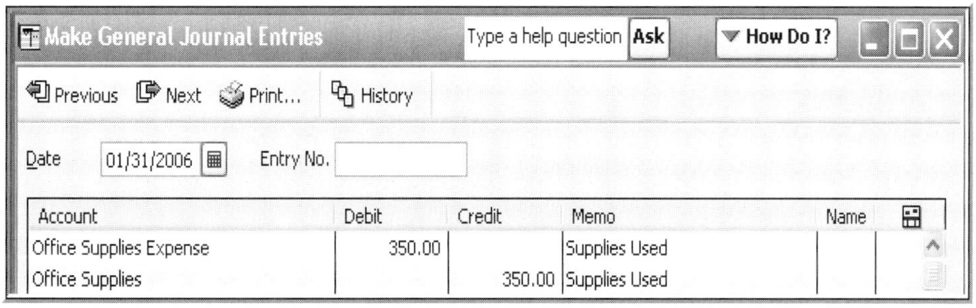

Click **Save & New**

ADJUSTING ENTRIES—DEPRECIATION

Using the accrual basis of accounting requires companies to record an expense for the amount of equipment used in the operation of the business. Unlike supplies—where you can actually see, for example, the paper supply diminishing—it is very difficult to see how much of a computer has been "used up" during the month. To account for the fact that machines do wear out and need to be replaced, an adjustment is made for depreciation. This adjustment correctly matches the expenses of the period against the revenue of the period.

The adjusting entry for depreciation can be made in the account register for Depreciation, or it can be made in the General Journal.

MEMO
DATE: January 31, 2006

Having received the necessary depreciation schedules, Consuelo records the adjusting entry for depreciation: Business Vehicles, $583 per month; Equipment, $142 per month.

Record a compound adjusting entry for depreciation of the equipment and the business vehicles in the **General Journal**:

If it is not automatically displayed, enter **01/31/06** as the **Date**
Entry No. is left blank

- Normally, the Debit portion of a Journal entry is entered first. However, in order to use the automatic calculation feature of QuickBooks Pro, you will enter the Credit entries first.

Tab to or click the **Account** column
Click the drop-down list arrow for **Account**, click **Depreciation** under **Business Vehicles**

- Make sure that you do not click the controlling account, Business Vehicles

Tab to or click **Credit**, enter **583**
Tab to or click **Memo**
Enter **Adjusting Entry January**
Tab to or click the **Account** column

- The amount of the 583 credit shows in the debit column temporarily.

Click the drop-down list arrow for **Account**, click **Depreciation** under **Office Furniture and Equipment**

- Again, make sure that you do not use the controlling account, Office Furniture and Equipment.

Tab to or click **Credit**
Enter **142**

- The 583 in the debit column is removed when you tab to or click **Memo**.

Tab to or click **Memo**
Enter **Adjusting Entry January**
Tab to or click the **Account** column
Click the drop-down list arrow for **Account**
Click **Depreciation Expense**
Debit column should automatically show **725**

- If 725 does not appear, enter it in the debit column.

Tab to or click **Memo**, enter **Adjusting Entry January**

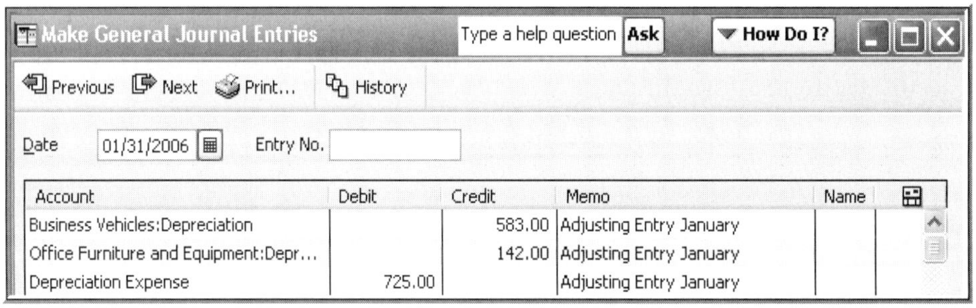

Click **Save & Close** to record the adjustment and close the **General Journal**

- If you get a message regarding Tracking Fixed Assets, click **OK.**

Close the **Chart of Accounts**, if necessary

VIEW GENERAL JOURNAL

Once transactions have been entered in the General Journal, it is important to view them. QuickBooks Pro also refers to the General Journal as the Journal and allows it to be viewed or printed at any time. Even with the special ways in which transactions are entered in QuickBooks

Pro through invoices, bills, checks, and account registers, the Journal is still the book of original entry. All transactions recorded for the company may be viewed in the Journal even if they were entered elsewhere.

View the Journal for January

Click **Reports** on the menu bar, point to **Accountant & Taxes,** click **Journal**
Enter the dates from **01/01/06** to **01/31/06**
Tab to generate the report

- Notice that the transactions do not begin with the adjustments entered directly into the Journal.
- The first transaction displayed is the entry for Invoice No. 1 to Jose Mendoza.
- If corrections or changes are made to entries, the transaction numbers may differ from the key. Since QuickBooks assigns transaction numbers automatically, disregard any discrepancies in transaction numbers.

Your Name Computer Consulting
Journal
January 2006

Trans #	Type	Date	Num	Name	Memo	Account	Debit	Credit
27	Invoice	01/02/2006	1	Mendoza, Jose, Esq.		Accounts Receivable	300.00	
				Mendoza, Jose, Esq.	10 Hours--Monthly Technical S...	Technical Support In...		300.00
							300.00	300.00
29	Invoice	01/05/2006	3	Jafrood, Kala	VOID:	Accounts Receivable	0.00	
				Jafrood, Kala	10 Hours--Monthly Technical S...	Technical Support In...	0.00	
							0.00	0.00
30	Invoice	01/05/2006	4	Steele, Rhoades, Whitcom...		Accounts Receivable	3,215.00	
				Steele, Rhoades, Whitcom...	Initial Hour of On-Site Training	Training Income		95.00
				Steele, Rhoades, Whitcom...	Additional Hours of On-Site Tra...	Training Income		3,120.00
							3,215.00	3,215.00
31	Invoice	01/05/2006	5	Grace, Anderson, and Bin...		Accounts Receivable	1,425.00	
				Grace, Anderson, and Bin...	Initial Hour of On-Site Training	Training Income		95.00
				Grace, Anderson, and Bin...	Additional Hours of On-Site Tra...	Training Income		880.00
				Grace, Anderson, and Bin...	15 Hours--Monthly Technical S...	Technical Support In...		450.00
							1,425.00	1,425.00

Partial Report

Scroll through the report to view all transactions recorded in the Journal
Verify the total Debit and Credit Columns of $46,530.29

- If your totals do not match, check for errors and make appropriate corrections.

Close the report without printing

OWNER WITHDRAWALS

In a sole proprietorship an owner cannot receive a paycheck because he or she owns the business. An owner withdrawing money from a business—even to pay personal expenses—is similar to withdrawing money from a savings account. A withdrawal simply decreases the owner's capital. QuickBooks Pro allows you to establish a separate account for owner withdrawals. If a separate account is not established, owner withdrawals may be subtracted directly from the owner's capital or investment account.

MEMO
DATE: January 31, 2006

Because you work in the business full time, you do not earn a paycheck. You prepare the check for your monthly withdrawal, $2,500.

Write Check No. 9 to yourself for $2,500 withdrawal

Open the **Write Checks - Checking** window:
Click **Banking** on the menu bar, click **Write Checks**
OR
Click the **Write Checks** icon in the Banking section of the Home Page
OR
Use the keyboard shortcut **Ctrl+W**
The Check No. should be **To Print**
- If not, click the check box **To be printed**

Date should be **01/31/06**
Enter **Your Name** on the **Pay to the Order of** line
Press the **Tab** key
- Because your name was not added to any list when the company was created, the **Name Not Found** dialog box appears on the screen.

Click **Quick Add** to add your name to a list

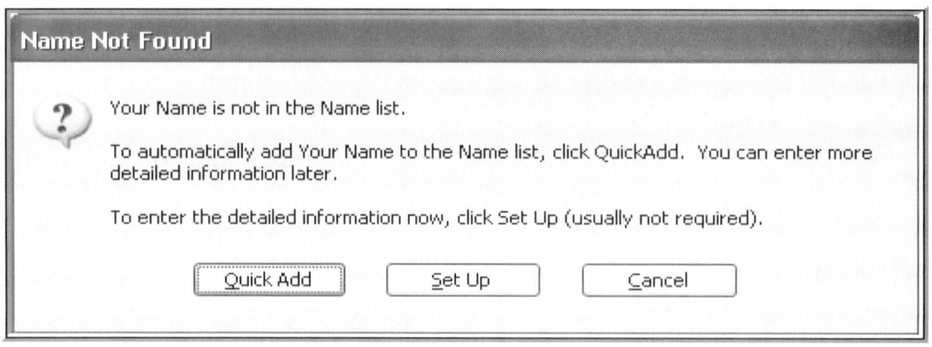

The **Select Name Type** dialog box appears
Click **Other**

Click **OK**

- Your name is added to a list of "Other" names, which are used for owners, partners, and other miscellaneous names.

Tab to or click in the area for the amount of the check

- If necessary, delete any numbers showing for the amount (0.00).

Enter **2500**
Tab to or click **Memo** on the check
Enter **Owner Withdrawal for January**
Tab to or click in the **Account** column at the bottom of the check
Click the drop-down list arrow, click the Equity account **Draws**

- The amount 2,500.00 should appear in the **Amount** column.
- If it does not, tab to or click in the **Amount** column and enter 2500.

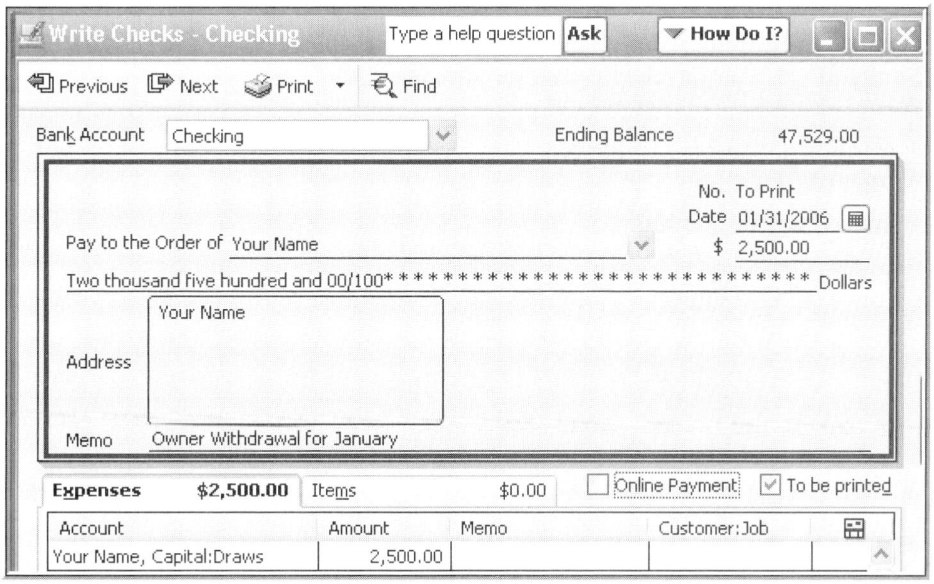

Click **Print** to print the check
The **Print Check** dialog box appears
Printed Check Number should be **9**

- If necessary, change the number to 9.

Click **OK**
Print the standard style check as previously instructed
Once the check has printed successfully, click **OK** to close the **Did check(s) print OK?** dialog box
Click **Save & Close** to record the check

ADDITIONAL CASH INVESTMENT BY OWNER

An owner may decide to invest more of his or her personal cash in the business at any time. The new investment is entered into the owner's investment account and into cash. The investment may be recorded in the account register for checking or in the register for the owner's investment account. It may also be recorded in the Journal.

MEMO
DATE: January 31, 2006

You received money from a certificate of deposit. Rather than reinvest in another certificate of deposit, you have decided to invest an additional $5,000 in the company.

Record the owner's additional cash investment in the Journal

Access the General Journal as previously instructed
The **Date** should be **01/31/06**

- Nothing is needed for Entry No.

Debit **Checking, $5,000**
Credit **Investments, $5,000**

- This account is listed as a subaccount of Your Name, Capital

The memo for both entries should be **Cash Investment**

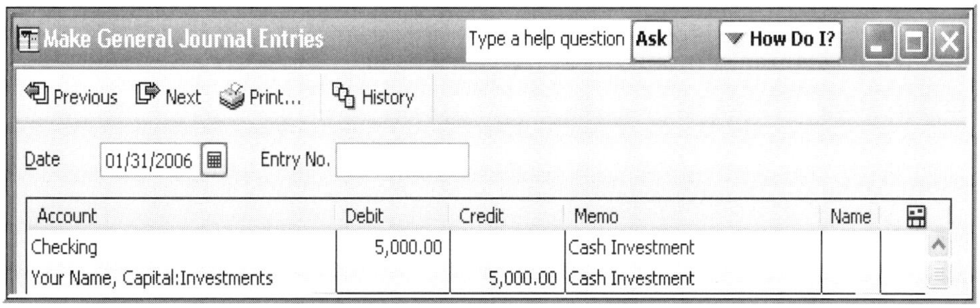

Click **Save & New** to record and go to the next blank **Make General Journal Entries** screen

NONCASH INVESTMENT BY OWNER

An owner may make investments in a business at any time. The investment may be cash; but it may also be something such as reference books, equipment, tools, buildings, and so on. Additional investments by an owner(s) are added to owner's equity. In the case of a sole proprietor, the investment is added to the Capital account for Investments.

MEMO
DATE: January 31, 2006

Originally, you planned to have an office in your home as well as in the company and purchased new office furniture for your home. Since then, you decided the business environment would appear more professional if the new furniture were in the office rather than your home. You gave the new office furniture to the company as an additional owner investment. The value of the investment is $3,000.

Record the non-cash investment in the Journal

The **Date** should be **01/31/06**
Nothing is needed for Entry No.
Debit **Office Furniture and Equipment: Original Cost, $3,000**

- Make sure you Debit the subaccount Original Cost not the controlling account Office Furniture and Equipment.

Credit **Investments, $3,000**

- This account is listed as a subaccount of Your Name, Capital

The memo for both entries should be **Investment of Furniture**

- If you wish to copy the memo for the second entry rather than retype it, drag through the memo text to highlight; press Ctrl+C; position the cursor in the memo area for the second entry; press Ctrl+V.

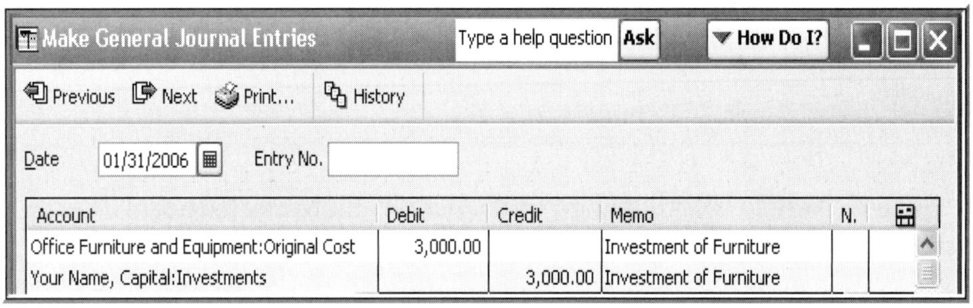

Click **Save & Close** to record and exit

- If you get a message regarding Tracking Fixed Assets, click **OK.**

VIEW BALANCE SHEET

Prior to the owner's making an additional investment in the business, there had been no withdrawals, and the drawing account balance was zero. Once the owner makes a withdrawal, that amount is carried forward in the owner's drawing account. Subsequent withdrawals are added to this account. When you view the Balance Sheet, notice the balance of the Drawing account after the check for the withdrawal was written. Also notice the Net Income account that appears in the equity section of the Balance Sheet. This account is automatically added by QuickBooks Pro to track the net income for the year.

View a Standard Balance Sheet:

Click **Reports** on the menu bar, point to **Company & Financial**, click **Balance Sheet Standard**
OR
Click the **Report Center** button, click **Company & Financial**, click **Balance Sheet Standard**
Tab to or click **As of**
Enter the date **01/31/06**
Tab to generate the report
Scroll through the report

- Notice the Equity section, especially Net Income.

Your Name Computer Consulting
Balance Sheet
As of January 31, 2006

		Jan 31, 06
Loan Payable		
Business Vehicles Loan	35,000.00	
Office Furniture/Equipment Loan	4,000.00	
Total Loan Payable		39,000.00
Total Long Term Liabilities		39,000.00
Total Liabilities		42,764.00
Equity		
Your Name, Capital		
Draws	-2,500.00	
Investments	33,000.00	
Your Name, Capital - Other	53,135.00	
Total Your Name, Capital		83,635.00
Net Income		4,385.71
Total Equity		88,020.71
TOTAL LIABILITIES & EQUITY		**130,784.71**

Partial Report

Close the report and, if necessary, the Report Center

BANK RECONCILIATION

Each month, the checking account should be reconciled with the bank statement to make sure that the balances agree. The bank statement will rarely have an ending balance that matches the balance of the checking account. This is due to several factors: outstanding checks (written by the business but not paid by the bank), deposits in transit (deposits that were made too late to be included on the bank statement), bank service charges, interest earned on checking accounts, collections made by the bank, and errors made in recording checks and/or deposits by the company or by the bank.

In order to have an accurate amount listed as the balance in the checking account, it is important that the differences between the bank statement and the checking account be reconciled. If something such as a service charge or a collection made by the bank appears on the bank statement, it needs to be recorded in the checking account.

Reconciling a bank statement is an appropriate time to find any errors that may have been recorded in the checking account. The reconciliation may be out of balance because a transposition was made (recording $94 rather than $49), a transaction was recorded backwards, a transaction was recorded twice, or a transaction was not recorded at all. If a transposition was made, the error may be found by dividing the difference by 9. For example, if $94 was recorded and the actual transaction amount was $49, you would subtract 49 from 94 to get 45. The number 45 can be divided by 9, so your error was a transposition. If the error can be evenly divided by 2, the transaction may have been entered backwards. For example, if you were out of balance $200, look to see if you had any $100 transactions. Perhaps you recorded a $100 debit, and it should have been a credit (or vice versa).

BEGIN RECONCILIATION

To begin the reconciliation, you need to open the Reconcile - Checking window. Verify the information shown for the checking account. The Opening Balance should match the amount of the final balance on the last reconciliation, or it should match the starting account balance.

MEMO
DATE: January 31, 2006

Received the bank statement from Sunshine Bank. The bank statement is dated January 31, 2006. Consuelo Alcampo needs to reconcile the bank statement and print a Detail Reconciliation Report for you.

Reconcile the bank statement for January

Open the **Begin Reconciliation** window and enter preliminary information
Open **Chart of Accounts** as previously instructed, click **Checking**, click **Activities**, click **Reconcile**
OR
Click the **Reconcile** icon in the Banking section of the Home Page
The **Account To Reconcile** should be **Checking**
If not, click the drop-down list arrow, click **Checking**
The Statement Date should be **013106**

- The Statement Date is entered automatically by the computer. If it the date is not shown at 01/31/06, change it.
- You may see several previous dates listed. Disregard them at this time.

Opening Balance should be **12,870**

- This is the same amount as the checking account starting balance.

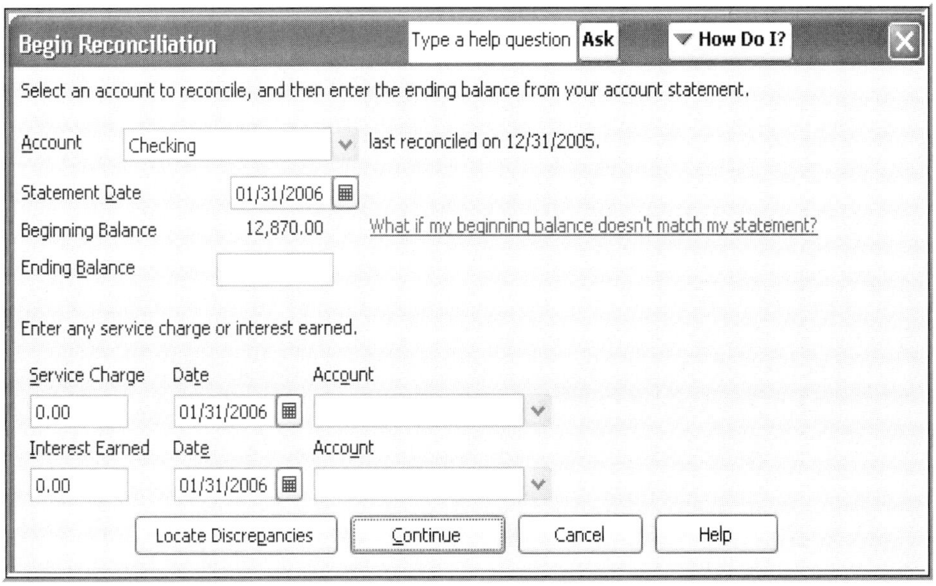

ENTER BANK STATEMENT INFORMATION FOR BEGIN RECONCILIATION

Some information appearing on the bank statement is entered into the Begin Reconciliation window as the next step. This information includes bank service charges and interest earned.

Continue to reconcile the following bank statement with the checking account

SUNSHINE BANK
12345 West Colorado Avenue
Woodland Hills, CA 91377
(818) 555-3880

BANK STATEMENT FOR:
Your Name Computer Consulting
2895 West Avenue
Woodland Hills, CA 91367

Acct. # 123-456-7890 **January 2006**

Beginning Balance 1/1/06			$12,870.00
01/02/06 Deposit	25,000.00		37,870.00
1/11/06 Deposit	13,840.00		51,710.00
1/26/06 Cash Transfer		110.00	51,600.00
1/26/06 Check 1		840.00	50,760.00
1/26/06 Check 2		195.00	50,565.00
1/26/06 Check 3		500.00	50,065.00
1/30/06 Vehicle Loan Pmt.: $467.19 Principal, $255.22 Interest		722.41	49,342.59
1/30/06 Office Equip. Loan Pmt.: $29.17 Principal, $53.39 Interest		82.56	49,260.03
1/30/06 Service Chg.		8.00	49,252.03
1/30/06 Interest	66.43		49,318.46
Ending Balance 1/30/06			49,318.46

Enter the **Ending Balance** from the Bank Statement, **49,318.46**
Tab to or click **Service Charge**
Enter **8.00**
Tab to or click Service Charge **Date**; if necessary, change to **01/31/2006**

- Don't forget to check the date. If you leave an incorrect date, you will have errors in your accounts and in your reports.

Tab to or click **Account**
Click the drop-down list arrow for **Account**
Click **Bank Service Charges**
Tab to or click **Interest Earned**, enter **66.43**
Tab to or click Interest Earned **Date**; if necessary, change to **01/31/2006**
Tab to or click **Account**
Click the drop-down list arrow for **Account**
Scroll through the list of accounts, click **Interest Income**

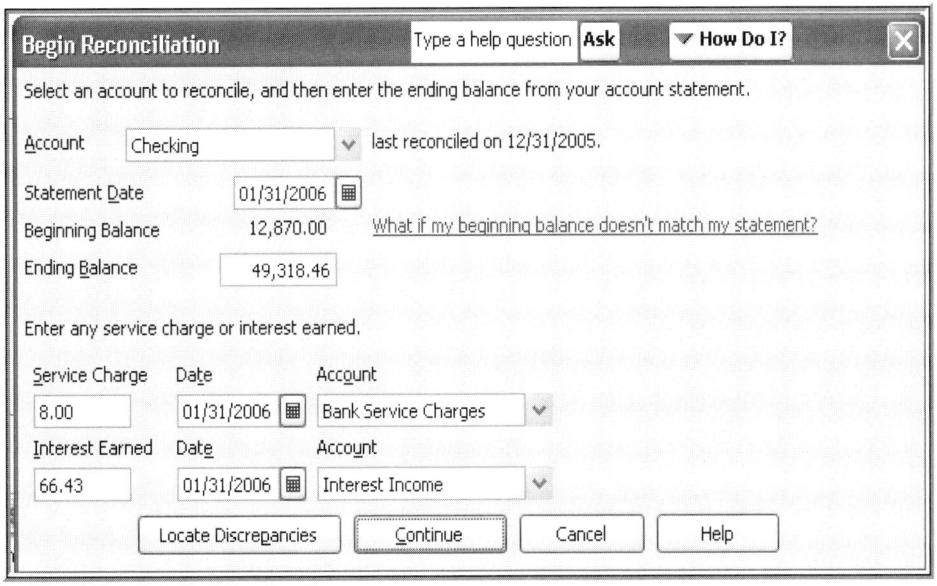

Click **Continue**

MARK CLEARED TRANSACTIONS FOR BANK RECONCILIATION

Once bank statement information for service charges and interest has been entered, compare the checks and deposits listed on the statement with the transactions for the checking account. Remember, the dates shown for the checks on the bank statement are the dates the checks were processed by the bank, not the dates the checks were written. If a deposit or a check is listed correctly on the bank statement and in the Reconcile - Checking window, it has cleared and should be marked. An item may be marked individually by positioning the cursor on the deposit or the check and clicking the primary mouse button. If all deposits and checks match, click the Mark All button. To remove all the checks, click the Unmark All button. To unmark an individual item, click the item to remove the check mark.

Mark cleared checks and deposits

Compare the bank statement with the **Reconcile - Checking** window
Click the items that appear on both statements

- *Note*: The date next to the check or the deposit on the bank statement is the date the check or deposit cleared the bank, not the date the check was written or the deposit was made.
- If you are unable to complete the reconciliation in one session, click the **Leave** button to leave the reconciliation and return to it later. Under no circumstances should you click **Reconcile Now** until the reconciliation is complete.

Include the Petty Cash transaction on 1/26/06 even though the bank statement shows 110 and the check register shows 100.

Look at the bottom of the **Reconcile - Checking** window

You have marked cleared:

4 Deposits, Interest and Other Credits for 38,906.43

- This includes interest earned and the voided check to Communication Telephone Co.

5 Checks, Payments, and Service Charges for 1,643.00

- This includes the $100 for petty cash and the $8 service charge.

The Ending Balance is 49,318.46

The Cleared Balance is 50,133.43

There is a Difference of -814.97

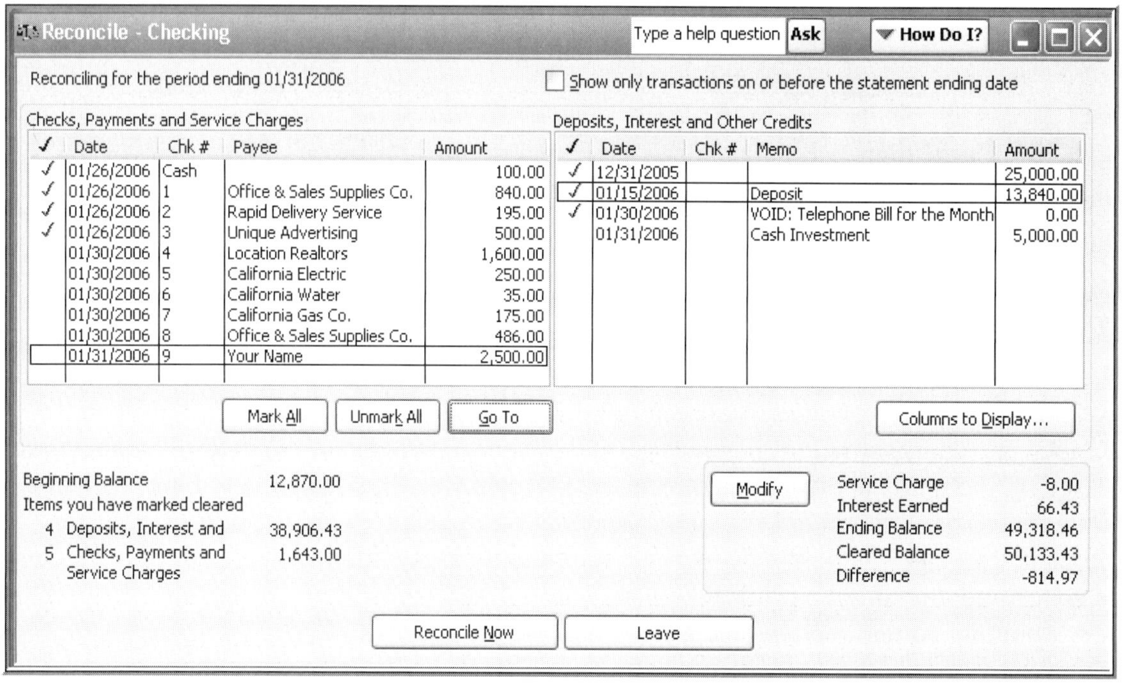

ADJUSTING AND CORRECTING ENTRIES—BANK RECONCILIATION

As you complete the reconciliation, you may find errors that need to be corrected or transactions that need to be recorded. Anything entered as a service charge or interest earned will be entered automatically when the reconciliation is complete and the Reconcile Now button is clicked. To correct an error such as a transposition, click on the entry, then click the Go To button. The original entry will appear on the screen. The correction can be made and will show in the Reconcile - Checking window. If there is a transaction, such as an automatic loan payment to the bank, you need to access the register for the account used in the transaction and enter the payment.

Correct the error on the transfer into Petty Cash and enter the automatic loan payments shown on the bank statement.

Correct the entry for the transfer of cash into Petty Cash:
In the section of the reconciliation for **Checks and Payments**, click the entry for **Cash** made on **01/26/06**

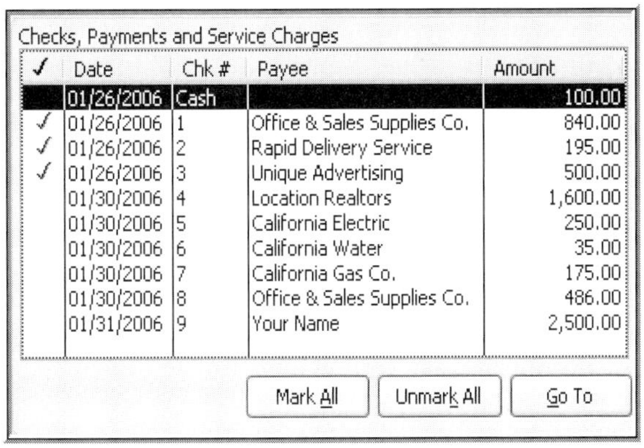

Click the **Go To** button
Change the amount on **Transfer Funds Between Accounts** from 100 to **110**

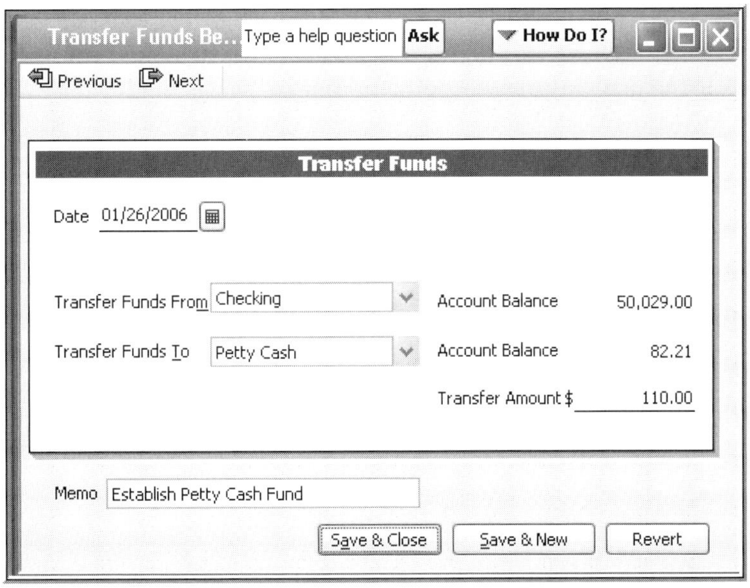

Click **Save & Close**
Click **Yes** on the **Change Transaction** dialog box

- Notice that the amount for the Petty Cash transaction now shows 110.

If necessary, click the Petty Cash transaction to mark it.

With the **Reconcile - Checking** window still showing, enter the automatic loan payments:

Click **Edit** on the menu bar, click **Use Register**

OR

Use the keyboard shortcut **Ctrl+R**

In the blank transaction at the bottom of the Checking register enter the **Date**, **01/31/06**

Tab to or click **Number**

Enter **Transfer**

Tab to or click **Payee**

Enter **Sunshine Bank**

Tab to or click the **Payment** column

- Because Sunshine Bank does not appear on any list, you will get a **Name Not Found** dialog box when you move to another field.

Click the **Quick Add** button to add the name of the bank to the Name list

Click **Other**

Click **OK**

- Once the name of the bank has been added to the Other list, the cursor will be positioned in the **Payment** column.

Enter **722.41** in the **Payment** column

Click the **Account** column

Click the **Splits** button at the bottom of the register

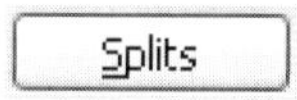

Click the drop-down list arrow for **Account**

Click **Interest on Loans** under Interest Expense

Tab to or click **Amount**, delete the amount 722.41 shown

Enter **255.22** as the amount of interest

Tab to or click **Memo**

Enter **Interest Business Vehicles Loan**

Tab to or click **Account**

Click the drop-down list arrow for **Account**

Click **Business Vehicles Loan** under Loan Payable

- The correct amount of principal, 467.19, should be showing for the amount.

Tab to or click **Memo**

Enter **Principal Business Vehicles Loan**

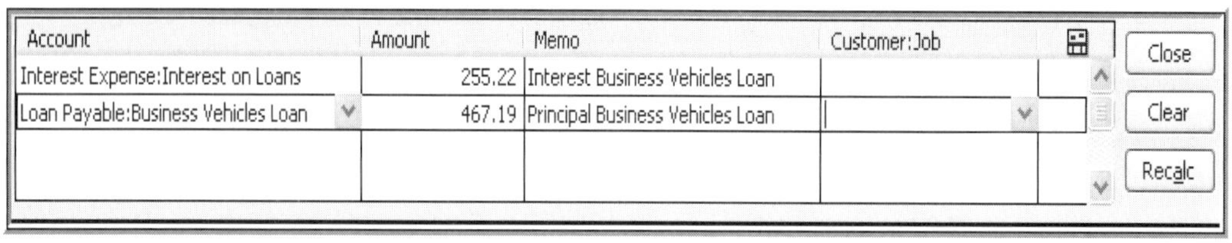

Click **Close**

- This closes the window for the information regarding the way the transaction is to be "split" between accounts.

For the **Memo** in the Checking Register, record **Loan Pmt., Business Vehicles**
Click the **Record** button to record the transaction

- Because the **Register** organizes transactions according to date, you will notice that the loan payment will not appear as the last transaction in the Register. You may need to scroll through the Register to see the transaction.

01/31/2006	Transfer	Sunshine Bank	722.41		46,796.59
	CHK	-split- Loan Pmt., Business Vehicles			

Repeat the procedures to record the loan payment for office equipment

- When you enter the Payee as Sunshine Bank, the amount for the previous transaction (722.41) appears in Amount.

Enter the new amount, **82.56**
Click **Splits** button
Click the appropriate accounts and enter the correct amount for each item

- Refer to the bank statement for details regarding the amount of the payment for interest and the amount of the payment applied to principal.
- *Note*: The amounts for the previous loan payment automatically appear. You will need to enter the amounts for both accounts in this transaction.

Account	Amount	Memo	Customer:Job
Interest Expense:Interest on Loans	53.39	Interest Office Equipment Loan	
Loan Payable:Office Furniture/Equipment Loan	29.17	Principal Office Equipment Loan	

Close | Clear | Recalc

Click **Close** to close the window for the information regarding the "split" between accounts
Enter the transaction Memo **Loan Pmt., Office Equipment**
Click **Record** to record the loan payment

01/31/2006	Transfer	Sunshine Bank	82.56		46,714.03
	CHK	-split- Loan Pmt., Office Equipment			

Close the **Checking** Register

- You should return to **Reconcile - Checking**.

Scroll to the top of **Checks and Payments**

- Notice the two entries for the payments in **Checks and Payments**.

Mark the two entries

- At this point, the **Ending Balance** and **Cleared Balance** should be equal—$49,318.46 with a difference of 0.00.

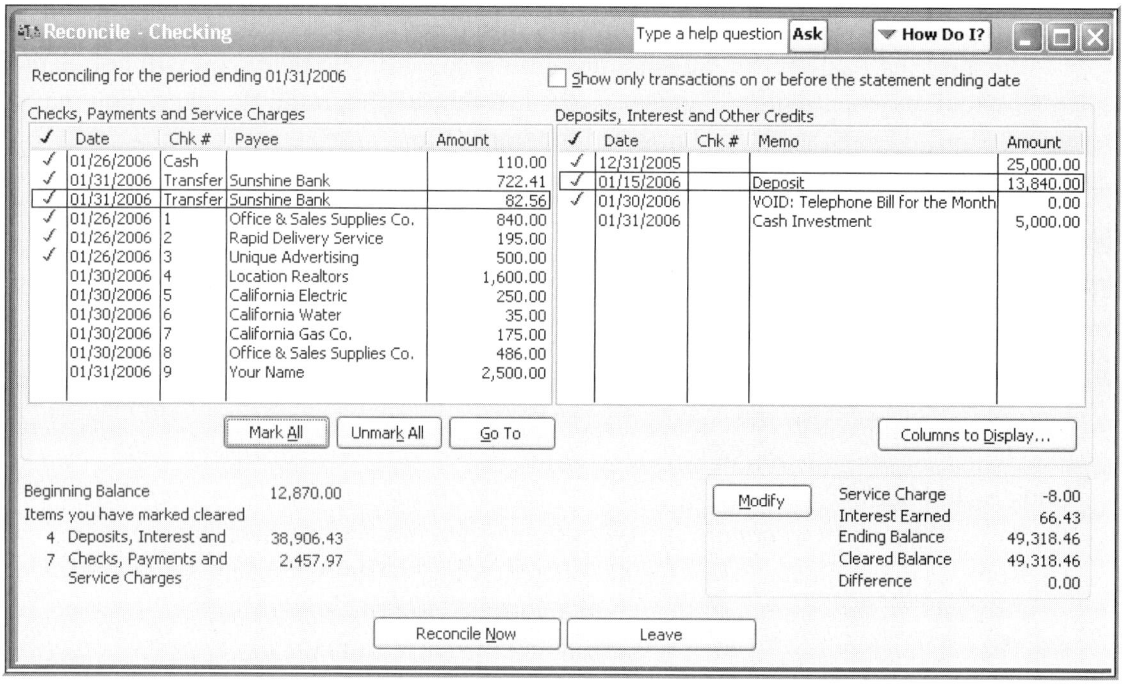

If your entries agree with the above, click **Reconcile Now** to finish the reconciliation

- If your reconciliation is not in agreement, do not click **Reconcile Now** until the errors are corrected.
- Once you click **Reconcile Now**, you may not return to this **Reconciliation - Checking** window.
- If you get an Information screen referring to online banking, click **OK**

PRINT A RECONCILIATION REPORT

As soon as the Ending Balance and the Cleared Balance are equal or when you finish marking and click Reconcile Now, a screen appears allowing you to select the level of Reconciliation report you would like to print. You may select Summary and get a report that lists totals only or Detail and get all the transactions that were reconciled on the report. You may print the report at the time you have finished reconciling the account or you may print the report later by returning to the Reconciliation window. QuickBooks Pro keeps your last two reconciliation reports in memory. If you think you may want to print the report again in the future, print the report to a file to save it permanently.

Print a **Detail Reconciliation Report**

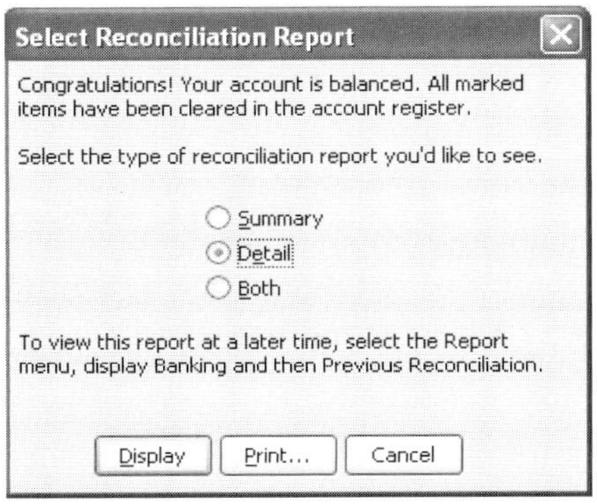

On the **Select Reconciliation Report** screen, click **Detail**

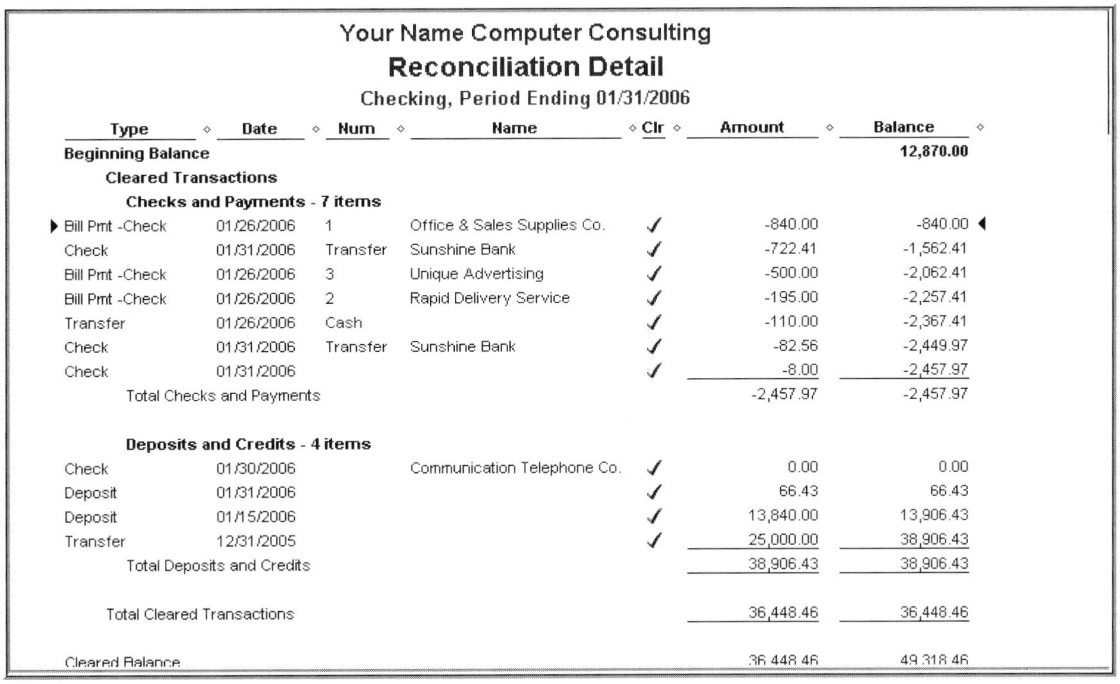

Your Name Computer Consulting
Reconciliation Detail
Checking, Period Ending 01/31/2006

Type	Date	Num	Name	Clr	Amount	Balance
Beginning Balance						**12,870.00**
Cleared Transactions						
Checks and Payments - 7 items						
Bill Pmt -Check	01/26/2006	1	Office & Sales Supplies Co.	✓	-840.00	-840.00
Check	01/31/2006	Transfer	Sunshine Bank	✓	-722.41	-1,562.41
Bill Pmt -Check	01/26/2006	3	Unique Advertising	✓	-500.00	-2,062.41
Bill Pmt -Check	01/26/2006	2	Rapid Delivery Service	✓	-195.00	-2,257.41
Transfer	01/26/2006	Cash		✓	-110.00	-2,367.41
Check	01/31/2006	Transfer	Sunshine Bank	✓	-82.56	-2,449.97
Check	01/31/2006			✓	-8.00	-2,457.97
Total Checks and Payments					-2,457.97	-2,457.97
Deposits and Credits - 4 items						
Check	01/30/2006		Communication Telephone Co.	✓	0.00	0.00
Deposit	01/31/2006			✓	66.43	66.43
Deposit	01/15/2006			✓	13,840.00	13,906.43
Transfer	12/31/2005			✓	25,000.00	38,906.43
Total Deposits and Credits					38,906.43	38,906.43
Total Cleared Transactions					36,448.46	36,448.46
Cleared Balance					36,448.46	49,318.46

Click the **Print** button
Print as previously instructed:
Printer should be default printer
Orientation is **Portrait**
Page Range is **All**
If your report printed correctly, close the report

- The uncleared information may be different than the report printed in the answer key. This is due to the fact that your computer's date may be different than January 31, 2006. As long as the cleared balance is $49,318.46, your report should be considered correct.

VIEW THE CHECKING ACCOUNT REGISTER

Once the bank reconciliation has been completed, it is wise to scroll through the Check register to view the effect of the reconciliation on the account. You will notice that the check column shows a check mark for all items that were marked as cleared during the reconciliation. If at a later date an error is discovered, the transaction may be changed, and the correction will be reflected in the Beginning Balance on the reconciliation.

View the register for the Checking account

Access the register as previously instructed
To display more of the register, click the check box for **1-Line**
Scroll through the register

- Notice that the transactions are listed in chronological order.

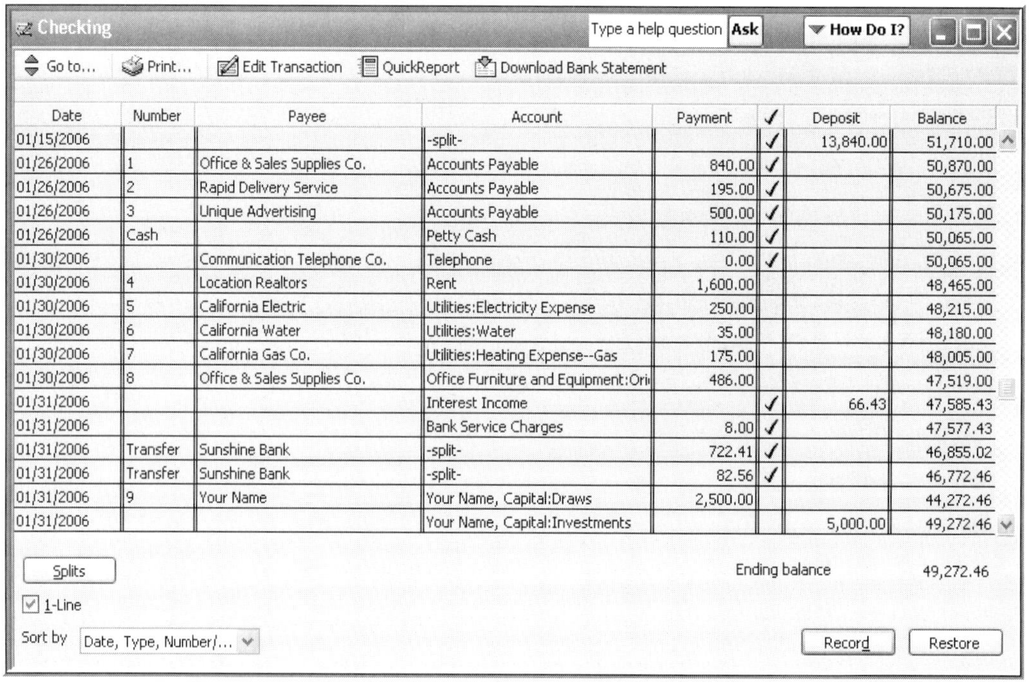

EDIT CLEARED TRANSACTIONS

Edit a transaction that was marked and cleared during the bank reconciliation:

Edit the **Petty Cash** transaction:
Click in the entry for the transfer of funds to **Petty Cash** on January 26
Change the **Payment** amount to **100**
Click **Record**

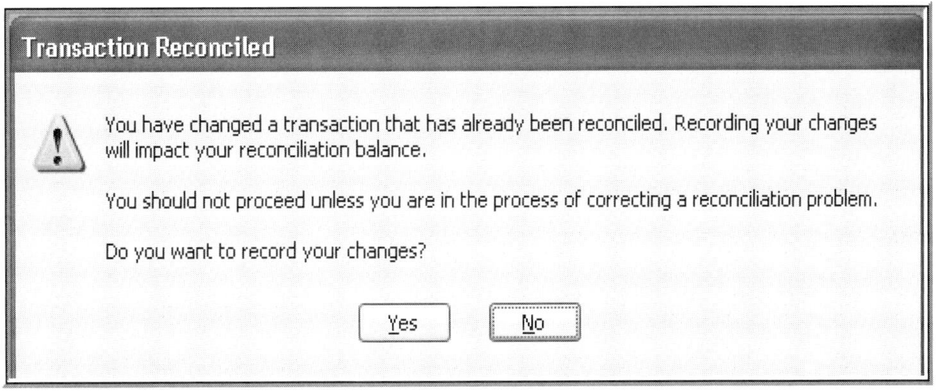

Click **Yes** on the **Transaction Cleared** dialog box

- The transaction amount has been changed.

Close the **Checking Register** and return to the Chart of Accounts

View the effects of the change to the Petty Cash transaction in the Begin Reconciliation window:

Display the **Begin Reconciliation** window by:

Making sure **Checking** is highlighted, clicking the **Activities** button, and clicking **Reconcile**

- Notice that the Opening Balance has been increased by $10 and shows $49,328.46.

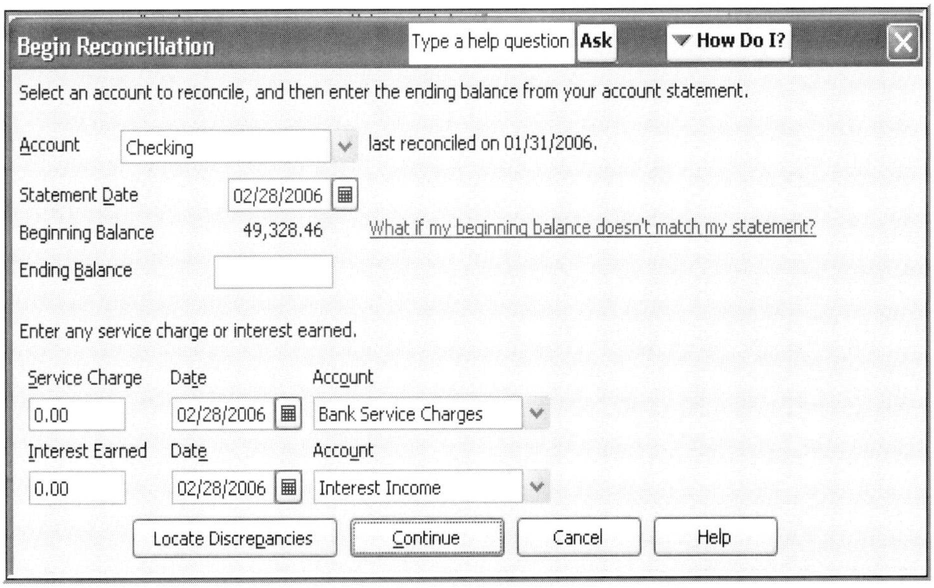

Click the **Cancel** button on the bottom of the **Begin Reconciliation** screen and return to the Chart of Accounts

Open the **Checking** account register

Change the amount for the **Petty Cash** transaction back to **110**

Click **Record** to record the change
Click **Yes** on the **Transaction Cleared** dialog box

01/26/2006	3	Unique Advertising	Accounts Payable	500.00	✓		50,175.00
01/26/2006	Cash	Payee	Petty Cash	110.00		Deposit	50,065.00
01/30/2006		Communication Telephone Co.	Telephone	0.00	✓		50,065.00

Close the **Checking Register** and the **Chart of Accounts**

VIEW THE JOURNAL

After entering several transactions, it is helpful to view the Journal. In the Journal, all transactions, regardless of the method of entry are shown in traditional debit/credit format.

View the **Journal** for January

Click the **Report Center** button, click **Accountant & Taxes** as the type of report, click **Journal**

- If you will be preparing several reports, using the Report Center is much more efficient.

Tab to or click **From**

- If necessary, delete existing date.

Enter **01/01/06**
Tab to or click **To**
Enter **01/31/06**
Tab to generate the report
Scroll through the report
Verify the total of $57,919.69

Your Name Computer Consulting
Journal
January 2006

Trans #	Type	Date	Num	Name	Memo	Account	Debit	Credit
73	Check	01/31/2006	Transfer	Sunshine Bank	Loan Pmt., Business Vehicles	Checking		722.41
				Sunshine Bank	Interest Business Vehicles ...	Interest on Loans	255.22	
				Sunshine Bank	Principal Business Vehicles...	Business Vehicles Loan	467.19	
							722.41	722.41
74	Check	01/31/2006	Transfer	Sunshine Bank	Loan Pmt., Office Equipment	Checking		82.56
				Sunshine Bank	Interest Office Equipment L...	Interest on Loans	53.39	
				Sunshine Bank	Principal Office Equipment L...	Office Furniture/Equipment Loan	29.17	
							82.56	82.56
75	Check	01/31/2006			Service Charge	Checking		8.00
					Service Charge	Bank Service Charges	8.00	
							8.00	8.00
76	Deposit	01/31/2006			Interest	Checking	66.43	
					Interest	Interest Income		66.43
							66.43	66.43
TOTAL							57,919.69	57,919.69

Close the **Journal** without printing
Do not close the Report Center

PREPARE TRIAL BALANCE

After all adjustments have been recorded and the bank reconciliation has been completed, it is wise to prepare the Trial Balance. As in traditional accounting, the QuickBooks Pro Trial Balance proves that debits equal credits.

MEMO
DATE: January 31, 2006

Because adjustments have been entered, prepare a Trial Balance.

Prepare a Trial Balance

Click **Trial Balance** on the Accountant & Taxes report
Enter the dates from **01/01/06** to **01/31/06**
Tab to generate the report
Scroll through the report and study the amounts shown

- Notice that the final totals of debits and credits are equal: $138,119.07.

Your Name Computer Consulting
Trial Balance
As of January 31, 2006

	Jan 31, 06	
	Debit	Credit
Income:Technical Support Income		900.00
Income:Training Income		7,850.00
Advertising Expense	260.00	
Bank Service Charges	8.00	
Business Vehicles Expense	588.88	
Depreciation Expense	725.00	
Dues and Subscriptions	79.00	
Equipment Rental	25.00	
Insurance:Business Vehicles Insurance	237.50	
Interest Expense:Interest on Loans	308.61	
Office Supplies Expense	368.57	
Postage and Delivery	195.34	
Rent	1,600.00	
Telephone	0.00	
Utilities:Electricity Expense	250.00	
Utilities:Heating Expense--Gas	175.00	
Utilities:Water	35.00	
Interest Income		66.43
TOTAL	138,119.07	138,119.07

USE QUICKZOOM IN TRIAL BALANCE

QuickZoom is a QuickBooks Pro feature that allows you to make a closer observation of transactions, amounts, and other entries. With QuickZoom you may zoom in on an item when the mouse pointer turns into a magnifying glass with a Z inside. If you point to an item and you do not get a magnifying glass with a Z inside, you cannot zoom in on the item. For example, if you point to Interest Expense, you will see the magnifying glass with the Z inside. If your Trial Balance had Retained Earnings and you pointed to the account, the mouse pointer would not change from the arrow. This means that you can see transaction details for Interest Expense but not for Retained Earnings.

Use QuickZoom to view the details of Interest Expense:

Scroll through the Trial Balance until you see Interest Expense
Position the mouse pointer over the amount of Interest Expense: Interest on Loans, **308.61**

- Notice that the mouse pointer changes to a magnifying glass with a Z.

Double-click the primary mouse button

- A Transactions by Account Report appears on the screen showing the payment of loan interest as of 01/31/2006.

Enter the From date **010106** and the To date **013106**
Tab to generate the report
Scroll through the report

Your Name Computer Consulting
Transactions by Account
As of January 31, 2006

Type	Date	Num	Name	Memo	Clr	Split	Amount	Balance
Interest Expense								
Interest on Loans								
Check	01/31/2006	Transfer	Sunshine Bank	Interest Business Vehicles Loan		Checking	255.22	255.22
Check	01/31/2006	Transfer	Sunshine Bank	Interest Office Equipment Loan		Checking	53.39	308.61
Total Interest on Loans							308.61	308.61
Total Interest Expense							308.61	308.61
TOTAL							**308.61**	**308.61**

Close the Transactions by Account report without printing

PRINT THE TRIAL BALANCE

Once the Trial Balance has been prepared, it may be printed.

Print the Trial Balance

Click the **Print** button at the top of the **Trial Balance**
Verify the **Settings** as previously instructed to print in Portrait Orientation
Click the **Preview** button to view a miniature copy of the report

- This helps determine the orientation and whether you need to select the feature to print one page wide.

Click **Close**
Click **Print**
Close the **Trial Balance**
Do not close the **Report Center**

SELECT ACCRUAL-BASIS REPORTING PREFERENCE

QuickBooks Pro allows a business to customize the program and select certain preferences for reports, displays, graphs, accounts, and so on. There are two report preferences available in QuickBooks Pro: Cash and Accrual. You need to choose the one you prefer. If you select Cash as the report preference, income on reports will be shown as of the date payment is received and expenses will be shown as of the date you pay the bill. If Accrual is selected, QuickBooks Pro shows the income on the report as of the date of the invoice and expenses as of the bill date. Prior to printing end-of-period reports, it is advisable to verify which reporting basis is selected. If cash has been selected and you are using the accrual method, it is imperative that you change your report basis.

MEMO
DATE: January 31, 2006

Prior to printing reports, check the report preference selected for the company. If necessary, choose Accrual. After the selection has been made, print a Standard Profit and Loss and a Standard Balance Sheet for Your Name Computer Consulting.

Select **Accrual** as the **Summary Reports Basis**

Click **Edit** on the menu bar, click **Preferences**
Scroll through the Preferences list until you see **Reports & Graphs**
Click **Reports & Graphs**

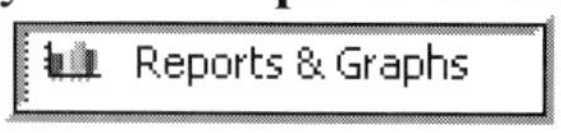

Click the **Company Preferences** tab
If necessary, click **Accrual** to select the **Summary Reports Basis**

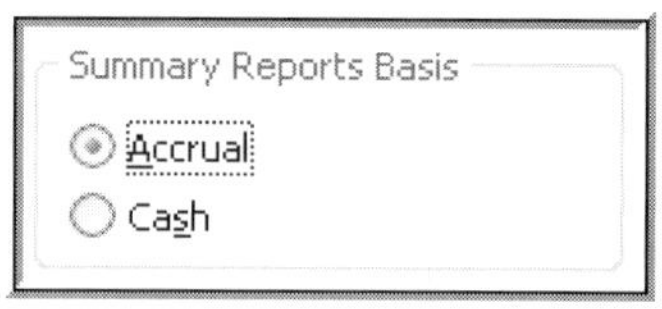

Click **OK** to close the **Preferences** window

PREPARE AND PRINT CASH FLOW FORECAST

In planning for the cash needs of a business, QuickBooks Pro can prepare a Cash Flow Forecast. This report is useful when determining the expected income and disbursement of cash. It is important to know if your company will have enough cash on hand to meet its obligations. A company with too little cash on hand may have to borrow money to pay its bills, while another company with excess cash may miss out on investment, expansion, or dividend opportunities. QuickBooks Pro Cash Flow Forecast does not analyze investments. It simply projects the amount you will be receiving if all those who owe you money pay on time and the amounts you will be spending to pay your accounts payable on time.

MEMO
DATE: January 31, 2006

Since this is the end of January, prepare Cash Flow Forecast for February 1-28, 2006.

Prepare Cash Flow Forecast for February

The Report Center should still be on the screen, if it is not, open it as previously instructed

Click **Company & Financial** in the type of reports section, scroll through the list of reports, click **Cash Flow Forecast**

Enter the **From** date of **02/01/06** and the **To** date of **02/28/06**

Tab to generate the report

- Notice that **Periods** show **Week**. Use Week, but click the drop-down list arrow to see the periods available for the report.
- Analyze the report for February: The Beginning Balance for Accounts Receivable shows the amounts due from customers as of 1/31/06.
- The amounts for A/R and A/P for the future weeks are for the customer payments you expect to receive and the bills you expect to pay. This information is based on the due dates for invoices and bills.
- The bank account amount for future weeks is based on deposits made or deposits that need to be made.
- Net Inflows summarizes the amounts that should be received and the amounts that should be paid to get a net inflow of cash.
- The projected balance is the total in all bank accounts if all customer and bill payments are made on time.

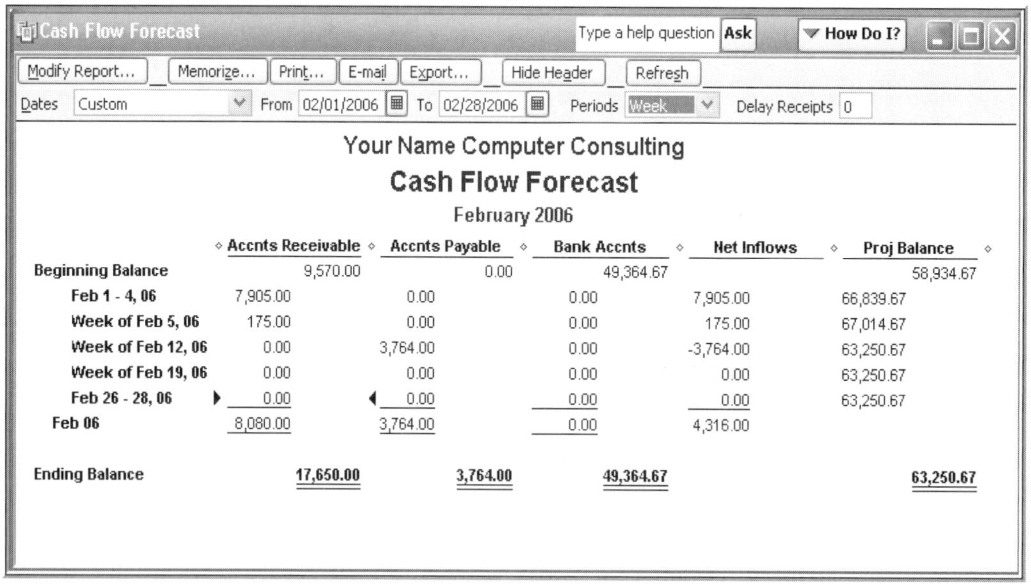

Your Name Computer Consulting

Cash Flow Forecast

February 2006

	Accnts Receivable	Accnts Payable	Bank Accnts	Net Inflows	Proj Balance
Beginning Balance	9,570.00	0.00	49,364.67		58,934.67
Feb 1 - 4, 06	7,905.00	0.00	0.00	7,905.00	66,839.67
Week of Feb 5, 06	175.00	0.00	0.00	175.00	67,014.67
Week of Feb 12, 06	0.00	3,764.00	0.00	-3,764.00	63,250.67
Week of Feb 19, 06	0.00	0.00	0.00	0.00	63,250.67
Feb 26 - 28, 06	0.00	0.00	0.00	0.00	63,250.67
Feb 06	8,080.00	3,764.00	0.00	4,316.00	
Ending Balance	**17,650.00**	**3,764.00**	**49,364.67**		**63,250.67**

Print the report for February in **Landscape**
Use **Preview** to determine if it is necessary to use **Fit report to one page wide**
Close the report
Do not close the Report Center

STATEMENT OF CASH FLOWS

Another report that details the amount of cash flow in a business is the Statement of Cash Flows. This report organizes information regarding cash in three areas of activities: Operating Activities, Investing Activities, and Financing Activities. The report also projects the amount of cash at the end of a period.

MEMO
DATE: January 31, 2006

Prepare Statement of Cash Flows for January 1-31, 2006.

Prepare Statement of Cash Flows for January

Click **Statement of Cash Flows** in the **Company & Financial** list of reports
Enter the **From** date of **01/01/06** and the **To** date of **01/31/06**

Tab to generate the report

Your Name Computer Consulting
Statement of Cash Flows
January 2006

	Jan 06
Accounts Payable	2,914.00
Net cash provided by Operating Activities	9,252.03
INVESTING ACTIVITIES	
Business Vehicles:Depreciation	583.00
Office Furniture and Equipment:Depreciation	142.00
Office Furniture and Equipment:Original Cost	-3,486.00
Net cash provided by Investing Activities	-2,761.00
FINANCING ACTIVITIES	
Loan Payable:Business Vehicles Loan	-467.19
Loan Payable:Office Furniture/Equipment Loan	-29.17
Your Name, Capital:Draws	-2,500.00
Your Name, Capital:Investments	8,000.00
Net cash provided by Financing Activities	5,003.64
Net cash increase for period	11,494.67
Cash at beginning of period	37,870.00
Cash at end of period	**49,364.67**

Print the report in Portrait mode following previous instructions
Close the report
Do not close the Report Center

PRINT STANDARD PROFIT AND LOSS STATEMENT

Because all income, expenses, and adjustments have been made for the period, a Profit and Loss Statement can be prepared. This statement is also known as the Income Statement. QuickBooks Pro has several different types of Profit and Loss statements available: Standard—summarizes income and expenses; Detail—shows the year-to-date transactions for each income and expense account; YTD Comparison—is like the Standard Profit and Loss but summarizes your income and expenses for this month and compares them to your income and expenses for the current fiscal year; Prev Year Comparison—is like the standard statement but summarizes your income and expenses for both this month and this month last year; By Job—is like the Standard Profit and Loss statement, but has columns for each customer and job and amounts for this year to date; By Class—is like the Standard Profit and Loss statement, but has columns for each class and sub-class with the amounts for this year to date, and Unclassified—is like the Standard Profit and Loss statement, but shows how much you are making or losing within segments of your business that are not assigned to a QuickBooks class.

Print a **Standard Profit and Loss Report**

Click **Standard** as the type of Profit & Loss (Income Statement) to prepare in the list of Company & Financial reports
Enter the dates From **01/01/06** to **01/31/06**
Tab to generate the report
Scroll through the report to view the income and expenses listed

Your Name Computer Consulting
Profit & Loss
January 2006

		Jan 06
Utilities		
Electricity Expense	250.00	
Heating Expense--Gas	175.00	
Water	35.00	
Total Utilities		460.00
Total Expense		4,855.90
Net Ordinary Income		4,069.10
Other Income/Expense		
Other Income		
Interest Income		66.43
Total Other Income		66.43
Net Other Income		66.43
Net Income		**4,135.53**

Partial Report

Print the report in **Portrait** orientation
Close the **Profit and Loss Report**
Do not close Report Center

PREPARE A STANDARD BALANCE SHEET

The Balance Sheet proves the fundamental accounting equation: Assets = Liabilities + Owner's Equity. When all transactions and adjustments for the period have been recorded, a balance sheet should be prepared. QuickBooks Pro has several different types of Balance Sheet statements available: Standard—shows as of today the balance in each balance sheet account with subtotals provided for assets, liabilities, and equity; Detail—which is a more detailed version of the standard balance sheet report; Summary—shows amounts for each account type but not for individual accounts; and Prev. Year Comparison—has columns for a year ago today, $ change, and % change. For each account, the report shows the starting balance at the beginning of last month, transactions entered in the account for this month to date, and the ending balance as of today.

Prepare a **Standard Balance Sheet Report**

Click **Standard** as the type of Balance Sheet to prepare in the list of Company & Financial reports
Tab to or click **As of**, enter **01/31/06**, tab to generate the report
Scroll through the report to view the assets, liabilities, and equities listed

- Notice the Net Income account listed in the Equity section of the report. This is the same amount of Net Income shown on the Profit and Loss Statement.

Your Name Computer Consulting
Balance Sheet
As of January 31, 2006

	Jan 31, 06	
Office Furniture/Equipment Loan	3,970.83	
Total Loan Payable		38,503.64
Total Long Term Liabilities		38,503.64
Total Liabilities		42,267.64
Equity		
Your Name, Capital		
Draws	-2,500.00	
Investments	33,000.00	
Your Name, Capital - Other	53,135.00	
Total Your Name, Capital		83,635.00
Net Income		4,135.53
Total Equity		87,770.53
TOTAL LIABILITIES & EQUITY		**130,038.17**

Partial Report

Do not close the **Standard Balance Sheet**

ADJUSTMENT TO TRANSFER NET INCOME/RETAINED EARNINGS INTO YOUR NAME, CAPITAL

Because Your Name Computer Consulting is a sole proprietorship, the amount of net income should appear as part of your capital account rather than set aside in Retained Earnings as QuickBooks Pro does automatically. In many instances, this is the type of adjustment the CPA makes on the Accountant's Copy of the QuickBooks Pro company files. The adjustment may be made before the closing date for the fiscal year, or it may be made after the closing has been performed. Because QuickBooks Pro automatically transfers Net Income into Retained Earnings, the closing entry will transfer the net income into the Owner's Capital account. This adjustment is made in a Journal entry that debits Retained Earnings and credits the Owner's Capital account. When you view a report before the end of the year, you will see an amount in Net Income and the same amount as a negative in Retained Earnings. If you view a report after the end of the year, you will not see any information regarding Retained Earnings or Net Income because the adjustment correctly transferred the amount to the Owner's Capital account.

If you prefer to use the power of the program and not make the adjustment, QuickBooks Pro simply carries the amount of Retained Earnings forward. Each year net income is added to Retained Earnings. On the Balance Sheet, Retained Earnings and/or Net Income appears as part of the equity section. The owner's drawing and investment accounts are kept separate from Retained Earnings at all times.

Transfer the net income into Your Name, Capital account

Open the General Journal by clicking on **Company** on the menu bar, and clicking **Make General Journal Entries**
Enter the date of **01/31/06**
The first account used is **Retained Earnings**
Debit **Retained Earnings**, **4,135.53**

- Note: if the entire General Journal disappears during the transaction entry, simply open the Journal again and continue recording the transaction.

For the Memo record, **Transfer Net Income into Capital**
The other account used is **Your Name, Capital**
4,135.53 should appear as the credit amount for **Your Name, Capital**
Enter the same Memo

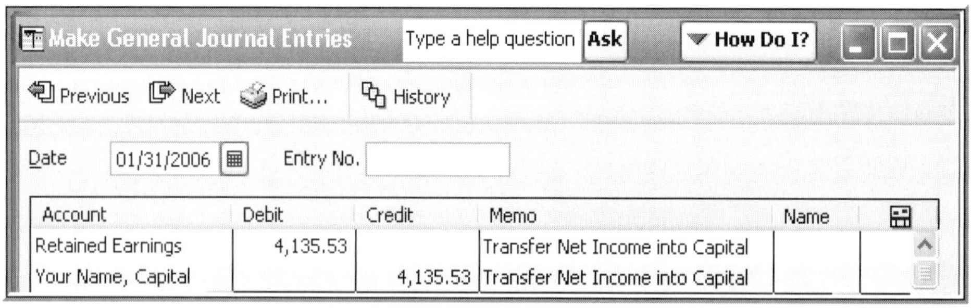

Click **Save & Close** to record and close the **General Journal**
If a Retained Earnings screen appears, click **OK**

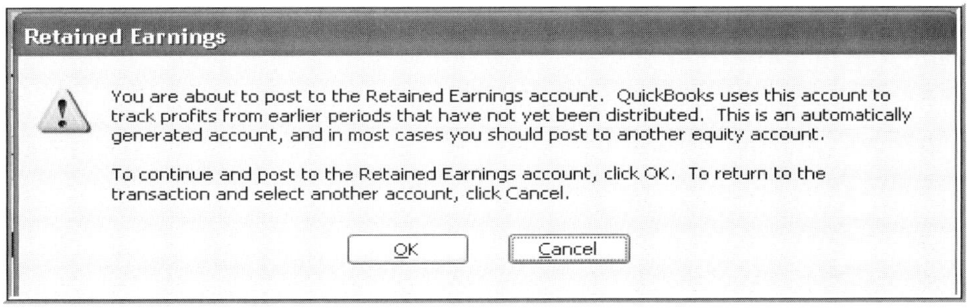

PRINT STANDARD BALANCE SHEET

Once the adjustment for Net Income/Retained Earnings has been performed, viewing or printing the Balance Sheet will show you the status of the Owner's Equity.

Print a **Standard Balance Sheet** for January 2006

The Standard Balance Sheet should still be showing on the screen
Scroll through the report

- Notice the Equity section, especially Retained Earnings and Net Income.

Prior to printing, change the title of the report by clicking **Modify Report**, clicking the **Header/Footer** tab, clicking at the end of **Balance Sheet** in the Report Title dialog box and keying **(After Transfer of Net Income)**, click **OK**

Your Name Computer Consulting
Balance Sheet (After Transfer of Net Income)
As of January 31, 2006

		Jan 31, 06
Total Loan Payable		38,503.64
Total Long Term Liabilities		38,503.64
Total Liabilities		42,267.64
Equity		
Retained Earnings		-4,135.53
Your Name, Capital		
Draws	-2,500.00	
Investments	33,000.00	
Your Name, Capital - Other	57,270.53	
Total Your Name, Capital		87,770.53
Net Income		4,135.53
Total Equity		87,770.53
TOTAL LIABILITIES & EQUITY		**130,038.17**

Partial Report After Adjusting Entry

Print the **Balance Sheet** for January 2006 in **Portrait** orientation

- The Balance Sheet shows on the screen after printing is complete.

Change the **As of** date to **01/31/07**

- Because you did not close the report, the title does not change
- Notice the Equity section.
- Nothing is shown for Retained Earnings or Net Income.
- The Net Income has been added to the account Your Name, Capital - Other.
- Verify this by adding the net income of 4,135.53 to 53,135.00, which was shown as the balance of the Your Name, Capital - Other account on the Balance Sheet prepared before the adjusting entry was made. The total should equal 57,270.53, which is the amount of Your Name, Capital - Other on the 2007 Balance Sheet.

Your Name Computer Consulting

Balance Sheet (After Transfer of Net Income)

As of January 31, 2007

	Jan 31, 07	
Business Vehicles Loan	34,532.81	
Office Furniture/Equipment Loan	3,970.83	
Total Loan Payable		38,503.64
Total Long Term Liabilities		38,503.64
Total Liabilities		42,267.64
Equity		
Your Name, Capital		
Draws	-2,500.00	
Investments	33,000.00	
Your Name, Capital - Other	57,270.53	
Total Your Name, Capital		87,770.53
Total Equity		87,770.53
TOTAL LIABILITIES & EQUITY		**130,038.17**

Partial Report

Print the **Balance Sheet** for January 2007
Close the **Balance Sheet**; do not close the Report Center

PRINT JOURNAL

It is always wise to have a printed or "hard copy" of the data on disk. After all entries and adjustments for the month have been made, print the Journal for January. This copy should be kept on file as an additional backup to the data stored on your disk. If something happens to your disk to damage it, you will still have the paper copy of your transactions available for re-entry into the system.

Print the Journal for January

With the Report Center on the screen, click **Accountant & Taxes** as the type of reports, click **Journal**

Enter the dates From **01/01/06** to **01/31/06**

- Notice that the report contains all the transactions from Chapters 2, 3, and 4

Verify that the final total for debits and credits is $62,055.22

- If it is not, make the necessary corrections to incorrect transactions. Frequent errors include incorrect dates, incorrect accounts used, and incorrect amounts.

Print in **Landscape** orientation, select **Fit report to one page wide**

Close the **Journal**

EXPORTING REPORTS TO EXCEL

Many of the reports prepared in QuickBooks Pro can be exported to Microsoft® Excel. This allows you to take advantage of extensive filtering options available in Excel, hide detail for some but not all groups of data, combine information from two different reports, change titles of columns, add comments, change the order of columns, and to experiment with "what if" scenarios. In order to use this feature of QuickBooks Pro you must also have Microsoft® Excel.

Optional Exercise: Export a report from QuickBooks Pro to Excel

With Report Finder on the screen, click **Trial Balance** in the Accountant & Taxes report listing

Enter the **From** date as **01/01/06** and the **To** date as **01/31/06**

Click the Export... button

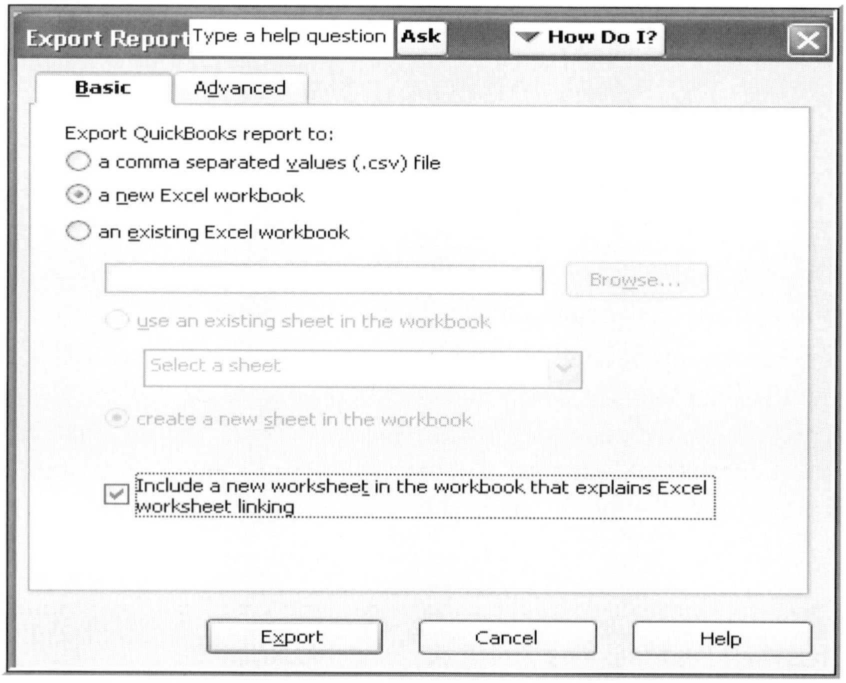

Make sure the Export QuickBooks Report to: is **a new Excel workbook**
Click **Export**

- The **Trial** Balance will be displayed in Excel.

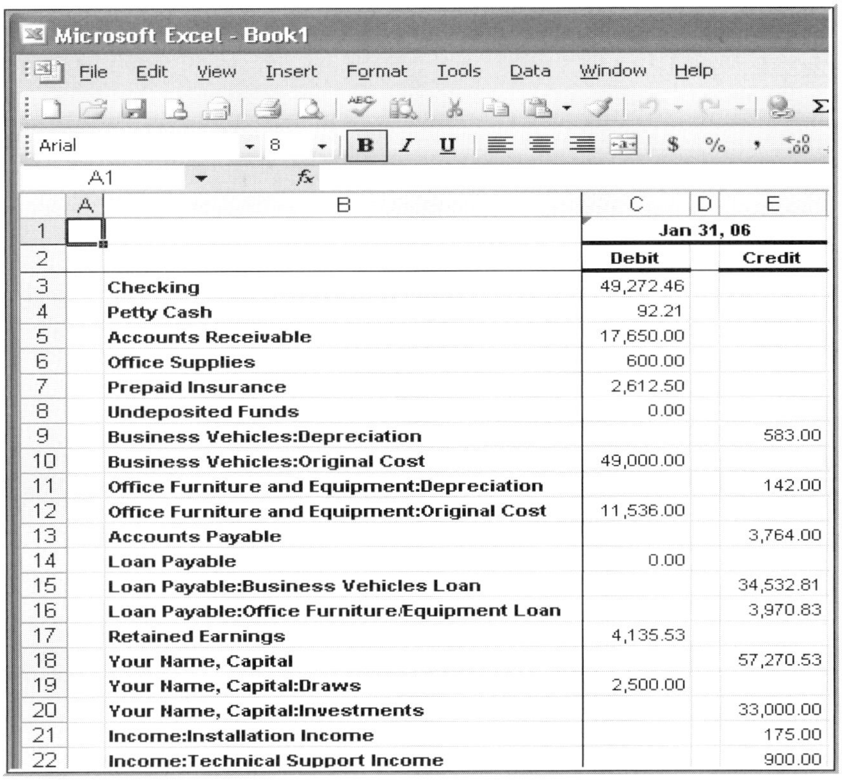

	A	B	C	D	E
1			Jan 31, 06		
2			Debit		Credit
3		Checking	49,272.46		
4		Petty Cash	92.21		
5		Accounts Receivable	17,650.00		
6		Office Supplies	600.00		
7		Prepaid Insurance	2,612.50		
8		Undeposited Funds	0.00		
9		Business Vehicles:Depreciation			583.00
10		Business Vehicles:Original Cost	49,000.00		
11		Office Furniture and Equipment:Depreciation			142.00
12		Office Furniture and Equipment:Original Cost	11,536.00		
13		Accounts Payable			3,764.00
14		Loan Payable	0.00		
15		Loan Payable:Business Vehicles Loan			34,532.81
16		Loan Payable:Office Furniture/Equipment Loan			3,970.83
17		Retained Earnings	4,135.53		
18		Your Name, Capital			57,270.53
19		Your Name, Capital:Draws	2,500.00		
20		Your Name, Capital:Investments			33,000.00
21		Income:Installation Income			175.00
22		Income:Technical Support Income			900.00

Partial Trial Balance in Excel

Click in Cell C1, change the heading by typing **JANUARY 31, 2006**
Click in Cell C2, type **DEBIT** to change Debit to all capitals
Click in Cell E2, type **CREDIT** to change Credit to all capitals

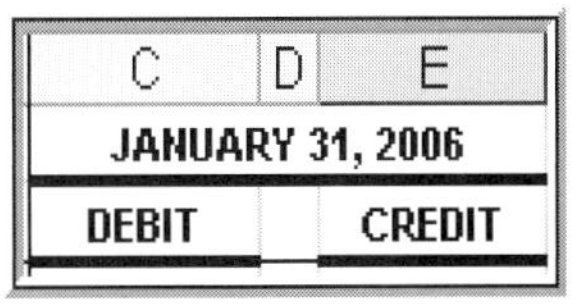

Click the **Close** button in the top right corner of the Excel title bar to close Excel

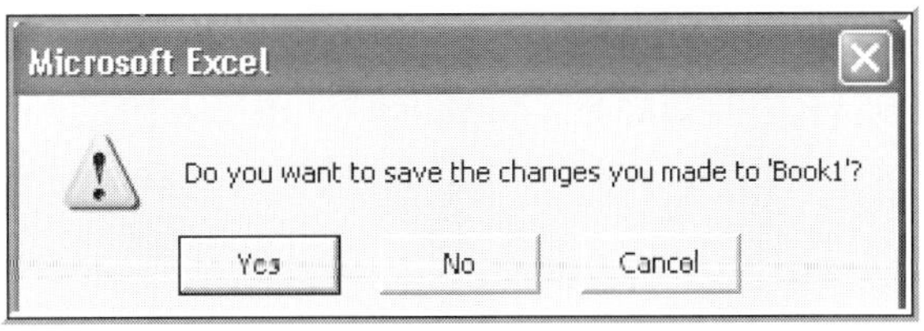

Click **No** to close Book1 without saving
Close the **Trial Balance** and the **Report Center**

END-OF-PERIOD BACKUP

Once all end-of-period procedures have been completed, a regular backup and a second backup of the company data should be made. The second backup should be filed as an archive copy. Preferably this copy will be located someplace other than on the business premises. The archive or file copy is set aside in case of emergency or in case damage occurs to the original and current backup copies of the company data.

Back up company data and prepare an archive copy of the company data

For training purposes, use your USB drive or put a blank disk should be in **A:**
Click **File** on the menu bar, click **Back Up**
In the **Name** text box enter **Computer Archive 1-31-06.qbb** as the name for the backup
Verify the storage location of your archive file

- In actual practice, the company (.qbw) file would be on your hard drive and the backup (.qbb) file would be stored on separate disk or USB drive. An archive file can be created on a floppy disk for separate storage.
- Check with your instructor for specific classroom procedures for creating an archive copy based on your individual classroom configuration. Also, if your disk becomes full, check with your instructor for alternate procedures.

Click **OK**
Once the backup has been made, click **OK** on the QuickBooks Pro Information dialog box to acknowledge the successful backup

PASSWORDS

Not every employee of a business should have access to all the financial records for the company. In some companies, only the owner will have complete access. In others, one or two key employees will have full access while other employees are provided limited access based on the jobs they perform. Passwords are secret words used to control access to data. QuickBooks Pro has several options available when assigning passwords.

In order to assign any passwords at all, you must have an administrator. The administrator has unrestricted access to all QuickBooks Pro functions, sets up users and user passwords for

QuickBooks and for Windows, and assigns areas of transaction access for each user. Areas of access can be limited to transaction entry for certain types of transactions or a user may have unrestricted access into all areas of QuickBooks Pro and company data. To obtain more information regarding QuickBooks' passwords, refer to the Help Index.

A password should be kept secret at all times. It should be something that is easy for the individual to remember, yet difficult for someone else to guess. Birthdays, names, initials, and similar devices are not good passwords because the information is too readily available. Never write down your password where it can be easily found or seen by someone else. Make sure your password is something you won't forget. Otherwise, you will not be able to access your Company file.

Since the focus of the text is in training in all aspects of QuickBooks Pro, no passwords will be assigned.

SET THE CLOSING DATE FOR THE PERIOD

A closing date assigned to transactions for a period prevents change to data from the period without acknowledging that a transaction has been changed for a closed period. This is helpful to discourage casual changes or transaction deletions to a period that has been closed. Setting the closing date is done by accessing Preferences in QuickBooks Pro.

MEMO
DATE: January 31, 2006

Consuelo, now that the closing transactions have been performed, protect the data by setting the closing date to 1/31/06.

➤ Assign the closing date of **01/31/06** to the transactions for the period ending 1/31/06

Click **Edit** on the menu bar, click **Preferences**
Scroll through the list of Preferences until you see **Accounting**
Click **Accounting**
Click **Company Preferences**
Enter **013106** as the date through which the books are closed
Do not assign a closing password at this time

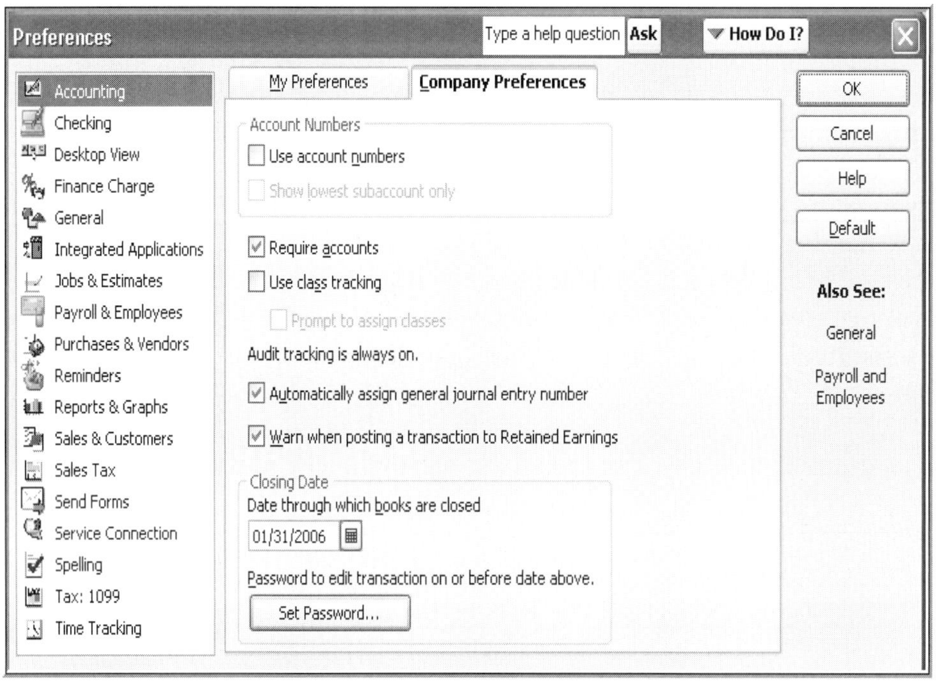

Click **OK** to close the period and to close Preferences

ACCESS TRANSACTION FOR PREVIOUS PERIOD

Even though the month of January has been "closed," transactions still appear in the account registers, the Journal, and so on. The transactions shown may not be changed unless you click Yes on the screen warning you that you have changed a transaction to a closed period.

Change Prepaid Insurance to 2,500

Access the **Chart of Accounts** as previously instructed
Double-click **Prepaid Insurance** to access the account Register
Click the **Increase** column showing **2,850** paid to Southern California Insurance Co.
Highlight 2,850, enter **2,500**
Click **Record**
The **QuickBooks** dialog box allowing the transaction to be changed appears

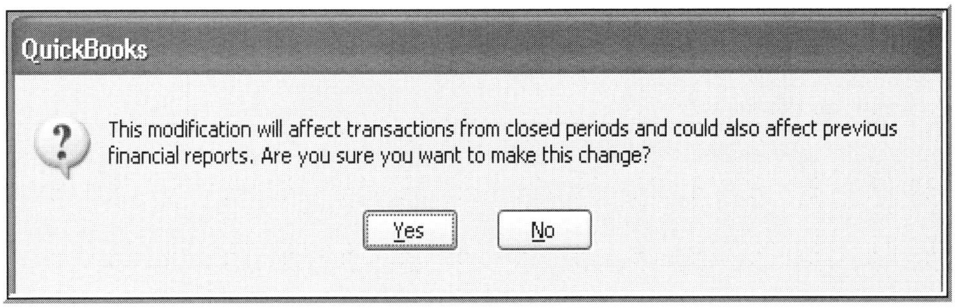

Click **No**
Click **Restore** to restore the transaction to the original 2,850
Close the **Prepaid Insurance** account
Do not close the **Chart of Accounts**

EDIT TRANSACTION FROM PREVIOUS PERIOD

If it is determined that an error was made in a previous period, QuickBooks Pro does allow the correction. Before it will record any changes for previous periods, QuickBooks Pro requires that Yes be clicked on the dialog box warning of the change to a transaction date that is prior to the closing date for the company. The adjusting entry used to transfer retained earnings/net income into the owner's capital account also needs to be adjusted as a result of any changes to transactions. Increasing the amount of supplies on hand by $25 will decrease the amount of expense incurred and will result in a $25 increase in net income/retained earnings.

MEMO
DATE: February 1, 2006

After reviewing the journal and reports printed at the end of January, You find that the amount of supplies used was $325, not $350. Make the correction to the adjusting entry of January 31.

Change Office Supplies adjusting entry to $325 from $350

Double-click the **Office Supplies** account to access the account Register
Click the **Decrease** column for the Adjusting Entry recorded to the account on 01/31/06
Change 350 to **325**
Click **Record**

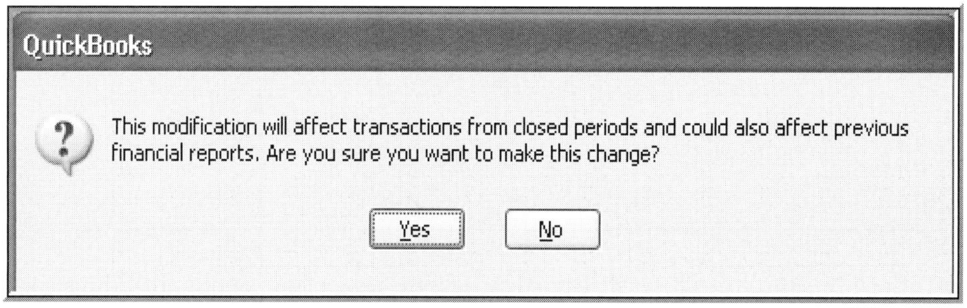

Click **Yes** on the QuickBooks screen

- The change to the transaction has been made.
- Notice that the Balance for the Office Supplies account now shows 625 instead of 600.

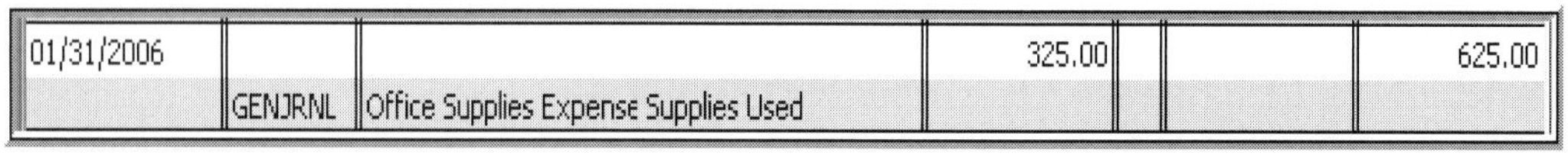

Close the **Register for Office Supplies**

- Since the correction to Office Supplies decreased the amount of the expense by $25, there is an additional $25 that will need to be included in the net income.

Click **Your Name, Capital**
Click **Activities** at the bottom of the **Chart of Accounts**
Click **Make General Journal Entries**
Click **Previous** until you find the entry adjusting Retained Earnings
Change the Debit to Retained Earnings from 4135.53 to **4160.53**
Change the Credit to Your Name, Capital from 4135.53 to **4160.53**

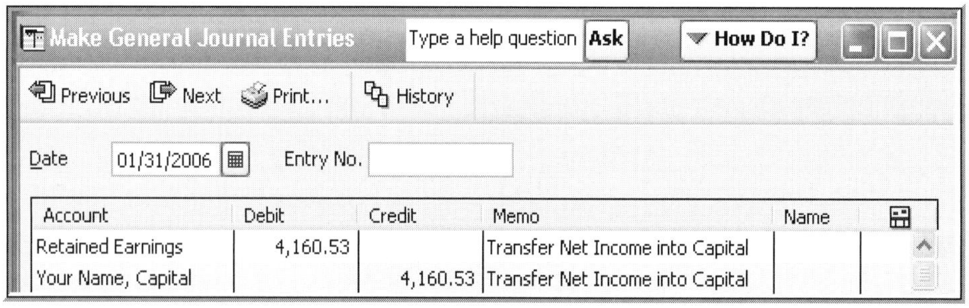

Click **Save & Close**
Click **Yes** on all of the **QuickBooks** dialog boxes
Close the **Chart of Accounts**

PRINT POST-CLOSING TRIAL BALANCE

After "closing" has been completed, it is helpful to print a Post-Closing Trial Balance. This proves that debits still equal credits.

MEMO
DATE: February 1, 2006

Print a Post-Closing Trial Balance, a Post-Closing Profit and Loss Statement, and a Post-Closing Balance Sheet for Your Name Computer Consulting. The dates should be as of or for 02/01/06.

Print a Post-Closing Trial Balance to prove debits still equal credits

Click the **Report Center** button, click **Accountant & Taxes** as the type of report, click **Trial Balance**
Enter the As of date **02/01/06**
Tab to generate the report
Change the Header so the report title is **Post-Closing Trial Balance**
Scroll through the report and study the amounts shown

- Notice that the final totals of debits and credits are equal.

Click the **Print** button at the top of the Trial Balance
Click **Preview** to view a miniature copy of the report

- Using Preview helps determine if you should still use Landscape orientation or change to Portrait. Preview also helps you determine whether you need to select the feature to print one page wide.

Your Name Computer Consulting
Trial Balance
As of February 1, 2006

	Feb 1, 06	
	Debit	Credit
Advertising Expense	260.00	
Bank Service Charges	8.00	
Business Vehicles Expense	588.88	
Depreciation Expense	725.00	
Dues and Subscriptions	79.00	
Equipment Rental	25.00	
Insurance:Business Vehicles Insurance	237.50	
Interest Expense:Interest on Loans	308.61	
Office Supplies Expense	343.57	
Postage and Delivery	195.34	
Rent	1,600.00	
Telephone	0.00	
Utilities:Electricity Expense	250.00	
Utilities:Heating Expense--Gas	175.00	
Utilities:Water	35.00	
Interest Income		66.43
TOTAL	142,279.60	142,279.60

Partial Report

Click **Close**
Print the report in **Portrait** orientation
Close the **Trial Balance**

PRINT POST-CLOSING PROFIT AND LOSS STATEMENT

Because February 1 is after the closing date of January 31, 2006, the Profit and Loss Statement for February 1 is the Post-Closing Profit and Loss Statement. To verify the closing, print a Profit and Loss statement for February 1.

Print a **Standard Profit and Loss Report** as the Post-Closing Profit and Loss report for February

Using the **Report Center**, click **Company & Financial** as the type of report, click **Profit & Loss Standard**
The dates are From **02/01/06** to **02/01/06**
Tab to generate the report
For clarity, change the Header so the report title is **Post-Closing Profit & Loss**

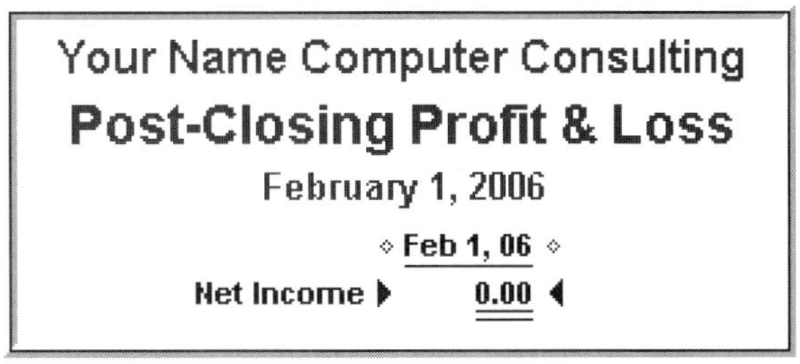

Print the report in **Portrait** orientation
Close the **Profit and Loss Report**
- The Net Income is **0.00**.

PRINT POST-CLOSING BALANCE SHEET

Proof that assets are equal to liabilities and owner's equity needs to be displayed in a Post-Closing Balance Sheet. The Balance Sheet for February 1 is considered to be a Post-Closing Balance Sheet because it is prepared after the closing of the period. Most of the adjustments were for the month of January 2006. Because this report is for a month, the adjustment to Retained Earnings and Net Income will result in both accounts being included on the Balance Sheet. If, however, this report were prepared for the year, neither account would appear.

Print a **Standard Balance Sheet Report** for February 1, 2006, and February 1, 2007

Prepare a **Standard Balance Sheet** as previously instructed
Tab to or click **As of**, enter **02/01/06**
Tab to generate the report
Change the Header so the report title is **Post-Closing Balance Sheet**
Scroll through the report to view the assets, liabilities, and equities listed
- Because this report is for a one-month period, both Retained Earnings and Net Income are included on this report.

Your Name Computer Consulting
Post-Closing Balance Sheet
As of February 1, 2006

		Feb 1, 06
Total Loan Payable		38,503.64
Total Long Term Liabilities		38,503.64
Total Liabilities		42,267.64
Equity		
Retained Earnings		-4,160.53
Your Name, Capital		
Draws	-2,500.00	
Investments	33,000.00	
Your Name, Capital - Other	57,295.53	
Total Your Name, Capital		87,795.53
Net Income		4,160.53
Total Equity		87,795.53
TOTAL LIABILITIES & EQUITY		**130,063.17**

Partial Report

Print the report in **Portrait** orientation
Change the date to **02/01/07**, tab to generate the report
Change the Header so the report title is **Balance Sheet**
Scroll through the report to view the assets, liabilities, and equities listed

- Because this report is prepared after the end of the fiscal year, neither Retained Earnings nor Net Income is included on this report.

Your Name Computer Consulting
Balance Sheet
As of February 1, 2007

	Feb 1, 07	
Business Vehicles Loan	34,532.81	
Office Furniture/Equipment Loan	3,970.83	
Total Loan Payable		38,503.64
Total Long Term Liabilities		38,503.64
Total Liabilities		42,267.64
Equity		
Your Name, Capital		
Draws	-2,500.00	
Investments	33,000.00	
Your Name, Capital - Other	57,295.53	
Total Your Name, Capital		87,795.53
Total Equity		87,795.53
TOTAL LIABILITIES & EQUITY		**130,063.17**

Partial Report

Print the report in **Portrait** orientation then close the **Balance Sheet** and **Report Center**

END-OF-CHAPTER BACKUP AND CLOSE COMPANY

As in previous chapters, you should back up your company and close the company.

Follow instructions previously provided to back up company files, close the company, and make a duplicate disk

SUMMARY

In this chapter, end-of-period adjustments were made, a bank reconciliation was performed, backup and archive disks were prepared, and a period was closed. The use of Net Income and Retained Earnings accounts was explored and interpreted for a sole proprietorship. Account name changes were made, and the effect on subaccounts was examined. Even though QuickBooks Pro focuses on entering transactions on business forms, a Journal recording each transaction is kept by QuickBooks Pro. This chapter presented transaction entry directly into the Journal. The differences between accrual-basis and cash-basis accounting were discussed. Company preferences were established for reporting preferences. Owner withdrawals and additional owner investments were made. Many of the different report options available in

QuickBooks Pro were examined, and the exporting of reports to Excel was explored. A variety of reports were printed. Correction of errors was explored, and changes to transactions in "closed" periods were made. The fact that QuickBooks Pro does not require an actual closing entry at the end of the period was examined.

END-OF-CHAPTER QUESTIONS

TRUE/FALSE

ANSWER THE FOLLOWING QUESTIONS IN THE SPACE PROVIDED BEFORE THE QUESTION NUMBER.

_____ 1. Accrual-basis accounting matches the income from the period and the expenses for the period in order to determine the net income or net loss for the period.

_____ 2. In QuickBooks Pro, the Journal is called the book of final entry.

_____ 3. An account may be deleted at any time.

_____ 4. In a sole proprietorship, an owner's name is added to the Vendor List for recording withdrawals.

_____ 5. Additional investments made by an owner may be cash or noncash items.

_____ 6. QuickBooks Pro keeps a Journal record of every transaction.

_____ 7. QuickBooks Pro keeps the last two Bank Reconciliation reports in memory.

_____ 8. Once an account has been used in a transaction, no changes may be made to the account name.

_____ 9. Anything entered as a service charge or as interest earned during a bank reconciliation will be entered automatically when the reconciliation is complete.

_____ 10. A Balance Sheet is prepared to prove the equality of debits and credits.

MULTIPLE CHOICE

WRITE THE LETTER OF THE CORRECT ANSWER IN THE SPACE PROVIDED BEFORE THE QUESTION NUMBER.

_____ 1. To close a period, you must ___.
A. have a closing password
B. change company preferences for Accounting
C. change company preferences for Reports
D. enter the traditional closing entries in debit/credit format in the General Journal

_____ 2. When an account name such as "cars" is changed to "automobile," the subaccount "car depreciation" ___.
A. needs to be changed to "automobile depreciation"
B. is automatically changed to "automobile depreciation"
C. cannot be changed
D. must be deleted and re-entered

_____ 3. The report that proves Assets = Liabilities + Owner's Equity is the ___.
A. Trial Balance
B. Income Statement
C. Profit and Loss Statement
D. Balance Sheet

_____ 4. If the adjusting entry to transfer net income/retained earnings into the owner's capital account is made prior to the end of the year, the Balance Sheet shows ___.
A. Retained Earnings
B. Net Income
C. both Net Income and Retained Earnings
D. none of the above because the income/earnings has been transferred into capital

_____ 5. The type of Profit and Loss Report showing year-to-date transactions instead of totals for each income and expense account is a(n) ___ Profit and Loss Report.
A. Standardized
B. YTD Comparison
C. Prev Year Comparison
D. Detailed

_____ 6. A bank statement may ___.
A. show service charges or interest not yet recorded
B. be missing deposits in transit or outstanding checks
C. both of the above
D. none of the above

_____ 7. The Journal shows ___.
- A. all transactions no matter where they were recorded
- B. only those transactions recorded in the General Journal
- C. only transactions recorded in account registers
- D. only those transactions that have been edited

_____ 8. A QuickBooks backup file ___.
- A. is a condensed file containing company data
- B. is prepared in case of emergencies or errors on current disks
- C. must be restored before information can be used
- D. all of the above

_____ 9. An error known as a transposition can be found by ___.
- A. dividing the amount out of balance by 9
- B. dividing the amount out of balance by 2
- C. multiplying the difference by 9, then dividing by 2
- D. dividing the amount out of balance by 5

_____ 10. The type of Balance Sheet Report showing information for today and a year ago is a(n) ___ Balance Sheet.
- A. Standard
- B. Summary
- C. Comparison
- D. Detailed

FILL-IN

IN THE SPACE PROVIDED, WRITE THE ANSWER THAT MOST APPROPRIATELY COMPLETES THE SENTENCE.

1. Bank reconciliations should be performed on a(n) ____________ basis.

2. Exporting report data from QuickBooks Pro to __________ can be made in order to perform "what if" scenarios.

3. An owner's paycheck is considered a(n) ____________.

4. The two types of reporting are ____________ basis and ____________ basis.

5. The Cash Flow Forecast _______________ column shows the total in all bank accounts if all customer and bill payments are made on time.

SHORT ESSAY

Describe the four types of Balance Sheet Reports available in QuickBooks Pro.

NAME____________________

TRANSMITTAL

CHAPTER 4: YOUR NAME COMPUTER CONSULTING

Attach the following documents and reports:

Check No. 9: You
Reconciliation Detail Report
Trial Balance, January 1-31, 2006
Cash Flow Forecast, February 1-28, 2006
Statement of Cash Flows, January 2006
Profit and Loss Statement, January 31, 2006
Balance Sheet (After Transfer of Net Income), January 31, 2006
Balance Sheet (After Transfer of Net Income), January 31, 2006
Journal, January 1-31, 2006
Post-Closing Trial Balance, February 1, 2006
Post-Closing Profit and Loss, February 1, 2006
Post-Closing Balance Sheet, February 1, 2006
Balance Sheet, February 1, 2007

END-OF-CHAPTER PROBLEM

YOUR NAME GARDEN & POOL MAINTENANCE

Chapter 4 continues with the end-of-period adjustments, bank reconciliation, archive disks, and closing the period for Your Name Garden & Pool Maintenance. The company does use a certified professional accountant for guidance and assistance with appropriate accounting procedures. The CPA has provided information for use in recording adjusting entries and so on.

INSTRUCTIONS

Continue to use the company file **Garden.qbw** that you used for Chapters 1, 2, and 3. Record the adjustments and other transactions as you were instructed in the chapter. Always read the transaction carefully and review the Chart of Accounts when selecting transaction accounts. Print the reports and journals as indicated.

RECORD TRANSACTIONS

January 31—Enter the following:

- Change the names of the following accounts:
    - **Student's Name, Capital** to **Your Name, Capital**
    - **Business Trucks** to **Business Vehicles** (also change the subaccounts so they reflect the name Business Vehicles)
    - **Automobile Expense** to **Business Vehicles Expense**
    - **Business Trucks Loan** to **Business Vehicles Loan**
    - **Auto Insurance Expense** to **Business Vehicles Insurance**
- Make the following accounts inactive:
    - **Recruiting**
    - **Travel & Ent**
- Delete the following accounts:
    - **Sales**
    - **Services**
    - **Amortization Expenses**
    - **Contributions**
    - **Interest Expense: Mortgage**
    - **Taxes: Property**
- Print the Chart of Accounts by clicking **Reports** on the menu bar, pointing to **List**, clicking **Account Listing.** Use Landscape orientation.

January 31—Enter the following:

- Enter adjusting entries in the Journal for:
  - Office Supplies Used, $185. Memo: Office Supplies Used for January
  - Business vehicles insurance expense for the month, $250. Memo: Insurance Expense January
  - Depreciation for the month (Use a compound entry), Memo: Depreciation January
    - Business Vehicles, $950
    - Equipment, $206.25
- Enter transactions for Owner's Equity:
  - Owner withdrawal $1,000. Memo: Withdrawal for January (Print the check.)
  - Additional cash investment by you, $2,000. Memo: Investment: Cash
  - Additional noncash investment by owner, $1,500 of lawn equipment. Memo: Investment: Equipment (Note: The value of the lawn equipment is the original cost of the asset.)
- Prepare Bank Reconciliation and Enter Adjustments for the Reconciliation for January 31, 2006 (Be sure to enter automatic payments, service charges, and interest. Pay close attention to the dates.)

SANTA BARBARA BANK
1234 Coast Highway
Santa Barbara, CA 93100 (805) 555-9310

BANK STATEMENT FOR
Your Name Garden & Pool Maintenance
18527 State Street
Santa Barbara, CA 93103
Acct. #987-352-9152 January 31, 2006

Beginning Balance, January 2, 2006			$23,850.00
1/18/06, Check 1		485.00	23,365.00
1/18/06, Check 2		375.00	22,990.00
1/18/06, Check 3		669.00	22,321.00
1/18/06, Check 4		180.00	22,141.00
1/31/06, Service Charge		10.00	22,131.00
1/31/06, Business Vehicles Loan Pmt.: Interest, 795.54; Principal, 160.64		956.18	21,174.82
1/31/06, Interest	59.63		21,234.45
Ending Balance, 1/31/06			$21,234.45

- Print a Detailed Reconciliation Report in Landscape orientation

- Change Preferences:
  Verify or change reporting preferences to accrual basis
- Print reports for January, 2006 or as of January 31, 2006 in Portrait orientation.
  - Trial Balance
  - Standard Profit & Loss Statement
- Transfer Net Income/Retained Earnings into Capital Account
- Prepare a Balance Sheet Standard, add **(After Transfer of Net Income)** to the header, and print
- Close the period. The closing date is **01/31/06**
- Edit a Transaction from a closed period: Discovered an error in the amount of office supplies used. The amount used should be **$175**, not $185. (Don't forget to adjust Retained Earnings and Capital.)

<u>February 1, 2006</u>—Print the following in Portrait orientation unless specified as Landscape:

- Journal for January, 2006 (Landscape orientation, Fit report to one page wide)
- Post-Closing Trial Balance, February 1, 2006 (Add the words **Post-Closing** to the report title)
- Cash Flow Forecast for February 1-30 (Landscape orientation), 2006
- Statement of Cash Flows, January 1-31, 2006
- Post-Closing Profit & Loss Statement, February 1, 2006 (Add the words **Post-Closing** to the report title)
- Post-Closing Balance Sheet, February 1, 2006 (Add the words **Post-Closing** to the report title)

<u>February 1, 2007</u>—Print the following:

- Standard Balance Sheet

- Backup your work to **Garden Ch 4.qbb**

NAME____________________

TRANSMITTAL

CHAPTER 4: YOUR NAME GARDEN & POOL MAINTENANCE

Attach the following documents and reports:

Account Listing, January 31, 2006
Check No. 8: Your Name
Reconciliation Report
Trial Balance, January 31, 2006
Profit and Loss, January 2006
Balance Sheet, January 31, 2006 (After Transfer of Net Income)
Journal, January 2006
Post-Closing Trial Balance, February 1, 2006
Cash Flow Forecast, February 2006
Statement of Cash Flows, January 2006
Post-Closing Profit and Loss, February 1, 2006
Post-Closing Balance Sheet, February 1, 2006
Balance Sheet, February 1, 2007

SECTION 1 PRACTICE SET: YOUR NAME HELPING HANDS

The following is a comprehensive practice set combining all the elements of QuickBooks Pro studied in the text. In this practice set, you will keep the books for a company for one month. Entries will be made to record invoices, receipt of payments on invoices, cash sales, receipt and payment of bills, credit memos for invoices and bills. Account names will be added, changed, deleted, and made inactive. Customer, vendor, and owner names will be added to the appropriate lists. Reports will be prepared to analyze sales, bills, and receipts. Formal reports including the Trial Balance, Profit and Loss Statement, and Balance Sheet will be prepared. Adjusting entries for depreciation, supplies used, and insurance expense will be recorded. A bank reconciliation will be prepared.

YOUR NAME HELPING HANDS

Located in Beverly Hills, California, Your Name Helping Hands is a service business providing assistance with errands, shopping, home repairs, simple household chores, and transportation for children and others who do not drive. Rates are on a per-hour basis and differ according to the service performed.

Your Name Helping Hands is a sole proprietorship owned and operated by you. You have one assistant, Gail Robbins, helping you with errands, scheduling of duties, and doing the bookkeeping for Your Name Helping Hands. In addition, a part-time employee, Virginia Gomez, works weekends for Your Name Helping Hands.

INSTRUCTIONS

To work with transactions for Your Name Helping Hands, copy the file **Hands.qbw** from the Prentice Hall Web site. Follow the steps presented in Chapter 1.

The following lists are used for all sales items, customers, and vendors. You will be adding additional customers and vendors as the company is in operation. When entering transactions, you are responsible for any memos or customer messages you wish to include in transactions. Unless otherwise specified, the terms for each sale or bill will be the terms specified on the Customer or Vendor List. (View the terms for the individual customers or vendors in the Customer Center and Vendor Center.)

Customers:

Student's Name Helping Hands
Customer & Job List
January 1, 2006

Customer	Balance Total
Appel, William Dr.	275.00
Avedisian, Tekko	750.00
Basil, Blanche	150.00
Carter, Cindy	0.00
Clark, Robert	250.00
Cunningham, Mary	600.00
Dubinskia, Stamos	450.00
Edwards, Brent	50.00
Jacobstein, Miriam	200.00
Minassian, Silas	1,000.00
Smith, Rick	500.00

Vendors:

Student's Name Helping Hands
Vendor List
January 1, 2006

Vendor	Balance Total
BH Stationers	350.00
Boulevard Flowers	25.00
Brentwood Auto Repairs	500.00
Employment Development	0.00
Neighborhood Gasoline	250.00
United States Treasury	0.00

Sales Items:

Student's Name Helping Hands
Item Listing
January 1, 2006

Item	Description	Type	Cost	Price
Errands	Household Errands	Service	0	25.00
Household	Household Chores	Service	0	15.00
Party	Party Planning and Supervision	Service	0	50.00
Pets	Pet Sitting	Service	0	25.00
Repairs	Repair Service	Service	0	50.00
Shopping	Client Shopping	Service	0	25.00
Transport	Transportation	Service	0	25.00

Each Item is priced per hour. Unless otherwise specified within the transactions, a minimum of one hour is charged for any service provided. As you can see, there is no difference in amount between the first hour of a service and subsequent hours of service.

RECORD TRANSACTIONS

Enter the transactions for Your Name Helping Hands and print as indicated. Always print invoices, sales receipts, checks, and so on as they are entered.

Week 1: January 1-6, 2006:

- ► Add your name to the company name. The company name will be **Your Name Helping Hands**. (Type your actual name, *not* the words *Your Name*.)
- ► Change Report Preferences: Reports should refresh automatically, Report Header/Footer should *not* include the Date Prepared, Time Prepared, or the Report Basis
- ► Change the Capital account to **Your Name, Capital**.
- ► Find all accounts with the name **Automobile** as part of the account name. Change every occurrence of Automobile to **Business Vehicle**.
- ► Find all accounts with the name **Office Equipment** as part of the account name. Change every occurrence of Office Equipment to **Office Furniture/Equipment**.
- ► Make the following inactive: **Interest Expense: Mortgage**, **Taxes: Property**, **Travel & Ent**
- ► Delete the following accounts: **Sales**, **Recruiting**, **Contributions**, **Amortization Expense,** and **Professional Development**
- ► Add **Petty Cash** to the Chart of Accounts. Transfer **$100** from checking to Petty Cash to fund the account.
- ► Print an Account Listing in Portrait orientation. (From the Report menu select List and Account Listing)
- ► Prior to recording any transactions, print a Trial Balance as of January 1, 2006.

1/1/06

- ► Cindy Carter is having a party in two weeks. Bill Cindy Carter for 3 hours of party planning. Refer to the Item Detail List for the appropriate sales item. Invoice No. 35, terms, Net 30. Print the invoice.
- ► Dr. Smith has arranged for you to feed and walk his dogs every day. Bill Dr. Smith for pet sitting, 1 hour per day for 7 days (put this all on one bill).
- ► We were out of paper, toner cartridges for the laser printer, computer disks, and various other office supplies that we need to have on hand. Received a bill—Invoice No. 1806-1—from BH Stationers for $350 for the office supplies we received today.
- ► Every week we put fresh flowers in the office in order to provide a welcoming environment for any customers who happen to come to the office. Received a bill—Invoice No. 887—from Boulevard Flowers for $25 for office flowers for the week. (Miscellaneous Expense)

1/2/06

- ► Dr. Appel almost forgot his anniversary. He called Your Name Helping Hands with an emergency request for assistance. The store will bill the doctor for the actual gift purchased. Bill Dr. William Appel, 3 hours of shopping for his wife's birthday gift.

- Blanche Basil needed to have her shelves relined. You did part of the house this week and will return next week to continue the work. Bill her for 5 hours of household chores for this week.

1/3/06

- Mr. Dubinskia's mother has several doctor appointments. He has asked Your Name Helping Hands to take her to these appointments. Bill Stamos Dubinskia for 3 hours of transportation.

1/4/06

- Received a bill—Invoice No. 81056—from Neighborhood Gasoline, $125 for the weekly gasoline charge.
- Received checks from the following customers on account: Dr. William Appel, Check No. 713 for $275; Robert Clark, Check No. 3381 for $250; Stamos Dubinskia, Check No. 6179 for $450; Silas Minassian, Check No. 38142 for $1000.

1/5/06

- Fionna Jacobstein has a birthday party to attend. Her mother, Miriam, has hired Your Name Helping Hands to take her to the party and stay with her while she is there. Bill Miriam Jacobstein 3 hours of transportation for the birthday party. (This transportation charge also includes the time at the party.)

1/6/06

- Prepare Sales Receipt No. 22 to record a cash sale. Received Check No. 2894 for 1 hour of errands for a new customer: Amy Ricardo, 18062A Camden Drive, Beverly Hills, CA 90210, 310-555-7206, Fax 310-555-6027, E-mail ARicardo@abc.com, terms Net 10 days. (*Note:* Remember to key the last name first for the customer name.) Print the sales receipt.
- Prepare Unpaid Bills Detail Report. Print the report.
- Pay bills for the amount owed to Boulevard Flowers and Neighborhood Gasoline on December 31. (Refer to the Vendor List shown on the second page of the practice set or to the Unpaid Bills Detail Report to determine the amounts for the checks. Remember that the due dates will not be 8/31/06.) Print the checks using a Standard check style—they may be printed on one page or individually.
- Make the bank deposit for the week. The date of the deposit is 1/6/06. Print a Deposit Summary.
- Print Trial Balance.
- Back up your work for the week. Use **Hands Week 1.qbb** as the file name.

Week 2: January 7-13, 2006

1/7/06

- Cindy Carter is having a party and has finalized the date for January 19. Bill Cindy Carter for 4 hours of party planning.

- ▶ Mr. Dubinskia's mother has several additional doctor appointments. He has asked Your Name Helping Hands to take her to these appointments. Bill Stamos Dubinskia for 4 hours of transportation.
- ▶ Dr. Smith was pleased with Your Name Helping Hands' service and has arranged to have Your Name Helping Hands feed and walk his dogs every day on a permanent basis. Bill Dr. Smith for pet sitting, 1 hour per day for 7 days.

1/8/06

- ▶ Mary Cunningham really likes the floral arrangements in the office of Your Name Helping Hands. She has asked that flowers be brought to her home and arranged throughout the house. When you complete the placement of the flowers in the house, Mary gives you Check No. 387 for $40. This is payment in full for 1 hour of errands and 1 hour of household chores.

1/9/06

- ▶ Received checks from the following customers: Dr. Smith, No. 7891, $500; Ms. Jacobstein, No. 97452, $200; Ms. Cunningham, No. 395, $600; Mr. Edwards, No. 178, $50; Mr. Avedisian, No. 3916, $750.
- ▶ Received a bill—Invoice No. 943—from Boulevard Flowers for $25 for office flowers for the week.
- ▶ Received a bill—Invoice No. 81085—from Neighborhood Gasoline, $100 for the weekly gasoline charge.

1/10/06

- ▶ Silas Minassian has arranged for Your Name Helping Hands to supervise and coordinate the installation of new tile in his master bathroom. Bill Mr. Minassian for 4 hours of repair service for hiring the subcontractor, scheduling the installation for 1/15 and 1/16, and contract preparation.

1/11/06

- ▶ Blanche Basil needed to have her shelves relined. You did part of the house last week and completed the work today. Bill Ms. Basil for 5 hours of household chores for this week.
- ▶ Returned faulty printer cartridge. Received Credit Memo No. 5 from BH Stationers, $75.

1/13/06

- ▶ Pay all bills for the amounts due on or before January 13. (*Hint:* Are there any credits to apply?) There should be three checks. Print the checks–all on one page or individually.
- ▶ Correct the invoice issued to Blanche Basil on 1/11/06. The number of hours billed should be 7 instead of 5. Print the corrected invoice.
- ▶ Make the bank deposit for the week. The date of the deposit is 1/13/06. Print a Deposit Summary.
- ▶ After depositing checks, print A/R Aging Detail Report as of 1/13/06. Use Landscape orientation.

- Back up your work for the week. Use **Hands Week 2.qbb** as the file name.

Week 3: January 14-20, 2006

1/14/06

- Cindy Carter is having a party the 19th. Bill Cindy Carter for 2 more hours of party planning.

1/15/06

- Pay postage due 64 cents. Use Petty Cash.
- Print Petty Cash Account QuickReport. Fit report to one page wide.
- Mary Cunningham was really pleased with the floral arrangements you did last week. She has asked that flowers be brought to her home and arranged throughout the house on a weekly basis. This week when you complete the placement of the flowers in the house, Mary gives you Check No. 421 for 1 hour of errands and 1 hour of household chores.

1/17/06

- Received a bill—Invoice No. 81109—from Neighborhood Gasoline, $150 for the weekly gasoline charge.
- Received a bill—Invoice No. 979—from Boulevard Flowers for $25 for office flowers for the week.
- The bathroom tile was installed on 1/15 and 1/16. The installation was completed to Mr. Minassian's satisfaction. Bill him for 16 hours of repair service.

1/18/06

- Mary Cunningham's neighbor, Dr. Patrick Goldin, really liked the flowers in Mary's house and asked you to bring flowers to his home and office. This week he gave you Check No. 90-163 for 1 hour of errands and 1 hour of household chores. Add him to the customer list: Dr. Patrick Goldin, 236 West Canon Drive, Beverly Hills, CA 90210, 310-555-0918, Net 10.

1/19/06

- Tonight is Cindy's big party. She has arranged for both you and Virginia to supervise the party from 3 p.m. until 1 a.m. Bill Cindy Carter for 20 hours of party planning and supervision.
- Print a Customer Balance Summary Report.

1/20/06

- Record the checks received from customers for the week: Mr. Dubinskia, No. 9165, $175; Ms. Basil, No. 7-303, $150; Dr. Smith, No. 89162, $175; Ms. Jacobstein, No. 5291, $75.
- Make the bank deposit for the week. The date of the deposit is 1/20/06. Print a Deposit Summary.
- Back up your work for the week. Use **Hands Week 3.qbb** as the file name.

Week 4: January 21-27, 2006

1/22/06

- Mary Cunningham gave you Check No. 439 for 1 hour of errands and 1 hour of household chores in payment for the flowers that were brought to her home and arranged throughout the house this week.

1/23/06

- Use Petty Cash to pay for a box of file folders to be used immediately in reorganizing some of the files in the office, $4.23. (This is an expense.)
- Print a Petty Cash Account QuickReport. Fit the report to one page wide.
- Cindy's party went so smoothly on the 19th that You went home at 11 p.m. rather than 1 a.m. Issue a Credit Memo to Cindy Carter for 2 hours of party planning and supervision. Apply the credit to Invoice 48 dated January 19, 2006.
- Brent Edwards arranged to have his pets cared for by Your Name Helping Hands during the past 7 days. Bill him for 1 hour of pet sitting each day. Brent wants to add a doggie door and a fenced area for his dog. Bill him 20 hours of repair service for the planning and overseeing of the project.

1/24/06

- You arranged for theater tickets and dinner reservations for Dr. Appel to celebrate his wife's birthday. Bill him for 1 hour of errands, 3 hours shopping for the gift, and 5 hours of party planning for the after-theater surprise party.
- Received a bill—Invoice No. 81116—from Neighborhood Gasoline, $110 for the weekly gasoline charge.
- Received a bill—Invoice No. 1002—from Boulevard Flowers for $25 for office flowers for the week.
- Write a check to BH Stationers for the purchase of a new printer for the office, $500. (*Note:* If you get a warning to use Pay Bills because we owe the company money, disregard the warning.) Print the check using standard-style checks.

1/27/06

- Dr. Smith has arranged for Your Name Helping Hands to feed and walk his dogs every day. Bill him for pet sitting, 1 hour per day for the past two weeks. In addition, Dr. Smith is going to have a party and wants Your Name Helping Hands to plan it for him. Bill him for 20 hours party planning. When the dogs were puppies they did some damage to the interior of the house. In order to prepare for the party several areas in the house need to be reorganized and repaired. Bill him for 15 hours of household chores and 15 hours of repairs.
- Write checks to pay bills for rent and utilities. The utility companies and the rental agent will need to be added to the Vendor List. Vendor information is provided in each transaction. Print the checks using standard-style checks. They may be printed as a batch or individually.
    - Monthly telephone bill: $192, Beverly Hills Telephone, 2015 Wilshire Boulevard, Beverly Hills, CA 90210, 310-555-8888, Net 30 days.

   - Monthly rent for office space: $1,500, Rentals for You, 3016 Robertson Boulevard, Beverly Hills, CA 90210, 310-555-1636, Net 30 days.
   - Monthly water bill: $153, California Water, 9916 Sunset Boulevard, Beverly Hills, CA 90210, 310-555-1961, Net 30 days.
   - Monthly gas and electric bill: $296, Beverly Hills Power, 10196 Olympic Boulevard, West Los Angeles, CA 90016, 310-555-9012, Net 30 days.
- ▶ Prepare and print in Portrait orientation an Unpaid Bills Detail Report for January 27.
- ▶ Pay bills for all amounts due on or before January 27.
- ▶ Prepare a Check Detail Report from 1/1/06 to 1/27/06. Use Landscape orientation and fit report to one page wide.
- ▶ Record payments received from customers: Ms. Carter, No. 4692, $150; Dr. Smith, No. 7942, $175; Mr. Edwards, No. 235, $175; Dr. Appel, No. 601, $75; Ms. Basil, No. 923-10, $75.
- ▶ Make the bank deposit for the week. The date of the deposit is 1/27/06. Print a Deposit Summary.
- ▶ Record the bill received from United Insurance, 7654 Western Avenue, Hollywood, CA 90721, 310-555-1598, Fax 310-555-8951, terms Net 30 for Business Vehicle Insurance for the year, $2,400.00, Invoice 2280.
- ▶ Print Customer Balance Detail Report in Portrait orientation. Fit report to one page wide.
- ▶ Record adjusting entries for:
   - Business Vehicle Insurance, $200
   - Office Supplies Used, $150
   - Depreciation: Business Vehicles, $500 and Office Furniture and Equipment, $92
- ▶ Write a check for a withdrawal by you, $1,000.
- ▶ Because a fax machine is a business necessity, you decided to give your new fax machine to Your Name Helping Hands. Record this additional $350 investment of equipment by you.
- ▶ Because they are remodeling the offices, Rentals for You decreased the amount of rent to $1,000 per month. Correct and reprint the check for rent.
- ▶ Back up your work for the week. Use **Hands Week 4.qbb** as the file name.

End of the Month: January 30, 2006

- ▶ Prepare the bank reconciliation using the following bank statement. Record any adjustments necessary as a result of the bank statement. Print a Detailed Reconciliation Report.

Beverly Hills Bank, 1234 Rodeo Drive, Beverly Hills, CA 90210

Your Name Helping Hands, 27800 Beverly Boulevard, Beverly Hills, CA 90210

Beginning Balance, 1/1/06			$15,350.00
1/1/06, Transfer		100.00	15,250.00
1/6/06, Deposit	2,000.00		17,250.00
1/7/06, Check 1		25.00	17,225.00
1/7/06, Check 2		250.00	16,975.00
1/13/06, Check 4		25.00	16,950.00
1/13/06, Deposit	2,140.00		19,090.00
1/15/06, Check 5		500.00	18,590.00
1/16/06, Check 3		275.00	18,315.00
1/20/06, Deposit	655.00		18,970.00
1/28/06, Check 6		500.00	18,470.00
1/29/06, Check 8		1,000.00	17,470.00
1/31/06, Payment: Business Vehicle Loan: interest $445.15; principal $86.06		531.21	16,938.79
1/31/06, Payment: Office Equipment Loan: interest $53.42; principal $10.33		63.75	16,875.04
1/31/06, Service Charge		15.00	16,860.04
1/31/06, Interest	42.50		16,902.54
1/31/06, Ending Balance			$16,902.54

- Print the following reports as of 1/31/06:
    - Trial Balance from 1/1/06 through 1/31/06 in Portrait orientation.
    - Cash Flow Forecast from 2/1/06 through 2/28/06 in Landscape orientation.
    - Statement of Cash Flows from 1/1/06 through 1/31/06 in Portrait orientation.
    - Standard Profit and Loss Statement from 1/1/06 through 1/31/06 in Portrait orientation.
    - Standard Balance Sheet for 1/31/06 in Portrait orientation.
- Transfer the net income/retained earnings to owner's capital account.
- Prepare a Standard Balance Sheet as of 1/31/06. Change the title to **Balance Sheet After Transfer of Net Income** and print
- Print the Journal from 1/1/06 through 1/31/06 in Landscape orientation and Fit to one page wide.
- Close the period as of 01-31-06. Do not use any passwords.
- Back up your work for the week. Use **Hands Complete.qbb** as the file name.

NAME ____________________

TRANSMITTAL

SECTION 1 PRACTICE SET: YOUR NAME HELPING HANDS

Attach the following documents and reports:

Week 1
Account Listing
Trial Balance, January 1, 2006
Invoice No. 35: Cindy Carter
Invoice No. 36: Rick Smith
Invoice No. 37: William Appel
Invoice No. 38: Blanche Basil
Invoice No. 39: Stamos Dubinskia
Invoice No. 40: Miriam Jacobstein
Sales Receipt No. 22: Amy Ricardo
Unpaid Bills Detail, January 6, 2006
Check No. 1: Boulevard Flowers
Check No. 2: Neighborhood Gasoline
Deposit Summary, January 6, 2006
Trial Balance, January 6, 2006

Week 2
Invoice No. 41: Cindy Carter
Invoice No. 42: Stamos Dubinskia
Invoice No. 43: Rick Smith
Sales Receipt No. 23: Mary Cunningham
Invoice No. 44: Silas Minassian
Invoice No. 45: Blanche Basil
Check No. 3: BH Stationers
Check No. 4: Boulevard Flowers
Check No. 5: Brentwood Auto Repairs
Invoice No. 45 (Corrected): Blanche Basil
Deposit Summary, January 13, 2006
A/R Aging Detail, January 13, 2006

Week 3

Invoice No. 46: Cindy Carter
Petty Cash QuickReport, January 15, 2006 (May be in Portrait or Landscape)
Sales Receipt No. 24: Mary Cunningham
Invoice No. 47: Silas Minassian
Sales Receipt No. 25: Patrick Goldin
Invoice No. 48: Cindy Carter
Customer Balance Summary
Deposit Summary, January 20, 2006

Week 4

Sales Receipt No. 26: Mary Cunningham
Petty Cash QuickReport, January 23, 2006 (May be in Portrait or Landscape)
Credit Memo No. 49: Cindy Carter
Invoice No. 50: Brent Edwards
Invoice No. 51: William Appel
Check No. 6: BH Stationers
Invoice No. 52: Rick Smith
Check No. 7: Beverly Hills Telephone
Check No. 8: Rentals for You
Check No. 9: California Water
Check No. 10: Beverly Hills Power
Unpaid Bills Detail, January 27, 2006
Check No. 11: Boulevard Flowers
Check Detail, January 1-27, 2006
Deposit Summary, January 27, 2006
Customer Balance Detail
Check 12 Your Name
Check No. 8 (Corrected): Rentals for You
Bank Reconciliation Report
Trial Balance, January 31, 2006
Cash Flow Forecast, February 2006
Statement of Cash Flows, January 2006
Profit and Loss, January 2006
Balance Sheet, January 31, 2006
Balance Sheet (After adjustment for net income), January 31, 2006
Journal, January 2006

SALES AND RECEIVABLES: MERCHANDISING BUSINESS

5

LEARNING OBJECTIVES

At the completion of this chapter, you will be able to:

1. Enter sales transactions for a retail business.
2. Prepare invoices that use sales tax, have sales discounts, and exceed a customer's credit limit.
3. Prepare transactions for cash sales with sales tax.
4. Prepare transactions for customers using credit cards.
5. Add new accounts to the Chart of Accounts and new sales items to the Item List.
6. Add new customers and modify existing customer records.
7. Delete and void invoices.
8. Prepare credit memos with and without refunds.
9. Record customer payments on account with and without discounts.
10. Deposit checks and credit card receipts for sales and customer payments.
11. Record a transaction for a NSF check.
12. Customize report preferences and prepare and print Customer Balance Detail Reports, Open Invoice Reports, and Sales Reports.
13. View a QuickReport and use the QuickZoom feature.
14. Use the Customer Center to obtain information regarding credit customers.

ACCOUNTING FOR SALES AND RECEIVABLES IN A MERCHANDISING BUSINESS

Rather than using a traditional Sales Journal to record transactions using debits and credits and special columns, QuickBooks Pro uses an invoice to record sales transactions for accounts receivable in the Accounts Receivable Register. Because cash sales do not involve accounts receivable, a Sales Receipt is prepared, and QuickBooks Pro puts the money from a cash sale into the Undeposited Funds account until a deposit to a bank account is made. Instead of being recorded within special journals, cash receipt transactions are entered as activities. However, all transactions, regardless of the activity, are placed in the Journal behind the scenes. A new account, sales item, or customer can be added *on the fly* as transactions are entered. Customer information may be changed by editing the Customer List.

For a retail business, QuickBooks Pro tracks inventory, maintains information on reorder limits, tracks the quantity of merchandise on hand, maintains information on the value of the inventory, and can inform you of the percentage of sales for each inventory item. Discounts to certain types of customers can be given as well as early-payment discounts. Different price levels may be created for sales items and/or customers.

Unlike many computerized accounting programs, QuickBooks Pro makes error correction easy. A sales form may be edited, voided, or deleted in the same window where it was created or via an account register. If a sales form has been printed prior to correction, it may be reprinted after the correction has been made.

A multitude of reports are available when using QuickBooks Pro. Accounts receivable reports include Customer Balance Summary and Customer Balance Detail reports. Sales reports provide information regarding the amount of sales by item. Transaction Reports by Customer are available as well as the traditional accounting reports such as Trial Balance, Profit and Loss, and Balance Sheet. QuickBooks Pro also has graphing capabilities so that you can see and evaluate your accounts receivable and sales at the click of a button. Reports created in QuickBooks Pro may be exported to Microsoft® Excel.

TRAINING TUTORIAL

The following tutorial is a step-by-step guide to recording receivables (both cash and credit) for a fictitious company with fictitious employees. This company is called Your Name Sports. In addition to recording transactions using QuickBooks Pro, you will prepare several reports and graphs for Your Name Sports. The tutorial for Your Name Sports will continue in Chapters 6 and 7, when accounting for payables, bank reconciliations, financial statement preparation, and closing an accounting period for a merchandising business will be completed.

COMPANY PROFILE: YOUR NAME SPORTS

Your Name Sports is a sporting goods store located in Mammoth Lakes, California. Previously, the company was open only during the winter. As a result Your Name Sports specializes in equipment, clothing, and accessories for skiing and snowboarding. You have plans to expand into year-round operation and will eventually provide merchandise for summer sports and activities. The company is a partnership between you and Tim Bailey. Each partner has a 50 percent share of the business, and both of you devote all of your efforts to Your Name Sports. You have several part-time employees who work in the evenings and on the weekends during ski season. There is a full-time bookkeeper and manager, Rose Spencer, who oversees purchases, maintains the inventory, and keeps the books for the company.

OPEN A COMPANY—YOUR NAME SPORTS

As in previous chapters, copy the Sports.qbw file from the Prentice Hall Web site, access QuickBooks Pro, and open the company.

Copy the file **Sports.qbw** from the Prentice Hall Web site as instructed in Chapter 1, open QuickBooks Pro, open Sports.qbw

ADD YOUR NAME TO THE COMPANY NAME

As with previous companies, each student in the course will be working for the same company and printing the same documents. Personalizing the company name to include your name will help identify many of the documents you print during your training.

Add your name to the company name

Click **Company** on the menu bar
Click **Company Info**
Drag through the words **Student's Name** to highlight
Type –**your real name**

- Type your real name, *not* the words *Your Real Name*. For example, Pamela Iverson would type—**Pamela Iverson**.

Click **OK**

- The title bar now shows Your Name Sports

VERIFYING AN OPEN COMPANY

Verify the title bar heading:

BEGINNING THE TUTORIAL

In this chapter you will be entering both accounts receivable transactions and cash sales transactions for a retail company that charges its customers sales tax. Much of the organization of QuickBooks Pro is dependent on lists. The two primary types of lists you will use in the tutorial for receivables are a Customer List and a Sales Item List.

The names, addresses, telephone numbers, credit terms, credit limits, balances, and tax terms for all established credit customers are contained in the Customer List. The Customer List is also the Accounts Receivable Ledger. You will be using the following Customer List for established credit customers:

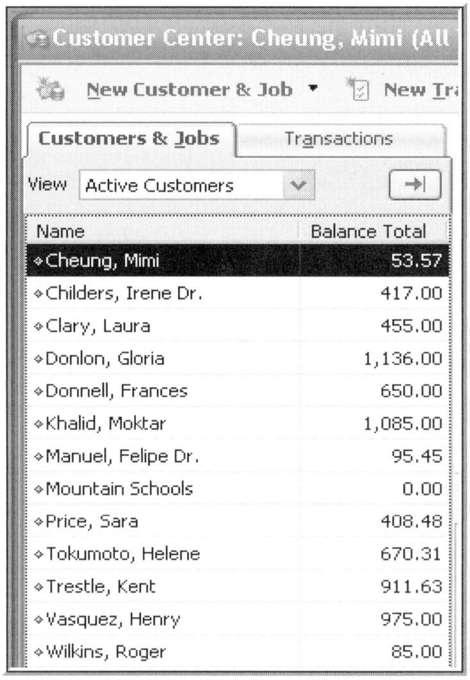

Sales are often made up of various types of income. In Your Name Sports there are several income accounts. In addition, there are sales categories within an income account. For example, each sales item represents an inventory item and is a subaccount of an income account—Ski Boots is a sales item and is a subaccount of Equipment Income. QuickBooks Pro uses lists to organize sales items. Using lists for sales items allows for flexibility in billing and a more accurate representation of the way in which income is earned. If the company charges a standard price for an item, the price of the item will be included on the list. In Your Name Sports, all items sell at different prices, so the price given for each item is listed at 0.00. In a retail business with an inventory, the number of units on hand can be tracked; and, when the amount on hand gets to a predetermined limit, an order can be placed. The following Item List for the various types of merchandise and sales categories will be used for Your Name Sports:

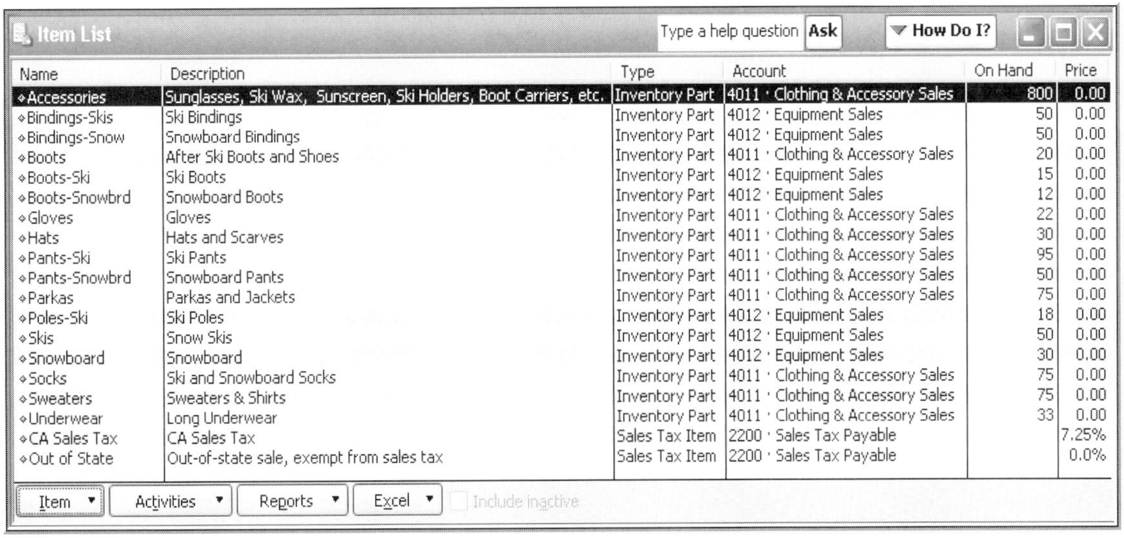

Item List

Name	Description	Type	Account	On Hand	Price
Accessories	Sunglasses, Ski Wax, Sunscreen, Ski Holders, Boot Carriers, etc.	Inventory Part	4011 · Clothing & Accessory Sales	800	0.00
Bindings-Skis	Ski Bindings	Inventory Part	4012 · Equipment Sales	50	0.00
Bindings-Snow	Snowboard Bindings	Inventory Part	4012 · Equipment Sales	50	0.00
Boots	After Ski Boots and Shoes	Inventory Part	4011 · Clothing & Accessory Sales	20	0.00
Boots-Ski	Ski Boots	Inventory Part	4012 · Equipment Sales	15	0.00
Boots-Snowbrd	Snowboard Boots	Inventory Part	4012 · Equipment Sales	12	0.00
Gloves	Gloves	Inventory Part	4011 · Clothing & Accessory Sales	22	0.00
Hats	Hats and Scarves	Inventory Part	4011 · Clothing & Accessory Sales	30	0.00
Pants-Ski	Ski Pants	Inventory Part	4011 · Clothing & Accessory Sales	95	0.00
Pants-Snowbrd	Snowboard Pants	Inventory Part	4011 · Clothing & Accessory Sales	50	0.00
Parkas	Parkas and Jackets	Inventory Part	4011 · Clothing & Accessory Sales	75	0.00
Poles-Ski	Ski Poles	Inventory Part	4012 · Equipment Sales	18	0.00
Skis	Snow Skis	Inventory Part	4012 · Equipment Sales	50	0.00
Snowboard	Snowboard	Inventory Part	4012 · Equipment Sales	30	0.00
Socks	Ski and Snowboard Socks	Inventory Part	4011 · Clothing & Accessory Sales	75	0.00
Sweaters	Sweaters & Shirts	Inventory Part	4011 · Clothing & Accessory Sales	75	0.00
Underwear	Long Underwear	Inventory Part	4011 · Clothing & Accessory Sales	33	0.00
CA Sales Tax	CA Sales Tax	Sales Tax Item	2200 · Sales Tax Payable		7.25%
Out of State	Out-of-state sale, exempt from sales tax	Sales Tax Item	2200 · Sales Tax Payable		0.0%

As in previous chapters, all transactions are listed on memos. The transaction date will be the same date as the memo date unless otherwise specified within the transaction. Customer names, when necessary, will be given in the transaction. Unless otherwise specified, all terms for customers on account are Net 30 days.

Even when you are instructed to enter a transaction step by step, you should always refer to the memo for transaction details. Once a specific type of transaction has been entered in a step-by-step manner, additional transactions will be made without having instructions provided. Of course, you may always refer to instructions given for previous transactions for ideas or for steps used to enter those transactions.

CUSTOMIZE REPORT FORMAT

The report format used in one company may not be appropriate for all companies that use QuickBooks Pro. The preferences selected in QuickBooks Pro are only for the current company. In Section 1 of the text, report preferences were changed for Your Name Computer Consulting, but those changes have no effect on Your Name Sports. The header/footer for reports in Your Name Sports must be customized to eliminate the printing of the date prepared, time prepared, and report basis as part of a report heading. In addition, QuickBooks can automatically refresh reports when a change is made. This feature may be selected as a preference as well.

MEMO

DATE: January 1, 2006

Before recording any transactions or preparing any reports, customize the report format by removing the date prepared, time prepared, and report basis from report headings. In addition, have reports refresh automatically.

Customize the report preferences as indicated in the memo

Click **Edit**, click **Preferences**

Scroll through the items listed on the left side of the screen until you get to **Reports and Graphs**

Click **Reports and Graphs**

On the **My Preferences** tab, click **Refresh automatically**

Click the **Company Preferences** tab

Click the **Format** button

Click the **Header/Footer** tab

Click **Date Prepared**, **Time Prepared**, and **Report Basis** to deselect

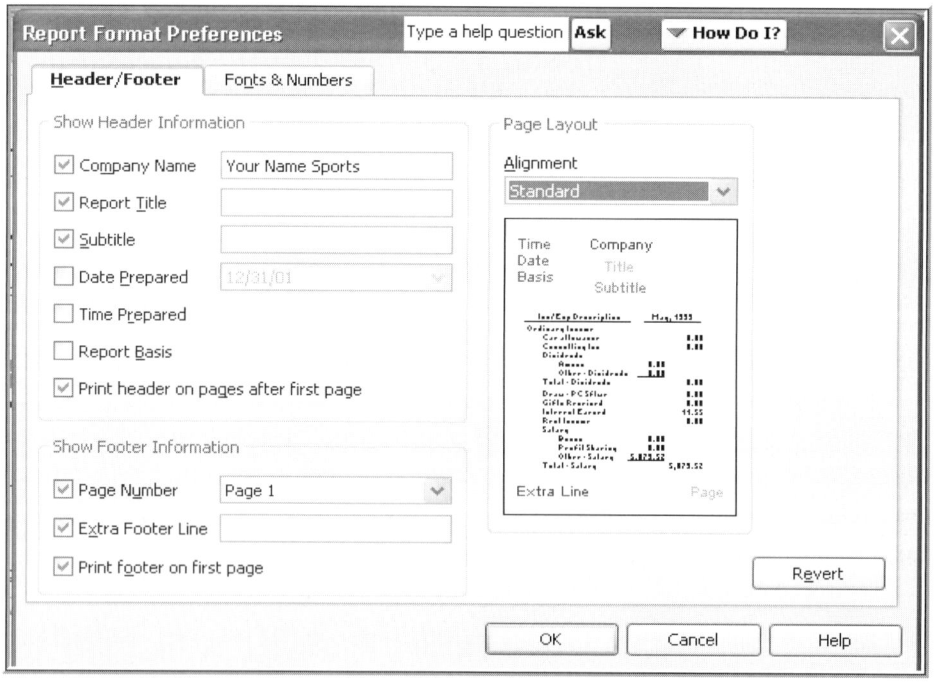

Click **OK** to save the change

Click **OK** to close **Preferences**

CUSTOMIZE BUSINESS FORMS

In QuickBooks it is possible to customize the business forms used in recording transactions. In earlier chapters some student names did not print on the same line as the company name. In order to provide more room for the company title, QuickBooks' Layout Designer must be used. When you access an invoice, for example, QuickBooks uses a ready-made form. This is called a *template*. In order to make changes to a template, you must first duplicate the template and then make changes to it. Other business forms may be changed without duplicating the form.

MEMO

DATE: January 2, 2006

Customize the Sales Receipt form, the Credit Memo form, and the template used for Product Invoices.

Customize the Sales Receipt and the Product Invoice

Open a **Sales Receipt** as previously instructed
Click the **Customize** button next to Template

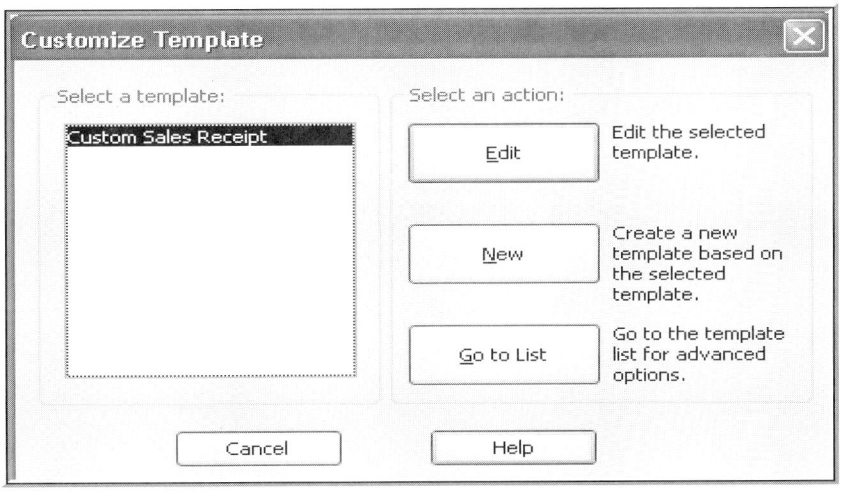

Click the **Edit** button on the Customize Template dialog box
Click the **Layout Designer** button on the Customize Sales Receipt screen
Point to the black squares (sizing handles) on the frame around Sales Receipt
When the cursor turns into a double arrow, hold the primary (left) mouse button and drag until the size of the frame begins at **6** on the ruler bar

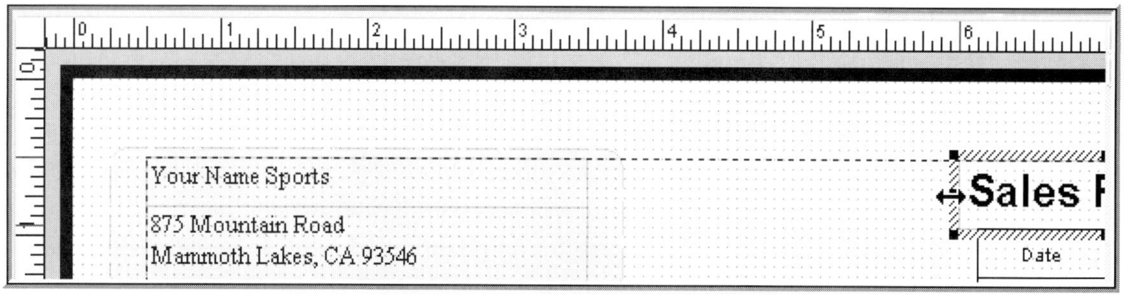

Click in the textbox for **Your Name Sports**
Drag the border of the frame until it is a **5 ¾** on the ruler bar

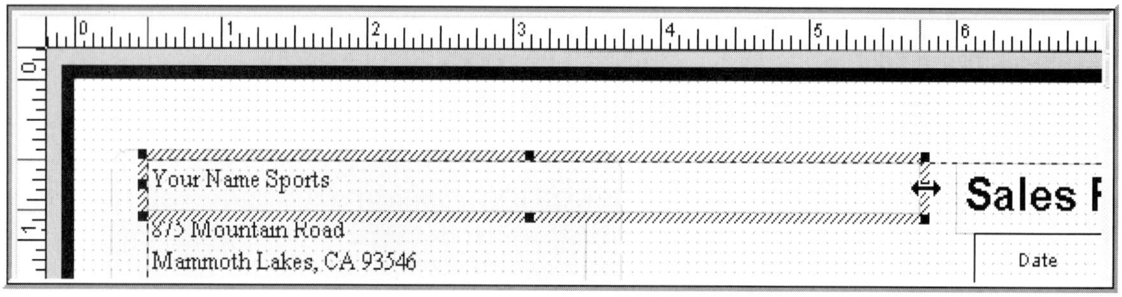

Click **OK** on Layout Designer
Click **OK** on Customize Sales Receipt
Close the **Enter Sales Receipts** screen
Repeat the steps previously listed to customize the Credit Memo
When finished with the customization of the Credit Memo, click **Lists** on the menu bar
Click **Templates**

- *Note:* The Custom Sales Receipt and Custom Credit Memo have been added to the Template list

From the Templates List, click **Intuit Product Invoice**
Click the **Templates** button
Click **Duplicate**

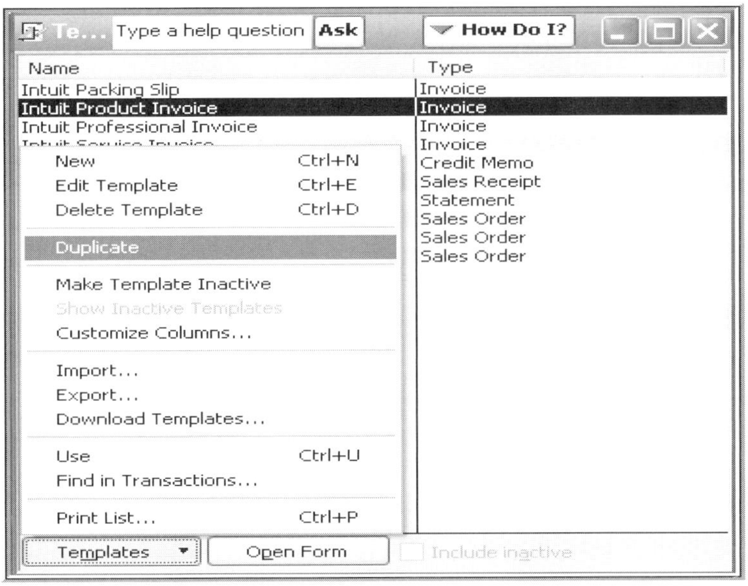

On the Select Template Type make sure Invoice is selected and click **OK**

Make sure **DUP: Intuit Product Invoice** is selected

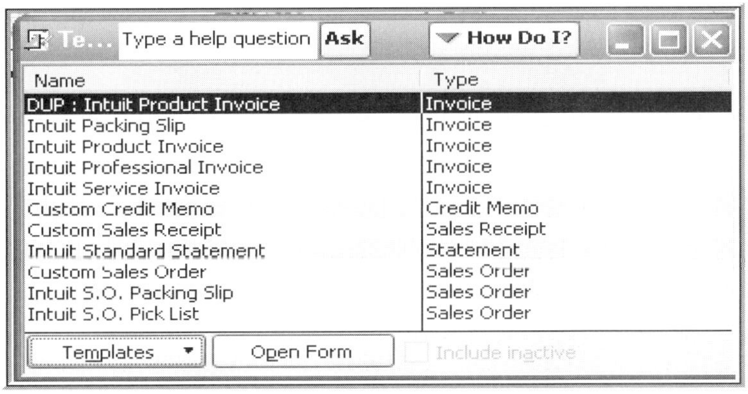

Click the **Templates** button, click **Edit Template**
Click the **Layout Designer** button and change the layout as instructed for Sales Receipts

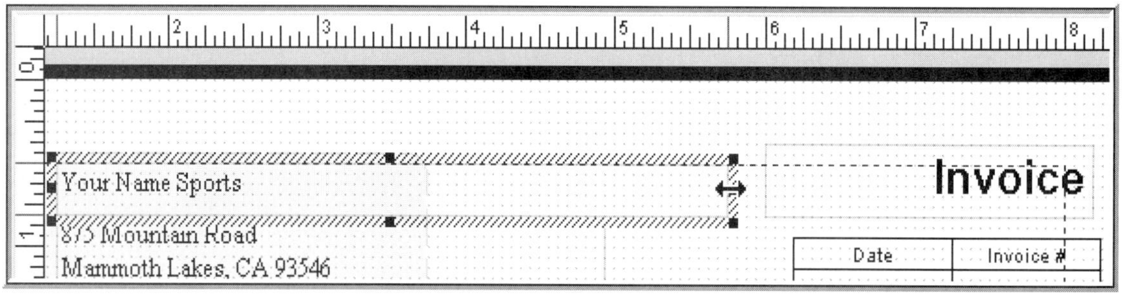

Click **OK** until you return to the Template List
Close the Template List

ENTER SALES ON ACCOUNT

Because QuickBooks Pro operates on a business form premise, a sale on account is entered via an invoice. When you sell merchandise on account, you prepare an invoice including sales tax and payment terms and QuickBooks Pro records the transaction in the Journal and updates the customer's account automatically. QuickBooks allows you to set up different price levels for customers. Since our small company has not established sales prices for each item it sells, we will not be using Price Levels in this tutorial. For information on Price Levels, refer to Appendix C.

MEMO
DATE: January 2, 2006

Bill the following: Invoice No. 1—An established customer, Roger Wilkins, purchased a pair of after-ski boots for $75.00 on account. Terms are Net 15.

Record the sale on account shown in the invoice above. This invoice is used to bill a customer for a sale using one sales item:

Access a blank invoice as previously instructed in Chapter 2
Click the drop-down list arrow next to **Customer:Job**
Click **Wilkins, Roger**
Click the drop-down list arrow next to Intuit Product Invoice
Click **DUP: Intuit Product Invoice** to use your customized invoice
Tab to **Date** and enter the date of **01/02/2006**

Invoice No. 1 should be showing in the **Invoice No.** box
There is no PO No. to record
Terms should be indicated as **Net 15**
Tab to or click **Quantity**
Type **1**

- The quantity is one because you are billing for one pair of after-ski boots.

Tab to or click the first line beneath **Item Code**
Click the drop-down list arrow next to **Item Code**

- Refer to the memo above and the Item list for appropriate billing information.

Click **Boots** to bill for one pair of after-ski boots

- The Description ***After Ski Boots and Shoes*** is automatically inserted.

Tab to or click **Price Each**
Type in the amount of the after-ski boots **75**

- Because the price on ski boots differs with each style, QuickBooks Pro has not been given the price in advance. It must be inserted during the invoice preparation. If you chose to set up separate sales items for each type of ski boot, sales prices could and should be assigned. In addition, different price levels could be given for the item.

Click in the box for **Customer Message**

- QuickBooks Pro will automatically calculate the total in the **Amount** column.
- Because this is a taxable item, QuickBooks Pro inserts **Tax** in the **Tax** column.

Click the drop-down list arrow next to **Customer Message**
Click **Thank you for your business.**

- Message is inserted in the **Customer Message** box.
- Notice that QuickBooks Pro automatically calculates the tax for the invoice and adds it to the invoice total.

EDIT AND CORRECT ERRORS

If an error is discovered while entering invoice information, position the cursor in the field containing the error. As in previous chapters, you may do this by positioning the mouse pointer in the field and clicking the primary key, by tabbing to move forward through each field, or pressing Shift+Tab to move back to the field containing the error. If the error is highlighted, type the correction. If the error is not highlighted, you can correct the error by pressing the Backspace or the Delete key as many times as necessary to remove the error, then typing the correction. (*Alternate method*: point to error, highlight by dragging the mouse through the error, then type the correction.)

If you are not comfortable correcting errors, do the following on Invoice No. 1:

Click the drop-down list arrow next to **Customer:Job**
Click **Cheung, Mimi**

- If the message, "Switching between customers may alter tax codes" appears, click **OK**.
- Name is changed in Customer:Job, and Bill To information is also changed.

Click to the left of the first number in the **Date**—this is **0**
Hold down primary mouse button and drag through the date to highlight.
Type **11/19/2006** as the date

- This removes the 01/02/2006 date originally entered.

Click to the right of the **1** in **Quantity**
Backspace and type a **2**, press the **Tab** key
To eliminate the changes made to Invoice No. 1, click the drop-down list arrow next to **Customer:Job**
Click **Wilkins, Roger**
Click the cursor so it is in front of the **1** in the **Date**
Press the **Delete** until the date is removed
Type **01/02/2006**
Click to the right of the **2** in **Quantity**
Backspace and type a **1**
Press the **Tab** key

- This will cause QuickBooks Pro to calculate the amount and the total for the invoice and will move the cursor to the **Description** field.
- Invoice No. 1 has been returned to the correct customer, date, and quantity.

Compare the information you entered with the information provided in the memo and on the following:

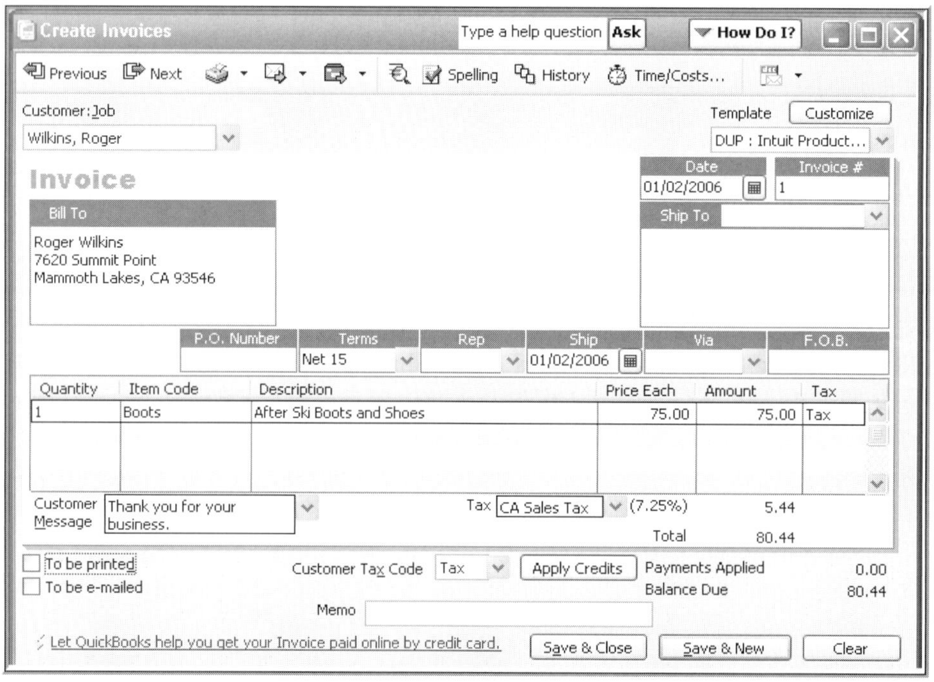

PRINT AN INVOICE

With Invoice No. 1 on the screen, print the invoice with lines around each field immediately after entering the corrected information

Follow the instructions given previously for printing invoices making the change to Do not print lines around each field

Do not print lines around each field check box: should not have a check mark

- If there is a check mark in the box, lines will not print around each field.
- If a check is not in the box, lines will print around each field.
- To save printing time and ink, your instructor may suggest that you do not print lines around each field. If this is the case, make sure there is a check mark in the check box.

Click the **Save & New** button on the bottom of the **Create Invoices** screen to record the invoice and go to a blank invoice

ENTER TRANSACTIONS USING MORE THAN ONE SALES ITEM AND SALES TAX

Frequently, sales to customers will be for more than one item. For example, new bindings are usually purchased along with a new pair of skis. Invoices can be prepared to bill a customer for several items at once.

MEMO

DATE: January 3, 2006

Bill the following: Invoice No. 2—Every year Dr. Felipe Manuel gets new ski equipment. Bill him for his equipment purchase for this year: skis, $425; bindings, $175; ski boots, $250; and ski poles, $75.

Record a transaction on account for a sale involving several taxable sales items:

Click the drop-down list arrow next to **Customer:Job**
Click **Manuel, Felipe Dr.**
Verify the Template as **DUP: Intuit Product Invoice**
Tab to or click **Date**
Type **01/03/06** as the date
Make sure the number **2** is showing in the **Invoice No.** box
There is no PO No. to record
Terms should be indicated as **2% 10 Net 30**

Tab to or click **Quantity**
Type **1**
Tab to or click the first line beneath **Item Code**
Click the drop-down list arrow next to **Item Code**
Click **Skis**

- **Skis** is inserted as the item code.
- **Snow Skis** is inserted as the **Description**.

Tab to or click **Price Each**
Enter **425**

- Notice that the **Customer is taxable** because the Customer Tax Code indicates **Tax**.
- Because Dr. Manuel is a taxable customer, sales tax is indicated by **Tax** in the **Tax** column.

Tab to or click the second line for **Quantity**
Type **1**
Click the drop-down list arrow next to **Item Code**
Click **Bindings-Skis**

- **Ski Bindings** is inserted as the **Description**.

Tab to or click **Price Each**
Enter **175**

- Notice that sales tax is indicated by **Tax** in the **Tax** column.

Repeat the above steps to enter the information for the ski boots and the ski poles
Click the drop-down list arrow next to **Customer Message**
Click **Thank you for your business.**

- Notice that QuickBooks Pro automatically calculates the tax for the invoice and adds it to the invoice total.

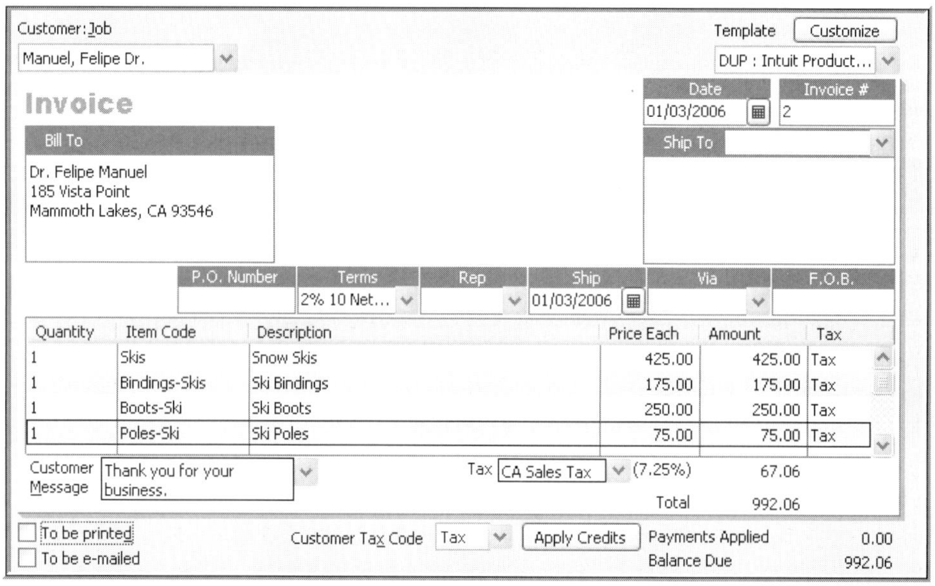

Print the invoice by following the instructions provided for Invoice No. 1
Do not close the invoice

E-MAIL INVOICES

In addition to printing and mailing invoices, QuickBooks® Pro 2006 allows invoices to be sent to customers via e-mail. While this text will not actually require sending invoice by e-mail, it is important to be aware of this time-saving feature of QuickBooks.

Explore e-mailing an invoice:

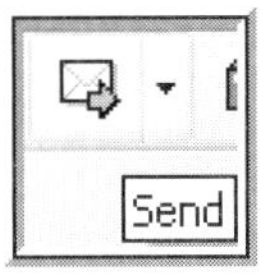

Click the drop-down list arrow next to **Send**
Click **E-mail Invoice**

- Notice that the e-mail text has automatically been completed.
- Look at the message that will accompany the electronic copy of the invoice.

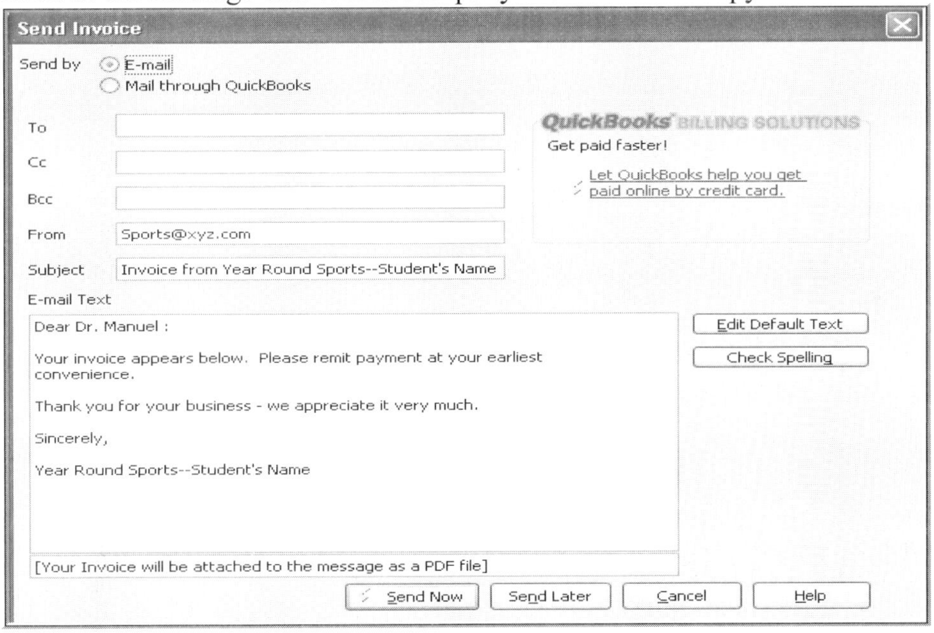

Click **Cancel**

PREPARE INVOICES WITHOUT STEP-BY-STEP INSTRUCTIONS

MEMO

DATE: January 3, 2006

Bill the following:

Invoice No. 3—We give Mountain Schools a special rate on equipment and clothing for the ski team. This year the school purchases 5 pairs of skis, $299 each; 5 pairs of bindings, $100 each; and 5 sets of ski poles, $29 each. Terms 2/10 Net 30.

Invoice No. 4—Sara Price purchased a new ski outfit: 1 parka, $249; a hat, $25; a sweater, $125; 1 pair of ski pants, $129; long underwear, $68; ski gloves, $79; ski socks, $15.95; sunglasses, $89.95; and a matching ski boot carrier, $2.95. Terms Net 15.

Invoice No. 5—Kent Trestle broke his snowboard when he was going down his favorite run, Dragon's Back. He purchased a new one without bindings for $499.95, Terms 1/10 Net 30.

Invoice No. 6—Roger Wilkins decided to buy some new powder skis and bindings. Bill him for snow skis, $599, and ski bindings, $179. Terms Net 15.

Prepare and print invoices without step-by-step instructions.

If Invoice 2 is still on the screen, click **Next**

Enter the four transactions in the memo above. Refer to instructions given for the two previous transactions entered.

- Always use the Item List to determine the appropriate sales items for billing.
- Use *Thank you for your business.* as the message for these invoices.
- If you make an error, correct it.
- If you get a suggestion from Spell check; i.e., **Snowboard**, and the word is spelled correctly, click **Ignore All**.
- Print each invoice immediately after you enter the information for it, and print lines around each field.
- To go from one invoice to the next, click **Save & New** at the bottom of the **Create Invoices** screen or click **Next** at the top of the invoice.

- Click **Save & New** after Invoice No. 6 has been entered and printed.

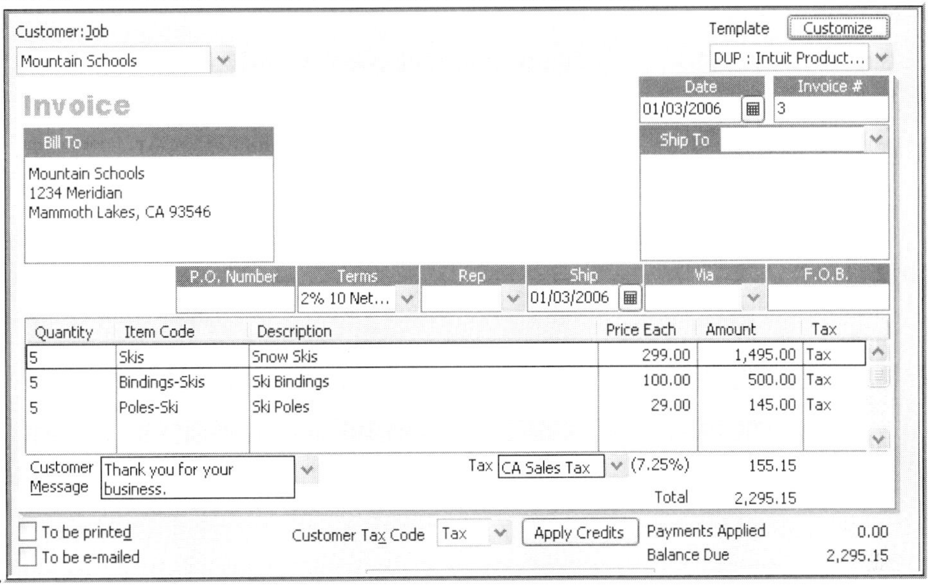

Customer:Job: Mountain Schools
Template: DUP : Intuit Product... Customize

Invoice

Date: 01/03/2006 Invoice #: 3

Bill To:
Mountain Schools
1234 Meridian
Mammoth Lakes, CA 93546

Ship To:

P.O. Number	Terms	Rep	Ship	Via	F.O.B.
	2% 10 Net...		01/03/2006		

Quantity	Item Code	Description	Price Each	Amount	Tax
5	Skis	Snow Skis	299.00	1,495.00	Tax
5	Bindings-Skis	Ski Bindings	100.00	500.00	Tax
5	Poles-Ski	Ski Poles	29.00	145.00	Tax

Customer Message: Thank you for your business.
Tax: CA Sales Tax (7.25%) 155.15
Total 2,295.15

To be printed
To be e-mailed
Customer Tax Code: Tax
Apply Credits
Payments Applied 0.00
Balance Due 2,295.15

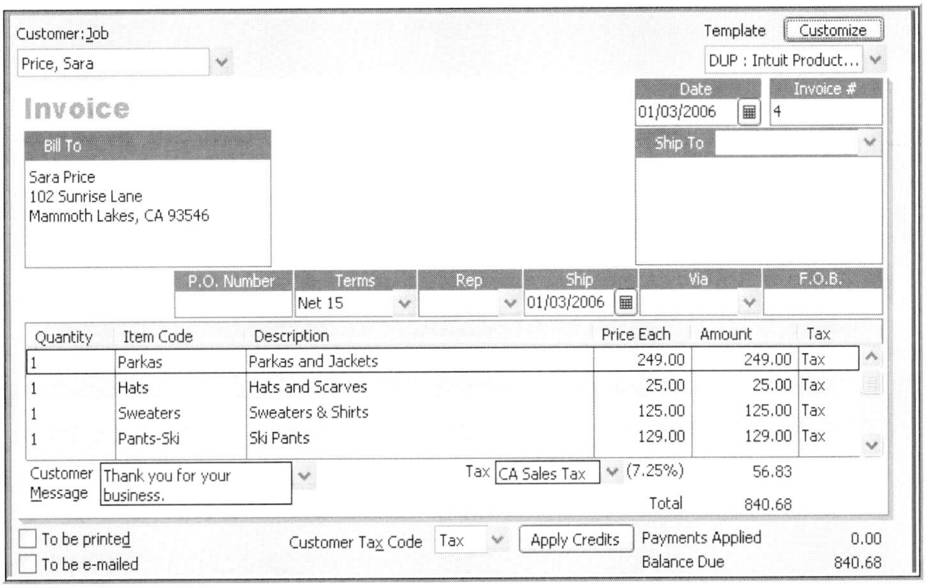

Customer:Job: Price, Sara
Template: DUP : Intuit Product... Customize

Invoice

Date: 01/03/2006 Invoice #: 4

Bill To:
Sara Price
102 Sunrise Lane
Mammoth Lakes, CA 93546

Ship To:

P.O. Number	Terms	Rep	Ship	Via	F.O.B.
	Net 15		01/03/2006		

Quantity	Item Code	Description	Price Each	Amount	Tax
1	Parkas	Parkas and Jackets	249.00	249.00	Tax
1	Hats	Hats and Scarves	25.00	25.00	Tax
1	Sweaters	Sweaters & Shirts	125.00	125.00	Tax
1	Pants-Ski	Ski Pants	129.00	129.00	Tax

Customer Message: Thank you for your business.
Tax: CA Sales Tax (7.25%) 56.83
Total 840.68

To be printed
To be e-mailed
Customer Tax Code: Tax
Apply Credits
Payments Applied 0.00
Balance Due 840.68

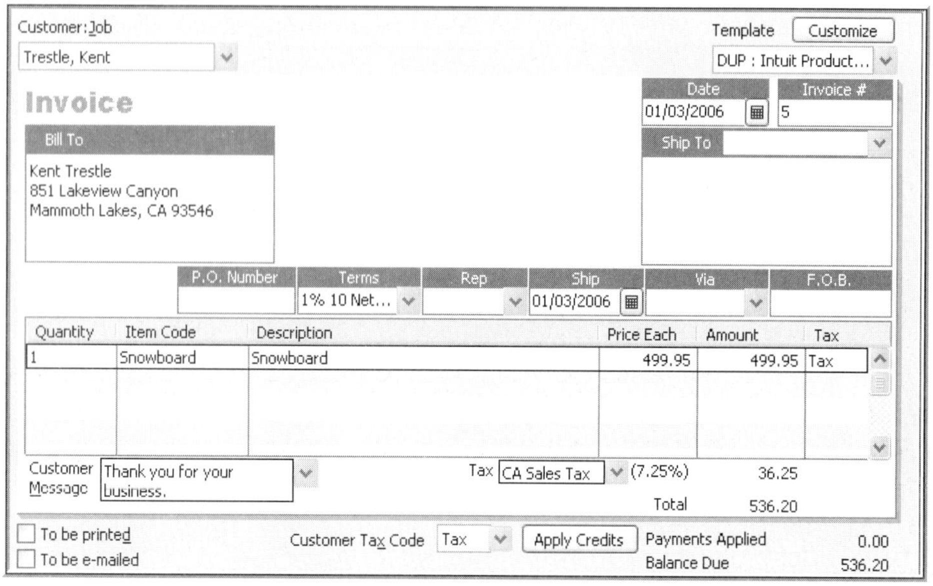

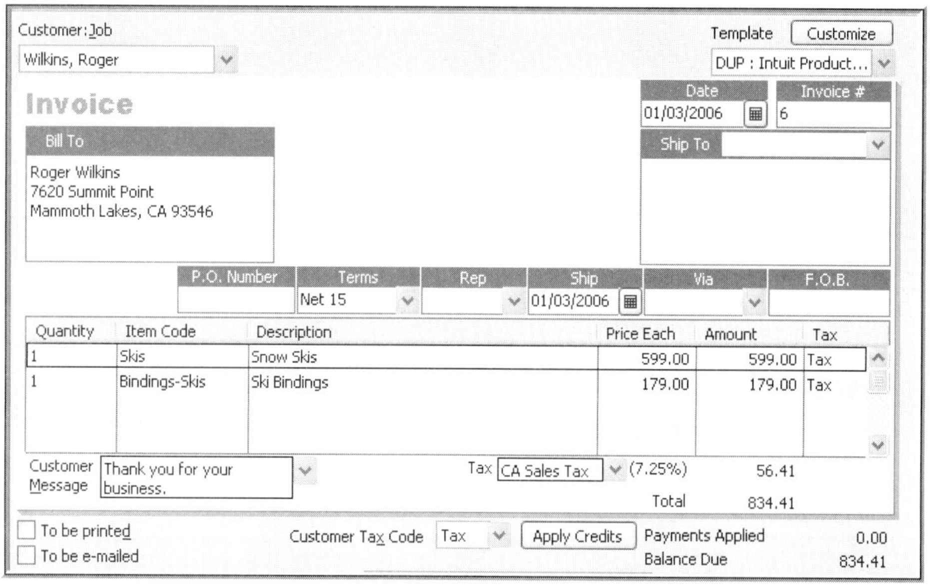

ENTER A TRANSACTION EXCEEDING A CUSTOMER'S CREDIT LIMIT AND ADD A WORD TO THE SPELLING DICTIONARY

When a customer is added to the Customer List and a complete setup is performed, the file tab for Additional Info will appear. Additional Info contains a dialog box in which a credit limit can be established for a customer. QuickBooks Pro does allow transactions for a customer to exceed the established credit limit, but a dialog box appears with information regarding the transaction amount and the credit limit for a customer.

MEMO
DATE: January 5, 2006

Prepare and print a Customer Balance Detail Report so that the owners can see exactly how much each customer owes to Your Name Sports.

Prepare a Customer Balance Detail Report for all customers for all transactions:

Click **Reports** on the menu bar, point to **Customers & Receivables**, click **Customer Balance Detail**
- *Note:* When preparing a single report, it is more convenient to use the Reports menu. When preparing several reports, using the Report Center is more efficient.

Dates should be **All**
- If not, click the drop-down list arrow next to the **Dates** text box, click **All**.
- Scroll through the report. See how much each customer owes for each invoice.
- Notice that the amount owed by Mimi Cheung for Invoice No. 7 is $1,017.68 and that her total balance is $1,071.25.

Do not close the **Customer Balance Detail Report**

USE THE QUICKZOOM FEATURE

QuickZoom is a feature of QuickBooks Pro that allows you to view additional information within a report. For example, an invoice may be viewed when the Customer Balance Detail Report is on the screen simply by using the QuickZoom feature.

MEMO
DATE: January 5, 2006

The bookkeeper, Rose Spencer, could not remember if Invoice No. 7 was for ski equipment or snowboard equipment. With the Customer Balance Detail Report on the screen, use QuickZoom to view Invoice No. 7.

Use QuickZoom to view Invoice No. 7

Position the cursor over any part of the report showing information about Invoice No. 7
- The cursor will turn into a magnifying glass with a letter **Z** inside.

Double-click

- Invoice No. 7 appears on the screen.
- Check to make sure the four items on the invoice are: Snowboard, Bindings-Snow, Boots-Snowbrd, and Accessories.

With Invoice No. 7 on the screen, proceed to the next section.

CORRECT AN INVOICE AND PRINT THE CORRECTED FORM

QuickBooks Pro allows corrections and revisions to an invoice even if the invoice has been printed. The invoice may be corrected by going directly to the original invoice or by accessing the original invoice via the Accounts Receivable Register. An invoice can be on view in QuickZoom and still be corrected.

MEMO
DATE: January 5, 2006

While viewing Invoice No. 7 for Mimi Cheung in QuickZoom, the bookkeeper, Rose Spencer, realizes that the snowboard should be $499.95, not the $489.95 that is on the original invoice. Make the correction and reprint the invoice.

Correct Invoice No. 7 while showing on the screen in QuickZoom

Click in the **Price Each** column
Change the amount to **499.95**
Press Tab to change the **Amount** calculated for the Snowboard
Print the corrected Invoice No. 7
Click **Save & Close** at the bottom of the **Create Invoice** screen to record and close the invoice
When the **Recording Transaction** message box appears regarding saving a changed transaction, click **Yes**
A **Recording Transaction** message box appears on the screen regarding the credit limit of $500 for Mimi Cheung

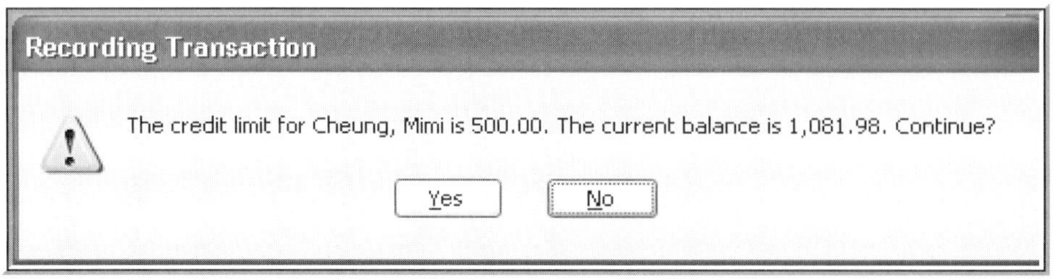

Click **Yes** to accept the current balance of $1,081.98

- This closes the invoice and returns you to the Customer Balance Detail Report.
- Notice that the total amount for Invoice No. 7 is $1,028.41 and that Mimi Cheung's total balance is $1,081.98

Click **Print** at the top of the **Customer Balance Detail Report** and print the report in Portrait orientation

Your Name Sports
Customer Balance Detail
All Transactions

Type	Date	Num	Account	Amount	Balance
Cheung, Mimi					
Invoice	12/31/2005		1200 · Accounts Receivable	53.57	53.57
Invoice	01/05/2006	7	1200 · Accounts Receivable	1,028.41	1,081.98
Total Cheung, Mimi				1,081.98	1,081.98
Childers, Irene Dr.					
Invoice	12/31/2005		1200 · Accounts Receivable	417.00	417.00
Total Childers, Irene Dr.				417.00	417.00
Clary, Laura					
Invoice	12/31/2005		1200 · Accounts Receivable	455.00	455.00
Total Clary, Laura				455.00	455.00
Donlon, Gloria					
Invoice	12/31/2005		1200 · Accounts Receivable	1,136.00	1,136.00
Total Donlon, Gloria				1,136.00	1,136.00

Partial Report

After the report is printed, click **Close** to close the **Customer Balance Detail Report**

ADDING NEW ACCOUNTS TO THE CHART OF ACCOUNTS

Because account needs can change as a business is in operation, QuickBooks Pro allows you to make changes to the Chart of Accounts at any time. Some changes to the Chart of Accounts require additional changes to other lists, such as the Item List. An account may be added by accessing the Chart of Accounts. It is also possible to add an account to the Chart of Accounts while adding an item to another list.

ADD NEW ITEMS TO LIST

In order to accommodate the changing needs of a business, all QuickBooks Pro lists allow you to make changes at any time. New items may be added to the list via the Item List or *on the fly* while entering invoice information. The Item List stores information about the items Your Name

Sports sells. Since Your Name Sports does not use price levels, it would be appropriate to have an item allowing for sales discounts. Having a discount item allows discounts to be recorded on the sales form. A discount can be a fixed amount or a percentage. A discount is calculated only on the line above it on the sales form. To allow the entire amount of the invoice to receive the discount, an item for a subtotal will also need to be added. When you complete the sales form, the subtotal item will appear before the discount item.

MEMO
DATE: January 5, 2006

Add an item for Sales Discounts and a Subtotal Item. Add a new expense account, 6130 Sales Discount, to the Chart of Accounts. The description for the account should be Discount on Sales.

Add new items and accounts

Click the **Items & Services** icon on the QuickBooks' Home Page
Click **Item** button at the bottom of the **Item List** screen
Click **New**
Item Type is **Discount**
Tab to or click **Item Name/Number**
Type **Nonprofit Discount**
Tab to or click **Description**
Type **10% Discount to Nonprofit Agencies**
Tab to or click **Amount or %**
Type in **10%**

- The % sign must be included in order to differentiate between a $10 discount and a 10% discount.

Click the drop-down list arrow for **Account**
Type **Sales Discounts**, press **Tab**

- **Account Not Found** dialog box appears on the screen.

Click **Set Up** on the **Account Not Found** dialog box
Complete the information for a New Account:
Type should be **Expense**

- If **not**, click the drop-down list arrow next to the text box for Type.
- **Click Expense**.

Tab to or click in the **Number** text box
Enter the Account Number **6130**
Tab to or click **Name**
Type **Sales Discounts**
Tab to or click **Description**
Enter **Discount on Sales**

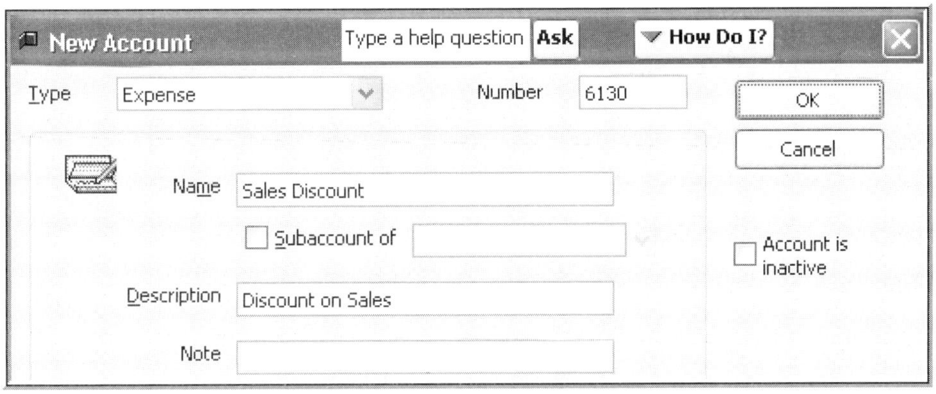

Click **OK** to add the **Sales Discounts** account, close the **New Account** dialog box, and return to the New Item screen

- At the bottom of the screen you should see the Tax Code as **Tax** and the statement **Discount is applied before sales tax** should be displayed.

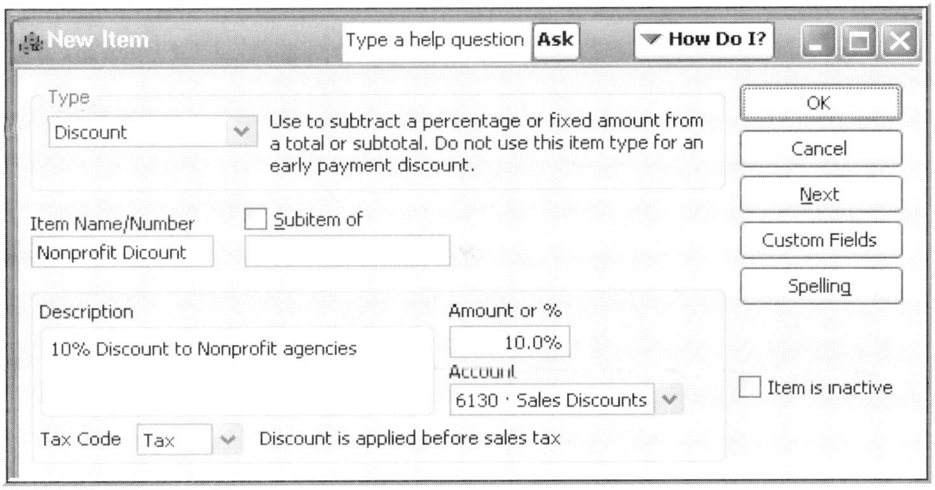

Click **Next** on the **New Item** dialog box

- A **discount** is calculated only on the line above it on the sales form. To allow the entire amount of the invoice to receive the discount, an item for a subtotal will also need to be added.

Repeat the steps for adding a New Item to add **Subtotal**
Type should be **Subtotal**
Item Name/Number is **Subtotal**
The description is **Subtotal**

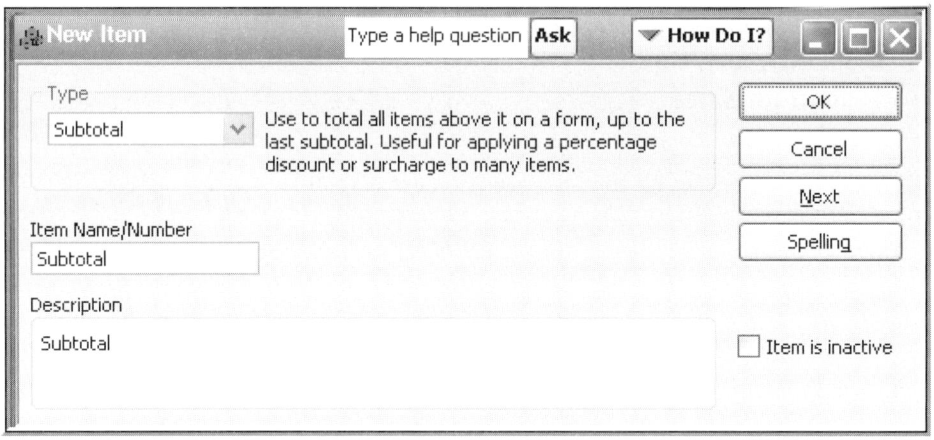

Click **OK** to add the new items and to close the **New Item** screen

- Verify the addition of Nonprofit Discount and Subtotal on the Item List. If everything is correct, close the **Item List**.
- If you find an error, click on the item with the error, click the **Item** button, click **Edit**, make corrections as needed.

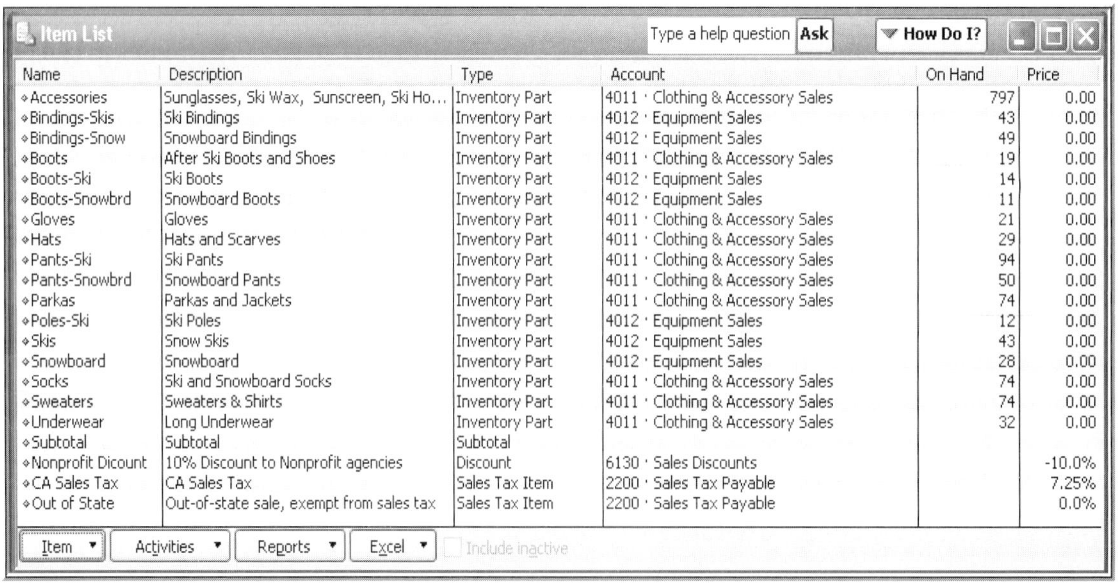

Name	Description	Type	Account	On Hand	Price
◊Accessories	Sunglasses, Ski Wax, Sunscreen, Ski Ho...	Inventory Part	4011 · Clothing & Accessory Sales	797	0.00
◊Bindings-Skis	Ski Bindings	Inventory Part	4012 · Equipment Sales	43	0.00
◊Bindings-Snow	Snowboard Bindings	Inventory Part	4012 · Equipment Sales	49	0.00
◊Boots	After Ski Boots and Shoes	Inventory Part	4011 · Clothing & Accessory Sales	19	0.00
◊Boots-Ski	Ski Boots	Inventory Part	4012 · Equipment Sales	14	0.00
◊Boots-Snowbrd	Snowboard Boots	Inventory Part	4012 · Equipment Sales	11	0.00
◊Gloves	Gloves	Inventory Part	4011 · Clothing & Accessory Sales	21	0.00
◊Hats	Hats and Scarves	Inventory Part	4011 · Clothing & Accessory Sales	29	0.00
◊Pants-Ski	Ski Pants	Inventory Part	4011 · Clothing & Accessory Sales	94	0.00
◊Pants-Snowbrd	Snowboard Pants	Inventory Part	4011 · Clothing & Accessory Sales	50	0.00
◊Parkas	Parkas and Jackets	Inventory Part	4011 · Clothing & Accessory Sales	74	0.00
◊Poles-Ski	Ski Poles	Inventory Part	4012 · Equipment Sales	12	0.00
◊Skis	Snow Skis	Inventory Part	4012 · Equipment Sales	43	0.00
◊Snowboard	Snowboard	Inventory Part	4012 · Equipment Sales	28	0.00
◊Socks	Ski and Snowboard Socks	Inventory Part	4011 · Clothing & Accessory Sales	74	0.00
◊Sweaters	Sweaters & Shirts	Inventory Part	4011 · Clothing & Accessory Sales	74	0.00
◊Underwear	Long Underwear	Inventory Part	4011 · Clothing & Accessory Sales	32	0.00
◊Subtotal	Subtotal	Subtotal			
◊Nonprofit Dicount	10% Discount to Nonprofit agencies	Discount	6130 · Sales Discounts		-10.0%
◊CA Sales Tax	CA Sales Tax	Sales Tax Item	2200 · Sales Tax Payable		7.25%
◊Out of State	Out-of-state sale, exempt from sales tax	Sales Tax Item	2200 · Sales Tax Payable		0.0%

Close the **Item List**

CORRECT AN INVOICE TO INCLUDE SALES DISCOUNT

MEMO
DATE: January 6, 2006

Now that the appropriate accounts for sales discounts have been created, use the Accounts Receivable Register to correct Invoice 3 for Mountain Schools to give the schools a 10% discount as a nonprofit organization.

Correct the invoice to Mountain Schools by opening the Chart of Accounts

Use the keyboard shortcut, **Ctrl+A**
In the Chart of Accounts, double-click **Accounts Receivable**

- Double-clicking opens the register
- The **Accounts Receivable Register** appears on the screen with information regarding each transaction entered into the account.

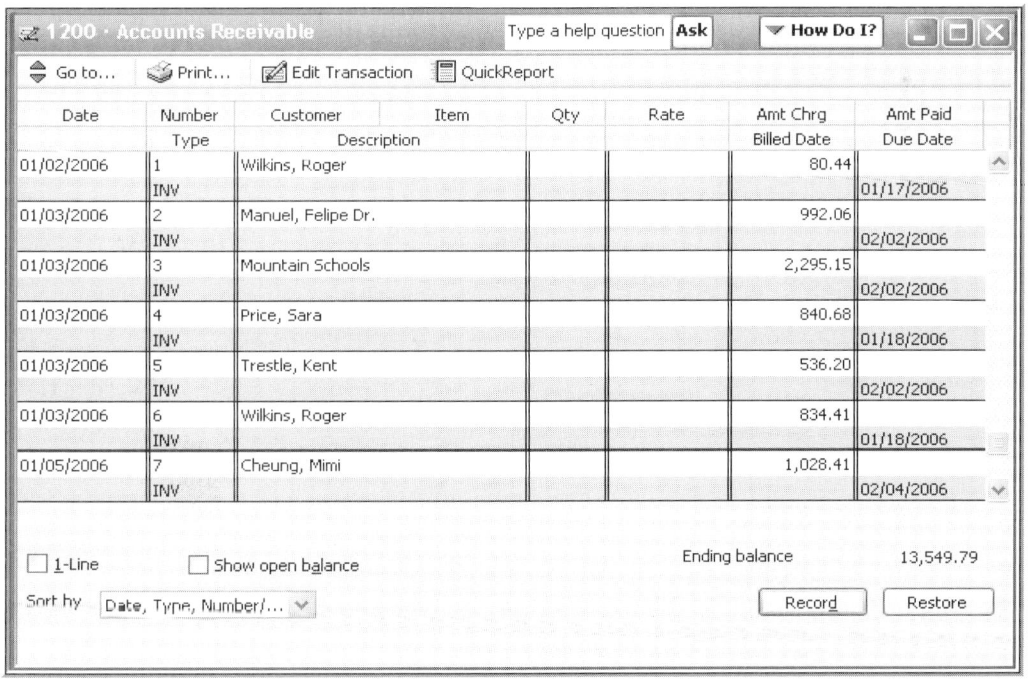

Date	Number / Type	Customer / Description	Item	Qty	Rate	Amt Chrg / Billed Date	Amt Paid / Due Date
01/02/2006	1 INV	Wilkins, Roger				80.44	01/17/2006
01/03/2006	2 INV	Manuel, Felipe Dr.				992.06	02/02/2006
01/03/2006	3 INV	Mountain Schools				2,295.15	02/02/2006
01/03/2006	4 INV	Price, Sara				840.68	01/18/2006
01/03/2006	5 INV	Trestle, Kent				536.20	02/02/2006
01/03/2006	6 INV	Wilkins, Roger				834.41	01/18/2006
01/05/2006	7 INV	Cheung, Mimi				1,028.41	02/04/2006

If necessary, scroll through the register until the transaction for **Invoice No. 3** is on the screen

- **Look** at the **Number/Type** column to identify the number of the invoice and the type of transaction.
- On the **Number** line you will see a check number or an invoice number.
- On **the Type** line **PMT** indicates a payment was received on account, and **INV** indicates a sale on account.

Click anywhere in the transaction for Invoice No. 3 to Mountain Schools
Click **Edit Transaction** at the top of the register

- Invoice No. 3 appears on the screen.

Click in **Item Code** beneath the last item, Poles-Ski
Click the drop-down list arrow for **Item Code**
Click **Subtotal**

- You may need to scroll through the Item List until you find Subtotal.
- Remember that QuickBooks Pro must subtotal the items on the invoice in order to calculate a discount on all items on the invoice.

Tab to or click the next blank line in **Item Code**
Click **Nonprofit Discount**

- You may need to scroll through the Item List until you find Nonprofit Discount.

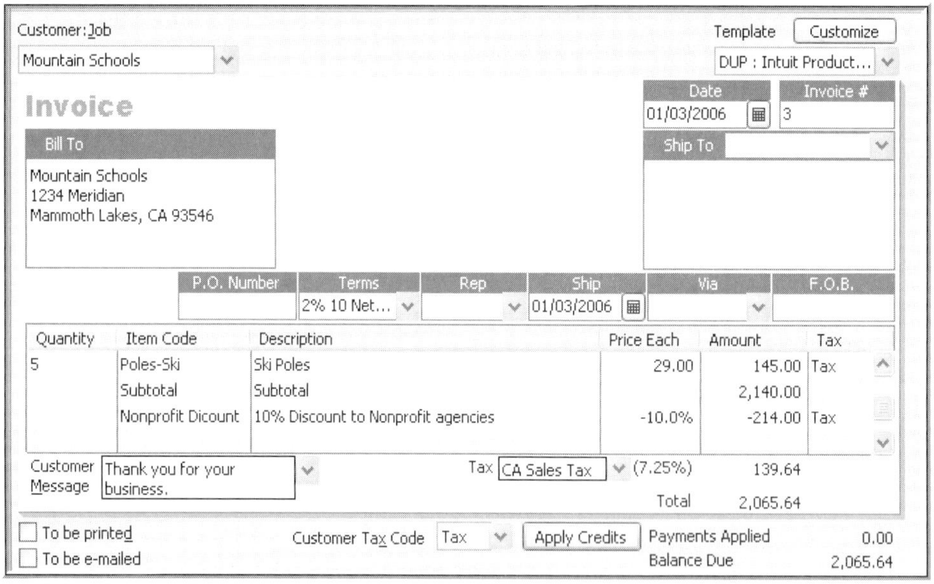

- Notice the subtotal of $2,140.00, the discount of $214, and the new invoice total of $2,065.64.

Click **Print** on the **Create Invoices** screen to print a corrected invoice
Click **Save & Close** on the **Create Invoices** screen to save the corrected invoice and return to the Accounts Receivable Register
Click **Yes** on the **Recording Transaction** screen

- Notice the new Amt Chg of $2,065.64 for Invoice No. 3 in the register.

Do not close the **Accounts Receivable Register**

VIEW A QUICKREPORT

After editing the invoice and returning to the register, you may get a detailed report regarding the customer's transactions by clicking the QuickReport button.

With the cursor in Invoice No. 3, click **QuickReport** button to view the **Mountain Schools** account

ANALYZE THE QUICKREPORT FOR MOUNTAIN SCHOOLS

Analyze the QuickReport

Your Name Sports
Register QuickReport
All Transactions

Type	Date	Num	Memo	Account	Paid	Open Balance	Amount
Mountain Schools							
Invoice	01/03/2006	3		1200 · Accounts Receivable	Unpaid	2,065.64	2,065.64
Total Mountain Schools						2,065.64	2,065.64
TOTAL						**2,065.64**	**2,065.64**

Notice that the total of Invoice No. 3 is $2,065.64
Close the **QuickReport** without printing
Close the **Accounts Receivable Register**
Close the **Chart of Accounts**

ADD A NEW CUSTOMER

QuickBooks Pro allows customers to be added at any time. They may be added to the company records through the Customer List, or they may be added *on the fly* as you create an invoice or sales receipt. When adding *on the fly*, you may choose between Quick Add (used to add only a customer's name) and Set Up (used to add complete information for a customer).

Memo

DATE: January 8, 2006

Rose was instructed to add a new customer. The information provided for the new customer is: Mountain Recreation Center, 985 Old Mammoth Road, Mammoth Lakes, CA 93546, Contact: Kathleene Clark, Phone: 909-555-2951, Fax: 909-555-1592, E-mail: mountainrec@abc.com Terms: 1%10 Net 30, Tax Code is Tax, Tax Item: CA Sales Tax, Credit Limit: 5,000, as of 1/8/2006 there is a 0.00 opening balance for the customer.

Add a new customer

Click the **Customer Center** icon at the top of the Home Page or the **Customers** button on the left side of the Home Page

With the Customer List showing on the screen

Use the keyboard shortcut **Ctrl+N** to create a new customer

In the **Customer** text box, enter **Mountain Recreation Center**

Tab to or click **Company Name**

Enter **Mountain Recreation Center**

Tab to or click the second line in **Bill To**

Enter the address listed above

Tab to or click **Contact**, enter the name of the person to contact

Tab to or click **Phone**, enter the telephone number

Tab to or click **FAX**, enter the fax number

Tab to or click **E-mail**, enter the e-mail address

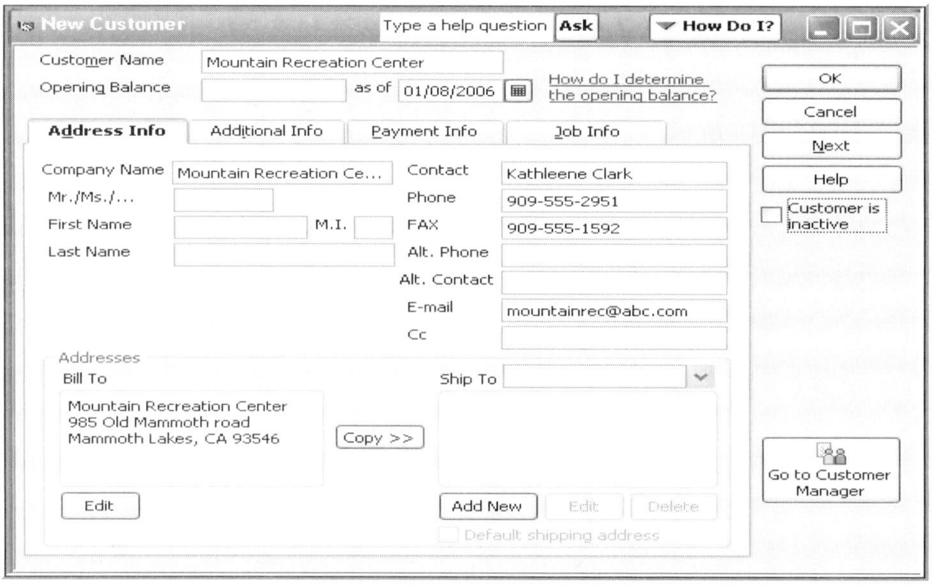

Click the **Additional Info** tab
Enter the terms and sales tax information for **Additional Info**

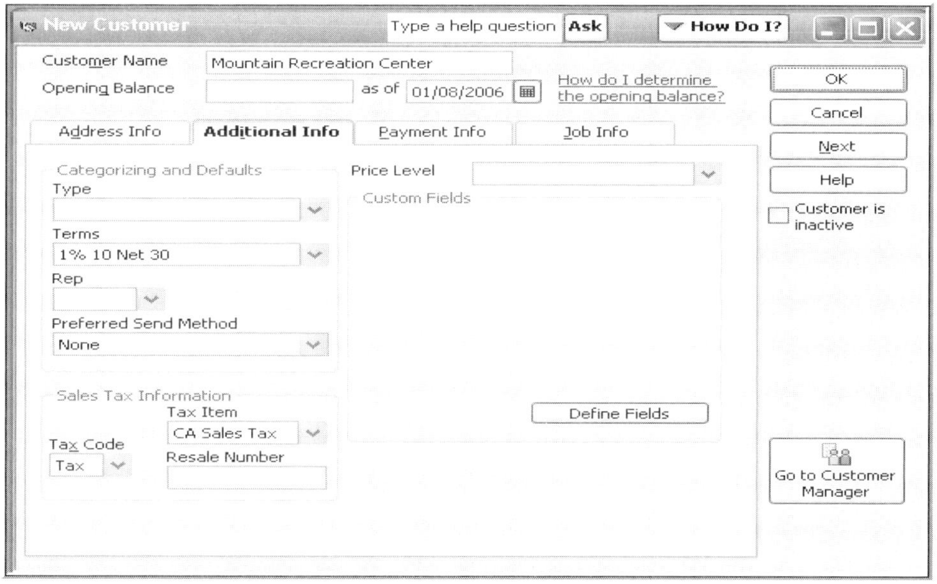

Click the **Payment Info** tab and enter the credit limit

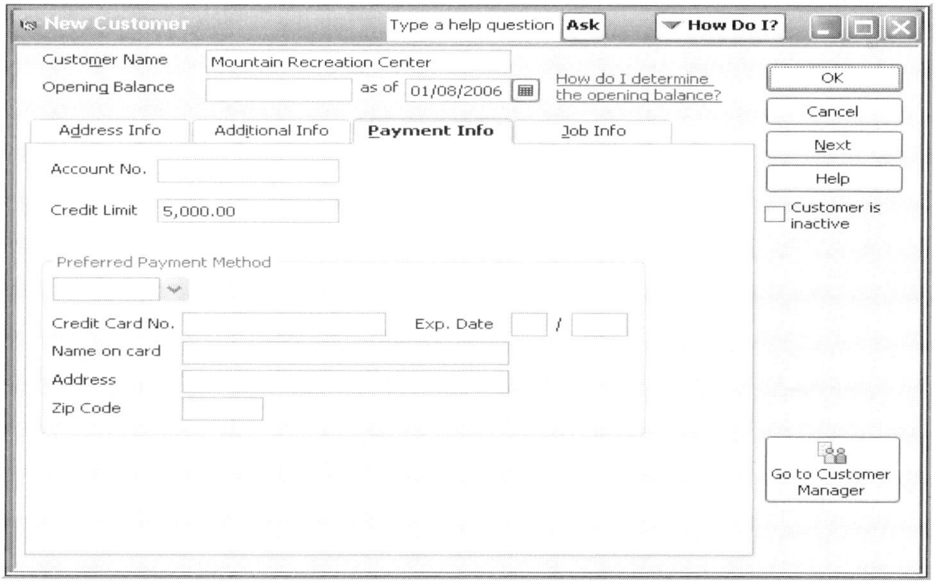

Click **OK** to complete the addition of Mountain Recreation Center as a customer

- Verify the addition of Mountain Recreation Center to the Customer:Job List.

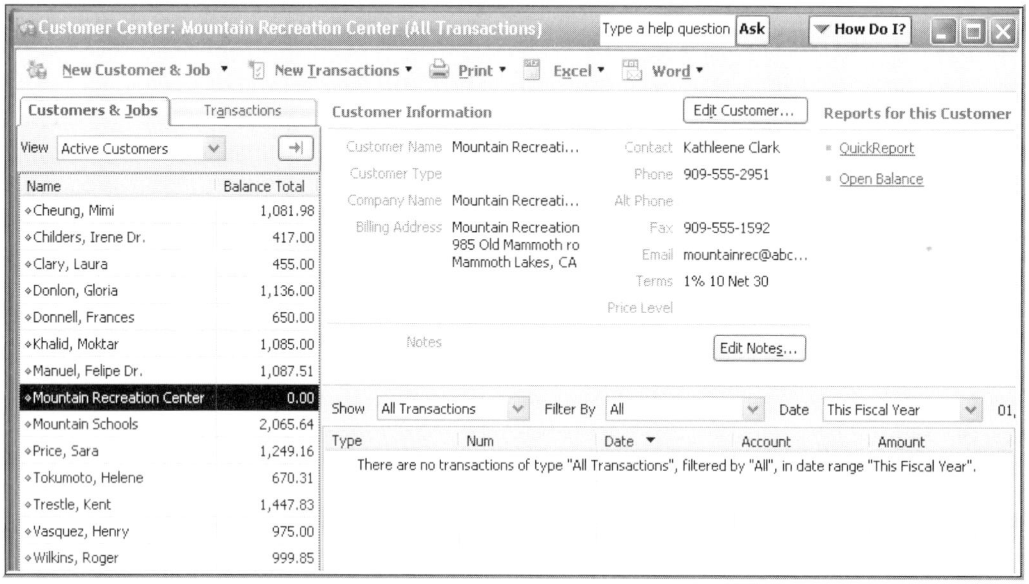

Close the **Customer Center**

RECORD A SALE TO A NEW CUSTOMER

Once a customer has been added, sales may be recorded for a customer.

MEMO
DATE: January 8, 2006

Record a sale of 5 sleds at $119.99 each and 5 toboggans at $229.95 each to Mountain Recreation Center. Because the sale is to a nonprofit organization, include a nonprofit discount.

Record the above sale on account to a new customer and add two new sales items

Access a blank invoice by using the keyboard shortcut **Ctrl+I**
Enter invoice information for **Mountain Recreation Center** as previously instructed
Date of the invoice is **01/08/2006**
Invoice No. is **8**
Tab to or click **Quantity**
Enter **5**
Tab to or click **Item Code**
Type **Sleds** for the **Item Code**, press **Enter**

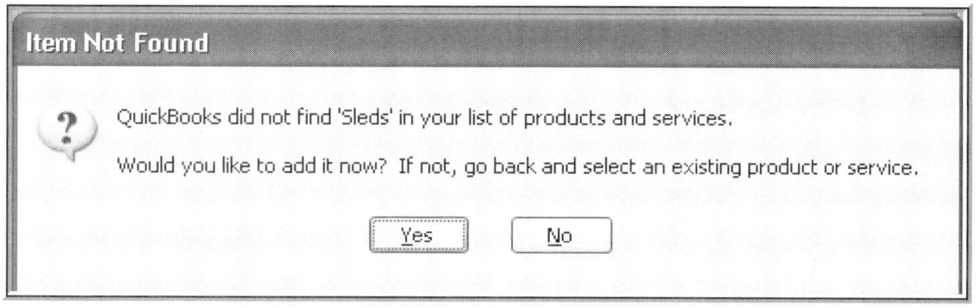

Click **Yes** to create the new item.
On the **New Item** screen, click **Inventory Part** for **Type**
- If necessary, click the drop-down list menu to get a list of choices for **Type**.

Item Name/Number should be **Sleds**
- If not, tab to or click in the text box for Item Name/Number, type **Sleds**.

Complete **Purchase Information**:
- This section provides information to be used for orders of sleds for Your Name Sports.

  Description on Purchase Transactions: enter **Sleds**
  Cost: **0.00**
  - Your Name Sports has elected to keep the item list simple and not use different items for different styles and models of sleds. Thus, sleds are purchased at different prices so the Cost is left at 0.00.

  COGS Account: **5000 Cost of Goods Sold**
  - If this account is not in the **COGS Account** text box, click the drop-down list arrow, click **5000 Cost of Goods Sold**.

  Preferred Vendor: Leave blank

Complete **Sales Information**:
- This section provides the information used when Your Name Sports sells sleds to customers.

Description on Sales Transactions: Should be **Sleds**
- If Sleds was not inserted at the same time as the Purchase Information Description, enter **Sleds** for the description.

  Sales Price: Leave 0.00
  - Your Name Sports has elected to keep the item list simple and not use different items for different styles and models of sleds. Thus, sleds are sold at different prices; and the Sales Price remains as 0.00.

  Tax Code: Should be **Tax**
  - If not, click the drop-down list arrow and click **Tax**.

  Click the drop-down list arrow for **Income Account**
  Click **4012 Equipment Sales**

Complete the **Inventory Information**:

- QuickBooks Pro uses this information to track the amount of inventory on hand and to provide reorder information.

Asset Account: Should be **1120 Inventory Asset**

- If this account is not in the Asset Account text box, click the drop-down list arrow, click **1120 Inventory Asset**.

Tab to or click **Reorder Point**
Enter **5**
Tab to or click **Qty on Hand**
Enter **10**
Tab to or click **Total Value**

- Five of the ten sleds were purchased by Your Name Sports for $75 each. The other five sleds were purchased for $60 each.

Enter **675** for the **Total Value**
Tab to or click **As of**
Enter the As of date of **01/08/06**

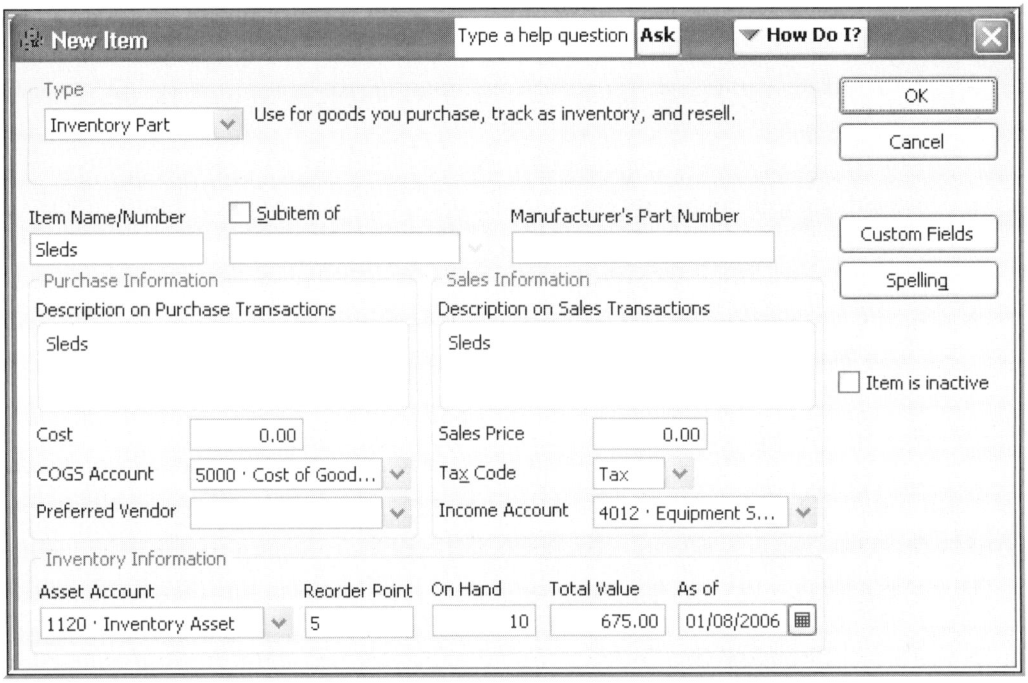

Click **OK** to add Sleds as a sales item
On the invoice, tab to or click **Price Each**
Enter **119.99**
Tab to or click the second line in **Quantity**
Enter **5**
Tab to or click **Item Code**
Click the drop-down list arrow for **Item Code**

- There is no item listed for Toboggans.

Click <**Add New**> at the top of the **Item List**
Complete the information for **New Item**
On the **New Item** screen, click **Inventory Part** for **Type**

- If necessary, click the drop-down list menu to get a list of choices for **Type**.

Tab to or click **Item Name/Number**
Enter **Toboggans**
Complete **Purchase Information**:
  Description on Purchase Transactions: Enter **Toboggans**
  Cost: **0.00**
  COGS Account: **5000 Cost of Goods Sold**
  Preferred Vendor: Leave blank
Complete **Sales Information**:
  Description on Sales Transactions: Should be **Toboggans**

  - If Toboggans was not inserted at the same time as the Purchase Information Description, enter **Toboggans** for the description.

  Sales Price: Leave **0.00**
  Tax Code: Should be **Tax**
  Click the drop-down list arrow for **Income Account**
  Click **4012 Equipment Sales**
Complete the **Inventory Information**:
  Asset Account: Should be **1120 Inventory Asset**

  - If this account is not in the **Asset Account** text box, click the drop-down list arrow, click **1120 Inventory Asset**.

  Tab to or click **Reorder Point**, enter **5**
  Tab to or click **Qty on Hand**, enter **10**
  Tab to or click **Total Value**

  - Five of the ten toboggans were purchased by Your Name Sports for $125 each. The other five toboggans were purchased for $150 each.

  Enter **1375** for the **Total Value**
  Tab to or click **As of**
  Enter the As of date of **01/08/06**
  Click **OK** to add Toboggans as a sales item

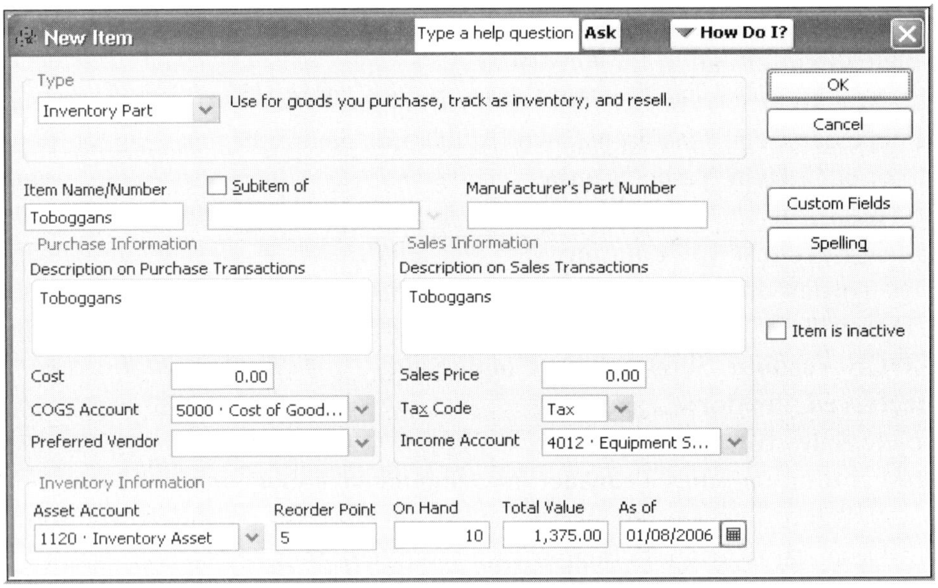

Complete the invoice

- Remember that Mountain Recreation Center is a nonprofit organization and is entitled to a Nonprofit Discount.

The message is **Thank you for your business.**

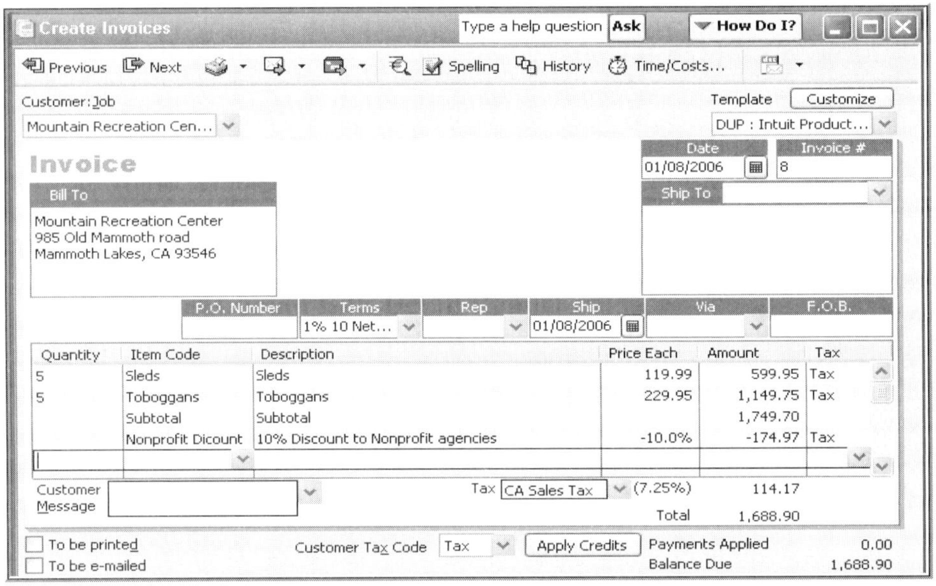

Print the invoice as previously instructed

Click **Save & Close** to record the invoice and close the transaction

MODIFY CUSTOMER RECORDS

Occasionally information regarding a customer will change. QuickBooks Pro allows customer accounts to be modified at any time by editing the Customer List.

MEMO
DATE: January 8, 2006

In order to update Mimi Cheung's account, change her credit limit to $2,500.00.

➤ Edit an account

Access the **Customer List** using the keyboard shortcut: **Ctrl+J**.
Double-click **Cheung, Mimi** on the Customer:Job List.
Click the **Payment Info** tab
Tab to or click **Credit Limit**
Enter **2500** for the amount
Click **OK** to record the change and exit the information for Mimi Cheung
Close the **Customer:Job List**

VOID AND DELETE SALES FORMS

Deleting an invoice or sales receipt permanently removes it from QuickBooks Pro without leaving a trace. If you want to correct financial records for an invoice that is no longer viable, it is more appropriate to void the invoice. When an invoice is voided, it remains in the QuickBooks Pro system, but QuickBooks Pro does not count it. Voiding an invoice should be used only if there have been no payments made on the invoice. If any payment has been received, a Credit Memo would be appropriate for recording a return.

Void an Invoice

MEMO
DATE: January 8, 2006

Roger Wilkins returned the after-ski boots he purchased for $80.44 including tax on January 2. He had not made any payments on this purchase. Void the invoice.

➤ Void the above transaction using **Advanced Find** to locate the invoice:

- **Advanced Find** is useful when you have a large number of invoices and want to locate an invoice for a particular customer.
- Using Advanced **Find** will locate the invoice without requiring you to scroll through all the invoices for the company. For example, if customer Sanderson's transaction was on Invoice No. 7 and the invoice on the screen was 784, you would not have to scroll through 777 invoices because Find would locate Invoice No. 7 instantly.

Click **Find** on the Edit menu, click the **Advanced** tab

In the list displayed under **Filter**, click **Name**

In the **Name** dialog box, click the drop-down list arrow, click **Wilkins, Roger**

Click the **Find** button on the **Find** dialog box

- QuickBooks Pro will find all transactions recorded for Roger Wilkins.

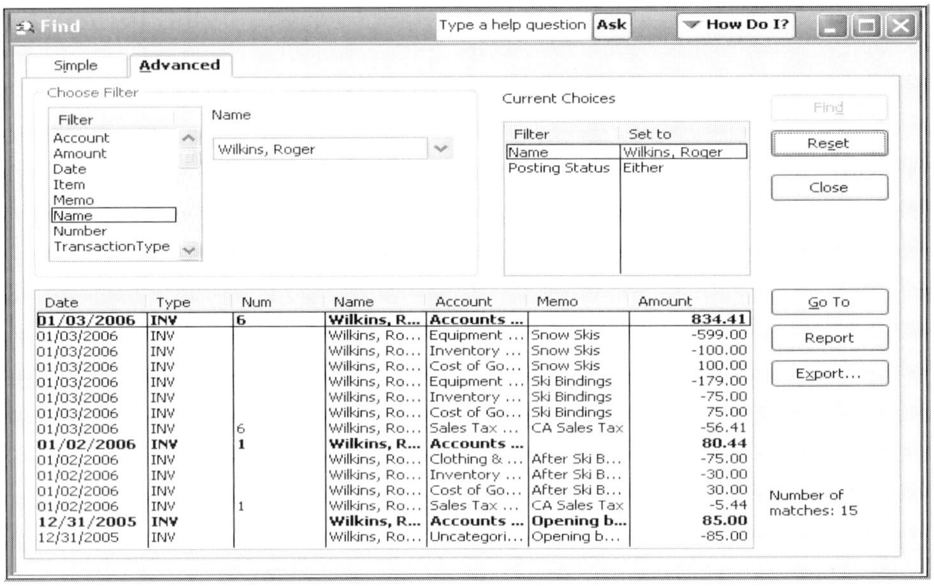

- Because there are several invoices, another filter would need to be defined in order to find the invoice with the exact amount of 80.44. This would be done by selecting a second filter.

Click **Amount** under **Filter**

Click the **Select** box in front of the = sign

Key in **80.44** in the text box

Press the **Tab** key

- The first two lines of the Current Choices Box shows *Filter: Amount* and *Set to: 80.44*: followed by *Filter: Name* and *Set to: Wilkins, Roger*.

Click the **Find** button on the **Find** dialog box

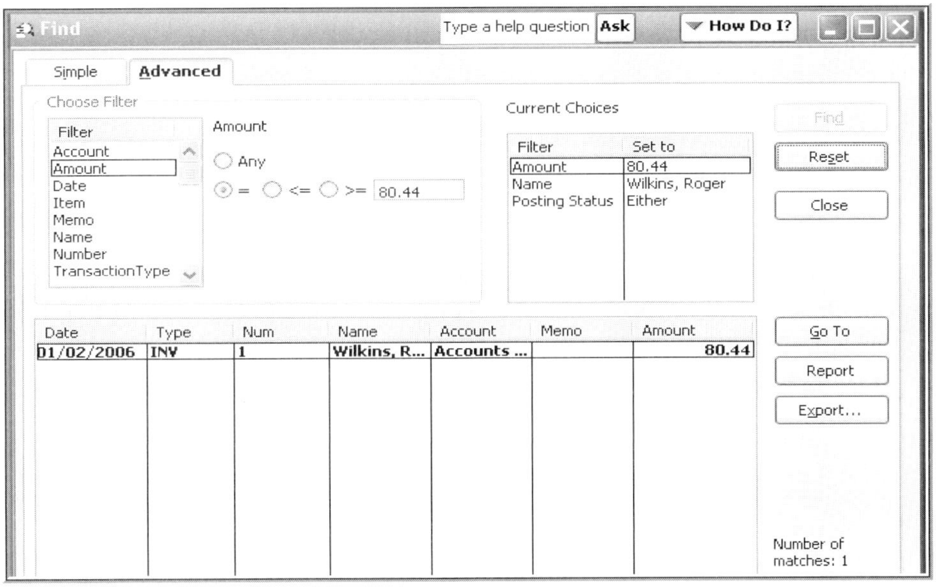

Click the line for **Invoice No. 1**
Click **Go To** button

- Invoice No. 1 appears on the screen.

With the invoice on the screen, click **Edit** menu, click **Void Invoice**

- Notice that the amount and the total for Invoice No. 1 are no longer 80.44. Both are **0.00**. Also note that the Memo box contains the word Void.

Click **Save & Close** button on the **Create Invoices** screen to close the invoice
Click **Yes** on the **Recording Transaction** screen

- Invoice No. 1 is no longer displayed on the **Advanced Find** screen.

Click **Close** button to close **Find**

Delete an Invoice

MEMO
DATE: January 8, 2006

Kent Trestle lost his part-time job. He decided to repair his old snowboard and return the new one he purchased from Your Name Sports. Delete Invoice No. 5.

Delete Invoice No. 5

Access Invoice No. 5 as previously instructed
Click the **Edit** menu, click **Delete Invoice**

Click **OK** in the **Delete Transaction** dialog box

- The cursor is now positioned on Invoice No. 6.

Click **Previous**

- Now the cursor is positioned on Invoice No. 4.

Click **Close** on the **Create Invoices** screen to close the invoice

View the **Customer Balance Detail Report**

Click **Reports** on the menu bar, point to **Customer & Accounts Receivable,** click **Customer Balance Detail**

Scroll through the report

- Look at Kent Trestle's account. Notice that Invoice No. 5 does not show up in the account listing. When an invoice is deleted, there is no record of it anywhere in the report.
- Notice that the Customer Balance Detail Report does not include the information telling you which amounts are opening balances.
- The report does give information regarding the amount owed on each transaction plus the total amount owed by each customer.
- Look at Roger Wilkins's account. The amount for Invoice No. 1 shows as **0.00**.

Your Name Sports

Customer Balance Detail

All Transactions

Type	Date	Num	Account	Amount	Balance
Tokumoto, Helene					
Invoice	12/31/2005		1200 · Accounts Receivable	670.31	670.31
Total Tokumoto, Helene				670.31	670.31
Trestle, Kent					
Invoice	12/31/2005		1200 · Accounts Receivable	911.63	911.63
Total Trestle, Kent				911.63	911.63
Vasquez, Henry					
Invoice	12/31/2005		1200 · Accounts Receivable	975.00	975.00
Total Vasquez, Henry				975.00	975.00
Wilkins, Roger					
Invoice	12/31/2005		1200 · Accounts Receivable	85.00	85.00
Invoice	01/02/2006	1	1200 · Accounts Receivable	0.00	85.00
Invoice	01/03/2006	6	1200 · Accounts Receivable	834.41	919.41
Total Wilkins, Roger				919.41	919.41
TOTAL				**14,392.54**	**14,392.54**

Close the report without printing

PREPARE CREDIT MEMOS

Credit memos are prepared to show a reduction to a transaction. If the invoice has already been sent to the customer, it is more appropriate and less confusing to make a change to a transaction by issuing a credit memo rather than voiding an invoice and issuing a new one. A credit memo notifies a customer that a change has been made to a transaction.

MEMOS
DATE: January 10, 2006

Prepare Credit Memo No. 9 for Mimi Cheung to show a reduction to her account for the return of the boot carrying case purchased for $49.95 on Invoice No. 7.

Prepare the Credit Memo shown above

Click the **Refunds and Credit** icon on the Home Page
Click the down arrow for the drop-down list box next to **Customer:Job**
Click **Cheung, Mimi**
Tab to **Template**

- It should say **Custom Credit Memo**.
- If not, click the drop-down list arrow and click **Custom Credit Memo**.

Tab to or click **Date**
Type in the date of the Credit Memo—**01/10/06**
The **Credit No.** field should show the number **9**

- Because Credit Memos are included in the numbering sequence for invoices, this number matches the number of the next blank invoice.

There is no PO No.
Tab to or click in **Item**
Click the drop-down list arrow next to **Item**, click **Accessories**
Tab to or click in **Quantity**, type in **1**
Tab to or click **Rate**, enter **49.95**
Press tab to enter 49.95 in the **Amount** column
Click the drop-down list arrow next to **Customer Message**
Click **Thank you for your business.**

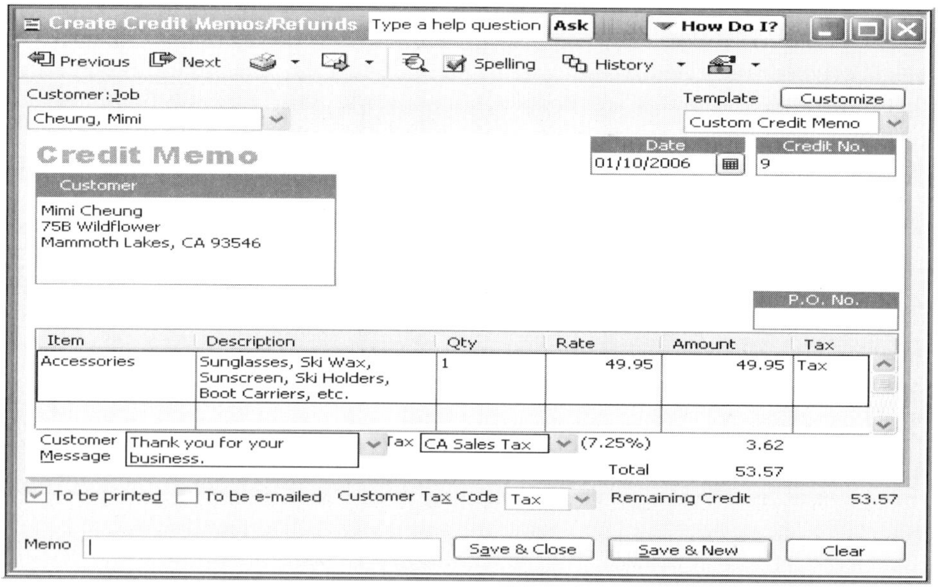

Print the credit memo with lines around each field as previously instructed
Click **Save & Close** on **Create Credit Memo/Refunds** to close the **Credit Memo**

- When saving the credit memo, you will get an **Available Credit** dialog box presenting options for handling the credit memo.
- Since the return was for an item purchased on Invoice 7, it is appropriate to apply the credit memo to Invoice 7

Click **Apply to an invoice**.

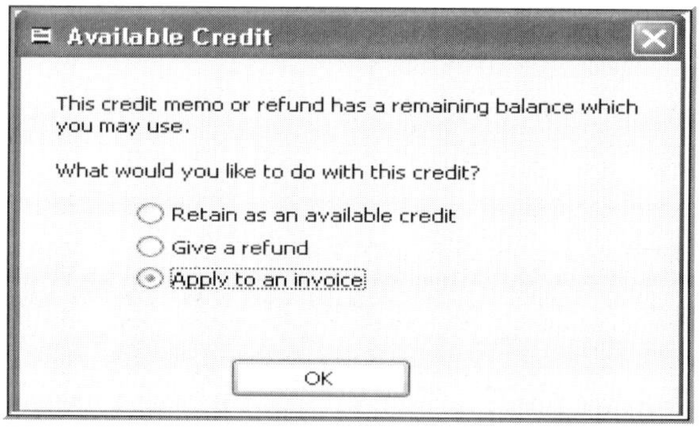

Click **OK**

- The Apply Credit to Open Invoices screen will appear. Because QuickBooks applies the credit to the oldest item, you will see a checkmark in the column next to the date of 12/31/2005, which is the Opening Balance.

Click the **Clear Selections** button
Click in the check column to mark Invoice 7 on 01/05/2006

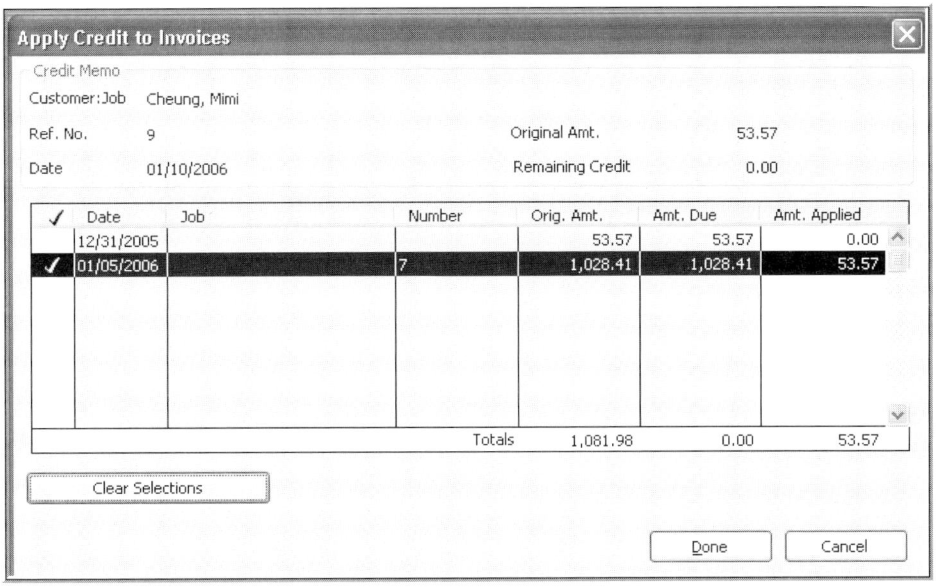

Click **Done**

PRINT OPEN INVOICES REPORT

To determine which invoices are still open—they have not been paid—QuickBooks Pro allows you to print a report titled Open Invoices. This report shows information regarding the type of transaction (Invoice or Credit Memo), the transaction date, the Invoice or Credit Memo number, a Purchase Order number (if there is one), terms of the sale, due date, aging, and the amount of the open balance. The total amount due from each customer for all open invoices less credit memos is also listed. If a credit memo has been applied to an invoice, the new total due is reflected in this report and the credit memo is not shown separately.

When you view and a print report, each column of information is separated by a diamond between the column headings. These diamonds may be used to change the size/width of a column. This is useful if the report is too wide to view on screen, if a column is taking up too much room, if a column is displayed too small, or a column does not contain any information.

MEMO

DATE: January 10, 2006

Rose needs to prepare and print an Open Invoices Report to give to the owners, Andy and Tim, so they can see which invoices are open. When preparing the report, eliminate the column for P.O. # and adjust the width of the columns. The report should be one page wide without selecting the print option *Fit report to one page wide*.

Prepare, resize, and print an Open Invoices Report

Click **Reports** menu, point to **Customers & Receivables**, click **Open Invoices**
Enter the date **011006**
Press the **Tab** key to generate the report

- Notice the amount due for Invoice 7. It now shows $974.84 as the total rather than $1,028.41. This verifies that the credit memo was applied to Invoice 7.

Click **Print**

- Be sure the orientation is Portrait and that *Fit report to one page wide* is not selected.

Click **Preview**
Click **Next Page** to see all of the pages in the report
Click **Zoom In** to see what information is contained in the report
Click **Close** to close the **Preview**
Click **Cancel** to close **Print Reports**
Hide columns or resize the width of the columns so the report will fit on one page wide

- The column for P.O. # does not contain any information.

To hide the column from view, position the cursor on the diamond between **P.O.** # and **Terms**

- The cursor turns into a plus with arrows pointing left and right.

Hold down the primary mouse button
Drag the cursor from the diamond between **P.O.** # and **Terms** to the diamond between **P.O.** # and **Num**

- You will see a dotted vertical line while you are dragging the mouse and holding down the primary mouse button.
- When you release the primary mouse button, the column for **P.O.** # will not show on the screen.

Click **Print**

- Verify that **Fit report to one page wide** is not selected.
- If it is selected, click the check box to remove the check mark.

Click **Preview**

- The report will now fit on one page wide.

Click **Close** to close the **Preview**
Click **Print**

Your Name Sports
Open Invoices
As of January 10, 2006

Type	Date	Num	Terms	Due Date	Aging	Open Balance
Cheung, Mimi						
Invoice	12/31/2005		Net 30	01/30/2006		53.57
Invoice	01/05/2006	7	Net 30	02/04/2006		974.84
Total Cheung, Mimi						1,028.41
Childers, Irene Dr.						
Invoice	12/31/2005		Net 30	01/30/2006		417.00
Total Childers, Irene Dr.						417.00
Clary, Laura						
Invoice	12/31/2005		Net 30	01/30/2006		455.00
Total Clary, Laura						455.00
Donlon, Gloria						
Invoice	12/31/2005		Net 30	01/30/2006		1,136.00
Total Donlon, Gloria						1,136.00

Close the **Open Invoices Report**

RECORD CASH SALES WITH SALES TAX

Not all sales in a business are on account. In many instances, payment is made at the time the merchandise is purchased. This is entered as a cash sale. Sales with cash, credit cards, or checks as the payment method are entered as cash sales. When entering a cash sale, you prepare a Sales Receipt rather than an Invoice. QuickBooks Pro records the transaction in the Journal and places the amount of cash received in an account called *Undeposited Funds*. The funds received remain in Undeposited Funds until you record a deposit to your bank account.

Memo
DATE: January 11, 2006

Record the following cash sale: Sales Receipt No. 1—Received cash from a customer who purchased a pair of sunglasses, $29.95; a boot carrier, $2.99; and some lip balm, $1.19. Use *Thank you for your business.* as the message.

Enter the above transaction as a cash sale to a cash customer

Click the **Create Sales Receipts** icon on the Home Page
Enter **Cash Customer** in the **Customer:Job** text box
Tab to **Template**

Because Your Name Sports does not have a customer named Cash Customer, a **Customer:Job Not Found** dialog box appears on the screen.

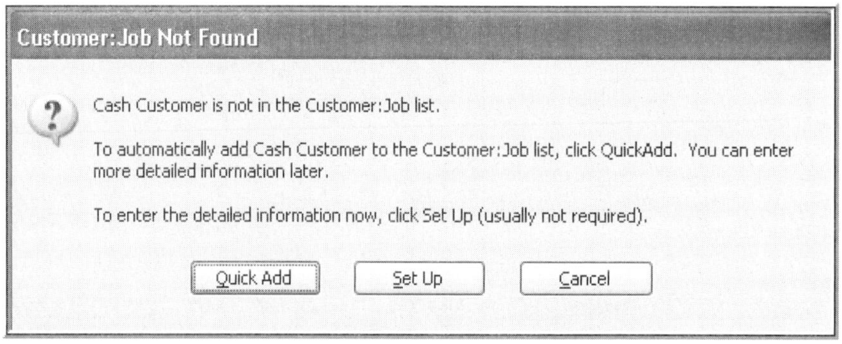

Click **Quick Add** to add the customer name Cash Customer to the Customer List

- Details regarding Cash Customer are not required, so Quick Add is the appropriate method to use to add the name to the list.
- Now that the customer name has been added to the Customer:Job List, the cursor moves to the **Template** field.

Template should be **Custom Sales Receipt**

- If not, click the drop-down list arrow and click Custom Cash Sales.

Tab to or click **Date**, type **01/11/06**
Sales No. should be **1**
Click the drop-down list arrow next to **Payment Method**, click **Cash**
Tab to or click beneath **Item**
Click the drop-down list arrow next to **Item**, click **Accessories**
Tab to or click **Qty**, type **1**
Tab to or click **Rate**, enter **29.95**
Tab to or click the next line in **Item**
Click the drop-down list arrow next to **Item**, click **Accessories**
Tab to or click **Qty**, type **1**
Tab to or click **Rate**, enter **2.99**
Repeat the steps above to enter $1.19 for the lip balm
Click the drop-down list arrow for Customer Message, click **Thank you for your business.**

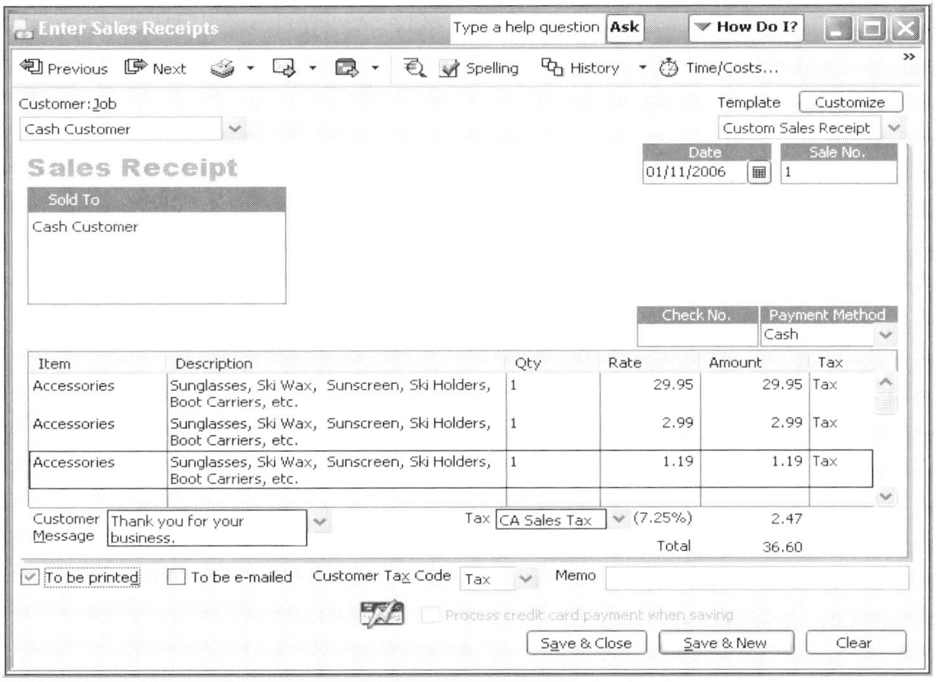

Print the Sales Receipt with lines around each field as previously instructed
Click **Save & New** on the bottom of the **Enter Sales Receipts** screen to save the Sales Receipt and go to the next one

ENTERING A CREDIT CARD SALE

A credit card sale is treated exactly like a cash sale. When you prepare the Sales Receipt, the payment method selected is credit card. The credit cards available on the Payment Method List are American Express, Discover, MasterCard, and Visa. Except for American Express, the credit card deposits are made into the checking or bank account, and bank fees for the charge cards are deducted directly from the bank account. Because American Express is not a *bank* charge card, charge receipts are sent to American Express, and American Express sends a check to the company for the amount of the charge, less American Express fees.

MEMO
DATE: January 11, 2006

Enter a sale to a cash customer using a Visa card. Identify the customer as Cash Customer. The sale was for a sled, $199.95. Use *Thank you for your business.* as the message.

Record the credit card sale

Click the drop-down list arrow next to **Customer:Job**, click **Cash Customer**
The date of the transaction is **01/11/06**
Sales No. should be **2**
Click the drop-down list arrow next to **Payment Method**, click **VISA**
Click the drop-down list arrow next to **Item**, click **Sleds**
Tab to or click **Qty**, type **1**
Tab to or click **Rate**, enter **199.95**
Click the drop-down list arrow for **Customer Message**, click **Thank you for your business.**

- If your business subscribes to the optional QuickBooks Merchant Accounts, you may click the check box for Process VISA payment when saving.

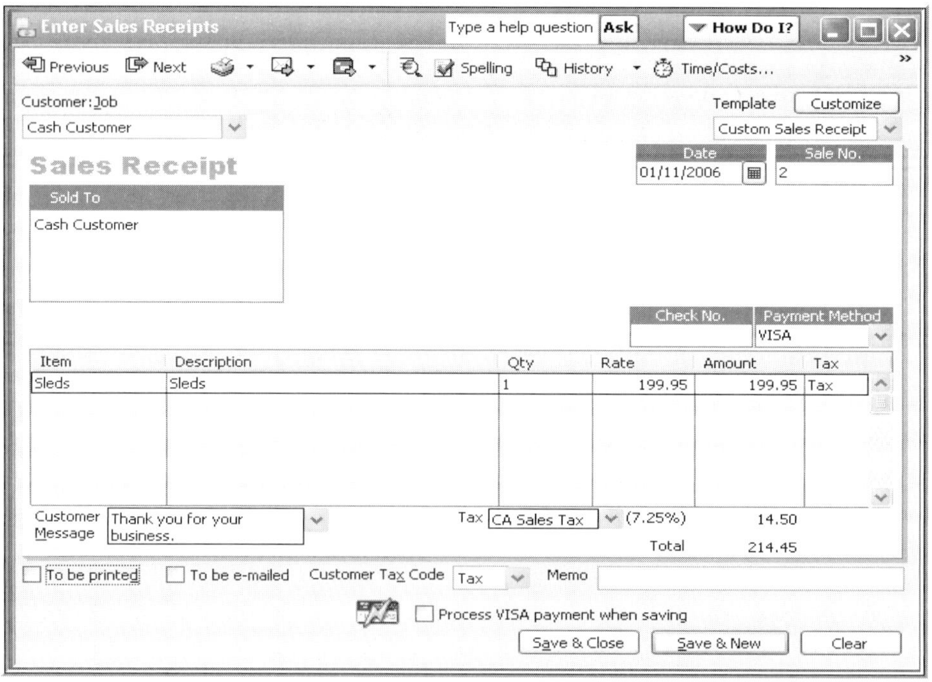

Print the sales receipt
Click **Next** to go to Sales Receipt No. 3

RECORD SALES PAID BY CHECK

A sale paid for with a check is considered a cash sale. A sales receipt is prepared to record the sale.

MEMO
DATE: January 11, 2006

We do take checks for sales even if a customer is from out of town. Record the sale of 2 pairs of socks at $15.99 each to a cash customer using Check No. 5589. The message for the Sales Receipt is *Thank you for your business.*

With Sales Receipt No. 3 on the screen, enter the information for the above transaction

Click the drop-down list arrow next to **Customer:Job**, click **Cash Customer**
The Date is **01/11/06**
Sales No. should be **3**
Tab to or click **Check No.**, type **5589**
Click the drop-down list arrow next to **Payment Method**, click **Check**
Click the drop-down list arrow next to **Item**, click **Socks**
Tab to or click **Qty**, type **2**
Tab to or click **Rate**, enter **15.99**
The **Customer Message** is **Thank you for your business.**
Print Sales Receipt No. 3

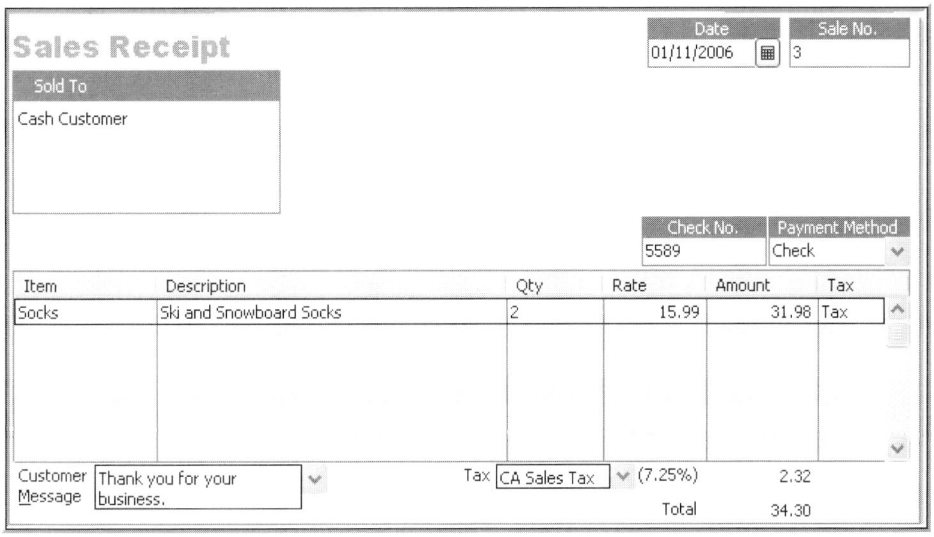
Sales Receipt

Date: 01/11/2006 Sale No.: 3

Sold To: Cash Customer

Check No.: 5589 Payment Method: Check

Item	Description	Qty	Rate	Amount	Tax
Socks	Ski and Snowboard Socks	2	15.99	31.98	Tax

Customer Message: Thank you for your business.
Tax: CA Sales Tax (7.25%) 2.32
Total 34.30

Click **Next** to go to Sales Receipt No. 4

ENTER CASH SALES TRANSACTIONS WITHOUT STEP-BY-STEP INSTRUCTIONS

MEMO

DATE: January 12, 2006

After a record snowfall, the store is really busy. Use Cash Customer as the customer name for the transactions. Record the following cash, check, and credit card sales:

Sales Receipt No. 4—A cash customer used Check No. 196 to purchase a ski parka, $249.95; ski pants, $129.95; and a ski sweater, $89.95.

Sales Receipt No. 5—A cash customer used a MasterCard to purchase a snow-board, $389.95; snowboard boots, $229.95; and snowboard bindings, $189.95.

Sales Receipt No. 6—A cash customer purchased a pair of gloves for $89.95.

Repeat the procedures used to enter Sales Receipt Nos. 1, 2, and 3 to record the additional transactions listed above

- Always use the Item List to determine the appropriate sales items for billing.
- Use **Thank you for your business.** as the message for these sales receipts.
- Print each Sales Receipt immediately after entering the information for it.
- If you get a Merchant Service message, click **Not Now**
- Click **Save & Close** after you have entered and printed Sales Receipt No. 6.

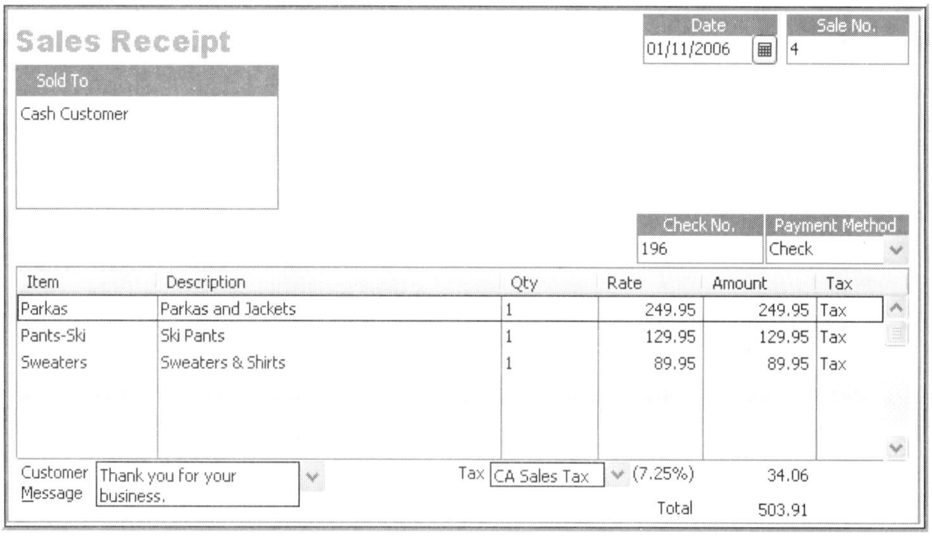

Sales Receipt

Date: 01/11/2006 Sale No.: 4

Sold To: Cash Customer

Check No.: 196 Payment Method: Check

Item	Description	Qty	Rate	Amount	Tax
Parkas	Parkas and Jackets	1	249.95	249.95	Tax
Pants-Ski	Ski Pants	1	129.95	129.95	Tax
Sweaters	Sweaters & Shirts	1	89.95	89.95	Tax

Customer Message: Thank you for your business.

Tax: CA Sales Tax (7.25%) 34.06

Total 503.91

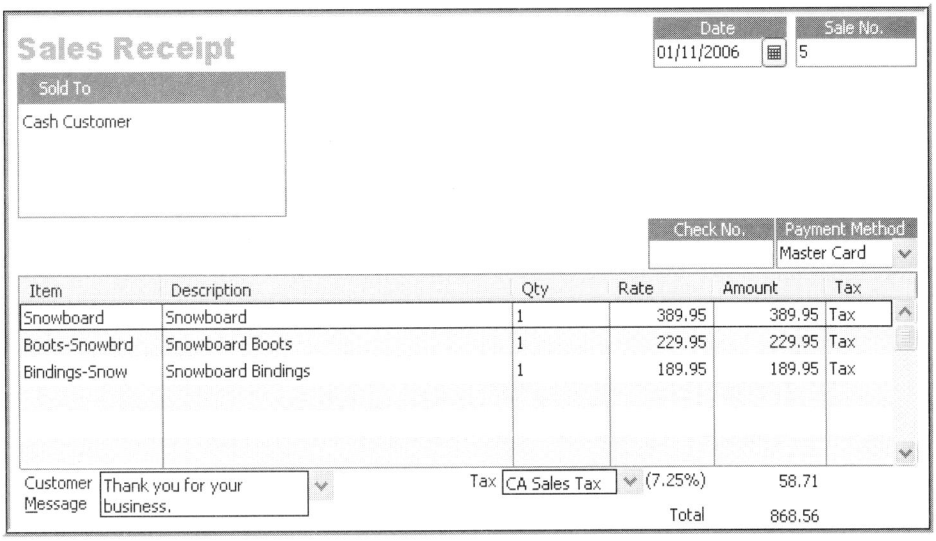

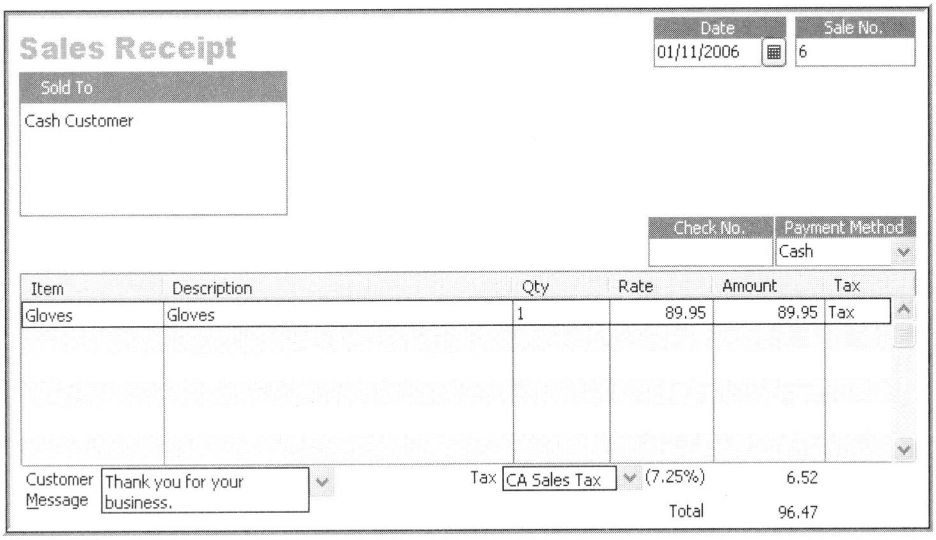

PRINT SALES BY ITEM SUMMARY REPORT

The Sales by Item Summary Report analyzes the quantity of merchandise on hand by item, gives the amount or value of the merchandise, gives the percentage of the total sales of each item, and calculates the average price per item, the cost of goods sold for each item, the average cost of goods sold for each item, the gross margin for each item, and the percentage of gross margin for each item. Information regarding the total inventory is also provided. This includes the value of the total inventory, the cost of goods sold for the inventory, and the gross margin for the inventory of merchandise.

MEMO

DATE: January 13, 2006

Near the middle of the month, Rose prepares a Summary Sales by Item Report to obtain information about sales, inventory, and merchandise costs. Prepare this report in landscape form for 1/1/2006-1/13/2006. Adjust the widths of the columns so the report prints on one page without selecting the print option *Fit report to one page wide*

Prepare the Summary Sales by Item report

Click **Reports** on the menu bar, point to **Sales Reports**, click **Sales by Item Summary**
The report dates are From **010106** To **011306**
Tab to generate the report
Scroll through the report
Click **Print**
Click **Landscape** to select **Orientation: Landscape**
Click **Preview**
Click **Next Page**

- Notice that the report does not fit on one page wide.

Click **Close** to close the Preview
Click **Cancel** to return to the report
Position the cursor on the diamond between columns
Drag to resize the columns

- The names of the column headings should appear in full and should not have **...** as part of the heading.

If you get a **Resize Columns** dialog box wanting to know if all columns should be the same size, click **No**

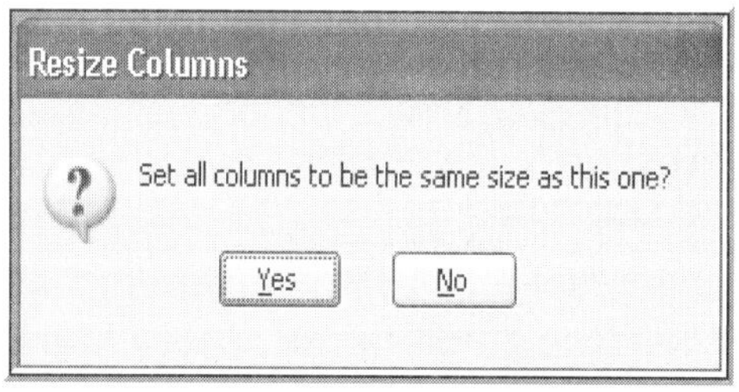

When the columns have been resized, click **Print** and **Preview**
When the report fits on one page wide, print the report

Your Name Sports

Sales by Item Summary

January 1 - 13, 2006

	Jan 1 - 13, 06							
	Qty	Amount	% of Sales	Avg Price	COGS	Avg COGS	Gross Margin	Gross Margin %
Inventory								
Accessories	5	127.03	1.5%	25.41	18.30	3.66	108.73	85.6%
Bindings-Skis	7	854.00	10%	122.00	525.00	75.00	329.00	38.5%
Bindings-Snow	2	349.94	4.1%	174.97	150.00	75.00	199.94	57.1%
Boots	0	0.00	0.0%	0.00	0.00	0.00	0.00	0.0%
Boots-Ski	1	250.00	2.9%	250.00	75.00	75.00	175.00	70.0%
Boots-Snowbrd	2	478.95	5.6%	239.48	150.00	75.00	328.95	68.7%
Gloves	2	168.95	2%	84.48	30.00	15.00	138.95	82.2%
Hats	1	25.00	0.3%	25.00	8.00	8.00	17.00	68.0%
Pants-Ski	2	258.95	3%	129.48	60.00	30.00	198.95	76.8%
Parkas	2	498.95	5.8%	249.48	116.66	58.33	382.29	76.6%
Poles-Ski	6	220.00	2.6%	36.67	180.00	30.00	40.00	18.2%
Skis	7	2,519.00	29.5%	359.86	700.00	100.00	1,819.00	72.2%
Sleds	6	799.90	9.4%	133.32	405.00	67.50	394.90	49.4%
Snowboard	2	889.90	10.4%	444.95	200.00	100.00	689.90	77.5%
Socks	3	47.93	0.6%	15.98	9.00	3.00	38.93	81.2%
Sweaters	2	214.95	2.5%	107.48	50.00	25.00	164.95	76.7%
Toboggans	5	1,149.75	13.5%	229.95	687.50	137.50	462.25	40.2%

CORRECT A SALES RECEIPT AND PRINT THE CORRECTED FORM

QuickBooks Pro makes correcting errors user friendly. When an error is discovered in a transaction such as a cash sale, you can simply return to the form where the transaction was recorded and correct the error. Thus, to correct a sales receipt, you could click Customers on the menu bar, click Enter Sales Receipts, click the Previous button until you found the appropriate sales receipt, and then correct the error. Since cash or checks received for cash sales are held in the Undeposited Funds account until the bank deposit is made, a sales receipt can be accessed through the Undeposited Funds account in the Chart of Accounts. Accessing the receipt in this manner allows you to see all the transactions entered in the account for Undeposited Funds.

When a correction for a sale is made, QuickBooks Pro not only changes the form, it also changes all Journal and account entries for the transaction to reflect the correction. QuickBooks Pro then allows a corrected sales receipt to be printed.

MEMO

DATE: January 13, 2006

After reviewing transaction information, you realize that the date for Sales Receipt No. 1 was entered incorrectly. Change the date to 1/8/2006.

➤ Use the Undeposited Funds account register to correct the error in the memo above, and print a corrected Sales Receipt

Open the **Chart of Accounts**, use the keyboard shortcut **Ctrl+A**
Double-click **Undeposited Funds**

- The register maintains a record of all the transactions recorded within the Undeposited Funds account.

Click anywhere in the transaction for **Sale No. 1**

- Look at the **Ref/Type** column to see the type of transaction.
- The number in the Ref column indicates the number of the sales receipt or the customer's check number.
- Type shows **RCPT** for a sales receipt.

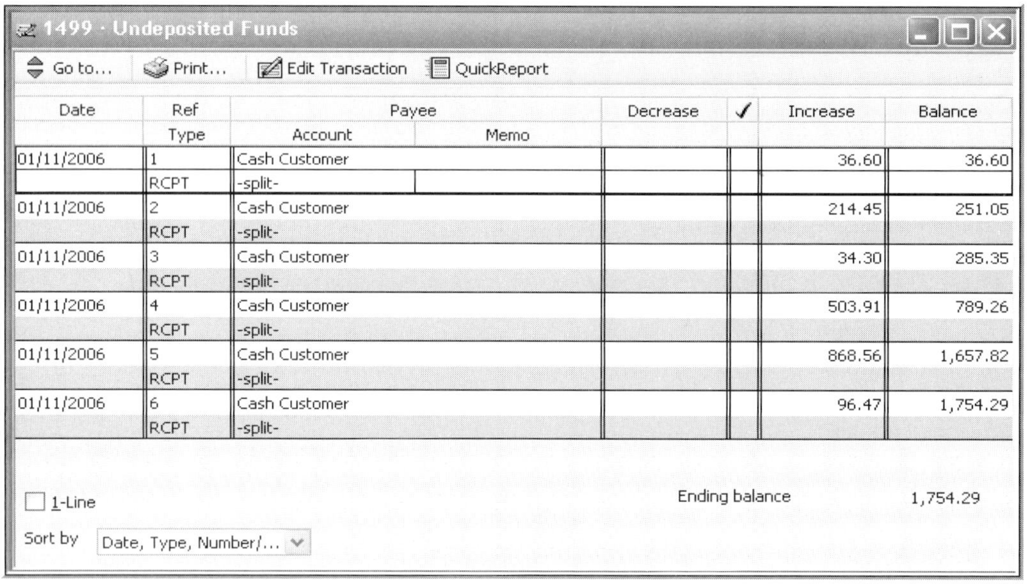

Click **Edit Transaction**

- The sales receipt appears on the screen.

Tab to or click **Date** field
Change the Date to **01/08/06**

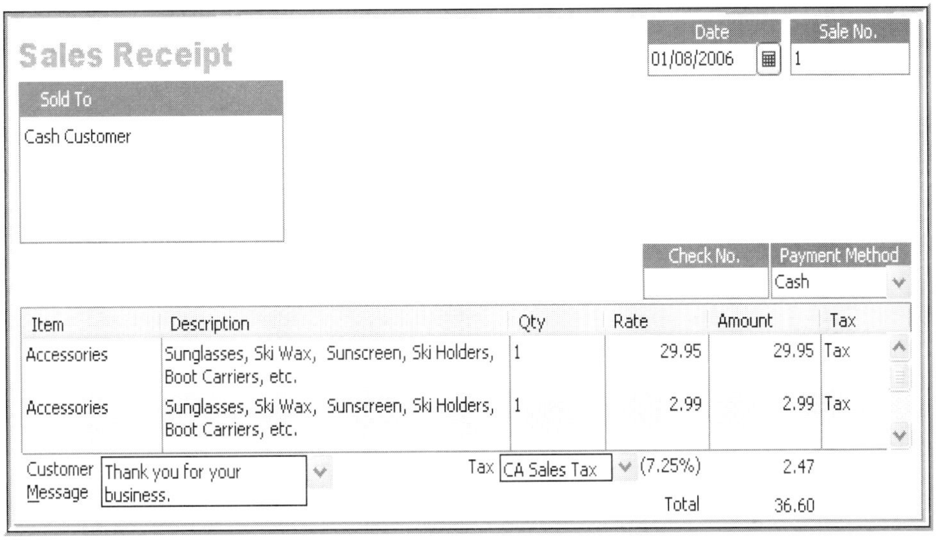

Print a corrected sales receipt as previously instructed

Click **Save & Close** on the **Enter Sales Receipts** screen to record changes, close the **Sales Receipt**, and return to the **Register for Undeposited Funds**

Click **Yes** on the **Recording Transactions** dialog box

Do not close the register

VIEW A QUICKREPORT

After editing the sales receipt and returning to the register, you may get a detailed report regarding the customer's transactions by clicking the QuickReport button. If you use Cash Customer for all cash sales, a QuickReport will be for all the transactions of Cash Customer.

Prepare a QuickReport for Cash Customer

After closing the sales receipt, you returned to the register for the Undeposited Funds account

Click the **QuickReport** button to display the Register QuickReport for **Cash Customer**

Because there are no entries in the Memo and Clr columns, drag the diamond between columns to eliminate the columns for **Memo** and **Clr**

Widen the **Account** column until the account name **Undeposited Funds** appears in full

Your Name Sports
Register QuickReport
All Transactions

Type	Date	Num	Account	Split	Amount
Cash Customer					
Sales Receipt	01/08/2006	1	1499 · Undeposited Funds	-SPLIT-	36.60
Sales Receipt	01/11/2006	2	1499 · Undeposited Funds	-SPLIT-	214.45
Sales Receipt	01/11/2006	3	1499 · Undeposited Funds	-SPLIT-	34.30
Sales Receipt	01/11/2006	4	1499 · Undeposited Funds	-SPLIT-	503.91
Sales Receipt	01/11/2006	5	1499 · Undeposited Funds	-SPLIT-	868.56
Sales Receipt	01/11/2006	6	1499 · Undeposited Funds	-SPLIT-	96.47
Total Cash Customer					1,754.29
TOTAL					**1,754.29**

ANALYZE THE QUICKREPORT FOR CASH CUSTOMER

Analyze the QuickReport

All transactions for Cash Customer appear in the report
- Notice that the date for Sales Receipt No. 1 has been changed to **01/08/2006**.

The account used is Undeposited Funds
The Split column contains the other accounts used in the transactions
- For all the transactions you see the word **-SPLIT-** rather than an account name.
- Split means that more than one account was used for this portion of the transaction.
- In addition to a variety of sales items, sales tax was charged on all sales, so each transaction will show **-SPLIT-** even if only one item was sold as in Sales Receipt No. 2.

View the accounts used for the Split by using QuickZoom to view the actual sales receipt
Use QuickZoom by double-clicking anywhere on the information for Sales Receipt No. 2
- The accounts used are Sleds and CA Sales Tax.

Close **Sales Receipt No. 2**
Close the report without printing
Close the register for **Undeposited Funds**
Do not close the **Chart of Accounts**

VIEW SALES TAX PAYABLE REGISTER

The Sales Tax Payable Register shows a detailed listing of all transactions with sales tax. The option of 1-Line may be selected in order to view each transaction on one line rather than the standard two lines. The account register provides information regarding the vendor and the account used for the transaction.

View the register for the Sales Tax Payable account

Click **Sales Tax Payable** in the Chart of Accounts
Use the keyboard shortcut, **Ctrl+R**
Once the register is displayed on the screen, click **1-Line** to view the transactions on single lines

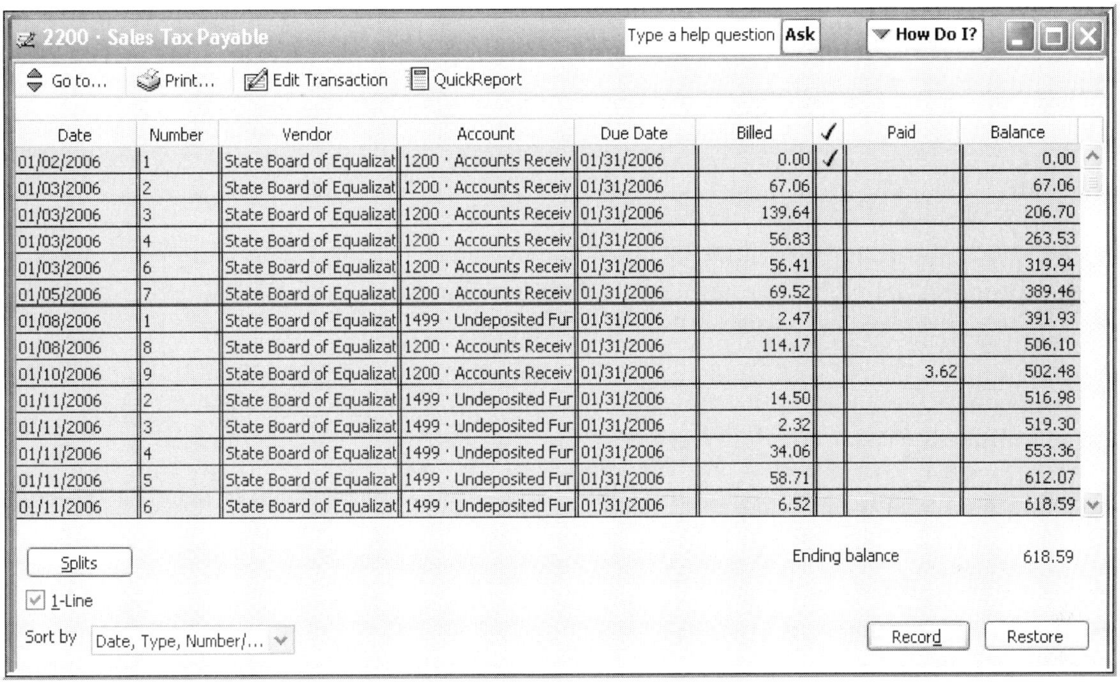

2200 · Sales Tax Payable

Type a help question Ask | How Do I?

Go to... | Print... | Edit Transaction | QuickReport

Date	Number	Vendor	Account	Due Date	Billed	✓	Paid	Balance
01/02/2006	1	State Board of Equalizat	1200 · Accounts Receiv	01/31/2006	0.00	✓		0.00
01/03/2006	2	State Board of Equalizat	1200 · Accounts Receiv	01/31/2006	67.06			67.06
01/03/2006	3	State Board of Equalizat	1200 · Accounts Receiv	01/31/2006	139.64			206.70
01/03/2006	4	State Board of Equalizat	1200 · Accounts Receiv	01/31/2006	56.83			263.53
01/03/2006	6	State Board of Equalizat	1200 · Accounts Receiv	01/31/2006	56.41			319.94
01/05/2006	7	State Board of Equalizat	1200 · Accounts Receiv	01/31/2006	69.52			389.46
01/08/2006	1	State Board of Equalizat	1499 · Undeposited Fur	01/31/2006	2.47			391.93
01/08/2006	8	State Board of Equalizat	1200 · Accounts Receiv	01/31/2006	114.17			506.10
01/10/2006	9	State Board of Equalizat	1200 · Accounts Receiv	01/31/2006			3.62	502.48
01/11/2006	2	State Board of Equalizat	1499 · Undeposited Fur	01/31/2006	14.50			516.98
01/11/2006	3	State Board of Equalizat	1499 · Undeposited Fur	01/31/2006	2.32			519.30
01/11/2006	4	State Board of Equalizat	1499 · Undeposited Fur	01/31/2006	34.06			553.36
01/11/2006	5	State Board of Equalizat	1499 · Undeposited Fur	01/31/2006	58.71			612.07
01/11/2006	6	State Board of Equalizat	1499 · Undeposited Fur	01/31/2006	6.52			618.59

Splits | Ending balance 618.59

1-Line

Sort by Date, Type, Number/... | Record | Restore

Close the register for **Sales Tax Payable**, and close the **Chart of Accounts**

RECORD CUSTOMER PAYMENTS ON ACCOUNT

Whenever money is received, whether it is for a cash sale or when customers pay the amount they owe on account, QuickBooks Pro uses the account called *Undeposited Funds* rather than a cash/checking account. The money stays in the account until a bank deposit is made. When you start to record a payment on account, you see the customer's balance, any credits made to the account, and a complete list of outstanding invoices. QuickBooks Pro automatically applies the payment received to the oldest invoice.

If a customer owes you money for a purchase made "on account" (an invoice) you record the payment in Receive Payments. If a customer made a "cash purchase" (a sales receipt) the amount received is recorded at the time the sales receipt is prepared.

MEMO

DATE: January 13, 2006

Record the following receipt of Check No. 765 for $975 from Henry Vasquez as payment in full on his account.

Record the above payment on account:

Click the **Receive Payments** icon on the QuickBooks Home Page
Click the drop-down list for **Received From**, click **Vasquez, Henry**

- Notice that the current date shows in the **Date** column and that the total amount owed appears as the Customer Balance.

Tab to or click **Date**, type **01/13/06**
Tab to or click **Amount**, enter **975**

- QuickBooks Pro will enter the **.00** when you tab to or click **Ref./Check No.**

Click the drop-down list arrow for **Pmt. Method**

- Notice that the cursor moves into the **Pmt. Method** text box and that the payment amount is entered in the **Payment** column for Outstanding Invoices/Statement Charges.

Click **Check**

- QuickBooks places a check mark in the check mark column to indicate the invoice for which the payment is received. When there is more than one open invoice, QuickBooks Pro automatically applies the payment to the oldest open invoice.

Tab to or click **Check No.**, enter **765**

- At the bottom of the **Receive Payments** screen, notice that the unpaid invoice for Henry Vasquez shows in the Applied To section of the screen.

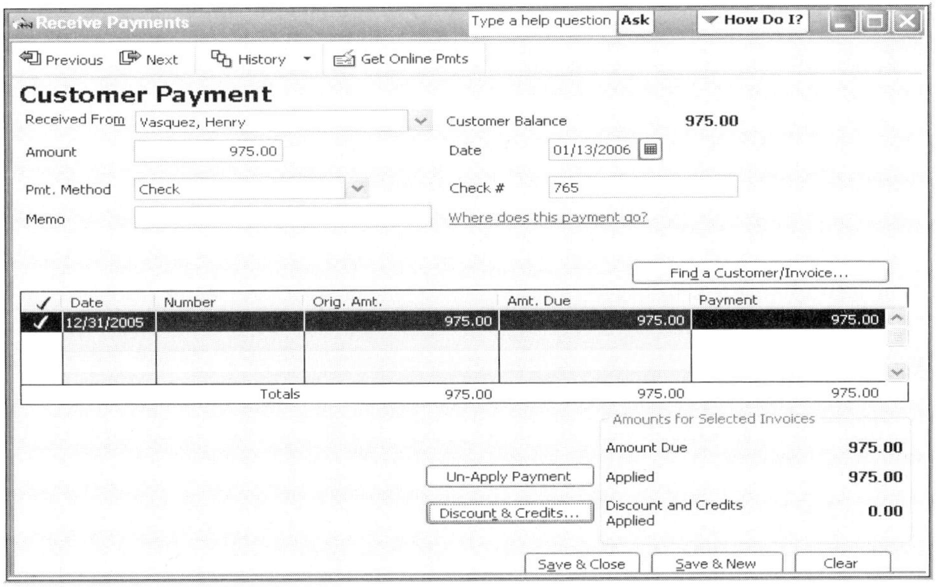

Click **Next** to record this payment and advance to the next **Receive Payments** screen

RECORD CUSTOMER PAYMENT ON ACCOUNT WHEN A CREDIT HAS BEEN APPLIED

If there are any existing credits (such as a Credit Memo) on an account that have not been applied to the account, they may be applied to a customer's account when a payment is made. If a credit was recorded and applied to an invoice, the total amount due on the invoice will reflect the credit.

MEMO
DATE: January 13, 2006

Mimi Cheung sent Check No. 1026 for $1,028.41 to pay her account in full. Apply unused credits when recording her payment on account.

Record the payment by Mimi Cheung and apply her unused credits

Click the drop-down list for **Received From**, click **Cheung, Mimi**

- Notice the Customer Balance shows the total amount owed by the customer.
- In the lower portion of the **Receive Payments** screen, notice the list of unpaid invoices for Mimi Cheung.

Tab to or click **Date**, type the date **01/13/06**

Tab to or click **Amount**, enter **1028.41**
Check should still show as the payment method
Tab to or click **Check No.**, enter **1026**

- Because the amount of the payment matched the amount due for the opening balance and Invoice 7, both have a check mark in the Applied to: column.
- Notice the Original Amount of the two transactions, the Amt. Due, and the Payment amounts. The Amt. Due for Invoice 7 reflects the $53.47 that was previously recorded on a credit memo.

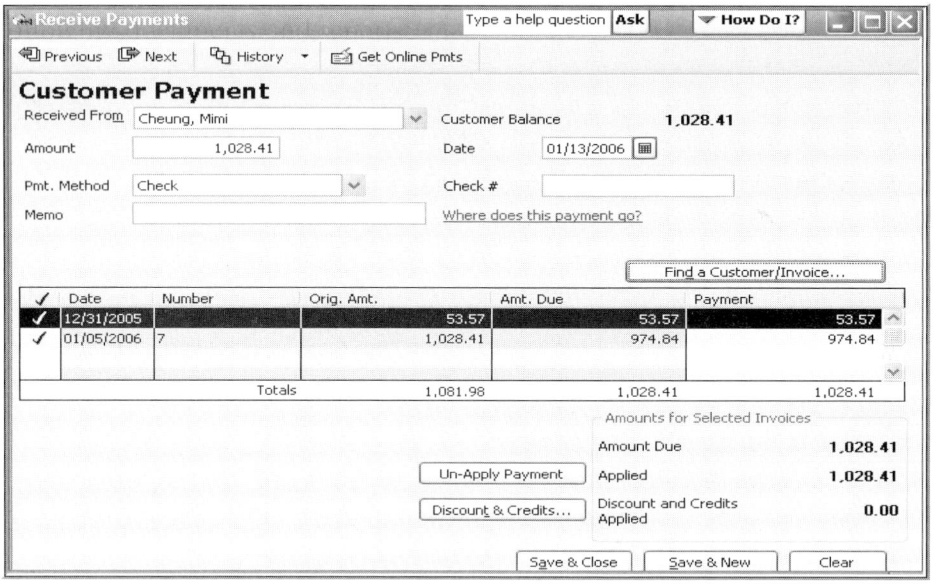

- If you did not apply a credit directly to an invoice, you may do so by clicking the invoice that should receive the credit (Invoice 7), clicking the Discount & Credits button, selecting the amount of credit to apply, and clicking the Done button.

Click **Next** to record this payment and to advance to the next **Receive Payments** screen.

RECORD PAYMENT ON ACCOUNT FROM A CUSTOMER QUALIFYING FOR AN EARLY-PAYMENT DISCOUNT

Each customer may be assigned terms as part of the customer information. When terms such as 1% 10 Net 30 or 2% 10 Net 30 are given, customers whose payments are received within ten days of the invoice date are eligible to deduct 1% or 2% from the amount owed when making their payments.

MEMO
DATE: January 13, 2006

Received payment from Mountain Recreation Center for Invoice No. 8. Check No. 981-13 for $1672.01 was received as full payment. Record the payment and the 1% discount for early payment under the invoice terms of 1% 10 Net 30.

Record the receipt of the check and apply the discount to the above transaction

Click the drop-down list for **Received From**
Click **Mountain Recreation Center**

- The total amount owed, $1,688.90, appears as the Customer Balance.
- In the lower portion of the **Receive Payments** screen, notice that the unpaid Invoice 8 for Mountain Recreation Center is shown

Tab to or click **Date**, type date **01/13/06**
Tab to or click **Amount**, enter **1672.01**

- Notice that this amount is different from the balance of $1,688.90.

You will get a message in the lower portion of Receive Payments

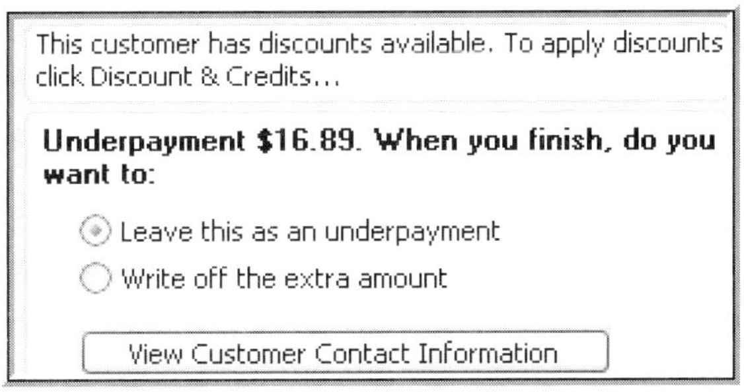

The **Pmt. Method** should show Check
Tab to or click **Check No.**, enter **981-13**

- Notice that the payment amount is entered in the **Payment** column for Invoice 8.

Tab to or click **Memo**, type **Includes Early Payment Discount**

- Since the column for Disc. Date is displayed, you will see that the Invoice is being paid within the discount date and is eligible to receive a discount

Click **Discounts & Credits** button

- QuickBooks displays the 1% discount amount, which was calculated on the total amount due

Click the drop-down list arrow for **Discount Account**, click **6130 Sales Discounts**

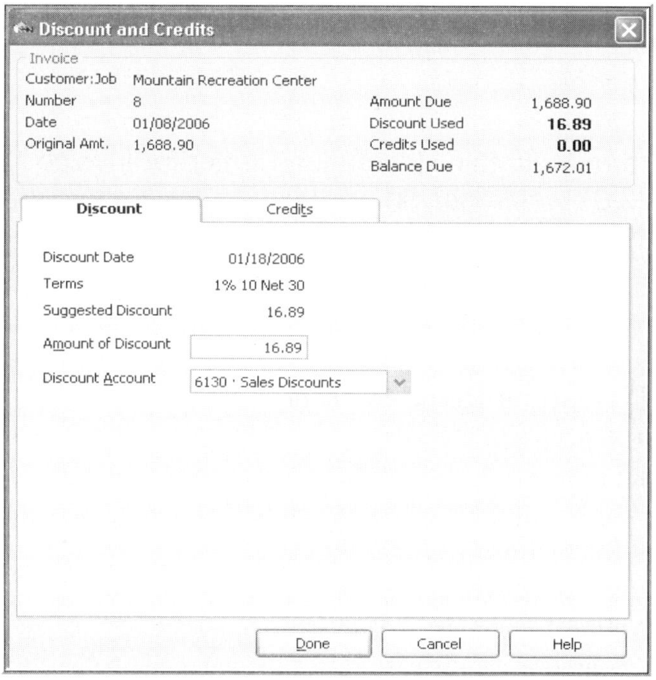

Click **Done** to apply the discount of $16.89

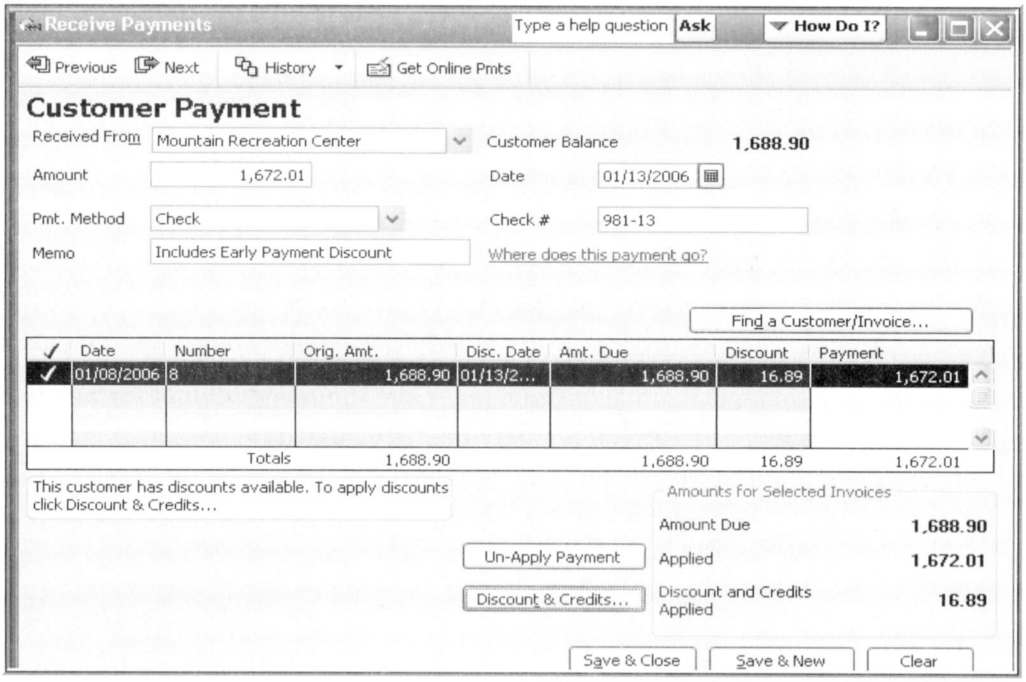

- Notice that the Original Amount stays the same, the Amount Due on Invoice No. 8 changes to $1,688.90, the discount amount of $16.89 shows in the Discount column, and the Payment shows $1,672.01.

- In the area for Amounts for Selected invoice, you will see the Amount Due, Amount Applied, and Amount of Discounts and Credits Applied.
- If you make an error in applying the discount, click the Clear and re-enter the transaction.

Click **Next** to record this payment and to advance to the next **Receive Payments** screen

RECORD ADDITIONAL PAYMENTS ON ACCOUNT WITHOUT STEP-BY-STEP INSTRUCTIONS

MEMO

DATE: January 14, 2006

Received Check No. 152 from Roger Wilkins for $919.41

Received Check No. 8252 dated January 11 and postmarked 1/12 for $2,024.33 from Mountain Schools. This receipt requires an item as a Memo. The memo is: *Includes Early Payment Discount.* Even though the date we are recording the payment is after the discount date, the check was postmarked within the discount period. Apply the discount for early payment to this transaction. Since the payment is being recorded after the discount date, you may need to enter the amount of the 2% discount when you click the Discounts & Credits button.

Received Check No. 3951 from Dr. Felipe Manuel for $1,087.51 (no discount).

Received Check No. 1051 for $500 from Gloria Donlon in partial payment of account. Record the memo: Partial Payment.

Received Check No. 563 from Sara Price for $408.48 in payment of the 12/31/2005 balance.

Received Check No. 819 from Kent Trestle for $100 in partial payment of his account.

Refer to the previous steps listed to enter the above payments:

- Any discounts or partial payments should be noted as a Memo.
- Be sure to apply any discounts.
- A partial payment should have *Leave this as an underpayment* marked.

Click the **Save & Close** button after all payments received have been recorded

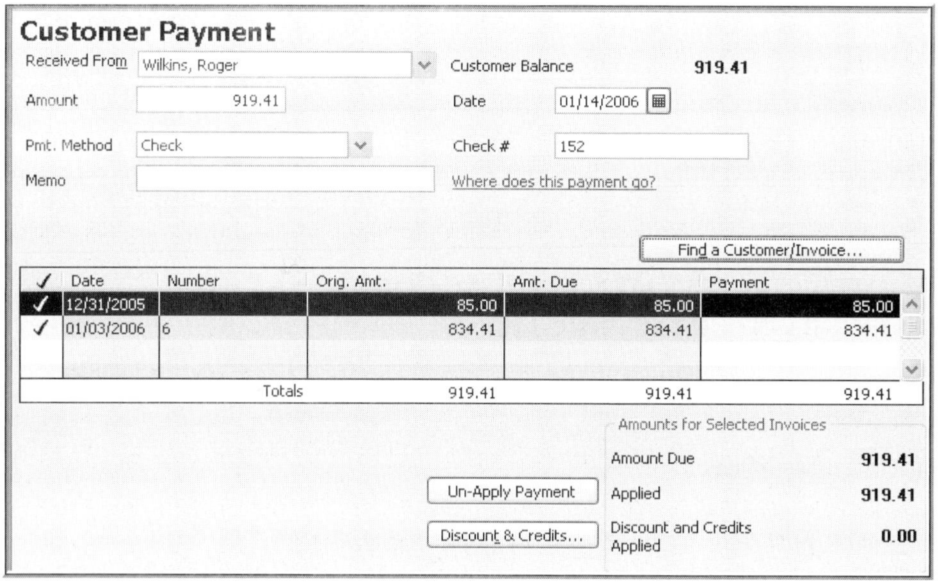
Customer Payment

Received From: Wilkins, Roger | Customer Balance: 919.41
Amount: 919.41 | Date: 01/14/2006
Pmt. Method: Check | Check #: 152
Memo: | Where does this payment go?

Find a Customer/Invoice...

✓	Date	Number	Orig. Amt.	Amt. Due	Payment
✓	12/31/2005		85.00	85.00	85.00
✓	01/03/2006	6	834.41	834.41	834.41
		Totals	919.41	919.41	919.41

Amounts for Selected Invoices
Amount Due 919.41
Un-Apply Payment | Applied 919.41
Discount & Credits... | Discount and Credits Applied 0.00

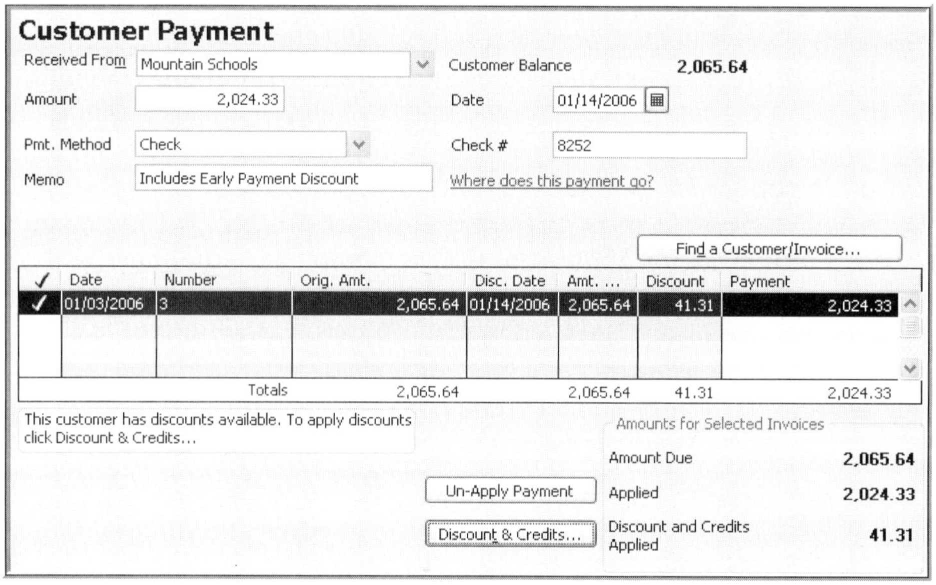
Customer Payment

Received From: Mountain Schools | Customer Balance: 2,065.64
Amount: 2,024.33 | Date: 01/14/2006
Pmt. Method: Check | Check #: 8252
Memo: Includes Early Payment Discount | Where does this payment go?

Find a Customer/Invoice...

✓	Date	Number	Orig. Amt.	Disc. Date	Amt. ...	Discount	Payment
✓	01/03/2006	3	2,065.64	01/14/2006	2,065.64	41.31	2,024.33
		Totals	2,065.64		2,065.64	41.31	2,024.33

This customer has discounts available. To apply discounts click Discount & Credits...

Amounts for Selected Invoices
Amount Due 2,065.64
Un-Apply Payment | Applied 2,024.33
Discount & Credits... | Discount and Credits Applied 41.31

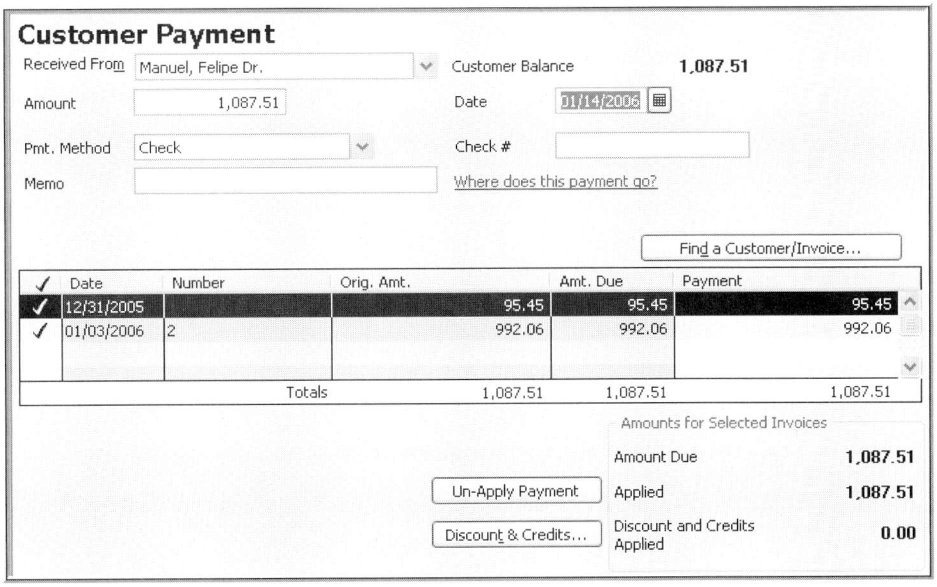
Customer Payment
Received From
Manuel, Felipe Dr.
Customer Balance
1,087.51
Amount
1,087.51
Date
01/14/2006
Pmt. Method
Check
Check #
Memo
Where does this payment go?
Find a Customer/Invoice...
Date
Number
Orig. Amt.
Amt. Due
Payment
12/31/2005
95.45
95.45
95.45
01/03/2006
2
992.06
992.06
992.06
Totals
1,087.51
1,087.51
1,087.51
Amounts for Selected Invoices
Amount Due
1,087.51
Applied
1,087.51
Discount and Credits Applied
0.00
Un-Apply Payment
Discount & Credits...

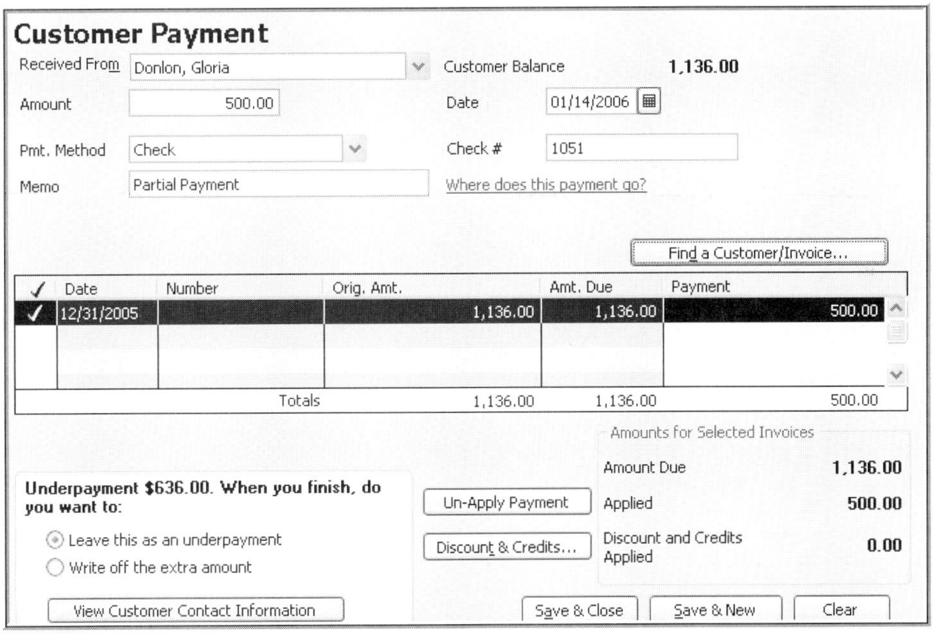
Customer Payment
Received From
Donlon, Gloria
Customer Balance
1,136.00
Amount
500.00
Date
01/14/2006
Pmt. Method
Check
Check #
1051
Memo
Partial Payment
Where does this payment go?
Find a Customer/Invoice...
Date
Number
Orig. Amt.
Amt. Due
Payment
12/31/2005
1,136.00
1,136.00
500.00
Totals
1,136.00
1,136.00
500.00
Amounts for Selected Invoices
Amount Due
1,136.00
Applied
500.00
Discount and Credits Applied
0.00
Underpayment $636.00. When you finish, do you want to:
Leave this as an underpayment
Write off the extra amount
View Customer Contact Information
Un-Apply Payment
Discount & Credits...
Save & Close
Save & New
Clear

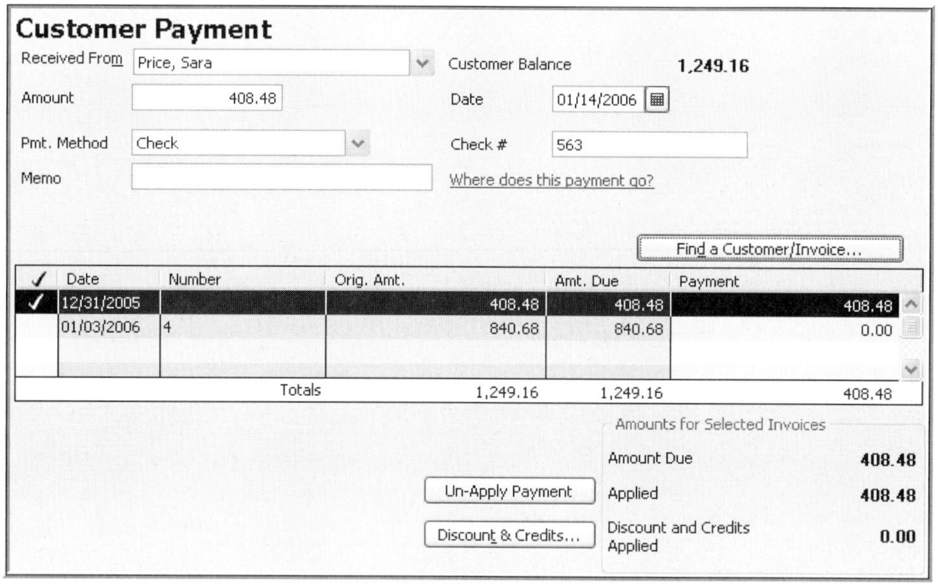

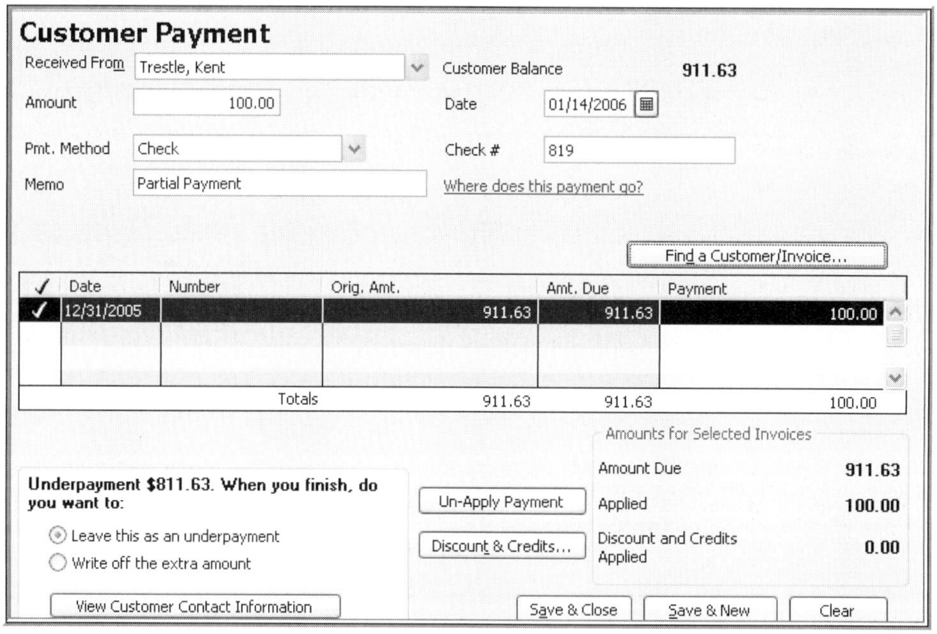

VIEW TRANSACTION LIST BY CUSTOMER

In order to see the transactions for customers, you need to prepare a report called Transaction List by Customer. This report shows all sales, credits, and payments for each customer on account and for the customer named Cash Customer. The report does not show the balance remaining on account for the individual customers.

➤ View the Transaction List by Customer

Click the **Report Center** button
Click **Customers & Receivables** as the type of report
Click **Transaction List by Customer**
Enter the dates from **01/01/06** to **01/14/06**
Tab to generate the report
Scroll through the report

- Information is shown for the Invoices, Sales Receipts, Credit Memos, and payments made on the accounts and the Num column shows the Invoice numbers, Sales Receipt numbers, Credit Memo numbers, and Check numbers.

Your Name Sports
Transaction List by Customer
January 1 - 14, 2006

Type	Date	Num	Memo	Account	Clr	Split	Amount
Cash Customer							
Sales Receipt	1/8/2006	1		1499 · Undeposited Funds		-SPLIT-	36.60
Sales Receipt	1/11/2006	2		1499 · Undeposited Funds		-SPLIT-	214.45
Sales Receipt	1/11/2006	3		1499 · Undeposited Funds		-SPLIT-	34.30
Sales Receipt	1/11/2006	4		1499 · Undeposited Funds		-SPLIT-	503.91
Sales Receipt	1/11/2006	5		1499 · Undeposited Funds		-SPLIT-	868.56
Sales Receipt	1/11/2006	6		1499 · Undeposited Funds		-SPLIT-	96.47
Cheung, Mimi							
Invoice	1/5/2006	7		1200 · Accounts Receivable		-SPLIT-	1,028.41
Credit Memo	1/10/2006	9		1200 · Accounts Receivable		-SPLIT-	-53.57
Payment	1/13/2006			1499 · Undeposited Funds		1200 · Accounts Receivable	1,028.41
Donlon, Gloria							
Payment	1/14/2006	1051	Partial Payment	1499 · Undeposited Funds		1200 · Accounts Receivable	500.00
Manuel, Felipe Dr.							
Invoice	1/3/2006	2		1200 · Accounts Receivable		-SPLIT-	992.06
Payment	1/14/2006			1499 · Undeposited Funds		1200 · Accounts Receivable	1,087.51
Mountain Recreation Center							
Invoice	1/8/2006	8		1200 · Accounts Receivable		-SPLIT-	1,688.90
Payment	1/13/2006	981-13	Includes Early Pa...	1499 · Undeposited Funds		1200 · Accounts Receivable	1,672.01
Mountain Schools							
Invoice	1/3/2006	3		1200 · Accounts Receivable		-SPLIT-	2,065.64
Payment	1/14/2006	8252	Includes Early Pa...	1499 · Undeposited Funds		1200 · Accounts Receivable	2,024.33
Price, Sara							
Invoice	1/3/2006	4		1200 · Accounts Receivable		-SPLIT-	840.68
Payment	1/14/2006	563		1499 · Undeposited Funds		1200 · Accounts Receivable	408.48
Trestle, Kent							
Payment	1/14/2006	819	Partial Payment	1499 · Undeposited Funds		1200 · Accounts Receivable	100.00
Vasquez, Henry							
Payment	1/13/2006	765		1499 · Undeposited Funds		1200 · Accounts Receivable	975.00
Wilkins, Roger							
Invoice	1/2/2006	1	VOID:	1200 · Accounts Receivable	X	-SPLIT-	0.00
Invoice	1/3/2006	6		1200 · Accounts Receivable		-SPLIT-	834.41
Payment	1/14/2006	152		1499 · Undeposited Funds		1200 · Accounts Receivable	919.41

Close the report without printing

PRINT CUSTOMER BALANCE SUMMARY

A report that will show you the balance owed by each customer is the Customer Balance Summary. The report presents the total balance owed by each customer as of a certain date.

MEMO
DATE: January 14, 2006

You and Tim want to see how much each customer owes to Your Name Sports. Print a Customer Balance Summary Report.

Prepare and print a **Customer Balance Summary** follow the steps given previously for printing the report in Portrait orientation

Your Name Sports
Customer Balance Summary
All Transactions

	Jan 14, 06
Childers, Irene Dr.	417.00
Clary, Laura	455.00
Donlon, Gloria	636.00
Donnell, Frances	650.00
Khalid, Moktar	1,085.00
Price, Sara	840.68
Tokumoto, Helene	670.31
Trestle, Kent	811.63
TOTAL	5,565.62

Close the report and the Report Center

DEPOSIT CHECKS AND CREDIT CARD RECEIPTS FOR CASH SALES AND PAYMENTS ON ACCOUNT

When cash sales are made and payments on accounts are received, QuickBooks Pro places the money received in the *Undeposited Funds* account. Once the deposit is recorded, the funds are transferred from *Undeposited Funds* to the account selected when preparing the deposit.

MEMO
DATE: January 14, 2006

Deposit all cash, checks and credit card receipts for cash sales and payments on account into the Checking account.

Deposit cash, checks and credit card receipts

Click the **Record Deposits** icon on the QuickBooks Home Page

The View payment method type should be **All types**

- The **Payments to Deposit** window shows all amounts received for cash sales (including bank credit cards) and payments on account that have not been deposited in the bank.
- Notice that the **check** column to the left of the Date column is empty.

Click the **Select All** button

- Notice the check marks in the check column.

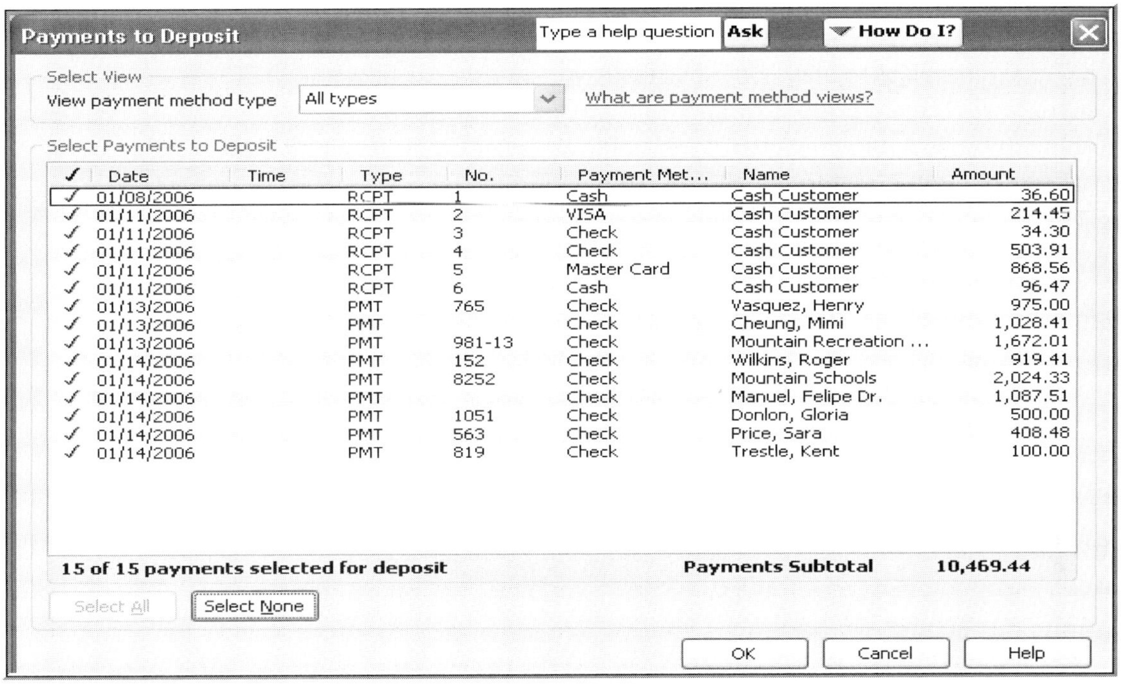

Payments to Deposit

Select View

View payment method type: All types — What are payment method views?

Select Payments to Deposit

✓	Date	Time	Type	No.	Payment Met...	Name	Amount
✓	01/08/2006		RCPT	1	Cash	Cash Customer	36.60
✓	01/11/2006		RCPT	2	VISA	Cash Customer	214.45
✓	01/11/2006		RCPT	3	Check	Cash Customer	34.30
✓	01/11/2006		RCPT	4	Check	Cash Customer	503.91
✓	01/11/2006		RCPT	5	Master Card	Cash Customer	868.56
✓	01/11/2006		RCPT	6	Cash	Cash Customer	96.47
✓	01/13/2006		PMT	765	Check	Vasquez, Henry	975.00
✓	01/13/2006		PMT		Check	Cheung, Mimi	1,028.41
✓	01/13/2006		PMT	981-13	Check	Mountain Recreation ...	1,672.01
✓	01/14/2006		PMT	152	Check	Wilkins, Roger	919.41
✓	01/14/2006		PMT	8252	Check	Mountain Schools	2,024.33
✓	01/14/2006		PMT		Check	Manuel, Felipe Dr.	1,087.51
✓	01/14/2006		PMT	1051	Check	Donlon, Gloria	500.00
✓	01/14/2006		PMT	563	Check	Price, Sara	408.48
✓	01/14/2006		PMT	819	Check	Trestle, Kent	100.00

15 of 15 payments selected for deposit — **Payments Subtotal 10,469.44**

Select All | Select None | OK | Cancel | Help

Click **OK** to close the **Payments to Deposit** screen and open the **Make Deposits** screen

On the **Make Deposits** screen, **Deposit To** should be **1100 Checking**

Date should be **01/14/2006**

- Tab to date and change if not correct.

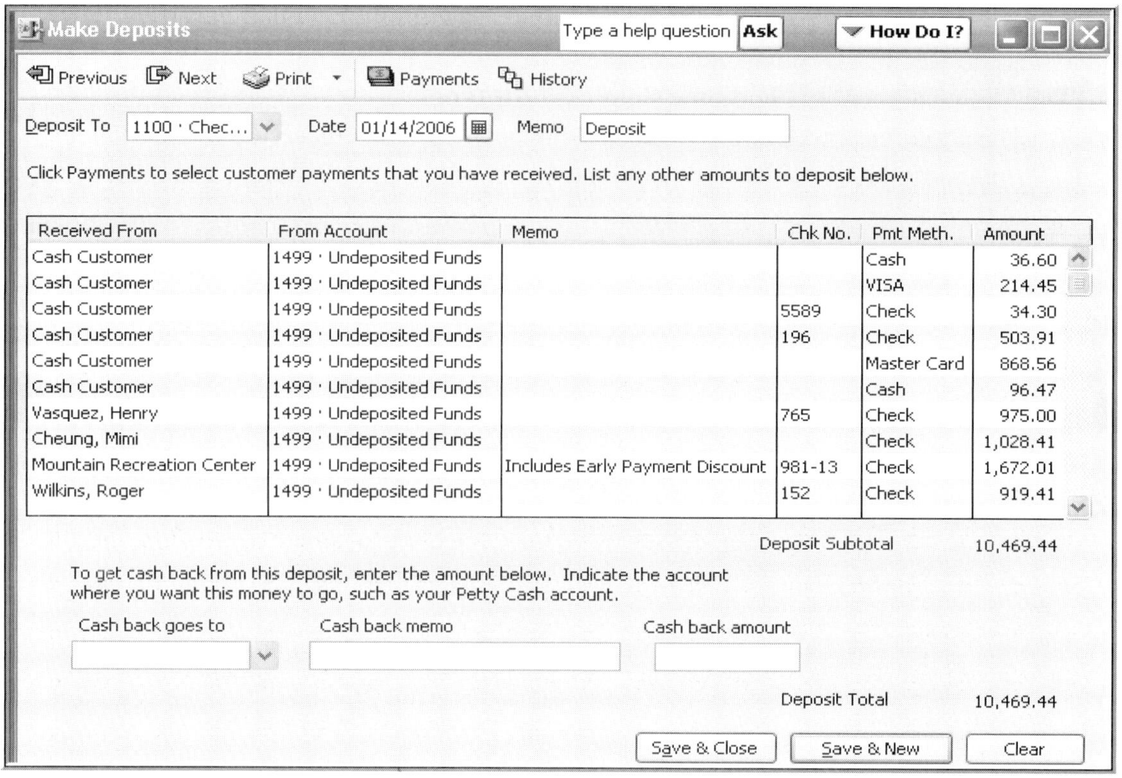

Click **Print** to print **Deposit Summary**
Select **Deposit summary only** and click **OK** on the **Print Deposit** dialog box

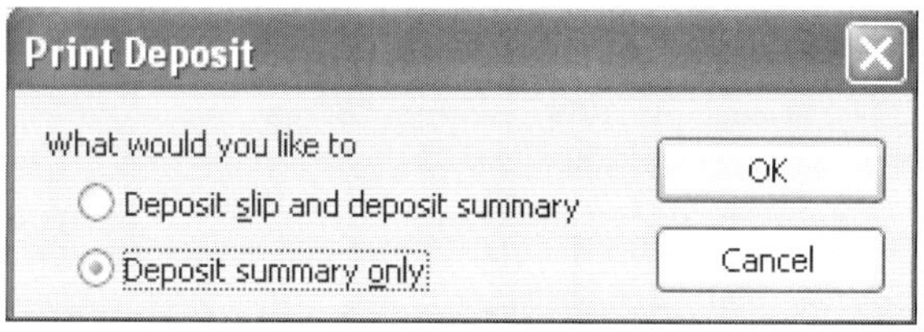

Click **Print** on the **Print Lists** dialog box
When printing is finished, click **Save & Close** on **Make Deposits**

RECORD THE RETURN OF A CHECK BECAUSE OF NONSUFFICIENT FUNDS

If a customer pays you with a check and the check cannot be processed by the bank because there are insufficient funds in the customer's bank account, the amount of the check and the associated bank charges need to be subtracted from the account where the check was deposited; and the Accounts Receivable account needs to be updated to show the amount the customer owes you for the check that "bounced." This type of check is also called *nonsufficient funds* or *NSF*. In order to track the amount of a bad check and to charge a customer for the bank charges and any penalties you impose, Other Charge items may need to be created and an invoice for the total amount due must be prepared..

MEMO

DATE: January 15, 2006

The bank returned Kent Trestle's Check No. 819 for $100 marked NSF. The bank imposed a $10 service charge for the NSF check. Your Name Sports charges a $15 fee for NSF checks. Record the NSF and related charges on an invoice to Kent Trestle. Add any necessary items for Other Charges to the Items List.

Prepare Invoice 10 to record the NSF check and related charges indicated above

Access invoices as previously instructed
Click the drop-down list arrow for **Customer:Job**, click **Trestle, Kent**
Tab to or click **Date**, enter **011506**
Click drop-down list arrow for **Terms**, click **Due on receipt**

- The invoice is prepared to increase the amount that Kent Trestle owes. That amount will include the bad check and the fees for the bad check.

Click the drop-down list arrow for **Item Code**

- You need to add an item that will identify the transaction as a bad check. Because you are preparing an invoice to record the NSF check, using this item will keep the bad check from being incorrectly identified as a sale.

Click **<Add New>**
Click **Other Charge**
Enter **Bad Check** as the **Item Name/Number**
Tab to or click **Description**
Enter **Check returned by bank**
Amount or % should be **0.00**
Click the drop-down-list arrow for **Tax Code**
Click **Non-Taxable**
Click the drop-down list arrow for **Account**
Click **1100 Checking**

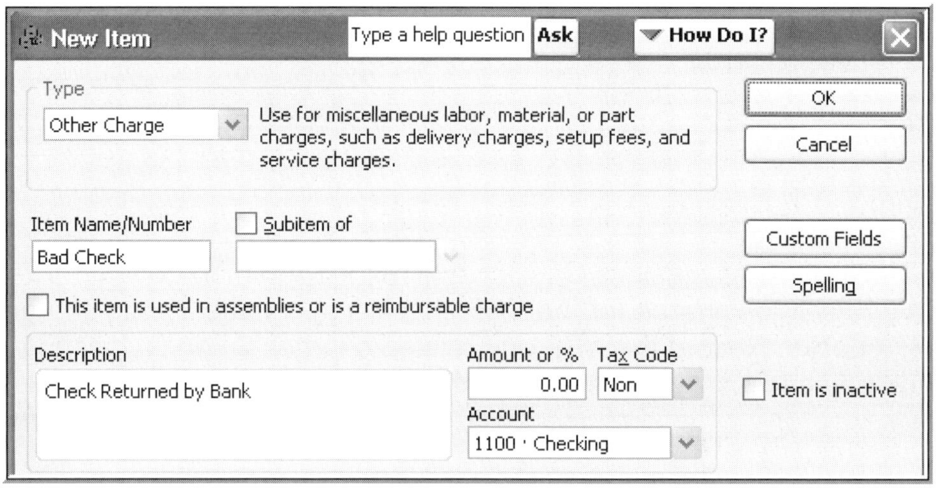

Click **OK**
Click or tab to **Price Each** on the Invoice
Enter **100**

- This is the amount of Kent's bad check.

Tab to or click the next line for **Item Code**, click the drop-down list arrow for **Item Code**

- Another item needs be added in order to identify the amount that Kent owes for the NSF charges from the bank and from Your Name Sports.

Click **<Add New>**

- The list for **Type** automatically appears.

Click **Other Charge** for **Type**
Tab to or click **Item Name/Number**
Enter **Bad Check Charges**
Tab to or click **Description**
Enter **Bank and other charges for returned check.**
Amount or % should be **0.00**
The **Tax Code** should be **Non-Taxable**
Click the drop-down list arrow for **Account**
Scroll through the list of accounts

- There are no appropriate accounts for this item.

Add a new account to the Chart of Accounts by clicking **<Add New>** at the top of the list for the Accounts
Type of account is **Income**

- This account is an income account because we will be receiving money for the charges. When the bank statement is reconciled, the amount of bank service charges will reduce the amount of income earned for the bad check charges leaving only the amount actually earned by Your Name Sports.

Enter **4040** for the **Number**
Tab to or click **Name**
Enter **Returned Check Service Charges**

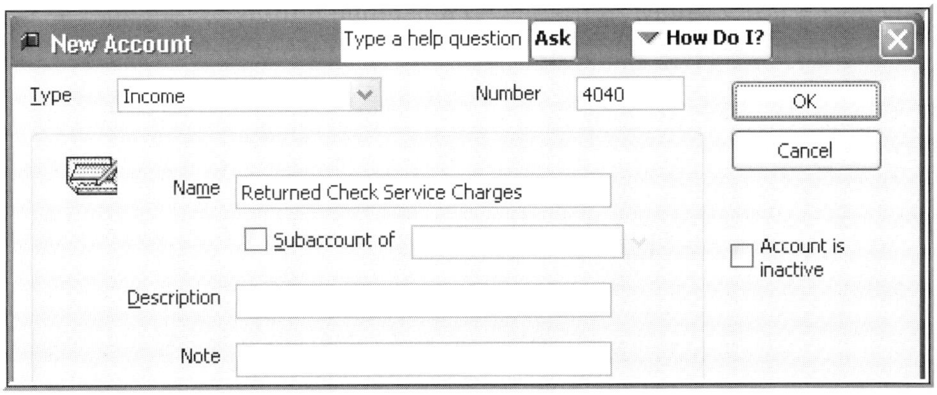

Click **OK** to record the new account in the **Chart of Accounts**
Account 4040 is inserted as the **Account** for the **New Item**

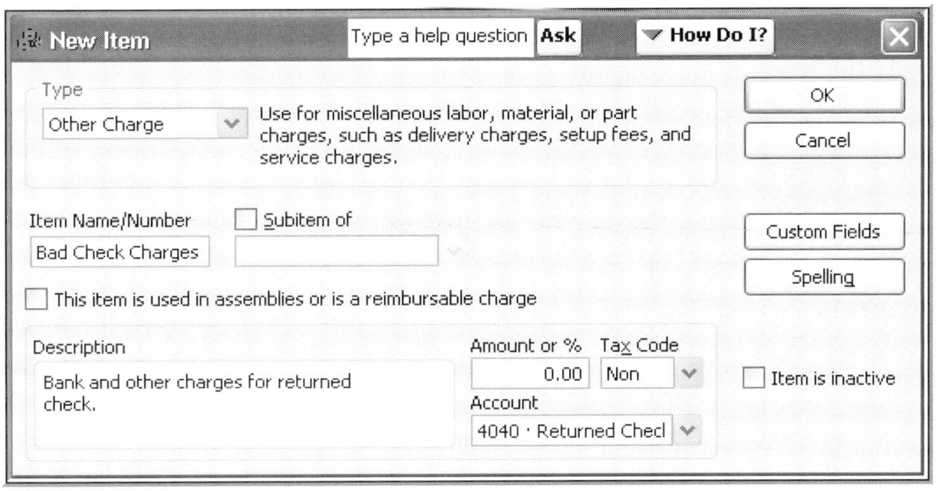

Click **OK** to add Bad Check Charges to the Item List
Tab to or click **Price Each** on the Invoice
Enter **25**

- This is the total amount of the charges Kent has incurred for the NSF check—$10 for the bank charges and $15 for Your Name Sports charges.

Click the drop-down list arrow for **Customer Message**, click **Please remit to above address.**

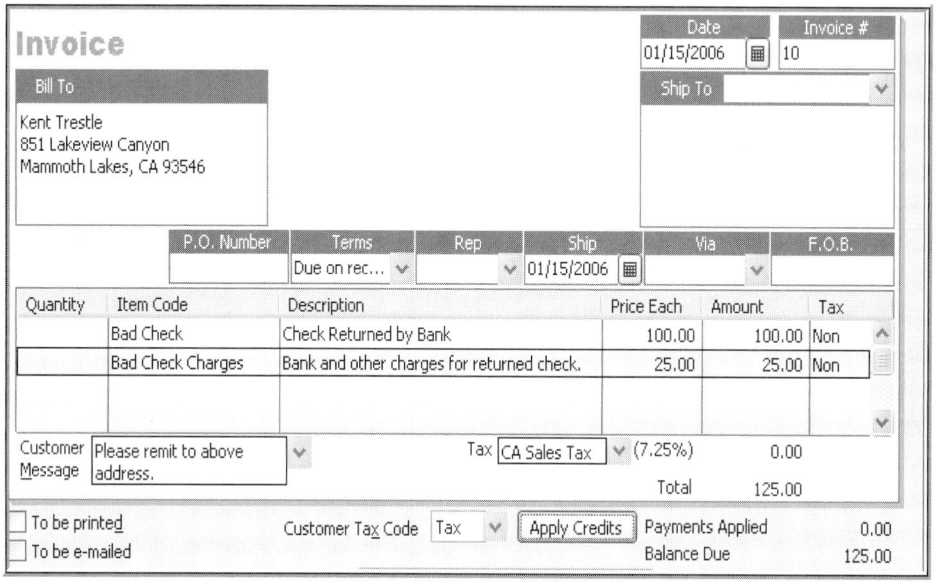

Print the Invoice
Click **Save & Close** to save and exit **Create Invoices**
- You may get a message box regarding the change in terms for Kent Trestle.

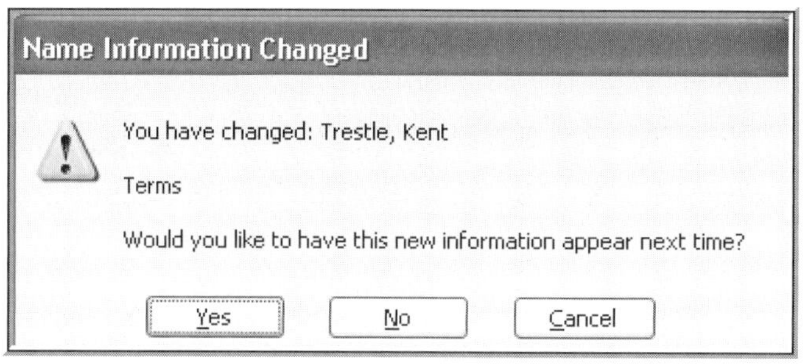

Click **No**

ISSUE A CREDIT MEMO AND A REFUND CHECK

If merchandise is returned and the invoice has been paid in full or the sale was for cash, a refund check may be issued at the same time as the credit memo is prepared. Simply clicking a Check Refund button instructs QuickBooks Pro to prepare the refund check for you.

Memo
DATE: January 15, 2006

Dr. Felipe Manuel returned the ski poles he purchased for $75 January 3 on Invoice No. 2. He has already paid his bill in full. Record the return and issue a check refunding the $75 plus tax.

Prepare a Credit Memo to record the return of the ski poles and issue a refund check

Issue a Credit Memo as previously instructed
Use the Customer Message **Thank you for your business.**
Click the drop-down list arrow for **Use Credit to**, click **Give Refund**.
The Issue a Refund dialog box appears.

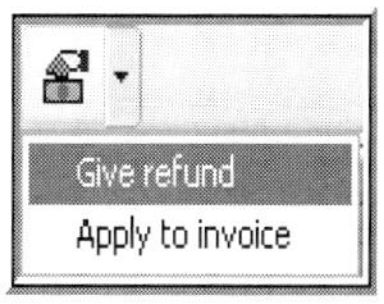

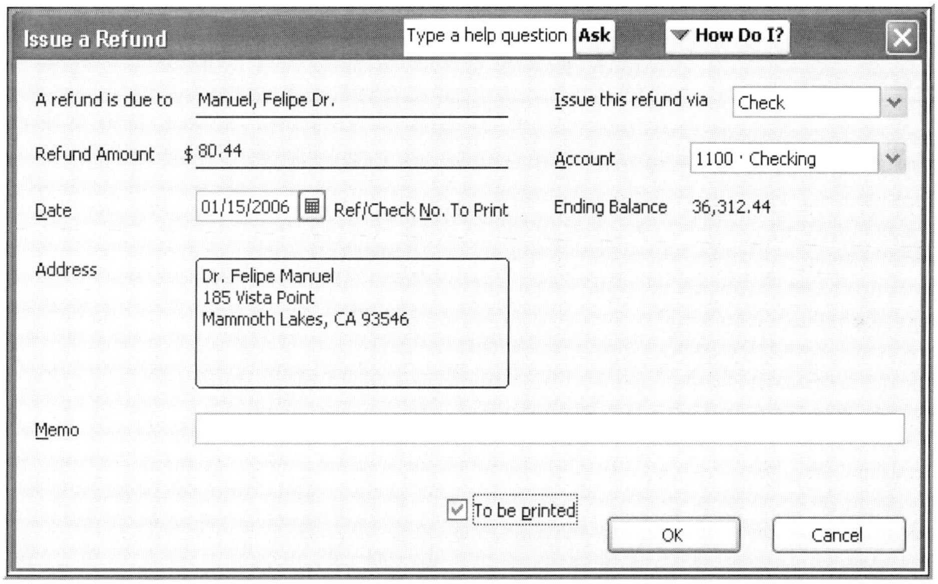

Verify the information and click **OK**.

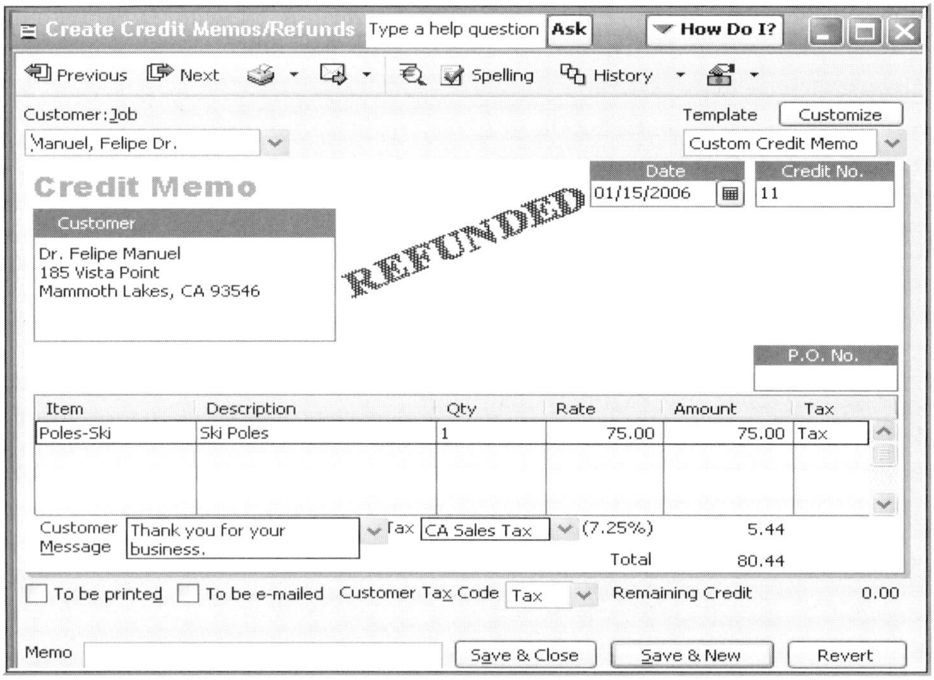

Print the Credit Memo.

- The Credit Memo is marked REFUNDED.

Click **Save & Close** to record the **Credit Memo** and exit

Click the **Write Checks** icon on the Home Page, click **Previous** until you get to the check for Dr. Manuel

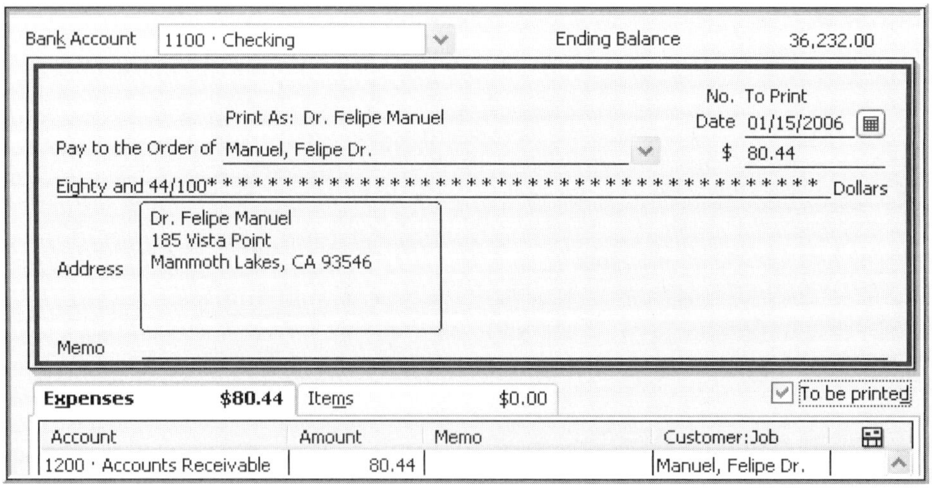

Print Check No. 1 in Standard format as previously instructed

Click **Save & Close** on the **Write Checks** screen

PRINT THE JOURNAL

Even though QuickBooks Pro displays registers and reports in a manner that focuses on the transaction—that is, entering a sale on account via an invoice rather than a Sales Journal or a General Journal—it still keeps a General Journal. The Journal records each transaction and lists the accounts and the amounts for debit and credit entries.

Print the Journal

Click the **Report Center** button, click **Accountant & Taxes** as the type of report, click **Journal** to select the report

The report date if from **01/01/06** to **01/15/06**

Scroll through the report to view the transactions

- For each item sold, you will notice that the Inventory Asset account is credited and the Cost of Goods Sold account is debited. This moves the value of the item out of your assets and into the cost of goods sold. The amount is not the same amount as the one in the transaction. This is because QuickBooks uses the average cost method of inventory valuation and records the transaction based on the average cost of an item rather than the specific cost of an item.

Resize the columns by positioning the cursor on the diamond and dragging so that the report will print on one-page wide without clicking Fit to one-page wide

- Make sure that the account names are displayed in full

Print the report in Landscape orientation

Use Print Preview to make sure that the report fits on one-page wide and that the account names are displayed in full

Your Name Sports
Journal
January 1 - 15, 2006

Trans #	Type	Date	Num	Name	Memo	Account	Debit	Credit
48	Invoice	01/02/2006	1	Wilkins, Roger	VOID:	1200 · Accounts Receivable	0.00	
				Wilkins, Roger	After Ski Boot...	4011 · Clothing & Accessory Sales	0.00	
				Wilkins, Roger	After Ski Boot...	1120 · Inventory Asset	0.00	
				Wilkins, Roger	After Ski Boot...	5000 · Cost of Goods Sold	0.00	
				State Board of Equaliza...	CA Sales Tax	2200 · Sales Tax Payable	0.00	
							0.00	0.00
49	Invoice	01/03/2006	2	Manuel, Felipe Dr.		1200 · Accounts Receivable	992.06	
				Manuel, Felipe Dr.	Snow Skis	4012 · Equipment Sales		425.00
				Manuel, Felipe Dr.	Snow Skis	1120 · Inventory Asset		100.00
				Manuel, Felipe Dr.	Snow Skis	5000 · Cost of Goods Sold	100.00	
				Manuel, Felipe Dr.	Ski Bindings	4012 · Equipment Sales		175.00
				Manuel, Felipe Dr.	Ski Bindings	1120 · Inventory Asset		75.00
				Manuel, Felipe Dr.	Ski Bindings	5000 · Cost of Goods Sold	75.00	
				Manuel, Felipe Dr.	Ski Boots	4012 · Equipment Sales		250.00
				Manuel, Felipe Dr.	Ski Boots	1120 · Inventory Asset		75.00
				Manuel, Felipe Dr.	Ski Boots	5000 · Cost of Goods Sold	75.00	
				Manuel, Felipe Dr.	Ski Poles	4012 · Equipment Sales		75.00
				Manuel, Felipe Dr.	Ski Poles	1120 · Inventory Asset		30.00
				Manuel, Felipe Dr.	Ski Poles	5000 · Cost of Goods Sold	30.00	

When the report is printed, close it
Do not close the Report Center

PRINT THE TRIAL BALANCE

When all sales transactions have been entered, it is important to print the trial balance and verify that the total debits equal the total credits.

Click **Trial Balance** to select the type of report on the Accountant & Taxes section the Report Center

The report dates are from **01/01/2006** to **01/15/2006**

Your Name Sports
Trial Balance
As of January 15, 2006

	Jan 15, 06	
	Debit	Credit
1340 · Prepaid Insurance	250.00	
1499 · Undeposited Funds	0.00	
1511 · Original Cost	5,000.00	
1521 · Original Cost	4,500.00	
2000 · Accounts Payable		8,500.00
2100 · Visa		150.00
2200 · Sales Tax Payable		613.15
2510 · Office Equipment Loan		3,000.00
2520 · Store Fixtures Loan		2,500.00
3000 · Retained Earnings	0.00	
3010 · Your Name & Bailey Capital		25,459.44
3011 · Your Name, Investment		20,000.00
3012 · Tim Bailey, Investment		20,000.00
4011 · Clothing & Accessory Sales		1,409.76
4012 · Equipment Sales		7,436.44
4040 · Returned Check Service Charges		25.00
5000 · Cost of Goods Sold	3,342.46	
6130 · Sales Discounts	447.17	
TOTAL	**89,093.79**	**89,093.79**

Print the Trial Balance in **Portrait** orientation
Close the report and the Report Center

CUSTOMER CENTER

In the Customer Center, you will see the customer list. As you click each customer, you will see the customer information and transaction details for the individual customer. You may also have transaction details for specific types of transactions by clicking the drop-down list arrow

View the Customer Center

Click the **Customer Center** button
View the information for Cash Customer
Click the drop-down list arrow next to **Show** to see the list of the types of transactions that may be displayed

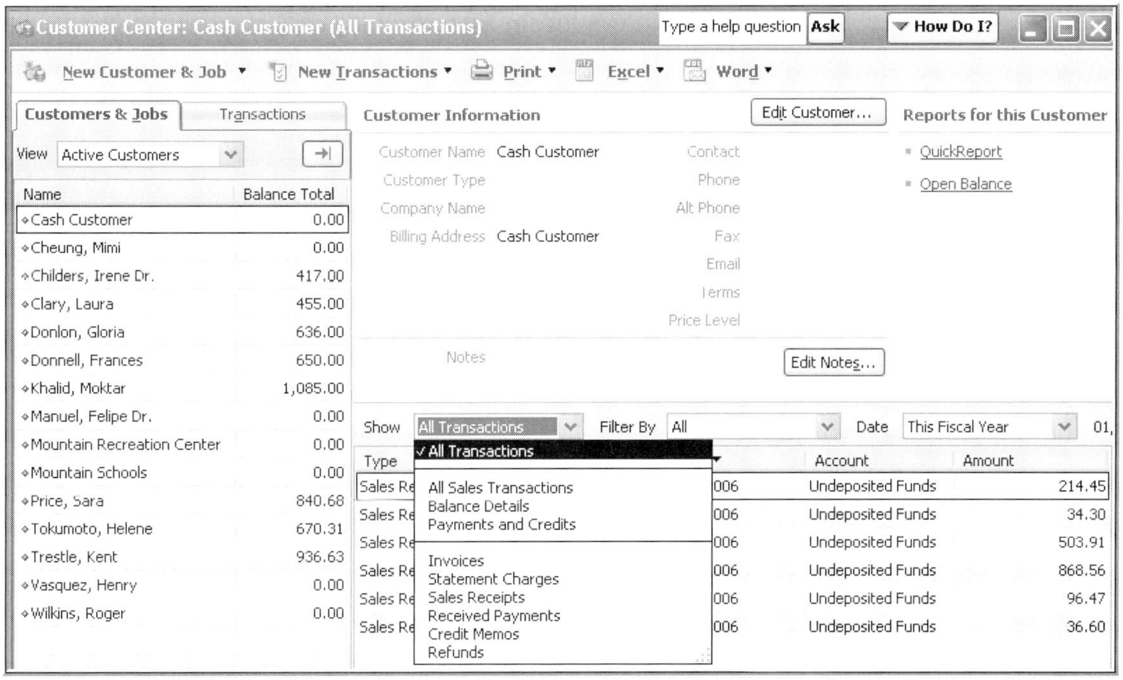

Close the Customer Center

BACK UP YOUR NAME SPORTS

Whenever an important work session is complete, you should always back up your data. If your data disk is damaged or an error is discovered at a later time, the backup disk may be restored and the information used for recording transactions. No matter what type of business, the backup procedure remains the same. In addition, it is always wise to make a duplicate of your data disk just in case the disk is damaged in some way.

Follow the instructions given in Chapters 1 to back up data for Your Name Sports. If you wish to make a duplicate disk, follow the instructions in Appendix A

SUMMARY

In this chapter, cash, bank charge card, and credit sales were prepared for Your Name Sports, a retail business, using sales receipts and invoices. Credit memos and refund checks were issued, and customer accounts were added and revised. Invoices and sales receipts were edited, deleted, and voided. Cash payments were received, and bank deposits were made. New accounts were added to the Chart of Accounts, and new items were added to the Item List while entering transactions. Inventory items were added and sold. All the transactions entered reinforced the QuickBooks Pro concept of using the business form to record transactions rather than entering information in journals. However, QuickBooks Pro does not disregard traditional accounting methods. Instead, it performs this function in the background. The Journal was accessed, analyzed, and printed. The importance of reports for information and decision-making was illustrated. Sales reports emphasized both cash and credit sales according to the customer or according to the sales item generating the revenue. Accounts receivable reports focused on amounts owed by credit customers. The traditional trial balance emphasizing the equality of debits and credits was prepared.

END-OF-CHAPTER QUESTIONS

TRUE/FALSE

ANSWER THE FOLLOWING QUESTIONS IN THE SPACE PROVIDED BEFORE THE QUESTION NUMBER.

_____ 1. If a return is made after an invoice has been paid in full, a refund check is issued along with a credit memo.

_____ 2. QuickBooks Pro automatically applies a payment received to the most current invoice.

_____ 3. Sales tax will be calculated automatically on an invoice if a customer is marked taxable.

_____ 4. A new sales item may be added only at the beginning of a period.

_____ 5. A new customer may be added *on the fly*.

_____ 6. Report formats may be customized.

_____ 7. The Discounts & Credits button on the Receive Payments window allows discounts to be applied to invoices being paid by clicking Cancel.

_____ 8. Cash sales are recorded in the Receive Payments window and marked paid.

_____ 9. If a customer issues a check that is returned marked NSF, you may charge the customer the amount of the bank charges and any penalty charges you impose.

_____ 10. Sales tax must be calculated manually and added to sales receipts.

MULTIPLE CHOICE

WRITE THE LETTER OF THE CORRECT ANSWER IN THE SPACE PROVIDED BEFORE THE QUESTION NUMBER.

_____ 1. Information regarding details of a customer's balance may be obtained by viewing .

A. the Trial Balance
B. the Customer's Balance Summary Report
C. the Customer's Balance Detail Report
D. an invoice for the customer

_____ 2. Even though transactions are entered via business documents such as invoices and sales receipts, QuickBooks Pro keeps track of all transactions ___.

A. in a chart
B. in the master account register
C. on a graph
D. in the Journal

_____ 3. If a transaction is ___, it will not show up in the Customer Balance Detail Report.

A. voided
B. deleted
C. corrected
D. canceled

_____ 4. A credit card sale is treated exactly like a ___.

A. cash sale
B. sale on account until reimbursement is received from a bank
C. sale on account
D. bank deposit

_____ 5. If the word -Split- appears in the Split column of a report rather than an account name, it means that the transaction is split between two or more ___.

A. accounts or items
B. customers
C. journals
D. reports

_____ 6. When adding a customer *on the fly*, you may choose to add just the customer's name by selecting ___.
A. Quick Add
B. Set Up
C. Condensed
D. none of the above—a customer cannot be added *on the fly*

_____ 7. The Item List stores information about ___.
A. each item that is out of stock
B. each item in stock
C. each customer with an account
D. each item a company sells

_____ 8. A report prepared to obtain information about sales, inventory, and merchandise costs is a ___.
A. Stock Report
B. Income Statement
C. Sales by Vendor Summary Report
D. Sales by Item Summary Report

_____ 9. If a customer has a balance for an amount owed and a return is made, a credit memo is prepared and ___.
A. a refund check is issued
B. the amount of the return may be applied to the balance owed at the time the invoice is paid
C. the customer determines whether to apply the amount to the balance owed or to get a refund check
D. all of the above

_____ 10. Purchase information regarding an item sold by the company is entered ___.
A. in the Invoice Register
B. when adding a sales item
C. only when creating the company
D. when the last item in stock is sold

FILL-IN

IN THE SPACE PROVIDED, WRITE THE ANSWER THAT MOST APPROPRIATELY COMPLETES THE SENTENCE.

1. A report showing all sales, credits, and payments for each customer on account but not the remaining balance on the account is the ____________ report.

2. When a customer with a balance due on an account makes a payment, it is recorded in the ____________.

3. If the Quantity and Price Each are entered on an invoice, pressing the ____________ key will cause QuickBooks Pro to calculate and enter the correct information in the Amount column of the invoice.

4. QuickBooks Pro allows you to view additional information within a report by using the ____________ feature.

5. When you receive payments from customers, QuickBooks Pro places the amount received in an account called ____________.

SHORT ESSAY

Describe the use of Find. Based on chapter information, what is used to instruct Find to limit its search?

____

____

____

____

____

NAME ______________________

TRANSMITTAL

CHAPTER 5: YOUR NAME SPORTS

Attach the following documents and reports:

Invoice No. 1: Roger Wilkins
Invoice No. 2: Felipe Manuel
Invoice No. 3: Mountain Schools
Invoice No. 4: Sara Price
Invoice No. 5: Kent Trestle
Invoice No. 6: Roger Wilkins
Invoice No. 7: Mimi Cheung
Invoice No. 7 (Corrected): Mimi Cheung
Customer Balance Detail
Invoice No. 3 (Corrected): Mountain Schools
Invoice No. 8: Mountain Recreation Center
Credit Memo No. 9: Mimi Cheung
Open Invoices by Customer, January 10, 2006
Sales Receipt No. 1: Cash Customer
Sales Receipt No. 2: Cash Customer
Sales Receipt No. 3: Cash Customer
Sales Receipt No. 4: Cash Customer
Sales Receipt No. 5: Cash Customer
Sales Receipt No. 6: Cash Customer
Sales by Item Summary, January 1-13, 2006
Sales Receipt No. 1 (Revised): Cash Customer, January 8, 2006
Customer Balance Summary
Deposit Summary
Invoice No. 10: Kent Trestle
Credit Memo No. 11: Felipe Manuel
Check No. 1: Felipe Manuel
Journal, January 1-15, 2006
Trial Balance, January 1-15, 2006

END-OF-CHAPTER PROBLEM

YOUR NAME CLOTHING

Your Name Clothing is a men's and women's clothing store located in San Luis Obispo, California, specializing in resort wear. The store is owned and operated by you and your partner Julie Lee. Julie keeps the books and runs the office for the store, and you are responsible for buying merchandise and managing the store. Both partners sell merchandise in the store, and they have some college students working part time during the evenings and on the weekends.

INSTRUCTIONS

As in previous chapters, copy **Clothing.qbw** from the Prentice Hall Web Site. Open the company, and record the following transactions using invoices and sales receipts. Your Name Clothing accepts cash, checks, and credit cards for *cash* sales. Make bank deposits as instructed. Print the reports as indicated. Add new accounts, items, and customers where appropriate.

When recording transactions, use the Item List to determine the item(s) sold. All transactions are taxable unless otherwise indicated. Terms for sales on account are the standard terms assigned to each customer individually. If a customer exceeds his or her credit limit, accept the transaction. When receiving payment for sales on account, always check to see if a discount should be given. A customer's beginning balance is not eligible for a discount. The date of the sale begins the discount period. A check should be received or postmarked within ten days of the invoice in order to qualify for a discount. If the customer has any credits to the account because of a return, apply the credits to the appropriate invoice. If the customer makes a return and does not have a balance on account, prepare a refund check for the customer. Invoices begin with number 15, are numbered consecutively, and have lines printed around each field. Sales Receipts begin with number 25, are also numbered consecutively, and have lines printed around each field. Each invoice and sales receipt should contain a message. Use the one you feel is most appropriate.

If you write any checks, keep track of the check numbers used. QuickBooks Pro does not always display the check number you are expecting to see. Remember that QuickBooks Pro does not print check numbers on checks because most businesses use checks with the check numbers preprinted.

If a transaction can be printed, print the transaction when it is entered.

LISTS

The Item List and Customer List are displayed for your use in determining which sales item and customer to use in a transaction.

ITEM LIST

Item List

Name	Description	Type	Account	On Hand	Price
Access-Belts	Belts	Inventory Part	4010 · Sales:4013 · Accessories Sales	40	0.00
Access-Shades	Sunglasses	Inventory Part	4010 · Sales:4013 · Accessories Sales	50	0.00
Access-Ties	Ties and Scarves	Inventory Part	4010 · Sales:4013 · Accessories Sales	100	0.00
Men-Pants	Men's Pants and Shorts	Inventory Part	4010 · Sales:4012 · Men's Clothing Sales	100	0.00
Men-Shirts	Men's Shirts	Inventory Part	4010 · Sales:4012 · Men's Clothing Sales	100	0.00
Men-Shoes	Men's Shoes	Inventory Part	4010 · Sales:4012 · Men's Clothing Sales	100	0.00
Women-Pants	Women's Pants and Shorts	Inventory Part	4010 · Sales:4011 · Women's Clothing Sales	30	0.00
Women-Shirts	Women's Shirts and Blouses	Inventory Part	4010 · Sales:4011 · Women's Clothing Sales	100	0.00
Women-Shoes	Women's Shoes	Inventory Part	4010 · Sales:4011 · Women's Clothing Sales	100	0.00
CA Sales Tax	CA Sales Tax	Sales Tax Item	2200 · Sales Tax Payable		7.25%
Out of State	Out-of-state sale, exempt from sales tax	Sales Tax Item	2200 · Sales Tax Payable		0.0%

CUSTOMER LIST

Customers & Jobs | Transactions

View: Active Customers

Name	Balance Total
Allen, Millie	1,359.00
Carter, Gail	325.00
Dezavala, Erwin	598.00
Kitasaki, Taka	785.00
Lewis, John	1,065.00
Lipari, Tom	0.00
Long, Alex	750.00
McBride, Steve	950.00
Mitchell, Koko	0.00
Patterson, Ellen	1,254.00
Ramirez, Tina	945.00
Sanders, Bruce	75.00
Van, Lincoln	450.00
Wayne, Andy	835.00
Webber, Madeline	375.00

RECORD TRANSACTIONS

January 3, 2007:

- ► Add your name to the company name. The company name will be **Your Name Clothing**—(Type your actual name, *not* the words *Your Name*.)
- ► Add your name to the owner's equity accounts. Replace "Student's Name" with your actual name.
- ► Customize the Product Invoice, the Sales Receipt, and the Credit Memo so that there is enough room to display your name in full on the same line as the company name. Change the

company preferences so that the date prepared, time prepared, and report basis do not print as part of the heading on reports. Have the reports refresh automatically.

- Prepare Invoice No. 15 to record the sale on account for 1 belt for $29.95, 1 pair of men's shorts for $39.95, and a man's shirt for $39.95 to Tom Lipari. Print the invoice.
- Received Check No. 3305 from Gail Carter for $325 in payment of her bill in full.
- Record the sale on account of 1 pair of sunglasses for $89.95 to Lincoln Van. (Remember to approve any transaction that exceeds a customer's credit limit.)
- Record the sale of one dress on account to Ellen Patterson for $79.95. (Add a new sales item: Women-Dress, Women's Dresses, preferred vendor is Fun Clothing, Income Account is 4011 Women's Clothing, Reorder Point is 20, Qty on Hand 25, Total Value $750, as of 01/01/2007.)
- Add a new customer: San Luis Obispo Rec Center, 451 Marsh Street, San Luis Obispo, CA 93407, Contact person is Katie Gregg, 805-555-2241, Credit Terms are 2% 10 Net 30, Credit Limit $1,000, they are taxable for CA Sales Tax.
- Sold 5 men's shirts on account to San Luis Recreation Center for $29.95 each, 5 pair of men's shorts for $29.95 each. Because San Luis Recreation Center is a nonprofit organization, include a subtotal for the sale and apply a 10% sales discount for a nonprofit organization. (Create any new sales items necessary by following the instructions given in the chapter. The nonprofit discount is marked Taxable so the discount is taken before adding sales tax. If you need to add a Sales Discounts account to the Chart of Accounts, assign account number 6130.)
- Sold 1 woman's blouse for $59.95 to Julee Gardener. Received Check No. 378 for the full amount including tax. Record the sale as a cash customer. (If necessary, refer to steps provided within the chapter for instructions on creating a cash customer.) Issue and print Sales Receipt No. 25 for this transaction.
- Received a belt returned by Andy Wayne. The original price of the belt was $49.95. Prepare a Credit Memo. Apply the credit to his Opening Balance.
- Sold a dress to a customer for $99.95. The customer paid with her Visa. Record the sale.
- Sold a scarf for $19.95 plus tax for cash. Record the sale.
- Received payments from the following customers:
  - Erwin Dezavala, $598.00, Check No. 145
  - Madeline Webber, $375, Check No. 4015
  - Alex Long, $750, Check No. 8915-02
  - Andy Wayne, $781.43, Check No. 6726

January 5, 2007:

Deposit all cash, checks, and credit card receipts. Print a Deposit Summary.

January 15, 2007:

- Received an NSF notice from the bank for the check for $325 from Gail Carter. Enter the necessary transaction for this nonsufficient funds check. The bank's charges are $15, and Your Name Clothing charges $15 for all NSF checks. (If necessary, refer to steps provided within the chapter for instructions on adding accounts or items necessary to record this transaction.)

- Alex Long returned a shirt he had purchased for $54.99 plus tax. Record the return. Check the balance of his account. If there is no balance, issue a refund check.
- Sold 3 men's shirts to Richard Ralph, a cash customer, for $39.95 each plus tax. Richard used his Master Card for payment.
- Sold on account 1 dress for $99.99, 1 pair of sandals for $79.95, and a belt for $39.95 to Taka Kitasaki.
- Sold 1 pair of women's shorts for $34.95 to a cash customer. Accepted Check No. 8160 for payment.
- Received a partial payment on account from John Lewis, $250, Check No. 2395.
- Received payment in full from Bruce Sanders, Check No. 9802.
- Received $1,338.03 from Ellen Patterson as payment in full on account, Check No. 2311. The payment was postmarked 1/11/2007. (Because both the 12/31/2006 Invoice for $1,254 and Invoice No. 17 are being paid with this check, the payment will be applied to both invoices. In order to apply the discount to Invoice No. 17, click both the beginning balance and Invoice No. 17 to deselect; then click in the check mark column for Invoice No. 17; click the Discounts & Credits button; calculate the 2 percent discount and enter the amount on the Discounts and Credits screen, select the appropriate account for the sales discount, click Done to apply the discount; and, finally, click in the check mark column for the 12/31/2006 invoice.)
- Sold 3 pairs of men's pants for $75.00 each, 3 men's shirts for $50.00 each, 3 belts for $39.99 each, 2 pairs of men's shoes for $90.00 each, 2 ties for $55.00 each, and 1 pair of sunglasses for $75.00 to Tina Ramirez on account. (If the amount of the sale exceeds Tina's credit limit, accept the sale anyway.)
- Sold on account 1 pair of sunglasses for $95.00, 2 dresses for $99.95 each, and 2 pairs of women's shoes for $65.00 each to Madeline Webber.
- Print Customer Balance Detail Report. Adjust column widths so the account names are shown in full and the report is one page wide without selecting Fit report to one page wide. The report length may be longer than one page.
- Print a Sales by Item Detail Report for 01/01/2007 to 01/15/2007 in Landscape orientation. Adjust column widths so the report fits on one page wide. Do not select Fit report to one page wide.
- Deposit all payments, checks, and charges received from customers. Print the Deposit Summary.
- Print a Trial Balance for 01/01/2007 to 01/15/2007.

NAME __________________________

TRANSMITTAL

CHAPTER 5: YOUR NAME CLOTHING

Attach the following documents and reports:

Invoice No. 15: Tom Lipari
Invoice No. 16: Lincoln Van
Invoice No. 17: Ellen Patterson
Invoice No. 18: San Luis Obispo Rec Center
Sales Receipt No. 25: Cash Customer
Credit Memo No. 19: Andy Wayne
Sales Receipt No. 26: Cash Customer
Sales Receipt No. 27: Cash Customer
Deposit Summary, January 5, 2007
Invoice No. 20: Gail Carter
Credit Memo No. 21: Alex Long
Check No. 1: Alex Long
Sales Receipt No. 28: Cash Customer
Invoice No. 22: Taka Kitasaki
Sales Receipt No. 29: Cash Customer
Invoice No. 23: Tina Ramirez
Invoice No. 24: Madeline Webber
Customer Balance Detail
Itemized Sales by Item Report, January 1-15, 2007
Deposit Summary, January 15, 2007
Trial Balance, January 1-15, 2007

PAYABLES AND PURCHASES: MERCHANDISING BUSINESS

6

LEARNING OBJECTIVES

At the completion of this chapter you will be able to:

1. Understand the concepts for computerized accounting for payables in a merchandising business.
2. Customize a Purchase Order template.
3. Prepare, view, and print purchase orders and checks.
4. Enter items received against purchase orders.
5. Enter bills, enter vendor credits, and pay bills.
6. Edit and correct errors in bills and purchase orders.
7. Add new vendors, modify vendor records, and add new accounts.
8. View accounts payable transaction history from the Enter Bills window.
9. View, use the QuickZoom feature, and/or print QuickReports for vendors, accounts payable register, and so on.
10. Record and edit transactions in the Accounts Payable Register.
11. Edit, void, and delete bills, purchase orders, and checks.
12. Use various payment options including writing checks, using Pay Bills to write checks, and company credit cards.
13. Display and print a Sales Tax Liability Report, an Accounts Payable Aging Summary Report, an Unpaid Bills Detail Report, and a Vendor Balance Summary Report.
14. Use the Vendor Detail Center to obtain information for an individual vendor.

ACCOUNTING FOR PAYABLES AND PURCHASES

In a merchandising business, much of the accounting for purchases and payables consists of ordering merchandise for resale and paying bills for expenses incurred in the operation of the business. Purchases are for things used in the operation of the business. Some transactions will be in the form of cash purchases; others will be purchases on account. Bills can be paid when they are received or when they are due. Merchandise received must be checked against purchase orders, and completed purchase orders must be closed. Rather than use cumbersome journals, QuickBooks Pro continues to focus on recording transactions based on the business document; therefore, you use the Enter Bills and Pay Bills features of the program to record the receipt and payment of bills. While QuickBooks Pro does not refer to it as such, the Vendor List is the same as the Accounts Payable Subsidiary Ledger.

QuickBooks Pro can remind you when inventory needs to be ordered and when payments are due. Purchase orders are prepared when ordering merchandise. The program automatically tracks inventory and uses the average cost method to value the inventory. QuickBooks Pro can calculate and apply discounts earned for paying bills early. Payments can be made by recording payments in the Pay Bills window or, if using the cash basis for accounting, by writing a check. Merchandise purchased may be paid for at the same time the items and the bill are received, or it may be paid for at a later date. A cash purchase can be recorded by writing a check, by using a credit card, or by using petty cash. Even though QuickBooks Pro focuses on recording transactions on the business forms used, all transactions are recorded behind the scenes in the General Journal.

As in previous chapters, corrections can be made directly on the bill or within the transaction journal. New accounts and vendors may be added *on the fly* as transactions are entered. Purchase orders, bills, or checks may be voided or deleted. Reports illustrating vendor balances, unpaid bills, accounts payable aging, sales tax liability, transaction history, and accounts payable registers may be viewed and printed.

TRAINING TUTORIAL AND PROCEDURES

The following tutorial will once again work with Your Name Sports. As in Chapter 5, transactions will be recorded for this fictitious company. Refer to procedures given in Chapter 5 to maximize training benefits. You will use the company file for Your Name Sports that contains your transactions for Chapter 5. As with the earlier training in a service company, the merchandising section of the text has you enter the transactions for all three chapters—5, 6, and 7—within the same company file.

OPEN QUICKBOOKS® PRO AND YOUR NAME SPORTS

Open QuickBooks Pro and Your Name Sports as instructed in previous chapters

Check the title bar to verify that Your Name Sports is the open company and that your name appears.

BEGINNING THE TUTORIAL

In this chapter you will be entering purchases of merchandise for resale in the business and entering bills incurred by the company in the operation of the business. You will also be recording the payment of bills and purchases using checks and credit cards.

The Vendor List keeps information regarding the vendors with which you do business. This information includes the vendor names, addresses, telephone number, fax number, e-mail address, payment terms, credit limits, and account numbers. You will be using the following list for vendors with which Your Name Sports has an account:

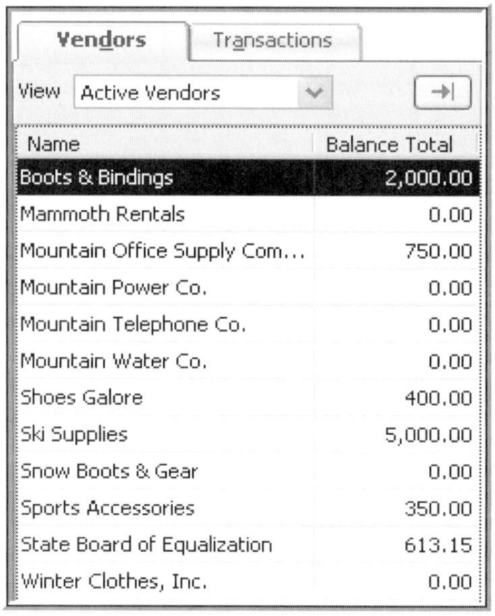

As in previous chapters, all transactions are listed on memos. The transaction date will be the same date as the memo date unless otherwise specified within the transaction. Vendor names, when necessary, will be given in the transaction. Unless otherwise specified, terms are 2% 10 Net 30. Once a specific type of transaction has been entered in a step-by-step manner, additional transactions of the same or a similar type will be made without having instructions provided. Of course, you may always refer to instructions given for previous transactions for ideas or for steps used to enter those transactions. To determine the account used in the transaction, refer to the Chart of Accounts. When entering account information on a bill, clicking the drop-down list arrow will show a copy of the Chart of Accounts.

VIEW THE REMINDERS LIST TO DETERMINE MERCHANDISE TO ORDER

QuickBooks Pro has a Reminders List that is used to remind you of things that need to be completed. The Company menu allows you to display the Reminders List. Information on the Reminders List may be displayed in summary (collapsed) form or in detailed (expanded) form.

MEMO

DATE: January 16, 2006

Display the Reminders List to determine which items need to be ordered.

Display the **Reminders List**

Click **Company** on the Menu bar
Click **Reminders**

- The Reminders List appears on the screen in Summary form.

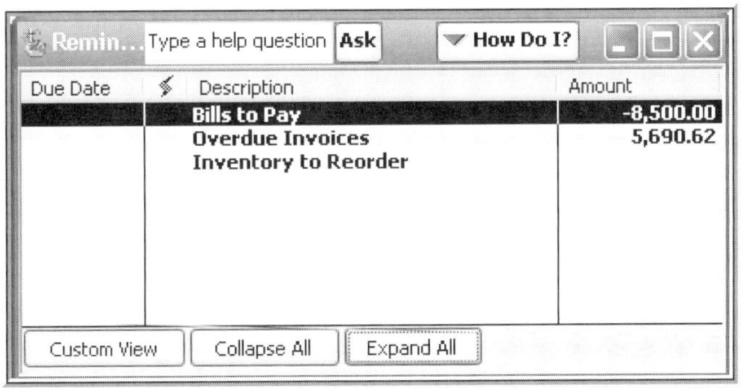

To view the list, click the **Expand All** button

- Note: Your Reminders List Summary (Collapsed) form and Reminders List Detail (Expanded) form may not match the ones displayed in the text. This is due to the fact that your computer date may be different from the date used in the chapter. Disregard any differences.
- The expanded view shows the bills that need to be paid as well as overdue invoices, inventory to reorder, any items that need to be printed, and alerts.

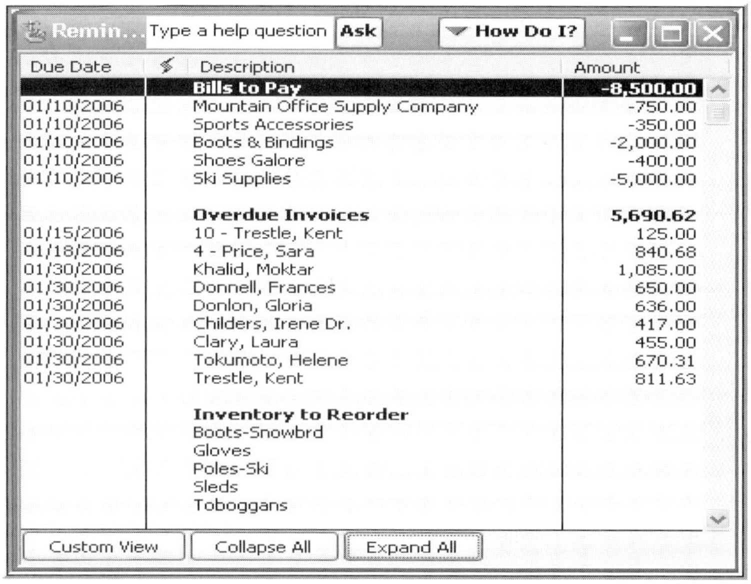

Close the Reminders List

PURCHASE ORDERS

Using the QuickBooks Pro Purchase Order feature helps you track your inventory. Information regarding the items on order or the items received may be obtained at any time. Once merchandise has been received, QuickBooks Pro marks the purchase order *Received in full*. The Purchase Order feature must be selected as a Preference when setting up the company, or it may be selected prior to processing your first purchase order. QuickBooks Pro will automatically set up an account called Purchase Orders in the Chart of Accounts. The account does not affect the balance sheet or the profit and loss statement of the company. As with other business forms, QuickBooks Pro allows you to customize your purchase orders to fit the needs of your individual company or to use the purchase order format that comes with the program.

VERIFY PURCHASE ORDERS ACTIVE AS A COMPANY PREFERENCE

Verify that the Purchase Order feature of QuickBooks Pro is active by checking the Company Preferences.

MEMO
DATE: January 16, 2006

Prior to completing the first purchase order, verify that Purchase Orders are active.

Verify that Purchase Orders are active by accessing the Company Preferences

Click **Edit** menu, click **Preferences**
Scroll through Preference List until you see **Purchases & Vendors**
Click **Purchases & Vendors**
Click the **Company Preferences** tab

- Make sure there is a check mark in the check box for **Inventory and purchase orders are active**.
- If not, click the check box to select.

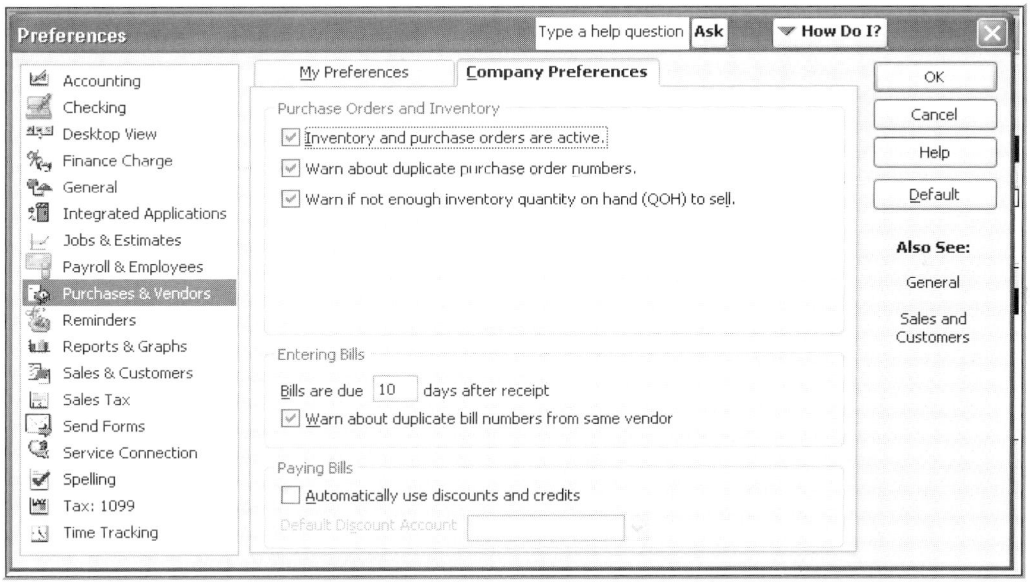

Click **OK** to accept and close

CUSTOMIZE PURCHASE ORDERS

As instructed in Chapter 5, business forms may be customized. Prior to recording your first purchase order, it should be customized.

Customize a Purchase Order

Click the **Purchase Orders** icon in the **Vendors** section of the Home Page
Click the **Customize** button next to **Template**
Click **Edit**
Click the **Layout Designer** button
Change the size for **Purchase Order** to begin at **5**
Expand the area for **Your Name Sports** to **4 ¾**
Click **OK** to close the Layout Designer
Click **OK** to close the Custom Purchase Order template
Do not close the Purchase Order

PREPARE PURCHASE ORDERS TO ORDER MERCHANDISE

Once the Purchase Order feature is selected, purchase orders may be prepared. Primarily, purchase orders are prepared to order merchandise; but they may also be used to order non-inventory items like supplies or services.

MEMO
DATE: January 16, 2006

With only 10 pairs of snowboard boots in stock in the middle of January, Tim and you decide to order an additional 25 pairs of boots in assorted sizes from Snow Boots & Gear for $75 per pair. Prepare Purchase Order No. 1.

Prepare Purchase Order No. 1 for 25 pairs of snowboard boots

Purchase Order 1 should be on the screen
- If not, click the **Purchases Order** icon on the Home Page

Click the drop-down list arrow for **Vendor**, click **Snow Boots & Gear**
Tab to or click **Date**, enter **01/16/2006**
- P.O. No. should be 1.
- If not, enter 1 as the P.O. No.

Tab to or click **Item**, click **Boots-Snowbrd**
Tab to or click **Qty**, enter **25**
- The cost of the item was entered when Boots-Snowbrd was created. The Rate should appear automatically as **75.00**

Tab to generate Amount
- Before printing, make sure that **To be printed** is selected and **To be e-mailed** is *not* selected

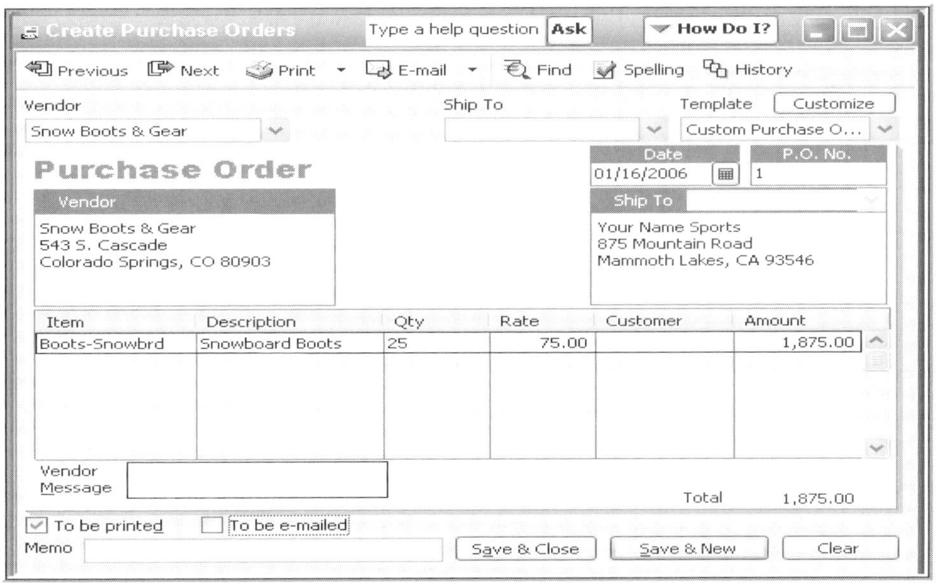

Click **Print** to print the **Purchase Order**

Check printer settings:

- Make sure the appropriate printer is selected.
- **Printer type** is Page-oriented (Single sheets).
- **Print on** Blank paper.
- Print lines around each field.

Click **Print**

After printing, click **Next** or **Save & New** to go to the next purchase order

PREPARE A PURCHASE ORDER FOR MORE THAN ONE ITEM

If more than one item is purchased from a vendor, all items purchased can be included on the same purchase order.

MEMO

DATE: January 16, 2006

Prepare a purchase order for 3 sleds @ $50 each, and 2 toboggans @ $110 each from a new vendor: Snowline Gear, 7105 Camino del Rio, Durango, CO 81302, Contact: Leo Jenkins, Phone: 303-555-7765, Fax: 303-555-5677, E-mail: Snowgear@ski.com, Terms: 2% 10 Net 30, Credit Limit: $2000.

Prepare a purchase order and add a new vendor

Click the drop-down list arrow for **Vendor**, click **< Add New >**
Enter **Snow Gear** for the **Vendor** name and the **Company** name
Click the second line of the address, enter **7105 Camino del Rio**
Click the third line of the address, enter **Durango, CO 81302**
Click Address Details

- Verify that **Show this window again when address is incomplete or unclear** has a check mark. This means that the **Edit Address Information** window will appear if the address is incomplete or unclear.

Click **OK**
Tab to or click **Contact**, enter **Leo Jenkins**
Tab to or click **Phone**, enter **303-555-7765**
Tab to or click **FAX**, enter **303-555-5677**
Tab to or click **E-mail**, enter **Snowgear@ski.com**
Click **Additional Info** tab, click the drop-down list arrow for **Terms**, click **2% 10 Net 30**
Tab to or click **Credit Limit**, enter **2000**
Click **OK** to add Vendor

- The **Date** should be **01/16/2006**. If it is not, delete the date shown and enter **01/16/06**.
- P.O. No. should be **2**. If it is not, enter **2**.

Tab to or click the first line in the column for **Item**
Click the drop-down list arrow for **Item**, click **Sleds**
Tab to or click **Qty**, enter **3**
Tab to or click **Rate**, enter **50**

- The purchase cost was not entered when the item was created, so it must be entered on the purchase order as the Rate.

Tab to generate the total for **Amount**

- If you get a message about the change an of item cost, click **No**

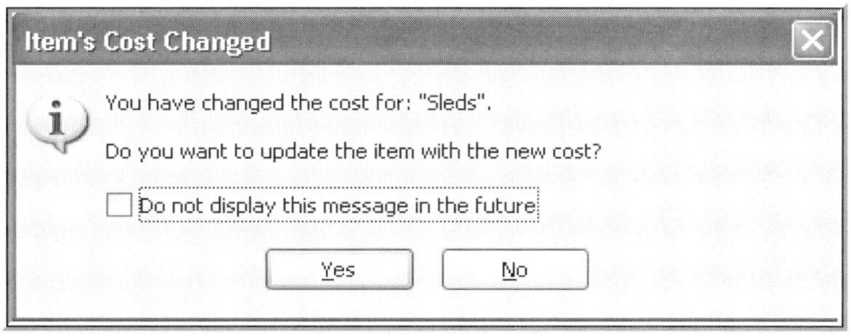

Repeat steps necessary to enter the information to order 2 toboggans at $110 each

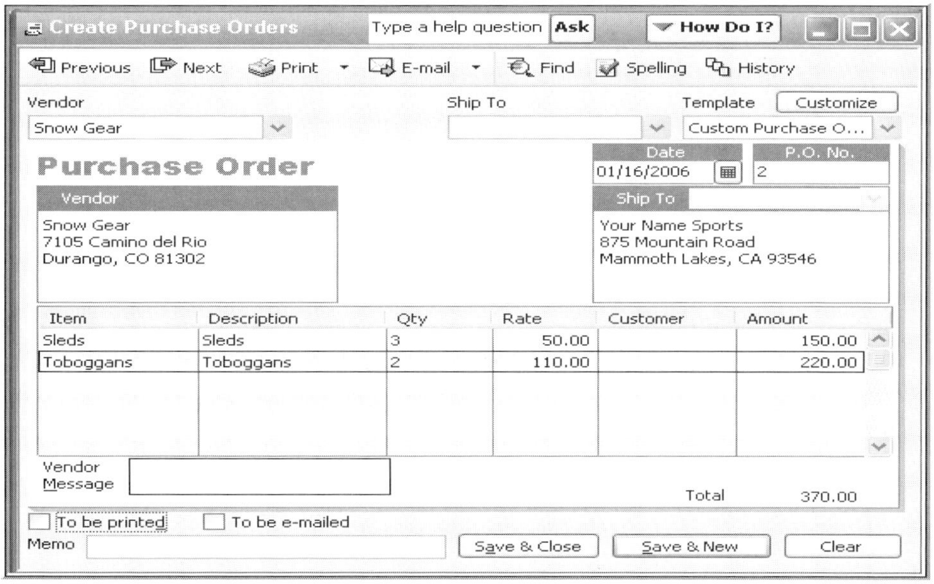

Print **Purchase Order No. 2**
Click **Next** to save **Purchase Order No. 2** and go to the next purchase order

ENTER PURCHASE ORDERS WITHOUT STEP-BY-STEP INSTRUCTIONS

MEMO
DATE: January 16, 2006

Prepare purchase orders for the following:
25 pairs of gloves @ 15.00 each from Winter Clothes, Inc.
12 sets of ski poles @ 30.00 each from Ski Supplies.

Prepare and print the purchase orders indicated above.

Compare your completed purchase orders with the ones below:

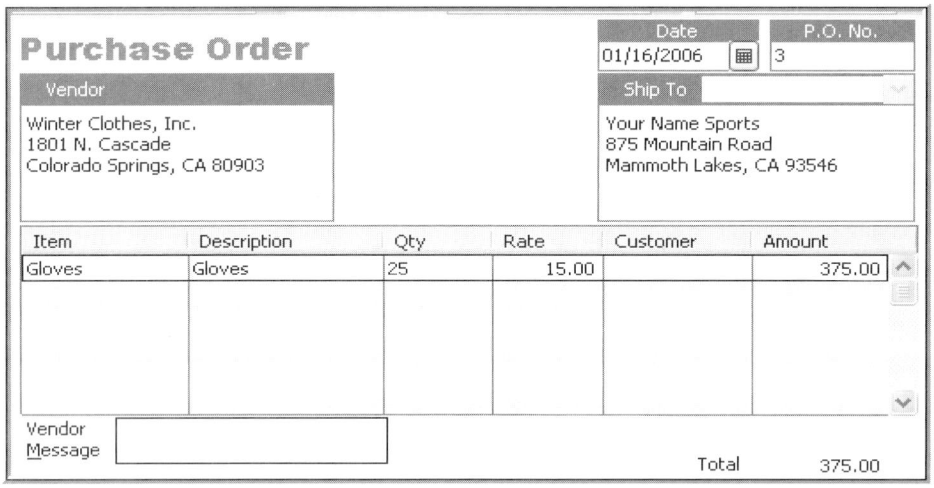

Purchase Order

Date: 01/16/2006 P.O. No.: 3

Vendor:
Winter Clothes, Inc.
1801 N. Cascade
Colorado Springs, CA 80903

Ship To:
Your Name Sports
875 Mountain Road
Mammoth Lakes, CA 93546

Item	Description	Qty	Rate	Customer	Amount
Gloves	Gloves	25	15.00		375.00

Vendor Message

Total 375.00

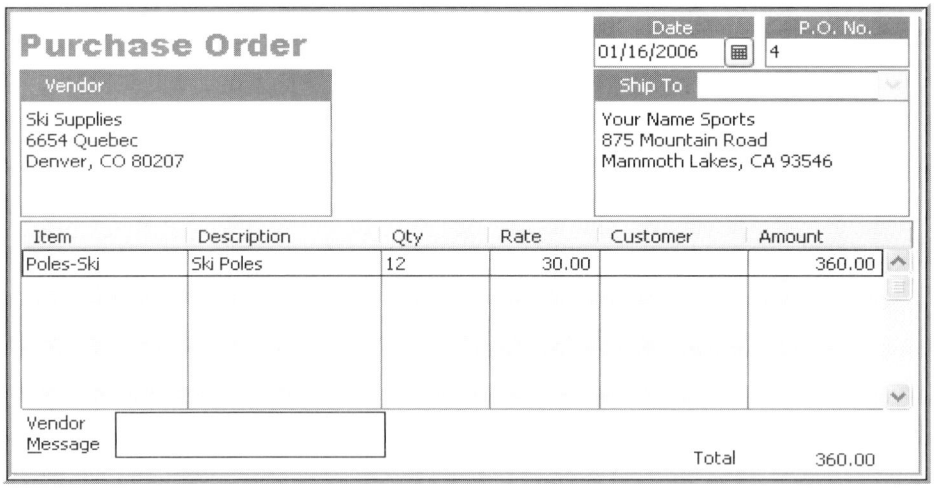

Purchase Order

Date: 01/16/2006 P.O. No.: 4

Vendor:
Ski Supplies
6654 Quebec
Denver, CO 80207

Ship To:
Your Name Sports
875 Mountain Road
Mammoth Lakes, CA 93546

Item	Description	Qty	Rate	Customer	Amount
Poles-Ski	Ski Poles	12	30.00		360.00

Vendor Message

Total 360.00

Save and Close the Purchase Orders

PREPARE AND PRINT A PURCHASE ORDERS QUICKREPORT

To see a list of purchase orders that have been prepared, open the Chart of Accounts, select Purchase Orders, click the Reports button, and choose QuickReport from the menu shown.

MEMO
DATE: January 16, 2006

You and Tim need to see which purchase orders are open. Prepare and print the Purchase Orders QuickReport.

View the open purchase orders for Your Name Sports

Click the **Chart of Accounts** icon on the Home Page
Scroll through the accounts until you see **Purchase Order Non-Posting**
Click the **Reports** button

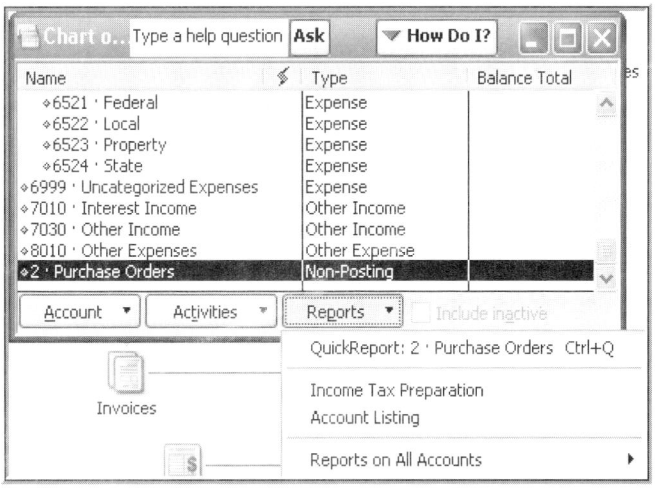

Click **QuickReport: 2 Purchase Orders**

- The list shows all open purchase orders, the date of the purchase order, the number of the purchase order, and the amount of the purchase order.

The dates are from **01/01/06** to **01/16/06**
Tab to generate the report
Resize the columns as previously instructed to:

Be able to view the account name in full in the **Split** column
Be able to print in Portrait orientation on one page without using Fit to one page wide
Click **Print** to print the report

Your Name Sports
Account QuickReport
As of January 16, 2006

Type	Date	Num	Name	Memo	Split	Amount
2 · Purchase Orders						
Purchase Order	01/16/2006	1	Snow Boots & Gear		1120 · Inventory Asset	-1,875.00
Purchase Order	01/16/2006	2	Snow Gear		-SPLIT-	-370.00
Purchase Order	01/16/2006	3	Winter Clothes, Inc.		1120 · Inventory Asset	-375.00
Purchase Order	01/16/2006	4	Ski Supplies		1120 · Inventory Asset	-360.00
Total 2 · Purchase Orders						-2,980.00
TOTAL						**-2,980.00**

Close the **Purchase Order QuickReport** and the **Chart of Accounts**

CHANGE MINIMUM REORDER LIMITS FOR AN ITEM

Any time that you determine your reorder limits are too low or too high, you can change the Reorder Point by editing the Item in the Item List.

MEMO
DATE: January 16, 2006

View the Item List to see the amount on hand for each item. In viewing the list, you and Tim determine that you should have a minimum of 35 sets of long underwear on hand at all times. Currently, there are 32 sets of long underwear in stock. Change the reorder point for long underwear to 35.

View the **Item List**

Click the **Items & Services** icon on the QuickBooks Home Page
Scroll through Item List, click **Underwear**
Click **Item** button at the bottom of the **Item List**, click **Edit Item**
Click in **Reorder Point**
Change 30 to **35**

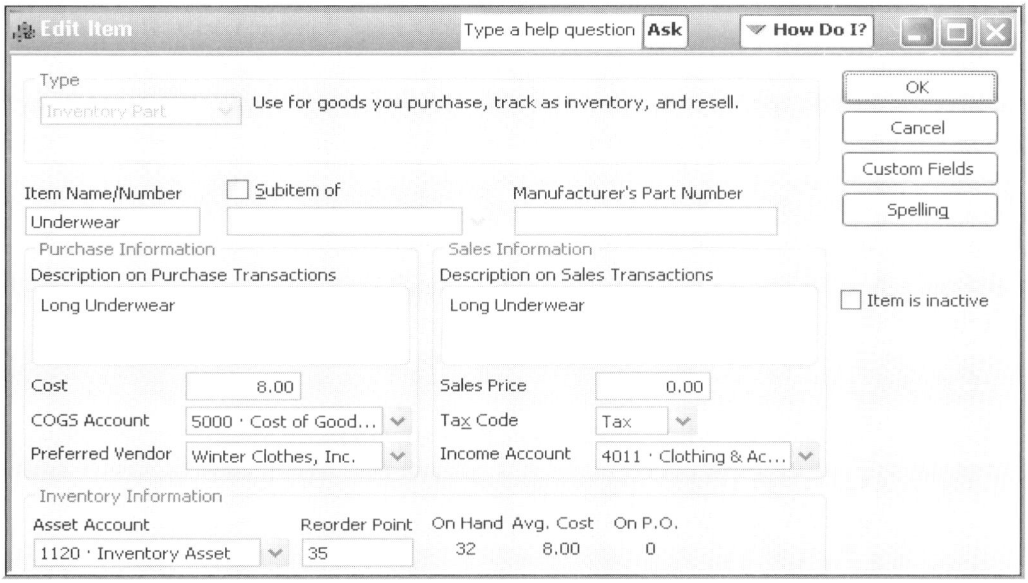

Click **OK** to save and exit
Close the **Item List**

VIEW EFFECT OF REORDER POINT ON REMINDERS LIST

Once the reorder point has been changed and the quantity on hand is equal to or falls below the new minimum, the item will be added to the Reminders List so you will be reminded to order it.

> **MEMO**
> **DATE:** January 16, 2006
>
> Look at the Reminders List to see what items need to be ordered.

Look at the **Reminders List**

Open **Reminders** as previously instructed
Expand the list

Close Reminders

VIEW INVENTORY STOCK STATUS BY ITEM REPORT

Several Inventory Reports are available for viewing and/or printing. One report is the Inventory Stock Status by Item report. This report provides information regarding the stock on hand, the stock on order, and the stock that needs to be reordered.

MEMO
DATE: January 16, 2006

More detailed information regarding the stock on hand, stock ordered, and stock needing to be ordered needs to be provided. View the report for Inventory Stock Status by Item.

View the **Inventory Stock Status by Item Report**

Click the **Reports** menu, point to **Inventory,** click **Inventory Stock Status by Item**
The dates are From **01/01/06** to **01/16/06**
Tab to generate the report

Your Name Sports
Inventory Stock Status by Item
January 1 - 16, 2006

	Item Description	Pref Vendor	Reorder Pt	On Hand	Order	On PO	Next Deliv	Sales/Week
Bindings-Snow	Snowboard Bindings	Boots & Bindings	5	48		0		0.9
Boots	After Ski Boots and Sh...	Shoes Galore	10	20		0		0
Boots-Ski	Ski Boots	Snow Boots & Gear	10	14		0		0.4
Boots-Snowbrd	Snowboard Boots	Snow Boots & Gear	10	10		25	01/16/2006	0.9
Gloves	Gloves	Winter Clothes, Inc.	20	20		25	01/16/2006	0.9
Hats	Hats and Scarves	Sports Accessories	20	29		0		0.4
Pants-Ski	Ski Pants	Winter Clothes, Inc.	10	93		0		0.9
Pants-Snowbrd	Snowboard Pants	Winter Clothes, Inc.	10	50		0		0
Parkas	Parkas and Jackets	Winter Clothes, Inc.	25	73		0		0.9
Poles-Ski	Ski Poles	Ski Supplies	15	13		12	01/16/2006	2.2
Skis	Snow Skis	Ski Supplies	15	43		0		3.1
Sleds	Sleds		5	4		3	01/16/2006	2.6
Snowboard	Snowboard	Ski Supplies	15	28		0		0.9
Socks	Ski and Snowboard So...	Snow Boots & Gear	25	72		0		1.3
Sweaters	Sweaters & Shirts	Winter Clothes, Inc.	25	73		0		0.9
Toboggans	Toboggans		5	5		2	01/16/2006	2.2
Underwear	Long Underwear	Winter Clothes, Inc.	35	32	✓	0		0.4

Scroll through the report

- Notice the items in stock.
- Notice the reorder point for items.
- Find the items marked as needing to be ordered.
- Notice the dates of the items that have been ordered.

Close the report without printing

RECEIVING ITEMS ORDERED

The form used to record the receipt of items in QuickBooks Pro depends on the way in which the ordered items are received. Items received may be recorded in three ways. If the items are received without a bill and you pay later, record the receipt on an item receipt. If the items are received at the same time as the bill, record the item receipt on a bill. If the items are received and paid for at the same time, record the receipt of items on a check or a credit card.

RECORD RECEIPT OF ITEMS NOT ACCOMPANIED BY A BILL

The ability to record inventory items prior to the arrival of the bill keeps quantities on hand, quantities on order, and the inventory up to date. Items ordered on a purchase order that arrive before the bill is received are recorded on an item receipt. When the bill arrives, it is recorded.

MEMO

DATE: January 18, 2006

The sleds and toboggans ordered from Snow Gear, arrive without a bill. Record the receipt of the 3 sleds and 2 toboggans.

Record the receipt of the items above

Click the **Receive Inventory** icon on the Home Page
Click **Receive Inventory without Bill**
Click the drop-down list arrow for **Vendor**, click **Snow Gear**

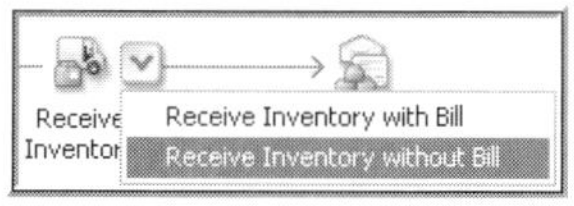

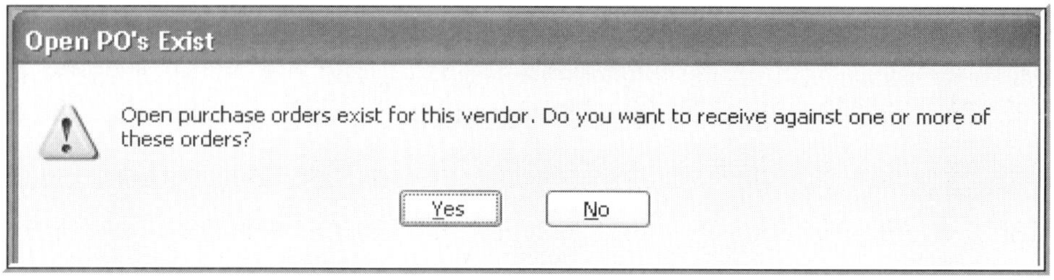

Click **Yes** on the **Open PO's Exist** message box

- An **Open Purchase Orders** dialog box appears showing all open purchase orders for the vendor, Snow Gear

Point to any part of the line for P.O. No. 2
Click to select **Purchase Order No. 2**

- This will place a check mark in the check mark column.

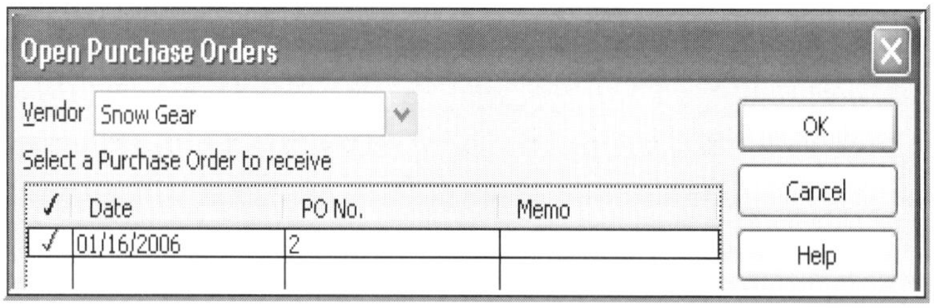

Click **OK**

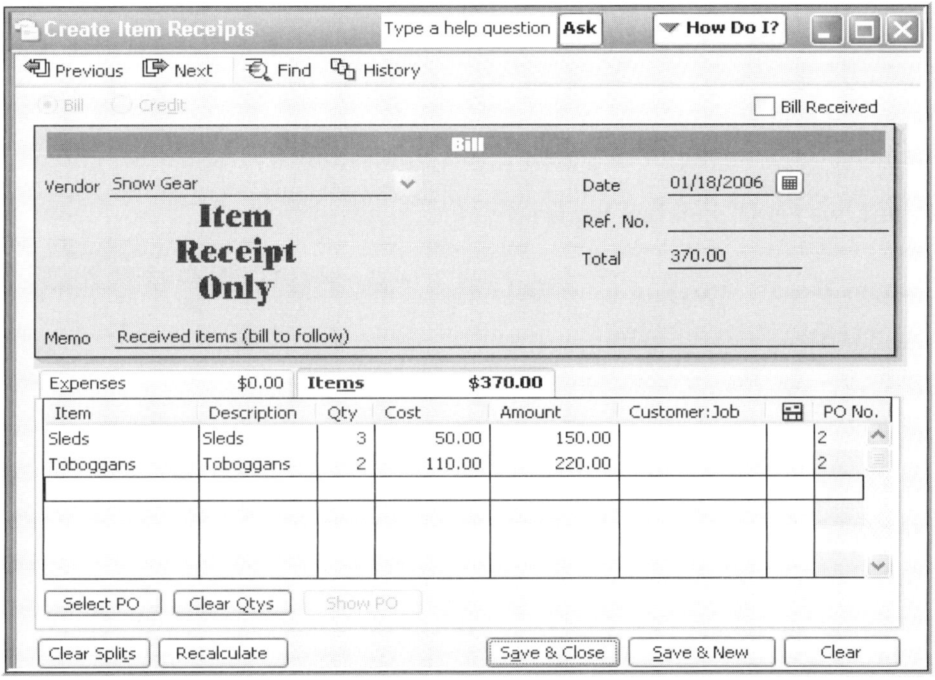

Change the date to **01/18/2006**.

- Notice the completed information for the **Items** tab indicating how many sleds and toboggans were received.
- Notice the **Memo** box beneath **Item Receipt Only**. It states *Received items (bill to follow).*

Click **Save & Close**

VERIFY THAT PURCHASE ORDER IS MARKED RECEIVED IN FULL

Once items have been marked as received, QuickBooks Pro stamps the Purchase Order *Received in Full* and marks each item received in full as *Clsd.*

MEMO
DATE: January 18, 2006

View the original Purchase Order No. 2 to verify that it has been stamped Received in Full and each item received is marked Clsd.

Verify that Purchase Order No. 2 is marked Received in Full and all items received are Closed

Access Purchase Orders as previously instructed
Click **Previous** until you get to **Purchase Order No. 2**

- The Purchase Order should be stamped **RECEIVED IN FULL.**
- Next to the **Amount** column, you will see two new columns: **Rcv'd** and **Clsd**. **Rcv'd** indicates the number of the items received. **Clsd** indicates that the number of items were received in full so the Purchase Order has been closed for that Item.

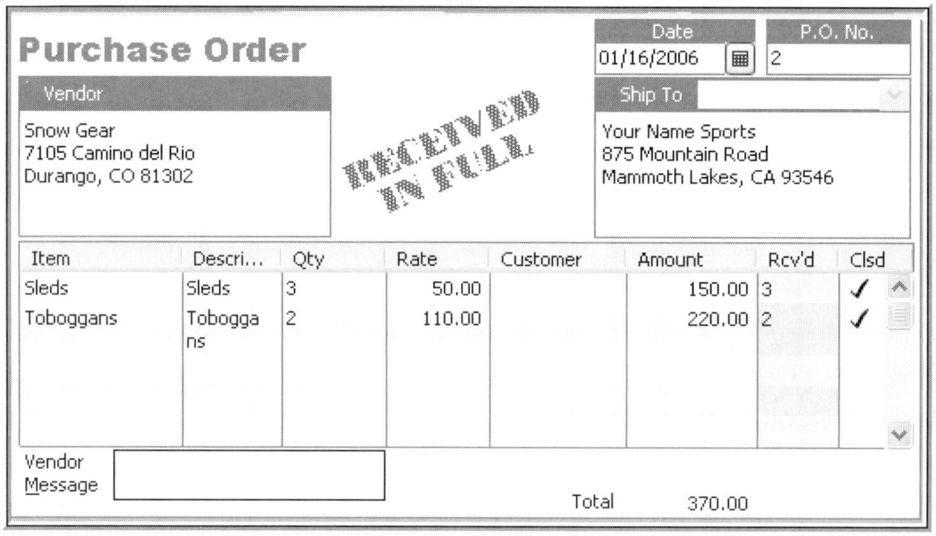
Purchase Order

Date: 01/16/2006 P.O. No.: 2

Vendor: Snow Gear, 7105 Camino del Rio, Durango, CO 81302

RECEIVED IN FULL

Ship To: Your Name Sports, 875 Mountain Road, Mammoth Lakes, CA 93546

Item	Descri...	Qty	Rate	Customer	Amount	Rcv'd	Clsd
Sleds	Sleds	3	50.00		150.00	3	✓
Toboggans	Toboggans	2	110.00		220.00	2	✓

Vendor Message

Total 370.00

Close **Create Purchase Orders** window

ENTER RECEIPT OF A BILL FOR ITEMS ALREADY RECEIVED

For items that have been received prior to the bill, the receipt of items is recorded as soon as the items arrive. When the bill is received, it must be recorded. To do this, indicate that the bill is for items received and mark the Receive Items List as bill received. When completing a bill for items already received, QuickBooks Pro fills in all essential information on the bill. A bill is divided into two sections: a vendor-related section (the upper part of the bill that looks similar to a check and has a memo text box under it) and a detail section (the area that has two tabs marked Items and Expenses). The vendor-related section of the bill is where information for the actual bill is entered, including a memo with information about the transaction. The detail section is where the information regarding the items ordered, the quantity ordered and received, and the amounts due for the items received is indicated.

MEMO
DATE: January 19, 2006

Record the bill for the sleds and toboggans already received from Snow Gear, Vendor's Invoice No. 97 dated 01/18/2006, Terms 2% 10 Net 30.

Record the above bill for items already received

Click the **Enter Bills Against Inventory** icon on the Home Page
On the **Select Item Receipt**, click the drop-down list arrow for **Vendor**, click **Snow Gear**
- Snow Gear is entered as the vendor.

Click anywhere on the line **01/18/2006 Received items (bill to follow)** to select the Item Receipt

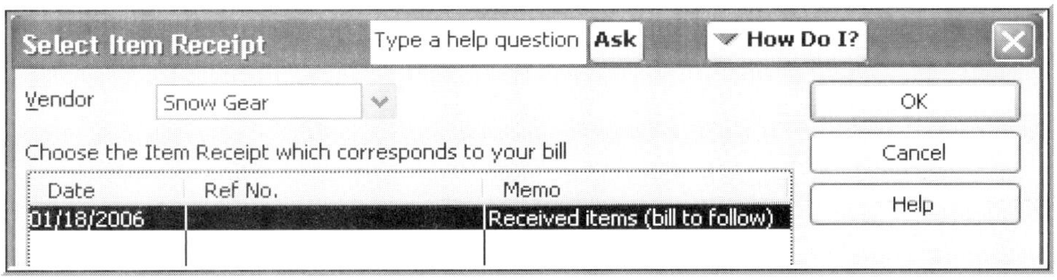

- The line for the item receipt will be highlighted.

Click **OK**
- QuickBooks Pro displays the **Enter Bills** screen and the completed bill for Snow Gear
- The date shown is the date the items were received **01/18/2006**.

Tab to or click **Ref No.**, type the vendor's invoice number **97**
- Notice that the **Amount Due** of **370** has been inserted.
- Terms of **2% 10 Net 30** and the Discount Date and the Due Date are shown.

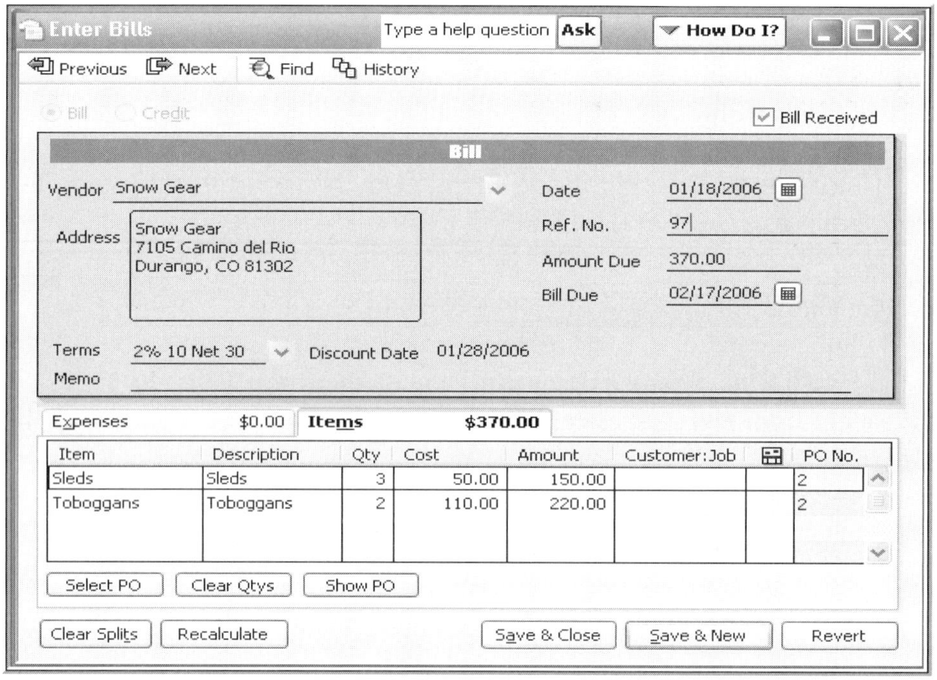

Click **Save & Close**

- If you get a Recording Transaction message box regarding the fact that the transaction has been changed, click **Yes**.

RECORD RECEIPT OF ITEMS AND A BILL

When ordered items are received and accompanied by a bill, the receipt of the items is recorded while entering the bill.

MEMO

DATE: January 19, 2006

Received 25 pairs of snowboard boots and a bill from Snow Boots & Gear. Record the bill dated 01/18/2006 and the receipt of the items.

Record the receipt of the items and the bill

Click **Receive Inventory** icon on the QuickBooks Home Page
Click **Receive Inventory with Bill**
Click the drop-down list for **Vendor**, click **Snow Boots & Gear**
Click **Yes** on the **Open PO's Exist** message box

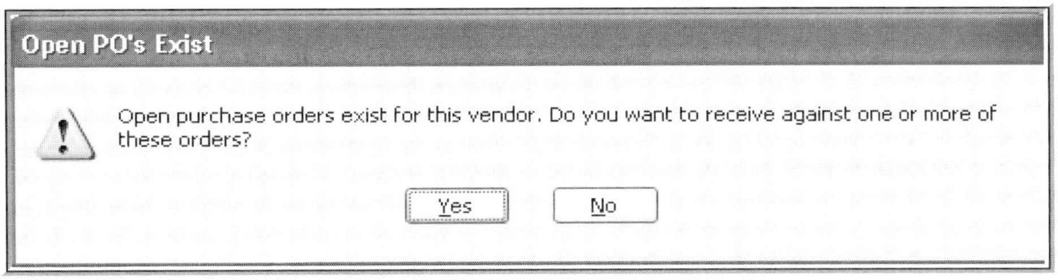

Click anywhere in P.O. No. 1 line to select and insert a check mark in the √column

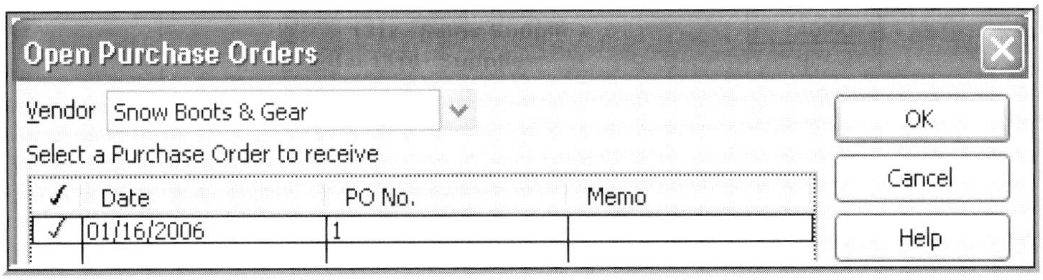

Click **OK**

- The bill appears on the screen and is complete.
- Because no invoice number was given in the transaction, leave the **Ref. No.** blank.

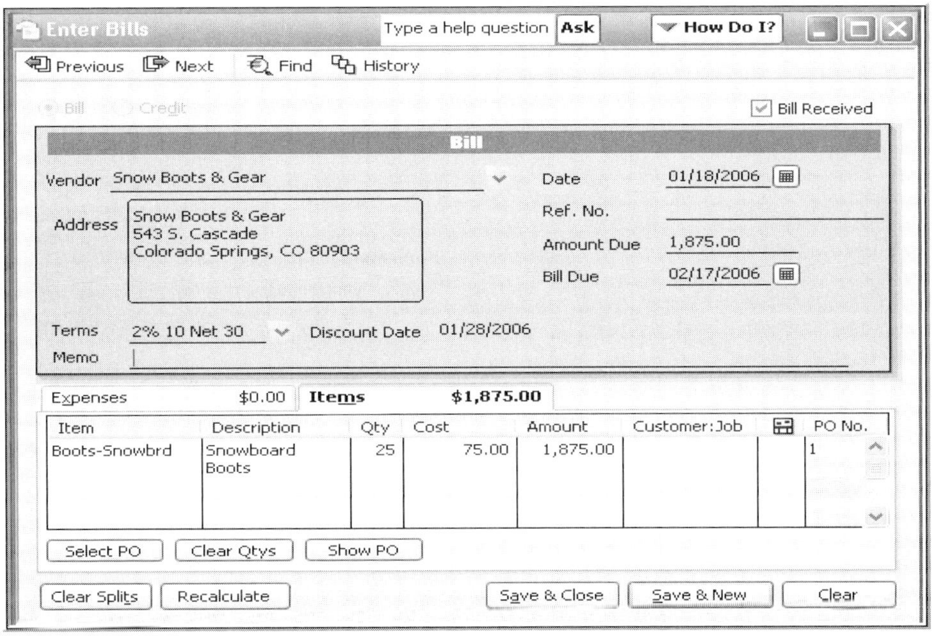

Click **Save & Close**

EDIT A PURCHASE ORDER

As with any other form, purchase orders may be edited once they have been prepared. Purchase orders may be accessed by clicking on the Purchase Order icon on the QuickBooks Home Page.

> **MEMO**
> **DATE:** January 19, 2006
>
> Rose realized that Purchase Order No. 4 should be for 15 pairs of ski poles. Change the purchase order and reprint.

Change Purchase Order No. 4

Access Purchase Order No. 4 as previously instructed
Click in **Qty**, change the number from 12 to **15**
Tab to recalculate the amount due for the purchase order

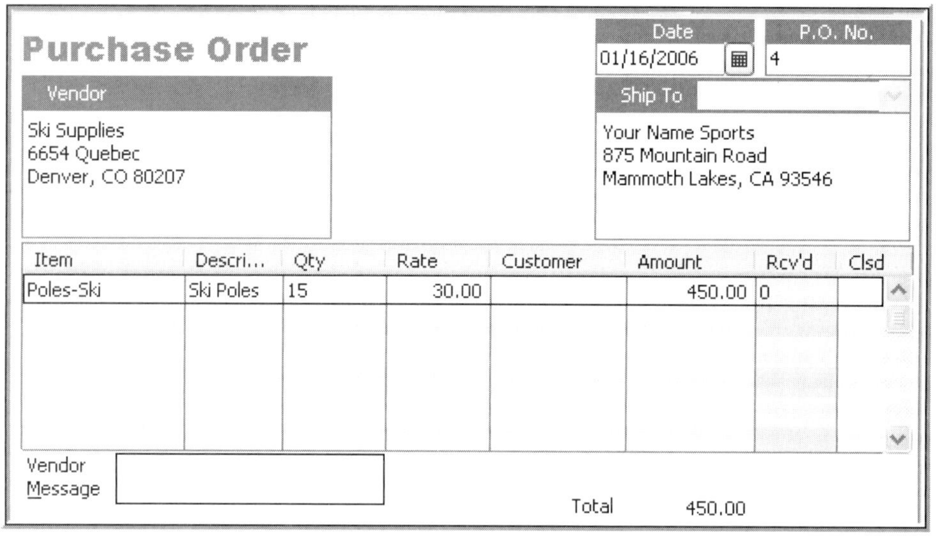

Purchase Order

Date: 01/16/2006 | P.O. No.: 4

Vendor:
Ski Supplies
6654 Quebec
Denver, CO 80207

Ship To:
Your Name Sports
875 Mountain Road
Mammoth Lakes, CA 93546

Item	Descri...	Qty	Rate	Customer	Amount	Rcv'd	Clsd
Poles-Ski	Ski Poles	15	30.00		450.00	0	

Vendor Message

Total 450.00

- Notice the columns for Rcv'd and Clsd. Those are included on the Purchase Order once it is saved.

Print the **Purchase Order** as previously instructed
Click **Save & Close** to record the changes and exit
Click **Yes** on the **Recording Transaction** dialog box to save the changes

RECORD A PARTIAL RECEIPT OF MERCHANDISE ORDERED

Sometimes when items on order are received, they are not received in full. The remaining items may be delivered as back-ordered items. This will usually occur if an item is out of stock, and you must wait for delivery until more items are manufactured and/or received by the vendor. With QuickBooks Pro you record the number of items you actually receive, and the bill is recorded for that amount.

> **MEMO**
> **DATE:** January 19, 2006
>
> Record the bill and the receipt of 20 pairs of gloves ordered on Purchase Order No. 3. On the purchase order, 25 pairs of gloves were ordered. Winter Clothes, Inc. will no longer be carrying these gloves, so the remaining 5 pairs of gloves on order will not be shipped. Manually close the purchase order. The date of the bill is 01/18/2006.

➤ Record the receipt of and the bill for 20 pairs of gloves from Winter Clothes, Inc.

Access **Receive Inventory with a Bill** as previously instructed
If necessary, change the **Date** of the bill to **01/18/2006**
Click the drop-down list arrow for **Vendor**, click **Winter Clothes, Inc.**
Click **Yes** on **Open PO's Exist** dialog box
Click anywhere in the line for **P.O. 3** on **Open Purchase Orders** dialog box
Click **OK**
Click the **Qty** column on the Items tab at the bottom of the Enter Bills window
Change the quantity to **20**
Tab to change **Amount** to **300**

- Notice the **Amount Due** on the bill also changes.

Click **Save & Close** to record the items received and the bill

CLOSE PURCHASE ORDER MANUALLY

If you have issued a purchase order and it is determined that you will not be receiving the items on order, a purchase order can be closed manually.

➤ Close Purchase Order No. 3 using **Find** to locate Purchase Order No. 3

Click **Find** on the Edit menu, then, if necessary, click the **Advanced Find** tab
Scroll through **Choose Filter**

- Filter helps to narrow the search for locating something.

Click **Transaction Type**, click the drop-down list arrow for **Transaction Type**, click **Purchase Order**
Click **Find**

- A list of all purchase orders shows on the screen.

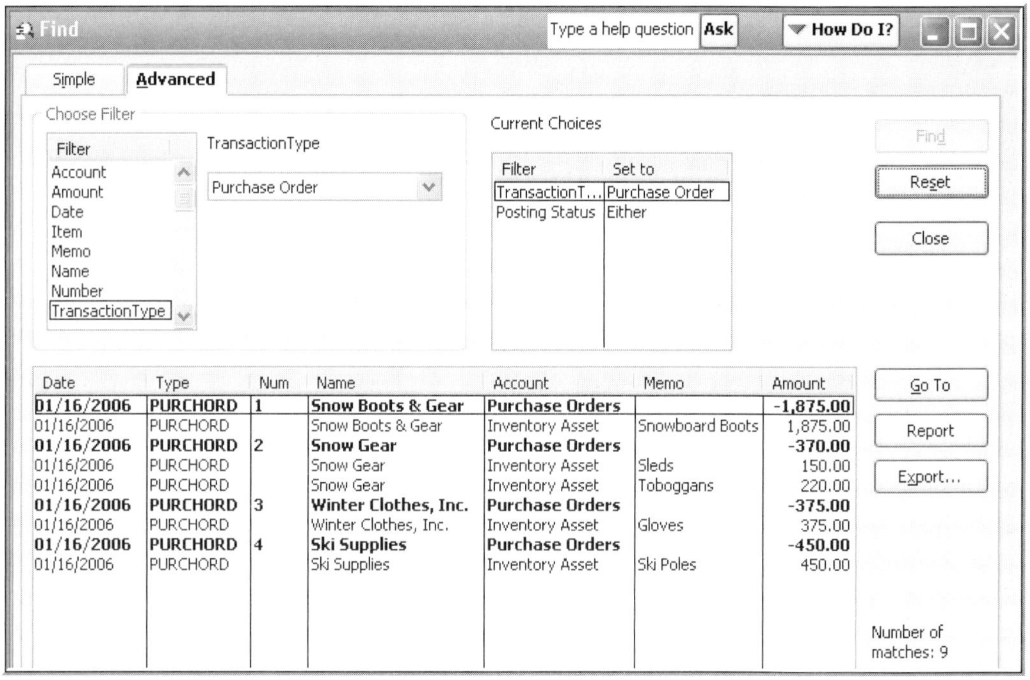

Click **Purchase Order No. 3** for **Winter Clothes, Inc.**
Click **Go To**
Click the **Clsd** column to mark and close the purchase order

- Notice that the ordered **Qty** is 25 and **Rcv'd** is 20.

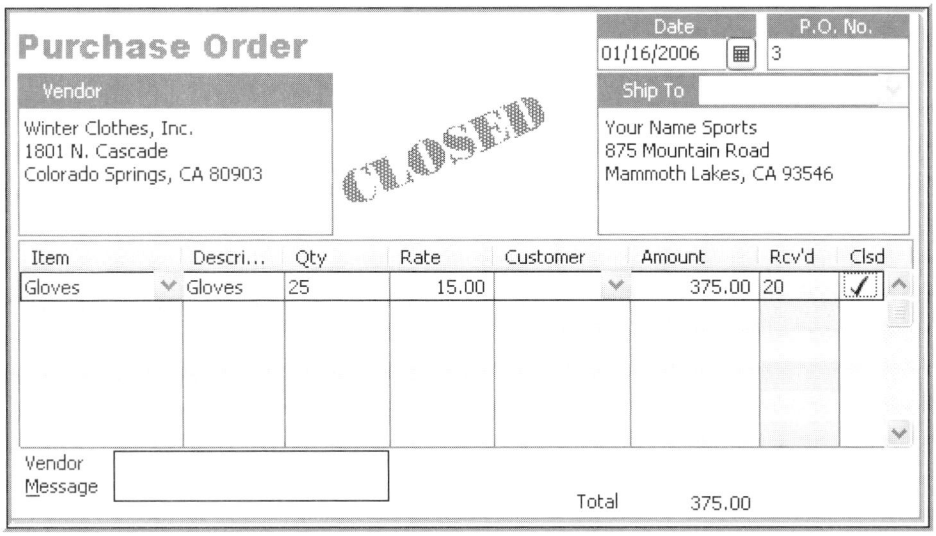

Purchase Order

Date: 01/16/2006
P.O. No.: 3

Vendor:
Winter Clothes, Inc.
1801 N. Cascade
Colorado Springs, CA 80903

CLOSED

Ship To:
Your Name Sports
875 Mountain Road
Mammoth Lakes, CA 93546

Item	Descri...	Qty	Rate	Customer	Amount	Rcv'd	Clsd
Gloves	Gloves	25	15.00		375.00	20	✓

Vendor Message

Total 375.00

Click **Save & Close** to close the purchase order
Close **Find**

ENTER A CREDIT FROM A VENDOR

Credit memos are prepared to record a reduction to a transaction. With QuickBooks Pro you use the Enter Bills window to record credit memos received from vendors acknowledging a return of or an allowance for a previously recorded bill and/or payment. The amount of a credit memo can be applied to the amount owed to a vendor when paying bills.

MEMO
DATE: January 21, 2006

Upon further inspection of merchandise received, Rose Spencer found that one of the sleds received from Snow Gear, was cracked. The sled was returned. Received Credit Memo No. 9912 from Snow Gear, for $50, the full amount on the return of 1 sled.

Check the **Item List** to verify how many sleds are currently on hand

Access **Item List** as previously instructed

- Look at Sleds to verify that there are 7 sleds in stock.

Close the **Item List**

Record the return of one sled

Access the **Enter Bills** window and record the credit memo shown above
On the **Enter Bills** screen, click **Credit** to select

- The word *Bill* changes to *Credit.*

Click the drop-down list arrow next to **Vendor**, click **Snow Gear**
Tab to or click the **Date**, type **01/21/06**
Tab to or click **Ref. No.**, type **9912**
Tab to or click **Credit Amount**, type **50**
Tab to **Memo**, enter **Returned 1 Sled**
Tab to or click the **Items** tab
Tab to or click the first line in the **Item** column, click the drop-down list arrow, click **Sleds**
Tab to or click **Qty**, enter **1**
Tab to or click **Cost**, enter **50**
Tab to enter the **50** for **Amount**
Click **No** on the Item Cost Changed message

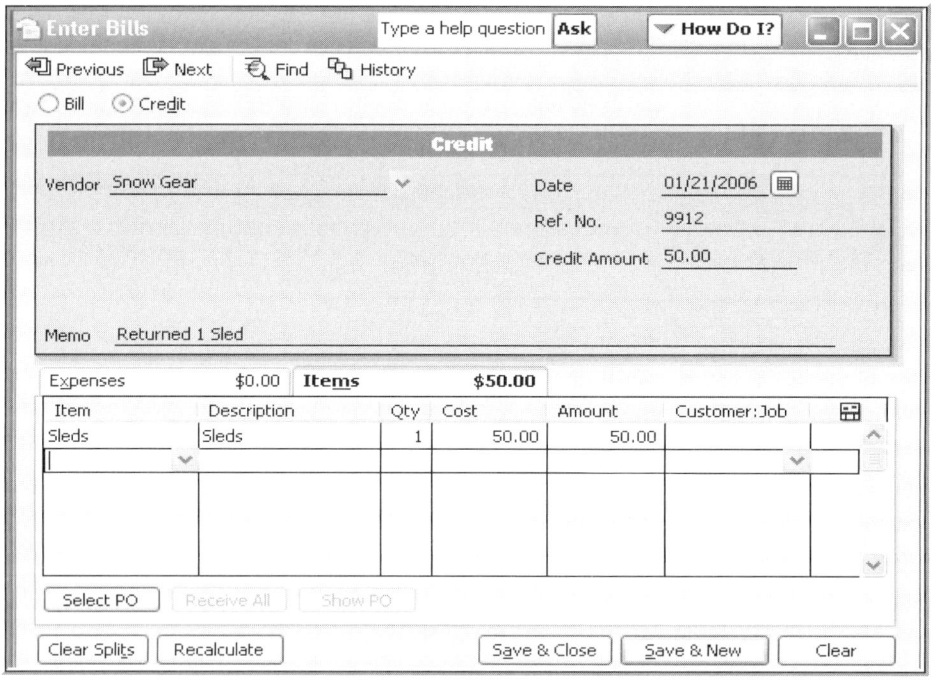

Click **Save & Close** to record the credit and exit the **Enter Bills** window

- QuickBooks Pro decreases the quantity of sleds on hand and creates a credit with the vendor that can be applied when paying the bill. The Credit Memo also appears in the Accounts Payable account in the **Paid** column, which decreases the amount owed and shows the transaction type as BILLCRED in the Accounts Payable register.

Verify that there are 6 sleds in stock after the return.

Access the **Item List**
Close the list

View the return in the Accounts Payable register

Access the **Chart of Accounts** as previously instructed, click **Accounts Payable**
Click the **Activities** button, click **Use Register**
Scroll through the register until you see the BILLCRED for Snow Gear

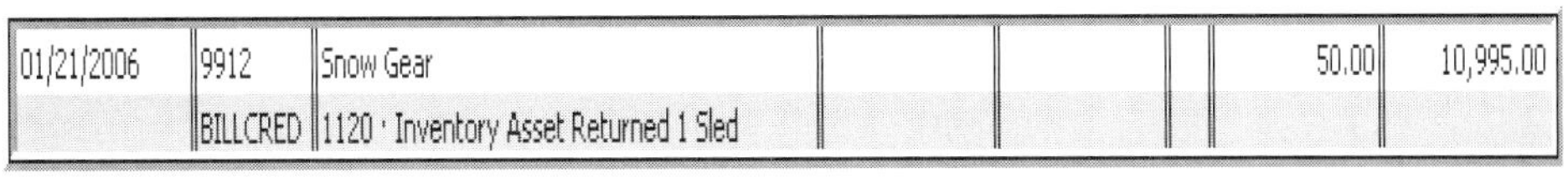

Close the **Accounts Payable Register**
Close the **Chart of Accounts**

MAKE A PURCHASE USING A CREDIT CARD

Some businesses use credit cards as an integral part of their finances. Many companies have a credit card used primarily for gasoline purchases for company vehicles. Other companies use credit cards as a means of paying for expenses or purchasing merchandise or other necessary items for use in the business.

> **MEMO**
> **DATE:** January 21, 2006
>
> Rose discovered that she was out of paper. She purchased a box of paper to have on hand to be used for copies, for the laser printer, and for the fax machine from Mountain Office Supply Company for $21.98. Rather than add to the existing balance owed to the company, Rose pays for the office supplies using the company's Visa card.

Purchase the above office supplies using the company's Visa card

Click the **Banking** menu, click **Enter Credit Card Charges**
Credit Card should indicate **2100 Visa**
Click the drop-down list arrow for **Purchased From**, click **Mountain Office Supply Company**

Click **OK** on the **Warning** screen

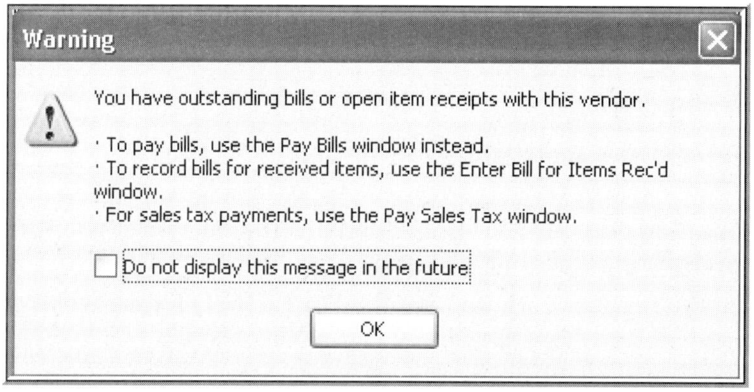

Date should be **01/21/2006**
Ref No. is blank
Tab to or click **AMOUNT**, enter **21.98**
Tab to or click **Memo**, enter **Purchase Paper**
Tab to or click the **Account** column on the **Expenses** tab, click the drop-down list arrow for **Account**, click **1311 Office Supplies**

- This transaction if for supplies to have on hand, so the asset Office Supplies is used.

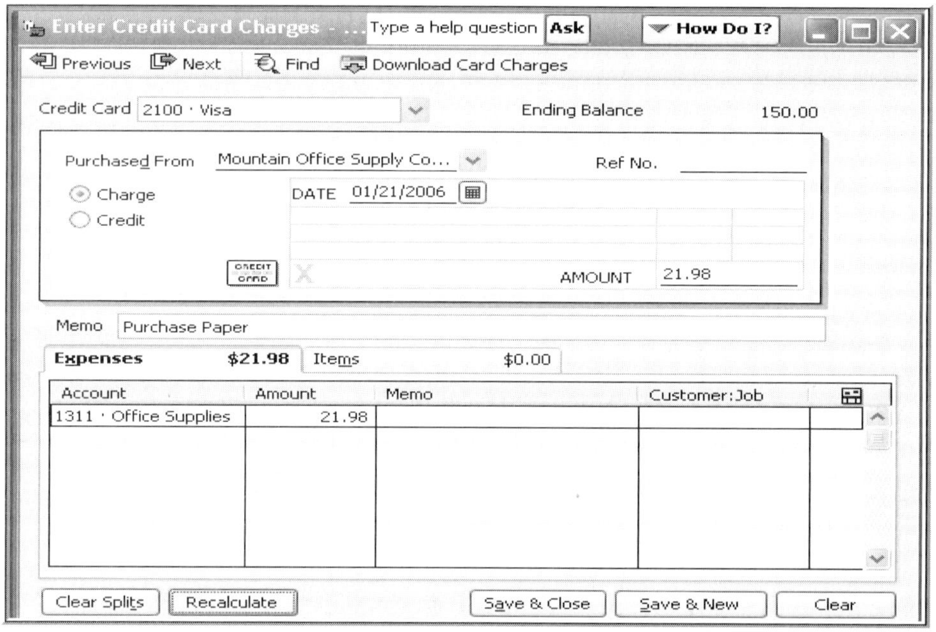

Click **Next** to record the charge and go to the next credit card entry

PAY FOR INVENTORY ITEMS ON ORDER USING A CREDIT CARD

It is possible to pay for inventory items using a credit card. The payment may be made using the Pay Bills window, or it may be made by recording an entry for Credit Card Charges. If you are purchasing something that is on order, you may record the receipt of merchandise on order first, or you may record the receipt of merchandise and the credit card payment at the same time.

MEMO
DATE: January 21, 2006

Note from You: Rose, record the receipt of 10 ski poles from Ski Supplies. Pay for the ski poles using the company's Visa.

Pay for the ski poles received using the Visa

Click the drop-down list for **Purchased From** click **Ski Supplies**
Click the **Yes** button on the **Open PO's Exist** message box

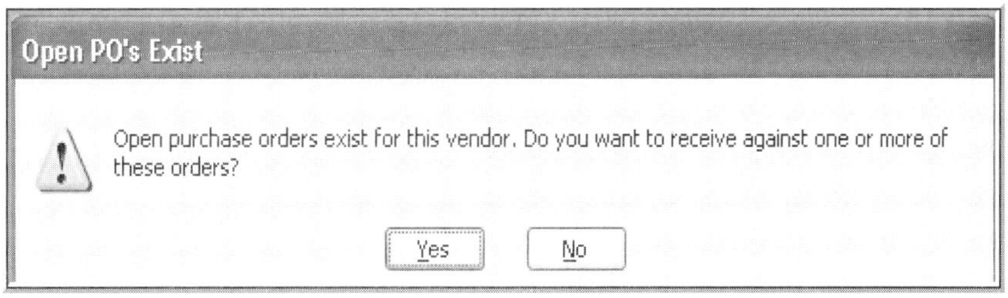

To select P.O. No. 4, click the line containing information regarding P.O. No. 4 on the **Open Purchase Orders** dialog box

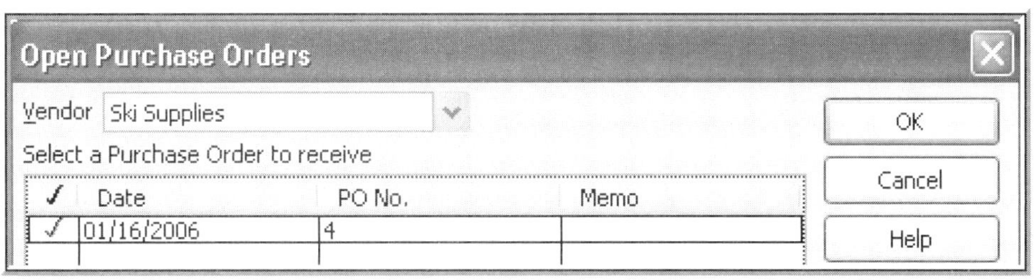

Click **OK**

- If you get a warning screen regarding outstanding bills, click **OK.**

Click the **Clear Qtys** button on the bottom of the screen to clear 15 from the Qty column
Tab to or click **Qty**, enter **10**

Tab to change the Amount to 300

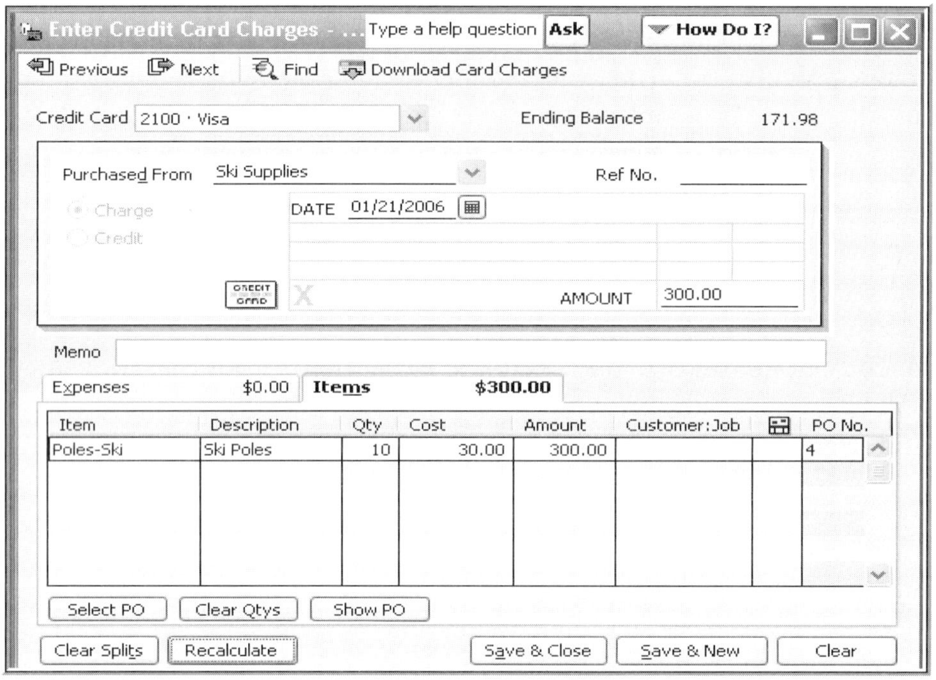

Click **Save & Close** to record and close the transaction

CONFIRM THE RECORDING OF THE SKI POLES RECEIVED ON PURCHASE ORDER NO. 4

MEMO
DATE: January 21, 2006

View Purchase Order No. 4 to determine whether or not the amount of ski poles received was recorded.

Access Purchase Order No. 4 as previously instructed

- The **Rcv'd** column should show **10**.
- Notice that the **Qty** column shows **15** and **Clsd** is not marked. This indicates that 5 sets of ski poles are still on order.

Close Purchase Order No. 4

ENTER BILLS

Whether the bill is to pay for expenses incurred in the operation of a business or to pay for merchandise to sell in the business, QuickBooks Pro provides accounts payable tracking for all vendors to which the company owes money. Entering bills as soon as they are received is an efficient way to record your liabilities. Once bills have been entered, QuickBooks Pro will be able to provide up-to-date cash flow reports, and QuickBooks Pro will remind you when it's time to pay your bills. As previously stated, a bill is divided into two sections: a vendor-related section (the upper part of the bill that looks similar to a check and has a memo text box under it) and a detail section (the area that is divided into columns for Account, Amount, and Memo). The vendor- related section of the bill is where information for the actual bill is entered, including a memo with information about the transaction. If the bill is for paying an expense, the Expenses tab is used for the detail section. Using this tab allows you to indicate the expense accounts for the transaction, to enter the amounts for the various expense accounts, and to provide transaction explanations. If the bill is for merchandise, the Items tab will be used to record the receipt of the items ordered.

MEMO

DATE: January 23, 2006

Took out an ad in the *Mammoth Lakes News* announcing our February sale. Received a bill for $95.00 from *Mammoth Lakes News*, Terms Net 30, Invoice No. 381-22. The newspaper is a new vendor. The address is 1450 Main Street, Mammoth Lakes, CA 93546, Contact: Fran Falco, Phone: 909-555-2525, Fax: 909-555-5252, E-mail: mammothlakesnews@ski.com.

Record the receipt of the bill from *Mammoth Lakes News* and add the newspaper as a new vendor

Click the **Enter Bills** icon on the Home Page
Complete the **Vendor-Related Section** of the bill:
Click the drop-down list arrow next to **Vendor**, click **<Add New>**
Enter the **Vendor** name as **Mammoth Lakes News**
Tab to or click **Company Name**, enter **Mammoth Lakes News**
Tab to or click the second line in the **Address**, enter **1450 Main Street**, press **Enter**
Key in **Mammoth Lakes, CA 93546**
Tab to or click **Contact**, key in **Fran Falco**
Tab to or click **Phone**, enter **909-555-2525**
Tab to or click **FAX**, enter **909-555-5252**

Tab to or click **E-mail**, enter **mammothlakesnews@ski.com**

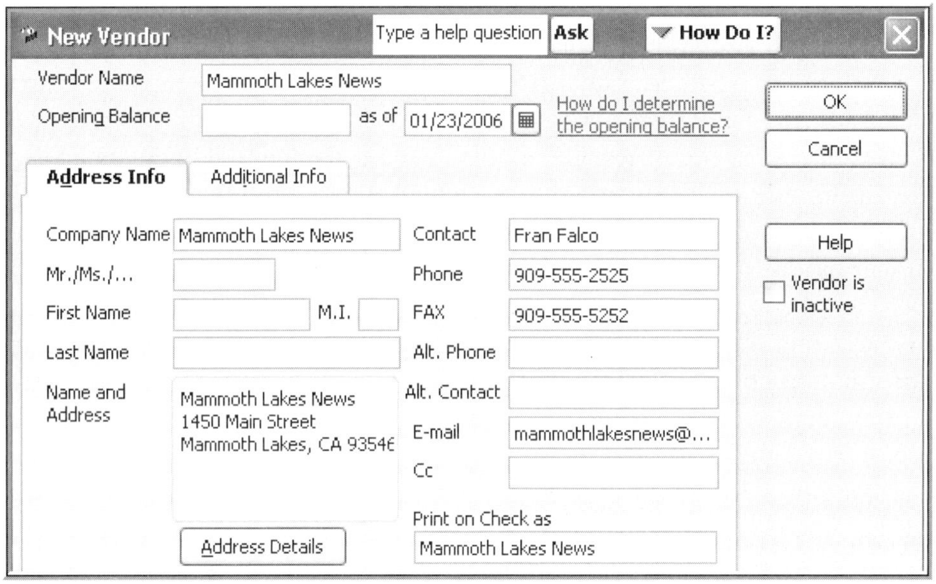

Click **OK** to exit and add the name to the Vendor List

- Mammoth Lakes News is entered as the vendor on the bill.

Tab to **Date**, type **01/23/06** as the date
Tab to **Ref No.**, type the vendor's invoice number **381-22**
Tab to **Amount Due**, type **95**
Tab to **Terms**, click the drop-down list arrow next to **Terms**, click **Net 30**

- QuickBooks Pro automatically changes the Bill Due date to show 30 days from the transaction date.
- At this time no change will be made to the Bill Due date, and nothing will be inserted as a memo.

Complete the **Detail Section** of the bill:

- If necessary, click the **Expenses** tab so it is the area of the detail section in use.

Tab to or click in the column for **Account**, click the drop-down list arrow next to **Account**, scroll through the list to find **Advertising Expense**
Because the account does not appear, click **<Add New>**

- **Type** of account should show **Expense**. If not, click drop-down list arrow and click **Expense**.

Enter **6140** as the account number in **Number**
Tab to or click **Name**, enter **Advertising Expense**

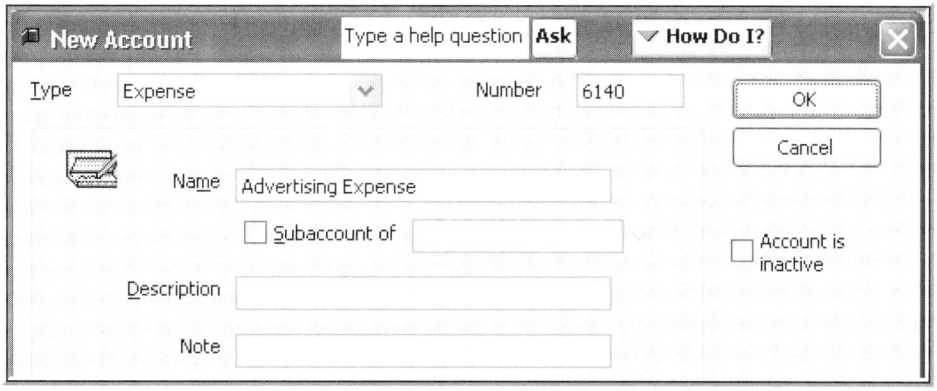

Click **OK**

6140 Advertising Expense shows as the Account

- Based on the accrual method of accounting, **Advertising Expense** is selected as the account for this transaction because this expense should be matched against the revenue of the period.
    - The Amount column already shows **95.00**—no entry required
- Tab to or click the first line in the column for **Memo**

Enter the transaction explanation of **Ad for February Sale**

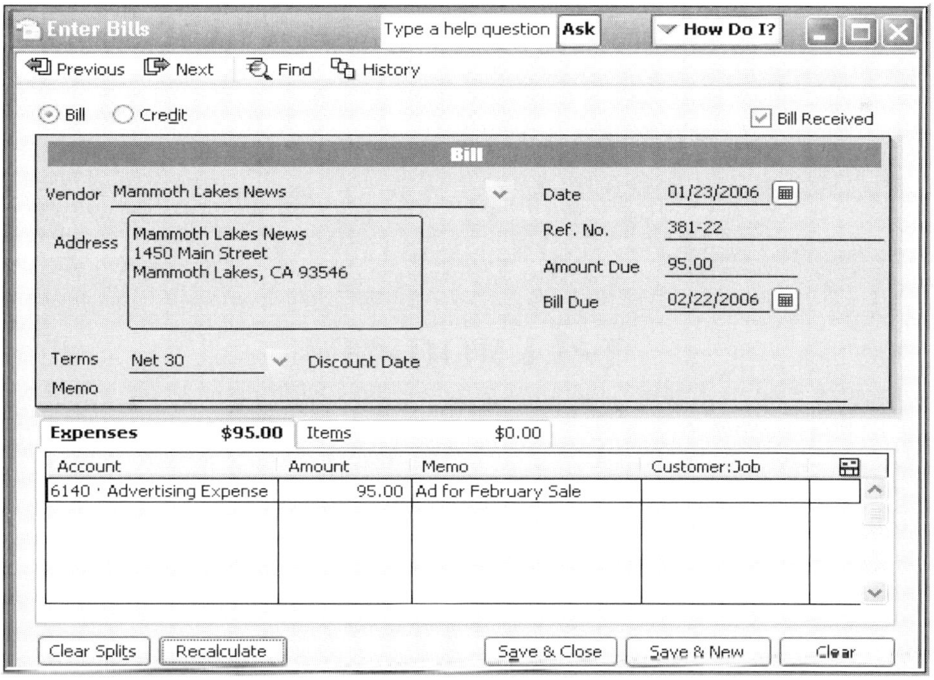

Click **Save & Close**

- If you get a dialog box for **Name Information Changed**, click **No**.

CHANGE EXISTING VENDORS' TERMS

Once a vendor has been established, changes can be made to the vendor's account information. The changes will take effect immediately and will be reflected in any transactions recorded for the vendor.

MEMO
DATE: January 23, 2006

Rose Spencer realizes that no terms were recorded for Mountain Power Company, Mountain Telephone Company, and Mountain Water Company when vendor accounts were established. Change the terms for the three companies to Net 30.

Change the terms for all of the vendors listed above

Access the **Vendor List** in the Vendor Center as previously instructed
Double-click on **Mountain Power Co.**
Click **Additional Info** tab
Click the drop-down list arrow for terms, click **Net 30**
Click **OK**
Repeat for the other vendors indicated in the memo above
Close the **Vendor Center** when all changes have been made

PREPARE BILLS WITHOUT STEP-BY-STEP INSTRUCTIONS

It is more efficient to record bills in a group or batch than it is to record them one at a time. If an error is made while preparing the bill, correct it. Your Name Sports uses the accrual basis of accounting. In the accrual method of accounting the expenses of a period are matched against the revenue of the period. Unless otherwise instructed, use the accrual basis of accounting when recording entries.

MEMO
DATE: January 25, 2006

Record the following bills:
Mountain Power Company electrical power for January, $359.00, Invoice No. 3510-1023, Net 30.
Mountain Telephone Company telephone service for January, $156.40, Invoice No. 7815-21, Net 30.
Mountain Water Company water for January, $35.00, Invoice No. 3105, Net 30.

Enter the three transactions in the memo above.

- Refer to the instructions given for previous transactions.
- Remember, when recording bills, you will need to determine the accounts used in the transaction. To determine the appropriate accounts to use, refer to the Chart of Accounts as you record the transactions.
- Enter information for Memos where transaction explanation is needed for clarification.
- To go from one bill to the next, click **Next** button at the top of the bill or the **Save & New** button at the bottom of the bill.
- After entering the last bill, click **Save & Close** to record and exit the **Enter Bills** screen.

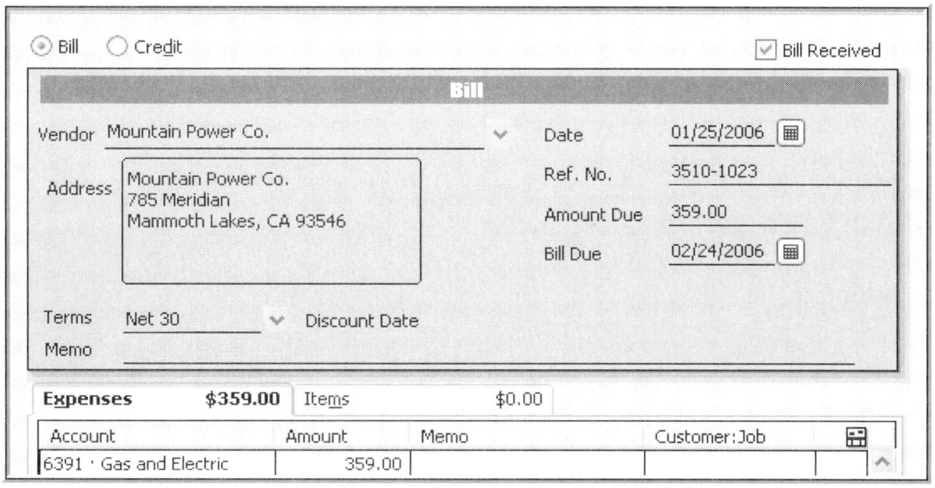

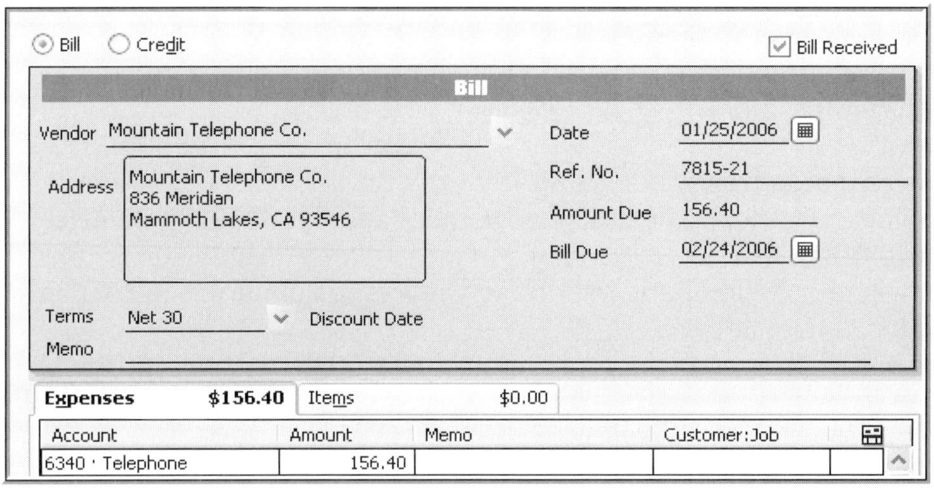

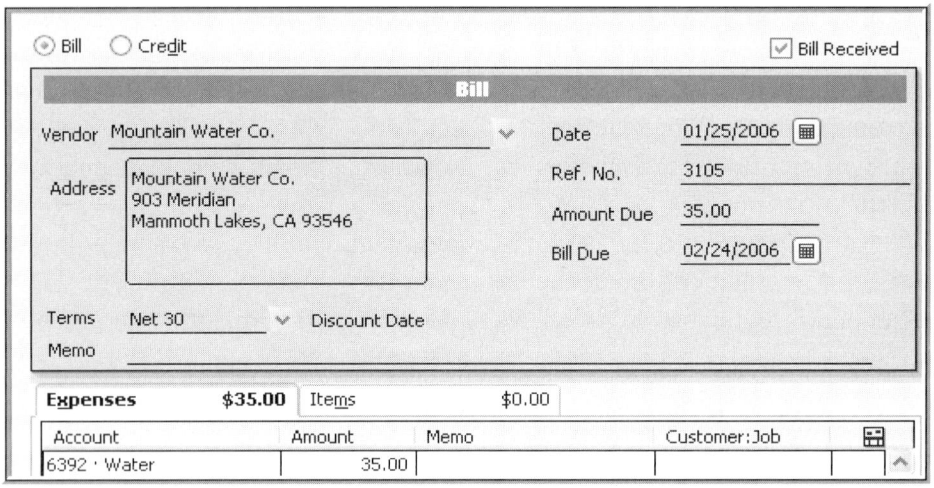

ENTER A BILL USING THE ACCOUNTS PAYABLE REGISTER

The Accounts Payable Register maintains a record of all the transactions recorded within the Accounts Payable account. Not only is it possible to view all of the account activities through the account's register, it is also possible to enter a bill directly into the Accounts Payable register. This can be faster than filling out all of the information through Enter Bills.

MEMO
DATE: January 25, 2006

Received a bill for the rent from Mammoth Rentals. Use the Accounts Payable Register and record the bill for rent of $950, Invoice No. 7164, due February 4, 2006.

Use the Accounts Payable Register to record the above transaction:

Use the keyboard shortcut, **Ctrl+A** to access the Chart of Accounts
Double-click **Accounts Payable** to open the Accounts Payable register
Click in the blank entry at the end of the register
The date is highlighted, key in **01/25/06** for the transaction date
The word *Number* is in the next column
Tab to or click **Number**

- The word *Number* disappears.

Enter the Invoice Number **7164**
Tab to or click **Vendor**, click the drop-down list arrow for the Vendor, click **Mammoth Rentals**
If necessary, Tab to or click **Due Date**, and enter the due date **02/04/06**
Tab to or click **Billed**, enter the amount **950**
Tab to or click **Account**, click the drop-down list arrow for **Account**
Determine the appropriate account to use for rent

- If all of the accounts do not appear in the drop-down list, scroll through the accounts until you find the one appropriate for this entry.

Click **6300 Rent**
Tab to or click Memo, key **Rent**
Click **Record** to record the transaction

01/25/2006	7164	Mammoth Rentals	02/04/2006	950.00			12,590.40
	BILL	6300 · Rent Rent					

Do not close the register

EDIT A TRANSACTION IN THE ACCOUNTS PAYABLE REGISTER

Because QuickBooks Pro makes corrections extremely user friendly, a transaction can be edited or changed directly in the Accounts Payable Register as well as on the original bill. By eliminating the columns for Type and Memo, it is possible to change the register to show each transaction on one line. This can make the register easier to read.

MEMO
DATE: January 25, 2006

Upon examination of the invoices and the bills entered, Rose discovers an error: The actual amount of the bill from the water company was **$85**, not $35. Change the transaction amount for this bill.

Correct the above transaction in the Accounts Payable Register

Click the check box for **1-line** to select
- Each Accounts Payable transaction will appear on one line.

Click the transaction for Mountain Water Co.
Change the amount of the transaction from $35.00 to **$85.00**
Click the **Record** button at the bottom of the register to record the change in the transaction

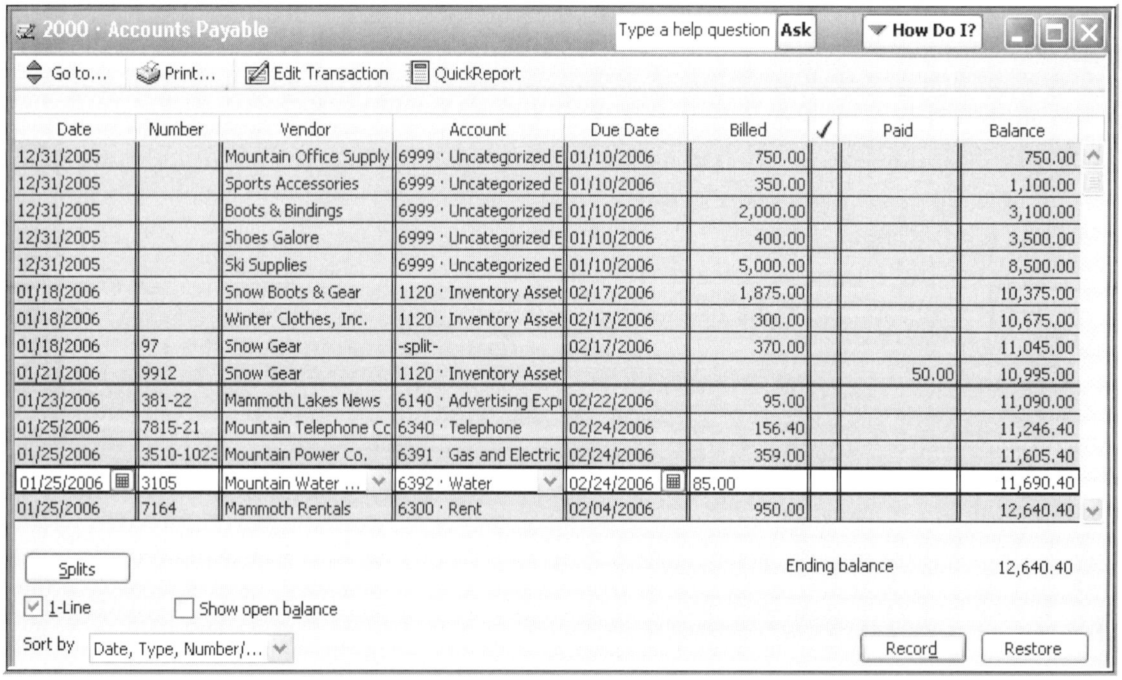

Do not close the register

PREVIEW AND PRINT A QUICKREPORT FROM THE ACCOUNTS PAYABLE REGISTER

After editing the transaction, you may want to view information about a specific vendor. Clicking the vendor's name within a transaction and clicking the QuickReport button at the top of the register can do this quickly and efficiently.

> **MEMO**
> **DATE:** January 25, 2006
>
> More than one transaction has been entered for Snow Gear. You and Tim, like to view transaction information for all vendors that have several transactions within a short period of time.

Prepare a QuickReport for Snow Gear

Click any field in any transaction for Snow Gear
Click the **QuickReport** button at the top of the Register
- The Register QuickReport for All Transactions for Snow Gear appears on the screen.

Resize the columns so the Account is shown in full and the report will print on one page in Landscape orientation
Click **Print**
Click **Preview** to view the report before printing
- The report appears on the screen as a full page.
- A full-page report usually cannot be read on the screen.

To read the text in the report, click the **Zoom In** button at the top of the screen
Use the scroll buttons and bars to view the report columns
Click the **Zoom Out** button to return to a full-page view of the report
When finished previewing the report, click **Close**
- You will return to the Print Reports Screen.
- If necessary, click **Cancel** and resize the columns so the reports will print on one-page wide.

When the columns are shown appropriately, Print the report

Your Name Sports
Register QuickReport
All Transactions

Type	Date	Num	Memo	Account	Paid	Open Balance	Amount
Snow Gear							
Bill	01/18/2006	97		2000 · Accounts Payable	Unpaid	370.00	370.00
Credit	01/21/2006	9912	Returned 1 Sled	2000 · Accounts Payable	Unpaid	-50.00	-50.00
Total Snow Gear						320.00	320.00
TOTAL						**320.00**	**320.00**

Click the **Close** button to close the report
Close the Accounts Payable register and the Chart of Accounts

PREPARE AND PRINT UNPAID BILLS DETAIL REPORT

It is possible to get information regarding unpaid bills by simply preparing a report. No more digging through tickler files, recorded invoices, ledgers, or journals. QuickBooks Pro prepares an Unpaid Bills Detail Report listing each unpaid bill grouped and subtotaled by vendor.

MEMO
DATE: January 25, 2006

Rose Spencer prepares an Unpaid Bills Report for you and Tim each week. Because Your Name Sports is a small business, you like to have a firm control over cash flow so you can determine which bills will be paid during the week.

Prepare and print an **Unpaid Bills Detail Report**

Click **Reports** on the menu bar, point to **Vendors & Payables**, click **Unpaid Bills Detail**
Enter the date of **01/25/06** as the report date
Tab to generate report

Your Name Sports

Unpaid Bills Detail

As of January 25, 2006

Type	Date	Num	Due Date	Aging	Open Balance
Snow Boots & Gear					
Bill	01/18/2006		02/17/2006		1,875.00
Total Snow Boots & Gear					1,875.00
Snow Gear					
Credit	01/21/2006	9912			-50.00
Bill	01/18/2006	97	02/17/2006		370.00
Total Snow Gear					320.00
Sports Accessories					
Bill	12/31/2005		01/10/2006	15	350.00
Total Sports Accessories					350.00
Winter Clothes, Inc.					
Bill	01/18/2006		02/17/2006		300.00
Total Winter Clothes, Inc.					300.00
TOTAL					**12,640.40**

Print in Portrait orientation
Click **Close** to close the report

PAYING BILLS

When using QuickBooks Pro, you may choose to pay your bills directly from the Pay Bills command and let QuickBooks Pro write your checks for you, or you may choose to write the checks yourself. If you recorded a bill, you should use the Pay Bills feature of QuickBooks Pro to pay the bill. If no bill was recorded, you should pay the bill by writing a check in QuickBooks Pro. Using the Pay Bills window enables you to determine which bills to pay, the method of payment—check, or credit card—and the appropriate account. When you are determining which bills to pay, QuickBooks Pro allows you to display the bills by due date, discount date, vendor, or amount. All bills may be displayed, or only those bills that are due by a certain date may be displayed. In addition, when a bill has been recorded and is paid using the Pay Bills feature of QuickBooks Pro, the bill will be marked *Paid in Full* and the amount paid will no longer be shown as a liability. If you record a bill and pay it by writing a check and *not* using the Pay Bills feature of QuickBooks, the bill won't be marked as paid and it will show up as a liability.

MEMO
DATE: January 25, 2006

Whenever possible, Rose Spencer pays the bills on a weekly basis. Show all the bills in the Pay Bills window. Select the bills, except the bill for Snow Gear, with discounts dates of 1/28/2006 for payment.

Pay the bills that are eligible for a discount

Click **Pay Bills** on the QuickBooks Home Page
Click **Show All Bills** to select
Sort Bills by **Due Date**

- If this is not showing, click the drop-down list arrow next to the **Sort Bills** text box, click **Due Date**.
- At the bottom of the **Pay Bills** window, verify the following items: **1100 Checking** is the account used, **Payment Method** shows **Check**, and **To be printed** is selected.

Tab to or click **Payment Date**, **enter 01/25/06**
Scroll through the list of bills

- The bills will be shown according to the date due.

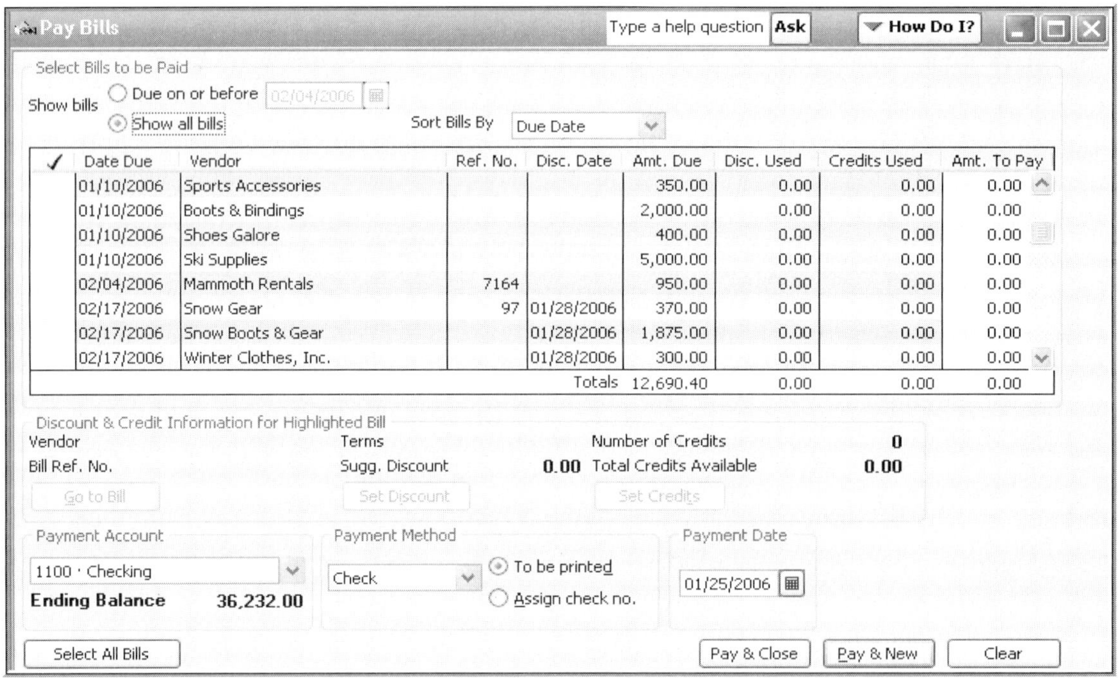

Select the bills to be paid and apply the discounts:

Click in the check mark column for the transaction for Snow Boots & Gear with a due date of 2/17/2006

Click the **Set Discount** button

- Verify the amount of the discount.

Click the drop-down list arrow for the Discount Account

- Scroll through the list of accounts. There is account 4030 Purchases Discounts but it is not appropriate for this transaction. It is used for purchases of things used by the business not for merchandise. There is 6130 Sales Discounts. This expense account is used when we give discounts to customers. The bill payment is for merchandise purchased to sell in the business. A cost of goods sold discount account needs to be created for merchandise discounts

Click **<Add New>**

Click **Cost of Good Sold** as the type of account

Enter **5100** as the account number

Enter the account name **Merchandise Discounts**

Click **Subaccount** and select **5000 Cost of Good Sold** as the account

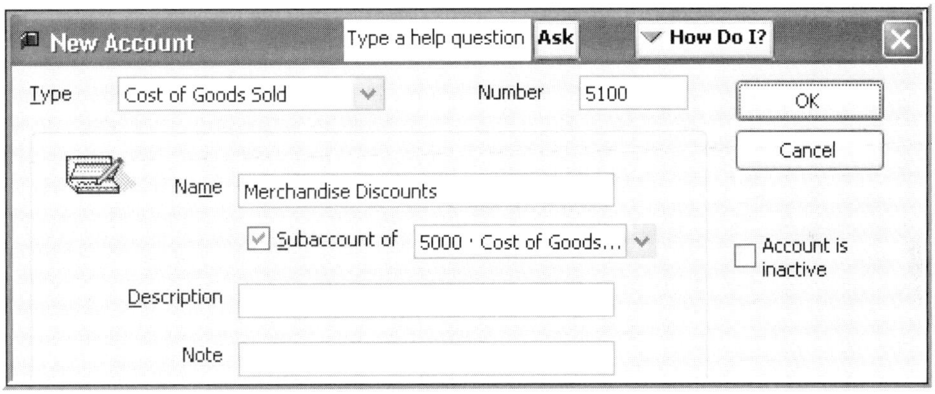

Click **OK**

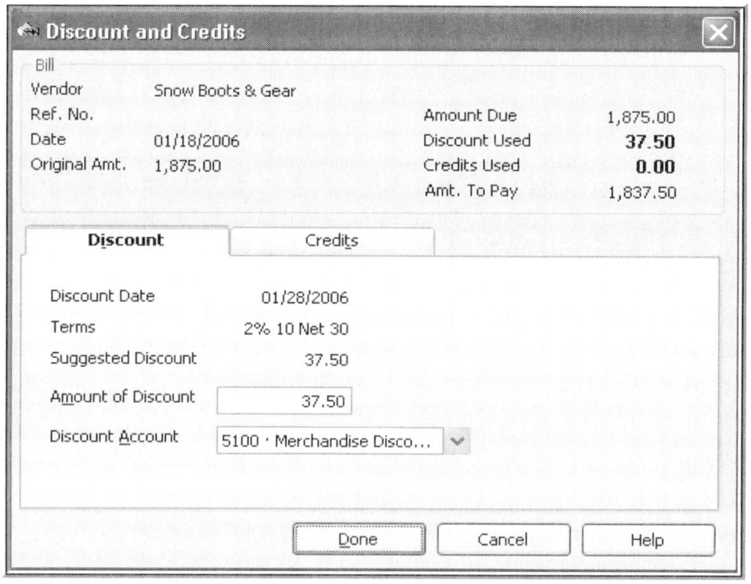

Click **Done** to record the discount
Repeat the steps for the bill from Winter Clothes that is eligible for a discount

	02/17/2006	Snow Gear	97	01/28/2006	370.00	0.00	0.00	0.00
✓	02/17/2006	Snow Boots & Gear		01/28/2006	1,875.00	37.50	0.00	1,837.50
✓	02/17/2006	Winter Clothes, Inc.		01/28/2006	300.00	6.00	0.00	294.00

- Once you click **Done** to accept the discount, the amount due and amount paid amounts change to reflect the amount of the discount taken.

Click **Pay & New** button to record the payments and go to the next **Pay Bills** screen

PAY A BILL QUALIFYING FOR A PURCHASE DISCOUNT AND APPLY CREDIT AS PART OF PAYMENT

When paying bills, it is a good idea to apply credits received for returned or damaged merchandise to the accounts as payment is made.

MEMO
DATE: January 25, 2006

As she is getting ready to pay bills, Rose looks for any credits that may be applied to the bill as part of the payment. In addition, Rose looks for bills that qualify for an early-payment discount. Apply the credit received from Snow Gear, as part of the payment for the bill, then apply the discount, and pay the bill within the discount period.

Apply the credit received from Snow Gear, as part of the payment for the bill and pay bill within the discount period

Verify **Payment Date** of **01/25/2006**
Verify the **Payment Method** as **Check** and **To be printed** is marked
Verify **1100 Checking** is the **Payment Account**
Select **Show all bills**
Click the drop-down list for **Sort Bills By**, click **Vendor**
Scroll through transactions until you see the transaction for Snow Gear
Click the transaction to select it

- *Note:* This must be completed before applying the discount or credit to the bill.
- Notice that both the Set Credits and Set Discount buttons are now active and that information regarding credits and discounts is displayed.

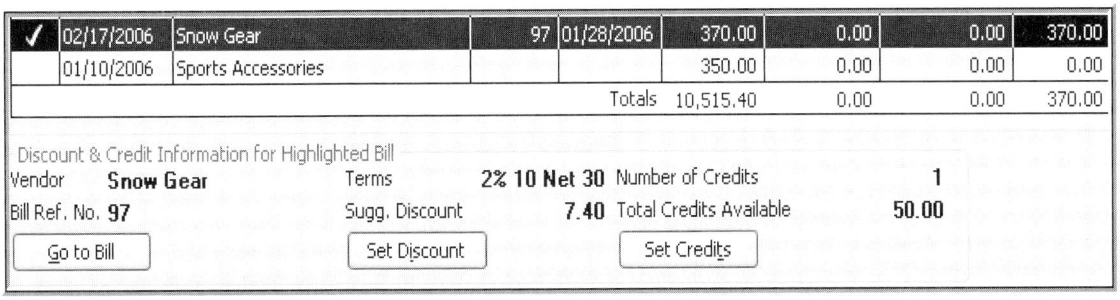

Click the **Set Discount** button

- Verify the amount of the discount **7.40** and the discount account **51 Merchandise Discounts**

Click the **Credits** tab
Click the Check column for the credit amount of **50.00**

- On the Discounts and Credits screen, verify the amount due of **370**, the discount used of **7.40**, and the credit used of **50.00**, leaving an amount to pay of **312.60**
- QuickBooks calculates the discount on the original amount of the invoice rather than the amount due after subtracting the credit. If you need to recalculate the discount on the amount due after the credit, you may change the amount of the discount on the

Discount screen. At this point in training, we will accept the discount calculated by QuickBooks.

Click the **Done** button

✓	Date Due	Vendor	Ref. No.	Disc. Date	Amt. Due	Disc. Used	Credits Used	Amt. To Pay
	02/04/2006	Mammoth Rentals	7164		950.00	0.00	0.00	0.00
	01/10/2006	Mountain Office Supply Company			750.00	0.00	0.00	0.00
	02/24/2006	Mountain Power Co.	3510-1...		359.00	0.00	0.00	0.00
	02/24/2006	Mountain Telephone Co.	7815-21		156.40	0.00	0.00	0.00
	02/24/2006	Mountain Water Co.	3105		85.00	0.00	0.00	0.00
	01/10/2006	Shoes Galore			400.00	0.00	0.00	0.00
	01/10/2006	Ski Supplies			5,000.00	0.00	0.00	0.00
✓	02/17/2006	Snow Gear	97	01/28/2006	370.00	7.40	50.00	312.60
				Totals	10,515.40	7.40	50.00	312.60

Click **Pay & Close** to record the payment

VERIFY THAT BILLS ARE MARKED PAID

Access **Enter Bills** as previously instructed

Click **Previous** and view all the bills that were paid in Pay Bills to verify that they are marked as paid

- Notice that the Credit for Snow Gear is *not* marked in any way to indicate that it has been used.

Close the Enter Bills screen

PRINT CHECKS TO PAY BILLS

Once bills have been selected for payment and any discounts taken or credits applied, the checks should be printed, signed, and mailed. QuickBooks Pro has two methods that may be used to print checks. Checks may be accessed and printed one at a time using the Write Checks window. This allows you to view the Bill Payment Information for each check. A more efficient way to print checks is to click the File menu and select checks from the Print Forms menu. This method will print all checks that are marked *To be printed* but will not allow you to view the bill payment information for any of the checks as you would if you printed each check separately. QuickBooks does not separate checks it writes in Pay Bills from the checks that are written when using the Write Checks feature of the program.

MEMO
DATE: January 25, 2006

Rose needs to print the checks for bills that have been paid. She decides to print checks individually so she can view bill payment information for each check while printing. When she finishes with the checks, she will give them to you for approval and signature.

Print the checks for bills that have been paid

Access the Write Checks window using the keyboard shortcut **Ctrl+W**

- A blank check will show on the screen.

Click **Previous** until you get to the check for **Winter Clothes, Inc.**

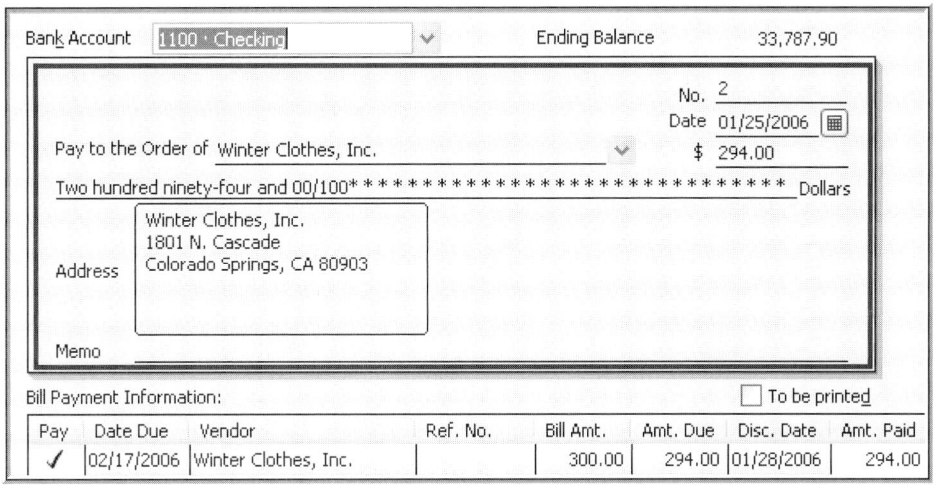

Click **Print** at the top of the window to print the check

Click **OK** on the Print Check screen to select Check No. 2

- Check No. 1 was issued in Chapter 5 to Dr. Felipe Manuel for a return. If Check No. 2 is not on the Print Check screen, change the screen so that the check number is 2.

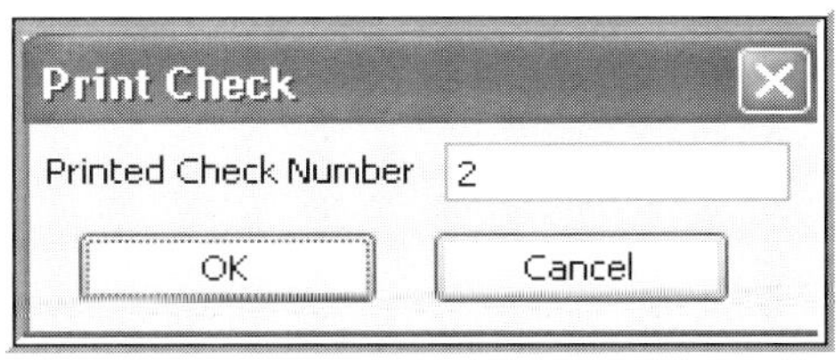

- On the **Print Checks** screen, verify the printer name, printer type, and the selection of Standard check style.

Print Company Name and Address should be selected

- If is not marked with a check, click the check box to insert a check mark and select.

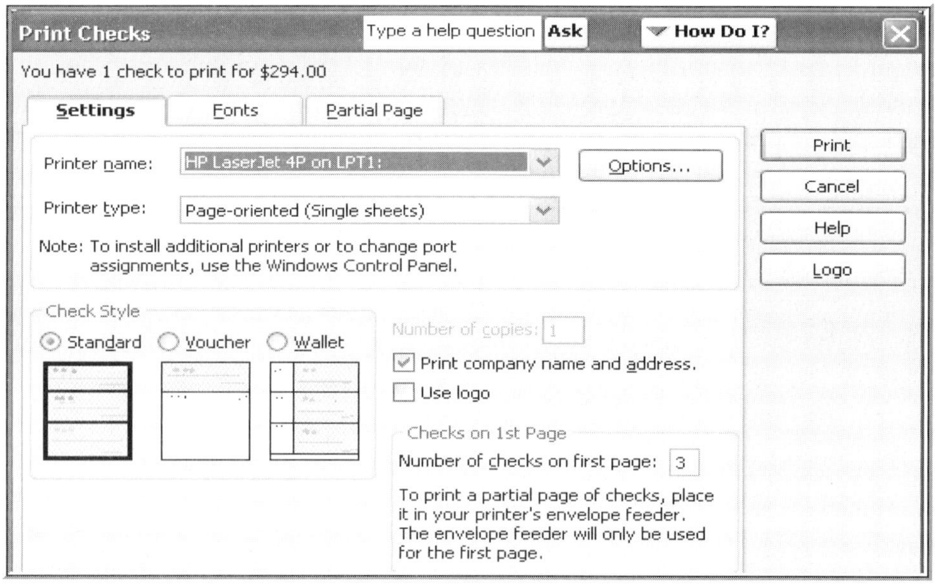

Click **Print** to print the check

Click **OK** on **Did check(s) print OK?**

- If you get a **Set Check Reminder** screen, click **No**

Click **Previous** or **Next** and repeat the steps to print Check No. 3 for Snow Boots & Gear, and Check No. 4 for Snow Gear

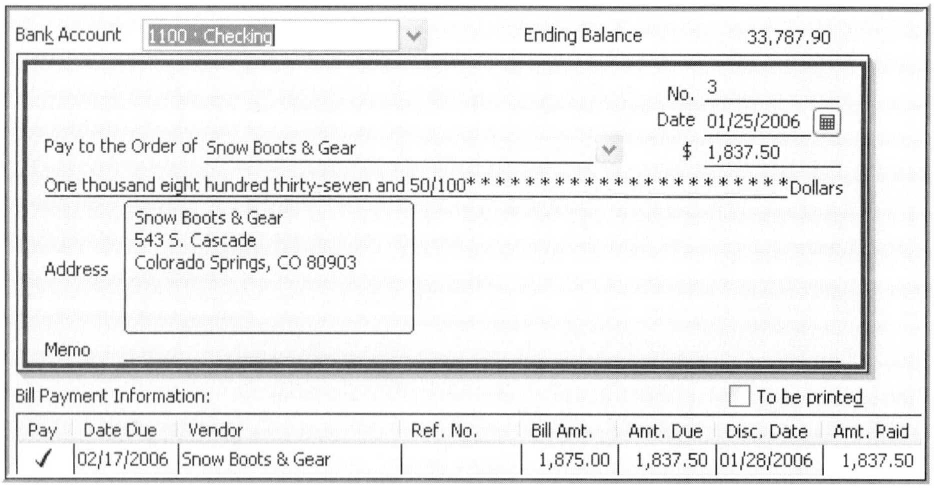

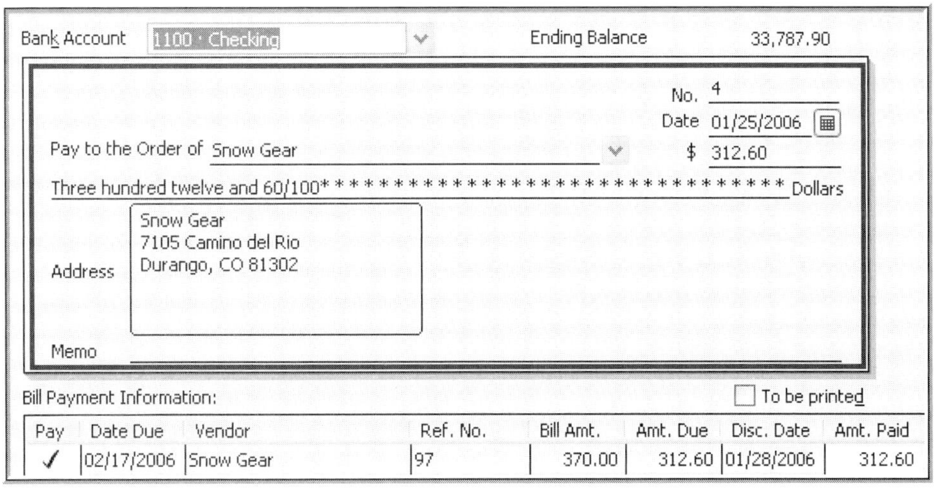

- Notice that the amount of the check to Snow Gear, is $312.60. This allows for the original bill of $370 less the return of $50 and the discount of $7.40.

Close the **Write Checks** window.

PAY BILLS USING A CREDIT CARD

A credit card may be used to pay a bill rather than a check. Use the Pay Bills feature, but select Pay By Credit Card rather than Pay By Check.

> **MEMO**
> **DATE:** January 25, 2006
>
> In viewing the bills due, you direct Rose to pay the bills to Sports Accessories and Shoes Galore using the Visa credit card.

➤ Pay the above bills with a credit card

Access **Pay Bills** as previously instructed

Select **Show all bills**

In **Payment Method** click the drop-down list arrow, click **Credit Card** to select

- Payment Account should show 2100 Visa. If it does not, click the drop-down list arrow and click **2100 Visa**.

Payment Date should be **01/25/2006**

Scroll through the list of bills and select **Shoes Galore** and **Sports Accessories** by clicking in the check mark column

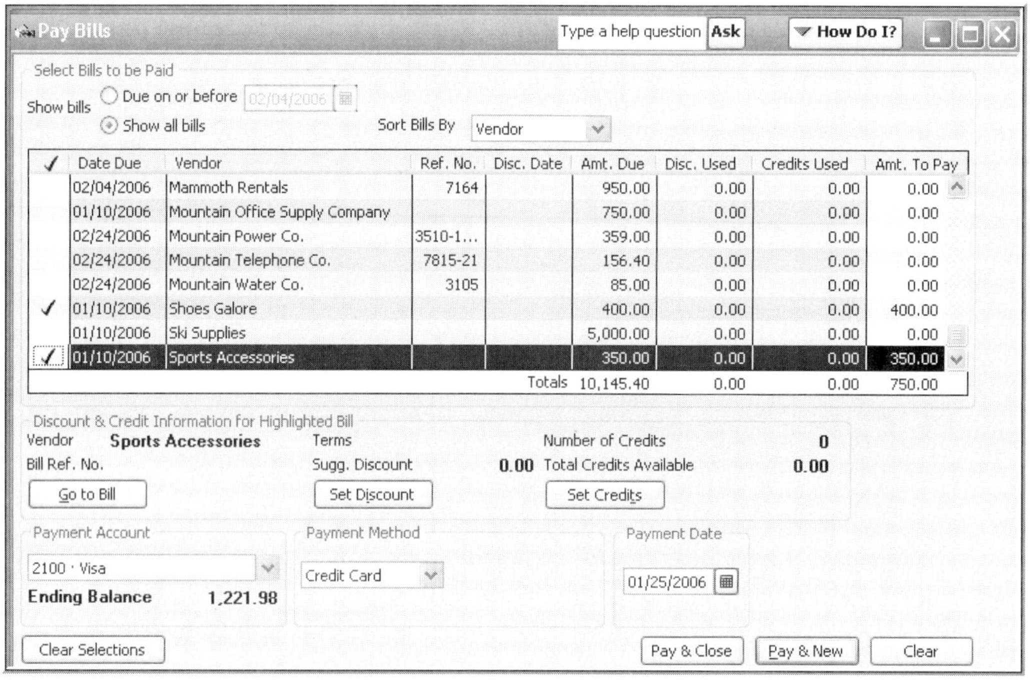

Click **Pay & Close** to record the payment

VERIFY THE CREDIT CARD PAYMENT OF BILLS

Paying bills with a credit card in Pay Bills automatically creates a Credit Card transaction in QuickBooks Pro. This can be verified through the Visa account register in the Chart of Accounts and through Enter Credit Card Charges. The entry into QuickBooks does not actually charge the credit card. It only records the transaction.

MEMO
DATE: January 25, 2006

Verify the credit card charges for Sports Accessories and Shoes Galore.

Verify the credit card charges

Access the Visa account register in the **Chart of Accounts**
Scroll through the register to see the charges for Shoes Galore and Sports Accessories

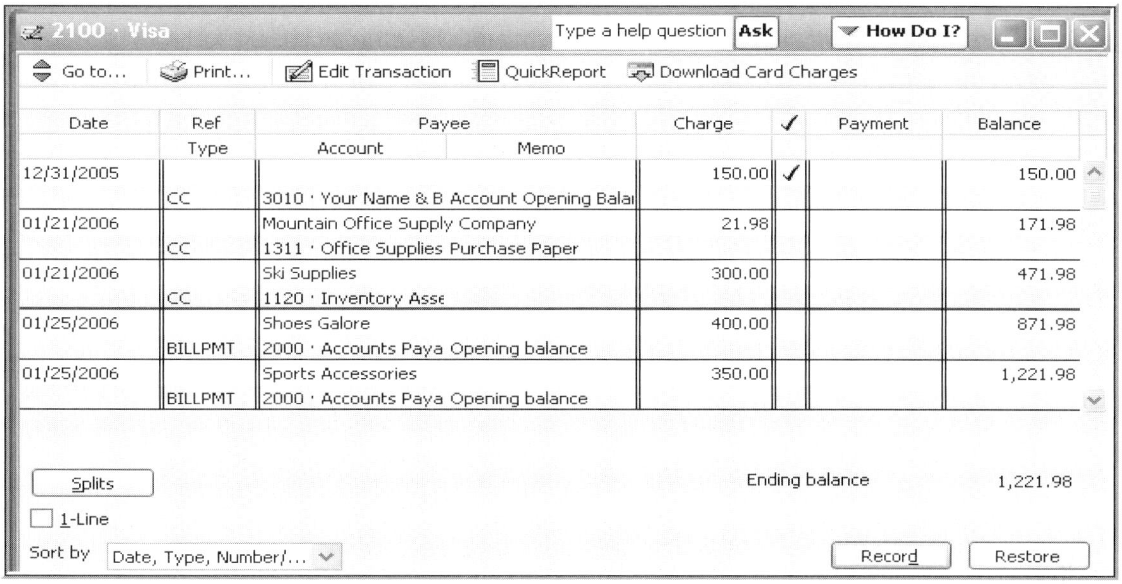

Close the register and the **Chart of Accounts**

SALES TAX

When a company is set up in QuickBooks Pro, a Sales Tax Payable liability account is automatically created if the company indicates that it charges sales tax on sales. The Sales Tax Payable account keeps track of as many tax agencies as the company needs. As invoices are written, QuickBooks Pro records the tax liability in the Sales Tax Payable account. To determine the sales tax owed, a Sales Tax Liability Report is prepared.

PRINT SALES TAX LIABILITY REPORT

The Sales Tax Liability Report shows your total taxable sales, the total nontaxable sales, and the amount of sales tax owed to each tax agency.

> **MEMO**
> **DATE:** January 25, 2006
>
> Prior to paying the sales tax, Rose prepares the Sales Tax Liability Report.

➤ Prepare the Sales Tax Liability Report

Click **Reports** on the Menu bar, point to **Vendors & Payables** as the type of report, click **Sales Tax Liability Report**

The Report Dates are **From 01/01/2006 To 01/25/2006**

- If necessary, adjust the column widths so the report will fit on one page.
- If you get a message box asking if all columns should be the same size as the one being adjusted, click **No**.

Your Name Sports

Sales Tax Liability

January 1 - 25, 2006

	Total Sales	Non-Taxable Sales	Taxable Sales	Tax Rate	Tax Collected	Sales Tax Payable As of Jan 25, 06
State Board of Equalization						
CA Sales Tax	8,582.23	125.00	8,457.23	7.25%	613.15	613.15
Total State Board of Equalization	8,582.23	125.00	8,457.23		613.15	613.15
TOTAL	**8,582.23**	**125.00**	**8,457.23**		**613.15**	**613.15**

Print in Landscape orientation

Close the report after printing

PAYING SALES TAX

Use the Pay Sales Tax window to determine how much sales tax you owe and to write a check to the tax agency. QuickBooks Pro will update the sales tax account with payment information.

MEMO

DATE: January 25, 2006

Note from Tim: Rose, pay the sales taxes owed.

Pay the sales taxes owed

Click the **Pay Sales Tax** icon in the Vendor section of the QuickBooks Home Page

Pay From Account is **1100 Checking**

Check Date is **01/25/2006**

Show sales tax due through is **01/25/2006**

To be printed should be selected with a check mark in the check box.

Click the **Pay All Tax** button

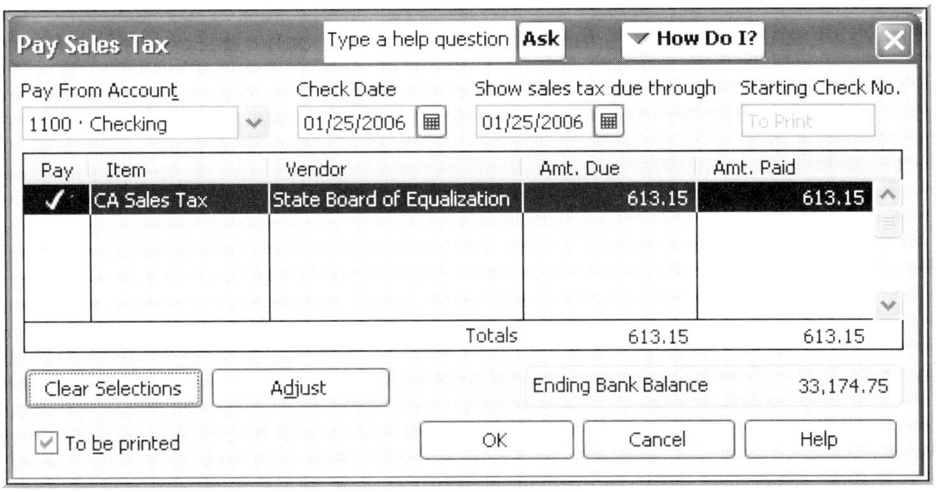

- Once **Pay All Tax** has been clicked and the item selected, the **Ending Bank Balance** changes to reflect the amount in checking after the tax has been paid.

Click **OK**

Print Check No. 5 for the payment of the Sales Tax

Click **File**, point to **Print Forms**, click **Checks**

- Verify the Bank Account 1100 Checking, the First Check No. 5, and the check mark in front of State Board of Equalization.

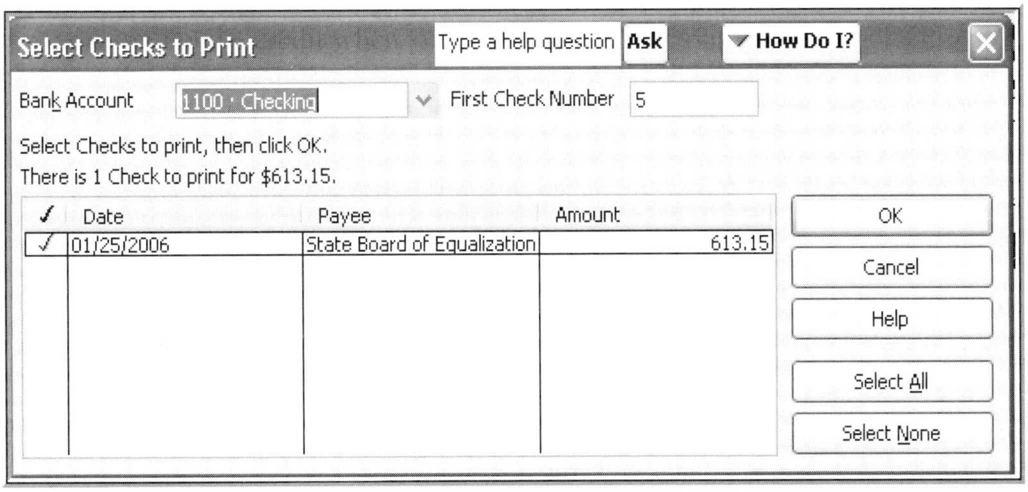

Click **OK**, click **Print**, click **OK** to answer *Did check(s) print Ok?*

VOIDING AND DELETING PURCHASE ORDERS, BILLS, CHECKS, AND CREDIT CARD PAYMENTS

QuickBooks Pro is so user friendly it allows any business form to be deleted. Some accounting programs do not allow error corrections, except as adjusting entries, once an entry has been made. As you learned in earlier chapters, QuickBooks Pro, allows a purchase order, a bill, a credit card payment, or a check to be voided or deleted. If a business form is voided, the form remains as a transaction. The transaction shows as a zero amount. This is useful when you want a record to show that an entry was made. If the form is deleted, all trace of the form is deleted. QuickBooks Pro allows a company to keep an audit trail if it wants a complete record of all transactions entered. The audit trail includes information regarding deleted transactions as well as transactions that appear on business forms, in the Journal, and in reports. An audit trail helps to eliminate misconduct such as printing a check and then deleting the check from the company records.

The procedures for voiding and deleting business forms are the same whether the business is a retail business or a service business. For actual assignments and practice in voiding and deleting business forms, refer to Chapters 2, 3, and 5.

VENDOR CENTER

The Vendor Center is used to obtain information regarding individual vendors. Once you open the vendor Center, clicking on a vendor in the Vendor List will display the Vendor Contact Information for the selected vendor. Click Edit/More Info to see further information about the vendor or to edit the information.

In the lower-right section of the Vendor Center, you will see transaction information displayed for the selected vendor.

Open the Vendor Center

Click the **Vendor Center** button
Click the vendor **Ski Supplies** in the Vendor List
Click the **Edit Vendor** button to change the vendor information for the company
Change the following information for Ski Supplies
Address: **1274 Boulder Avenue, Lafayette, CO 80026**
Contact: **Robert Carrillo**
Telephone: **303-555-1263**
FAX: **303-555-6321**
E-mail: **supplies@co.com**
Click **OK**
View the changes to the Vendor

Look at the transactions displayed for Ski Supplies

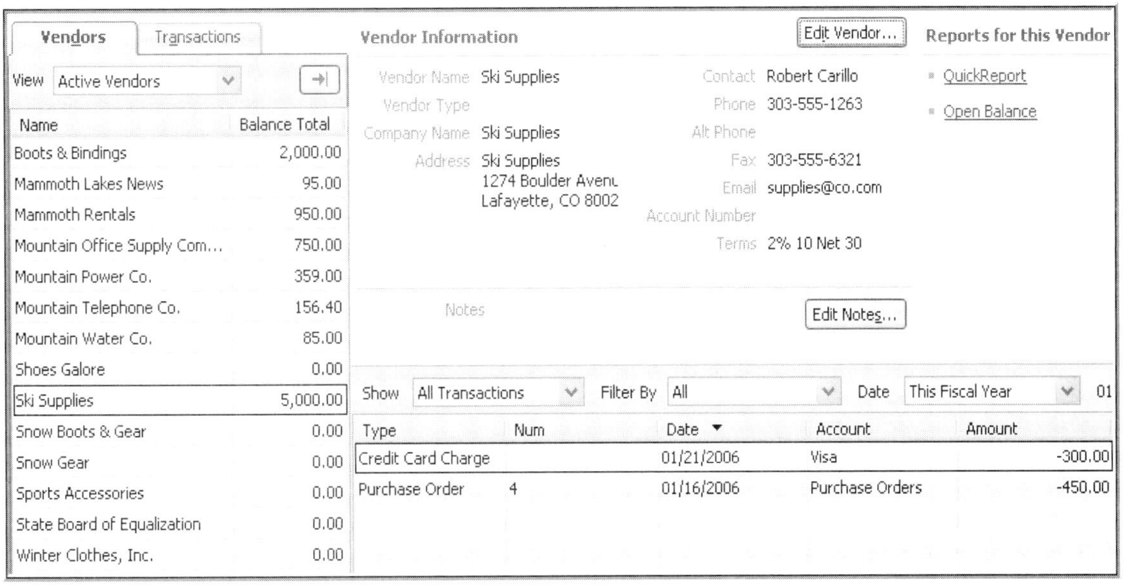

Close the **Vendor Center**

BACK UP YOUR NAME SPORTS

Follow the instructions given in previous chapters to back up data for Your Name Sports, use the file name **Sports Ch 6.qbb**, and follow the instructions in Appendix A to prepare a duplicate disk.

SUMMARY

In this chapter, purchase orders were completed, inventory items were received, and bills were recorded. Payments for purchases and bills were made by cash and by credit card. Sales taxes were paid. Vendors, inventory items, and accounts were added while transactions were being recorded. Various reports were prepared to determine unpaid bills, account and vendor QuickReports, and sales tax liability.

END-OF-CHAPTER QUESTIONS

TRUE/FALSE

ANSWER THE FOLLOWING QUESTIONS IN THE SPACE PROVIDED BEFORE THE QUESTION NUMBER.

_____ 1. Receipt of purchase order items is never recorded before the bill arrives.

_____ 2. A bill can be paid by check or credit card.

_____ 3. The Cost of Goods Sold account Merchandise Discounts is used to record discounts to customers.

_____ 4. Voiding a purchase order removes all trace of the purchase order from the company records.

_____ 5. The Vendor Center displays the vendor list and information about individual vendors.

_____ 6. A single purchase order can be prepared and sent to several vendors.

_____ 7. A Sales Tax account is automatically created if a company indicates that it charges sales tax on sales.

_____ 8. A credit received from a vendor for the return of merchandise can be applied to a payment to the vendor.

_____ 9. A new vendor cannot be added while recording a transaction.

_____ 10. A purchase order is closed automatically when a partial receipt of merchandise is recorded.

MULTIPLE CHOICE

WRITE THE LETTER OF THE CORRECT ANSWER IN THE SPACE PROVIDED BEFORE THE QUESTION NUMBER.

_____ 1. If you change the minimum quantity for an item, it becomes effective ___.
A. immediately
B. the beginning of next month
C. as soon as outstanding purchase orders are received
D. the beginning of the next fiscal year

_____ 2. If an order is received with a bill but is incomplete, QuickBooks Pro will ___.
A. record the bill for the full amount ordered
B. record the bill only for the amount received
C. not allow the bill to be prepared until all the merchandise is received
D. close the purchase order

_____ 3. The Purchase Order feature must be selected as a preference ___.
A. when setting up the company
B. prior to recording the first purchase order
C. is automatically set when the first purchase order is prepared
D. either A or B

_____ 4. A faster method of entering bills can be entering the bills ___.
A. while writing the checks for payment
B. in the Pay Bills window
C. in the Accounts Payable Register
D. none of the above

_____ 5. When items ordered are received with a bill, you record the receipt ___.
A. on an item receipt form
B. on the bill
C. on the original purchase order
D. in the Journal

_____ 6. Sales tax is paid by using the ___ window.
A. Pay Bills
B. Pay Sales Tax
C. Write Check
D. Credit Card

_____ 7. A Purchase Order may be customized using the ___.
A. Layout Designer
B. Drawing menu
C. Customize Form button on the Home Page
D. a form may not be changed

_____ 8. Checks to pay bills may be printed ___.
A. individually
B. all at once
C. as the checks are written
D. all of the above

_____ 9. When recording a bill for merchandise received, you click the ___ tab on the vendor section of the bill.
A. Memo
B. Expenses
C. Items
D. Purchase Order

_____ 10. The ___ matches income for the period against expenses for the period.
A. cash basis of accounting
B. credit basis of accounting
C. accrual basis of accounting
D. debit/credit basis of accounting

FILL-IN

IN THE SPACE PROVIDED, WRITE THE ANSWER THAT MOST APPROPRIATELY COMPLETES THE SENTENCE.

1. Orders for merchandise are prepared using the QuickBooks Pro __________________ form.

2. Information on the Reminders List may be displayed in _________ or __________ form.

3. The _______________ Report shows the total taxable sales and the amount of sales tax owed.

4. A purchase order can be closed __________ or __________.

5. To see the bill payment information, checks must be printed _______________.

SHORT ESSAY

Describe the cycle of obtaining merchandise. Include the process from ordering the merchandise through paying for it. Include information regarding the QuickBooks Pro forms prepared for each phase of the cycle, the possible ways in which an item may be received, and the ways in which payment may be made.

NAME________________________

TRANSMITTAL

CHAPTER 6: YOUR NAME SPORTS

Attach the following documents and reports:

Purchase Order No. 1: Snow Boots & Gear
Purchase Order No. 2: Snow Gear
Purchase Order No. 3: Winter Clothes, Inc.
Purchase Order No. 4: Ski Supplies
Account QuickReport, Purchase Orders, January 16, 2006
Purchase Order No. 4 (Revised): Ski Supplies
Register Quick Report, Snow Gear
Unpaid Bills Detail, January 25, 2006
Check No. 2: Winter Clothes, Inc.
Check No. 3: Snow Boots & Gear
Check No. 4: Snow Gear
Sales Tax Liability Report, January 1-25, 2006
Check No. 5: State Board of Equalization

END-OF-CHAPTER PROBLEM

YOUR NAME CLOTHING

Chapter 6 continues with the transactions for purchase orders, merchandise receipts, bills, bill payments, and sales tax payments. Julie prints the checks, purchase orders, and any related reports; and you sign the checks. This procedure establishes cash control procedures and lets both owners know about the checks being processed.

INSTRUCTIONS

Continue to use the copy of Your Name you used in Chapter 5. Open the company—the file used is **Clothing.qbw**. Record the purchase orders, bills, payments, and other purchases as instructed within the chapter. Always read the transactions carefully and review the Chart of Accounts when selecting transaction accounts. Print reports and graphs as indicated. Add new vendors and minimum quantities where indicated. Print all purchase orders and checks issued. The first purchase order used is Purchase Order No. 1. When paying bills, always check for credits that may be applied to the bill, and always check for discounts.

In addition to the Item List and the Chart of Accounts, you will need to use the Vendor List when ordering merchandise and paying bills.

RECORD TRANSACTIONS

January 5, 2007:

- Customize a Purchase Order template so the Company Name is expanded to **5 ¼** and Purchase Order begins at **5 ½**.
- Change the reorder point for dresses from 20 to 25.
- Change the reorder point for women's pants to 30.

- Prepare and print an Inventory Stock Status by Item Report for January 1-5, 2007 in Landscape orientation. Manually adjust column widths so the item descriptions and the vendors' names are shown in full and the report prints on one page.
- Prepare Purchase Orders for all items marked Order on the Stock Status by Item Inventory Report. Refer to the Stock Status by Item Report for vendor information. The quantity for each item ordered is 10. The rate is $35 for dresses and $20 for pants. Print purchase orders with lines around each field.
- Order an additional 10 dresses from a new vendor: Clothes Time, 9382 Grand Avenue, San Luis Obispo, CA 93407, Contact person is Mitchell Rogers, 805-555-5512, Fax is 805-555-2155, E-mail is clothestime@slo.com, Credit terms are 2% 10 Net 30, Credit limit is $2000. The rate for the dresses is $25.
- Print a Purchase Order QuickReport in Landscape orientation for January 1-5. Adjust column widths so all columns are displayed in full and the report prints on one page.

January 8, 2007:

- Received pants ordered from California Clothing Supply, Inc. without the bill. Enter the receipt of merchandise. The transaction date is 01/08/2007.
- Received dresses from Fun Clothes with Bill C309. Enter the receipt of the merchandise and the bill.
- Received 8 dresses from Clothes Time. Enter the receipt of the merchandise and Bill 406.
- After recording the receipt of merchandise, view the three purchase orders. Notice which ones are marked Received in Full and Clsd.

January 9, 2007:

- Received Bill 239 from California Clothing Supply, Inc. for the pants received on 01/08/07. The bill was dated 01/08/2007.
- Pay for the dresses from Clothes Time with a credit card. (Take a purchase discount if the transaction qualifies for one. Use a Cost of Goods Sold account 5100 Merchandise Discounts for the discount.)

January 10, 2007:

- Discovered unstitched seams in two pairs of women's pants ordered on PO 2. Return the pants for credit. Use 2340 as the Reference number.

January 15, 2007:

- Record bill for rent of $1150. (Vendor is SLO Rental Company, 301 Marsh Street, San Luis Obispo, CA 93407, Contact person is Matt Ericson, 805-555-4100, Fax 805-555-0014, Terms Net 30.)
- Record bill for telephone service of $79.85. (Vendor is SLO Telephone Co., 8851 Hwy. 58, San Luis Obispo, CA 93407, 805-555-1029. No terms or credit limits have been given.)

January 18, 2007:

- Pay all bills that are eligible for a discount. Take any discounts for which you are eligible. Take the full amount of the discount even if you have a credit to apply. If there are any credits to an account, apply the credit prior to paying the bill. Pay the bill(s) by check.
- Print Check Nos. 2 and 3 for the bills that were paid.

January 25, 2007:

- Purchase office supplies to have on hand for $250 with a credit card from Office Masters, 8330 Grand Avenue, Arroyo Grande, CA 93420, Contact person is Larry Thomas, 805-555-9915, Fax 805-555-5199, E-mail OfficeMasters@slo.com, Terms Net 30, Credit limit $500.
- Print Unpaid Bills Detail Report in Portrait orientation.
- Pay bills for rent and telephone. Print the checks prepared for these bills.

January 30, 2007:

- Prepare Sales Tax Liability Report from 01/01/2007 to 01/30/2007. Print the report in Landscape orientation. Change columns widths, if necessary, so the report will fit on one page.
- Pay Sales Tax and print the check.
- Prepare a Vendor Balance Detail Report as of 01/30/2007. Print in Portrait orientation. Adjust column widths so the report will display the account names in full and will print on one page without selecting Fit report on one page wide.
- Print a Trial Balance for 01/01/2007 to 01/30/2007.
- Back up data.

NAME____________________

TRANSMITTAL

CHAPTER 6: YOUR NAME CLOTHING

Attach the following documents and reports:

Inventory Stock Status by Item, January 1-5, 2007
Purchase Order No. 1: Fun Clothes
Purchase Order No. 2: California Clothing Supply, Inc.
Purchase Order No. 3: Clothes Time
Account QuickReport, Purchase Orders
Check No. 2: Fun Clothes
Check No. 3: California Clothing Supply, Inc.
Unpaid Bills Detail, January 25, 2007
Check No. 4: SLO Rental Company
Check No. 5: Telephone Service Company
Sales Tax Liability Report
Check No. 6: State Board of Equalization
Vendor Balance Detail, January 30, 2007
Trial Balance, January 1-30, 2007

GENERAL ACCOUNTING AND END-OF-PERIOD PROCEDURES: MERCHANDISING BUSINESS

7

LEARNING OBJECTIVES

At the completion of this chapter, you will be able to:

1. Complete the end-of-period procedures.
2. Change the name of existing accounts in the Chart of Accounts, view the account name change, and view the effect of an account name change on subaccounts.
3. Delete an existing account from the Chart of Accounts.
4. Enter the adjusting entries required for accrual-basis accounting.
5. Record depreciation and an adjustment for Purchases Discounts.
6. Understand how to record owners' equity transactions for a partnership.
7. Enter a transaction for owner withdrawals, and transfer owner withdrawals and net income to the owners' capital accounts.
8. Reconcile the bank statement, record bank service charges, and mark cleared transactions.
9. Reconcile a credit card statement.
10. Undo a reconciliation and customize the layout of the reconciliation screen.
11. Print the Journal.
12. Print reports such as Trial Balance, Profit and Loss Statement, and Balance Sheet.
13. Export a report to Microsoft® Excel and import data from Excel
14. Perform end-of-period backup, close a period, record transactions in a closed period, and adjust inventory quantities.

GENERAL ACCOUNTING AND END-OF-PERIOD PROCEDURES

As stated in previous chapters, QuickBooks Pro operates from the standpoint of the business document rather than an accounting form, journal, or ledger. While QuickBooks Pro does incorporate all of these items into the program, in many instances they operate behind the scenes. Many accounting programs require special closing procedures at the end of a period. QuickBooks Pro does not require special closing procedures at the end of a period. At the end of the fiscal year, QuickBooks Pro transfers the net income into the Retained Earnings account and allows you to protect the data for the year by assigning a closing date to the period. All of the transaction detail is maintained and viewable, but it will not be changed unless OK is clicked on a warning screen.

Even though a formal closing does not have to be performed within QuickBooks Pro, when using accrual-basis accounting, several transactions must be recorded in order to reflect all expenses and income for the period accurately. For example, bank statements and credit cards must be reconciled; and any charges or bank collections need to be recorded. An adjustment to transfer purchase discounts from income to cost of goods sold needs to be made. Other adjusting entries such as depreciation, office supplies used, and so on will also need to be made. These adjustments may be recorded by the CPA or by the company's accounting personnel. At the end of the year, net income for the year and the owner withdrawals for the year should be transferred to the owners' capital accounts.

As in a service business, the CPA for the company will review things such as account names, adjusting entries, depreciation schedules, owner's equity adjustments, and so on. There are several ways for accountant entries to be made.

If the CPA makes the changes and adjustments, they may be made on the Accountant's Review Copy of the business files. This disk is then merged with the company files that are used to record day-to-day business transactions. All adjustments made by the CPA are added to the current company files. There are certain restrictions to the types of transactions that may be made on an accountant's copy of the business files. Using this method enables you to continue recording your day-to-day transactions.

In some instances, the accountant will make adjustments on a backup copy of the company data. In addition, a portable company file may be e-mailed to your accountant for changes. Either of these methods may be used because there are no restrictions on the types of entries that may be made. If the backup is used, the transactions entered by the accountant on backup company files will also need to be entered in the company files used to record day-to-day transactions. The two sets of company files cannot be merged. If a portable file is used, it must be used in place of your company file.

Another method to use for an accountant is to allow your accountant to access your QuickBooks company file remotely. This may be done if your accountant is using QuickBooks® Premier: Accountant Edition. When a file is accessed remotely, the accountant may enter the appropriate transactions directly into your company file. During the session, the accountant controls QuickBooks on your computer. All the transactions are shown on your screen in real-time. When the session is complete, your company file contains all the transactions made by the accountant.

Once necessary adjustments have been made, reports reflecting the end-of-period results of operations should be prepared. For archive purposes, at the end of the fiscal year, an additional backup disk is prepared and stored.

TRAINING TUTORIAL AND PROCEDURES

The following tutorial will once again work with Your Name Sports. As in Chapters 5 and 6, transactions will be recorded for this fictitious company. Refer to procedures given in Chapter 5 to maximize training benefits.

OPEN QUICKBOOKS® PRO AND YOUR NAME SPORTS

➤ Open **QuickBooks Pro** and **Your Name Sports** as instructed in previous chapters

BEGINNING THE TUTORIAL

In this chapter you will be recording end-of-period adjustments, reconciling bank and credit card statements, changing account names, and preparing traditional end-of-period reports. Because QuickBooks Pro does not perform a traditional closing of the books, you will learn how to close the period to protect transactions and data recorded during previous accounting periods.

As in previous chapters, all transactions are listed on memos. The transaction date will be the same as the memo date unless otherwise specified within the transaction. To determine the account used in the transaction, refer to the Chart of Accounts.

CHANGE THE NAME OF EXISTING ACCOUNTS IN THE CHART OF ACCOUNTS

Even though transactions have been recorded during the month of January, QuickBooks Pro makes it a simple matter to change the name of an existing account. Once the name of an account has been changed, all transactions using the old name are updated and show the new account name.

> **MEMO**
> **DATE:** January 31, 2006
>
> On the recommendation of the company's CPA, you decided to change the account named Freight Income to Delivery Income.

➤ Change the account name of Freight Income

Access the Chart of Accounts using the keyboard shortcut **Ctrl+A**

Scroll through accounts until you see Freight Income, click **Freight Income**
Use the keyboard shortcut **Ctrl+E**
On the **Edit Account** screen, highlight **Freight Income**
Enter the new name **Delivery Income**
Change the description from **Freight Income** to **Delivery Income**
Click **OK** to record the name change and to close the **Edit Account** screen

- Notice that the name of the account appears as Delivery Income in the Chart of Accounts.

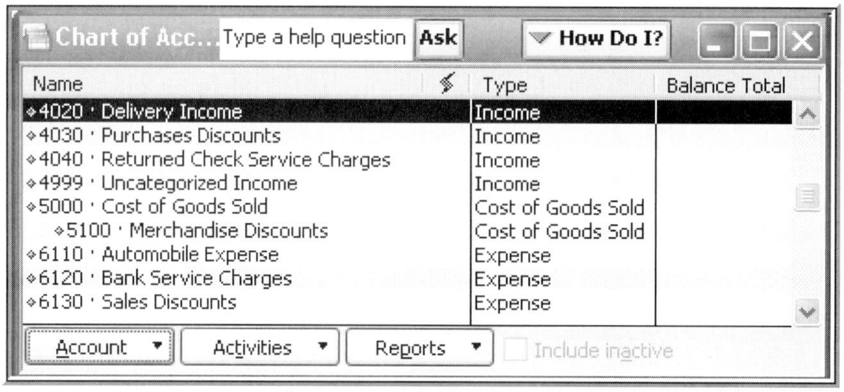

Do not close the **Chart of Accounts**

MAKE AN ACCOUNT INACTIVE

If you are not using an account and do not have plans to do so in the near future, the account may be made inactive. The account remains available for use, yet it does not appear on your Chart of Accounts unless you check the Show All check box.

> **MEMO**
> **DATE:** January 31, 2006
>
> At this time, Your Name Sports does not plan to rent any equipment. The account Equipment Rental should be made inactive. In addition, the company does not plan to use Franchise Fees. Make these accounts inactive.

Make the accounts listed above inactive

Click **Equipment Rental**
Click the **Account** button at the bottom of the Chart of Accounts, click **Make Inactive**

- The account no longer appears in the Chart of Accounts.

Make **Franchise Fees** inactive
Click **Franchise Fees**
Use the keyboard shortcut **Ctrl+E**
On the Edit Account screen, click the **Account is inactive** check box
Click **OK**

- If you wish to view all accounts, including the inactive ones, click the **Include Inactive** check box at the bottom of the Chart of Accounts, and all accounts will be displayed.
- Notice the icons that mark Equipment Rental and Franchise Fees as inactive accounts.

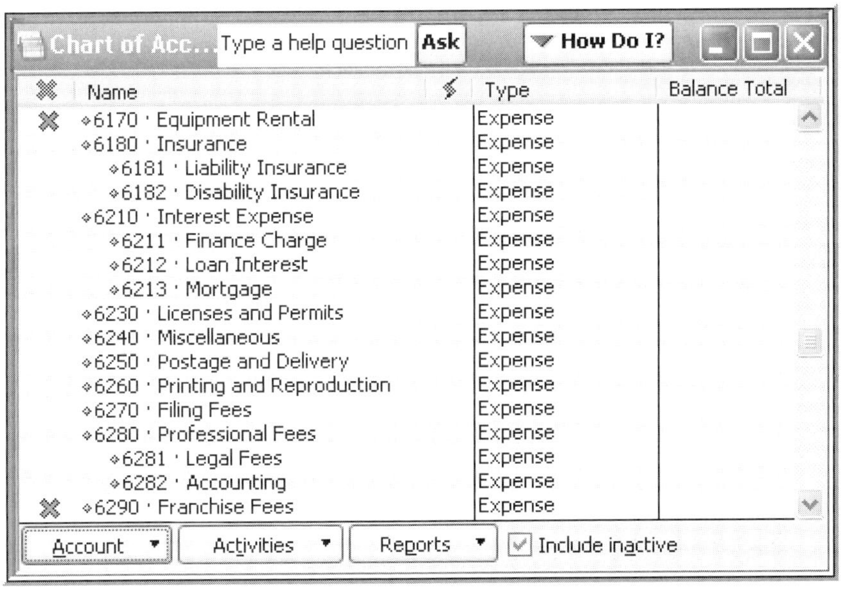

Do not close the **Chart of Accounts**

DELETE AN EXISTING ACCOUNT FROM THE CHART OF ACCOUNTS

If you do not want to make an account inactive because you have not used it and do not plan to use it at all, QuickBooks Pro allows the account to be deleted at anytime. However, as a safeguard, QuickBooks Pro does prevent the deletion of an account once it has been used even if it simply contains an opening or an existing balance.

MEMO
DATE: January 31, 2006

In addition to previous changes to account names, you find that you do not use nor will they use the expense accounts: Interest Expense: Mortgage, Taxes: Property, and Travel & Ent. Delete these accounts from the Chart of Accounts.

Delete the accounts listed in the memo

Scroll through Chart of Accounts until you see Interest Expense: Mortgage, click **Interest Expense: Mortgage**
Click the **Account** button at the bottom of the Chart of Accounts, click **Delete**
Click **OK** on the **Delete Accounts** dialog box
- The account has now been deleted.

Use the keyboard shortcut **Ctrl+D** to delete **Taxes: Property**
Also follow the same procedures to delete the subaccounts of **Travel & Ent.**
- *Note:* Whenever an account has subaccounts, the subaccounts must be deleted before QuickBooks Pro will let you delete the main account. This is what you must do before you can delete Travel & Ent. A subaccount is deleted the same as any other account. In fact, Taxes: Property was a subaccount of Taxes.

When the subaccounts of Travel & Ent. have been deleted, delete **Travel & Ent.**
Close the **Chart of Accounts**

FIXED ASSET MANAGEMENT

QuickBooks contains a Fixed Asset Manager in the program. When you purchase fixed assets that you need for your business, it's important to keep good records so you can track their cost, the cost of repairs and upgrades, and how much they depreciate from year to year. These amounts affect the worth of your business and the size of your tax bill.

Fixed asset items provide a way to keep important information about your assets in one convenient place.

You can create an item to track a fixed asset at several points during the asset's life cycle; however, it is recommended that you create the item when you buy the asset or setup the company.

You can create a fixed asset item from the Fixed Asset List or from a Transaction.

MEMO

DATE: January 31, 2006

When Your Name Sports was setup in QuickBooks, Office Equipment and Store Fixtures were designated as Fixed Assets but were not added to the Fixed Asset List. To work with the Fixed Asset List, the Fixed Assets need to be added to the list.

Create a fixed asset list

Click **Lists** on the menu bar
Click **Fixed Asset Item List**
Use the keyboard shortcut **Ctrl+N** to create a new item
Complete the information for the new item:
The **Asset Name** is **Store Fixtures**
The Item is **new**
The **Purchase Description** should be **Store Fixtures**
The **Date** is **12/31/05**
The **Cost** is **4500**
The **Asset Account** is **1520**
The **Asset Description** is **Store Fixtures**

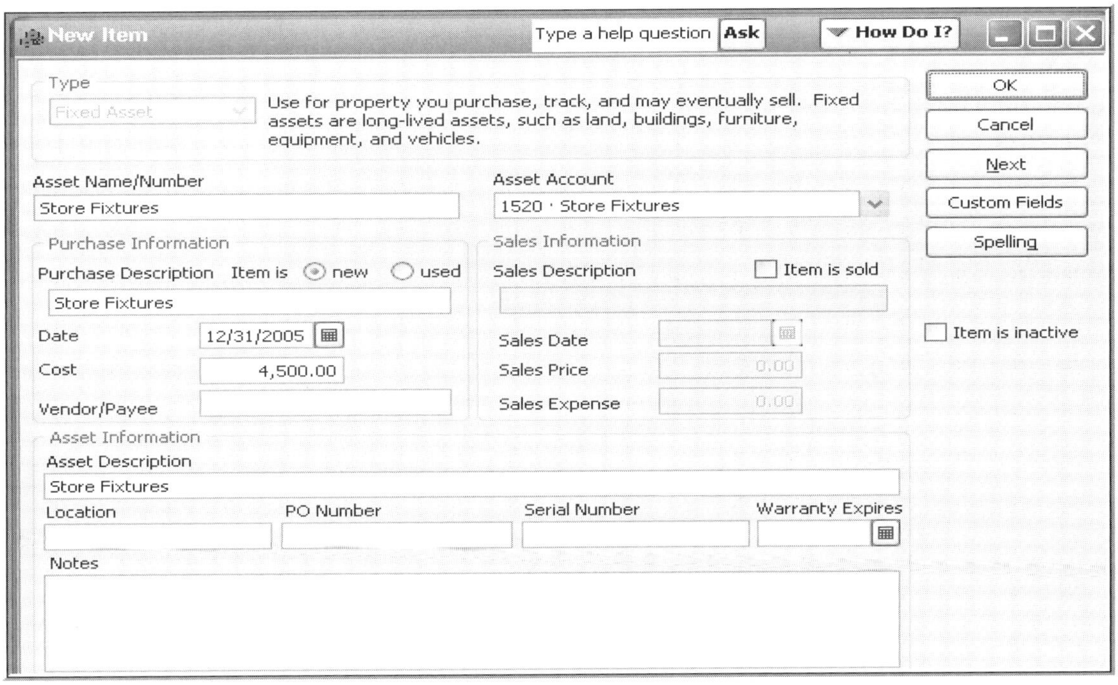

- Look at the bottom of the screen. If you want to add information for the items location, PO Number, Serial Number, and Warranty, fields are provided. There is also room to add Notes about the item.

When the information is entered for Store Fixtures, click **Next**
Repeat to add the Office Equipment with a cost of $5,000.00 to the list

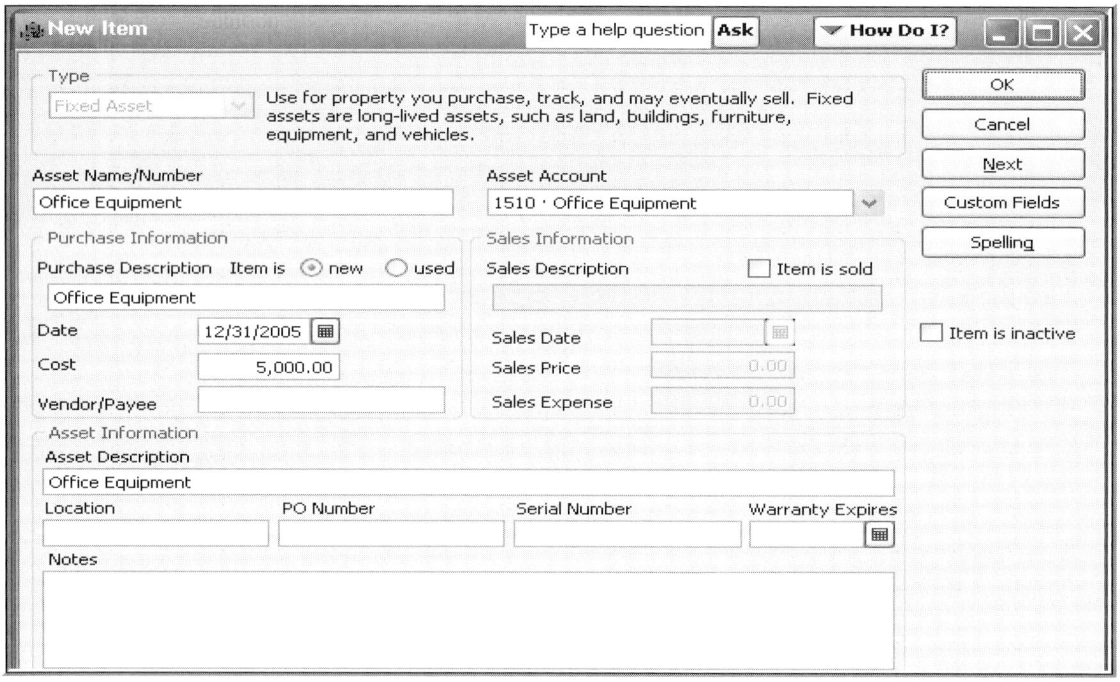

Click **OK**

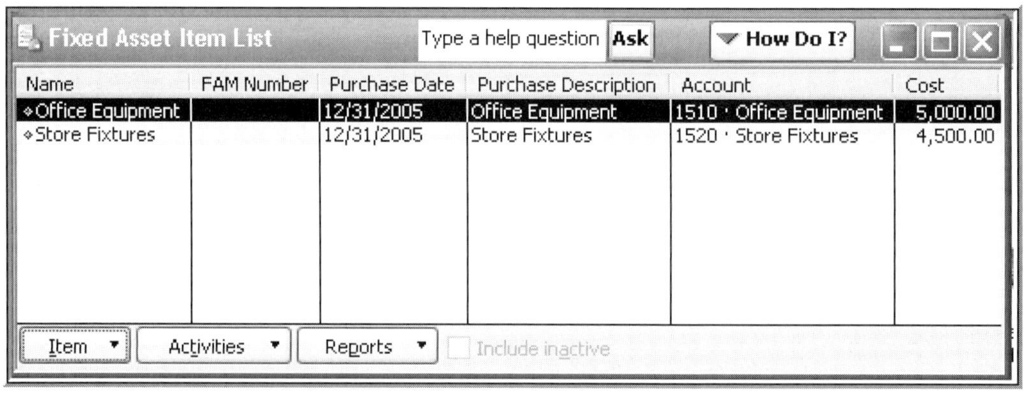

Close the Fixed Asset List

ADJUSTMENTS FOR ACCRUAL-BASIS ACCOUNTING

In accrual-basis accounting, the income from a period is matched against the expenses of a period in order to arrive at an accurate figure for net income. Thus, the revenue is earned at the time the service is performed or the sale is made regardless of when the cash is actually received. The same holds true when a business buys things or pays bills. In the accrual basis of accounting, the expense is recorded at the time the bill is received or the product or service is delivered regardless of the actual payment date. The cash basis of accounting records income or revenue at the time cash is received regardless of when the sale was made or the service performed. In cash-basis accounting, the expense is not recorded until it is paid.

There are several internal transactions that must be recorded when using the accrual basis of accounting. These entries are called adjusting entries. For example, equipment does wear out and will eventually need to be replaced. Rather than waiting until replacement to record the use of the equipment, an adjusting entry is made to allocate the use of equipment as an expense for a period. This is called *depreciation*. Certain items used in a business are paid for in advance. As these are used, they become expenses of the business. For example, insurance for the entire year would be used up month by month and should, therefore, be a monthly expense. Commonly, the insurance is billed and paid for the entire year. Until the insurance is used, it is an asset. Each month the portion of the insurance used becomes an expense for the month.

ADJUSTING ENTRIES—PREPAID EXPENSES

During the operation of a business, companies purchase supplies to have on hand for use in the operation of the business. In accrual-basis accounting, the supplies are considered to be assets (something the business owns) or prepaid expenses until they are used in the operation of the business. As the supplies are used, the amount used becomes an expense for the period. The same rationale applies to other things paid for in advance, such as insurance. At the end of the period, an adjusting entry must be made to allocate correctly the amount of prepaid assets to expenses.

The transactions for these adjustments may be recorded in the register for the account by clicking on the prepaid asset in the Chart of Accounts, or they may be made in the General Journal.

MEMO
DATE: January 31, 2006

NOTE from Tim: Rose, remember to record the monthly adjustment for Prepaid Insurance. The $250 is the amount we paid for two months of liability insurance coverage. Also, we have a balance of $521.98 in office supplies and a balance of $400 in sales supplies. Please adjust accordingly.

Record the adjusting entries for insurance expense, office supplies expense, and sales supplies expense in the General Journal.

Access the **General Journal**:
Click **Company,** click **Make General Journal Entries**
Record the adjusting entry for Prepaid Insurance
Click **OK** on the Assigning Numbers to Journal Entries screen
Enter **01/31/06** as the **Date**

- Entry No. is left blank unless you wish to record a specific number.
- Because all transactions entered for the month have been entered in the Journal as well as on an invoice or a bill, all transactions automatically have a Journal entry number. When the Journal is printed, your transaction number may be different from the answer key. Disregard the transaction number because it can change based on how many times you delete transactions, etc.

Tab to or click the **Account** column, click the drop-down list arrow for **Account**, click **6181 Liability Insurance Expense**
Tab to or click **Debit**

- The $250 given in the memo is the amount for two months.

Use the QuickBooks Calculator do determine the amount of the adjustment for the month:
Press the + sign
QuickBooks calculator shows and adding machine tape
Delete the 0.00 and enter **250**
Press / for division
Key **2**
Press **Enter**

- The calculation is performed and the amount is entered in the Debit column.

Tab to or click the **Memo** column, type **Adjusting Entry, Insurance**
Tab to or click **Account**, click the drop-down list arrow for Account, click **1340 Prepaid Insurance**

- The amount for the **Credit** column should have been entered automatically. If not, enter **125**.

Enter the Memo information by using the copy command:

Click the **Memo** column for the Debit entry
Drag through the memo **Adjusting Entry, Insurance**
When the memo is highlighted, use the keyboard command **Ctrl+C** to copy the memo
Click in the **Memo** column for the Credit entry
Use the keyboard command **Ctrl+V** to paste the memo into the column

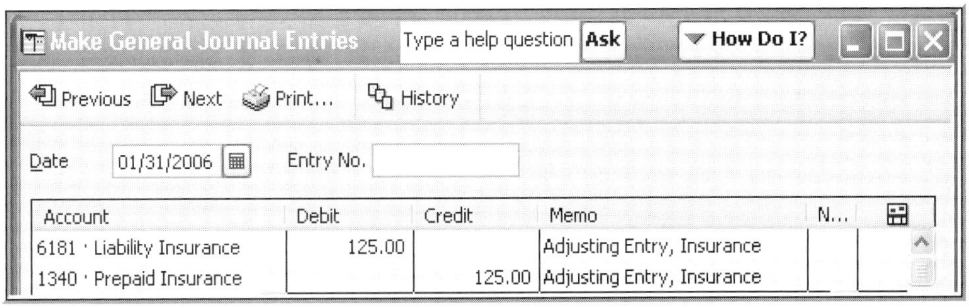

Click **NEXT** to record the adjustment and to advance to the next General Journal Entry screen
Repeat the above procedures to record the adjustment for the office supplies used

- The amount given in the memo is the balance of the account after the supplies have been used.
- The actual amount of the supplies used in January must be calculated.

Determine the balance of the Office Supplies account by using the keyboard shortcut **Ctrl+A** to access the Chart of Accounts
Use the QuickBooks Calculator or the Windows Calculator to determine the amount of the adjustment

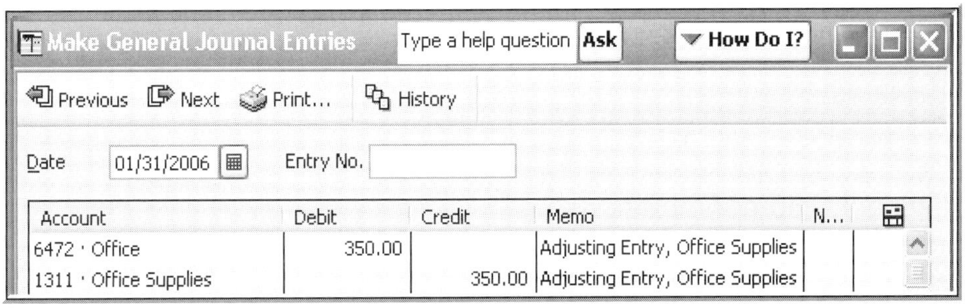

When the entry is complete, click **Next**
Repeat the above procedures to record the adjustment for the sales supplies used

- The amount given in the memo is the balance of the account after the supplies have been used. The actual amount of the supplies used in January must be calculated.

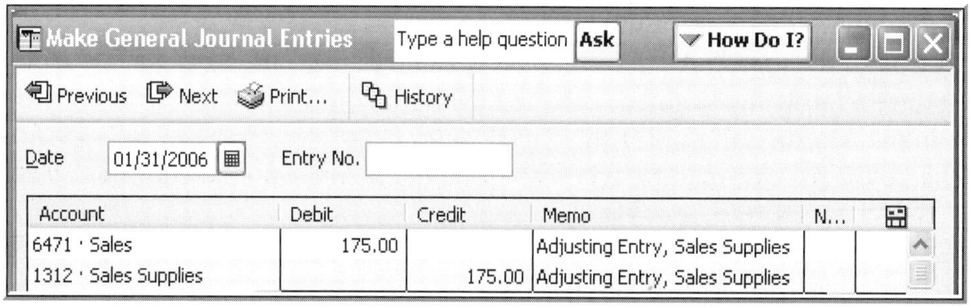

When the entry is complete, click **Save & New**

ADJUSTING ENTRIES—DEPRECIATION

Using the accrual basis of accounting requires companies to record an expense for the amount of equipment used in the operation of the business. Unlike supplies, where you can actually see the paper supply diminishing, it is very difficult to see how much of a cash register has been used up during the month. To account for the fact that machines do wear out and need to be replaced, an adjustment is made for depreciation. This adjustment correctly matches the expenses of the period against the revenue of the period.

The adjusting entry for depreciation can be made in the depreciation account register, or it can be made in the General Journal.

MEMO
DATE: January 31, 2006

Having received the necessary depreciation schedules, Rose records the adjusting entry for depreciation:

Office Equipment, $85 per month
Store Fixtures, $75 per month

Record a compound adjusting entry for depreciation of the office equipment and the store fixtures in the General Journal:

The Date is **01/31/06**
Entry No. is left blank

- In order to use the automatic calculation feature of QuickBooks Pro, the credit entries will be entered first.

Tab to or click the **Account** column, click the drop-down list arrow for **Account**, click **1512 Depreciation** under **Office Equipment**

Tab to or click **Credit**, enter **85**

Tab to or click **Memo**, enter **Adjusting Entry, Depreciation**

Tab to or click the **Account** column, click the drop-down list arrow for **Account**, click **1522 Depreciation** under **Store Fixtures**

- Disregard the 85 that shows as a debit. Entering an amount in the credit column and pressing the tab key will eliminate the debit.

Tab to or click **Credit**, enter **75**

Tab to or click **Memo**, enter **Adjusting Entry, Depreciation**

Tab to or click the **Account** column, click the drop-down list arrow for **Account**, click **6150 Depreciation Expense**

Debit column should automatically show **160**

Tab to or click **Memo**, enter **Adjusting Entry, Depreciation**

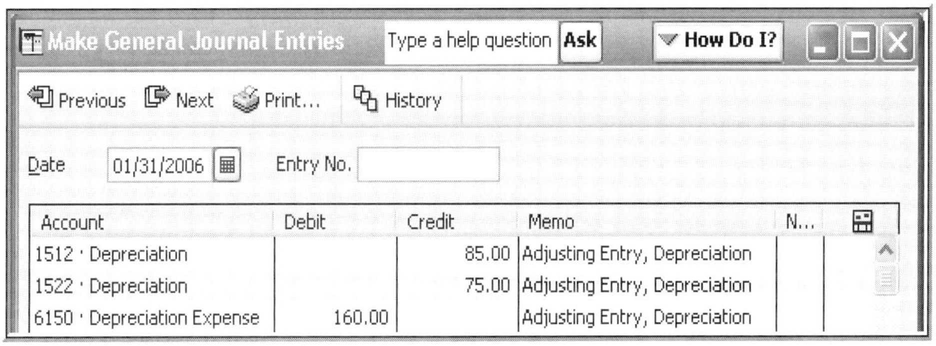

Click **Save & Close** to record the adjustment and close the General Journal

- If you get a message regarding tracking fixed assets on journal entries, click **OK**.

VIEW GENERAL JOURNAL

Once transactions have been entered in the General Journal, it is important to view them. QuickBooks Pro also refers to the General Journal as the Journal and allows it to be viewed or printed at any time. Even with the special ways in which transactions are entered in QuickBooks Pro through invoices, bills, checks, and account registers, the Journal is still the book of original entry. All transactions recorded for the company may be viewed in the Journal even if they were entered elsewhere.

View the Journal for January

Click **Reports** on the menu bar, point to **Accountant & Taxes**, click **Journal**

The Dates are from **01/01/06** to **01/31/06**

Tab to generate the report

Your Name Sports
Journal
January 2006

Type	Date	Num	Name	Memo	Account	Debit	Credit
				Adjusting Entry, Insurance	1340 · Prepaid Insurance		125.00
						125.00	125.00
General Journal	01/31/2006			Adjusting Entry, Office Supplies	6472 · Office	350.00	
				Adjusting Entry, Office Supplies	1311 · Office Supplies		350.00
						350.00	350.00
General Journal	01/31/2006			Adjusting Entry, Sales Supplies	6471 · Sales	175.00	
				Adjusting Entry, Sales Supplies	1312 · Sales Supplies		175.00
						175.00	175.00
General Journal	01/31/2006			Adjusting Entry, Depreciation	1512 · Depreciation		85.00
				Adjusting Entry, Depreciation	1522 · Depreciation		75.00
				Adjusting Entry, Depreciation	6150 · Depreciation Expe...	160.00	
						160.00	160.00
						43,875.91	**43,875.91**

Scroll through the report to view all transactions recorded in the Journal

- Only the transactions made from January 1 through January 31, 2006 are displayed. Since opening balances have also been entered during the creation of the company, note that the first transaction shown is 48—Invoice No. 1.
- Viewing the Journal and checking the accounts used in transactions, the dates entered for transactions, and the amounts recorded for the transactions is an excellent way to discover errors and determine corrections that need to be made.

Close the report without printing

DEFINITION OF A PARTNERSHIP

A partnership is a business owned by two or more individuals. Because it is unincorporated, each partner owns a share of all the assets and liabilities. Each partner receives a portion of the profits based on the percentage of his or her investment in the business or according to any partnership agreement drawn up at the time the business was created. Because the business is owned by the partners, they do not receive a salary. Any funds obtained by the partners are in the form of withdrawals against their share of the profits. QuickBooks Pro makes it easy to set up a partnership and create separate accounts, if desired, for each partner's equity, investment, and withdrawals.

OWNER WITHDRAWALS

In a partnership, owners cannot receive a paycheck because they own the business. An owner withdrawing money from a business—even to pay personal expenses—is similar to an individual withdrawing money from a savings account. A withdrawal simply decreases the owners' capital. QuickBooks Pro allows you to establish a separate account for owner withdrawals for each owner. If a separate account is not established, owner withdrawals may be subtracted directly from each owner's capital or investment account.

MEMO
DATE: January 31, 2006

Because both partners work in the business full time, they do not earn a paycheck. Prepare checks for your monthly withdrawal of $1,000 and Tim's monthly withdrawal of $1,000.

Write the checks for the owner withdrawals

Usc the keyboard shortcut **Ctrl+W** to open the **Write Checks - Checking** window:
Click the check box **To be printed**, the Check No. should be **To Print**
Date should be **01/31/06**
Enter **Your Name** on the **Pay to the Order of** line, press the **Tab** key

- Because your name was not added to any list when the company was created, the **Name Not Found** dialog box appears on the screen.

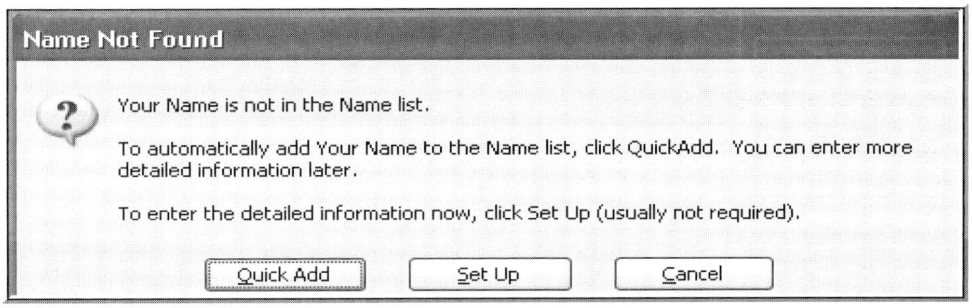

Click **Quick Add** to add your name to a list
The **Select Name Type** dialog box appears
Click **Other**

Click **OK**

- Your name is added to a list of *Other* names, which is used for owners, partners, and other miscellaneous names.

Tab to or click in the area for the amount of the check

- If necessary, delete any numbers showing for the amount (0.00).

Enter **1000**

Tab to or click **Memo**, enter **Owner Withdrawal for January**

Tab to or click in the Account column at the bottom of the check, click the drop-down list arrow, click the Equity account **3013 Your Name, Drawing**

- The amount 1,000.00 should appear in the Amount column.
- If it does not, tab to or click in the Amount column and enter 1000.
- Make sure To be printed is selected.

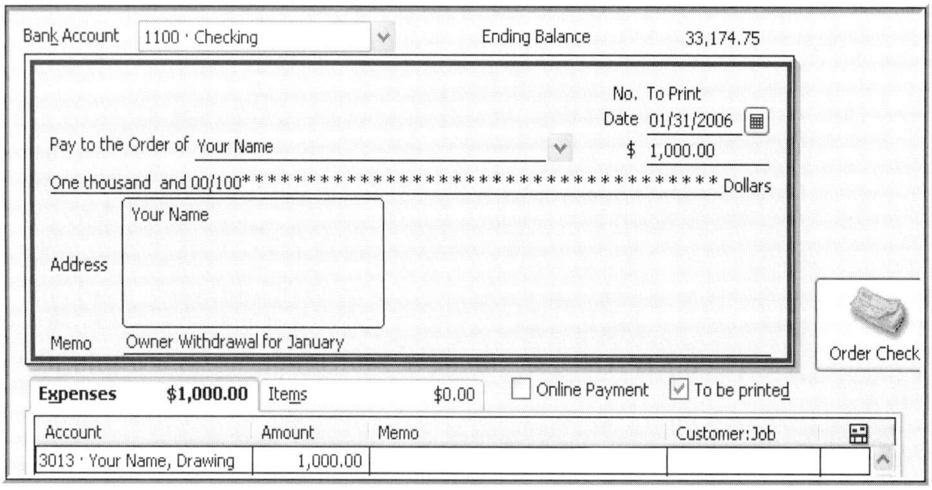

Click **Next** to record the check and advance to the next check

Repeat the above procedures to prepare Check No. 7 for Tim Bailey for $1,000 withdrawal

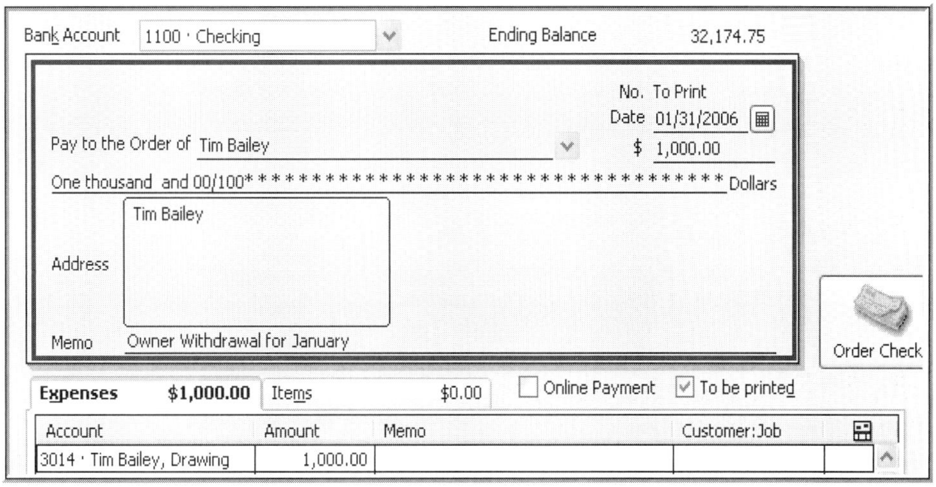

Click **Next**
Click the drop-down list arrow for **Print**
Click **Print Batch**
The **Select Checks to Print** dialog box appears
The **First Check Number** should be **6**

- If necessary, change the number to **6**.

If both checks have a check mark, click **OK**, if not, click **Select All** and then click **OK**

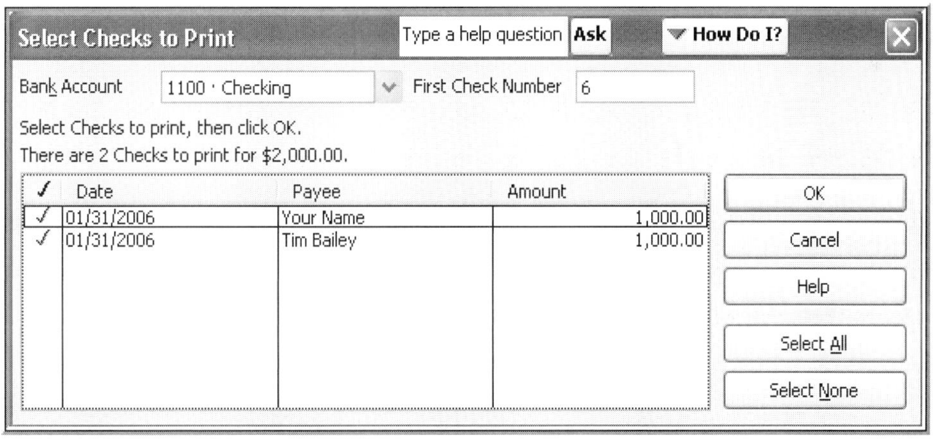

The Check style should be Standard
Once the check has printed successfully, click **OK** to close **Did check(s) print OK?** dialog box
Close **Write Checks - Checking**

PREPARE BALANCE SHEET

A balance sheet proves that assets equal liabilities plus owners' equity; however, the owners' equity in a partnership may be organized in a manner that is more meaningful than is currently shown.

▶ View the Balance Sheet for January 31, 2006

Click **Reports** on the menu bar, point to **Company & Financial**, click **Balance Sheet Standard**
Enter **01/31/06** for the date
Tab to generate the report
Scroll through the report

- Notice the Equity section, especially the Investment and Drawing accounts for each owner.
- Also notice the Your Name & Bailey Capital account balance. When the capital for both owners is combined into one account, the report does not indicate how much of the capital is for each owner.

Your Name Sports
Balance Sheet
As of January 31, 2006

		Jan 31, 06
Equity		
3010 · Your Name & Bailey Capital		
3011 · Your Name, Investment	20,000.00	
3012 · Tim Bailey, Investment	20,000.00	
3013 · Your Name, Drawing	-1,000.00	
3014 · Tim Bailey, Drawing	-1,000.00	
3010 · Your Name & Bailey Capital - Other	25,459.44	
Total 3010 · Your Name & Bailey Capital		63,459.44
Net Income		2,667.07
Total Equity		66,126.51
TOTAL LIABILITIES & EQUITY		**82,243.89**

Do not close the report

CREATE AN INDIVIDUAL CAPITAL ACCOUNT FOR EACH OWNER

A better display of owners' equity would be to show all equity accounts for each owner grouped together by owner. In addition, each owner should have an individual capital account.

MEMO
DATE: January 31, 2006

Change the account number of Your Name & Bailey, Capital, to 3100. Create separate Capital accounts for Your Name and Tim Bailey. Name the accounts 3110 Your Name, Capital, and 3120 Tim Bailey, Capital. In addition, renumber Your Name Investment account to 3111 and your Drawing account to 3112. Make these subaccounts of Your Name, Capital. Do the same for Tim's accounts: 3121 Investment and 3122 Drawing.

Create separate Capital accounts and change subaccounts for existing owners' equity accounts

Access the **Chart of Accounts** as previously instructed
Click **3010 Your Name & Bailey, Capital**
Click **Account** at the bottom of the **Chart of Accounts**, click **Edit**
Change the account number to **3100**
Click **OK**
Click **Account** at the bottom of the **Chart of Accounts**, click **New**
Click the drop-down list arrow for **Type**, click **Equity**
Tab to or click **Number**, enter **3110**
Tab to or click **Name**, enter **Your Name, Capital**
Click **Subaccount**, click the drop-down list arrow next to **Subaccount**, click **3100 Your Name & Bailey, Capital**
Click **OK**
Click **Your Name, Investment**
Edit the account following steps previously listed
Change the account number to **3111**
Make this a subaccount of **3110 Your Name, Capital**
Click **OK** when the changes have been made
Make the following changes to **Your Name, Drawing**: Account number is **3112**, Subaccount of **3110**
Create the Equity account **3120 Tim Bailey, Capital**: Account 3120 is a subaccount of **3100**
Change **3012 Tim Bailey, Investment** to **3121**: Account 3121 is a subaccount of **3120**
Change **3014 Tim Bailey, Drawing** to **3122**: Account 3122 is a subaccount of **3120**

◆3000 · Retained Earnings	Equity	
◆3100 · Your Name & Bailey Capital	Equity	63,459.44
◆3110 · Your Name, Capital	Equity	19,000.00
◆3111 · Your Name, Investment	Equity	20,000.00
◆3112 · Your Name, Drawing	Equity	-1,000.00
◆3120 · Tim Bailey, Capital	Equity	19,000.00
◆3121 · Tim Bailey, Investment	Equity	20,000.00
◆3122 · Tim Bailey, Drawing	Equity	-1,000.00

Close the **Chart of Accounts**

- Since the Balance Sheet is still on the screen, the changes made to the Capital accounts will be shown in the report. If you get a screen asking if you would like to refresh the report, click **Yes**.
- Notice the change in the Equity section of the Balance Sheet.

Your Name Sports
Balance Sheet
As of January 31, 2006

		Jan 31, 06	
Equity			
3100 · Your Name & Bailey Capital			
3110 · Your Name, Capital			
3111 · Your Name, Investment	20,000.00		
3112 · Your Name, Drawing	-1,000.00		
Total 3110 · Your Name, Capital		19,000.00	
3120 · Tim Bailey, Capital			
3121 · Tim Bailey, Investment	20,000.00		
3122 · Tim Bailey, Drawing	-1,000.00		
Total 3120 · Tim Bailey, Capital		19,000.00	
3100 · Your Name & Bailey Capital - Other		25,459.44	
Total 3100 · Your Name & Bailey Capital			63,459.44
Net Income			2,667.07
Total Equity			66,126.51
TOTAL LIABILITIES & EQUITY			**82,243.89**

Do not close the report

DISTRIBUTE CAPITAL TO EACH OWNER

As you view the Balance Sheet, you will notice that the balance for Your Name & Bailey, Capital, is $25,459.44. The report does not indicate how much of the capital should be distributed to each partner because Your Name & Bailey, Capital, is a combined Capital account. In order to clarify this section of the report, the capital should be distributed between the two owners. Each owner has contributed an equal amount as an investment in the business, so the capital should be divided equally between Tim and you.

Make an adjusting entry to distribute capital between the two owners

Access the **General Journal Entry** screen as previously instructed

Transfer the amount in the account **3100 Your Name & Bailey, Capital –Other** to the owners' individual capital accounts by debiting Account **3100** for **25459.44**

Memo for all entries in the transaction is **Transfer Capital to Individual Accounts**

Transfer one-half of the amount debited to **3110 Your Name, Capital**, by crediting this account

- To determine one-half of the amount use QuickMath as follows: Click after the credit amount, press /, enter **2,** and press **Enter**.

Credit **3120 Tim Bailey, Capital**, for the other half of the amount

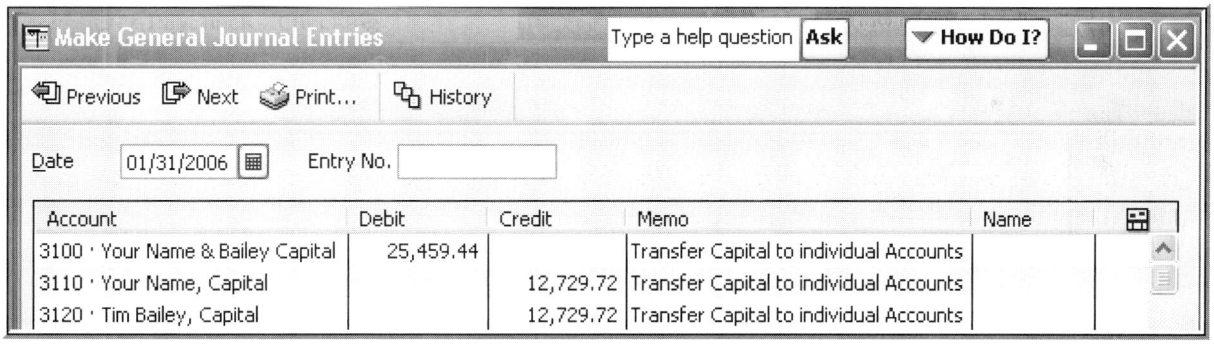

Click **Save & Close** to record and return to the Balance Sheet

- Notice the change in the Equity section of the Balance Sheet.
- Total of 3100 Your Name & Bailey, Capital, is still 63,459.44; however, accounts 3110 Your Name, Capital-Other and 3120 Tim Bailey, Capital-Other each show 12,729.72, which is the amount of capital for each owner.

Your Name Sports
Balance Sheet
As of January 31, 2006

		Jan 31, 06	
Equity			
3100 · Your Name & Bailey Capital			
3110 · Your Name, Capital			
3111 · Your Name, Investment	20,000.00		
3112 · Your Name, Drawing	-1,000.00		
3110 · Your Name, Capital - Other	12,729.72		
Total 3110 · Your Name, Capital		31,729.72	
3120 · Tim Bailey, Capital			
3121 · Tim Bailey, Investment	20,000.00		
3122 · Tim Bailey, Drawing	-1,000.00		
3120 · Tim Bailey, Capital - Other	12,729.72		
Total 3120 · Tim Bailey, Capital		31,729.72	
Total 3100 · Your Name & Bailey Capital			63,459.44
Net Income			2,667.07
Total Equity			66,126.51
TOTAL LIABILITIES & EQUITY			**82,243.89**

Close the report

BANK RECONCILIATION

Each month the Checking account should be reconciled with the bank statement to make sure both balances agree. The bank statement will rarely have an ending balance that matches the balance of the Checking account. This is due to several factors: outstanding checks (written by the business but not paid by the bank), deposits in transit (deposits that were made too late to be included on the bank statement), bank service charges, interest earned on checking accounts, collections made by the bank, errors made in recording checks and/or deposits by the company or by the bank, etc.

In order to have an accurate amount listed as the balance in the Checking account, it is important that the differences between the bank statement and the Checking account be reconciled. If something such as a service charge or a collection made by the bank appears on the bank statement, it needs to be recorded in the Checking account.

Reconciling a bank statement is an appropriate time to find any errors that may have been recorded in the Checking account. The reconciliation may be out of balance because a transposition was made (recording $45 rather than $54), a transaction was recorded backwards, a transaction was recorded twice, or a transaction was not recorded at all.

OPEN RECONCILE – CHECKING

To begin the reconciliation, the Reconcile - Checking window needs to be opened. Verify the information shown for the Checking account. The Beginning Balance should match the amount of the final balance on the last reconciliation, or it should match the starting account balance.

The Begin Reconciliation screen initiates the account reconciliation. On this screen, information regarding the ending balance, service charges, and interest earned is entered.

MEMO
DATE: January 31, 2006

Received the bank statement from Old Mammoth Bank. The bank statement is dated January 31, 2006. Rose needs to reconcile the bank statement and print a Reconciliation Report for Tim and you.

➤ Reconcile the bank statement for January

ENTER BANK STATEMENT INFORMATION AND COMPLETE BEGIN RECONCILIATION

Information appearing on the bank statement is entered into the Begin Reconciliation window as the first step in the reconciliation process. The information entered includes the ending balance, bank service charges, and interest earned.

OLD MAMMOTH BANK
12345 Old Mammoth Road
Mammoth Lakes, CA 93546
(909) 555-3880

Your Name Sports
875 Mountain Road
Mammoth Lakes, CA 93546

Acct. # 123-456-7890 **January 2006**

Beginning Balance 1/1/06	25,943.00		$25,943.00
1/18/06 Deposit	10,469.44		36,412.44
1/20/06 NSF Returned Check		100.00	36,312.44
1/20/06 Check 1		80.44	36,232.00
1/25/06 Check 2		294.00	35,938.00
1/25/06 Check 3		1,837.50	34,100.50
1/25/06 Check 4		312.60	33,787.90
1/25/06 Check 5		613.15	33,174.75
1/31/06 Office Equip. Loan Pmt.: $10.33 Principal, $53.42 Interest		63.75	33,111.00
1/31/06 Store Fixtures Loan Pmt.: $8.61 Principal, $44.51 Interest		53.12	33,057.88
1/31/06 Service Chg.		8.00	33,049.88
1/31/06 NSF Charge		10.00	33,039.88
1/31/06 Interest	54.05		33,093.93
Ending Balance 1/31/06			33,093.93

Open the **Reconcile - Checking** window and enter preliminary information on the Begin Reconciliation screen

Click **Reconcile** on the QuickBooks Home Page

- *Note:* If you need to exit the Begin Reconciliation screen before it is complete, click **Cancel**.

The **Account To Reconcile** should be **1100 Checking**

- If not, click the drop-down list arrow, click **Checking**.

The **Statement Date** should be **01/31/06**

Beginning Balance should be **25,943.00**

- This is the same amount as the Checking account starting balance.

Enter the **Ending Balance** from the bank statement, **33,093.93**
Tab to or click **Service Charge**, enter the **Service Charge**, **18.00**

- Note that this includes both the service charge of $8.00 and the $10.00 charge for Kent Trestle's NSF check in Chapter 5.

Tab to or click Service Charge **Date**, the date should be **01/31/06;** if not, change it
Tab to or click **Account**, click the drop-down list arrow for **Account**, click **6120 Bank Service Charges**
Tab to or click **Interest Earned**, enter **54.05**
Tab to or click Interest Earned **Date**, the date should be **01/31/06**; if not, change it
Tab to or click **Account**, enter the account number **7010** for Interest Income

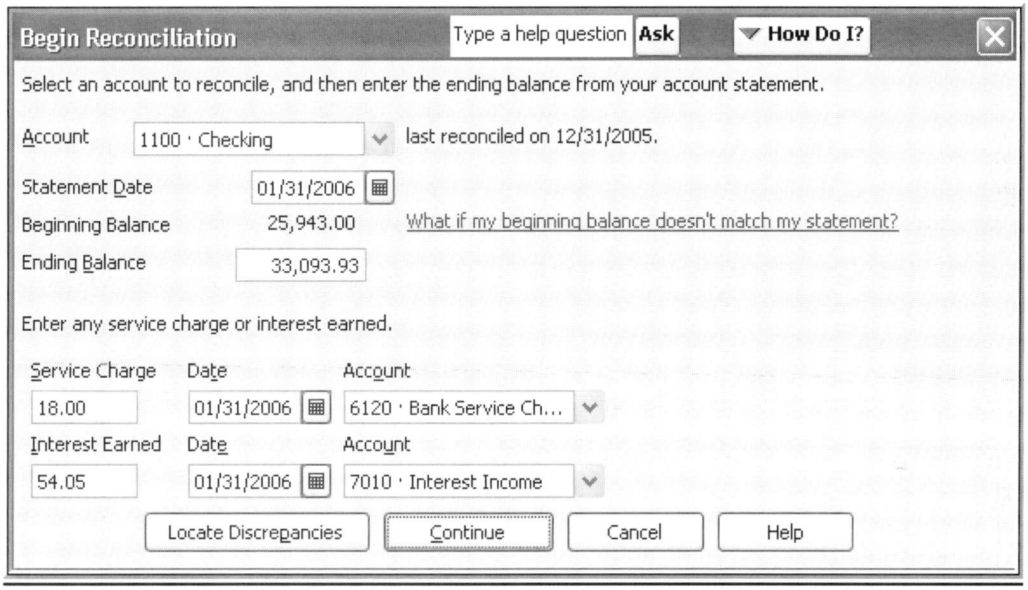

Click **Continue**

MARK CLEARED TRANSACTIONS FOR BANK RECONCILIATION

Once bank statement information for the ending balance, service charges, and interest has been entered, compare the checks and deposits listed on the statement with the transactions for the Checking account. If a deposit or a check is listed correctly on the bank statement and in the Reconcile - Checking window, it has cleared and should be marked. An item may be marked individually by positioning the cursor on the deposit or the check and clicking the primary mouse button. If all deposits and checks match, click the Mark All button to mark all the deposits and checks at once. To remove all the checks, click the Unmark All button. To unmark an individual item, click the item to remove the check mark.

Mark cleared checks and deposits

- *Note:* If you need to exit the Reconcile - Checking screen before it is complete, click **Leave**. If you click **Reconcile Now**, you must Undo the reconciliation and start over.
- If you need to return to the Begin Reconciliation window, click the **Modify** button.

Compare the bank statement with the **Reconcile - Checking** window
Click the items that appear on both statements
Look at the bottom of the **Reconcile - Checking** window
You have marked cleared:
2 Deposits and Other Credits for 10,523.49

- This includes interest earned.

7 Checks and Payments for 3,255.69

- This includes the $100 NSF check returned, the $10 charge for the return of the NSF check, and the $8 service charge.

The Ending Balance is 33,093.96
The Cleared Balance is 33,210.80
There is a Difference of -116.87

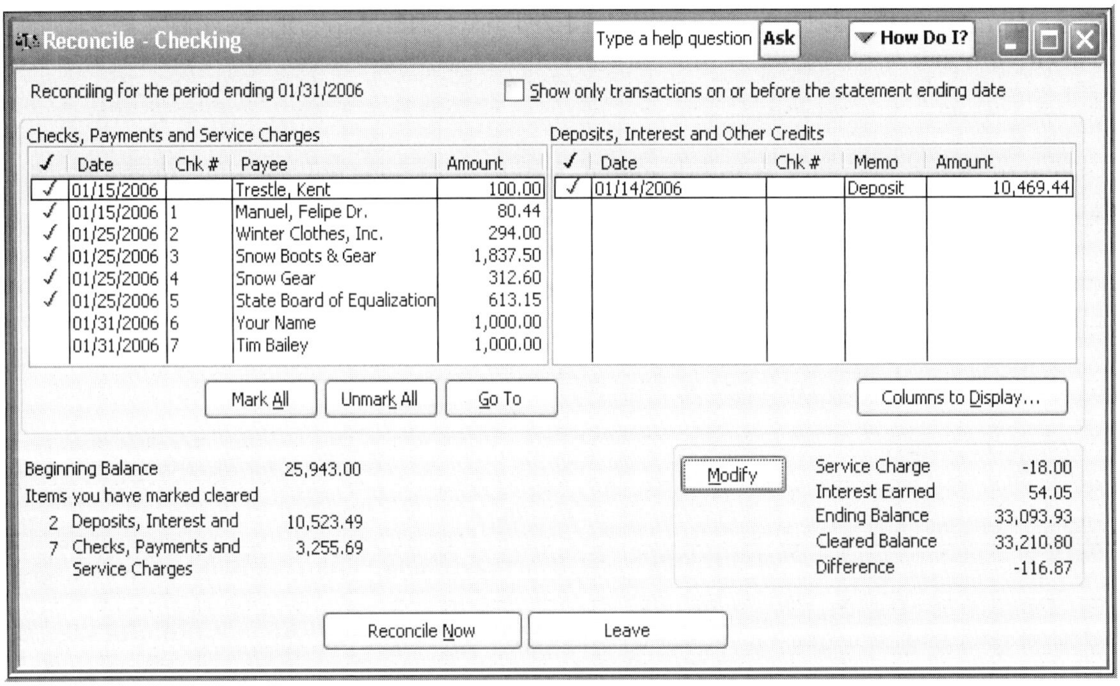

The bank statement should remain on the screen while you complete the next section

ADJUSTING AND CORRECTING ENTRIES—BANK RECONCILIATION

As you complete the reconciliation, you may find errors that need to be corrected or transactions that need to be recorded. Anything entered as a service charge or interest earned will be entered automatically when the reconciliation is complete and the Reconcile Now button is clicked. To correct an error such as a transposition, click on the entry then click the Go To button. The original entry will appear on the screen. The correction can be made and will show in the Reconcile - Checking window. If there is a transaction, such as an automatic loan payment to the bank, access the register for the account used in the transaction and enter the payment.

Enter the automatic loan payments shown on the bank statement

Use the keyboard shortcut **Ctrl+R** to open the register for the **1100 Checking** account:
In the blank transaction at the bottom of the register, enter the **Date**, **01/31/06**
Tab to or click **Number**, enter **Transfer**
Tab to or click **Payee**, enter **Old Mammoth Bank**
Tab to or click the **Payment** column

- Because Old Mammoth Bank does not appear on any list, you will get a **Name Not Found** dialog box when you move to another field.

Click the **Quick Add** button to add the name of the bank to the Name List
Click **Other**
Click **OK**

- Once the name of the bank has been added to the Other List, the cursor will be positioned in the **Payment** column.

Enter **63.75** in the **Payment** column
Click the **Account** column
Click **Splits** at the bottom of the register
Click the drop-down list arrow for **Account**, click **6212 Loan Interest**
Tab to or click **Amount**, delete the amount 63.75 shown
Enter **53.42** as the amount of interest
Tab to or click **Memo**, enter **Interest Office Equipment Loan**
Tab to or click **Account**, click the drop-down list arrow for **Account**, click **2510 Office Equipment Loan**

- The correct amount of principal, 10.33, should be shown as the amount.
- Tab to or click **Memo**, enter **Principal Office Equipment Loan**

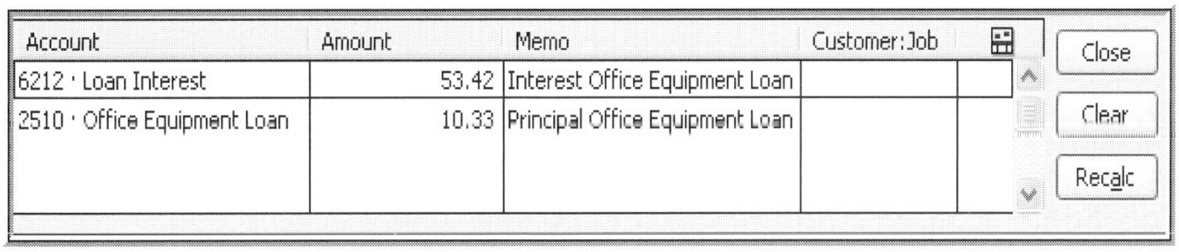

Click **Close**

- This closes the window for the information regarding the way the transaction is to be "split" between accounts.

For the **Memo** in the Checking Register, record **Loan Payment Office Equipment**
Click the **Record** button to record the transaction

- Notice that the loan payment does not appear as the last transaction in the register.

01/31/2006	Transfer	Old Mammoth Bank	63.75			33,111.00
	CHK	-split- Loan Payment Office Equipment				

Repeat the procedures to record the loan payment for store fixtures

- When you enter the Payee as Old Mammoth Bank, the amount for the previous transaction (63.75) appears in amount.

Enter the new amount **53.12**
Click **Splits**
Click the appropriate accounts and enter the correct amount for each item

- The accounts used for the office equipment loan payment may appear. Click the drop-down list arrow and select the appropriate accounts for the store fixture loan payment.
- Refer to the bank statement for details regarding the amount of the payment for interest and the amount of the payment applied to principal.

Account	Amount	Memo	Customer:Job
6212 · Loan Interest	44.51	Interest Store Fixtures Loan	
2520 · Store Fixtures Loan	8.61	Principal Store Fixtures Loan	

Close | Clear | Recalc

Click **Close** to close the window for the information regarding the "split" between accounts
Enter the transaction **Memo**
Click **Record** to record the loan payment

01/31/2006	Transfer	Old Mammoth Bank	53.12			33,057.88
	CHK	-split- Loan Payment Store Fixtures				

Close the **Checking Register**

- You should return to **Reconcile - Checking**.

Scroll to the top of **Checks and Payments**

- Notice the two entries for the payments in Checks and Payments.

Mark the two entries

- At this point the Ending Balance and Cleared Balance should be equal—$33,093.93 with a difference of 0.00.

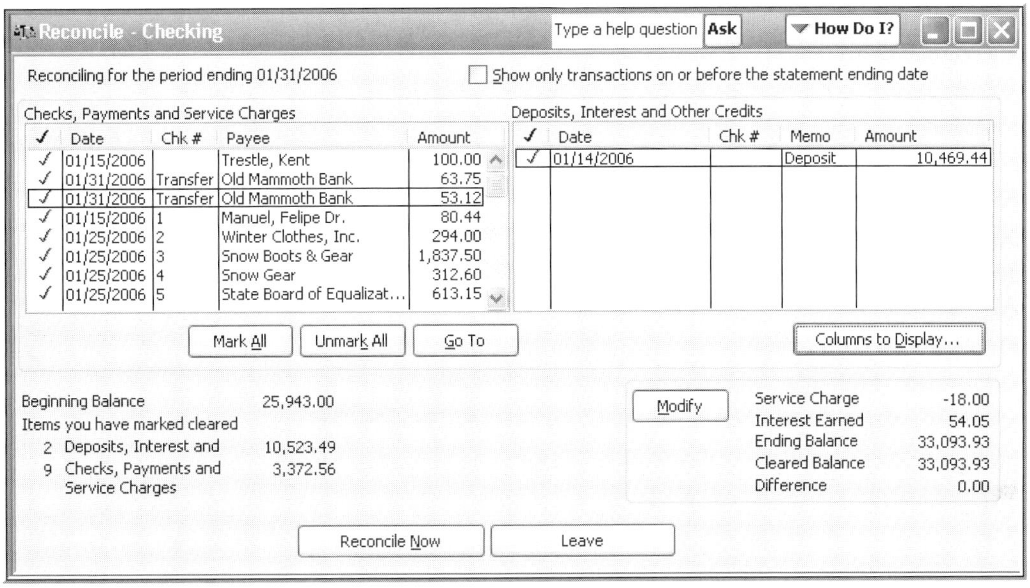

If your entries agree with the above, click **Reconcile Now** to finish the reconciliation

- If your reconciliation is not in agreement, do not click **Reconcile Now** until the errors are corrected.
- Once you click **Reconcile Now**, you may not return to this **Reconciliation - Checking** window. You would have to Undo the reconciliation and start over.

PRINT A RECONCILIATION REPORT

As soon as the Ending Balance and the Cleared Balance are equal or when you finish marking and click Reconcile Now, a screen appears allowing you to select the level of Reconciliation Report you would like to print. You may select Detail, which shows all the transactions that were reconciled, or Summary, which shows the beginning balance, the totals of the deposits and checks, and the ending balance. You may print the report at the time you have finished reconciling the account, or you may print the report later by returning to the Reconciliation window. QuickBooks Pro keeps your last two Reconciliation Reports in memory. If you think you may want to print the report after it is no longer one of the two reconciliation reports in memory, you can print the report to a file to save it permanently.

Print a Detail Reconciliation report

On the **Reconciliation Complete** screen, click **Detail**, click **Display**

Adjust the column widths so the report will print on one page and all information is displayed in full

Your Name Sports

Reconciliation Detail

1100 · Checking, Period Ending 01/31/2006

Type	Date	Num	Name	Clr	Amount	Balance
Beginning Balance						**25,943.00**
Cleared Transactions						
Checks and Payments - 9 items						
Bill Pmt -Check	01/25/2006	3	Snow Boots & Gear	✓	-1,837.50	-1,837.50
Sales Tax Payment	01/25/2006	5	State Board of Equalization	✓	-613.15	-2,450.65
Bill Pmt -Check	01/25/2006	4	Snow Gear	✓	-312.60	-2,763.25
Bill Pmt -Check	01/25/2006	2	Winter Clothes, Inc.	✓	-294.00	-3,057.25
Invoice	01/15/2006	10	Trestle, Kent	✓	-100.00	-3,157.25
Check	01/15/2006	1	Manuel, Felipe Dr.	✓	-80.44	-3,237.69
Check	01/31/2006	Transfer	Old Mammoth Bank	✓	-63.75	-3,301.44
Check	01/31/2006	Transfer	Old Mammoth Bank	✓	-53.12	-3,354.56
Check	01/31/2006			✓	-18.00	-3,372.56
Total Checks and Payments					-3,372.56	-3,372.56
Deposits and Credits - 2 items						
Deposit	01/31/2006			✓	54.05	54.05
Deposit	01/14/2006			✓	10,469.44	10,523.49
Total Deposits and Credits					10,523.49	10,523.49
Total Cleared Transactions					7,150.93	7,150.93
Cleared Balance					7,150.93	33,093.93

Print as previously instructed in Portrait orientation
When the report finishes printing, close the report

VIEW THE CHECKING ACCOUNT REGISTER

Once the bank reconciliation has been completed, it is wise to scroll through the Check Register to view the effect of the reconciliation on the account. You will notice that the check column shows a check mark for all items that were marked as cleared during the reconciliation. If at a later date an error is discovered, the transaction may be changed, and the correction will be reflected in the Beginning Balance on the reconciliation.

View the register for the Checking account

Access the register as previously instructed
To display more of the register, click the check box for **1-Line**
Scroll through the register

- Notice that the transactions are listed in chronological order. Even though the bank reconciliation transactions were recorded after the checks written on January 31, the bank reconciliation transactions appear before the checks because they were recorded as a Transfer.

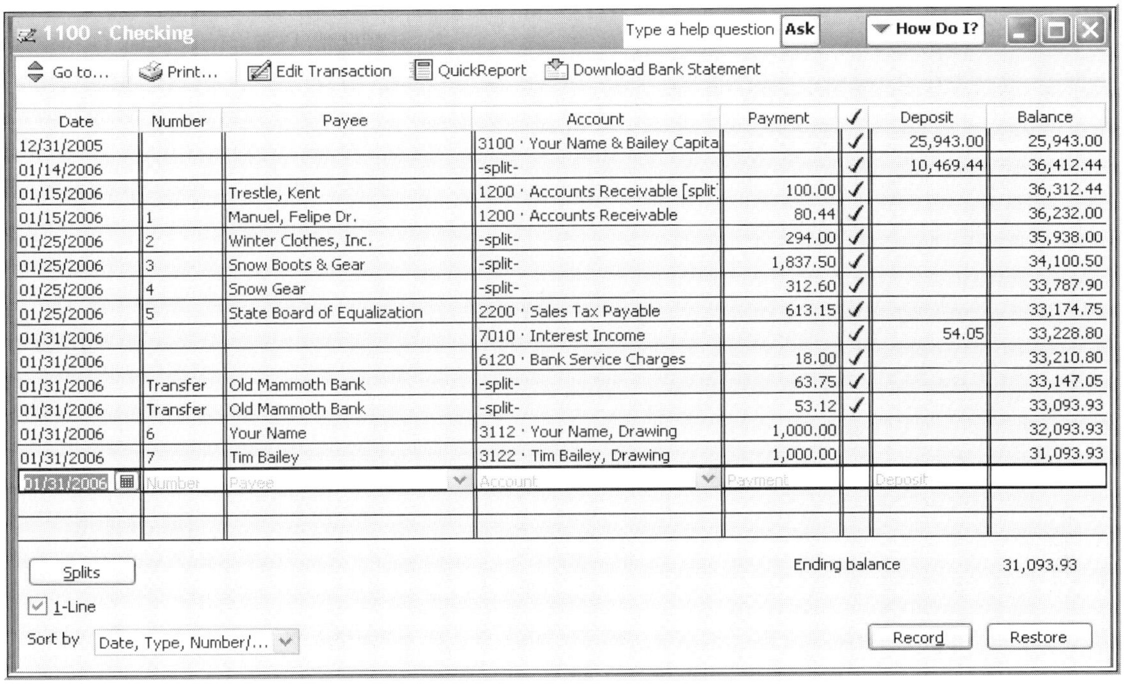

1100 · Checking

Date	Number	Payee	Account	Payment	✓	Deposit	Balance
12/31/2005			3100 · Your Name & Bailey Capita		✓	25,943.00	25,943.00
01/14/2006			-split-		✓	10,469.44	36,412.44
01/15/2006		Trestle, Kent	1200 · Accounts Receivable [split]	100.00	✓		36,312.44
01/15/2006	1	Manuel, Felipe Dr.	1200 · Accounts Receivable	80.44	✓		36,232.00
01/25/2006	2	Winter Clothes, Inc.	-split-	294.00	✓		35,938.00
01/25/2006	3	Snow Boots & Gear	-split-	1,837.50	✓		34,100.50
01/25/2006	4	Snow Gear	-split-	312.60	✓		33,787.90
01/25/2006	5	State Board of Equalization	2200 · Sales Tax Payable	613.15	✓		33,174.75
01/31/2006			7010 · Interest Income		✓	54.05	33,228.80
01/31/2006			6120 · Bank Service Charges	18.00	✓		33,210.80
01/31/2006	Transfer	Old Mammoth Bank	-split-	63.75	✓		33,147.05
01/31/2006	Transfer	Old Mammoth Bank	-split-	53.12	✓		33,093.93
01/31/2006	6	Your Name	3112 · Your Name, Drawing	1,000.00			32,093.93
01/31/2006	7	Tim Bailey	3122 · Tim Bailey, Drawing	1,000.00			31,093.93

Ending balance 31,093.93

- Notice that the final balance of the account is $31,093.93.

Close the register

Leave the Chart of Accounts open

CREDIT CARD RECONCILIATION

Any account used in QuickBooks Pro may be reconciled. As with a checking account, it is a good practice to reconcile the Credit Card account each month. When the credit card statement is received, the transactions entered in QuickBooks Pro should agree with the transactions shown on the credit card statement. A reconciliation of the credit card should be completed on a monthly basis.

> **MEMO**
> **DATE:** January 31, 2006
>
> The monthly bill for the Visa has arrived and is to be paid. Prior to paying the monthly credit card bill, reconcile the Credit Card account.

➡ Reconcile and pay the credit card bill

Click **2100 Visa** in the Chart of Accounts, click the **Activities** button, click **Reconcile Credit Card**

The Beginning Balance should be **150.00**

OLD MAMMOTH BANK
VISA
12345 Old Mammoth Road
Mammoth Lakes, CA 93546
(619) 555-3880

Your Name Sports
875 Mountain Road
Mammoth Lakes, CA 93546 **Acct. # 098-776-4321**

Beginning Balance 1/1/06		150.00	$150.00
1/23/06 Mountain Office Supply Company		21.98	171.98
1/23/06 Ski Supplies		300.00	471.98
1/25/06 Sports Accessories		350.00	821.98
1/25/06 Shoes Galore		400.00	1,221.98
Ending Balance 1/31/06			1,221.98

Minimum Payment Due: $50.00 Payment Due Date: February 15, 2006

Compare the credit card statement with the **Reconcile Credit Card - Visa**

Enter the **Statement Date** of **01/31/06**

Enter the **Ending Balance** of **1,221.98** in the **Begin Reconciliation** window

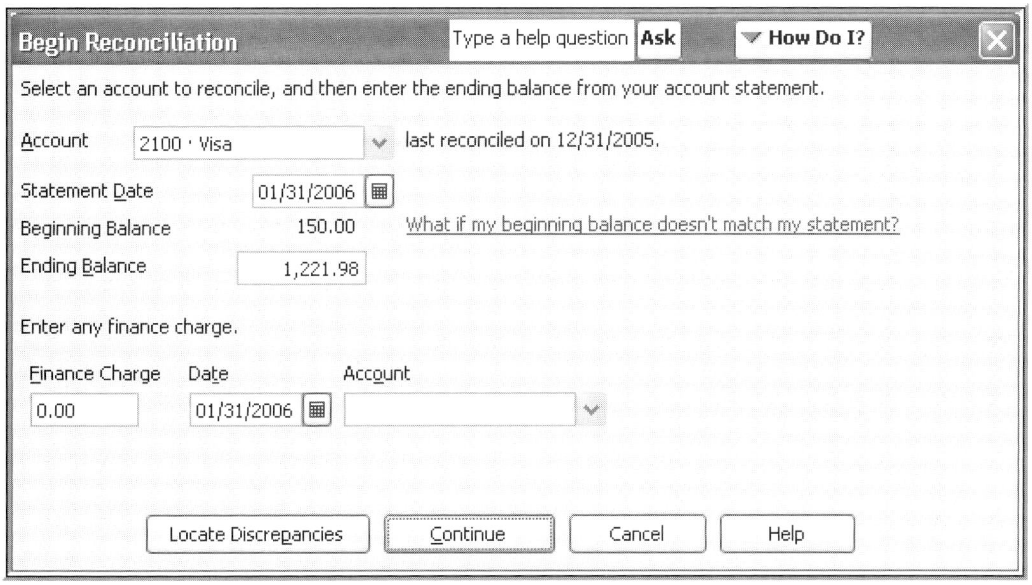

Click **Continue**

Mark each item that appears on both the statement and in the reconciliation EXCEPT for the $**400** transaction for Shoes Galore

RECORD AN ADJUSTMENT TO A RECONCILIATION

In QuickBooks Pro 2006, adjustments to reconciliations may be made during the reconciliation process. In addition, account reconciliations may be eliminated by clicking an Undo button.

Verify that all items are marked EXCEPT the charge for **$400** for Shoes Galore

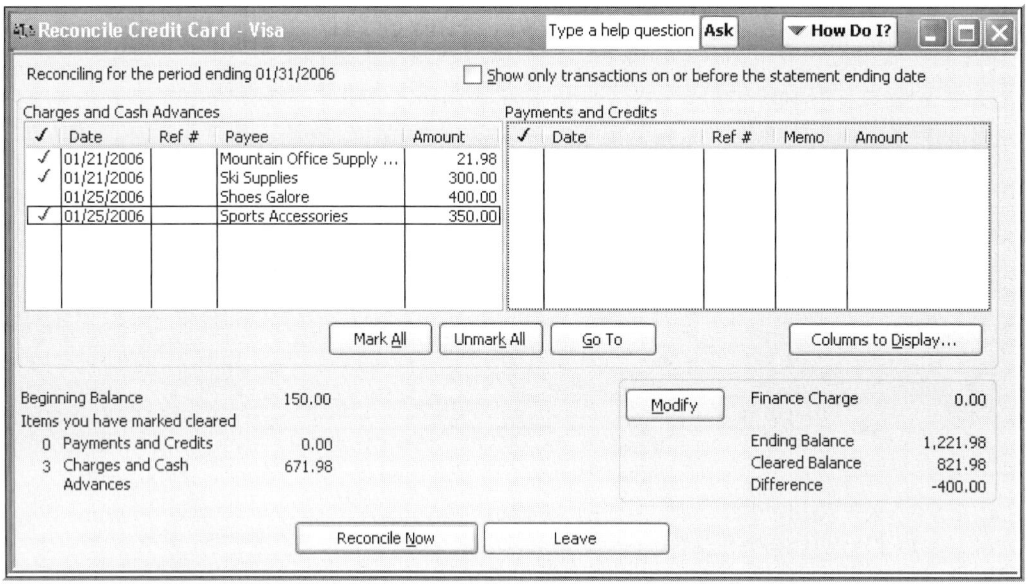

Click **Reconcile Now**

- The Reconcile Adjustment screen appears because there was a $400 Difference shown at the bottom of the reconciliation.
- Even though the error on the demonstration reconciliation is known, an adjustment will be entered and then deleted at a later time.

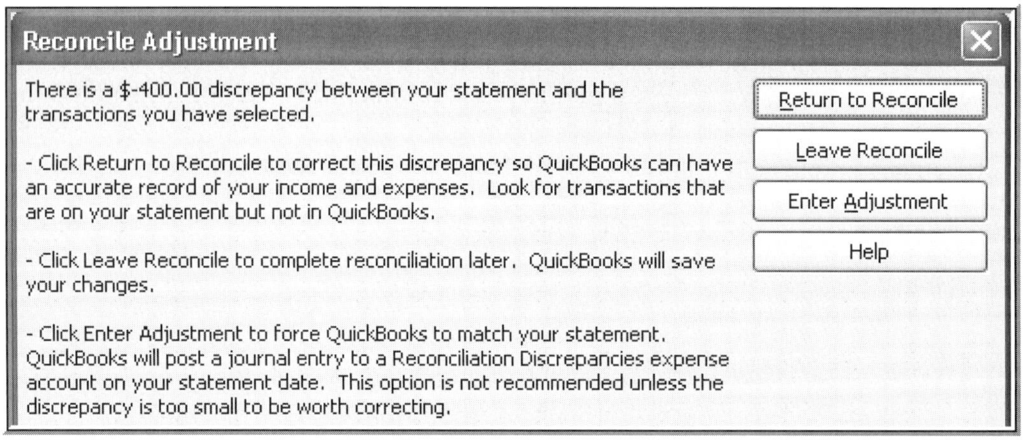

Click **Enter Adjustment**
Click **Cancel** on the Make Payment screen

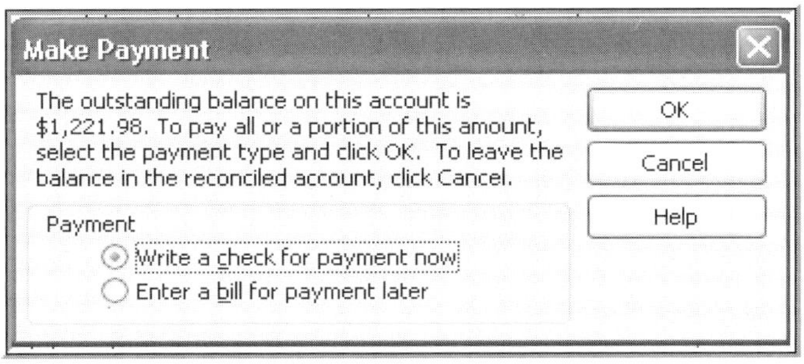

- The Reconciliation report is generated

Display the Detail report

Your Name Sports
Reconciliation Detail
2100 · Visa, Period Ending 01/31/2006

Type	Date	Num	Name	Clr	Amount	Balance
Beginning Balance						**150.00**
Cleared Transactions						
Checks and Payments - 4 items						
General Journal	01/31/2006			✓	-400.00	-400.00
Bill Pmt -CCard	01/25/2006		Sports Accessories	✓	-350.00	-750.00
Credit Card Charge	01/21/2006		Ski Supplies	✓	-300.00	-1,050.00
Credit Card Charge	01/21/2006		Mountain Office Supply Company	✓	-21.98	-1,071.98
Total Checks and Payments					-1,071.98	-1,071.98
Total Cleared Transactions					-1,071.98	-1,071.98
Cleared Balance					1,071.98	1,221.98
Uncleared Transactions						
Checks and Payments - 1 item						
Bill Pmt -CCard	01/25/2006		Shoes Galore		-400.00	-400.00
Total Checks and Payments					-400.00	-400.00
Total Uncleared Transactions					-400.00	-400.00
Register Balance as of 01/31/2006					1,471.98	1,621.98

- Notice that there is a General Journal entry for $400 in the Cleared Transactions section of the report. This is the Adjustment made by QuickBooks.
- Also note that Uncleared Transactions shows the $400 for Shoes Galore.

Close the Reconciliation Detail report without printing

- When you return to the chart of Accounts, you will see a new account, **4000 Reconciliation Discrepancies**

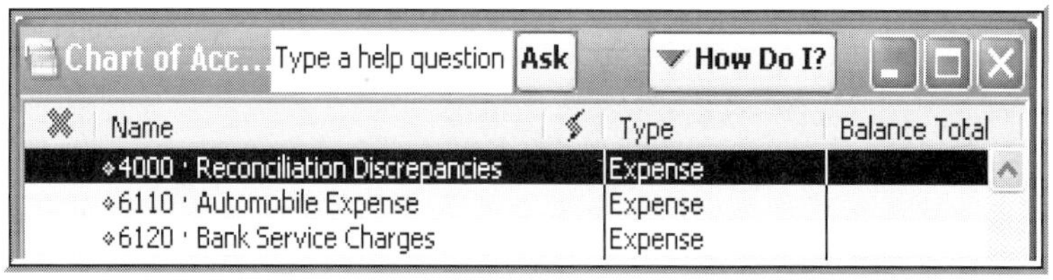

UNDO A PREVIOUS RECONCILIATION, DELETE AN ADJUSTMENT, AND REDO A RECONCILIATION

If an error is discovered after an account reconciliation has been completed, the reconciliation may be removed by using the Undo Reconciliation feature located on the Locate Discrepancies screen. If an adjusting entry for a reconciliation has been made, it may be deleted. This is useful if you had a discrepancy when making the reconciliation and found the error at a later date.

Undo the credit card reconciliation and delete the adjusting entry made by QuickBooks

Access the **Reconcile Credit Card** window as previously instructed
Click **Locate Discrepancies** on the Begin Reconciliation screen

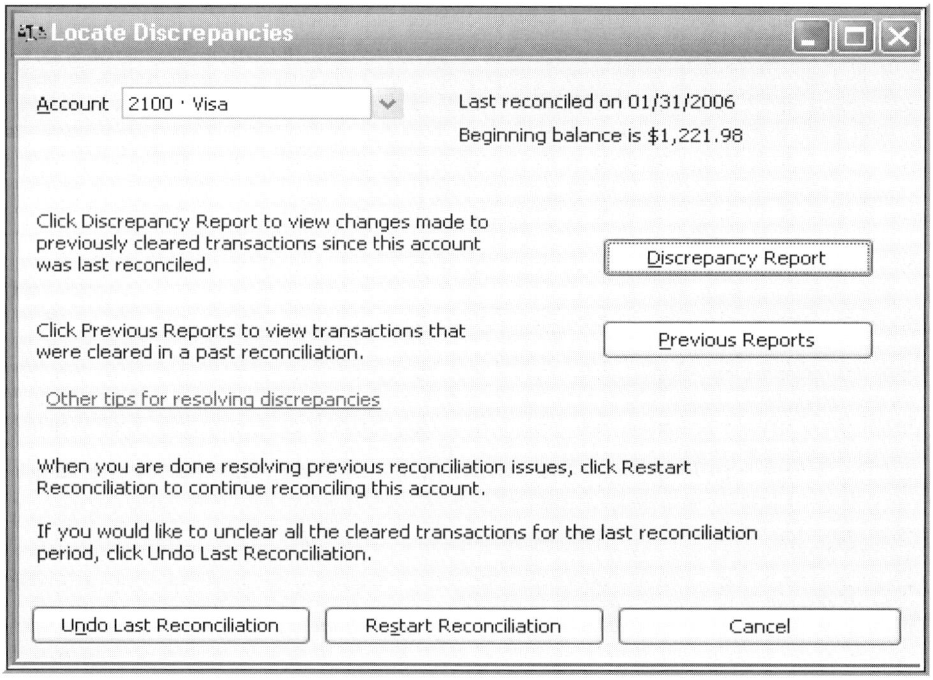

Click the **Undo Last Reconciliation** button

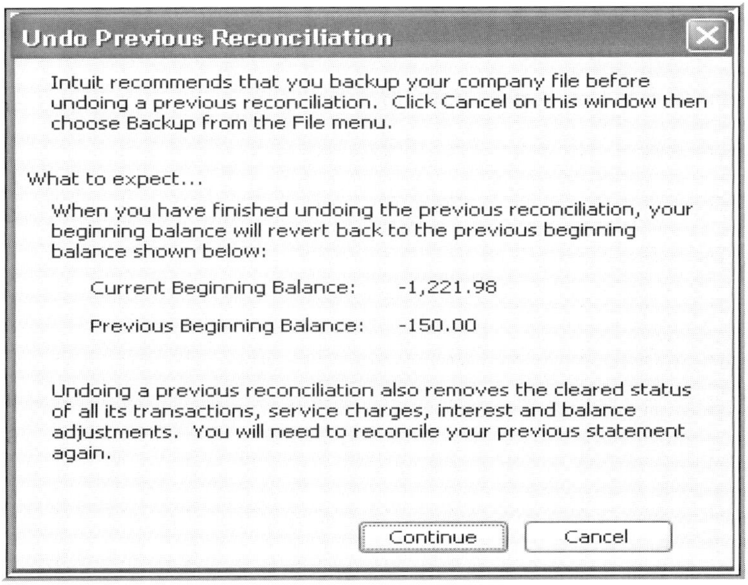

Click **Continue** on the Undo Previous Reconciliation screen

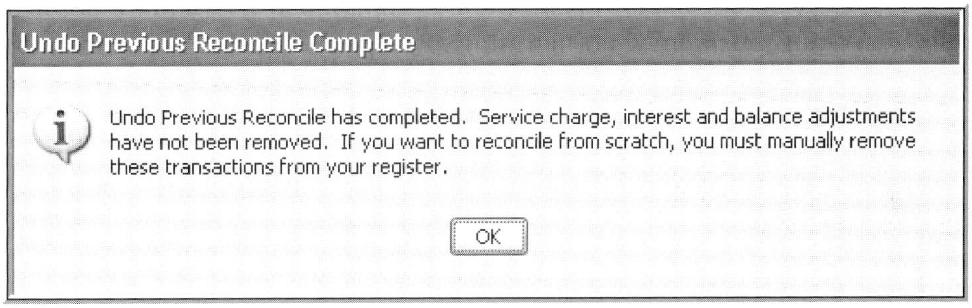

Click **OK** on the Undo Previous Reconcile Complete screen

- Remember that service charges, interest, and balance adjustments are not removed. If you have entered any of these items on the previous reconciliation, they will need to be deleted from the Journal manually. None of the items were entered on the previous reconciliation so there is nothing to be deleted.

Click the **Restart Reconciliation** button on the Locate Discrepancies screen

- You will return to the Begin Reconciliation screen.

Make sure the **Statement Date** is **01/31/06**
Enter the **Ending Balance** of **1221.98**
Click **Continue**
Mark all the items listed on the Credit Card Statement INCLUDING the $400 for Shoes Galore
Click the Adjusting entry for 01/31/06

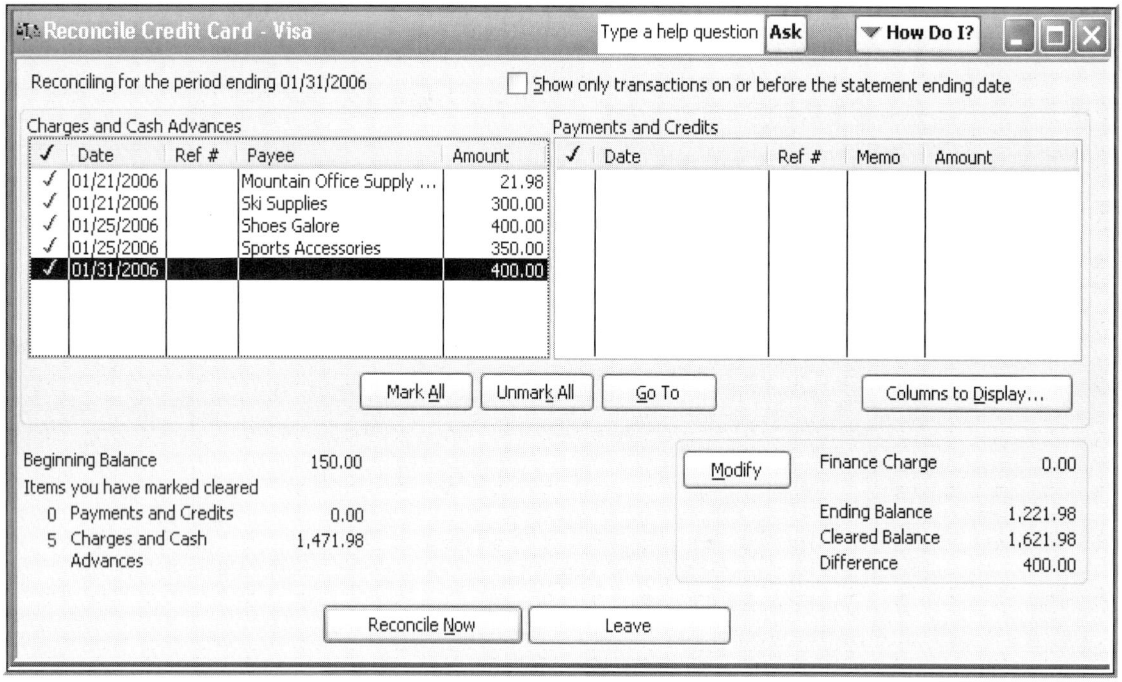

Click **Go To**

- You will go to the Make General Journal Entries screen

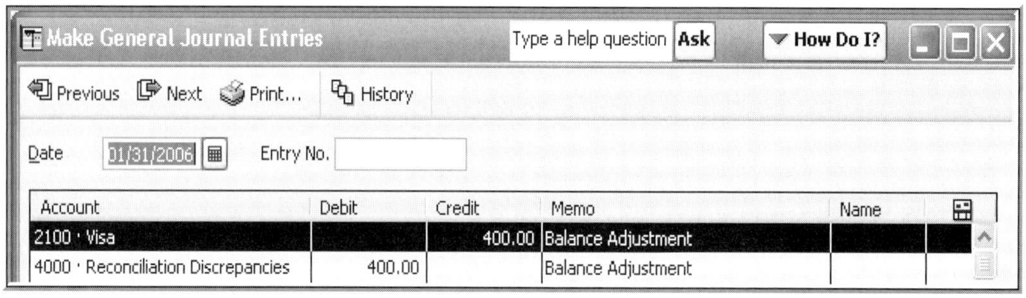

Use the keyboard shortcut **Ctrl+D** to delete the entry

After the adjustment has been deleted, close the Journal

Verify that the adjusting entry has been deleted and that the Ending and Cleared Balances are 1,221.98 and the Difference is 0.00

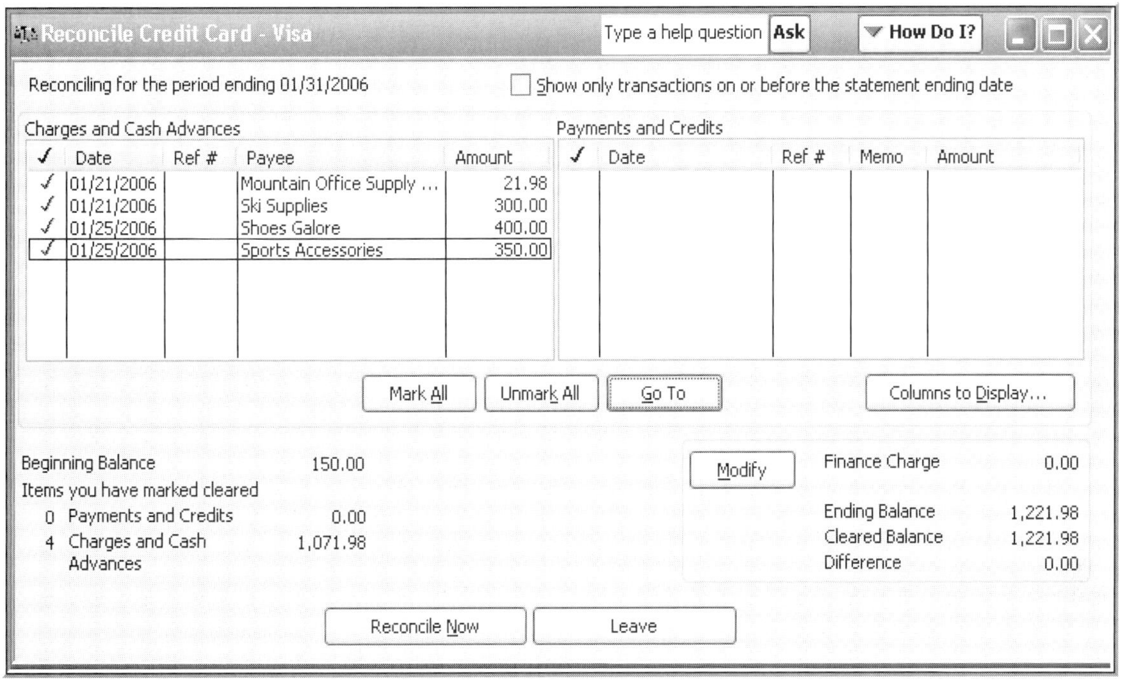

Click **Reconcile Now**

When the **Make Payment** dialog box appears on the screen

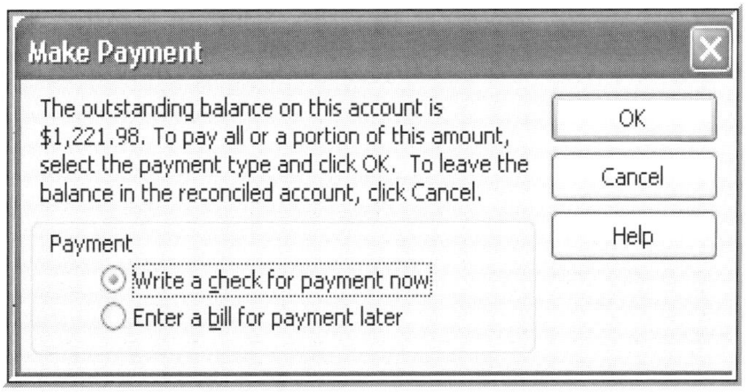

Make sure **Write a check for payment now** is selected, click **OK**

- If it is not selected, click **Write a check for payment now** to select, then click **OK**.

Display and print a **Reconciliation Detail Report** following the procedures given for the Bank Reconciliation Report

Your Name Sports
Reconciliation Detail
2100 · Visa, Period Ending 01/31/2006

Type	Date	Num	Name	Clr	Amount	Balance
Beginning Balance						**150.00**
Cleared Transactions						
Checks and Payments - 4 items						
Bill Pmt -CCard	01/25/2006		Shoes Galore	✓	-400.00	-400.00
Bill Pmt -CCard	01/25/2006		Sports Accessories	✓	-350.00	-750.00
Credit Card Charge	01/21/2006		Ski Supplies	✓	-300.00	-1,050.00
Credit Card Charge	01/21/2006		Mountain Office Supply Company	✓	-21.98	-1,071.98
Total Checks and Payments					-1,071.98	-1,071.98
Total Cleared Transactions					-1,071.98	-1,071.98
Cleared Balance					1,071.98	1,221.98
Register Balance as of 01/31/2006					1,071.98	1,221.98
Ending Balance					**1,071.98**	**1,221.98**

Close the Reconciliation Detail report
The payment check should appear on the screen
Enter **8** as the check number
The **Date** of the check should be **01/31/06**
Click the drop-down list next to **Pay to the Order of**, click **Old Mammoth Bank**

- If you get a dialog box for **Auto Recall**, click **No**.

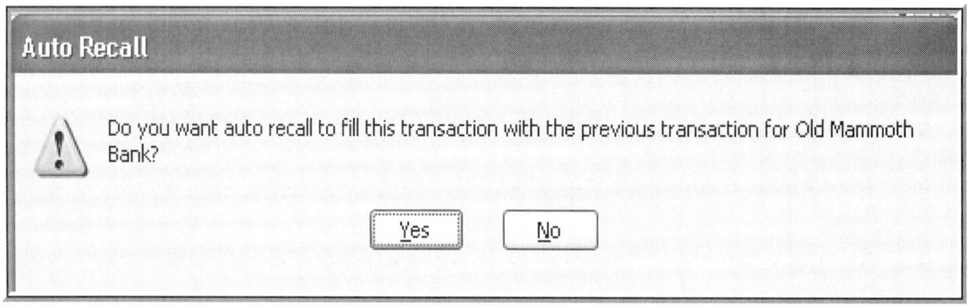

Tab to or click **Memo** on the bottom of the check
Enter **January Visa Payment** as the memo

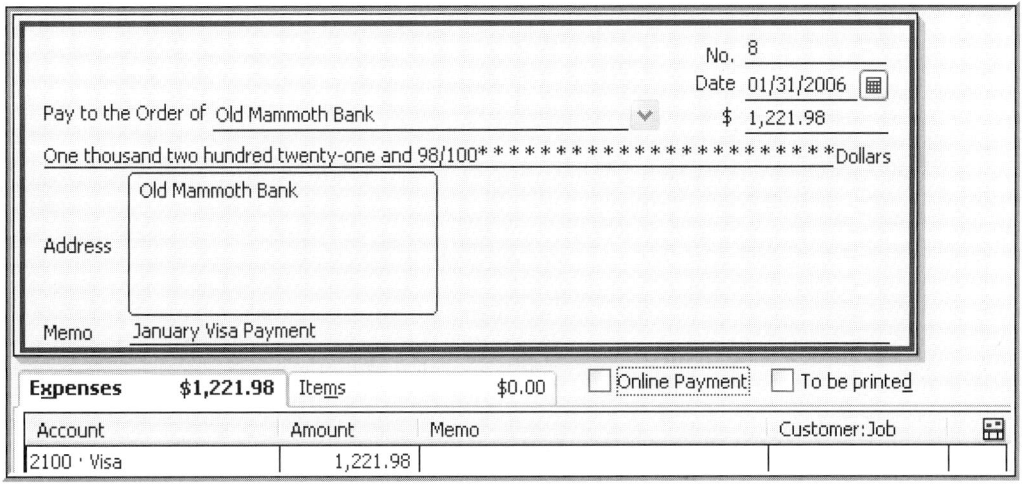

Print the standard-style check as previously instructed
When the check has printed successfully, click **Save & Close** to record and exit **Write Checks**
Close the Chart of Accounts

VIEW THE JOURNAL

After entering several transactions, it is helpful to view the Journal. In the Journal all transactions regardless of the method of entry are shown in traditional debit/credit format.

View the **Journal** for January

Since you will be preparing several reports, click the **Report Center** button
Click **Accountant & Taxes** as the type of report, click **Journal**
The dates are from **01/01/06** to **01/31/06**, press **Tab**
Scroll through the Journal and view all the transactions that have been made

Your Name Sports
Journal
January 2006

Trans #	Type	Date	Num	Name	Memo	Account	Debit	Credit
107	Check	01/31/2006	Transfer	Old Mammoth Bank	Loan Payment Store Fix...	1100 · Checking		53.12
				Old Mammoth Bank	Interest Store Fixtures L...	6212 · Loan Interest	44.51	
				Old Mammoth Bank	Principal Store Fixtures ...	2520 · Store Fixtures Loan	8.61	
							53.12	53.12
108	Check	01/31/2006			Service Charge	1100 · Checking		18.00
					Service Charge	6120 · Bank Service Charges	18.00	
							18.00	18.00
109	Deposit	01/31/2006			Interest	1100 · Checking	54.05	
					Interest	7010 · Interest Income		54.05
							54.05	54.05
111	Check	01/31/2006	8	Old Mammoth Bank	January Visa Payment	1100 · Checking		1,221.98
				Old Mammoth Bank	January Visa Payment	2100 · Visa	1,221.98	
							1,221.98	1,221.98
TOTAL							72,746.25	72,746.25

Close the **Journal** without printing
The **Report Center** should remain on the screen

PREPARE TRIAL BALANCE

After all adjustments have been recorded and the bank reconciliation has been completed, it is wise to prepare the Trial Balance. As in traditional accounting, the QuickBooks Pro Trial Balance proves that debits equal credits.

MEMO
DATE: January 31, 2006

Because adjustments have been entered, prepare a Trial Balance.

Prepare a trial balance using the Report Center

Verify that the type of report is **Accountant & Taxes**
Click **Trial Balance**

- If necessary, enter the dates **From 01/01/06** and **To 01/31/06**

Scroll through the report and study the amounts shown

- Notice that the final totals of debits and credits are equal: $89,472.05.

Do not close the report

USE QUICKZOOM IN TRIAL BALANCE

QuickZoom is a QuickBooks Pro feature that allows you to make a closer observation of transactions, amounts, etc. With QuickZoom you may zoom in on an item when the mouse pointer turns into a magnifying glass with a Z inside. For example, if you point to Store Fixtures Loan, you will see the magnifying glass with the Z inside. If you point to an item and you do not get a magnifying glass with a Z inside, you cannot zoom in on the item.

Use QuickZoom to view the details of Office Supplies:

Scroll through the Trial Balance until you see **1311 Office Supplies**
Position the mouse pointer over the amount of Office Supplies, **521.98**
- Notice that the mouse pointer changes to a magnifying glass with a Z.

Double-click the primary mouse button
- A **Transactions by Account Report** appears on the screen showing the two transactions entered for office supplies.

Scroll through the report

Your Name Sports
Transactions by Account
As of January 31, 2006

Type	Date	Num	Name	Memo	Clr	Split	Amount	Balance
1310 · Supplies								**850.00**
1311 · Office Supplies								**850.00**
Credit Card Charge	01/21/2006		Mountain Office Supply Company	Purchase Paper		2100 · Visa	21.98	871.98
General Journal	01/31/2006			Adjusting Entry...		6472 · Office	-350.00	521.98
Total 1311 · Office Supplies							-328.02	521.98
Total 1310 · Supplies							-328.02	521.98
TOTAL							**-328.02**	**521.98**

Close the report

PRINT THE TRIAL BALANCE

Once the trial balance has been prepared, it may be printed.

Print the **Trial Balance** in Portrait orientation as previously instructed

Click **Preview** to view a miniature copy of the report

- This helps determine the orientation, whether you need to select the feature to print one page wide, or whether you need to adjust the column widths.

Print in Portrait orientation
Close the **Trial Balance**
Do not close the **Report Center**

SELECT ACCRUAL-BASIS REPORTING PREFERENCE

QuickBooks Pro allows a business to customize the program and select certain preferences for reports, displays, graphs, accounts, and so on. There are two report preferences available in QuickBooks Pro: Cash and Accrual. You need to select the preference you prefer. If you select Cash as the report preference, income on reports will be shown as of the date payment is received, and expenses will be shown as of the date you pay the bill. If Accrual is selected, QuickBooks Pro shows the income on the report as of the date of the invoice and expenses as of the bill date. Prior to printing end-of-period reports, it is advisable to verify which reporting basis is selected. If Cash has been selected and you are using the Accrual method, it is imperative that you change your report basis.

MEMO
DATE: January 31, 2006

Prior to printing the Balance Sheet, Profit and Loss or Income Statement, or any other reports, check the report preference. If necessary, choose Accrual. After the selection has been made, print a Standard Profit and Loss and a Standard Balance Sheet for Your Name Sports.

Select **Accrual** as the Summary Report Basis

Click **Edit** on the menu bar, click **Preferences**
Scroll through the Preferences List until you see **Reports & Graphs**
Click **Reports & Graphs** and the **Company Preferences** tab

- If necessary, click **Accrual** to select the Summary Reports Basis

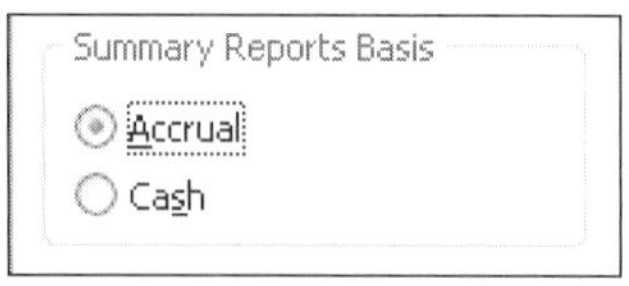

Click **OK** to close the **Preferences** window

PRINT STANDARD PROFIT AND LOSS STATEMENT

Because all income, expenses, and adjustments have been made for the period, a Profit and Loss Statement can be prepared. This statement is also known as the Income Statement. QuickBooks Pro has several different types of Profit and Loss Statements available: Standard—summarizes income and expenses; Detail—shows year-to-date transactions for each income and expense account; YTD Comparison—like the Standard Profit and Loss but summarizes your income and expenses for this month and compares them to your income and expenses for the current fiscal year; Prev Year Comparison—summarizes your income and expenses for both this month and this month last year and shows $ change and % change; By Job—like the Standard Profit and Loss statement, but with columns for each customer and job and amounts for this year to date; and By Class—like the Standard Profit and Loss statement, but with columns for each class and subclass with the amounts for this year to date. Unclassified shows how much you are making or losing within segments of your business that are not assigned to a QuickBooks class.

Print a **Standard Profit and Loss Report**

In the Report Center, click **Company & Financial** as the type of report, click **Profit & Loss Standard**

The dates are from **01/01/06** to **01/31/06**, press **Tab** to generate the report

Your Name Sports

Profit & Loss

January 2006

	Jan 06	
6392 · Water	85.00	
Total 6390 · Utilities		444.00
6470 · Supplies Expense		
6471 · Sales	175.00	
6472 · Office	350.00	
Total 6470 · Supplies Expense		525.00
Total Expense		3,018.50
Net Ordinary Income		2,551.14
Other Income/Expense		
Other Income		
7010 · Interest Income		54.05
Total Other Income		54.05
Net Other Income		54.05
Net Income		2,605.19

Scroll through the report to view the income and expenses listed

Print the report using **Portrait** orientation

Close the **Profit and Loss Report**

VIEW A STANDARD BALANCE SHEET

The Balance Sheet proves the fundamental accounting equation: Assets = Liabilities + Owners' Equity. When all transactions and adjustments for the period have been recorded, a Balance Sheet should be prepared. QuickBooks Pro has several different types of Balance Sheet statements available: Standard—shows as of today the balance in each Balance Sheet account with subtotals provided for assets, liabilities, and equity; Detail—This report is a more detailed version of the Standard Balance Sheet Report, Summary—shows amounts for each account type but not for individual accounts; and Comparison—has columns for today, a year ago today, $ change, and % change;. For each account, the report shows the starting balance at the beginning of last month, transactions entered in the account for this month to date, and the ending balance as of today.

View a **Standard Balance Sheet Report**

Click **Balance Sheet Standard**
Tab to or click **As of,** enter **01/31/06**
Tab to generate the report
Scroll through the report to view the assets, liabilities, and equities listed

- Notice the Net Income account listed in the **Equity** section of the report. This is the same amount of Net Income shown on the Profit and Loss Statement.

Your Name Sports
Balance Sheet
As of January 31, 2006

	Jan 31, 06		
Equity			
3100 · Your Name & Bailey Capital			
3110 · Your Name, Capital			
3111 · Your Name, Investment	20,000.00		
3112 · Your Name, Drawing	-1,000.00		
3110 · Your Name, Capital - Other	12,729.72		
Total 3110 · Your Name, Capital		31,729.72	
3120 · Tim Bailey, Capital			
3121 · Tim Bailey, Investment	20,000.00		
3122 · Tim Bailey, Drawing	-1,000.00		
3120 · Tim Bailey, Capital - Other	12,729.72		
Total 3120 · Tim Bailey, Capital		31,729.72	
Total 3100 · Your Name & Bailey Capital			63,459.44
Net Income			2,605.19
Total Equity			66,064.63
TOTAL LIABILITIES & EQUITY			**80,941.09**

Do not close the report

ADJUSTMENT TO TRANSFER NET INCOME/RETAINED EARNINGS INTO YOUR NAME, CAPITAL, AND TIM BAILEY, CAPITAL

Because Your Name Sports is a partnership, the amount of net income should appear as part of each owner's capital account rather than appear as Retained Earnings. In many instances, this is the type of adjustment the CPA makes on the Accountant's Copy of the QuickBooks Pro company files. The adjustment may be made before the closing date for the fiscal year, or it may be made after the closing has been performed. Because QuickBooks Pro automatically transfers the amount in the Net Income account into Retained Earnings, the closing entry for a partnership will transfer the net income into each owner's capital account. This adjustment is made by debiting Retained Earnings and crediting the owners' individual capital accounts. When you view a report before the end of the year, you will see an amount in Net Income and the same amount as a negative in Retained Earnings. If you view a report after the end of the year, you will not see any information regarding Retained Earnings or Net Income because the adjustment correctly transferred the amount to the owners' capital accounts.

If you prefer to use the power of the program and not make the adjustment, QuickBooks Pro simply carries the amount of Retained Earnings forward. Each year the amount of net income is added to Retained Earnings.

On the Balance Sheet, Retained Earnings and/or Net Income appear as part of the equity section. The owners' Drawing and Investment accounts are kept separate from Retained Earnings at all times

➤ Evenly divide and transfer the net income into the Your Name, Capital, and Tim Bailey, Capital, accounts after year end:

Open the **General Journal** as previously instructed
The **Date** is **01/31/06**
The first account used is **3000 Retained Earnings**
Debit **3000 Retained Earnings**, **2,605.19**
For the Memo record **Transfer Net Income into Capital**
The other accounts used are **3110 Your Name, Capital**, and **3120 Tim Bailey, Capital**
1,302.60 should be entered as the credit amount for **3110 Your Name, Capital**

- QuickBooks Pro enters **1,302.59** as the credit amount for **3120 Tim Bailey, Capital**.
- Because QuickBooks Pro accepts only two numbers after a decimal point, the cents must be rounded. Thus, there is a 1¢ difference in the distribution between the two owners. If there is an uneven amount in the future, Tim will receive the extra amount.

Enter the same Memo as entered for Retained Earnings

Make General Journal Entries

Date 01/31/2006 Entry No.

Account	Debit	Credit	Memo	Name
3000 · Retained Earnings	2,605.19		Transfer Net Income into Capital	
3110 · Your Name, Capital		1,302.60	Transfer Net Income into Capital	
3120 · Tim Bailey, Capital		1,302.59	Transfer Net Income into Capital	

Click **Save & Close** to record and close the **General Journal**

- Since you did not close the report, the Balance Sheet should still be on the screen.

Your Name Sports
Balance Sheet
As of January 31, 2006

			Jan 31, 06
Equity			
3000 · Retained Earnings			-2,605.19
3100 · Your Name & Bailey Capital			
3110 · Your Name, Capital			
3111 · Your Name, Investment	20,000.00		
3112 · Your Name, Drawing	-1,000.00		
3110 · Your Name, Capital - Other	14,032.32		
Total 3110 · Your Name, Capital		33,032.32	
3120 · Tim Bailey, Capital			
3121 · Tim Bailey, Investment	20,000.00		
3122 · Tim Bailey, Drawing	-1,000.00		
3120 · Tim Bailey, Capital - Other	14,032.31		
Total 3120 · Tim Bailey, Capital		33,032.31	
Total 3100 · Your Name & Bailey Capital			66,064.63
Net Income			2,605.19
Total Equity			66,064.63
TOTAL LIABILITIES & EQUITY			**80,941.09**

- Notice the change in the **Equity** section of the Balance Sheet.
- Not all companies have a profit each month. If your business has a negative amount for net income, the appropriate adjustment would be to debit each owner's individual capital account and to credit Retained Earnings. For example, if Net Income was -500.00, you would record the following: 3110 Your Name, Capital—debit 250; 3120 Tim Bailey, Capital—debit 250; and 3000 Retained Earnings—credit 500.

Do not close the report

PRINT STANDARD BALANCE SHEET

Once the adjustment for Net Income/Retained Earnings has been performed, viewing or printing the Balance Sheet will show you the status of the Owners' Equity.

To see the effect of the adjustment, print a **Standard Balance Sheet** for **January 2007**

Change the **As of** date to **01/31/2007**, press **Tab**

Your Name Sports
Balance Sheet
As of January 31, 2007

	Jan 31, 07		
Equity			
3100 · Your Name & Bailey Capital			
3110 · Your Name, Capital			
3111 · Your Name, Investment	20,000.00		
3112 · Your Name, Drawing	-1,000.00		
3110 · Your Name, Capital - Other	14,032.32		
Total 3110 · Your Name, Capital		33,032.32	
3120 · Tim Bailey, Capital			
3121 · Tim Bailey, Investment	20,000.00		
3122 · Tim Bailey, Drawing	-1,000.00		
3120 · Tim Bailey, Capital - Other	14,032.31		
Total 3120 · Tim Bailey, Capital		33,032.31	
Total 3100 · Your Name & Bailey Capital			66,064.63
Total Equity			66,064.63
TOTAL LIABILITIES & EQUITY			**80,941.09**

Print the report in Portrait Orientation

- The Balance Sheet still appears on the screen after printing is complete.
- Notice the Equity section. Nothing is shown for Retained Earnings or Net Income.
- The net income has been added to the owners' Capital accounts.

Do not close the report

Change the **As of** date for the Balance Sheet to **01/31/06**

CLOSE DRAWING AND TRANSFER INTO OWNERS' CAPITAL ACCOUNTS

In traditional accrual-basis accounting, there are four entries that need to be made at the end of a fiscal year. These entries close income, expenses, and the drawing accounts and transfer the net income into owners' equity. When preparing reports during the next fiscal year, QuickBooks Pro will not show any amounts in the income and expense accounts for the previous year. However, QuickBooks Pro does not close the owners' drawing accounts, nor does it transfer the net income into the owners' Capital accounts. If you prefer to use the power of the program and omit the last two closing entries, QuickBooks Pro will keep a running account of the owner withdrawals, and it will put net income into a Retained Earnings account. However, transferring the net income and drawing into the owners' Capital accounts provides a clearer picture of the value of the owners' equity.

The entry transferring the net income into the owners' Capital accounts has already been made. While this is not the actual end of the fiscal year for Your Name Sports, the closing entry for the Drawing accounts will be entered at this time so that you will have experience in recording this closing entry.

MEMO
DATE: January 31, 2006

Record the closing entry to close 3112 Your Name, Drawing, and 3122 Tim Bailey, Drawing, into each owner's Capital account.

Record the closing entry for each owner's Drawing account

Access the **General Journal** as previously instructed
Debit **3110 Your Name, Capital**, for the amount of the drawing account **1,000**
The Memo for the transaction is **Close Drawing**
Credit **3112 Your Name, Drawing**, for **1,000**
Use the same Memo for this portion of the transaction

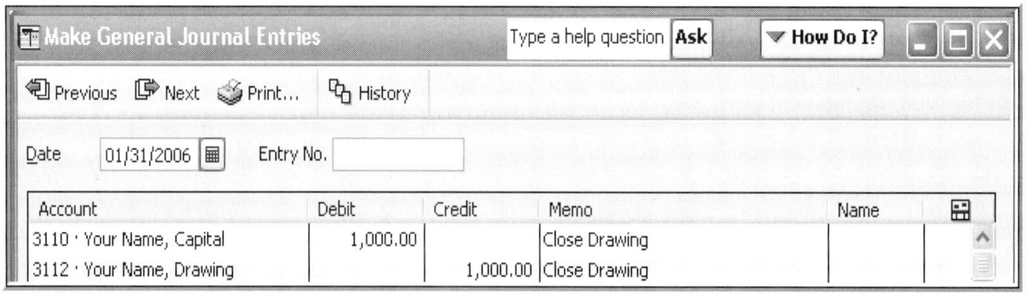

Click **Next**
Repeat the above steps to close **3122 Tim Bailey, Drawing**

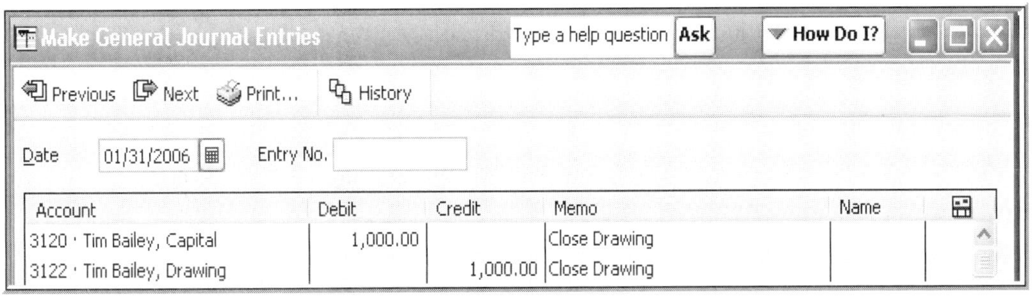

Click **Save & Close** and return to the Balance Sheet

- Notice the change in the **Equity** section of the Balance Sheet.

Change the Header/Footer so the title is **Balance Sheet After Equity Adjustments**

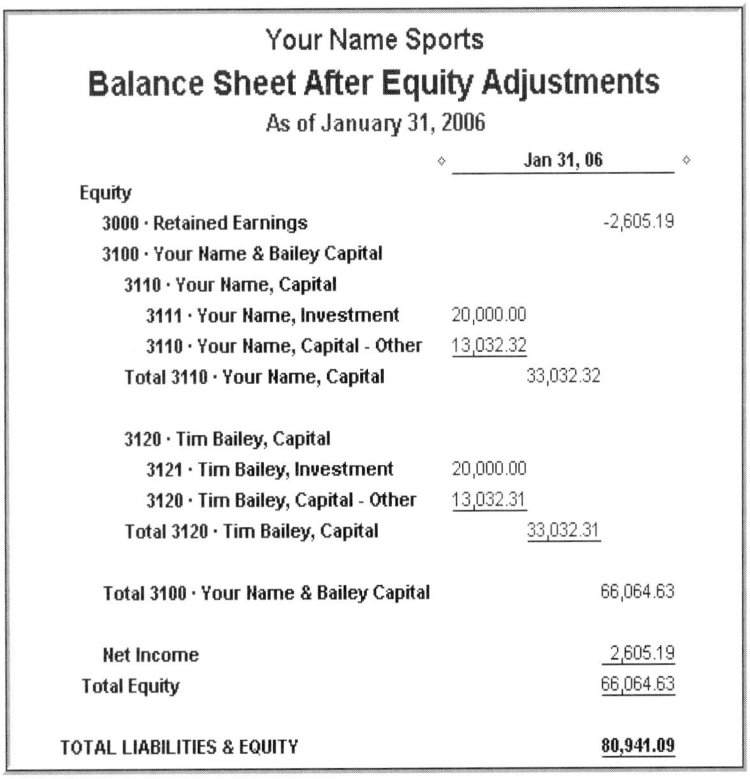

Your Name Sports

Balance Sheet After Equity Adjustments

As of January 31, 2006

			Jan 31, 06
Equity			
3000 · Retained Earnings			-2,605.19
3100 · Your Name & Bailey Capital			
3110 · Your Name, Capital			
3111 · Your Name, Investment	20,000.00		
3110 · Your Name, Capital - Other	13,032.32		
Total 3110 · Your Name, Capital		33,032.32	
3120 · Tim Bailey, Capital			
3121 · Tim Bailey, Investment	20,000.00		
3120 · Tim Bailey, Capital - Other	13,032.31		
Total 3120 · Tim Bailey, Capital		33,032.31	
Total 3100 · Your Name & Bailey Capital			66,064.63
Net Income			2,605.19
Total Equity			66,064.63
TOTAL LIABILITIES & EQUITY			**80,941.09**

Print the **Balance Sheet**

Do not close the report if you are going to do the following optional exercise

EXPORTING REPORTS TO EXCEL

Many of the reports prepared in QuickBooks Pro can be exported to Microsoft® Excel. This allows you to take advantage of extensive filtering options available in Excel, hide detail for some but not all groups of data, combine information from two different reports, change titles of columns, add comments, change the order of columns, and experiment with "what if" scenarios. In order to use this feature of QuickBooks Pro you must also have Microsoft Excel.

Optional Exercise: Export a report from QuickBooks Pro to Excel

With the **Balance Sheet After Equity Adjustments** showing on the screen, click the **Export** button

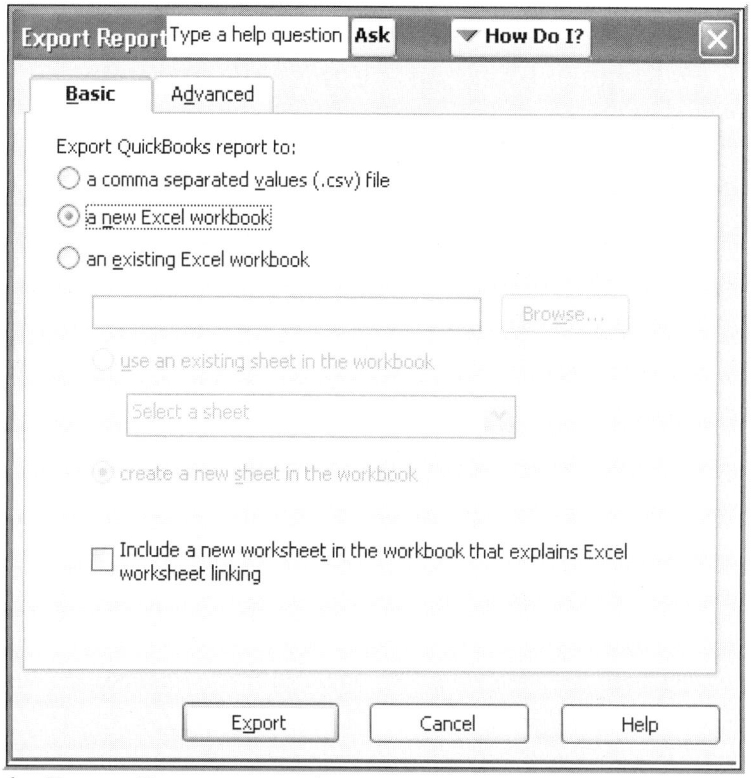

Make sure the Export Report screen has **a new Excel workbook** selected as the File option and that **Include a new worksheet in the workbook that explains Excel worksheet linking** is not selected

Click **Export**

- The Balance Sheet will be displayed in Excel.

	Jan 31, 06
ASSETS	
Current Assets	
Checking/Savings	
1100 · Checking	29,871.95
Total Checking/Savings	29,871.95
Accounts Receivable	
1200 · Accounts Receivable	5,690.62
Total Accounts Receivable	5,690.62
Other Current Assets	
1120 · Inventory Asset	34,991.54
1310 · Supplies	
1311 · Office Supplies	521.98
1312 · Sales Supplies	400.00
Total 1310 · Supplies	921.98
1340 · Prepaid Insurance	125.00
Total Other Current Assets	36,038.52
Total Current Assets	71,601.09

Scroll through the report and click in Cell A60
Type **BALANCE SHEET EXPORTED TO EXCEL**

Arial 10 B I U

F65 fx

	A B C D E	F
1		Jan 31, 06
50	3121 · Tim Bailey, Investment	20,000.00
51	3120 · Tim Bailey, Capital - Other	13,032.31
52	Total 3120 · Tim Bailey, Capital	33,032.31
53	Total 3100 · Your Name & Bailey Capital	66,064.63
54	Net Income	2,605.19
55	Total Equity	66,064.63
56	TOTAL LIABILITIES & EQUITY	80,941.09
57		
58		
59		
60	BALANCE SHEET EXPORTED TO EXCEL	

Click the **Close** button in the upper right corner of the Excel title bar to close **Excel**

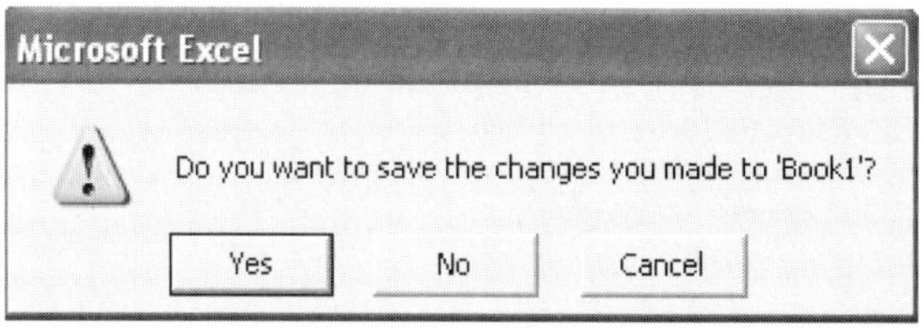

Click **No** to close **Book1** without saving
Return to QuickBooks, close the Balance Sheet, and the Report Center

IMPORTING DATA FROM EXCEL

You may have Excel or .csv (comma separated value) files that contain important business information about customers, vendors, and sales that are not contained in your QuickBooks Company File. That information can now be imported directly into QuickBooks and customized as desired. An import file must conform to a specific structure for QuickBooks to interpret the data in the file correctly.

It is recommended that you set up your import file correctly in order to transfer the data properly and avoid errors. This includes preparing the file for import into QuickBooks, mapping the data from your file to QuickBooks, and previewing the imported data. QuickBooks has a built in Reference Guide for Importing Files that may be accessed and printed through Help.

JOURNAL FOR JANUARY

It is always wise to have a printed or hard copy of the data on disk. After all entries and adjustments for the month have been made, print the Journal for January. This copy should be kept on file as an additional backup to the data stored on your disk. If something happens to your disk to damage it, you will still have the paper copy of your transactions available for re-entry into the system. Normally, the Journal would be printed before closing the period; however, we will print the Journal at the end of the chapter so that all entries are included.

END-OF-PERIOD BACKUP

Once all end-of-period procedures have been completed, in addition to a regular backup copy of company data and a duplicate disk, a second duplicate disk of the company data should be made and filed as an archive disk. Preferably, this copy will be located someplace other than on the business premises. The archive disk or file copy is set aside in case of emergency or in case damage occurs to the original and current backup copies of the company data.

Back up company data and prepare an archive copy of the company data

Prepare a Back Up as previously instructed

- In the **File** Name text box enter **Sports Archive 1-31-06.qbb** as the name for the backup

Also prepare a duplicate disk as instructed in Appendix A

- Label this disk **Sports Archive, 1-31-06**

PASSWORDS

Not every employee of a business should have access to all the financial records. In some companies, only the owner(s) will have complete access. In others, one or two key employees will have full access while other employees are provided limited access based on the jobs they perform. Passwords are secret words used to control access to data. QuickBooks Pro has several options available to assign passwords.

In order to assign any passwords at all, you must have an administrator. The administrator has unrestricted access to all QuickBooks Pro functions and sets up users, user passwords, and assigns areas of transaction access for each user. Areas of access can be limited to transaction entry for certain types of transactions or a user may have unrestricted access into all areas of QuickBooks Pro and company data.

A password should be kept secret at all times. It should be something that is easy for the individual to remember, yet difficult for someone else to guess. Birthdays, names, initials, and other similar devices are not good passwords because the information is too readily available. Never write down your password where it can be easily found or seen by someone else.

Even though the password feature is available, we will not be assigning passwords during training. If a password is forgotten, QuickBooks cannot be accessed until the appropriate password is entered.

SET THE CLOSING DATE FOR THE PERIOD

A closing date assigned to transactions for a period prevents change to data from the period without acknowledging that a transaction has been changed for a closed period. This is helpful to discourage casual changes or transaction deletions to a period that has been closed. Setting the closing date is done by accessing Accounting Preferences in QuickBooks Pro.

MEMO
DATE: January 31, 2006

Now that the closing transactions have been performed, you want to protect the data by setting the closing date to 1/31/06.

Assign the closing date of **01/31/06** to the transactions for the period ending 1/31/06

Click **Edit** on the menu bar, click **Preferences**
Click **Accounting**
Click **Company Preferences**
Enter **01/31/06** as the closing date in the Closing Date section of the Company Preferences for Accounting

Click **OK**

ENTER A CORRECTION TO A CLOSED PERIOD

If it is determined that an error was made in a previous period, QuickBooks Pro does allow the correction. Before it will record any changes for previous periods, QuickBooks Pro requires that Yes is clicked on the dialog box warning of the change to a transaction date that is prior to the closing date for the company.

MEMO
DATE: January 31, 2006

After entering the closing date, Rose reviews the Journal and reports printed at the end of January. She finds that $25 of the amount of Office Supplies should have been recorded as Sales Supplies. Record an entry in the Journal to transfer $25 from Office Supplies to Sales Supplies.

Transfer $25 from Office Supplies to Sales Supplies

Access the **General Journal** as previously instructed
Enter the date of **01/31/06**
Tab to or click **Account**, click the drop-down list arrow for **Account**, click **1312 Sales Supplies**
Enter the debit of **25.00**
Enter the Memo **Correcting Entry**
Tab to or click **Account**, click the drop-down list arrow for Account, click **1311 Office Supplies**

- A credit amount of 25.00 should already be in the credit column. If not, enter the amount.

Enter the Memo **Correcting Entry**

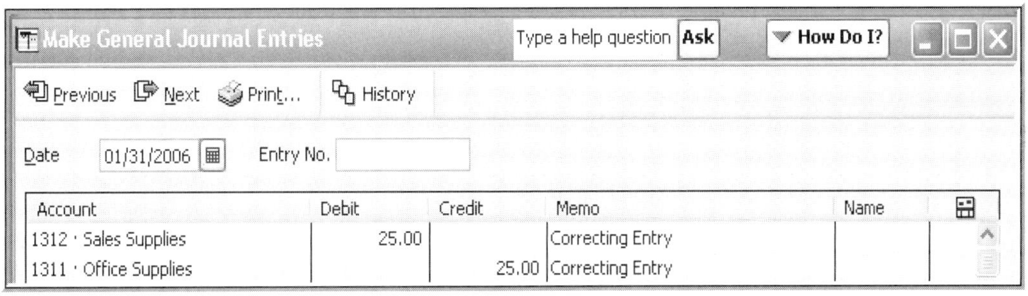

Click **Save & Close**

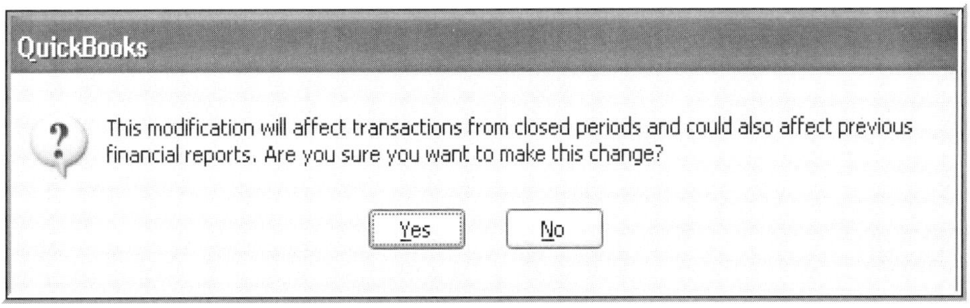

Click **Yes** on the **QuickBooks** dialog box

VERIFY THE CORRECTION TO OFFICE AND SALES SUPPLIES

Once the correction has been made, it is important to view the change in the accounts. The transfer of an amount of one asset into another will have no direct effect on the total assets in your reports. The account balances for Office Supplies and Sales Supplies will be changed. To view the change in the account, open the Chart of Accounts and look at the balance of each account. You may also use the account register to view the correcting entry as it was recorded in each account.

MEMO
DATE: January 31, 2006

Access the Chart of Accounts and view the change in the account balances and the correcting entry in each account's register.

View the correcting entry in each account

If necessary, open the **Chart of Accounts** as previously instructed

- Notice that the balance for Office Supplies has been changed from 521.98 to 496.98.
- Notice that the balance for Sales Supplies has been changed from 400.00 to 425.00.

Account	Type	Balance
◆1310 · Supplies	Other Current Asset	921.98
◆1311 · Office Supplies	Other Current Asset	496.98
◆1312 · Sales Supplies	Other Current Asset	425.00

Double-click **Office Supplies** to open the account register

- Verify that the correcting entry was recorded for Office Supplies.

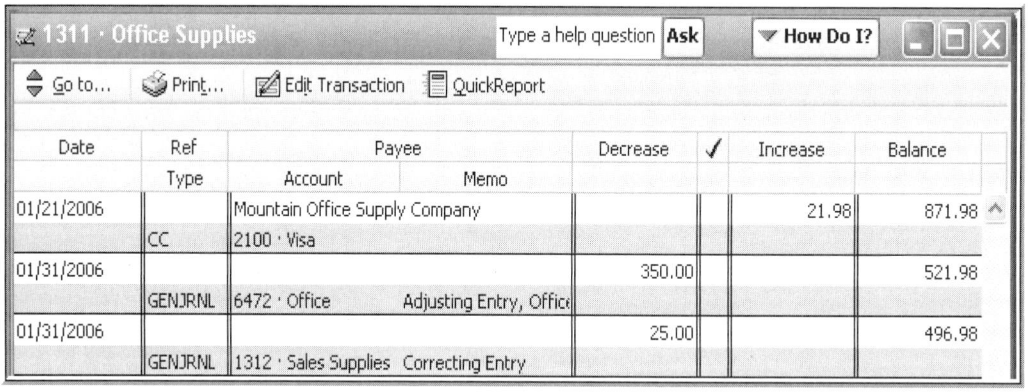

Date	Ref / Type	Payee / Account	Memo	Decrease	✓	Increase	Balance
01/21/2006		Mountain Office Supply Company				21.98	871.98
	CC	2100 · Visa					
01/31/2006				350.00			521.98
	GENJRNL	6472 · Office	Adjusting Entry, Offic				
01/31/2006				25.00			496.98
	GENJRNL	1312 · Sales Supplies	Correcting Entry				

Close the **Office Supplies Register**

Repeat the steps to view the correcting entry in Sales Supplies

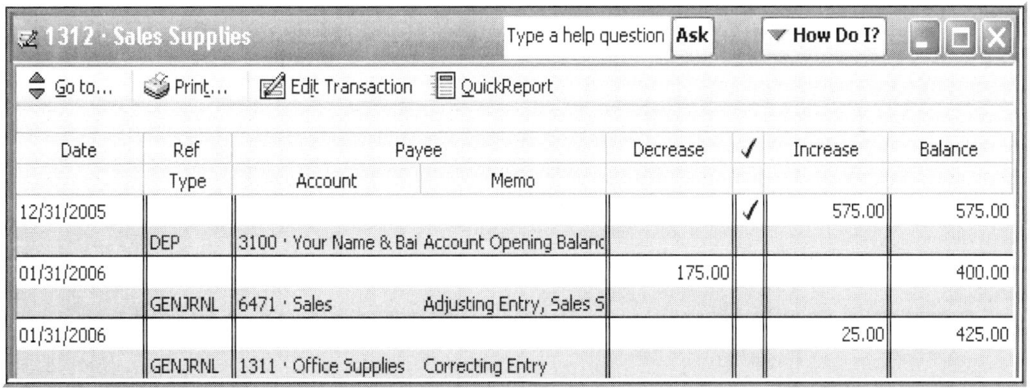

Date	Ref / Type	Payee / Account	Memo	Decrease	✓	Increase	Balance
12/31/2005					✓	575.00	575.00
	DEP	3100 · Your Name & Bai Account Opening Balanc					
01/31/2006				175.00			400.00
	GENJRNL	6471 · Sales	Adjusting Entry, Sales S				
01/31/2006						25.00	425.00
	GENJRNL	1311 · Office Supplies	Correcting Entry				

Close the **Sales Supplies Register**
Close the **Chart of Accounts**

INVENTORY ADJUSTMENTS

In a business that has inventory, it is possible that the number of items on hand is different from the quantity shown in QuickBooks Pro when a physical inventory is taken. This can be caused by a variety of items: loss due to theft, fire, or flood; damage to an item in the stockroom; an error in a previous physical inventory. Even though QuickBooks Pro uses the average cost method of inventory valuation, the value of an item can be changed as well. For example, assume that several pairs of after-ski boots are discounted and sold for a lesser value during the summer months. QuickBooks Pro allows the quantity and value of inventory to be adjusted.

> **MEMO**
> **DATE:** January 31, 2006
>
> After taking a physical inventory, you discover two hats were placed next to the cleaning supplies and are discolored because bleach was spilled on them. These hats must be discarded. Record this as an adjustment to the quantity of inventory. Use the Expense account 6190 Merchandise Adjustments to record this adjustment.

Adjust the quantity of hats

Click the **Adjust Qty on Hand** icon on the QuickBooks Home Page
Enter the adjustment date of **013106**
Click the drop-down list arrow next to **Adjustment Account**
Click **<Add New>**
Enter the new account information:
Type **Expense**

Number **6190**
Name **Merchandise Adjustments**
Click **OK** to add the account
Click in the **New Qty** column for Hats
Enter **27**
Tab to enter the change

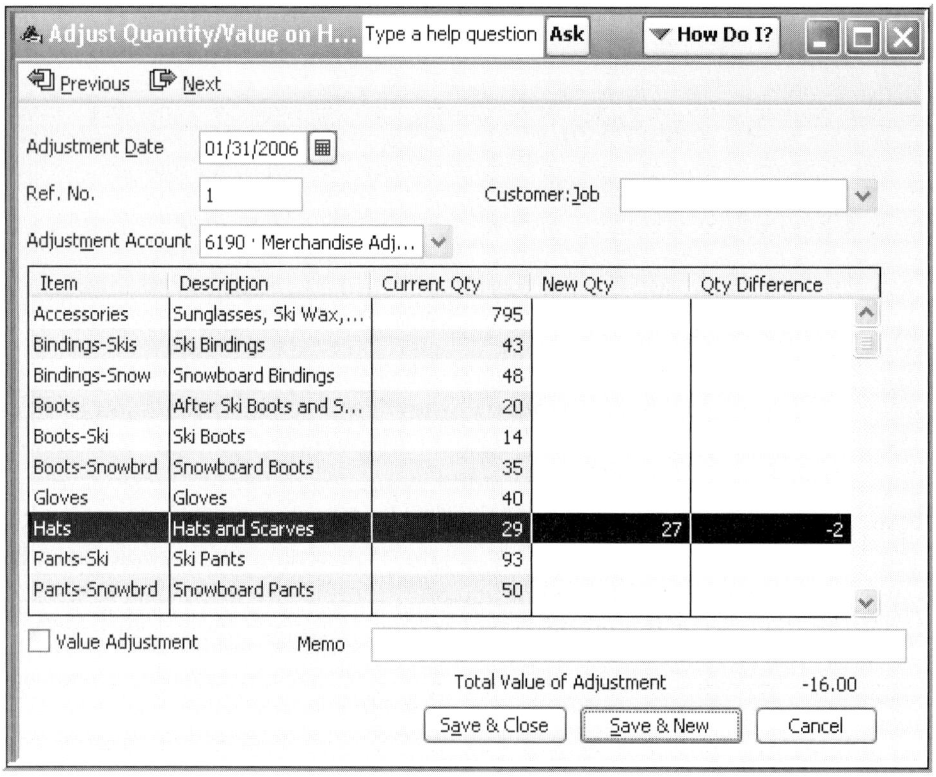

Click **Save & Close**
Click **Yes** on the **QuickBooks** dialog box

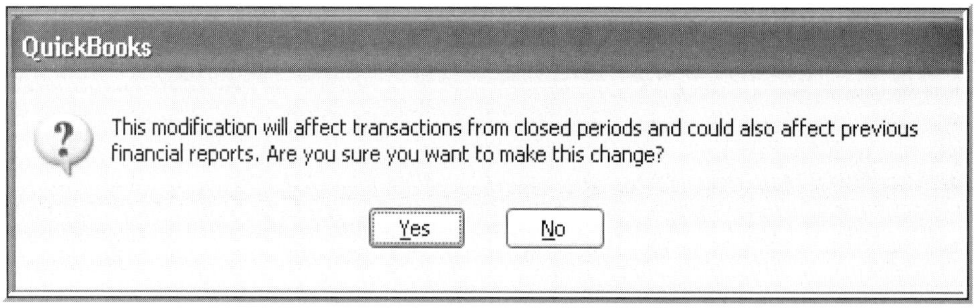

ADJUST THE JOURNAL ENTRY FOR NET INCOME/RETAINED EARNINGS

The adjustment to inventory reduced the value of the inventory asset by $16.00 and increased the expenses of the business by $16.00. The change decreased the net income by $16.00; thus, the adjusting entry for net income/retained earnings made previously needs to be changed.

Adjust the net income

Access **General Journal** transactions as previously instructed
Click **Previous** until you get to the entry debiting Retained Earnings for 2,605.19
Reduce the amount by $16.00 so change the debit to Retained Earnings to **2,589.19**
Change the credit amount for Your Name to **1,294.60**
Change the credit amount for Tim Bailey to **1,294.59**

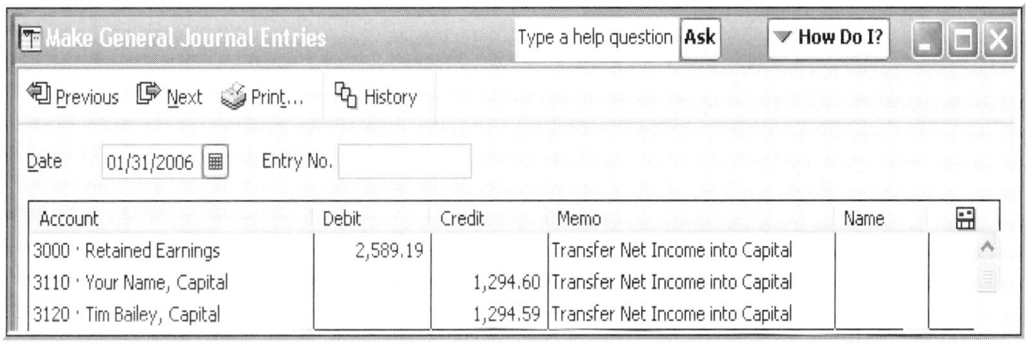

Account	Debit	Credit	Memo	Name
3000 · Retained Earnings	2,589.19		Transfer Net Income into Capital	
3110 · Your Name, Capital		1,294.60	Transfer Net Income into Capital	
3120 · Tim Bailey, Capital		1,294.59	Transfer Net Income into Capital	

Click **Save & Close**
Click **Yes** to save the changed transaction and to record a transaction for a closed period

PRINT POST-CLOSING TRIAL BALANCE

After closing has been completed, it is helpful to print a Post-Closing Trial Balance. This proves that debits still equal credits. Printing the Trial Balance on February 1 is printing the Post-Closing Trial Balance for January 31.

MEMO
DATE: February 1, 2006

Print a Post-Closing Trial Balance, a Post-Closing Profit and Loss Statement, and a Post-Closing Balance Sheet for Your Name Sports. The dates should be as of or for 02/01/06.

Print a **Post-Closing Trial Balance** to prove debits still equal credits

Prepare a **Trial Balance** as previously instructed
The dates are from **02/01/06** to **02/01/06**
Scroll through the report and study the amounts shown

- Notice that the final totals of debits and credits are equal.

Change the Header/Footer so the report title is **Post-Closing Trial Balance**

Your Name Sports
Post-Closing Trial Balance
As of February 1, 2006

	Feb 1, 06	
	Debit	Credit
6120 · Bank Service Charges	18.00	
6130 · Sales Discounts	447.17	
6140 · Advertising Expense	95.00	
6150 · Depreciation Expense	160.00	
6181 · Liability Insurance	125.00	
6190 · Merchandise Adjustments	16.00	
6212 · Loan Interest	97.93	
6300 · Rent	950.00	
6340 · Telephone	156.40	
6391 · Gas and Electric	359.00	
6392 · Water	85.00	
6471 · Sales	175.00	
6472 · Office	350.00	
7010 · Interest Income		54.05
TOTAL	90,061.24	90,061.24

Print in Portrait orientation
Close the **Trial Balance**

PRINT POST-CLOSING PROFIT AND LOSS STATEMENT

Because February 1 is after the closing date of January 31, 2006, the Profit and Loss Statement for February 1 is the Post-Closing Profit and Loss Statement. To verify the closing, print a Profit and Loss Statement for February 1.

Print a **Standard Profit and Loss Report** for February

Prepare a Standard Profit and Loss Report as previously instructed
The dates are from **02/01/06** to **02/01/06**
Change the Header/Footer so the report title is **Post-Closing Profit & Loss**

- The Net Income is **0.00**.

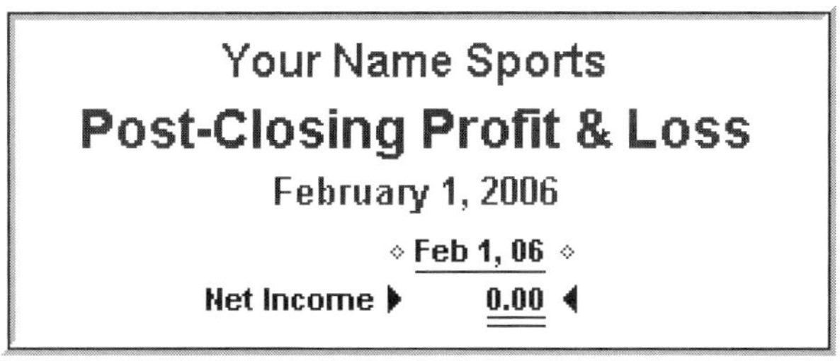
Your Name Sports
Post-Closing Profit & Loss
February 1, 2006

	Feb 1, 06
Net Income	0.00

Print the report in **Portrait** orientation
Close the Report

PRINT POST-CLOSING BALANCE SHEET

The proof that assets equal liabilities and owners' equity after the closing entries have been made needs to be displayed in a Post-Closing Balance Sheet. The Balance Sheet for February 1 is considered to be a Post-Closing Balance Sheet because it is prepared after the closing of the period. Most of the adjustments were for the month of January 2006. Because this report is for a month, the adjustment to Retained Earnings and Net Income will result in both of the accounts being included on the Balance Sheet. If, however, this report were prepared for the year, neither account would appear.

Print a Standard Balance Sheet report for February 1, 2006

Prepare a **Standard Balance Sheet** as previously instructed
If necessary, enter the as of date as **02/01/06**
Change the Header/Footer so the report title is **Post-Closing Balance Sheet**
Scroll through the report to view the assets, liabilities, and equities listed

- Because this report is for a one-month period, both Retained Earnings and Net Income are included on this report.

Your Name Sports
Post-Closing Balance Sheet
As of February 1, 2006

	Feb 1, 06		
3100 · Your Name & Bailey Capital			
3110 · Your Name, Capital			
3111 · Your Name, Investment	20,000.00		
3110 · Your Name, Capital - Other	13,024.32		
Total 3110 · Your Name, Capital		33,024.32	
3120 · Tim Bailey, Capital			
3121 · Tim Bailey, Investment	20,000.00		
3120 · Tim Bailey, Capital - Other	13,024.31		
Total 3120 · Tim Bailey, Capital		33,024.31	
Total 3100 · Your Name & Bailey Capital			66,048.63
Net Income			2,589.19
Total Equity			66,048.63
TOTAL LIABILITIES & EQUITY			**80,925.09**

Print the report, orientation is **Portrait**
Close the **Balance Sheet**

PRINT JOURNAL

Since the Journal was not printed before closing the period, it should be printed at this time. This will give a printed copy of all the transactions made in Chapters 5, 6, and 7.

Print the **Journal** for January

Access the Journal as previously instructed
The dates are from **01/01/06** to**01/31/06**
Tab to generate the report
Resize the columns so all names and accounts are shown in full and the report prints on one-page wide
Print the report in **Landscape** orientation
Close the **Journal** and the **Report Center**

SUMMARY

In this chapter, end-of-period adjustments were made, a bank reconciliation and a credit card reconciliation were performed, backup (duplicate) and archive disks were prepared, and adjusting entries were made. The use of Drawing, Net Income, and Retained Earnings accounts were explored and interpreted for a partnership. The closing date for a period was assigned. Account names were changed, and new accounts were created. Even though QuickBooks Pro focuses on entering transactions on business forms, a Journal recording each transaction is kept by QuickBooks Pro. This chapter presented transaction entry directly into the Journal. The difference between accrual-basis and cash-basis accounting was discussed. Company preferences were established for accrual-basis reporting preferences. Owner withdrawals and distribution of capital to partners were examined. Many of the different report options available in QuickBooks Pro were explored, and a report was exported to Microsoft® Excel. A variety of reports were printed. Correction of errors was analyzed, and corrections were made after the period was closed and adjustments were made to inventory. The fact that QuickBooks Pro does not require an actual closing entry at the end of the period was addressed.

END-OF-CHAPTER QUESTIONS

TRUE/FALSE

ANSWER THE FOLLOWING QUESTIONS IN THE SPACE PROVIDED BEFORE THE QUESTION NUMBER.

_____ 1. The owner's Drawing account should be transferred to capital each week.

_____ 2. Even if entered elsewhere, all transactions are recorded in the Journal.

_____ 3. You must access the General Journal in order to close a period.

_____ 4. If Show All is selected, inactive accounts will not appear in the Chart of Accounts.

_____ 5. When you reconcile a bank statement, anything entered as a service charge will automatically be entered as a transaction when the reconciliation is complete.

_____ 6. Once an account has been used, the name cannot be changed.

_____ 7. The adjusting entry for depreciation may be made in the Depreciation account register.

_____ 8. At the end of the year, QuickBooks Pro transfers the net income into retained earnings.

_____ 9. A withdrawal by an owner in a partnership reduces the owner's capital.

_____ 10. As with other accounting programs, QuickBooks Pro requires that a formal closing be performed at the end of each year.

MULTIPLE CHOICE

WRITE THE LETTER OF THE CORRECT ANSWER IN THE SPACE PROVIDED BEFORE THE QUESTION NUMBER.

_____ 1. To print a Reconciliation Report that lists only totals, select ___.
- A. none
- B. summary
- C. detail
- D. complete

_____ 2. The report that proves debits equal credits is the ___.
- A. Sales Graph
- B. Balance Sheet
- C. Profit and Loss Statement
- D. Trial Balance

_____ 3. If reports are prepared as of January 31, net income will appear in the ___.
- A. Profit and Loss Statement
- B. Balance Sheet
- C. both A and B
- D. neither A nor B

_____ 4. In QuickBooks Pro, you export reports to Microsoft® Excel in order to ___.
- A. print the report
- B. explore "what if" scenarios with data from QuickBooks Pro
- C. prepare checks
- D. all of the above

_____ 5. QuickBooks Pro uses the ___ method of inventory valuation
- A. LIFO
- B. average cost
- C. FIFO
- D. Actual Cost

_____ 6. If a transaction is recorded in the Journal, it may be viewed ___.
- A. in the Journal
- B. in the register for each account used in the transaction
- C. by preparing an analysis graph
- D. both A and B

_____ 7. Entries for bank collections ___.
A. are automatically recorded at the completion of the bank reconciliation
B. must be recorded after the bank reconciliation is complete
C. should be recorded while one is reconciling the bank statement
D. should be recorded on the first of the month

_____ 8. The account(s) that may be reconciled are ___.
A. Checking
B. Credit Card
C. both A and B
D. the Customer list account

_____ 9. The closing entry for drawing transfers the balance of an owner's drawing account into the ___ account.
A. Retained Earnings
B. Net Income
C. Capital
D. Investment

_____ 10. A Balance Sheet that shows amounts for each account type but not for individual accounts is the ___ Balance Sheet.
A. Standard
B. Summary
C. Detail
D. Comparison

FILL-IN

IN THE SPACE PROVIDED, WRITE THE ANSWER THAT MOST APPROPRIATELY COMPLETES THE SENTENCE.

1. __________-basis accounting matches income and expenses against a period, and ________-basis accounting records income when the money is received and expenses when the purchase is made or the bill is paid.

2. The __________ proves that Assets = Liabilities + Owners' Equity.

3. In a partnership, each owner has a share of all the __________ and __________ based on the percentage of his or her investment in the business or according to any partnership agreements.

4. In order to close a period, a closing __________ must be provided.

5. No matter where transactions are recorded, they all appear in the __________.

SHORT ESSAY

Describe the entry that is made to transfer net income into the owner's capital account. Include the reason this entry should be made and how income will be listed if it is not made.

____

____

____

____

____

NAME______________________

TRANSMITTAL

CHAPTER 7: YOUR NAME SPORTS

Attach the following documents and reports:

Check No. 6: Your Name
Check No. 7: Tim Bailey
Bank Reconciliation Detail Report, January 30, 2006
Credit Card Reconciliation Detail Report, January 31, 2006
Check No. 8: Old Mammoth Bank
Trial Balance, January 31, 2006
Standard Profit and Loss Statement, January 2006
Standard Balance Sheet, January 31, 2007
Standard Balance Sheet, January 31, 2006 (After Equity Adjustments)
Post-Closing Trial Balance, February 1, 2006
Post-Closing Profit and Loss, February 1, 2006
Post-Closing Balance Sheet, February 1, 2006
Journal, January 2006

END-OF-CHAPTER PROBLEM

YOUR NAME CLOTHING

Chapter 7 continues with the end-of-period adjustments, bank and credit card reconciliations, archive disks, and closing the period for Your Name Clothing. The company does use a certified public accountant for guidance and assistance with appropriate accounting procedures. The CPA has provided information for Julie to use for adjusting entries, etc.

INSTRUCTIONS

Continue to use the copy of Your Name you used in the previous chapters. Open the company—the file used is **Clothing.qbw**. Record the adjustments and other transactions as you were instructed in the chapter. Always read the transaction carefully and review the Chart of Accounts when selecting transaction accounts. Print the reports and journals as indicated.

RECORD TRANSACTIONS

January 31, 2007—Enter the following:

- ► Change the names and/or the account numbers of the following accounts. Make sure the account description is appropriate for the new account name.
  - o **6260 Printing and Reproduction** to **6260 Printing and Duplication**
  - o **6350 Travel & Ent** to **6350 Travel**
  - o **3010 Your Name & Lee Capital** to **3100 Your Name & Lee, Capital**
- ► Add the following accounts:
  - o Equity account **3110 Your Name, Capital** (subaccount of **3100**)
  - o Equity account **3120 Julie Lee, Capital** (subaccount of **3100**)
- ► Change the following accounts:
  - o **3011 Your Name, Investment** to **3111 Your Name, Investment** (subaccount of **3110**) (Note: Since 3110 is a subaccount of 3100, you may not see the entire name of the subaccount listing. Cursor through the subaccount name to read it completely.)
  - o **3013 Your Name, Drawing** to **3112 Your Name, Drawing** (subaccount of **3110**)
  - o **3012 Julie Lee, Investment** to **3121 Julie Lee, Investment** (subaccount of **3120**)
  - o **3014 Julie Lee, Drawing** to **3122 Julie Lee, Drawing** (subaccount of **3120**)
- ► Make the following accounts inactive:
  - o **6291 Building Repairs**
  - o **6351 Entertainment**
- ► Delete the following accounts:
  - o **6182 Disability Insurance**
  - o **6213 Mortgage**
  - o **6823 Property**

- Print the Chart of Accounts (Do *not* show inactive accounts. Use the File menu to print the list.)
- Create a Fixed Asset Item List for:
  - Office Equipment, Date is 12/31/06, Cost is $8,000, Account is 1510
  - Store Fixtures, Date is 12/31/06, Cost is $9,500, Account is 1520
- Enter adjusting entries in the Journal and use the memo Adjusting Entry for the following:
  - Office Supplies Used, the amount used is $35
  - Sales Supplies Used, account balance (on hand) at the end of the month is $1,400
  - Record a compound entry for depreciation for the month: Office Equipment, $66.67 and Store Fixtures, $79.17
  - The amount of insurance remaining in the Prepaid Insurance account is for six months of liability insurance. Record the liability insurance expense for the month
- Each owner withdrew $500. (Memo: Withdrawal for January) Print Check Nos. 7 and 8 for the owners' withdrawals.
- Prepare Bank Reconciliation and Enter Adjustments for the Reconciliation: (Refer to the chapter for appropriate Memo notations)

CENTRAL COAST BANK
1234 Coast Highway
San Luis Obispo, CA 93407
(805) 555-9300

Your Name Clothing
784 Marsh Street
San Luis Obispo, CA 93407

Acct. # 987-352-9152 January 31, 2007

Beginning Balance, January 1, 2007			$32,589.00
1/15/07, Deposit	3,022.33		35,611.33
1/15/07, Deposit	1,829.05		37,440.38
1/15/07, NSF Returned Check		325.00	37,115.38
1/15/07, Check 1		58.98	37,056.40
1/18/07, Check 2		156.00	36,900.40
1/18/07, Check 3		343.00	36,557.40
1/25/07, Check 4		1,150.00	35,407.40
1/25/07, Check 5		79.85	35,327.55
1/31/07, Service Charge		10.00	35,317.55
1/31/07, NSF Charge		15.00	35,302.55
1/31/07, Office Equipment Loan Pmt.: $44.51 Interest, $8.61 Principal		53.12	35,249.43
1/31/07, Store Fixtures Loan Pmt.: $53.42 Interest, $10.33 Principal		63.75	35,185.68
1/31/07, Interest	73.30		35,258.98
Ending Balance, 1/31/07			35,258.98

- Print a Detailed Reconciliation Report. Adjust column widths so the report fits on one page
- Reconcile the Visa account

CENTRAL COAST BANK
1234 Coast Highway
San Luis Obispo, CA 93407

Your Name Clothing
784 Marsh Street
San Luis Obispo, CA 93407
VISA Acct. # 9187-52-9152 **January 31, 2007**

		Balance
Beginning Balance, January 2, 2007		0.00
1/9/07, The Clothes Rack	196.00	196.00
1/18/07, Office Masters	250.00	446.00
Ending Balance, 1/31/07		446.00

Minimum Payment Due: $50.00 **Payment Due Date: February 5, 2007**

- Print a Detailed Reconciliation Report. Pay Central Coast Bank for the Visa bill using Check No. 9. Print Check No. 9
- Distribute capital to each owner: divide the balance of 3100 Your Name & Lee, Capital equally between the two partners. Record an entry to transfer each owner's portion of capital to her individual capital account. (Memo: Transfer Capital to Individual Accounts)
- Verify or change reporting preferences to accrual basis
- Print the following for January 1-31, 2007, or as of January 31, 2007:
  - Trial Balance
  - Standard Profit and Loss Statement
- Divide in half and transfer Net Income/Retained Earnings into owners' individual Capital accounts.
- Close Drawing accounts into owner's individual Capital accounts
- Print a Standard Balance Sheet
- Close the period as of January 31, 2007
- Edit a transaction from a closed period: Discovered an error in the amount of Office Supplies and Sales Supplies: Transfer $40 from Office Supplies to Sales Supplies on 01/31/07
- Found one damaged tie. Adjust the quantity of ties on 01/31/07 using the Expense account 6190 Merchandise Adjustments
- Change the net income/retained earnings adjustment to reflect the merchandise adjustment for the ties

February 1, 2007

- Print the following:
  - Journal for 01/01/07-02/01/07 (Landscape orientation, Fit to one page wide)
  - Post-Closing Trial Balance, February 1, 2007
  - Post-Closing Standard Profit and Loss Statement, February 1, 2007
  - Post-Closing Standard Balance Sheet, February 1, 2007

February 1, 2008

- Print the following:
  - Standard Balance Sheet, February 1, 2008

NAME_______________________

TRANSMITTAL

CHAPTER 7: YOUR NAME CLOTHING

Attach the following documents and reports:

Chart of Accounts (Revised)
Check No. 7: Your Name
Check No. 8: Julie Lee
Bank Reconciliation, January 31, 2007
Visa Reconciliation, January 31, 2007
Check No. 9: Central Coast Bank
Trial Balance, January 31, 2007
Standard Profit and Loss, January 2007
Standard Balance Sheet, January 31, 2007
Standard Balance Sheet, January 31, 2007
Journal, January 1-February 1, 2007
Post-Closing Trial Balance, February 1, 2007
Post-Closing Profit and Loss, February 1, 2007
Post-Closing Balance Sheet, February 1, 2007
Balance Sheet, February 1, 2008

YOUR NAME GOLF SHOP PRACTICE SET: MERCHANDISING BUSINESS

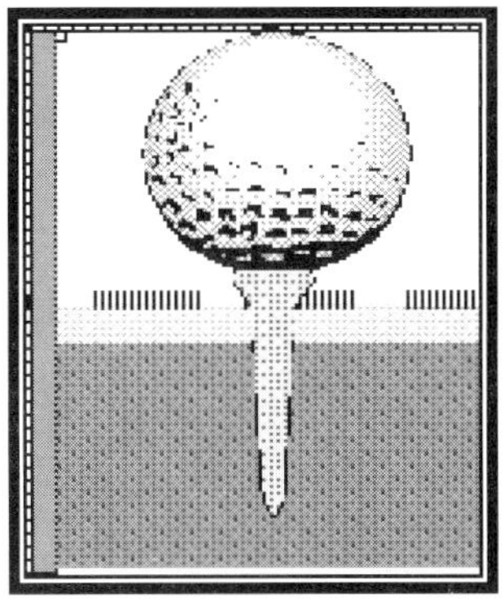

The following is a comprehensive practice set combining all the elements of QuickBooks Pro studied in the merchandising section of the text. In this practice set you will keep the books for a company for the month of January 2007. Entries will be made to record invoices, receipt of payments on invoices, cash sales, credit card sales, receipt and payment of bills, orders and receipts of merchandise, credit memos for invoices and bills, sales tax payments, and credit card payments. Account names will be added, changed, deleted, and made inactive. Customer, vendor, owner names, and fixed assets will be added to the appropriate lists. Reports will be prepared to analyze sales, bills, receipts, and items ordered. Formal reports including the Trial Balance, Profit and Loss Statement, and Balance Sheet will be prepared. Adjusting entries for depreciation, supplies used, insurance expense, and automatic payments will be recorded. Both bank and credit card reconciliations will be prepared. Entries to display partnership equity for each partner will be made. The owners' Drawing accounts will be closed and the period will be closed.

YOUR NAME GOLF SHOP

Located in Palm Springs, California, Your Name Golf Shop is a full-service golf shop that sells golf equipment and golf clothing. Your Name Golf Shop is a partnership owned and operated by Annie Andrews and you. Each partner contributed an equal amount to the partnership. You buy the equipment and manage the store. Annie buys the clothing and accessory items and keeps the books for Your Name Golf Shop. There are several part-time employees working for Your Name Golf Shop selling merchandise.

INSTRUCTIONS

Copy the file **Golf.qbw** from the Web site as previously instructed. The following lists are used for all sales items, customers, and vendors. You will be adding additional customers and vendors as the company is in operation. When entering transactions, you are responsible for any memos you wish to include in transactions. Unless otherwise specified, the terms for each sale or bill will be the term specified on the Customer or Vendor List. (Choose edit for the individual customers or vendors and select the Additional Info tab to see the terms for each customer or vendor.) Customer Message is usually *Thank you for your business*. However, any other message that is appropriate may be used. If a customer's order exceeds the established credit limit, accept the order and process it. If the terms allow a discount for a customer, make sure to apply the discount if payment is made within the discount period. Use 6130 Sales Discounts as the discount account. On occasion, a payment may be made within the discount period but not received or recorded within the discount period. Information within the transaction will indicate whether or not the payment is equivalent to a full payment. For example, if you received $98 for an invoice for $100 shortly after the discount period and the transaction indicated payment in full, apply the discount. If a customer has a credit and has a balance on the account, apply the credit to the appropriate invoice for the customer. If there is no balance for a customer and a return is made, issue a credit memo and a refund check. Always pay bills in time to take advantage of purchase discounts. Use the Cost of Goods Sold Account 5010 Merchandise Discounts for the discount account. Remember that the discount due date will be ten days from the date of the bill.

Invoices, purchase orders, and other business forms should be printed as they are entered. Print with lines around each field. Most reports will be printed in Portrait orientation; however, if the report (such as the Journal) will fit across the page using Landscape, use Landscape orientation. Whenever possible, adjust the column widths so that reports fit on one page wide *without* selecting Fit report to one page wide.

Back up your work at the end of each week.

Sales Items:

Item List

Name	Description	Type	Account	On Hand	Price
Bags	Golf Bags	Inventory Part	4000 · Sales:4010 · Accessory Sales	15	0.00
Clubs-Irons	Golf Clubs: Irons	Inventory Part	4000 · Sales:4030 · Equipment Sales	150	0.00
Clubs-Sets	Golf Clubs: Sets	Inventory Part	4000 · Sales:4030 · Equipment Sales	50	0.00
Clubs-Woods	Golf Clubs: Woods	Inventory Part	4000 · Sales:4030 · Equipment Sales	150	0.00
Gift Sets	Golf Gift Sets	Inventory Part	4000 · Sales:4010 · Accessory Sales	10	0.00
Gloves	Golf Gloves	Inventory Part	4000 · Sales:4010 · Accessory Sales	35	0.00
Golf Balls	Golf Balls	Inventory Part	4000 · Sales:4010 · Accessory Sales	60	0.00
Hats	Golf Hats	Inventory Part	4000 · Sales:4010 · Accessory Sales	20	0.00
Men's Jackets	Men's Jackets	Inventory Part	4000 · Sales:4020 · Clothing Sales	12	0.00
Men's Pants	Men's Pants	Inventory Part	4000 · Sales:4020 · Clothing Sales	15	0.00
Men's Shirts	Men's Shirts	Inventory Part	4000 · Sales:4020 · Clothing Sales	15	0.00
Men's Shoes	Men's Shoes	Inventory Part	4000 · Sales:4020 · Clothing Sales	18	0.00
Men's Shorts	Men's Shorts	Inventory Part	4000 · Sales:4020 · Clothing Sales	12	0.00
Tees	Golf Tees	Inventory Part	4000 · Sales:4010 · Accessory Sales	30	0.00
Towels	Golf Towels	Inventory Part	4000 · Sales:4010 · Accessory Sales	10	0.00
Women's Jacket	Women's Jackets	Inventory Part	4000 · Sales:4020 · Clothing Sales	12	0.00
Women's Pants	Women's Pants	Inventory Part	4000 · Sales:4020 · Clothing Sales	12	0.00
Women's Shirt	Women's Shirts	Inventory Part	4000 · Sales:4020 · Clothing Sales	12	0.00
Women's Shoes	Women's Shoes	Inventory Part	4000 · Sales:4020 · Clothing Sales	20	0.00
Women's Short	Women's Shorts	Inventory Part	4000 · Sales:4020 · Clothing Sales	15	0.00
CA Sales Tax	CA Sales Tax	Sales Tax Item	2200 · Sales Tax Payable		7.25%
Out of State	Out-of-state sale, exempt from sales tax	Sales Tax Item	2200 · Sales Tax Payable		0.0%

Note: Individual golf clubs are categorized as irons or woods. A complete set of clubs would be categorized as a set. The type of material used in a golf club makes no difference in a sales item. For example, graphite is a material used in the shaft of a golf club. A set of graphite clubs would refer to a set of golf clubs. Titanium is a type of metal used in the head of a golf club. A titanium wood would be sold as a wood. Golf balls are sold in packages called sleeves; thus, a quantity of one would represent one package of golf balls.

Vendors:

Vendors | Transactions

View: Active Vendors

Name	Balance Total
Golf Clubs, Inc.	15,000.00
Golf Supplies & Equipment	500.00
Shoe Suppliers	500.00
Sports Attire	5,000.00
State Board of Equalization	0.00

Customers:

Customers & Jobs | Transactions

View: Active Customers

Name	Balance Total
Azizi, Tekin	1,575.00
Brown, Derek	1,850.00
Chan, Colleen	1,700.00
Cooper, Mary	0.00
Duncan, Mitchell	850.00
Hamid, Farzad	0.00
Ling, Jozu	375.00
Mills, Judy	550.00
Nakamura, Burt	450.00
Osborn, Doreen	850.00
Poltash, George	1,200.00
Ricardo, Lon	750.00
Shumway, Steve	950.00
Stephens, Lucy	75.00
Stoval, Wayne	150.00
Tompkins, Julie	350.00
Torres, Ed	1,200.00
Winston, Jennifer	0.00

RECORD TRANSACTIONS:

Enter the transactions for Your Name Golf Shop and print as indicated.

Week 1—January 2-8, 2007:

► Add your name to the company name. The company name will be **Your Name Golf Shop**. (Type your actual name *not* the words Student's Name.)

- ► Change Preferences: Reports should refresh automatically, the Report Header/Footer should *not* include the Date Prepared, Time Prepared, or Report Basis. Inventory and purchase orders should be active
- ► Change the names and, if necessary, the descriptions of the following accounts:
    - o **4200 Sales Discounts** to **4200 Purchases Discounts**
    - o **6130 Cash Discounts** to **6130 Sales Discounts**
    - o **6350 Travel & Ent** to **6350 Travel**
    - o **6381 Marketing** to **6381 Sales** (this is a subaccount of 6380 Supplies Expense)
- ► Delete the following accounts:
    - o **4050 Reimbursed Expenses**
    - o **4070 Resale Discounts**
    - o **4090 Resale Income**
    - o **4100 Freight Income**
    - o **6140 Contributions**
    - o **6182 Disability Insurance**
    - o **6213 Mortgage**
    - o **6265 Filing Fees**
    - o **6285 Franchise Fees**
    - o **6351 Entertainment**
- ► Make the following accounts inactive:
    - o **6311 Building Repairs**
    - o **6413 Property**
- ► Add the following accounts:
    - o Equity account: **3010 Your Name, Capital** (subaccount of **3000**)
    - o Equity account: **3020 Annie Andrews, Capital** (subaccount of **3000**)
    - o Cost of Goods Sold account: **5010 Merchandise Discounts** (subaccount of **5000**)
- ► Change the following accounts:
    - o **Your Name, Investment** to **3011 Your Name, Investment** (subaccount of **3010**)
    - o **Your Name, Drawing** to **3012 Your Name, Drawing** (subaccount of **3010**)
    - o **Annie Andrews, Investment** to **3021 Annie Andrews, Investment** (subaccount of **3020**)
    - o **Annie Andrews, Drawing** to **3022 Annie Andrews, Drawing** (subaccount of **3020**)
- ► Print the Chart of Accounts using print lists on the File menu. Do *not* show inactive accounts.
- ► Create Fixed Asset List
    - o Office Equipment, New, Description Office Equipment, Purchase Date 12/31/06, Cost 5,000.00, Asset Account 1510 Office Equipment
    - o Store Fixtures, New, Description Store Fixtures, Purchase Date 12/31/06, Cost 6,000.00, Asset Account 1520 Store Fixtures
- ► Prior to recording any transactions, print a Trial Balance as of January 1, 2007.
- ► Customize Sales Receipts, Invoices, and Purchase Orders so your name will print on the same line as the company name.
- ► Print invoices, checks, and other items as they are entered in the transactions.

1/2/2007

- ▶ Sold 2 pairs of women's shorts @ $64.99 each, 2 women's shirts @ $59.99 each, 1 women's jacket @ $129.99, and 1 pair of women's shoes @ $179.99 to Jennifer Winston. (Remember: Print Invoice No. 1 when the transaction is entered.)
- ▶ Having achieved her goal of a handicap under 30, Mary treated herself to the new clubs she had been wanting. Sold 1 set of graphite clubs for $750, 1 golf bag for $129.95, and 5 sleeves (packages) of golf balls @ $6.95 each to Mary Cooper. (Remember to accept sales that are over the credit limit.)
- ▶ Farzad heard that titanium would give him extra yardage with each shot. Sold 4 titanium woods to Farzad Hamid @ $459.00 each.
- ▶ Sold 5 golf bags @ $59.99 each and 5 sets of starter clubs @ $159.99 each to Palm Springs Schools for the high school golf team. Palm Springs Schools located at 99-4058 South Palm Canyon Drive, Palm Springs, CA 92262 is a nonprofit organization. The telephone number is 760-555-4455, and the contact person is Claudia Colby. The terms are Net 30. Even though this is a nonprofit organization, it does pay California Sales Tax on all purchases. The credit limit is $1,500. Include a subtotal for the sale and apply a 10% sales discount for a nonprofit organization. (Create any new sales items necessary.)
- ▶ Correct the invoice to Mary Cooper. The price of the golf bag should be $179.95. Reprint the invoice.
- ▶ Received Check No. 2285 from Tekin Azizi in full payment of his account.
- ▶ Received Check No. 102-33 from Ed Torres, $600, in partial payment of his account.

1/3/2007

- ▶ Sold 3 gift sets @ $14.99 each and 3 sleeves (packages) of golf balls @ $8.95 each to Lucy Stevens to be given away as door prizes at an upcoming ladies' club tournament.
- ▶ Sold 2 pairs of men's shorts @ $49.95 each, 2 men's shirts @ $59.99 each, and 1 pair of golf shoes @ $119.99 to Wayne Stoval.
- ▶ Received Check No. 815 from Mitchell Duncan for $850 in full payment of his account.
- ▶ Sold 2 golf towels @ $9.95 each to a cash customer. (Cash is the payment method. Remember to print Sales Receipt No. 1.)
- ▶ Sold 1 pair of women's golf shoes @ $149.95 to a new customer: Laura Hansen, 45-2215 PGA Drive, Rancho Mirage, CA 92270, 760-555-3322, Terms 1% 10 Net 30, taxable customer for California Sales Tax, Credit Limit $1,000
- ▶ Received Check No. 2233 for $950 from George Poltash in partial payment of his account.
- ▶ Sold a golf bag for $99.95 to a cash customer using a Visa card.

1/5/2007

- ▶ Prepare and print an Inventory Stock Status by Item Report for January 1-5 in Landscape orientation.
- ▶ Prepare Purchase Orders for all items marked Order on the Inventory Stock Status by Item Report. Place all orders with the preferred vendors. Prepare only one purchase order per vendor. For all items ordered, the Qty on Hand should exceed the Reorder Point by 10 when the new merchandise is received. (For example, if the reorder point is 5 and you have 4 items

on hand, you will need to order 11 items. This would make the quantity 15 when the order is received. This would exceed the reorder point by 10.) The cost of golf bags are $40 each, gift sets are $3 each, men's shorts are $20 each, towels are $2 each, and women's shirts are $20 each. (Remember to print the purchase orders.)

- ▶ Order 5 women's hats @ $10.00 each from a new vendor: Hats and More, 45980 West Los Angeles Street, Los Angeles, CA 90025, Contact Chris Griswald, Phone 310-555-8787, Fax 310-555-7878, E-mail hats@la.com, Terms 2% 10 Net 30, Credit Limit $500. Add a new inventory sales item: Women's Hats with Hats and More as the preferred vendor. The purchase and sales description is Women's Golf Hats. The COGS account is 5000. Leave the sales price at 0.00. The hats are taxable. The Income account is 4000-Sales: 4010-Accessory Sales. The Asset account is 1120-Inventory Asset. The reorder point is 10. Quantity on Hand is 0 as of 01/05/2007.
- ▶ Change the current sales item Hats from Item Name: Hats to Men's Hats. The purchase and sales descriptions should be Men's Golf Hats. Change the reorder point from 15 to 12.
- ▶ Print a Purchase Order QuickReport in Landscape orientation for January 1-5.

1/8/2007

- ▶ Received Check No. 1822 for a cash sale of 2 men's golf hats @ $49.95 each.
- ▶ Deposit all receipts (checks, credit cards, and/or cash) for the week. Print the Deposit Summary.
- ▶ Backup your work for Week 1. Name your backup file **Golf Week 1.qbb**

Week 2—January 9-15:

1/10/2007

- ▶ Received the order from Hats and More without the bill.
- ▶ Received the orders from Golf Supplies & Equipment and Sports Attire, along with the bills for the merchandise received. All items were received in full except the golf bags. Of the 12 bags ordered, only 8 were received. Use 01/10/2007 for the bill date for both transactions.
- ▶ Lucy Stevens returned 1 of the gift sets purchased on January 3. Issue a credit memo and apply to Invoice 5.
- ▶ Mitchell Duncan returned 1 pair of men's golf shorts that had been purchased for $59.95. (The shorts had been purchased previously and were part of his $850 opening balance.) Issue the appropriate items.
- ▶ Sold 1 complete set of golf clubs on account to Burt Nakamura for $1,600.00.
- ▶ Sold a graphite sand wedge and a graphite gap wedge @ $119.95 each to a customer using a Visa card. (Both clubs are classified as irons.)

1/12/2007

- ▶ Received the telephone bill for the month, $85.15 from Desert Telephone Co., 11-092 Highway 111, Palm Springs, CA 92262, 760-555-9285. The bill is due January 25.

- ► Purchased $175 of office supplies to have on hand from Indio Office Supply, 3950 46th Avenue, Indio, CA 92201, Contact Cheryl Lockwood, Phone 760-555-1535, Fax 760-555-5351. Used the company Visa card for the purchase.

1/14/2007

- ► Received the bill for the order from Hats and More. Use 01/14/2007 for the bill date.
- ► Received a bill from the Sunshine Electric Co., 995 Date Palm Drive, Cathedral City, CA 92234, 760-555-4646 for the monthly electric bill. The bill is for $275.00 and is due January 30.
- ► Received the monthly water bill for $65 from Indian Wells Water, 84-985 Jackson Street, Indian Wells, CA 92202, 760-555-5653. The bill is due January 30.
- ► Sold a set of golf clubs on account to Laura Hansen for $895.00.
- ► Received Check No. 3801 for $1,949.42 from Farzad Hamid in full payment of his bill. (The payment includes the discount since the check was dated 01/10/07.)
- ► Received Check No. 783 for $594.53 from Jennifer Winston in full payment of her bill. (The payment includes the discount since the check was dated 01/11/07.)
- ► Deposit all receipts (checks, credit cards, and/or cash) for the week. Print the Deposit Summary.
- ► Back up your work for the week.

Week 3—January 16-22:

1/17/2007

- ► Received Check No. 1822 back from the bank. This check was for $107.14 from a cash customer: William Jones, 8013 Desert Drive, Desert Hot Springs, CA 92270, 760-555-0100. Payment is due on receipt. Charge William the bank charge of $15 plus Your Name Golf Shop's own NSF charge of $15. Add any necessary customers, items and/or accounts. (Returned check service charges should be Income account 4040.)
- ► Received Check No. 67-086 for $135.95 from Lucy Stevens in full payment of her account.
- ► Received the remaining 4 golf bags and the bill from Golf Supplies & Equipment on earlier purchase order. The date of the bill is 01/16/2007.

1/18/2007

- ► Pay all bills that are eligible to receive a discount if paid between January 18 and 22. Use account 5010 Merchandise Discounts as the Discount Account. (Print the checks. You may use Print Forms or you may print the checks individually.)
- ► Sold 1 golf bag @ $199.95, 1 set of graphite golf clubs @ $1,200.00, 1 putter @ $129.95 (record the putter as Golf Clubs: Irons), and 3 sleeves of golf balls @ $9.95 each to Lucy Stevens.
- ► Returned 2 men's shirts that had poorly stitched seams at a cost of $20 each to Sports Attire Received a credit memo from the company.

1/20/2007

- Sold 1 men's golf hat @ $49.95 and 1 men's golf jacket at $89.95 to a customer using a Master Card.
- Sold 1 towel @ $9.95, 2 packages of golf tees @ $1.95 each, and 1 sleeve of golf balls at $5.95 to a customer for cash.
- Received Check No. 1256 in full payment of account from Colleen Chan.
- George Poltash bought a starter set of golf clubs for his son @ $250.00 and a new titanium driver for himself @ $549.95 (a driver is categorized as Golf Club: Woods).
- A businessman in town with his wife bought them each a set of golf clubs @ $1,495.00 per set and a new golf bag for each of them @ $249.95 per bag. He purchased 1 men's jacket for $179.95. His wife purchased 1 pair of golf shoes for $189.99 and 1 women's jacket for $149.99. He used his Visa to pay for the purchases.
- Prepare and print an Inventory Stock Status by Item Report for January 1-20.
- Prepare Purchase Orders to order any inventory items indicated on the report. As with earlier orders, use the preferred vendor, issue only one purchase order per vendor, and order enough to have 10 more than the minimum quantity of the ordered items on hand. (Golf balls cost $3.50 per sleeve, men's and women's jackets cost $20 each, and women's hats cost $10 each.)
- Deposit all receipts (checks, credit cards, and/or cash) for the week. Print the Deposit Summary.
- Back up your work for the week.

Week 4 and End of Period—January 23-31:
1/23/2007

- Pay all bills eligible to receive a discount if paid between January 23 and 30 and pay the telephone bill in full.
- Lucy Stevens was declared Club Champion and won a prize of $500. She brought in the $500 cash as a payment to be applied to the amount she owes on her account.
- Sold Lucy Stevens 5 Women's Golf Hats @ $25.99 each to give away as prizes at her next ladies' club tournament.

1/24/2007

- Received the bill and all the items ordered from Sports Attire, and Golf Supplies & Equipment. The bills are dated 01/23/2007.
- Received Check No. 5216 from Derek Brown as payment in full on his account.
- Received Check No. 1205 from Mary Cooper as payment in full on her account.
- Received a letter of apology for the NSF check and a new check for $137.14 from William Jones to pay his account in full. The new check is Check No. 9015.

1/25/2007

- Received the bill and all the hats ordered from Hats and More. The date of the bill is 01/23/2007.

- ▶ Received the bill for $3,000 rent from Palm Springs Rentals, 11-2951 Palm Canyon Drive, Palm Springs, CA 92262, Contact Tammi Moreno, Phone 760-555-8368, Fax 760-555-8638. The rent is due February 4.
- ▶ Purchased sales supplies to have on hand for $150 from Indio Office Supply. Used the company Visa for the purchase.
- ▶ Prepare an Unpaid Bills Detail Report for January 25, 2007. Print the report.
- ▶ Pay Bills
  - o $1,000 to Sports Attire, for the amount owed on 12/31/2006. (NOTE: Select the bill you want to pay. Apply the credit you have from Sports Attire, because of returned merchandise. You want to pay $1,000 plus use the $40 credit and reduce the amount owed by $1,040, *not* $960. Once the credit is applied, you will see the amount owed as $4,960. Since you are not paying the full amount owed, click in Amt. Paid column and enter the amount you are paying. In this case, enter 1,000 as the amount you are paying. When the payment is processed, $1,000 will be deducted from cash to pay for this bill and the $40 credit will be applied.)
  - o Pay $5,000 to Golf Clubs, Inc. toward the amount owed on 12/31/2006
  - o Pay $500 to Golf Supplies & Equipment to pay the amount owed on 12/31/2006
  - o Pay $500 to Shoe Suppliers to pay the amount owed on 12/31/2006
  - o Pay the rent
  - o Pay the electric bill
  - o Pay the water bill.

1/26/2007

- ▶ Prepare and print an Unpaid Bills Detail Report by Vendor for January 26, 2007. (*Note:* check Sports Attire, the amount owed should be $4,360. If your report does not show this, check to see how you applied the credit when you paid bills. If necessary, QuickBooks Pro does allow you to delete the previous bill payment and redo it. If this is the case, be sure to apply the credit, and record $1,000 as the payment amount.)
- ▶ Received $1,000 from Burt Nakamura, Check No. 3716, in partial payment of his account.
- ▶ Received payment in full from Ed Torres, Check No. 102-157.
- ▶ Sold 15 sleeves of golf balls @ $5.95 each to a cash customer to use as prizes in a retirement golf tournament for an employee of his company. Paid with Check No. 2237.

1/29/2007

- ▶ Deposit all checks and credit card receipts for the week.

1/30/2007

- ▶ Prepare Sales Tax Liability Report from January 1-30, 2007. Adjust the column widths and print the report in Landscape orientation. The report should fit on one page.
- ▶ Pay sales tax and print the check.
- ▶ Print a Sales by Item Summary Report for January 1-30. Use Landscape orientation and, if necessary, adjust column widths so the report fits on one page wide.
- ▶ Print a Trial Balance for January 1-30 in Landscape orientation.

- ► Enter the following adjusting entries:
  - Office Supplies Used for the month is $125.
  - The balance of the Sales Supplies is $650 on January 30.
  - The amount of Prepaid Insurance represents the liability insurance for 12 months. Record the adjusting entry for the month of January.
  - Depreciation for the month is: Office Equipment, $83.33, and Store Fixtures, $100.
- ► Record the transactions for owner's equity:
  - Each owner's withdrawal for the month of January is $2,000.
  - Divide the amount in account 3000-Your Name & Andrews, Capital, and transfer one-half the amount into each owner's individual Capital account. Prepare a Standard Balance Sheet for January 30 to determine the amount to divide.

01/31/2007

- ► Use the following bank statement to prepare a bank reconciliation. Enter any adjustments. Print a Reconciliation Detail Report.

DESERT BANK
1234-110 Highway 111
Palm Springs, CA 92270
(760) 555-3300

Your Name Golf Shop
55-100 PGA Boulevard
Palm Springs, CA 92270
Acct. # 9857-32-922
January 2007

Beginning Balance, January 1, 2007			$35, 275.14
1/8/2007, Deposit	4,210.68		39,485.82
1/10/2007, Check 1		64.30	39,421.52
1/14/2007, Deposit	2,801.24		42,222.76
1/16/2007, NSF Check		107.14	42,115.62
1/18/2007, Check 2		365.54	41,750.08
1/25/2007, Check 3		392.00	41,358.08
1/23/2007, Check 4		85.15	41,272.93
1/23/2007, Check 5		156.80	41,116.13
1/23/2007, Check 6		49.00	41,067.13
1/25/2007, Deposit	6,307.77		47,374.90
1/25/2007, Check 7		1,000.00	46.374.90
1/25/2007, Check 13		275.00	46,099.90
1/25/2007, Check 12		500.00	45,599.90
1/25/2007, Check 11		3,000.00	42,599.90
1/25/2007, Check 8		5,000.00	37,599.90
1/25/2007, Check 9		500.00	37,099.90
1/25/2007, Check 10		65.00	37,034.*0
1/31/2007, Service Charge, $15, and NSF Charge, $15		30.00	37,004.90
1/31/2007, Store Fixtures Loan Pmt.: $89.03 Interest, $17.21 Principal		106.24	36,898.66
1/31/2007, Office Equipment Loan Pmt: $53.42 Interest, $10.33 Principal		63.75	36,834.91
1/31/2007, Interest	76.73		36,911.64
Ending Balance, 1/31/2007			36,911.64

► Received the Visa bill. Prepare a Credit Card Reconciliation and pay the Visa bill. Print the check for payment to Desert Bank and a Reconciliation Summary Report

DESERT BANK
VISA DEPARTMENT
1234-110 Highway 111
Palm Springs, CA 92270 (760) 555-3300

Your Name Golf Shop
55-100 PGA Boulevard
Palm Springs, CA 92270
VISA Acct. # 9287-52-952 January 2007

Beginning Balance, January 1, 2007			0.00
1/12/2007, Indio Office Supply		175.00	175.00
1/25/2007, Indio Office Supply		150.00	325.00
Ending Balance, 1/25/2007			325.00
Minimum Payment Due, $50.00		Payment Due Date: February 7, 2007	

► Make sure the reporting preference is for accrual basis.
► Print the following reports for January 1-31, 2007, or as of January 31, 2007:
  - o Standard Profit & Loss Statement
  - o Standard Balance Sheet
► Divide the Net Income/Retained Earnings in half and transfer one-half into each owner's individual capital account.
► Close the drawing account for each owner into the owner's individual capital account.
► Print a Standard Balance Sheet for January 31, 2007.
► Close the period using the closing date of 01/31/2007.
► Edit a transaction from the closed period: Discovered an error in the Supplies accounts. Transfer $50 from 1320-Sales Supplies to 1310-Office Supplies.
► Adjust the number of tees on hand to 24. Use the expense account 6190 for Merchandise Adjustments. Be sure to correct the adjustment for net income/ retained earnings.

2/1/2007
► Print the following:
  - o Journal (Landscape orientation, Fit on one page wide) for January 1, 2007-February 1, 2007
  - o Post-Closing Trial Balance, February 1, 2007 (Landscape orientation)
  - o Post-Closing Standard Profit and Loss Statement, February 1, 2007
  - o Post-Closing Standard Balance Sheet, February 1, 2007

2/1/2008
► Print a Standard Balance Sheet for February 1, 2008
► Back up your work to **Golf Complete.qbb**

NAME____________________

TRANSMITTAL

YOUR NAME GOLF SHOP: PRACTICE SET MERCHANDISING BUSINESS

Attach the following documents and reports:

Week 1
Chart of Accounts
Trial Balance, January 1, 2007
Invoice No. 1: Jennifer Winston
Invoice No. 2: Mary Cooper
Invoice No. 3: Farzad Hamid
Invoice No. 4: Palm Springs Schools
Invoice No. 2 (Corrected): Mary Cooper
Invoice No. 5: Lucy Stevens
Invoice No. 6: Wayne Stoval
Sales Receipt No. 1: Cash Customer
Invoice No. 7: Laura Hansen
Sales Receipt No. 2: Cash Customer
Inventory Stock Status by Item Report, January 1-5, 2007
Purchase Order No. 1: Golf Supplies & Equipment
Purchase Order No. 2: Sports Attire
Purchase Order No. 3: Hats and More
Purchase Order QuickReport, January 5, 2007
Sales Receipt No. 3: Cash Customer
Deposit Summary, January 8, 2007

Week 2
Credit Memo No. 8: Lucy Stevens
Credit Memo No. 9: Mitchell Duncan
Check No. 1: Mitchell Duncan
Invoice No. 10: Burt Nakamura
Sales Receipt No. 4: Cash Customer
Invoice No. 11: Laura Hansen
Deposit Summary, January 14, 2007

Week 3
Invoice No. 12: William Jones
Check No. 2: Golf Supplies & Equipment
Check No. 3: Sports Attire
Invoice No. 13: Lucy Stevens
Sales Receipt No. 5: Cash Customer
Sales Receipt No. 6: Cash Customer
Invoice No. 14: George Poltash
Sales Receipt No. 7: Cash Customer
Inventory Stock Status by Item, January 1-20, 2007
Purchase Order No. 4: Golf Supplies & Equipment
Purchase Order No. 5: Sports Attire
Purchase Order No. 6: Hats and More
Deposit Summary, January 20, 2007

Week 4 and End of Period
Check No. 4: Desert Telephone
Check No. 5: Golf Supplies & Equipment
Check No. 6: Hats and More
Invoice No. 15: Lucy Stevens
Unpaid Bills Detail, January 25, 2007
Check No. 7: Sports Attire
Check No. 8: Golf Clubs, Inc.
Check No. 9: Golf Supplies & Equipment
Check No. 10: Indian Wells Water
Check No. 11: Palm Springs Rentals
Check No. 12: Shoe Suppliers
Check No. 13: Sunshine Electric Co.
Unpaid Bills Detail, January 26, 2007
Sales Receipt No. 8: Cash Customer
Deposit Summary, January 30, 2007
Sales Tax Liability Report, January 1-30, 2007
Check No. 14: State Board of Equalization
Sales by Item Summary, January 1-30, 2007
Trial Balance, January 30, 2007
Check No. 15: Your Name
Check No. 16: Annie Andrews
Bank Reconciliation, January 31, 2007
Credit Card Reconciliation, January 31, 2007
Check No. 17: Desert Bank
Standard Profit and Loss, January 2007
Standard Balance Sheet, January 31, 2007
Standard Balance Sheet After Owner Equity Adjustments, January 31, 2007
Journal, January 2007
Post-Closing Trial Balance, February 1, 2007
Post-Closing Standard Profit and Loss Statement, February 1, 2007
Post-Closing Standard Balance Sheet, February 1, 2007
Standard Balance Sheet, February 1, 2008

PAYROLL

8

LEARNING OBJECTIVES

At the completion of this chapter, you will be able to:

1. Create, preview, and print payroll checks.
2. Adjust pay stub information.
3. Correct, void, and delete paychecks.
4. Change employee information and add a new employee.
5. Print a Payroll Summary by Employee Report.
6. View an Employee Earnings Summary Report.
7. Print a Payroll Liabilities Report.
8. Pay Taxes and Other Liabilities.
9. Prepare and print forms 941 and 940
10. Prepare and preview W-2 forms
11. Print a Journal

PAYROLL

Many times, a company begins the process of computerizing its accounting system simply to be able to do the payroll using the computer. It is much faster and easier to let QuickBooks Pro look at the tax tables and determine how much withholding should be deducted for each employee than to have an individual perform this task. Because tax tables change frequently, QuickBooks Pro requires its users to enroll in a payroll service plan. In order to enroll in a payroll service plan, you must have a company tax identification number and a registered copy of QuickBooks. QuickBooks Pro has two types of payroll service plans: QuickBooks Standard Payroll and QuickBooks Enhanced Payroll. These are available for an additional charge. If you do not subscribe to a payroll plan, you must calculate and enter the payroll taxes manually.

The QuickBooks Standard Payroll includes tools, tables, and federal forms to help you run payroll, pay payroll taxes, and prepare federal tax forms. The QuickBooks Enhanced Payroll adds state tax forms, tools for tracking workers compensation costs, tolls for calculating bonuses, and tools for entering hours for a large number of employees more quickly. In addition, the QuickBooks Enhanced Payroll also comes in an accountant's version and allows payroll to be processed for up to 50 businesses.

Since all of our businesses in this text are fictitious, we will not be subscribing to any of the QuickBooks Pro Payroll Services; therefore, we will be entering all tax information for paychecks manually based on data provided in the text. Calculations will be made for vacation pay, sick pay, medical and dental insurance deductions, and so on. Paychecks will be created, printed, corrected, and voided. Tax reports, tax payments, and tax forms will be prepared.

TRAINING TUTORIAL

The tutorial will work with Your Name Workout Co. As in all the previous chapters, you should download the company file **Workout.qbb** from the Prentice Hall Web Site. Once you open your copy of the company file, transactions will be recorded for the fictitious company. To maximize training benefits, you should follow the procedures listed in earlier chapters.

You have four employees Matthew Bayless, who provides the management and supervision of the gym; Rex McCarthy, who is a personal trainer; Louise Rodriguez, who manages and runs the boutique shop and is the bookkeeper; and Lyndsey Wilson, who is the pilates instructor.

Matthew Bayless and Louise Rodriguez are salaried employees. Rex McCartney and Lyndsey Wilson are paid on an hourly basis, and any hours in excess of 160 for the pay period will be paid as overtime. Paychecks for all employees are issued on a monthly basis.

ADD YOUR NAME TO THE COMPANY NAME

As with previous companies, each student in the course will be working for the same company and printing the same documents. Personalizing the company name to include your name will help identify many of the documents you print during your training.

➤ Add your name to the company name

Click **Company** on the menu bar
Click **Company Info**
Drag through the words **Student's Name** to highlight
Type –**your real name**

- Type your real name, *not* the words *Your Real Name*. For example, Susan Smith would type—**Susan Smith**.

Click **OK**

- The title bar now shows Your Name Workout Co.

CHANGE THE NAME OF THE CAPITAL ACCOUNTS

Since the owner's equity accounts have the words Student's Name as part of the account name, replace *Student's Name* with your actual name.

Change the owner equity account names as previously instructed

Access the **Chart of Accounts**
Change **Student's Name, Capital** to **Your Name, Capital**
Change **Student's Name, Investment** to **Your Name, Investment**
Change **Student's Name, Drawing** to **Your Name, Drawing**
Close the Chart of Accounts

SELECT A PAYROLL OPTION

Before entering any payroll transactions, QuickBooks Pro must be informed of the type of payroll service you are selecting. Once QuickBooks Pro knows what type of payroll process has been selected for the company, you will be able to create paychecks. In order to create paychecks manually, you must go through the Help menu to designate this choice.

Select a **Manual** payroll option

Press **F1** to access Help
Click the **Index** tab
Type **payroll**
Scroll through the list of payroll items
Click **without a payroll service subscription**
Click the **Display** button

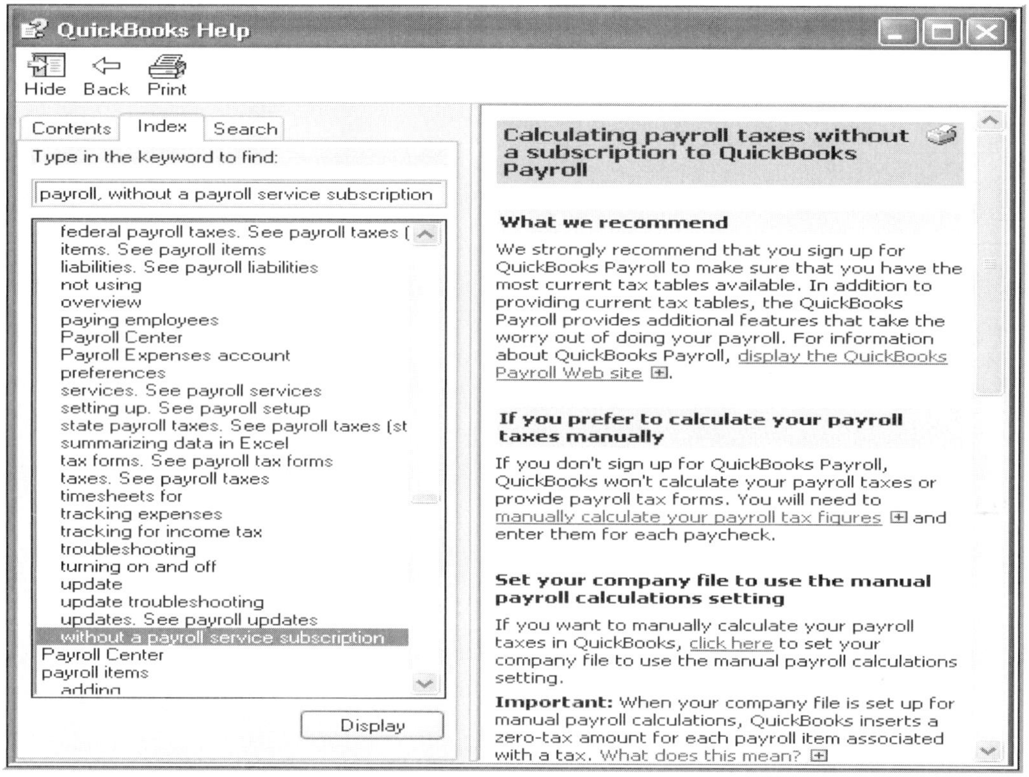

In the "Set **your company file to use the manual payroll calculations setting"** section, click the words **<u>manual payroll calculations</u>**

In the section **"Are you sure you want to set your company file to use manual calculations"**, click **<u>Set my company file to use manual calculations</u>**

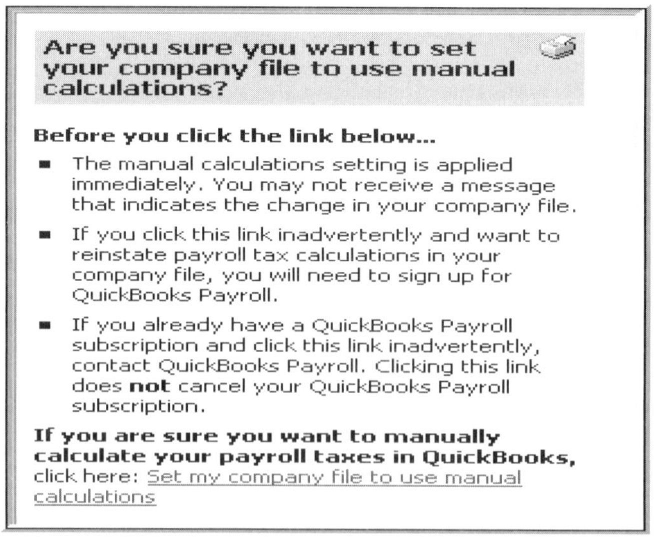

Once QuickBooks processes the selection, you will get a message

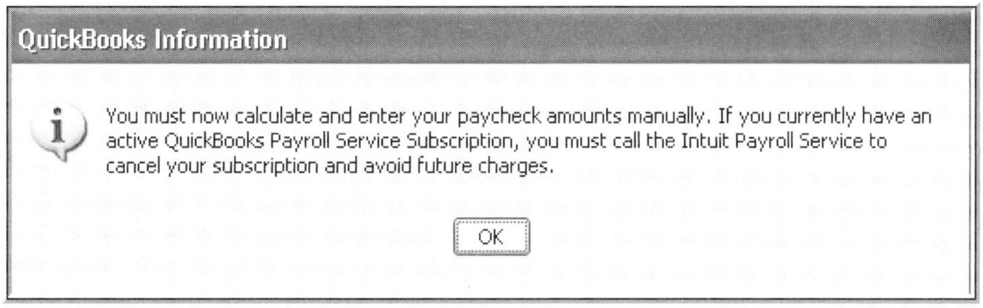

Click **OK**
Close Help

CHANGE EMPLOYEE INFORMATION

Whenever a change occurs for an employee, it may be entered at any time.

MEMO
DATE: January 30, 2006

Effective today, Matthew Bayless will receive a pay raise to $30,000 annually. In addition, all employees will be paid on a monthly basis.

Change the salary for Matthew

Click the **Employee Center** icon
Click **Matthew Bayless**
Click the **Edit Employee** button
Click the drop-down list arrow for **Change Tabs**
Click **Payroll and Compensation Info**
On the **Payroll Info** tab, change the **Hourly/Annual Rate** to **30,000**
Click the drop-down list arrow for Pay Period, click **Monthly**

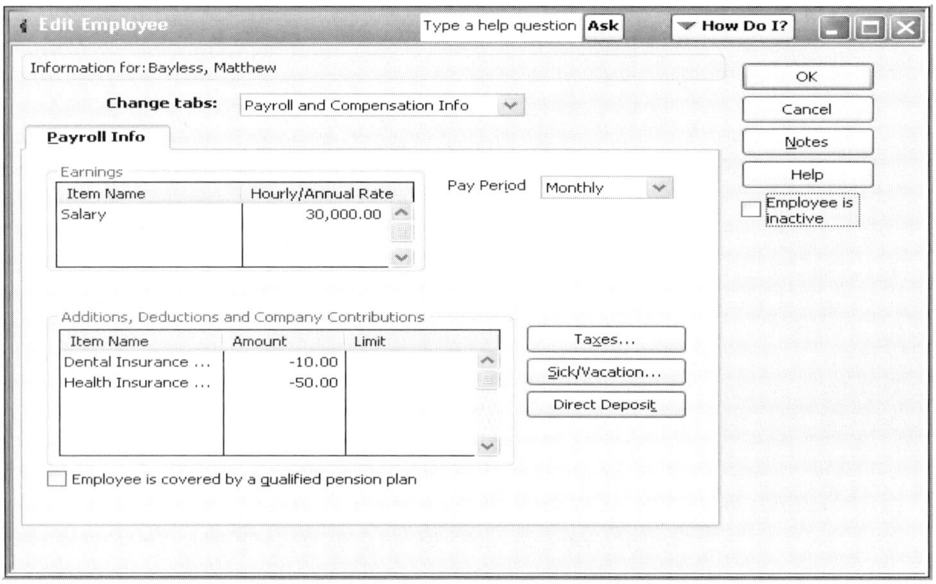

Click **OK**
Do *not* close the **Employee Center**

Change the other three employees to a monthly Pay Period

Edit each employee and change the pay period to Monthly by following the procedures listed above

ADD A NEW EMPLOYEE

As new employees are hired, they should be added.

MEMO
DATE: January 30, 2006

Effective 01/30/06 hired a part-time employee to teach yoga classes. Ms. Penny Benson, SS. No. 100-55-6936, Female, Birth date 02/14/80, 2379 Bayshore Drive, Venice, CA 90405, 310-555-6611. Paid an hourly rate of $15.00 monthly and an overtime rate of $22.50. Federal and state withholding: Single, 0 Allowances. No local taxes, dental insurance, medical insurance, sick time, or vacation time.

Add the new employee, Penny Benson

Click the **New Employee** button at the top of the Employee Center

On the **Personal** tab, click in the text box for **Mr./Ms./...**, enter **Ms.**

Using the information provided, tab to or click in each field and enter the information for the **Personal** tab

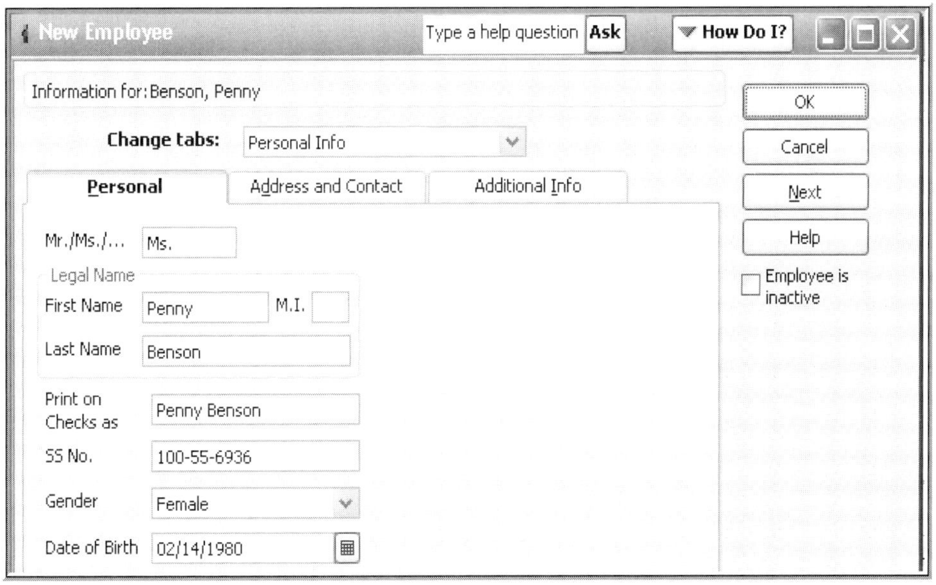

Click the **Address and Contact** tab and continue to enter the information provided

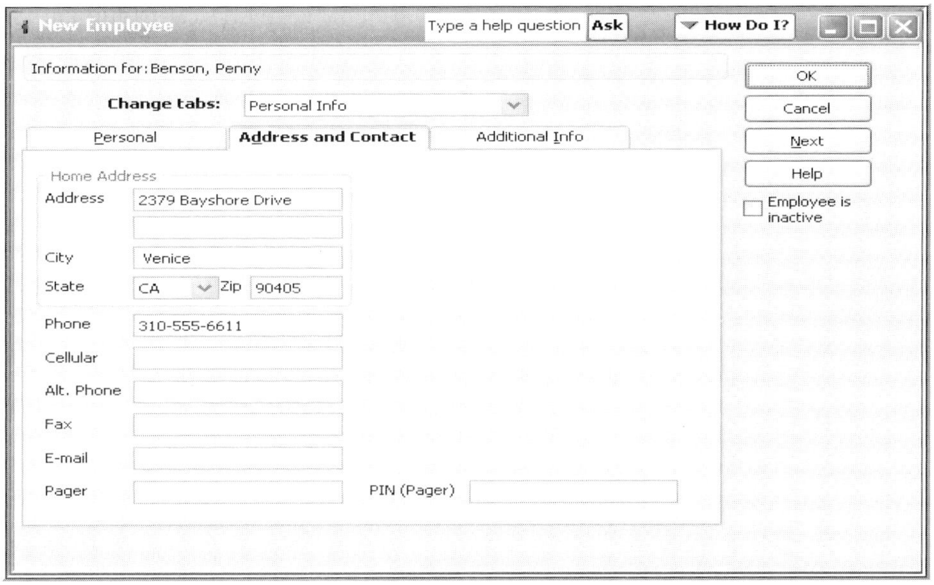

Click the drop-down list arrow for Change Tabs and select **Payroll and Compensation Info**

Click **Item Name** column under **Earnings**, click the drop-down list arrow that appears, click **Hourly Regular Rate**

Tab to or click **Hourly/Annual Rate**, enter the hourly rate she will be paid

Click **Item Name** column under **Hourly Regular Rate**, click the drop-down list arrow that appears, click **Overtime Rate**

- QuickBooks enters the rate of 22.50.

Select a **Monthly** pay period

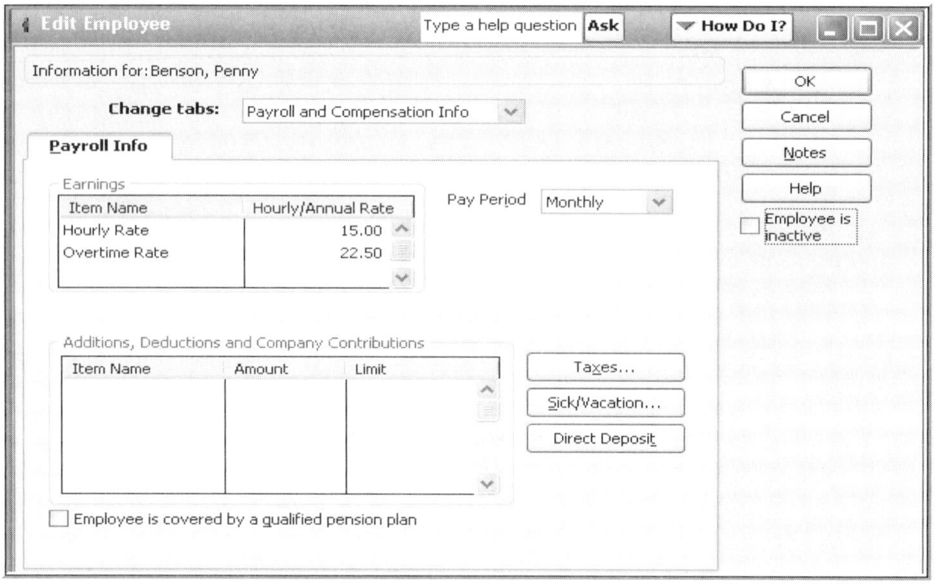

Click the **Taxes** button and complete the tax information

Federal taxes should show Filing Status: **Single,** Allowances: **0,** Extra Withholding: **0.00,** Subject to **Medicare**, **Social Security**, and **Federal Unemployment Tax (Company Paid)** should have a check mark

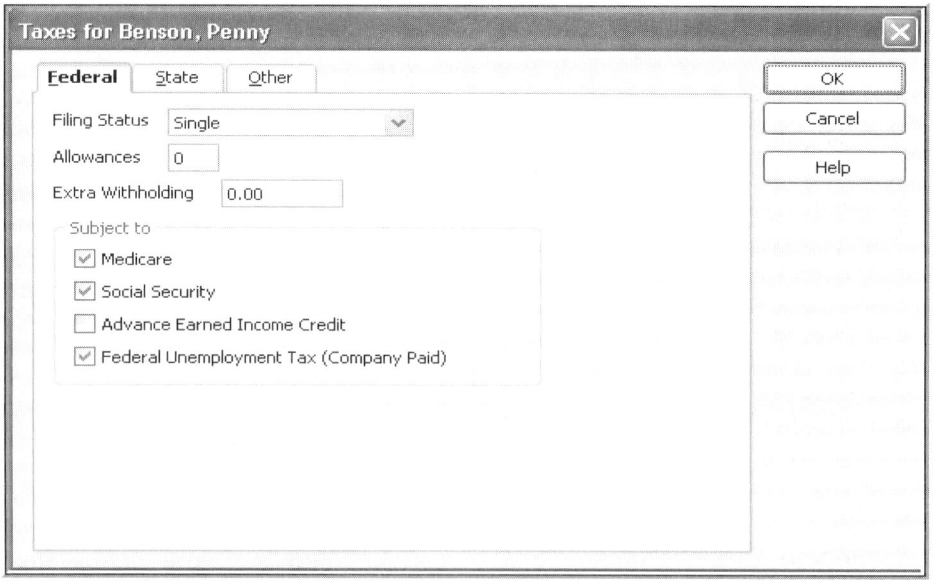

Click the **State** tab
State Worked: **CA**, **SUI** and **SDI** should be selected
State Subject to Withholding: **CA**, Filing Status: **Single**, Allowances: **0**, Extra Withholding: **0.00**; Estimated Deductions: **0**

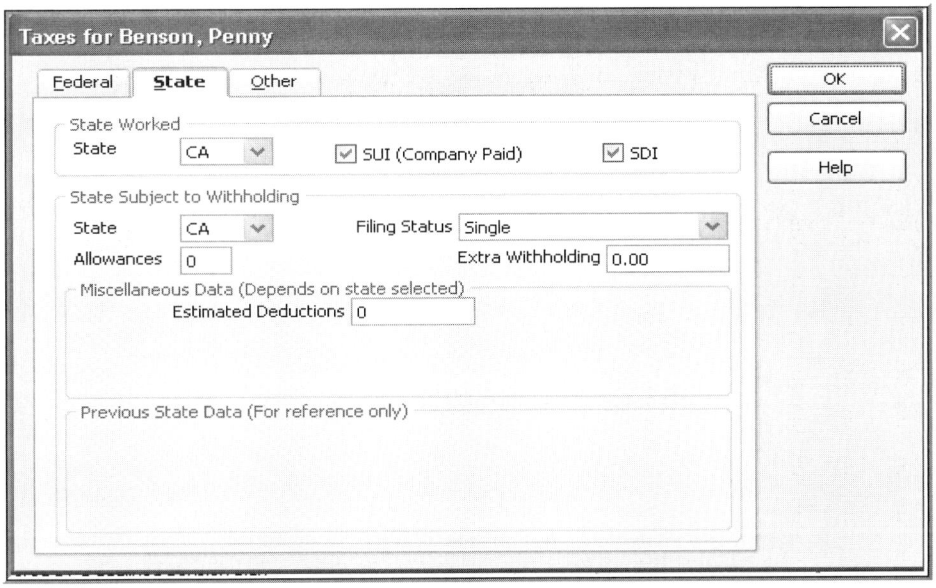

Click the **Other** tab
Click the drop-down list arrow for **Item Name**
Click **CA-Employment Training Tax**

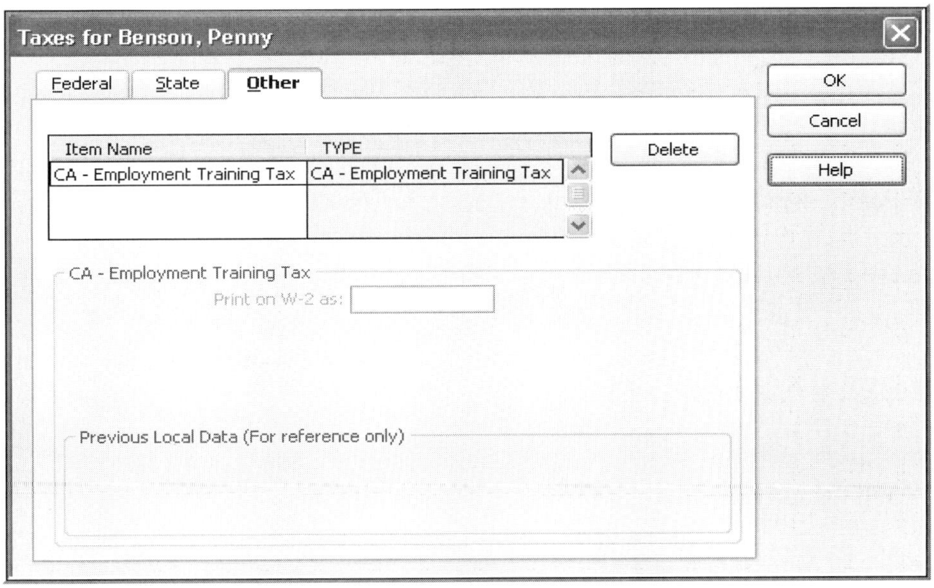

Click **OK** to complete the tax information
Click the drop-down list arrow for **Change Tabs**

Click **Employment Info**
The **Hire Date** should be **01/30/06** and **Employment Details Type** should be **Regular**

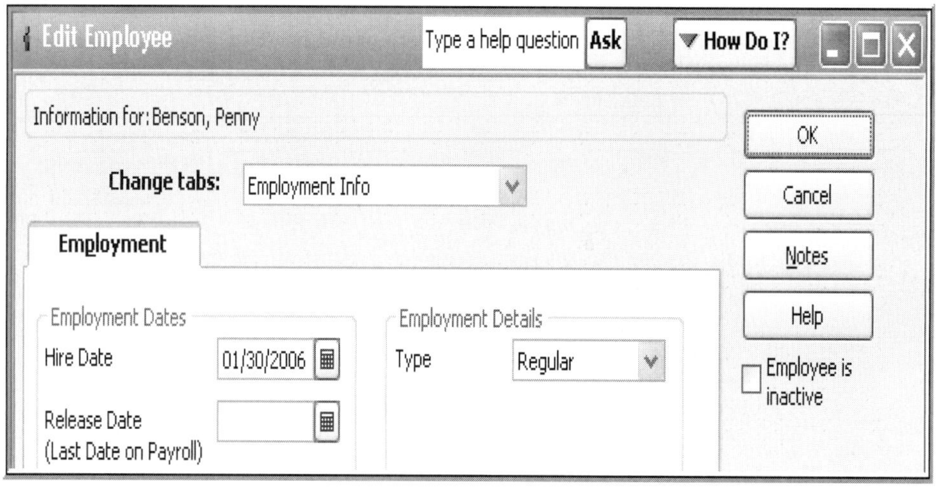

Click **OK** to complete the addition of the new employee

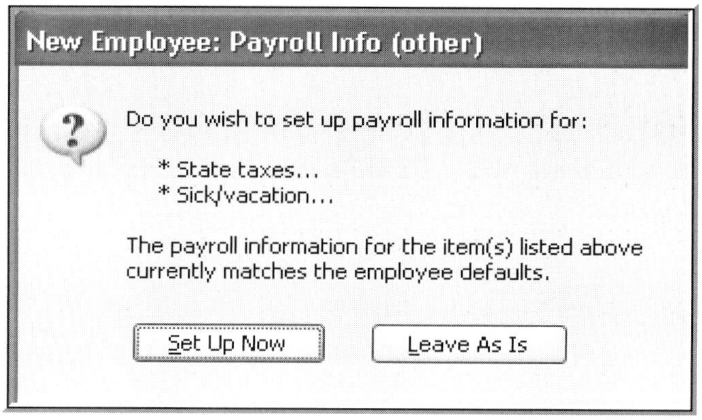

Since Penny does not have any sick/vacation hours, click **Leave As Is** on the New Employee: Payroll Info (other)
Close the Employee Center

VIEW THE PAYROLL ITEM LIST

Prior To processing employee paychecks, it is helpful to view the Payroll Item list to see the payroll items and the tax amounts.

View the Payroll Item List

Click **Employees** on the Menu bar

Click **Payroll Item List**
Click **No** on the Payroll Service Message regarding signing up for payroll services

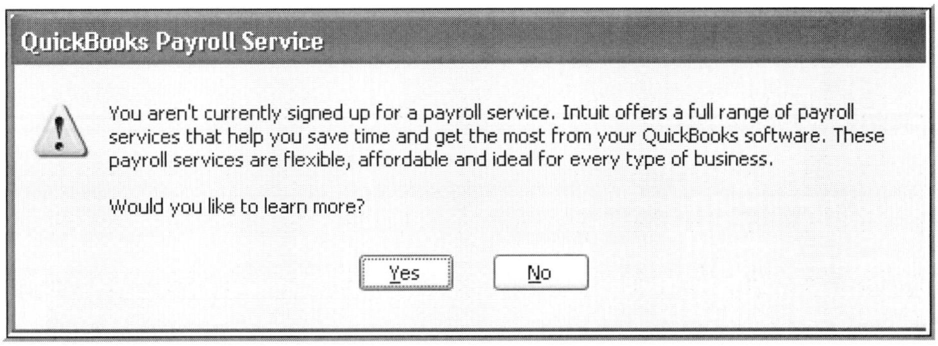

- Since you have not signed up for Payroll Services through QuickBooks, you will frequently see this message. Whenever it appears, click **No**
- The Payroll Item List displays

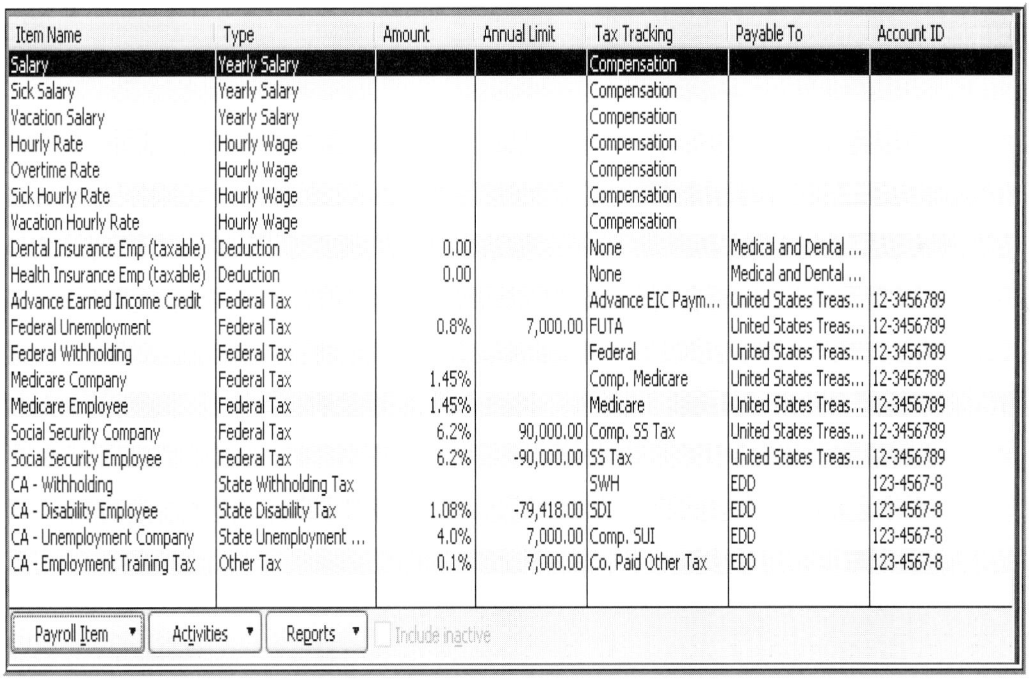

Item Name	Type	Amount	Annual Limit	Tax Tracking	Payable To	Account ID
Salary	Yearly Salary			Compensation		
Sick Salary	Yearly Salary			Compensation		
Vacation Salary	Yearly Salary			Compensation		
Hourly Rate	Hourly Wage			Compensation		
Overtime Rate	Hourly Wage			Compensation		
Sick Hourly Rate	Hourly Wage			Compensation		
Vacation Hourly Rate	Hourly Wage			Compensation		
Dental Insurance Emp (taxable)	Deduction	0.00		None	Medical and Dental ...	
Health Insurance Emp (taxable)	Deduction	0.00		None	Medical and Dental ...	
Advance Earned Income Credit	Federal Tax			Advance EIC Paym...	United States Treas...	12-3456789
Federal Unemployment	Federal Tax	0.8%	7,000.00	FUTA	United States Treas...	12-3456789
Federal Withholding	Federal Tax			Federal	United States Treas...	12-3456789
Medicare Company	Federal Tax	1.45%		Comp. Medicare	United States Treas...	12-3456789
Medicare Employee	Federal Tax	1.45%		Medicare	United States Treas...	12-3456789
Social Security Company	Federal Tax	6.2%	90,000.00	Comp. SS Tax	United States Treas...	12-3456789
Social Security Employee	Federal Tax	6.2%	-90,000.00	SS Tax	United States Treas...	12-3456789
CA - Withholding	State Withholding Tax			SWH	EDD	123-4567-8
CA - Disability Employee	State Disability Tax	1.08%	-79,418.00	SDI	EDD	123-4567-8
CA - Unemployment Company	State Unemployment ...	4.0%	7,000.00	Comp. SUI	EDD	123-4567-8
CA - Employment Training Tax	Other Tax	0.1%	7,000.00	Co. Paid Other Tax	EDD	123-4567-8

View the Payroll Item list to see the item names, types, amounts, annual limits, tax tracking, payable to, and account id
Close the report without printing

CREATE PAYCHECKS

Once the manual payroll option has been selected, paychecks may be created. You may enter hours and preview the checks before creating them, or, if using a payroll service, you may create the checks without previewing. Once the payroll has been processed, checks may be printed.

MEMO
DATE: January 31, 2006

Since you chose to process the payroll manually, you will enter the payroll data for withholdings and deductions rather than have QuickBooks Pro automatically calculate the amounts for you. QuickBooks Pro will still enter other payroll items such as medical and dental insurance deductions, and it will calculate the total amount of the checks. Create and print paychecks for January 31, 2006. Use the above date as the pay period ending date and the check date. Pay all employees using the hours and deductions listed in the following table.

Use the following information to record the payroll for January

PAYROLL TABLE: JANUARY 31, 2006					
	Matthew Bayless	**Penny Benson**	**Rex McCartney**	**Louise Rodriguez**	**Lyndsey Wilson**
HOURS					
REGULAR	160	8	72	140	160
OVERTIME					8
SICK			8		
VACATION				20	
DEDUCTIONS OTHER PAYROLL ITEMS: EMPLOYEE					
DENTAL INS.	10.00			10.00	
MEDICAL INS.	50.00			50.00	
DEDUCTIONS: COMPANY					
CA-EMPLOYMENT TRAINING TAX	2.50	0.00	2.00	1.67	2.58
SOCIAL SECURITY	155.00	7.44	124.00	103.33	159.96
MEDICARE	36.25	1.74	29.00	24.17	37.41
FEDERAL UNEMPLOYMENT	20.00	0.00	16.00	13.33	20.64
CA-UNEMPLOYMENT	100.00	4.80	80.00	66.67	103.20
DEDUCTIONS: EMPLOYEE					
FEDERAL WITHHOLDING	375.00	18.00	300.00	249.90	387.00
SOCIAL SECURITY	155.00	7.44	124.00	103.33	159.96
MEDICARE	36.25	1.74	29.00	24.17	37.41
CA-WITHHOLDING	100.00	4.80	80.00	66.64	103.20
CA-DISABILITY	27.00	1.30	21.60	17.99	27.86

Create checks for the above employees

Click **Pay Employees** on the **Employees** menu
If you get a message regarding QuickBooks Payroll Service, click **No**
On the Pay Employees message, click **Pay employees anyway**

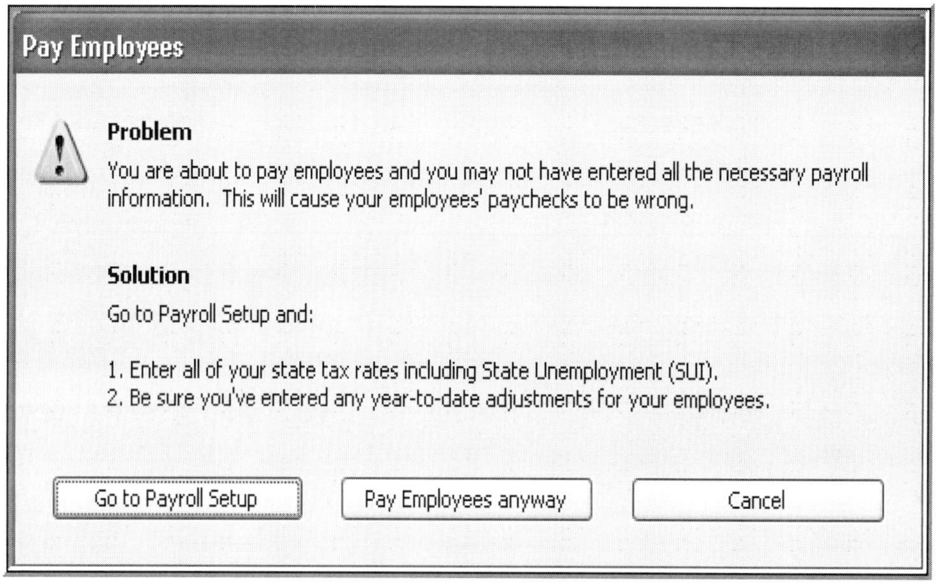

The **Select Employees to Pay** screen should use **Checking** as the bank account

- If not, click the drop-down list for Bank Account and select Checking

Click **To be printed**

Select **Enter hours and tax amounts before creating paychecks**

Check Date is **01/31/06** and the **Pay Period Ends 01/31/06**

Click **Mark All** to select all employees to be paid

- Notice the check mark in front of each employee name.

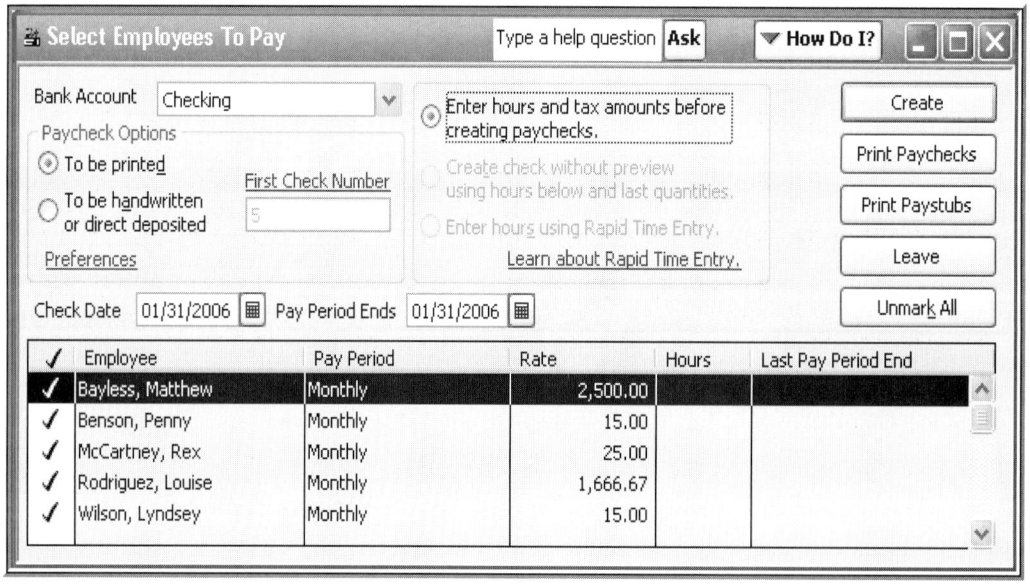

Click the **Create** button

The **Preview Paycheck** screen for Matthew Bayless appears.

- As you record the information for each employee, refer to the payroll chart listed earlier in the chapter.
- Remember, if you subscribe to QuickBooks Pro payroll services you will not enter the taxes manually. QuickBooks Pro will calculate them and enter them for you. Since tax tables change frequently, the taxes calculated by QuickBooks Pro may not be the same as the amounts listed on the Payroll Table in the text.

Tab to or click **Hours**, enter **160**

The section for Other Payroll Items is completed by QuickBooks Pro

Complete the Company Summary information:

Click in the **Amount** column for **CA-Employment Training Tax,** enter **2.50**

Click in the **Amount** column for **Social Security Company**, enter **155.00**

For **Medicare Company** enter **36.25**

Federal Unemployment is **20.00**

CA-Unemployment Company is **100.00**

Complete the Employee Summary information:

Click in the **Amount** column for **Federal Withholding**, enter **375.00**

For **Social Security Employee** enter **155.00**

Medicare Employee is **36.25**

CA-Withholding is **100.00**

CA-Disability Employee is **27.00**, press **Tab**

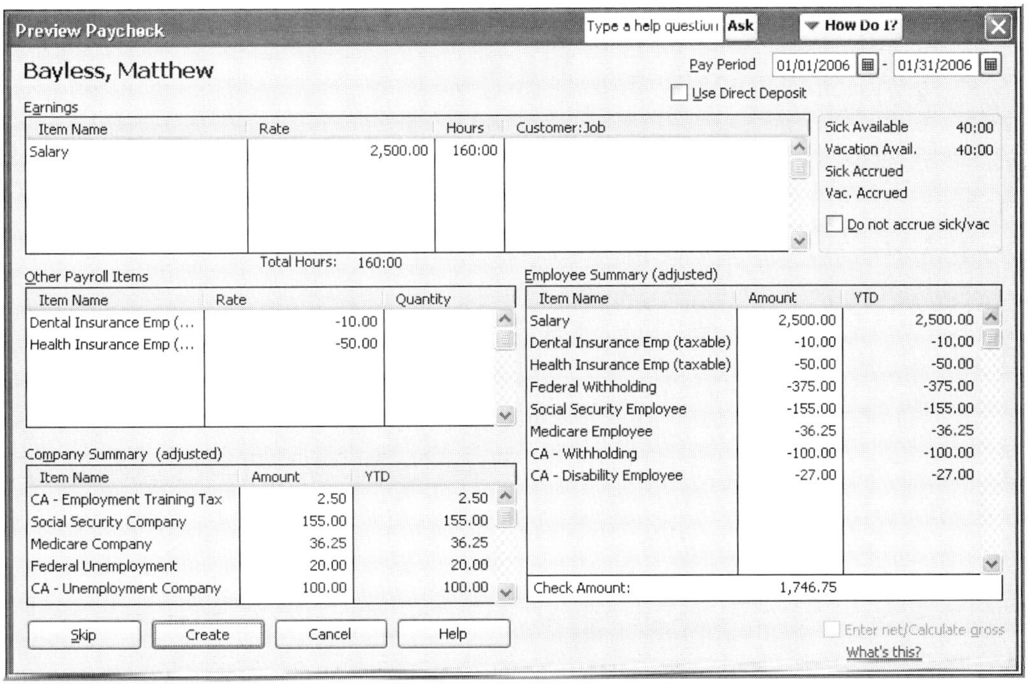

- Notice that QuickBooks calculated the monthly salary based on the annual salary and automatically entered the amount of Dental and Health Insurance paid by the employee.

After verifying that everything was entered correctly, click **Create**
The next Preview Paycheck screen should be for **Penny Benson**
Tab to or click the **Hours** column next to **Hourly Regular Rate** for **Penny Benson**, enter **8**
Refer to the Payroll Table for January 31, 2006, and enter the company and employee deductions for Penny

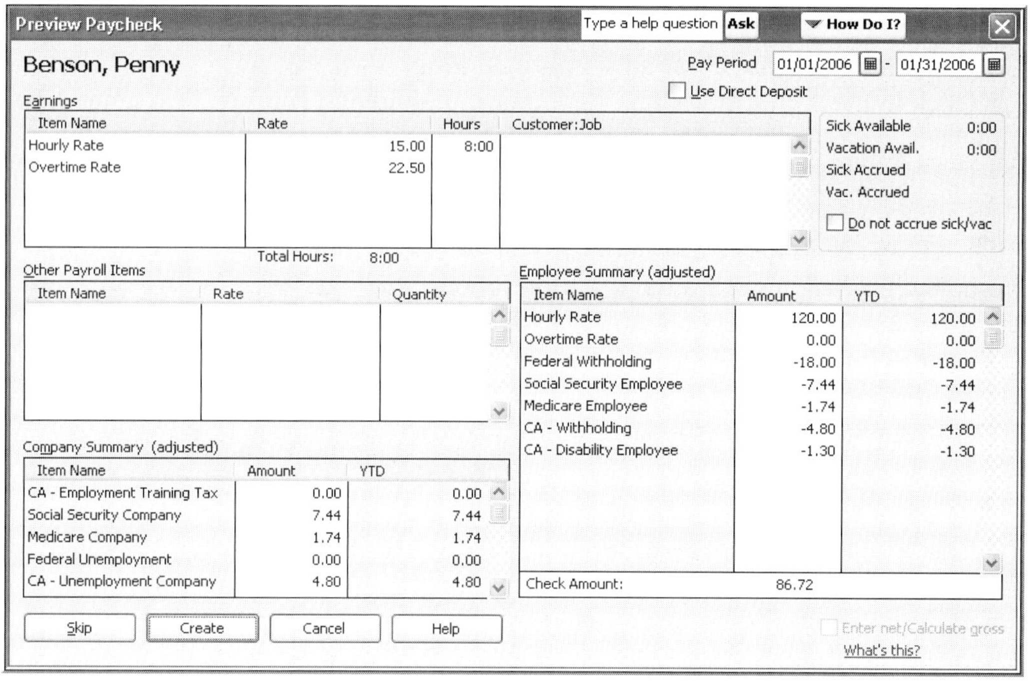

Click **Create**
Pay **Rex McCartney** for **72** hours of **Hourly Regular Rate**
Click in the **Item Names** section for **Earnings**
Click the drop-down list arrow, click **Sick Hourly Rate**
Enter **8** for the number of hours Rex was out sick
Following the steps previously indicated, enter the company and employee deductions from the Payroll Table for January 31, 2006

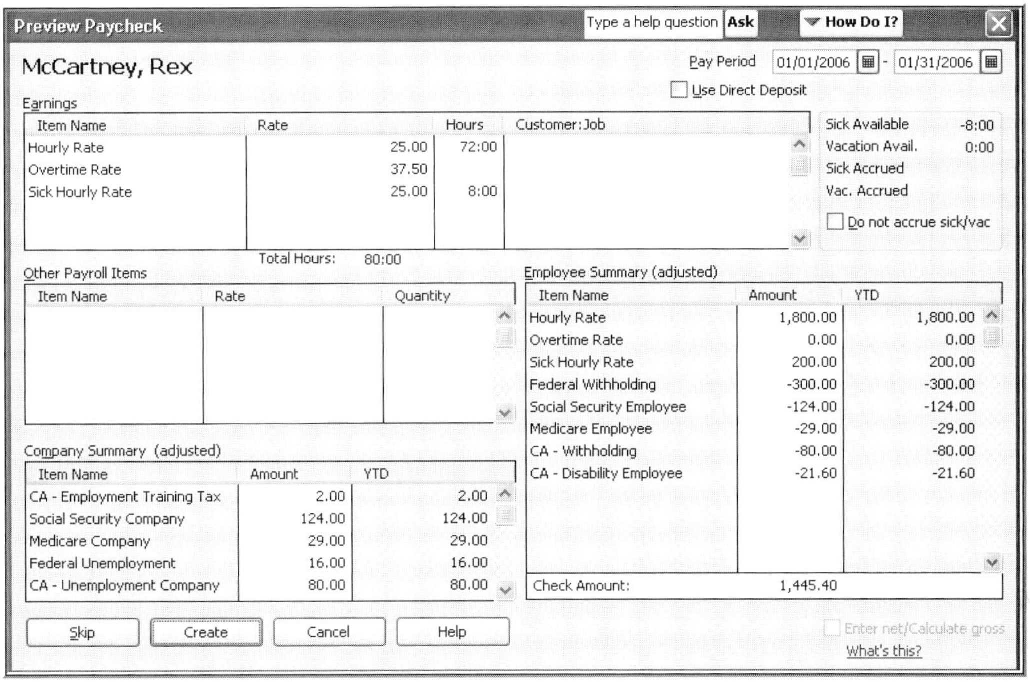

Click **Create**

Pay **Louise Rodriguez** for **140** hours of **Salary**

- Notice that thc number of Vacation Hours listed in **Vacation Available** is **20.00**.

In the **Item Name** column under **Earnings**, click on the blank line beneath Salary, click the drop-down list arrow that appears, click **Vacation Salary**, tab to or click the **Hours** column, enter **20**

- The Vacation Hours will show 0.00.

Complete the paycheck information

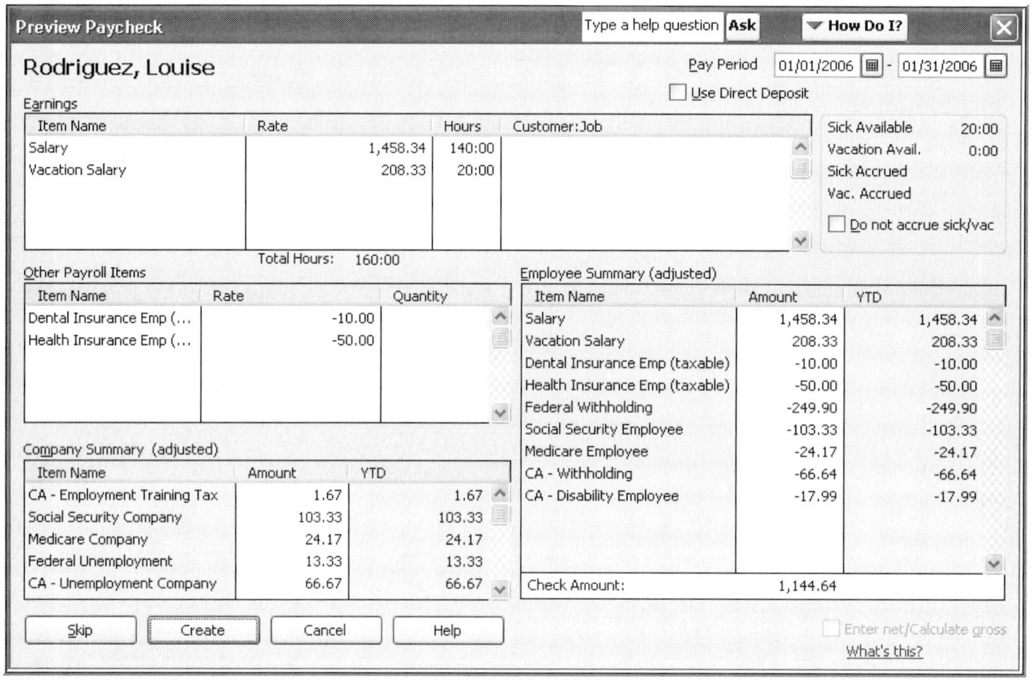

Click **Create**

Process the paycheck for **Lyndsey Wilson**

Record **160** for her Hourly Rate Hours

Record **8** as her Overtime Rate Hours

Using the Payroll Table provided, enter the remaining payroll information as previously instructed

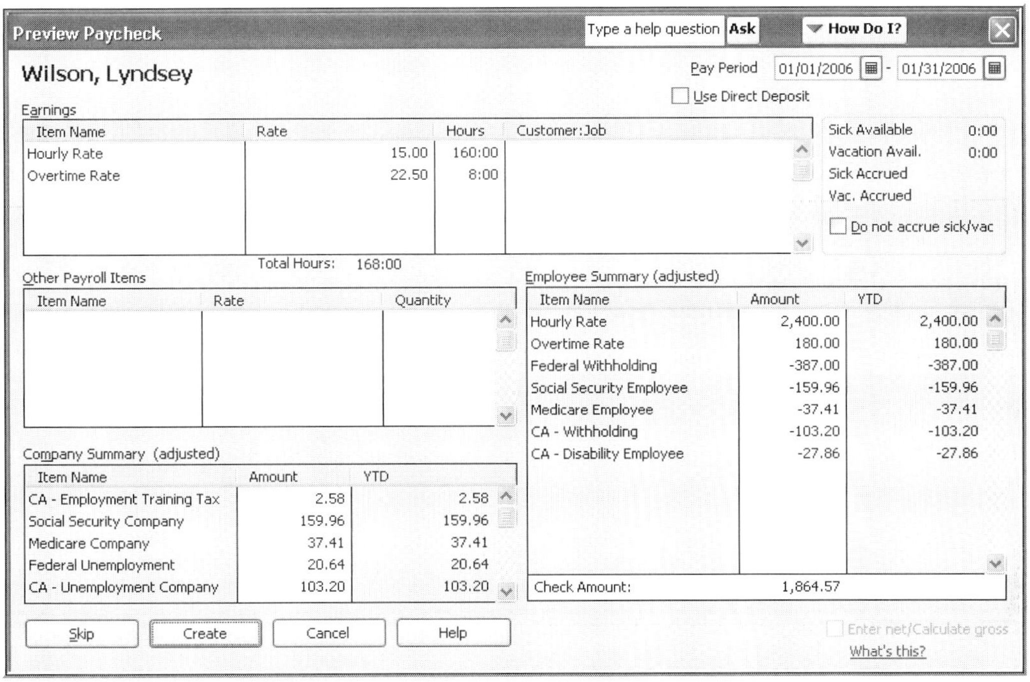

Click **Create**

- **Select Employees To Pay** appears on the screen. Notice that the check marks have been removed, the Hours column has the hours for each employee, and the Last Pay Period End is 01/31/2006 for all employees.

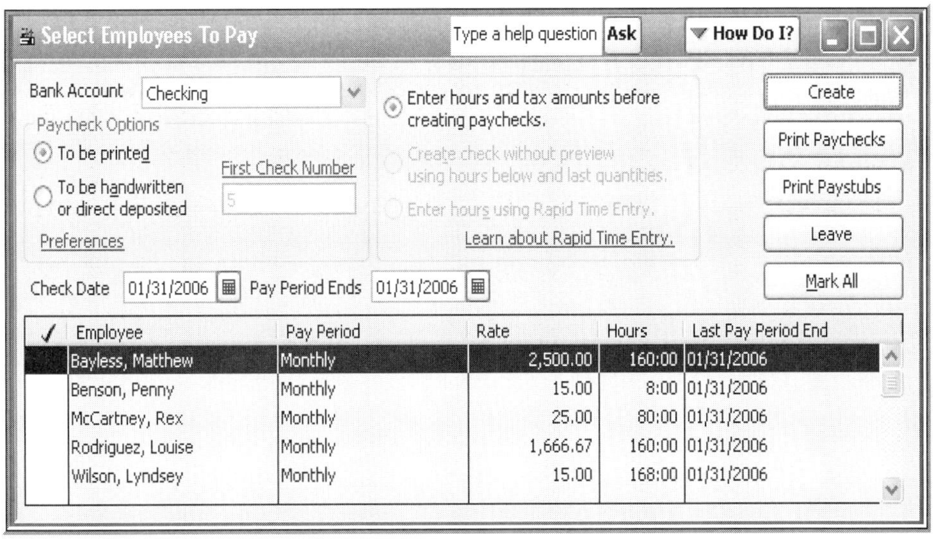

Do not close the Select Employees to Pay Screen

PRINT PAYCHECKS

Paychecks may be printed one at a time or all at once. You may use the same printer setup as your other checks in QuickBooks Pro or you may print using a different printer setup. If you use a voucher check, the pay stub is printed as part of the check. If you do not use a voucher check, you may print the pay stub separately. The pay stub information includes the employee's name, address, Social Security number, the pay period start and end dates, pay rate, the hours, the amount of pay, all deductions, sick and vacation time used and available, net pay, and year-to-date amounts.

MEMO

DATE: January 31, 2006
Print the paychecks for all employees using a voucher-style check with 2 parts. Print the company name on the checks.

Print the January 31 paychecks

Click **Print Paychecks** on the **Select Employees To Pay** screen
Bank Account should be **Checking**; if it is not, click the drop-down list for Bank Account, click Payroll Checking.
Select All employees, **First Check Number** is **1**; if it is not, change it to 1

- Notice that there are 5 Paychecks to be printed for a total of $6,288.08.
- QuickBooks can process payroll for direct deposit or printed paychecks. Even though we are not processing direct deposit paychecks, leave **Show** as **Both**

Click the **Preferences** button and verify that all items for Payroll Printing Preferences for Paycheck Vouchers and Paystubs have been selected

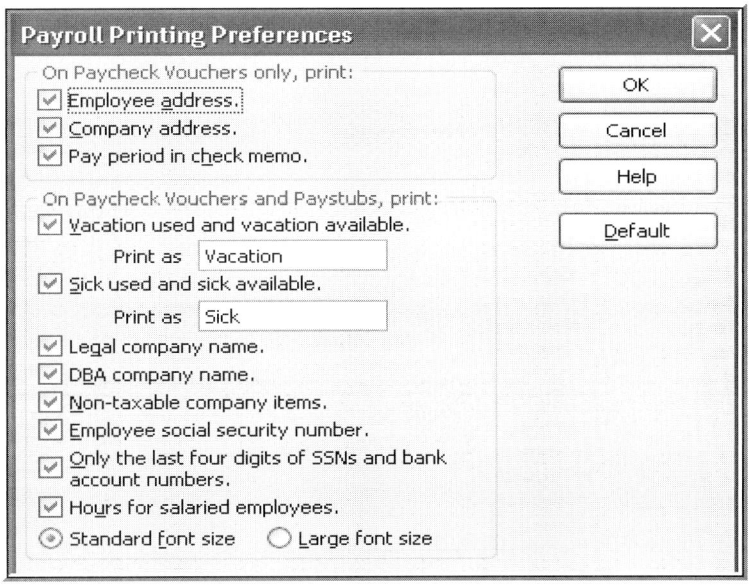

Click **OK**

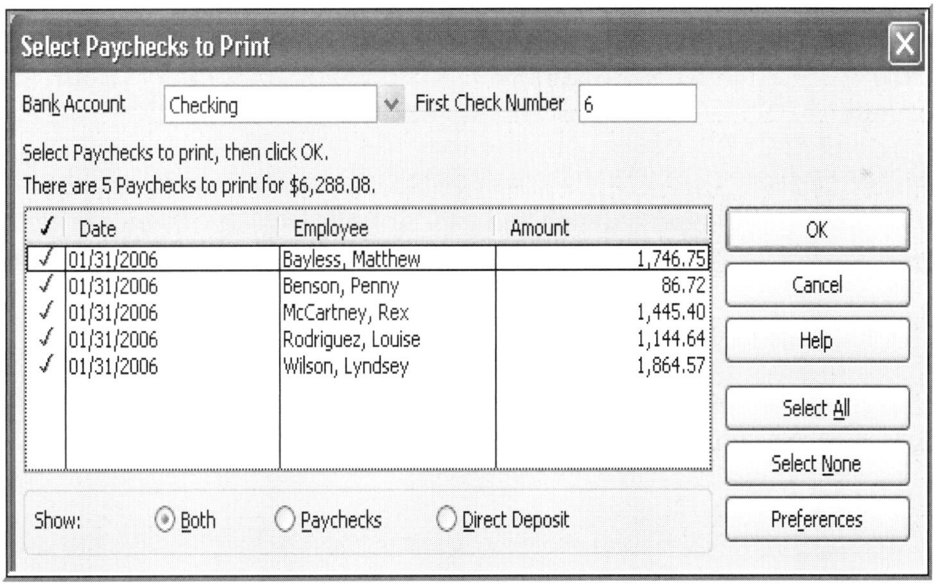

Click **OK** on the Select Paychecks to Print screen

- Printer Name and Printer Type will be the same as in the earlier chapters.

Click **Voucher Checks** to select as the check style

- If necessary, click **Print company name and address** to select. There should not be a check mark in Use logo. **Number of copies** should be **1**.

Click **Print**, click **OK** for **Did checks print OK?**

- *Note*: The pay stub information may be printed on the check two times. This is acceptable.

When the checks have been printed, click **Leave** on **Select Employees To Pay**

VIEW CHECKS, MAKE CORRECTIONS, AND PRINT CHECKS INDIVIDUALLY

As in earlier chapters, checks may be viewed individually and printed one at a time. A paycheck differs from a regular check. Rather than list accounts and amounts, it provides a Payroll Summary and an option to view Paycheck Detail at the bottom of the screen. When you are viewing the paycheck detail, corrections may be made and will be calculated for the check.

MEMO

DATE: January 31, 2006

After reviewing the printed checks, you notice that Rex McCartney shows -8.00 for Available Sick time. He should have had 20 hours Available. Change his employee information to show 12.00 hours of Available Sick Time. He should also have 20 hours of vacation time available as of January 31, 2006. Change this to 20 hours as well.

Lyndsey Wilson should have been paid for 10 hours overtime. Change her deductions as follows: CA-Employment Training Tax 2.63, Social Security (Company and Employee) 162.75, Medicare (Company and Employee) 38.25, Federal Unemployment 21.00, CA-Unemployment 105.00, Federal Withholding 393.75, CA Withholding 105.00, and CA Disability 28.35.

View the changes to the two checks and reprint both.

View, correct, and print the paychecks as indicated

To change the Available Sick time for Rex McCartney, click **Employee Center**
Click **Rex McCartney**, click the **Edit Employee** button
Click the drop-down list arrow for Change tabs
Click **Payroll and Compensation Info**
Click the **Sick/Vacation** button
Enter **12:00** for the Sick Hours available as of **01/31/06**
Enter **20:00** for the Vacation Hours available as of **01/31/06**

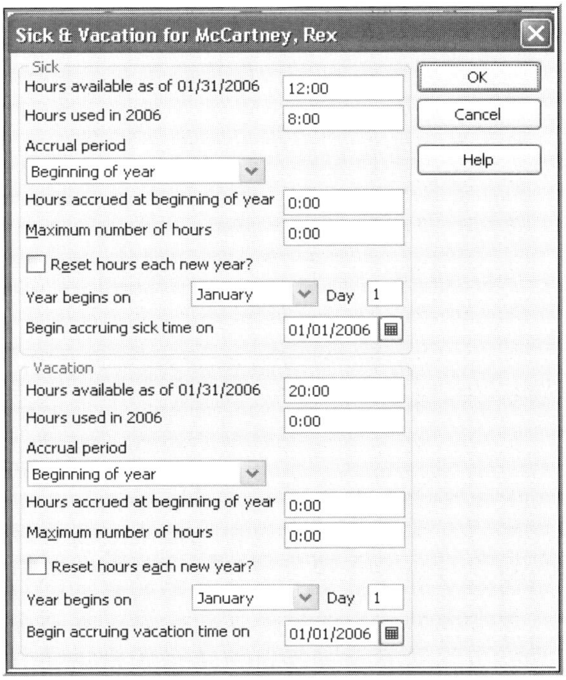

Click **OK** for Sick/Vacation, and click **OK** on the Edit Employee Screen
Close the Employee Center
To view the paychecks, click **Write Checks** in the Banking section of the Home Page
Click **Previous** until you get to the check for **Rex McCartney** for **01/31/06**
Click **Paycheck Detail** button to view the withholding details

- Notice that the Sick Available shows 12 rather than -8.
- Vacation Avail. Shows 20.

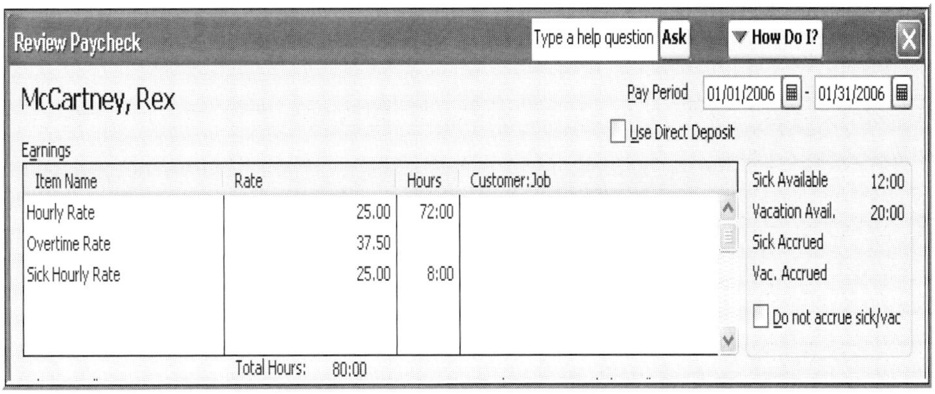

Click **OK**

- Even though the amount of the check is not changed by this adjustment, the check should be reprinted so the correct sick leave information is shown.

Reprint Check **3**
Click **Print**

If 3 is not shown as the check number, enter **3**

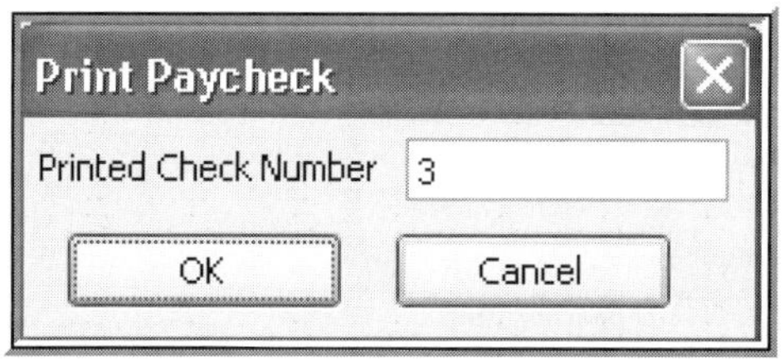

Click **OK**
Verify the information on the Print Checks screen including the selection of Voucher checks
Click **Print**
Click **Next** until you get to **Lindsey Wilson's** paycheck
Click **Paycheck Detail**
Change the Overtime Rate Hours to **10**
Press the **Tab** key
You may get a message regarding Net Pay Locked

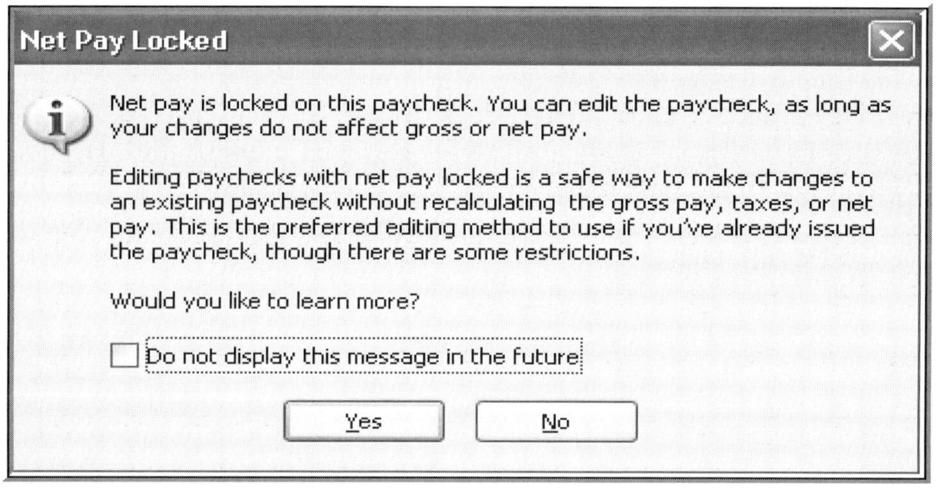

Click **No**
At the bottom of the paycheck, click **Unlock Net Pay**

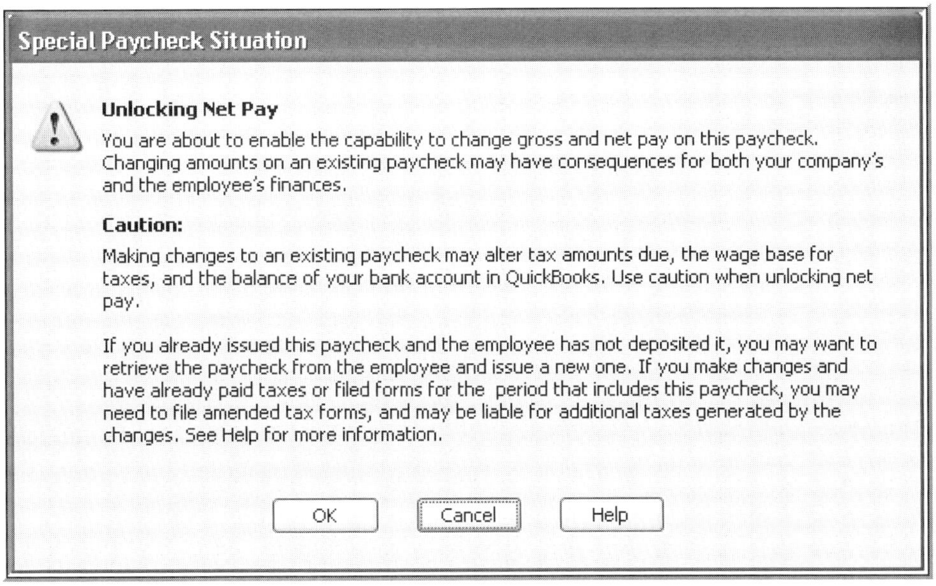

- Since paychecks have not been distributed to the employees until after they are reviewed, it is acceptable to change this paycheck rather than voiding and reissuing a new one.

Click **OK**

Enter the changes to the tax amounts as indicated in the Memo

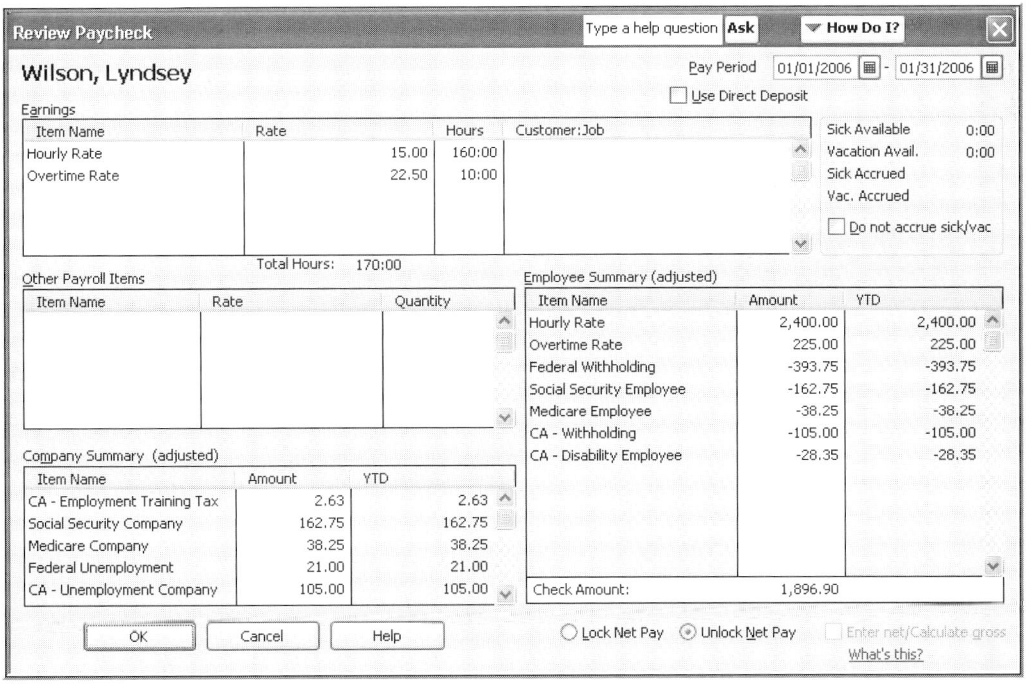

Click **OK**

- If you return to the Paycheck Detail, you will find that Lock Net Pay is once again selected.

Reprint Check 5
Do not close the Paycheck-Checking window

VOIDING AND DELETING CHECKS

As with regular checks, paychecks may be voided or deleted. A voided check still remains as a check, but it has an amount of 0.00 and a Memo that says VOID. If a check is deleted, it is completely removed from the company records. The only way to have a record of the deleted check would be if an audit trail had been selected as a company preference. If you have prenumbered checks and the original check is misprinted, lost, or stolen, you should void the check. If an employee's check is lost or stolen and needs to be replaced and you are not using prenumbered checks, it may be deleted and reissued. For security reasons, it is better to void a check than to delete it.

MEMO
DATE: January 31, 2006

The checks have been distributed and Penny Benson spilled coffee on her paycheck for the January 31 pay period. Void the check, issue and print a new one. Remember that she worked 8 hours.

Void Penny's January 31 paycheck and issue a new one

Click **Previous** until Penny's paycheck appears on the screen, click **Edit** menu, click **Void Paycheck**

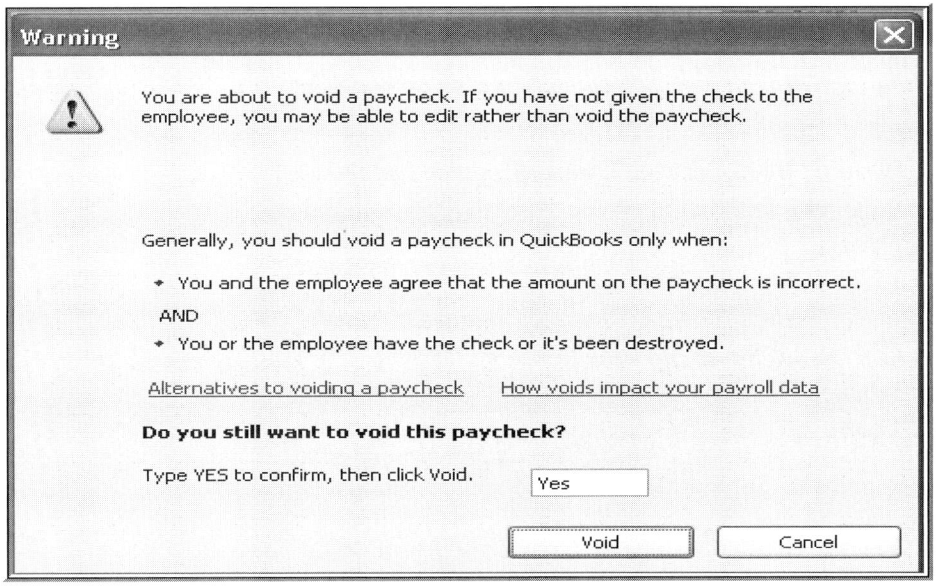

Enter **Yes** on the Warning Screen and click **Void**
Notice that the amount is 0.00 and that the Memo is VOID:.
Print the voided check as Check No. 2

- Notice that the check now shows "Cleared"

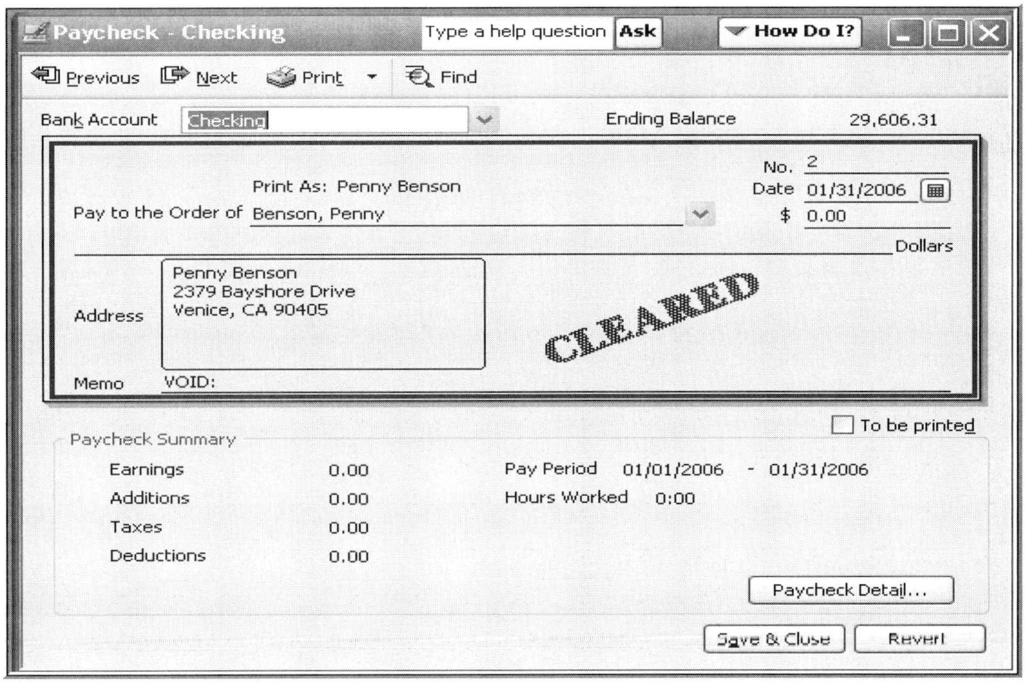

To issue Penny's replacement check, click **Save & Close** on Paycheck-Checking screen, click **Pay Employees** in the Employees section of the Home Page
The Bank Account is **Checking**

Select: **To be printed** and **Enter hours and tax amounts before creating paychecks**
The Check Date is **01/31/06** and the Pay Period Ends **01/31/06**
Select **Penny Benson**, click **Create**
Pay Period is **01/01/06 - 01/31/06**
Penny worked **8** hours at the Hourly Regular Rate
Enter the deductions listed on the Payroll Table for January 31, 2006
Click **Create**
Click **Print Paychecks**
Print the replacement check as Check No. **6**
Click **OK** on the **Select Paychecks to Print** screen
Print the check
Click **Leave**

MISSING CHECK REPORT

Since the same account is used for paychecks and regular checks, the Missing Check report will provide data regarding all the checks issued by Your Name Workout Co. After entering a number of checks, it is wise to review this report.

View the Missing Check report

Click **Report Center**, click **Banking** for the type of report, click **Missing Checks**
Specify the account as **Checking**

Your Name Workout Co.
Missing Checks
All Transactions

Type	Date	Num	Name	Memo	Account	Split	Amount
Paycheck	01/31/2006	1	Bayless, Matthew		Checking	-SPLIT-	-1,746.75
Paycheck	01/31/2006	2	Benson, Penny	VOID:	Checking	-SPLIT-	0.00
Paycheck	01/31/2006	3	McCartney, Rex		Checking	-SPLIT-	-1,445.40
Paycheck	01/31/2006	4	Rodriguez, Louise		Checking	-SPLIT-	-1,144.64
Paycheck	01/31/2006	5	Wilson, Lyndsey		Checking	-SPLIT-	-1,896.90
Paycheck	01/31/2006	6	Benson, Penny		Checking	-SPLIT-	-86.72

Review the report and close without printing
Do not close the Report Center

PAYROLL SUMMARY REPORT

The Payroll Summary Report shows gross pay, sick and vacation hours and pay, deductions from gross pay, adjusted gross pay, taxes withheld, deductions from net pay, net pay, and employer-paid taxes and contributions for each employee individually and for the company.

Print the Payroll Summary Report for January

Since the Report Center is on the screen, click **Employees & Payroll** to select the type of report
Click **Payroll Summary**
Enter the report dates from **01/01/06** to **01/31/06**
- View the information listed for each employee and for the company.

Remove the Date Prepared and Time Prepared from the header
Print the report in Landscape orientation; if necessary, adjust the column widths
Close the report

PREPARE THE EMPLOYEE EARNINGS SUMMARY REPORT

The Employee Earnings Summary Report lists the same information as the Payroll Summary Report above. The information for each employee is categorized by payroll items.

Prepare the Employee Earnings Summary report

Click **Employee Earnings Summary** as the report
Use the dates from **01/01/06** to **01/31/06**
Scroll through the report
- Notice the way in which payroll amounts are grouped by item rather than employee.

Do not print the report

PAYROLL LIABILITY BALANCES REPORT

The third payroll report is the Payroll Liability Balances Report. This report lists the company's payroll liabilities that are unpaid as of the report date. This report should be prepared prior to paying any payroll taxes.

Prepare and print the Payroll Liability Balances report

Click **Payroll Liability Balances** as the report
The report dates should be **01/01/06** to **01/31/06**
Remove the Date Prepared and Time Prepared from the header
Print the report in Portrait orientation

Your Name Workout Co.
Payroll Liability Balances
January 2006

	BALANCE
Payroll Liabilities	
Federal Withholding	1,336.65
Medicare Employee	129.41
Social Security Employee	552.52
Federal Unemployment	70.33
Medicare Company	129.41
Social Security Company	552.52
CA - Withholding	356.44
CA - Disability Employee	96.24
CA - Unemployment Company	356.47
CA - Employment Training Tax	8.80
Dental Insurance Emp (taxable)	20.00
Health Insurance Emp (taxable)	100.00
Total Payroll Liabilities	**3,708.79**

Close the report and the Report Center

PAY TAXES AND OTHER LIABILITIES

QuickBooks Pro keeps track of the payroll taxes and other payroll liabilities that you owe. When it is time to make your payments, QuickBooks Pro allows you to choose to pay all liabilities or to select individual liabilities for payment. When the liabilities to be paid have been selected, QuickBooks Pro will consolidate all the amounts for one vendor and prepare one check for that vendor.

MEMO
DATE: January 31, 2006

Based on the information in the Payroll Liabilities Report, pay all the payroll liabilities.

Pay all the payroll liabilities

Click **Pay Liabilities** in Employees section of the Home Page
Enter the dates of **01/01/06** to **01/31/06** on the **Select Date Range For Liabilities** screen

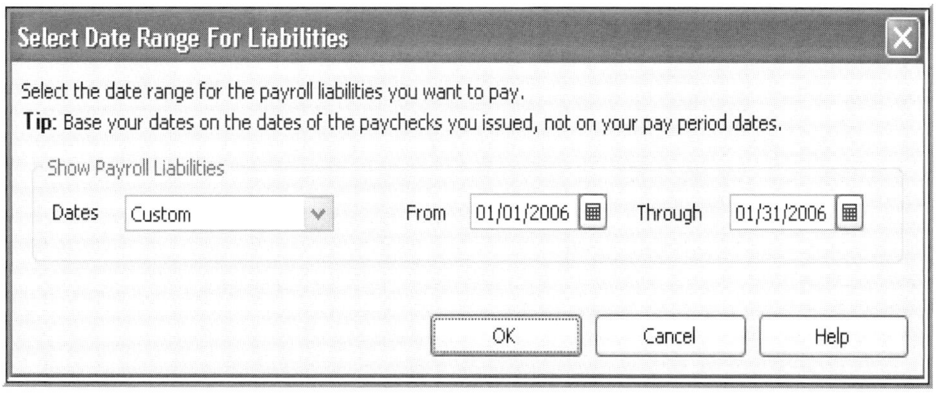

Click **OK**
If necessary, select **To be printed**
Bank Account should be **Checking**; if it is not, select it from the drop-down list.
Check Date is **01/31/06**
Show payroll liabilities from **01/01/06** to **01/31/06**
Sort by **Payable To**
Create liability check without reviewing should be selected
Click in the check column to place a check mark next to each liability listed; be sure to scroll through the list to view and mark each liability

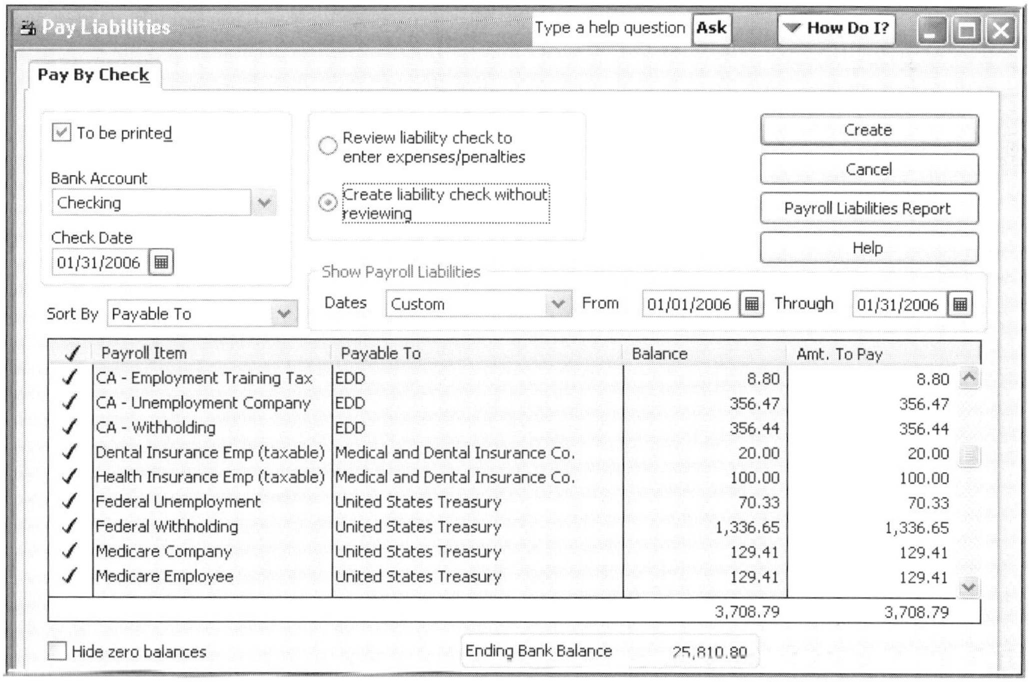

Click **Create**
To print the checks, access **Write Checks** as previously instructed
Click the drop-down list arrow next to **Print** at the top of the window

Click **Print Batch**, on the **Select Checks to Print** screen
The first check number should be **7**
The names of the agencies receiving the checks and the check amounts should be listed and marked with a check.
Click **OK**
Change the style of checks to **Standard**, click **Print**
When the checks have printed successfully, click **OK** on the screen asking if checks printed correctly

- Standard style checks print three to a page so all three checks will print on one page.
- If you wish to have each check printed separately, you would go to each check and print individually as previously instructed.

Close the Checks window

FILE PAYROLL TAX FORMS

QuickBooks Pro creates and prints your Form 941—Employer's Quarterly Federal Tax Return, Schedule B—Employer's Record of Federal Tax Liability, and your Form 940—Employer's Annual Federal Unemployment Tax Return. These forms are accurate and updated with each release of QuickBooks Pro. You may also create a custom tax form that may be submitted in conjunction with any state taxes paid. Because each state has different reporting requirements, we will not create a customized state form in this chapter. If you want QuickBooks to generate State Tax Forms for you, you must subscribe to the Enhanced Payroll service. Even though the forms are for the quarter and for the year, we will prepare them for the month of January to provide experience in the preparation of these items. Please note that as Intuit provides updates to QuickBooks, the appearance of the forms may change; however, the procedures will still be similar to the instructions provided in the text.

PREPARE AND PRINT FORM 941 AND SCHEDULE B

MEMO
DATE: January 31, 2006

Prepare Form 941—Employer's Quarterly Federal Tax Return, and Schedule B—Employer's Record of Federal Tax Liability.

Prepare Form 941 and Schedule B

Click **Process Payroll Forms** in the Employees section of the Home Page
You must select the type of form you want to prepare. Federal form should already be selected, if not, click to select.

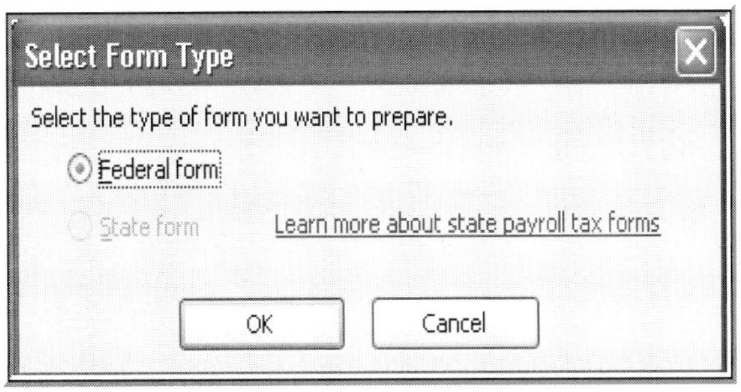

Click **OK**
Click **Quarterly Form 941/Schedule B**
The Filing Period should be 2006, if necessary, change the Year to **2006**
Click the drop-down list arrow for Quarter, click **Custom**
Enter the date of **01/31/06**

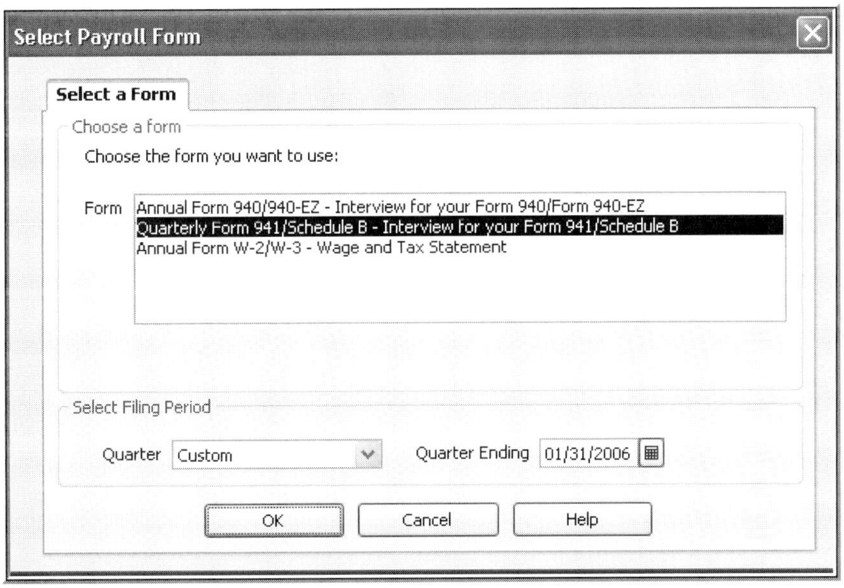

Click **OK**

- If you get a screen regarding a QuickBooks Payroll Tip, click **No, and turn off pop-up messages for products and services**, click **OK**

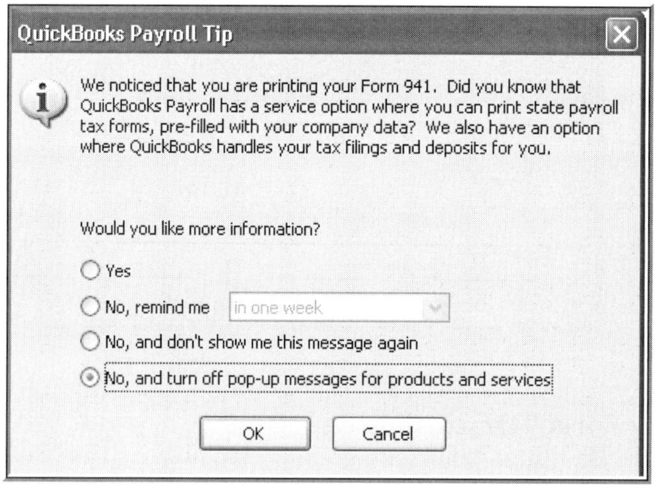

Since Your Name Workout Co. has not accumulated $100,000 or more in tax liability, we do not need to file a Schedule B, the **No** box for "Do you need a Schedule B?"

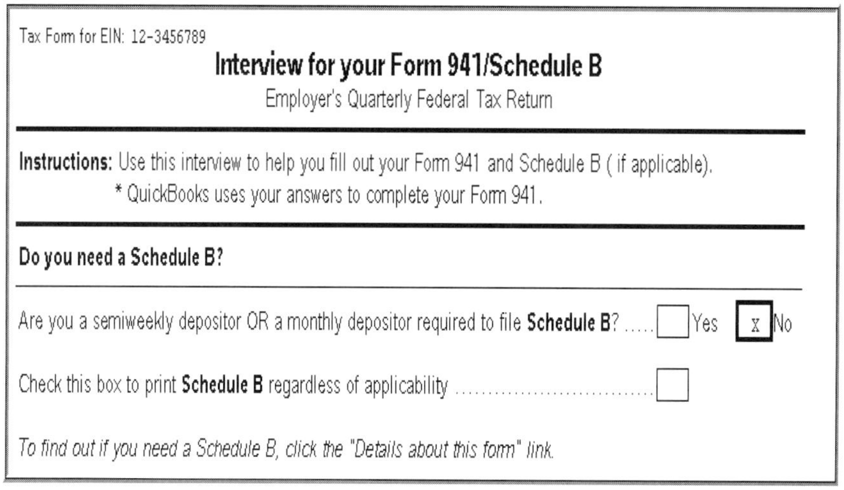
Tax Form for EIN: 12-3456789

Interview for your Form 941/Schedule B

Employer's Quarterly Federal Tax Return

Instructions: Use this interview to help you fill out your Form 941 and Schedule B (if applicable).
* QuickBooks uses your answers to complete your Form 941.

Do you need a Schedule B?

Are you a semiweekly depositor OR a monthly depositor required to file **Schedule B**? ..... ☐ Yes ☒ No

Check this box to print **Schedule B** regardless of applicability .... ☐

To find out if you need a Schedule B, click the "Details about this form" link.

In the section "Answer the following Questions for Form 941, enter **CA** as the state

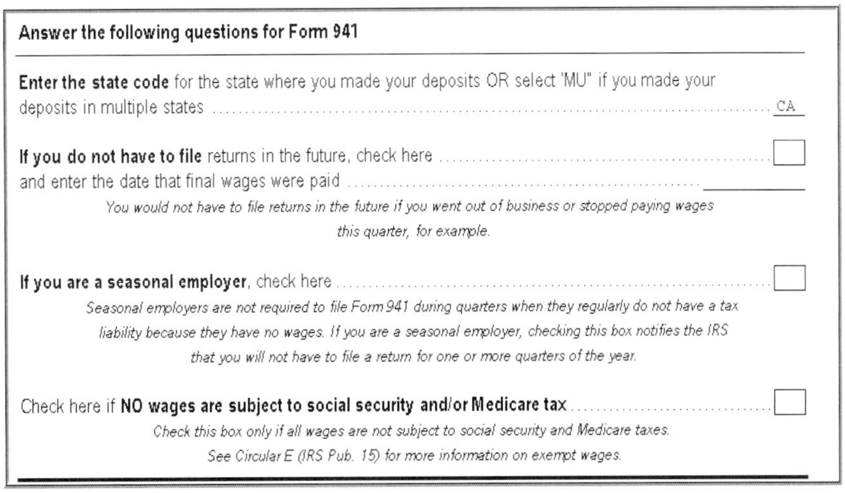

Answer the following questions for Form 941

Enter the state code for the state where you made your deposits OR select 'MU" if you made your deposits in multiple states .... CA

If you do not have to file returns in the future, check here .... ☐
and enter the date that final wages were paid .... ______

You would not have to file returns in the future if you went out of business or stopped paying wages this quarter, for example.

If you are a seasonal employer, check here .... ☐

Seasonal employers are not required to file Form 941 during quarters when they regularly do not have a tax liability because they have no wages. If you are a seasonal employer, checking this box notifies the IRS that you will not have to file a return for one or more quarters of the year.

Check here if **NO wages are subject to social security and/or Medicare tax** .... ☐

Check this box only if all wages are not subject to social security and Medicare taxes. See Circular E (IRS Pub. 15) for more information on exempt wages.

Scroll through and read the section regarding the adjustments QuickBooks makes for you
Click **Next** at the bottom of the screen
Scroll down through Form 941
The number of employees shows as 0, click the **0**
Enter **5** as the number of employees

- You will get a pop-up message regarding overriding QuickBooks.

Right-click on the **0**
Click **Override**

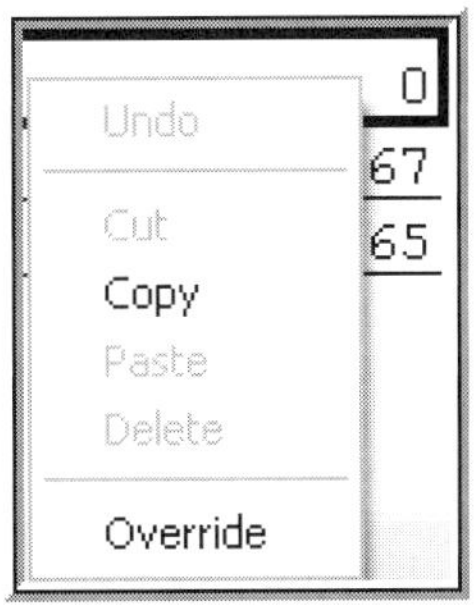

Enter **5**, press **Tab**

- QuickBooks will automatically complete the Employer's Quarterly Federal Tax Return

Part 1 – Answer These Questions For This Quarter

		Column 1		Column 2	Line	Amount
1	Number of employees who received wages, tips, or other compensation for the pay period including March 12 (Quarter 1), June 12 (Quarter 2), September 12 (Quarter 3), December 12 (Quarter 4)				1	5
2	Wages, tips, and other compensation				2	8,911.67
3	Total income tax withheld from wages, tips, and other compensation				3	1,336.65
4	If no wages, tips, and other compensation are subject to social security or Medicare tax, check here and go to line 6 ☐					
5	Taxable social security and Medicare wages and tips:					
a	Taxable social security wages	8,911.67	x .124 =	1,105.05		
b	Taxable social security tips		x .124 =			
c	Taxable Medicare wages and tips	8,911.67	x .029 =	258.44		
d	Total social security and Medicare taxes (Column 2, lines 5a + 5b + 5c = line 5d)				5d	1,363.49
6	Total taxes before adjustments (lines 3 + 5d = line 6)				6	2,700.14
7	Tax adjustments:					
a	Current quarter's fractions of cents		7a	0.37		
b	Current quarter's sick pay		b			

Before printing and saving the form, click the **Check for Errors** button at the bottom of the report

- If you had made an error, QuickBooks would indicate the error in the above screen.

Click **Close Errors**
Click **Print Forms** at the bottom of the screen
Tax form(s) and filing instructions should be selected

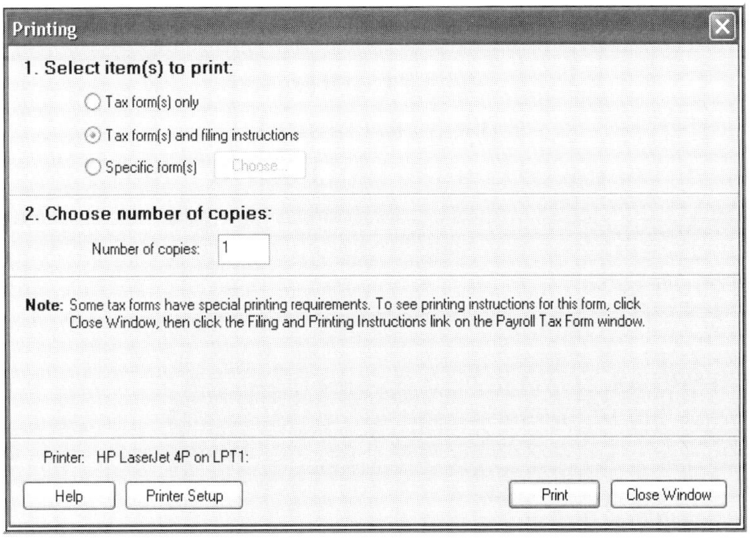

Click **Print**

- Your form may show the year 2005. If it does, do not worry about the year displayed.

When finished printing, click **Save & Close**

Read the Next Steps screen

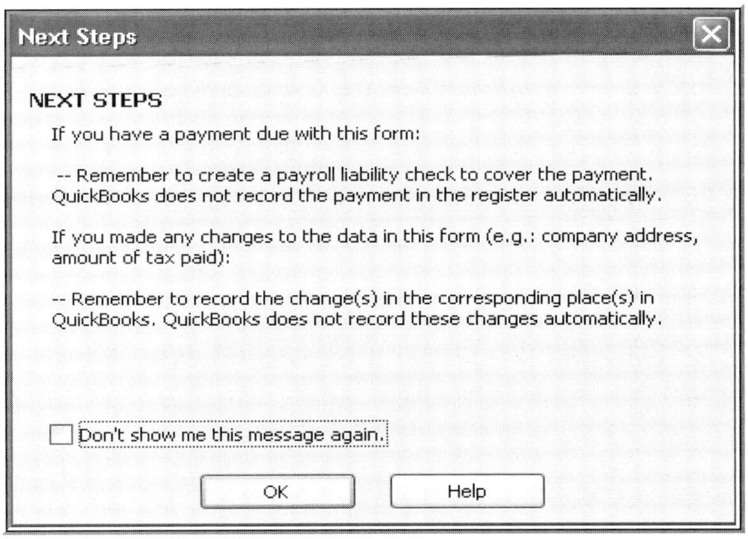

Click **OK**

PREPARE AND PRINT FORM 940

The preparation of Form 940 for the Employer's Annual Federal Unemployment Tax Return (FUTA) is similar to the preparation of Form 941.

> **MEMO**
> **DATE:** January 31, 2006
>
> Even though Form 940 for FUTA is filed as an annual tax return, prepare this form for January.

Prepare and print Form 940

Click **Process Payroll Forms**
Federal form should already be selected on the Select Form Type screen, if not, click to select.
Click **OK**
Click **Annual Form 940/940EZ**
Enter the year as **2006**
Click **OK**
If you get a Warning screen for Payroll Tax Form, click **OK**

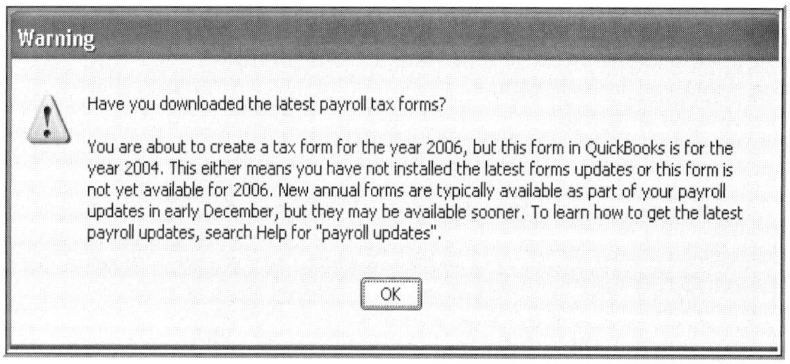

Complete the Interview sheet by clicking in the **Yes** box for questions A, B, C, and D

Which form do you want to use: Form 940 or Form 940-EZ?

To figure out which form you should use, answer the following questions:

A	Are you required to pay unemployment contributions to only one state? .... *If you paid unemployment taxes in only one state, click Yes. Otherwise, click No.* (If 'No', skip questions B and C.)	[X] Yes	[ ] No
B	Did you pay all state unemployment contributions by January 31, 2005? .... *IRS rules state that you can also check Yes if either of the following apply:* *– You deposited your total FUTA (Federal Unemployment tax) by its due date AND you paid your state unemployment contributions by February 10, 2005.* *– Your state granted you a 0% experience rate.* (If 'No', skip question C.)	[X] Yes	[ ] No
C	Were all wages that were taxable for FUTA tax also taxable for your state unemployment tax? .... *– For information on question D, click "Details about this form"*	[X] Yes	[ ] No
D	Did you pay all wages in a state other than New York?	[X] Yes	[ ] No

If you answered 'No' to any of these questions, you must file Form 940. Otherwise, you may use Form 940-EZ.

QuickBooks will mark that you need to use Form 940EZ
Click **Next** at the bottom of the page
Scroll through the form
The Taxable Wages and FUTA Tax should appear as follows:

Part I **Taxable Wages and FUTA Tax**

1	Total payments (including payments shown on lines 2 and 3) during the calendar year for services of employees			1	8911.67
2	Exempt payments. (Explain all exempt payments, attaching additional sheets if necessary.) ►	2	0.00		
3	Payments of more than $7,000 for services. Enter only amounts over the first $7,000 paid to each employee	3	0.00		
4	Add lines 2 and 3			4	0.00
5	**Total taxable wages** (subtract line 4 from line 1) .... ►			5	8911.67
6	**FUTA tax.** Multiply the wages on line 5 by .008 and enter here. **(If the result is over $100, also complete Part II.)**			6	71.29
7	Total FUTA tax deposited for the year, including any overpayment applied from a prior year			7	70.33
8	**Balance due** (subtract line 7 from line 6) .... ► If you owe more than $100, see **Depositing FUTA tax** in the instructions.			8	0.96
9	**Overpayment** (subtract line 6 from line 7). Check if it is to be: [ ] **Applied to next return** or [ ] **Refunded** .... ►			9	

Check for Errors as you did on Form 941
Click **Print Forms** at the bottom of the screen
Repeat the procedures used to print Form 941
When finished printing, click **Save & Close**
Read the Next Steps screen, click **OK**

PREPARE AND PREVIEW EMPLOYEES' W-2 FORMS

The W-2 form is prepared at the end of the year, mailed to each employee, and mailed to the Social Security Administration. The wages earned and taxes withheld for the individual employee for the year are shown on the form. A W-3 form is a summary of all the W-2 forms you are submitting to the federal government and cannot be printed unless the W-2s have been printed. QuickBooks Pro is set up to fill in this information on blank W-2 and W-3 forms. You may not print the W-2s on blank paper unless you subscribe to a QuickBooks payroll service. Electronic filing of W-2s for companies employing 250 or more is required. QuickBooks Pro does not support electronic filing of W-2s unless you subscribe to a QuickBooks payroll service.

MEMO
DATE: January 31, 2006

W-2s and the corresponding W-3 are prepared at the end of the year. However, for experience with this procedure, you will prepare and review the W-2s for each employee. Because the W-3 cannot be viewed and cannot be printed unless all W-2s have been printed, we will not prepare this form.

Prepare and review the W-2s

Click **Process Payroll Forms**
Select Federal forms as done previously
Click **Annual Form W-2/W3**
The year should be **2006**
Click **OK**
If you get a warning screen regarding tax tables, click **OK**
On the Select Employees for Form W2/W3, click the **Review/Edit** button

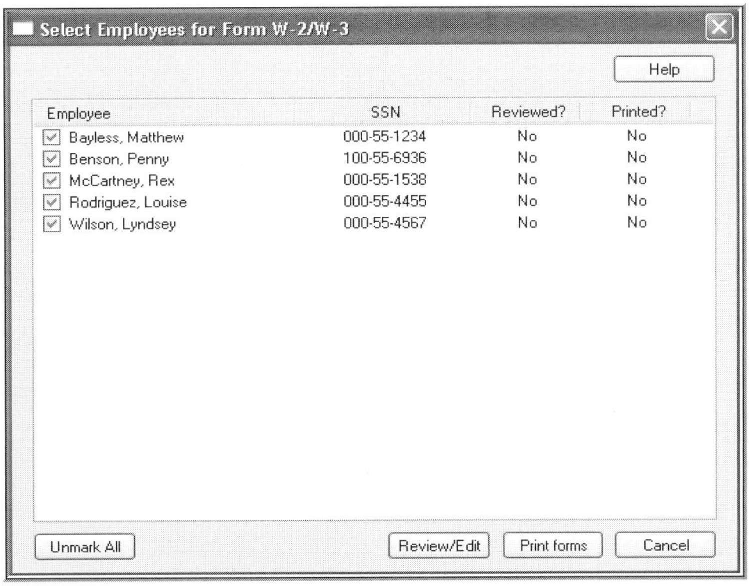

Read the information presented in the Interview section of the form
Click **Next**

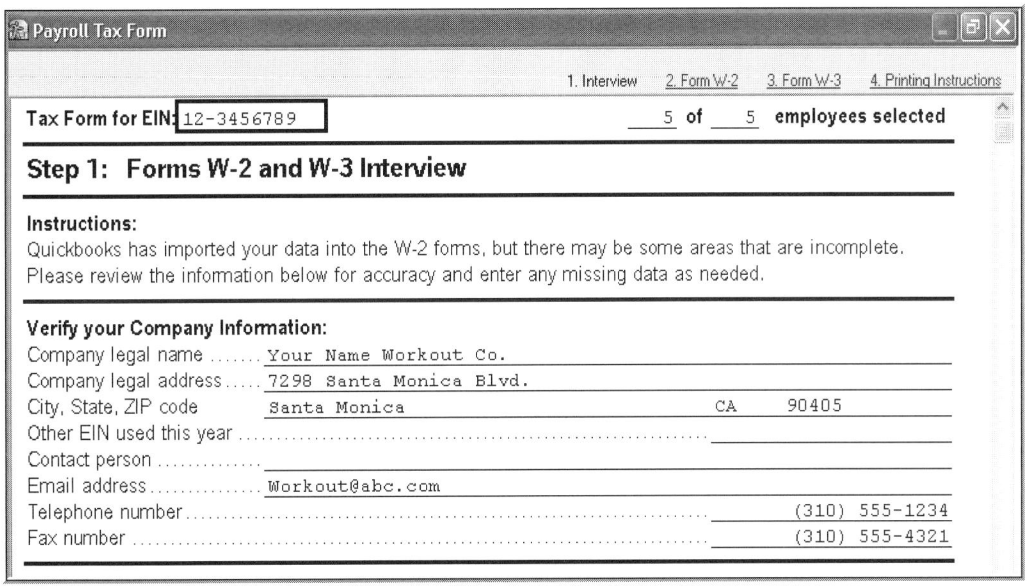

Read the information presented in the Form W-2 section of the form
Click **Next**

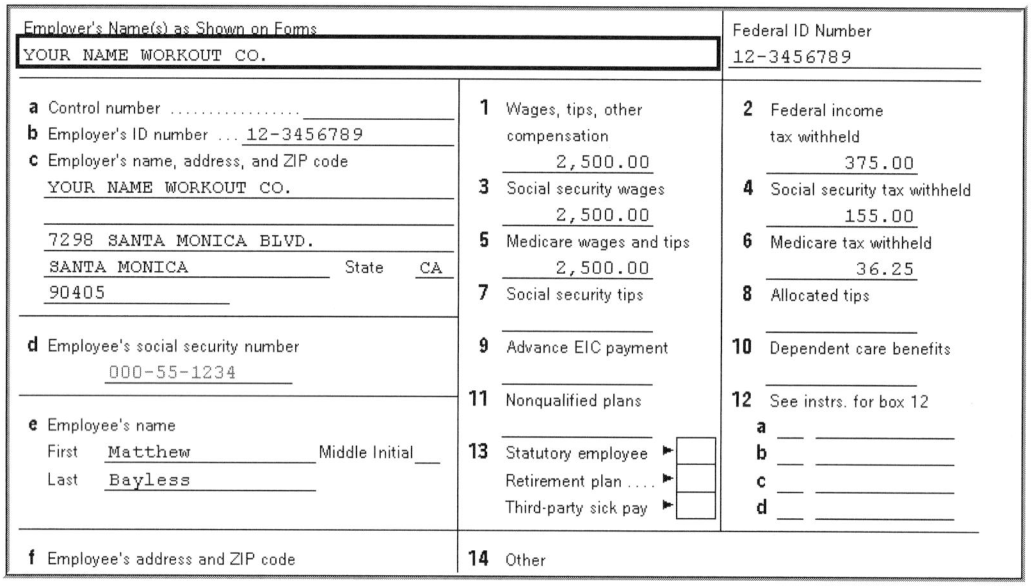

Employer's Name(s) as Shown on Forms: YOUR NAME WORKOUT CO.
Federal ID Number: 12-3456789

a Control number
b Employer's ID number 12-3456789
c Employer's name, address, and ZIP code
YOUR NAME WORKOUT CO.
7298 SANTA MONICA BLVD.
SANTA MONICA State CA
90405
d Employee's social security number 000-55-1234
e Employee's name
First Matthew Middle Initial
Last Bayless
f Employee's address and ZIP code

1 Wages, tips, other compensation 2,500.00
2 Federal income tax withheld 375.00
3 Social security wages 2,500.00
4 Social security tax withheld 155.00
5 Medicare wages and tips 2,500.00
6 Medicare tax withheld 36.25
7 Social security tips
8 Allocated tips
9 Advance EIC payment
10 Dependent care benefits
11 Nonqualified plans
12 See instrs. for box 12 a b c d
13 Statutory employee / Retirement plan / Third-party sick pay
14 Other

Review Matthew Bayless's W-2, click **Next**
Repeat the procedures to view the W-2 for each employee

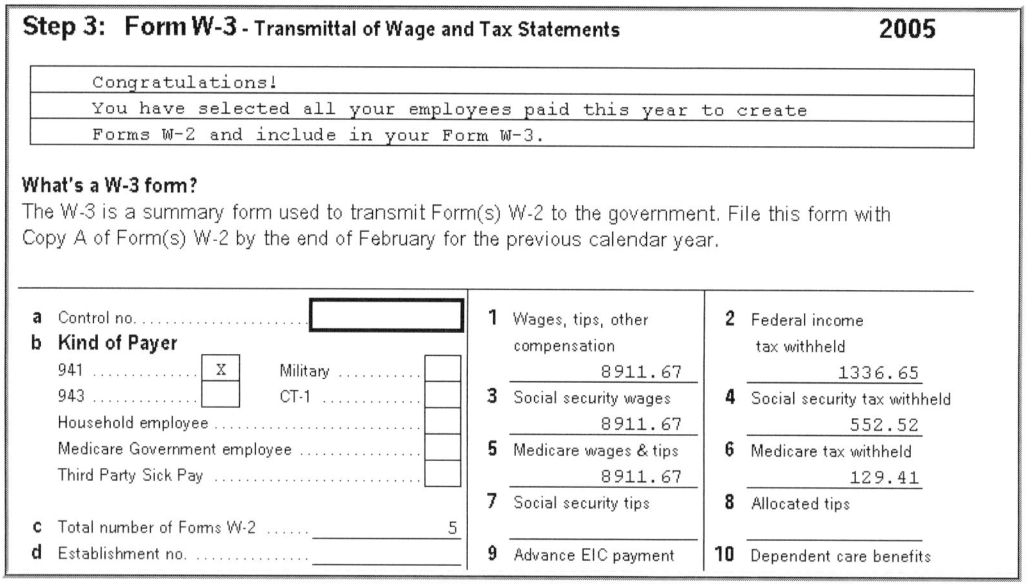

Step 3: Form W-3 - Transmittal of Wage and Tax Statements **2005**

Congratulations!
You have selected all your employees paid this year to create
Forms W-2 and include in your Form W-3.

What's a W-3 form?
The W-3 is a summary form used to transmit Form(s) W-2 to the government. File this form with Copy A of Form(s) W-2 by the end of February for the previous calendar year.

a Control no.
b Kind of Payer
941 X Military
943 CT-1
Household employee
Medicare Government employee
Third Party Sick Pay
c Total number of Forms W-2 5
d Establishment no.

1 Wages, tips, other compensation 8911.67
2 Federal income tax withheld 1336.65
3 Social security wages 8911.67
4 Social security tax withheld 552.52
5 Medicare wages & tips 8911.67
6 Medicare tax withheld 129.41
7 Social security tips
8 Allocated tips
9 Advance EIC payment
10 Dependent care benefits

When the final screen appears, click **Save & Close** without printing
Click **OK** on the Next Steps screen

PRINT THE JOURNAL

As in the previous chapters, it is always a good idea to print the Journal to see all of the transactions that have been made. If, however, you only want to see the transactions for a particular date or period of time, you can control the amount of data in the report by restricting the dates.

Print the Journal for January 31 in landscape orientation

Prepare the report as previously instructed
Use the dates from **01/31/06** to **01/31/06**

BACK UP

Follow the instructions provided in previous chapters to make a backup file. Refer to Appendix A to make a duplicate disk.

SUMMARY

In this chapter, paychecks were generated for employees who worked their standard number of hours, took vacation time, took sick time, and were just hired. Rather than have QuickBooks Pro calculate the amount of payroll deductions, a table was provided and deductions to paychecks were inserted manually. Changes to employee information were made, and a new employee was added. Payroll reports were printed and/or viewed, and payroll liabilities were paid. Federal Forms 940, 941, and W-2's were viewed and/or printed.

END-OF-CHAPTER QUESTIONS

TRUE/FALSE

ANSWER THE FOLLOWING QUESTIONS IN THE SPACE PROVIDED BEFORE THE QUESTION NUMBER.

_____ 1. You cannot enter payroll deductions manually on paychecks.

_____ 2. Once a paycheck has been printed, you may not edit it.

_____ 3. Paychecks may be printed only as a batch.

_____ 4. A payroll check may never be deleted.

_____ 5. Checks may be created and previewed or created without previewing when entering the payroll manually.

_____ 6. An employee may be added at anytime.

_____ 7. If several taxes are owed to a single agency, QuickBooks Pro generates a separate check to the agency for each tax liability item.

_____ 8. If a salaried employee uses vacation pay, QuickBooks Pro will automatically distribute the correct amount of earnings to Vacation Salary once the number of vacation hours has been entered.

_____ 9. Processing the Payroll Liabilities Report also generates the checks for payment of the liabilities.

_____ 10. All payroll reports must be printed before payroll liabilities may be paid.

MULTIPLE CHOICE

WRITE THE LETTER OF THE CORRECT ANSWER IN THE SPACE PROVIDED BEFORE THE QUESTION NUMBER.

_____ 1. When completing paychecks manually, you ___.
   A. provide the information about hours worked
   B. provide the amounts for deductions
   C. preview all checks
   D. all of the above

_____ 2. To change the amount of a deduction entered on an employee's check that has been created, you ___.
   A. must void the check and issue a new one
   B. adjust the next check to include the change
   C. change the Paycheck Detail for the check and reprint it
   D. must delete the check

_____ 3. When paying tax liabilities, you may ___.
   A. pay all liabilities at one time
   B. select individual tax liabilities and pay them one at a time
   C. pay all the tax liabilities owed to a vendor
   D. all of the above

_____ 4. A new employee may be added ___.
   A. at any time
   B. only at the end of the week
   C. only at the end of the pay period
   D. only when current paychecks have been printed

_____ 5. Pay stub information may be printed ___.
   A. as part of a voucher check
   B. separate from the paycheck
   C. only as an individual employee report
   D. both A and B

_____ 6. The form sent to the government as a summary of the forms sent to all the individual employees of the company is the ___ form.
   A. W 2
   B. 940
   C. W-3
   D. 941

_____ 7. A voided check ___.
A. shows an amount of 0.00
B. has a Memo of VOID
C. remains as part of the company records
D. all of the above

_____ 8. When the payroll liabilities to be paid have been selected, QuickBooks Pro will ___.
A. create a separate check for each liability
B. consolidate the liabilities paid and create one check for each vendor
C. automatically process a Payroll Liability Balances Report
D. prepare any tax return forms necessary

_____ 9. The Journal may be prepared ___.
A. for any range of dates
B. for a specific month
C. for a specific day
D. all of the above

_____ 10. Changes made to an employee's pay rate will become effective ___.
A. immediately
B. at the end of the next payroll period
C. at the end of the quarter
D. after a W-2 has been prepared for the employee

FILL-IN

IN THE SPACE PROVIDED, WRITE THE ANSWER THAT MOST APPROPRIATELY COMPLETES THE SENTENCE.

1. In the ____________, the individual employees name, address, and telephone number is displayed in the Employee Information area.

2. The ____________ is the report that lists transactions in debit/credit format.

3. The reports that show an employee's gross pay, sick and vacation hours and pay, deductions, taxes, and other details are the ____________ and the ____________.

4. When the Employee Center is on the screen, the ____________ button is used to add a new employee.

5. The report listing the company's unpaid payroll liabilities as of the report date is the ____________ Report.

SHORT ESSAY

What is the difference between voiding a paycheck and deleting a paycheck? Why should a business prefer to void paychecks rather than delete them?

NAME ____________________

TRANSMITTAL

CHAPTER 8: YOUR NAME WORKOUT CO.

Attach the following documents and reports:

Check No. 1: Matthew Bayless
Check No. 2: Penny Benson
Check No. 3: Rex McCartney
Check No. 4: Louise Rodriguez
Check No. 5: Lyndsey Wilson
Check No. 3: Rex McCartney After Editing Sick Time
Check No. 5: Lyndsey Wilson After Editing Over Time
Check No. 2: Penny Benson Voided Check
Check No. 6: Penny Benson Replacement Check
Payroll Summary, January 2006
Payroll Liability Balances, January 2006
Check No. 7: EDD
Check No. 8: Medical and Dental Insurance Co.
Check No. 9: United States Treasury
Form 941/B
Form 940
Journal, January 31, 2006

END-OF-CHAPTER PROBLEM

YOUR NAME POOL MAINTENANCE & SUPPLIES

You will be working with a company called Your Name Pool Maintenance & Supplies. Transactions for employees, payroll, and payroll liabilities will be completed.

INSTRUCTIONS

For Chapter 8 download the company file **Pool.qbw** as previously instructed. You will select a manual payroll option; record the addition of and changes to employees; create, edit, and void paychecks; pay payroll liabilities; and prepare payroll reports.

RECORD TRANSACTIONS:

January 30, 2006

► Add your name to the company name and the owner equity accounts
► Turn off the Date Prepared, Time Prepared, and Report Basis in the Header/Footer
► Choose a Payroll Option and Select Manual processing
► Add a new employee, Suzy Akbar to help with pool supply sales. Social Security No. 100-55-2145; female, Date of Birth 04/23/1977. Her address is: 2325 Summerland Road, Summerland, CA 93014, 805-555-9845. Suzy is an hourly employee at $7.00 per hour with an overtime rate of $10.50. She is paid monthly, is single, claims no exemptions or allowances, is subject to Federal Taxes: Medicare, Social Security, and Federal Unemployment Tax, State Taxes: SUI, and SDI; Other Taxes: CA-Employment Training Tax. Suzy does not accrue vacation or sick leave and does not pay for medical or dental insurance.
► Doreen Samuels changed her telephone number to 805-555-5111. Edit the employee on the employee list and record the change.

January 31, 2006

► Use the following Payroll Table to prepare and print checks for the monthly pay period from January 1-January 31, 2006: Checking is the appropriate account to use. (Remember, you may get a screen regarding signing up for QuickBooks Payroll service. You should say No. In addition, on the Pay Employees screen, click "Pay Employees Anyway.")

PAYROLL TABLE: JANUARY 31, 2006				
	Doreen Samuels	Jerry Mitchell	Mannie Mendoza	Suzy Akbar
HOURS				
Regular	120	152	160	8
Overtime			20	
Sick		8		
Vacation	40			
DEDUCTIONS OTHER PAYROLL ITEMS: EMPLOYEE				
Dental Ins.	25.00	25.00	25.00	
Medical Ins.	25.00	25.00	25.00	
DEDUCTIONS: COMPANY				
CA-Employment Training Tax	2.60	2.42	1.71	0.00
Social Security	161.20	149.83	106.00	3.47
Medicare	37.70	35.04	24.80	.81
Federal Unemployment	20.80	19.33	13.68	0.00
CA-Unemployment	104.00	96.67	68.40	2.24
DEDUCTIONS: EMPLOYEE				
Federal Withholding	390.00	362.50	256.50	0.00
Social Security	161.20	149.83	106.00	3.47
Medicare	37.70	35.04	24.80	.81
CA-Withholding	104.00	96.67	68.40	0.00
CA-Disability	28.08	26.10	18.47	0.00

- ► Print the company name and address on the voucher checks. Checks begin with number 1.
- ► Change Mannie Mendoza's check to correct the overtime hours. (Remember to Unlock Net Pay before recording the changes.) He worked 12 hours overtime. Because of the reduction in overtime pay, his deductions change as follows: CA-Employment Training Tax: 1.60; Social Security Company and Employee: 99.32; Medicare Company and Employee: 23.23; Federal Unemployment: 12.82; CA-Unemployment: 64.08; Federal Withholding: 240.30; CA-Withholding: 64.08; and CA-Disability: 17.30. Reprint Check No. 3.
- ► Suzy spilled coffee on her check. Void her Check No. 4 for January 31, print the voided check, reissue the paycheck, and print it using Check No. 5.

- ► Prepare and print the Payroll Summary Report for January 1-31, 2006 in Landscape orientation.
- ► Prepare and print the Payroll Liability Balances Report for January 1-31, 2006 in Portrait orientation.
- ► Pay all the taxes and other liabilities for January 1-31, 2006; and print the checks using a Standard check style with the company name and address.
- ► Prepare and print Federal Forms 941/B and 940
- ► Prepare and print the Journal for January 31, 2006 in Landscape orientation.

NAME ____________________

TRANSMITTAL

CHAPTER 8: YOUR NAME POOL MAINTENANCE & SUPPLIES

Attach the following documents and reports:

Check No. 1: Doreen Samuels
Check No. 2: Jerry Mitchell
Check No. 3: Mannie Mendoza
Check No. 4: Suzy Akbar
Check No. 3: Mannie Mendoza (Corrected)
Check No. 4: Suzy Akbar (Voided)
Check No. 5: Suzy Akbar
Payroll Summary, January, 2006
Payroll Liability Balances, January 2006
Check No. 6: Dental and Medical Ins.
Check No. 7: Employment Development Department
Check No. 8: United States Treasury
Form 941/B
Form 940
Journal, January 31, 2006

CREATING A COMPANY IN QUICKBOOKS

9

LEARNING OBJECTIVES

At the completion of this chapter, you will be able to:

1. Set up a company using the EasyStep Interview.
2. Establish a Chart of Accounts for a company.
3. Set up Company Info and start dates.
4. Create lists for receivables, payables, items, customers, vendors, employees, and others.
5. Complete the Payroll setup and create payroll items and employee defaults.
6. Customize reports and company preferences.

COMPUTERIZING A MANUAL SYSTEM

In previous chapters, QuickBooks Pro was used to record transactions for businesses that were already set up for use in the program. In this chapter, you will actually set up a business, create a chart of accounts, create various lists, add names to lists, and delete unnecessary accounts. QuickBooks Pro makes setting up the records for a business user-friendly by going through the process using the EasyStep Interview. Once the basic accounts, items, lists, and other items are established via the EasyStep Interview, you will make some refinements to accounts, add detail information regarding customers and vendors, transfer Uncategorized Income and Expenses to the owner's equity account, customize report and company preferences, and customize a business form.

TRAINING TUTORIAL

The following tutorial is a step-by-step guide to setting up the fictitious company Your Name Movies, Etc. Company information, accounts, items, lists, and other items must be provided before transactions may be recorded in QuickBooks Pro. The EasyStep Interview will be used to set up company information. Once the basic company information has been entered via the EasyStep Interview, changes and modifications to the company data will be made. As in earlier chapters, information for the company setup will be provided in memos. Information may also be shown in lists or within the step-by-step instructions provided.

COMPANY PROFILE: YOUR NAME MOVIES, ETC.

Your Name Movies, Etc. is a fictitious company that sells and rents DVDs. In addition, Your Name Movies, Etc. has a repair department that cleans, conditions, and repairs DVD players. Your Name Movies, Etc. is located in San Diego, California, and is a sole proprietorship owned by you. You are involved in all aspects of the business. Your Name Movies, Etc. has one full-time employee who is paid a salary: Yvonne Benson whose duties include placing all the orders, managing the office, and keeping the books. There is one full-time hourly employee: Jaime Hernandez, who works in the store and performs all the services in the repairs department,

CREATE A NEW COMPANY

Since Your Name Movies, Etc. is a new company, it does not appear as a company file if you select Open Company on the File menu. A new company may be created by clicking New Company on the File menu.

MEMO
DATE: January 1, 2006

Because this is the beginning of the fiscal year for Your Name Movies, Etc., it is an appropriate time to set up the company information in QuickBooks Pro. Use the EasyStep Interview in QuickBooks Pro.

Open QuickBooks Pro as previously instructed

Insert a USB drive as previously instructed or use the storage location you have been using throughout the text
Click **File** menu, click **New Company**

The first screen of the EasyStep Interview will appear on the screen.

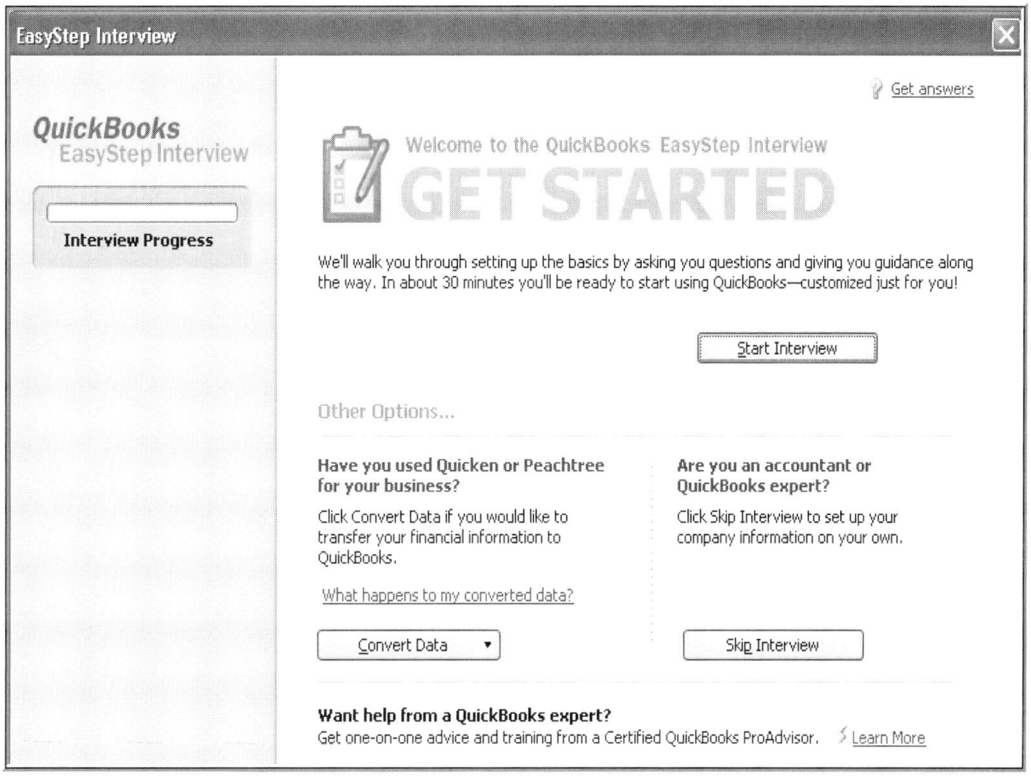

THE EASYSTEP INTERVIEW

The EasyStep Interview is a step-by-step guide to entering your company information as of a single date called a start date. It also provides tips regarding a chart of accounts, standard industry practices, and other items for the type of company indicated. During the Interview, general company information is entered; you may select a preset Chart of Accounts; indicate preferences such as payroll, inventory, time tracking, and employees; and select a start date.

Once a screen has been read and any required items have been filled in or questions answered, the Next button is clicked to tell QuickBooks Pro to advance to the next screen. If you need to return to a previous screen, click the Previous button. If you need to stop the Interview before completing everything, you may exit by clicking the Leave button in the bottom right corner of the screen or by clicking the close button at the top right corner of the EasyStep Interview screen

Begin the Interview

Click the **Start Interview** button

COMPLETE THE EASYSTEP INTERVIEW

The EasyStep Interview provides a series of screen with questions that, when answered, enables QuickBooks to set up the company file, create a Chart of Accounts designed for your specific type of business, and establish the beginning of a company's fiscal year and income tax year.

MEMO
DATE: January 1, 2006

Use the following information to complete the EasyStep Interview for Your Name Movies, Etc.:

Company and Legal Name: Your Name Movies, Etc (*Key in your actual name*)
Federal Tax ID: 15-9888654
Address: 8795 Mission Bay Drive, San Diego, CA 92109
Telephone: 760-555-7979; Fax: 760-555-9797
E-mail: YourNameMoviesEtc@info.com
Web: www.MoviesEtc.com
Do not use Passwords
File Name: Your Name Movies, Etc.qbw
Type of Business: Retail
Record each sale individually, do charge sales tax
Do not sell online
Do use sales receipts and invoices (do not use progress invoicing)
Do accept credit cards and debit cards
Do not use estimates, statements, or track time
Do track bills
Inventory: Yes
Employees: Yes, W-2 Employees
Use QuickBooks to set up the Chart of Accounts
Start Date: 01/01/2006
Bank account name Checking, account number 123-456-78910, opened before 01/01/2006. Last bank statement 12/31/2005, ending balance 29,385.00
First Month in Tax and Fiscal Year: January
Income Tax form: None

Complete the Company Info screen

Enter the Company Name **Your Name Movies, Etc.**, press the Tab key

- Your Name Movies, Etc. is entered as the Legal name when the Tab key is pressed. Do not actually enter the words "Your Name" as part of the company name. Instead, type your own name. For example, Selma Anderson would have **Selma Anderson Movies, Etc.** This makes it easier for you to identify your work when you print.

Tab to or click **Tax ID number**, enter **159-88-8654**

Enter the Company Address information in the spaces provided, tab to or click in the blanks to move from item to item

For the state, California, type C and QuickBooks Pro will fill in the rest or click the drop-down list arrow for State.

- The country is automatically filled in as US.

Enter the telephone number, fax number, e-mail address, and Web address as given in the Memo

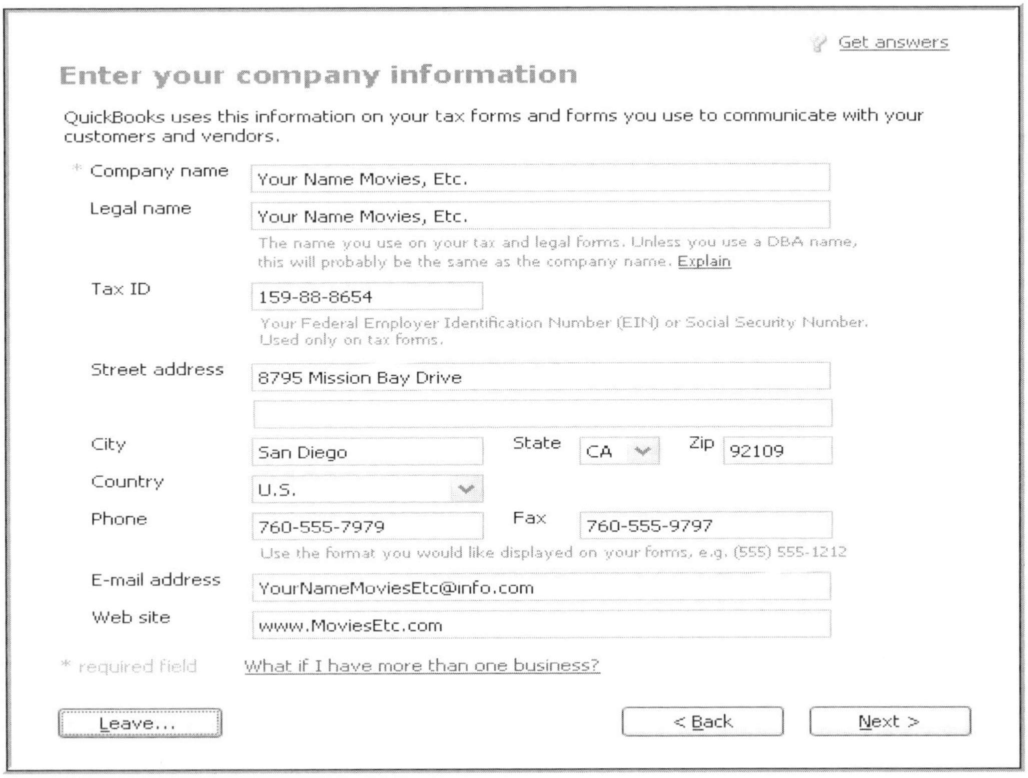

Click **Next**

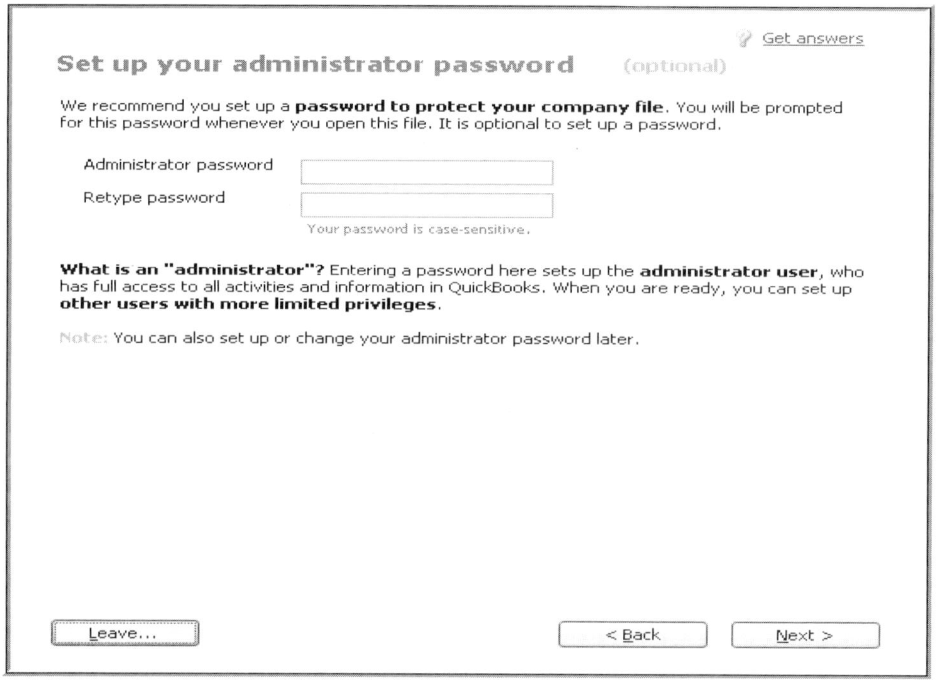

You are not going to assign passwords, click **Next**

Read the screen to Create your company file, click **Next**

Click the drop-down list for **Save in:** and click the storage location you have been instructed to use (The example provided shows a USB drive in F:/ as the storage location.)

The File name is **Your Name Movies, Etc**.

Save as type: should show QuickBooks Files (*.QBW, *.QBA)

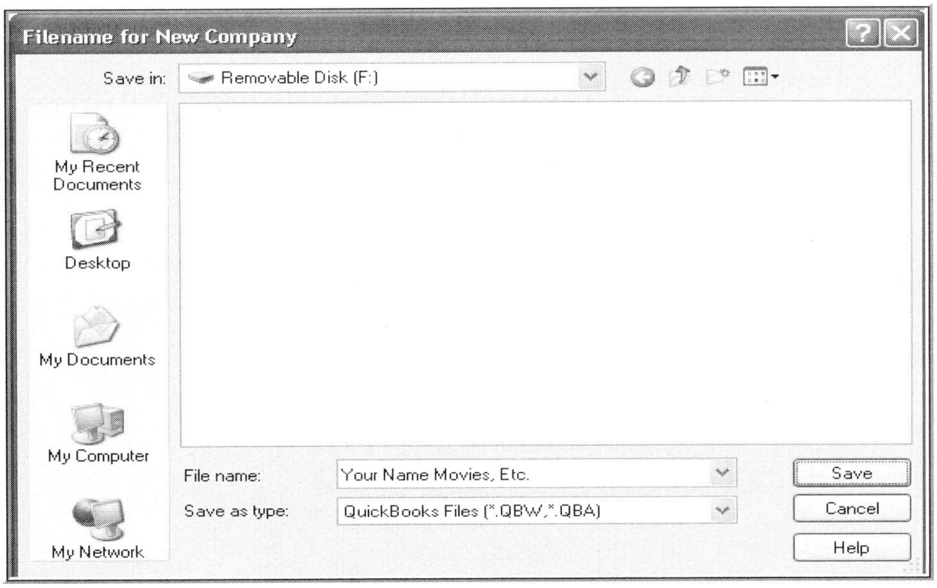

Click **Save**

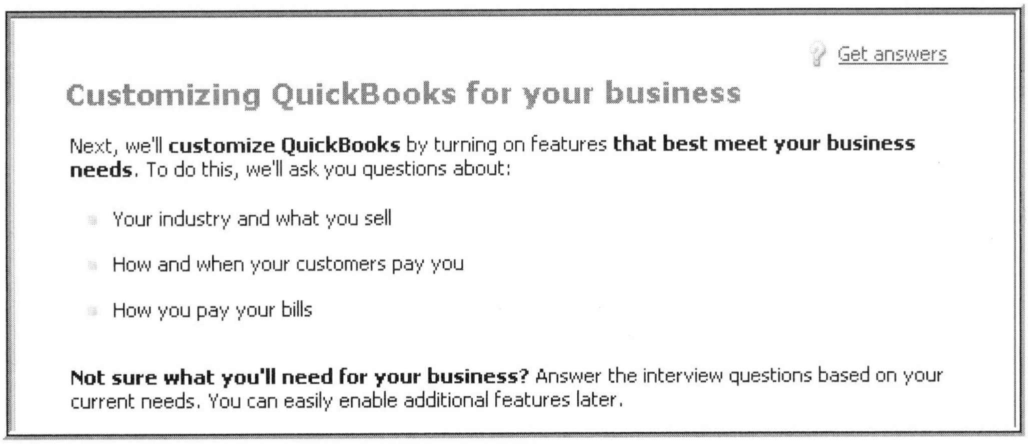

Click **Next**
Scroll through the list of industries
Click **Retail**

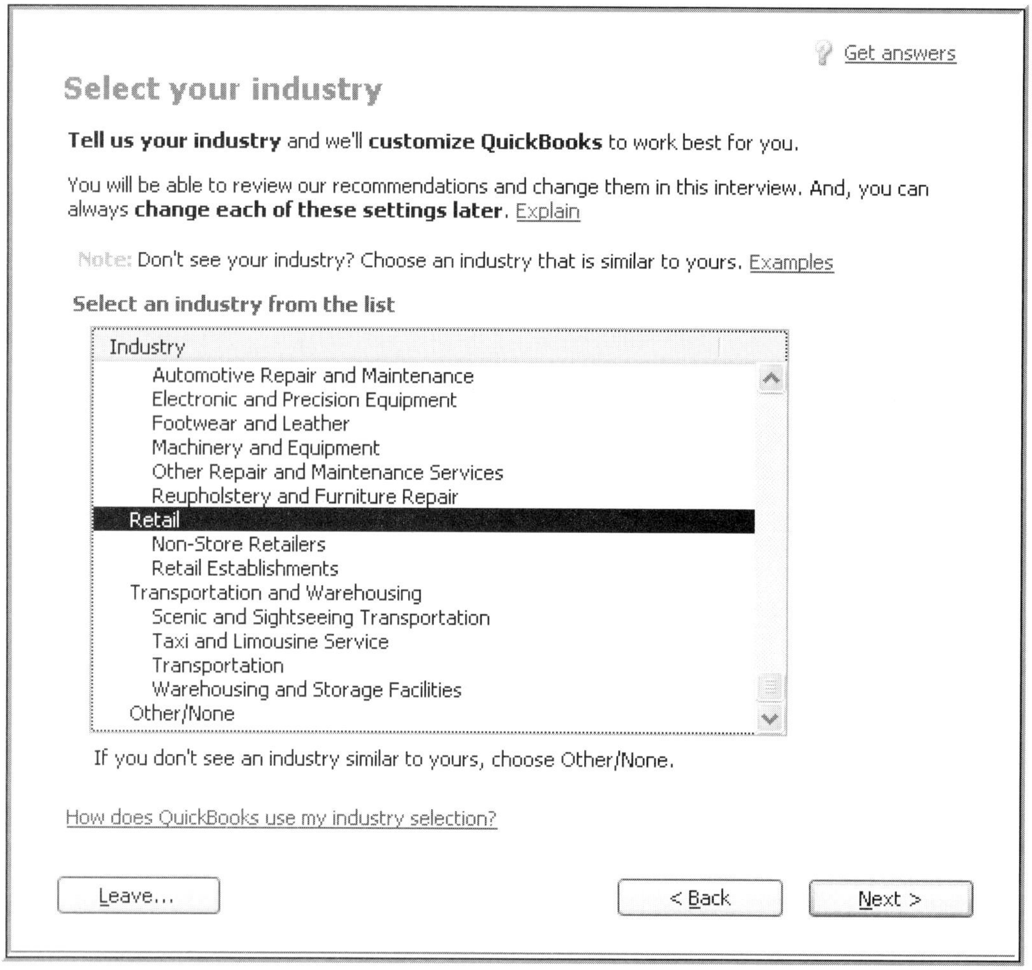

Click **Next**

Click **Both services and products** on the “What do you sell?” screen

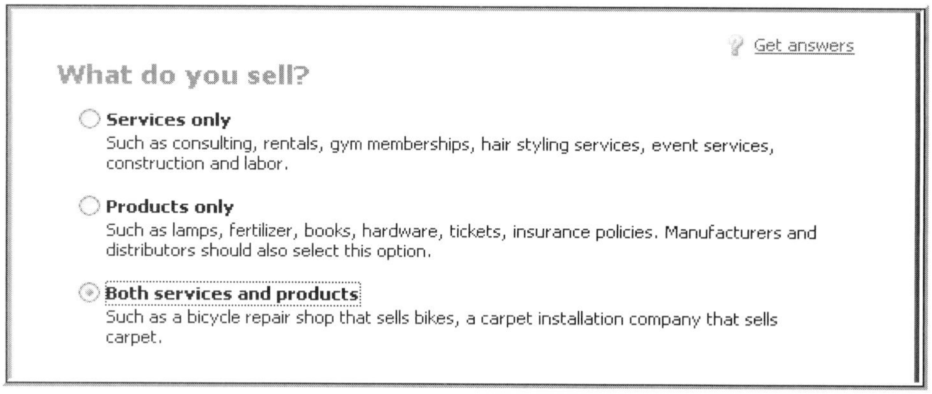

Click **Next**

Click **Record each sale individually** on the "How will you enter sales in QuickBooks" screen

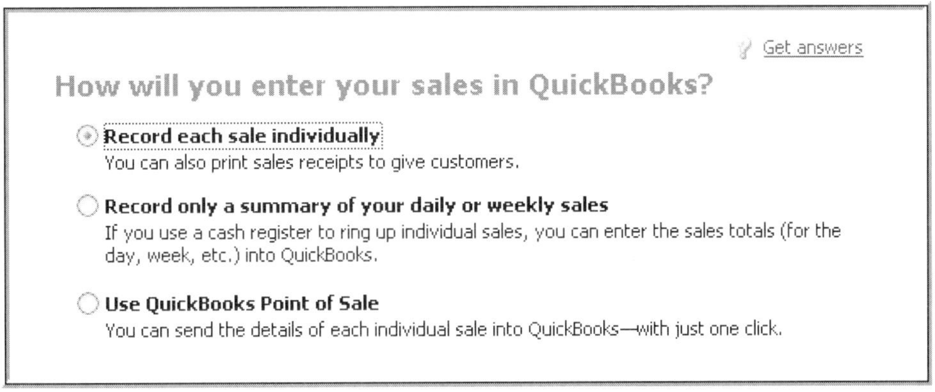

Click **Next**

At this point you are not planning to sell products online so click **I don't sell online and I am not interested in doing so** on the "Do you sell products online?" screen

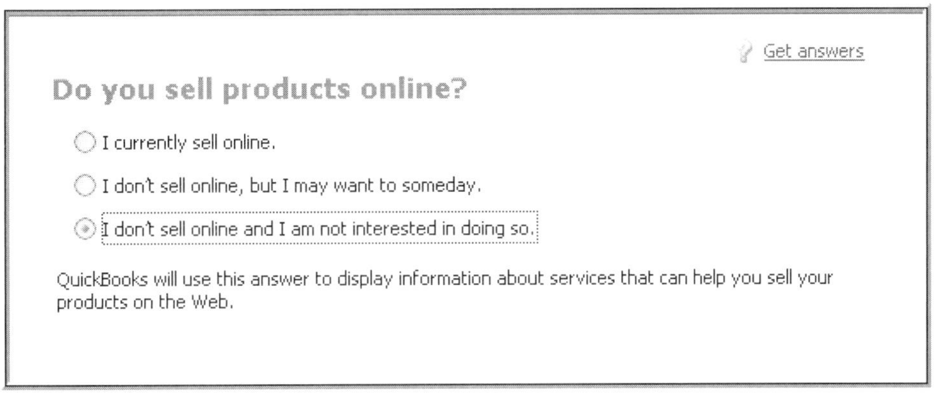

Click **Next**

You do plan to charge sales tax, click **Yes** on the "Do you charge sales tax?" screen

Click **Next**

Click **No** on the "Do you want to create estimates in QuickBooks?" screen

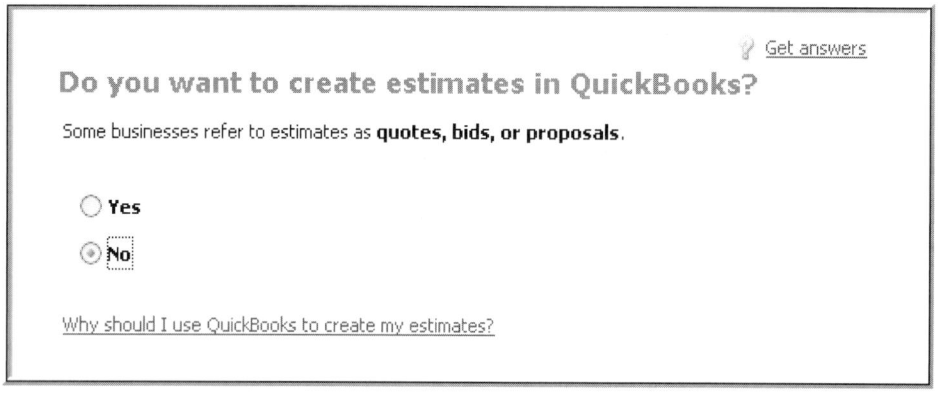

Click **Next**
Click **Yes** on the "Using sales receipts in QuickBooks" screen

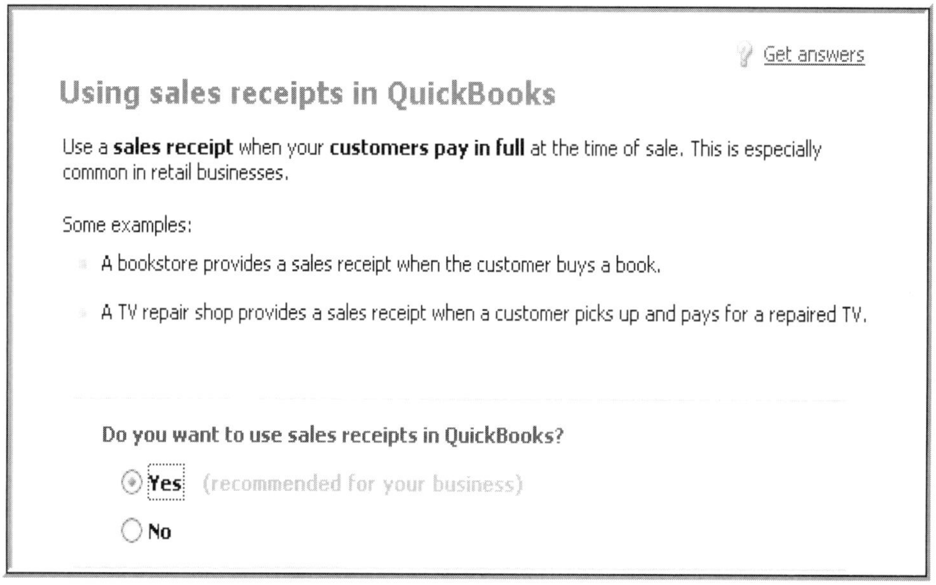

Click **Next**
You do not plan to send statements, click **No** on the "Using statements in QuickBooks" screen

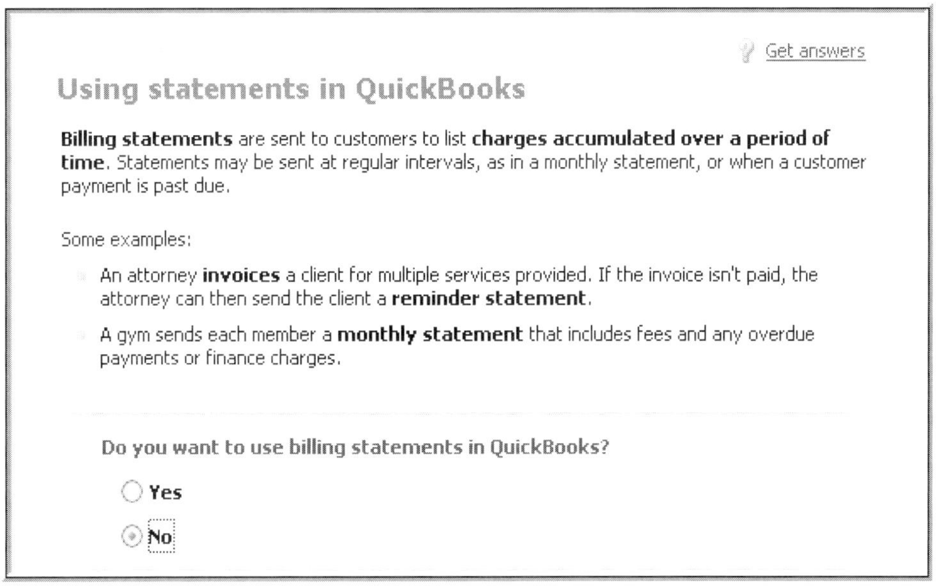

Click **Next**

Since you plan to use invoices to record sales on account, click **Yes** on the "Using invoices in QuickBooks" screen

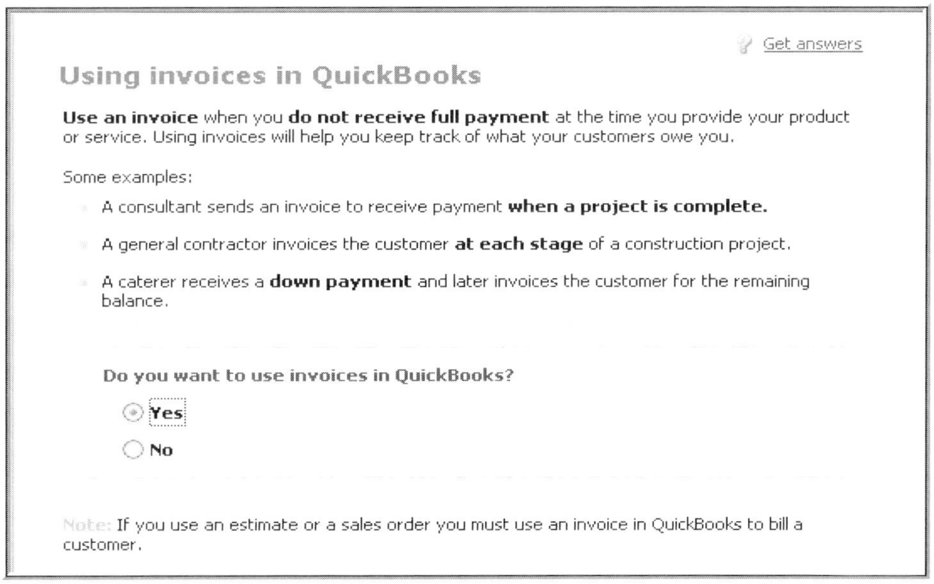

Click **Next**

Click **No** on the "Using progress invoicing" screen

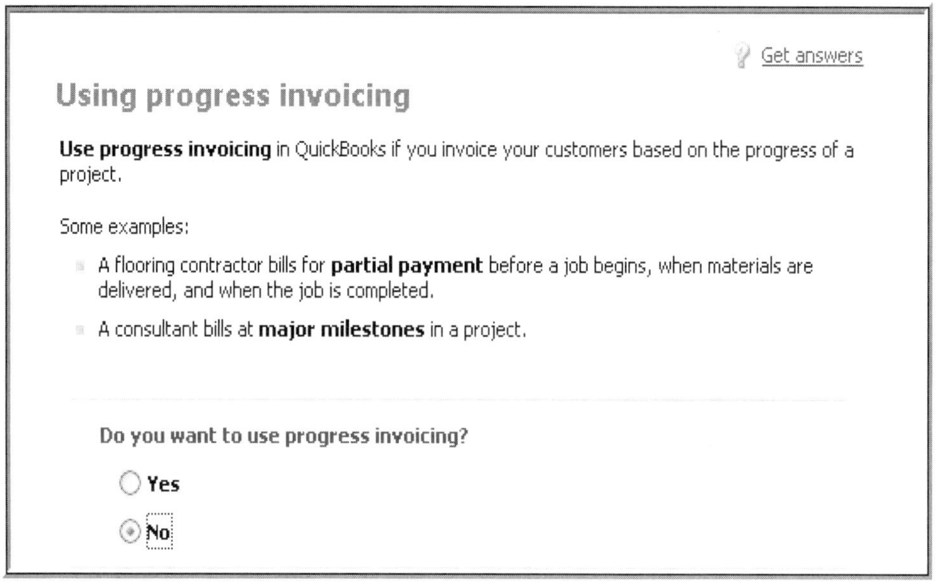

Click **Next**

You do want to keep track of the bills you owe, click **Yes** on the "Managing bills you owe" screen

Click **Next**

You have inventory and plan to use QuickBooks to track it, click **Yes** on the "Tracking inventory in QuickBooks" screen

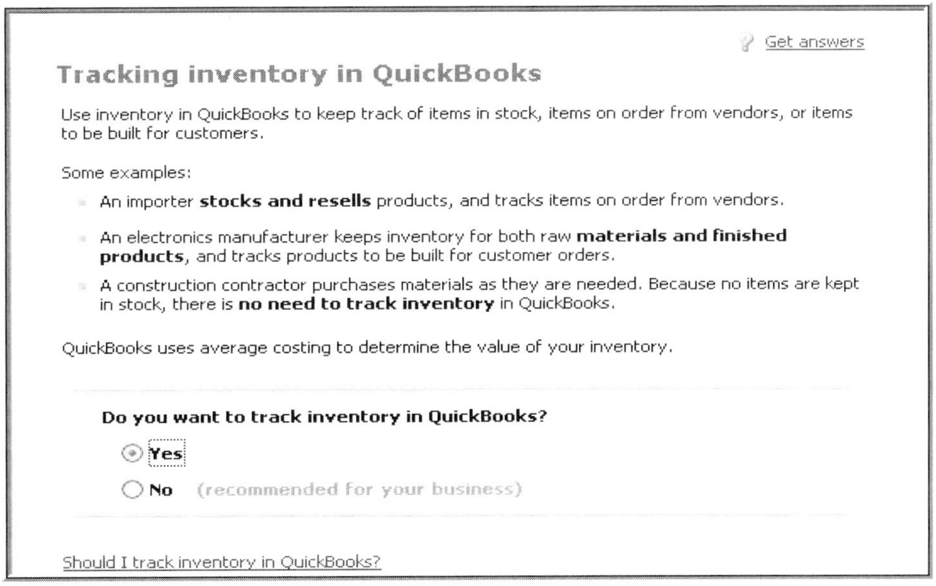

Click **Next**

You accept credit cards, click **I accept credit cards and debit cards.** on the "Do you accept credit cards" screen

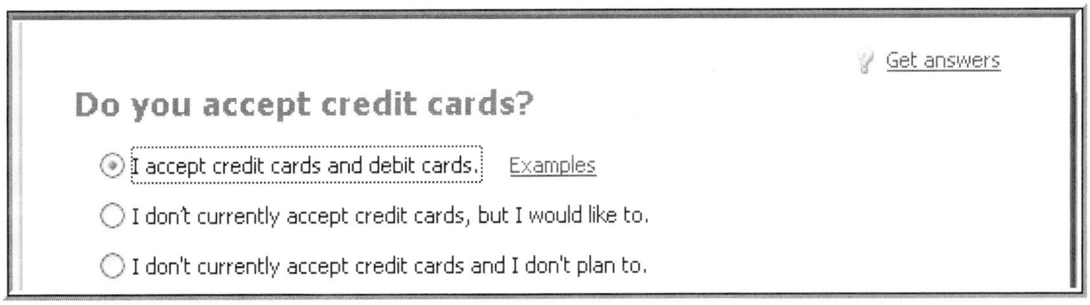

Click **Next**

Tracking time is used to keep track of the time spent on a particular job or with a particular client, which is not done in your company; so click **No** on the "Tracking time in QuickBooks" screen

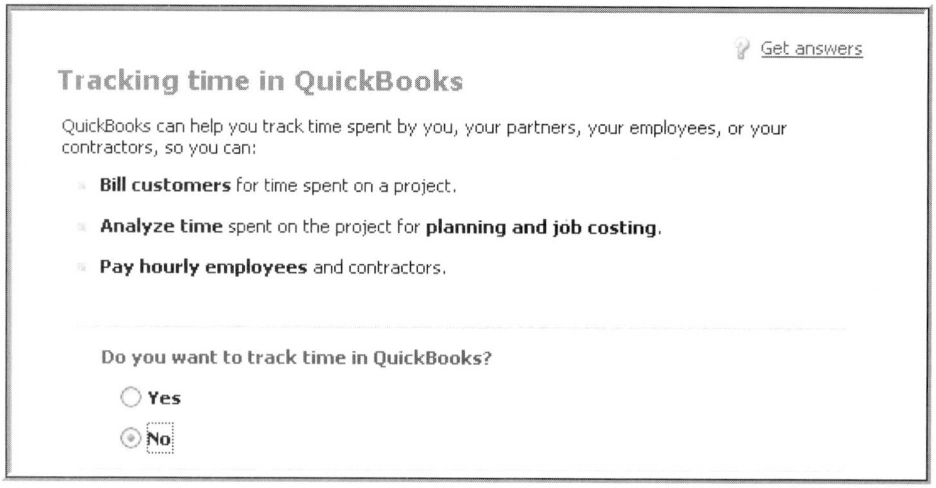

Click **Next**

There are two employees who work for us so click **Yes** and **We have W-2 employees.**

On the "Do you have employees?" screen

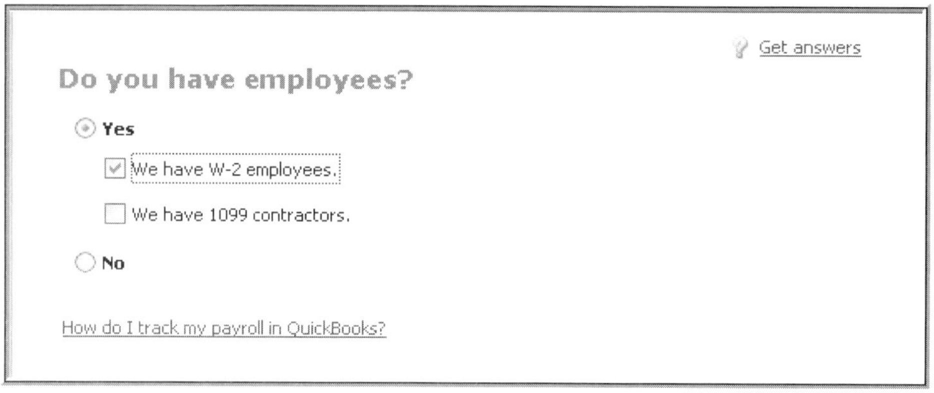

Click **Next**

You want to use QuickBooks to set up the Chart of Accounts

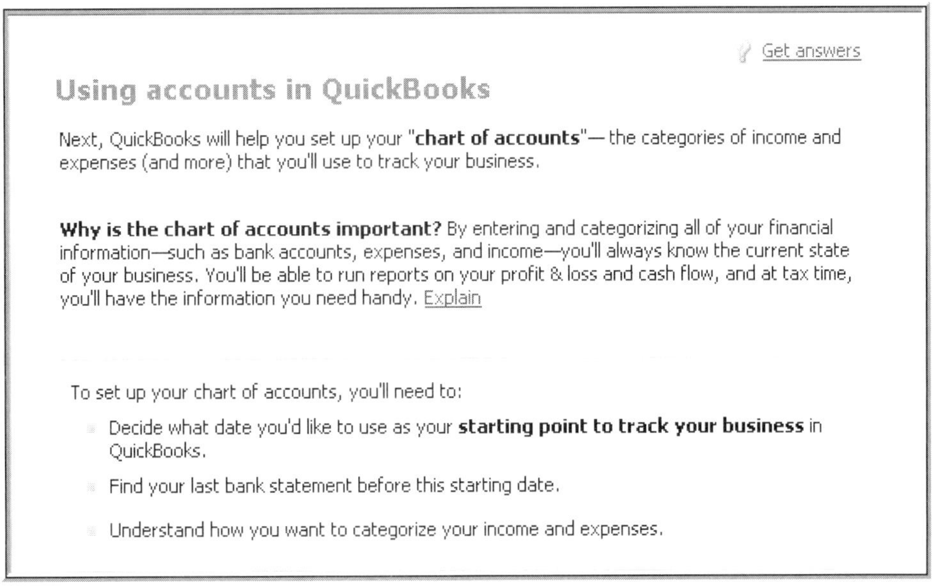

Click **Next**
Enter **01/01/2006** as the Start date for keeping records in QuickBooks

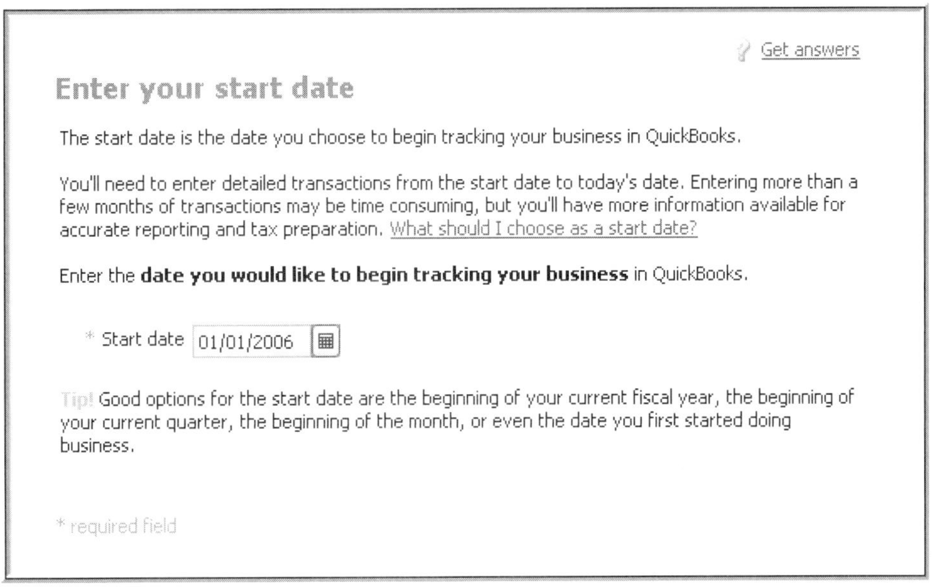

Click **Next**
Click **Yes** to add your bank account

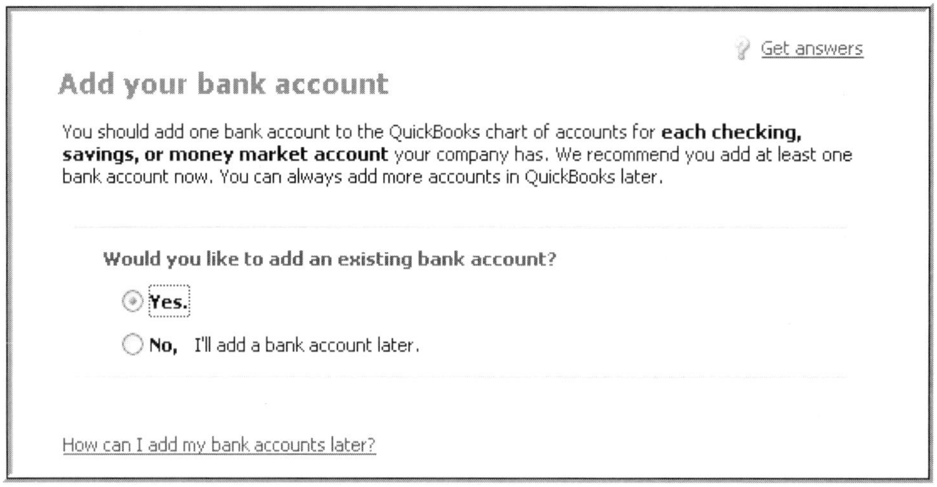

Click **Next**

Enter the bank account information: name is **Checking**, the number is **123-456-78910**, opened **Before 01/01/2006**

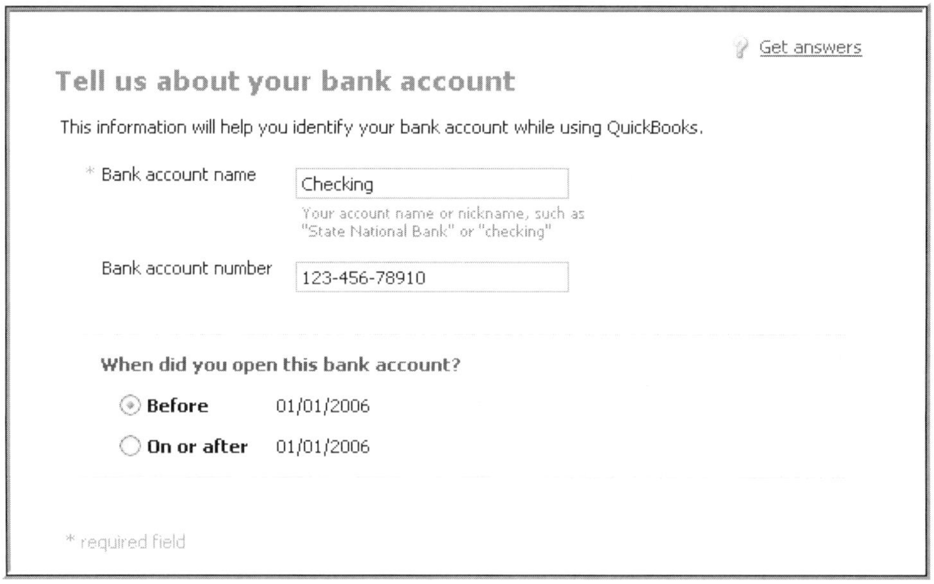

Click **Next**

Enter the ending date of the last bank statement **12/31/2005** and the ending balance **29,385**

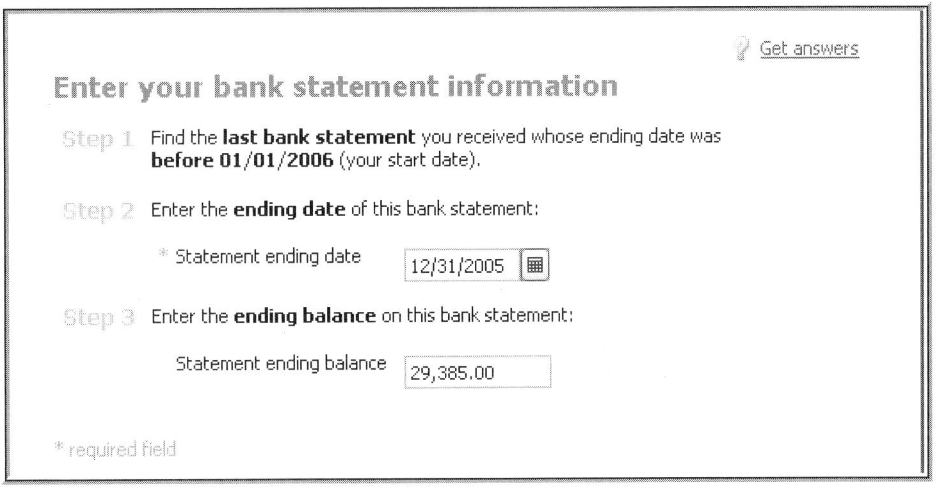

Click **Next**

Review the bank account name, **No** should be selected for adding another bank account

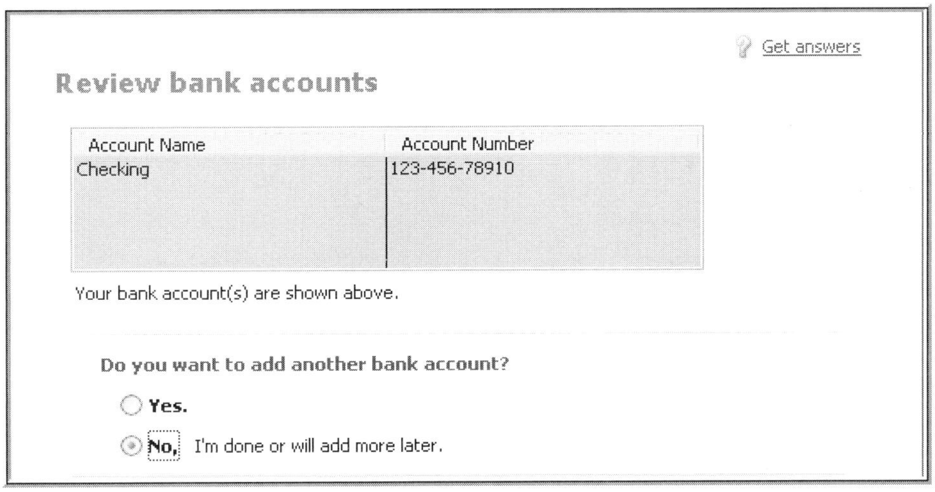

Click **Next**

Scroll through the list of Expense accounts created by QuickBooks, select **Yes** to start with these accounts

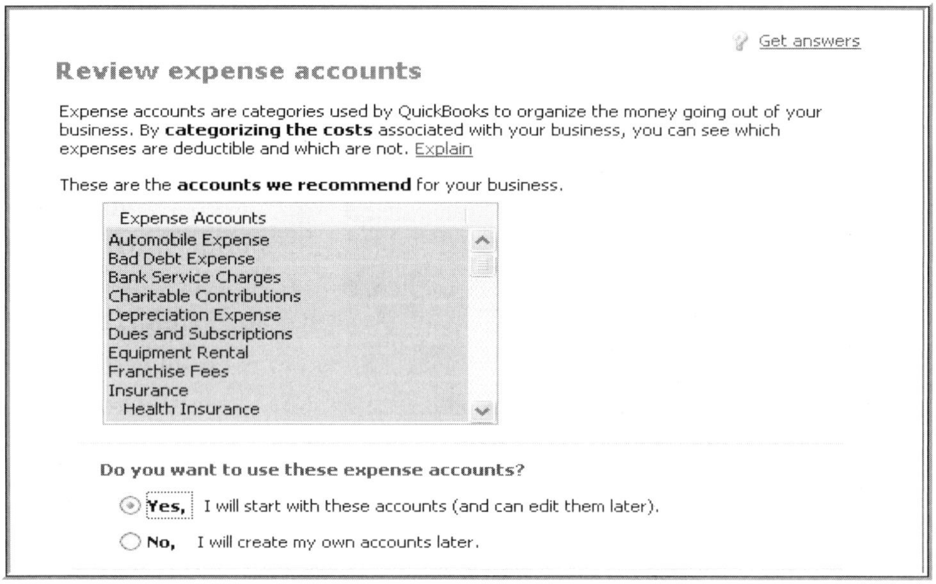

Click **Next**

Scroll through the list of Income accounts created by QuickBooks, select **Yes** to start with these accounts

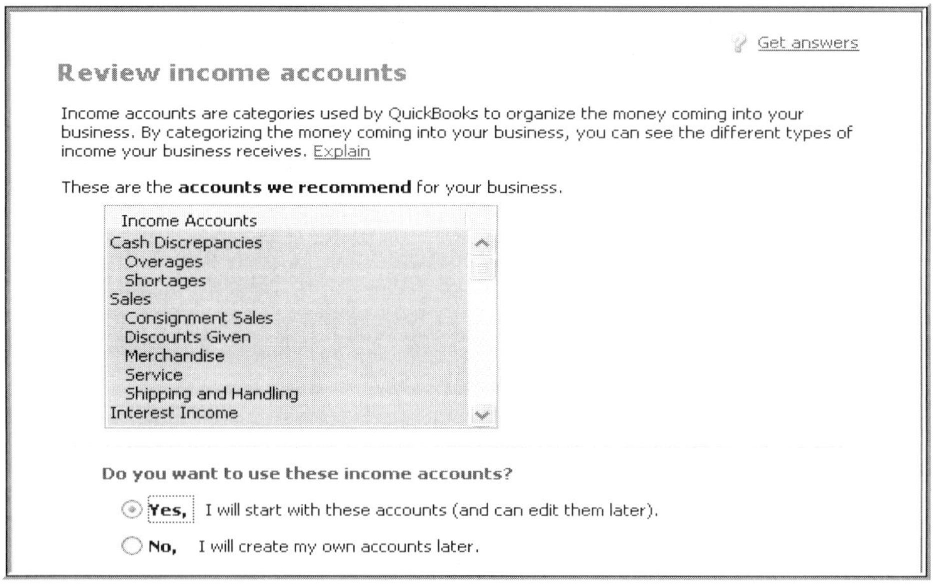

Click **Next**

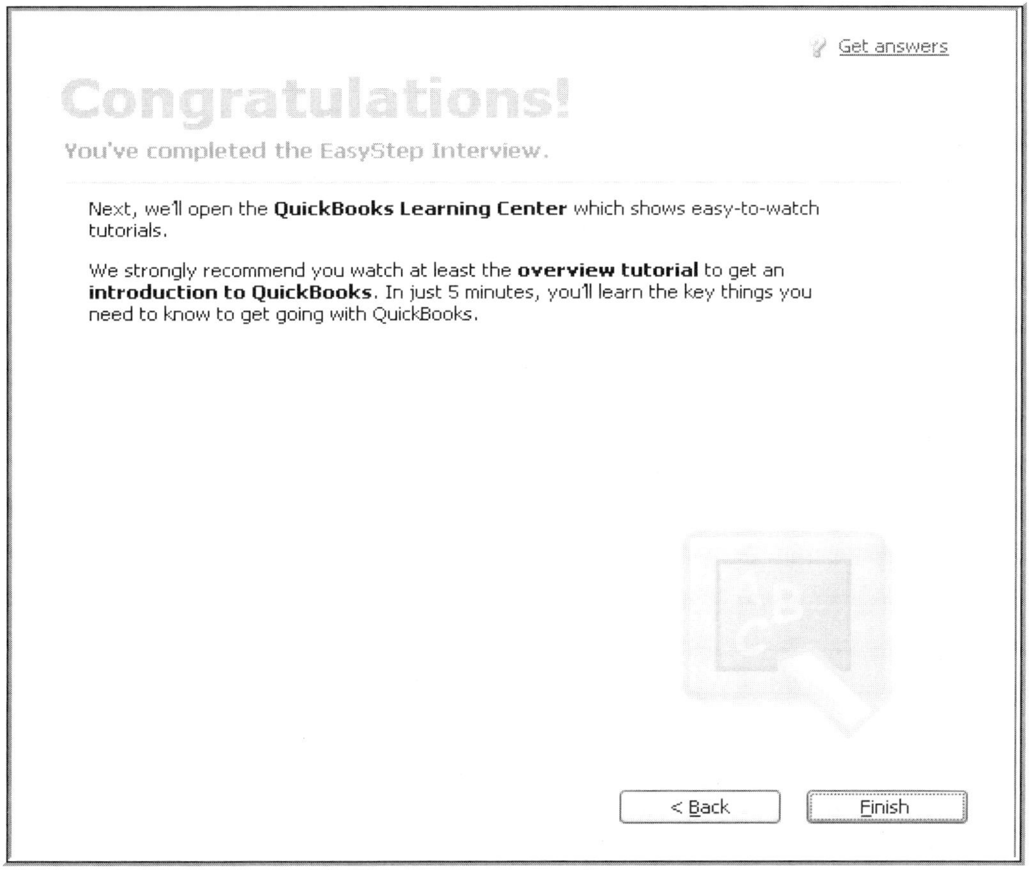

Click the **Finish** button

On the QuickBooks Learning Center, click **Show this window at startup** to remove the check mark

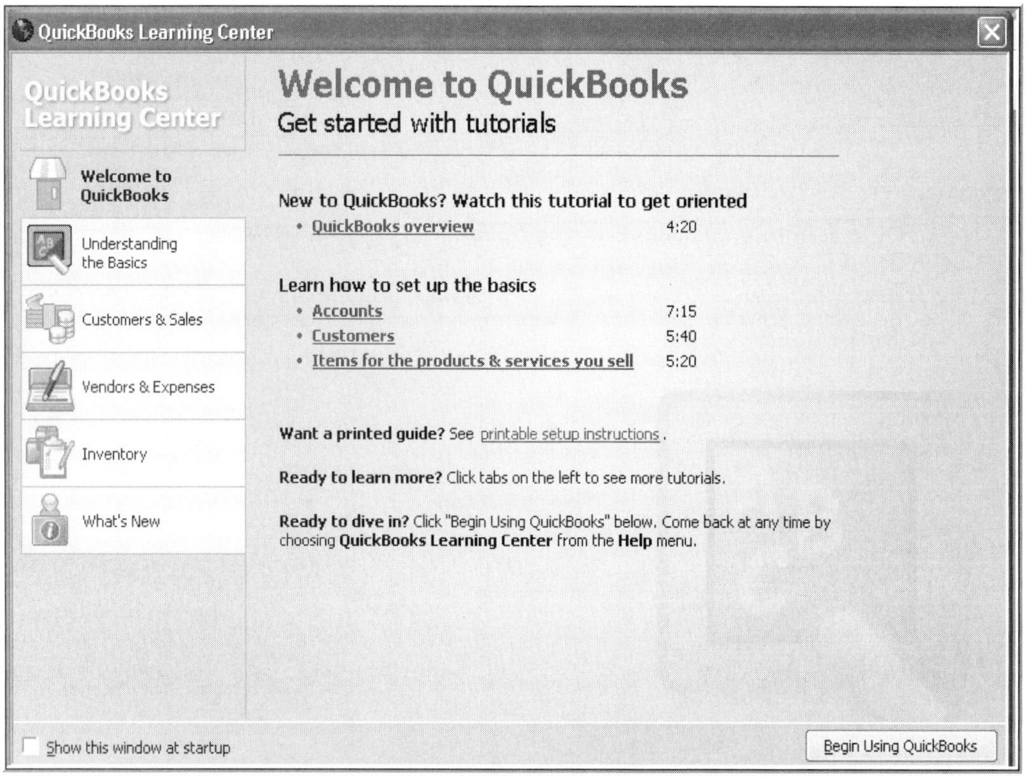

Click the **Begin Using QuickBooks** button

COMPLETE COMPANY INFORMATION

Once the EasyStep Interview has been completed, other information for the company must be entered. Information such as tax forms, Federal Employer Identification numbers, and payroll processing information may need to be provided. Customers, vendors, employees, sales items, and preferences need to be entered. In addition, the chart of accounts will need to be refined.

MEMO
DATE: January 1, 2006

The information necessary to complete the Company information is the Federal Employer Identification number. The number is 15-9888654.

Enter the Federal Employer Identification number

Click **Company Info** on the Company menu

Click in the Federal Employer Identification number text box, enter 15-9888654

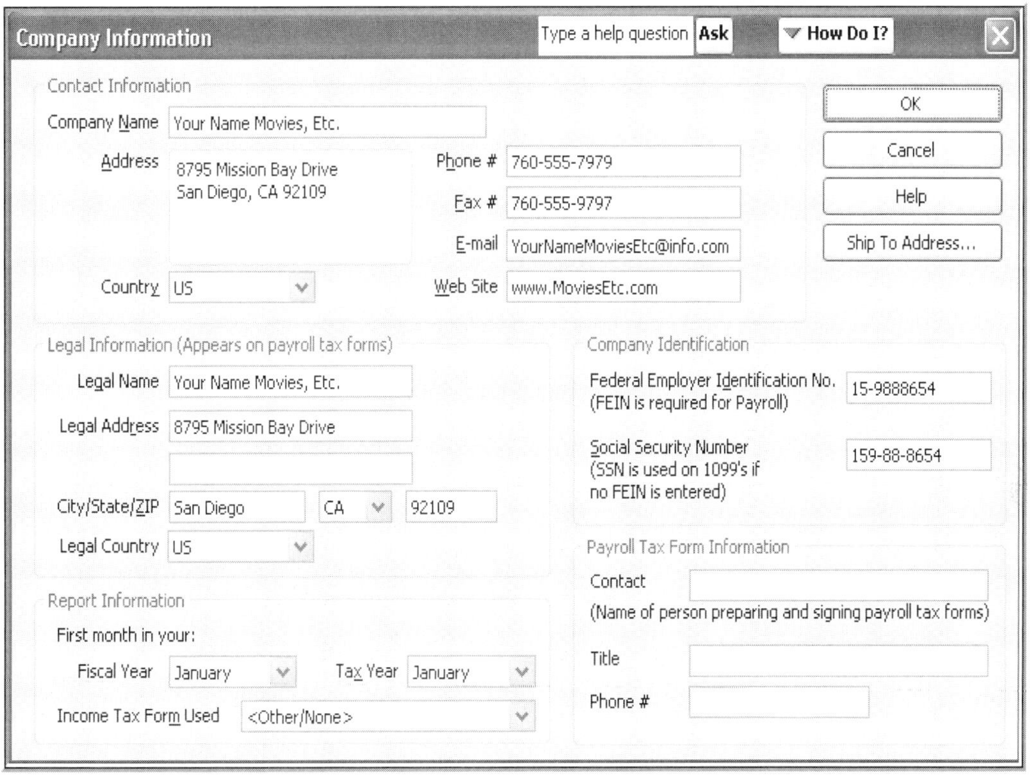

- View the other information on the page. Notice that the Report Information shows the Fiscal Year and Tax Year as January. There is no Income Tax Form selected. The Contact Information and Legal Information appear as it was entered during the EasyStep Interview. Do not make any other changes to the Company Information.

Click **OK**

ITEMS LIST

The Items list contains information about all of the items sold or services performed by the business. The Items used to track services performed and products sold for income are created. The Items List is used in conjunction with the income accounts previously created.

January 1, 2006			
Type	Service	Service	Service
Item Name	DVD Rental	DVD Repair	DVD Service
Description	DVD Rental	DVD Repair	DVD Service
Rate	3.95	0.00	39.95
Tax Code	Yes	Non-taxable	Non-taxable
Account	Sales: Rental	Sales: Service	Sales: Service

Add the three service items above to the Items List

Click **Lists** on the menu bar, click **Item List**
Click the **Item** button at the bottom of the list
Click **New**

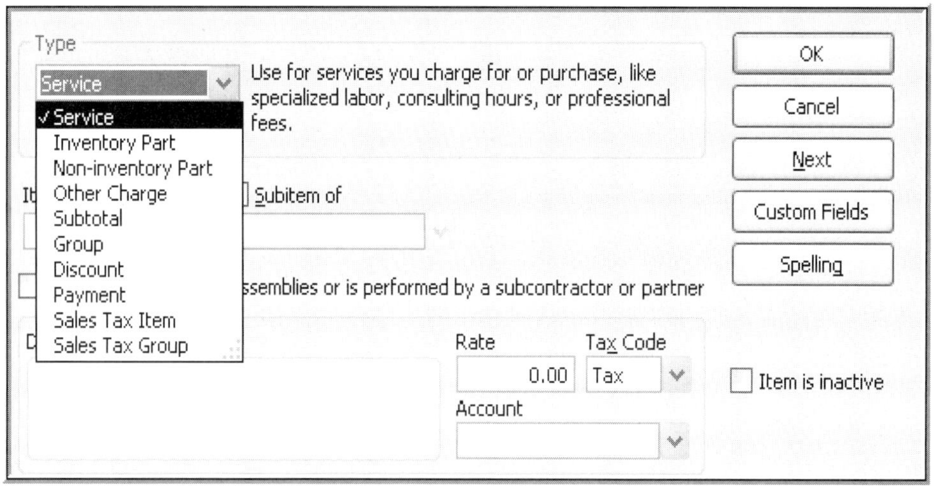

Click **Service**
Tab to or click Item Name/Number
Enter Item Name **DVD Rental**
Tab to or click Description, enter **DVD Rental**
Tab to or click Rate, enter **3.95**
The Tax Code should be **Tax**
Click the drop-down list arrow for Account
Since Sales: Rental Income does not appear in the account list, scroll to the top of the list and click **<Add New>**
The type of account is **Income**
The name is **Rental**
The account is a subaccount of **Sales**

The description is **Rental Income**

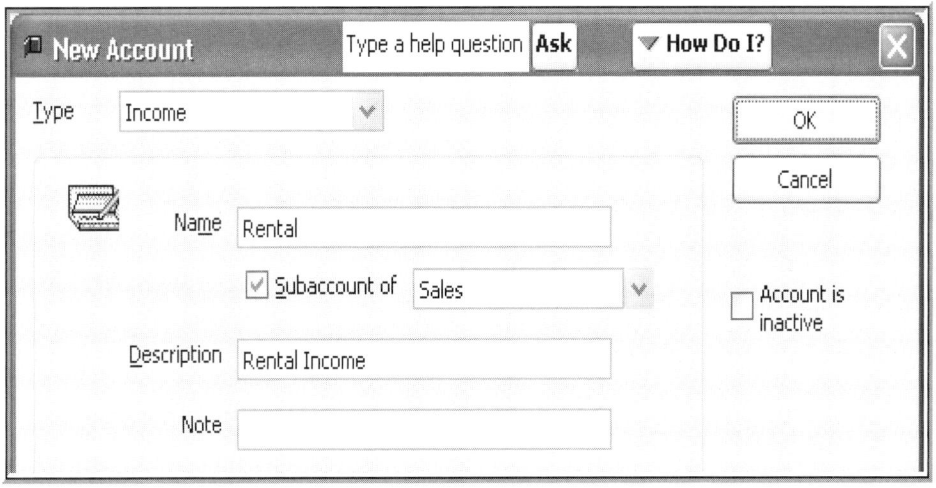

Click **OK**

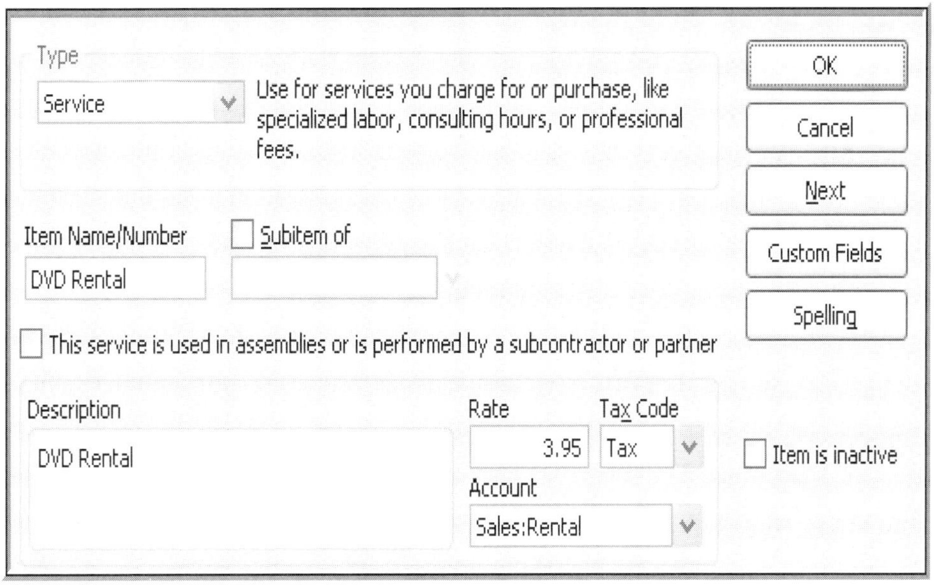

The information for DVD Rental is complete, click **Next** to add the sales item for DVD repair

DVD does not appear in QuickBooks spell check so the Check Spelling on Form screen appears

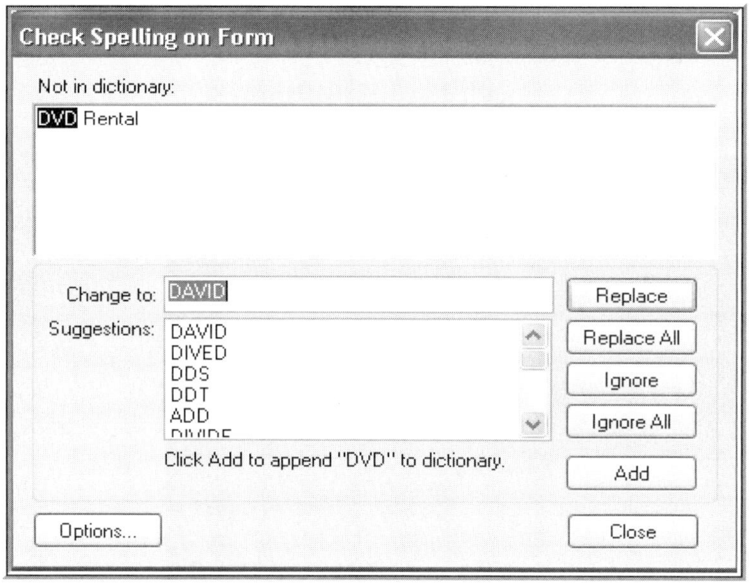

Click **Add** to add the word to the dictionary

Complete the information for DVD repair using the information provided in the memo

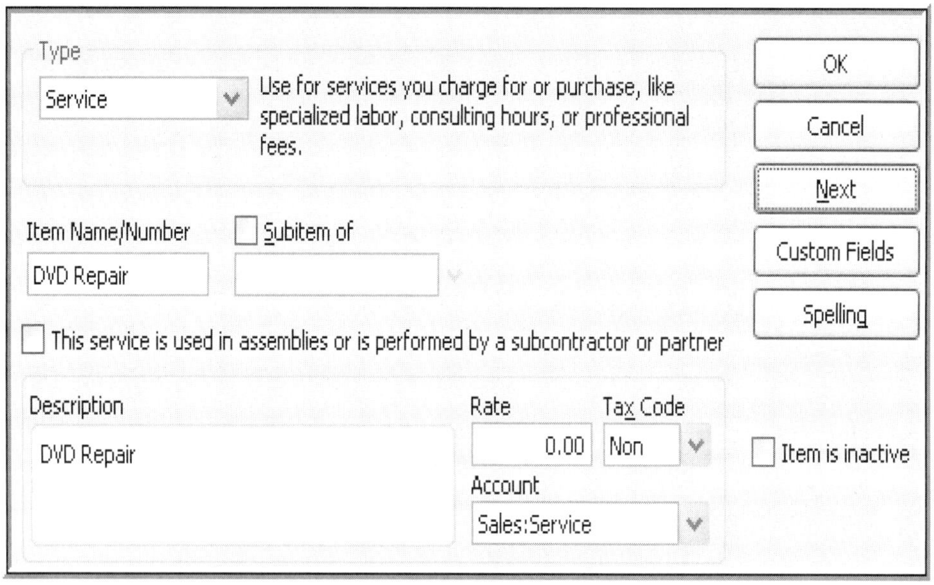

Add the third service item, DVD service

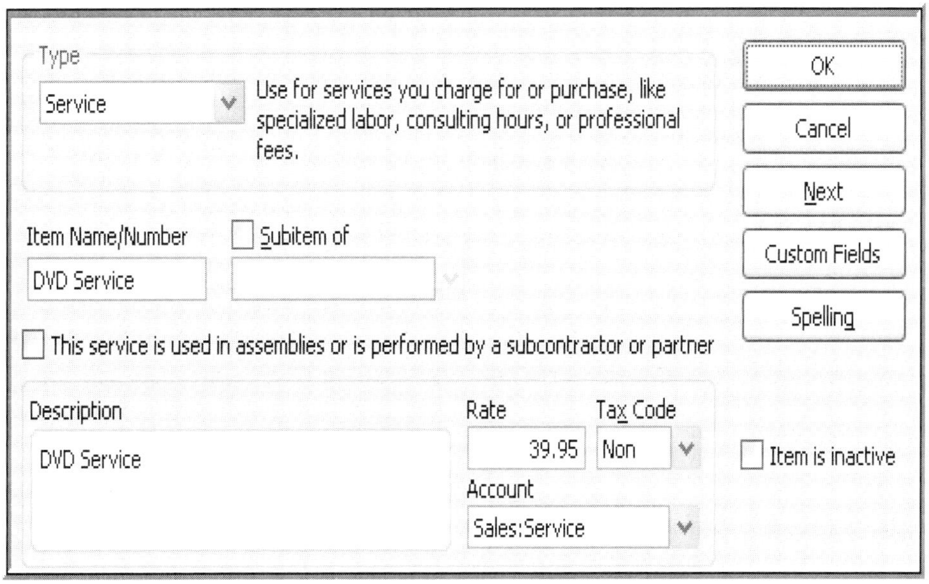

Click **OK**

Once the service items have been added, the Inventory part items should be entered. Inventory part items are the things you purchase, hold in inventory, and then sell.

January 1, 2006				
Type	Inventory Part	Inventory Part	Inventory Part	Inventory Part
Item Name	Action DVD	Children DVD	Comedy DVD	Drama DVD
Purchase Description	Action DVD	Children DVD	Comedy DVD	Drama DVD
Cost	0.00	0.00	0.00	0.00
COGS Account	Cost of Goods Sold	Cost of Goods Sold	Cost of Goods Sold	Cost of Goods Sold
Preferred Vendor				
Sales Description	Action DVD	Children DVD	Comedy DVD	Drama DVD
Sales Price	0.00	0.00	0.00	0.00
Tax Code	Tax	Tax	Tax	Tax
Income Account	Sales: Merchandise	Sales: Merchandise	Sales: Merchandise	Sales: Merchandise
Asset Account	Inventory Asset	Inventory Asset	Inventory Asset	Inventory Asset
Reorder Point	100	100	100	100
On-Hand	2550	1250	1500	1450
Total Value	12,750	6,250	7,500	7,250
As Of	01/01/06	01/01/06	01/01/06	01/01/06

Use the information above to add the Inventory Part Items

Click the **Item** button at the bottom of the Item List screen
Click **New**
Click **Inventory Part**
Enter **Action DVD** as the Item Name
Tab to or click Description on Purchase Transactions, enter **Action DVD**

- Since the purchase price of the DVDs vary, the Cost is **0.00**
- The COGS Account is **Cost of Goods Sold**
- There is no Preferred Vendor, so leave this blank

Enter the Description on Sales Transactions **Action DVD**

- Because DVDs are sold for different amounts, Sales Price remains **0.00**
- The Tax Code should be **Tax**

Click the drop-down list arrow for Income Account, click **Merchandise,** which is a subaccount of Sales

- The Asset Account is **Inventory Asset**

Enter the Reorder Point of **100**
Tab to On Hand, enter **2,550**
Enter the Total Value of **12,750**, and the As of date **01/01/2006**

- The only time a Total Value may be entered is at the time the Inventory Part item is created.

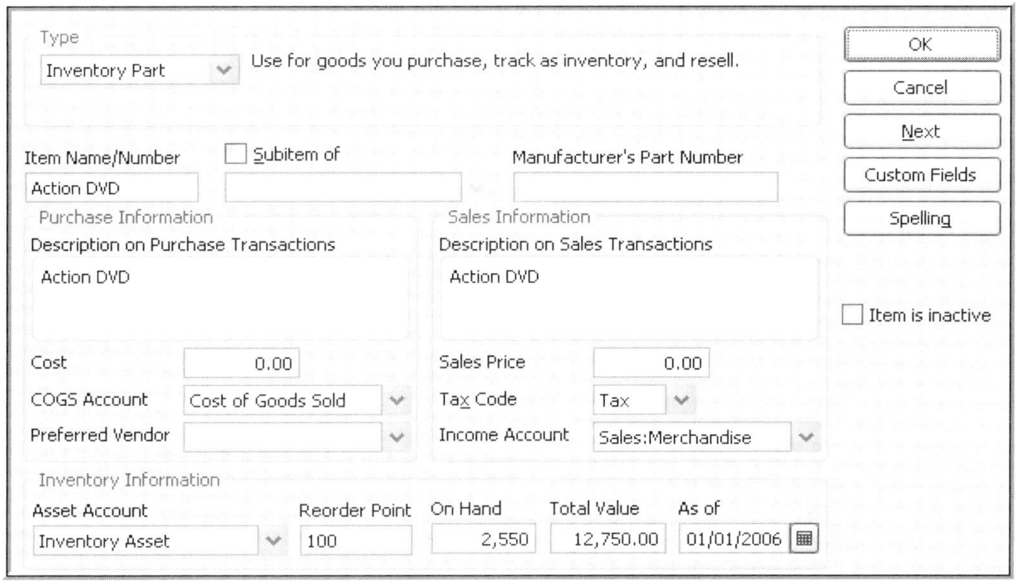

Click **Next** and enter the information for Children DVD

Click **Next** and enter the information for Comedy DVD

Click **Next** and enter the information for Drama DVD

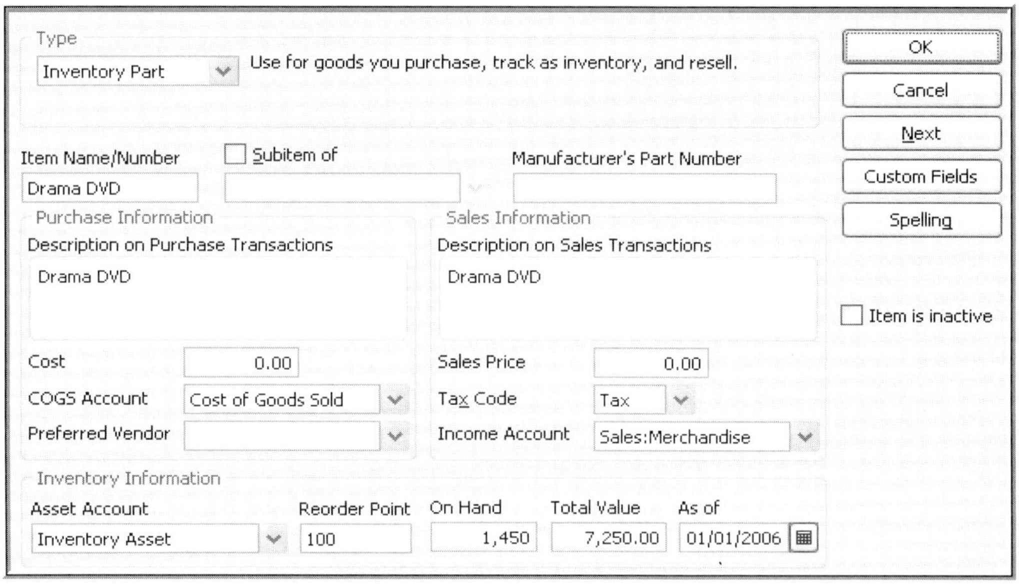

Click **OK**

The Item List shows some items that we will not be using. These items need to be deleted.

Delete the following sales items: Service Item, Inventory Item 1, Inventory Item 2, Consignment Item, and Non-Inventory Item

Click **Service Item** in the Item list

Click the **Item** button at the bottom of the Item List
Click **Delete Item**

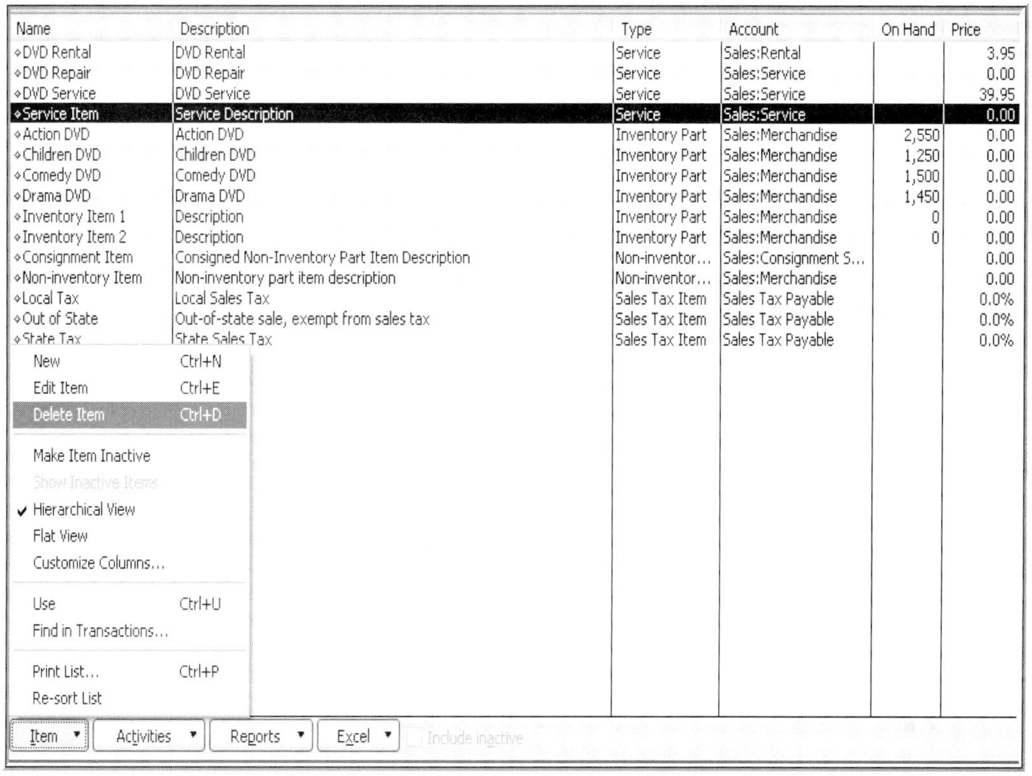

Click **Delete Item**

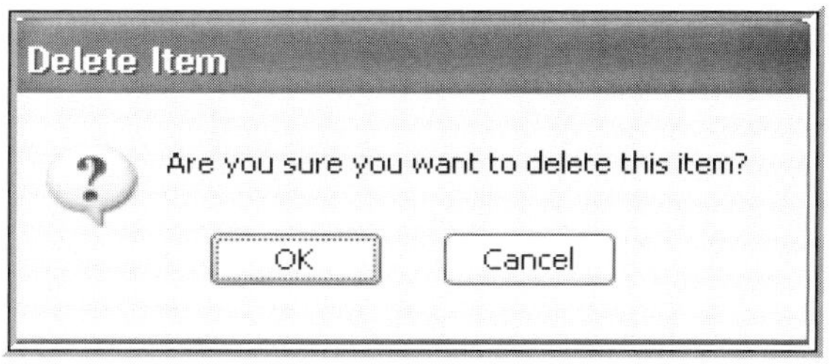

Click **OK**
Repeat the procedures for the remaining items
Your Item List should match the following

◆DVD Rental	DVD Rental	Service	Sales:Rental		3.95
◆DVD Repair	DVD Repair	Service	Sales:Service		0.00
◆DVD Service	DVD Service	Service	Sales:Service		39.95
◆Action DVD	Action DVD	Inventory Part	Sales:Merchandise	2,550	0.00
◆Children DVD	Children DVD	Inventory Part	Sales:Merchandise	1,250	0.00
◆Comedy DVD	Comedy DVD	Inventory Part	Sales:Merchandise	1,500	0.00
◆Drama DVD	Drama DVD	Inventory Part	Sales:Merchandise	1,450	0.00
◆Local Tax	Local Sales Tax	Sales Tax Item	Sales Tax Payable		0.0%
◆Out of State	Out-of-state sale, exempt from sales tax	Sales Tax Item	Sales Tax Payable		0.0%
◆State Tax	State Sales Tax	Sales Tax Item	Sales Tax Payable		0.0%

ENTER SALES TAX INFORMATION

As you view the Item List, you will notice that the State Sales Tax shows 0,0%. This should be changed to show the appropriate amount of sales tax deducted for the state. If you also collect local sales tax, this amount needs to be provided as well. In addition to the amount of tax collected, the Tax Agency needs to be identified. The Tax Agency is added to the company's vendor list.

MEMO

DATE: January 1, 2006

The information necessary to complete the CA State Sales Tax: A tax rate of 7.25% paid to State Board of Equalization, 7800 State Street, Sacramento, CA 94267.

➤ Enter the amount of sales tax and the sales tax agency information for State Sales Tax

Click **State Tax** in the Item List
Click the **Item** button
Click **Edit Item**
Change the Item Name to **CA State Tax**
Enter **7.25%** as the tax rate
Click the drop-down list arrow for Tax Agency
Click **<Add New>**
Enter **State Board of Equalization** as the Vendor name
Enter **State Board of Equalization** as the Company name
Tab to or click in the address text box, if necessary enter **State Board of Equalization**, press Enter
Enter **7800 State Street**, press Enter
Type **Sacramento, CA 94265**, press Tab

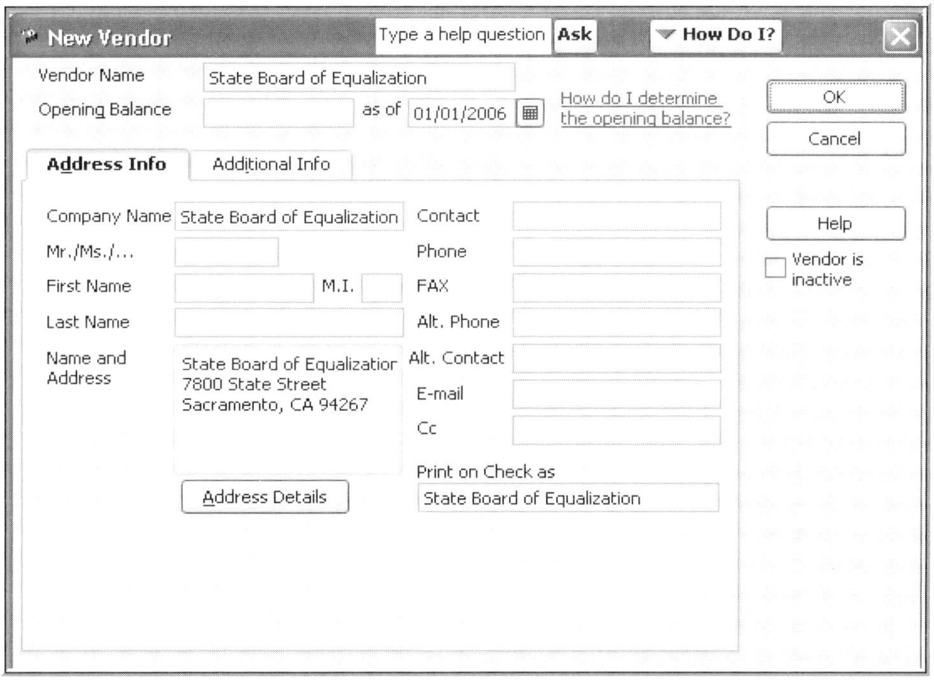

Click **OK**

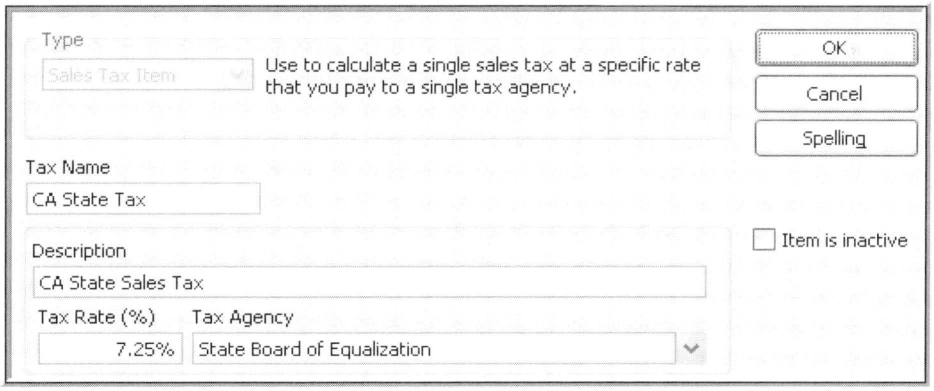

Click **OK** to close the Sales Tax Item

◆DVD Rental	DVD Rental	Service	Sales:Rental		3.95
◆DVD Repair	DVD Repair	Service	Sales:Service		0.00
◆DVD Service	DVD Service	Service	Sales:Service		39.95
◆Action DVD	Action DVD	Inventory Part	Sales:Merchandise	2,550	0.00
◆Children DVD	Children DVD	Inventory Part	Sales:Merchandise	1,250	0.00
◆Comedy DVD	Comedy DVD	Inventory Part	Sales:Merchandise	1,500	0.00
◆Drama DVD	Drama DVD	Inventory Part	Sales:Merchandise	1,450	0.00
◆CA State Tax	CA State Sales Tax	Sales Tax Item	Sales Tax Payable		7.25%
◆Local Tax	Local Sales Tax	Sales Tax Item	Sales Tax Payable		0.0%
◆Out of State	Out-of-state sale, exempt from sales tax	Sales Tax Item	Sales Tax Payable		0.0%

Note the change to the State Tax on the Item List
To print the list in Landscape orientation and fit to one-page wide, click the **Reports** button at the bottom of the screen

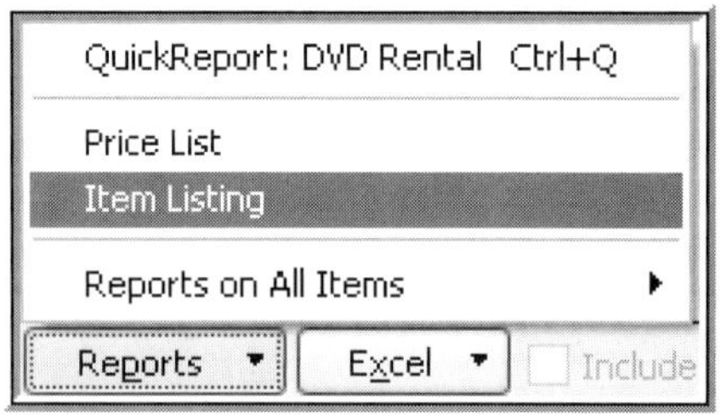

Click **Item Listing**
Click the **Modify Report** button, click Date Prepared and Time Prepared to remove from the report heading, click **OK**
Click **Print**
Click **Landscape** and **Fit report to 1 page wide**, click the **Print** button
Close the report and close the Item List

CUSTOMER LIST

The Customer List is created in the Customer Center. The list includes a customer's name, opening balance, address, telephone and fax numbers, credit terms, credit limits, and sales tax information. The Customer List is also known as the Accounts Receivable Subsidiary Ledger. Whenever a transaction is entered for a customer, it is automatically posted to the General Ledger account and the Accounts Receivable Subsidiary Ledger account.

January 1, 2006				
Customer Name	Gorst, George	Morgan, Elena	Nakamura Day Care Center	Walsh, Bob
Opening Balance	500	800	1,500	150
As Of	01/01/06	01/01/06	01/01/06	01/01/06
Address	1980 A Street	719 4th Avenue	2190 State Street	2210 Columbia Street
City, State, Zip	San Diego, CA 92101	San Diego, CA 92101	San Diego, CA 92101	San Diego, CA 92101
Telephone	760-555-8763	760-555-8015	760-555-1275	760-555-2594
Terms	Net 30	Net 30	Net 30	Net 30
Tax Code	Yes	Yes	Yes	Yes
Tax Item	CA State Tax	CA State Tax	CA State Tax	CA State Tax
Credit Limit	500	1,000	1,500	500

Add the customers and their information to create the Customer List

Click the icon for **Customer Center**
Click **New Customer & Job**
Click **New Customer**
Enter **Gorst, George**

- QuickBooks will organize the Customer List by alphabetizing the first letter shown for the Customer Name.

Enter the Opening Balance of **500** as of **01/01/06**

- This is the only time you are able to enter the opening balance for a customer.

Enter **George** in the text box for First Name
Enter **Gorst** in the text box for Last Name
Tab to or click in the text box for Address
The cursor should appear after George Gorst in the first line of the address, press Enter
Enter the street address **1980 A Street**, press Enter
Enter the city, state and Zip **San Diego, CA 92101**, press Tab
Enter the telephone number **760-555-8763**

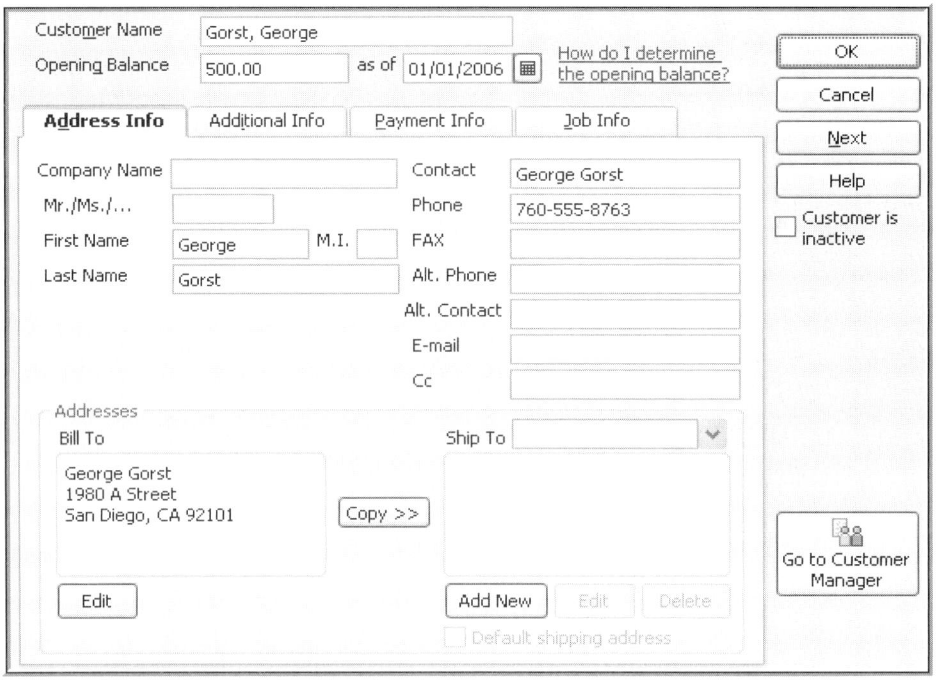

Click the **Additional Info** tab
Click the drop-down list arrow for Terms, click **Net 30**
Click the drop-down list arrow for Tax Code, click **Tax**
Click the drop-down list arrow for Tax Item, click **CA State Tax**

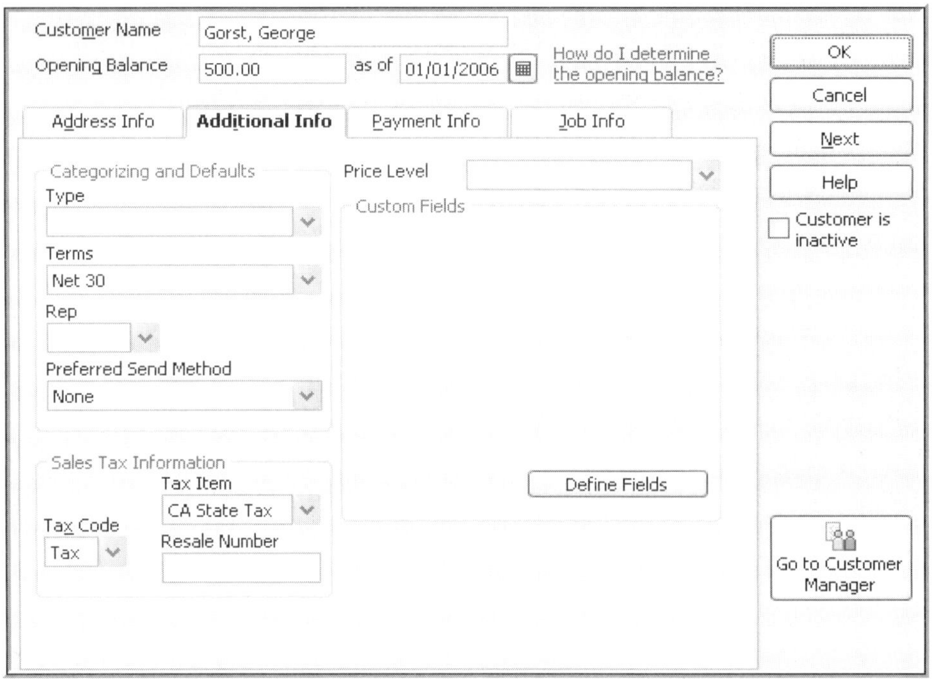

Click the **Payment Info** tab
Enter the Credit Limit of **500**

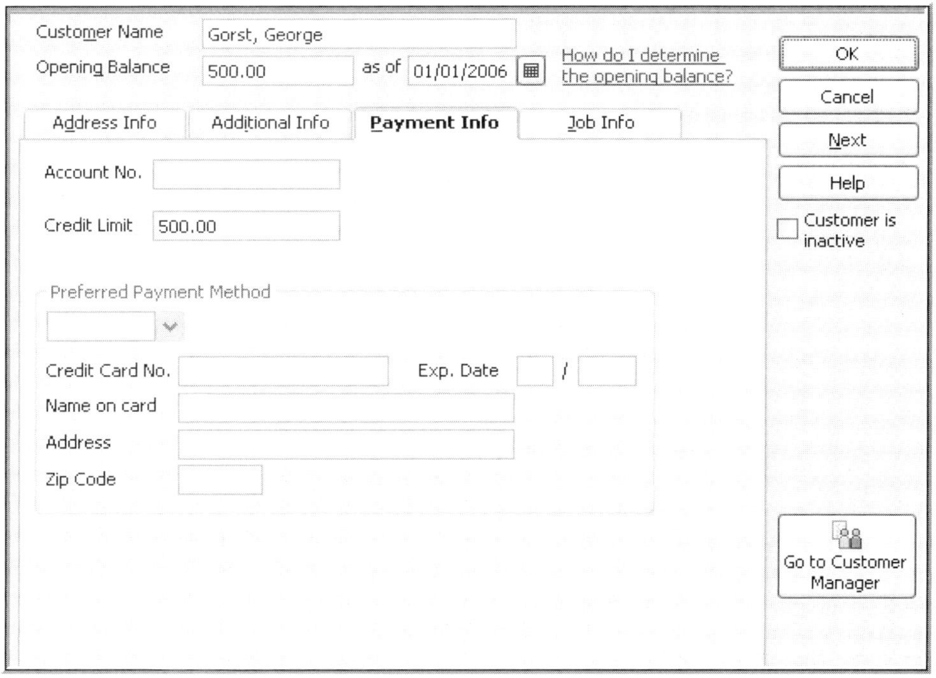

Click **Next** to add the next customer
Repeat the steps above to add each customer
Click **OK** after adding the last customer

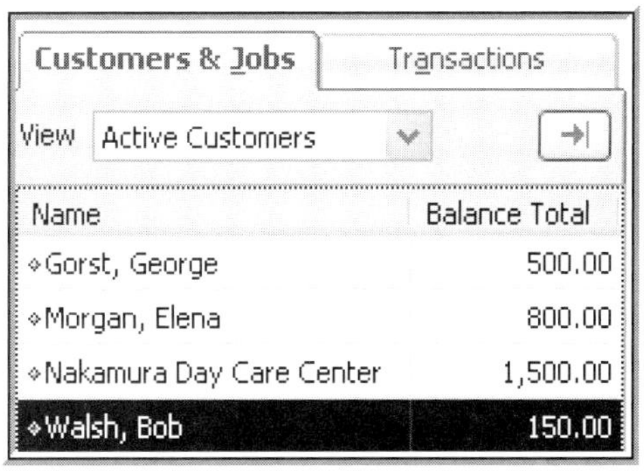

Print the Customer:Job List in Portrait orientation, click **Print** at the top of the screen, click **Customer & Job List**,

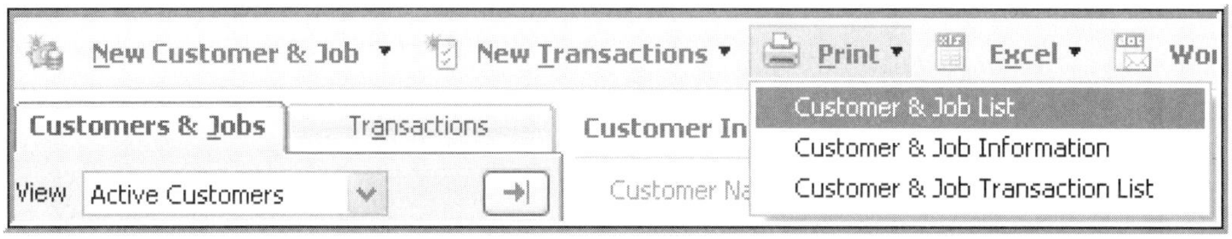

Click **OK** on the List Reports screen

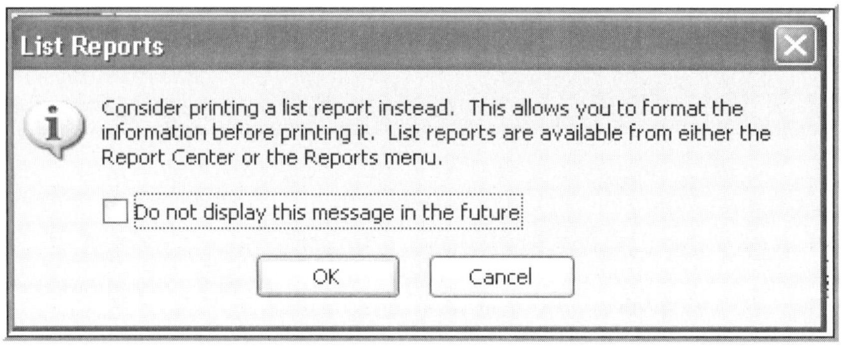

Check the print to information, select **Portrait** orientation and make sure you are not using **Fit report to 1 page wide**
Click **Print**

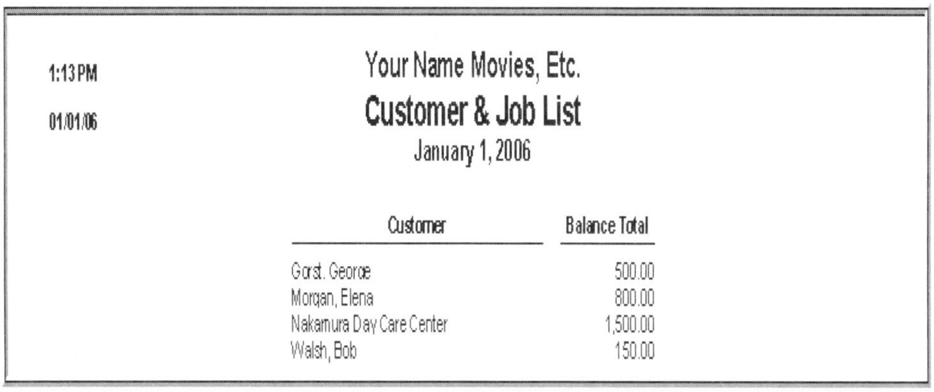

1:13 PM
01/01/06

Your Name Movies, Etc.
Customer & Job List
January 1, 2006

Customer	Balance Total
Gorst, George	500.00
Morgan, Elena	800.00
Nakamura Day Care Center	1,500.00
Walsh, Bob	150.00

- Notice the Time and Date Prepared are shown at the top of the report. Your time and date will reflect the current date and time of your computer and may not match the illustration. The customers and balances should match the illustration.

Close the report and close the Customer Center

VENDOR LIST

QuickBooks Pro keeps detailed information regarding vendors. This includes the vendor's name, opening balance, address, contact person, telephone and fax numbers, credit terms, and credit limits. The Vendor List is also known as the Accounts Payable Subsidiary Ledger. Whenever a transaction is entered for a vendor, it is automatically posted to the General Ledger account and the Accounts Payable Ledger account. Some vendors are those from whom you purchase merchandise, while others are vendors you use to pay tax and withholding payments

January 1, 2006			
Vendor Name	DVD Supplies	Disks Galore	Movie Sales
Opening Balance	3,000	2,000	0.00
As Of	01/01/06	01/01/06	01/01/06
Address	10855 Western Avenue	7758 Broadway Avenue	1970 College Boulevard
City, State, Zip	Los Angeles, CA 90012	San Diego, CA 92101	Hollywood, CA 90028
Contact Person	Dennis Gonzalez	Doris Collins	Chrystal Levy
Phone	310-555-6971	760-555-2951	310-555-6464
Fax	310-555-1796	760-555-1592	310-555-4646
Terms	2% 10, Net 30	2% 10, Net 30	Net 30
Credit Limit	1,500	10,000	5,000

Add the vendors that sell us merchandise and their information to create part of the Vendor List

Click the icon for **Vendor Center**
- Notice that the State Board of Equalization already appears as a vendor.

Click **New Vendor**
Enter **DVD Supplies** for the Vendor Name
Enter the Opening Balance of **3,000** as of **01/01/06**
- This is the only time you are able to enter the opening balance for a vendor.

Enter **DVD Supplies** as the Company Name
Click after DVD Supplies in the Address, press Enter
Enter **10855 Western Avenue**, press Enter
Enter **Los Angeles, CA 90012**
Tab to Contact, enter **Dennis Gonzalez**
Tab to or click Phone, enter **310-555-6974**
Tab to or click Fax, enter **310-555-4796**

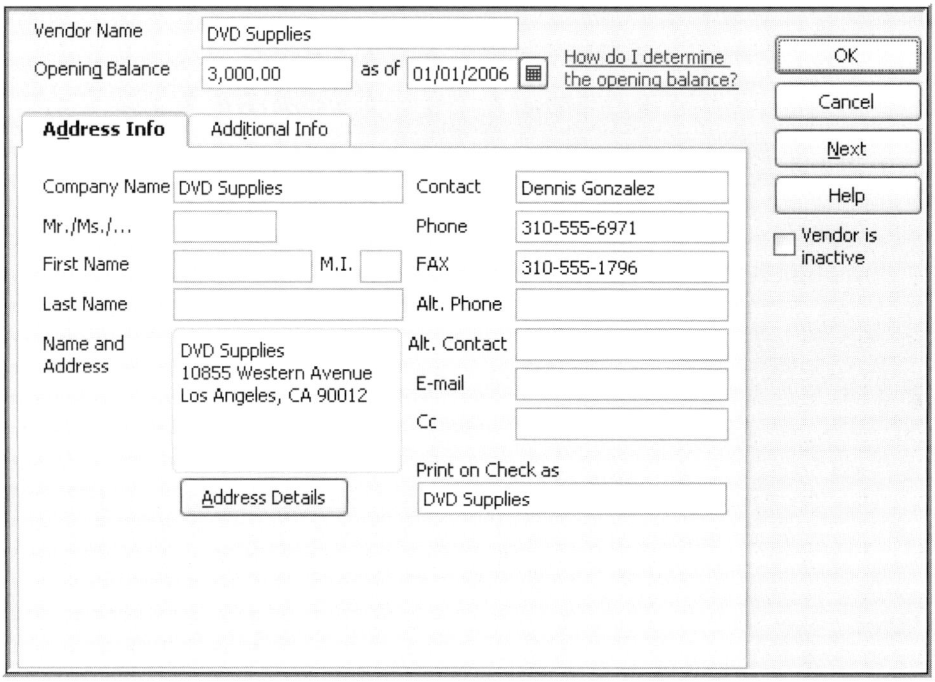

Click the **Additional Info** tab
Click the drop-down list arrow for Terms, click **2% 10 Net 30**
Enter the Credit Limit **1,500**

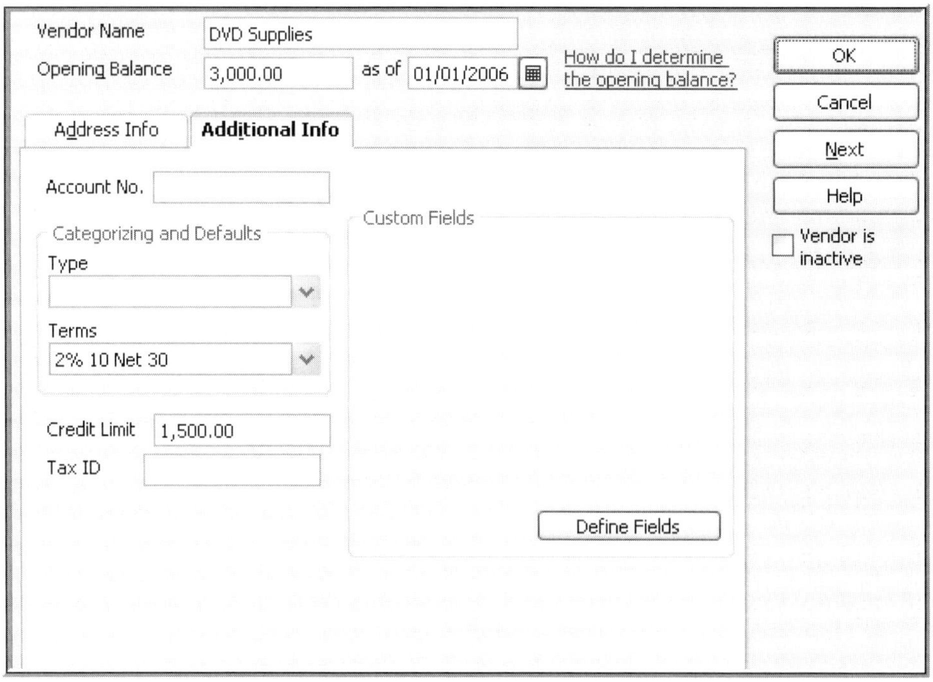

Click **Next** and repeat for each vendor
When complete, refer to the next table for information regarding vendors used for tax and withholding payments

JANUARY 1, 2006			
Vendor Name	Employment Development Department	Beach Cities Bank	Health Ins., Inc.
Address	11033 Wilshire Boulevard	350 Second Street	2085 Wilshire Boulevard
City, State, Zip	Los Angeles, CA 90007	San Diego, CA 92114	Los Angeles, CA 90007
Phone	310-555-8877	760-555-9889	310-555-7412
Fax	310-555-7788	760-555-9988	310-555-2147

Add the vendors that we use for tax and withholding payments to the Vendor List

Follow the steps previously provided to enter the vendors
Click **OK** after adding the last vendor

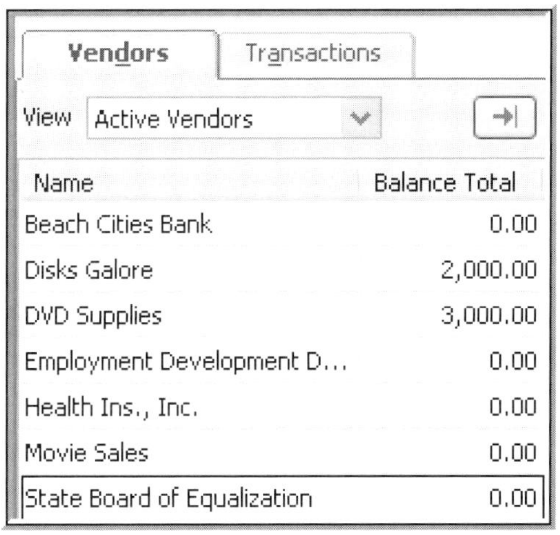

Print the Vendor List in Portrait orientation, click **Print** at the top of the screen, click **Vendor List**

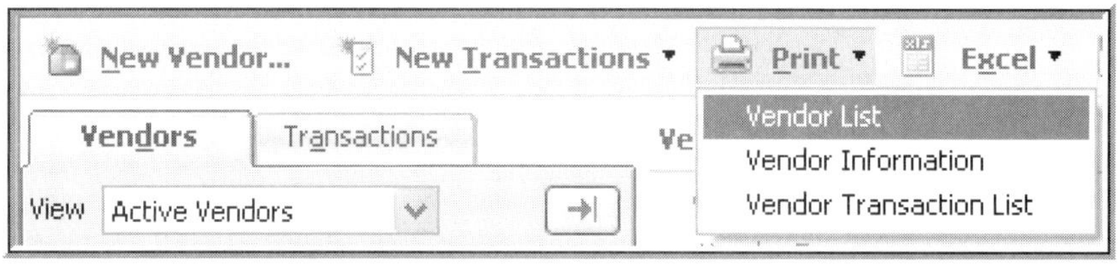

Click **OK** on the List Reports screen

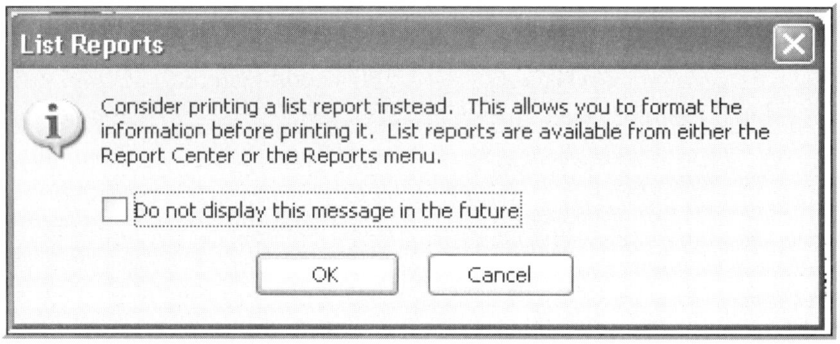

Check the print to information, select **Portrait** orientation and make sure you are not using **Fit report to 1 page wide**

Click **Print**

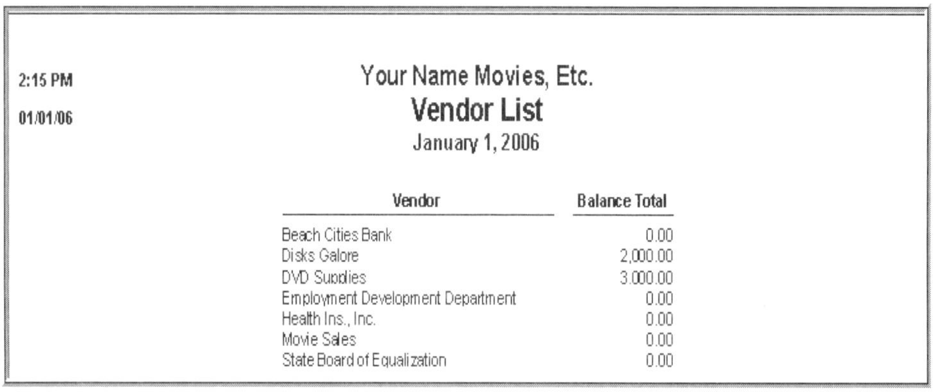

2:15 PM
01/01/06

Your Name Movies, Etc.
Vendor List
January 1, 2006

Vendor	Balance Total
Beach Cities Bank	0.00
Disks Galore	2,000.00
DVD Supplies	3,000.00
Employment Development Department	0.00
Health Ins., Inc.	0.00
Movie Sales	0.00
State Board of Equalization	0.00

- Notice the Time and Date Prepared are shown at the top of the report. Your time and date will reflect the current date and time of your computer and may not match the illustration. The customers and balances should match the illustration.

Close the report and close the Vendor Center

CHART OF ACCOUNTS

Using the EasyStep Interview to set up a company is a user-friendly way to establish the basic structure of the company. However, the Chart of Accounts created by QuickBooks Pro may not be the exact Chart of Accounts you wish to use in your business. In order to customize your chart of accounts, additional accounts need to be created, balances need to be entered for balance sheet accounts, some account names need to be changed, and some accounts need to be deleted or made inactive

The Chart of Accounts is not only a listing of the account names and balances but also the General Ledger used by the business. As in textbook accounting, the General Ledger/Chart of Accounts is the book of final entry.

MEMO
DATE: January 1, 2006

Set up the following Balance Sheet accounts and balances:

Long-term liability: Store Equipment Loan, Opening Balance $2,000,
Long-term liability: Store Fixtures Loan, Opening Balance $2,500,
Other Current Asset: Prepaid Insurance, Opening Balance $1,200
Other Current Asset: Office Supplies, Opening Balance $350
Other Current Asset: Sales Supplies, Opening Balance $500
Fixed Asset: Store Equipment
Fixed Asset: Store Equipment Original Cost, Subaccount of Store Equipment, Opening Balance $8,000 as of 01/01/06,
Fixed Asset: Store Equipment Depreciation, Subaccount of Store Equipment, Opening Balance -$800 as of 01/01/06
Fixed Asset: Store Fixtures
Fixed Asset: Store Fixtures Original Cost, Subaccount of Store Fixtures, Opening Balance $15,000 as of 01/01/06,
Fixed Asset: Store Fixtures Depreciation, Subaccount of Store Fixtures, Opening Balance -$1,500 as of 01/01/06
Expense: Store Supplies

Add the accounts and balances listed above

Click **Chart of Accounts** in the Company section of the Home Page
Click the **Account** button at the bottom of the Chart of Accounts
Click **New**
Click the drop-down list arrow for **Type**, click **Long-term liability**

Tab to or click in the textbox for **Name**
Enter **Store Equipment Loan** as the Name
Tab to or click **Opening Balance**, enter **2,000** as of **01/01/2006**,

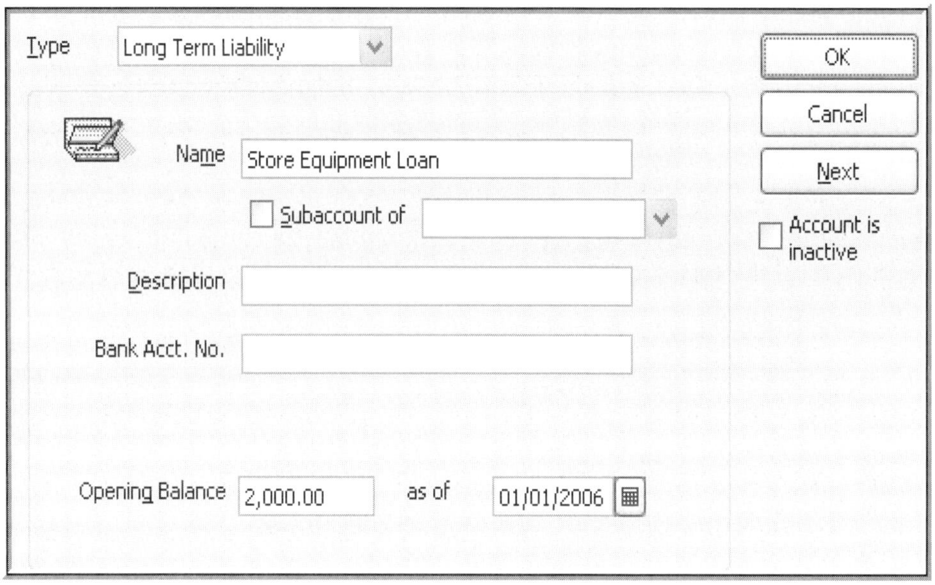

Click **Next** and add the Store Fixtures Loan account

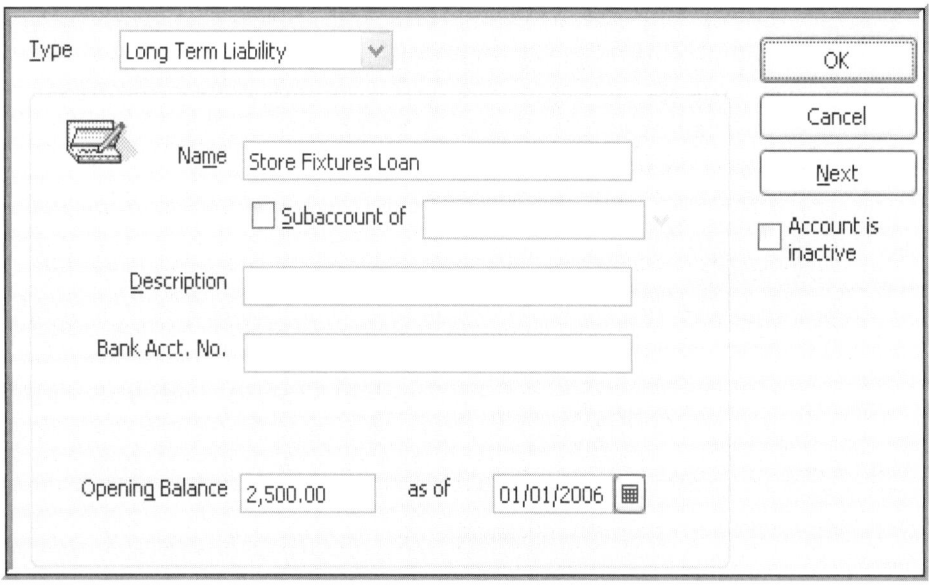

Click **Next** add the Other Current Asset **Prepaid Insurance**
Click the drop-down list arrow for Type
Click **Other Current Asset**
Enter **Prepaid Insurance** as the Name

Enter the Opening Balance **1,200** as of **01/01/06**

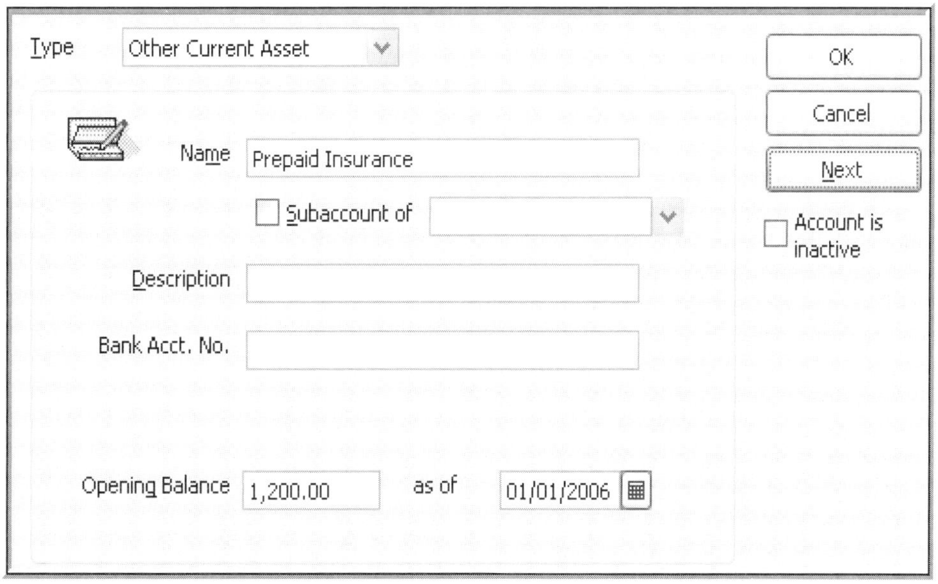

Add the Other Current Asset accounts, Office Supplies and Sales Supplies, listed in the Memo

Add the Fixed Asset accounts listed in the Memo

Click the drop-down list arrow for **Type**, click **Fixed Asset**

Enter **Store Equipment** as the Name

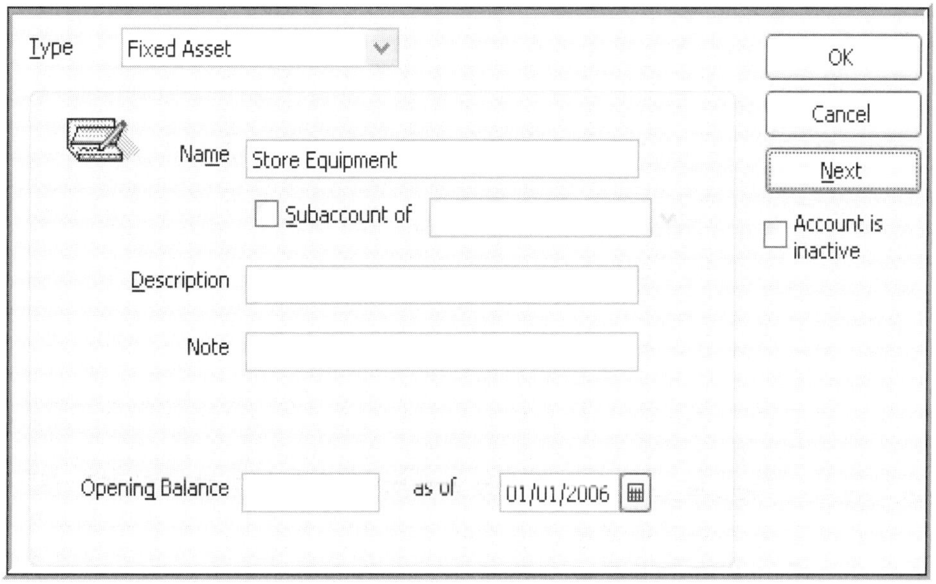

Click **Next**

The type of account is still Fixed Asset, enter **Store Equipment Original Cost** as the Name

Click **Subaccount of** to enter a check mark

Click the drop-down list arrow for Subaccount

Click **Store Equipment**

Enter the Opening Balance **8,000** as of **01/01/06**

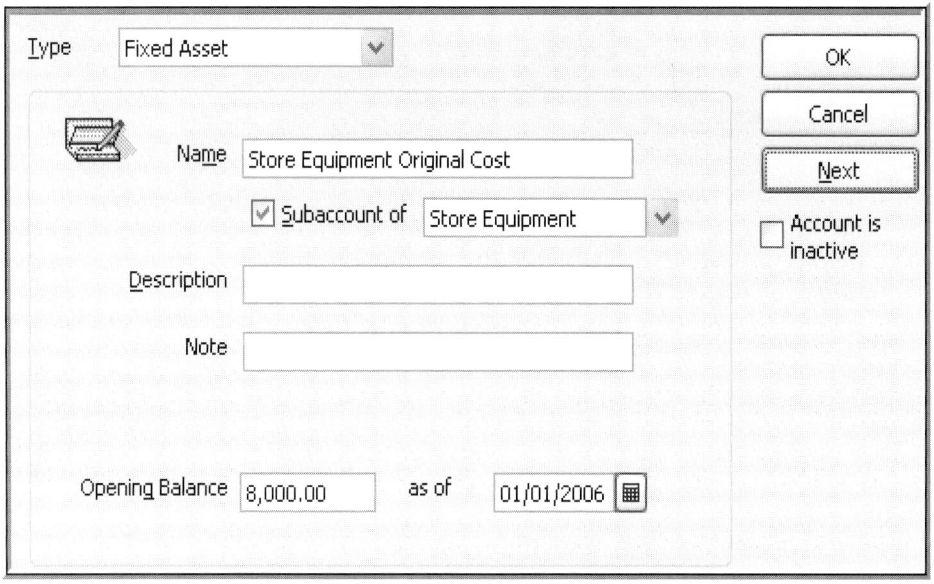

Repeat the procedure and add **Store Equipment Depreciation** as a Subaccount of Store Equipment with an Opening Balance of **-800** as of **01/01/06**

- Be sure to use a minus (-) sign in front of the 800. Remember, depreciation reduces the value of the asset.

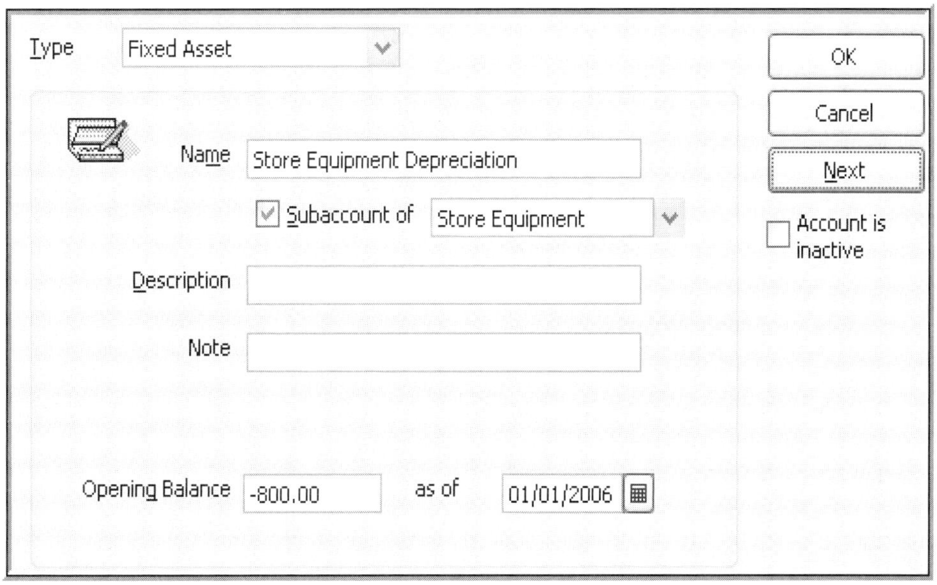

Add the other fixed asset, **Store Fixtures**

- Also be sure to add the accounts for **Original Cost** and **Depreciation**

Add the Expense account **Store Supplies**

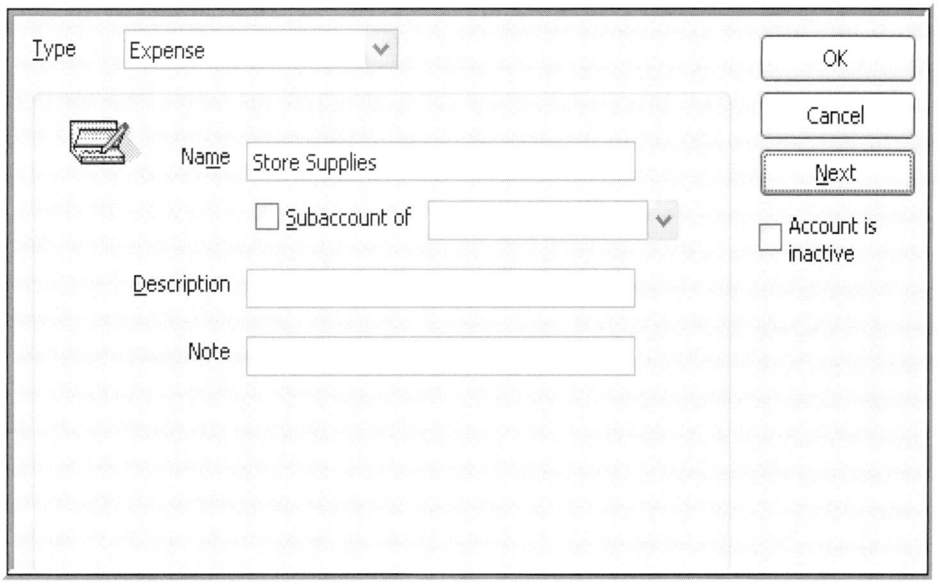

- As you can see, an expense account does not have an opening balance. Only balance sheet accounts—assets, liabilities, and owner's equity accounts—have opening balances.

When finished, click **OK**

View the Chart of Accounts

Account	Type	Balance
◆Checking	Bank	29,385.00
◆Accounts Receivable	Accounts Receivable	2,950.00
◆Inventory Asset	Other Current Asset	33,750.00
◆Inventory on Consignment	Other Current Asset	0.00
◆Office Supplies	Other Current Asset	350.00
◆Prepaid Insurance	Other Current Asset	1,200.00
◆Sales Supplies	Other Current Asset	500.00
◆Undeposited Funds	Other Current Asset	0.00
◆Store Equipment	Fixed Asset	7,200.00
◆Store Equipment Depreciation	Fixed Asset	-800.00
◆Store Equipment Original Cost	Fixed Asset	8,000.00
◆Store Fixtures	Fixed Asset	13,500.00
◆Store Fixtures Depreciation	Fixed Asset	-1,500.00
◆Store Fixtures Original Cost	Fixed Asset	15,000.00
◆Accounts Payable	Accounts Payable	5,000.00
◆Payroll Liabilities	Other Current Liability	0.00
◆Sales Tax Payable	Other Current Liability	0.00
◆Store Equipment Loan	Long Term Liability	2,000.00
◆Store Fixtures Loan	Long Term Liability	2,500.00
◆Opening Bal Equity	Equity	81,385.00
◆Retained Earnings	Equity	

- Note the value of Store Equipment and Store Fixtures.

Do not close the Chart of Accounts

MEMO

DATE: January 1, 2006

Since Your Name Movies, Etc. the Chart of Accounts/General Ledger should be customized. Make the following changes to the accounts:

Delete: Inventory on Consignment, Sales: Consignment Sales, Sales: Shipping and Handling, Automobile Expense, Franchise Fees, Travel & Ent. including subaccounts (Remember to delete the subaccounts of Travel & Ent. before deleting the account.).
Change name: Equity Account: Opening Bal Equity to **Your Name, Capital**;
Make inactive: Merchant Fees
Add Equity Accounts: **Your Name, Investment**; Subaccount of Your Name, Capital; Opening Balance $25,000 as of 01/01/06
Your Name, Withdrawals; Subaccount of Your Name, Capital; Opening Balance, $0.00 as of 01/01/06

Make the changes indicated above

Click the account **Inventory on Consignment** to highlight, use the keyboard **Ctrl+D** to delete the account, click **OK** to delete

Repeat to delete the other accounts listed in the memo

Position the cursor on **Opening Bal Equity**, click the **Account** button, click **Edit**, enter **Your Name, Capital** as the account name, click **OK**

Repeat basic procedures to rename the other accounts listed in the memo

Position the cursor on **Merchant Fees**, click the **Account** button, click **Make Inactive**

Click **Account** button, click **New**, click drop-down list arrow next to **Type**, click **Equity**, tab to or click **Name**, enter **Your Name, Investment**, click **Subaccount**, click **Your Name, Capital**, tab to or click **Balance**, enter **25,000** (if necessary, enter **01/01/06** as the date), click **Next**

Add the withdrawal account

When all changes have been made, print the **Chart of Accounts** in Portrait orientation

Click the **Report** button at the bottom of the Chart of Accounts, click **Account Listing**

Click the **Modify Report** button, click the **Header/Footer** button, click **Date Prepared** and **Time Prepared** to remove from the heading, click **OK**

Click the **Print** button, select **Portrait** orientation, click **Fit report to 1 page wide**

When finished printing, close the Account Listing report and the Chart of Accounts

PREFERENCES

Many preferences for the use of QuickBooks Pro are selected during the EasyStep Interview. However, there may be some preferences you would like to select in addition to those marked during the interview. The Preferences section has tabs where you may indicate your preferences or company preferences. Some areas that may be customized include: Accounting, Checking, Desktop View, Finance Charge, General, Integrated Applications, Jobs & Estimates, Payroll & Employees, Purchases & Vendors, Reminders, Reports & Graphs, Sales & Customers, Sales Tax, Send Forms, Service Connection, Spelling, Tax: 1099, and Time Tracking. Not all the possible changes will be discussed in this chapter; however, some changes will be made.

MEMO

DATE: January 1, 2006

Open the Preferences screen and explore the choices available for each of the areas. When you get to the following preferences, make the changes indicated below:

Checking Preferences: My Preferences—Select Default Accounts to use should be Checking for Open Write Checks, Open Pay Bills, Open Pay Sales Tax, and Open Make Deposits; Company Preferences— Select Default Accounts to use should be Checking for Create Paychecks and Pay Payroll Liabilities

Payroll & Employees: Company Preferences—Display Employee List by Last Name

Reports & Graphs: My Preferences—Refresh reports automatically, Company Preferences—modify the report Format for the Header/Footer to remove the Date Prepared, Time Prepared, and Report Basis from reports

Sales Tax: Company Preferences—Most common sales tax is CA State Tax

In the following sections the Preferences are shown in the exact order listed on the Preferences screen. Click the icons for each category and explore the choices available on both the My Preferences tabs and the Company tabs. When you get to a Preference that needs to be changed, make the changes indicated in the textbox above.

Access Preferences from the Edit menu

ACCOUNTING PREFERENCES

The Company Preferences screen is accessed to select the use of account numbers. Selecting Use Account Numbers provides an area for each account to be given a number during editing. Use audit trail is an important choice if you want QuickBooks Pro to track all transactions (including any and all changes made to transactions). This allows an owner to see everything that has been entered, including deleted transactions, error corrections, etc. This is an important choice if there is a possibility of an employee making unauthorized changes. This screen instructs QuickBooks to automatically assign general journal entry numbers and to warn when posting a transaction to Retained Earning. The closing date for a period is entered on the Company Preferences tab for Accounting Preferences.

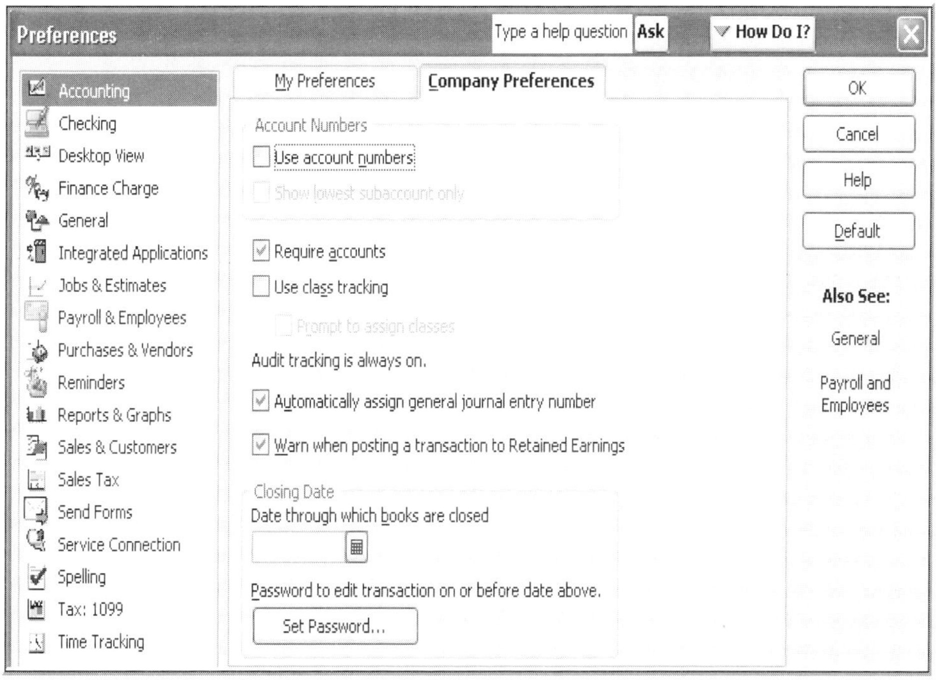

CHECKING PREFERENCES

The preferences listed for checking allows QuickBooks Pro to print account names on check vouchers, warn of duplicate check numbers, change the check date when a check is printed, start with the payee field on a check, and set default accounts to use for checks.

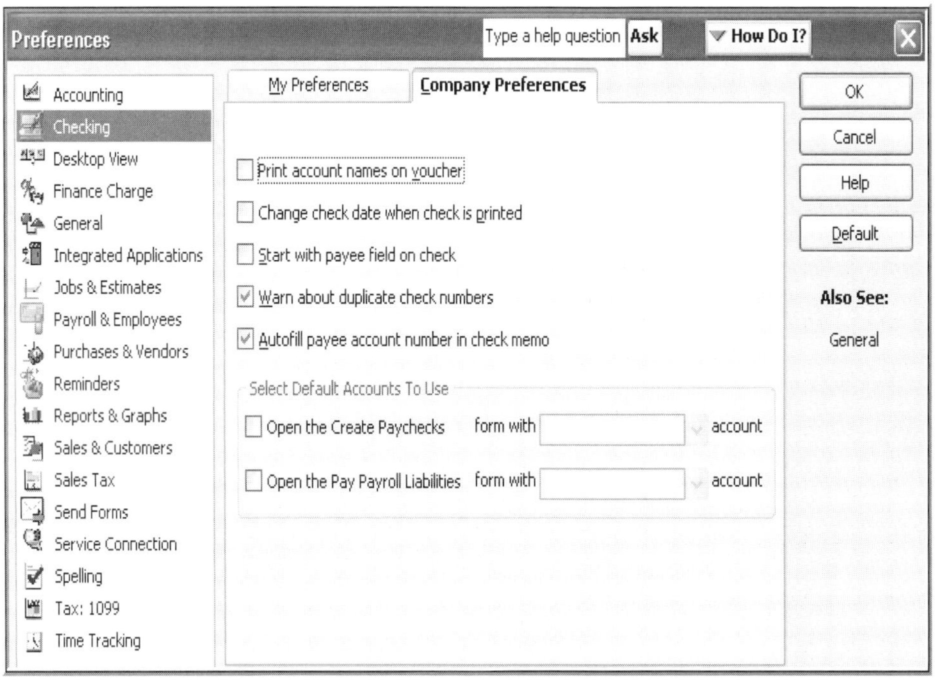

Select Default Accounts to use Checking

Click **My Preferences Tab**
Click the Check box for Open the Write Checks to select
Click the drop-down list arrow for Account
Click **Checking**
Repeat for Open the Pay Bills, Open the Pay Sales Tax, and Open the Make Deposits

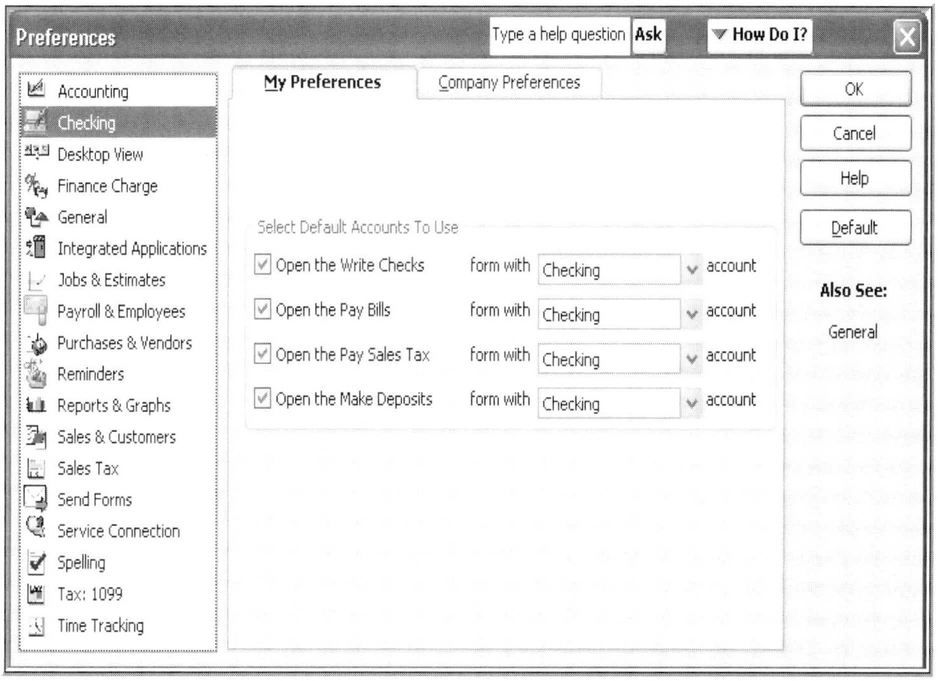

Click the **Company Preferences** tab

Click the check box for **Open the Create Paychecks**, **Checking** on the drop-down list for account

Repeat for **Pay Payroll Liabilities**

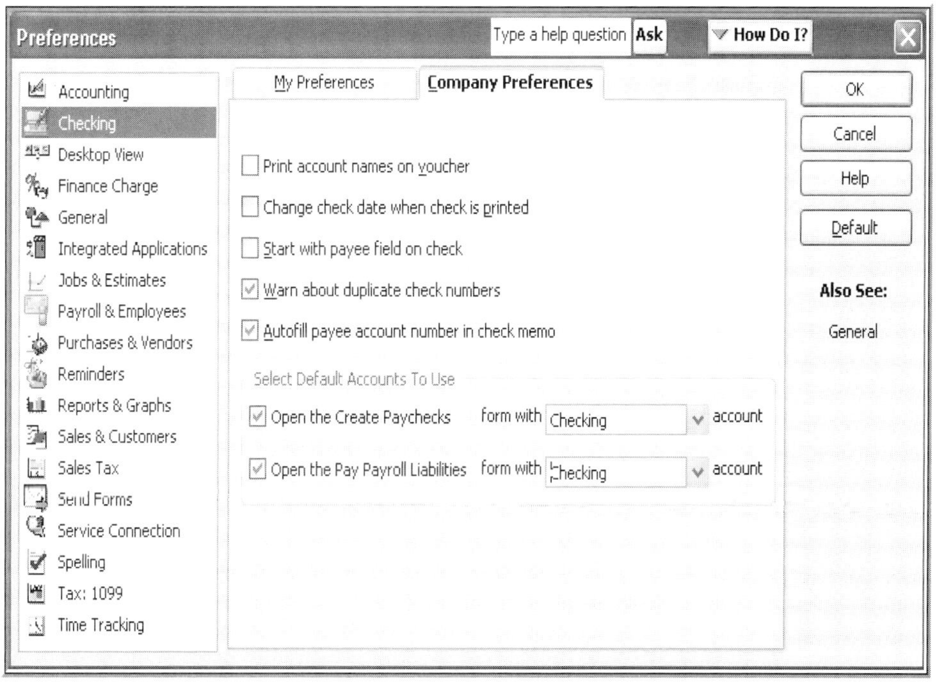

DESKTOP VIEW PREFERENCES

The Desktop View preference allows you to set My Preferences to customize your QuickBooks screens, to display the Home Page, to save the desktop, select color schemes, and sounds. Company Preferences allow you to select features that you want to show on the Home Page and to explore Related Preferences.

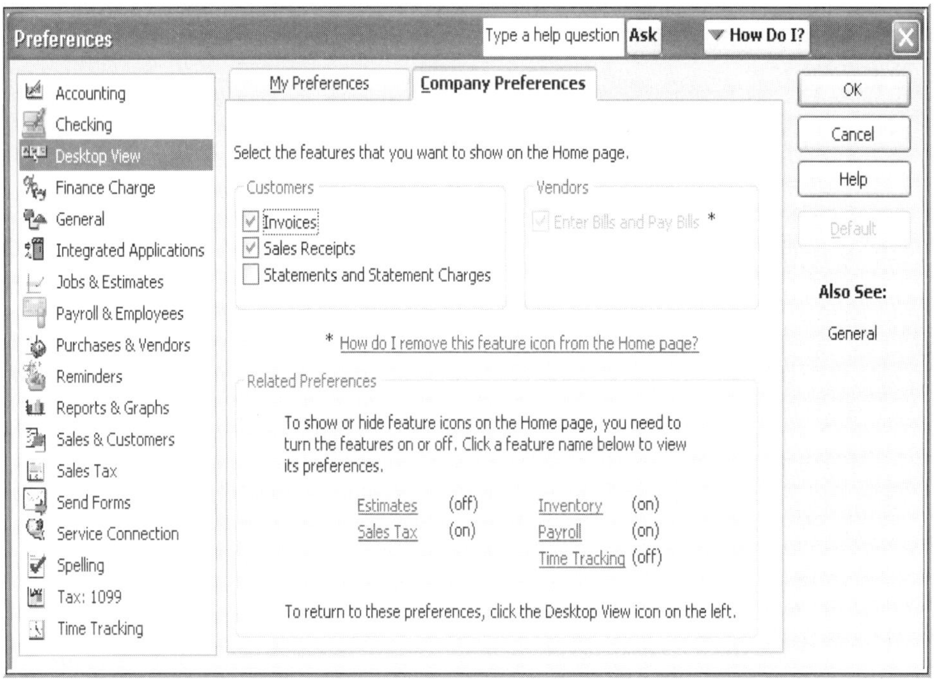

FINANCE CHARGE PREFERENCES

This preference allows you to provide information about finance charges if they are collected. You can even tell QuickBooks Pro if you want to collect finance charges. The information you may provide includes the annual interest rate, the minimum finance charge, the grace period, the finance charge account, and whether to calculate finance charges from the due date or from the invoice/billed date.

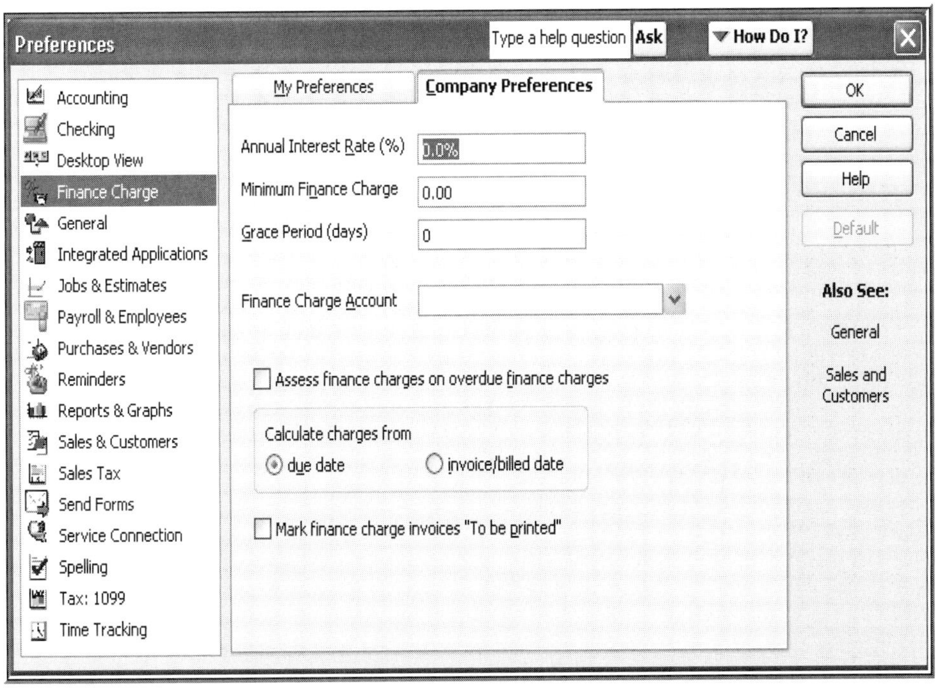

GENERAL PREFERENCES

General preferences uses the Company Preferences tab to set the time format, to display the year as four digits. My Preferences tab is used to indicate decimal point placement, to set warning screens and beeps, to turn on messages, and to automatically recall the last transaction for a name.

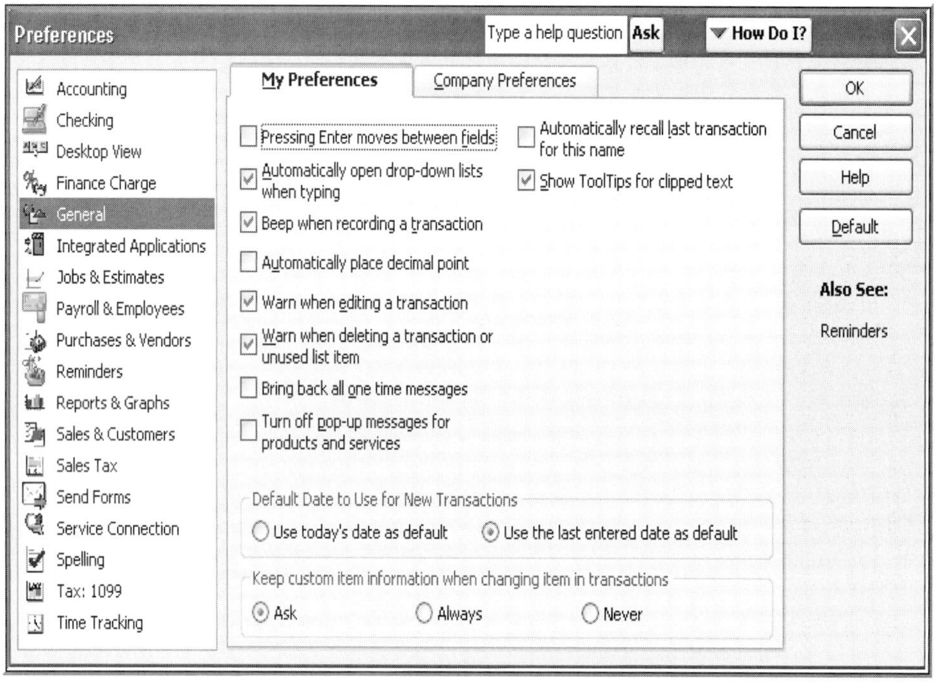

INTEGRATED APPLICATIONS PREFERENCES

Integrated preferences are used to manage all applications that interact with the current QuickBooks company file.

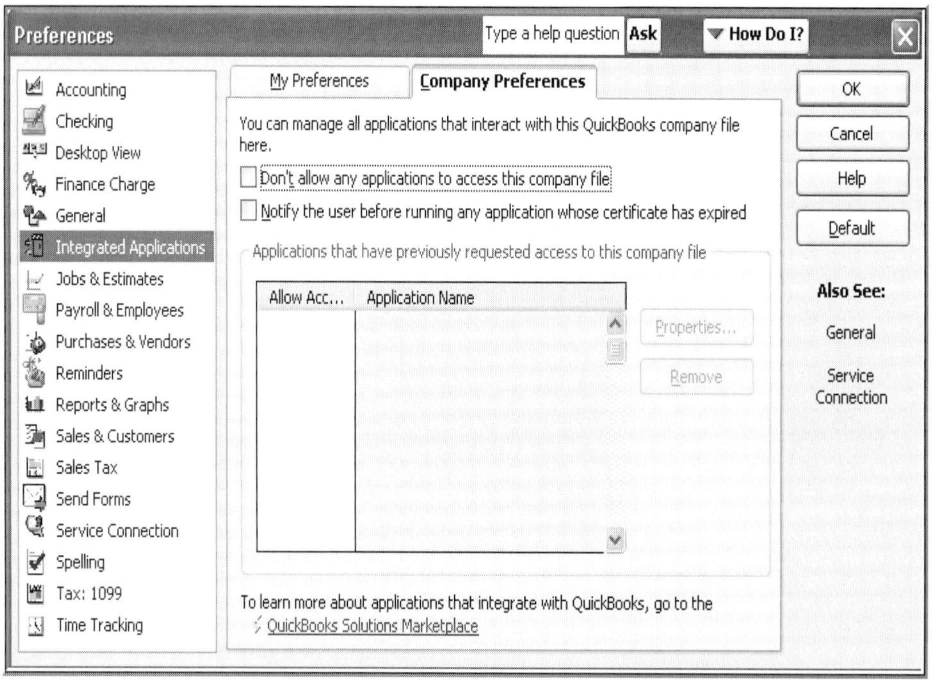

JOBS & ESTIMATES PREFERENCES

This preference allows you to indicate the status of jobs and to choose whether or not to use estimates.

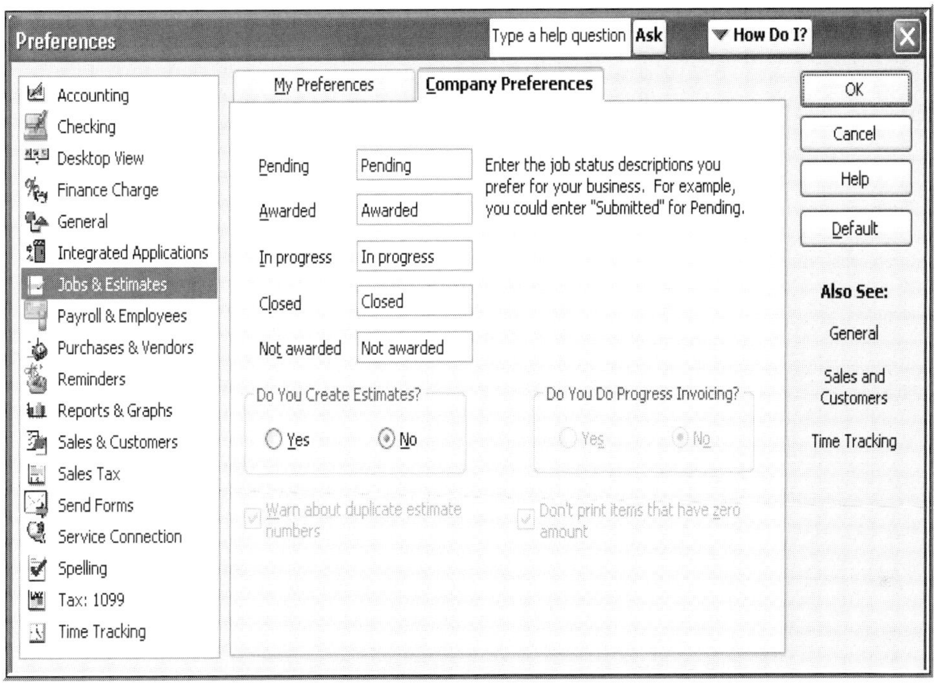

PAYROLL & EMPLOYEES PREFERENCES

Payroll preferences include selecting the payroll features, if any, you wish to use. Items for printing on checks and vouchers are selected. You may choose the method by which employees are sorted. Employee Defaults may be accessed from this screen. Once accessed, the Employee Defaults may be changed and/or modified.

Change the Display Employee List to Last Name

Click **Payroll & Employees** to select
Click the **Company Preferences** tab
Click **Last Name** in the section for Display Employee List by

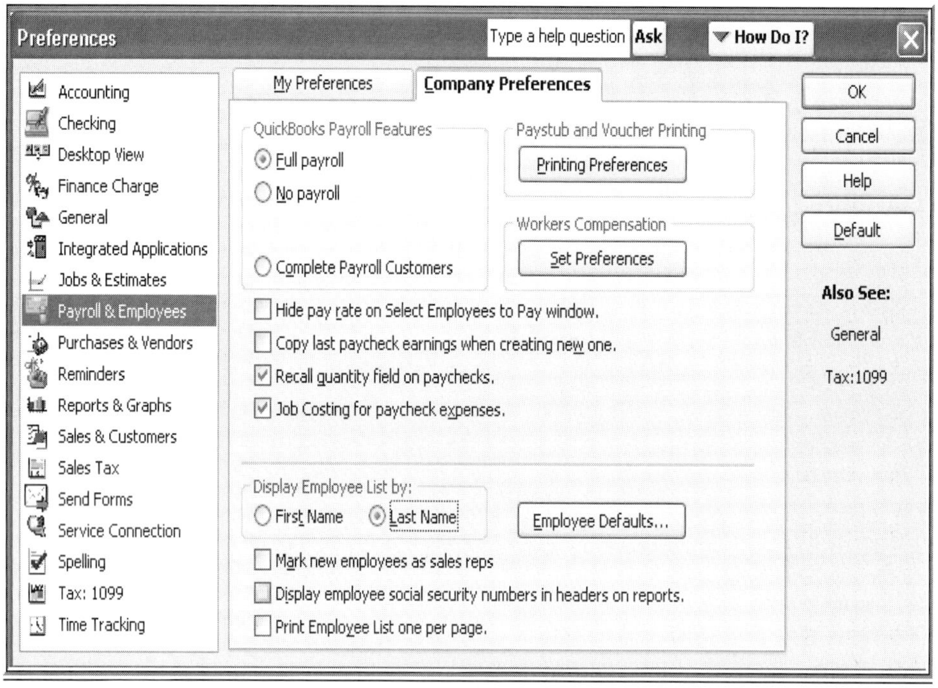

Click **Purchases & Vendors** to go to the next Preference area

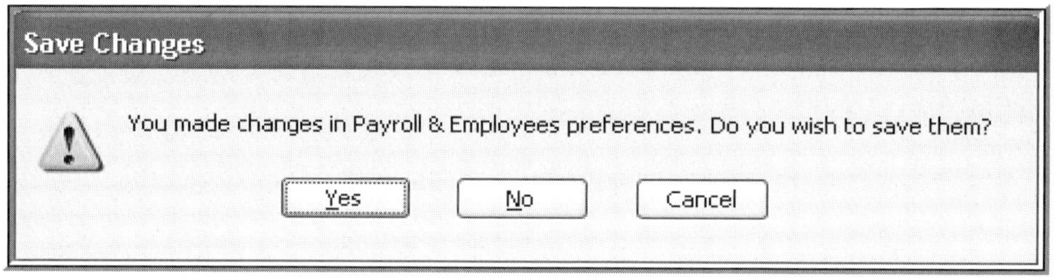

Click **Yes**

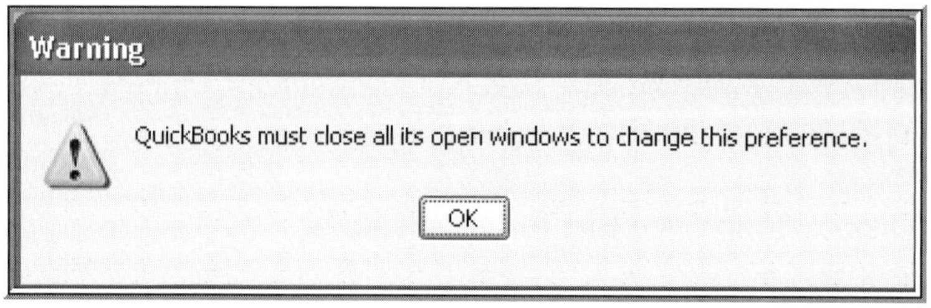

Click **OK** on the Warning screen

- Preferences should reopen automatically. If it does not, click the Edit menu, click Preferences, click Purchases & Vendors.

PURCHASES & VENDORS PREFERENCES

This section allows you to activate the inventory and purchase orders feature of the program. Have QuickBooks provide warnings if there is not enough inventory to sell, if there are duplicate purchase order numbers, and warnings if there are duplicate bills. The number of days for bill due dates is also selected in the Purchases & Vendors preferences. QuickBooks can be instructed to automatically apply discounts and credits.

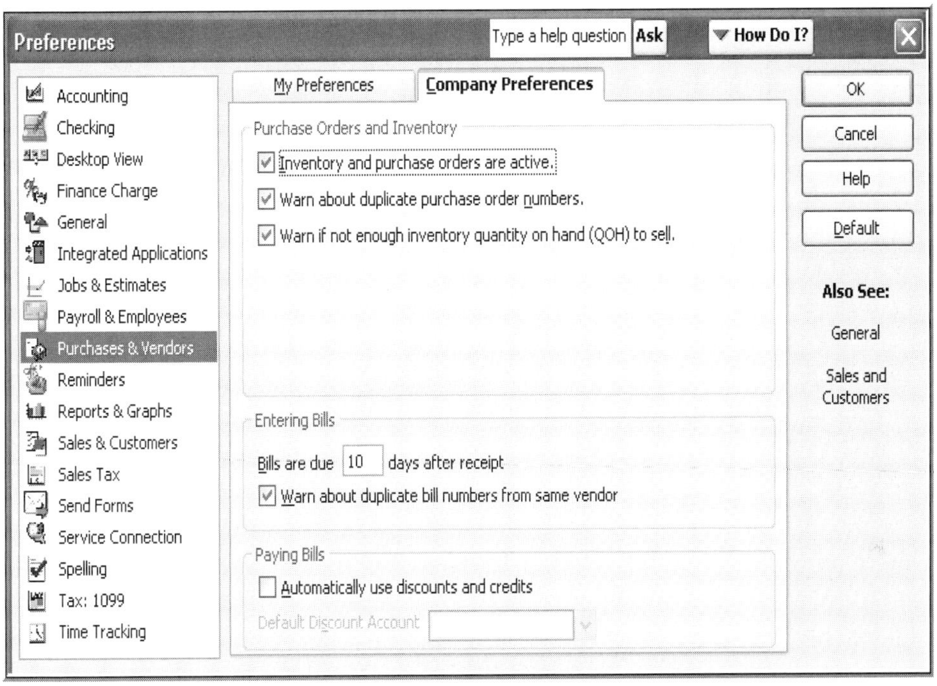

REMINDERS PREFERENCES

In this section you may use My Preferences to select whether or not to have the Reminders List appear when the QuickBooks Pro program is started. If you chose to have Reminders displayed, Company Preferences is used to select the items included on the Reminders List.

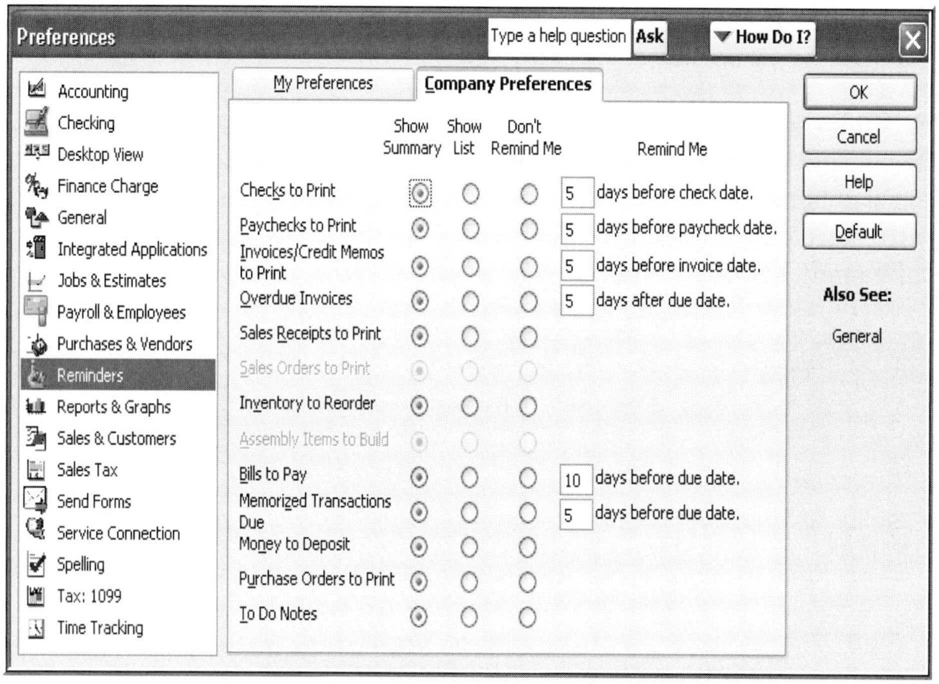

REPORTS & GRAPHS PREFERENCES

My Preferences tab allows you to select whether to show a prompt to refresh reports and graphs or to refresh them automatically and whether to draw graphs in 2D or use patterns. The Company Preferences tab allows the selection of accrual or cash reporting. Preferences for report aging and account display within reports are selected in this section. We can tell QuickBooks assign accounts to the sections of the Statement of Cash Flows. In addition, report formats may be customized on this screen.

Change My Preferences to have the reports refresh automatically

Click **My Preferences** tab
Click **Refresh Automatically**

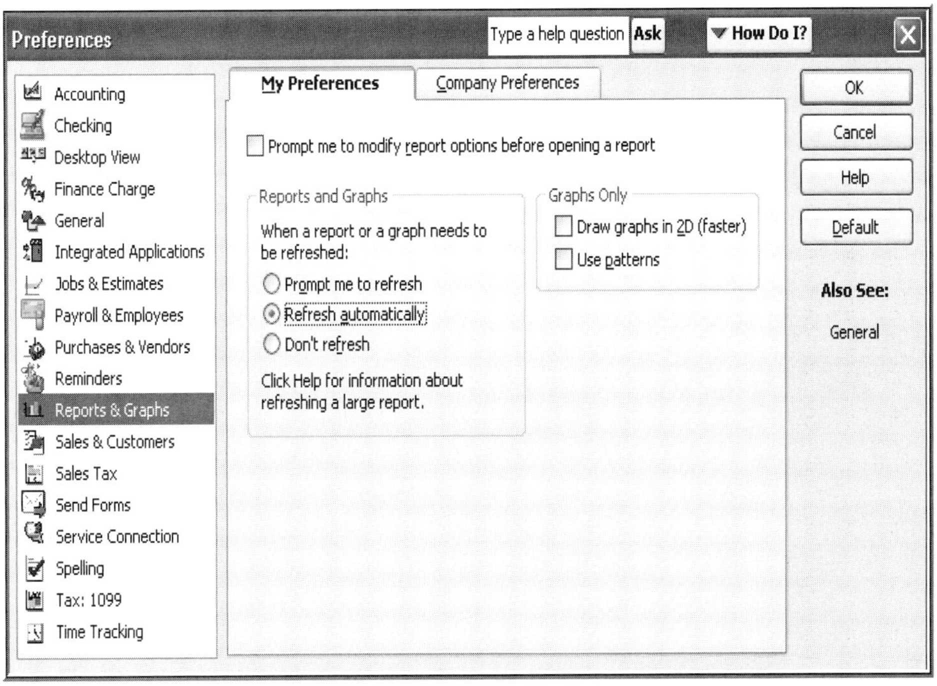

Modify the report format to remove the Date Prepared, Time Prepared, and Report Basis

Click **Company Preferences**
Click the **Format** button
On the Header/Footer tab, click **Date Prepared**, **Time Prepared**, and **Report Basis** to remove the check marks

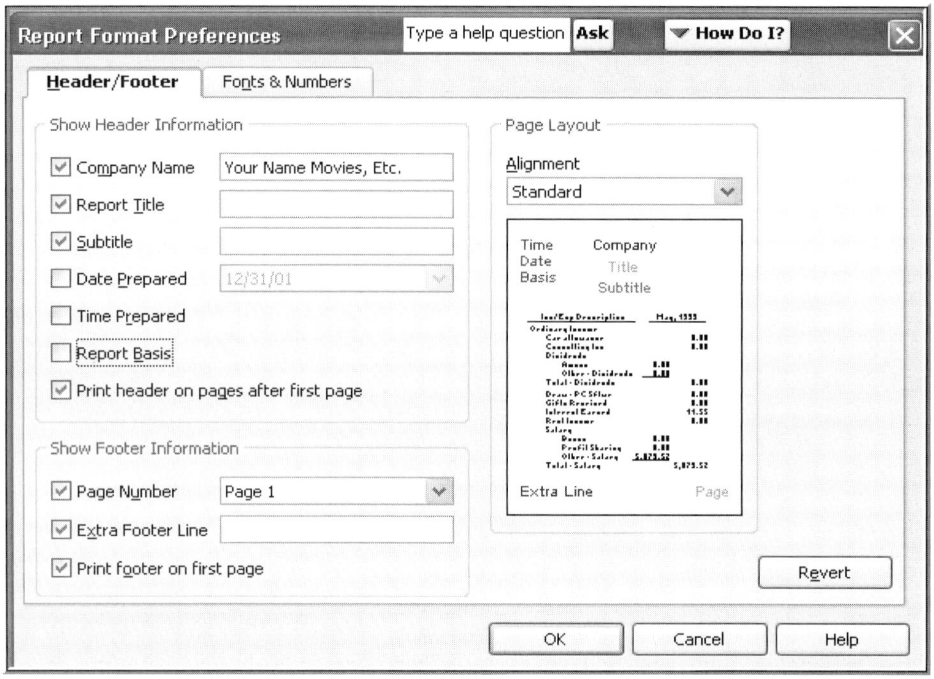

Click **OK**

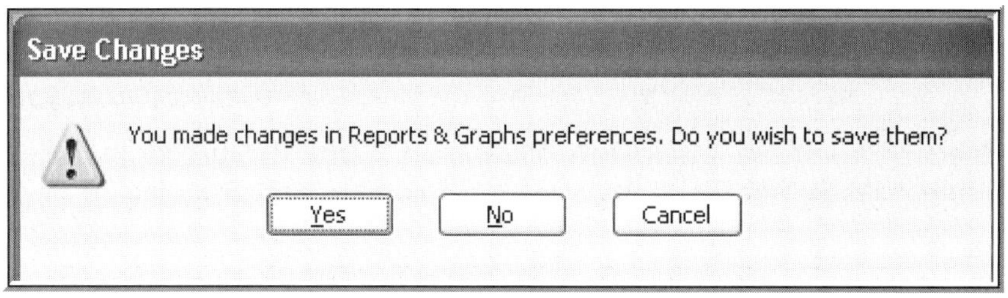

Click **Yes**

SALES & CUSTOMERS PREFERENCES

Shipping methods, markup percentages, and usual FOB (free on board) preferences may be indicated on this screen. In addition, selections to automatically apply and calculate payments, to use Undeposited Funds as the default deposit account, to track reimbursed expenses as income, to warn about duplicate invoice numbers, and whether or not to use price levels are made in this section.

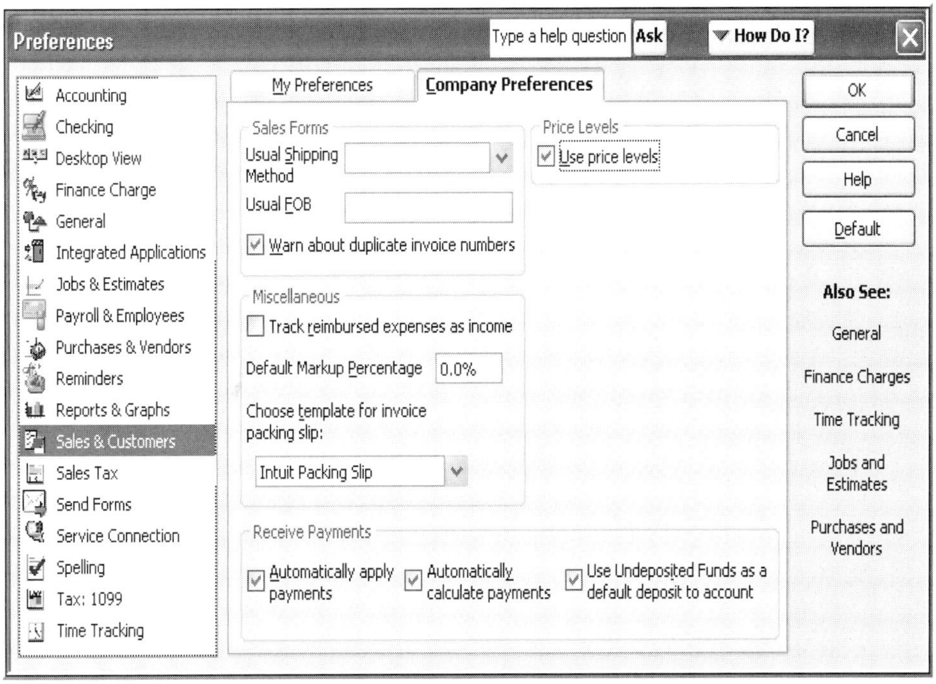

SALES TAX PREFERENCES

The Sales Tax preferences indicate whether or not you charge sales tax. If you do collect sales tax, the default sales tax codes, when you need to pay the sales tax, when sales tax is owed, the most common sales tax, and whether or not to mark taxable amounts are selected on this screen.

Change the default for the Most common sales tax to CA State Tax

Click the drop-down list arrow for **Most common sales tax**
Click **CA State Tax**

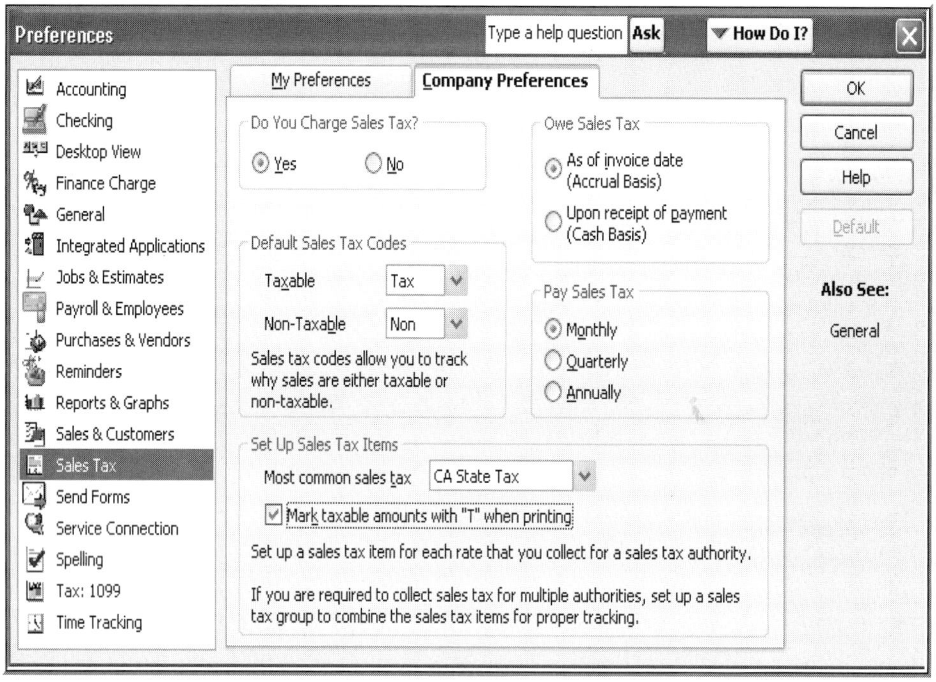

Click **Yes** to save the change

SEND FORMS PREFERENCES

Default text is provided and may be changed for invoices, estimates, statements, sales orders, sales receipts, credit memos, purchase orders and reports for business documents that are sent by e-mail.

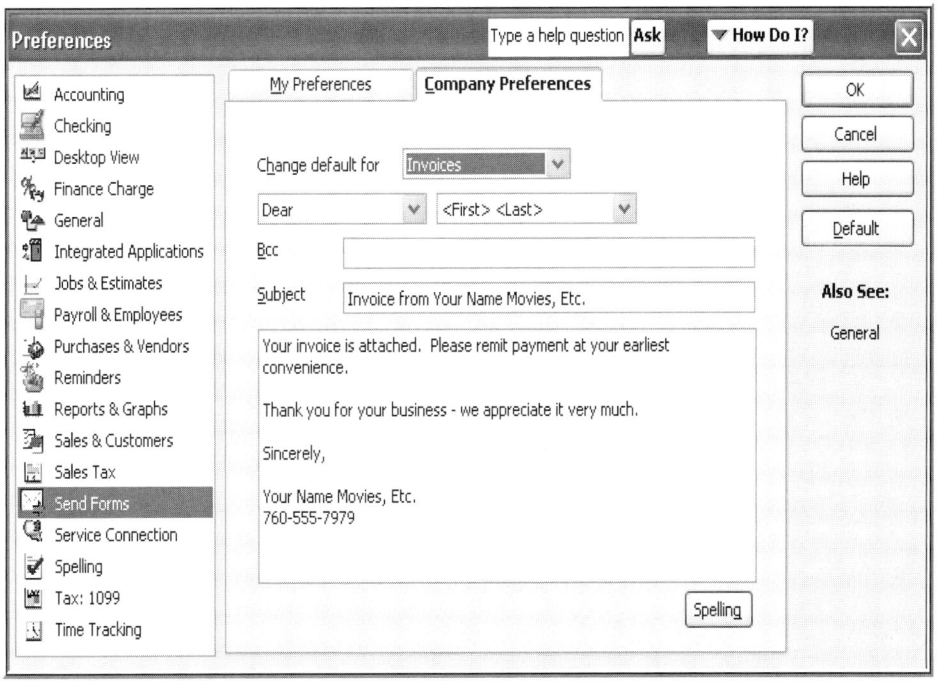

SERVICE CONNECTION PREFERENCES

You can specify how you and other company file users log in to QuickBooks Business Services. You may select to automatically connect to QuickBooks Business Services network without passwords or require passwords before connecting. This preference is used to select whether or not Service updates are automatically downloaded from the Intuit server to your computer.

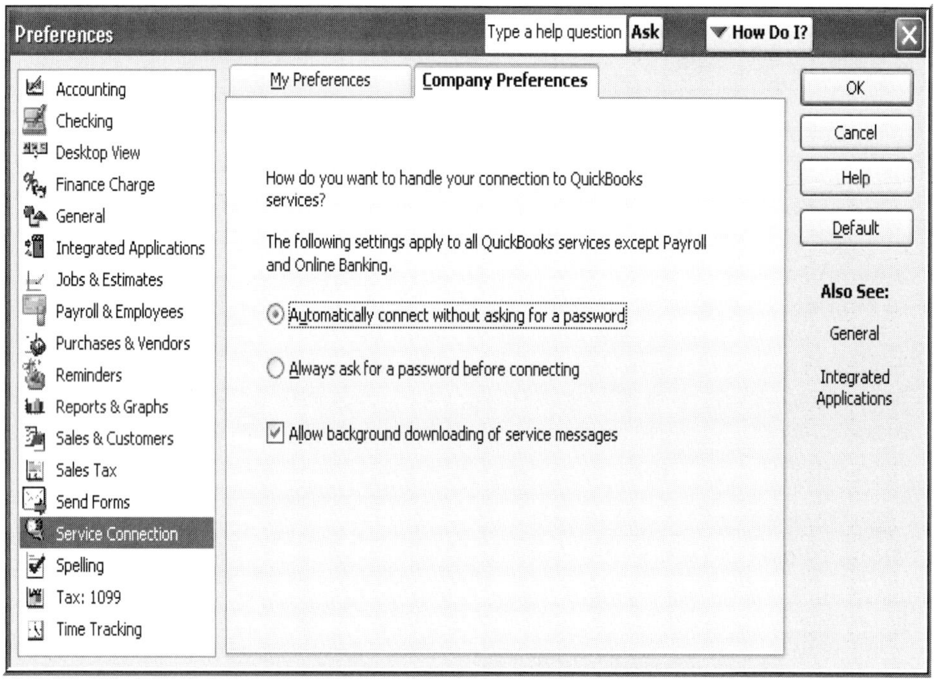

SPELLING PREFERENCES

You can check the spelling in the Description, Memo, Text fields, and Message fields of most sales forms including invoices, estimates, sales receipts, credit memos, purchase orders, and lists. You can run Spell Checker automatically or change the preference and run the Spell Checker manually. There is also a selection for words to ignore.

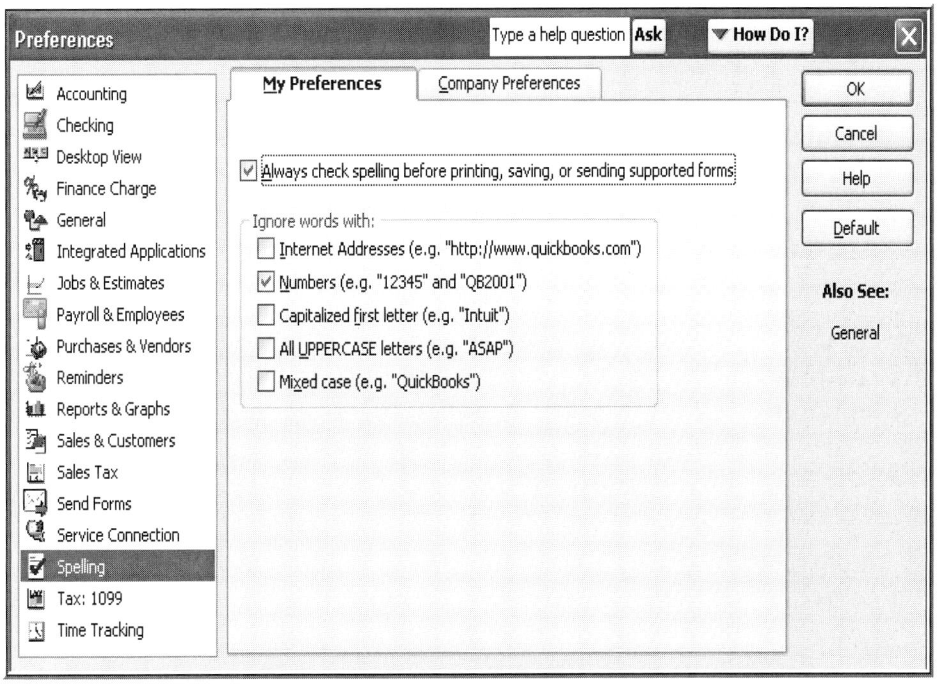

TAX: 1099 PREFERENCES

This preference is used to indicate whether or not you file 1099-MISC forms. If you do file 1099s, you are given categories; you may select accounts and thresholds for the categories on this screen.

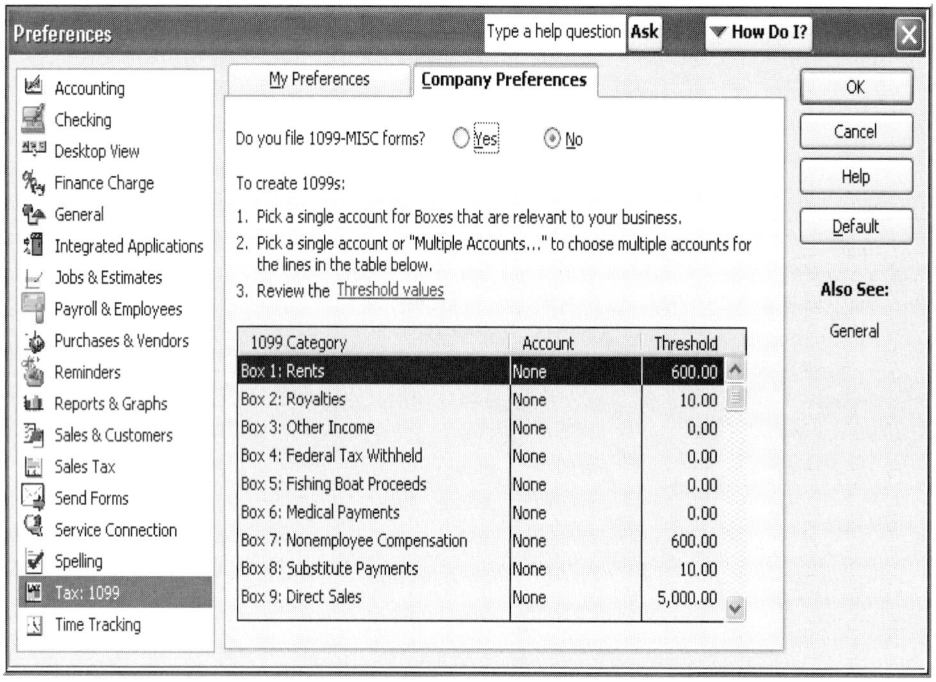

TIME TRACKING PREFERENCES

The Time Tracking preference is used to tell QuickBooks Pro to track time. Tracking time is useful if you bill by the hour.

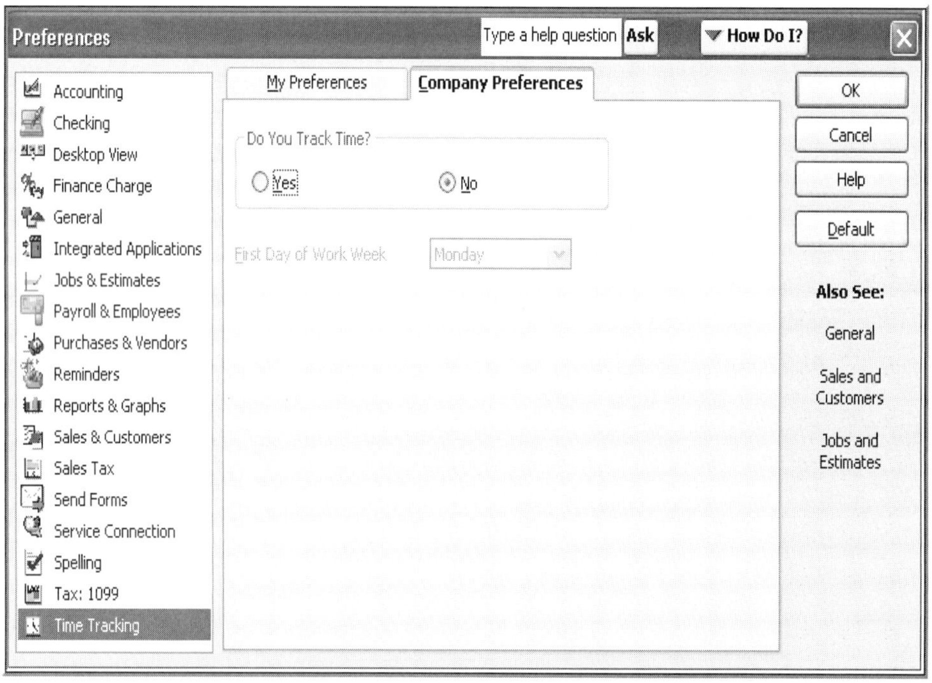

To close the Preferences screen, click **OK**

PAYROLL

When you completed the tutorial in Chapter 8, you paid the employees who worked for the company. In order to use QuickBooks to process payroll, you need to complete the Payroll Set up Interview and add your employees.

SELECT A PAYROLL OPTION

Before entering any payroll transactions, QuickBooks Pro must be informed of the type of payroll service you are selecting. Once QuickBooks Pro knows what type of payroll process has been selected for the company, you will be able to create paychecks. In order to create paychecks manually, you must go through the Help menu to designate this choice.

Select a **Manual** payroll option

Press **F1** to access Help
Click the **Index** tab
Type **payroll**
Scroll through the list of payroll items
Click **without a payroll service subscription**
Click the **Display** button

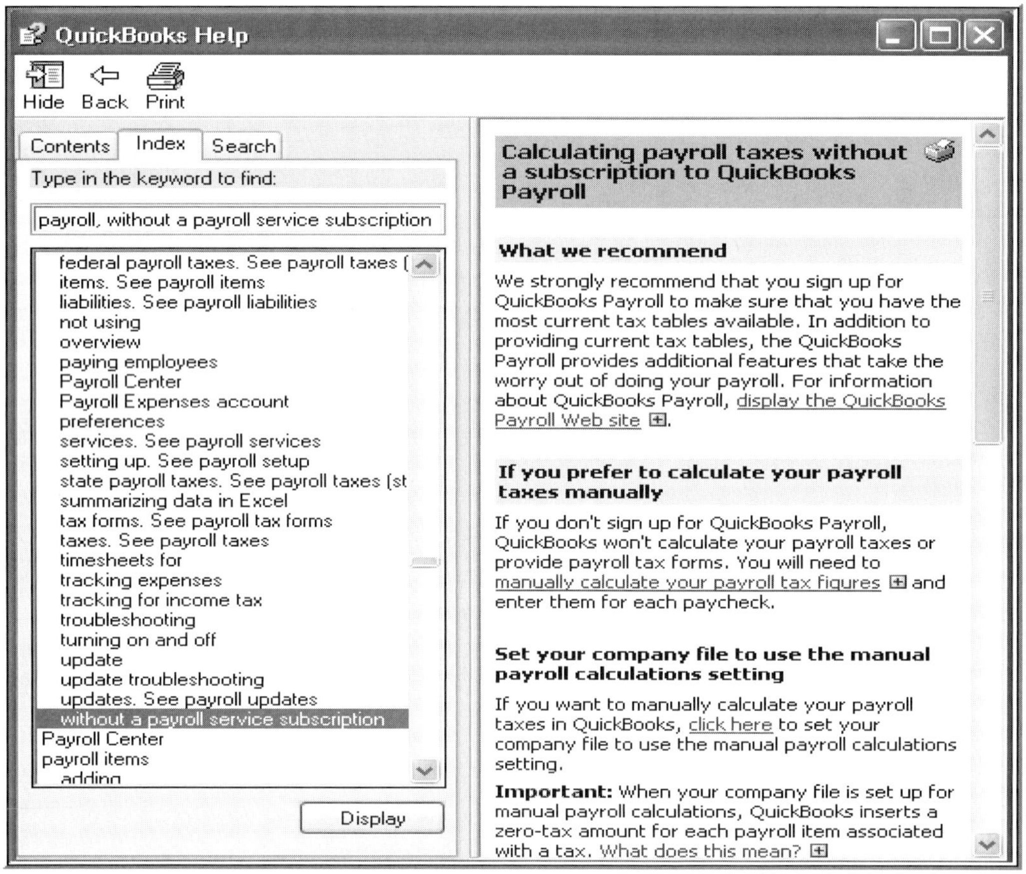

In the *"Set your company file to use the manual payroll calculations setting"* section, click the words **manual payroll calculations**

In the section *"If you are sure you want to manually calculate your payroll taxes in QuickBooks"*, click **Set my company file to use manual calculations**

Once QuickBooks processes the selection, you will get a message

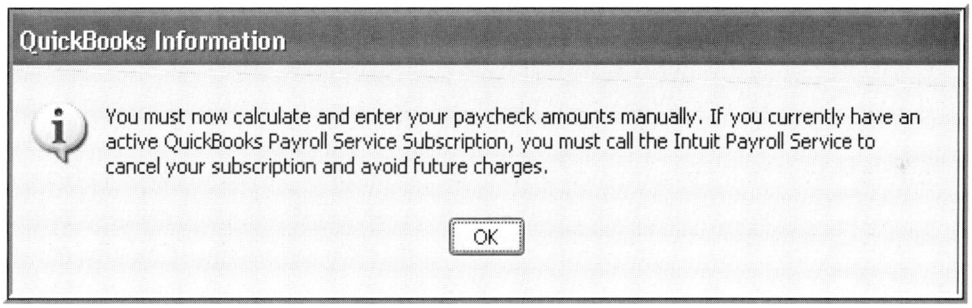

Click **OK**
Close Help

GENERAL NOTES ON PAYROLL SETUP

Before adding employees, you complete the payroll setup interview. The original release of QuickBooks Pro 2006 had five sections in the Payroll setup—no Payroll History section—and a slightly different arrangement of some of the screens and/or information provided on the screens. The payroll setup shown below was written after updating QuickBooks Pro 2006 in February, 2006.

QuickBooks is setup with Automatic Update turned on. Periodically, Intuit will send out program updates via the Internet that will be downloaded to your computer. It is important to note that sometimes information in the program changes as it did with the Payroll Setup. If your screens differ from the ones shown, do not be alarmed, you will enter the same information; but, perhaps, in a slightly different format or order.

THE PAYROLL SETUP INTERVIEW

There are six sections in the Payroll Setup to guide you through the process of setting up the payroll in QuickBooks.

The first section is an introductory screen. This is followed by the Company Setup for payroll. This section helps you identify and setup your methods of compensation, benefits your company offers, and additions and deductions your employees might have.

The third section leads you through setting up individual employees. When establishing the Employee Defaults, you will specify which payroll items apply to all or most of the employees of the company. Payroll items are used to identify and/or track the various amounts that affect a paycheck. There are items for salaries and wages, each kind of tax, each type of other deduction, commissions, and company-paid benefits.

The fourth section, Taxes, automatically sets up the payroll items for federal taxes, state taxes, and local taxes. Payroll tax liabilities and payroll withholding items need to be associated with a vendor in order to have payments processed appropriately.

The fifth section, Payroll History, earnings and withholdings for the employees for the current year are entered and payroll liability payments are recorded. This is important if you are installing QuickBooks and have already made payroll payments during the calendar year.

The final section Finishes the Payroll Setup and takes companies that subscribe to QuickBooks Payroll Services to the Payroll Center. Since we do not subscribe to a payroll service, we will go to the Employee Center or to the Home Page.

BEGIN THE PAYROLL SETUP

➤ Click the **Employees** menu, click **Payroll Setup**

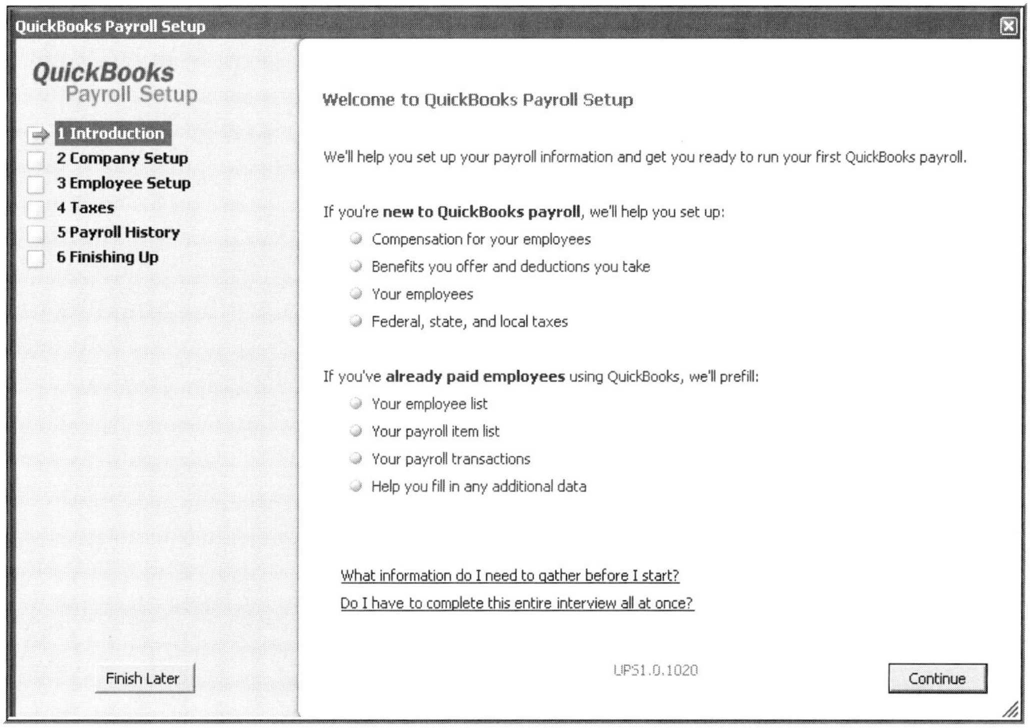

Read the screen, click **Continue**

COMPANY SECTION OF THE PAYROLL SETUP

In this section of the Payroll Setup, information about the methods of paying employees, deductions, and benefits is entered.

MEMO
DATE: January 1, 2006

Complete the Company portion of the Payroll Setup Interview:

Payroll List Items for Wages, Tips, and Taxable Fringe Benefits: Salary, Hourly Wage and Overtime
Insurance Benefits: Health Insurance, Dental Insurance Both are fully paid by the employee after taxes have been deducted
Retirement Benefits: None
Paid Time Off: Sick Time and Vacation Time
Other Payments and Deductions: None

Complete the Company portion of the Payroll Setup

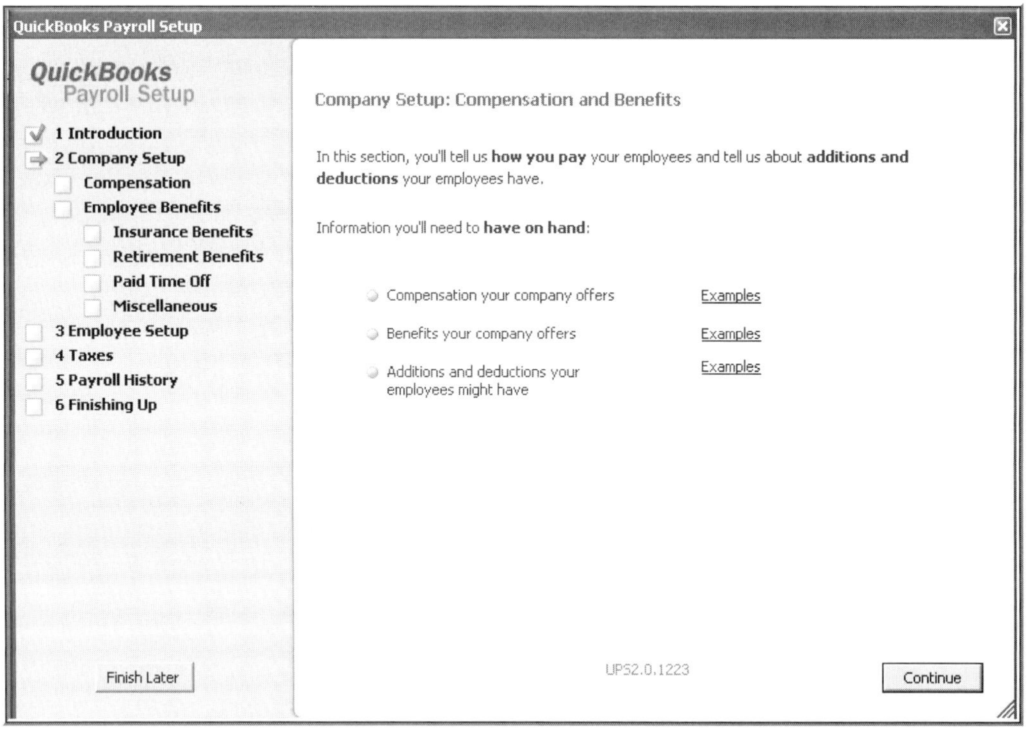

Click **Examples** to view each area of examples provided for the Company Setup

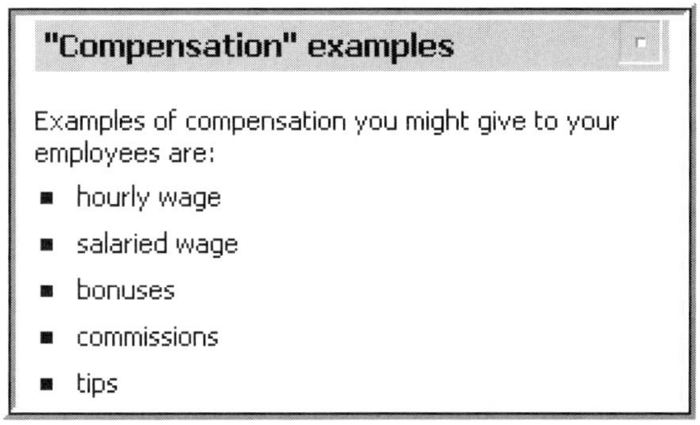

Click **Continue**
Click **Bonus, award, or one-time compensation** to unmark

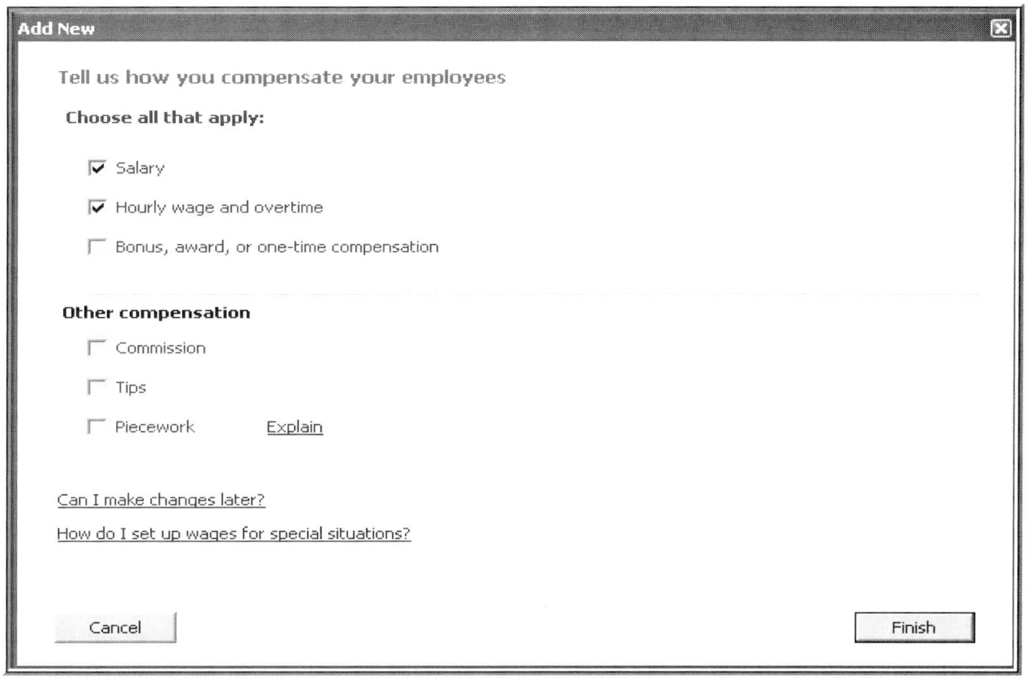

Click **Finish**
Review the Compensation List

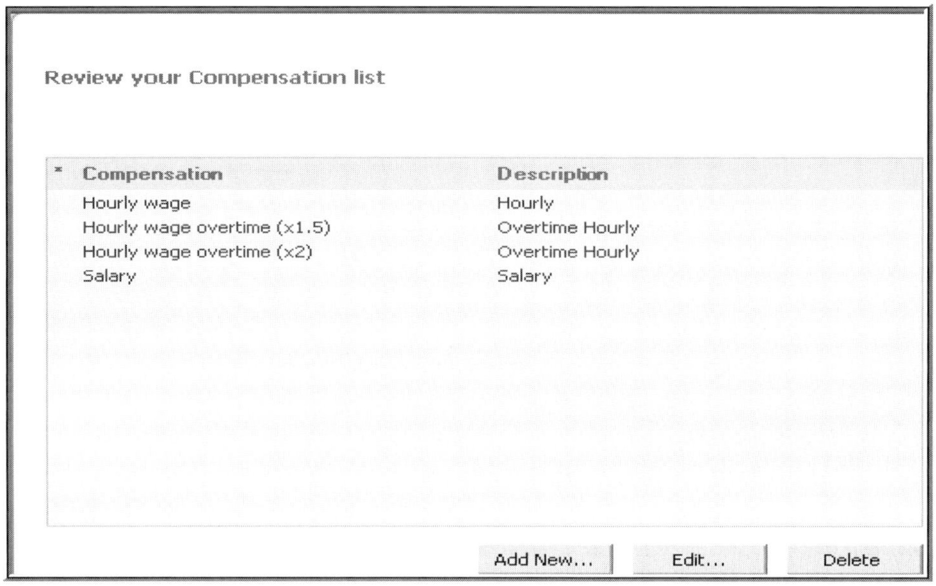

Click **Continue**

Read the screen regarding Set up employee benefits

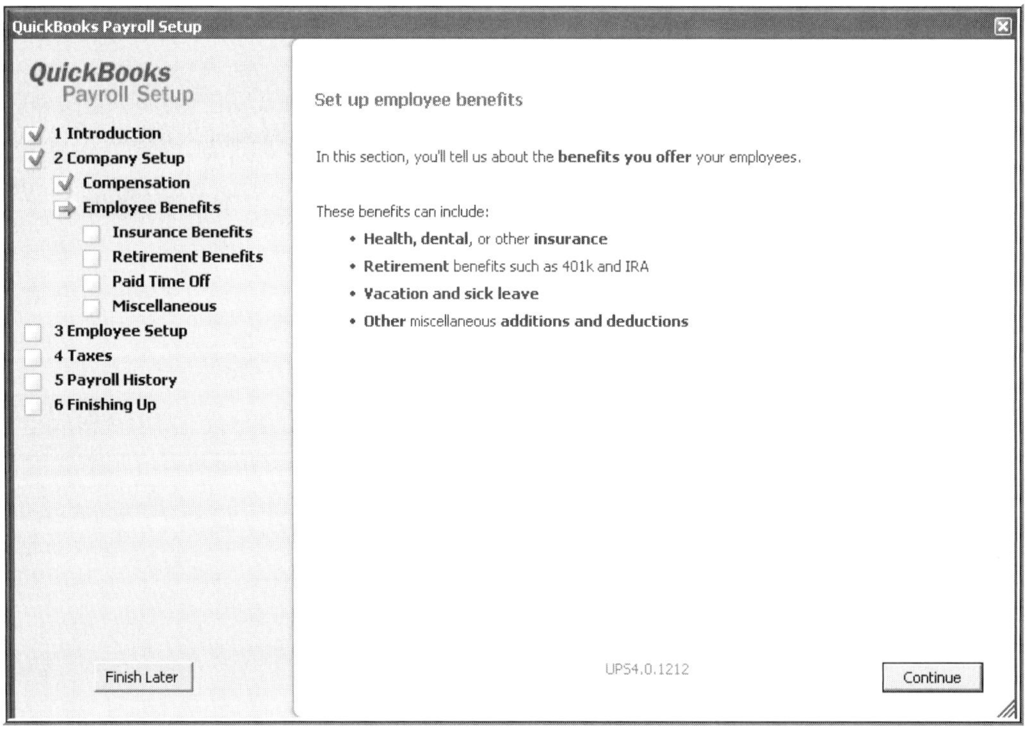

Click **Continue**

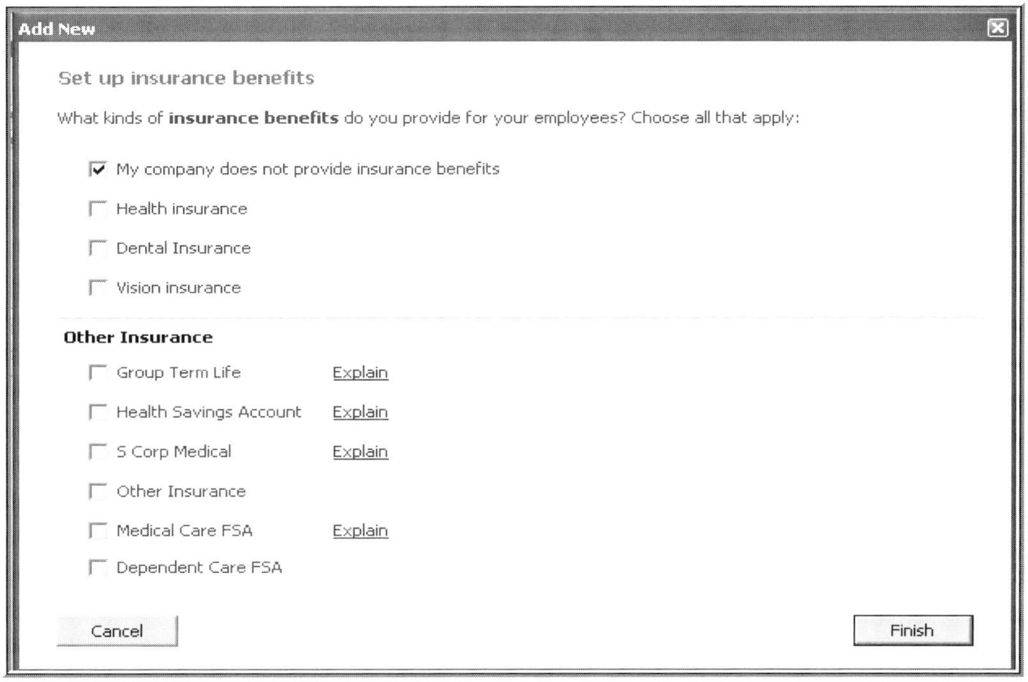

Click **My company does not provide insurance benefits** to remove the check mark
Click **Health insurance** and **Dental insurance** to select

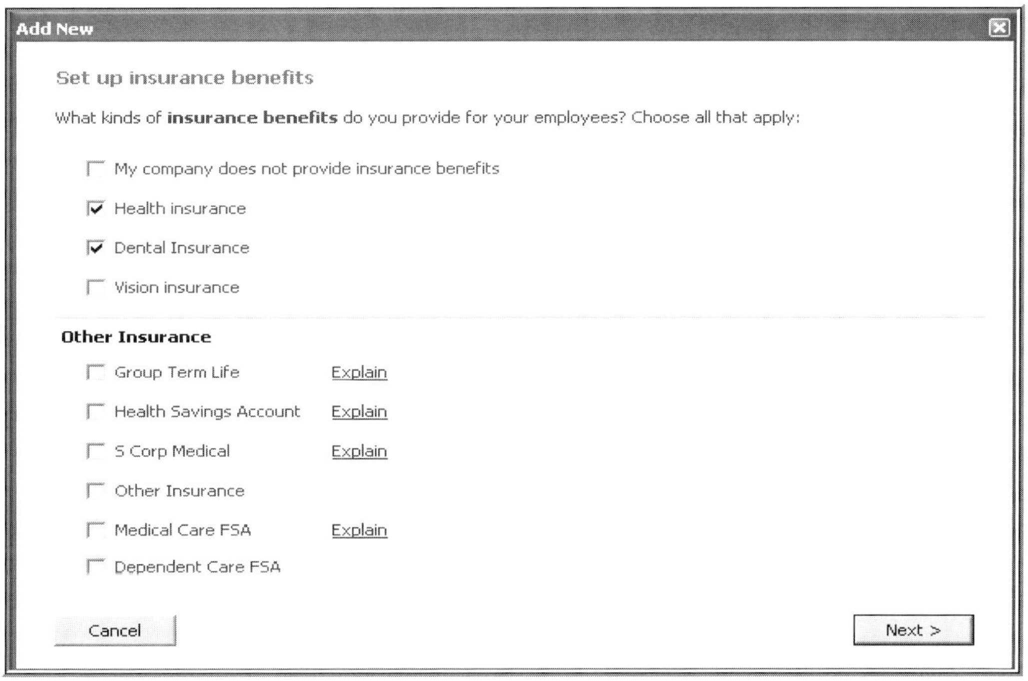

Click **Next**

On the Health Insurance screen, click **Employee pays for all of it** and **Payment is deducted after taxes**

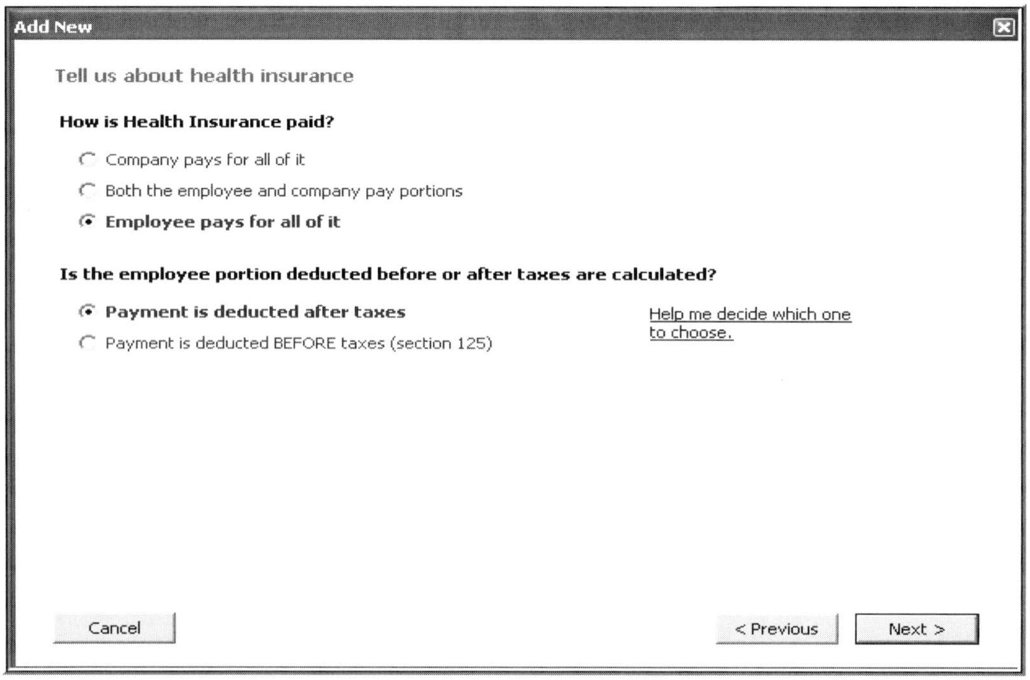

Click **Next**

On The Dental Insurance screen, click **Employee pays for all of it** and **Payment is deducted after taxes**

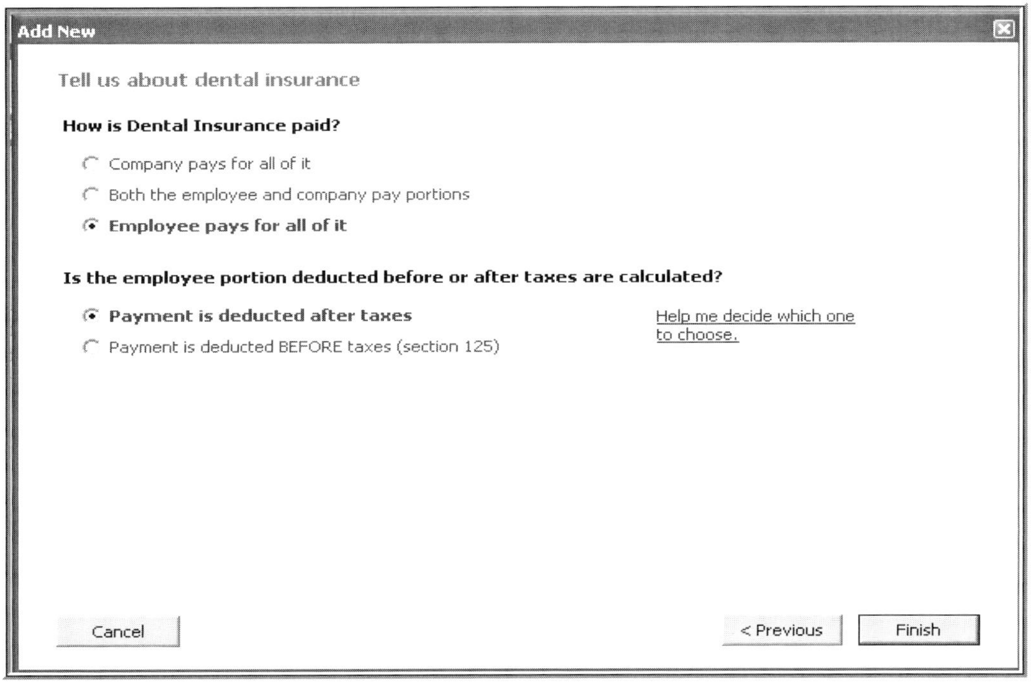

Click **Finish**
Review your Insurance Benefits list

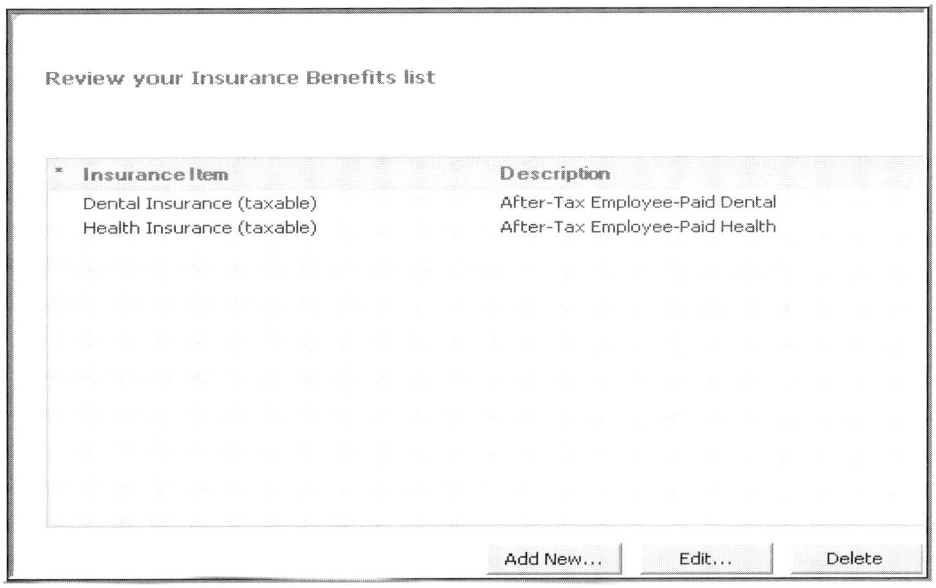

Click **Continue**
The next screen allows you to select retirement benefits.
We do not provide any retirement benefits for our employees

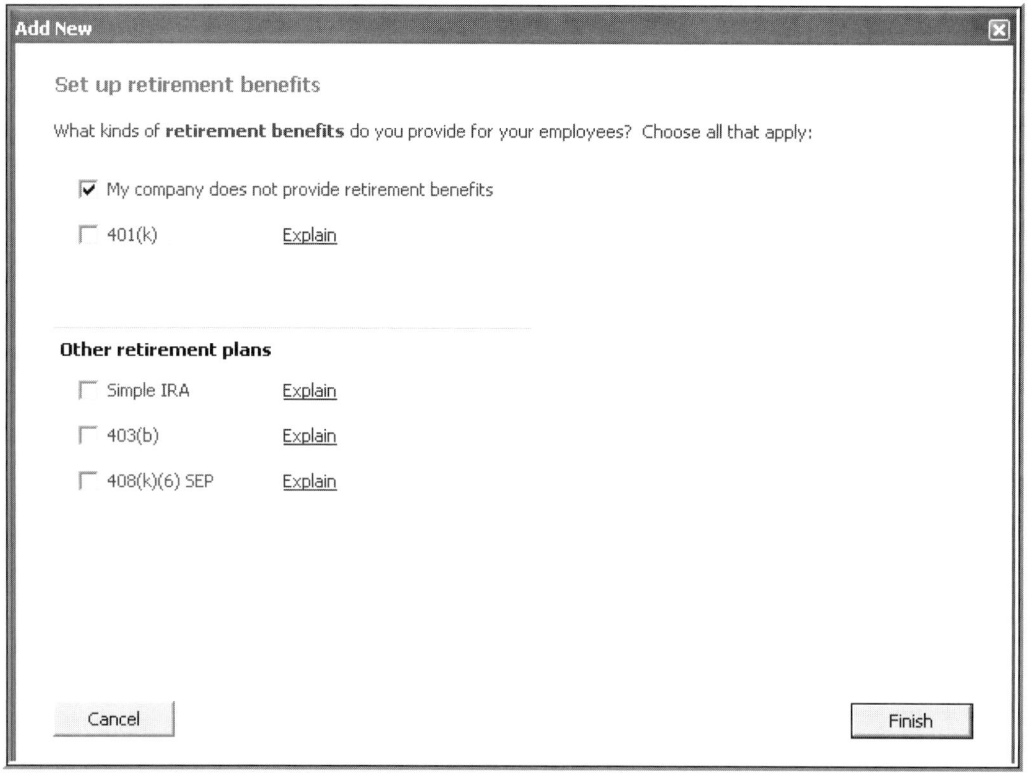

Click **Finish**, click **Continue**

For Paid Time Off, we do provide paid time off for Sick Leave and Vacation Leave, click **Paid sick time off** and **Paid vacation time off** to select

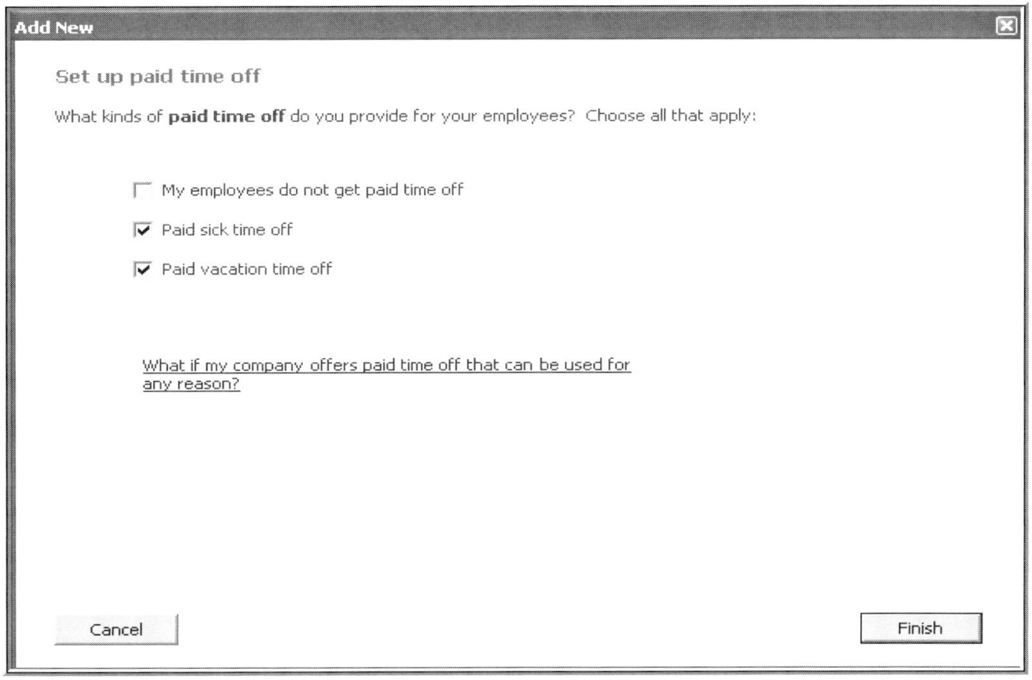

Click **Finish**

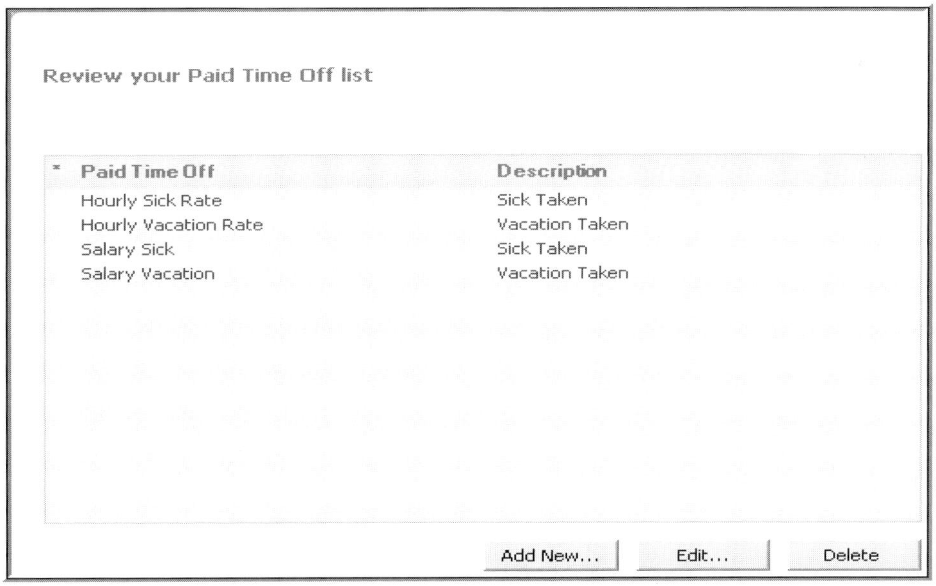

Review the Paid Time Off list, click **Continue**
We do not have any other Additions or Deductions

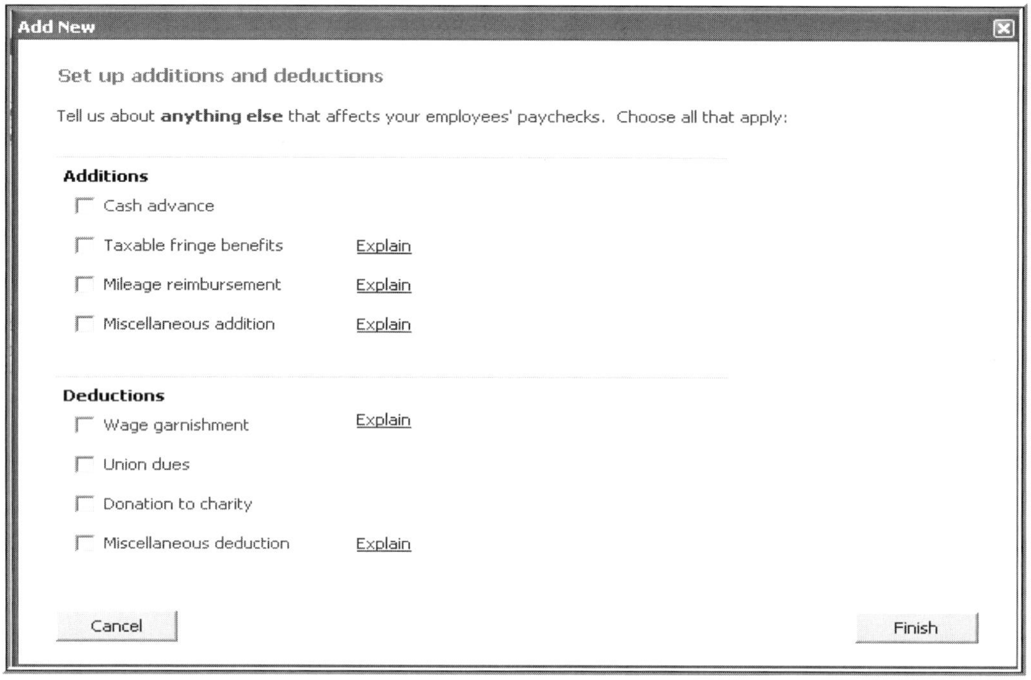

Click **Finish**

The Company Setup is complete, click **Continue** to complete the Employee Section of the Payroll Setup

EMPLOYEE SECTION OF THE PAYROLL SETUP

During the Employee section of the Payroll Setup, individual employees are added and information about their payroll items will be identified.

- When you print the Summary for each employee, check the beginning date for accruing sick and vacation time. It should show the Hire date; however, if it does not, change it by editing the employee(s) in the Employee Center after the Payroll Setup Interview is complete.

EMPLOYEES January 1, 2006 Yvonne Benson and Jaime Hernandez		
Name	Yvonne Benson	Jaime Hernandez
Status	Active	Active
Street Address	1077 Columbia Street	2985 A Street
City, State Zip	San Diego, CA 92101	San Diego, CA 92101
Phone	760-555-1232	760-555-9874

EMPLOYEES January 1, 2006 Yvonne Benson and Jaime Hernandez		
Employee Tax Type	Regular	Regular
Social Security No.	100-55-2525	100-55-9661
Hire Date	04/23/1996	06/30/2004
Birth Date	12/28/1949	04/23/1977
Gender	Female	Male
Pay Period	Monthly	Monthly
Salary	$26,000 per year	$15.50 per hour $23.25 per 1.5 overtime $31.00 per 2 x overtime
Health Insurance	$50 per month, annual maximum $600	$25 per month, annual maximum $300
Dental Insurance	$10 per month, annual maximum $120	$10 per month, annual maximum $120
Sick Time Earns	40:00 per year	40:00 per year
Unused Hours	Have an accrual limit	Have an accrual limit
Maximum Hours	120:00	120:00
Earns	Time off currently	Time off currently
Hours Available as of 01/01/06	20:00	50:00
Begin Accruing Time On	04/23/1996	06/30/2004
Vacation Time Earns	40:00 per year	40:00 per year
Unused Hours	Have an accrual limit	Have an accrual limit
Maximum Hours	120:00	120:00
Earns	Time off currently	Time off currently
Hours Available as of 01/01/06	20:00	40:00
Begin Accruing Time On	04/23/1996	06/30/2004
Direct Deposit	No	No
State Subject to Withholding	CA	CA
State Where Employee Works	CA	CA
Live or Work in Another State in 2006	No	No
Federal Filing Status	Single	Married
Allowances	0	2

EMPLOYEES January 1, 2006 Yvonne Benson and Jaime Hernandez		
Subject to	Medicare Social Security Federal Unemployment	Medicare Social Security Federal Unemployment
State Filing Status	Single	Married (2 incomes)
Standard Deductions	0	2
Subject to	CA-Unemployment CA-Employment Training Tax CA-Disability	CA-Unemployment CA-Employment Training Tax CA-Disability
Local Taxes	No	No

Complete the Employee portion of the Payroll Setup

Read the screen about the Employee Setup

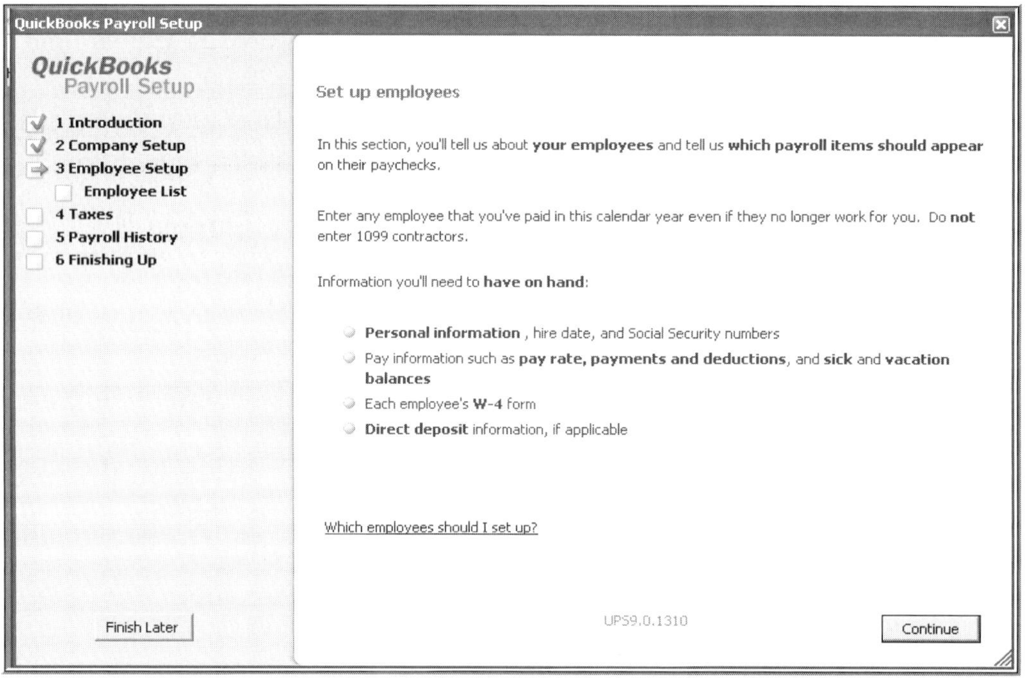

Click **Continue**

Enter the name, address, and phone for Yvonne Benson using the information provided in the memo

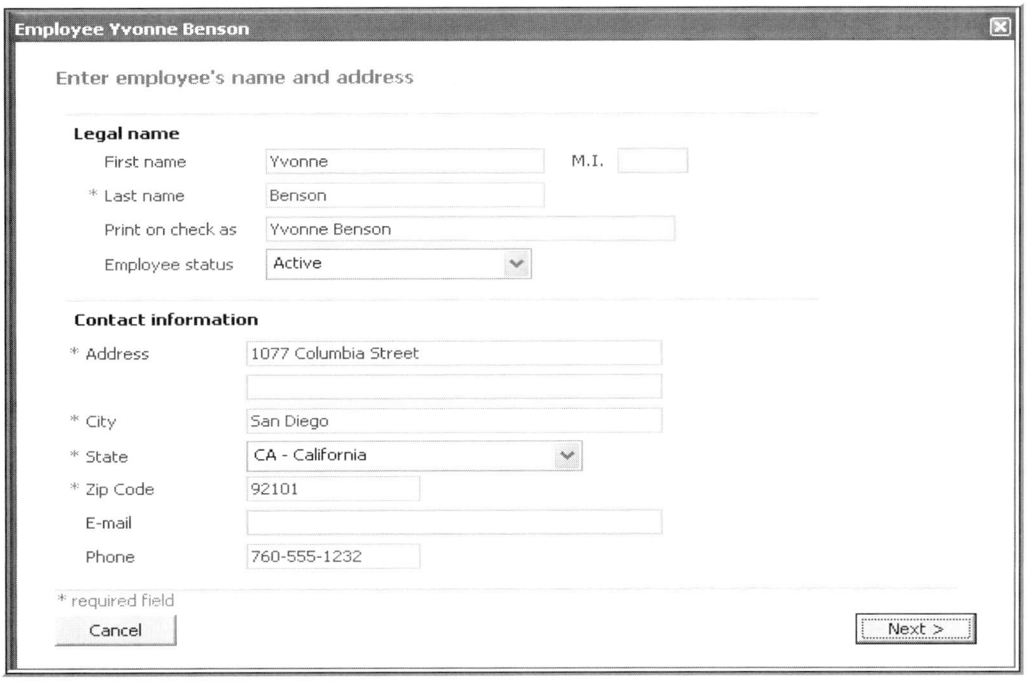

Click **Next**

Enter Yvonne's hiring information as given in the memo

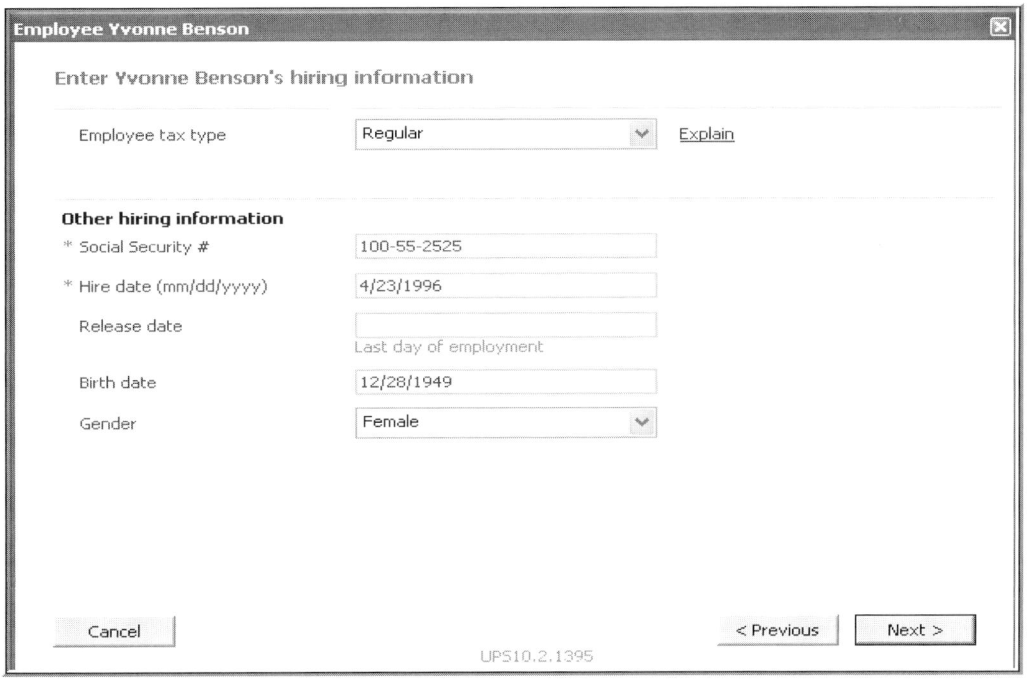

Click **Next**

Yvonne is paid monthly and has a salary of $26,000 per year, complete the screen for compensation

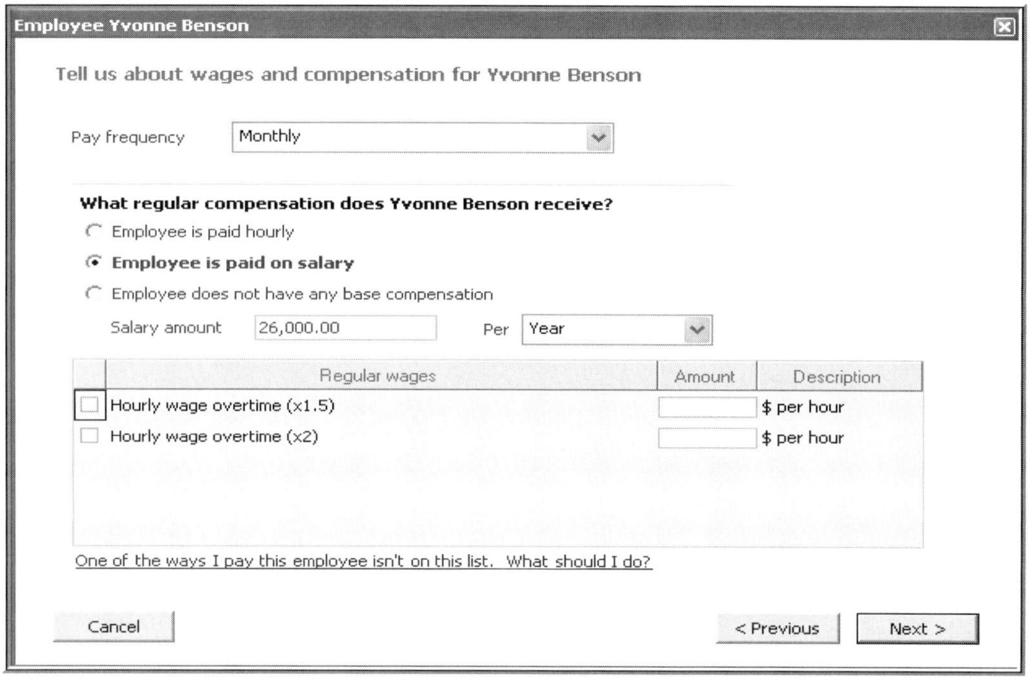

Click **Next**

Click the **Use** box for **Health Insurance**, enter **50** as the amount per paycheck and **600** as the annual maximum

Click the **Use** box for **Dental Insurance**, enter **10** as the amount per paycheck and **120** as the annual maximum

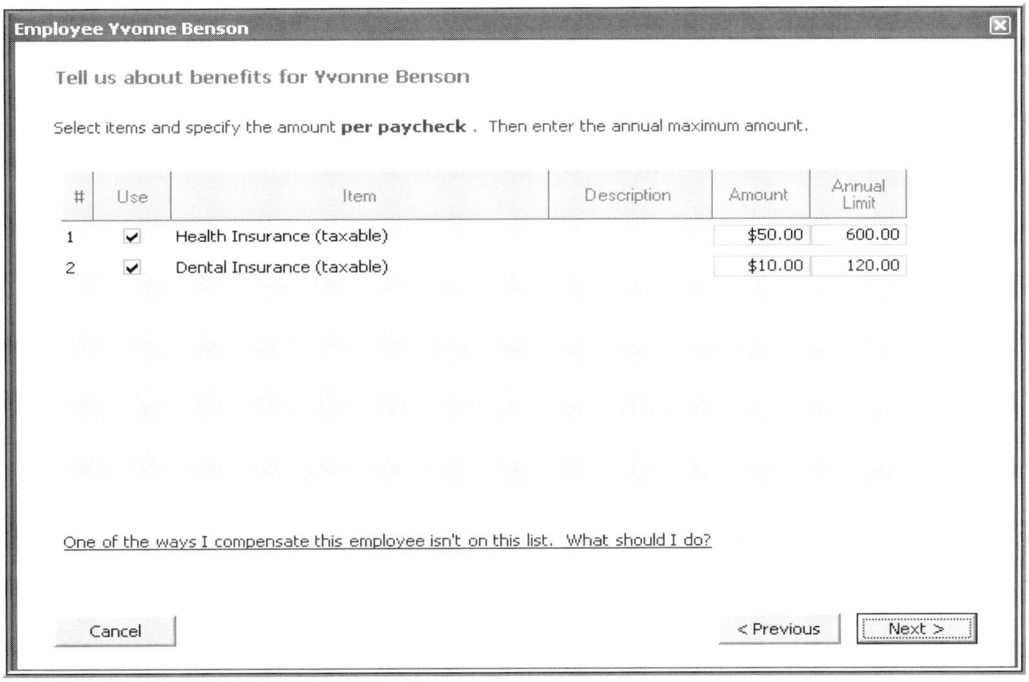

Click **Next**

Enter the information about Yvonne's sick time

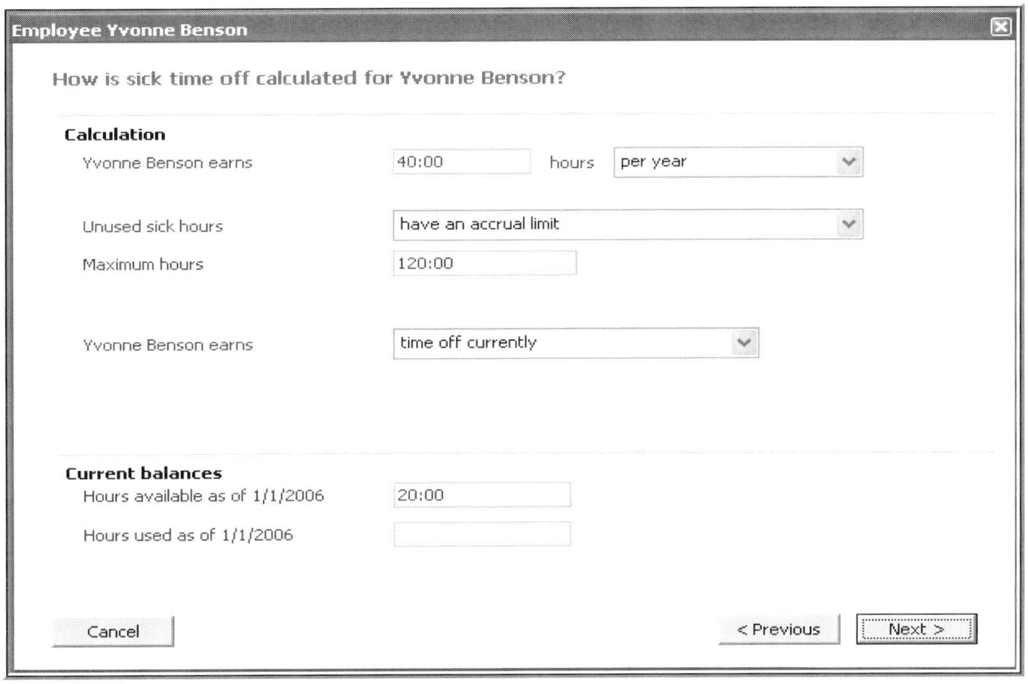

Click **Next**

Enter the information regarding Yvonne's vacation time

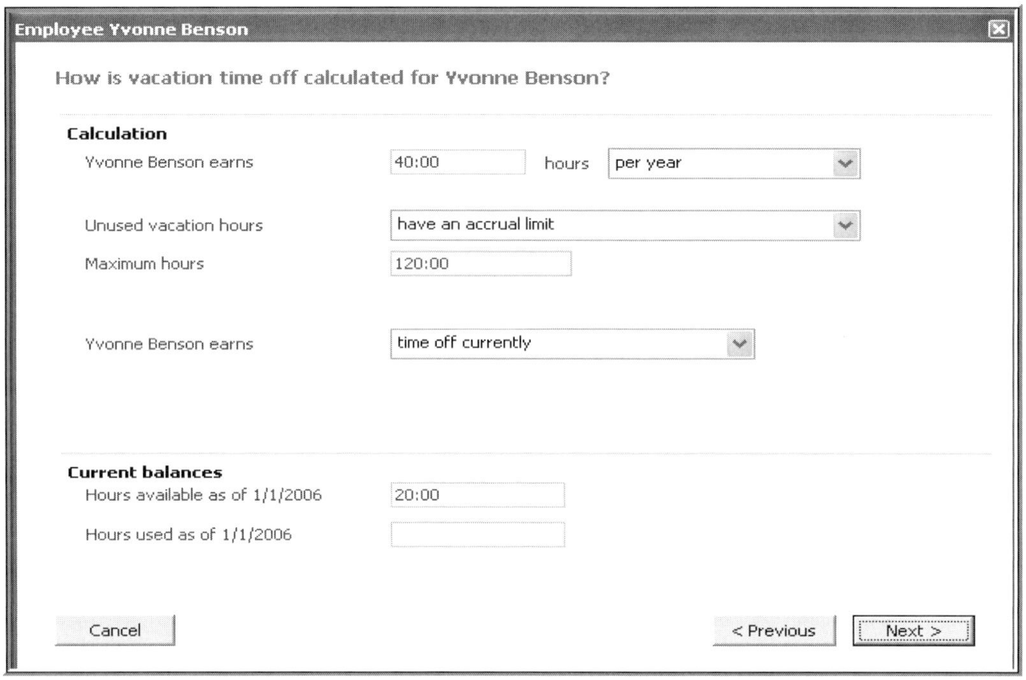

Click **Next**

There is no Direct Deposit for Yvonne

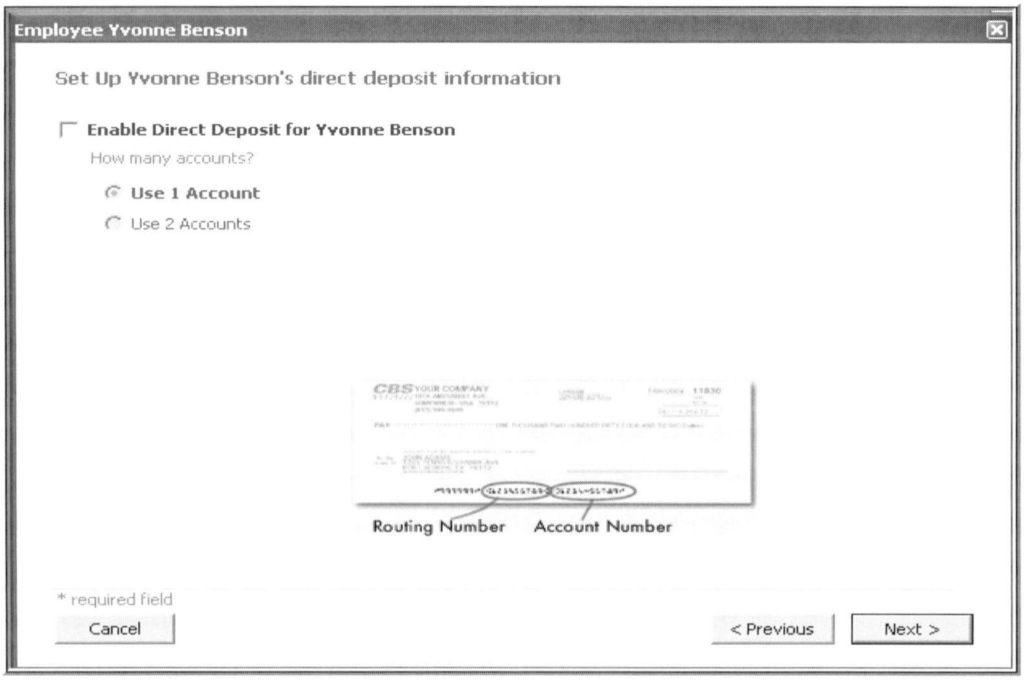

Click **Next**

Enter California as the state where Yvonne lives and works. She has not lived or worked in another state in 2006

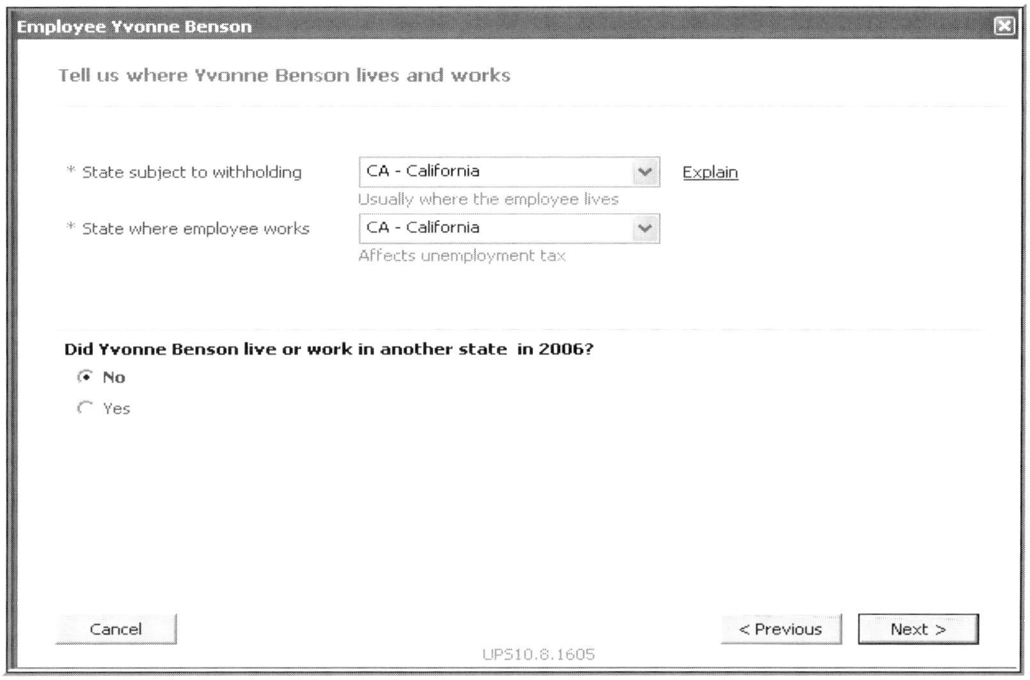

Click **Next**

Enter the federal tax information for Yvonne

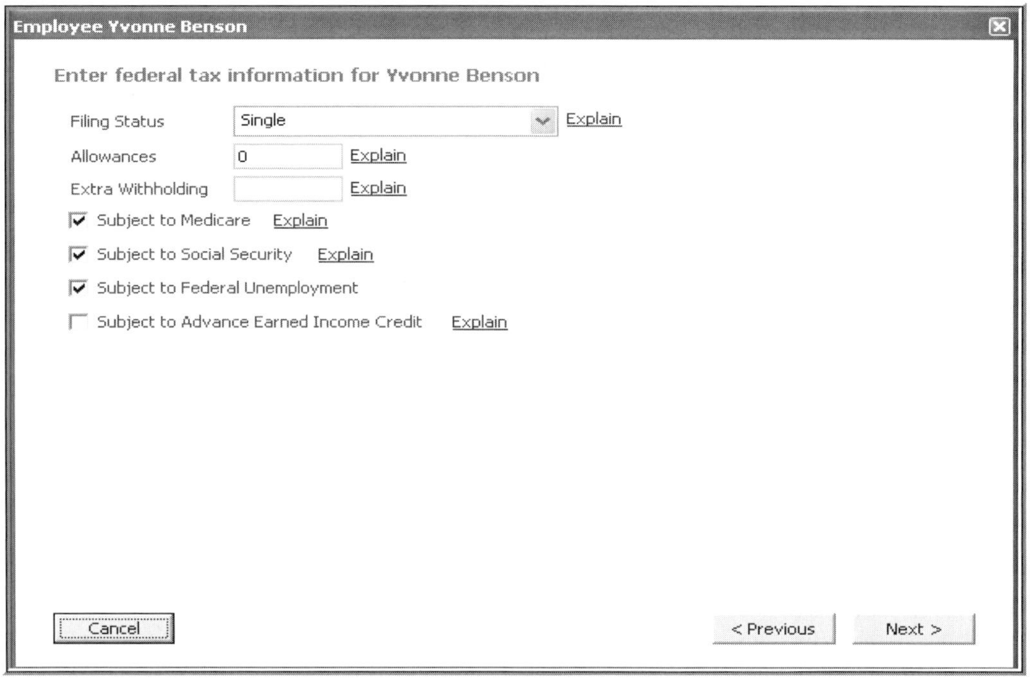

Click **Next**
Enter the state tax information for Yvonne; she is not subject to any special local taxes

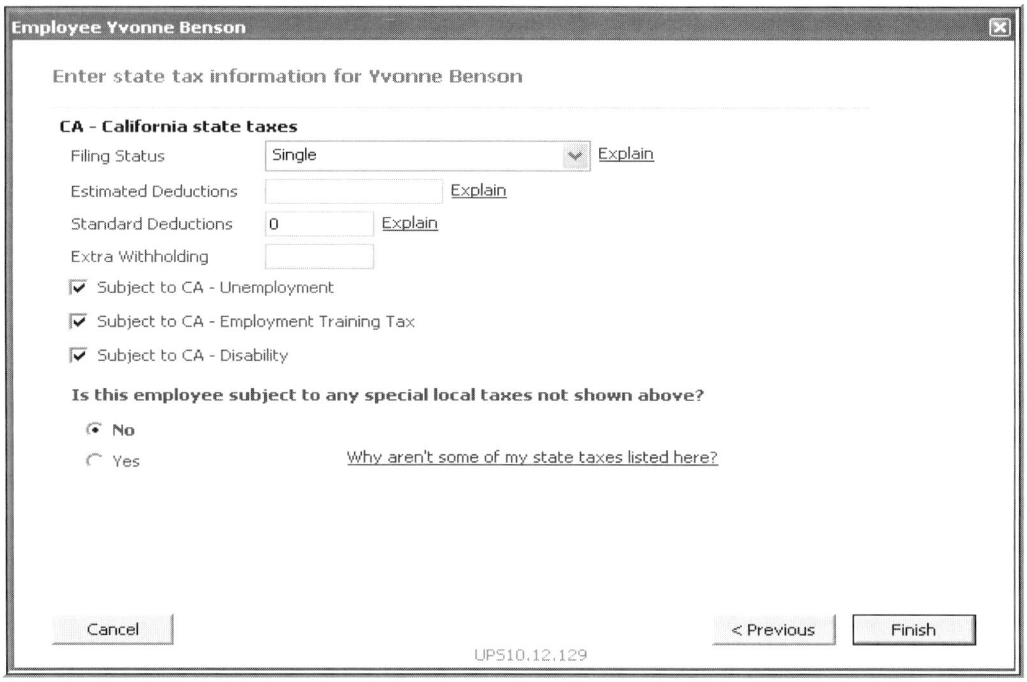

Click **Finish**
Click the **Summary** button to view the information entered for Yvonne Benson

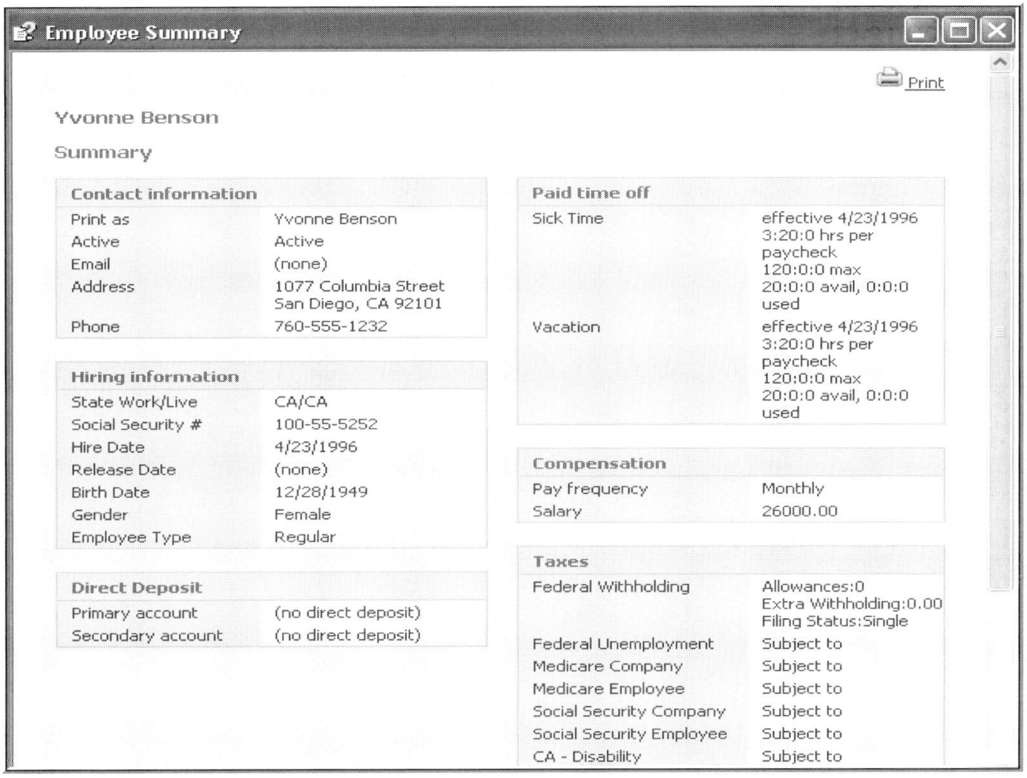

Click **Print** on the Summary screen and print Yvonne's information

Close the **Employee summary** window for Yvonne

Click the **Add New** button on the Employee List

Add Jaime Hernandez using the information provided in the memo and following the steps provided for Yvonne Benson

When you complete the wages and compensation section for Jaime, click **Employee is paid hourly**, enter **15.50**

Click **Hourly wage overtime (x1.5)** to select, enter the amount **23.25**, click **Hourly wage overtime (x2)** to select, enter **31.00**

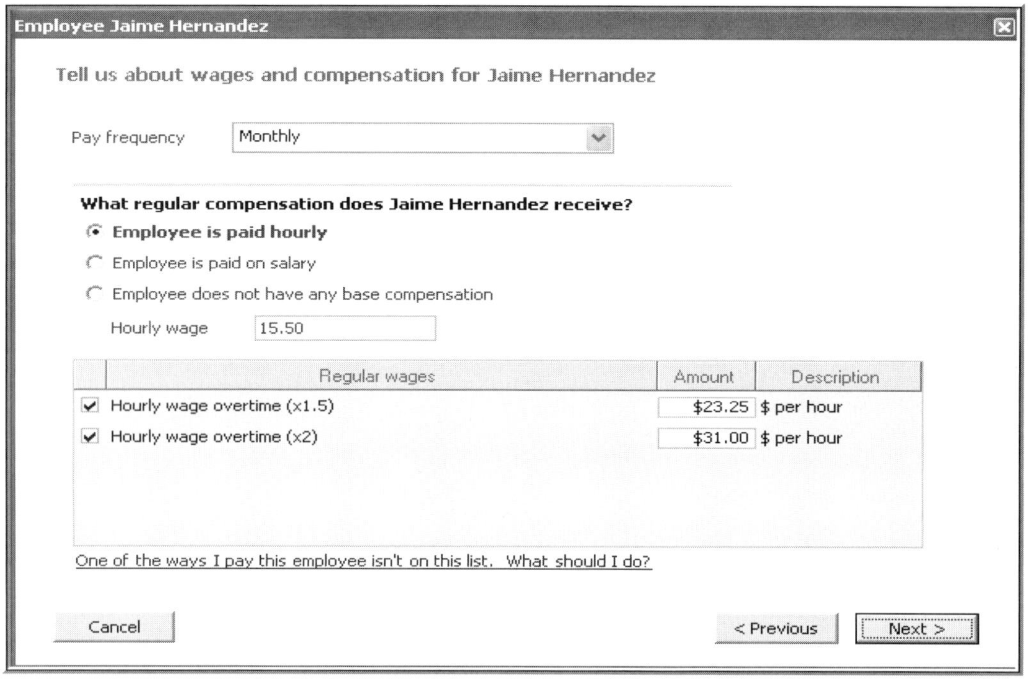

Complete the employee setup for Jaime Hernandez
Review the Employee List

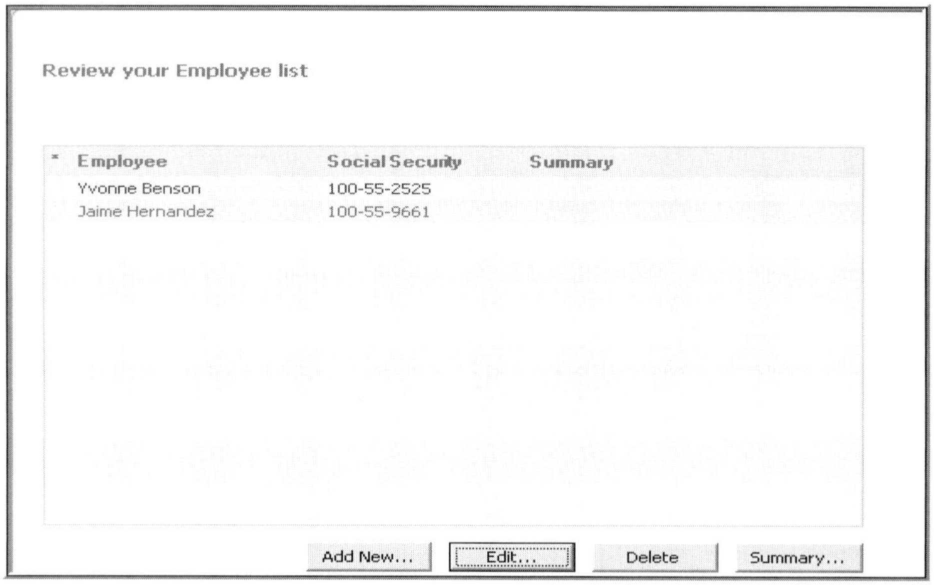

With Jaime Hernandez highlighted in the employee list, click the **Summary** button

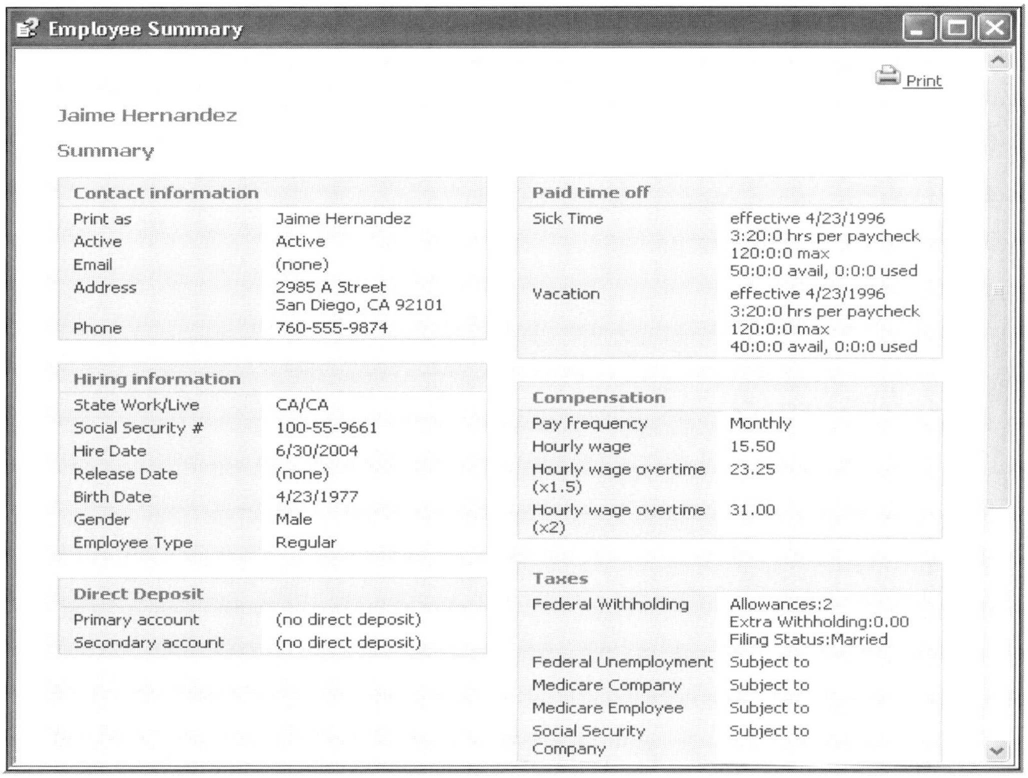

Print Jaime's Summary, close the Summary
Click **Continue**

TAXES SECTION OF THE PAYROLL SETUP

The Taxes section of the Payroll setup allows you to identify federal, state, and local tax payments and agencies.

Complete the Taxes section of the Payroll setup

Read the screen for "Set up your payroll taxes"

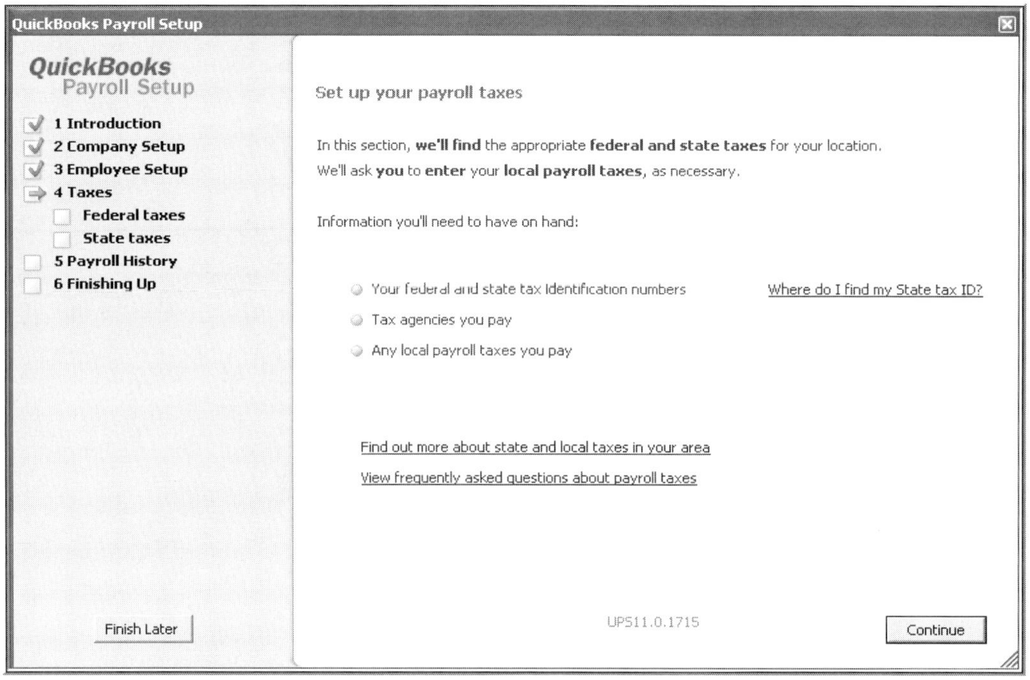

Click **Continue**

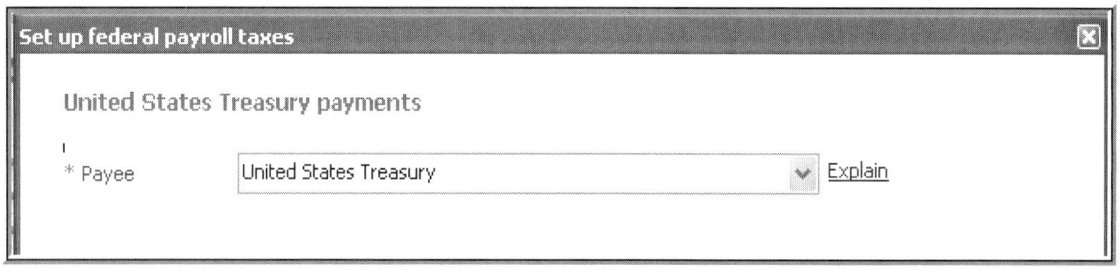

Click **Finish**

Review the list of taxes

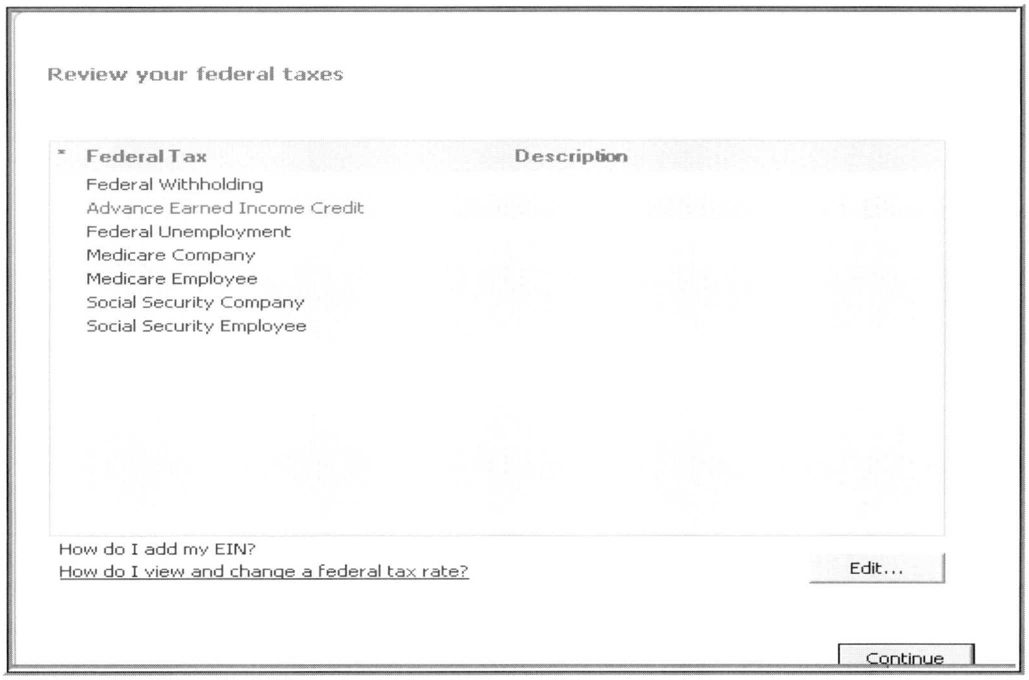

Click **Continue**

Complete the information for CA-EDD Payments:

Click the drop-down list arrow for Payee, click **Employment Development Department**

Tab to or click in the textbox for California EDD Employer Account, enter **999-9999-9**

Tab to or click the textbox for California-Unemployment Company Rate, enter **4%**

The rate for CA-Employment Training Tax Company Rate should be shown as 0.1% and the rate for CA-Disability Employee Rate should be shown as 1.08%, if not change as necessary

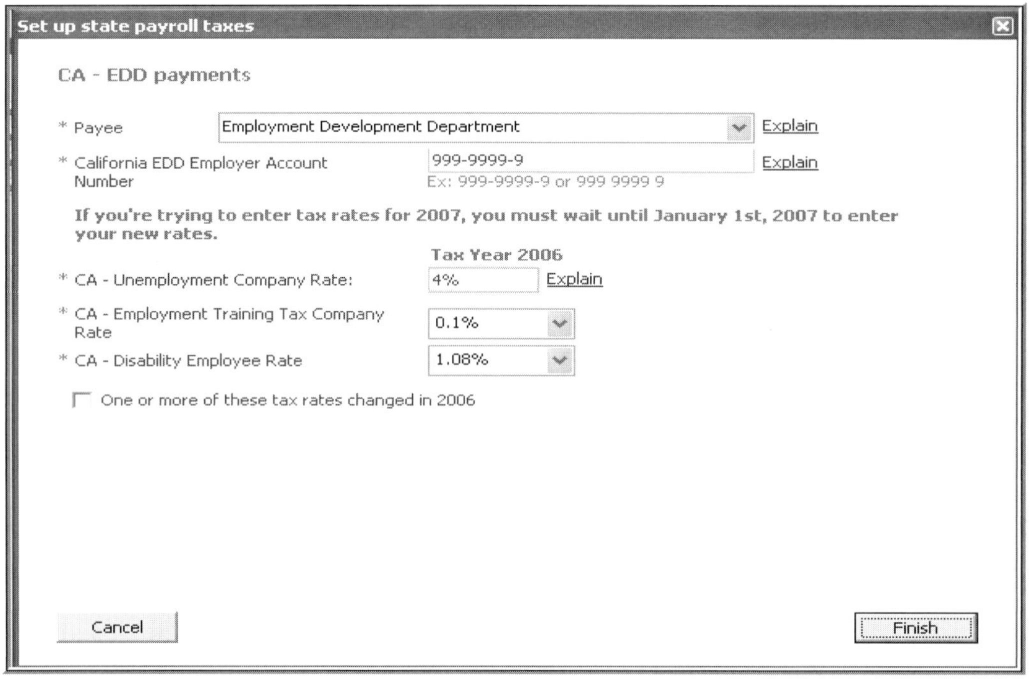

Click **Finish**

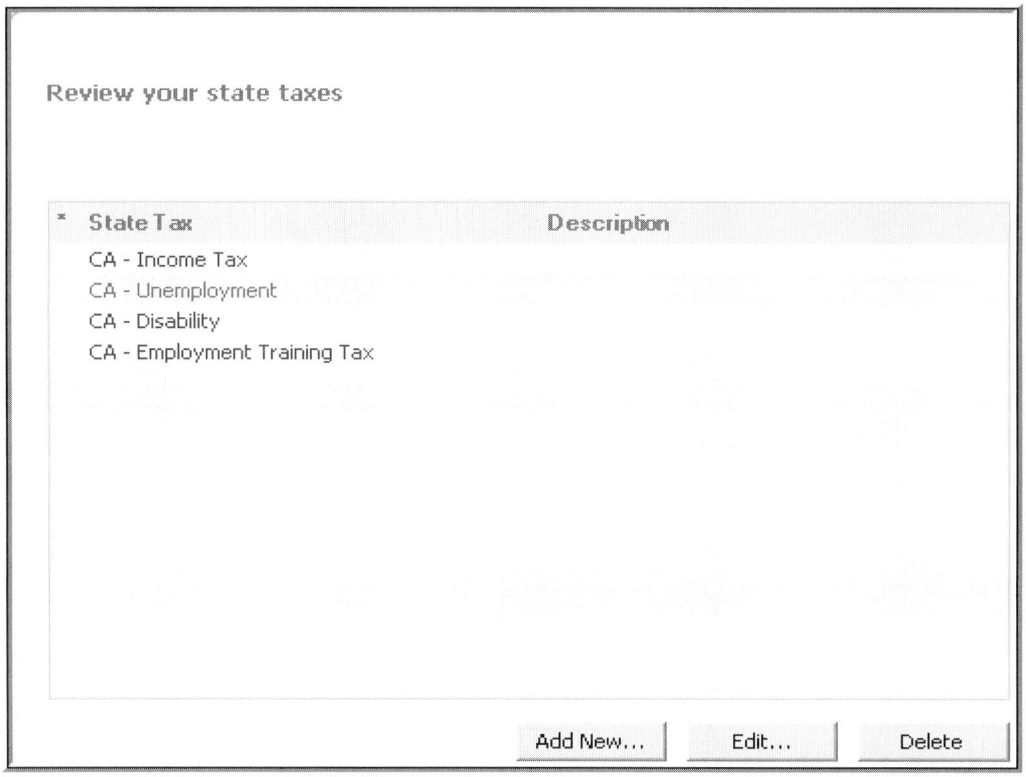

Review the state taxes, click **Continue**

PAYROLL HISTORY SECTION OF THE PAYROLL SETUP

The Payroll History is completed to enter year-to-date amounts for employees and to identify liability payments you made.

Even though we have not processed paychecks for the employees, use the following chart to enter the payroll history for the month of December, 2005 with a pay date of January 1, 2006

PAYROLL HISTORY		
	Yvonne Benson	**Jaime Hernandez**
Paid	Yes	Yes
Paycheck Date	01/01/06	01/01/06
Payroll Date From	12/01/05	12/31/05
Payroll Date To	12/31/05	12/31/05
Report Hours	No	No
	EARNINGS	
Salary/Hourly Wages	$2,166.66	$2,480.00
	WITHHOLDING	
Withholding Dental	10.00	10.00
Withholding Health	50.00	50.00
Federal Withholding	375.00	387.00
Medicare Employee	36.25	37.41
Social Security Employee	155.00	159.96
CA-Disability	27.00	27.86
CA-Income Tax	100.00	103.20
	COMPANY TAXES	
Federal Unemployment	20.00	20.64
Medicare Company	36.25	37.41
Social Security Company	155.00	159.96
CA-Unemployment	100.00	103.20
CA-Employee Training Tax	2.50	2.58

Complete the Payroll History for the employees

Read the screen, click **Continue**

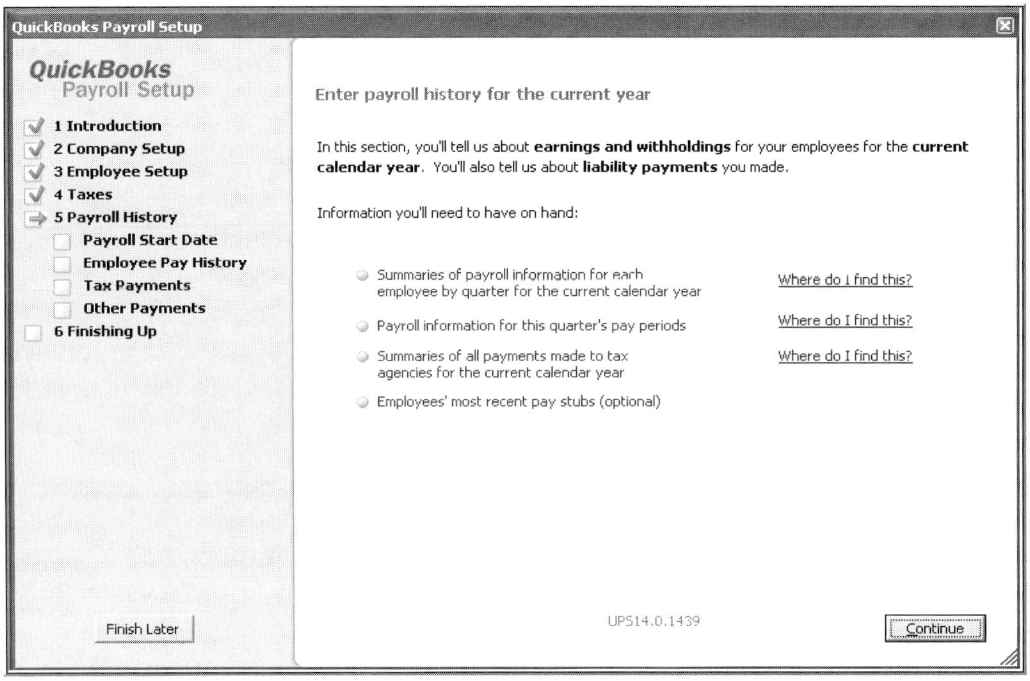

On the screen to determine whether you need to add payroll history, click **Yes**

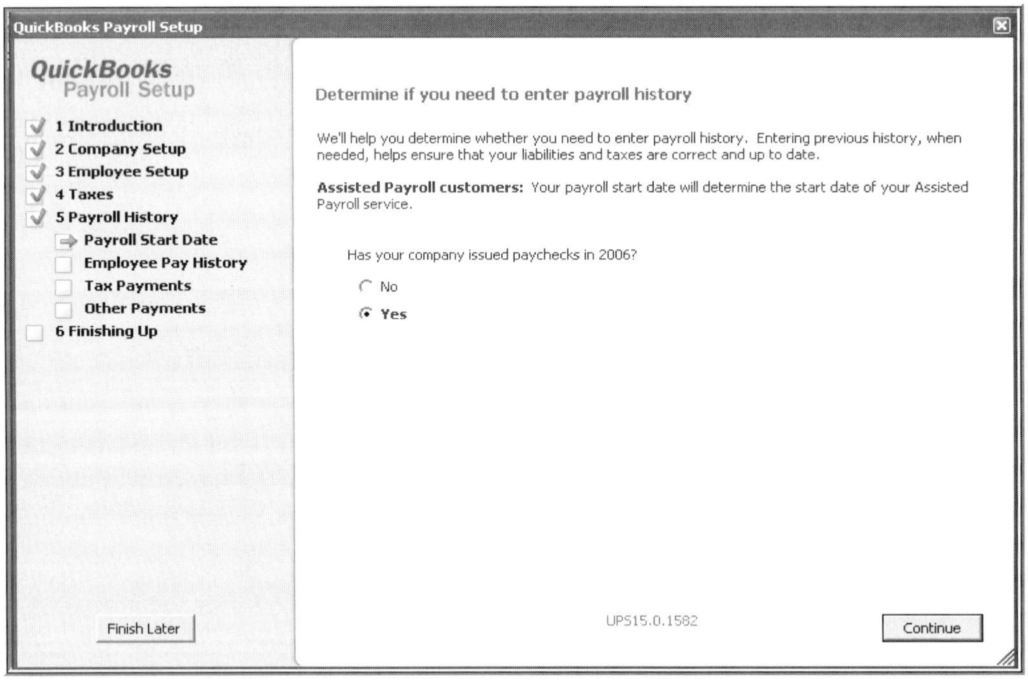

Click **Continue**

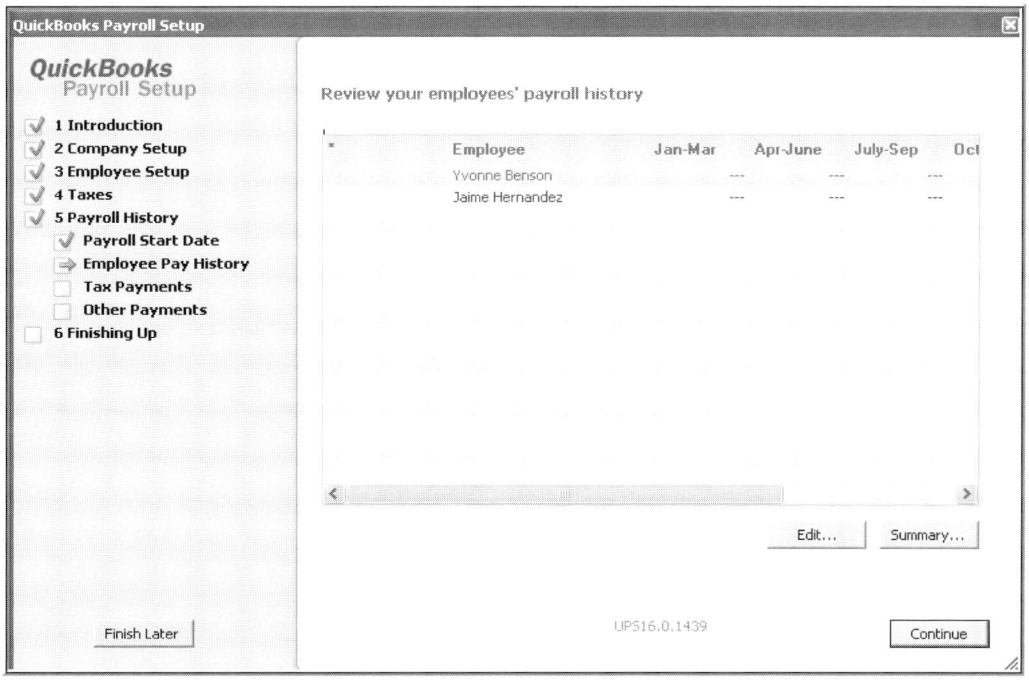

Click the **Edit** button

Enter the pay information as provided in the Payroll Table for the Paycheck date and pay period dates

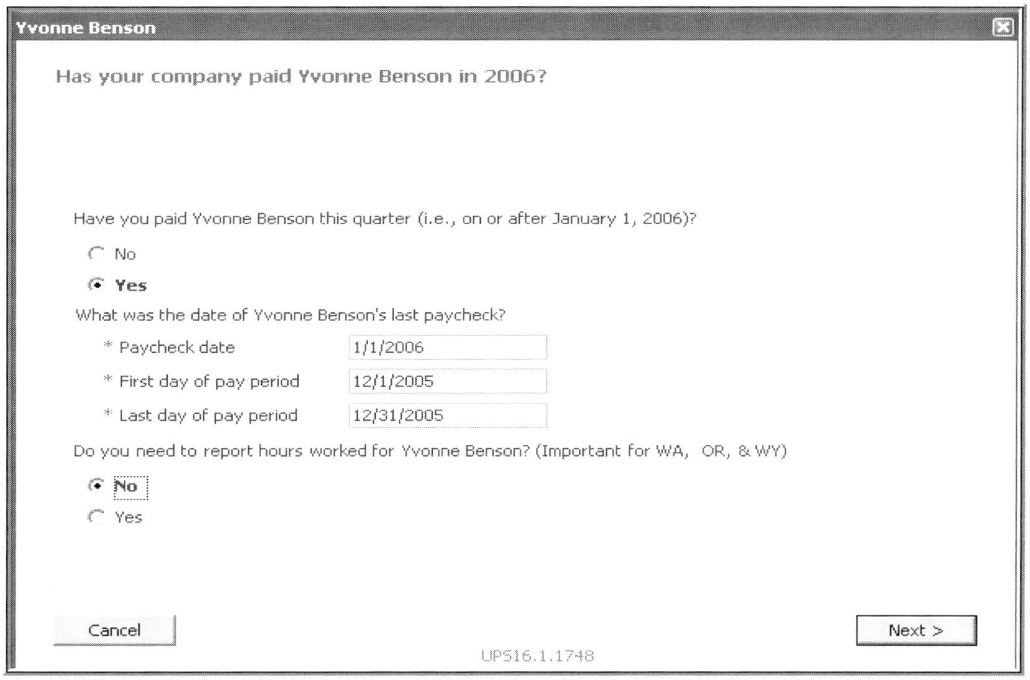

Click **Next**

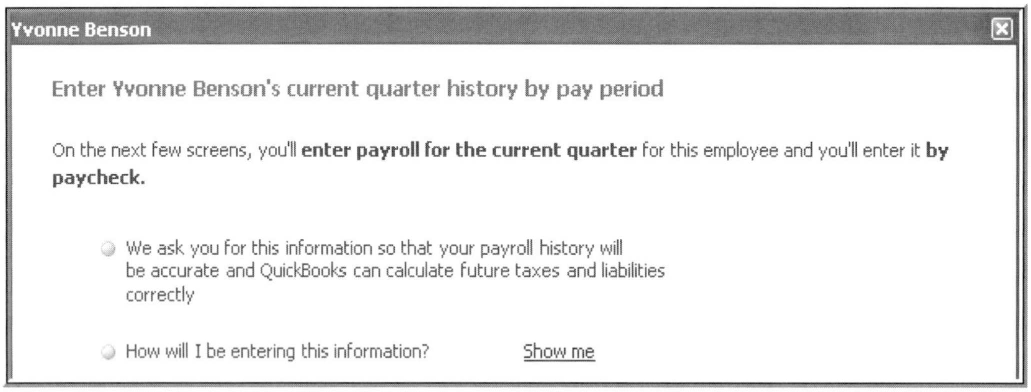

After you have read the screen above, click **Next**, verify the January Paycheck Dates of **1/1/2006**, if necessary, enter the date

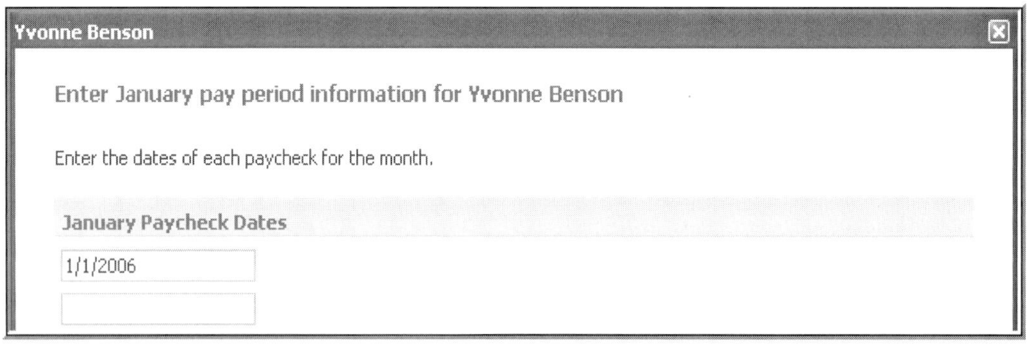

Click **Next**, enter the Salary earnings of **2,166.66**

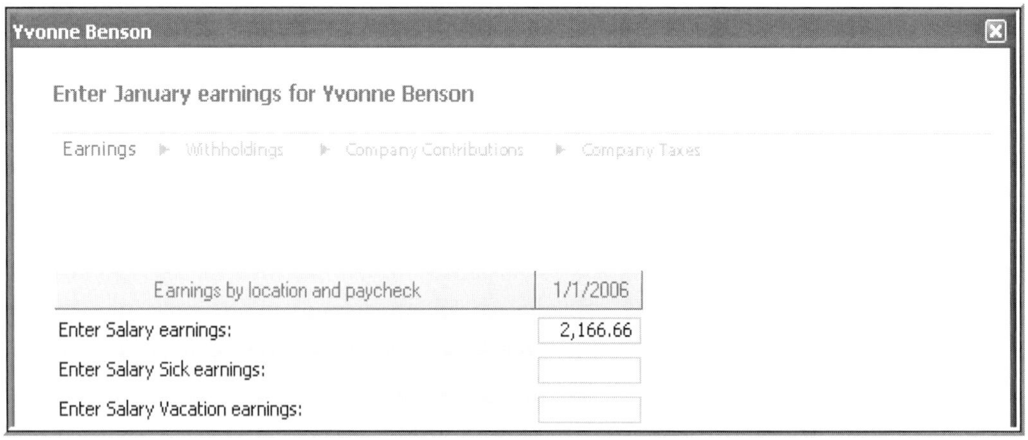

Click **Next**

Refer to the Payroll Table and enter the amounts for withholding by paycheck

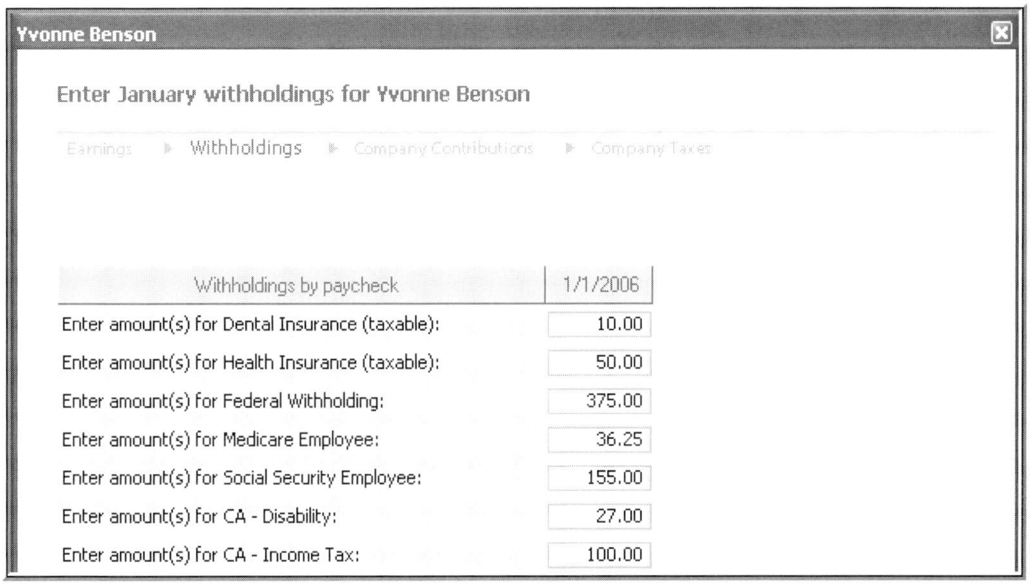

Click **Next**, enter the Company taxes for Yvonne

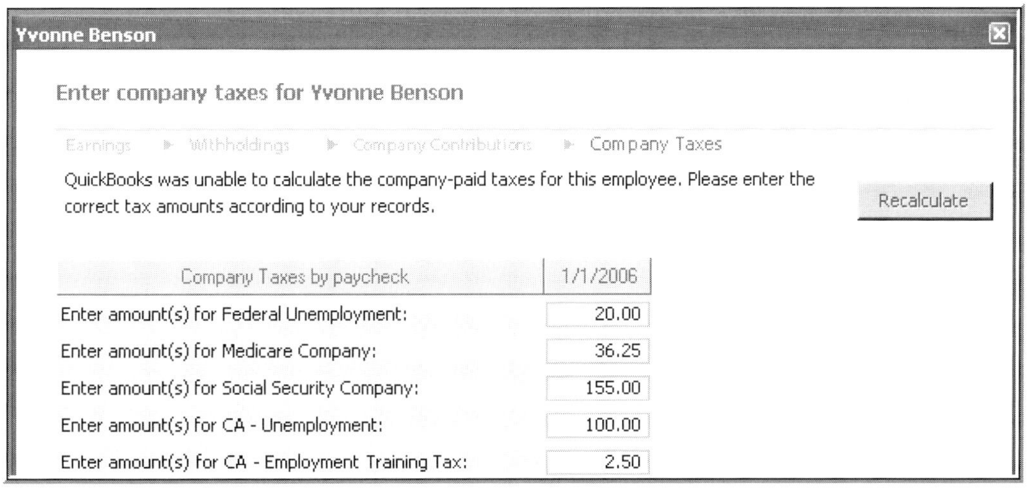

Click **Finish**

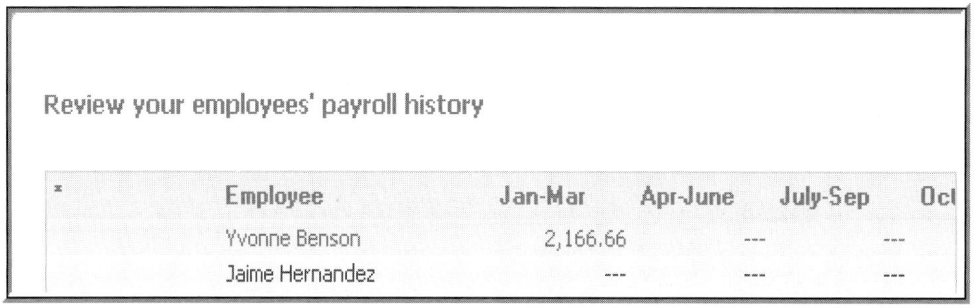

Review your employees' payroll history

Employee	Jan-Mar	Apr-June	July-Sep	Oct
Yvonne Benson	2,166.66	---	---	
Jaime Hernandez	---	---	---	

Click the **Summary** button to review the information entered for Yvonne
Click **Print** and print her summary information

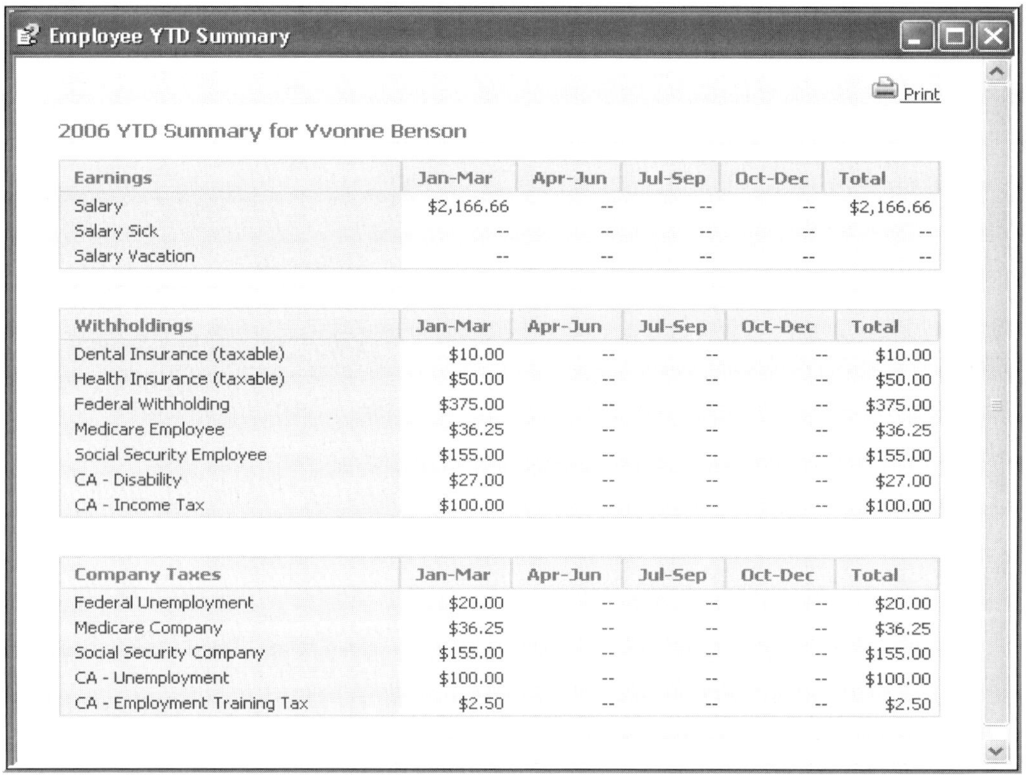

Employee YTD Summary

Print

2006 YTD Summary for Yvonne Benson

Earnings	Jan-Mar	Apr-Jun	Jul-Sep	Oct-Dec	Total
Salary	$2,166.66	--	--	--	$2,166.66
Salary Sick	--	--	--	--	--
Salary Vacation	--	--	--	--	--

Withholdings	Jan-Mar	Apr-Jun	Jul-Sep	Oct-Dec	Total
Dental Insurance (taxable)	$10.00	--	--	--	$10.00
Health Insurance (taxable)	$50.00	--	--	--	$50.00
Federal Withholding	$375.00	--	--	--	$375.00
Medicare Employee	$36.25	--	--	--	$36.25
Social Security Employee	$155.00	--	--	--	$155.00
CA - Disability	$27.00	--	--	--	$27.00
CA - Income Tax	$100.00	--	--	--	$100.00

Company Taxes	Jan-Mar	Apr-Jun	Jul-Sep	Oct-Dec	Total
Federal Unemployment	$20.00	--	--	--	$20.00
Medicare Company	$36.25	--	--	--	$36.25
Social Security Company	$155.00	--	--	--	$155.00
CA - Unemployment	$100.00	--	--	--	$100.00
CA - Employment Training Tax	$2.50	--	--	--	$2.50

After reviewing the information for Yvonne, click **Jaime Hernandez**, click the **Edit** button and enter his information for Payroll History and print his Summary information

Employee YTD Summary

Print

2006 YTD Summary for Jaime Hernandez

Earnings	Jan-Mar	Apr-Jun	Jul-Sep	Oct-Dec	Total
Hourly wage	$2,480.00	--	--	--	$2,480.00
Hourly wage overtime (x1.5)	--	--	--	--	--
Hourly wage overtime (x2)	--	--	--	--	--
Hourly Sick Rate	--	--	--	--	--
Hourly Vacation Rate	--	--	--	--	--

Withholdings	Jan-Mar	Apr-Jun	Jul-Sep	Oct-Dec	Total
Dental Insurance (taxable)	$10.00	--	--	--	$10.00
Health Insurance (taxable)	$50.00	--	--	--	$50.00
Federal Withholding	$387.00	--	--	--	$387.00
Medicare Employee	$37.41	--	--	--	$37.41
Social Security Employee	$159.96	--	--	--	$159.96
CA - Disability	$27.86	--	--	--	$27.86
CA - Income Tax	$103.20	--	--	--	$103.20

Company Taxes	Jan-Mar	Apr-Jun	Jul-Sep	Oct-Dec	Total
Federal Unemployment	$20.64	--	--	--	$20.64
Medicare Company	$37.41	--	--	--	$37.41
Social Security Company	$159.96	--	--	--	$159.96
CA - Unemployment	$103.20	--	--	--	$103.20
CA - Employment Training Tax	$2.58	--	--	--	$2.58

Click **Continue**, click **No** for payment of payroll taxes

- Since the payroll taxes withheld from the employee paychecks were for the Oct-Dec, 2005 quarter, there are no payroll taxes that have been withheld for 2006.

2006 Tax Payments

2006 Tax Payments

Have you paid any payroll taxes in 2006?

(•) No

( ) Yes

Click **Finish**, click **Continue**

Click **No** for Dental Payments

2006 Other Payments

Enter all payments to your dental insurance provider

Have you made any payments to your dental insurance provider in 2006?

(•) No

( ) Yes

Click **Next**, click **No** for payments to health insurance provider

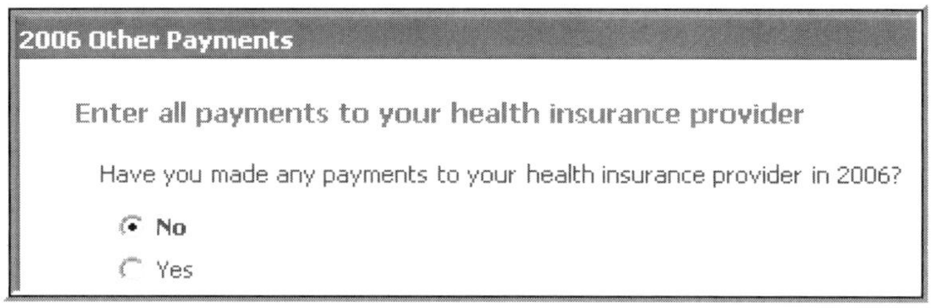

Click **Finish**, then click **Continue**

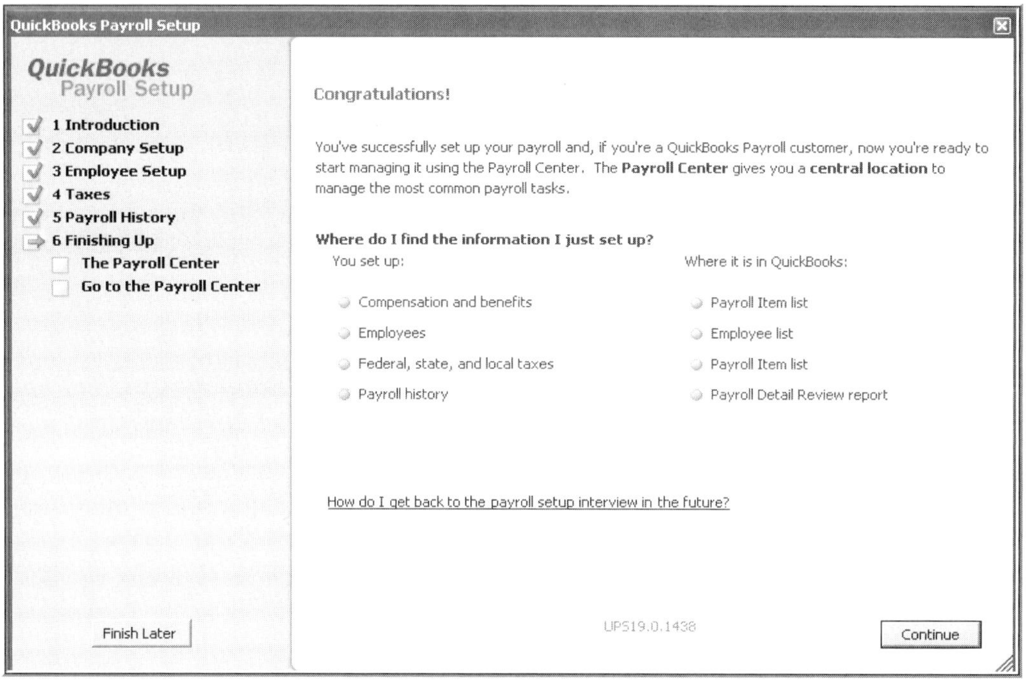

Click **Continue**

- You will see an example of QuickBooks Payroll Center for those companies using QuickBooks Payroll services

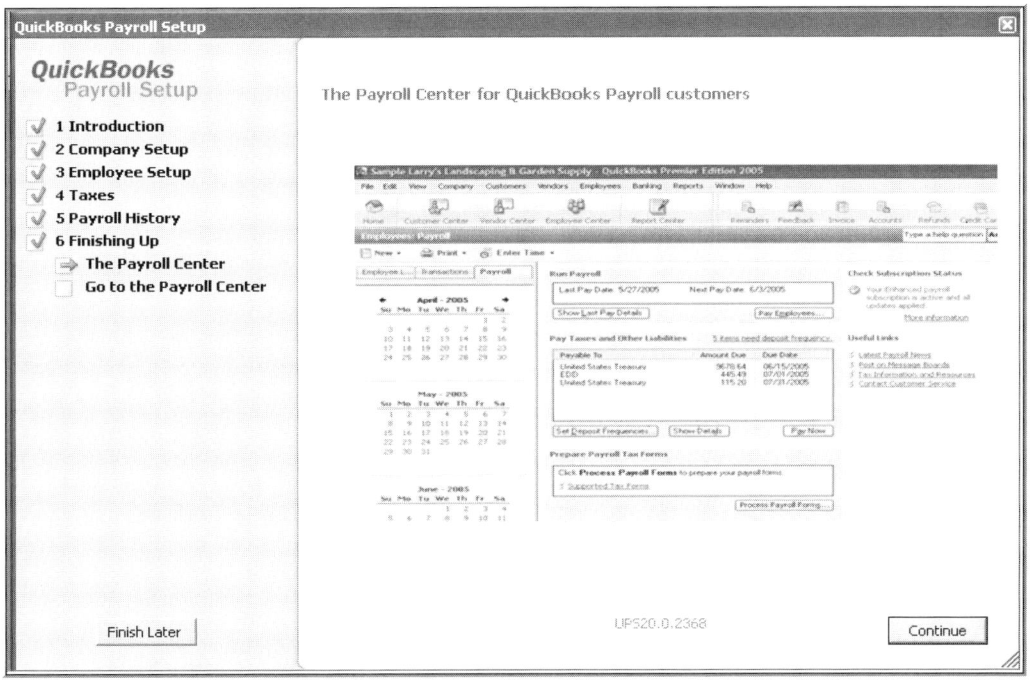

Click **Continue**

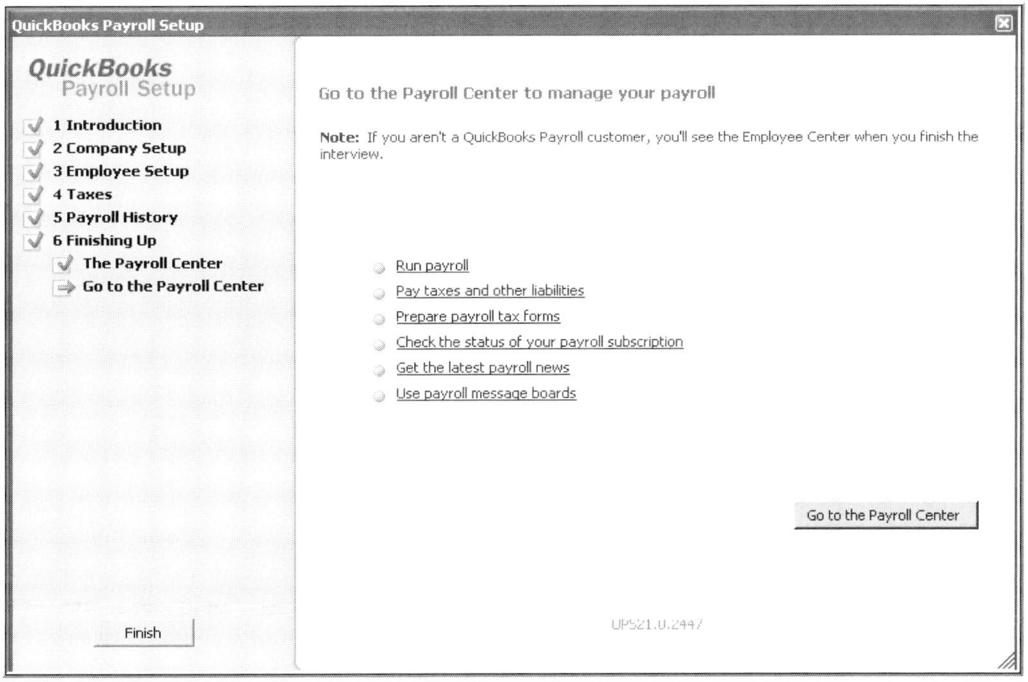

Click **Finish** to end the Payroll Setup Interview

PRINT THE PAYROLL ITEM LISTING

To verify the payroll items used and the information regarding the employees entered, it is wise to print a listing of the Payroll Items and the Employees Contact List. There are also reports available to print information regarding the employees withholding and paid time off.

Print the **Payroll Item Listing** for January 1, 2006

Click **Report Center** at the top of the Home Page
Click **Lists**
Click **Payroll Item Listing**
Click **No** on the Payroll Services screen
Print the report in landscape orientation; and, if necessary, fit to one-page wide
Close the report and the Report Center

ADJUSTING ENTRIES

When the EasyStep Interview is completed, all existing balances are placed into the Uncategorized Income and Uncategorized Expenses accounts so that the amounts listed will not be interpreted as income or expenses for the current period. This adjustment transfers the amount of income and expenses recorded prior to the current period into the owner's capital account. In actual practice this adjustment would be made at the completion of the EasyStep Interview. In traditional accounting, Income is credited to the owner's capital account and expenses are debited. The same process is used in recording a Journal entry in QuickBooks.

MEMO
DATE: January 1, 2006

Make the adjusting entry to transfer Uncategorized Income and Uncategorized Expenses to Your Name, Capital.

Transfer the Uncategorized Income and Expenses to the owner's capital account

Click **Chart of Accounts** in the Company Section of the Home Page
Double-click on the account **Uncategorized Income**, enter the to and from dates as **01/01/06**, tab to generate the report, note the amount of Uncategorized Income **$2,950.00**

Your Name Movies, Etc.
Account QuickReport
January 1, 2006

Type	Date	Num	Name	Memo	Split	Amount
Uncategorized Income						
Invoice	01/01/2006		Gorst, George	Opening balance	Accounts Receivable	500.00
Invoice	01/01/2006		Morgan, Elena	Opening balance	Accounts Receivable	800.00
Invoice	01/01/2006		Nakamura Day Care Center	Opening balance	Accounts Receivable	1,500.00
Invoice	01/01/2006		Walsh, Bob	Opening balance	Accounts Receivable	150.00
Total Uncategorized Income						2,950.00
TOTAL						**2,950.00**

Close the QuickReport
Repeat the steps given to determine the balance of the Uncategorized Expenses account

Your Name Movies, Etc.
Account QuickReport
January 1, 2006

Type	Date	Num	Name	Memo	Split	Amount
Uncategorized Expenses						
Bill	01/01/2006		DVD Supplies	Opening balance	Accounts Payable	3,000.00
Bill	01/01/2006		Disks Galore	Opening balance	Accounts Payable	2,000.00
Total Uncategorized Expenses						5,000.00
TOTAL						**5,000.00**

Close the QuickReport
Click the **Activities** button at the bottom of the Chart of Accounts, click **Make General Journal Entries**
Enter the date **01/01/06**
Tab to or click **Account**, click the drop-down list arrow, click **Uncategorized Income**, tab to or click **Debit** enter **2950**, tab to or click **Account**, click the drop-down list arrow, click **Your Name, Capital**

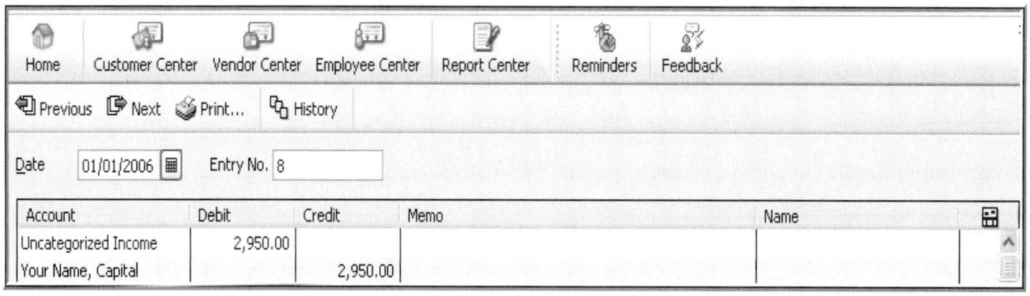

Click **Save & New**

Enter the adjustment to transfer the amount of **Uncategorized Expenses** to **Your Name, Capital**

- Remember, you will debit the Capital account and credit the Uncategorized Expenses account.

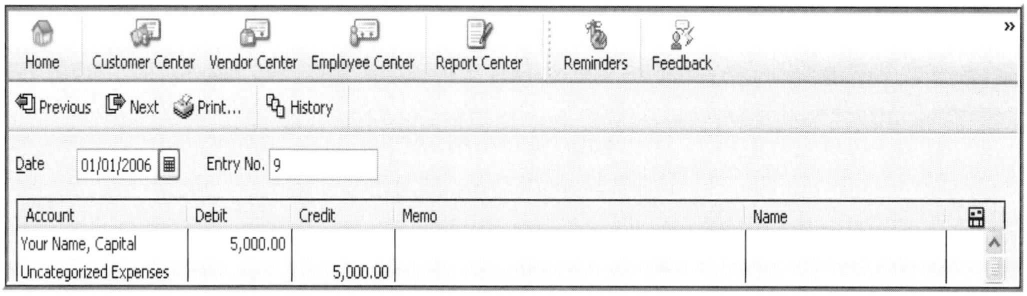

Click **Save & Close**

Close the Chart of Accounts

Print a Standard Balance Sheet for January 1, 2006 in Portrait orientation

BACKUP

As in previous chapters, a backup of the data file for Your Name Movies, Etc. should be made.

Back up the company file to **Movies.qbb** as instructed in earlier chapters and make a duplicate disk as instructed in Appendix A.

SUMMARY

In this chapter a company was created using the EasyStep Interview provided by QuickBooks Pro. Once the interview was complete, the Chart of Accounts/General Ledger was customized. Detailed information was given for customers and vendors. Preferences were customized. The Payroll Setup was completed, and employees were added. Adjusting entries were made.

END-OF-CHAPTER QUESTIONS

TRUE/FALSE

ANSWER THE FOLLOWING QUESTIONS IN THE SPACE PROVIDED BEFORE THE QUESTION NUMBER.

_____ 1. You must use the EasyStep Interview to add customers and vendors.

_____ 2. The EasyStep Interview is used to add employees and year-to-date earnings.

_____ 3. The Company Info screen in the EasyStep Interview is where the company name, address, and Tax ID number is entered.

_____ 4. Permanently removing the date prepared and time prepared from a balance sheet heading is done the first time you complete a balance sheet.

_____ 5. The start date is the date you select to give QuickBooks Pro the financial information for your company.

_____ 6. The EasyStep Interview allows you to have QuickBooks generate a chart of accounts.

_____ 7. When the EasyStep Interview is complete, the Uncategorized Expenses account contains a balance that reflects the total amount of all receivables accounts..

_____ 8. When using the EasyStep Interview to set up income and expenses, you must type in the name of every income and expense account you use.

_____ 9. The Item List is automatically generated in the Easy Step Interview.

_____ 10. Customer names, addresses, credit terms, and credit limits are entered after the EasyStep Interview.

MULTIPLE CHOICE

WRITE THE LETTER OF THE CORRECT ANSWER IN THE SPACE PROVIDED BEFORE THE QUESTION NUMBER.

_____ 1. Send forms preferences contain default text for business documents sent by ___.
A. Fax
B. E-mail
C. Fed-Ex
D. All of the above

_____ 2. Adjusting entries that must be made after the company setup are ___.
A. Close Uncategorized Income to Capital
B. Close Uncategorized Expenses to Capital
C. Both of the above
D. None of the above

_____ 3. When creating the employee list, you use the ___.
A. Payroll Setup Interview
B. Employee File
C. Employee Roster
D. Payroll Menu

_____ 4. The EasyStep Interview is accessed on the ___.
A. File menu
B. QuickBooks Company Preferences screen
C. Activities menu
D. all of the above

_____ 5. In order to create paychecks manually, you must go through the __ to designate this choice.
A. Payroll menu
B. Help menu
C. EasyStep Interview
D. Company Configuration

_____ 6. The Company File uses a _____ extension as part of the name
A. .qbb
B. .qbi
C. .qbp
D. .qbw

_____ 7. When an __ account is created, you must provide an opening balance.
A. Income
B. Expense
C. Asset
D. Posting

_____ 8. Select to display employee names by last name on the ___.
A. Payroll & Employees Preferences
B. Employee List
C. Employee Center
D. none of the above

_____ 9. Employee deductions for medical and dental insurance may be selected ___.
A. during the EasyStep Interview
B. during the Payroll Setup Interview
C. by clicking the Reports button at the bottom of the employee list
D. on the Employee Menu

_____ 10. Sales tax is listed on the ___..
A. Vendor List
B. Company List
C. Banking List
D. Item List

FILL-IN

IN THE SPACE PROVIDED, WRITE THE ANSWER THAT MOST APPROPRIATELY COMPLETES THE SENTENCE.

1. The asset account used for Inventory sales items is ____________.

2. In the Chart of Accounts, only ____________ accounts have opening balances.

3. Accounts that are listed individually but are grouped together under a main account are called ____________.

4. ____________ Preferences warns you of duplicate check numbers

5. The ____________ section of the Payroll Setup Interview allows information for earnings, withholding, and payroll liabilities to be entered for the year-to-date.

SHORT ESSAY

List the six sections in the Payroll Setup and describe the purpose of each section.

____

____

____

____

NAME______________________

TRANSMITTAL

▶ CHAPTER 9: YOUR NAME MOVIES, ETC.

Attach the following documents and reports:

Item Listing
Customer:Job List
Vendor List
Account Listing
Payroll Information Summary, Yvonne Benson
Payroll Information Summary, Jaime Hernandez
Payroll History Summary, Yvonne Benson
Payroll History Summary, Jaime Hernandez
Payroll Item Listing
Balance Sheet, January 1, 2006

END-OF-CHAPTER PROBLEM

YOUR NAME COFFEE

Your Name Coffee is a fictitious company that sells coffee and pastries. You also provide catering service for meetings and lunches. The company is located in San Francisco, California, and is a sole proprietorship owned by you. You are involved in all aspects of the business. There is one full-time employee who is paid a salary Ms. Alexis Toms, who manages the store, is responsible for the all the employees, and keeps the books. There is one full-time hourly employee, who works in the shop and provides the catering service, Sharon Akbar.

CREATE A NEW COMPANY

► Use the following information to complete the EasyStep Interview for Your Name Coffee.

Your Name Coffee *(Use your actual name)* is used for both the Company Name and the Legal Name
Federal Tax ID 45-6221346
Address: 550 Powell Street, San Francisco, CA 94102
Phone: 415-555-4646; Fax: 415-555-6464
E-mail: YourNameCoffee@info.com
Web: www.YourNameCoffee.com
Do not use passwords
File Name: YourNameCoffee.qbw
Type of business: Retail
Record each sale individually, do charge sales tax
Do not sell online
Do use sales receipts and invoices (do not use progress invoicing)
Do accept credit cards and debit cards
Do not use estimates, statements, or track time
Do track bills
Inventory: Yes
Employees: Yes, W-2 Employees
Use QuickBooks to set up the chart of Accounts (Accept all the accounts provided by QuickBooks. They will be edited later.)
Start Date: 01/01/2006
Bank account name: Checking; account number 123-654-98755; opened before 01/01/2006; last bank statement 12/31/2005; ending balance $35,871

COMPANY INFORMATION

► Verify the company information. Make sure the Federal Employer Identification number is 45-6221346, First Month in Tax and Fiscal Year: January, Income Tax form: None

ITEMS LIST

► Add the service item and any required account

SERVICE ITEM	
Type	Service
Item Name	Catering
Description	Catering
Rate	$50 per hour
Tax Code	Non-taxable
Account	Catering
Subaccount of	Sales
Account Description	Catering Sales

► Add the inventory items and any required accounts

INVENTORY ITEMS		
Type	Inventory Part	Inventory Part
Item Name	Coffee	Pastry
Purchase Description	Coffee	Pastry
Cost	0.00	0.00
COGS Account	Cost of Goods Sold	Cost of Goods Sold
Preferred Vendor		
Sales Description	Coffee	Pastry
Sales Price	0.00	0.00
Tax Code	Tax	Tax
Income Account	Coffee	Pastry
Subaccount Of	Sales	Sales
Account Description	Coffee Sales	Pastry Sales
Asset Account	Inventory Asset	Inventory Asset
Reorder Point	100	100
On-Hand	1,500	1,750
Total Value	12,000	1,750
AS Of	01/01/06	01/01/06

► Delete the following sales items: Service Item, Inventory Item 1, Inventory item 2, Consignment Item, and Non-Inventory Item

COMPLETE SALES TAX INFORMATION

► Edit the State Sales Tax item. The name and description should be **CA State Sales Tax** The rate is 7.25% and is paid to the State Board of Equalization, 7800 State Street, Sacramento, CA 94267

► Print the Item List in Landscape orientation. Modify the Header so the Date Prepared and Time Prepared are not shown.

CUSTOMER LIST

► Use the following information to add customers. Remember to use Jones, Sandra, Inc. as the customer name and use Sandra Jones, Inc. in the Bill To address.

CUSTOMER LIST		
Customer Name	Jones, Sandra, Inc.	Training, Inc.
Opening Balance	1,500.00	5,245.00
As Of	01/01/2006	01/01/2006
Company Name	Sandra Jones, Inc.	Training, Inc.
Address	785 Mason Street	490 Harvard Street
City, State Zip	San Francisco, CA 94102	San Francisco, CA 94102
Phone	415-555-1248	415-555-8762
Terms	Net 30	Net 30
Tax Code	Tax	Tax
Tax Item	CA State Sales Tax	CA State Sales Tax
Credit Limit	2,000.00	8,000.00

► Print the Customer:Job List in Portrait orientation. (Since you are printing from the Customer Center, you will have the date and time prepared as the header. Your date and time may not be the same as the one shown in the answer key.)

VENDOR LIST

► Use the following Vendor List as you add individual vendors

VENDOR LIST		
Vendor Name	Coffee Deluxe	Pastry Delights
Opening Balance	1,000.00	$500
As Of	01/01/2006	01/01/2006
Address	195 N. Market Street	701 7th Street
City, State Zip	San Francisco, CA 94103	San Francisco, CA 94104
Contact Person	Ron Richards	Katie Collins
Phone	415-555-3614	415-555-8712
Fax	415-555-4163	415-555-2178
Terms	2% 10, Net 30	2% 10, Net 30
Credit Limit	3,000.00	2,500.00

► Use the following information to add vendors who receive tax and withholding payments. There are no credit terms.

VENDOR LIST			
Vendor Name	Employment Development Department	Hill Street Bank	Insurance Organization of California
Company Name	Employment Development Department	Hill Street Bank	Insurance Organization of California
Address	10327 Washington Street	205 Hill Street	20951 Oakmont Avenue
City, State Zip	San Francisco, CA 94107	San Francisco, CA 94104	San Francisco, CA 94103
Phone	415-555-5248	415-555-9781	415-555-2347
Fax	415-555-8425	415-555-1879	415-555-7432

► Print the Vendor List in Portrait orientation. (Since you are printing from the Vendor Center, you will have the date and time prepared as the header. Your date and time may not be the same as the one shown in the answer key.)

CHART OF ACCOUNTS

► Set up the following Balance Sheet accounts and balances. The Opening Balance date is **01/01/2006**.

CHART OF ACCOUNTS			
Account Type	**Account Name**	**Sub-Account of**	**Opening Balance**
Long-Term Liability	Store Fixtures Loan		$2,000.00
Other Current Asset	Prepaid Insurance		$1,200.00
Other Current Asset	Office Supplies		$950.00
Other Current Asset	Sales Supplies		$1,800.00
Fixed Asset	Store Fixtures		
Fixed Asset	Store Fixtures Original Cost	Store Fixtures	$18,000
Fixed Asset	Store Fixtures Depreciation	Store Fixtures	$-1,800
Expense	Store Supplies		
Equity	Your Name, Investment	Opening Bal Equity	$35,000
Equity	Your Name, Withdrawals	Opening Bal Equity	

► Customize the Chart of Accounts provided by QuickBooks.

- Delete: Inventory on Consignment, Sales: Consignment Sales, Sales: Shipping and Handling, Franchise Fees, Travel & Ent (including subaccounts, which must be deleted before Travel & Ent can be deleted)
- Change Name: Equity Account: Opening Bal Equity to **Your Name, Capital** (Your Name Investment and Your Name, Withdrawals will now be subaccounts of Your Name Capital.)
- Make Inactive: Merchant Fees

► Print an Account Listing in Landscape orientation. Use the Report Center to print a List report for Account Listing. Remove the Date and Time Prepared from the Header.

CUSTOMIZE PREFERENCES

► Make the following changes to Preferences.

- Checking Preferences: Company Preferences—Select Default Accounts for Payroll and Pay Payroll Taxes to Checking; My Preferences—Select Default Accounts for Open the Write Checks, Open the Pay Bills, Open the Pay Sales Tax, and Open the Make Deposits to Checking
- Payroll & Employees: Company Preferences—Display Employee List by Last Name
- Reports & Graphs: My Preferences—Refresh reports automatically
- Reports & Graphs: Company Preferences—modify the report Format for the Header/Footer to remove the Date Prepared, Time Prepared, and Report Basis from reports
- Sales Tax: Company Preferences—Most common sales tax is CA State Tax

PAYROLL SETUP

► Prior to completing the Payroll Setup Interview, select a **Manual** payroll option

PAYROLL SETUP INTERVIEW

► Complete the **Company** portion of the Payroll Setup Interview.

- Payroll List Items for Wages, Tips, and Taxable Fringe Benefits: Salary, Hourly Wage, and Overtime (If any other items appear on the list, delete them.)
- Insurance Benefits: Health Insurance, Dental Insurance (both are fully paid by the employee after taxes have been deducted)
- Retirement Benefits: None
- Paid Time Off: Sick Time and Vacation Time
- Other Payments and Deductions: None

► Use the following information to complete the **Employee** portion of the Payroll Setup Interview. Print a Summary Report for each employee

- When you print the Summary for each employee, check the beginning date for accruing sick and vacation time. It should show the Hire date; however, if it does not, change it by editing the employee(s) in the Employee Center after the Payroll Setup Interview is complete.

EMPLOYEES January 1, 2006 Alexis Toms and Sharon Akbar		
Name	Alexis Toms	Sharon Akbar
Status	Active	Active
Street Address	9077 Harvard Avenue	1808 17th Street
City, State Zip	San Francisco, CA 94101	San Francisco, CA 94103
Phone	415-555-7801	415-555-7364
Employee Tax Type	Regular	Regular
Social Security No.	100-55-5201	100-55-9107
Hire Date	02/19/2001	06/30/2005
Birth Date	09/29/1975	07/17/1980
Gender	Female	Female
Pay Period	Monthly	Monthly
Salary	$21,000 per year	$9.50 per hour $14.25 per 1.5 overtime $19.00 per 2 x overtime
Health Insurance	$35 per month, annual maximum $420	$25 per month, annual maximum $300
Dental Insurance	$10 per month, annual maximum $120	$10 per month, annual maximum $120
Sick Time Earns	40:00 per year	40:00 per year
Unused Hours	Have an accrual limit	Have an accrual limit
Maximum Hours	120:00	120:00
Earns	Time off currently	Time off currently
Hours Available as of 01/01/06	30:00	20:00
Begin Accruing Sick Time On	02/19/2001	06/30/2005
Vacation Time Earns	40:00 per year	40:00 per year
Unused Hours	Have an accrual limit	Have an accrual limit
Maximum Hours	120:00	120:00
Earns	Time off currently	Time off currently
Hours Available as of 01/01/06	40:00	20:00
Begin Accruing Time On	02/19/2001	06/30/2005
State Subject to Withholding	CA	CA
State Where Employee	CA	CA

EMPLOYEES January 1, 2006 Alexis Toms and Sharon Akbar		
Works		
Live or Work in Another State in 2006	No	No
Federal Filing Status	Single	Married
Allowances	0	2
Subject to	Medicare Social Security Federal Unemployment	Medicare Social Security Federal Unemployment
State Filing Status	Single	Married (2 incomes)
Standard Deductions	0	2
Subject to	CA-Unemployment CA-Employment Training Tax CA-Disability	CA-Unemployment CA-Employment Training Tax CA-Disability
Local Taxes	No	No

► Complete the **Taxes** section of the Payroll Setup Interview.

- Federal Payroll Taxes—Payee United States Treasury
- State Payroll Taxes—Payee: Employee Development Department; California EDD Employer Account 123-1234-4; California-Unemployment Company Rate: 4%; CA-Employment Training Tax Company Rate: 0.1%; CA-Disability Employee Rate: 1.08%

► Complete the **Payroll History** section of the Payroll Setup Interview. Print a Summary Report for each employee

PAYROLL HISTORY		
	Alexis Toms	**Sharon Akbar**
Paid	Yes	Yes
Paycheck Date	01/01/06	01/01/06
Payroll Date From	12/01/05	12/31/05
Payroll Date To	12/31/05	12/31/05
Report Hours	No	No
EARNINGS		
Salary/Hourly Wages	$1,750.00	$1,520.00
WITHHOLDING		
Withholding Dental	10.00	10.00
Withholding Health	35.00	35.00
Federal Withholding	325.00	307.00
Medicare Employee	32.25	37.41
Social Security Employee	148.00	139.50
CA-Disability	24.00	22.86
CA-Income Tax	98.00	93.20
COMPANY TAXES		
Federal Unemployment	19.00	18.64
Medicare Company	32.25	37.41
Social Security Company	148.00	139.50
CA-Unemployment	92.00	87
CA-Employee Training Tax	2.50	2.42

► No payroll tax payments, dental insurance payments, or health insurance payments were made in 2006

► After completing the Payroll Setup, print the Payroll Item Listing in Landscape orientation using the Report menu or Report Center

MAKE ADJUSTMENTS AND PRINT THE BALANCE SHEET

► Record the adjusting entry to transfer Uncategorized Income and Uncategorized Expenses to Your Name, Capital

► Print the Balance Sheet for January 1, 2006 in Portrait orientation

BACKUP

► Backup your company file to **Coffee Ch 9.qbb**

NAME________________________

TRANSMITTAL

CHAPTER 9: YOUR NAME COFFEE

Attach the following documents and reports:

Item Listing
Customer: Job List
Vendor List
Account Listing
Payroll Information Summary, Sharon Akbar
Payroll Information Summary, Alexis Toms
Payroll History Summary, Sharon Akbar
Payroll History Summary, Alexis Toms
Payroll Item Listing
Balance Sheet, January 1, 2006

COMPREHENSIVE PRACTICE SET: YOUR NAME BOOKS

The following is a comprehensive practice set combining all the elements of QuickBooks studied throughout the text. In this practice set you will set up a company and keep the books for January 2007. You will use the EasyStep Interview to create Your Name Books. Once the company has been created, detailed information will be provided for items, customers, vendors, and employees. The Payroll Setup Interview will be completed. Adjustments will be made to accounts and various items, and transactions will be recorded.

During the month, new customers, vendors, and employees will be added. When entering transactions, you are responsible for any memos you wish to include in transactions. Unless otherwise specified, the terms for each sale or bill will be the term specified on the Customer or Vendor List. The Customer Message is usually *Thank you for your business*. However, any other message that is appropriate may be used. If a customer's order exceeds the established credit limit, accept the order and process it. If the terms allow a discount for a customer, make sure to apply the discount if payment is received in time for the customer to take the discount. Remember, the discount period starts with the date of the invoice. If an invoice or bill date is not provided, use the transaction date to begin the discount period. Use Sales Discounts as the discount account. If a customer has a credit and has a balance on the account, apply the credit to the invoice used for the sale. If there is no balance for a customer and a return is made, issue a credit memo and a refund check. Always pay bills in time to take advantage of purchase discounts.

Invoices, purchase orders, and other similar items should be printed without lines around each field. Most reports will be printed in Portrait orientation; however, if the report (such as the Journal) will fit across the page using Landscape orientation, use Landscape. Whenever possible, adjust the column widths so that reports fit on one-page wide without selecting Fit report to one page wide.

YOUR NAME BOOKS

Your Name Books is a fictitious company that provides a typing service and sells books and educational supplies. Your Name Books is located in Sacramento, California, and is a sole proprietorship owned by you. You do all the purchasing and are involved in all aspects of the business. Your Name Books has one full-time employee who is paid a salary, Ms. Aimee Nelson, who manages the store, is responsible for the all the employees, and keeps the books.

Caitlin Ellis is a full-time hourly employee who works in the shop. The store is currently advertising for a part-time employee who will provide word processing/typing services.

CREATE A NEW COMPANY

► Use the following information to complete the EasyStep Interview for Your Name Books

- Company and Legal Name: Your Name Books (*Key in your actual name*)
- Federal Tax ID: 466-52-1446
- Address: 1055 Front Street, Sacramento, CA 95814.
- Telephone: 916-555-9876; Fax: 916-555-6789
- E-mail: YourNameBooks@reader.com
- Web: www.YourNameBooks.com
- Do not use Passwords
- File Name: Books.qbw
- Type of Business: Retail
- Sell Both Services and Products
- Record each sale individually, do charge sales tax
- Do not sell online
- Do use sales receipts and invoices (do not use progress invoicing)
- Do accept credit cards and debit cards
- Do not use estimates, statements, or track time
- Do track bills
- Inventory: Yes
- Employees: Yes, W-2 Employees
- Use QuickBooks to set up the Chart of Accounts
- Start Date: 01/01/2007
- Bank account name Checking, account number 123-456-78910, opened before 01/01/2007. Last bank statement 12/31/2006, ending balance 35,870.25
- First Month in Tax and Fiscal Year: January
- Income Tax form: None

COMPLETE THE COMPANY INFORMATION

► Add the Federal Employer Identification number 46-6521146 to the Company Information

CHANGE PREFERENCES

► Change the following preferences:

- Checking Preferences: My Preferences—Select Default Accounts to use should be Checking for Open Write Checks, Open Pay Bills, Open Pay Sales Tax, and Open Make Deposits; Company Preferences— Select Default Accounts to use should be Checking for Create Paychecks and Pay Payroll Liabilities
- Payroll & Employees: Company Preferences—Display Employee List by Last Name
- Reports & Graphs: My Preferences—Refresh reports automatically, Company Preferences—modify the report Format for the Header/Footer to remove the Date Prepared, Time Prepared, and Report Basis from reports
- Sales Tax: Company Preferences—Most common sales tax is CA State Tax

CUSTOMER LIST

► Use the following Customer List to add customers. Those customers who are individuals should be added last name first for Customer:Job but first name then last name on the Bill to address. *Note:* Remember that the only time an opening balance may be entered is when the customer is created. An opening balance is not eligible for a discount. The terms given are for future sales to a customer.

CUSTOMER LIST

Customer Name	**Complete Training, Inc.**	**Newton, Lora**	**Nichols, Violet**	**Sacramento Schools**	**Simpson, Gene**	**Watson, Charles**
Opening Balance	$1,450	$100	$0.00	$1,000	$0.00	$350
As Of	01/01/07	01/01/07	01/01/07	01/01/07	01/01/07	01/01/07
Address	785 Harvard Street	8025 Richmond Street	6784 Front Street	1085 2nd Street	158 16th Street	253 Mason Street
City, State, Zip	Sacramento, CA 95814	Sacramento, CA 95814	Sacramento, CA 95814	Sacramento, CA 95814	Sacramento, CA 95814	Sacramento, CA 95814
Contact	Sharon Jackson	Lora Newton	Violet Nichols	Alicia Vincent	Dr. Gene Simpson	Charles Watson
Telephone	916-555-8762	916-555-8961	916-555-6487	916-555-1235	916-555-3693	916-555-2264
Fax	916-555-2678					
Terms	Net 30	2% 10 Net 30	Net 30	2% 10 Net 30	Net 30	Net 30
Tax Code	Yes	Yes	Yes	Yes	Yes	Yes
Tax Item	CA State Tax	CA State Tax	CA State Tax	CA State Tax	CA State Tax	CA State Tax
Credit Limit	$1,500	$500	$100	$5,000	$100	$350

- Print a Customer List

VENDOR LIST

► Use the following Vendor Lists to add vendors that sell us merchandise and that are used for tax and withholding payments. *Note:* Remember that the only time an opening balance may be entered is when the customer is created. An opening balance is not eligible for a discount. The terms given are for future purchases from a vendor.

- Use the following list to add the vendors that sell merchandise to us:

VENDOR LIST			
Vendor Name	**Books & Texts Co.**	**Exotic Pens**	**Supplies Co.**
Opening Balance	$1,000	$500	$800
As Of	01/01/07	01/01/07	01/01/07
Address	559 4th Street	2785 Market Street	95 8th Street
City, State, Zip	Sacramento, CA 95814	San Francisco, CA 94103	Sacramento, CA 95814
Contact Person	Al Daruty	Dennis Johnson	Raymond Ahrens
Phone	916-555-2788	415-555-3224	916-555-5759
Fax	916-555-8872	415-555-4223	916-555-9575
Terms	2% 10, Net 30	2% 10, Net 30	2% 10, Net 30
Credit Limit	$15,000	$5,000	$15,000

- Use the following list to add the vendors that are used for tax and withholding payments:

VENDOR LIST			
Vendor Name	**Employment Development Department**	**State Bank**	**Medical Ins., Inc.**
Address	1037 California Street	102 8th Street	20865 Oak Street
City, State, Zip	Sacramento, CA 95814	Sacramento, CA 95814	San Francisco, CA 94101
Phone	916-555-8877	916-555-9889	415-555-4646
Fax	916-555-7788	916-555-9988	415-555-6464

- Print a Vendor List

ITEMS LIST

► Create the Items List

- There is only one service item for Your Name Books: Item Name: WP/Typing, Sales Description: Word Processing/Typing Service, Price: 0.00, not Taxable, Income Account: Word Processing/Typing Service Income and is a subaccount of Sales
- There are no subcontracted items, non-inventory parts, or other charges.
- Use the following Inventory Items List and balances to add inventory items.

INVENTORY ITEMS					
Item Name	**Textbooks**	**Paperback Books**	**Paper**	**Stationery**	**Pens, etc.**
Purchase Description	Textbooks	Paperback Books	Paper Supplies	Stationery	Pens, etc.
Cost	0.00	0.00	0.00	0.00	0.00
COGS Account	Cost of Goods Sold	Cost of Goods Sold	Cost of Goods Sold	Cost of Goods Sold	Cost of Goods Sold
Preferred Vendor	Books & Texts Co.	Books & Texts Co.	Supplies Co.	Supplies Co.	Exotic Pens
Sales Description	Textbooks	Paperback Books	Paper Supplies	Stationery	Pens, etc.
Sales Price	0.00	0.00	0.00	0.00	0.00
Tax Code	Tax	Tax	Tax	Tax	Tax
Income Account	Book Sales (Subaccount of Sales)	Book Sales (Subaccount of Sales)	Supplies Sales (Subaccount of Sales)	Supplies Sales (Subaccount of Sales)	Supplies Sales (Subaccount of Sales)
Asset Account	Inventory Asset	Inventory Asset	Inventory Asset	Inventory Asset	Inventory Asset
Reorder Point	100	30	100	25	50
Quantity on Hand	2,000	45	200	30	50
Value	10,000	180	3,000	150	100

- Delete the following sales items: Service Item, Inventory Item 1, Inventory Item 2, Consignment Item, and Non-Inventory Item
- Enter the amount of sales tax and the sales tax agency information for State Sales Tax on the Item List: CA State Sales Tax: A tax rate of 7.25% paid to State Board of Equalization, 7800 State Street, Sacramento, CA 94267
- Print an Item Listing (If necessary use Fit to 1-page wide)

CHART OF ACCOUNTS

► Use the following chart of accounts and balances to customize Your Name Books chart of accounts.

- Add additional accounts and balances for balance sheet accounts.
- Chart Abbreviations for account types: C.A.=Current Asset, F.A.=Fixed Asset; C.L.=Current Liability; Long Term L.=Long Term Liability; COGS=Cost of Goods Sold.
- *** means that QuickBooks will enter the account balance
- Change account names where appropriate, make inactive or delete any unused accounts.
- Print an Account Listing in Landscape orientation when finished.

YOUR NAME BOOKS
CHART OF ACCOUNTS

ACCOUNT	TYPE	BALANCE	ACCOUNT	TYPE
Checking (01/01/07)	Bank	35,870.25	Fire Insurance	Expense
Accounts Receivable	Accts. Rec.	***	Health Insurance	Expense
Inventory Asset	Other C.A	***	Liability Insurance	Expense
Office Supplies	Other C.A.	450.00	Interest Expense	Expense
Prepaid Insurance	Other C.A.	1,200.00	Marketing and Advertising	Expense
Sales Supplies	Other C.A.	900.00	Miscellaneous	Expense
Undeposited Funds	Other C.A.	0.00	Office Expenses	Expense
Store Equipment	F.A.	6,000.00	Postage and Delivery	Expense
Store Equipment: Depreciation	F.A.	0.00	Printing and Reproduction	Expense
Store Equipment: Original Cost	F.A.	6,000.00	Payroll Expenses	Expense
Store Fixtures	F.A.	10,000.00	Professional Fees	Expense
Store Fixtures: Depreciation	F.A.	0.00	Accounting	Expense
Store Fixtures: Original Cost	F.A.	10,000.00	Legal Fees	Expense
Accounts Payable	Acct. Pay.	***	Rent	Expense
MasterCard (01/31/07)	Credit Card	50.00	Repairs	Expense
Payroll Liabilities	Other C.L.	0.00	Building Repairs	Expense
Sales Tax Payable	Other C.L.	0.00	Computer Repairs	Expense
Store Equipment Loan	Long Term L.	1,500.00	Equipment Repairs	Expense
Store Fixtures Loan	Long Term L.	4,500.00	Sales Discounts	Expense
Retained Earnings	Equity	***	Supplies	Expense
Your Name, Capital	Equity	***	Office	Expense
Your Name, Drawing	Equity	0.00	Sales	Expense
Your Name, Investment	Equity	10,000.00	Taxes	Expense
Purchases Discounts	Income		Federal	Expense
Sales and Services	Income		Local	Expense
Book Sales	Income		State	Expense
Supplies Sales	Income		Telephone	Expense
Word Processing/Typing Service	Income		Uncategorized Expenses	Expense
Uncategorized Income	Income		Utilities	Expense
Cost of Goods Sold	COGS		Gas and Electric	Expense
Merchandise Discounts	COGS		Water	Expense
Bank Service Charges	Expense		Interest Income	Other Income
Depreciation Expense	Expense		Other Income	Other Income
Dues and Subscriptions	Expense		Other Expenses	Other Expense
Equipment Rental	Expense			
Insurance Expense	Expense			
Disability Insurance	Expense			

PAYROLL

- ▶ Select Manual as the payroll option
- ▶ Complete the Payroll Setup
- o Complete the Company portion of the setup
    - Payroll List Items for Wages, Tips, and Taxable Fringe Benefits: Salary, Hourly Wage and Overtime
    - Insurance Benefits: Health Insurance, Dental Insurance Both are fully paid by the employee after taxes have been deducted
    - Retirement Benefits: None
    - Paid Time Off: Sick Time and Vacation Time
    - Other Payments and Deductions: None
- o Use the Employee List to enter the employees and the appropriate information

EMPLOYEE LIST Caitlin Ellis and Aimee Nelson		
Name	Caitlin Ellis	Aimee Nelson
Status	Active	Active
Street Address	833 Oak Avenue	1777 Watt Avenue
City, State Zip	Sacramento, CA 95814	Sacramento, CA 95814
Phone	916-555-7862	916-555-1222
Employee Tax Type	Regular	Regular
Social Security No.	100-55-6886	100-55-5244
Hire Date	04/03/96	02/17/95
Birth Date	12/07/70	11/28/49
Gender	Female	Female
Pay Period	Monthly	Monthly
Salary	$10.00 per hour $15.00 per 1.5 overtime $20.00 per 2 x overtime	$26,000 per year
Health Insurance	$20 per month, annual maximum $300	$30 per month, annual maximum $600
Dental Insurance	$20 per month, annual maximum $360	$30 per month, annual maximum $360
Sick Time Earns	40:00 per year	40:00 per year
Unused Hours	Have an accrual limit	Have an accrual limit
Maximum Hours	120:00	120:00
Earns	Time off currently	Time off currently

EMPLOYEE LIST Caitlin Ellis and Aimee Nelson		
Hours Available as of 01/01/07	40:00	40:00
Begin Accruing Time On	04/03/96	02/17/95
Vacation Time Earns	40:00 per year	40:00 per year
Unused Hours	Have an accrual limit	Have an accrual limit
Maximum Hours	120:00	120:00
Earns	Time off currently	Time off currently
Hours Available as of 01/01/07	40:00	40:00
Begin Accruing Time On	04/03/96	02/17/95
Direct Deposit	No	No
State Subject to Withholding	CA	CA
State Where Employee Works	CA	CA
Live or Work in Another State in 2007	No	No
Federal Filing Status	Married	Single
Allowances	1	0
Subject to	Medicare Social Security Federal Unemployment	Medicare Social Security Federal Unemployment
State Filing Status	Married (one income)	Single
Standard Deductions	1	0
Subject to	CA-Unemployment CA-Employment Training Tax CA-Disability	CA-Unemployment CA-Employment Training Tax CA-Disability
Local Taxes	No	No

- Print the Summary for each employee

o Enter Payroll Tax information

- The Payee for Federal Payroll taxes is **United States Treasury**
- The Payee for California taxes is **Employment Development Department**, the Employer Account is **999-9999-9**, the California-Unemployment Company Rate is **4%**, the rate for CA-Employment Training Tax Company Rate is 0.1% and the rate for CA-Disability Employee Rate is 1.08%

o Enter the Payroll History

PAYROLL HISTORY Caitlin Ellis and Aimee Nelson		
	Caitlin Ellis	**Aimee Nelson**
Paid	Yes	Yes
Paycheck Date	01/01/07	01/01/07
Payroll Date From	12/31/06	12/01/06
Payroll Date To	12/31/06	12/31/06
Report Hours	No	No
	EARNINGS	
Salary/Hourly Wages	$1,600.00	$2,166.66
	WITHHOLDING	
Withholding Dental	20.00	30.00
Withholding Health	20.00	30.00
Federal Withholding	126.00	292.00
Medicare Employee	23.20	31.42
Social Security Employee	97.53	134.33
CA-Disability	8.00	10.00
CA-Income Tax	56.05	63.30
	COMPANY TAXES	
Federal Unemployment	9.33	9.33
Medicare Company	23.20	31.42
Social Security Company	97.53	134.33
CA-Unemployment	46.67	46.67
CA-Employee Training Tax	2.58	2.50

- There are no payroll taxes, dental or medical payments for 2007
- Print the Summary for each employee

MAKE ADJUSTMENTS

► Transfer the Uncategorized Income and Uncategorized Expenses to the owner's Your Name account

o Print a Balance Sheet as of January 1, 2007.

► Customize the Invoice: Use a duplicate of a Product Invoice. Use Layout Designer to make the area for the company name wide enough for your name. Customize Sales Receipts, and Purchase Orders so they have the same format as the invoice. Finally, duplicate and customize a Return Receipt (used for Credit Memos). On the Header tab, replace the Default Title of Return Receipt with Credit Memo. Then, use the Layout Designer to widen the area for the company name.

ENTER TRANSACTIONS

- ► Print invoices, sales receipts, purchase orders, checks, and other items as they are entered in the transactions. Use the product invoice for all invoices, voucher checks for payroll, and standard checks for all other checks. Create new items, accounts, customers, vendors, etc., as necessary. Refer to information given at the beginning of the problem for additional transaction details and information.
- ► Prepare an Inventory Stock Status by Item Report every five days as the last transaction of the day to see if anything needs to be ordered. If anything is indicated, order enough so you will have 10 more than the minimum number of items. (For example, if you needed to order textbooks and the minimum number on hand is 100, you would order enough books to have 110 on hand.) For this problem, the price per book ordered is $15 per textbook and $5 per paperback; pens are $2.50 each, paper is $2.00 per ream, and stationery is $4.00 per box.
- ► Full-time employees usually work 160 hours during a payroll period. Hourly employees working in excess of 160 hours in a pay period are paid overtime. Normally, there is a separate Payroll Checking account used when paying employees; however, this problem uses the regular checking account to pay employees.
- ► Check every five days to see if any bills are due and eligible for a discount. If any bills can be paid and a discount received, pay the bills; otherwise, wait for instructions to pay bills. Remember that an opening balance is not eligible for a discount.

January 1

► Add a new part-time hourly employee:

- o Kristin King
- o Social Security No. 100-55-3699
- o Gender Female
- o Birthday 1/3/76
- o Active Status
- o 1177 Florin Road, Sacramento, CA 95814
- o 916-555-7766
- o Pay Period Monthly; Hourly Regular Rate $6.50, 1.5 x Overtime $9.75, 2 x Overtime $13.00
- o Dental and Health Insurance: None
- o Sick and Vacation Hours Available 0, Sick and Vacation Hours Accrued 20 at the beginning of the year, Maximum Sick and Vacation Hours 40
- o Federal and State Filing Status: Single, 0 Allowance
- o State Subject to Withholding, State Worked, and State Lived is California
- o Subject to Medicare, Social Security, Federal Unemployment, CA Unemployment, CA Training Tax, and CA Disability taxes

January 2:

- Cash sale of one $40 textbook.
- Complete Training purchased 30 copies of a textbook on account for $40 each.
- Sold three paperback books at $6.99 each to a cash customer.
- Received Check No. 1096 from Lora Newton for $100 as payment in full on her account.
- Sold 25 pens on account at $8.99 each to Sacramento Schools for awards to students.
- Sold five textbooks at $39.99 each for the new quarter to a student using a Visa.
- Prepare and print an Inventory Stock Status by Item report to see if anything needs to be ordered.
- Prepare and print Purchase Orders for any merchandise that needs to be ordered.
- Check bills for discount eligibility between January 1-4. Pay any bills that qualify for a discount. (Opening balances do not qualify for an early payment discount.)

January 3:

- Received Check No. 915 for $350 from Charles Watson for the full amount due on his account.
- Sold five pens at $12.99 each to Lora Newton.
- Received payment of $1,450 from Complete Training, Inc., Check No. 7824.

January 4:

- Kristin typed a five-page paper for a student at the rate of $5 per page. Received Check No. 2951 for $25 as full payment.
- Sold two textbooks on account at $40 each to a new customer: Brian Scott, 478 Front Street, Sacramento, CA 95814, Phone: 916-555-6841, E-mail: bScott@email.com, Terms Net 10 (Do you need to add a new Standard Term for Net 10?), Credit Limit $100, Taxable.

January 5:

- Received the pens ordered from Exotic Pens with the bill.
- Sold five boxes of stationery at $10.99 per box to Violet Nichols.
- Sold five reams of paper at $4.99 per ream to Sacramento Schools.
- Prepare and print Stock Status by Item Inventory Report for January 1-5, 2007. Order any items indicated.
- Check bills for discount eligibility. Pay any bills that qualify for a discount between January 5-9.
- Deposit all cash, checks, and credit card payments received.

January 7:

- The nonprofit organization, State Schools, bought a classroom set of 30 computer training textbooks for $40.00 each. Add the new customer: State Schools, 451 State Street, Sacramento, CA 95814, Contact Allison Hernandez, 916-555-8787, Fax 916-555-7878, Terms Net 30, Taxable, Credit Limit $2000. Include a subtotal for the sale and apply a 10%

sales discount for a nonprofit organization. (Create any new sales items necessary.)

- Add a new sales item for Gift Ware, Purchase Description: Gift Ware, Cost: 0.00, COGS Account: Cost of Goods Sold, Preferred Vendor: Gift Gallery (125 Oak Street, Sacramento, CA 95814, Contact: Mary Ellen Morrison, 916-555-5384, Fax 916-555-4835, E-mail gifts@abc.com, Terms Net 30, Credit Limit $500, Sales Description: Gift Ware, Sales Price: 0.00, Taxable: Yes, Income Account: Supplies Sales, Asset Account: Inventory Asset, Reorder Point: 15, Quantity on Hand: 0, Value: 0.00,
- Order 15 gift items at $5.00 each from the Gift Gallery.

January 8:

- Sold ten reams of paper to Gene Simpson at $3.99 per ream.
- Received Check No. 10525 from Complete Training, Inc., $1,000 as partial payment on account.
- Lora Newton returned two pens purchased on January 3. She did not like the color. Apply the credit to the invoice and print after you apply the credit to the invoice.
- Paid Books & Texts Co. full amount owed on account. This is the opening balance for the vendor. Print Check No. 1 using Standard Checks.

January 10:

- Sold three pens at $14.95 each, two sets of stationery at $9.99 each, and three paperback books at $6.99 each to a cash customer.
- Kristin typed a 15-page report at $5.00 per page for Violet Nichols.
- Sold eight additional computer textbooks to Sacramento Schools at $40 each.
- Received Check No. 825 as payment from Sacramento Schools for the 01/02/07 transaction for $236.22, the full amount due, less discount.
- Deposit all cash, checks, and credit card receipts.
- Prepare Stock Status by Item Inventory Report for January 1-10, 2007. Order any items indicated. (If an item is marked to order but is on order, do not re-order the item.)
- Check bills for discount eligibility. Pay any bills that qualify for a discount between January 10-14. (Remember opening balances do not qualify for a discount.)

January 11:

- Sold ten paperback books at $6.99 each and two pens at $5.99 each to a customer using a Visa.
- Sold ten reams of paper to a cash customer at $4.99 each. Received Check No. 8106.

January 12:

- Received gift ware ordered from Gift Gallery. A bill was not included with the order.
- Sold one pen at $8.99 and a box of stationery at $9.99 to a cash customer.
- Kristin typed a one-page letter with an envelope for Charles Watson, $8.00. (Qty is 1.)

January 13:

- ▶ Received Check No. 1265 from Lora Newton in payment for full amount due, $40.41. Apply any discounts.
- ▶ Received a notice from the bank that Check No. 915 from Charles Watson was marked NSF and returned. Record the NSF check and charge Charles the bank's $25 fee for the bad check plus Your Name Books' fee of $15. Payment is due on receipt. Add any necessary items and/or accounts. Record charges for returned checks in an account called Bad Check Charges.

January 14:

- ▶ Received Check No. 870 from Sacramento Schools for $26.22 as payment in full for Invoice No. 6.
- ▶ Received Check No. 10-283 for $85.80 from Brian Scott in payment of Invoice No. 4.

January 15:

- ▶ Received all but three boxes of stationery ordered. The bill was included with the stationery and the three missing boxes are on back order. (Did you order 10 boxes?)
- ▶ Received Charles Watson's new Check No. 304 for payment in full of his account including all NSF charges.
- ▶ Sold five paperback books to a customer using a Visa. The books were $6.99 each.
- ▶ Deposit all cash, checks, and credit card receipts.
- ▶ Check to see if any bills qualify for a discount between January 15 and 19. If any qualify, take the discount and pay them.
- ▶ Prepare and print a Stock Status by Item Inventory Report for January 1-15 in Landscape orientation. Prepare Purchase Orders for all items marked Order on the Stock Status by Item Inventory Report. Place all orders with preferred vendors.

January 17:

- ▶ Sold eight textbooks at $50 each to State Schools, which is a nonprofit organization.
- ▶ Brian Scott returned one textbook he had purchased for $40.
- ▶ Received Credit Memo No. 721 from Supplies Co. for the return of ten reams of paper. (Be sure to apply the credit when you pay your bill.)

January 18:

- ▶ Print a Stock Status by Item Report after recording the return of the paper. Print in Landscape.
- ▶ Sold three paperback books to Charles Watson at $8.99 each.

January 20:

- ▶ Received the bill and the three boxes of stationery that were on back order with Supplies Co..
- ▶ A cash customer purchased four textbooks at $59.99 each using Check No. 289.
- ▶ Received Check No. 891 from Sacramento Schools for $336.34 for payment in full of Invoice No. 11.

- ► Prepare Stock Status by Item Inventory Report. Order any items indicated.
- ► Check to see if any bills qualify for a discount between January 20 and 24. If any qualify, pay them.

January 21:
- ► Sold one textbook for $89.95. Customer used a VISA card to pay for the purchase.
- ► Kristin typed an eight-page exam for a professor at $5 per page. Add Professor John Smith, 1052 Florin Avenue, Sacramento, CA 95814, 916-555-8741, Terms Net 30, Taxable, Credit Limit $100.
- ► Received the bill from Gift Gallery for the gift ware ordered and received January 12. Date the bill January 21.
- ► Deposit all cash, checks , and credit card receipts.

January 22:
- ► Sold one gift ware item at $15.99 to a cash customer. Received Check No. 105.
- ► Sold five gift ware items at $9.99 each to Lora Newton.

January 24:
- ► Sold three pens at $8.99 each to Brian Scott.
- ► Received Check No. 127 for $42.79 as payment in full from Gene Simpson.

January 25:
- ► Prepare Stock Status by Item Inventory Report. Order any items indicated.
- ► Check to see if any bills qualify for a discount between January 25 and 29. If any qualify, accept the discount offered by QuickBooks, and pay them. If there any credits to apply to any bill payments, be sure to use them. (Print a voucher-style check so you can see the discounts and credits used.)
- ► Deposit all cash, checks, and credit card receipts.

January 27:
- ► Received the bill and all of the paperback books ordered from Books & Texts Co..

January 29:
- ► Received Check No. 4325 for $133.93 from Violet Nichols.
- ► Received Bill No. 1092-5 and pens on order from Exotic Pens.
- ► Sold 60 textbooks to Complete Training, Inc., for $59.95 each.
- ► Sold 45 textbooks to Sacramento Schools for $49.99 each.

January 30:
- ► Prepare Stock Status by Item Inventory Report. Order any items indicated.
- ► Deposit all checks, cash, and credit card receipts.

- ► Pay balance due to Supplies Co. as well as any bills eligible for a discount between January 30 and February 4. Print using a standard style check.
- ► Pay $900 rent to the CA Rental Agency, 1234 Front Street, Sacramento, CA 95814, Contact: Gail Ruiz, 916-555-1234, Fax 916-555-4321, Terms Net 30.
- ► Pay gas and electricity bill of $257 to State Utilities, 8905 Richmond, Sacramento, CA 95814, 916-555-8523, Terms Net 30.
- ► Pay the telephone bill of $189 to Sacramento Telephone Company, 3899 Oak Avenue, Sacramento, CA 95814, 916-555-8741, Terms Net 30.

January 31:

- ► Pay the payroll: Use the information in the following table and print the paychecks using a voucher-style check.

PAYROLL TABLE: JANUARY 31, 2007			
	Caitlin Ellis	**Kristin King**	**Aimee Nelson**
HOURS			
Regular	144	80	158
Overtime	3		
Sick	16		2
Vacation			
DEDUCTIONS OTHER PAYROLL ITEMS: EMPLOYEE			
Dental Ins.	20.00		30.00
Medical Ins.	20.00		30.00
DEDUCTIONS: COMPANY			
CA Employment Training Tax	2.58	1.40	2.50
Social Security	97.53	63.33	134.34
Medicare	23.20	15.08	31.42
Federal Unemployment	9.33	6.75	9.33
CA-Unemployment	46.67	30.40	46.67
DEDUCTIONS: EMPLOYEE			
Federal Withholding	126.00	56.00	292.00
Social Security	52.39	46.12	67.17
Medicare	23.20	18.77	31.42

PAYROLL TABLE: JANUARY 31, 2007			
	Caitlin Ellis	**Kristin King**	**Aimee Nelson**
CA-Withholding	56.05	37.00	63.30
CA-Disability	8.00	6.30	10.00

- ▶ Before distributing paychecks, you realize that the Social Security Employee Deductions for each employee are incorrect. Go to the checks, unlock them and change the amount of Social Security Employee Deductions for Aimee to 134.34, for Caitlin to 97.53, and for Kristin to 63.33. Reprint the checks using Voucher style.
- ▶ Prepare and print the Payroll Summary Report for January in Landscape orientation. (Adjust column widths to print the report on one page.)
- ▶ Prepare and print the Payroll Liabilities Balances Report for January in Portrait orientation. (If you need to enter a vendor for the Liability payment for Dental Insurance and Medical Insurance, follow the screens and select Medical Ins. Inc. as the vendor. No other changes need to be entered. Click Next until you can click Finish.)
- ▶ Pay all the payroll taxes and other payroll liabilities for January. Print the checks.
- ▶ Prepare and print Forms 941: Use 01/31/2007 as the date the quarter ended. You do not have to file a Schedule B for Form 941. The state is California. There are three employees employed. Select Apply to Next Return for the overpayment. Assume there are no adjustments to be made to either report. Print the Tax Form only.
- ▶ Prepare and print Form 940: Deposits are made monthly. When preparing Form 940, the year is 2007. Answer Yes to Questions A, B, C, and D. Apply any overpayment to the next return. Print the Tax Form only.
- ▶ Prepare Sales Tax Liability Report for January 1-30, 2007. Print in Landscape orientation. Adjust column widths so the report fits on one page, maintains the same font, and has column headings shown in full.
- ▶ Pay Sales Tax and print the check.
- ▶ Print a Sales by Item Summary Report for January in Landscape orientation. Adjust column widths so report fits on one-page wide.
- ▶ Print a Trial Balance for January 1-31 in Portrait orientation.
- ▶ Enter adjusting entries: Depreciation—Store Equipment $100, Store Fixtures $166.66. Supplies used—Office Supplies $150, Sales Supplies $250. Insurance a total of $100—$50 fire Insurance, $50 Liability Insurance. (Use a compound entry to record insurance adjustment.)
- ▶ Record the owner withdrawal for the month $1,500.
- ▶ Prepare a bank reconciliation and record any adjustments. Be sure to use the date of 01/31/07 for the bank statement date, service charges, and interest earned.

STATE BANK
102 8th Street
Sacramento, CA 95814
(916) 555-9889

BANK STATEMENT FOR:

Your Name Books
1055 Front Street
Sacramento, CA 95814 Acct. # 97-1132-07922 January 2007

Beginning Balance, January 1, 2007			$35,870.25
1/5/2007, Deposit	2,204.84		38,075.09
1/9/2007, Check 1		1,000.00	37,075.09
1/10/2007, Deposit	1,328.24		38,403.33
1/13/2007, NSF Check		350.00	38,053.33
1/15/2007, Deposit	749.61		38,802.94
1/16/2007, Check 2		85.75	38,717.19
1/18/2007, Check 3		42.90	38,674.29
1/21/2007, Deposit	690.17		39,364.46
1/25/2007, Check 4		7.44	39,357.02
1/25/2007, Deposit	59.94		39,416.96
1/30/2007, Service Charge, $15, and NSF Charge, $25		40.00	39,379.96
1/30/2007, Store Fixtures Loan Pmt.: $80.12 Interest, $15.49 Principal		95.61	39,281.35
1/30/2007, Store Equipment Loan Pmt.: $26.71 Interest, $5.16 Principal		31.87	39,249.48
1/30/2007, Interest	94.03		39,343.51
Ending Balance, 1/31/2007			$39,343.51

- ► Print the Detail Reconciliation Report.
- ► Print a Standard Profit and Loss Statement.
- ► Close the Drawing account
- ► Transfer the Net Income/Retained Earnings into the capital account
- ► Print the following for January Standard Balance Sheet
- ► Print Statement of Cash Flows for January
- ► Adjust the Merchandise Item of Gift Ware for 1 Gift Set that was damaged. (Use the expense account Merchandise Adjustments.)
- ► Correct the Amount of Net Income to reflect the merchandise adjustment
- ► Print a Standard Balance Sheet
- ► Close the period with a closing date of 01/31/07

► Print the Journal (Landscape, adjust column width to fit to one-page wide with the standard font)

NAME________________________

TRANSMITTAL

COMPREHENSIVE PRACTICE SET: YOUR NAME BOOKS

Attach the following documents and reports:

Customer:Job List
Vendor List
Item Listing
Account Listing
Employee Summary for Caitlin Ellis
Employee Summary for Aimee Nelson
Payroll History Summary for Caitlin Ellis
Payroll History Summary for Aimee Nelson
Standard Balance Sheet, January 1, 2007
Sales Receipt No. 1: Cash Customer
Invoice No. 1: Complete Training, Inc.
Sales Receipt No. 2: Cash Customer
Invoice No. 2: Sacramento Schools
Sales Receipt No. 3: Cash Customer
Inventory Stock Status by Item, January 1, 2007
Purchase Order No. 1: Exotic Pens
Invoice No. 3: Lora Newton
Sales Receipt No. 4: Cash Customer
Invoice No. 4: Brian Scott
Invoice No. 5: Violet Nichols
Invoice No. 6: Sacramento Schools
Inventory Stock Status by Item, January 1-5, 2007
Purchase Order No. 2: Supplies Co.
Deposit Summary, January 5, 2007
Invoice No. 7: State Schools
Purchase Order No. 3: Gift Gallery
Invoice No. 8: Gene Simpson
Credit Memo No. 9: Lora Newton
Check No. 1: Books & Texts Co.
Sales Receipt No. 5: Cash Customer

Invoice No. 10: Violet Nichols
Invoice No. 11: Sacramento Schools
Deposit Summary, January 10, 2007
Inventory Stock Status by Item, January 1-10, 2007
Sales Receipt No. 6: Cash Customer
Sales Receipt No. 7: Cash Customer
Sales Receipt No. 8: Cash Customer
Invoice No. 12: Charles Watson
Invoice No. 13: Charles Watson
Sales Receipt No. 9: Cash Customer
Deposit Summary, January 15, 2007
Check No. 2: Exotic Pens
Inventory Stock Status by Item, January 1-15, 2007
Purchase Order No. 4: Gift Gallery
Purchase Order No. 5: Books & Texts Co.
Invoice No. 14: State Schools
Check No. 3: Brian Scott
Credit Memo No. 15: Brian Scott,
Inventory Stock Status by Item, January 1-18, 2007
Invoice No. 16: Charles Watson
Sales Receipt No. 10: Cash Customer
Inventory Stock Status by Item, January 1-20, 2007
Sales Receipt No. 11: Cash Customer
Invoice No. 17: John Smith
Deposit Summary, January 21, 2007
Sales Receipt No. 12: Cash Customer
Invoice No. 18: Lora Newton
Invoice No. 19: Brian Scott
Inventory Stock Status by Item, January 1-25, 2007
Purchase Order No. 6: Exotic Pens
Check No. 4: Supplies Co.
Deposit Summary, January 25, 2007
Invoice No. 20: Complete Training, Inc.
Invoice No. 21: Sacramento Schools
Inventory Stock Status by Item, January 1-30, 2007
Deposit Summary, January 30, 2007
Check No. 5: Supplies Co.
Check No. 6: CA Rental Agency
Check No. 7: State Utilities
Check No. 8: Sacramento Telephone Company
Check No. 9: Aimee Nelson

Check No. 10: Kristin King
Check No. 11: Caitlin Ellis
Check No. 9: Aimee Nelson (Corrected)
Check No. 10: Kristin King (Corrected)
Check No. 11: Caitlin Ellis (Corrected)
Payroll Summary, January 2007
Payroll Liability Balances, January 30, 2007
Check No. 12: Employment Development Department
Check No. 16: Medical Ins., Inc.
Check No. 14: State Bank
Employer's Quarterly Federal Tax Return, Form 941
Employer's Annual Federal Unemployment (FUTA) Tax Return
Sales Tax Liability Report, January 2007
Check No. 15: State Board of Equalization
Sales by Item Summary, January 2007
Trial Balance, January 31, 2007
Check No. 16: Your Name
Bank Reconciliation Report
Standard Profit and Loss, January 2007
Balance Sheet After Adjustments, January 31, 2007
Statement of Cash Flows, January 2007
Balance Sheet, January 31, 2007, (After Adjustment of Merchandise Inventory)
Journal, January 2007

INTRODUCTION TO WINDOWS® AND DISK MANAGEMENT

A

INTRODUCTION TO WINDOWS®

When you turn on the computer, Windows will automatically be in use and icons will be visible on the desktop. (Some computer laboratories require the use of passwords in order to access Windows and the various application programs available. Check with your instructor regarding the configuration of your classroom computers.) Currently, there are several versions of Windows in use. Most things will work in a similar manner so only one set of screen shots will be displayed in this appendix. These screen shots are from Windows® XP.

➤ If needed, turn on your computer and monitor

Windows will begin running, and the desktop will be displayed on the screen

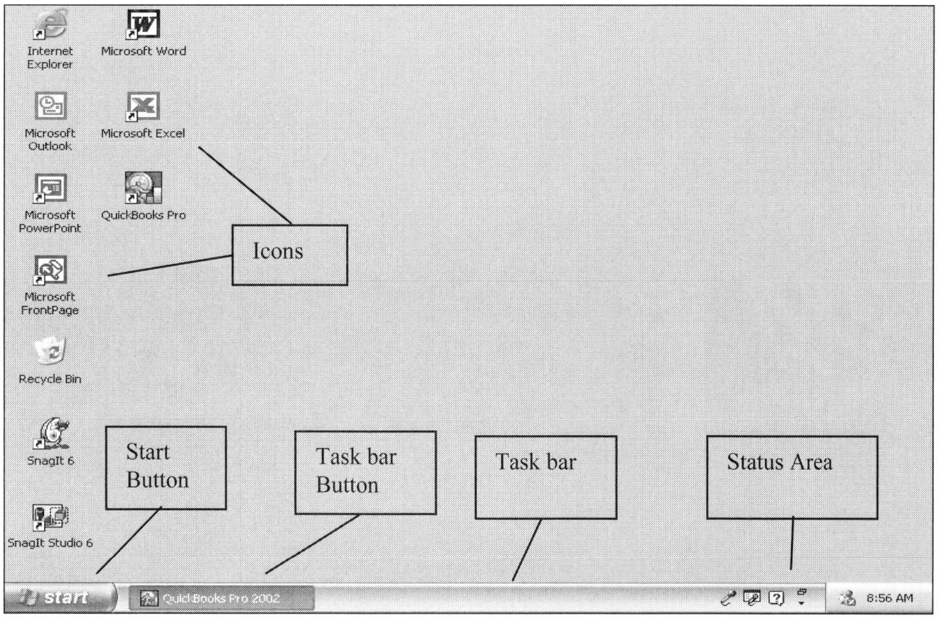

In order to use Windows effectively, it is helpful to understand the terminology used in describing the various Windows elements.

Desktop is the primary work area and covers the entire screen.

Icons are pictorial representations of objects. Some icons on the desktop are "shortcuts" used to access programs and/or documents. Other icons are used to access information regarding your computer or to delete files/programs from the computer.

Taskbar is the major focal point of Windows. It usually appears at the bottom of your screen. The taskbar contains the Start button, which is used to launch (open) programs, access documents, alter the appearance of the desktop, and shut down the computer when you are finished working.

Taskbar buttons indicate the names of any programs/files that are currently open.

Status area is on the taskbar. Programs can place information or notification of events in the status area. Windows places information in the status area: the time and (if available on your computer) a sound icon, which is used to control the volume of the computer's sound system.

ToolTip is a definition, instruction, or information that pops up when you point to something. For example, pointing to the time in the status area of the taskbar gives you a ToolTip that displays the full date; pointing to the Start button gives you the ToolTip "Click here to begin."

Start button is used to access the primary menu in Windows. This menu lists the main functions available.

All Programs is a menu listing the application programs available on your system. Frequently, you must make selections from several menus to access a program. For example, to access Calculator, which is a Windows Accessory Program, you point to the **All Programs** menu, then point to the **Accessories** menu, and finally point to and click on **Calculator**.

My Documents lists the names of documents stored on the hard disk of the computer. (In a classroom environment, documents may be stored on an external floppy disk, USB, or on a network. Always check with your instructor prior to saving any work.)

My Pictures lists the names of pictures stored on the hard disk of the computer.

My Music lists the names of music files stored on the hard disk of the computer.

My Computer provides access to and gives information about disk drives and other hardware connected to your computer.

My Network Places gives access to and provides information about files and folders on other computers.

Control Panel provides options for computer customization, adding or removing programs, and setting up network connections and adding user accounts.

Connect To is used for Internet connection.

Help and Support opens a central location for Help topics.

Search opens a window in which you can select search options and work with search results.

Run Opens a program, folder, document, or Web site. Run also allows you to execute a program by name.

Turn Off Computer is *always* used to exit Windows or restart the computer.

Once you have opened a program and are ready to work, Windows will provide several items that are similar to those shown in the following QuickBooks Pro window.

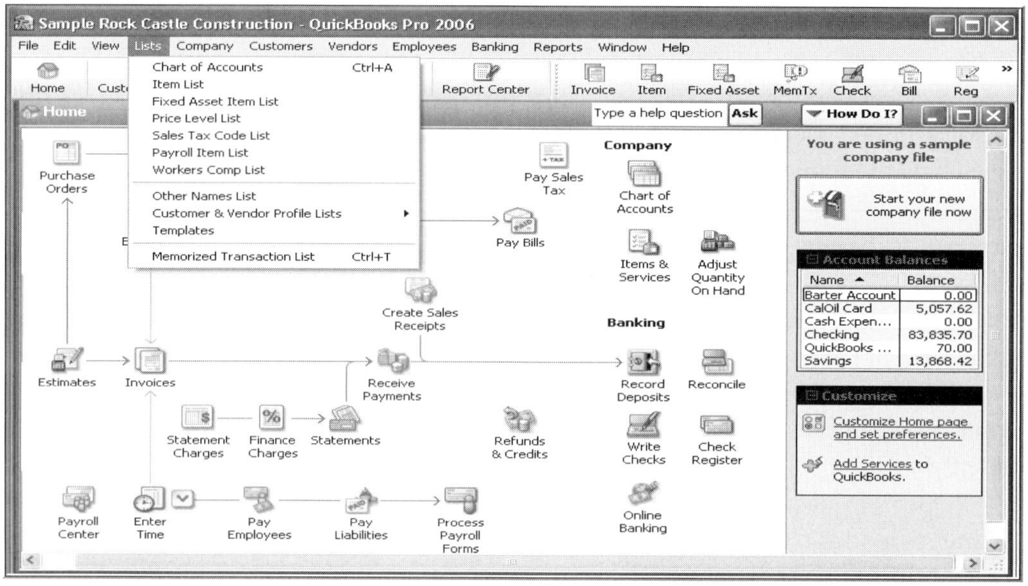

Control menu icon is always in the upper left corner of every window. Clicking on this allows you to access a drop-down menu, which is used for resizing, moving, maximizing, minimizing, closing, or switching a window.

Title bar indicates the name of the program and the file in use.

Minimize button is located on the upper right side of the screen. It appears as a button with a minus sign. Clicking on this allows you to shrink or minimize a window into a button, which appears on the taskbar. When a window is minimized, the program/document is still open and usable; it is just placed on the taskbar as a button so it is out of the way.

Maximize button is a button with a single window as the icon. This is the middle button on the right side of the title bar. Clicking on this allows you to fill the entire screen with the contents of the window. (This is not shown on the QuickBooks window above.)

Restore button appears when a window is maximized, the maximize button changes into a button with two windows. (This is shown on the QuickBooks window above). Clicking on this restores the window to its previous size.

Close button is on the far right side of the title bar. This button has an **X** on it. Clicking on this button closes both the document and the program. (The document window may also have its own minimize, maximize, and close buttons to be used only with the document. If so, these buttons will usually appear below the program minimize, maximize, and close buttons.)

Windows borders are the borders around the outside of open windows. You may point to a border, get a double arrow, then hold down the primary mouse button and drag the border to resize a window.

Menu bar will drop down a menu when clicked. These different menus allow you to access most of the commands within a program.

Dialog box is a box that appears in the middle of your screen and presents information to you or requests information from you.

Message box is a type of dialog box that informs you of a condition—a question, information, or a critical error. Most message boxes require you to confirm, cancel, or retry an action by clicking on a command button.

Command button is a button used to answer the questions within a dialog box.

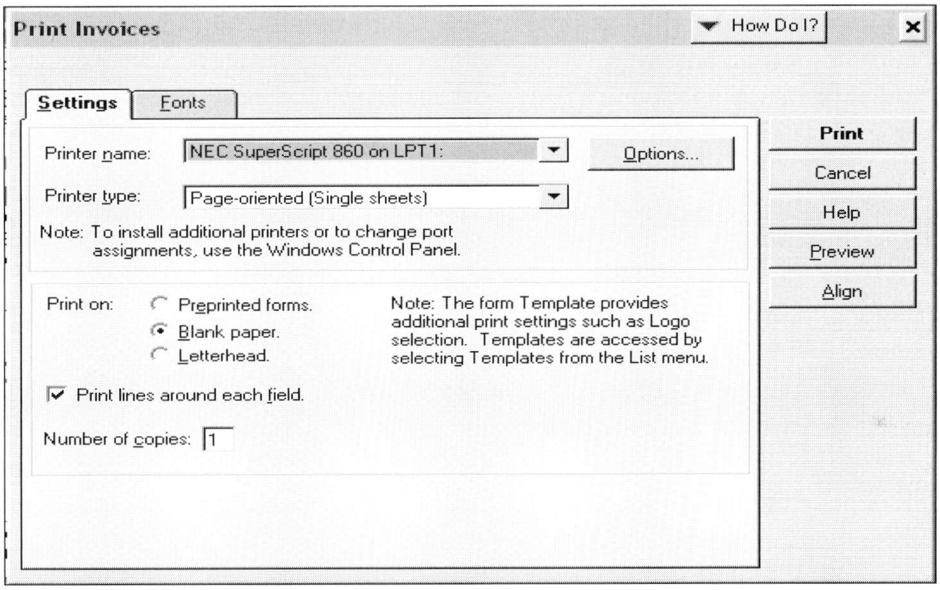

Other items in dialog boxes are:

Drop-down list or box contains the default choice. If you wish to make another selection, click the arrow next to the drop-down list box. If your choice is displayed, simply click on the desired item. (Look at the arrow next to the text box for "Printer name" in the "Print One Invoice" dialog box above.)

Option buttons present more than one choice; however, only one item may be chosen. The selected option contains a black dot. Options that are unavailable are dimmed. (Look at the section for "Print On" in the "Print One Invoice" dialog box.)

Text box allows you to key in information. (Look at the box next to "Printer name.")

Check box provides a choice that may be enabled or disabled. More than one item may be selected. If an option is unavailable, it is dimmed. (Look at the check box for "Do not print lines around each field.")

Spin box allows you to key in a number or to click on up or down arrows to increase or decrease a number. (This is not shown on the illustration.)

HOW TO USE A MOUSE

A mouse is an input device that is primarily used to issue commands within a software program. When working in a graphical user interface environment such as Windows, the user sends instructions to programs by simply using the mouse to position the mouse pointer and clicking either the right or left mouse button. A mouse pointer is an arrow that can be used to point to an icon. When you are in a document or a dialog box that requires typing, the mouse pointer turns into an I-beam so it may be positioned more easily.

MOUSE TERMINOLOGY

When using a mouse, terms such as "click," "double-click," "right-click," "drag," and "drag and drop" will be used.

Mouse pointer is the arrow used when pointing to icons.

I-beam is the shape of the mouse pointer when being positioned within a document or a dialog box requiring typing.

Click means pressing the primary (usually left) mouse button one time.

Right-click means pressing the secondary (usually right) mouse button one time.

Double-click means to press the primary (usually left) mouse button two times very quickly.

Drag means to hold down the primary mouse button while dragging the mouse pointer through something (usually text) to highlight.

Right drag means to hold down the secondary mouse button while dragging the mouse pointer through something. Releasing the secondary mouse button will frequently cause Windows to display a popup menu.

Drag and drop means to reposition something. This is achieved by pointing to an object or highlighted text with the mouse pointer, holding down the primary mouse button, and moving the mouse pointer/object by moving the mouse. When the item is repositioned, release the mouse button to "drop" the item into the new position.

Right drag and drop means to reposition something. This is achieved by pointing to an object or highlighted text with the mouse pointer, holding down the secondary mouse button, and moving the mouse pointer/object by moving the mouse. When the item is repositioned, release the mouse button to "drop" the item into the new position. Releasing the secondary mouse button will frequently cause Windows to display a popup menu.

DUPLICATING A DISK

When working with any computer program, it is essential to make a backup disk of your work. In QuickBooks Pro you regularly make a backup file of the company on the same disk as your work. This is not a backup disk; it is a backup of company data that must be restored to a company file before it can be used. A backup file has an extension of .qbb and as indicated it must be restored to a company file with an extension of .qbw.

A backup or duplicate disk is extremely important to have available for use. If something happens to your company disk, you no longer have any of your work. Thus, it is a good practice to make a complete copy of all the files on your company disk to a separate disk. This is usually called a backup disk. For the sake of clarity, this text calls this a duplicate disk.

The size of QuickBooks Pro backup files necessitates the use of a USB drive. If you are using a USB drive (F:, G:, etc. drive), you will use a drag and drop procedure.

➤ Create a duplicate disk using USB drives

Insert the USB containing your company file in the **F:** drive (or whatever drive location you are using)

Insert a second USB drive in the **G:** drive (or whatever drive location you are using)

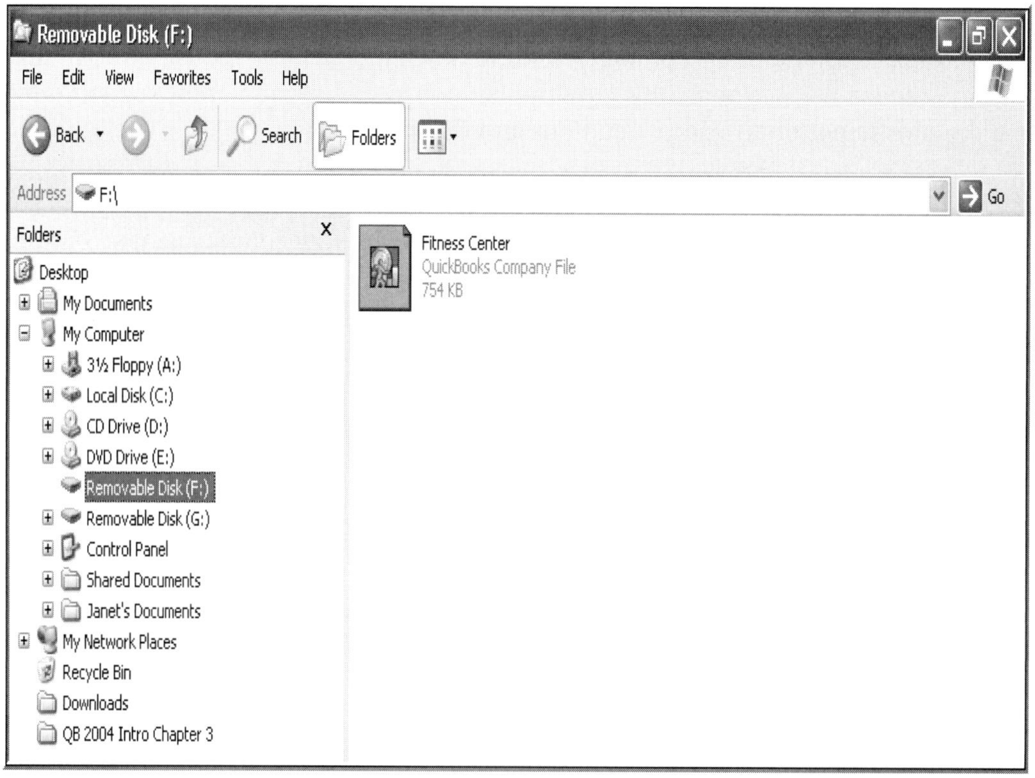

Click the Company file name located on the right side of the screen

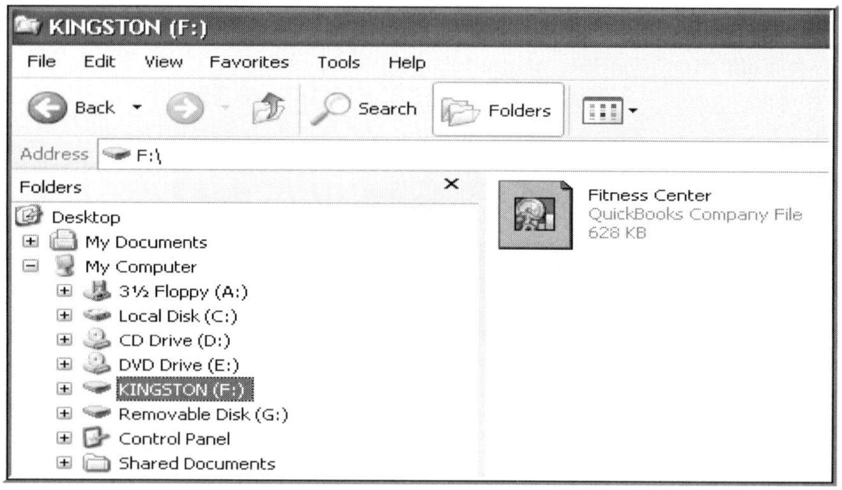

Point to the file, hold down the right mouse button, drag until Removable Disk (G:) is highlighted

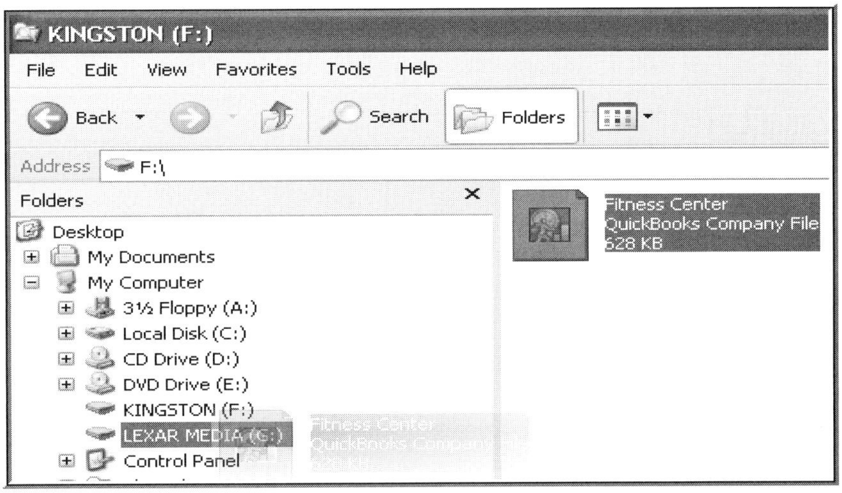

Release the mouse, click **Copy Here**

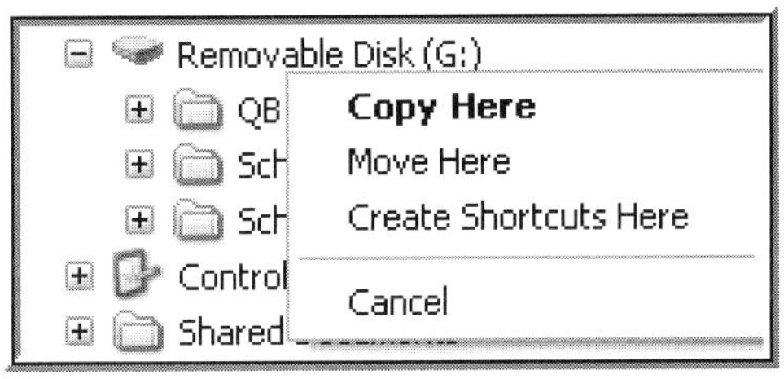

The file will be copied from F: to G:

Once the disk has been copied successfully, click **G:** to verify that the file is on the disk

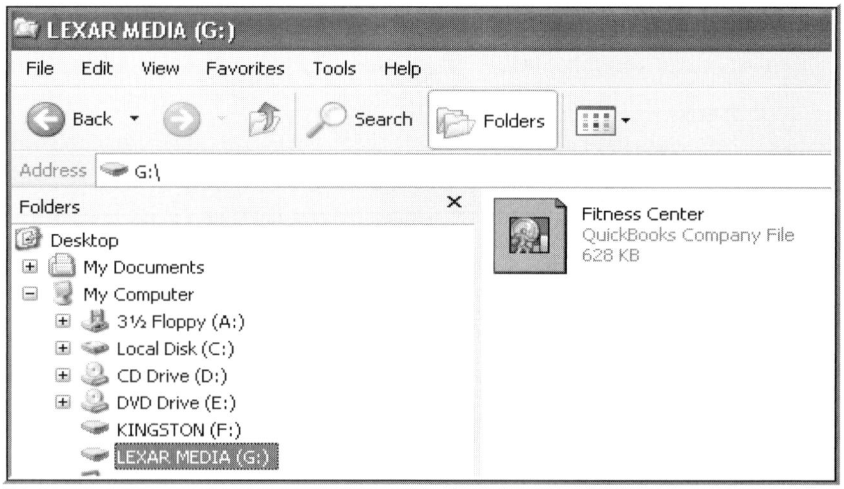

Label this USB as **Duplicate Company Disk**

- It is important to reduplicate your disk at the end of each chapter. It is a better practice to duplicate your disk at the end of each computer work session. If your original disk is lost or becomes damaged, you have the duplicate disk that you can use.
- Repeat the above procedures to copy any backup files you have on your disk

To copy more than one file at a time, click one file, hold down the Ctrl key and click the second file, repeat for any additional files

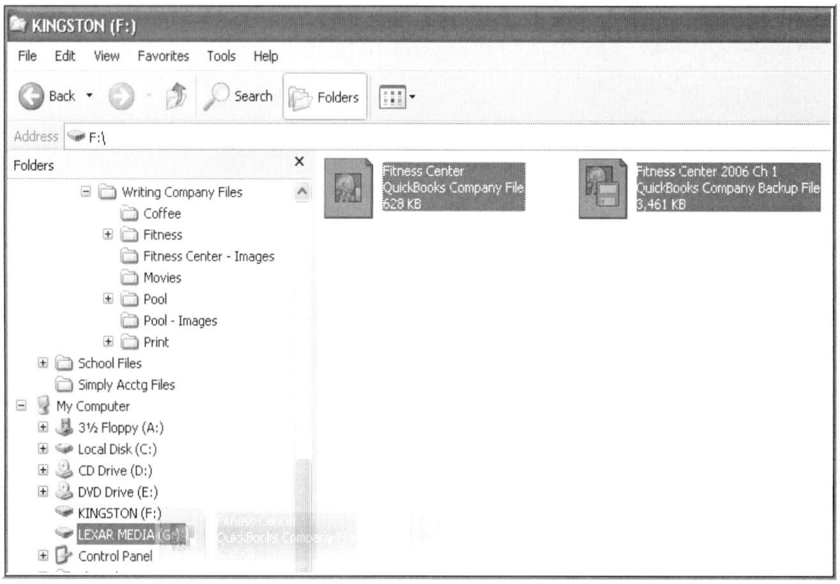

Follow the same procedures as previously illustrated

When you create a duplicate disk at the completion of a subsequent work session or chapter, you will get a screen asking you if you want to replace the file on the G: drive.

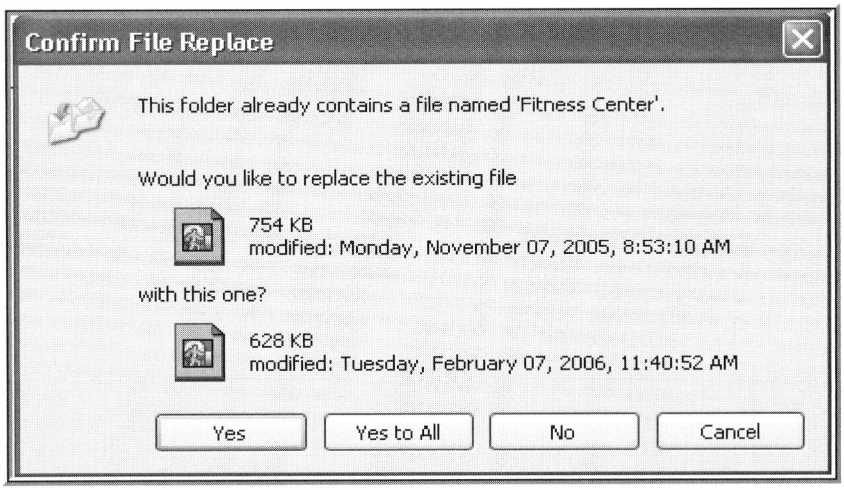

Click **Yes**

HOW TO CREATE A QUICKBOOKS® PRO BACKUP FILE

As you work with a company and record transactions, it is important to back up your work. This allows you to keep the information for a particular period separate from current information. A backup also allows you to restore information in case your data disk becomes damaged. There are two different ways in which you can make a backup of your data. If you use Windows Explorer you can make a duplicate disk (as illustrated in this Appendix). In Windows, this is called making a backup. If you use QuickBooks Pro to make a backup, you are actually asking QuickBooks Pro to create a condensed file that contains the essential transaction and account information. This file has a **.qbb** extension and is not usable unless it is restored to a company file that has a **.qbw** extension. Before entering transactions for Your Name Computer Consulting in Chapter 1, make a QuickBooks Pro backup of the company data from the Computer.qbw file.

Make a QuickBooks Pro backup of the company data for Your Name Computer Consulting.

Open QuickBooks as instructed in Chapter 1
Open the company file **Computer.qbw**
Click **File** on the Menu Bar
Click **Back Up...**

- If you get a message for a Portable Company file, click the check box **Do not display this message in the future** to turn off the message, then click **OK**

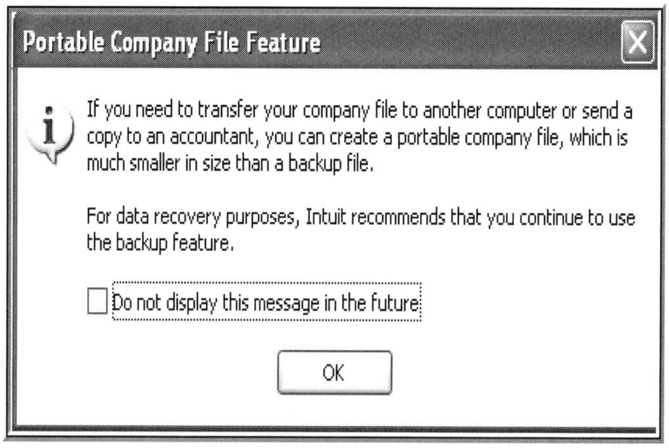

• QuickBooks Backup has two tabs: Back Up Company File and Schedule Backup. The **Back Up Company File** tab should be active

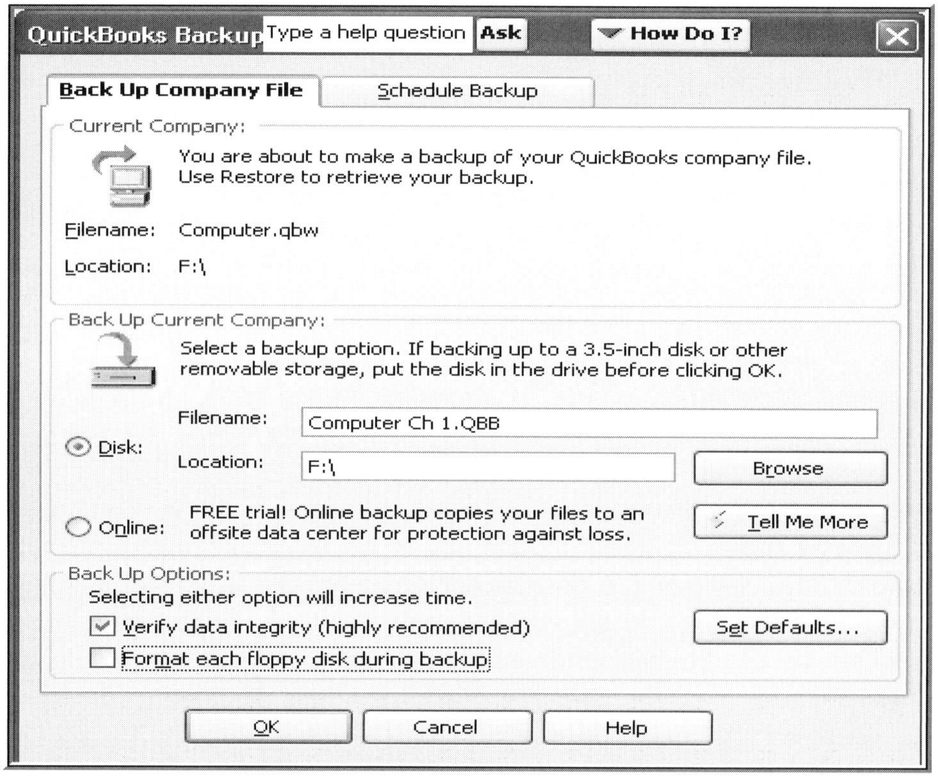

Verify the Current Company information:

Filename is Fitness Center.qbw

Location is F:\ or the location where your "working" file is stored

Backup Current Company should be to Disk

The circle in front of Disk should have a black dot in it

Enter the filename **Computer Ch 1.qbb**
Location should be F:\ or the location where you want to store your backup file
- If it is not, click in the text box and enter the storage location

Click **OK**
- QuickBooks Pro will back up the information for Your Name Computer Consulting on the USB disk

Click the **OK** button in the dialog box stating that the backup was successful.

HOW TO RESTORE A QUICKBOOKS® PRO BACKUP FILE

If you make an error in your training, you may find it beneficial to restore your .qbb backup file. The only way in which a .qbb backup file may be used is by restoring it to a .qbw company file. Using QuickBooks' Restore command on the File menu restores a backup file. A restored backup file replaces the current data in your company file with the data in the backup file so any transactions recorded after the backup was made will be erased.

Practice restoring a backup file

Click **File** on the menu bar
Click **Restore...**
Complete the **Get Company Backup From:** area of the screen
Insert **Computer Ch 1.qbb** for the Filename
Insert the Location as **F:** (or the location you are using for your files)
Complete the **Restore Company Backup To:** area of the screen
Insert **Computer.qbw** for the Filename
Insert the Location as **F:** (or the location you are using for your files)

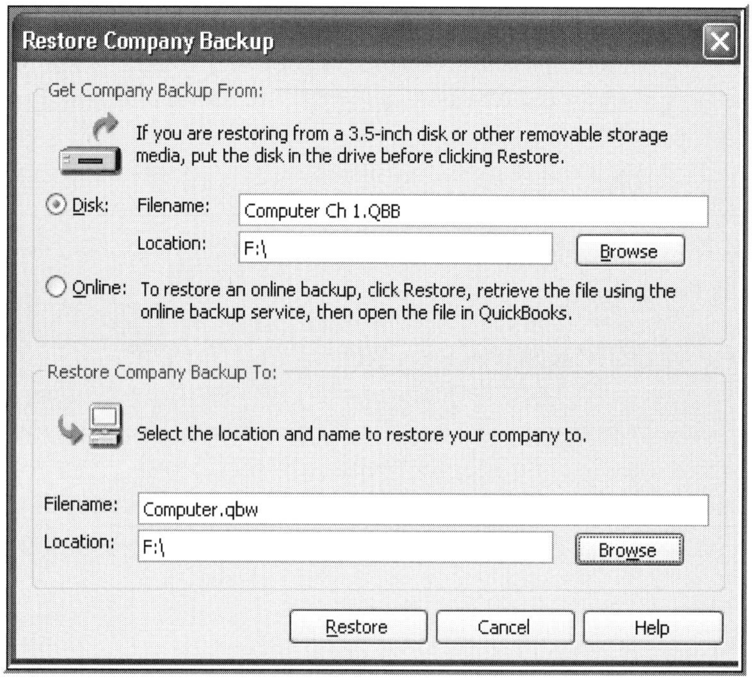

Click the **Restore** button

You will get a warning that you are choosing to overwrite an existing company file

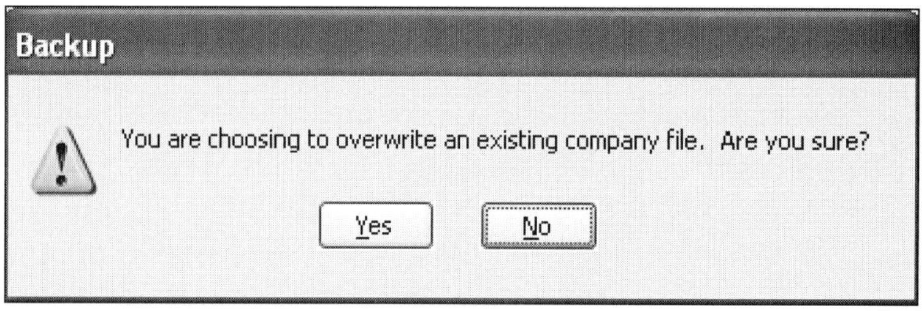

Click **Yes**

- You will get a screen telling you how much space you have available on the disk

Click **OK**

- You will get a **Delete Entire File** warning screen

Enter the word **Yes** and click **OK**

- When you restore a file to an existing company file, all the data contained in the company file will be replaced with the information in the backup file.

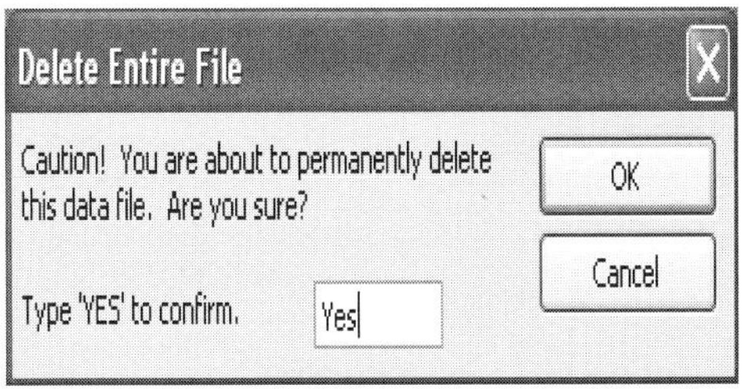

When the file has been restored, you will get the following

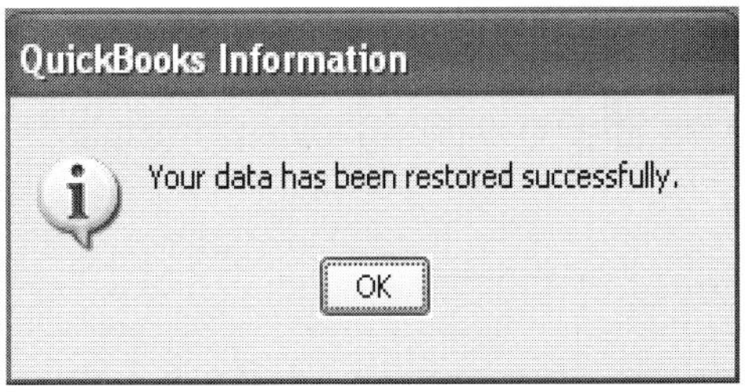

Press Enter or click **OK**

HOW TO EXIT QUICKBOOKS® PRO AND REMOVE YOUR USB DRIVE

When you complete your work, you need to exit the QuickBooks Pro program. If you are saving work on a separate data disk or USB drive, you must not remove your disk until you exit the program. Following the appropriate steps to close and exit a program is extremely important. There are program and data files that must be closed in order to leave the program and company data so that they are ready to be used again. It is common for a beginning computer user to turn off the computer without exiting a program. This can cause corrupt program and data files and can make a disk or program unusable.

Close the company file for Your Name Computer Consulting, close QuickBooks, and stop the USB

Close the company file by clicking **File** on the menu bar and clicking **Close Company**
Close QuickBooks by clicking the **Close** button in upper right corner of title bar

Click the icon for the USB drive in the lower right portion of the Taskbar 

Click on the message 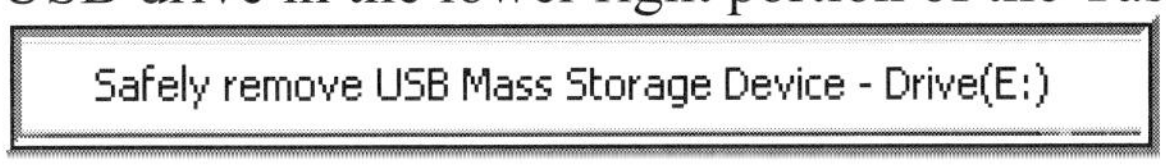

When you get the message that it is safe to remove hardware, remove your USB

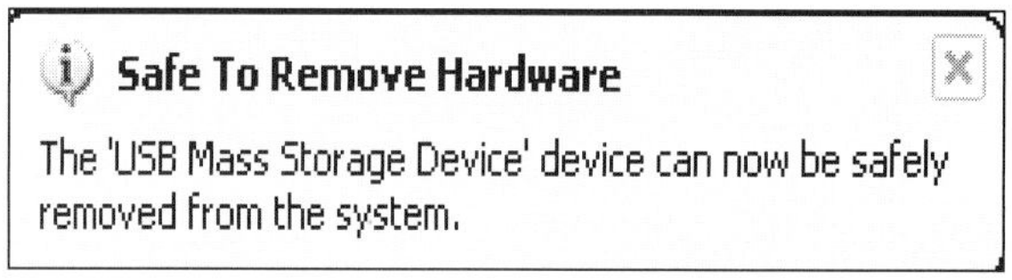

HOW TO CLOSE OR SHUT DOWN WINDOWS®

When you have exited your application program and are ready to close Windows, you need to follow proper exit/closing procedures. Simply turning off the machine is *not* the method to follow when exiting Windows. This might corrupt files that are needed to make the program work properly. When you close or shut down, Windows must close certain files and write information to disk so it will be ready for use the next time the computer is needed. Always be sure to follow the appropriate steps for closing/shutting down Windows. Follow the procedures illustrated unless instructed differently.

Shut Down Windows

Click **Start**
Click **Turn Off Computer** or **Shut Down**

Click **Turn Off** or **Shut down**

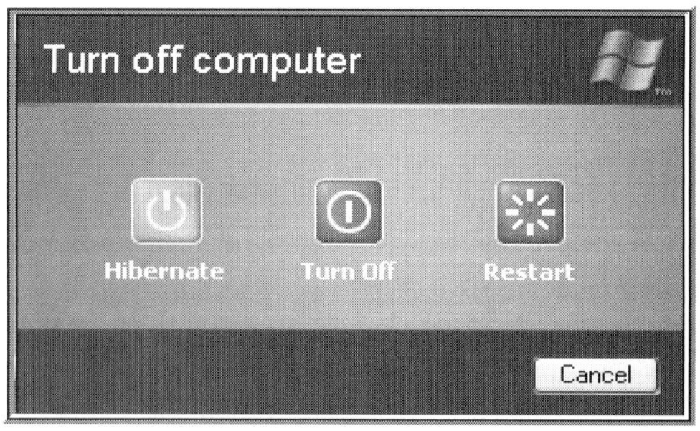

B

QUICKBOOKS PROGRAM INTEGRATION WITH MICROSOFT® WORD AND EXCEL

QuickBooks Pro and QuickBooks Premier are integrated to work in conjunction with Microsoft Word and Excel to prepare many different types of letters or send QuickBooks reports directly to an Excel workbook. QuickBooks Basic does not have this feature. In order to use the integration features of the program, you must have Microsoft Word 2000 (or higher) and Microsoft Excel 2000 (or higher) installed on your computer

QUICKBOOKS LETTERS

There are many times in business when you need to write a letter of one type or another to your customers. This is an important feature because QuickBooks will insert information, such as the amount a customer owes, from your customer files directly into a letter. We will use the sample company, Larry's Landscaping, to work with QuickBooks Letters and prepare a collection letter for David Hughes.

Prepare a Collection Letter for David Hughes

To open the Sample Company file for a Service Business, open QuickBooks
On the **No Company Open** window, click the button for **Open a Sample File**
Click **Sample service-based business**

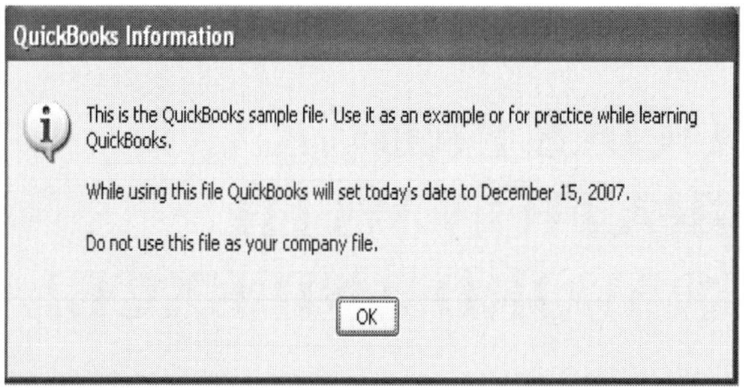

Click **OK** on the QuickBooks Information screen
Click the **Customers Center** icon
Click the **Word** button
Click **Prepare Collection Letters**
Complete the screen to Choose the Recipients

- Include listed customers or jobs that are: **Both**
- Create a letter for each: **Customer**
- Limit letters to customers or jobs with payments overdue by: **1 Day or More**

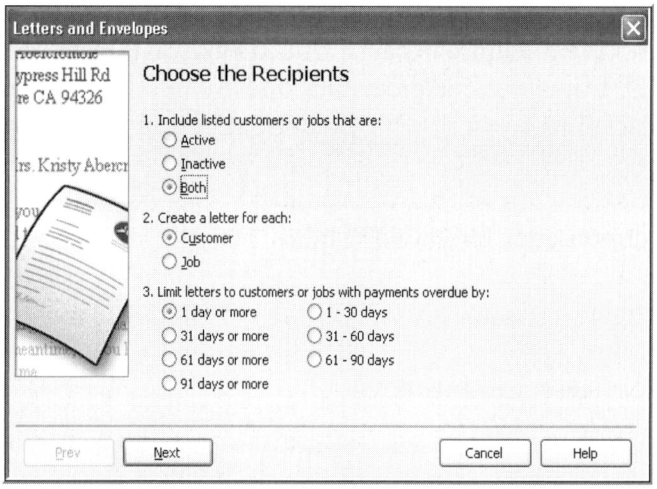

Click **Next**
Click **Unmark All** button, then click in the check column to select David Hughes
Click **Next**
Click **Friendly Collection** as the type of letter

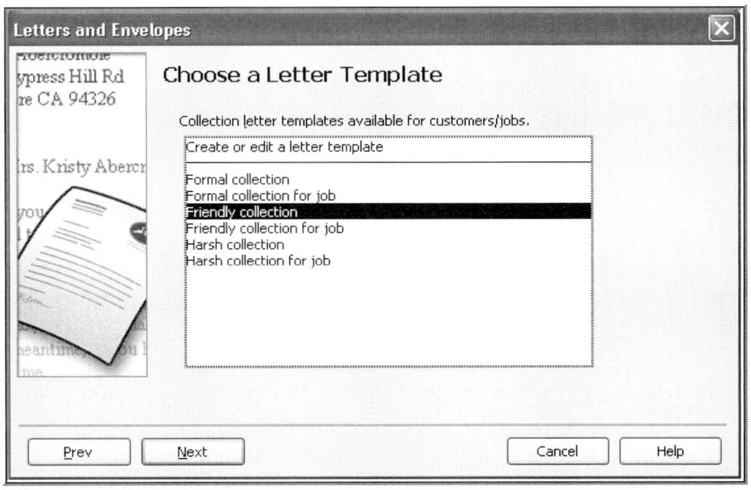

Click **Next**

Enter **Your Name** (your actual name not the words your name) for the name at the end of the letter

Enter your title as **President**

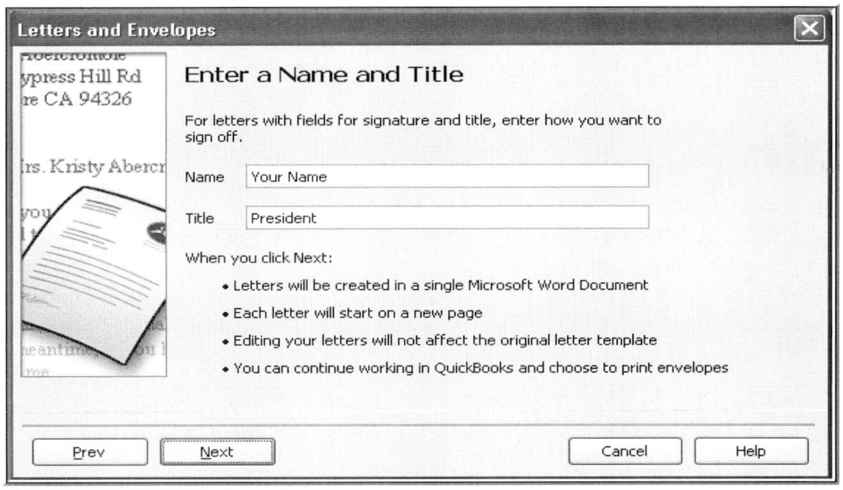

Click **Next**.

$ When the letter is created, Microsoft Word will be opened and the collection letter for David Hughes will appear on the screen.

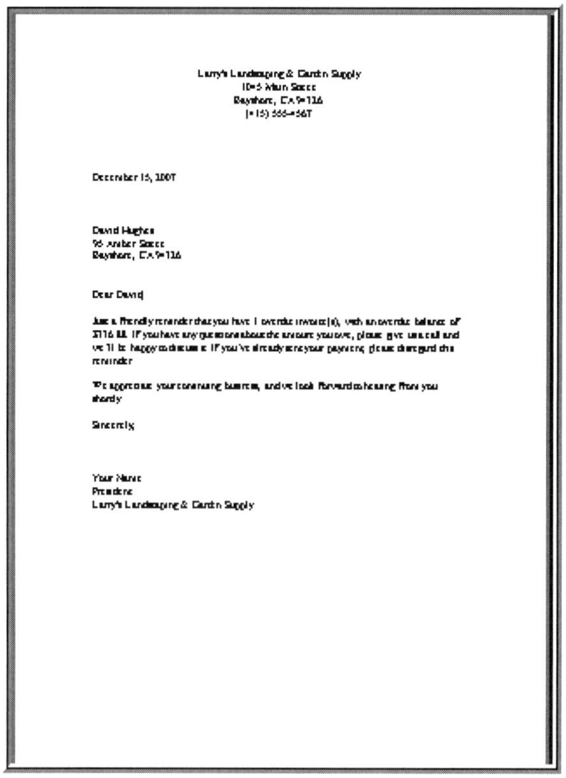

To make the short letter appear more balanced:
Press **Ctrl+A** to select the entire document
Click **File** menu, **Page Setup**
Change the Left and Right margins to **2"**

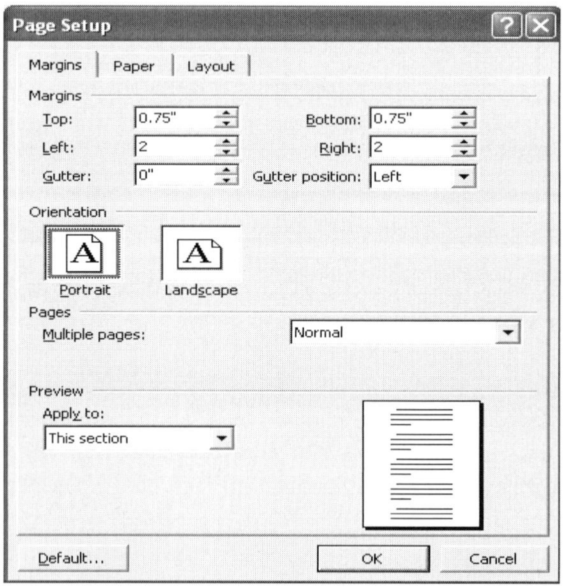

Click **OK**
Position the cursor between the date and the letter address
Press the **Enter** key **5** times so there are 8 blank lines between the date and the letter address
Delete one of the blank lines between the letter address and the salutation

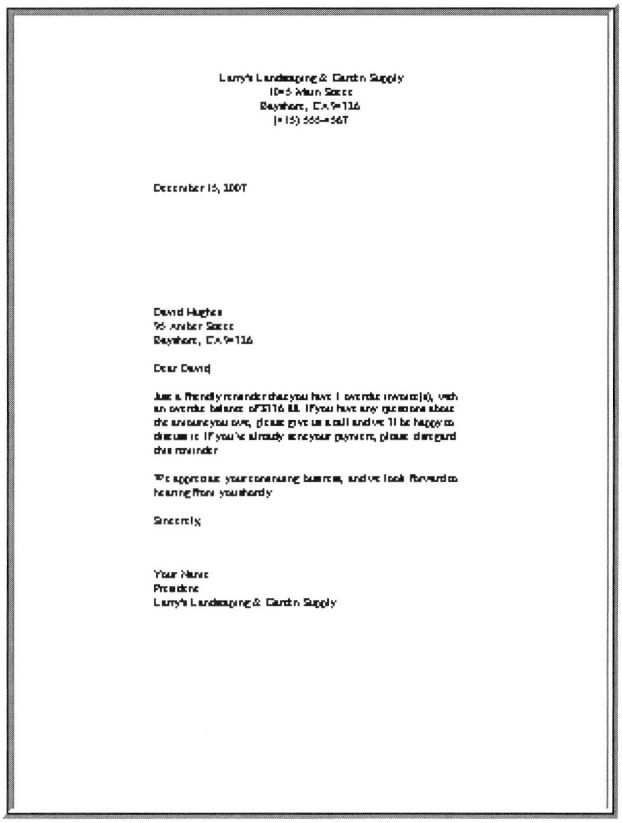
Larry's Landscaping & Garden Supply
[illegible] Main Street
Bayshore, CA [illegible]
[illegible]

December 15, [illegible]

David Hughes
[illegible] Amber Street
Bayshore, CA [illegible]

Dear David

Just a friendly reminder that you have 1 overdue invoice(s), with an overdue balance of [illegible]. If you have any questions about the amount you owe, please give us a call and we'll be happy to discuss it. If you've already sent your payment, please disregard this reminder.

We appreciate your continuing business, and we look forward to hearing from you shortly.

Sincerely,

Your Name
President
Larry's Landscaping & Garden Supply

$ Your letter should look like the one above.
Close Word without saving the letter
Click **Cancel** to cancel the Letters to Customers, close the **Customer Center**

EXPORTING REPORTS TO EXCEL

Many of the reports prepared in QuickBooks Pro can be exported to Microsoft® Excel. This allows you to take advantage of extensive filtering options available in Excel, hide detail for some but not all groups of data, combine information from two different reports, change titles of columns, add comments, change the order of columns, and experiment with *what if* scenarios. In order to use this feature of QuickBooks Pro you must also have Microsoft Excel 2000 or higher.

Continue to use the sample company: Larry's Landscaping and Export a report to Excel

Click **Report Center**
With the Report Center on the screen, click **Company and Financial**
Click **Balance Sheet Standard**
Enter the date **12/15/07**
Click the **Export** button at the top of the report

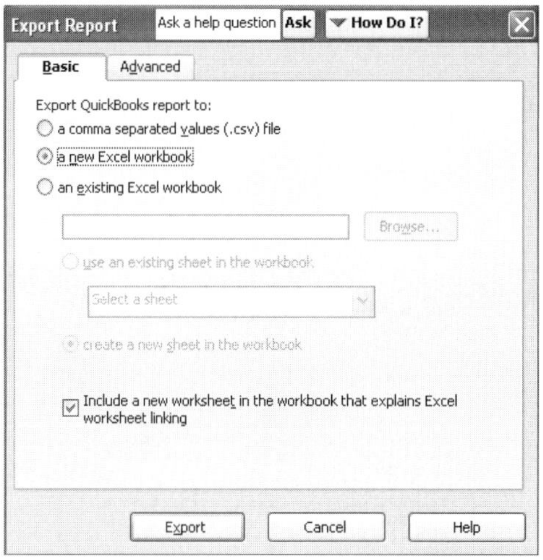

Make sure the Export QuickBooks Report to has **a new Excel workbook** selected as the File option
Click **Export**
$ The Balance Sheet will be displayed in Excel.

	A	B	C	D	E	F	G
1							Dec 15, 07
2	ASSETS						
3		Current Assets					
4			Checking/Savings				
5				Checking			102,893.52
6				Cash Expenditures			225.23
7				Savings			5,887.50
8			Total Checking/Savings				109,006.25
9			Accounts Receivable				
10				Accounts Receivable			35,810.02
11			Total Accounts Receivable				35,810.02
12			Other Current Assets				
13				Prepaid Insurance			500.00
14				Employee advances			100.00
15				Inventory Asset			6,937.08
16				Undeposited Funds			110.00
17			Total Other Current Assets				7,647.08
18		Total Current Assets					152,463.35

Scroll through the report and click in Cell A60

Type **BALANCE SHEET IMPORTED TO EXCEL**

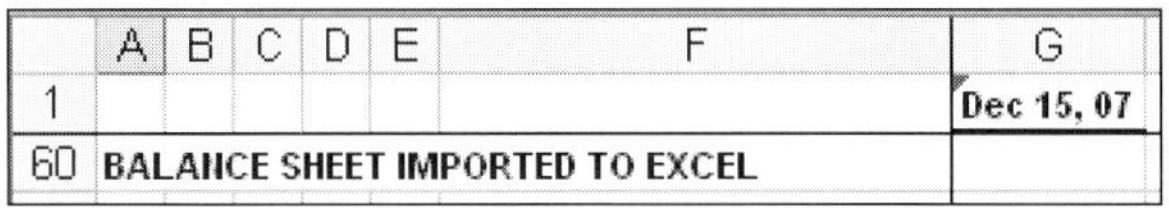

Click the **Close** button in the upper right corner of the Excel title bar to close **Excel**
Click **No** to close **Book1** without saving

IMPORTING DATA FROM EXCEL

Another feature of QuickBooks is the ability to import data from Excel into QuickBooks. You may have Excel or .csv (comma separated value) files that contain important business information about customers, vendors, and sales that are not contained in your QuickBooks Company File. That information can be imported directly into QuickBooks and customized as desired. An import file must conform to a specific structure for QuickBooks to interpret the data in the file correctly.

It is recommended that you set up your import file correctly in order to transfer the data properly and avoid errors. This includes preparing the file for import into QuickBooks, mapping the data from your file to QuickBooks, and previewing the imported data. QuickBooks has a built-in Reference Guide for Importing Files that may be accessed and printed through Help.

Since importing data is not reversible, we will not do this procedure at this time. However, procedures to follow include:

- In the Customer or Vendor Center, select the Customers & Jobs or Vendors tab. Then, go to the Excel menu and click Import from Excel.
- In the Item list, click Excel at the bottom of the list and then click Import Items.
- Go to the File menu, choose Utilities, click Import, and then click Excel Files.
- Set up the import by specifying the import file and how the contents of the file should be mapped to your QuickBooks data.
- Click the Preferences tab and specify how QuickBooks should handle errors and duplicate entries.
- Preview the data and make any necessary corrections.
- Click Import.
- If any errors occur during import, you will be prompted to save an error log.
- Use the error log to correct any errors. There are two ways to correct the records that contain errors: Correct the records directly in the import error log and then import the error log (recommended). Or, correct the records in the original import file and then re-import the file.

C

QUICKBOOKS® FEATURES: NOTES, TIME TRACKING, JOB COSTING AND TRACKING, MAILING SERVICES, SHIPPING, AND PRICE LEVELS

The QuickBooks Program contains many areas that were not explored during the training chapters of the text. Some of these areas are time tracking, job costing and tracking, price levels, and notes. To Do Notes, customer notes, vendor notes, employee notes, other names notes, and customer:job classifications are available in all versions of QuickBooks while the other features listed are available only in QuickBooks Pro and QuickBooks Premier. This appendix will use the sample company. Rock Castle Construction, to provide information regarding the features mentioned in the appendix title. Since saving the demonstration transactions will make permanent changes to the sample company and the company file will not fit on a separate floppy disk, you will not need to do the demonstration transactions unless they are assigned by your instructor.

QUICKBOOKS NOTES

QuickBooks allows you to use several types of notes. These are To Do notes, Customer notes, Vendor notes, and Time Tracking notes.

To Do Notes

To Do notes are available in all the versions of QuickBooks. To Do's are accessed by clicking To Do List on the Company menu. The To Do List is QuickBooks version of a tickler file, which is used to remind you to do something on a particular date.

Steps to Create a To Do Note:

Click **To Do List** on the Company menu
Click **To Do** button, click **New**
Enter the text of the note
Enter the **Remind me on date**

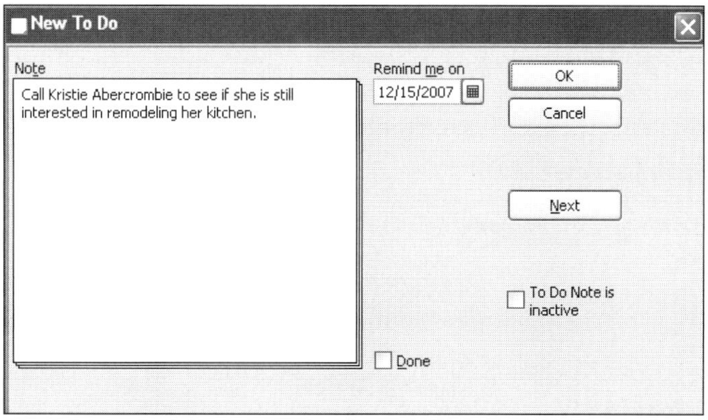

Click **OK**

- The note will be added to the list of To Do notes

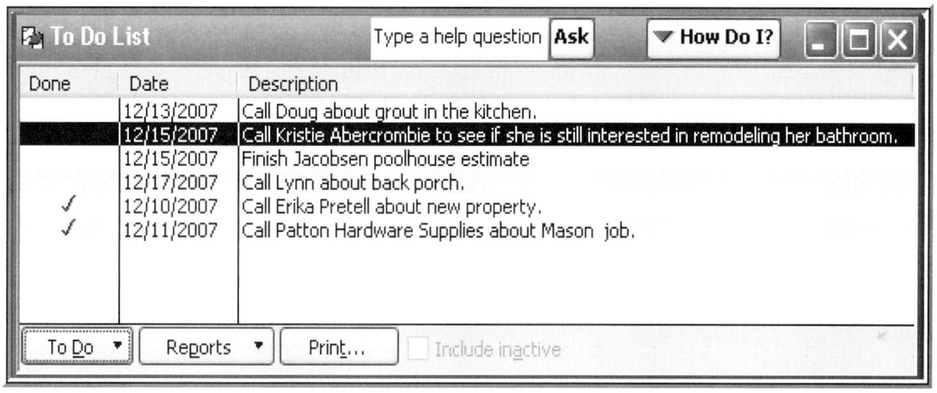

Customer Notes

The customer list contains information about each customer and/or job. One of the columns available is the Notes column. QuickBooks provides a notepad for recording notes about a customer or job. Approximately ten windows worth of text can be displayed on each customer's notepad. You can also write on the customer notepad when viewing a customer's record or when entering a transaction. When using the customer notepad, an entry may be date stamped, To Do notes may be accessed, and the note may be printed.

Steps to Create Customer or Job Notes

Open the **Customer Center**
Click on the Customer you wish to view or add notes (Kristie Abercrombie)
Click the **Edit Notes** button
Click at the bottom of the list of notes, press **Enter**, click the **Date Stamp** button and QuickBooks will enter the date of the note, then type the note

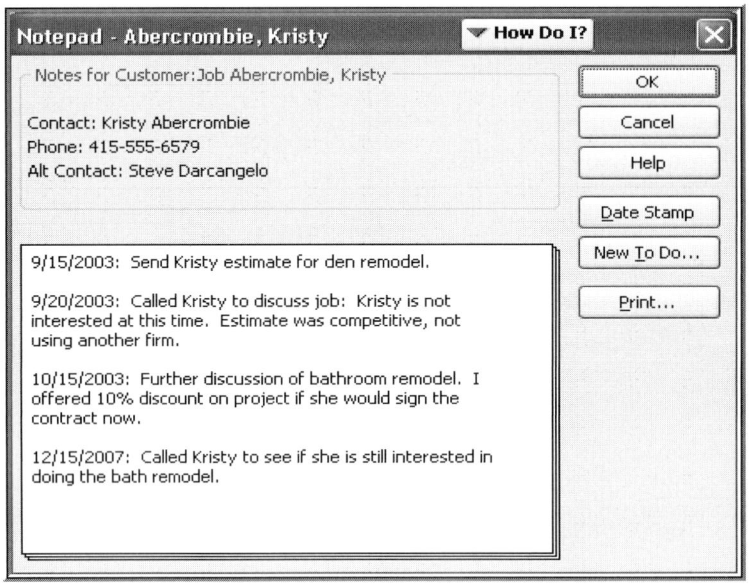

Click **OK** to save and exit the notepad

Vendor, Employee, and Other Names Notes

Vendor notes are recorded on the notepad for individual vendors in the Vendor Center. As with customer notes, this is where important conversations and product information would be recorded. The vendor notepad can be accessed from the Vendor Center. When using the vendor notepad, an entry may be date stamped, To Do notes may be accessed, and the note may be printed. Each entry on your Vendor, Employee, and Other Names lists has its own notepad where you can keep miscellaneous notes to yourself about that vendor, employee, or name. The procedures followed for vendors, employees, or other names are the same as illustrated for customers and vendors and will not be demonstrated.

Notes for Time Tracking

The Timer is a separate program that is installed and works in conjunction with QuickBooks Pro and Premier. Time Tracking will be discussed separately later in this appendix. Notes regarding the time spent working on a task are entered when using the stopwatch.

Steps to Create Notes for Time Tracking

Click the **Employees** menu, point to **Enter Time**
Click **Time/Enter Single Activity**
Click the drop-down list arrow for **Name** and select the employee (Dan T. Miller)
Click the drop-down list arrow for **Customer:Job** and select the customer (Kristie Abercrombie)

Click the drop-down list arrow for **Service Item**, click the item (Blueprint Changes)
Click in the **Notes** section of the window
Enter the note: **Revise plan for bathroom remodel**

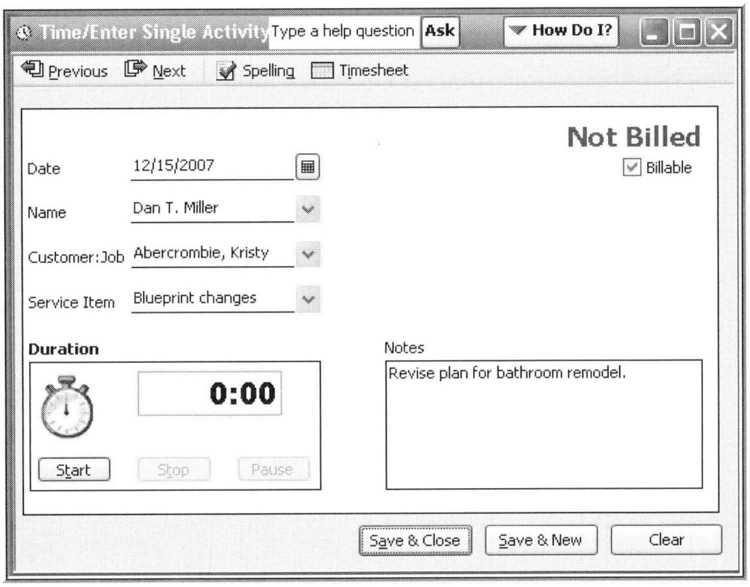

Click **Save & Close**

TRACKING TIME

Many businesses bill their customers or clients for the actual amount of time they spend working for them. In this case you would be tracking billable time. When you complete the invoice to the customer, you can add the billable time to the invoice with a few clicks. In other situations, you may not want to bill for the time; but you may want to track it. For example, you may want to find out how much time you spend working on a job that was negotiated at a fixed price. This will help you determine whether or not you estimated the job correctly. Also, you may want to track the amount of time employees spend on various jobs, whether or not you bill for the time.

Both QuickBooks Pro and Premier come with a separate Timer program. Timer can be run on any computer whether or not it has QuickBooks. You have a choice between tracking time via the Timer and then transferring the time data to QuickBooks, using the Stopwatch on the Time/Enter Single Activity window, or entering time directly into QuickBooks manually on the Weekly Timesheet window or the Time/Enter Single Activity window.

Steps to Track Time as a Single Activity

Click the **Employees** menu, point to **Enter Time**

Click **Time/Enter Single Activity**
Enter the date or accept the date the computer provides
Click the drop-down list arrow for **Name** and select the employee (Dan T. Miller)
Click the drop-down list arrow for **Customer:Job** and select the customer (Kristie Abercrombie) for whom time is being recorded
Click the drop-down list arrow for **Service Item**, click the item (Blueprint Changes)
Indicate whether or not the time recorded is billable

- A check in the billable box means that this is recorded as billable time. No check means that the time is being tracked but not billed.

Click the drop-down list arrow for **Payroll Item**
Indicate the payroll item for the time
Enter any notes regarding the work being performed
Click **Start** on the timer
When finished with the work, click **Stop** on the timer

- If work is stopped at any time, you may click Pause when stopping and click Start when resuming work.

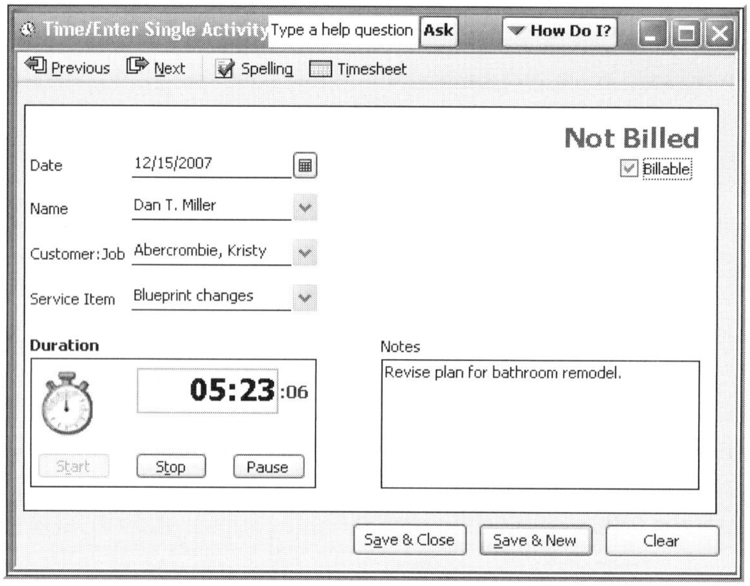

When finished, click **Stop** and **Save & Close**

Steps to Track Time on a Timesheet

Click **Employees** menu, point to **Enter Time**
Click **Use Weekly Timesheet**
Click the drop-down list arrow for **Name**, and click the name of the employee doing the work (Dan T. Miller)
Enter the date, accept the date the computer provides, or click the **Set Date** button

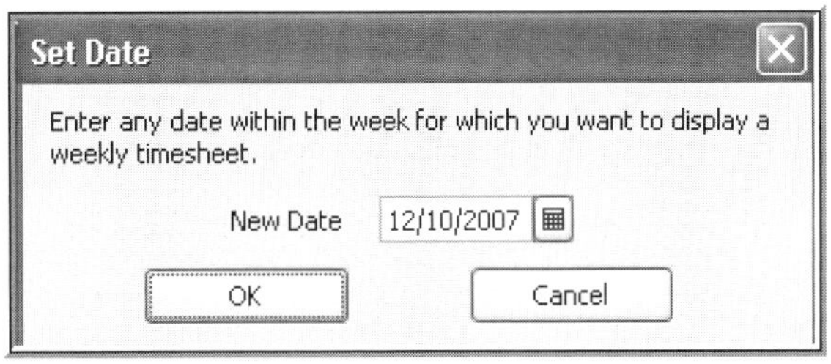

- Any work completed as a Single Activity will appear on the time sheet

If you need to enter the information for the time period, in the Customer column, click the drop-down list arrow for Customer:Job

Click the name of the customer for whom work is being performed

Click the drop-down list arrow for **Service Item**

Click the name of the service item

Enter any notes regarding the work

Enter the number of hours worked in the appropriate columns for the days of the week

If the information is the same as the previous timesheet, click Copy Last Sheet

- The information for the previous timesheet will be entered for this time period.

Indicate whether or not the hours are billable

- QuickBooks Timer records all hours as billable unless otherwise indicated. The icons in the last column indicate whether or not the items are billable, have been billed on a previous invoice, or are not billable.

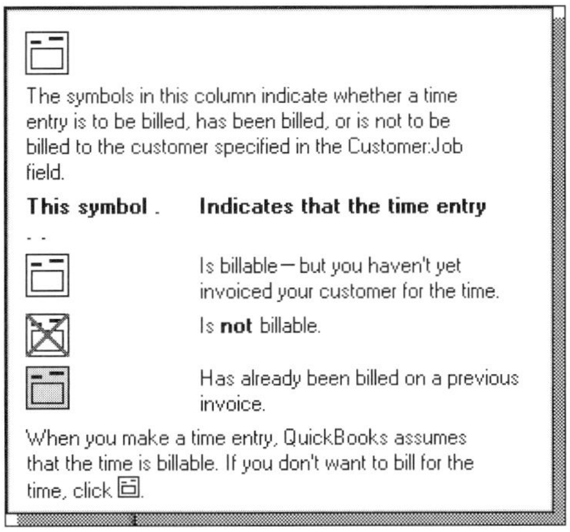

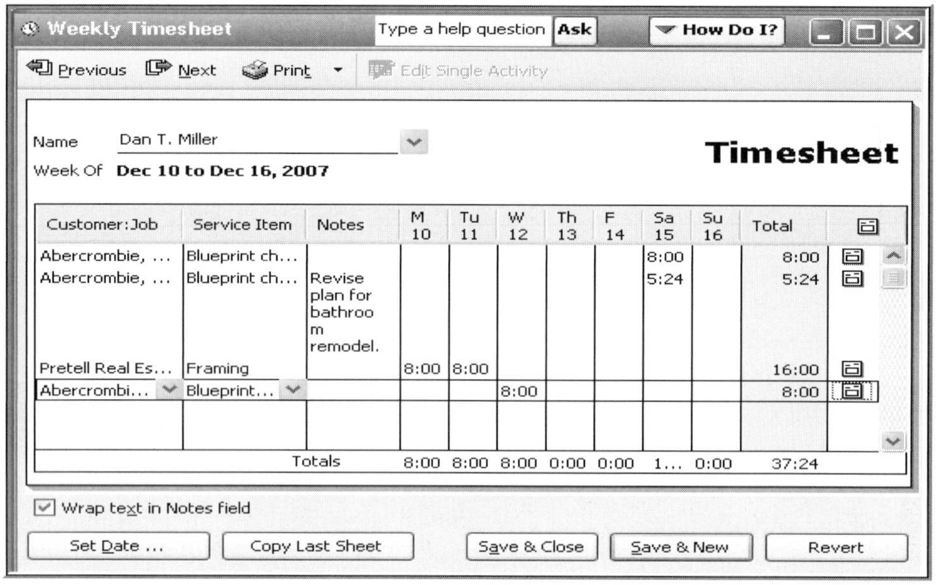

When the timesheet is complete, click **Save & Close**

<u>Prepare an Invoice Using Billable Hours</u>

Click the **Invoice** icon on the Customer Navigator
Enter the name of the **Customer:Job**

- QuickBooks will search for any estimates to be billed to the Customer:Job. If necessary, select the estimate to be billed. Indicate whether the estimate should be billed in full or in part. Complete this section of the invoice.

Since we do not want to bill for estimates, click **Cancel** to go to the invoice and not bill for the estimates.

- A Time & Expense Invoice will appear. It has a column for Class. When the Time appears for the customer, there will not be the same number shown as in the screen shot following the next steps.

Click the **Time/Costs** button on the top of the Create Invoices screen
Click the **Time** tab
Scroll through the list of Time and Costs for the customer
Click the time you wish to bill

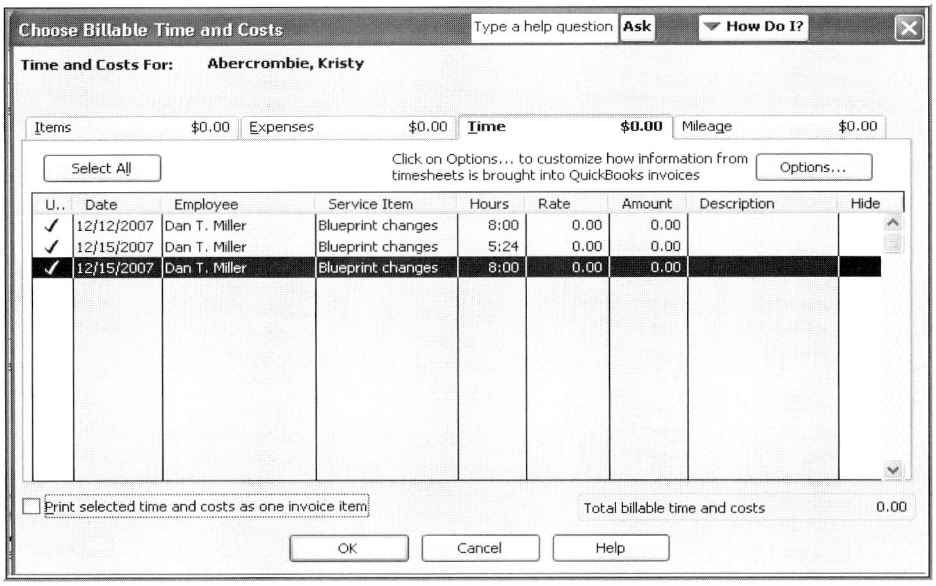

Click **OK**

- The time will be entered on the invoice.

Complete the invoice as previously instructed

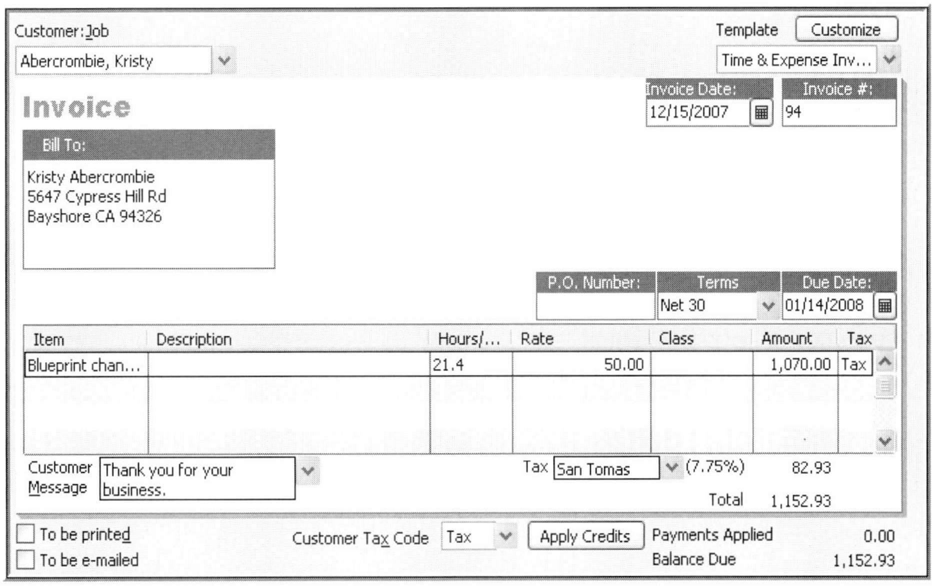

- The time clock keeps time in minutes but enters time on the invoice in tenths of an hour.

Click **Save & Close**

JOB COSTING AND TRACKING

Many companies complete work based on a job for a customer rather than just the customer. In QuickBooks, a job is a project done for a particular customer. You must always associate a job with a customer. However, if you are only doing one job for the customer, you do not have to add a new job to the Customer:Job list. Instead, you can use the Job Info tab to track the status of the job. This tab is available in the New Customer (or Edit Customer) window when you have not set up any jobs for the customer. You may also track several jobs for one customer.

When tracking jobs, there are nineteen reports that may be prepared. These reports use the information provided when tracking the jobs and display information. These reports answer questions about how well you estimate jobs, how much time you spend on jobs, how profitable jobs are, and mileage costs for the jobs. Some of the reports available are:

Job profitability summary: This report summarizes how much money your company has made or lost on each job for each customer

Job profitability detail: This report shows how much money your company has made to date on the customer or job whose name you entered. The report lists costs and revenues for each item you billed to the customer so you can see which parts of the job were profitable and which parts were not.

Job estimates vs. actuals summary: This report summarizes how accurately your company estimated job-related costs and revenues. The report compares estimated cost to actual cost and estimated revenue to actual revenue for all customers.

Job estimates vs. actuals detail: This report shows how accurately your company estimated costs and revenues for the customer or job whose name you entered. The report compares estimated and actual costs and estimated and actual revenues for each item that you billed. That way, you can see which parts of the job you estimated accurately and which parts you did not.

Time by job summary: This report shows how much time your company spent on various jobs. For each customer or job, the report lists the type of work performed (service items). Initially, the report covers all dates from your QuickBooks records, but you can restrict the period covered by choosing a different date range from the Dates list.

Time by job detail: This report lists each time activity (that is, work done by one person for a particular customer or job on a specific date) and shows whether the work is billed, unbilled, or not billable. The report groups and subtotals the activities first by customer and job and then by service item.

Mileage by vehicle summary: The report lists the total miles and mileage expenses for each vehicle used by the company.

Steps to Create a Job for a Customer

Open the **Customer Center**

Select the customer for whom you want to add a job

Click the **New Customer & Job** button, click **Add Job**
In the New Job window, enter a name for this job
On the **Job Info** tab, choose a job status (Pending, Awarded, etc.) from the drop-down list.
(Optional) Enter a start date and an end date (projected or actual) for the job
(Optional) Enter a job description and a job type

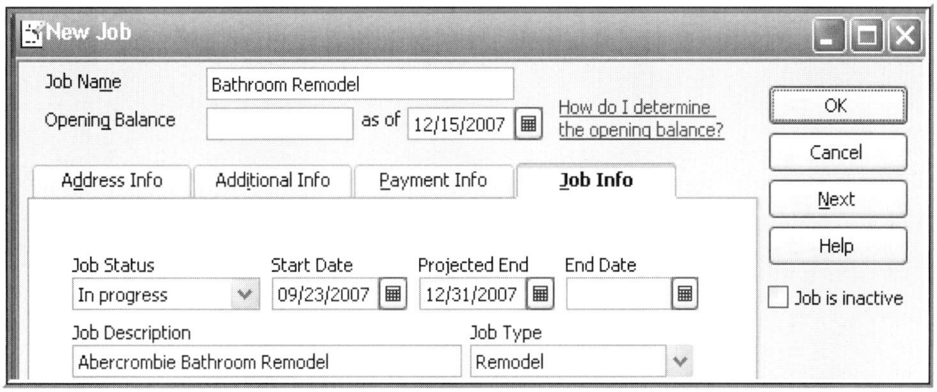

Click **OK** to record the new job.
The job is added to the customer or the Customer List

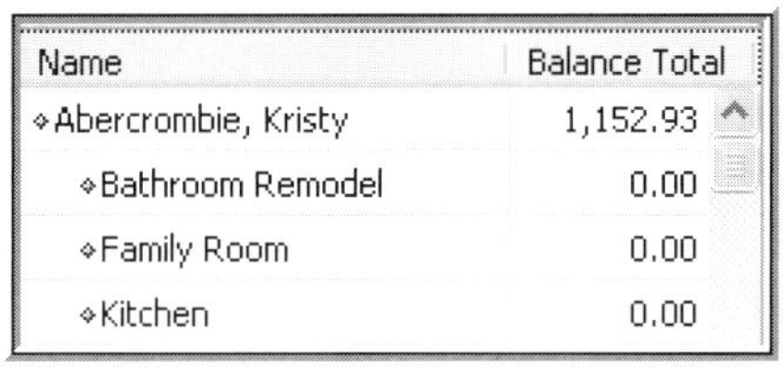

Steps to Create a Bill Received for Expenses Incurred on a Job and Items Purchased for a Job

Enter the bill information as instructed in Chapter 6
Click the drop-down list arrow for Customer:Job
Click the appropriate Customer:Job
Enter the date and amount of the bill
Enter the expense on the Expenses tab

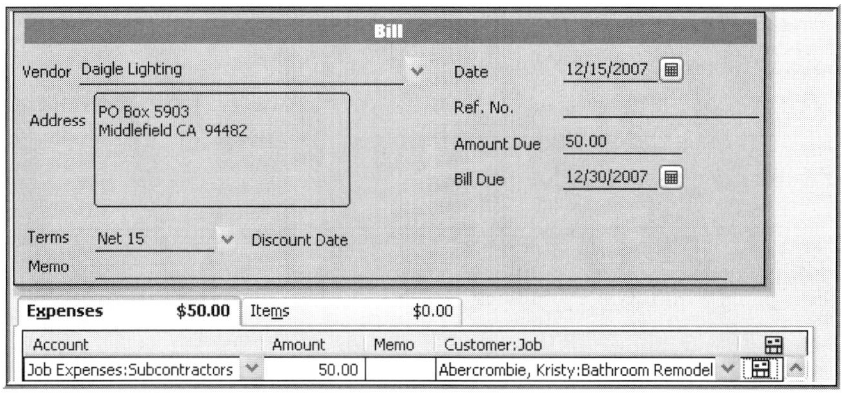

To prepare a bill for both expenses and items, click the Items tab and enter the appropriate information.

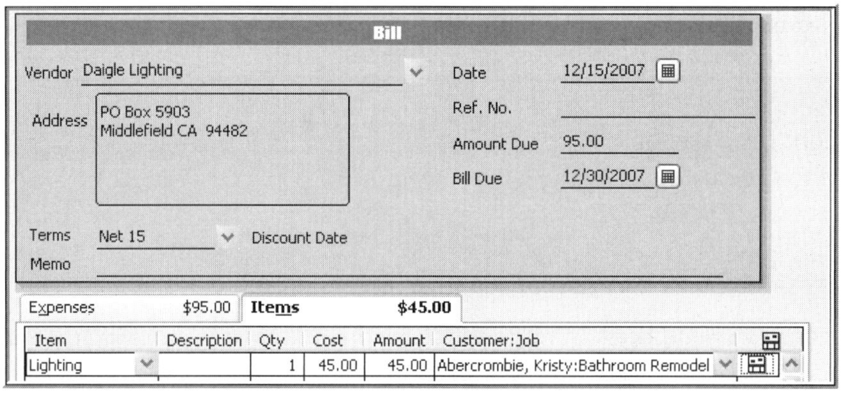

Click **Save & Close**

Steps to Create an Invoice for Items and/or Expenses Billed for a Job

Open an Invoice as previously instructed
Indicate the Customer:Job as previously instructed
Click **Time/Costs** at the top of the Create Invoices window
Click the **Items** tab
Select the Item by clicking in the **Use** column

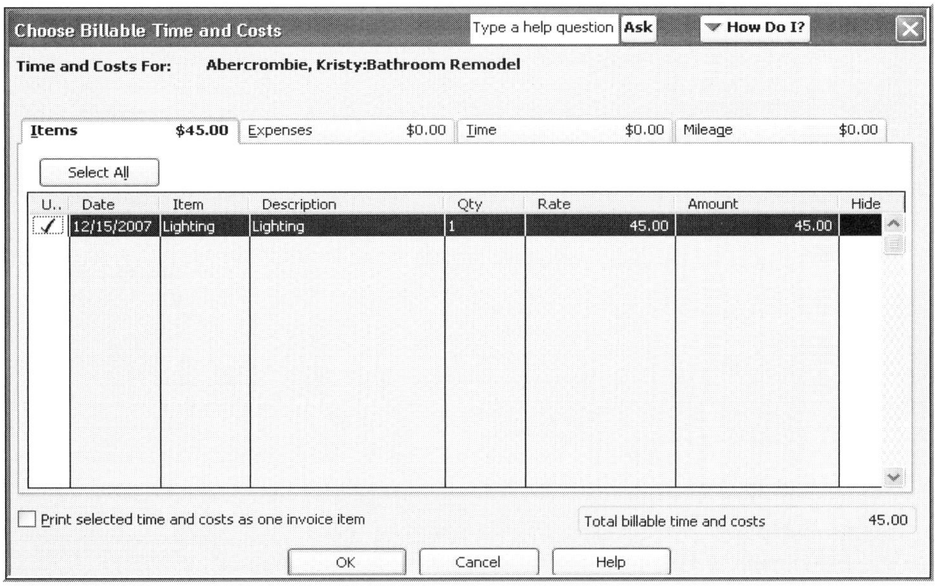

Indicate whether or not you have a markup percentage and the account associated with markups
Click the **Expenses** tab
Click the Expense in the Use column to select

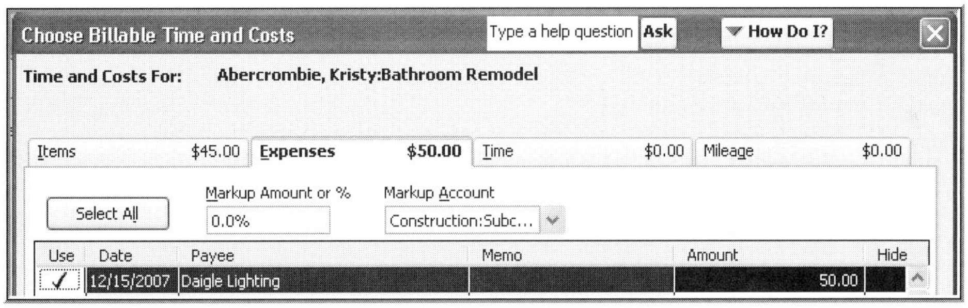

Click **OK**
Complete the Invoice

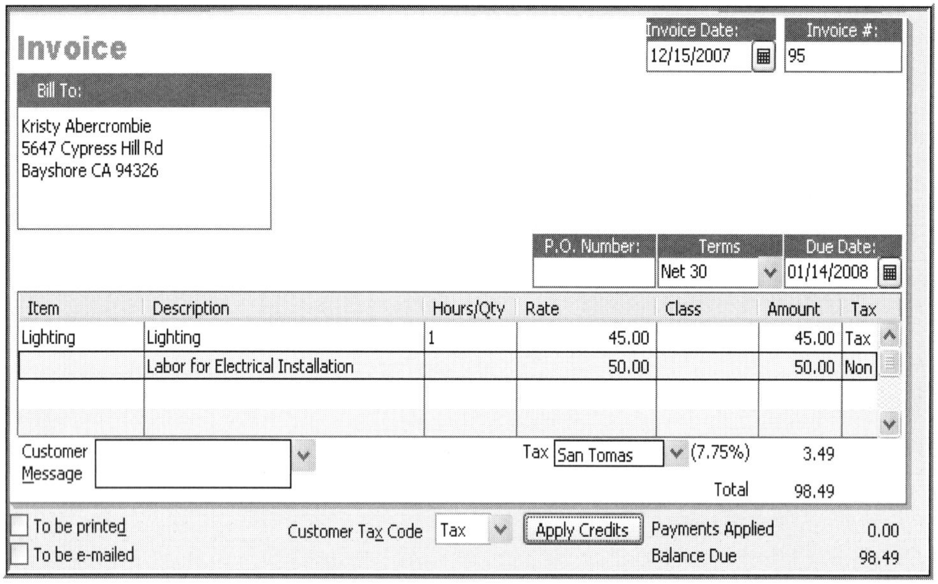

Invoice

Invoice Date: 12/15/2007 | Invoice #: 95

Bill To:
Kristy Abercrombie
5647 Cypress Hill Rd
Bayshore CA 94326

P.O. Number: | Terms: Net 30 | Due Date: 01/14/2008

Item	Description	Hours/Qty	Rate	Class	Amount	Tax
Lighting	Lighting	1	45.00		45.00	Tax
	Labor for Electrical Installation		50.00		50.00	Non

Customer Message | Tax San Tomas (7.75%) 3.49
Total 98.49

To be printed
To be e-mailed
Customer Tax Code Tax | Apply Credits | Payments Applied 0.00
Balance Due 98.49

Click **Save & Close**

<u>Creating Reports Using Jobs and Time</u>

Use **Report Center** or the Reports Menu
Click **Jobs & Time**
Click the report you wish to prepare
If preparing the report from the menu, enter the Dates as a range or enter the **From** and **To** dates at the top of the report and Tab

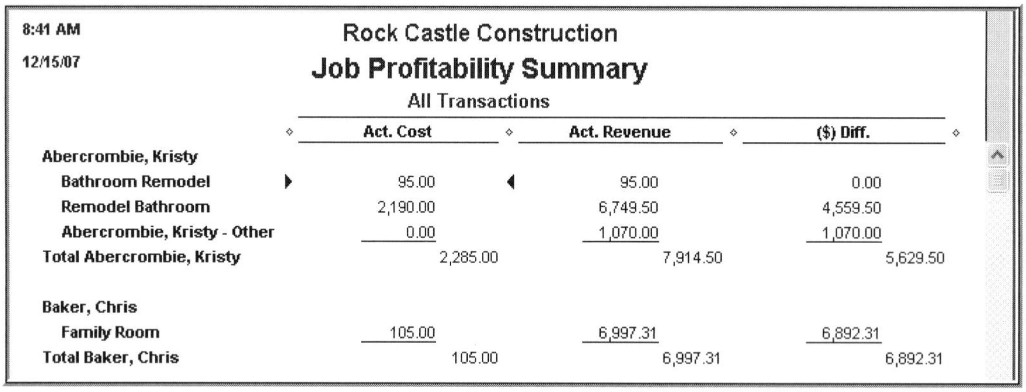

8:41 AM
12/15/07

Rock Castle Construction
Job Profitability Summary
All Transactions

	Act. Cost		Act. Revenue		($) Diff.	
Abercrombie, Kristy						
Bathroom Remodel	95.00		95.00		0.00	
Remodel Bathroom	2,190.00		6,749.50		4,559.50	
Abercrombie, Kristy - Other	0.00		1,070.00		1,070.00	
Total Abercrombie, Kristy		2,285.00		7,914.50		5,629.50
Baker, Chris						
Family Room	105.00		6,997.31		6,892.31	
Total Baker, Chris		105.00		6,997.31		6,892.31

Scroll through the report to evaluate the information

SENDING MERCHANDISE USING QUICKBOOKS SHIPPING MANAGER

QuickBooks has a shipping manager that works in conjunction with FedEx or UPS. In order to send merchandise to a customer, you must set up the shipping manager and have an account with FedEx. Since we are working for a fictitious company we will not do this. The steps listed below will illustrate the setup of the Shipping Manager but will not complete the shipping procedure.
To set up the Shipping Manager, you would click the **Ship** button at the top of an invoice
Click **Ship a Package**
Complete or change the information on the QuickBooks Shipping Manager FedEx form

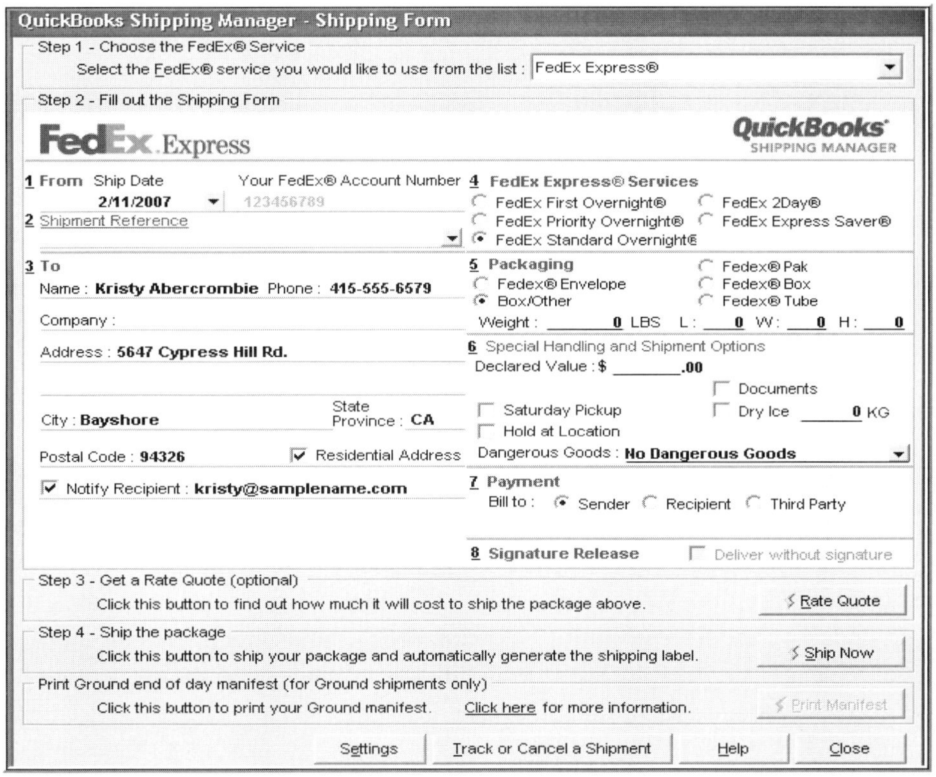

Click **Rate Quote** to find out the cost for shipment
Click **Ship Now** to ship the package and automatically generate the shipping label
For this demonstration click **Close**, when asked if you would like to cancel this shipment, click **Yes**
To ship using UPS click **Ship UPS Package**

- Since a UPS account has not been created for the sample company, you would need to complete the Shipping Manager setup wizard to establish an account.

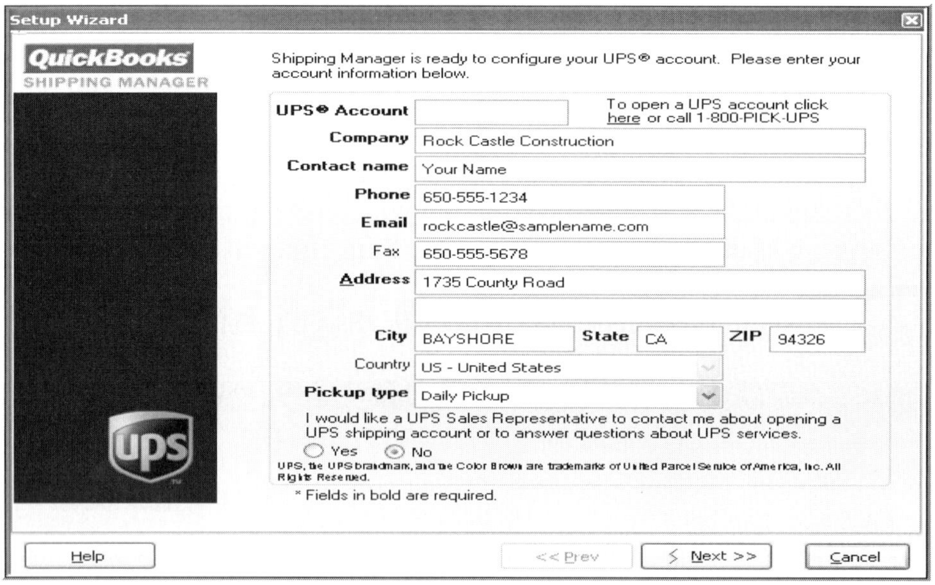

In a business you would click Next and continue the setup, since this is a practice company, click **Cancel**

PRICE LEVELS

In QuickBooks Pro and Premier you can create price levels. Price levels are created to increase or decrease inventory, non-inventory, and service item prices. For each price level you create, you assign a name and percentage of increase or decrease. You can use price levels on invoices, sales receipts, or credit memos. When you apply a price level to an item on a sales form, the adjusted price appears in the Rate column. You can assign price levels to customers and jobs. Then, whenever you use that customer and job on a sales form, the associated price level is automatically used to calculate the item price.

Create a Price Level List

From the Lists menu, choose **Price Level List**
From the Price Level menu, choose **New**
In the New Price Level window, enter the name of the new price level
In the area for **This price level will**, select either Increase sales price by or Reduce sales price by
In the Percentage % field, enter the percent number by which the item price will be increased or reduced.

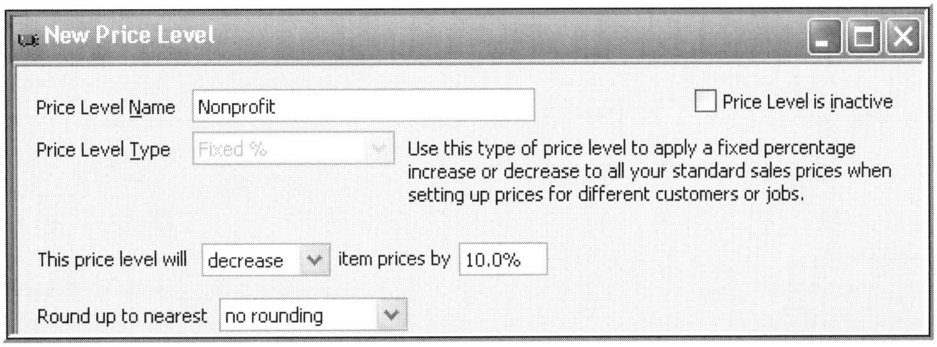

Click **OK** to go back to the Price Levels list.

Apply a Price Level on an Invoice

Fill out the invoice as previously instructed
In the Rate column, click the drop-down button

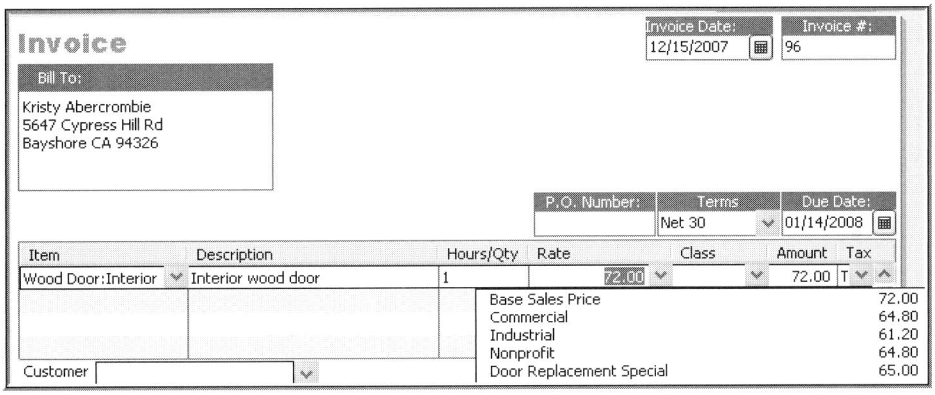

Choose a price level to apply to the item

- The amount shown next to each price level is the adjusted amount of the item

Save the invoice

Associate a Price Level with a Customer

Access the Customer Center, select the **Customer**
Click the **Edit Customer** button
Click the **Additional Info** tab
From the Price Level drop-down list, select the price level you want to associate with the customer

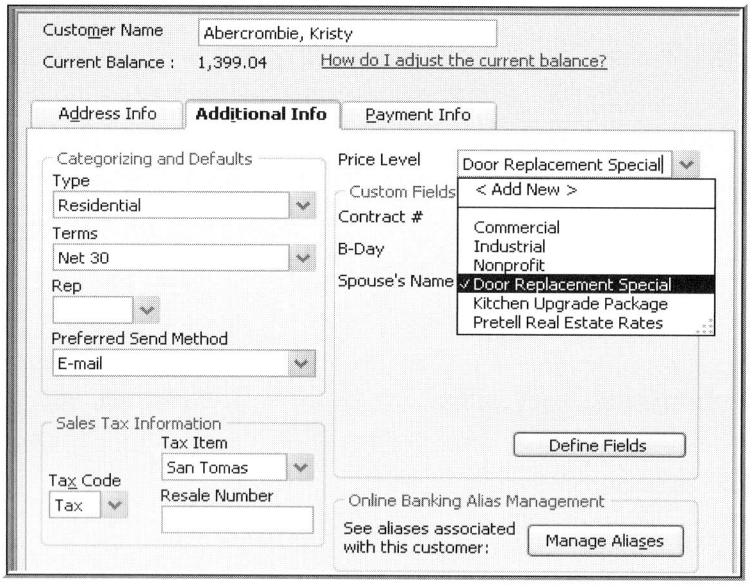

Click **OK**

When preparing an invoice, items will automatically appear at the price level selected for the customer

To verify this, click the drop-down list arrow for Price Each and notice that the price for the interior wood door has been entered at the price level selected for the customer (Door Replacement Special).

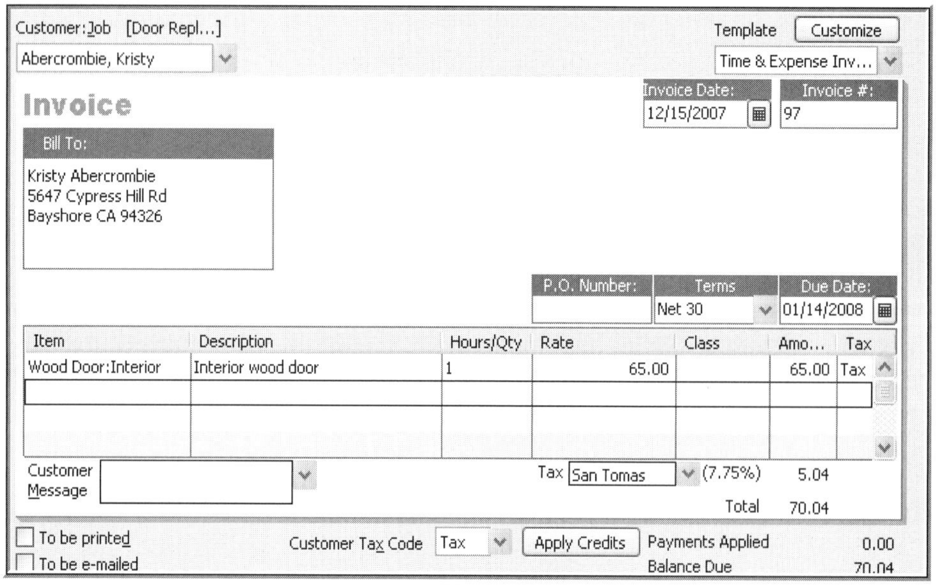

Click **Save & Close**

QUICKBOOKS® PRO ONLINE FEATURES

D

QuickBooks Pro is up-to-date in its online capabilities. It has integrated Internet access built into the program and Internet Explorer is included on the QuickBooks Pro CD-ROM. It performs online updates to the program, subscribers to the Basic Payroll Services can receive online updates to tax tables, Trial Versions of the program can be downloaded, and online banking can be performed within the program. In addition, through QuickBooks.com you can obtain product support, access training resources, find a professional advisor in your area, access user-to-user forums, obtain information about business resources, access Intuit's Home Page, and order checks and business forms online.

In addition to the included online items, there are several online subscription programs that may be used in conjunction with QuickBooks. These include processing credit card payments, credit check services, a QuickBooks credit card, a shipping manager, bill pay, and others. Intuit also offers the QuickBooks Solutions Marketplace that brings together over 100 companies that have integrated their software products with QuickBooks Pro, Premier and QuickBooks Enterprise Solutions.

This Appendix will explore some of the online options listed above.

INTUIT AND THE INTERNET

At Intuit's Web site you may get up-to-date information about QuickBooks Pro and other products by Intuit. You can access the Intuit Web site at www.Intuit.com through your browser.

QUICKBOOKS® PRO UPDATES

Intuit has a service that is free of charge and allows you to check the Web site to download messages and updates for QuickBooks Pro. You may have QuickBooks Pro do this automatically, or it will remind you to update periodically. QuickBooks Pro provides two methods for updating—automatic and immediate. Both methods require an Internet connect and may be used concurrently.

Update QuickBooks Pro Automatically

With this method, updates of your choice are automatically downloaded from the Intuit server to your computer. QuickBooks Pro periodically checks the Intuit server for new updates, and proceeds to download information gradually at times when your open Internet connection is not being used by another process or application.

The advantages of updating QuickBooks Pro automatically are:

- Updates are downloaded to your computer unobtrusively, without interrupting a QuickBooks Pro session or other tasks that you perform with your computer.
- Updating occurs whether or not QuickBooks Pro is running.
- You can disconnect from the Internet anytime and not worry about updating. When you reconnect to the Internet, QuickBooks Pro resumes downloading updates at the point where it was previously halted.

QuickBooks Pro continues to download updates automatically until you turn off the Automatic Update option. Even with the Automatic Update option turned on, you can still download all available updates immediately whenever you choose to do so.

If you have several different copies of QuickBooks Pro running and you share data, it is essential that computers be updated at the same time so they all have the same exact version of the program in operation. If you update QuickBooks Pro on one computer and not another, QuickBooks Pro may not be able to read the company file on the computer that did not receive the update.

Update QuickBooks Pro Immediately

With this method, updates of your choice are downloaded immediately from the Intuit server to your computer. You can use this method at any time—even when your computer is configured to download updates automatically.

To download immediately, click the **Help** menu, click **Update QuickBooks**, click the **Update Now** tab

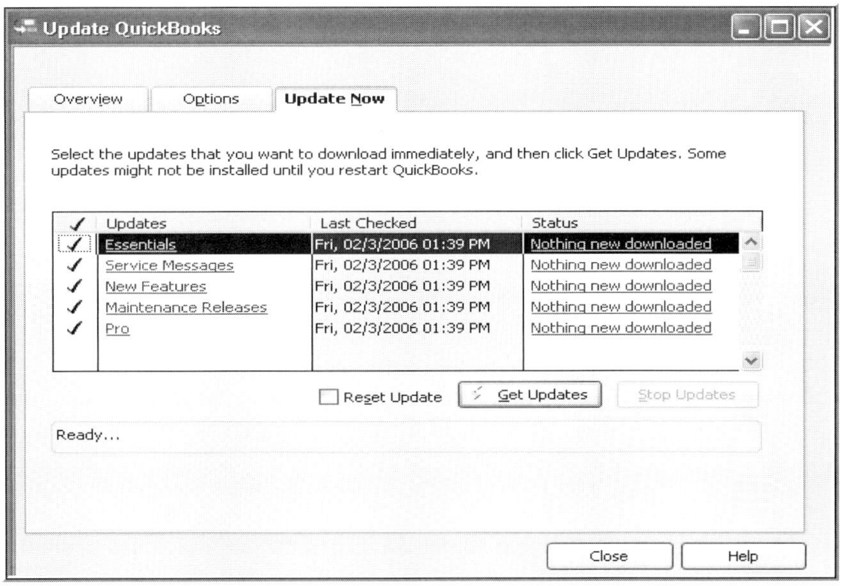

Click **Get Updates**

<u>Select or Deselect Automatic Updates</u>

To select or deselect automatic updates, click the **Help** menu, click **Update QuickBooks**, click the **Options** tab

To select Automatic Update, click **Yes**, click **Select All** to choose updates of New Features and Maintenance Releases

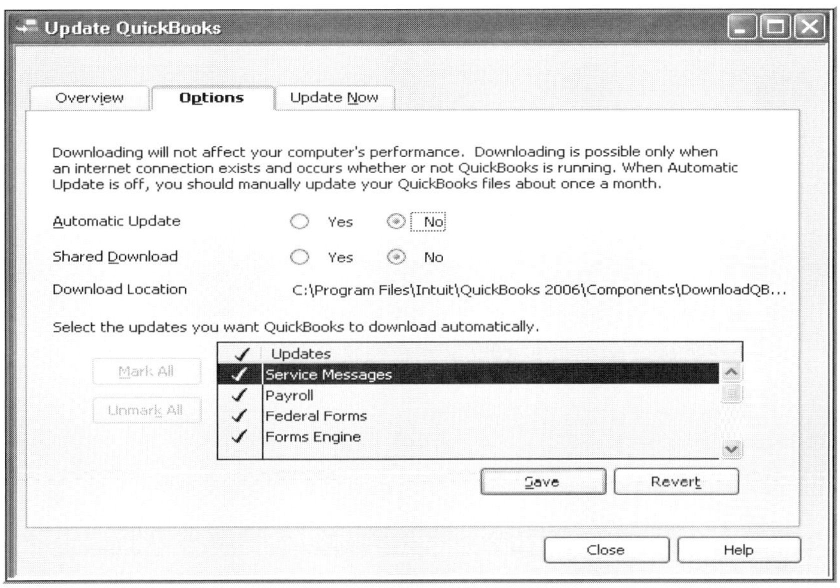

To deselect automatic update, click **No** and **Save**

- In a classroom configuration and for students using QuickBooks other than in the classroom, it is recommended that Automatic Updates be turned off. If a computer with an updated program is used to record transactions and a different computer without an updated program is used later, QuickBooks may not recognize the company file. To update, all computers in use should be updated at the same time.

CONNECTING TO THE INTERNET IN QUICKBOOKS® PRO

Before connecting to Intuit's using QuickBooks, you must have the QuickBooks Pro program and a company open. In addition, you must have a modem for your computer, and the modem must be connected to a telephone line or cable. Once the modem is connected and QuickBooks Pro and a company are open, you may establish your Internet connection.

QuickBooks Pro has a step-by-step tutorial that will help you do this. Clicking Internet Connection Setup on the Help menu allows you to identify an internet connection and complete the setup. The first screen you see informs QuickBooks Pro of your choice for your Internet connection. You may tell QuickBooks Pro that you have an existing dial-up Internet connection, that you plan to use a direct connection through a network at school or work, or that you want to sign up for an Internet account with limited access.
Click the **Help** menu, click **Internet Connection Setup**

To Use an Established Internet Connection

Click **Use the following connection**, click the connection, click **Next**

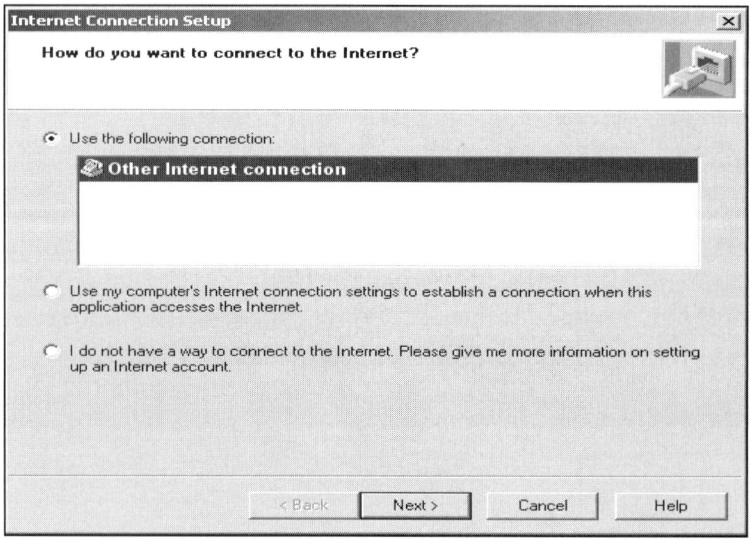

Verify the information provided, click **Done**

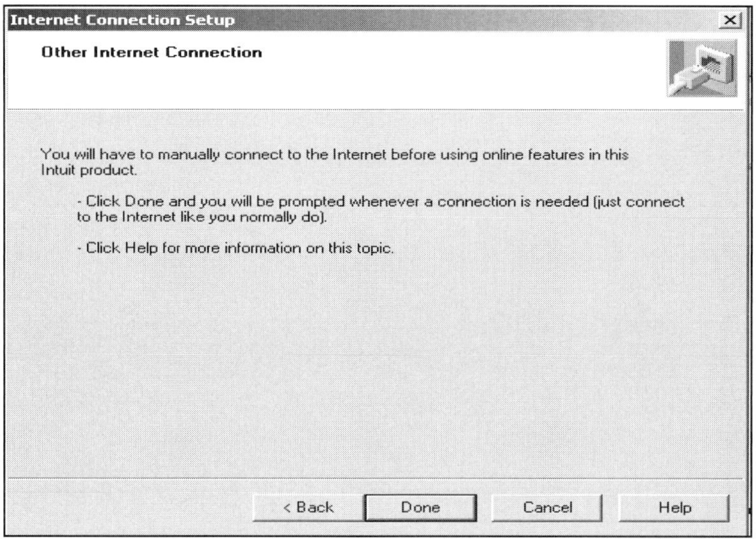

To Use a Computer's Internet Connection

If you have a direct Internet connection, select **Use my computer's Internet connection settings to establish a connection when this application accesses the Internet**, click **Next**

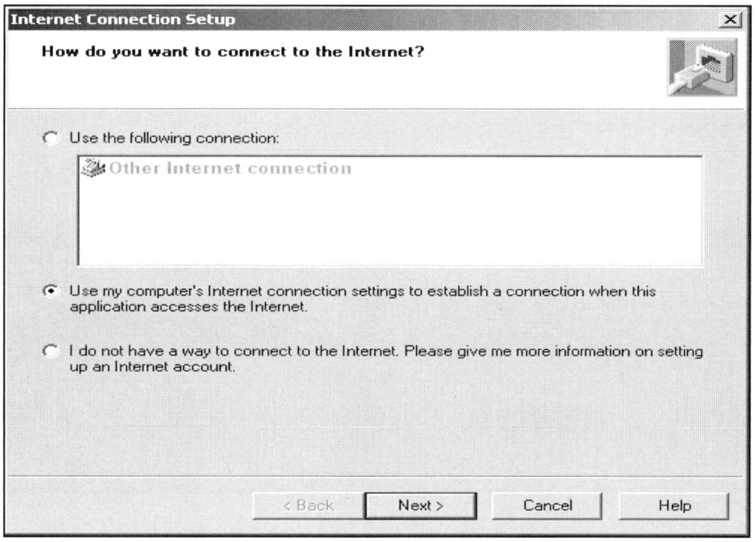

Verify the information, click **Done**

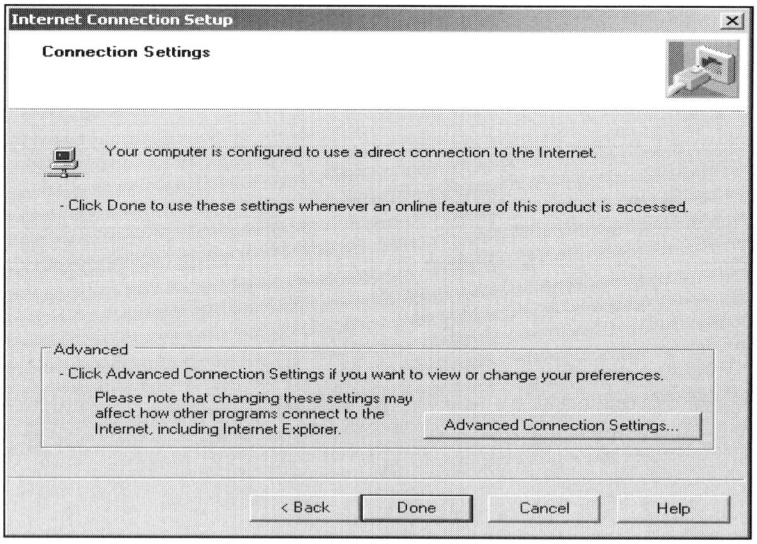

To Establish an Internet Provider and Connection

If you do not have an Internet provider, click **I do not have a way to connect to the Internet. Please give me more information on setting up an Internet account**

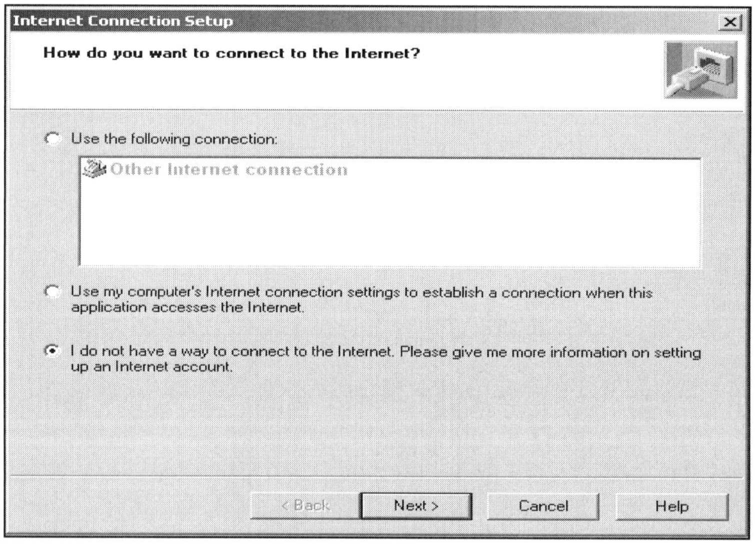

Click **Next**

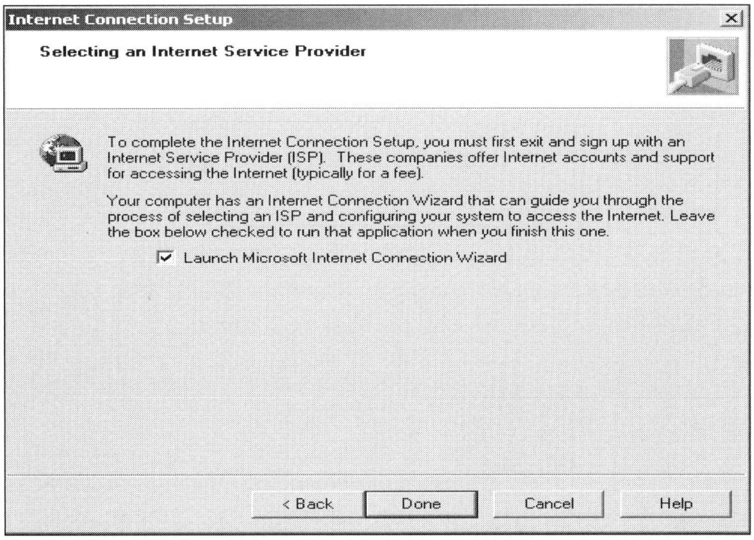

Click **Done** and complete the steps listed in the Microsoft Internet Connection Wizard

ACCESS QUICKBOOKS®' ONLINE FEATURES

Anytime you see a lightning bolt, this denotes information or services that require an Internet connection. Click on the lightning bolt.

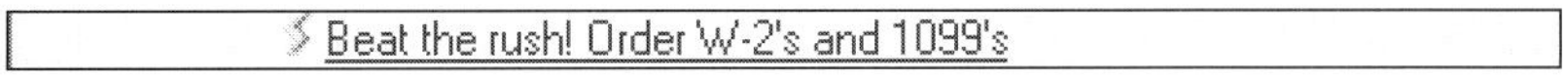

If you have a direct Internet connection, you will go directly to the QuickBooks Web site
If you use a dial-up service to connect to the Internet, you may get the following screen.

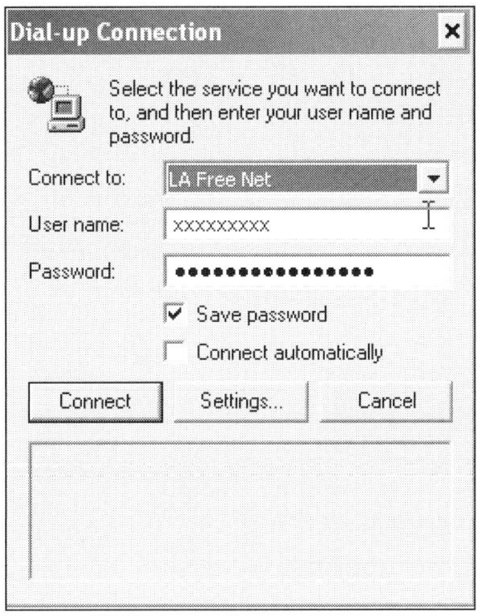

If necessary, click **Connect**

When you are connected, you will go to the areas requested. For example, on the Home Page, I clicked

QuickBooks connected to the Web and brought up a screen describing services available for subscription and used in conjunction with QuickBooks

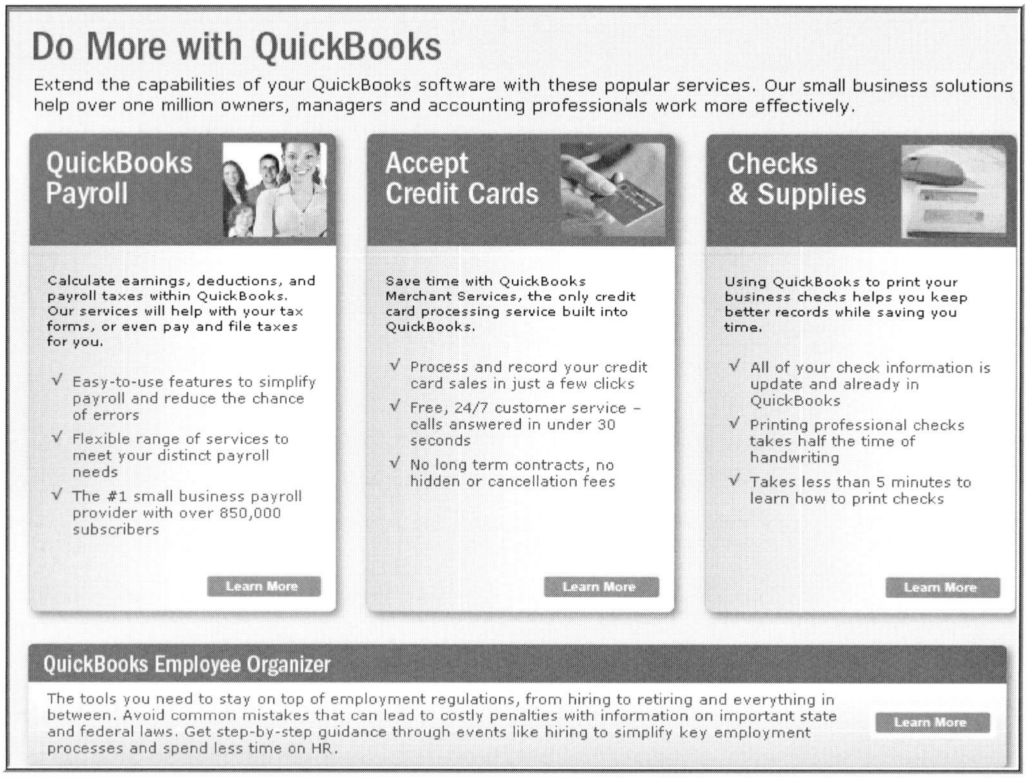

If you position the cursor on the any of the Learn More buttons, the cursor will turn into a hand. This means you can click on any of these items and get item descriptions and ordering information.

ONLINE BANKING AND PAYMENTS

Online banking and payment services are offered through QuickBooks Pro in conjunction with a variety of financial institutions. You must apply for this service through your financial institution. If you bank with or make payments to more than one institution, you must sign up with each institution separately. Most banks will charge a fee for online services and may not offer both online banking and online payment services. Many financial institutions provide online services.

Online Banking

Online account access allows you to download transactions from a checking, savings, money market, or credit or charge account. You can also transfer money online and send e-mail to your financial institution.

To use the online banking services for account access or payment, you need access to the Internet and an account at a participating financial institution. You must also apply for the service through QuickBooks or through a participating financial service. To see a list of participating financial institutions, click the Banking menu, point to Online Banking, and click **Available Financial Institutions**

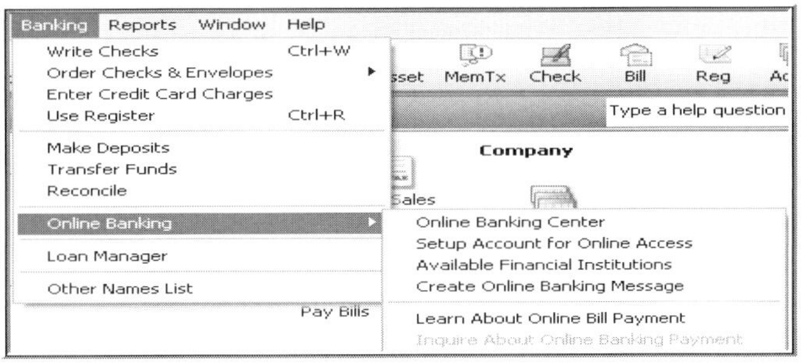

QuickBooks connects to the Internet and a list of banks appears

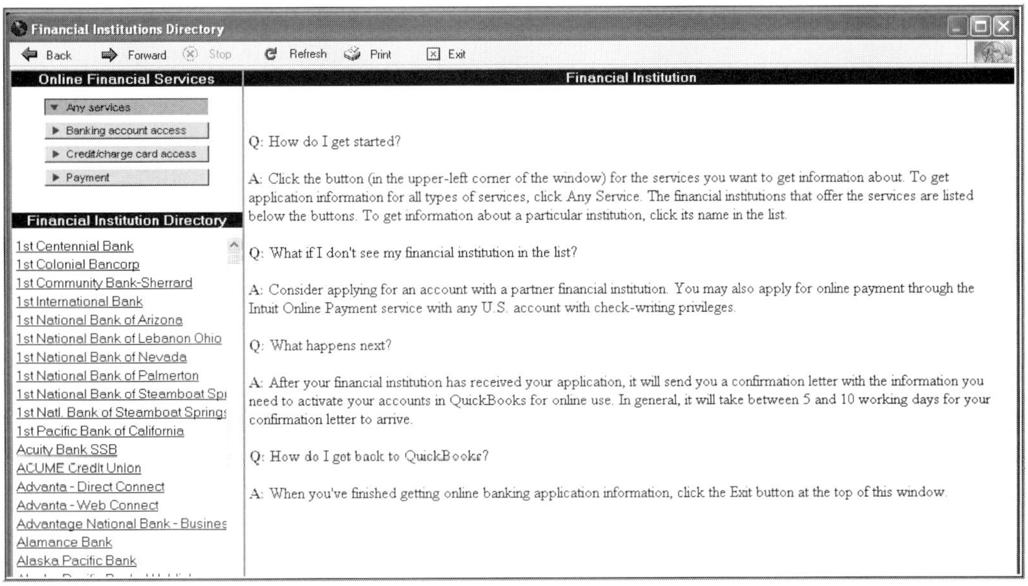

In order to provide security and confidentiality in online services, QuickBooks uses state-of-the-art encryption and authentication security features. All of your online communications with your financial institution require a Personal Identification Number (PIN) or password, which only you possess. You may also use passwords within QuickBooks Pro.

For this appendix, we will use Larry's Landscaping as our business and use ANYTIME Financial services as our financial institution

Set Up Online Banking

To apply for an online account, click the **Banking** menu bar
Point to Online Banking, click **Setup Account for Online Banking Access**
Complete the Online Setup Interview

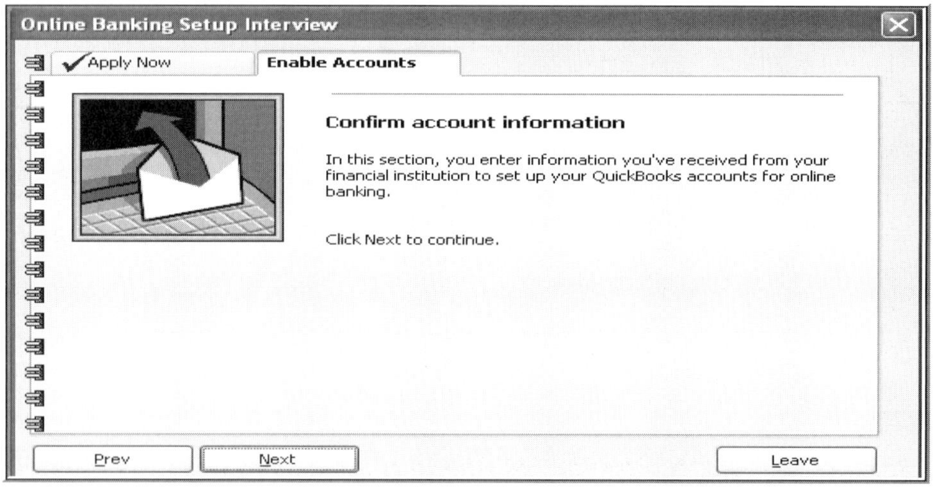

Click **Next**
Click the drop-down list arrow for **I would like to enter information for my accounts at:**
Click **ANYTIME Financial**

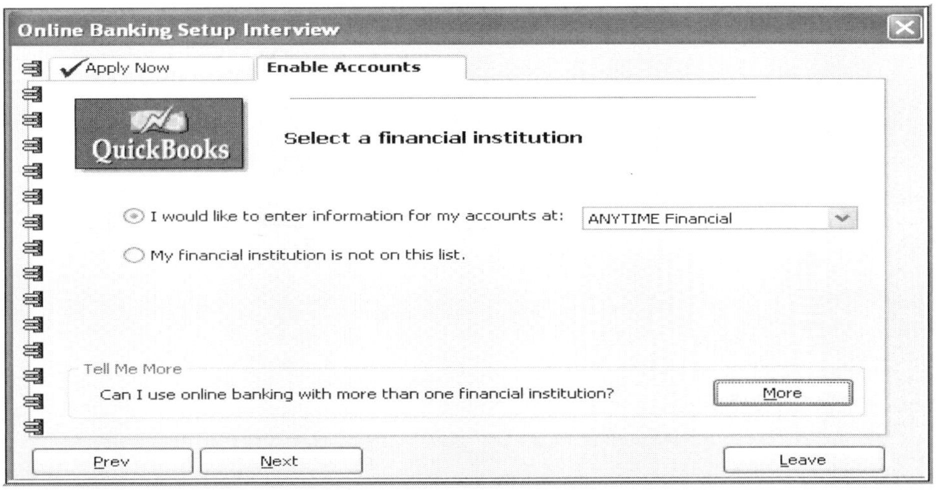

Click **Next**
Review the account information provided
Make any necessary changes

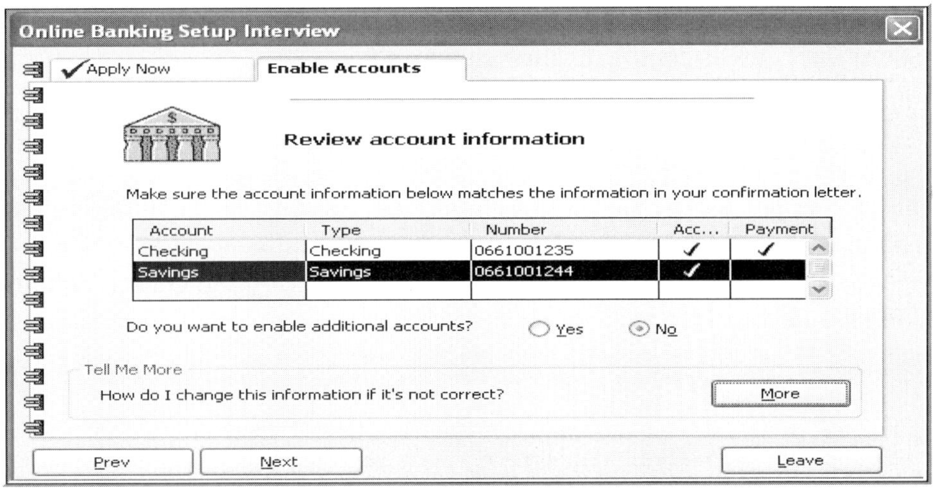

Click **Next**, and read the Service Agreement Information screen

Click **OK**
You do not wish to enable accounts at another institution
Click **Next**

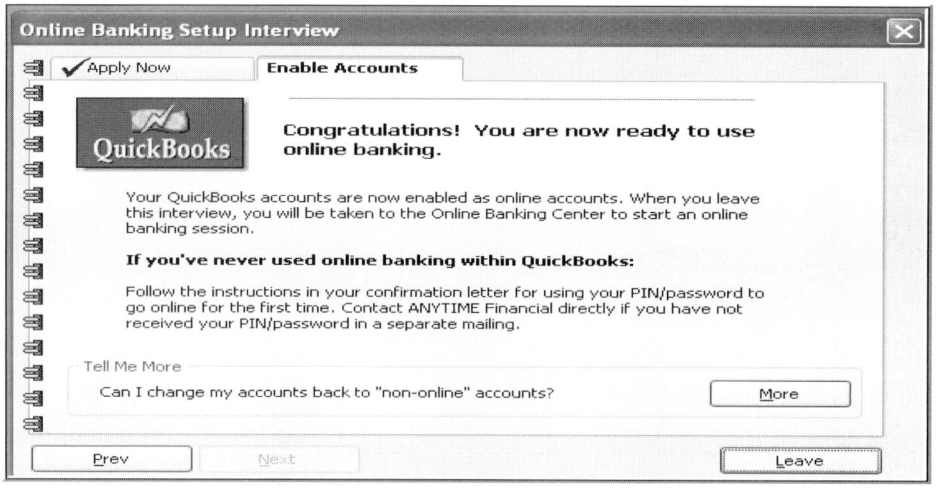

The Online Setup Interview is complete, click **Leave**

Using Online Banking

Online banking allows you to download current information from and send messages to your financial institution. This can include transactions, balances, online messages, and transfer of funds. To use online banking, click **Banking** on the menu bar, point to Online Banking, click **Online Banking Center**.

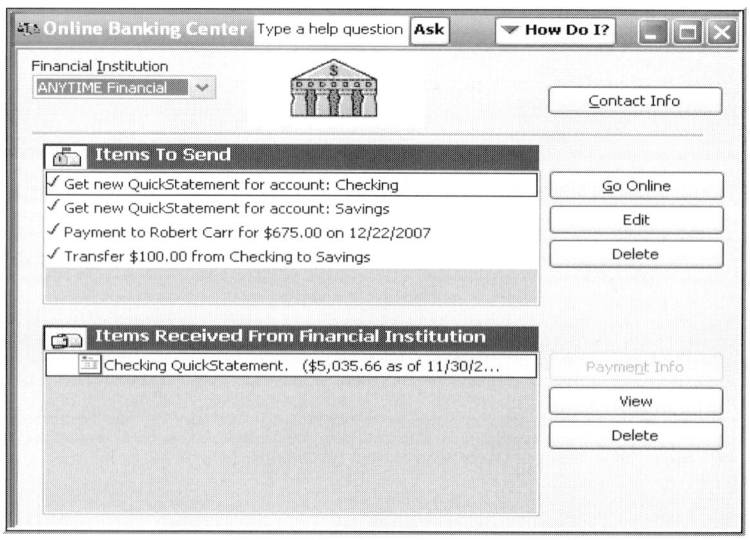

You can automatically compare the downloaded transactions with those in your register. QuickBooks Pro will match downloaded transactions to those in your register and note any unmatched transactions so that they may be entered into your register.
Click the **View** button

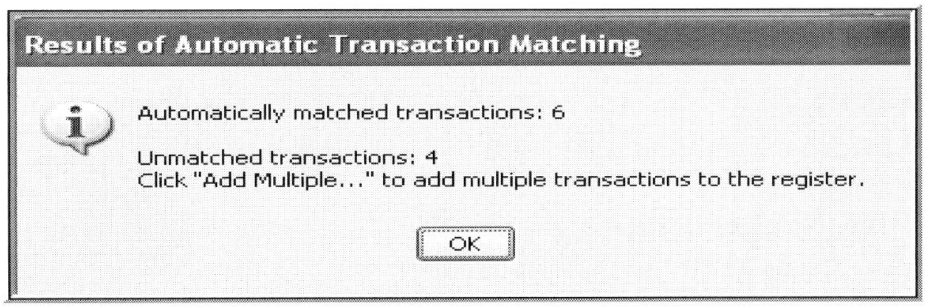

Click **OK**
The QuickStatement shown lists the transactions that occurred since your last download and any transactions that were not matched from previous downloads. The QuickStatement does not replace your paper statement. You will receive your usual paper statement by mail from your financial institution listing your monthly account transactions.
Note: Even the year for the sample company is 2007, many of the transactions have the year 2003.

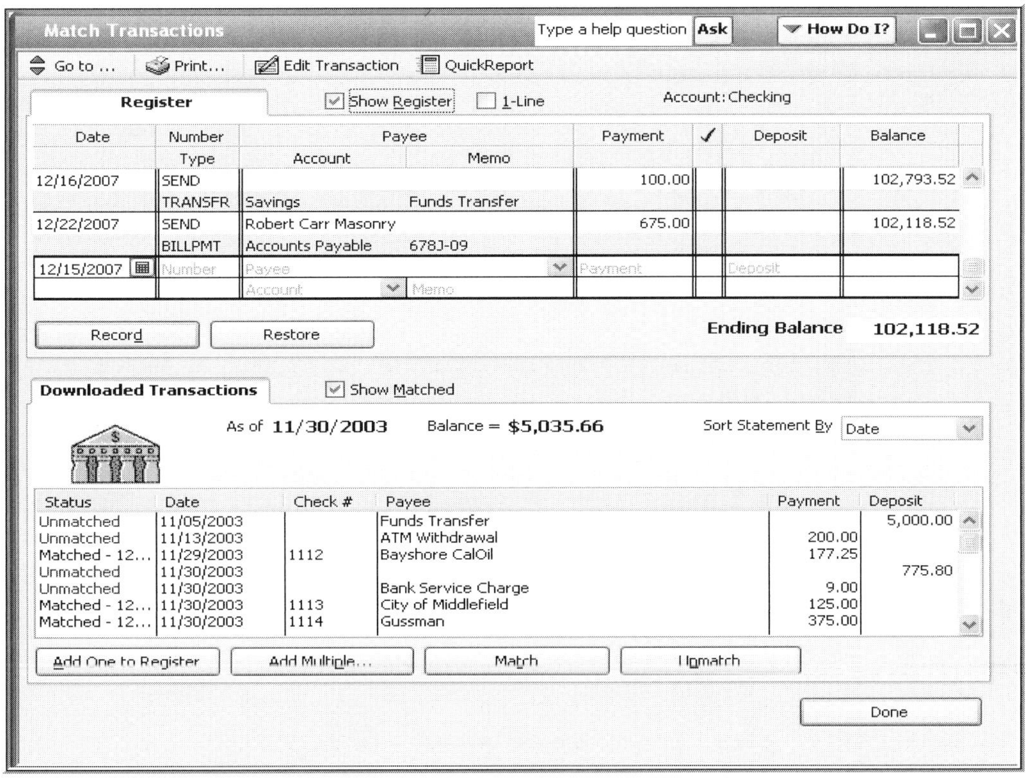

To match the ATM Withdrawal to the QuickStatement, you must add the transaction to the register.

Click the **Unmatched ATM Withdrawal** transaction in the lower portion of the screen, click the **Add One to Register** button.

Click **Add To Register** on the Unmatched Transaction screen

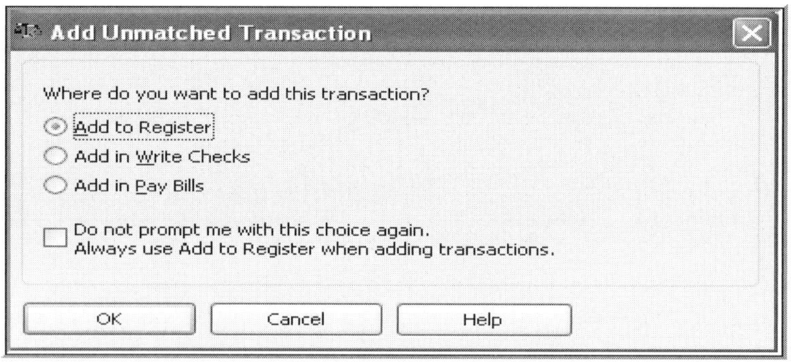

Click **OK**

Click the drop-down list arrow for Account, click **Owner's Draw** from the list of accounts.

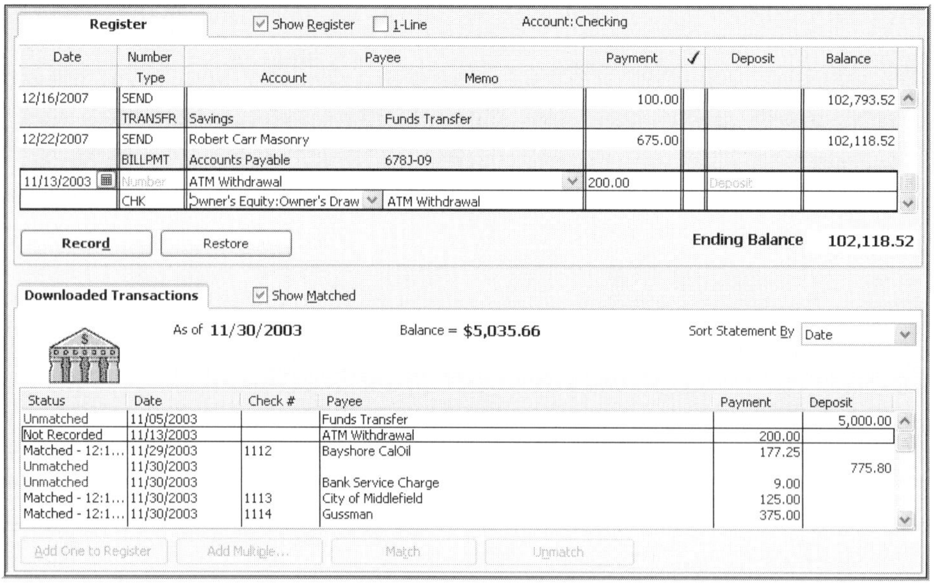

Click **Record**

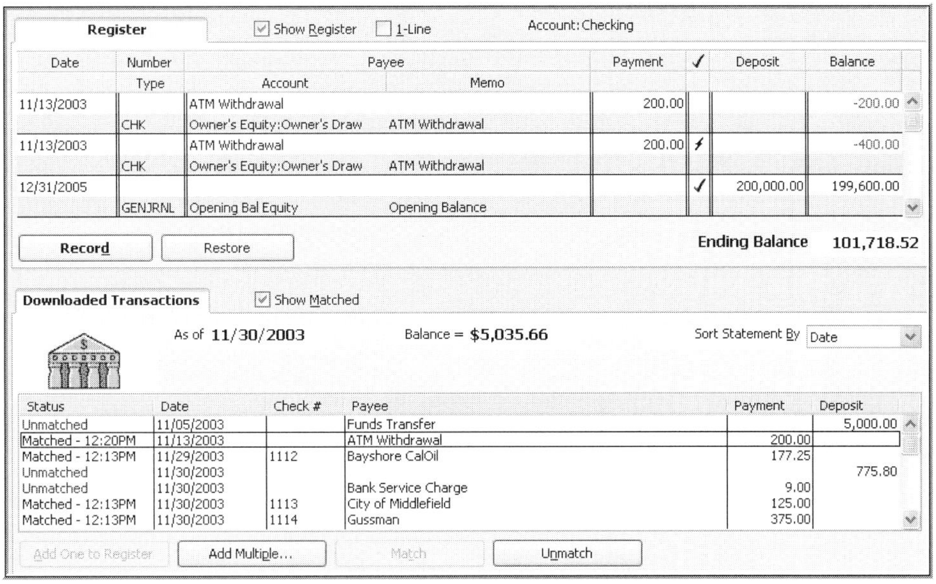

The transaction status is Matched

Click **Done**, if you get a message that not all transactions are matched, click **Yes**

Online Payments

You may use the online payment services to create online payment instructions for one or more payments, then send the instructions via your modem. You may schedule a payment to arrive on a certain date, inquire about online payments, and cancel them if need be. You can record and pay your bills at the same time, all from within QuickBooks.

Online banking through QuickBooks uses state-of-the-art encryption technology and requires a PIN to send transactions. You can use online payment with any U.S. bank account with check-writing privileges.

With online payment you can:

- Pay bills without writing checks or going to the post office.
- Attach additional information to the payment (such as invoice number and invoice date) so your vendor knows which bill to apply it to.
- Schedule a payment in advance, to be delivered on or before the date you specify.
- Apply for online payment services online.

There are three ways to send an online payment:

- From the Pay Bills window
- From the Write Checks window
- From an online account register

You use these methods the same way you always do, except that you designate the transaction as an online transaction and send the payment instructions to your financial institution.

To use online payments, you need to set up a payee. Once the payee is set up, you may either send an electronic funds transfer (EFT) to the payee's institution or have your financial institution print a check and send it to the payee. An electronic funds transfer deducts money from your account and transfers it into the payee's account electronically. This usually takes one or two business days. This is called lead time and must be considered when sending online payments. If you have your institution mail checks to payees, you should allow four days lead time.

A check used to send an online payment will use Send as the No. and will have a checkmark for Online Bank Payment.

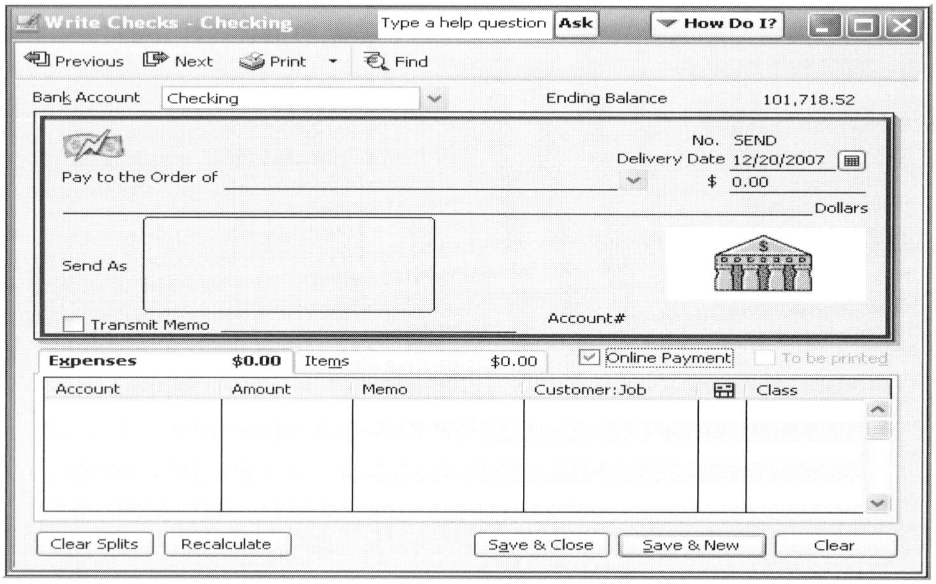

QUICKBOOKS BILLING SOLUTIONS

QuickBooks offers an invoice e-mail service that will instantly e-mail easy-to-read PDF files of invoices, statements and estimates from QuickBooks. It also has a mailing service that will print, fold, and mail invoices to customers. In addition, payment reminders, online e-mail tracking, and customer online payment options are also included. Customers can pay invoices and statements online by entering their credit card information in the Customer Account Center, a secure Web site hosted by Intuit. Charges are processed through the QuickBooks Merchant Service. This requires signing up for the optional QuickBooks Billing Solutions and QuickBooks Merchant Service.

If enrolled in the services, invoices may be e-mailed, faxed, or mailed in the US mail. Customers may pay for their invoices online using a credit card in the password protected online Customer Account Center. When a customer pays online, an online receipt will be provided. Online payments are downloaded and matched to customer invoices in the QuickBooks in the receive payments window.

QUICKBOOKS MERCHANT SERVICES

QuickBooks Merchant Services allows your business to accept credit cards from customers. As a subscriber to QuickBooks Merchant Services, credit card charges are processed and deposited into your designated bank account. Funds will be generally deposited into your account within two to three business days depending on your financial institution and your Demand Deposit Account. Everything needed to process credit cards is built right into QuickBooks. This enables you to offer customers more payment options, process credit cards in QuickBooks or remotely. Credit card payments may be entered manually into QuickBooks or by swiping the credit card by using a card reader purchased separately. You can also process recurring charges and bill customers online.

Enter credit card transactions

When a transaction is processed for a credit card payment, sales receipt or customer payment is recorded as usual. The checkbox for Process Credit Card Payment should be selected.

When receiving payments by credit card, click the History button and assign the payment to the invoice, then click **Go To** to see the invoice being paid.

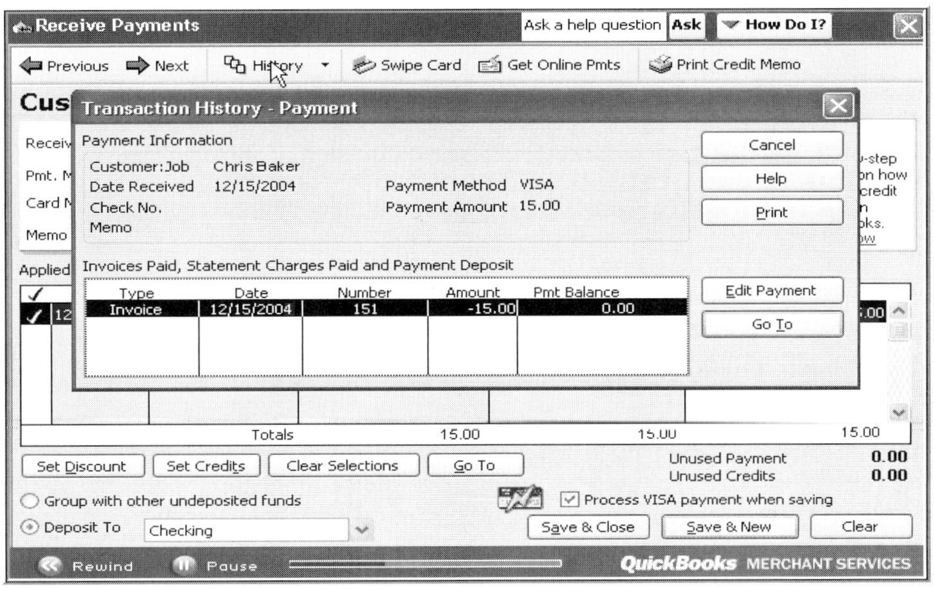

You may also sign up for and attach a credit card reader that will enable you to swipe a card and have the transaction entered directly into QuickBooks.

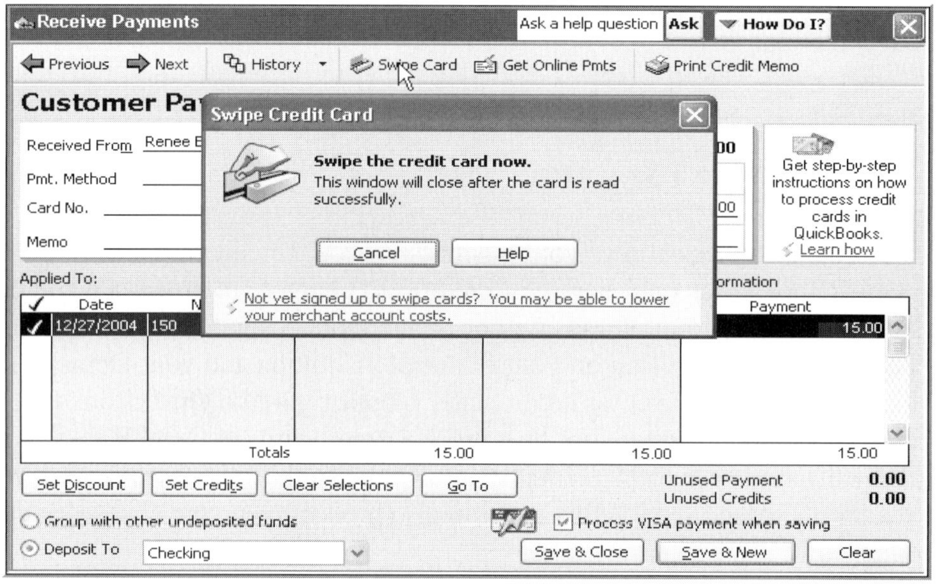

Once a credit card transaction has been entered, you will get a notice of approval.

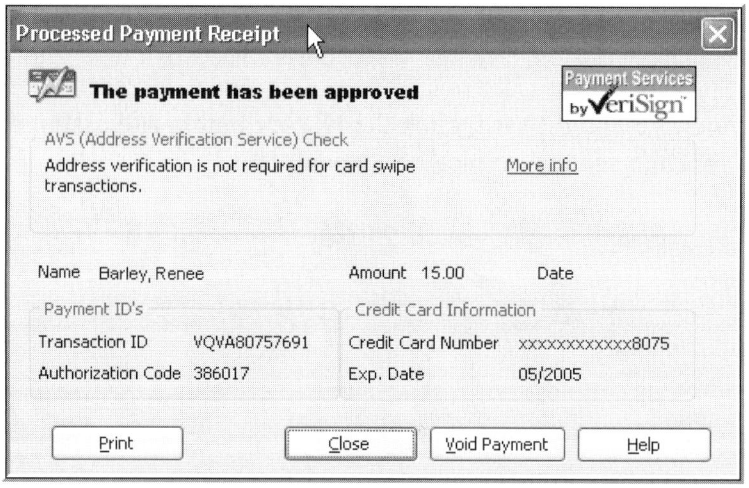

In addition, you may use a virtual terminal to process credit card receipts. This enables transactions to be entered without employees directly accessing the company's QuickBooks files.

Use may set up automatic recurring charges and integrate with Billing Solutions so customers can also pay online. QuickBooks credit card processing also enables credit card fees to be included on the Make Deposits window.

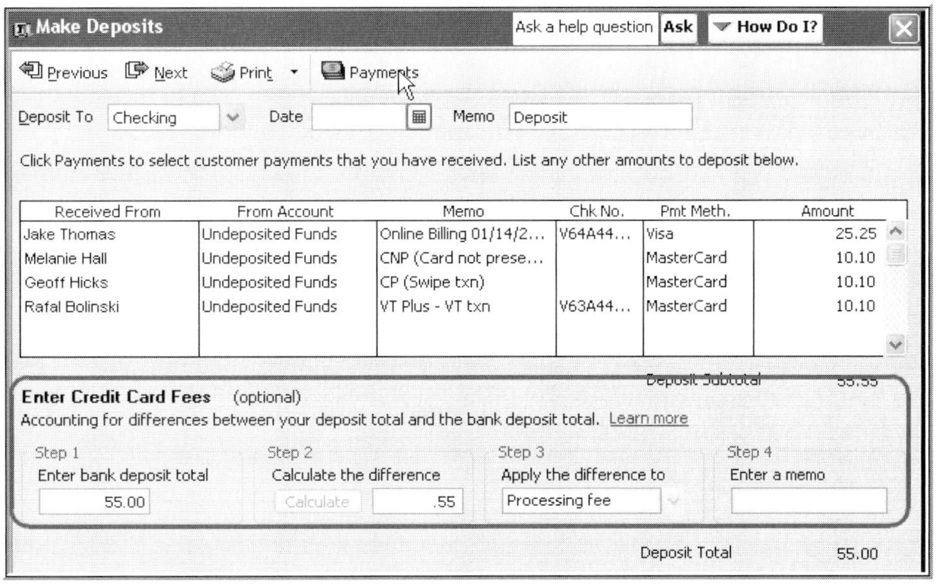

Automatic Credit Card Billing

QuickBooks Merchant Account Services also has an Automatic Credit Card Billing feature that allows you to bill a customer's credit card a fixed amount at regular intervals for recurring services, such as membership fees, insurance premiums, or subscriptions. Prior to setting up a recurring charge, you must have written authorization from your customer.

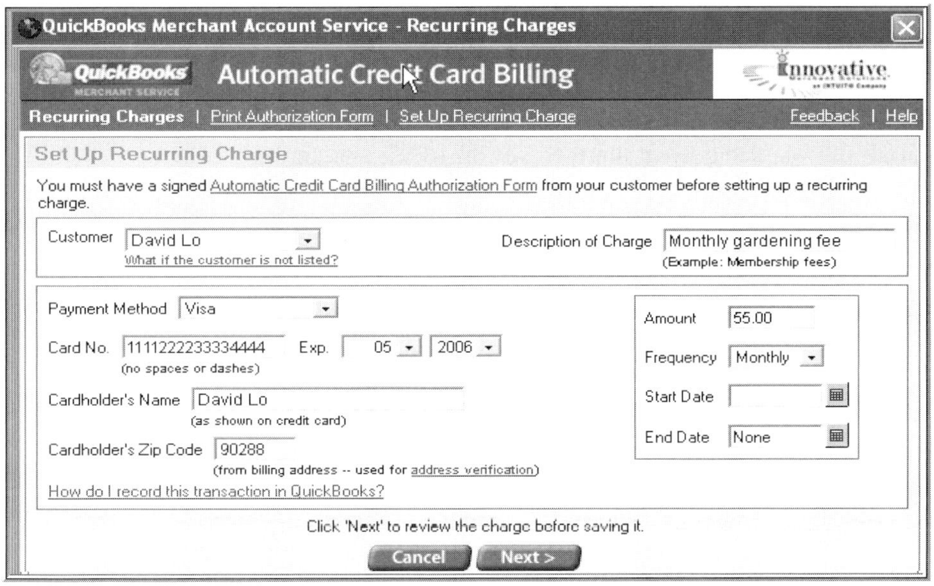

ONLINE BACKUP SERVICES

In addition to having a backup stored in the office, having an offsite backup copy of your company data files is extremely important. This is necessary in case something happens to your computer or your office. For a monthly fee, you may subscribe to QuickBooks Online Backup Service. Files are compressed, encrypted, and securely transferred across the Internet then stored at mirrored off-site data centers managed by IT experts.

Files may be selected for backup automatically or manually. You schedule the days and times for your backups.

When backing up data files online, the same procedure is followed as instructed in Appendix A. The only change is that you click Online rather than Disk.

DIRECT DEPOSIT

Rather than mail or give paychecks to your employees, you may sign up for Direct Deposit if you have a subscription to QuickBooks Payroll. You will go to the Employees menu and click Payroll Service Activities. Some of the information you need to do this is your federal employer identification number, the company's principal name, the company's legal name and address, your financial institution routing and account numbers, and your QuickBooks registration number.

You also need to set up those employees who wish to receive their checks by direct deposit. This is done by:

- Accessing the Employee Center.
- Double-click the employee you want to set up for direct deposit.
- In the Edit Employee window, click the "Change Tabs" drop-down list and choose Payroll and Compensation Info.
- Click the Direct Deposit button.
- Select Use Direct Deposit for this employee.
- Select whether to deposit the paycheck into one or two accounts.
- Enter the employee's financial institution information.

Index

C

D

E

F

G

M

N

O

P

Q

R

S

T

U

V

W

Y